"...a political earthquake... an exceptic
the anti-freedom crowd is not going to like *Supreme Court Gun Cases*.

Larry Pratt, Executive Director, Gun Owners of America

"...wonderful... groundbreaking...
belongs on the bookshelf of every practitioner of constitutional law...
Gun rights are an integral part of each American's
fundamental constitutional liberties."

Thomas C. Patterson, M.D., Chairman, Goldwater Institute

"...dynamite...
Sometimes people need to defend themselves while we're responding to a 911 call. Law enforcement officers know that firearms in the hands of decent people are a deterrent to crime... It's good to know the Supreme Court has been this positive about gun rights and self defense... pulls the rug out from under politicians who want you to believe you have no right to defend yourself or own a gun."

Joe Arpaio, "America's Toughest Sheriff"

"Academics and judges will be surprised (no actually shocked) by how many times the Supreme Court has issued decisions bearing on private gun ownership. The extremely careful attention to documenting all the decisions will make it very difficult for future court decisions not to be affected by this work. The number of precedents is truly overwhelming."

John R. Lott, Jr., Ph.D., Resident Scholar, American Enterprise Institute

"...a stunning accomplishment...
will change the political landscape on the gun-rights debate."

Evan Nappen, Attorney and Author

"...shows that scores of Supreme Court decisions recognize the legal, theoretical and practical logic of private firearms ownership... entertainingly explains the amazing true stories and profound ideals that rise from time-honored American gun rights."

Aaron Zelman, Jews for the Preservation of Firearms Ownership

"The dream team of American gun-law experts has driven a stake through the heart of the anti-rights gun-ban lobby... gun haters will need to manufacture new lies... The individual right to keep and bear arms is an American tradition with roots as deep as the nation itself."

Alan Gottlieb, Chairman, Second Amendment Foundation

"Right in the face of unrelenting media distortion and anti-gun propaganda, *Supreme Court Gun Cases* proves beyond any doubt that the Court has explicitly upheld the legal and historical record of private firearms ownership and armed self-defense. This book proves what NRA has been saying all along—the Second Amendment protects an individual's right to keep and bear arms—a freedom existing before America's founding and enshrined in our Bill of Rights."

Wayne R. LaPierre, Executive Vice President
National Rifle Association

"It is fundamentally sound, sorely needed research that supports the basic human and civil right to protect what's yours."

Lawrence E. Tahler, Executive Director, American Self-Defense Institute

"...the rights of man are endowed by their Creator, but ensured by the state... Each responsible citizen must consider himself to be the custodian of his own liberty, and thus it is incumbent upon him to understand the processes by which such liberty is ensured. This text covers that subject at appropriate length."

Lt. Col. Jeff Cooper, USMC (Ret.)
"The Father of the Modern Techniques of Shooting"

"While the Supremes have directly acknowledged the Second Amendment as an individual right, this new book unearths 92 gun-related cases where the High Court upheld, among other things, armed self-defense of person, family and community—the heart of the Second Amendment. The synopsis of the *Miller* case is the best I have ever read."

Neal Knox, Gun-Rights Activist and Writer, The Firearms Coalition

"...strikes a powerful blow for freedom... I'm particularly gratified to learn how vigorous the Court has been in supporting the right to self defense. If more states accepted this, countless innocent lives would be saved. My hope and prayer is that your book will supply the brain-cell ammunition necessary to continue our battle against those who would deny Americans such a basic human right."

Suzanna Gratia Hupp, Texas State Representative
Survivor of Luby's Massacre and Mother

"My interviews of gun-control spokespeople show they either don't know or won't tell the truth about how the Supreme Court has consistently ruled in favor of a strong Second Amendment. This book, in the Court's own words, should convince anyone that the right to own firearms is at least as strong as the right to free speech. Bravo on an important scholastic work that is easy to read and understand."

Tom Gresham, Nationally Syndicated Radio Talk Show Host

SUPREME COURT GUN CASES

Two Centuries of Gun Rights Revealed

Featuring plain-English summaries and every word of every key case

— ◆ —

Plus the nearly forgotten self-defense cases

Attorney David B. Kopel
Attorney Stephen P. Halbrook, Ph.D.
Alan Korwin

BLOOMFIELD PRESS
Phoenix, Arizona

BLOOMFIELD PRESS
4718 E. Cactus #440 • Phoenix, AZ 85032
602-996-4020 Offices • 602-494-0679 Fax
1-800-707-4020 Order Hotline
gunlaws.com

The State Constitution citations were researched and compiled by
Prof. Eugene Volokh of UCLA Law School

Front cover photograph courtesy of Franz Jantzen
Collections Manager, United States Supreme Court

Trade paperback ISBN: 1-889632-05-8
Library/Lawyer's hardcover edition ISBN: 1-889632-12-0
Library of Congress Control Number: 2003107806

ATTENTION
Contact the publisher for information on quantity discounts!

Printed and bound in the United States of America
At Central Plains Book Manufacturing, Winfield, Kansas

First Edition

TABLE OF CONTENTS

ACKNOWLEDGMENTS

This book would not have happened if not for the work of Jerod Tufte. After my interminable efforts to assemble the ever-increasing full body of cases over a period of many years (in a myriad of formats), I had reached the end of my rope. He stepped in and compiled, cleaned, proofed and did the basic edit on the text of the cases, as well as early sketches on the gists. He completed these tasks during the time he was studying for his bar exam, an amazing feat. A native of West Fargo, North Dakota, Jerod graduated first in his class at the Arizona State University College of Law in 2002. He also holds a degree in Computer Engineering from Case Western Reserve University in Cleveland, Ohio. His student article on Arizona's constitutional right to arms provision was published in 2001 in the *Arizona State Law Journal,* 33 Ariz. St. L.J. 341. He is now a member of the Arizona bar, and will enter private practice in Phoenix upon completing his clerkship with the Eighth Circuit U.S. Court of Appeals. Jerod, you have earned my deepest gratitude. –Alan Korwin

The patience, love and endurance shown me by my precious wife Cheryl and my wonderful daughter Tyler got me through the hardest parts of the struggle.

This book was also made possible by the willing cooperation, advice, hard work and moral support of so many companies and individuals over such a very long period of time that it would be unfair to attempt to attribute the precise contributions of each one whose name accumulated for recognition in my boxes and boxes of files. My dream of publishing *Supreme Court Gun Cases* would never have taken place without their assistance:

Michael P. Anthony, Attorney at Law; The Arizona State University Law Library; The Arizona Supreme Court Law Library; Mitchell Bard; Stuart Burnett; Gary Christensen; The Citizens Committee for the Right to Keep and Bear Arms; Clark, Boardman, Callaghan; Charles Curley; Robert Dowlut, Attorney at Law; Karen Earley; Becky Fenger; Findlaw; Charles Finger; Sandy Froman; Melissa Funk; Richard Gardiner, Attorney at Law; Alan Gottlieb; Charly Gullett; Gun Owners of America; Handgun Control, Inc.; Charles Heller; Dennis Henigan, Attorney at Law; Gwen Henson; The Independence Institute; The Institute for Legislative Action; Jews for the Preservation of Firearms Ownership; Cal Knickerbocker; Lisa Liddy; Steve Maniscalco; The Maricopa County Law Library; Jordan Meschkow, Attorney at Law; Mark Moritz, Attorney at Law; The National Rifle Association; The National Rifle Association Foundation; Wendy Nelson; The Second Amendment Foundation; Lisa Halbrook-Stevenson; Vin Suprynowicz; Thompson Legal Publishing; C.D. Tavares; The United States Supreme Court; Paul J. Updike; Westlaw.

Edited by Candice M. DeBarr

Indexing by Enid Zafran, Indexing Partners

Cover design by Ralph Richardson

FOREWORD

WARNING! • DON'T MISS THIS!

This book is not "the law," and is not a substitute for the law. The law includes all the legal obligations imposed on you, a much greater volume of work than the mere Supreme Court decisions contained in this book. You are fully accountable under the exact wording and current official interpretations of all applicable laws, regulations, court precedents, executive orders and more, when you deal with firearms under any circumstances.

Many people find laws hard to understand, and gathering all the relevant ones is a lot of work. This book helps you with these chores. Collected in one volume are copies, reproduced with great care, of the principal Supreme Court decisions affecting private gun ownership, possession and use in America.

A variety of scholarly and popular analysis and description of the High Court's rulings are included for your convenience. However, legal interpretation of Supreme Court decisions is a matter for the courts, **no guarantee of accuracy is expressed or implied, and the explanatory sections of this book are not to be considered as legal advice or a restatement of law.**

In explaining the general meanings of various cases, using plain English, differences inevitably arise, so **you must always check the actual cases. Some of the cases reproduced in this book are edited excerpts only.** The actual and complete cases are published by the U.S. Government Printing Office and by commercial publishers. The authors and publisher of this book expressly disclaim any liability whatsoever arising out of reliance on information contained in this book.

New laws and regulations may be enacted at any time by the authorities, and courts at every level are constantly interpreting the laws and regulations. **The author and publisher make no representation that this book includes all cases requirements, prohibitions and rules that may exist.**

FIREARMS LAWS AND PRECEDENTS ARE CONSTANTLY CHANGING. You are strongly urged to consult with a qualified attorney and local authorities to determine the current status and applicability of the law to specific situations that you may encounter.

Some people may feel that certain laws are unconstitutional and invalid, but remember that while they are laws they are enforceable, and remain so until overturned by the legislature or future test cases. Being able to cite the perfect test case may not matter to a police officer at the side of your car.

Guns are deadly serious business and require the highest level of responsibility from you. Firearm ownership, possession and use are long-recognized rights that carry awesome responsibility. Unfortunately, **what the law says and what the authorities and courts do aren't always an exact match.** You must remember that each legal case is different and may lack prior court precedents. A decision to prosecute a case and the charges brought may involve a degree of discretion from the authorities involved. Sometimes, there just isn't a plain, clear-cut answer you can rely upon. Abuses, ignorance, carelessness, human frailties and plain fate subject you to legal risks, which can be exacerbated when firearms are involved. Take nothing for granted, recognize that legal risk is attached to everything you do, and **ALWAYS ERR ON THE SIDE OF SAFETY.**

The Second Amendment to the United States Constitution

"A well regulated Militia,
being necessary to the security of a free State,
the right of the people to keep and bear Arms,
shall not be infringed."

In the hope that we preserve
the good thing we have here in America

About the Supreme Court's Gun Cases

by Alan Korwin

One of the biggest problems with law today is that there is so much of it. Congress doesn't stop legislating, it seems, sometimes heedless of its delegated authority or any real need to do so. The federal courts at every level churn out stupefying quantities of interpretation of legislative activity, practically legislating on their own in case after case. All 50 states do the same. Every county and every city contributes to the glut.

> **"Law is an institution of the most pernicious tendency. The institution, once begun, can never be brought to a close. No action of any man was ever the same as any other action, ever had the same degree of utility or injury. As new cases occur, the law is perpetually found to be deficient. It is therefore perpetually necessary to make new laws. The volume in which justice records her prescriptions is forever increasing, and the world would not contain the books that might be written. The consequences of the infinitude of law is its uncertainty." –William Godwin**

All the components that constitute law have already grown so large they are functionally inaccessible to the general public on which they act. The informed electorate that the Founding Fathers hoped for, in too many respects, has fallen beyond the pale of human endeavor:

> **"It will be of little avail to the people that the laws are made by men of their own choice, if the laws be so voluminous that they cannot be read, or so incoherent that they cannot be understood; if they be repealed or revised before they are promulgated, or undergo such incessant changes that no man who knows what the law is to-day can guess what it will be to-morrow." –James Madison, The Federalist Papers, #62**

The Supreme Court's steady activity contributes to this difficulty, though its work is perhaps more well organized and (sometimes) better thought out. The full official bound set requires 95 feet of shelf space.

It is the goal of *Supreme Court Gun Cases* to make accessible one tiny fragment of that august body's work, namely the High Court's decisions that have a bearing on private gun ownership in America today. What does the Supreme Court say about your right to keep arms and your right to bear arms?

Few other subjects have sparked such a firestorm of debate—but a mostly recent debate it turns out, which takes place all too often in abject darkness, or replete with lies, deceit, myths, politically motivated balderdash, statistical work from The Three Stooges, and outright self-evident silliness.

It is the self-evident silliness that is hardest to accept—if we are ever to reach any rational conciliation on crucial issues, surely it must be by exercising our intellect. Even absent an infallible agreed-upon set of facts, we should be able to apply our critical thinking to proceed in a straight line.

Nowhere are the self-evident errors more pronounced than in the new (recent decades) argument that the Second Amendment does not protect the rights of individual people, but rather protects the "right" of the states to run a militia. The ability of a state to organize its militia is not a right, it is a power delegated to the state by the people.

Even a casual glance at history shows there are and have always been gun dealers selling to citizens who are not in the National Guard (which didn't even exist as a concept until 1903). More than 94,000 words of federal statute regulate well this activity (q.v., *Gun Laws of America*). How could all the people and all the authorities possibly have gotten it so wrong for so long, and only now be discovering their mistake?

The answer of course is that we and they didn't get it wrong. Through the efforts of Stephen Halbrook we know that the collective-rights argument—the one that proclaims you have no rights—first appears out of nowhere in the federal judiciary in *U.S. v. Tot,* as he notes in his section, later in this book (citations omitted here):

> **The "collective rights" theory originated in *U.S. v. Tot,* (1943). The historical references in *Tot* simply do not support its thesis. See Halbrook, *That Every Man Be Armed* 189-191 (1984). Subsequent cases merely string cite to earlier cases which are ultimately traceable to *Tot.***

Another source of distortion over the years has been flagrant use of out-of-context quotations, and with this book that farce ends. For too long, *Cruikshank* has been held up as flatly dismissing your rights, with these pulled phrases referring to the Second Amendment:

> **The right there specified is that of "bearing arms for a lawful purpose." This is not a right granted by the Constitution.**

Sure, the Supreme Court actually said that. What is all too frequently omitted however is the very next line:

> **Neither is it in any manner dependent upon that instrument for its existence.**

The High Court goes on to explain, in its now-awkward nineteenth century legalese, that the individual right to arms embodied in the Second Amendment (as well as certain other basic individual rights), existed before the Constitution. These are inherent natural rights of free people, recognized but certainly not created by the Founders, which the Constitution merely established as off-limits for federal intrusion.

The United States operates the way it does because the Second Amendment means what it always used to mean—individual people can and do indeed keep arms and bear arms for their personal safety, defense of the common good, and every other legitimate purpose, if they so choose. The idea that you don't have these rights is something new and aberrant, and represents a total reversal of what has been the case in America so far. Feel how you wish about an armed people's deterrence to tyranny, or personal gun possession in public, or resisting crime, or firearm education at school, or proper safety measures for anything you keep at your home. But in order to adopt the logically bankrupt notion that the Constitution does not protect your individual right to arms, you must deny the reality surrounding you.

The individual right to arms is clearly borne out in the copious decisions of the Supreme Court, which have been obscured from public view until now.

The Supreme Court's gun cases were not heretofore referred to as plentiful in public discourse. That is one of the breakthroughs of this book. It is also the reason this book took six years to complete.

I thought myself pretty clever when I approached Dave Kopel at a convention with my concept for an easy and unique book about the Supreme Court. We would take the popular essays Dave had already written for Mike Dillon's magazine-catalog ("magalog") the *Blue Press,* reproduce the actual cases he discussed, and create a relatively thin text pretty quickly. Dillon's publication of those fascinating essays was the genesis of the book you now hold. The early burst of enthusiasm that set this task on its course anticipated an easy compilation of less than a dozen cases, believing, as we all did back then, that the Supreme Court has said little with respect to guns. The number of cases to be included unedited was small enough to be pitched on the draft of the back cover from 1997:

U.S. v. Cruikshank, 1876
Presser v. Illinois, 1886
Miller v. State of Texas, 1894
U.S. v. Miller, 1939
Lewis v. U.S., 1980
U.S. v. Thompson/Center, 1992
U.S. v. Lopez, 1995
Printz/Mack v. U.S., 1997

The shocking realization that this was in fact an enormous body of work (44 cases are included unedited) pulled the rug out from under the effort. The project alternately languished behind every other pressing exigency of modern life, or pressed ahead in fits and starts as batches of new cases were unearthed. In the interim I used my discovery of a dozen self-defense cases for a section of Tanya Metaksa's book, *Safe, Not Sorry* (Harper Collins). David published "The Supreme Court's Thirty-Five *Other* Gun Cases," in the *St. Louis University Public Law Review* (1999), and other material based on our unfinished research crept into scholarly and popular work for years.

On top of 36 cases that actually mention or quote the Second Amendment, we began to recognize that guns are a bigger subject than the Amendment itself. We kept discovering cases that addressed firearms from other perspectives—search and seizure, sentence enhancements, taxes, states' rights, double jeopardy, definitions, statutory interpretation, due process and more. My faith and motivation waned more than once. Finally, I could no longer stand the continued darkness and applied the afterburners in mid 2002. I thought for sure I would finish by New Years, but the project just soaked up the hours and I sit here in July 2003 still trying to nail it all down.

My friend Steve Cascone has advice that rings true here—you don't finish a book, you declare an ending. But I couldn't do that until I had examined every case for quotable lines (and found 1,068). Then I felt compelled to simmer each case down to the identifying questions in the special Descriptive Index. And of course a few new cases sprang up near the end (*Simpson* on armed robbery, *Busic* on armed assault of officials, and even *Terry v. Ohio*, on frisks).

It was common for writers of every stripe to refer to the mere few pronouncements of the High Court, but now that ends. As you can see for yourself, 92 decisions have a bearing on the issue, and at least seven others (see *Miranda*) are often cited. Reduced to a common measurement, these 337,141 words with a bearing on your gun rights are three times more case law on guns than federal statutory law (a tidy 94,333 words as of 2003).

Interesting word counts within the case text:
(all variant spellings are included)

Word	Count	Word	Count
firearm	1,380	ammunition	77
arms	621	shotgun	61
gun	362	handgun	53
rifle	134	revolver	47
pistol	135	keep and bear arms	37
armed	125	Second Amendment	38
self defense	123	bear arms	27
machinegun	112	Winchester	5

The "few" cases most writers were referring to was just a mass mental blockage passed down from one lazy parrot to another, and I include myself in that class. How much other claptrap passes for fact unobserved, you have to wonder. The few-cases fallacy perhaps reflects an interest by some people in seeing this inconvenient Amendment up and leave—an interest so strong mere facts are not normally enough to contain it.

•

Part of the liberty and freedom Americans have cherished since the country began is the freedom to own weapons as free adults, for their own safety as well as the nation's. There was no more need to state the obvious—you have the right to have the guns you have—than to state that you have a right to own a pen, a point the High Court has never found the need to actually say.

Possession of private property, in this case firearms, without some external overt wrongdoing, is not a crime. All the shouting about the rights to arms

Americans share as a culture is new, a modern debate working to eliminate or reduce rights already extant, for reasons we needn't dwell upon here.

No where is this more evident than in the practically forgotten Supreme Court self-defense cases from the 1890s, where time after time the Justices take for granted that the people have guns. The Court focuses instead solely on when and how the people used their guns, and if such use was proper.

It was understood as normal, reasonable and expectable for a small man to go home and get his gun, as in *Gourko,* when publicly threatened with death by a much larger man. And no, it was not premeditated murder when Gourko used his gun in the ensuing confrontation. Time and again, the Court easily and calmly presumes that gun ownership is normative behavior. American people own and use guns for all the legitimate purposes that make guns so important in a peace-loving society. That's them talking, not me.

No less than nine fundamental elements of self defense are defined by these cases, and can be categorized roughly thus:

Innocence
Logan 1892; Beard 1895; Rowe 1896; Brown 1921

Reasonable Belief & Grounds For Belief
Beard 1895; Allen, Acers, Alberty, Wallace 1896

Intent
Gourko 1894; Thompson 1894; Allen, Wallace 1896

Actions Not Words
Allison 1895; Allen, Acers, Alberty 1896

Necessity
Logan 1892; Starr 1894; Beard 1895; Rowe 1896

Equal Force
Logan 1892; Beard 1895; Allen, Alberty 1896

Immediacy Ends
Acers 1896; Brown 1921

Retreat
Beard 1895; Rowe, Alberty 1896; Brown 1921

Chase
Garner 1995

Garner has not been previously thought of as a self-defense case, but it exists nonetheless on an important fringe of that issue. When a criminal exits your home at a high rate of speed carrying your valuables, is deadly force permissible to retain your property, as so many staunch gun owners wish? A continuum exists on types of criminal flight, from kidnapping and car-jacking where innocent life is at risk, to escape of known dangerous characters, to the mere loss of property or escape of suspects. *Garner,* which applies specifically to police, is the only Supreme Court case known to address this at all. Many states have codified the use of deadly force to prevent escape, but folk wisdom has a place here—better a criminal goes free than a lien on your home.

Later cases generally have better English, at least to the modern ear, but all the important things were settled early on. Cases in modern times often pick at minutiae related to statutory construction, the constitutionality of a provision, or quite often, the possession of guns in connection with the war on some drugs. That war takes up much of the back half of this book. Statements about the rights each American has with regard to personal possession and use of firearms were established matters of law by the early 1900s.

Cases since then restate or reinforce the American right to arms, directly and by implication. The question now seems to be how much infringement is tolerable, a question that unfortunately will always dog us. The relationship between rights and controls is a dynamic balance, not a bright line.

When you think about it, no rights are limitless. Put simply, your right to swing your arms stops where my nose begins. The right to arms does not include a right to wave a gun around wildly and terrify people, or to stick up a liquor store. Even the absolute pronouncement at the front of the First Amendment, "Congress shall make no law..." allows for laws against fraud, slander, impersonating an officer, threatening the President, bomb jokes in airports and the classic, falsely shouting fire in a crowded theater and creating a panic. Justice Holmes created the wonderful theater metaphor in a case that convicted a man for circulating leaflets about resisting the military draft, a less than beautiful example in retrospect.

With the word *gun* used in some form in these decisions 2,910 times, they can't all be part of the holding in each case. Many expressions of the individual right to keep arms and to bear arms are in *dicta,* the discussion portions of the decisions that are not legally binding. Serious lawyers scoff at dicta, uh, except when it strongly supports their cases. They dismiss it totally when the other side claims the Court's words mean something.

I guess I'm the champion of dicta. I like dicta. In it I find the life of America, the depth of the decisions, a window into what reality was like at the time. I give great credit to those writers of words, they had something to say, and they could turn a phrase. The statute might give you the rules about liquor, cigarettes and guns, but dicta tells you what it was like at the party.

Experts may not even agree on where dicta ends and the holding begins, except for occasional brief statements such as, "The holding of the court below is reversed." While dicta is not binding, it is persuasive, and that is the nub. With so much "between the lines" evidence available and all basically pointed in the same direction, it can only logically be read to support the decisions themselves, which are consistent with the individual private gun ownership in place in America since Day One. A portion of the record may only be dicta, but have mercy, there are 500 pages of it.

Whether you "have" any legal rights or not is immaterial in the larger picture of human survival. You *can* defend against predatory attack, you *can* slay an adversary, and if you survive in today's world, you get to take what comes next from the people generally known as officials, for better or worse. Your neighbors, being by and large rational, will typically celebrate your survival, when you persevere in the stark face of unprovoked assault, regardless of law books on a shelf somewhere. And so it has been since time immemorial. Nothing in the natural order of the jungle can require you to stand idle and let the lion eat you or your family, with or without some musty old parchment curtain between you and the powers that be.

The Supreme Court has upheld the legal tradition and historical record of self-defense in both law and logic, which has existed as a principle, unbroken, since the Code of Hamurabai, the first written law drafted 4,000 years ago. In America, you have a right to armed self defense. The Court describes it explicitly, repeatedly.

Those well buttressed pronouncements are under assault, as increasingly strident calls are made to denounce the protection the Second Amendment has traditionally afforded us, e.g., police need guns but you don't, because they face dangerous criminals and you, umm, well... that line of thought does fall a bit short in the logic department. Such arguments are generally designed to incrementally disarm the freely armed public we observe today, and to ban or severely discourage personal responsibility for your own safety.

Three main reasons are put forth in advocating such a radical departure from the historical and legal record. The first simply suggests that you're too stupid and guns are too dangerous for a citizen to handle. This requires accepting a bizarre paradox—guns should be banned because they make murder easy but are way too complex for effective self defense. (See dozens of similar paradoxes by M.Z. Williamson posted at KeepAndBearArms.com). The second reason is seemingly benign and sometimes presented as the "common sense" approach to public disarmament—as an attempt to control crime. Since guns cause crime, or so the thinking goes, ban the guns and crime will go away. The fact that guns are already totally banned for criminals doesn't enter the equation, and only the guns of people who don't commit crimes are targeted. Both arguments are easily dismissed on common sense grounds.

The mainstream media though inexplicably adopts these as a frame of reference and abandons any semblance of balance, casting nearly all gun-related reports to imply that guns and crime are inextricably linked, and that firearms serve little other than criminal purposes. Research showing millions of DGUs (defensive gun uses) each year are completely suppressed by America's "unbiased" mainstream reporters. John Lott's latest book, *The Bias Against Guns,* documents how *The New York Times,* for example, ran 50,745 words about crimes with guns in 2001, and one story of 163 words on a gun being used (by a retired cop) to prevent a crime. The "paper of record" shamelessly deceives the public. The scandal caused by one lying reporter on its staff is meaningless, a smokescreen to obscure its institutionalized distortions.

Certainly, the gun-friendly sense of early Americans and their Supreme Court is not what appears on nightly news broadcasts or the morning newspaper. The facts that guns save lives, guns stop crime, guns keep you safe, and guns are why America is still free, are not found in the "news." This contributes to why tens of millions of gun-friendly people today have good reason to distrust the media. And why many unsuspecting members of the public have come to dislike—or have even been manipulated into viciously hating guns—the very thing that helps guarantee their freedom.

The third and darkest motive, according to an increasing number of observers, is for more sinister purposes involving stricter management of the population and the incremental demise of a self-governing republic that was founded with populist arms two-and-a-quarter centuries ago. Nah, couldn't possibly happen here.

Still, no issue as large as this is absolute. The anti-rights argument can draw some support from cases like *Lewis, Maryland, Miller* (which everyone claims as their own) and a few others, plus occasional dissents that take a strong statist view.

The question of what might occur in the future if the Supremes were to hear a case about the personal, individual, historically extant right to the means of self and national defense that you and your forbearers have always had, is addressed next.

The question of where the Supreme Court has stood thus far on the issue is addressed in the body of this work, for all to see.

The Fall of the Second Amendment

The past speaks for itself. In this country, individual free people have always had the right and the ability to keep arms and to bear arms. In recent times, restrictions on this right and ability have grown. Challenges to the civil right itself have been introduced in courts and the public debate.

Things change. Why not the Second Amendment? We asked if slavery should continue and said no. We asked if women should be allowed to vote and said yes. We asked if liquor should be outlawed and said yes, then no. We even asked if sovereignty should stand in the way of forcing the Bill of Rights on the several states and eventually said why not. So why not private gun ownership—should "they" allow "us" to keep and bear arms?

What if the Supreme Court were to hear yet another case addressing the Second Amendment's current protection of the individual right to both keep arms and to bear arms? Should people continue to have the right to arms they currently have, or should the right be taken away by the very government this right is intended to keep in check?

And let's assume the High Court unequivocally answers the question to the satisfaction of the most skeptical critic, instead of being unclear, waffling around, or addressing only tangents, as the most ardent critics might argue they have done, even in the face of the research presented in this book. I can't even find a perfect way to frame the bottom-line question if that case appeared today. Are the people the militia? Do individual people in the United States have a right to keep and bear arms which shall not be infringed? Yes or no?

The results of such a case are so intense, and could so shift or rend the fabric of America—adjusting the balances of power in ways no one can foresee—that both sides in the gun-rights debate have been reluctant to take the chance. They have actually backed off when cases presented themselves, arguing the case wasn't airtight enough, or the bench was not in their favor. They each have too much to lose.

The Court itself has shown repeated reluctance to address the issue, refusing to review many cases that might answer, from its desk at least, The Big Question. So the status quo remains—most anyone can stroll into a gun store and go shopping, while infringements of all flavors continue to mount.

The Supreme Court is unlikely to one day jump in and decide that, yes, the Second Amendment does indeed protect an uninfringeable right to individually arm yourself if you so choose, and any laws violating that freedom would be invalid. That's not going to happen because, as we've already seen, reasonable boundaries are defined around all rights. There's also the practical problem of defining each word, not just answering some single question—what are arms, how does "regulated" differ from "well regulated," what exactly is "keep," and "bear"—the human condition, and the rules by which we govern ourselves, do not conveniently reduce down to a yea or nay.

Even if the Court once again says yes, the Second Amendment basically means what the gunnies say it means, nothing substantial is invented. Gun stores will open the very next day, the same as the previous day. Here comes the new boss, same as the old boss.

The loudest of the "gun bigots," from huge non-profits to people who are actually in Congress sworn to uphold the Constitution, would be missing their main subject matter. The mass media would be out on a limb trying to spin the decision to the masses, since it would conflict with the bulk of what the news has been saying for the past several decades.

The valid debate must then become how much regulation constitutes infringement. This is in fact the direction policy debates are now taking, as overwhelming scholarly evidence and the book you are holding begin to force anti-rights advocates into rethinking their untenable positions. Disarmament advocates would have to shift to the less deceitful policy question of whether people should *continue* to run around with this right to keep arms and right to bear arms intact.

Otherwise, and here's the surprise, life would pretty much be business as usual, with guns for sale during regular business hours, shooting ranges handling the usual crowds, honorable people handling firearms in honorable ways, and 99+% of all guns involved in no wrongdoing or inherent evil, exactly as things are today. Oh, I suppose some people would drink beer till dawn, and feel woozy for a few days.

Crooks would essentially be unaffected, since guns are already totally prohibited as far as they're concerned, and all the existing anti-criminal laws would still be in place, with neither more nor less resources for enforcement than are available now.

Challenges would be mounted against many of the more egregious infringing laws at the state and federal levels, and there are some real doozies. The juggernaut of social fabric would ponderously lumber ahead. People terrified of guns (*hoplophobes*, from the Greek *hoplites*, weapon) would shriek about blood in the streets, gun owners would remain skeptical of course, and we'd all get to see what really happens.

On the other hand, well-meaning Justices sometimes choose to use their power and perceived notions of the public good, instead of plain evaluation of law or the Constitution, as a basis for their decisions. A High Court peopled with enough Justices of this philosophical bent could conceivably decide that, no, there is no protection in the Second Amendment for individuals to keep arms, or to bear arms, or at least there won't be anymore, despite the historical, social and judicial record. The Supreme Court can essentially decide to reverse what is.

If you doubt this possibility, see the dissenting opinion in *Adams v. Williams,* where Justices Douglas and Marshall see no problem with outright bans. With three more similarly oriented people on the bench, gun rights could be abolished, on paper at least, regardless of precedent.

Voices of increasing authority and volume are grousing that the Constitution no longer adequately constrains the Congress. Why should the uninfringeable right to arms be any different.

There would be elation in some circles, a euphoria of perceived safety, and I suppose some folks would sip tea and converse in giddy tones until quite late. And we might expect that a substantial and already discomfited armed portion of the public would feel further alienated. The political right would be sweating bullets, and the far right, armed to the teeth, might begin to figure we're doomed.

But one of the surprising results if the personal protection of the Second Amendment were to fall by Supreme Court decree (or even by legislative decree, for a bill to repeal the Second Amendment has been introduced by a Congressman from New York) is that all of the honest gun ownership, possession and use we see in every fiber of American life today would not suddenly become illegal. The collapse of the Second Amendment is not a ban on anything. It might open a floodgate of attempts at new regulation, but the current status quo rights would not, of themselves, up and disappear. The complex bundle of rights merely become vulnerable to attack on the grounds that they are no longer specifically protected by the Second Amendment as they had always been thought to be. We would be back to floor fights in all the legislatures over every new proposal for either side. Just like now.

If the Second Amendment is suddenly found to only guarantee the gun "rights" of the state, or only the gun "rights" of the National Guard, or some sort of gun rights of organized collectives of people, then the Constitution suddenly falls almost totally silent on the gun rights of individual people and privately held arms.

Then the Ninth Amendment suddenly rears its forgotten head, and reminds us that any rights that aren't specifically granted (which the fall of the Second could be interpreted as), belong to the people. The people. That's us. It's hard to imagine a winning argument proposing that "the people" in the Ninth Amendment means the National Guard or the states:

"The enumeration in the Constitution of certain rights shall not be construed to deny or disparage others retained by the people."

Then too, states have their own Constitutions, most of which embed their own rendition of the Second Amendment, and often in far more direct terms. These would remain standing, wholly unaffected by any abrogation of the Bill of Rights' apparent protections of gun ownership. Consider Arizona's take, where I currently make my home:

> **"The right of the individual citizen to bear arms in defense of himself or the state shall not be impaired, but nothing in this section shall be construed as authorizing individuals or corporations to organize, maintain, or employ an armed body of men."**

It's hard to imagine a court exercising legitimate authority and determining that the Second Amendment does not mean what it always used to mean, with language like Arizona's in a Constitution drafted as late as 1912 (the last of the 48 contiguous states). If you consider each states' statements and their historical evolution—the list compiled by Professor Volokh of UCLA Law School is included in this book—it leaves little room for rationally arguing against the individual rights to arms. These may give rise to a debate on the degree to which privately held arms may be regulated, but they are simultaneously clear that such a right exists. For example:

> **Connecticut: Every citizen has a right to bear arms in defense of himself and the state.**

> **Delaware: A person has the right to keep and bear arms for the defense of self, family, home and State, and for hunting and recreational use.**

> **Wyoming: The right of citizens to bear arms in defense of themselves and of the state shall not be denied.**

Never forget that a complete collapse of 10% of the Bill of Rights (the Second Amendment) would leave untouched and unaffected the Constitutions of the individual States.

There is also the inconvenient question of what to do with all the existing gun laws. For just as laws regulate what you cannot do, they often stipulate what's allowed as well. Federal statutes would be subject to refreshed attack from pro-rights and anti-rights groups and individuals. But those 94,333 words of federal gun law describe how to become a gun dealer, what age you must reach before you can buy this gun or that gun, ammunition sales, and even how to buy, sell and trade fully automatic firearms like the Army and National Guard routinely use.

Statutes tell you how to walk into your local gun shop on a nice sunny day and buy pretty much anything that's legal to own, even if that legality was no more guaranteed by the Constitution than buying chewing gum or floor tile. Owning nice cars isn't specifically constitutionally guaranteed but you certainly can build quite a collection.

The analogy is a strong one. The Court cannot today meaningfully say you have a right to own a car, and be saying anything of substance, since that right is endemic to citizenry, and well manifested. It can only say you have no right to own a car, and affect change. Imagine a world gone to such a weird future place that for reasons of safety, or crime control, or speed control, or to avert some other perceived disaster, a Supreme Court might consider finding citizens have no right to own a car, and having to defend your commute to work on Ninth Amendment grounds.

The work necessary to unhinge all the federal and state laws that guarantee and administer private ownership of arms could take decades, against a populace that might appear somewhat less than receptive and who are, after all, heavily armed. All this contributes to making sudden dramatic change from the centuries-long status quo of a free fully armed public unlikely. The true specter of loss of our rights and freedom comes from more subtle foes:

> **There are more instances of the abridgment of the freedom of the people by the gradual and silent encroachment of those in power, than by violent and sudden usurpation.** –James Madison

> **The greatest dangers to liberty lurk in insidious encroachment by men of zeal, well-meaning but without understanding.**
> –Justice Louis Brandeis

> **If a nation values anything more than freedom, it will lose its freedom; and the irony of it is that if it is comfort or money that it values more, it will lose that, too.** –Somerset Maugham

> **The saddest epitaph which can be carved in memory of a vanished liberty is that it was lost because its possessors failed to stretch forth a saving hand while yet there was time.** –Justice George Sutherland

> **They that can give up liberty to obtain a little temporary safety deserve neither liberty nor safety.** –Benjamin Franklin

> **Guard with jealous attention the public liberty. Suspect everyone who approaches that jewel. Unfortunately, nothing will preserve it but downright force. Whenever you give up that force, you are ruined.**
> –Patrick Henry

> **Today, we need a nation of Minutemen: citizens who are not only prepared to take arms, but citizens who regard the preservation of freedom as the basic purpose of their daily life and who are willing to consciously work and sacrifice for that freedom.** –John F. Kennedy

> **The natural progress of things is for liberty to yield and government to gain ground.** –Thomas Jefferson

It kind of makes the Second Amendment seem a little less vulnerable, because ultimately, the right to defend what's yours doesn't depend on the Constitution for its existence, as *Cruikshank* makes so elegantly clear. It depends on the valiant courage of the people, and the forces of nature, which the Constitution merely recognizes in this particular case.

> **Life, liberty, and property do not exist because men have made laws. On the contrary, it was the fact that life, liberty, and property existed beforehand that caused men to make laws in the first place.**
> –Frederic Bastiat

Understanding the Citation System

When you first come upon Supreme Court cases you have to marvel at the craftsmanship. These are not idle musings, or the "opinions" that, like part of the anatomy, everyone has. No, these are meticulously crafted and scholarly renderings of the highest order. They actually take into account every case that has ever come before and which they feel has a bearing on the matter at hand, naming each one with exquisite precision. These citations are flatly inserted into the text with no other indication at all, which is startling to the newcomer, but eventually become second nature and are remarkably efficient. Just the system necessary to catalog each prior case, and the precedent it sets for the future, is a science and artform without equal.

Majority decisions become the law of the land, as much as any signed piece of legislation. You can only hope we have the most competent people up there acting to the highest order of performance. Though the majority carries the day, dissenting opinions are usually as well reasoned as the majority decisions, and often quite as compelling. These may even more closely reflect the prevailing beliefs of the public, if such a thing could be known. The dissenting Justices have a point, just not the numbers to sway the determining vote. In some cases, the dissent is compelling enough to sway future arguments. In more than one case, a previous dissent has been adopted verbatim in a later decision, making it law.

The overall logic and precision of the dissents can be as hard to ignore as the holding of the majority. They *both* have a point. It's like the old joke where, on hearing the defense argument, a trial judge says, "You're right," and then on hearing the prosecution, the judge says, "You're right." "But they can't both be right, your honor," the bailiff implores. "You're right too," comes the dry judicial reply.

A tad of tempest can occasionally be seen in the Justices' remarks toward each other's conclusions. The Justices circulate and review all the drafts before a final version is released, and sometimes address each others' concerns in the published document.

In producing the decisions, these individuals we call Justices don't merely decide the fate of the people in the case before them, although those folks' fates are as bindingly sealed as we can make them in this society. No, these nine people decide what the very fabric of America looks like, where the different weaves and colors and textures are to be placed. They are defining who we are as a people, and they bring to it a level of thought and care that is unmatched anywhere in our national being.

Threads entrusted to these individuals, in the cloth of twin hapless players drawn into a prolonged legal battle, comprise the greatest drama we have to proffer. The controversies are as fundamental as any we know.

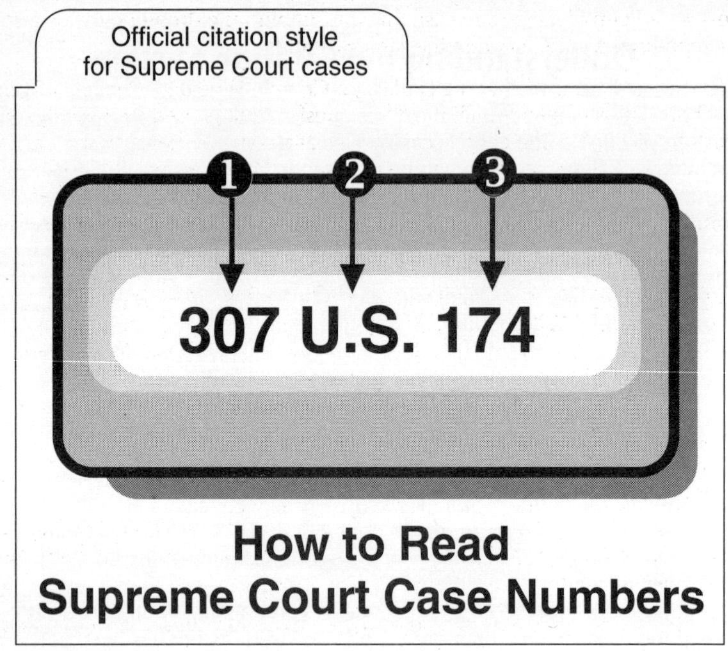

❶ The Volume Number **307** U.S. 174

Every Supreme Court case is printed and bound into an official set of books by the U.S. Government. Once bound into the set, the book number of each court case never changes, and becomes the first point of reference. The case cited above is found in volume number 307. The volume numbers are printed on the book spines.

❷ The Book Name Abbreviation 307 **U.S.** 174

Many of the numbering systems in U.S. law use a three-part notation like Supreme Court citations, where the middle element is an abbreviation for the name of the series of books. "U.S." stands for *United States Reports,* the official set of Supreme Court cases. Many of the abbreviations seem alien at first, with mixtures of numbers, capital and lower case letters, and punctuation no public school class ever hinted at, but they become eminently familiar with use, and you get to know most of the main ones by heart. Law libraries have lists of all the abbreviations used.

Since 1879, the bound set of Supreme Court decisions has been abbreviated simply "U.S.". The earlier sets, however, were known by the name of the person who assembled them. So the earliest case citations have a volume number, the name of the "reporter" and a page number. The very first case is *1 Dallas 1* and, as it was produced on a volunteer basis for a court that in its infancy didn't require written decisions, it isn't even a Supreme Court case—it's a Pennsylvania state case that this ambitious entrepreneur was also busy reporting, and included in the same volume.

The volume names following Dallas are Cranch, Wheaton, Peters, Howard, Black and Wallace, after which the "U.S." designation is used exclusively. No records from some of the earliest cases exist, and some of the earliest committed to writing are known to be unreliable. Wheaton was the first reporter to be federally paid, and is generally credited with upgrading the reporting system to a reliable professional science, a process that continues to this day.

Only one Supreme Court gun case in this book dates back before the "U.S." terminology, and that is 5 Wheaton 1, (abbreviated, as many of the reporters' names are, 5 Wheat. 1). It is the case of *Houston v. Moore*, 1820, that establishes when an individual person leaves private citizenship and becomes a member of the nationalized militia for purposes cited in the Constitution, subject to the President's call.

❸ The Page Number 307 U.S. **174**

Because each Supreme Court case is permanently bound into the official set of books, it's starting page number never changes, and this is the third and final element needed to zero in precisely on any given case.

To summarize, the case cited here will be found in volume 307 of *United States Reports* on page 174. What could be simpler.

When writing their opinions, the Supreme Court Justices refer frequently to other cases by using this system, and indicate the precise page they are referring to. So while the citation for this example case (which happens to be *U.S. v. Miller*, 1939) is correct as shown (307 U.S. 174), it would also be valid to cite 307 U.S. 177, to make a point about something that appears on that page, or more commonly (though perhaps less intuitively) 307 U.S. 174, 177. After identifying a case, subsequent consecutive references may simply refer back to a page number by simply saying, "at 177."

Also imbedded within many cases are indicators for the original page breaks, where they fall in the official version. This allows you to make sense of any internal references a case makes to its own pages. The "imbedded page numbers" are contained within brackets, are not part of the language of the decision, take the form, "[307 U.S. 176]" and are placed precisely where the original page breaks occur (making for some occasionally weird looking typesetting). For complex technological reasons, these are not included in *Supreme Court Gun Cases,* though you may see them in online or other printed versions of the cases.

Other Systems

The numbering system described above, used by the government, is the primary one used in this book. To keep things interesting, it turns out there are fully three printed editions of Supreme Court decisions, each with its own numbering system.

It seems that several companies have figured out that with something as important as the Supreme Court, there was room for more than just the government version, and it turns out they were right.

The other editions added their own head notes—summary comments preceding the official decision, prepared by the company instead of the Court's staff (the official summary is known as the *syllabus*). This is not law but is usually easier to read than the decisions and is all that some people review (including many lawyers, and often the news media) when trying to figure out the sometimes voluminous decisions of the Court.

So there are three different sets of head notes, all fascinating, all offering slightly different takes on what the cases are about. With the publication of this edition there is a fourth version, at least on the cases included here. Our system attempts to be the most convenient for use and reference by our audience, but only the official U.S. version counts in matters at law.

Each of the published editions is typeset slightly differently. Sometimes the break of a paragraph or the arrangement of the remarks affects the sense of the words. Sometimes the words themselves are different, though not by much (one version says "Justice Soandso dissents," another says "Justice Soandso dissenting,") and typos are known to occur in all three versions.

In what appears to be the worst typo in this entire set of cases, Justice Story quotes the Second Amendment in a proper context, yet refers to it as the Fifth, in *Houston v. Moore,* 18 U.S. (5 Wheat.) 1 (1820).

Whenever there is a discrepancy, the *United States Reports* version rules. That version is the most spacious, with large type and wide margins, taking four times the number of pages for the same content. For example, *Houston v. Moore* fills 75 pages in U.S., but only 19 pages in S.Ct., the West Co. edition.

Our version attempts to be as compact as reasonable, using slightly less ink on smaller characters, and conveniently saving trees in the process. By editing each case to its essentials for the theme of this book, *Houston v. Moore* is a scant three pages in SCGC. This is a sword that cuts both ways, and if you haven't read the unedited originals, you don't know what you're missing. The very same financial forces that motivate other commercial publishers and which the government seems to more or less ignore, affect Bloomfield Press and its comparatively small scope of operations.

When making citations,
the official government edition is:
United States Reports
307 U.S. 174

The West Co. edition is:
Supreme Court Reporter
59 S.Ct. 816

The Lawyer's Edition is:
United States Supreme Court Reports
83 L.Ed. 1206

The citations above all refer to the same case, *United States v. Miller*, 1939, and in many contexts you will see this cited as simply *Miller.* Sometimes cross-references within a case will include more than one citation to be thorough. Citations appear without warning or controlling punctuation, imbedded in the text right where they apply, in an off-putting, confusing but highly efficient way. Footnote reference numbers are similarly bluntly inserted. Hey, they didn't ask me if I thought it made good sense. Try to think of it as style.

To the novice eye, the text has an imposing impossible look to it. Once you acclimatize however, the eye has a natural ability to scan past the numbers and follow the threads of text. When you get *really* good at it, you take notice of the cite, quickly recollect the essence of the case it refers to, and read on, adding an entire dimension to your understanding of these marvelous writings.

Rumor has it that law students and even attorneys use whatever's available online, and then cite to *U.S. Reports*. The difference between the versions can be pronounced, and though we considered documenting some of the more interesting anomalies we found, we left that task for someone else.

Bloomfield Press refers to its own books by acronyms:

Supreme Court Gun Cases: **SCGC**

Gun Laws of America: **GLOA**
(unabridged edition of federal firearms statutes)

The Arizona Gun Owner's Guide: **AGOG**
(comprehensive guide to state firearms laws)

and when specifying a page:
SCGC-357, GLOA-223, AGOG-38

Another great challenge for newcomers, or the average member of the gun hobby, is all the Latin that gets thrown around in these decisions. As if 100-year-old legalese isn't bad enough, the Justices rely on a language that has been on life-support for 2,000 years for added clarity. The obvious solution, as I began this project, was to build a glossary of terms. When it became obvious I was recreating *Black's Law Dictionary,* I instead got one, and you should too.

With time and care you can spot the Court's bewildering uses of actual English words like defendant, respondent, petitioner, prisoner, plaintiff, plaintiff in error, and victim to mean the same thing. Don't be surprised to learn that some cases cannot be read, they must be studied. In a few, I had to make a cast of characters and draw diagrams to get it straight. Don't worry, be happy. Look at it this way—it keeps life interesting.

The Right to Keep and Bear Arms As Provided for in State Constitutions

Compiled by *Prof. Eugene Volokh*, UCLA Law School

Editor's Note: Can anything be deduced about the Founders' intentions, the Supreme Court's decisions, or the current rights Americans have to arms, from the firearm provisions of the state Constitutions? One must assume the Supreme Court Justices would be aware of these state constitutional provisions, being adopted and amended even as the High Court was deciding case after case with guns in the mix. The assembled statements below provide a backdrop against which the cases in this book may be gauged.

Alabama: That every citizen has a right to bear arms in defense of himself and the state. Art. I, § 26 (enacted 1819, art. I, § 23, with "defence" in place of "defense," spelling changed 1901).

Alaska: A well-regulated militia being necessary to the security of a free state, the right of the people to keep and bear arms shall not be infringed. The individual right to keep and bear arms shall not be denied or infringed by the State or a political subdivision of the State. Art. I, § 19 (first sentence enacted 1959, second sentence added 1994).

Arizona: The right of the individual citizen to bear arms in defense of himself or the State shall not be impaired, but nothing in this section shall be construed as authorizing individuals or corporations to organize, maintain, or employ an armed body of men. Art. II, § 26 (enacted 1912).

Arkansas: The citizens of this State shall have the right to keep and bear arms for their common defense. Art. II, § 5 (enacted 1868, art. I, § 5).

1836: "That the free white men of this State shall have a right to keep and to bear arms for their common defence." Art. II, § 21.

California: No provision.

Colorado: The right of no person to keep and bear arms in defense of his home, person and property, or in aid of the civil power when thereto legally summoned, shall be called in question; but nothing herein contained shall be construed to justify the practice of carrying concealed weapons. Art. II, § 13 (enacted 1876, art. II, § 13).

Connecticut: Every citizen has a right to bear arms in defense of himself and the state. Art. I, § 15 (enacted 1818, art. I, § 17). The original 1818 text came from the Mississippi Constitution of 1817.

Delaware: A person has the right to keep and bear arms for the defense of self, family, home and State, and for hunting and recreational use. Art. I, § 20 (enacted 1987).

Florida: (a) The right of the people to keep and bear arms in defense of themselves and of the lawful authority of the state shall not be infringed, except that the manner of bearing arms may be regulated by law.

(b) There shall be a mandatory period of three days, excluding weekends and legal holidays, between the purchase and delivery at retail of any handgun. For the purposes of this section, "purchase" means the transfer of money or other valuable consideration to the retailer, and "handgun" means a firearm capable of being carried and used by one hand, such as a pistol or revolver. Holders of a concealed weapon permit as prescribed in Florida law shall not be subject to the provisions of this paragraph.

(c) The legislature shall enact legislation implementing subsection (b) of this section, effective no later than December 31, 1991, which shall provide that anyone violating the provisions of subsection (b) shall be guilty of a felony.

(d) This restriction shall not apply to a trade in of another handgun. Art. I, § 8 (sections (b)-(d) added in 1990).

1838: "That the free white men of this State shall have a right to keep and to bear arms for their common defence." Art. I, § 21.

1865: Clause omitted.

1868: "The people shall have the right to bear arms in defence of themselves and of the lawful authority of the State." Art. I, § 22.

1885: "The right of the people to bear arms in defence of themselves and the lawful authority of the State, shall not be infringed, but the Legislature may prescribe the manner in which they may be borne." Art. I, § 20.

1968: "The right of the people to keep and bear arms in defense of themselves and of the lawful authority of the state shall not be infringed, except that the manner of bearing arms may be regulated by law."

Georgia: The right of the people to keep and bear arms shall not be infringed, but the General Assembly shall have power to prescribe the manner in which arms may be borne. Art. I, § 1, ¶ VIII (enacted 1877, art. I, § XXII).

1865: "A well-regulated militia, being necessary to the security of a free State, the right of the people to keep and bear arms shall not be infringed." Art. I, § 4.

1868: "A well-regulated militia being necessary to the security of a free people, the right of the people to keep and bear arms shall not be infringed; but the general assembly shall have power to prescribe by law the manner in which arms may be borne." Art. I, § 14.

Hawaii: A well regulated militia being necessary to the security of a free state, the right of the people to keep and bear arms shall not be infringed. Art. I, § 17 (enacted 1950).

Idaho: The people have the right to keep and bear arms, which right shall not be abridged; but this provision shall not prevent the passage of laws to govern the carrying of weapons concealed on the person nor prevent passage of legislation providing minimum sentences for crimes committed while in possession of a firearm, nor prevent the passage of legislation providing penalties for the possession of firearms by a convicted felon, nor prevent the passage of any legislation punishing the use of a firearm. No law shall impose licensure, registration or special taxation on the ownership or possession of firearms or ammunition. Nor shall any law permit the confiscation of firearms, except those actually used in the commission of a felony. Art. I, § 11 (enacted 1978).

1889: "The people have the right to bear arms for their security and defense; but the Legislature shall regulate the exercise of this right by law." Art. I, § 11.

Illinois: Subject only to the police power, the right of the individual citizen to keep and bear arms shall not be infringed. Art. I, § 22 (enacted 1970).

Indiana: The people shall have a right to bear arms, for the defense of themselves and the State. Art. I, § 32 (enacted 1851, art. I, § 32).

1816: That the people have a right to bear arms for the defense of themselves and the State, and that the military shall be kept in strict subordination to the civil power. Art. I, § 20.

Iowa: No provision.

Kansas: The people have the right to bear arms for their defense and security; but standing armies, in time of peace, are dangerous to liberty, and shall not be tolerated, and the military shall be in strict subordination to the civil power. Bill of Rights, § 4 (enacted 1859, art. I, § 4).

Kentucky: All men are, by nature, free and equal, and have certain inherent and inalienable rights, among which may be reckoned:

First: The right of enjoying and defending their lives and liberties. . . .

Seventh: The right to bear arms in defense of themselves and of the State, subject to the power of the General Assembly to enact laws to prevent persons from carrying concealed weapons. §1 (enacted 1891).

1792: "That the right of the citizens to bear arms in defense of themselves and the State shall not be questioned." Art. XII, § 23.

1799: "That the rights of the citizens to bear arms in defense of themselves and the State shall not be questioned." Art. X, § 23.

1850: "That the rights of the citizens to bear arms in defense of themselves and the State shall not be questioned; but the General Assembly may pass laws to prevent persons from carrying concealed arms." Art. XIII, § 25.

Louisiana: The right of each citizen to keep and bear arms shall not be abridged, but this provision shall not prevent the passage of laws to prohibit the carrying of weapons concealed on the person. Art. I, § 11 (enacted 1974).

1879: "A well regulated militia being necessary to the security of a free State, the right of the people to keep and bear arms shall not be abridged. This shall not prevent the passage of laws to punish those who carry weapons concealed." Art. 3.

Maine: Every citizen has a right to keep and bear arms and this right shall never be questioned. Art. I, § 16 (enacted 1987, after a collective-rights interpretation of the original provision).

1819: "Every citizen has a right to keep and bear arms for the common defence; and this right shall never be questioned." Art. I, § 16.

Maryland: No provision.

Massachusetts: The people have a right to keep and to bear arms for the common defence. And as, in time of peace, armies are dangerous to liberty, they ought not to be maintained without the consent of the legislature; and the military power shall always be held in an exact subordination to the civil authority, and be governed by it. Pt. 1, art. 17 (enacted 1780).

Michigan: Every person has a right to keep and bear arms for the defense of himself and the state. Art. I, § 6 (enacted 1835).

Minnesota: No provision.

Mississippi: The right of every citizen to keep and bear arms in defense of his home, person, or property, or in aid of the civil power when thereto legally summoned, shall not be called in question, but the legislature may regulate or forbid carrying concealed weapons. Art. III, § 12 (enacted 1890, art. 3, § 12).

1817: "Every citizen has a right to bear arms, in defence of himself and the State." Art. I, § 23.

1832: "Every citizen has a right to bear arms in defence of himself and of the State." Art. I, § 23.

1868: "All persons shall have a right to keep and bear arms for their defence." Art. I, § 15.

Missouri: That the right of every citizen to keep and bear arms in defense of his home, person and property, or when lawfully summoned in aid of the civil power, shall not be questioned; but this shall not justify the wearing of concealed weapons. Art. I, § 23 (enacted 1945).

1820: "That the people have the right peaceably to assemble for their common good, and to apply to those vested with the powers of government for redress of grievances by petition or remonstrance; and that their right to bear arms in defence of themselves and of the State cannot be questioned." Art. XIII, § 3.

1865: Same as above, but with "the lawful authority of the State" instead of "the State." Art. I, § 8.

1875: "That the right of no citizen to keep and bear arms in defense of his home, person and property, or in aid of the civil power, when thereto legally summoned, shall be called into question; but nothing herein contained is intended to justify the practice of wearing concealed weapons." Art. II, § 17.

Montana: The right of any person to keep or bear arms in defense of his own home, person, and property, or in aid of the civil power when thereto legally summoned, shall not be called in question, but nothing herein contained shall be held to permit the carrying of concealed weapons. Art. II, § 12 (enacted 1889).

Nebraska: All persons are by nature free and independent, and have certain inherent and inalienable rights; among these are life, liberty, the pursuit of happiness, and the right to keep and bear arms for security or defense of self, family, home, and others, and for lawful common defense, hunting, recreational use, and all other lawful purposes, and such rights shall not be denied or infringed by the state or any subdivision thereof. To secure these rights, and the protection of property, governments are instituted among people, deriving their just powers from the consent of the governed. Art. I, § 1 (right to keep and bear arms enacted 1988).

Nevada: Every citizen has the right to keep and bear arms for security and defense, for lawful hunting and recreational use and for other lawful purposes. Art. I, § 11(1) (enacted 1982).

New Hampshire: All persons have the right to keep and bear arms in defense of themselves, their families, their property and the state. Pt. 1, art. 2-a (enacted 1982).

New Jersey: No provision.

New Mexico: No law shall abridge the right of the citizen to keep and bear arms for security and defense, for lawful hunting and recreational use and for other lawful purposes, but nothing herein shall be held to permit the carrying of concealed weapons. No municipality or county shall regulate, in any way, an incident of the right to keep and bear arms. Art. II, § 6 (first sentence enacted in 1971, second sentence added 1986).

1912: "The people have the right to bear arms for their security and defense, but nothing herein shall be held to permit the carrying of concealed weapons."

New York: No provision.

North Carolina: A well regulated militia being necessary to the security of a free State, the right of the people to keep and bear arms shall not be infringed; and, as standing armies in time of peace are dangerous to liberty, they shall not be maintained, and the military shall be kept under strict subordination to, and governed by, the civil power. Nothing herein shall justify the practice of carrying concealed weapons, or prevent the General Assembly from enacting penal statutes against that practice. Art. 1, § 30 (enacted 1971).

1776: "That the people have a right to bear arms, for the defence of the State; and, as standing armies, in time of peace, are dangerous to liberty, they ought not to be kept up; and that the military should be kept under strict subordination to, and governed by, the civil power." Bill of Rights, § XVII.

1868: "A well-regulated militia being necessary to the security of a free State, the right of the people to keep and bear arms shall not be infringed; and, as standing armies, in time of peace, are dangerous to liberty, they ought not to be kept up, and the military should be kept under strict subordination to, and governed by, the civil power." Art. I, § 24.

1875: Same as 1868, but added "Nothing herein contained shall justify the practice of carrying concealed weapons, or prevent the Legislature from enacting penal statutes against said practice."

North Dakota: All individuals are by nature equally free and independent and have certain inalienable rights, among which are those of enjoying and defending life and liberty; acquiring, possessing and protecting property and reputation; pursuing and obtaining safety and happiness; and to keep and bear arms for the defense of their person, family, property, and the state, and for lawful hunting, recreational, and other lawful purposes, which shall not be infringed. Art. I, § 1 (right to keep and bear arms enacted 1984).

Ohio: The people have the right to bear arms for their defense and security; but standing armies, in time of peace, are dangerous to liberty, and shall not be kept up; and the military shall be in strict subordination to the civil power. Art. I, § 4 (enacted 1851).

1802: "That the people have a right to bear arms for the defence of themselves and the State; and as standing armies, in time of peace, are dangerous to liberty, they shall not be kept up, and that the military shall be kept under strict subordination to the civil power." Art. VIII, § 20.

Oklahoma: The right of a citizen to keep and bear arms in defense of his home, person, or property, or in aid of the civil power, when thereunto legally summoned, shall never be prohibited; but nothing herein contained shall prevent the Legislature from regulating the carrying of weapons. Art. II, § 26 (enacted 1907).

Oregon: The people shall have the right to bear arms for the defence of themselves, and the State, but the Military shall be kept in strict subordination to the civil power[.] Art. I, § 27 (enacted 1857, art. I, § 28).

Pennsylvania: The right of the citizens to bear arms in defence of themselves and the State shall not be questioned. Art. 1, § 21 (enacted 1790, art. IX, § 21).

1776: That the people have a right to bear arms for the defence of themselves and the state; and as standing armies in the time of peace are dangerous to liberty, they ought not to be kept up; And that the military should be kept under strict subordination, to, and governed by, the civil power. Declaration of Rights, cl. XIII.

Rhode Island: The right of the people to keep and bear arms shall not be infringed. Art. I, § 22 (enacted 1842).

South Carolina: A well regulated militia being necessary to the security of a free State, the right of the people to keep and bear arms shall not be infringed. As, in times of peace, armies are dangerous to liberty, they shall not be maintained without the consent of the General Assembly. The military power of the State shall always be held in subordination to the civil authority and be governed by it. Art. 1, § 20 (enacted 1895).

1868: "The people have a right to keep and bear arms for the common defence. As, in times of peace . . . ." Art. I, § 28.

South Dakota: The right of the citizens to bear arms in defense of themselves and the state shall not be denied. Art. VI, § 24 (enacted 1889).

Tennessee: That the citizens of this State have a right to keep and to bear arms for their common defense; but the Legislature shall have power, by law, to regulate the wearing of arms with a view to prevent crime. Art. I, § 26 (enacted 1870).

1796: "That the freemen of this State have a right to keep and bear arms for their common defence." Art. XI, § 26.

1834: "That the freemen of this State have a right to keep and bear arms for their common defence." Art. I, § 26.

Texas: Every citizen shall have the right to keep and bear arms in the lawful defense of himself or the State; but the Legislature shall have power, by law, to regulate the wearing of arms, with a view to prevent crime. Art. I, § 23 (enacted 1876).

1836: "Every citizen shall have the right to bear arms in defence of himself and the republic. The military shall at all times and in all cases be subordinate to the civil power." Declaration of Rights, cl. 14.

1845: "Every citizen shall have the right to keep and bear arms in lawful defence of himself or the State." Art. I, § 13.

1868: "Every person shall have the right to keep and bear arms in the lawful defence of himself or the State, under such regulations as the legislature may prescribe." Art. I, § 13.

Utah: The individual right of the people to keep and bear arms for security and defense of self, family, others, property, or the state, as well as for other lawful purposes shall not be infringed; but nothing herein shall prevent the legislature from defining the lawful use of arms. Art. I, § 6 (enacted 1984).

1896: "The people have the right to bear arms for their security and defense, but the legislature may regulate the exercise of this right by law."

Vermont: That the people have a right to bear arms for the defence of themselves and the State -- and as standing armies in time of peace are dangerous to liberty, they ought not to be kept up; and that the military should be kept under strict subordination to and governed by the civil power. Ch. I, art. 16 (enacted 1777, ch. I, art. 15).

Virginia: That a well regulated militia, composed of the body of the people, trained to arms, is the proper, natural, and safe defense of a free state, therefore, the right of the people to keep and bear arms shall not be infringed; that standing armies, in time of peace, should be avoided as dangerous to liberty; and that in all cases the military should be under strict subordination to, and governed by, the civil power. Art. I, § 13 (enacted 1776 without explicit right to keep and bear arms; "therefore, the right to keep and bear arms shall not be infringed" added in 1971).

Washington: The right of the individual citizen to bear arms in defense of himself, or the state, shall not be impaired, but nothing in this section shall be construed as authorizing individuals or corporations to organize, maintain or employ an armed body of men. Art. I, § 24 (enacted 1889).

West Virginia: A person has the right to keep and bear arms for the defense of self, family, home and state, and for lawful hunting and recreational use. Art. III, § 22 (enacted 1986).

Wisconsin: No provision.

Wyoming: The right of citizens to bear arms in defense of themselves and of the state shall not be denied. Art. I, § 24 (enacted 1889).

Firearms Law Deskbook

By Stephen P. Halbrook, Ph.D.

Noted Second Amendment attorney Stephen Halbrook's Firearms Law Deskbook *provides comprehensive analyses of federal and state firearms laws for legal practitioners. It shows defense attorneys how to use an array of defenses to federal, state and local gun control laws. It directs prosecutors to the law that can help them bring an indictment. It is an important tool and source of tactics to attorneys and prosecutors nationwide, though it is a virtual secret as far as the public is concerned. Reproduced below, by permission of West Group, is the first chapter of this amazing book, which looks at the overall jurisprudence of the Second Amendment, including many Supreme Court precedents. Annual updates to the* Deskbook *are available from West Group, see their contact info on page two of this book.*

Right to Keep and Bear Arms

Sec. 1:1 General rule

The Second Amendment to the United States Constitution provides: "A well regulated Militia, being necessary to the security of a free State, the right of the people to keep and bear Arms, shall not be infringed." Historically, the Second Amendment was adopted as an individual right so that the people could maintain a balance with government, which the framers believed had the potential for oppression. Supreme Court jurisprudence establishes that militia arms are protected and that "the people" include individuals. However, in the last quarter of a century, some appellate courts have interpreted the Second Amendment to protect only a "collective" right of states to maintain militias, not an individual right.

The Fourteenth Amendment was intended to protect federal Bill of Rights guarantees from state deprivation. The Supreme Court has not resolved whether the Second Amendment is incorporated into the Fourteenth Amendment so as to prevent the states from infringing on the right to keep and bear arms.

Some forty-three state constitutions protect the right to keep and bear arms for defense of self and state or other purposes. In a number of instances, state courts have declared statutes or ordinances to violate these guarantees. State courts differ on the extent to which the right is considered to be fundamental.

Sec. 1:2 Intent of the framers

The Supreme Court has held that "when we do have evidence that a particular law would have offended the Framers, we have not hesitated to invalidate it on that ground alone."[1] The Constitution must be construed as

1. *Minneapolis Star and Tribune Co. v. Minnesota Com'r of Revenue*, 460 U.S. 575, 584, 103 S. Ct. 1365, 75 L. Ed. 2d 295 (1983).

intended by the framers and by the people adopting it.[2] "In the construction of the language of the Constitution . . . we are to place ourselves as nearly as possible in the condition of the men who framed that instrument. Undoubtedly, the framers . . . had for a long time been absorbed in considering the arbitrary encroachments of the Crown on the liberty of the subject."[3]

When the Constitution was proposed in 1787 without a bill of rights, the federalists argued that one was unnecessary, since Congress had no enumerated power to control rights such as a free press and bearing arms. Keeping and bearing arms was seen as an individual right which would not be infringed.[4]

In *The Federalist Papers,* James Madison, contending that "the ultimate authority . . . resides in the people alone,"[5] predicted that encroachments by the federal government would provoke "plans of resistance" and an "appeal to a trial of force."[6] To a regular army of the United States government "would be opposed a militia amounting to near half a million citizens with arms in their hands." Alluding to "the advantage of being armed, which the Americans possess over the people of almost every other nation," Madison continued, "Notwithstanding the military establishments in the several kingdoms of Europe, which are carried as far as the public resources will bear, the governments are afraid to trust the people with arms."[7] If the people were armed and organized into militia, "the throne of every tyranny in Europe would be speedily overturned in spite of the legions which surround it."[8]

Noah Webster, the influential federalist whose name still appears on dictionaries, stated:

> Before a standing army can rule, the people must be disarmed; as they are in almost every kingdom in Europe. The supreme power in America cannot enforce unjust laws by the sword; because the whole body of the people are armed, and constitute a force superior to any band of regular troops that can be, on any pretence, raised in the United States.[9]

The antifederalists insisted that these promises be made in writing. Advocating a bill of rights, Richard Henry Lee wrote that "to preserve liberty, it is essential that the whole body of the people always possess arms, and be taught alike, especially when young, how to use them."[10] The Supreme Court has noted: "The remarks of Richard Henry Lee are typical of the rejoinders of the

---

2. *Whitman v. National Bank of Oxford,* 176 U.S. 559, 20 S. Ct. 477, 44 L. Ed. 587 (1900). *See Puerto Rico v. Branstad,* 483 U.S. 219, 229, 107 S. Ct. 2802, 2809, 97 L. Ed. 2d 187 (1987).

3. *Ex parte Bain,* 121 U.S. 1, 12, 7 S. Ct. 781, 30 L. Ed. 849 (1887).

4. On the historical background of the Second Amendment, *see* Halbrook, *That Every Man Be Armed: The Evolution of a Constitutional Right* 7-54 (1984) (political classics and common law); Malcolm, *To Keep and Bear Arms: The Origins of an Anglo-American Right* (1994) (common law); Halbrook, "Encroachments of the Crown on the Liberty of the Subject: Pre-Revolutionary Origins of the Second Amendment," 15 Univ. Dayton L. Rev. 91 (1989) (colonial origins); Halbrook, "The Right of the People or the Power of the State: Bearing Arms, Arming Militias, and the Second Amendment," 26 Valparaiso U. L. Rev. 131 (1991) (proposal and ratification of Second Amendment). For congressional interpretations of the Second Amendment, see Halbrook, "Personal Security, Personal Liberty, and 'the Constitutional Right to Bear Arms': Visions of the Framers of the Fourteenth Amendment," 5 Seton Hall Const. L.J. 341 (Spring 1995); Halbrook, "Congress Interprets the Second Amendment: Declarations by a Co-Equal Branch on the Individual Right to Keep and Bear Arms," 62 Tenn. L. Rev. 597 (Spring 1995).

5. *The Federalist* No. 46, Madison, Hamilton, & Jay, *The Federalist Papers* 294 (Arlington House ed. n.d.).

6. *Id.* at 298.

7. *Id.* at 299.

8. *Id.* at 300.

9. Webster, "An Examination into the Leading Principles of the Federal Constitution," in *Pamphlets on the Constitution of the United States* 56 (Ford ed. 1888).

10. Lee, *Additional Letters from the Federal Farmer* 170 (1788).

Antifederalists. . . . The concerns voiced by the Antifederalists led to the adoption of the Bill of Rights. . . . The fears of the Antifederalists were well founded."[11]

Ten days after James Madison introduced the Bill of Rights in the U.S. House of Representatives in 1789, federalist leader Tench Coxe wrote of what became the Second Amendment:

> As civil rulers, not having their duty to the people duly before them, may attempt to tyrannize, and as the military forces which must be occasionally raised to defend our country, might pervert their power to the injury of their fellow-citizens, the people are confirmed by the next article in their right to keep and bear their private arms.[12]

Madison endorsed Coxe's analysis, which was reprinted without contradiction.[13]

What became the Second Amendment was seen as embodying the proposal drafted by Samuel Adams "that the said constitution be never construed to authorize congress . . . to prevent the people of the United States, who are peaceable citizens, from keeping their own arms."[14]

St. George Tucker, the first major commentator on the Bill of Rights,[15] explained the Second Amendment as follows: "The right of self-defense is the first law of nature. . . . Wherever . . . the right of the people to keep and bear arms is, under any color or pretext whatsoever, prohibited, liberty, if not already annihilated, is on the brink of destruction."[16]

Tactical Tip:

Unlike other Bill of Rights provisions, the intent of the Framers of the Second Amendment is not definitively analyzed in any published judicial decision, including any by the Supreme Court. Ample scholarly sources are available in the *Index to Legal Periodicals*. It may be unpredictable whether judicial aversion to the Second Amendment in a specific case will occasion or preclude actual reliance on the intent of the framers.

Sec. 1:3 Jurisprudence of the second amendment

The U.S. Supreme Court has analyzed the Second Amendment as guaranteeing an individual right to keep and bear arms.[17] It has also held that explicitly guaranteed constitutional rights are fundamental. However, Supreme Court jurisprudence on the Second Amendment is undeveloped, and bears a resemblance to the scanty jurisprudence on the First Amendment until the

---

11. *Minneapolis Star and Tribune Co. v. Minnesota Com'r of Revenue*, 460 U.S. 575, 584, 103 S. Ct. 1365, 75 L. Ed. 2d 295 (1983).

12. "Remarks on the First Part of the Amendments to the Federal Constitution," Federal Gazette, June 18, 1789, at 2, col. 1. *See* Halbrook and Kopel, "Tench Coxe and the Right to Keep and Bear Arms, 1787-1823," 7 William & Mary Bill of Rights Journal, Issue 2, 347-99 (Feb. 1999).

13. *See* 12 *Madison Papers* at 239-40, 257 (1979).

14. Independent Gazetteer (Philadelphia), Sept. 9, 1789, at 2, col. 2.

15. *New York Times Co. v. Sullivan*, 376 U.S. 254, 296-97, 84 S. Ct. 710, 11 L. Ed. 2d 686, 95 A.L.R.2d 1412 (1964).

16. Tucker, 1 *Blackstone's Commentaries* 300 (1803). Henry St. George Tucker, another major commentator, wrote that "the right of bearing arms" was one of the "protections or barriers [which] have been erected which serve to maintain inviolate the three primary rights of personal security, personal liberty, and private property." Tucker, 1 *Commentaries on the Laws of Virginia* 43 (1831).

17. D. Kopel, "The Supreme Court's Thirty-Five *Other* Gun Cases: What the Supreme Court Has Said About the Second Amendment," 28 St. Louis Univ. Public Law Rev., No. 1, 99 (1999).

1920s.[18] On three occasions when the right was perceived as being endangered, Congress passed statutes reaffirming the right as a fundamental, individual liberty which may not be infringed.

From the time the Second Amendment was adopted by Congress in 1789 and ratified by the states in 1791, little controversy surrounded the right to keep and bear arms. In the Dred Scott decision, the Supreme Court conceded that if African-Americans were citizens, they would be "entitled to the privileges and immunities of citizens" and would be exempt from the special "police regulations" applicable to them. "It would give to persons of the negro race, who were recognized as citizens in any one State of the Union, the right to enter every other State whenever they pleased, singly or in companies . . .; and it would give them the full liberty of speech . . .; to hold public meetings upon political affairs, and to keep and carry arms wherever they went."[19]

When the slaves were freed as a result of the Civil War, the southern states reenacted the slave codes which made it illegal for blacks to exercise basic civil rights, including the keeping and bearing of firearms. Congress responded by passing the Freedmen's Bureau Act of 1866, which provided:

> [T]he right . . . to have full and equal benefit of all laws and proceedings concerning personal liberty, personal security, and the acquisition, enjoyment, and disposition of estate, real and personal, including the constitutional right to bear arms, shall be secured to and enjoyed by all the citizens of such State or district without respect to race or color or previous condition of slavery.[20]

> Since it passed as a veto override, the Act was approved by over two-thirds of Congress. The same two-thirds of Congress adopted the Fourteenth Amendment, which was intended to protect the above rights.

At the end of Reconstruction, the Supreme Court stated that the rights of the people "peaceably to assemble for lawful purposes" and "of bearing arms for a lawful purpose" were not "granted" by the Constitution because they existed long before its adoption.[21] The amendments which recognize these rights serve to "restrict the powers of the National government."[22] A later opinion again recognized "the right of the people to keep and bear arms" and repeated that the Second Amendment is a limitation "upon the power of Congress and the National government."[23]

Robertson v. Baldwin analyzed regulation of Bill of Rights freedoms as follows:

> The law is perfectly well settled that the first ten Amendments to the constitution, commonly known as the Bill of Rights, were not intended to lay down any novel principle of government, but simply to embody certain guarantees and immunities which we had inherited from our English ancestors, and which had from time immemorial been subject to certain well-recognized exceptions arising from the

18. van Alstyne, "The Second Amendment and the Personal Right to Arms," 43 Duke L.J. 1236, 1238-41 (1994).

19. *Dred Scott v. Sandford*, 60 U.S. 393, 19 How. 393, 15 L. Ed. 691 (1856). "Nor can Congress deny the people the right to keep and bear arms, nor the right to trial by jury, nor compel anyone to be a witness against himself in a criminal proceeding." *Dred Scott v. Sandford*, 60 U.S. 393, 19 How. 393, 15 L. Ed. 691 (1856).

20. 14 Statutes at Large 176-77 (July 16, 1866). For the legislative history of this provision, *see* Halbrook, "Personal Security, Personal Liberty, and 'the Constitutional Right to Bear Arms': Visions of the Framers of the Fourteenth Amendment," 5 Seton Hall Const. L.J. 341 (Spring 1995).

21. *U.S. v. Cruikshank*, 92 U.S. 542, 551, 23 L. Ed. 588 (1875).

22. *Id.* at 553.

23. *Presser v. People of State of Ill.*, 116 U.S. 252, 265, 6 S. Ct. 580, 29 L. Ed. 615 (1886). *Miller v. State of Texas*, 153 U.S. 535, 538, 14 S. Ct. 874, 38 L. Ed. 812 (1894), repeats that the Second and Fourth Amendments restrict "the Federal power."

> necessities of the case. In incorporating those principles into the fundamental law there was no intention of disregarding the exceptions, which continued to be recognized as if they had been formally expressed. Thus, the freedom of speech and of the press (article 1) does not permit the publication of libels, blasphemous or indecent articles or other publications injurious to public morals or private reputations; the right of the people to keep and bear arms (article 2) is not infringed by laws prohibiting the carrying of concealed weapons.[24]

In *United States v. Miller*,[25] the Court avoided determining whether a short-barreled shotgun may be taxed and subjected to stringent registration requirements under the National Firearms Act consistent with the Second Amendment. The district court had declared the Act unconstitutional on its face as in violation of the Second Amendment,[26] and thus no evidence was in the record that such shotgun was an ordinary military arm. The Supreme Court remanded the case for fact-finding based on the following:

> In the absence of any evidence tending to show that possession or use of a "shotgun having a barrel of less than eighteen inches in length" at this time has some reasonable relationship to the preservation or efficiency of a well regulated militia, we cannot say that the Second Amendment guarantees the right to keep and bear such an instrument. Certainly it is not within judicial notice that this weapon is any part of the ordinary military equipment or that its use could contribute to the common defense. *Aymette v. State*, 21 Tenn. 154, 2 Hum. 154, 158, 1840 WL 1554 (1840).[27]

The *Miller* court did not suggest that the possessor must be a member of the militia or National Guard, asking only whether the arms could have militia use. The private, individual character of the right protected by the Second Amendment went unquestioned.

The *Aymette* opinion was a Tennessee case which stated on the page cited above by the U.S. Supreme Court:

> [T]he *arms*, the right to keep which is secured, are such as are usually employed in civilized warfare, and that constitute the ordinary military equipment. If the citizens have these arms in their hands, they are prepared in the best possible manner to repel any encroachments on their rights by those in authority.[28]

Referring to the militia clause of the Constitution, the Supreme Court stated that "to assure the continuation and render possible the effectiveness of such forces the declaration and guarantee of the Second Amendment were made."[29]

The court then surveyed colonial and state militia laws to demonstrate that "the Militia comprised all males physically capable of acting in concert for the common defense" and that "these men were expected to appear bearing arms supplied by themselves and of the kind in common use at the time."[30]

The *Miller* court noted that most states "have adopted provisions touching the right to keep and bear arms" but that differences in language meant variations in "the scope of the right guaranteed."[31]

---

24. *Robertson v. Baldwin*, 165 U.S. 275, 281-82, 17 S. Ct. 326, 41 L. Ed. 715 (1897).
25. *U.S. v. Miller*, 307 U.S. 174, 59 S. Ct. 816, 83 L. Ed. 1206 (1939).
26. 26 F. Supp. 1002, 1003 (W.D. Ark. 1939).
27. 307 U.S. at 178. Since no factual record was made in the trial court that a "sawed-off" shotgun could have militia uses, and defendant Miller did not even appear and file a brief in the Supreme Court, the Court did not consider whether the tax and related registration requirements of the National Firearms Act violated the Second Amendment.
28. *Aymette v. State*, 21 Tenn. 154, 2 Hum. 154, 158, 1840 WL 1554 (1840).
29. 307 U.S. at 178.
30. *Id.* at 179.
31. *Id.* at 182.

State precedents cited by the court are divided mainly over whether the respective state guarantees protect all arms or only militia-type arms.[32]

Miller also cites approvingly the commentaries of Joseph Story and Thomas M. Cooley.[33] Justice Story stated:

> The right of the citizens to keep and bear arms has justly been considered, as the palladium of the liberties of the republic; since it offers a strong moral check against usurpation and arbitrary power of the rulers; and will generally, even if these are successful in the first instance, enable the people to resist and triumph over them.[34]

Judge Cooley stated in the reference cited by *Miller:*

> Among the other safeguards to liberty should be mentioned the right of the people to keep and bear arms. . . . The alternative to a standing army is 'a well-regulated militia'; but this cannot exist unless the people are trained to bearing arms. The federal and state constitutions therefore provide that the right of the people to bear arms shall not be infringed.[35]

Rifles would seem to pass the *Miller* test because they are appropriate for militia use, even though the Armed Forces currently use fully automatic machine guns.[36] Pistols and shotguns have also always been militia equipment.

In 1941, two years after *Miller* was decided, Congress enacted legislation to authorize the President to requisition broad categories of property with military uses from the private sector on payment of fair compensation. Known as the

---

32. *U.S. v. Miller*, 307 U.S. 174, 182, 59 S. Ct. 816, 83 L. Ed. 1206 (1939). Among the cases cited by the Supreme Court are the following: *Fife v. State*, 31 Ark. 455, 458, 1876 WL 1562 (1876) ("[t]he arms which it guarantees American citizens the right to keep and to bear, are such as are needful to, and ordinarily used by a well regulated militia, and such as are necessary and suitable to a free people, to enable them to resist oppression, prevent usurpation, repel invasion, etc., etc"); *People v. Brown*, 253 Mich. 537, 235 N.W. 245, 246, 82 A.L.R. 341 (1931) ("[s]ome courts have . . . held that the constitutional protection covers the bearing of such arms only as are a customary part of the equipment of a militiaman. . . . On the other hand, some courts . . . have extended the protection to weapons of all descriptions"); *State v. Duke*, 42 Tex. 455, 458-59, 1875 WL 7460 (1875) ("[t]he arms which every person is secured the right to keep and bear (in the defense of himself or the State, subject to legislative regulation), must be such arms as are commonly kept, according to the customs of the people, and are appropriate for open and manly use in self-defense, as well as such as are proper for the defense of the State"); *State v. Workman*, 35 W. Va. 367, 373, 14 S.E. 9, 11 (1891) ("[i]n regard to the kind of arms referred to in the [second] amendment, it must be held to refer to the weapons of warfare to be used by the militia, such as swords, guns, rifles, and muskets,—arms to be used in defending the state and civil liberty").

33. 307 U.S. at 182 n.3.

34. Story, 2 *Commentaries on the Constitution* 646 (5th ed. 1891). "One of the ordinary modes, by which tyrants accomplish their purpose without resistance is, by disarming the people, and making it an offense to keep arms." Story, *A Familiar Exposition of the Constitution of the United States* 264 (1893).

35. Cooley, *Constitutional Limitations* 729. Cooley, *General Principles of Constitutional Law* 281-82 (2d ed. 1891) states further:

> The right declared was meant to be a strong moral check against the usurpation and arbitrary power of rulers, and as a necessary and efficient means of regaining rights when temporarily overturned by usurpation.
>
> The right is General—It may be supposed from the phraseology of this provision that the right to keep and bear arms was only guaranteed to the militia; but this would be an interpretation not warranted by the intent ... But the law may make provision for the enrollment of all who are fit to perform military duty, or of a small number only, or it may wholly omit to make any provision at all; and if the right were limited to those enrolled, the purpose of this guaranty might be defeated altogether by the action or neglect to act of the government it was meant to hold in check. The meaning of the provision undoubtedly is that the people from whom the militia must be taken shall have the right to keep and bear arms, and they need no permission or regulation of law for the purpose.

36. The rifle might be considered the militia arm par excellence. The language of the Second Amendment resulted in "the deference and immunity extended to rifles in the earliest enactments." *People v. Raso*, 9 Misc. 2d 739, 170 N.Y.S.2d 245, 248-49 (County Ct. 1958). *People ex rel. Darling v. Warden of City Prison*, 154 A.D. 413, 139 N.Y.S. 277, 284 (1st Dep't 1913) states: "If the Legislature had prohibited the keeping of arms, it would have been clearly beyond its power."

Property Requisition Act, the legislation included the following provision to reaffirm Second Amendment rights:

> Nothing contained in this Act shall be construed—
>
> (1) to authorize the requisitioning or require the registration of any firearms possessed by any individual for his personal protection or sport (and the possession of which is not prohibited or the registration of which is not required by existing law), [or]
>
> (2) to impair or infringe in any manner the right of any individual to keep and bear arms.[37]

The reason for the above was explained by the House Committee on Military Affairs as follows:

> In view of the fact that certain totalitarian and dictatorial nations are now engaged in the willful and wholesale destruction of personal rights and liberties, our committee deem it appropriate for the Congress to expressly state that the proposed legislation shall not be construed to impair or infringe the constitutional right of the people to bear arms. In so doing, it will be manifest that, although the Congress deems it expedient to grant certain extraordinary powers to the Executive in furtherance of the common defense during critical times, there is no disposition on the part of this Government to depart from the concepts and principles of personal rights and liberties expressed in our Constitution.[38]

For the next forty years, both the Court and Congress were by and large silent on the Second Amendment. In *Lewis v. United States,* the Supreme Court held of a conviction for receipt of a firearm by a convicted felon: "These legislative restrictions [i.e., a felon may not receive a firearm in interstate commerce] on the use of firearms are neither based upon constitutionally suspect criteria, nor do they trench upon any constitutionally protected liberties."[39] Since "a legislature constitutionally may prohibit a convicted felon from engaging in activities far more fundamental than the possession of a firearm"—including the exercise of other civil liberties, and may even deprive a felon of life itself—felons have no fundamental right to keep and bear arms.[40] *Lewis* explicitly reaffirmed the *Miller* rule that the Second Amendment protects possession of "a firearm" with a militia nexus, and does not merely protect a person with a militia nexus.[41]

Elsewhere, the Supreme Court has stated that if a right is explicitly guaranteed by the Constitution, it is a fundamental right.[42] The Court has denied that some Bill of Rights freedoms "are in some way less 'fundamental' than" others. "Each establishes a norm of conduct which the Federal Government is bound to honor—to no greater or lesser extent than any other inscribed in the Constitution. Moreover, we know of no principled basis on which to create a hierarchy of constitutional values."[43] As stated by the Court:

---

37. Pub. L. No. 274, 77th Cong., 1st Sess., Ch. 445, 55 Stat., pt. 1, 742 (Oct. 16, 1941). For the legislative history of this provision, *see* Halbrook, "Congress Interprets the Second Amendment: Declarations by a Co-Equal Branch on the Individual Right to Keep and Bear Arms," 62 Tenn. L. Rev. 597, 618-31 (Spring 1995).

38. H.R. Rep. No. 1120 [to accompany S. 1579], House Committee on Military Affairs, 77th Cong., 1st Sess., at 2 (Aug. 4, 1941).

39. *Lewis v. U.S.*, 445 U.S. 55, 65 n.8, 100 S. Ct. 915, 63 L. Ed. 2d 198 (1980).

40. *Id.* at 66 n.8.

41. *Id.* at 65.

42. *San Antonio Independent School Dist. v. Rodriguez,* 411 U.S. 1, 33, 93 S. Ct. 1278, 36 L. Ed. 2d 16 (1973) (a right is "fundamental" if it is "explicitly or implicitly guaranteed by the Constitution").

43. *Valley Forge Christian College v. Americans United for Separation of Church and State, Inc.*, 454 U.S. 464, 484, 102 S. Ct. 752, 70 L. Ed. 2d 700 (1982).

> This constitutional protection must not be interpreted in a hostile or niggardly spirit. . . . Such a view does scant honor to the patriots who sponsored the Bill of Rights as a condition to acceptance of the Constitution by the ratifying States. . . .
>
> As no constitutional guarantee enjoys preference, so none should suffer subordination or deletion. . . . To view a particular provision of the Bill of Rights with disfavor inevitably results in a constricted application of it. This is to disrespect the Constitution.[44]

The fourth and most recent time Congress passed a constitutional amendment or legislation in support of the right to keep and bear arms was in 1986. The preamble to the Firearms Owners' Protection Act of 1986 states:

> The Congress finds that—(1) the rights of citizens—(A) to keep and bear arms under the second amendment to the United States Constitution . . . and (D) against unconstitutional exercise of authority under the ninth and tenth amendments; require additional legislation to correct existing firearms statutes and enforcement policies.[45]

The Supreme Court has discussed the Second Amendment in the context of other fundamental rights. In *United States v. Verdugo-Urquidez,* a Fourth Amendment case, the Court made clear that all law-abiding Americans are protected by the Second Amendment as follows:

> "The people" seems to have been a term of art employed in select parts of the Constitution. . . . The Second Amendment protects "the right of the people to keep and bear Arms," and the Ninth and Tenth Amendments provide that certain rights and powers are retained by and reserved to "the people." See also U.S. Const., Amdt. 1, ("Congress shall make no law . . . abridging . . . *the right of the people* peaceably to assemble"); Art. I, §2, cl. 1 ("The House of Representatives shall be composed of Members chosen every second year *by the People of the several States*") (emphasis added). While this textual exegesis is by no means conclusive, it suggests that "the people" protected by the Fourth Amendment, and by the First and Second Amendments, and to whom rights and powers are reserved in the Ninth and Tenth Amendments, refers to a class of persons who are part of a national community or who have otherwise developed sufficient connection with this country to be considered part of that community.[46]

The Second Amendment was treated in a parallel fashion in *Planned Parenthood v. Casey,* which stated:

> Neither the Bill of Rights nor the specific practices of States at the time of the adoption of the Fourteenth Amendment marks the outer limits of the substantive sphere of liberty which the Fourteenth Amendment protects. See U.S. Const., Amend. 9 . As the second Justice Harlan recognized: "[T]he full scope of the liberty guaranteed by the Due Process Clause cannot be found in or limited by the precise terms of the specific guarantees elsewhere provided in the Constitution . . . [such as] the freedom of speech, press, and religion; the right to keep and bear arms. . . . It is a rational continuum which, broadly

---

44. *Ullmann v. U.S.*, 350 U.S. 422, 426-29, 76 S. Ct. 497, 100 L. Ed. 511, 53 A.L.R.2d 1008 (1956).

45. Pub. L. No. 99-308, 100 Stat. 449, §1(b) (May 19, 1986). The congressional finding that the Second Amendment guarantees "the rights of citizens" to keep and bear arms was supported by "The Right to Keep and Bear Arms: Report of the Subcommittee on the Constitution," Senate Judiciary Committee, 97th Cong., 2d Sess., at 12 (1982), which states:

> The conclusion is thus inescapable that the history, concept, and wording of the second amendment to the Constitution of the United States, as well as its interpretation by every major commentator and court in the first half-century after its ratification, indicates that what is protected is an individual right of a private citizen to own and carry firearms in a peaceful manner.

On the Ninth Amendment, *see* Johnson, "Beyond the Second Amendment: An Individual Right to Arms Viewed Through the Ninth Amendment," 24 Rutgers L.J. 1 (1992).

46. *U.S. v. Verdugo-Urquidez*, 494 U.S. 259, 265, 110 S. Ct. 1056, 1060-61, 108 L. Ed. 2d 222, 232-33 (1990) (holding the Fourth Amendment warrant requirement inapplicable to the search of a home in a foreign country).

> speaking, includes a freedom from all substantial arbitrary impositions and purposeless restraints. . . ."[47]

A 1990 Supreme Court opinion has relevance to the twentieth century argument that the Second Amendment protects only the "right" of a state to maintain a militia, and that the "militia" is restricted to the National Guard. In *Perpich v. Department of Defense*,[48] the Court recognized that the National Guard is part of the Armed Forces of the United States and that the reserve militia includes all able-bodied citizens.[49]

The issue was whether the militia clause allows the President to order members of the National Guard to train outside the United States without the consent of a state governor.[50] The opinion fails to mention the Second Amendment at all, and refers to the state power over the militia as being recognized only in "the text of the Constitution":

> Two conflicting themes, developed at the Constitutional Convention and repeated in debates over military policy during the next century, led to a compromise in the text of the Constitution and in later statutory enactments. On the one hand, there was a widespread fear that a national standing Army posed an intolerable threat to individual liberty and to the sovereignty of the separate States, while, on the other hand, there was a recognition of the danger of relying on inadequately trained soldiers as the primary means of providing for the common defense. Thus, Congress was authorized both to raise and support a national army and also to organize "the Militia."[51]

The Court then reviewed Congress's various militia enactments. The first, passed in 1792, provided that "every able-bodied male citizen between the ages of 18 and 45 be enrolled [in the militia] and equip himself with appropriate weaponry."[52] In 1903, legislation divided able-bodied male citizens "into an 'organized militia' to be known as the National Guard of the several States, and the remainder of which was then described as the 'reserve militia,' and which later statutes have termed the 'unorganized militia.'"[53] Both of the above were passed under the Militia Clauses of the Constitution.[54]

By contrast, in legislation dating to 1916, "the statute expressly provided that the Army of the United States should include not only 'the Regular Army,' but also 'the National Guard while in the service of the United States'."[55] Thus, today's National Guard came into being through exercise by Congress of the power to raise armies, not the power to organize the militia.

The Court referred to "the traditional understanding of the militia as a part-time, nonprofessional fighting force,"[56] and as "a body of armed citizens trained to military duty, who may be called out in certain cases, but may not be kept on service like standing armies, in time of peace."[57] The Court also recognized the existence of "all portions of the 'militia'—organized or not."[58]

---

47. *Planned Parenthood of Southeastern Pennsylvania v. Casey*, 505 U.S. 833, 841, 112 S. Ct. 2791, 120 L. Ed. 2d 674 (1992).
48. *Perpich v. Dept. of Defense*, 496 U.S. 334, 110 S. Ct. 2418, 110 L. Ed. 2d 312 (1990).
49. *Id.* at 342-43.
50. *Id.* at 336.
51. *Id.* at 339.
52. *Id.* at 341.
53. *Id.* at 342.
54. *Id.* at 342-43.
55. *Id.* at 344.
56. *Id.* at 347.
57. *Id.* at 347, quoting *Dunne v. People*, 94 Ill. 120, 1879 WL 8671 (1879).
58. *Id.* at 352.

The Court concluded that "there is no basis for an argument that the federal statutory scheme deprives [a state] of any constitutional entitlement to a separate militia of its own."[59] The Second Amendment was never mentioned as having any relevance to the state power to maintain a militia.

It has been suggested that to "bear arms" refers to a soldier carrying arms and does not include a citizen carrying arms. However, in *Muscarello v. United States* (1998), which concerned a prohibition on carrying a firearm during and in relation to drug trafficking, the Supreme Court noted that "carrying" a firearm in a narrow sense means "'bearing' or (in slang) 'packing' (as in 'packing a gun')."[60] Black's Law Dictionary defines "carry arms or weapons" as: "To wear, bear or carry them upon the person or in the clothing or in a pocket, for the purpose of use, or for the purpose of being armed and ready for offensive or defensive action in case of a conflict with another person." "No one doubts that one who bears arms on his person 'carries a weapon.'"[61]

In her dissenting opinion, joined by Justices Rehnquist, Scalia, and Souter, Justice Ginsberg wrote about the meaning of "carry":

> Surely a most familiar meaning is, as the Constitution's Second Amendment ("keep and bear Arms") (emphasis added) and Black's Law Dictionary, at 214, indicate: "wear, bear, or carry . . . upon the person or in the clothing or in a pocket, for the purpose . . . of being armed and ready for offensive or defensive action in a case of conflict with another person."[62]

In contrast to the Supreme Court's jurisprudence, some federal appellate courts have decided (albeit without historical support) that the Second Amendment does not protect the right of persons to keep and bear arms, but protects the "collective right" of states to form militias.[63] While the denials of an individual right have been often repeated, the ramifications of the holistic "collective right" theory have not been explored.

Some federal courts have recognized the Second Amendment to protect an individual right.[64] The Fifth Circuit noted about the federal prohibition on

---

59. *Id.* "[The Constitution left] under the sway of the states undelegated the control of the militia to the extent that such control was not taken away by the exercise by Congress of its power raise armies." *Id.* at 354, quoting *Arver v. U.S.*, 245 U.S. 366, 383, 38 S. Ct. 159, 62 L. Ed. 349 (1918).

60. *Muscarello v. U.S.*, 524 U.S. 125, 118 S. Ct. 1911, 141 L. Ed. 2d 111, 116 (1998).

61. *Id.*

62. *Id.*

63. The "collective rights" theory originated in *U.S. v. Tot*, 131 F.2d 261, 266 (C.C.A. 3d Cir. 1942) *rev'd on other grounds*, *cert. granted*, 317 U.S. 623, 63 S. Ct. 441, 87 L. Ed. 504 (1943) and *judgment rev'd*, 319 U.S. 463, 63 S. Ct. 1241, 87 L. Ed. 1519 (1943). The historical references in *Tot* simply do not support its thesis. *See* Halbrook, *That Every Man Be Armed* 189-191 (1984).

Subsequent cases merely string cite to earlier cases which are ultimately traceable to *Tot.* E.g., *U.S. v. Nelsen*, 859 F.2d 1318 (8th Cir. 1988); *U.S. v. Warin*, 530 F.2d 103, 37 A.L.R. Fed. 687 (6th Cir. 1976); *U.S. v. Johnson*, 497 F.2d 548 (4th Cir. 1974). The Eighth Circuit has not been consistent. *See U.S. v. Wiley*, 309 F. Supp. 141, 145 (D. Minn. 1970), *judgment aff'd*, 438 F.2d 773 (8th Cir. 1971), *judgment vacated*, 404 U.S. 1009, 92 S. Ct. 686, 30 L. Ed. 2d 657 (1972). None of these opinions reflect any serious argument by counsel or include any scholarly analysis supportive of the "collective rights" thesis. *E.g., Johnson*, 497 F.2d at 550 (court appointed attorney argued that Second Amendment protects felon's purchase of firearm; unsupported dictum about "a collective right").

64. Felons are "a separate class whose individual right to bear arms may be prohibited." *U.S. v. Wiley*, 309 F. Supp. 141, 145 (D. Minn. 1970), *judgment aff'd*, 438 F.2d 773 (8th Cir. 1971), *judgment vacated*, 404 U.S. 1009, 92 S. Ct. 686, 30 L. Ed. 2d 657 (1972). "Although an individual's right to bear arms is constitutionally protected, *see U.S. v. Miller*, 307 U.S. 174, 178-79, 59 S. Ct. 816, 83 L. Ed. 1206 (1939), the possession of a gun, especially by anyone who has been convicted of a violent crime, is nevertheless a highly regulated activity, and everyone knows it." *U.S. v. Hutzell*, 217 F.3d 966, 969 (8th Cir. 2000), *reh'g and reh'g en banc denied*, (Sept. 12, 2000) and *cert. denied*, 532 U.S. 944, 121 S. Ct. 1408, 149 L. Ed. 2d 349 (2001). *See U.S. v. Bowdach*, 414 F. Supp. 1346, 1353 & n.11 (S.D. Fla. 1976), *judgment aff'd*, 561 F.2d 1160 (5th Cir. 1977) ("possession of the shotgun by a non-felon has no legal consequences. U.S. Const. Amend. II"), aff'd, 561 F.2d 1160 (5th Cir. 1977); *Gilbert Equipment Co., Inc. v. Higgins*, 709 F. Supp. 1071, 1090 (S.D. Ala. 1989), *judgment aff'd*, 894 F.2d 412 (11th Cir.

possession of a firearm in a school zone, defined to include the transportation of a firearm by any person in a vehicle on a public road within 1,000 feet of a school:

> It is also conceivable that some applications of section 922(q) might raise Second Amendment concerns. *Lopez* does not raise the Second Amendment and thus we do not now consider it. Nevertheless, this orphan of the Bill of Rights may be something of a brooding omnipresence here. For an argument that the Second Amendment should be taken seriously, see Levinson, *The Embarrassing Second Amendment,* 99 Yale L.J. 637 (1989).[65]

The Fifth Circuit took notice of Congress's recognition in the Firearms Owners' Protection Act of 1986 of "the rights of citizens . . . to keep and bear arms under the second amendment."[66]

As is suggested in the above reference to Professor Levinson's work, the historical view that the Second Amendment protects individual rights, and is a deterrent to governmental tyranny, is undergoing a contemporary revival.[67]

It remains to be seen whether the "collective rights" circuits will reevaluate their holdings.

As on other issues, the large Ninth Circuit is in conflict with itself on the Second Amendment. In *Hickman v. Block,* the Ninth Circuit held that an unsuccessful applicant for a concealed weapon permit has no standing to sue because "the Second Amendment is a right held by the states."[68] Besides failing to address the Constitution's consistent linguistic usage that the states have "powers" and "the people" have "rights,"[69] the opinion stated that "the Second Amendment is not incorporated into the Bill of Rights."[70] The opinion was later revised to delete "into the Bill of Rights" and to insert "against the states."[71]

Just six days after *Hickman* was decided, *United States v. Gomez* (1996),[72] in an opinion by Judge Kozinski, upheld a justification defense for a felon in

---

1990) (Second Amendment "guarantees to all Americans 'the right to keep and bear arms'"), aff'd, 894 F.2d 412 (11th Cir. 1990) (mem.); *U.S. v. Swinton*, 521 F.2d 1255, 32 A.L.R. Fed. 937 (10th Cir. 1975) ("there is no absolute constitutional right of an individual to possess a firearm") (emphasis added); *Cases v. U.S.*, 131 F.2d 916, 921 (C.C.A. 1st Cir. 1942) (statute "undoubtedly curtails to some extent the right of individuals to keep and bear arms"); *U.S. v. Atlas*, 94 F.3d 447, 452 (8th Cir. 1996) (Arnold, C.J., dissenting) ("possession of a gun, in itself, is not a crime. [Indeed, though the right to bear arms is not absolute, it finds explicit protection in the Bill of Rights.]"); *U.S. v. Gambill*, 912 F. Supp. 287, 290 (S.D. Ohio 1996), *aff'd*, 129 F.3d 1265 (6th Cir. 1997) (reference to "an activity, such as keeping and bearing arms, that arguably implicates the Bill of Rights.").

65. *U.S. v. Lopez*, 2 F.3d 1342, 1364 n.46, 85 Ed. Law Rep. 647 (5th Cir. 1993), *cert. granted*, 511 U.S. 1029, 114 S. Ct. 1536, 128 L. Ed. 2d 189 (1994) and *judgment aff'd*, 514 U.S. 549, 115 S. Ct. 1624, 131 L. Ed. 2d 626, 99 Ed. Law Rep. 24 (1995).

66. *Id.* at 1355 n.46.

67. *See* Amar, "The Bill of Rights as a Constitution," 100 Yale L. Rev. 1131, 1162-73 (1991); Scarry, "War and the Social Contract: Nuclear Policy, Distribution, and the Right to Bear Arms," 139 U. Pa. L. Rev. 1257 (1991).

68. *Hickman v. Block*, 81 F.3d 98, 101 (9th Cir. 1996), *cert. denied*, 519 U.S. 912 (1996); *accord, United States v. Hancock*, 231 F.3d 557, 566 (9th Cir. 2000).

69. However, Judge Noonan, who was a member of the *Hickman* panel, wrote in an earlier opinion:

> Donald Douglas Brier is a hobbyist who has been turned into a criminal by the too vivid zeal of government agents and prosecutors. Like many other hobbyists—stamp collectors for example—he swapped parts of his collection and sold and bought other parts. Admittedly guns are more dangerous than stamps, and Congress has seen fit to regulate gun dealers. But unlike stamps, guns are the subject of constitutional protection: "the right of the people to keep and bear arms shall not be infringed." United States Constitution, Amendment II. Congress has regulated guns, sensitive to the Second Amendment and to the difference between hobbyists and those making a living out of the gun business.

U.S. v. Breier, 827 F.2d 1366 (9th Cir. 1987) (Noonan, J., dissenting from denial of rehearing). The panel opinion made no reference to the Second Amendment. *See U.S. v. Breier*, 813 F.2d 212 (9th Cir. 1987).

70. *Hickman v. Block*, 81 F.3d at 101, 103 n.10 (first publication).

71. *Id.* (bound volume).

72. *U.S. v. Gomez*, 81 F.3d 846 (9th Cir. 1996), opinion *amended and superseded on denial of reh'g*, 92 F.3d 770 (9th Cir. 1996).

possession of a firearm. Because the felon had assisted the government, a drug trafficking gang was actively seeking to murder the felon, but the government refused to provide protection. The government then prosecuted the felon because he armed himself to protect his life.[73]

Holding that the death threats were sufficient justification to defeat the charge of being a felon in possession of a firearm, the Ninth Circuit opined:

> Indeed, 18 U.S.C. §922(g)(1) might not pass constitutional muster were it not subject to a justification defense. The Second Amendment embodies the right to defend oneself and one's home against physical attack. Nelson Lund, *The Second Amendment, Political Liberty, and the Right to Self-Preservation,* 39 Ala. L.Rev. 103, 117-120, 130 (1987) (Second Amendment guarantees right to means of self-defense); *see* Sanford Levinson, *The Embarrassing Second Amendment,* 99 Yale L.J. 637, 645-46 (1989) ("[I]t seems tendentious to reject out of hand the argument that one purpose of the [Second] Amendment was to recognize an individual's right to engage in armed self-defense against criminal conduct."). In modern society, the right to armed self-defense has become attenuated as we rely almost exclusively on organized societal responses, such as the police, to protect us from harm. . . . The possession of firearms may therefore be regulated, even prohibited, because we are "compensated" for the loss of that right by the availability of organized societal protection. The tradeoff becomes more dubious, however, when a citizen makes a particularized showing that the organs of government charged with providing that protection are unwilling or unable to do so. . . . At that point, the Second Amendment might trump a statute prohibiting the ownership and possession of weapons that would be perfectly constitutional under ordinary circumstances.[74]

Whatever the validity of the above suggestion that the Second Amendment right may be infringed in a crime-free society, it is a clear statement that the Amendment protects the individual right to have arms. The above opinion was originally unanimous. However, in an amended opinion, Judge Hall, who authored *Hickman,* disagreed with the above statement because it was in conflict with *Hickman,*[75] and Judge Hawkins would leave the question for another day.[76]

Interesting dictum by the D.C. Circuit is set forth in two opinions it rendered in a challenge by the Fraternal Order of Police to a ban, as applied to police officers, on possession of a firearm by a person convicted of misdemeanor domestic violence. While resolving the issue on other grounds, *FOP I* notes that the FOP argued that the ban violated the right to bear arms, while the government contended that the right does not belong to individuals but to state militias. The court responded:

> Analysis of the Second Amendment right has recently burgeoned. . . . Despite the intriguing questions raised, we will not attempt to resolve the status of the Second Amendment right, for we find that the 1996 amendments fall into the narrow class of provisions that fail even the most permissive, "rational basis," review.[77]

On rehearing, *FOP II* decided that the law had a rational basis after all. However, the Second Amendment issue had not been properly raised. The court explains:

---

73. *Id.* at 848-49.
74. *Id.* at 850.
75. *Hickman,* 92 F.3d at 778-79 (Hall, J., concurring).
76. *U.S. v. Gomez,* 81 F.3d 846 (9th Cir. 1996), *opinion amended and superseded on denial of reh'g,* 92 F.3d 770, 779 (9th Cir. 1996) (Hawkins, J., concurring).
77. *Fraternal Order of Police v. U.S.,* 152 F.3d 998, 1002 (D.C. Cir. 1998), *reh'g granted,* 159 F.3d 1362 (D.C. Cir. 1998) and *on reh'g,* 173 F.3d 898 (D.C. Cir. 1999) (*"FOP I"*), citing, *inter alis,* Akhil Reed Amar, *The Bill of Rights* 257-67 (1998). Amar takes the individual-rights interpretation.

> First we note that on appeal FOP also raises an independent Second Amendment claim. But as it did not do so in the district court we do not address it in that form. We must confess, however, that we are mystified by the decision to advance a substantive due process claim based on an explicit Second Amendment right in preference to a simple assertion of the explicit right itself. It is not apparent how a claim might be strengthened by being tucked into the catch-all of substantive due process.[78]

In other words, FOP's argument was convoluted in that it asserted that the law interfered with bearing arms and thus violated due process, rather than alleging that the law infringed on the right to bear arms. *FOP II* continues:

> In any event, the claim obviously requires us to consider the Second Amendment right, on which the Supreme Court's guidance has been notoriously scant. The government argues that FOP's claim fails because FOP has not "alleged, much less proven, that section 922(g)(9) has any relationship to the 'preservation or efficiency of a well regulated militia.'" . . . . Since *Miller* dealt with Congress's authority to prohibit ownership of short-barreled shotguns, FOP could have challenged the test's applicability by arguing that it serves only to separate weapons covered by the amendment from uncovered weapons. It did not do so, and we thus assume the test's applicability.[79]

According to the above, FOP failed to argue that the firearms its members have a right to possess are constitutionally protected arms, in contrast to arms which may not be so protected. Indeed, FOP presented no evidence that such firearms would be useful to a militia:

> But we are not altogether clear what kind of "relationship"—or, to quote *Miller* more precisely, "reasonable relationship," id.—is called for here. This *Miller* test appears in some sense to invert the commercial speech test, which requires the government to show that legislation restricting such speech bears a reasonable relationship to some "legitimate" or "substantial" goal. . . . We suppose *Miller* would be met by evidence supporting a finding that the disputed rule would materially impair the effectiveness of a militia, though perhaps some other showing could suffice. We need not fix the exact form of the required relationship, however, because FOP has presented no evidence on the matter at all.[80]

Rather than presenting evidence of the militia uses of the firearms possessed by the police, the FOP argued that policemen could be needed in state militias. To this *FOP II* responds:

> Instead FOP simply argues that, in "most" states, police officers can be called into service as militia members. But none of the nine states' provisions it cites appears to make police officers any more susceptible to such service than ordinary citizens (or in some cases, than males between the ages of 17 and 45). In any event, §922(g)(9) does not hinder the militia service of all police officers, only of domestic violence misdemeanants whose convictions have not been expunged, etc. FOP never indicates how restrictions on the latter, relevant class would have a material impact on the militia.

The above makes clear that, at least in the D.C. Circuit, a Second Amendment challenge to a firearms prohibition should be framed in terms of whether an arm is constitutionally protected, which would entail an evidentiary showing that the arm is ordinary military equipment or could be used for militia purposes. The mere claim that a plaintiff may be liable for militia service is insufficient.

Aside from the dicta about the Second Amendment quoted above, the U.S. Supreme Court has not rendered any decision on the topic since the 1939 *Miller*

---

78. *Fraternal Order of Police v. U.S.*, 173 F.3d 898, 905-06 (D.C. Cir. 1999) (*"FOP II"*).

79. *Id.* at 906.

80. *Miller* itself was predicated on "the absence of any evidence" that a short-barreled shotgun was "ordinary military equipment," a matter which was "not within judicial notice." *Miller*, 307 U.S. at 178.

opinion. However, certain individual Justices have written on the right to bear arms recently. In *A Matter of Interpretation* (1997), Justice Antonin Scalia wrote:

> So also, we value the right to bear arms less than did the Founders (who thought the right of self-defense to be absolutely fundamental), and there will be few tears shed if and when the Second Amendment is held to guarantee nothing more than the state National Guard. But this just shows that the Founders were right when they feared that some (in their view misguided) future generation might wish to abandon liberties that they considered essential, and so sought to protect those liberties in a Bill of Rights. We may . . . *like* the elimination of the right to bear arms; but let us not pretend that these are not *reductions of rights*.[81]

Justice Scalia found the militia clause no obstacle to his "interpretation of the Second Amendment as a guarantee that the federal government will not interfere with the individual's right to bear arms for self-defense."[82] The term "Militia" refers not to a select group, but to "the body of the people, trained to arms."[83]

The Second Amendment's militia clause, a prologue, does not limit the arms right, a "categorical guarantee"; it is "rather like saying 'police officers being necessary to law and order, the right of the people to carry handguns shall not be infringed.'"[84] Justice Scalia concluded:

> It would also be strange to find in the midst of a catalog of the rights of *individuals* a provision securing to the states the right to maintain a designated "Militia." Dispassionate scholarship suggests quite strongly that the right of the people to keep and bear arms meant just that.[85]

Justice Clarence Thomas discussed the Second Amendment in his concurring opinion in *Printz v. United States* (1997), which held that the Brady Act's command that local law enforcement officers conduct background checks on handgun purchasers violated the powers of the States under the Tenth Amendment.[86] Justice Thomas noted that "the Constitution, in addition to delegating certain enumerated powers to Congress, places whole areas outside the reach of Congress' regulatory authority." Like the First Amendment, "the Second Amendment similarly appears to contain an express limitation on the government's authority."[87] The Court had not considered the nature of the substantive right safeguarded by the Second Amendment since the 1939 *Miller* case, which decided that "the Second Amendment did not guarantee a citizen's right to possess a sawed-off shotgun because that weapon had not been shown to be 'ordinary military equipment' that could 'contribute to the common defense.'"[88]

---

81. Antonin Scalia, *A Matter of Interpretation*, 43 (Princeton, N.J.: Princeton University Press, 1997).

82. *Id.* at 136 n.13.

83. *Id.*, quoting Virginia Bill of Rights (1776), *see* Joyce Lee Malcolm, *To Keep and Bear Arms* 136, 148 (1994). Justice Scalia continued:

> This was also the conception of "militia" entertained by James Madison, who, in arguing that it would provide a ready defense of liberty against the standing army that the proposed Constitution allowed, described the militia as "amounting to near half a million of citizens with arms in their hands."

Id., quoting *The Federalist* No. 46, at 322 (Jacob E. Cooke ed., 1961).

84. *Id.* at 137 n.13.

85. *Id.*, citing Joyce Lee Malcolm, *To Keep and Bear Arms* 136, 148 (1994) and William Van Alstyne, "The Second Amendment and the Personal Right to Arms," 43 Duke L.J. 1236 (1994). Scalia quoted Madison as looking contemptuously upon the governments of Europe that "are afraid to trust the people with arms." *U.S. v. Miller*, 307 U.S. 174, 178, 59 S. Ct. 816, 83 L. Ed. 1206 (1939), citing *The Federalist* No. 46.

86. *Printz v. U.S.*, 521 U.S. 898, 117 S. Ct. 2365, 138 L. Ed. 2d 914 (1997).

87. 521 U.S. at 937-38.

88. *Id.* at 938, citing *U.S. v. Miller*, 307 U.S. 174, 178, 59 S. Ct. 816, 83 L. Ed. 1206 (1939). As noted above, *Miller* found that judicial notice could not be taken that a short barreled shotgun was a militia arm and remanded the case for fact-finding on that issue.

Justice Thomas continued: "If, however, the Second Amendment is read to confer a *personal* right to 'keep and bear arms,' a colorable argument exists that the Federal Government's regulatory scheme, at least as it pertains to the purely intrastate sale or possession of firearms, runs afoul of that Amendment's protections." He added in a footnote that, "Marshaling an impressive array of historical evidence, a growing body of scholarly commentary indicates that the 'right to keep and bear arms' is, as the Amendment's text suggests, a personal right."[89]

Noting that the parties did not raise the Second Amendment and it thus was not considered by the Court, Justice Thomas concluded with the challenge: "Perhaps, at some future date, this Court will have the opportunity to determine whether Justice Story was correct when he wrote that the right to bear arms 'has justly been considered, as the palladium of the liberties of a republic.'"[90]

A district court, invalidating a municipal prohibition on gun shows as preempted by state law, suggested that "traffic in guns may be afforded greater constitutional protection than traffic in air-tight plastic food containers."[91] The analogy referred to Supreme Court precedent that Tupperware parties entailed commercial speech protected by the First Amendment, which implied that commercial transactions at gun shows were likewise protected.[92]

In a 1998 dissent in another case, Justice John Paul Stevens mentioned the right to bear arms. Arguing for liberal standards of habeas corpus review, he noted the continuing injury caused by a criminal conviction: "It may result in tangible harms such as imprisonment, loss of the right to vote or to bear arms, and the risk of greater punishment if another crime is committed."[93] Bearing arms, whatever its scope, is recognized as a "right."

The Sixth Circuit has mentioned the Second Amendment in a similar context. The court held that, where the jury did not specify the amount of drugs possessed by the defendant, and the amount affected whether the offense was a felony or a misdemeanor, the judge could not impose a felony sentence. The court reasoned:

> It is a serious matter, obviously, to deprive an American citizen of civil rights as important as the right to vote, the right to keep and bear arms, and the right to engage in a chosen business or profession. For a sentencing judge to effect such a deprivation by factual findings that convert what would otherwise be a misdemeanor into a felony seems to us an impermissible usurpation of the historic role of the jury.[94]

---

89. *Id.*, citing, *inter alia*, J. Malcolm, *To Keep and Bear Arms: The Origins of an Anglo-American Right* 162 (1994); S. Halbrook, *That Every Man Be Armed, The Evolution of a Constitutional Right* (1984).

90. 521 U.S. at 939, citing 3 J. Story, *Commentaries* §1890, p. 746 (1833).

91. *HC Gun & Knife Shows, Inc. v. City of Houston*, 201 F.3d 544 (5th Cir. 2000).

92. *HC Gun & Knife Shows, Inc. v. City of Houston*, Civil No. H-96-0536, S.D. Texas, Jan. 23, 1997, at 13. *See Nordyke v. Santa Clara County*, 110 F.3d 707 (9th Cir. 1997) (commercial speech at gun shows protected by First Amendment).

93. *Spencer v. Kemna*, 523 U.S. 1, 118 S. Ct. 978, 140 L. Ed. 2d 43 (1998) (Stevens, J., dissenting).

94. *U.S. v. Sharp*, 12 F.3d 605, 608 (6th Cir. 1993). *Accord, U.S. v. Allen*, 190 F.3d 1208, 1212 (11th Cir. 1999) ("Because conviction of a felony results in the loss of constitutional rights important to each United States citizen, such as the rights to vote, to bear arms, and to engage in a profession, 'for a sentencing judge to effect such a deprivation by factual findings that convert what would otherwise be a misdemeanor into a felony seems . . . an impermissible usurpation of the historic role of the jury.'").

Sec. 1:4 The Fifth Circuit's *Emerson* decision and the Justice Department's policy

The most remarkable development in Second Amendment jurisprudence is the Fifth Circuit case *of United States v. Emerson.*[95] In that case, the district invalidated a provision of the Gun Control Act as violative of the Second Amendment. The Fifth Circuit agreed that the Second Amendment guarantees the individual right to keep and bear arms, but upheld the provision. In briefs filed in the Supreme Court, the Justice Department changed years of denial and conceded that the Second Amendment does indeed protect personal rights. While the Supreme Court denied Emerson's petition for certiorari, the decision of the Court of Appeals and the new policy of the Justice Department alters the landscape significantly.

In its 1999 decision in *Emerson,* the U.S. District Court for the Northern District of Texas held that a ban on possession of a firearm by a person who is subject to a domestic restraining order infringes on the right to keep and bear arms. The opinion began by contrasting the individual rights position, known as the Standard Model in the academic literature, from the "collective rights" view. The text of the amendment consists of the first, subordinate clause, and the second, independent clause. The right belongs to "the people," not "the States." The first clause states the purpose, but the right in the second clause is independent of the militia.[96]

Emerson analyzed the historical development of the right, beginning with the English antecedents, colonial understanding, the ratification debates, and the drafting of the Second Amendment.[97] It found that the structure of the amendment in the Bill of Rights indicates that the right is individual, and that this was supported by Supreme Court precedent.[98] It rejected a prudential or consequentialist argument that the social costs of the amendment outweigh its utility.[99] This was the first opinion in the history of American jurisprudence on the Second Amendment to be based on a thorough review of the academic literature.

Applying the above to the law at issue, the district court in *Emerson* held: "18 U.S.C. § 922(g)(8) is unconstitutional because it allows a state court divorce proceeding, without particularized findings of the threat of future violence, to automatically deprive a citizen of his Second Amendment rights."[100] The provision was less offensive in imposing the ban where particularized judicial findings of a threat to physical safety are made, but the ban also automatically comes into play if an order prohibiting use of force against an intimate partner is entered. "All that is required for prosecution under the Act is a boilerplate order with no particularized findings. Thus, the statute has no real safeguards against an arbitrary abridgement of Second Amendment rights."[101] The court opined:

> Under this statute, a person can lose his Second Amendment rights not because he has committed some wrong in the past, or because a judge finds he may commit some

95. *United States v. Emerson,* 46 F. Supp.2d 598 (N.D. Tex. 1999), *rev'd,* 270 F.3d 203 (5th Cir. 2001), *cert. denied* (June 11, 2002).
96. *Id.* at 600-01.
97. *Id.* at 602-07.
98. *Id.* at 607.
99. *Id.* at 609.
100. *Id.* at 610.
101. *Id.* at 611.

> crime in the future, but merely because he is in a divorce proceeding. Although he may not be a criminal at all, he is stripped of his right to bear arms as much as a convicted felon. Second Amendment rights should not be so easily abridged.[102]

In the most comprehensive decision ever on the Second Amendment by any court in United States history, the U.S. Court of Appeals for the 5th Circuit decided in 2001 that the right of the people to keep and bear arms is a fundamental right of every law-abiding person. Its decision in *Emerson* concluded: "the Second Amendment protects the right of individuals to privately keep and bear their own firearms that are suitable as individual, personal weapons and are not of the general kind or type excluded by *Miller*, regardless of whether the particular individual is then actually a member of a militia."[103]

Relying on the "considerable academic endorsement" that has appeared in the last two decades, the court found the above to be dictated by the Amendment's text, the intent of the Framers, and Supreme Court precedent. The court rejected the "collective rights" view that the Second Amendment only protects a state power to have a militia and the "sophisticated collective rights" view that it only protects bearing arms during militia duty.[104]

The court closely analyzed the Supreme Court's decision in *United States v. Miller* (1939), which held the test to be whether the firearm at issue was ordinary military ordnance, and was not concerned with whether its possessor was a member of the militia. (*Miller* found that it was not within judicial notice that a short-barreled shotgun was military ordnance and remanded the case for fact finding.) *Miller* in fact "cuts against the government's position."[105] Further, all other Supreme Court opinions mentioning the Second Amendment presuppose it to protect individual rights.

Most telling is the text of the Amendment itself as compared with other provisions of the Constitution. *Emerson* explained:

> the words "the people" have precisely the same meaning within the Second Amendment as without. And, as used throughout the Constitution, "the people" have "rights" and "powers," but federal and state governments only have "powers" or "authority", never "rights." Moreover, the Constitution's text likewise recognizes not only the difference between the "militia" and "the people" but also between the "militia" which has not been "call[ed] forth" and "the militia, when in actual service."[106]

Further, the term "bear arms" is not limited to military use, but includes the carrying of arms in general. No one even argued that "keep arms" is limited to the military, for it clearly applies to individuals.

The Amendment's preamble declares that "a well regulated Militia, being necessary to the security of a free State." "The Second Amendment's substantive guarantee, read as guaranteeing individual rights, may as so read reasonably be understood as being a guarantee which tends to enable, promote or further the existence, continuation or effectiveness of that 'well-regulated Militia' which is 'necessary to the security of a free State.'"[107] Moreover, a "well-regulated Militia" means the militia as a whole, not a select militia. The collective-rights

---

102. *Id.*
103. *United States v. Emerson*, 270 F.3d 203, 265 (5th Cir. 2001).
104. *Id.* at 220-22.
105. *Id.* at 226.
106. *Id.* at 227-28.
107. *Id.* at 233.

argument seeks to use the preamble to "torture" the substantive guarantee, but the preamble fully supports the individual-rights view.[108]

The opinion proceeds exhaustively to review the actual statements of the Framers of the Constitution and Bill of Rights, which were unanimous in their intent that the right to keep and bear arms is a personal right. The anti-federalist fears, the federalist response, and the state ratifications all prompted realization of the need that an individual right be recognized. Madison's proposal of the Amendment and debate thereon in the House and Senate, and the understanding as expressed in the public forum, also unanimously point to a private right. Nineteenth century legal commentaries were in accord with this view. Based on all of the following, *Emerson* decided:

> We reject the collective rights and sophisticated collective rights models for interpreting the Second Amendment. We hold, consistent with *Miller,* that it protects the right of individuals, including those not then actually a member of any militia or engaged in active military service or training, to privately possess and bear their own firearms, such as the pistol involved here, that are suitable as personal, individual weapons and are not of the general kind or type excluded by *Miller.*[109]

The pistol at issue was a Beretta semiautomatic. Weapons excluded by *Miller* are those with no militia utility. While *Emerson* does not probe far into the issue, it is clear that rifles, pistols, and shotguns in general are constitutionally-protected arms.

However, *Emerson* concluded that the law at issue as applied to the defendant *Emerson* did not violate the Second Amendment. That law, 18 U.S.C. § 922(g)(8)(C)(ii), prohibits possession of a firearm (with an interstate commerce nexus) by a person who is subject to a restraining order that prohibits the use of physical force against an intimate partner or child that would reasonably be expected to cause bodily injury. The prohibition exists only if the person receives notice and opportunity to participate at the court hearing, which includes the right to counsel and to cross examine witnesses. Such an order was issued in this case.

The district court in *Emerson* invalidated this provision because it does not require the court to make express findings of fact, and the order in this case seemed to be a routine, boiler plate divorce order. The Court of Appeals upheld the provision by interpreting Texas law to require higher procedural safeguards. Specifically, such a restraining order "may not properly issue unless the issuing court concludes, based on adequate evidence at the hearing, that the party restrained would otherwise pose a realistic threat of imminent physical injury to the protected party, and this is so regardless of whether or not Texas law requires the issuing court to make on the record express or explicit findings to that effect."[110] To the extent that a court might issue a restraining order without sufficient factual basis, the person may seek further judicial review.

Thus, the opinions of the district court and the court of appeals in *Emerson* differ not in how they interpret the Second Amendment, but in the standards for issuing a restraining order under Texas law. The latter concludes that "the nexus between firearm possession by the party so enjoined and the threat of lawless violence, is sufficient, though likely barely so, to support the deprivation, while

108. *Id.* at 236.
109. *Id.* at 261.
110. *Id.* at 264.

the order remains in effect, of the enjoined party's Second Amendment right to keep and bear arms."[111]

Concurring specially, one judge of the three-judge panel in *Emerson* argued that the court did not need to decide the nature of the Second Amendment. However, the two-judge majority found a decision on the merits to be necessary, and thus their view of the Second Amendment is a holding which is binding on all courts in the Fifth Circuit.

As a result of the decision in *Emerson*, it seems likely that courts will be more careful in issuing restraining orders so as faithfully to abide by the standards that Texas law actually imposes, and in view of the fact that issuance means serious consequences for a firearms owner. In broader terms, *Emerson* is a path-breaking precedent which establishes that the Second Amendment recognizes a fundamental, individual right which is subject only to "limited, narrowly tailored specific exceptions," but only as long as they are "not inconsistent with the right of Americans generally to individually keep and bear their private arms as historically understood in this country."[112]

Emerson is binding only in the Fifth Circuit, which encompasses Texas, Louisiana, and Mississippi. It may be persuasive authority in the circuits which have not rendered any opinion on the Second Amendment. The circuits which have adopted the "collective rights" view did so typically in two or three paragraphs which contain no meaningful analysis of the text or the Framers' intent. The analysis in *Emerson* is so overwhelming that those circuits might be persuaded to reconsider their precedents.

When *Emerson* was before the district court and the court of appeals, the Justice Department argued that the Second Amendment was a "collective" militia right only and did not protect any individual right. However, the Brief for the United States in Opposition to the petition for a writ of certiorari favorably quotes *Emerson* to the effect that the right is subject to "limited, narrowly tailored specific exceptions or restrictions for particular cases that are reasonable and not inconsistent with the right of Americans generally to individually keep and bear their private arms as historically understood in this country."[113] It argues that the 5th Circuit correctly held that a prohibition on firearm possession "by persons who have been judicially determined to pose a credible threat to the physical safety of a spouse or child" is permissible. No known case exists in which this or "any other federal statutory restriction on private gun possession" has been held "violative of the Second Amendment."[114] It adds in a footnote:

> In its brief to the court of appeals, the government argued that the Second Amendment protects only such acts of firearm possession as are reasonably related to the preservation or efficiency of the militia. The current position of the United States, however, is that the Second Amendment more broadly protects the rights of individuals, including persons who are not members of any militia or engaged in active military service or training, to possess and bear their own firearms, subject to reasonable restrictions designed to prevent possession by unfit persons or to restrict the possession of types of firearms that are particularly suited to criminal misuse.[115]

111. *Id.* at 264.
112. *Id.* at 261.
113. Brief for the United States in Opposition, *Emerson v. United States*, No. 01-8780, U.S. Supreme Court, May 2002, at 19.
114. *Id.*
115. *Id.* at 19-20 n.3.

In response to Emerson's argument that *Emerson* failed to apply strict scrutiny, the brief noted that the court "did not purport to apply a relaxed standard of review," specifically referring to "limited, narrowly tailored specific exceptions."[116] Since the court which issued the restraining order found a real threat of violence, *Emerson* "conclude[d] that the nexus between firearm possession by the party so enjoined and the threat of lawless violence, is sufficient, though likely barely so, to support the deprivation, while the order remains in effect, of the enjoined party's Second Amendment right to keep and bear arms." The brief concluded that, since the law was upheld and no circuit conflict existed, further review was unwarranted.[117]

Attached to the brief was a Memorandum to all United States Attorneys from the Attorney General, Re: *United States v. Emerson*, dated November 9, 2001. It expresses pleasure that the law was upheld and commits to "vigorously enforce and defend existing firearms laws." It praised the *Emerson* opinion as based on "a scholarly and comprehensive review" and as concluding that the Second Amendment "protects the right of individuals, including those not then actually a member of any militia or engaged in active military service or training, to privately possess and bear their own firearms." Restrictions on unfit persons and firearms particularly suited to criminal misuse are consistent with this interpretation. "In my view, the *Emerson* opinion, and the balance is strikes, generally reflect the correct understanding of the Second Amendment."

The memorandum promised to defend "all existing federal firearms laws" as consistent with the Second Amendment. "The Department has a solemn obligation both to enforce federal law *and* to respect the constitutional rights guaranteed to Americans." U.S. Attorney's offices were directed to advise the Criminal Division "of all cases in which Second Amendment issues are raised," and to coordinate briefing with the Criminal Division and the Solicitor General's office. It is better that justice be served than that the prosecution win every case, concludes the memorandum, which admonishes that federal law must be enforced "in a manner that heeds the commands of the Constitution."

Since the specific law at issue was upheld, the *Emerson* decision did not result in a circuit split. Not surprisingly, the Supreme Court denied certiorari. At this point it is likely that a body of precedent will percolate in the Fifth Circuit and elsewhere and that, at some indefinite point, the issue will be decided by the Supreme Court.

Emerson is beginning to be discussed outside the Fifth Circuit. A district court in Tennessee upheld the prohibition on possession of a firearm in furtherance of drug trafficking as follows:

> Defendant also asserts § 924(c)(1)(A) is unconstitutional because it treads on an individual's right to bear arms. In support of this argument, Defendant cites a recent holding of the United States Court of Appeals for the Fifth Circuit. *United States v. Emerson*, 270 F.3d 203 (5th Cir. 2001). In *Emerson* the Fifth Circuit did state the Second Amendment to the United States Constitution guarantees to citizens an individual right and like all the other rights in the Bill of Rights is subject to reasonable limitations. Based upon the reasoning of the *Emerson* court, this Court is confident that § 924(c)(1)(A) would pass muster even under that decision.[118]

116. *Id.* at 21.
117. *Id.*
118. *United States v. Helton*, No. 1:01-CR-89-2, D. Tenn. (Dec. 10, 2001), at 3, *appeal pending* (6th Cir.).

The *Emerson* precedent and the shift in the position of the Justice Department open a new chapter in Second Amendment litigation. While violent criminals will find no solace in this saga, challenges to firearm prohibitions which are victimless crimes and which restrict law-abiding persons will be greatly encouraged.

Although the case does not involve the Second Amendment, the Supreme Court has recently made clear that the alleged presence of a firearm does not extinguish other constitutional rights. In *Florida v. J.L.*,[119] the Court held unanimously that an anonymous tip that a person is carrying a gun is not, without more, sufficient to justify a police officer's stop and frisk of that person. An anonymous caller told police that a black male at a bus stop was carrying a concealed firearm. Officers frisked him and discovered a firearm, and thereafter charged him will carrying a concealed weapon without a license and juvenile possession of a handgun. "All the police had to go on in this case was the bare report of an unknown, unaccountable informant who neither explained how he knew about the gun nor supplied any basis for believing he had inside information about J. L."[120]

The government argued for a "firearm exception" to the rule set forth in *Terry v. Ohio* that, to justify a stop and frisk, police must have reasonable suspicion of criminal activity and that the suspects may be armed and dangerous.[121] Rejecting such an exception, the Court explained:

> Firearms are dangerous, and extraordinary dangers sometimes justify unusual precautions. Our decisions recognize the serious threat that armed criminals pose to public safety; *Terry's* rule, which permits protective police searches on the basis of reasonable suspicion rather than demanding that officers meet the higher standard of probable cause, responds to this very concern. . . . But an automatic firearm exception to our established reliability analysis would rove too far. Such an exception would enable any person seeking to harass another to set in motion an intrusive, embarrassing police search of the targeted person simply by placing an anonymous call falsely reporting the target's unlawful carriage of a gun. Nor could one securely confine such an exception to allegations involving firearms. Several Courts of Appeals have held it per se foreseeable for people carrying significant amounts of illegal drugs to be carrying guns as well.[122]

The Court declined to fashion a universal rule applicable to all instrumentalities. For instance, it did not purport to resolve whether "a report of a person carrying a bomb need bear the indicia of reliability we demand for a report of a person carrying a firearm before the police can constitutionally conduct a frisk."[123]

A different result may also obtain at airports, schools, and other places where a reasonable expectation of privacy may not exist.

The published opinion did not discuss the fact that Florida law provides for licensees to carry concealed firearms. This issue was discussed at oral argument. Even with a reliable tip that a person has a concealed firearm, is this evidence of criminal activity in a State where a considerable portion of the population have licenses to carry firearms?

---

119. *Florida v. J.L.*, 529 U.S. 266, 120 S. Ct. 1375, 146 L. Ed. 2d 254 (2000).

120. *Id.* at 271.

121. *Terry v. Ohio*, 392 U.S. 1, 88 S. Ct. 1868, 20 L. Ed. 2d 889 (1968). Even where the search is proper under *Terry*, the scope of the search is limited to whether a weapon is present. *U.S. v. Miles*, 247 F.3d 1009, 1014-15 (9th Cir. 2001) (suppressing cartridges discovered in tiny box which could not have been a weapon and which the officer shook and opened).

122. *Florida v. J.L.*, 529 U.S. 266, at 272-73, 120 S. Ct. 1375, 146 L. Ed. 2d 254 (2000).

123. *Florida v. J.L.*, 529 U.S. 266, 120 S. Ct. 1375, 146 L. Ed. 2d 254, 262 (2000).

Tactical Tip:

Most judicial decisions which denigrate the Second Amendment were litigated by criminal defense attorneys thoughtlessly seeking a last ditch defense of a felon in possession of a firearm, or by pro se defendants. Given the adverse case law created by cases not properly prepared, a decision to litigate the Second Amendment should be carefully considered by experienced counsel.

Sec. 1:5 The Fourteenth Amendment

The same two-thirds of Congress that adopted the Fourteenth Amendment to the United States Constitution also adopted the Freedmen's Bureau Act, which protected the "full and equal benefit of all laws and proceedings concerning personal liberty, personal security, and . . . estate . . ., including the constitutional right to bear arms."[124] Does the Fourteenth Amendment, which protects the individual rights to personal security and personal liberty from State violation,[125] incorporate the Second Amendment, so as to protect the right to keep and bear arms from state infringement?[126]

The Fourteenth Amendment provides: "No State shall make or enforce any law which shall abridge the privileges or immunities of citizens of the United States; nor shall any State deprive any person of life, liberty, or property, without due process of law." Senator Jacob Howard, when introducing the amendment in Congress in 1866, explained that its purpose was to protect "personal rights" such as "the right to keep and bear arms" from state infringement.[127]

In three cases decided in the last quarter of the nineteenth century, the United States Supreme Court stated in dicta that the First, Second, and Fourth Amendments do not directly limit state action, but did not rule on whether the Fourteenth Amendment prohibited state violations of the rights therein declared.[128] Since then, the Supreme Court has held that most Bill of Rights freedoms are incorporated into the Fourteenth Amendment, with little analysis and no discussion of the intent of the framers of that amendment,[129] but has

124. Act of July 16, 1866, 14 *Statutes at Large* 173, 176. For the legislative history of this provision, *see* Halbrook, "Personal Security, Personal Liberty, and 'the Constitutional Right to Bear Arms': Visions of the Framers of the Fourteenth Amendment," 5 Seton Hall Const. L.J. 341 (Spring 1995).

125. *Griswold v. Connecticut*, 381 U.S. 479, 485, 85 S. Ct. 1678, 14 L. Ed. 2d 510 (1965).

126. *See generally* Halbrook, *Freedmen, the Fourteenth Amendment, and the Right to Bear Arms*, 1866-1876 (Westport, Conn.: Praeger Publishers, 1998). On the applicability of the Second Amendment to the District of Columbia, *see* Halbrook, "Second-Class Citizenship and the Second Amendment in the District of Columbia," 5 Geo. Mason U. Civ. Rts. L.J. 601 (1995).

127. Cong. Globe, 39th Cong., 1st Sess. at 2765 (May 23, 1866).

128. *U.S. v. Cruikshank*, 92 U.S. 542, 551, 23 L. Ed. 588 (1875) (private harm to rights to assemble and bear arms held not to be a federal offense); *Presser v. People of State of Ill.*, 116 U.S. 252, 265, 6 S. Ct. 580, 29 L. Ed. 615 (1886) (city's requirement of license for armed march on public streets held not to violate right to assemble or bear arms); *Miller v. State of Texas*, 153 U.S. 535, 538, 14 S. Ct. 874, 38 L. Ed. 812 (1894) (refusal to consider whether Fourteenth Amendment protects Second and Fourth Amendment rights because claim not made in trial court). *See* Halbrook, *That Every Man Be Armed* 155-64 (1984); Halbrook, "The Right of Workers to Assemble and to Bear Arms: *Presser v. Illinois*, One of the Last Holdouts Against Application of the Bill of Rights to the States," 76 University of Detroit Mercy Law Review 943-89 (Summer 1999).

129. *E.g., Chicago, B. & Q.R. Co. v. City of Chicago*, 166 U.S. 226, 238-39, 17 S. Ct. 581, 41 L. Ed. 979 (1897) (just compensation); *Gitlow v. People of State of New York*, 268 U.S. 652, 666, 45 S. Ct. 625, 69 L. Ed. 1138 (1925) (speech and press); *De Jonge v. State of Oregon*, 299 U.S. 353, 364, 57 S. Ct. 255, 81 L. Ed. 278 (1937) (assembly); *Wolf v. People of the State of Colo.*, 338 U.S. 25, 27-28, 69 S. Ct. 1359, 93 L. Ed. 1782 (1949) (overruled by, *Mapp v. Ohio*, 367 U.S. 643, 81 S. Ct. 1684, 6 L. Ed. 2d 1081, 86 Ohio L. Abs. 513, 84 A.L.R.2d 933 (1961)) (search and seizure); *Robinson v. California*, 370 U.S. 660, 666, 82 S. Ct. 1417, 8 L. Ed. 2d 758 (1962) (cruel and unusual punishment); *Gideon v. Wainwright*, 372 U.S. 335, 341, 83 S. Ct. 792, 9 L. Ed. 2d 799, 93 A.L.R.2d 733 (1963) (counsel).

failed to decide whether the Second Amendment is so incorporated, despite the specific declaration of two-thirds of Congress in the Freedmen's Bureau Act.[130]

United States v. Emerson (5th Cir. 2001), referring to the three above nineteenth century cases, stated: "As these holdings all came well before the Supreme Court began the process of incorporating certain provisions of the first eight amendments into the Due Process Clause of the Fourteenth Amendment, and as they ultimately rest on a rationale equally applicable to all those amendments, none of them establishes any principle governing any of the issues now before us."[131] *Emerson* cited recent Supreme Court opinions on the Fourteenth Amendment which position the Second Amendment in an equal status with the other provisions of the first eight amendments.[132] Given *Emerson's* holding that the Second Amendment guarantees an individual right, it would be illogical not to incorporate it into the Fourteenth Amendment.

The first local and state prohibitions in American history on firearms possession by the citizenry at large—the Morton Grove, Illinois handgun ban, and California's prohibition on "assault weapons" (primarily repeating rifles)—were upheld by the United States Courts of Appeals for the Seventh and Ninth Circuits in 1982 and 1992 respectively. Both opinions rejected any reliance on the intent of the framers of the Fourteenth Amendment, and interpreted Supreme Court precedent to reject incorporation of the right to keep and bear arms into that amendment.[133]

Scholarly studies document that the framers of the Fourteenth Amendment did intend to protect Bill of Rights freedoms in general,[134] and the right to keep and bear arms in particular.[135] Critics have argued that speeches by individual framers of the Fourteenth Amendment are insufficient to demonstrate a consensus to incorporate the Bill of Rights.[136] Bearing arms was the only right declared as a right of personal security and personal liberty by over two-thirds of the same Congress which proposed the Fourteenth Amendment.[137]

The above language of the Freedmen's Bureau Act and related evidence was never acknowledged in any judicial opinion until the year 2000, in the

---

130. On the logic of incorporation under existing Supreme Court precedents, *see* Halbrook, *That Every Man Be Armed* 170-78 (1984).

131. *United States v. Emerson*, 270 F.3d 203, 221 n.13 (5th Cir. 2001), *cert. denied* (June 11, 2002).

132. *Id.* at 221. *See also id.* at 229 n.27 (quoting remarks of Senator Howard introducing the Fourteenth Amendment and stating that it would "person right" such as "the right to keep and to bear arms").

133. *Quilici v. Village of Morton Grove*, 695 F.2d 261, 270 n.8 (7th Cir. 1982) ("the debate surrounding the adoption of the second and fourteenth amendments . . . has no relevance on the resolution of the controversy before us"); *Fresno Rifle and Pistol Club, Inc. v. Van De Kamp*, 965 F.2d 723, 730 (9th Cir. 1992) (refusing to consider "remarks by various legislators during passage of the Freedmen's Bureau Act of 1866, the Civil Rights Act of 1866, and the Civil Rights act of 1871").

134. Amar, "The Bill of Rights and the Fourteenth Amendment," 101 Yale L.J. 1193 (1992) [hereinafter cited as Amar]; Curtis, *No State Shall Abridge: the Fourteenth Amendment and the Bill of Rights* (1986) [hereinafter cited as Curtis]; Flack, *The Adoption of the Fourteenth Amendment* (1908) [hereinafter cited as Flack].

135. Halbrook, *Freedmen, the Fourteenth Amendment, and the Right to Bear Arms* (Praeger Publishers 1998); Halbrook, "Personal Security, Personal Liberty, and 'The Constitutional Right to Bear Arms': Visions of the Framers of the Fourteenth Amendment," 5 Seton Hall Const. L.J. Book 341 (1994) [hereinafter cited as Halbrook, "Personal Security"]; Cottrol & Diamond, "The Second Amendment: Toward an Afro-Americanist Reconsideration," 80 Georgetown L.J. 309 (1991); Halbrook, *That Every Man Be Armed: The Evolution of a Constitutional Right* 107-53 (1984); "The Right to Keep and Bear Arms: Report of the Subcommittee on the Constitution," Senate Judiciary Committee, 97th Cong., 2d Sess. at 68-82 (1982).

136. *Compare* Fairman, "Does the Fourteenth Amendment Incorporate the Bill of Rights?", 2 Stanford L. Rev. 5 (1949) *with* Crosskey, "Charles Fairman, 'Legislative History,' and the Constitutional Limitations on State Authority," 22 U. Chi. L. Rev. 1 (1954).

137. The significance of this declaration to support incorporation of the Second Amendment as well as other parts of the Bill of Rights into the Fourteenth Amendment is the focus of Halbrook, "Personal Security," and is recognized in three of the best studies on the Fourteenth Amendment. *See* Amar at 1245 n.228; Curtis at 72; Flack at 17.

concurring opinion of Justice Brown in an opinion of the California Supreme Court.[138] Quoting the language of the Act and this author, Justice Brown states:

> Halbrook concludes the Freedman's Bureau Act, the Civil Rights Act of 1866, and the Fourteenth Amendment leave no doubt that "'the constitutional right to bear arms' is included among the 'laws and proceedings concerning personal liberty, personal security,' and property, and that 'the free enjoyment of such immunities and rights' is to be protected" . . . under the Fourteenth Amendment, which would confer citizenship on all persons born in the United States and imbue them with every right of citizenship, including the right to keep and bear arms.[139]

In a manner unique in judicial discussion of the Second Amendment but which captures the ultimate purpose of the right, Justice Brown responded to the argument that "the right of the people to keep and bear arms (if any such right exists) is outweighed by the right of the public to be safe" as follows:

> I suspect the freedmen of the Reconstruction Era would vehemently disagree. So would the Armenians facing the Ottoman Turks in 1915, the embattled Jews of the Warsaw Ghetto in 1943, and the victims of Pol Pot's killing fields.
>
> The media keep the horrific visions of gun violence ever before our eyes. These acts of individual madness are undeniably tragic and totally unacceptable in a civilized society. But there are other horrific visions—the victims of which number in the millions—perpetrated by governments against unarmed populations. . . .
>
> The framers could have had no conception of the massive scale on which government-sanctioned murder would be committed in the twentieth century, but they had a keen appreciation of the peril of being defenseless. That wariness is reflected in the Constitution.[140]

Tactical Tip:

No need may exist to raise the issue of whether the Fourteenth Amendment incorporates the Second Amendment in the forty-three states which have an arms guarantee, unless the courts of a particular state have interpreted the state arms guarantee not to protect anyone (such as in Massachusetts). States with the most stringent firearms prohibitions (such as New Jersey and California) have no constitutional protection for the right to keep and bear arms.

---

138. *Kasler v. Lockyer*, 23 Cal. 4th 472, 503-10, 97 Cal. Rptr. 2d 334, 2 P.3d 581, 601-05, (2000), *cert. denied*, 531 U.S. 1149, 121 S. Ct. 1090, 148 L. Ed. 2d 964 (2001) (Brown, J., concurring).

139. 23 Cal. 4th at 506, quoting Halbrook, "Second Class Citizenship and the Second Amendment in the District of Columbia," 5 Geo. Mason U. Civ. Rts. L.J. 105, 150 (1995). Justice Brown also wrote:

> Curiously, in the current dialectic, the right to keep and bear arms—a right expressly guaranteed by the Bill of Rights—is deemed less fundamental than implicit protections the court purports to find in the penumbras of other express provisions. . . . But surely, the right to preserve one's life is at least as fundamental as the right to preserve one's privacy.
>
> The founding generation certainly viewed bearing arms as an individual right based upon both English common law and natural law, a right logically linked to the natural right of self-defense. Blackstone described self-defense as the "primary law of nature," which could not be taken away by the law of society.

Slip opinion at 2-3, quoting Blackstone and Thomas Paine.

140. *Kasler v. Lockyer*, 23 Cal. 4th 472, 510, 97 Cal. Rptr. 2d 334, 2 P.3d 581, 601-05, (2000), *cert. denied*, 531 U.S. 1149, 121 S. Ct. 1090, 148 L. Ed. 2d 964 (2001).

Sec. 1:6 State jurisprudence

Some forty-three state constitutions explicitly recognize the right to keep and bear arms for defense of self and state or other purposes.[141] In at least twenty-one reported cases, state statutes or local ordinances have been held to violate constitutional guarantees of the right to keep arms or to bear arms.[142] As in the case of other constitutional rights, the courts are more prone to uphold the validity of an enactment than to declare it unconstitutional.

Traditionally, rifles, pistols, and shotguns have been considered to be constitutionally protected arms. Bearing concealed arms could be regulated, but the mere keeping of arms was unquestioned. In time, prohibitions on certain blunt objects and edged instruments were passed, following which machine guns and short-barreled rifles and shotguns came to be highly restricted. Only in very recent times have limited prohibitions on handguns and semiautomatic firearms been enacted. The following analyzes some representative cases to illustrate the constitutional issues which arise.

The high court of Kentucky, the first state court to rule a statute invalid under an arms guarantee, held that a prohibition on wearing concealed weapons was void because it questioned the right of a citizen to bear arms.[143] The state constitution was amended to authorize the regulation of the carrying of concealed weapons. Today, Vermont remains the only state in which a prohibition on carrying concealed weapons without a permit is deemed unconstitutional.[144]

Some other states thereafter adopted explicit constitutional authorizations to regulate the bearing of concealed weapons, giving rise to the implication that no legislative power existed to prohibit the keeping of arms. The courts of several states have held that the right to keep arms protects possession of militia-type firearms.[145]

---

141. On the adoption of the first state bills of rights and their evolution thereafter, *see* Halbrook, *A Right to Bear Arms: State and Federal Bills of Rights and Constitutional Guarantees* (1989). State judicial decisions on various state constitutional arms guarantees are analyzed in Dowlut, "Federal and State Constitutional Guarantees to Arms," 15 U. Dayton L. Rev. 59 (1989); Dowlut & Knoop, "State Constitutions and the Right to Keep and Bear Arms," 7 Okla. City U. L. Rev. 177 (1982); Halbrook, *That Every Man be Armed* 93-99, 179-87 (1984); Halbrook, "The Right to Bear Arms in Texas," 41 Baylor L. Rev. 629 (1989).

142. *State ex rel. City of Princeton v. Buckner*, 180 W. Va. 457, 377 S.E.2d 139 (1988) (pistol carrying statute); *Barnett v. State*, 72 Or. App. 585, 695 P.2d 991 (1985) (prohibition on possession of black jack); *State v. Delgado*, 298 Or. 395, 692 P.2d 610, 47 A.L.R.4th 643 (1984) (prohibition on possession of switchblade knife); *State v. Blocker*, 291 Or. 255, 630 P.2d 824 (1981) (prohibition on carrying club); *State v. Kessler*, 289 Or. 359, 614 P.2d 94 (1980) (prohibition on possession of club); *Junction City v. Mevis*, 226 Kan. 526, 601 P.2d 1145 (1979) (gun carrying ordinance); *Lakewood v. Pillow*, 180 Colo. 20, 501 P.2d 744 (1972) (ordinance requiring license for sale, possession, and carrying firearm); *City of Las Vegas v. Moberg*, 82 N.M. 626, 485 P.2d 737 (Ct. App. 1971) (gun carrying ordinance); *People v. Nakamura*, 99 Colo. 262, 62 P.2d 246 (1936) (prohibition on possession of firearm by alien); *Glasscock v. City of Chattanooga*, 157 Tenn. 518, 11 S.W.2d 678 (1928) (gun carrying ordinance); *People v. Zerillo*, 219 Mich. 635, 189 N.W. 927, 24 A.L.R. 1115 (1922) (statute prohibiting possession of firearm); *State v. Kerner*, 181 N.C. 574, 107 S.E. 222 (1921) (pistol carrying license and bond requirement statute); *In re Reilly*, 23 Ohio N.P. (n.s.) 65, 31 Ohio Dec. 364, 1919 WL 1022 (C.P. 1919) (ordinance forbidding hiring armed guard to protect property); *State v. Rosenthal*, 75 Vt. 295, 55 A. 610 (1903) (pistol carrying ordinance); *In re Brickey*, 8 Idaho 597, 70 P. 609 (1902) (gun carrying statute); *Jennings v. State*, 5 Tex. App. 298, 1878 WL 9108 (Ct. App. 1878) (statute requiring forfeiture of pistol after misdemeanor conviction); *Wilson v. State*, 33 Ark. 557, 1878 WL 1301 (1878) (pistol carrying statute); *Andrews v. State*, 50 Tenn. 165, 3 Heisk. 165, 1871 WL 3579 (1871) (pistol carrying statute); *Smith v. Ishenhour*, 43 Tenn. 214, 3 Cold. 214, 1866 WL 1804 (1866) (firearm confiscation law); *Nunn v. State*, 1 Ga. 243, 1846 WL 1167 (1846) (pistol carrying statute); *Bliss v. Com.*, 12 Ky. 90, 2 Litt. 90, 1822 WL 1085 (1822) (concealed weapon statute).

143. *Bliss v. Com.*, 12 Ky. 90, 2 Litt. 90, 1822 WL 1085 (1822).

144. *State v. Rosenthal*, 75 Vt. 295, 299, 55 A. 610, 611 (1903).

145. "[T]he term 'arms' as used means such arms as are recognized in civilized warfare." *State v. Swanton*, 129 Ariz. 131, 629 P.2d 98, 99 (Ct. App. Div. 2 1981). "The intention was to embrace the 'arms', an acquaintance with whose use was necessary for their protection against the usurpation of illegal power—such as rifles,

The North Carolina Supreme Court invalidated a prohibition on the unlicensed open carrying of pistols, explaining the criteria for which arms are constitutionally protected as follows:

> To him [the ordinary private citizen] the rifle, the musket, the shotgun, and the pistol are about the only arms which he could be expected to "bear," and his right to do this is that which is guaranteed by the Constitution. To deprive him of bearing any of these arms is to infringe upon the right guaranteed to him by the Constitution.
>
> It would be mockery to say that the Constitution intended to guarantee him the right to practice dropping bombs from a flying machine, to operate a cannon throwing missiles perhaps for a hundred miles or more, or to practice in the use of deadly gases. . . .
>
> . . . The intention was to embrace the "arms," an acquaintance with whose use was necessary for their protection against the usurpation of illegal power—such as rifles, muskets, shotguns, swords, and pistols.[146]

The West Virginia Supreme Court declared unconstitutional that state's prohibition on the carrying of a pistol without a license.[147] The defendant in that case allegedly carried a .22 caliber semiautomatic pistol in his pocket. The court held:

> W.Va.Code, 61-7-1 [1975] is written as a total proscription of the carrying of a dangerous or deadly weapon without a license or other authorization. W.Va.Code, 61-7-1 [1975] thus prohibits the carrying of weapons for defense of self, family, home and state without a license or statutory authorization. Article III, section 22 of the West Virginia Constitution, however, guarantees that a person has the right to bear arms for those defensive purposes. Thus, the statute operates to impermissibly infringe upon this constitutionally protected right to bear arms for defensive purposes.[148]

The West Virginia Court noted that the right to bear arms is not "absolute" and may be regulated.[149] "We stress, however, that the legitimate governmental purpose in regulating the right to bear arms cannot be pursued by means that broadly stifle the exercise of this right where the governmental purpose can be more narrowly achieved."[150]

Besides criminal prosecutions, civil suits seeking to obtain permits to carry pistols result in expositions of the nature of the right to bear arms. Ordering the issuance of a license, the Indiana Court of Appeals stated:

> We think it clear that our constitution provides our citizenry the right to bear arms for their self defense. . . .
>
> . . . The superintendent decided the application on the basis that the statutory reference to "a proper reason" vested in him the power and duty to subjectively evaluate an

---

muskets, shotguns, swords, and pistols." *State v. Kerner*, 181 N.C. 574, 107 S.E. 222, 224-25 (1921). "Under this head, with a knowledge of the habits of our people, and of the arms in the use of which a soldier should be trained, we would hold that the rifle of all descriptions, the shot-gun, the musket and repeater are such arms; and that under the constitution the right to keep such arms cannot be infringed or forbidden by the legislature." *Andrews v. State*, 50 Tenn. 165, 179, 3 Heisk. 165, 1871 WL 3579 (1871). *See Hill v. State*, 53 Ga. 472, 474, 1874 WL 3112 (1874) ("the word 'arms,' evidently means the arms of a militiaman, the weapons ordinarily used in battle, to-wit; guns of every kind, swords, bayonets, horseman's pistols, etc."); *Fife v. State*, 31 Ark. 455, 458, 1876 WL 1562 (1876) ("the arms which it guarantees American citizens the right to keep and to bear, are such as are needful to, and ordinarily used by a well regulated militia, and such as are necessary and suitable to a free people, to enable them to resist oppression").

146. *State v. Kerner*, 181 N.C. 574, 107 S.E. 222, 224 (1921).

147. *State ex rel. City of Princeton v. Buckner*, 180 W. Va. 457, 377 S.E.2d 139 (1988).

148. *Id.* at 144.

149. 377 S.E.2d at 145.

150. *State ex rel. City of Princeton v. Buckner*, 180 W. Va. 457, 377 S.E.2d 139, 146 (1988).

> assignment of "self-defense" as a reason for desiring a license and the ability to grant or deny the license upon the basis of whether the applicant "needed" to defend himself.
>
> Such an approach contravenes the essential nature of the constitutional guarantee. It would supplant a right with a mere administrative privilege which might be withheld simply on the basis that such matters as the use of firearms are better left to the organized military and police forces even where defense of the individual citizen is involved.[151]

Restrictions placed on the scope of a handgun concealed carry licensing scheme may violate constitutional provisions. The New Mexico Constitution provides: "No law shall abridge the right of the citizen to keep and bear arms for security and defense, for lawful hunting and recreational use and for other lawful purposes, but nothing herein shall be held to permit the carrying of concealed weapons. No municipality or county shall regulate, in any way, an incident of the right to keep and bear arms."[152] A State statute providing for licenses to carry concealed handguns but which authorized a locality to refuse to recognize licenses. The New Mexico Supreme Court declared the statute unconstitutional due to the local opt out provision: "The manner in which a person 'bears' a weapon, whether concealed or in plain view, is an incident of the right to bear arms."[153] The court explained:

> The Act purports to allow municipalities and counties to prohibit the carrying of concealed weapons and, in so doing, delegates to them the power to regulate an incident of the right to keep and bear arms. The broad language of Article II, Section 6 of our Constitution prohibiting municipalities and counties from regulating an "incident" of the right to keep and bear arms "in any way" indicates an intent to preclude piecemeal administration at a local level and to ensure uniformity in the regulation of firearms throughout the State of New Mexico.[154]

The Ohio Constitution, Section 4, Article I, provides: "The people have the right to bear arms for their defense and security . . . ." State statutes prohibit carrying a concealed weapon, subject to the affirmative defenses that it is carried for defensive purposes while engaged in a lawful business at a time and place that renders the citizen "particularly susceptible to criminal attack," such that a "prudent person" would be justified in going armed. The Ohio Court of Appeals invalidated the prohibition as a ban on the right to bear arms. If one bears arms openly, one would be arrested for inducing panic or disorderly conduct. If one bears arms concealed, one is arrested without regard to the affirmative defenses, which are vague. "No Ohioan can exercise the constitutional right to bear arms, whether concealed or unconcealed, without risking jail. The exercise of no other fundamental right subjects a citizen to arrest."[155] This decision has been appealed to the Ohio Supreme Court, which issued a stay of the injunction against the enforcement of the concealed weapon prohibition.[156]

An early Texas case held that the Texas arms guarantee "protects only the right to 'keep' such 'arms' as are used for purposes of war."[157] It added:

---

151. *Schubert v. DeBard*, 398 N.E.2d 1339, 1341 (Ind. Ct. App. 3d Dist. 1980).
152. N. Mex. Const., Article II, Section 6.
153. *Baca v. New Mexico Dept. of Public Safety*, 47 P.3d 441, 444 (N.M. 2002).
154. *Id.*
155. *Klein v. Leis*, 146 Ohio App. 3d 526, 767 N.E.2d 286 (1st Dist. Hamilton County 2002).
156. *Klein v. Leis*, 95 Ohio St. 3d 1433, 766 N.E.2d 999 (2002).
157. *English v. State*, 35 Tex. 473, 475, 1872 WL 7422 (1872).

> The word "arms" in this connection we find it in the constitution of the United States, refers to the arms of a militiaman or soldier, and the word is used in its military sense. The arms of the infantry soldier are the musket and bayonet; of cavalry and dragoons, the sabre, holster pistols and carbine.[158]

However, the Texas Supreme Court expanded that holding to include all personal weapons, not just military arms:

> The arms which every person is secured the right to keep and bear (in the defense of himself or the State, subject to legislative regulation), must be such arms as are commonly kept, according to the customs of the people, and are appropriate for open and manly use in self-defense, as well as such as are proper for the defense of the State.[159]

Upholding the conviction of a felon who possessed a blackjack, the Michigan Supreme Court noted that legislation "cannot constitutionally result in the prohibition of the possession of those arms which, by the common opinion and usage of law-abiding people, are proper and legitimate to be kept upon private premises for the protection of person and property."[160]

The Colorado Constitution provides that "the right of no person to keep and bear arms in defense of his home, person and property . . . shall be questioned." The Colorado Supreme Court invalidated a local ordinance which prohibited the possession of a revolver, pistol, shotgun or rifle, except within one's domicile or at a target range, unless licensed by the city, as "unconstitutionally overbroad":

> An analysis of the foregoing ordinance reveals that it is so general in its scope that it includes within its prohibitions the right to carry on certain businesses and to engage in certain activities which cannot under the police power be reasonably classified as unlawful and thus, subject to criminal sanctions. As an example, we note that this ordinance would prohibit gunsmiths, pawnbrokers and sporting goods stores from carrying on a substantial part of their business. Also, the ordinance appears to prohibit individuals from transporting guns to and from such places of business for the purpose of self-defense. Several of these activities are constitutionally protected, Colo. Const. art. II, §13. Depending upon the circumstances, all of these activities and others may be entirely free of any criminal culpability yet the ordinance in question effectively includes them within its prohibitions and is therefore invalid.[161]

The court explained why a prohibition on unlicensed possession of firearms is not proper under the police power as follows:

> A governmental purpose to control or prevent certain activities, which may be constitutionally subject to state or municipal regulation under the police power, may not be achieved by means which sweep unnecessarily broadly and thereby invade the area of protected freedoms. . . . Even though the governmental purpose may be legitimate and substantial, that purpose cannot be pursued by means that broadly stifle fundamental personal liberties when the end can be more narrowly achieved.[162]

By contrast, the Colorado Supreme Court upheld the state prohibition on possession of weapons by violent felons, who "cannot invoke the same constitutionally protected right to bear arms as could [a law-abiding person] for . . . the right of a convicted felon to bear arms is subject to reasonable legislative

---

158. *Id.* at 476-77.
159. *State v. Duke*, 42 Tex. 455, 458-59, 1875 WL 7460 (1875).
160. *People v. Brown*, 253 Mich. 537, 235 N.W. 245, 82 A.L.R. 341 (1931). An electrical shocking device (stun gun) is not a commonly possessed, constitutionally protected arm. *See People v. Smelter*, 175 Mich. App. 153, 437 N.W.2d 341, 342 (1989).
161. *City of Lakewood v. Pillow*, 180 Colo. 20, 501 P.2d 744, 745 (1972).
162. *Id.*

regulation and limitation."[163] "The statute simply limits the possession of guns and other weapons by persons who are likely to abuse such possession."[164] Nonetheless, the court held in a later case, a felon "who presents competent evidence showing that his purpose in possessing weapons was the defense of his home, person, and property thereby raises an affirmative defense."[165]

Under a traditional theory, a Texas appellate court ruled that "a machine gun is not a weapon commonly kept, according to the customs of the people and appropriate for open and manly use in self defense."[166] Other jurisdictions have upheld bans on unregistered machine guns, short shotguns, and similar weapons.[167]

The Oregon Supreme Court has set forth a detailed analysis of which "arms" are constitutionally protected and which are not:

> Therefore, the term "arms" as used by the drafters of the constitutions probably was intended to include those weapons used by settlers for both personal and military defense. . . .
>
> The term "arms" would not have included cannon or other heavy ordnance not kept by militiamen or private citizens. . . .
>
> These advanced weapons of modern warfare have never been intended for personal possession and protection. When the constitutional drafters referred to an individual's "right to bear arms," the arms used by the militia and for personal protection were basically the same weapons. Modern weapons used exclusively by the military are not "arms" which are commonly possessed by individuals for defense, therefore, the "arms" in the constitution does not include such weapons.
>
> If the text and purpose of the constitutional guarantee relied exclusively on the preference for a militia "for defense of the State" then the term "arms" most likely would include only the modern day equivalents of the weapons used by colonial militiamen. The Oregon provision, however, guarantees a right to bear arms "for defense of themselves and the State." The term arms in our constitution therefore would include weapons commonly used for either purpose, even if a particular weapon is unlikely to be used as a militia weapon.[168]

Until recently, semiautomatic firearms seem to have been universally considered constitutionally protected.[169] The Florida Supreme Court rejected broad construction of a statute to avoid its unconstitutionality:

> But such a construction might run counter to the historic constitutional right of the people to keep and bear arms. . . . We, therefore, hold that the statute does not prohibit the ownership, custody and possession of weapons not concealed upon the person, which, although designed to shoot more than one shot semi-automatically, are commonly kept and used by law-abiding people for hunting purposes or for the

---

163. *People v. Blue*, 190 Colo. 95, 544 P.2d 385, 390 (1975).

164. *Id.* at 391.

165. *People v. Ford*, 193 Colo. 459, 568 P.2d 26, 28 (1977).

166. *Morrison v. State*, 170 Tex. Crim. 218, 339 S.W.2d 529, 531 (1960).

167. *State v. Hamlin*, 497 So. 2d 1269, 1369-70 (La. 1986); *Carson v. State*, 241 Ga. 622, 247 S.E.2d 68, 72 (1978); *State v. Astore*, 258 So. 2d 33 (Fla. Dist. Ct. App. 2d Dist. 1972); *State v. LaChapelle*, 234 Neb. 458, 451 N.W.2d 689 (1990); *State v. Fennell*, 95 N.C. App. 140, 382 S.E.2d 231 (1989). The statutes of these states exempt these firearms if registered with federal or state authorities.

168. *State v. Kessler*, 289 Or. 359, 614 P.2d 94, 98-99 (1980).

169. *Taylor v. McNeal*, 523 S.W.2d 148, 150 (Mo. Ct. App. 1975), found "pistols and ammunition clips" (which feed ammunition into semiautomatic firearms) to be protected because "every citizen has the right to keep and bear arms in defense of his home, person and property."

> protection of their persons and property, such as semi-automatic shotguns, semiautomatic pistols and rifles.[170]

The Washington Supreme Court stated of "a CAR 15 semiautomatic rifle (civilian version of the military's M-16)": "Constitutionally protected behavior cannot be the basis of criminal punishment. . . . The State can take no action which will unnecessarily 'chill' or penalize the assertion of a constitutional right and the State may not draw adverse inferences from the exercise of a constitutional right."[171] While the prosecution labeled the CAR 15 "an assault weapon," the defendant used it for hunting varmints.[172] Ruling a death sentence to be invalid because the jury heard evidence of possession of arms unrelated to the murder, the court explained:

> Here, the challenged evidence directly implicates defendant's right to bear arms. Const. art. 1, §24 provides:
>
> The right of the individual citizen to bear arms in defense of himself, or the state, shall not be impaired. . . .
>
> Defendant's behavior—possession of legal weapons—falls squarely within the confines of the right guaranteed by Const. art. 1, §24. Defendant was thus entitled under our constitution to possess weapons, without incurring the risk that the State would subsequently use the mere fact of possession against him in a criminal trial unrelated to their use.[173]

The Oregon Supreme Court invalidated a prohibition on mere possession of switchblade knives under the test "whether a kind of weapon, as modified by its modern design and function, is of the sort commonly used by individuals for personal defense during either the revolutionary and post-revolutionary era, or in 1859 when Oregon's constitution was adopted."[174] The court's comments would apply to a variety of firearms and other weapons:

> At one time the single-action, single-shot handgun was carried by many men for defense. Did the development of the double-action feature of the handgun or the addition of the revolving cylinder which enabled one to fire the gun several times without pausing to reload, as a matter of law, transform the handgun from a defensive weapon to an offensive weapon? Obviously, the gun, both before and after such changes, could be used for either defense or offense.[175]

A county in Oregon prohibited possession of an "assault weapon in a public place" unless it is unloaded, disassembled into major component parts, and locked in a case.[176] While it could have disposed of the case on the narrow ground that the ordinance was not a prohibition on possession per se,[177] the

170. *Rinzler v. Carson*, 262 So. 2d 661, 666 (Fla. 1972). While the court held machine guns not to be constitutionally protected, Florida allowed possession of machine guns registered under federal law, and thus a local ordinance purporting to ban machine guns was preempted and invalid. *Id.* at 667-68.

171. *State v. Rupe*, 101 Wash. 2d 664, 683 P.2d 571, 594 (1984).

172. *Id.* at 594-95.

173. *Id.* at 596.

174. *State v. Delgado*, 298 Or. 395, 400-1, 692 P.2d 610, 47 A.L.R.4th 643 (1984).

175. *Id.* at 400.

176. *Oregon State Shooting Ass'n v. Multnomah County*, 122 Or. App. 540, 858 P.2d 1315, 1330 (1993).

177. For instance, *State v. Boyce*, 61 Or. App. 662, 658 P.2d 577, 578 (1983), held:

> The statute [found unconstitutional in Kessler] proscribed the "mere possession" of certain weapons, and that was the characteristic that made it unconstitutional. The Portland ordinance, on the other hand, does not proscribe the mere possession of anything. Under it, an individual may possess both a firearm and ammunition. He may even possess a loaded firearm, so long as he is not in a public place. In a public place, he may possess both a firearm and ammunition, so long as the ammunition is not in the chamber, cylinder, clip or magazine.

Oregon Court of Appeals held the firearms involved not to be constitutionally protected "arms"[178] because the Oregon Constitution was adopted in 1859, and repeating rifles did not become common until 1860-1862.[179]

The concurring and dissenting judges argued that "the listed weapons are the 'sort of' weapons commonly used for personal defense in 1859. They are rifles, pistols and shotguns."[180] The majority opinion "will come as a great shock to the many gun owners in Oregon who have possessed semi-automatic rifles and pistols for decades."[181] However, the ordinance did not unreasonably interfere with the right to bear arms because it is not "a complete ban on the possession of the listed firearms in public places" and "does not interfere with a citizen's defense capacity in their homes or other private places."[182]

Tactical Tip:

Persuasive arguments regarding a specific State constitution should depend on the language of the guarantee, the intent of its framers, and subsequent judicial interpretation. Of these, the intent of the framers is often neglected, but may have rejected the very law being challenged. In mounting a challenge, counsel should consult the entire constitutional history of a provision within a state.

Sec. 1:7 Is the right to bear arms fundamental?

The states have generally followed the formulation by the U.S. Supreme Court that a constitutional right is a "fundamental" right, which thereby triggers the "strict scrutiny" test for legislation rather than the mere "rational relation" test.[183]

While some states have no arms guarantee,[184] state arms guarantees have traditionally been accorded the same interpretive methodology as other state bill of rights provisions.

Because the right was explicitly recognized in the state constitution, a Connecticut court held in a handgun licensing case: "It appears that a Connecticut citizen, under the language of the Connecticut constitution, has a fundamental right to bear arms in self-defense, a liberty interest which must be protected by procedural due process."[185]

America's first handgun ban, that of Morton Grove, Illinois, passed in 1981, was upheld by the U.S. Court of Appeals for the Seventh Circuit.[186] The language of the Illinois guarantee is more limited than that of other states—it actually states that the right is "subject to the police power"—and was explained by one of its framers as allowing a handgun ban.[187] While the majority opinion contained little discussion of the fundamental rights doctrine, the dissenting opinion states:

---

178. As "evidence" of the nature of the prohibited firearms, the majority relied on the New York Times Magazine. 858 P.2d at 1321 ns.8, 9.

179. *Oregon State Shooting Ass'n v. Multnomah County*, 122 Or. App. 540, 858 P.2d 1315, 1321-22 (1993).

180. *Id.* at 1325.

181. *Id.* at 1327.

182. *Id.* at 1329-30.

183. *San Antonio Independent School Dist. v. Rodriguez*, 411 U.S. 1, 33, 93 S. Ct. 1278, 36 L. Ed. 2d 16 (1973) (a right is "fundamental" if it is "explicitly or implicitly guaranteed by the Constitution").

184. *E.g., City of Minneapolis v. Wurtele*, 291 N.W.2d 386, 398 (Minn. 1980) ("the Minnesota Constitution, unlike that of other states, contains no express reference to the right to bear arms for self defense").

185. *Rabbitt v. Leonard*, 36 Conn. Supp. 108, 413 A.2d 489, 491 (Super. Ct. 1979).

186. *Quilici v. Village of Morton Grove*, 695 F.2d 261, 266 (7th Cir. 1982).

187. *Id.* at 266-67.

> The majority cavalierly dismisses the argument that the right to possess commonly owned arms for self-defense and the protection of loved ones is a fundamental right protected by the Constitution. . . . Surely nothing could be more fundamental to the "concept of ordered liberty" than the basic right of an individual, within the confines of the criminal law, to protect his home and family from unlawful and dangerous intrusions.[188]

Rejecting the above decision and upholding a civil rights claim for violation of the right to bear handguns, the Supreme Court of Indiana held:

> The right of Indiana citizens to bear arms for their own self-defense and for the defense of the state is an interest in both liberty and property which is protected by the Fourteenth Amendment to the Federal Constitution. . . . This interest is one of liberty to the extent that it enables law-abiding citizens to be free from the threat and danger of violent crime.[189]

State courts with restrictive views of the constitutional guarantee to keep and bear arms have posed three different arguments in response to the general rule that explicitly guaranteed rights are fundamental rights. First, this right is the lone exception; it is explicitly guaranteed but is not fundamental. Second, this right is fundamental, but a rational relation test, not a strict scrutiny test, applies, thereby validating "reasonable" firearms prohibitions. Third, it need not be determined whether the right is fundamental, and any "reasonable" prohibition is valid.

The first argument was used by the Illinois Supreme Court in upholding the Morton Grove handgun ban. All constitutional rights are fundamental, it seems, except the right to keep and bear arms.[190]

The second argument was used by the Ohio Supreme Court in upholding Cleveland's prohibition on "assault weapons."[191] The Court recognized that the Ohio guarantee "secures to every person a fundamental *individual* right to bear arms for 'their *defense and security*.'"[192] Instead of the strict scrutiny test for fundamental rights as exists in other jurisdictions, in Ohio a constitutional right may be limited by a "reasonable" exercise of the police power.[193]

The dissenting opinion argued that the strict scrutiny standard applied, "particularly where the legislation prescribes an outright prohibition of possession as opposed to mere regulation of possession."[194] Moreover, the dissent opined, the plaintiffs were entitled to introduce evidence to demonstrate that the ordinance is arbitrary and unreasonable:

> Use of the term "assault weapon" generates emotional responses and inherent bias. Whether the weapons banned by the Cleveland ordinance are primarily antipersonnel or whether they are equally suitable for defensive or sporting purposes has yet to be demonstrated. . . . The mere declaration by Cleveland Council that it finds the primary purpose of assault weapons to be antipersonnel . . . is, standing alone, insufficient to satisfy the government's burden when such legislation infringes upon a fundamental right.[195]

The third above argument was used by the Colorado Supreme Court in upholding Denver's prohibition on "assault weapons" (other than portions found to be vague). Although the preamble to the Colorado Bill of Rights states that it

---

188. *Id.* at 278.
189. *Kellogg v. City of Gary*, 562 N.E.2d 685, 694 (Ind. 1990).
190. *Kalodimos v. Village of Morton Grove*, 103 Ill. 2d 483, 83 Ill. Dec. 308, 470 N.E.2d 266, 277-78 (1984).
191. *Arnold v. Cleveland*, 67 Ohio St. 3d 35, 616 N.E.2d 163, 166 (1993).
192. *Id.* at 169.
193. *Id.* at 172.
194. *Id.* at 176.
195. *Id.* at 177.

will "proclaim the principles upon which our government is founded," and the arms guarantee which follows declares that the right shall not "be called in question,"[196] the court decided: "While it is clear that this right is an important constitutional right, it is equally clear that this case does not require us to determine whether that right is fundamental. . . . The state may regulate the exercise of that right under its inherent police power so long as the exercise of that power is reasonable."[197]

It would appear that, at least in some states, jurisprudence on the right to keep and bear arms is in constant flux, if not disarray. General constitutional interpretive methodologies may be held not to apply, and established precedents may be swept away. The proliferation of ever more complex and intrusive firearms prohibitions may well test the limits of interpretation of rights under the State bills of rights in the coming decades.

Tactical Tip:

The constitutional convention debates and minutes of a state should not be neglected in reference to whether a right is fundamental or even exists under a state guarantee. While a court may choose to ignore such references, they may be decisive.

Sec. 1:8 Equal protection issues

Aside from whether a law may violate a right to keep and bear arms, it may make classifications which are without rational basis. Where no rational relation exists between a regulation and a legitimate governmental purpose, the regulation may deny the equal protection of the laws, in violation of the Fourteenth Amendment or, as applied to the federal government, the equal protection component of the Fifth Amendment's due process clause.

The Seventh Circuit upheld a prohibition on handguns with an exception for handguns "validly registered to a current owner in the City of Chicago prior to the effective date of this Chapter."[198]

However, the court noted that "the courts must certainly scrutinize grandfather clauses to learn whether they are masks for exploitation or invidious discrimination."[199]

The court found that the purpose of the grandfather clause was "the protection of the reliance interests of those who purchased handguns legally before the effective date of the ordinance."[200] It proceeded to uphold the grandfather clause as follows:

> The purpose of protecting those who relied on prior laws—and only to the extent they relied on prior laws—is a matter of simple fairness. Governments enact laws which invite citizens to invest their money and time and to arrange their affairs in reliance upon those laws. . . . We conclude, therefore, that the city's purpose in protecting the reliance interests of those who purchased and registered handguns in Chicago was a legitimate

196. Colo. Const., Art. II, preamble and §13.

197. *Robertson v. City and County of Denver*, 874 P.2d 325, 328, 29 A.L.R.5th 837 (Colo. 1994). *Accord State v. Mendoza*, 82 Haw. 143, 920 P.2d 357, 367-68 (1996).

198. *Sklar v. Byrne*, 727 F.2d 633, 635 & n.2 (7th Cir. 1984).

199. *Id.* at 639. The court added: "Where plaintiff can show that a grandfather provision impinges on a fundamental personal right . . ., or that the provision is a substitute for a suspect form of discrimination, courts should apply the compelling governmental interest standard." *Sklar v. Byrne*, 727 F.2d 633, 639 (7th Cir. 1984).

200. *Id.* at 641.

> purpose. The ordinance rationally furthers that purpose with its grandfather provisions tailored to fit the extent of the reliance.[201]

Put differently, "the council chose to protect the interests of those who had relied on prior Chicago laws permitting them to own handguns. . . . The fact that the ordinance stopped short of a complete ban and protected those who relied on prior law does not violate the equal protection clause."[202] Under this principle, where a law irrationally protects the reliance interests of some persons and not the reliance interests of others, all of whom relied on prior laws permitting them to own firearms, the law runs afoul of the equal protection guarantee. For instance:

> If the ordinance had said that all residents of Chicago on the effective date could own handguns and that all those who moved later to Chicago could not, the classification would be unlikely to survive constitutional challenge. . . . It is difficult to conceive of a legitimate state purpose for such a classification.[203]

Irrational classifications among firearms purchasers were held violative of equal protection under the rational basis test in a Third Circuit opinion.[204] A state law required firearm purchasers to be identified by two freeholders; leaseholders would not do. The court opined:

> While it may be true that Delaware could ban the sale of all deadly weapons, it does not follow that the State, having abrogated its power to effect a total ban, can arbitrarily establish categories of persons who can or cannot buy the weapons. Clearly, Delaware could not limit the sale of firearms to men only or to members of certain religious groups. The question then is whether it is rational for Delaware to limit sales to persons who know two Delaware freeholders and can produce them as witnesses. We think that this question must be answered in the negative.[205]

A prohibition on firearms businesses which were on leased property and which were within a half mile of a school or park was held violative of equal protection.[206] Exempted were firearms businesses on premises owned by the business and chain stores which sold general merchandise as well as firearms. "There is no rational reason to distinguish between a gun sold within .5 miles of a school or park by a person who owns the premises on which the gun shop is operated and a gun sold by a person who leases the premises on which a gun shop is operated. In both instances, guns will be sold near areas where children congregate and play."[207]

An irrational classification among firearms possessors in the Gun Control Act was held violative of equal protection and due process.[208] Federal law prohibited firearm possession by felons and by persons who had ever been committed to a mental institution; the law allowed felons, but not ex-mental patients, to have their rights restored. Finding that the law failed the rational basis test, the court held:

---

201. *Id.* at 641-42.

202. *Id.* at 642.

203. *Id. See Cincinnati v. Langan*, 94 Ohio App. 3d 22, 640 N.E.2d 200, 207-8 (1st Dist. Hamilton County 1994), *dismissed, appeal not allowed*, 70 Ohio St. 3d 1425, 638 N.E.2d 87 (1994) (no equal protection violation found where "the city council decided to ban the entry of semiautomatic weapons into the city after a certain date. Those persons already possessing the weapons were not stripped of their property, but were asked to register").

204. *Hetherton v. Sears, Roebuck & Co.*, 652 F.2d 1152, 1157-59 (3d Cir. 1981).

205. *Id.* at 1157-58.

206. *Illinois Sporting Goods Ass'n v. County of Cook*, 845 F. Supp. 582, 590 (N.D. Ill. 1994).

207. *Id.* at 591.

208. *Galioto v. Department of Treasury, Bureau of Alcohol, Tobacco and Firearms*, 602 F. Supp. 682 (D.N.J. 1985), *judgment vacated*, 477 U.S. 556, 106 S. Ct. 2683, 91 L. Ed. 2d 459 (1986) (statute amended to cure defect).

> The failure of the statute to provide former mental patients with the opportunity to contest their firearms disability is irrational in two ways that offend the due process and equal protection components of the fifth amendment. First, the statute offends the equal protection rights of former mental patients by treating them differently than other similarly situated, viz, ex-convicts, without any logical justification for doing so. Second, the statute offends the due process rights of these individuals because it deprives them permanently and without any rational basis of the opportunity to demonstrate that they are no longer, or never were, incapable of handling firearms safely.[209]

Similarly, another court invalidated as violative of equal protection a law allowing persons convicted of felonies, but not former mental patients, to obtain a permit to carry a concealed weapon.[210] The individual right to bear arms may be restricted as applied to mental patients, but the law here had no rational basis.[211]

Finally, a New York court found that a prohibition on firearm models by specified manufacturers violates the equal protection clause of the Fourteenth Amendment.[212]

The name listings were simply not relevant to the reasons stated by the legislative body for the prohibition. Accordingly, the court held:

> Careful review of the exhibits reveal no support for the notion that there is a difference in the danger posed to society by identical guns produced by different manufacturers, and no such distinction can be found through an exercise of reason. Therefore, to the extent that [the ordinance] names individual weapons, and excludes others that are identical, it is a violation of the equal protection clause of the United States Constitution.[213]

Issues involving other constitutional rights may arise in the equal protection context. New Jersey prohibits "assault firearms," but exempts certain persons who were members of certain rifle or pistol clubs.[214] The statute preconditions a continued liberty and property right not on lawful ownership of the property before a specified date, but on membership in certain private clubs before a specified date. Is this an irrational discrimination against persons who were not members of such clubs, and does it violate their right to freedom of association?

A district court invalidated, as violative of equal protection and freedom of association, a federal statute which preconditioned entitlement of a citizen to purchase an M1 semiautomatic rifle from the U.S. Department of Defense on membership in the National Rifle Association.[215] The court held:

> Among the rights protected by the First Amendment is that to freedom of association . . . and its corollary, the freedom not to be required to associate with groups holding views which an individual regards as obnoxious.[216]

While the purpose of the federal statute was to promote marksmanship, "it is obviously possible to become a competent marksman on an individual basis,"

---

209. *Id.* at 687-88.

210. *Morris v. Blaker*, 118 Wash. 2d 133, 821 P.2d 482, 489-91 (1992).

211. *Id.* at 488.

212. *Citizens for a Safer Community v. City of Rochester*, 164 Misc. 2d 822, 627 N.Y.S.2d 193, 203-4 (Sup 1994). While invalidating another ordinance on vagueness grounds, *Springfield Armory, Inc. v. City of Columbus*, 29 F.3d 250, 252, 1994 FED App. 239P (6th Cir. 1994), in language typical of an equal protection analysis, also found the ordinance to be irrational.

213. *Id.* at 204. For a more detailed analysis of this case, *see* §10:6 *infra*. On the California case, *see* §10:10 *infra*.

214. New Jersey Statutes, §§2C:39-5f, 2C:58-12b(4).

215. *Gavett v. Alexander*, 477 F. Supp. 1035, 1044 (D.D.C. 1979).

216. *Id.* at 1045, citing *Shelton v. Tucker*, 364 U.S. 479, 485-86, 81 S. Ct. 247, 5 L. Ed. 2d 231 (1960); *National Ass'n for Advancement of Colored People v. State of Ala. ex rel. Patterson*, 357 U.S. 449, 460, 78 S. Ct. 1163, 2 L. Ed. 2d 1488 (1958).

and marksmanship "is capable of achievement outside an organizational framework."[217] By analogy, regarding the New Jersey law, a citizen who was not a gun club member on a specified date would seem to be just as trustworthy a citizen as one who was. Nonetheless, a district court has rejected the argument that this violates the rights to equal protection and freedom of association.[218]

In sum, even where firearms may constitutionally be regulated, irrational discrimination may not be made among types of purchasers, sellers, owners, or firearms. Where such irrational classifications exist, the equal protection clause may be violated.

Sec. 1:9 Litigation checklist

☐ What bearing do the debates in the period of the ratification of the Constitution and Bill of Rights have on understanding the constitutional text? If you are arguing the intent of the framers of the Second Amendment, have you obtained access to all of the law review articles and scholarly books? [1:2]

☐ What distinctions do the cases decided by the Supreme Court make in regard to who are "the people" in the Second Amendment? Consider *Dred Scott* (citizens), *Lewis* (nonfelons), and *Verdugo-Urquidez* (members of the national community). What light does the discussion of the National Guard in *Perpich* shed on the subject? [1:3]

☐ How viable in your circuit is the *Miller* test that the Second Amendment protects militia arms? Would the Supreme Court adopt this same test today? Are there alternative tests? [1:3]

☐ Have you studied all Supreme Court cases on the Second Amendment? It may not be possible to read all First Amendment opinions in a free press case, but one can count the number of Supreme Court cases on the Second Amendment on two hands. [1:3]

☐ Has your circuit taken a position on the "collective rights" theory of the Second Amendment? Is any reference thereto merely dictum, such as in a felon-in-possession case? Where that theory has been favorably received, is there a realistic possibility that modern scholarship and Supreme Court statements such as are set forth in *Verdugo-Urquidez* would persuade a three-judge appellate panel or would lead to an en banc rehearing? [1:3]

☐ How persuasive is the case for arguing that the Fourteenth Amendment incorporates the Second Amendment, so as to protect the right to keep and bear arms from state infringement? Is there any reason to make this argument in any of the forty-three states that have a state constitution with an arms guarantee? [1:4]

☐ How strong is the wording of a particular state's arms guarantee? Has the state judiciary given the guarantee a broad or a narrow reading? To what extent will the current high court of a state follow precedent? [1:5]

217. 477 F. Supp. at 1048.

218. *Coalition of New Jersey Sportsmen, Inc. v. Whitman*, 44 F. Supp. 2d 666, 687-90 (D.N.J. 1999), *aff'd*, 263 F.3d 157 (3d Cir. 2001), *cert. denied*, 122 S. Ct. 613, 151 L. Ed. 2d 537 (U.S. 2001).

- ☐ Does the state statute or local ordinance in question permissibly regulate the bearing of arms, whether openly or concealed, or does it virtually prohibit the right altogether? Is the right to keep arms in the home broader than the right to carry arms outside the home? [1:5]

- ☐ How persuasive are the various tests for what is a constitutionally protected arm under a state guarantee, including the text of the guarantee (e.g., arms that an individual could "keep and bear" for self defense), common use by persons for lawful purposes, utility for personal defense and militia purposes, the status of being a rifle, pistol, or shotgun, or not being exclusively used by the military? [1:5]

- ☐ Are constitutionally guaranteed rights "fundamental"? What rationales have certain state courts suggested to exempt arms guarantees from the general rule? To what extent have the courts of a given state consistently held that fundamental constitutional rights are not subject to a merely rational relation test? [1:6]

The Supreme Court's Thirty-Five *Other* Gun Cases:

What the Supreme Court Has Said About the Second Amendment

by David B. Kopel*

Among legal scholars, it is undisputed that the Supreme Court has said almost nothing about the Second Amendment.[1] This article suggests that the Court has not been so silent as the conventional wisdom suggests.

While the meaning of the Supreme Court's leading Second Amendment case, the 1939 *United States v. Miller*[2] decision remains hotly disputed, the dispute about whether the Second Amendment guarantees an individual right can be pretty well settled by looking at the thirty-five other Supreme Court cases which quote, cite, or discuss the Second Amendment. These cases suggest that the Justices of the Supreme Court do now and usually have regarded the Second Amendment "right of the people to keep and bear arms" as an individual right, rather than as a right of state governments.

Chief Justice Melville Fuller's Supreme Court (1888-1910) had the most cases involving the Second Amendment: eight. So far, the Rehnquist Court is in second place, with six. But Supreme Court opinions dealing with the Second Amendment come from almost every period in the Court's history, and almost all of them assume or are consistent with the proposition that the Second Amendment is an individual right.

Part I of this Article discusses the opinions from the Rehnquist Court. Part II looks at the Burger Court, and Part III at the Warren, Vinson, and Hughes Courts. Part IV groups together the cases from the Taft, Fuller, and Waite Courts, while Part V consolidates the Chase, Taney, and Marshall Courts.

But first, let us quickly summarize what modern legal scholarship says about the Second Amendment, and why the Court's main Second

---

* Research Director, Independence Institute, Golden, Colorado, davekopel.org; J.D. 1985 University of Michigan Law School; B.A. in History, 1982, Brown University. Author of Gun Control and Gun Rights (NYU Press, 2001).
I would like to thank Paul Blackman, Clayton Cramer, Brannon Denning, Billie J. Grey, David Hunt, Dolores Kopel, Glenn Harlan Reynolds, Eugene Volokh, and the Cincinnati Law Library Association for very helpful comments. Any errors in this article are the fault of society, and cannot be blamed on an individual. This article originally appeared in the St. Louis University Public Law Review, Vol. 18, No. 1 (1999). That issue also includes a reply to this article by David Yassky and Kopel's response to Yassky.

1. See, e.g., Sanford Lewinson, Is the Second Amendment Finally Becoming Recognized as Part of the Constitution? Voices from the Courts, 1998 B.Y.U. Rev. 127.

2. United States v. Miller, 307 U.S. 174 (1939).

Amendment decision—*United States v. Miller*—does not by itself settle the debate.

Dennis Henigan, lead attorney for Handgun Control, Inc., argues that the Supreme Court has said so little about the Second Amendment because the fact that the Second Amendment does not protect the right of ordinary Americans to own a gun is "perhaps the most well-settled point in American law."[3] Henigan argues that the Second Amendment was meant to restrict the Congressional powers over the militia granted to Congress in Article I of the Constitution—although Henigan does not specify what the restrictions are.[4] One of Henigan's staff criticizes the large number of American history textbooks which "contradict[] a nearly unanimous line of judicial decisions by suggesting the meaning of the Second Amendment was judicially unsettled."[5]

Similarly, Carl Bogus argues that the only purpose of the Second Amendment was to protect state's rights to use their militia to suppress slave insurrections—although Bogus too is vague about exactly how the Second Amendment allegedly restricted Congressional powers.[6] This article refers to the State's Rights theory of the Second Amendment as the "Henigan/Bogus theory," in honor of its two major scholarly proponents.[7]

In contrast to the State's Rights theory is what has become known as the Standard Model.[8] Under the Standard Model, which is the consensus of most modern legal scholarship on the Second Amendment, the Amendment

---

3. Dennis Henigan, *The Right to Be Armed: A Constitutional Illusion*, S.F. BARRISTER, Dec. 1989, ¶ 19, *available online at* <http://www.handguncontrol.org/legalaction/C2/c2rtarms.htm>. The late Dean Griswold of Harvard, who was a member of the board of Henigan's group, expressed a nearly identical thought: "that the Second Amendment poses no barrier to strong gun laws is perhaps the most well-settled proposition in American constitutional law." Erwin N. Griswold, *Phantom Second Amendment 'Rights'*, WASH. POST, Nov. 4, 1990, at C7

4. DENNIS A. HENIGAN ET AL., GUNS AND THE CONSTITUTION: THE MYTH OF SECOND AMENDMENT PROTECTION FOR FIREARMS IN AMERICA (1995); Keith A. Ehrman & Dennis A. Henigan, *The Second Amendment in the Twentieth Century: Have You Seen Your Militia Lately?*, 15 U. DAYTON L. REV. 5 (1989); Dennis A. Henigan, *Arms, Anarchy and the Second Amendment*, 26 VAL. U. L. REV. 107 (1991) [hereinafter Henigan, *Arms, Anarchy*]

5. Mark Polston, *Obscuring the Second Amendment*, 34 VIRGINIA RESOLVES, No. 32 (Spring 1994), http://www.handguncontrol.org/legalaction/dockets/A1/obscure.htm.

6. Carl T. Bogus, *Race, Riots, and Guns*, 66 S. CAL. L. REV. 1365 (1993); Carl T. Bogus, *The Hidden History of the Second Amendment*, 31 U.C. DAVIS L. REV. 309 (1998). For a response to the latter article, *see* David B. Kopel, *The Second Amendment in the Nineteenth Century*, 1998 BYU. L. REV. 1359, 1515-29.

Some other scholarly sources rejecting individual rights are: ROBERT J. SPITZER, THE POLITICS OF GUN CONTROL (1995); George Anastaplo, *Amendments to the Constitution of the United States: A Commentary*, 23 LOY. U. CHI. L.J. 631, 687-93 (1992); Michael A. Bellesiles, *The Origins of Gun Culture in the United States, 1760-1865*, 83 J. AM. HIST. 425 (1996); Lawrence Delbert Cress, *An Armed Community: The Origins and Meaning of the Right to Bear Arms*, 71 J. AM. HIST. 22 (1984); Samuel Fields, *Guns, Crime and the Negligent Gun Owner*, 10 N.KY. L. REV. 141 (1982); Andrew D. Herz, *Gun Crazy: Constitutional False Consciousness and Dereliction of Dialogic Responsibility*, 75 B.U. L. REV. 57 (1995); Michael J. Palmiotto, *The Misconception of the American Citizen's Right to Keep and Bear Arms*, 4 J. ON FIREARMS & PUB. POL'Y 85 (1992); Warren Spannaus, *State Firearms Regulation and the Second Amendment*, 6 HAMLINE L. REV. 383 (1983).

7. For an effort to trace the potential contours of a State's Rights Second Amendment, see Glenn Harlan Reynolds & Don B. Kates, *The Second Amendment and States' Rights: A Thought Experiment*, 36 WM. & MARY L. REV. 1737 (1995) (arguing that a State's Rights Second Amendment would give each state legislature the power to arm its militia as it saw best, and thus the power to negate—within the borders of that state—federal bans on particular types of weapons).

8. Glenn Harlan Reynolds, *A Critical Guide to the Second Amendment*, 62 TENN. L. REV. 461, 463 (1995): *Perhaps surprisingly, what distinguishes the Second Amendment scholarship from that relating to other constitutional rights, such as privacy or free speech, is that there appears to be far more agreement on the general outlines of Second Amendment theory than exists in those other areas. Indeed, there is sufficient consensus on many issues that one can properly speak of a "Standard Model" in Second Amendment theory, much as physicists and cosmologists speak of a "Standard Model" in terms of the creation and evolution of the Universe. In both cases, the agreement is not complete: within both Standard Models are parts that are subject to disagreement. But the overall framework for analysis, the questions regarded as being clearly resolved, and those regarded as still open, are all generally agreed upon. This is certainly the case with regard to Second Amendment scholarship.*

guarantees a right of individual Americans to own and carry guns.[9] This modern Standard Model is similar to the position embraced by every known

9. *See, e.g.*, SENATE SUBCOMMITTEE ON THE CONSTITUTION OF THE COMMITTEE ON THE JUDICIARY, 97TH CONG., 2D SESS., THE RIGHT TO KEEP AND BEAR ARMS (Comm. Print 1982); AKHIL AMAR, THE BILL OF RIGHTS (1998); Robert J. Cottrol, *Introduction* to 1 GUN CONTROL AND THE CONSTITUTION: SOURCES AND EXPLORATIONS ON THE SECOND AMENDMENT at ix (Robert J. Cottrol ed., 1993); Robert J. Cottrol & Raymond T. Diamond, *Public Safety and the Right to Bear Arms, in* THE BILL OF RIGHTS IN MODERN AMERICA: AFTER 200 YEARS 72 (David J. Bodenhamer & James W. Ely, Jr., eds., 1993); Robert J. Cottrol, *Second Amendment, in* THE OXFORD COMPANION TO THE SUPREME COURT OF THE UNITED STATES 763 (Kermit L. Hall et al. eds., 1992); CLAYTON CRAMER, FOR THE DEFENSE OF THEMSELVES AND THE STATE at xv (1994); 4 ENCYCLOPEDIA OF THE AMERICAN CONSTITUTION 1639-40 (Leonard W. Levy et al. eds., 1986); ERIC FONER, RECONSTRUCTION: AMERICA'S UNFINISHED REVOLUTION, 1863-1876 (1989); STEPHEN HALBROOK, FREEDMEN, THE FOURTEENTH AMENDMENT, AND THE RIGHT TO BEAR ARMS: 1866-1876 (1998); STEPHEN HALBROOK, A RIGHT TO BEAR ARMS: STATE AND FEDERAL BILLS OF RIGHTS AND CONSTITUTIONAL GUARANTEES (1989); STEPHEN P. HALBROOK, THAT EVERY MAN BE ARMED: THE EVOLUTION OF A CONSTITUTIONAL RIGHT (1984); Edward F. Leddy, *Guns and Gun Conrtol*, *in* READER'S COMPANION TO AMERICAN HISTORY 477-78 (Eric Foner & John A. Garraty eds., 1991); Leonard W. Levy, ORIGINAL INTENT AND THE FRAMERS' CONSTITUTION 341 (1988); Leonard Levy, Origins of the Bill of Rights (1999); JOYCE LEE MALCOLM, TO KEEP AND BEAR ARMS: THE ORIGINS OF AN ANGLO-AMERICAN RIGHT (1994); Laurence H. Tribe, I American Constitutional Law 894-903 (3d ed. 2000). Akhil Reed Amar, *The Bill of Rights and the Fourteenth Amendment*, 101 YALE L.J. 1193 (1992); Akhil Reed Amar, *The Bill of Rights as a Constitution*, 100 YALE L.J. 1131, 1164 (1991); Randy E. Barnett & Don B. Kates, *Under Fire: The New Consensus on the Second Amendment*, 45 EMORY L.J. 1139, 1141 (1996); Bernard J. Bordenet, *The Right to Possess Arms: The Intent of the Framers of the Second Amendment*, 21 U. WEST L.A. L. REV. 1, 28 (1990); David I. Caplan, *The Right of the Individual to Bear Arms: A Recent Judicial Trend*, 1982 DET. C.L. REV. 789, 790; David I. Caplan, *The Right to Have Arms and Use Deadly Force Under the Second and Third Amendments*, 2.1 J. ON FIREARMS & PUB. POL'Y 165 (1990); Robert J. Cottrol & Raymond T. Diamond, *The Second Amendment: Toward an Afro-Americanist Reconsideration*, 80 GEO. L.J. 309 (1991); Brannon P. Denning, *Can the Simple Cite Be Trusted?: Lower Court Interpretations of* United States v. Miller *and the Second Amendment*, 26 CUMB. L. REV. 961 (1995-96) [hereinafter Denning, *Simple Cite*]; Brannon P. Denning, *Gun Shy: The Second Amendment as an "Underenforced Constitutional Norm"*, 21 HARV. J.L. & PUB. POL'Y 719 (1998); Anthony J. Dennis, *Clearing the Smoke From the Right to Bear Arms and the Second Amendment*, 29 AKRON L. REV. 57 (1995); Robert Dowlut, *Federal and State Constitutional Guarantees to Arms*, 15 U. DAYTON L. REV. 59 (1989); Robert Dowlut, *The Current Relevancy of Keeping and Bearing Arms*, 15 U. BALT. L.F. 32 (1984); Robert Dowlut, *The Right to Arms: Does the Constitution or the Predilection of Judges Reign?*, 36 OKLA. L. REV. 65 (1983); Robert Dowlut, *The Right to Keep and Bear Arms: A Right to Self-Defense Against Criminals and Despots*, 8 STAN. L. & POL'Y REV. 25 (1997); Richard E. Gardiner, *To Preserve Liberty—A Look at the Right to Keep and Bear Arms*, 10 N. Ky. L. Rev. 63 (1982); Alan M. Gottlieb, *Gun Ownership: A Constitutional Right*, 10 N. KY. L. REV. 113 (1982); Stephen P. Halbrook, *Congress Interprets the Second Amendment: Declarations by a Co-Equal Branch on the Individual Right to Keep and Bear Arms*, 62 TENN. L. REV. 597 (1995); Stephen Halbrook, *The Right of Workers to Assemble and to Bear Arms: Presser v. Illinois, Last Holdout Against Application of the Bill of Rights to the States*, 76 U. DET. MERCY L. REV (no. 4, 1999, forthcoming); Stephen P. Halbrook, *Encroachments of the Crown on the Liberty of the Subject: Pre-Revolutionary Origins of the Second Amendment*, 15 U. DAYTON L. REV. 91 (1989); Stephen P. Halbrook, *Personal Security, Personal Liberty, and "The Constitutional Right to Bear Arms": Visions of the Framers of the Fourteenth Amendment*, 5 SETON HALL CONST. L.J. 341 (1995); Stephen P. Halbrook, *Second-Class Citizenship and the Second Amendment in the District of Columbia*, 5 GEO. MASON U. CIV. RTS. L.J. 105 (1995); Stephen P. Halbrook, *The Jurisprudence of the Second and Fourteenth Amendments*, 4 GEO. MASON L. REV. 1 (1981); Stephen P. Halbrook, *The Right of the People or the Power of the State: Bearing Arms, Arming Militias, and the Second Amendment*, 26 VAL. U. L. REV. 131 (1991); Stephen P. Halbrook, *What the Framers Intended: A Linguistic Analysis of the Right to "Bear Arms"*, 49 LAW & CONTEMP. PROBS. 151 (1986); Stephen P. Halbrook & David B. Kopel, *Tench Coxe and the Right to Keep and Bear Arms in the Early Republic, 7* WM. & MARY BILL OF RTS. J. (1998); David G. Hardy, *Armed Citizens, Citizen Armies: Toward a Jurisprudence of the Second Amendment*, 9 HARV. J.L. & PUB. POL'Y 559 (1986); David G. Hardy, *The Second Amendment and the Historiography of the Bill of Rights*, 4 J.L. & POL. 1 (1987); Nicholas J. Johnson, *Principles and Passions: The Intersection of Abortion and Gun Rights*, 50 RUTGERS L. REV. 97 (1997); Don B. Kates, Jr., *Handgun Prohibition and the Original Meaning of the Second Amendment*, 82 MICH. L. REV. 204 (1983); Don B. Kates, Jr., *The Second Amendment: A Dialogue*, 49 LAW & CONTEMP. PROBS. 143 (1986); Don Kates, *The Second Amendment and the Ideology of Self-Protection*, 9 CONST. COMMENTARY 87 (1992); Kopel, *The Second Amendment in the Nineteenth Century*, *supra* note 7; David B. Kopel & Christopher C. Little, *Communitarians, Neorepublicans, and Guns: Assessing the Case for Firearms Prohibition*, 56 MD. L. REV. 438 (1997); Stephanie A. Levin, *Grassroots Voices: Local Action and National Military Policy*, 40 BUFF. L. REV. 321, 346-47 (1992); Sanford Levinson, *The Embarrassing Second Amendment*, 99 YALE L.J. 637 (1989); Nelson Lund, *The Ends of Second Amendment Jurisprudence: Firearms Disabilities and Domestic Violence Restraining Orders*, 4 TEX. REV. L. & POLITICS 157 (1999); Nelson Lund, *The Past and Future of the Individual's Right to Arms*, 31 GA. L. REV. 1 (1996); Nelson Lund, *The Second Amendment, Political Liberty, and the Right to Self-Preservation*, 39 ALA. L. REV. 103 (1987); Joyce Lee Malcolm, *The Right of the People to Keep and Bear Arms: The Common Law Tradition*, 10 HASTINGS CONST. L.Q. 285 (1983); Thomas B. McAffee & Michael J. Quinlan, *Bringing Forward the Right to Keep and Bear Arms: Do Text, History, or Precedent Stand in the Way?*, 75 N.C. L. REV. 781 (1997); Thomas M. Moncure, Jr., *The Second Amendment Ain't About Hunting*, 34 HOW. L.J. 589 (1991); Thomas M. Moncure, Jr., *Who is the Militia—The Virginia Ratification Convention and the Right to Bear Arms*, 19 LINCOLN L.

legal scholar in the nineteenth century who wrote about the Second Amendment: the Amendment guarantees an individual right, but is subject to various reasonable restrictions.[10]

Both the Standard Model and the State's Right theory claim that Supreme Court precedent, particularly the case of *United States* v. *Miller*, supports their position.

Two other scholarly theories about the Second Amendment are interesting, but their theories have little to do with Supreme Court precedent. Garry Wills argues that the Second Amendment has "no real meaning," and was merely a clever trick that James Madison played on the Anti-Federalists.[11] David Williams argues that the Second Amendment once guaranteed an individual right, but no longer does so because the American people are no longer virtuous and united, and hence are no longer "the people" referred to in the Second Amendment.[12] Neither the Wills Nihilism theory nor the Williams Character Decline theory make claims which depend on the Supreme Court for support, or which could be refuted by Supreme Court decisions.

REV. 1 (1990); James Gray Pope, *Republican Moments: The Role of Direct Popular Power in the American Constitutional Order*, 139 U. PA. L. REV. 287 (1990); L.A. Powe, Jr., *Guns, Words, and Constitutional Interpretation*, 38 WM. & MARY L. REV. 1311 (1997); Michael J. Quinlan, *Is There a Neutral Justification for Refusing to Implement the Second Amendment or is the Supreme Court Just "Gun Shy"?*, 22 CAP. U. L. REV. 641 (1993); Glenn Harlan Reynolds, *A Critical Guide to the Second Amendment*, 62 TENN. L. REV. 461 (1995); Glenn Harlan Reynolds, *The Right to Keep and Bear Arms Under the Tennessee Constitution: A Case Study in Civic Republican Thought*, 61 TENN. L. REV. 647 (1994) (discussing the Second Amendment as related to the Tennessee Constitution); Elaine Scarry, *War and the Social Contract: Nuclear Policy, Distribution, and the Right to Bear Arms*, 139 U. PA. L. REV. 1257 (1991); J. Neil Schulman, *The Text of the Second Amendment*, 4 J. ON FIREARMS & PUB. POL'Y 159 (1992); Robert E. Shalhope, *The Armed Citizen in the Early Republic*, 49 LAW & CONTEMP. PROBS. 125 (1986); Robert E. Shalhope, *The Ideological Origins of the Second Amendment*, 69 J. AM. HIST. 599 (1982); William Van Alstyne, *The Second Amendment and the Personal Right to Arms*, 43 DUKE L.J. 1236 (1994); David E. Vandercoy, *The History of the Second Amendment*, 28 VAL. U. L. REV. 1007 (1994); Eugene Volokh, *The Amazing Vanishing Second Amendment*, 73 N.Y.U. L. REV. 831 (1998); Eugene Volokh, *The Commonplace Second Amendment*, 73 N.Y.U. L. REV. 793 (1998); Scott Bursor, Note, *Toward a Functional Framework for Interpreting the Second Amendment*, 74 TEX. L. REV. 1125 (1996); Robert J. Cottrol & Raymond T. Diamond, *The Fifth Auxiliary Right*, 104 YALE L.J. 995 (1995) (reviewing JOYCE LEE MALCOLM, TO KEEP AND BEAR ARMS: THE ORIGINS OF AN ANGLO-AMERICAN RIGHT (1994)); Brannon P. Denning, *Professional Discourse, The Second Amendment, and the "Talking Head Constitutionalism" Counterrevolution: A Review Essay*, 21 S. ILL. U. L.J. 227 (1997) (reviewing DENNIS A. HENIGAN ET AL., GUNS AND THE CONSTITUTION: THE MYTH OF SECOND AMENDMENT PROTECTION FOR FIREARMS IN AMERICA (1996)); T. Markus Funk, *Is the True Meaning of the Second Amendment Really Such a Riddle? Tracing the Historical "Origins of an Anglo-American Right"*, 39 HOW. L.J. 411 (1995) (reviewing JOYCE LEE MALCOM, TO KEEP AND BEAR ARMS: THE ORIGINS OF AN ANGLO-AMERICAN RIGHT (1994)); David B. Kopel, *It Isn't About Duck Hunting: The British Origins of the Right to Arms*, 93 MICH. L. REV. 1333 (1995) (reviewing JOYCE LEE MALCOLM, TO KEEP AND BEAR ARMS: THE ORIGINS OF AN ANGLO-AMERICAN RIGHT (1994)); F. Smith Fussner, Book Review, 3 Const. Commentary 582 (1986) (reviewing STEPHEN P. HALBROOK, THAT EVERY MAN BE ARMED: THE EVOLUTION OF A CONSTITUTIONAL RIGHT (1984)); Joyce Lee Malcolm, Book Review, 54 GEO. WASH. L. REV. 452 (1986) (reviewing STEPHEN P. HALBROOK, THAT EVERY MAN BE ARMED: THE EVOLUTION OF A CONSTITUTIONAL RIGHT (1984)); *cf.* Nicholas J. Johnson, *Beyond the Second Amendment: An Individual Right to Arms Viewed through the Ninth Amendment*, 24 RUTGERS L.J. 1 (1992) (arguing that the Ninth Amendment supports an individual right to arms). For a list of all law review articles of firearms policy or the Second Amendment, See David B. Kopel, *Comprehensive Bibliography of the Second Amendment in Law Review*, 11 J. Firearms & Pub. Pol. 5 (1999), http://www.Saf.org/ALLLawReviews.htm.

10. The nineteenth century scholars were (in roughly chronological order): St. George Tucker; William Rawle; Joseph Story (see *infra* text at note 354); Henry St. George Tucker; Benjamin Oliver; James Bayard; Francis Lieber; Thomas Cooley (see note 25 *infra*); Joel Tiffany; Timothy Farrar; George W. Paschal; Joel Bishop; John Norton Pomeroy; Oliver Wendell Holmes, Jr.; Herbert Broom; Edward A. Hadley; Hermann von Holst; John Hare; George Ticknor Curtis; John C. Ordronaux; Samuel F. Miller; J.C. Bancroft Davis; Henry Campbell Black; George S. Boutwell; James Schouler; John Randolph Tucker; and William Draper Lewis. They are discussed in detail in David B. Kopel, *The Second Amendment in the 19th Century*, 1998 BYU. L. REV. 1359.

11. Garry Wills, *Why We Have No Right to Bear Arms*, N.Y. REV. BOOKS, Sept. 21, 1995 at 62, 72.

12. *See* David C. Williams, *Civic Republicanism and the Citizen Militia: The Terrifying Second Amendment*, 101 YALE L.J. 551 (1991); David C. Williams, *The Militia Movement and Second Amendment Revolution: Conjuring with the People*, 81 CORNELL L. REV. 879 (1996); David C. Williams, *The Unitary Second Amendment*, 73 N.Y.U. L. REV. 822 (1998).

Like the scholars, the lower federal courts are split on the issue, although their split is the opposite of the scholarly one: most federal courts which have stated a firm position have said that the Second Amendment is *not* an individual right.[13] The federal courts which follow the academic Standard Model are in the minority, although the ranks of the minority have grown in recent years.[14] The courts on both sides, like the scholars, insist that they are following the Supreme Court.

One approach to untangling the conflict has been to see if the lower federal courts have actually been following *Miller*. In *Can the Simple Cite be Trusted?*, Brannon Denning makes a persuasive argument that some lower courts have cited *Miller* for propositions which cannot reasonably be said to flow from *Miller*.[15] But part of the problem with deciding whether the courts or the scholars are being faithful to *Miller* is that *Miller* is such an opaque opinion.

Miller grew out of a 1938 prosecution of two bootleggers (Jack Miller and Frank Layton) for violating the National Firearms Act by possessing a sawed-off shotgun without having paid the required federal tax. The federal district court dismissed the indictment on the grounds that the National Firearms Act violated the Second Amendment.[16] Freed, Miller and Layton promptly absconded, and thus only the government's side was heard when the case was argued before the Supreme Court.[17]

---

13. *See, e.g.*, Hickman v. Block, 81 F.3d 98, 101 (9th Cir. 1996) ("the Second Amendment is a right held by the states"); United States v. Nelson, 859 F.2d 1318, 1320 (8th Cir. 1988) ("Later cases have analyzed the Second Amendment purely in terms of protecting state militias, rather than individual rights."); Quilici v. Morton Grove, 695 F.2d 261, 270 (7th Cir. 1982) (upholding city's ban on handguns; "the debate surrounding the adoption of the Second and Fourteenth Amendments. . .has no relevance to the resolution of the controversy before us"); United States v. Warin, 530 F.2d 103, 106 (6th Cir. 1976) ("it is clear that the Second Amendment guarantees a collective rather than an individual right"); Eckert v. Philadelphia, 477 F.2d 610 (3d Cir. 1973); United States v. Johnson, 441 F.2d 1134, 1136 (5th Cir. 1971) ("the Second Amendment only confers a collective right of keeping and bearing arms"); United States v. Tot, 131 F.2d 261, 266 (3d Cir. 1942) ("not adopted with individual rights in mind, but as a protection for the States in the maintenance of their militia organizations"), *rev'd on other grounds*, 319 U.S. 463 (1943).

14. *See, e.g*, Runnebaum v. Nationsbank of Maryland, N.A., 123 F.3d 156 n. 8 (4th Cir. 1997) (en banc, plurality opinion) ("Neither gathering in a group nor carrying a firearm are one of the major life activities under the ADA [Americans with Disabilities Act], though individuals have the constitutional right to peaceably assemble, *see* U.S. CONST. amend. I; and to 'keep and bear Arms,' U.S. CONST. amend. II."); United States v. Atlas, 94 F.3d 447, 452 (8th Cir. 1996) (Arnold, C.J., dissenting) ("possession of a gun, in itself, is not a crime. [Indeed, though the right to bear arms is not absolute, it finds explicit protection in the Bill of Rights.]"); Cases v. United States, 131 F.2d 916, 921 (1st Cir. 1942) (federal law restricting gun possession by persons under indictment "undoubtedly curtails to some extent the right of individuals to keep and bear arms." *Miller* test rejected because it would prevent federal government from restricting possession of machine guns by "private persons."); United States v. Emerson, 46 F. Supp.2d 598 (N.D. Tex. 1999) (dismissing criminal prosecution of defendant for violation of 18 U.S.C. 922(g)(8) because the provision violates the Second Amendment; case presents the most thorough exposition of the competing views of the Second Amendment ever presented in a federal court decision); Zappa v. Cruz, 30 F. Supp. 2d 123, 138 (D. P.R. 1998):

These individual liberties, aside from abridging the governments' ability to impose upon individual citizens—e.g., by protecting freedom of religion, prohibiting the quartering of troops and the taking [of] property for public use without compensation, and guaranteeing due process of law—enhance the citizenry's ability to police the government—e.g., by protecting speech, press, the right to assemble, and the right to bear arms.

See also United States v. Gambill, 912 F. Supp. 287, 290 (S.D. Ohio 1996) ("an activity, such as keeping and bearing arms, that arguably implicates the Bill of Rights."); Gilbert Equipment Co. v. Higgins, 709 F. Supp. 1071, 1090 (S.D. Ala. 1989) (Second Amendment "guarantees to all Americans 'the right to keep and bear arms'", but the right is not absolute and it does not include right to import arms), *aff'd* 894 F.2d 412 (11th Cir. 1990) (mem.).

15. *See* Denning, *Simple Cite*, *supra* note 9.

16. United States v. Miller, 26 F. Supp. 1002, 1003 (W.D. Ark, 1939) (sustaining demurrer to prosecution, because "The court is of the opinion that this section is invalid in that it violates the Second Amendment to the Constitution of the United States providing, 'A well regulated militia being necessary to the security of a free state, the right of the people to keep and bear arms, shall not be infringed.'")

17. Since a federal statute had been found unconstitutional, the federal government was allowed to take the case directly to the Supreme Court, under the law of the time.

Unfortunately, *Miller* was written by Justice James McReynolds, arguably one of the worst Supreme Court Justices of the twentieth century.[18] The opinion nowhere explicitly says that the Second Amendment does (or does not guarantee) an individual right. The key paragraph of the opinion is this:

> *In the absence of any evidence tending to show that possession or use of a "shotgun having a barrel of less than eighteen inches in length" at this time has some reasonable relationship to the preservation or efficiency of a well regulated militia, we cannot say that the Second Amendment guarantees the right to keep and bear such an instrument. Certainly it is not within judicial notice that this weapon is any part of the ordinary military equipment or that its use could contribute to the common defense. Aymette v. State, 2 Humphreys (Tenn.) 154, 158.*[19]

This paragraph can plausibly be read to support either the Standard Model or the State's Rights theory. By the State's Right theory, the possession of a gun by any individual has no constitutional protection; the Second Amendment only applies to persons actively on duty in official state militias.

In contrast, the Standard Model reads the case as adopting the "civilized warfare" test of nineteenth century state Supreme Court cases: individuals have a right to own arms, but only the type of arms that are useful for militia service; for example, ownership of rifles is protected, but not ownership of Bowie knives (since Bowie knives were allegedly useful only for fights and brawls).[20] The case cited by the *Miller* Court, *Aymette v. State*[21], is plainly in the Standard Model, since it interprets the Tennessee Constitution's right to arms to protect an individual right to own firearms, but only firearms suitable for militia use; in *dicta*, *Aymette* states that the Second Amendment has the same meaning.[22]

While scholars can contend for different meanings, it is true that, as a matter of pure linguistics, the *Miller* decision does not foreclose either the Standard Model or the State's Rights theory.

And what is one to make of the opinion's penultimate paragraph, stating, "In the margin some of the more important opinions and comments by writers are cited."[23] In the attached footnote, the opinion cites two prior U.S. Supreme Court opinions and six state court opinions, all of which treat the Second Amendment or its state analogue as an individual right, even as the opinions uphold particular gun controls.[24] The footnote likewise cites

18. *See* L.A. Powe, Jr., *Guns, Words, and Constitutional Interpretation*, 38 WM. & MARY L. REV. 1311, 1331 (1997), *supra* note 10.

19. *Miller*, 307 U.S. at 177.

20. *See, e.g.*, English v. State, 24 Tex. 394, 397 (1859); Cockrum v. State, 24 Tex. 394, 397 (1859). A typical formulation is found in the West Virginia case *State v. Workman*, which construed the Second Amendment to protect an individual's right to own:

the weapons of warfare to be used by the militia, such as swords, guns, rifles, and muskets—arms to be used in defending the State and civil liberty—and not to pistols, bowie-knives, brass knuckles, billies, and such other weapons as are usually employed in brawls, street-fights, duels, and affrays, and are only habitually carried by bullies, blackguards, and desparadoes, to the terror of the community and the injury of the State.

State v. Workman, 35 W. Va. 367, 372 (1891).

21. Aymette v. State, 21 Tenn. (2 Hum.) 154 (1840).

22. *Id.* at 158.

23. *Miller*, 307 U.S. at 182.

24. Presser v. Illinois, 116 U.S. 252 (1886) (Second Amendment not violated by ban on armed parades; *see infra*) text at notes 310-20; Robertson v. Baldwin, 165 U.S. 275 (1897) (Second Amendment not violated by ban on carrying concealed weapons, *see infra* text at notes 290-96); Fife v. State, 31 Ark. 455 (Second Amendment does not apply to the states; state right to arms not violated by ban on brass knuckles); People v. Brown, 253 Mich. 537, 235 N.W. 245 (1931) (Michigan state constitution right to arms applies to all citizens, not just militiamen; right is not violated by ban on carrying blackjacks); Aymette v. State, 21 Tenn. (2 Hum.) 154 (1840)

treatises by Justice Joseph Story and Thomas Cooley explicating the Second Amendment as an individual right.[25] But the same *Miller* footnote also cites a Kansas Supreme Court decision which is directly contrary; that case holds that the right to arms in Kansas belongs only to the state government, and in *dicta* makes the same claim about the Second Amendment.[26]

The *Miller* footnote begins with the phrase "Concerning the militia—" but several of the cases cited have nothing to do with the militia. For example, *Robertson* v. *Baldwin* (discussed *infra*) simply offers *dicta* that laws which forbid the carrying of concealed weapons by individuals do not violate the Second Amendment.[27]

If *Miller* were the only source of information about the Second Amendment, the individual right vs. government right argument might be impossible to resolve conclusively. Fortunately, the Supreme Court has addressed the Second Amendment in thirty-four other cases—although most of these cases appear to have escaped the attention of commentators on both

---

(Tennessee state constitution right to arms and U.S. Second Amendment right belong to individual citizens, but right includes only the types of arms useful for militia service); State v. Duke, 42 Tex. 455 (1874) (Second Amendment does not directly apply to the states; Texas constitution protects "arms as are commonly kept, according to the customs of the people, and are appropriate for open and manly use in self-defense, as well as such as are proper for the defense of the State."); State v. Workman, *supra* note 20.

25. "COOLEY'S CONSTITUTIONAL LIMITATIONS, VOL. 1, p. 729":

Among the other defences to personal liberty should be mentioned the right of the people to keep and bear arms. A standing army is particularly obnoxious in any free government, and the jealousy of one has at times been demonstrated so strongly in England as almost to lead to the belief that a standing army recruited from among themselves was more dreaded as an instrument of oppression than a tyrannical king, or any foreign power. So impatient did the English people become of the very army which liberated them from the tyranny of James II, that they demanded its reduction, even before the liberation could be felt to be complete; and to this day, the British Parliament renders a standing army practically impossible by only passing a mutiny bill from session to session. The alternative to a standing army is "a well-regulated militia," but this cannot exist unless the people are trained to bear arms. How far it is in the power of the legislature to regulate this right, we shall not undertake to say, as happily there has been little occasion to discuss that subject by the courts.

In a later treatise, Cooley elaborated on how the right to arms ensures the existence of the militia:

The Right is General. — *It may be supposed from the phraseology of this provision that the right to keep and bear arms was only guaranteed to the militia; but this would be an interpretation not warranted by the intent. The militia, as has been elsewhere explained, consists of those persons who, under the law, are liable to the performance of military duty, and are officered and enrolled for service when called upon. But the law may make provision for the enrolment of all who are fit to perform military duty, or of a small number only, or it may wholly omit to make any provision at all; and if the right were limited to those enrolled, the purpose of this guaranty might be defeated altogether by the action or neglect to act of the government it was meant to hold in check. The meaning of the provision undoubtedly is, that the people, from whom the militia must be taken, shall have the right to keep and bear arms, and they need no permission or regulation of law for the purpose. But this enables the government to have a well-regulated militia; for to bear arms implies something more than the mere keeping; it implies the learning to handle and use them in a way that makes those who keep them ready for their efficient use; in other words, it implies the right to meet for voluntary discipline in arms, observing in doing so the laws of public order.*

THOMAS M. COOLEY, THE GENERAL PRINCIPLES OF CONSTITUTIONAL LAW IN THE UNITED STATES OF AMERICA 281-82 (Boston, Little, Brown 2d ed. 1891).

The other scholar cited in the *Miller* footnote is "Story on The Constitution, 5th Ed., Vol. 2, p. 646":

The right of the citizens to keep and bear arms has justly been considered as the palladium of the liberties of a republic; since it offers a strong moral check against the usurpation and arbitrary power of rulers; and will generally, even if these are successful in the first instance, enable the people to resist and triumph over them.

And yet, though this truth would seem so clear, and the importance of a well regulated militia would seem so undeniable, it cannot be disguised that, among the American people, there is a growing indifference to any system of militia discipline, and a strong disposition, from a sense of its burdens, to be rid of all regulations. How it is practicable to keep the people duly armed, without some organization, it is difficult to see. There is certainly no small danger that indifference may lead to disgust, and disgust to contempt; and thus gradually undermine all the protection intended by this clause of our national bill of rights.

For more on Justice Story, see text at notes 351 to 355, *infra*.

26. Salina v. Blaksley, 72 Kan. 230, 83 P. 619 (1905) (right to arms in Kansas Bill of Rights is only an affirmance of the state government's supremacy over the militia; the Second Amendment means the same). Another cited case, Jeffers v. Fair, 33 Ga. 347 (1862), is a Confederate draft case.

27. *Infra* text at note 280.

sides of the issue. This article ends the bipartisan scholarly neglect of the Supreme Court's writings on the Second Amendment.[28]

The neglected cases are not, of course, directly about the Second Amendment. Rather, they are about other issues, and the Second Amendment appears as part of an argument intended to make a point about something else.[29] Nevertheless, all the *dicta* may be revealing. If Henigan and Bogus are correct, then the *dicta* should treat the Second Amendment as a right which belongs to state governments, not to American citizens. And if the Standard Model is correct, then the Amendment should be treated as an individual right. Moreover, the line between *dicta* and *ratio decendi* is rarely firm,[30] and one day's dicta may become another day's holding.[31]

C.S. Lewis observed that proofs (or disproofs) of Christianity found in apologetic documents are sometimes less convincing than offhand remarks made in anthropology textbooks, or in other sources where Christianity is only treated incidentally. The Supreme Court cases in which the Supreme Court mentions the Second Amendment only in passing are similarly illuminating.[32]

Before commencing with case-by-case analysis, let me present a chart which summarizes the various cases. The columns in chart are self-explanatory, but I will explain two of them anyway. A "yes" answer in the "Supportive of individual right in 2d Amendment?" column means only that the particular case provides support for the individual rights theory; although the part of the case addressing the Second Amendment might make sense only if the Second Amendment is considered an individual right, the case will not directly state that proposition. If the case is labeled "ambiguous," then the language of the case is consistent with both the Standard Model and with State's Rights.

The next column asks, "Main clause of 2d A. quoted without introductory clause?" The National Rifle Association and similar groups are frequently criticized for quoting the main clause of the Second Amendment

28. One reason for the neglect of the cases may be mistaken claims that the cases do not exist. "Issue Brief", Handgun Control, Inc. website claims, "Since *Miller*, the Supreme Court has addressed the Second Amendment in two cases." Actually, there have been 19 such cases after *Miller*. *The Second Amendment*, http://www.handguncontrol.org/myth.htm.

29. That the Court has discussed the Second Amendment relatively rarely, compared to the First or Fourth Amendments, does not necessarily mean that the Second Amendment is unimportant. Until recent decades, there was almost no federal gun control to speak of (except for the 1934 National Firearms Act, which was upheld in *Miller*). That Congress hardly ever passed legislation which arguably infringed the Second Amendment (and which would generate a challenge invoking judicial review) is itself proof of the Second Amendment's influence. "A principle of law is not unimportant because we never hear of it; indeed we may say that the most efficient rules are those of which we hear least, they are so efficient that they are not broken." FREDERIC W. MAITLAND, THE CONSTITUTIONAL HISTORY OF ENGLAND 481-82 (11th ed.) (Cambridge: Cambridge Univ. Pr., 1948).

Similarly, the Third Amendment has received little attention from the Court, but that is not because the Third Amendment can be violated with impunity; to the contrary, the Third Amendment has needed little discussion because it is has been universally respected, and, except in one case, never violated. Engblom v. Carey, 677 F. 2d 957 (2d Cir. 1982), *on remand*, 572 F. Supp. 44 (S.D. N.Y. 1983), *aff'd. per curiam*, 724 F.2d 28 (2d Cir. 1983).

30. Michael C. Dorf, *Dicta and Article III*, 142 U. PA. L. REV. 1997, 2050 (1994) ("All the words used by a court to explain its result contribute to its justification, and parsing the opinion into holding and dictum attributes a degree to precision to the enterprise of judicial decision-making that it lacks in actual practice.")

31. United States v. Rabinowitz, 339 U.S. 56, 75 (1950) (Frankfurter, J., dissenting) ("These decisions do not justify today's decision. They merely prove how a hint becomes a suggestion, is loosely turned into dictum, and finally elevated to a decision.").

32. The technique of using broader context to understand isolated statements is not unique to analysis of Supreme Court cases. Biblical scholars, for example, often refer to many different parts of the Bible in order to explain a passage which is confusing or ambiguous in isolation.

Because this article is only about the Second Amendment, it does not analyze Supreme Court cases involving gun control or the militia in which the Second Amendment was not mentioned ("the right of the people to keep and bear Arms, shall not be infringed") without quoting the introductory clause ("A well-regulated Militia, being necessary to the security of a free State").[33] The critics argue that the introductory, militia, clause controls the meaning of the main, right to arms, clause. They contend that to omit the introductory clause is to distort completely the Second Amendment's meaning. (And if, as these critics argue, the Second Amendment grants a right to state governments rather than to individuals, then omission of the introductory clause is indeed quite misleading.) On the other hand, if the Second Amendment is about a right of people (the main clause), and the introductory clause is useful only to resolve gray areas (such as what kind of arms people can own), then it is legitimate sometimes to quote the main clause only. As the chart shows, the Supreme Court has quoted the main clause alone much more often than the Supreme Court has quoted both clauses together.

This Supreme Court quoting pattern is consistent with the theory Eugene Volokh's article, *The Commonplace Second Amendment*, which argues that the Second Amendment follows a common pattern of constitutional drafting from the Early Republic: there is a "purpose clause," followed by a main clause.[34] For example, Rhode Island's freedom of the press provision declared: "The liberty of the press being essential to the security of freedom in a state, any person may publish sentiments on any subject, being responsible for the abuse of that liberty."[35] This provision requires judges to protect every person's right to "publish sentiments on any subject"—even when the sentiments are not "essential to the security of freedom in a state," or when they are detrimental to freedom or security.

Similarly, the New Hampshire Constitution declared: "Economy being a most essential virtue in all states, especially in a young one; no pension shall be granted, but in consideration of actual services, and such pensions ought to be granted with great caution, by the legislature, and never for more than one year at a time."[36] This provision makes all pensions of longer than one year at a time void—even if the state is no longer "a young one" and no longer in need of economy. Volokh supplies dozens of similar examples from state constitutions.[37]

Of the twenty-nine U.S. Supreme Court opinions (including *Miller*) which have quoted the Second Amendment, twenty-three contain only a partial quote. This quoting pattern suggests that, generally speaking, Supreme Court justices have not considered the "purpose clause" at the beginning of the Second Amendment to be essential to the meaning of the main clause.

---

33. Handgun Control, Inc., *The Second Amandment Myth & Meaning* <*http://www.handgun control.org*/legalactiona/C2/C2amdbro.htm>:

How many times have you heard an opponent of gun control cite the "right to keep and bear arms" without mentioning the introductory phrase "A well regulated Militia, being necessary to the security of a free state. . ."? In fact, some years ago, when the NRA placed the words of the Second Amendment near the front door of its national headquarters in Washington, D.C., it omitted that phrase entirely!

The NRA's convenient editing is not surprising; the omitted phrase is the key to understanding that the Second Amendment guarantees only a limited right that is not violated by laws affecting the private ownership of firearms.

34. *See* Eugene Volokh, *The Commonplace Second Amendment*, 73 N.Y.U. L. REV. 793 (1998).
35. R.I. CONST. art. I, § 20 (1842).
36. N.H. CONST. pt. I, art. XXXVI (1784).
37. Volokh, *supra* note 35, at 810.

Case name and year.	*Main issue in case*	*Opinion by*	*Type of opinion*	*Supportive of individual right in 2d Amendment?*	*Main clause of 2d A. quoted without introductory clause?*	*Page of this article*
Spencer v. Kemna. 1998	Article III case or controversy.	Stevens	Dissent from denial of cert.	Yes, but could possibly be read as referring to rights under state constitutions	No quote.	86
Muscarello v. U.S. 1998	Fed stat. interp.	Ginsburg	Dissent	Yes.	Partial quote.	87
Printz v. U.S. 1997	Federalism	Thomas	Concur	Says that *Miller* did not decide the issue. Thomas appears to support individual right.	Full quote.	90
Albright v. Oliver. 1994	14th A. and § 1983	Stevens	Dissent	Yes.	Partial quote.	93
Planned Parenthood v. Casey. 1992.	14th A.	O'Connor	Majority	Yes.	Partial quote.	95
U.S. v. Verdugo-Urquidez. 1990.	4th A. applied to foreign national.	Rehnquist	Majority	Yes.	Partial quote.	95
Lewis v. U.S. 1980.	Statutory interp. of Gun Control Act of 1968	Blackmun	Majority	Ambiguous, but probably not. If an individual right, less fundamental than some others.	Full quote.	98
Moore v. East Cleveland. 1976.	14th A.	Powell	Plurality	Yes. (But contrary opinion expressed by Justice Powell after retirement.)	Partial quote.	101
" "	" "	White	Dissent.	Yes.	Partial quote.	102
Adams v. Williams. 1972	4th A.	Douglas	Dissent	No.	Full quote.	104
Roe v. Wade. 1973	14th A.	Stewart	Concur	Yes.	Partial quote.	106
Laird v. Tatum. 1972.	Justiciability	Douglas	Dissent	Ambiguous.	Partial quote.	107
Burton v. Sills. 1969.	Challenge to state gun licensing law	Per curiam	Summary affirm.	Ambiguous.	No quote.	108
Duncan v. Louisiana. 1968.	Incorporation of 6th Amendment.	Black	Concur	Yes.	Partial quote.	110
Malloy v. Hogan. 1964.	Incorporation of 5th Amend.	Brennan	Majority	Yes.	No quote.	110

Konigsberg v. State Bar. 1961.	1st Amendment	Harlan	Majority	Yes.	Partial quote.	111
Poe v. Ullman. 1961.	14th Amendment	Harlan	Dissent	Yes	Partial quote.	112
" "	" "	Douglas	Dissent	Yes, but implicitly abandoned in *Adams*.	No quote.	113
Knapp v. Schweitzer. 1958.	Incorp. of 5th Amendment	Frankfurter	Majority	Yes	Partial quote.	114
Johnson v. Eisentrager. 1950.	5th A. applied to trial of enemy soldier.	Jackson	Majority	Yes	Partial quote.	115
Adamson v. Calif. 1947.	Incorp. of 5th Amendment	Black	Dissent	Yes	Partial quote.	117
Hamilton v. Regents. 1935.	Conscientious objector.	Butler	Majority	No, but not necessarily inconsistent with an individual right.	No quote.	120
U.S. v. Schwimmer. 1929.	Immigration laws	Butler	Majority	Ambiguous	Full quote.	123
Stearns v. Wood. 1915.	Article III case or controversy.	McReynolds	Majority	Ambiguous, since court refuses to hear any of plaintiff's claims	No quote.	124
Twining v. N.J. 1908.	Incorp. of 5th A self-incrim.	Moody	Majority	Yes.	Partial quote	124
Trono v. U.S. 1905	5th A. in the Philippines.	Peckham	Majority	Yes.	Partial quote.	126
Kepner v. U.S. 1904.	" "	Day	Majority	Yes. Same as *Trono*.	Partial quote.	126
Maxwell v. Dow. 1899.	Incorp. of 5th A. jury trial	Peckham	Majority	Yes.	Partial quote.	125
Robertson v. Baldwin. 1897.	13th Amend.	Brown	Majority	Yes.	Partial quote.	127
Brown v. Walker. 1896.	5th Amend.	Field.	Dissent	Yes.	Partial quote.	128
Miller v. Texas. 1894.	14th Amendment	Brown	Majority	Yes.	Partial quote.	129
Logan v. U.S. 1892.	Cong. Power from 14th A.	Gray	Majority	Yes.	Partial quote.	131
Presser v. Illinois. 1886.	2d A.	Woods	Majority	Yes.	Full quote.	133

U.S. v. Cruikshank 1876.	Cong. Power under 14th Amendment	Waite	Majority	Yes. A basic human right which pre-exists the Constitution, and is guaranteed by the Constitution, exactly like the 1st A. right to assembly.	No quote.	136
Scott v. Sandford. 1857.	Citizenship; Cong. powers over territories.	Taney	Majority	Yes.	Partial quote.	137
Houston v. Moore. 1820.	State powers over militia.	Story	Dissent	Yes, but also supportive of a state's right. (A later treatise written by Story is for individual right only.)	No quote.	140

I. The Rehnquist Court

Since William Rehnquist was appointed Chief Justice in 1986, six different opinions have addressed the Second Amendment. The authors of the opinions include the small left wing of the Court (Justices Stevens and Ginsburg), the Court's right wing (Justices Thomas and Rehnquist), and the Court's centrist Justice O'Connor. Every one of the opinions treats the Second Amendment as an individual right. Except for Justice Breyer, every sitting Supreme Court Justice has joined in at least one of these opinions—although this joinder does not prove that the joiner necessarily agreed with what the opinion said about the Second Amendment. Still, five of the current Justices have written an opinion in which the Second Amendment is considered an individual right, and three more Justices have joined such an opinion.

A. Spencer v. Kemna

After serving some time in state prison, Spencer was released on parole.[38] While free, he was accused but not convicted of rape, and his parole was revoked.[39] He argued that his parole revocation was unconstitutional.[40] But before his constitutional claim could be judicially resolved, his sentence ended, and he was released.[41] The majority of the Supreme Court held that

38. Spencer v. Kemna, 523 U.S. 1, 4 (1998).
39. *Id.* at 5.
40. *Id.* at 10.
41. *Id.* at 36. (Stevens, J., dissenting).

since Spencer was out of prison, his claim was moot, and he had no right to pursue his constitutional lawsuit.

Justice Stevens, in dissent, argued that being found to have perpetrated a crime (such as the rape finding implicit in the revocation of Spencer's parole) has consequences besides prison:

> *An official determination that a person has committed a crime may cause two different kinds of injury. It may result in tangible harms such as imprisonment, loss of the right to vote or to bear arms, and the risk of greater punishment if another crime is committed. It may also severely injure the person's reputation and good name.*[42]

A person can only lose a right upon conviction of a crime if a person had the right before conviction. Hence, if an individual can lose his right "to bear arms," he must possess such a right. Justice Stevens did not specifically mention the Second Amendment, so it is possible that his reference to the right to bear arms was to a right created by state constitutions, rather than the federal one. (Forty-four states guarantee a right to arms in their state constitution.[43]) When particular gun control laws are before the Supreme Court for either statutory or constitutional interpretation, Justice Stevens is a reliable vote to uphold the law in question, often with language detailing the harm of gun violence.[44] It is notable, then, that Justice Stevens recognizes a right to bear arms as an important constitutional right, whose deprivation should not be shielded from judicial review.[45]

B. Muscarello v. United States

Federal law provides a five year mandatory sentence for anyone who "carries a firearm" during a drug trafficking crime.[46] Does the sentence enhancement apply when the gun is merely contained in an automobile in which a person commits a drug trafficking crime—such as when the gun is in the trunk? The Supreme Court majority said "yes."[47] In dissent, Justice Ginsburg—joined by Justices Rehnquist, Scalia[48], and Souter—argued that "carries a firearm" means to carry it so that it is ready to use.[49] In support for

---

42. *Id.* (emphasis added). Numerous state and federal statutes outlaw firearms possession by persons convicted of felonies or certain misdemeanors. Generally speaking, the federal prohibitions are broader than their state counterparts.

43. The entire set of state constitutional right-to-arms statements, originally appearing here as a footnote, has been included in *Supreme Court Gun Cases* as its own chapter, q.v.

In addition, New York State's Civil Right Law has a statutory provision which is a word for word copy of the Second Amendment. N.Y. CIV. RIGHTS § 4.

44. *See* United States v. Thompson/Center Arms Co., 504 U.S. 505,526 (1992); Printz v. United States, 521 U.S. 898 (1997) (Stevens, J., dissenting); United States v. Lopez, 512 U.S. 1286 (1994) (Stevens, J., dissenting).

45. Contrast Justice Stevens' view with that of Justice Blackmun in the *Lewis* case, *infra* notes 94-113; the Blackmun opinion suggests that the right to arms is so unimportant that a person may be imprisoned for the exercise of that right after conviction of a crime—even if the conviction is concededly unconstitutional.

46. 18 U.S.C. § 924(c)(1).

47. United States v. Muscarello, 524 U.S. 125 (1998).

48. Justice Scalia has not written an opinion on the Second Amendment, but he has expressed his views out of court:

So also, we value the right to bear arms less than did the Founders (who thought the right to self-defense to be absolutely fundamental), and there will be few tears shed if and when the Second Amendment is held to guarantee nothing more than the state National Guard. But this just shows the Founders were right when they feared that some (in their view misguided) future generation might wish to abandon liberties that they considered essential, and so sought to protect those liberties in a Bill of Rights. We may. . .like elimination of the right to bear arms; but let us not pretend that these are not reductions of rights.

ANTONIN SCALIA, A MATTER OF INTERPRETATION 43 (1997).

49. *Muscarello*, 524 U.S. at 139-50 (Ginsburg, J., dissenting).

her view, Justice Ginsburg pointed to the Second Amendment "keep and bear arms" as an example of the ordinary meaning of carrying a firearm:

> *It is uncontested that §924(c)(1) applies when the defendant bears a firearm, i.e. , carries the weapon on or about his person "for the purpose of being armed and ready for offensive or defensive action in case of a conflict." Black's Law Dictionary 214 (6th ed. 1990) (defining the phrase "carry arms or weapons"); see ante, at 5. The Court holds that, in addition, "carries a firearm," in the context of §924(c)(1), means personally transporting, possessing, or keeping a firearm in a vehicle, anyplace in a vehicle.*
>
> *Without doubt, "carries" is a word of many meanings, definable to mean or include carting about in a vehicle. But that encompassing definition is not a ubiquitously necessary one. Nor, in my judgment, is it a proper construction of "carries" as the term appears in §924(c)(1). In line with Bailey and the principle of lenity the Court has long followed, I would confine "carries a firearm," for §924(c)(1) purposes, to the undoubted meaning of that expression in the relevant context. I would read the words to indicate not merely keeping arms on one's premises or in one's vehicle, but bearing them in such manner as to be ready for use as a weapon.*
>
> . . .
>
> *Unlike the Court, I do not think dictionaries, surveys of press reports, or the Bible tell us, dispositively, what "carries" means embedded in §924(c)(1). On definitions, "carry" in legal formulations could mean, inter alia, transport, possess, have in stock, prolong (carry over), be infectious, or wear or bear on one's person. At issue here is not "carries" at large but "carries a firearm." The Court's computer search of newspapers is revealing in this light. Carrying guns in a car showed up as the meaning "perhaps more than one third" of the time. Ante, at 4. One is left to wonder what meaning showed up some two thirds of the time. Surely a most familiar meaning is, as the Constitution's Second Amendment ("keep and bear Arms") (emphasis added) and Black's Law Dictionary, at 214, indicate: "wear, bear, or carry . . . upon the person or in the clothing or in a pocket, for the purpose . . . of being armed and ready for offensive or defensive action in a case of conflict with another person."*[50]

Perhaps no word in the Second Amendment is as hotly contested as the word "bear." The Standard Model scholars, following the usage of Webster's Dictionary,[51] the 1776 Pennsylvania Constitution,[52] and the 1787 call for a Bill of Rights from the dissenters at the Pennsylvania Ratification Convention read the word "bear" as including ordinary types of carrying.[53] Thus, a

50. *Id.* (footnotes omitted).

51. First: "[t]o support; to sustain; as, to *bear* a weight or burden" Second: "To carry; to convey; to support and remove from place to place". 3:"[t]o wear; to bear as a mark of authority or distinction; as, to *bear* a sword, a badge, a name; to *bear* arms in a coat." NOAH WEBSTER, AN AMERICAN DICTIONARY OF THE ENGLISH LANGUAGE (1828) (emphasis in originagl).

52. Volokh, *supra* note 35, at 810.

53. *Id.*

person carrying a gun for personal protection could be said to be bearing arms. If individuals can "bear arms," then the right to "bear arms" must belong to individuals.

In contrast, Garry Wills (who argues that the Second Amendment has "no real meaning"[54]) argues that "bear" has an exclusively military context.[55] It is impossible, he writes, to "bear arms" unless once is engaged in active militia service. Hence, the right to "bear arms" does not refer to a right of individuals to carry guns.[56]

Justice Ginsburg's opinion plainly takes the former approach. She believes that "to bear arms" is to wear arms in an ordinary way.[57]

---

54. Garry Wills, *Why We Have No Right to Bear Arms*, N.Y. REV. BOOKS, Sept. 21, 1995, at 62.
55. *Id.*
56. *Id.* at 64.
57. During the Senate Judiciary Committee hearings on Ruth Bader Ginsburg's nomination to the Supreme Court, Senator Dianne Feinstein (a strong supporter of gun prohibition) asked Mrs. Ginsburg about the Second Amendment. Mrs. Ginsburg politely refused to say anything, except that the Amendment had not been incorporated.

Sen. Feinstein:

Let me begin with the Second Amendment. I first became concerned about what does the Second Amendment mean with respect to guns in 1962 [sic] when President Kennedy was assassinated. . .

Judge Ginsburg:

Senator Feinstein, I can say on the Second Amendment only what I said earlier, the one thing that the court has held, that it is not incorporated in the Bill of Rights [sic, 14th Amendment], it does not apply to the states. The last time the Supreme Court spoke to this question is in 1939. You summarized what that was and you also summarized the state of law in the lower courts. But this is a question that may well be before again, and all I can do is to acknowledge what I understand to be the current case law, that this is not incorporated in—that this is not one of the provisions binding on the states. The last time the Supreme Court spoke to it is in 1939, and because of where I sit, it would be inappropriate for me to say anything more than that. I would have to consider, as I've said many times today, the specific case, the briefs and the arguments that would be made, and it would be injudicious for me to say anything more with respect to the Second Amendment.

. . . .

Sen. Feinstein:

[C]ould you talk at all about the methodology you might apply, what factors you might look at in discussing Second Amendment cases should Congress, say, pass a ban on assault weapons?

Judge Ginsburg:

I wish I could, Senator, but all I can tell you is that this is an amendment that has not been looked at the by the Supreme Court since 1939, and it—apart from the specific context, I can't—I really can't expound on it. It's an area of law in which my court has had no business and one I had no acquaintance as a law teacher. So really feel that I'm not equipped beyond what I already told you, that it isn't an incorporated amendment. The Supreme Court has not dealt with it since 1939. And I would proceed with the care I would give to any serious constitutional question.

At Justice Breyer's confirmation hearing, Senator Feinstein raised similar issues. He answered:

As you recognize, Senator, the Second Amendment does—is in the Constitution. It provides a protection. As you also have recognized, the Supreme Court law on the subject is very, very, very few cases. This really hasn't been gone into in any depth by the Supreme Court at all. Like you, I've never heard anyone even argue that there's some kind of constitutional right to have guns in a school. And I know that every day—not every day; I don't want to exaggerate—but every week or every month for the last 14 years I've sat on case after case in which Congress has legislated rules, regulations, restrictions of all kinds on weapons.

That is to say there are many, many circumstances in which carrying weapons of all kinds is punishable by very, very, very severe penalties. And Congress often—I mean by overwhelming majorities—has passed legislation imposing very severe additional penalties on people who commit all kinds of crimes with guns, even various people just possessing guns under certain circumstances.

And in all those 14 years, I've never heard anyone seriously argue that any of those was unconstitutional in a serious way. I shouldn't say never, because I don't remember every case in 14 years.

So, obviously, it's fairly well conceded across the whole range of society, whatever their views about gun control legislatively and so forth that there's a very, very large area for government to act. At the same time, as you concede and others, there's some kind of protection given in the Second Amendment.

Now that's, it seems to me, where I have to stop, and the reason that I have to stop is we're in a void in terms of what the Supreme Court has said. There is legislation likely to pass or has recently passed that will be challenged, and therefore I, if I am on that Court, have to listen with an open mind to the arguments that are made in the particular context.

Sen. Feinstein:

*Well, would you hold that the 1939 decision [*Miller*] is good law?*

Justice Breyer:

I've not heard it argued that it's not, but I haven't reviewed the case and I don't know the argument that would really come up. I know that it's been fairly limited, what the Supreme Court has said. And I know that it's been fairly narrow. I also know that other people make an argument for a somewhat more expanded view. But nobody

C. Printz v. United States

In *Printz v. United States*, the Supreme Court voted 5 to 4 to declare part of the Brady Act unconstitutional, because the Act ordered state and local law enforcement officials to perform a federal background check on handgun buyers.[58] While the *Printz* decision was not a Second Amendment case, *Printz* did result in some Second Amendment language from Justice Clarence Thomas's concurring opinion.

Justice Thomas joined in Justice Scalia's five-person majority opinion, but he also wrote a separate concurring opinion—an opinion which shows that all the Second Amendment scholarship in the legal journals is starting to be noticed by the Court.

The Thomas concurrence began by saying that, even if the Brady Act did not intrude on state sovereignty, it would still be unconstitutional.[59] The law was enacted under the congressional power "to regulate commerce. . .among the several states."[60] But the Brady Act applies to commerce that is purely *intra*state—the sale of handgun by a gun store to a customer in the same state.[61] Justice Thomas suggested that although the interstate commerce clause has, in recent decades, been interpreted to extend to purely intrastate transactions, that interpretation is wrong.[62]

Even if the Brady Act were within the Congressional power over interstate commerce, Justice Thomas continued, the Act might violate the Second Amendment:

> *. . . .Even if we construe Congress' authority to regulate interstate commerce to encompass those intrastate transactions that "substantially affect" interstate commerce, I question whether Congress can regulate the particular transactions at issue here. The Constitution, in addition to delegating certain enumerated powers to Congress, places whole areas outside the reach of Congress' regulatory authority. The First Amendment, for example, is fittingly celebrated for preventing Congress from "prohibiting the free exercise" of religion or "abridging the freedom*

---

that I've heard makes the argument going into these areas where there is quite a lot of regulation already. I shouldn't really underline no one, because you can find, you know, people who make different arguments. But it seems there's a pretty broad consensus there.

Sen. Feinstein:

Would you attach any significance to the framers of the Second Amendment, where it puts certain things in capital letters?

Justice Breyer:

I'm sure when you interpret this you do go back from the text to the history and try to get an idea of what they had in mind. And if there is a capital letter there, you ask why is there this capital letter there, somebody had an idea, and you read and try to figure out what the importance of that was viewed at the time and if that's changed over time.

Sen. Judiciary Comm., Confirmation Hearing for Stephen Breyer, July 13, 1994, Federal News Service Lexis library.

58. Printz v. United States, 521 U.S. 898 (1997)

59. *Id.* at 937 (Thomas, J., concurring).

60. The Civil Rights Act of 1964 used the interstate commerce power to regulate parties to commercial transactions, such as hotel or restaurant guests and owners. But the Brady Act attempted to expand the interstate commerce power even further, by forcing third parties to become involved in the commercial transaction. The Brady Act commandeered local sheriffs and police to perform background checks on a commercial act—the retail sale of a handgun. It was as if the Civil Rights Act had compelled state and local government employees to serve as race sensitivity mediators in hotel and restaurants. It was one thing to use the interstate commerce power to regulate commerce. It is another thing use that power to force people who are stranger to the commercial transaction to get involved. *See* David B. Kopel, *The Brady Bill Comes Due: The Printz Case and State Autonomy*, GEO. MASON UNIV. CIV. RIGHTS L.J. 189 (1999).

61. *Printz*, 521 U.S. at 937-38 (Thomas, J., concurring).

62. *Id*.

of speech." The Second Amendment similarly appears to contain an express limitation on the government's authority. That Amendment provides: "[a] well regulated Militia, being necessary to the security of a free State, the right of the people to keep and bear arms, shall not be infringed." This Court has not had recent occasion to consider the nature of the substantive right safeguarded by the Second Amendment. [n.1] If, however, the Second Amendment is read to confer[63] a personal *right to "keep and bear arms," a colorable argument exists that the Federal Government's regulatory scheme, at least as it pertains to the purely intrastate sale or possession of firearms, runs afoul of that Amendment's protections. [n.2] As the parties did not raise this argument, however, we need not consider it here. Perhaps, at some future date, this Court will have the opportunity to determine whether Justice Story was correct when he wrote that the right to bear arms "has justly been considered, as the palladium of the liberties of a republic." 3 J. Story, Commentaries §1890, p. 746 (1833). In the meantime, I join the Court's opinion striking down the challenged provisions of the Brady Act as inconsistent with the Tenth Amendment.*[64]

There are several notable elements in the Thomas concurrence. First, Justice Thomas equates the Second Amendment with the First Amendment. This is consistent with the rule from the *Valley Forge* case that all parts of the Bill of Rights are on equal footing; none is preferred (or derogated).[65] He implicitly rejected second-class citizenship for the Second Amendment.

Justice Thomas then suggests that the Brady Act could be invalid under the Second Amendment.[66] Regarding right to bear arms provisions in state constitutions, some state courts have upheld various gun restrictions as long as all guns are not banned.[67] Justice Thomas plainly does not take such a weak position in defense of the Second Amendment.[68] His implication is that by requiring government permission and a week-long prior restraint on the right to buy a handgun, the Brady Act infringed the Second Amendment.

And of course by recognizing that handguns are a Second Amendment issue, Justice Thomas implicitly rejects the argument that the Second Amendment merely protects "sporting weapons" (usually defined as a subset of rifles and shotguns).[69]

Noting that the Second Amendment was not at issue in the case before the Court (the case was brought by sheriffs who did not want to be subject to federal commands, rather by gun buyers or gun dealers), Justice Thomas gently urges the rest of the Court to take up a Second Amendment case in the future. And he leaves no doubt about his personal view of the issue, as he quotes the 19th century legal scholar and Supreme Court Justice Joseph

---

63. In contrast to the suggestion that the Bill of Rights might "confer" the right to bear arms, the Supreme Court in the 1875 case of *United States v. Cruikshank* stated that the Second Amendment, like the First Amendment, does not confer rights on anyone. Rather, those Amendments simply *recognized* and protected pre-existing human rights. *See* text at notes 321 to 328.

64. *Printz*, 521 U.S. at 938-39 (Thomas, J., concurring).

65. *See* Valley Forge Christian College v. Americans United for Separation of Church and State, Inc., 454 U.S. 464 (1982).

66. *Printz*, 521 U.S. at 938 (Thomas, J., concurring).

67. *See* Robertson v. Denver, 874 P.2d 325 (Colo. 1994); Arnold v. City of Cleveland, 616 N.E.2d 163 (Ohio 1993). For a discussion of these cases, see David Kopel, Clayton Cramer & Scott Hattrup, *A Tale of Three Cities: The Right to Bear Arms in State Supreme Courts*, 68 TEMP. L. REV. 1177 (1995).

68. *Printz*, 521 U.S. at 938-39 (Thomas, J., concurring).

69. *Id.*

Story, who saw the right to bear arms "as the palladium of the liberties of a republic."[70]

There are two footnotes in the Second Amendment portion of the Thomas concurrence. In the first footnote, the Justice states that the Supreme Court has not construed the Second Amendment since the 1939 case *United States v. Miller* (which upheld the National Firearms Act's tax and registration requirement for short shotguns[71]). He added that the Supreme Court has never directly ruled on the individual rights issue.

> *1 Our most recent treatment of the Second Amendment occurred in* United States *v.* Miller, *307 U.S. 174 (1939), in which we reversed the District Court's invalidation of the National Firearms Act, enacted in 1934. In* Miller, *we determined that the Second Amendment did not guarantee a citizen's right to possess a sawed off shotgun because that weapon had not been shown to be "ordinary military equipment" that could "contribute to the common defense."* Id., *at 178. The Court did not, however, attempt to define, or otherwise construe, the substantive right protected by the Second Amendment.*

The second footnote addressed the growing scholarship on the Second Amendment:

> *2 Marshaling an impressive array of historical evidence, a growing body of scholarly commentary indicates that the "right to keep and bear arms" is, as the Amendment's text suggests, a personal right. See,* e.g., *J. Malcolm, To Keep and Bear Arms: The Origins of an Anglo American Right 162 (1994); S. Halbrook, That Every Man Be Armed, The Evolution of a Constitutional Right (1984); Van Alstyne, The Second Amendment and the Personal Right to Arms, 43 Duke L. J. 1236 (1994); Amar, The Bill of Rights and the Fourteenth Amendment, 101 Yale L. J. 1193 (1992); Cottrol & Diamond, The Second Amendment: Toward an Afro Americanist Reconsideration, 80 Geo. L. J. 309 (1991); Levinson, The Embarrassing Second Amendment, 99 Yale L. J. 637 (1989); Kates, Handgun Prohibition and the Original Meaning of the Second Amendment, 82 Mich. L. Rev. 204 (1983). Other scholars, however, argue that the Second Amendment does not secure a personal right to keep or to bear arms. See,* e.g., *Bogus, Race, Riots, and Guns, 66 S. Cal. L. Rev. 1365 (1993); Williams, Civic Republicanism and the Citizen Militia: The Terrifying Second Amendment, 101 Yale L. J. 551 (1991); Brown, Guns, Cowboys, Philadelphia Mayors, and Civic Republicanism: On Sanford Levinson's The Embarrassing Second Amendment, 99 Yale L. J. 661 (1989); Cress, An Armed Community: The Origins and Meaning of the Right to Bear Arms, 71 J. Am. Hist. 22 (1984). Although somewhat overlooked in our jurisprudence, the Amendment has certainly engendered considerable academic, as well as public, debate.*

In the second footnote, Justice Thomas points out that the text of the Second Amendment (which refers to "the right of the people") suggests that the Second Amendment right belongs to individuals, not the government.

---

70. *Id.* at 939 (citing 3 J. STORY, COMMENTARIES § 1890, p. 746 (1833)).
71. *See* United States v. Miller, 307 U.S. 174 (1939).

As Justice Thomas notes, a large body of legal scholarship in the last fifteen years has examined the historical evidence, and found very strong proof that the Second Amendment guarantees an individual right.[72]

The Supreme Court does not always follow the viewpoint of the legal academy. But for most of this century, the Court has always been influenced by the academy's opinion. In the 1940s, for example, legal scholars paid almost no attention to the Second Amendment, and neither did the Supreme Court; in that decade, the Second Amendment was mentioned only once, and that mention was in a lone dissent.[73] But starting in the late 1970s, a Second Amendment revolution began to take place in legal scholarship. That an intellectual revolution was in progress became undeniable after the *Yale Law Journal* published Sanford Levinson's widely influential article *The Embarrassing Second Amendment* in 1989.[74] Since then, scholarly attention to the Second Amendment has grown even more rapidly. And more importantly, for purposes of this article, the Supreme Court Justices have raised the Second Amendment in six different cases in 1990-98. Six mentions in nine years hardly puts the Second Amendment on the same plane as the First Amendment; but six times in one decade is a rate six times higher than in the 1940s.

D. Albright v. Oliver

Albright involved a Section 1983 civil rights lawsuit growing out of a malicious decision to prosecute someone for conduct which was not crime under the relevant state law.[75] The issue before the Supreme Court was whether the prosecutor's action violated the defendant's Fourteenth Amendment Due Process rights. The majority said "no," in part because the claim (growing out of the victim's unlawful arrest) would be better presented as a Fourth Amendment claim.[76]

Justice Stevens dissented, and was joined by Justice Blackmun; part of the dissent quoted Justice Harlan's analysis of the meaning of the Fourteenth Amendment, and the Fourteenth Amendment's protection of the "right to keep and bear arms":

> *At bottom, the plurality opinion seems to rest on one fundamental misunderstanding: that the incorporation cases have somehow "substituted" the specific provisions of the Bill of Rights for the "more generalized language contained in the earlier cases construing the Fourteenth Amendment." Ante, at 7. In fact, the incorporation cases themselves rely on the very "generalized language" the Chief Justice would have them displacing. Those cases add to the liberty protected by the Due Process Clause most of the specific guarantees of the first eight Amendments, but they do not purport to take anything away; that a liberty interest is not the subject of an incorporated provision of the Bill*

72. *Printz*, 521 U.S. at 939 (Thomas, J., concurring). See note 9 *supra*.
73. See Adamson v. California, 332 U.S. 46, 78 (Black, J., dissenting).
74. See Levinson, *supra* note 9.
75. Albright v. Oliver, 510 U.S. 266 (1994). The only evidence against the person falsely accused came from a paid informant who had provided false information more than 50 times before. *Id.* at 292 (Stevens, J., dissenting). For more on the degradation of law enforcement caused by over-reliance on informants, especially in drug and gun cases, *see generally* David B. Kopel and Paul H. Blackman, *The Unwarranted Warrant: The Waco Warrant and the Decline of Law Enforcement*, 18 HAMLINE J. PUB. L. & POL 1 (1999).
76. *Albright*, 510 U.S. at 274-275.

> *of Rights does not remove it from the ambit of the Due Process Clause. I cannot improve on Justice Harlan's statement of this settled proposition:*
>
> "The full scope of the liberty guaranteed by the Due Process Clause cannot be found in or limited by the precise terms of the specific guarantees elsewhere provided in the Constitution. This "liberty" is not a series of isolated points pricked out in terms of the taking of property; the freedom of speech, press, and religion; the right to keep and bear arms; the freedom from unreasonable searches and seizures; and so on. It is a rational continuum which, broadly speaking, includes a freedom from all substantial arbitrary impositions and purposeless restraints . . . and which also recognizes, what a reasonable and sensitive judgment must, that certain interests require particularly careful scrutiny of the state needs asserted to justify their abridgment." Poe v. Ullman, 367 U.S. 497, 543 (1961) (dissenting opinion).[77]
>
> I have no doubt that an official accusation of an infamous crime constitutes a deprivation of liberty worthy of constitutional protection. The Framers of the Bill of Rights so concluded, and there is no reason to believe that the sponsors of the Fourteenth Amendment held a different view. The Due Process Clause of that Amendment should therefore be construed to require a responsible determination of probable cause before such a deprivation is effected. [78]

In *Poe v. Ullman*, the second Justice Harlan construed the "liberty" protected by the Fourteenth Amendment.[79] Although Justice Harlan's words originally were written in dissent, they have been quoted in later cases as the opinion of the Court.[80] Fourteenth Amendment "liberty" of course belongs to individuals, not to state governments. The point of the Fourteenth Amendment was to protect individual liberty from state infringement.

This "liberty" is not limited to "the specific guarantees elsewhere provided in the Constitution" including "the right to keep and bear arms." These individual rights in the Harlan list, like other individual rights in the Bill of Rights, *might* be included in the Fourteenth Amendment's protection of "liberty" against state action. The point made by Justice Harlan (and Justice Stevens, quoting Justice Harlan), is that Fourteenth Amendment "liberty" includes things which are not part of the Bill of Rights, and does not necessarily include every individual right which is in the Bill of Rights.

While the Harlan quote makes no direct claim about whether the individual Bill of Rights items should be incorporated in the Fourteenth Amendment, Justice Harlan was plainly saying that simply because an individual right is protected in the Bill of Rights does not mean that it is protected by the Fourteenth Amendment. (Justice Black's view was directly opposite.[81]) Therefore, although the Harlan quote is not dispositive, the quote could appropriately be used to argue against incorporating the Second Amendment into the Fourteenth.

---

77. *Id.* at 306-08 (Stevens, J., dissenting).
78. *Id.* at 307 (Stevens, J., dissenting) (footnote marker omitted) (emphasis added).
79. Poe v. Ullman, 367 U.S. 497, 523 (1961) (Harlan, J., dissenting).
80. See discussions of Planned Parenthood v. Casey, *infra* text at notes 82-84; Moore v. East Cleveland, *infra* text at notes 115-36; Roe v. Wade, *infra* text at notes 146-53.
81. *Infra* note 180.

At the same time, the quote obviously treats the Second Amendment as an individual right. That is why Justice Harlan used the Second Amendment (along with the religion, speech, press, freedom from unreasonable searches, and property) to make a point about what kind of individual rights are protected by the Fourteenth Amendment.

As we shall see below, Justice Harlan's words are the words about the Second Amendment which the Supreme Court has quoted most often.

E. Planned Parenthood v. Casey

Planned Parenthood was a challenge to a Pennsylvania law imposing various restrictions on abortion.[82] In discussing the scope of the Fourteenth Amendment, Justice Sandra Day O'Connor's opinion for the Court approvingly quoted Justice Harlan's earlier statement that "the right to keep and bear arms" is part of the "full scope of liberty" contained in the Bill of Rights, and made applicable to the state by the Fourteenth Amendment.[83] Although the *Planned Parenthood* decision was fractured, with various Justices joining only selected portions of each others' opinions, the portion where Justice O'Connor quoted Justice Harlan about the Fourteenth and Second Amendments was joined by four other Justices, and represented the official opinion of the Court.

Planned Parenthood is the second of the four Supreme Court opinions that quote the Harlan dissent in *Poe*. (The other two will be discussed *infra*.) Had the authors of those opinions chosen to delete the "right to keep and bear arms" words, by using ellipses, they certainly could have done so. As we shall see when we come to the original Harlan opinion in *Poe v. Ullman*, the full Harlan analysis of the scope of Fourteenth Amendment liberty includes important material which later Justices carefully avoided quoting.[84]

F. United States v. Verdugo-Urquidez

United States v. Verdugo-Urquidez[85] involved American drug agents' warrantless search of a Mexican's homes in Mexicali and San Felipe, Mexico. When Verdugo-Urquidez was prosecuted in a United States court for distribution of marijuana, his attorney argued that the evidence seized from his homes could not be used against him.[86] If the homes in question had been located in the United States and owned by an American, the exclusionary rule clearly would have forbade the introduction of the evidence. But did the U.S. Fourth Amendment protect Mexican citizens in Mexico?

---

82. Planned Parenthood v. Casey, 505 U.S. 833, 848-49 (1992).
83. *Id.* at 841.
84. *Infra* at notes 200 to 204.
85. United States v. Verdugo-Urquidez , 494 U.S. 259 (1990).
86. The evidence was some of Verdugo-Urquidez's personal papers. Under the original intent of the Fourth and Fifth Amendments, the seizure of such papers would be seen as particularly inappropriate. The English government's use of diaries and other personal papers in prosecution of dissidents was widely regarded in America as one of the great outrages of British despotism. See AKHIL AMAR, THE BILL OF RIGHTS 65-67 (1998). Under *Boyd v.United States*, the Court affirmed that private papers could not be introduced against a defendant, because the use of such papers would violate the Fourth and Fifth Amendments. Boyd v. United States, 116 U.S. 616 (1886). Unfortunately, a later Supreme Court abandoned this rule; thus, Independent Counsel Kenneth Starr was well within the letter of the law when his staff subpoenaed and read the diaries of Monica Lewinsky and her friends.

Chief Justice Rehnquist's majority opinion said "no." Part of the Court's analysis investigated who are "the people" protected by the Fourth Amendment:

> *"[T]he people" seems to have been a term of art employed in select parts of the Constitution. The preamble declares that the Constitution is ordained and established by "the People of the United States." The Second Amendment protects "the right of the people to keep and bear Arms," and the Ninth and Tenth Amendment provide that certain rights and power are retained by and reserved to "the people." See also U.S. Const., Amdt. 1 ("Congress shall make no law. . .abridging. . .*the right of the people *peaceably to assemble")(emphasis added); Art I, § 2, cl. 1 ("The House of Representatives shall be composed of Members chosen every second Year* by the People of the Several States *")(emphasis added). While this textual exegesis is by no means conclusive, it suggests that "the People" protected by the Fourth Amendment, and by the First and Second Amendment, and to whom rights are reserved in the Ninth and Tenth Amendments, refers to a class of persons who are part of a national community or who have otherwise developed sufficient connection with this country to be considered part of that community.*[87]

By implication therefore, if "the people" whose right to arms is protected by the Second Amendment are American people, then "the right of the people" in the Second Amendment does not mean "the right of the states."[88]

---

87. *Verdugo-Urquidez*, 494 U.S. at 265.

88. *Verdugo* is of course a Fourth Amendment case, not a Second Amendment case. But there is no reason to believe that the Court did not mean what it said about the Second Amendment in *Verdugo*.

Oddly, some of the same persons who want the public to ignore what the Supreme Court said about the Second Amendment in the *Verdugo* case instead want the public to rely on what a retired justice said about the Second Amendment in a forum with much less precedential value than a Supreme Court decision or a law journal: an article in *Parade* magazine.

While on the Supreme Court, Chief Justice Warren Burger never wrote a word about the Second Amendment. After retirement, he wrote an article for *Parade* magazine that is the only extended analysis by any Supreme Court Justice of why the Second Amendment does not guarantee an individual right. Warren Burger, *The Right to Bear Arms*, PARADE, Jan. 14, 1990, at 4-6.

Chief Justice Burger argued that the Second Amendment is obsolete because we "need" a large standing army, rather than a well-armed citizenry. But the notion that constitutional rights can be discarded because someone thinks they are obsolete is anathema to a written Constitution. If a right is thought "obsolete," the proper approach is to amend the Constitution and remove it. After all, the Seventh Amendment guarantees a right to a jury trial in all cases involving more than twenty dollars. U.S. CONST. amend. VII. In 1791, twenty dollars was a lot of money; today it is little more than pocket change. Nevertheless, courts must (and do) enforce the Seventh Amendment fully.

And while the Second Amendment certainly drew much of its original support from fear of standing armies, its language is not limited to that issue. "Legislation, both statutory and constitutional, is enacted,. . .from an experience of evils. . .its general language should not, therefore, be necessarily confined to the form that evil had heretofore taken. . .[A] principle to be vital must be capable of wider application than the mischief which gave it birth." Weems v. United States, 217 U.S. 349, 373 (1910).

Yet after attacking the Second Amendment as obsolete, Chief Justice Burger's essay affirmed that "Americans have a right to defend their homes." If this right does not derive from the Second Amendment, does it come from the Ninth Amendment, as Nicholas Johnson has argued? *See* Nicholas Johnson, *Beyond the Second Amendment: An Individual Right to Arms Viewed Through the Ninth Amendment*, 24 RUTGERS L.J. 1, 49 (1992). The Burger essay does not say.

Next comes the real shocker: "Nor does anyone seriously question that the Constitution protects the right of hunters to own and keep sporting guns for hunting game any more than anyone would challenge the right to own and keep fishing rods and other equipment for fishing—or to own automobiles."

In a single sentence, the former Chief Justice asserts that three "Constitutional rights"—hunting, fishing, and buying cars—are so firmly guaranteed as to be beyond question. Yet no Supreme Court case has ever held any of these activities to be Constitutionally protected.

What part of the Constitution protects the right to fish? The 1776 Pennsylvania Constitution guaranteed a right to fish and hunt, and the minority report from the 1789 Pennsylvania ratifying convention made a similar call. Various common law sources (such as St. George Tucker's enormously influential American edition of Blackstone) likewise support hunting rights. 3 WILLIAM BLACKSTONE, COMMENTARIES 414 n.3 (St. George

To adopt the Henigan/Bogus theory, and find that the Second Amendment "right of the people" belongs to state governments would require a rejection of *Verdugo's* explication of who are "the people" of the Second Amendment and the rest of the Constitution.

The dissent by Justice Brennan would have given "the people" a broader reading: "'The People' are 'the governed.'"[89] The dissent's reading is likewise consistent only with the Standard Model, and not with the State's Rights view. If "the people" of the Second Amendment are "the governed," then the "right of the people" must belong to people who are governed, and not to governments.[90]

Interestingly, the majority opinion's analysis of "the people" protected by the Bill of Rights was an elaboration of a point made by the dissenting opinion from the Ninth Circuit Court of Appeals, when the majority had held that Mr. Verdugo was entitled to Fourth Amendment protections.[91] When

---

Tucker ed., Lawbook Exchange, Ltd. 1996) (1803). And some state Constitutions guarantee a right to arms for hunting, among other purposes. *See, e.g.,* the state constitutions of New Mexico, Nevada, West Virginia, and Wisconsin, *supra* note 43.

But the Supreme Court has never recognized such a right, and its lone decision on the subject is to the contrary. Patsone v. Pennsylvania, 232 U.S. 138 (1914) (ban on possession of hunting guns by aliens is legitimate, because the ban does not interfere with gun possession for self-defense; the Court did not discuss the Second Amendment).

Similarly, the "right" to own automobiles could, arguably, be derived from the right to interstate travel but it is hardly a settled matter of law, despite what the Chief Justice seemed to say.

Chief Justice Burger contrasted "recreational hunting" guns with "Saturday Night Specials" and "machine guns," implying that the latter two are beyond the pale of the Constitution. Thus, according to the *Parade* essay, some unidentified part of the Constitution (but not the Second Amendment) guarantees a right to own guns for home defense, a right to own hunting guns, a right to fishing equipment, and a right to buy automobiles. But the Constitution does not guarantee the right to own inexpensive handguns or machine guns.

Chief Justice Burger's "machine gun" comment was particularly odd in light of what he was pictured holding on the front cover of *Parade*: an assault weapon. The Chief Justice displayed his grandfather's rifled musket, with which his grandfather had killed or attempted to kill people during the Civil War. While the musket seems quaint and non-threatening today, it was a state of the art assault weapon in its time. Under the *Miller* test (arms suitable for militia use; see *supra* text at note 19), the nineteenth century rifled musket and the twentieth century machine gun would seem to be much closer to the core of the Second Amendment than would "recreational hunting guns."

After writing the *Parade* essay, Chief Justice Burger participated in an advertising campaign for Handgun Control, Inc., in which he called the NRA's view of the Second Amendment "a fraud." Given that the Chief Justice *agreed* with the NRA that the Constitution protects a right to own home defense guns and recreational sporting guns, and disagreed with the NRA about "Saturday Night Specials," the "fraud" rhetoric was rather extreme. Was it reasonable to call the NRA fraudulent for locating the right in the Second Amendment, as opposed to the other (unknown) part of the Constitution that the Chief Justice would prefer?

89. *Verdugo-Urquidez*, 494 U.S. at 282 (Brennan, J., dissenting).

90. Handgun Control explains *Verdugo* thusly:

But the issue of whether the right to bear arms is granted to "the people" only in connection with militia service is not even addressed in the Verdugo-Urquidez *decision. At most, the decision implies that the Second Amendment right extends only to U.S. citizens; it does not address the precise scope of the right granted. In no way does the Court's ruling contradict the idea that the right of the people to bear arms is exercised only through membership in a "well regulated Militia."*

Handgun Control, *Exploding the NRA's Second Amendment Indeology: A Guide for Gun Control Advocates*, http://www.handguncontrol.org/legalaction/C2/C2myth.htm. Here, Henigan is apparently adopting an alternative theory of the Second Amendment. Rather than the Second Amendment guaranteeing a right to state governments (as Henigan claimed in his law review articles), the Second Amendment is now a right that does belong to people (rather than to state governments), but this right only applies to people in a well-regulated militia. This is also the view of Herz. *See generally* Herz, *supra* note 6. But neither Henigan nor Herz explain what this right might mean. Does a National Guardsman have a legal cause of action when the federal government takes away his rifle? Even though the rifle is owned by the federal government? *See* 32 U.S.C. § 105(a)(1).

If a disarmed National Guardsman does not have a cause of action, then who else could exercise the Second Amendment right to be armed in "a well-regulated militia"? The fundamental problem with Henigan's theories (and with those of his followers) is that the theories are not meant as an actual explanation of anything. They are meant to convince people that the Second Amendment places no restraint on gun control, but the theories are not meant to describe what the Second Amendment *does* protect.

91. United States v. Verdugo-Urquidez, 856 F. 2d 1214, 1239 (9th Cir. 1988) (Wallace, J., dissenting), *rev'd* 494 U.S. 259 (1990) ("Besides the fourth amendment, the name of 'the people' is specifically invoked in the first, second, ninth, and tenth amendment. Presumably, 'the people' identified in each amendment is coextensive with 'the people' cited in the other amendments.")

the *Verdugo* case went to the Supreme Court, the Solicitor General's office quoted from Ninth Circuit's dissent, but used ellipses to remove the dissent's reference to the Second Amendment.[92] The Supreme Court majority, of course, put the Second Amendment back in.

II. The Burger Court

The Second Amendment record of the Burger Court is more complex than that of the Rehnquist Court. The Rehnquist Court *dicta* about the Second Amendment points exclusively to the Second Amendment as an individual right. Indeed, except for Justice Thomas's observation that *Miller* did not resolve the individual rights issue, nothing in the Rehnquist Court's record contains even a hint that the Second Amendment might not be an individual right. In contrast, the Burger Court's *dicta* are not so consistent.

A. Lewis v. United States

The one Supreme Court majority opinion which is fully consistent with the Henigan/Bogus state's rights theory is *Lewis* v. *United States*.[93] Interestingly, the same advocates who dismiss *Verdugo* because it was not a Second Amendment case rely heavily on *Lewis* even though it too is not a Second Amendment case. The issue in *Lewis* was primarily statutory interpretation, and secondarily the Sixth Amendment. A federal statute imposes severe penalties on persons who possess a firearm after conviction for a felony.[94] In 1961, Lewis had been convicted of burglary in Florida[95]; since Lewis was not provided with counsel, his conviction was invalid under the rule of *Gideon* v. *Wainright*.[96] The question for the Court was whether Congress, in enacting the 1968 law barring gun possession by a person who "has been convicted by a court of the United States or of a State. . .of a felony," meant to include persons whose convictions had been rendered invalid by the 1963 *Gideon* case. Writing for a six-justice majority, Justice Blackmun held that the statutory language did apply to person with convictions invalid under *Gideon*.[97]

Given the non-existent legislative history on the point, Justice Blackmun was forced to be rather aggressive in his reading of Congressional intent. For example, Senator Russell Long, the chief sponsor of the Gun Control Act of 1968, had explained that "every citizen could possess a gun until the commission of his first felony. Upon his conviction, however, Title VII would deny. . .the right to possess a firearm. . . ."[98] This supposedly showed Congressional intent to disarm people like Lewis, since the Senator had

92. 494 U.S. 259 (1990).
93. Lewis v. United States, 445 U.S. 55 (1980).
94. 18 U.S.C. App. § 1202(a)(1).
95. *Lewis*, 445 U.S. at 57-58.
96. *Id.* (citing Gideon v. Wainright, 372 U.S. 335 (1963)).
97. Gideon v. Wainright, 372 U.S. 335, 345 (1963).
98. *Lewis*, 445 U.S. at 62-63 (citing 114 CONG. REC. 14773 (1968)).

"stressed conviction, not a 'valid' conviction."[99] By this reasoning, the Gun Control Act of 1968 would likewise apply to Scottsboro Boys; they had been tortured into confessing a crime which they did not commit, but they did indeed have a "conviction" for murder, even if not "a valid conviction."[100] Justice Brennan's dissent pointed out that the majority's reasoning would impose the Gun Control Act even on people whose convictions had been overturned by an appellate court.[101]

Did the Gun Control Act (as interpreted by the Court) violate equal protection?

> *Congress could rationally conclude that any felony conviction, even an allegedly invalid one, is a sufficient basis on which to prohibit possession of a firearm. See, e.g., United States v. Ransom, 515 F.2d 885, 891-892 (CA5 1975), cert. Denied, 424 U.S. 944 (1976). This Court has repeatedly recognized that a legislature constitutionally may prohibit a convicted felon from engaging in activities far more fundamental than the possession of a firearm. See Richardson v. Ramirez, 418 U.S. 24 (1974)(disenfranchisement); De Veau v. Braisted, 363 U.S. 144, 363 U.S. 144 (1960)(proscription against holding office in a waterfront labor organization); Hawker v. New York, 170 U.S. 189 (1898)(prohibition against the practice of medicine).*[102]

From this, it is reasonable to infer that possession of a firearm is a "right," but a right which is far less "fundamental" than voting, serving as an officer in a union, or practicing medicine. As to whether possessing a firearm is a constitutional right, the opinion does not say. But the opinion could certainly be cited for support that arms possession is not "fundamental" enough to be protected by the Fourteenth Amendment's due process clause.

In a footnote of the section supporting the rationality of a statute disarming convicted felons, Justice Blackmun wrote:

> *These legislative restrictions on the use of firearms are neither based upon constitutionally suspect criteria, nor do they trench upon any constitutionally protected liberties. See United States v. Miller, 307 U.S. 174, 178 (the Second Amendment guarantees no right to keep and bear a firearm that does not have "some reasonable relationship to the preservation or efficiency of a well-regulated militia"); United States v. Three Winchester 30-30 Caliber Lever Action Carbines, 504 F. 2d 1288, 1290, n. 5 (CA7 1974); United States v. Johnson, 497 F.2d 548 (CA4 1974); Cody v. United States, 460 F.2d 34 (CA8), cert. denied, 409 U.S. 1010 (1972)(the latter three cases holding, respectively, that 1202(a)(1), 922(g), and 922(a)(6) do not violate the Second Amendment).*[103]

Attorney Stephen Halbrook (the successful plaintiffs' attorney in the Supreme Court gun cases of Printz v. United States[104], and United States v. Thompson/Center[105]) reads *Lewis* as reflecting the principle that since a

99. *Id*. at 62.
100. Powell v. Alabama, 287 U.S. 45 (1932).
101. *Lewis*, 445 U.S. at 69 (Brennan, J., dissenting).
102. *Id.* at 66.
103. *Id.* at 65-66, n. 8
104. Printz v. United States, 521 U.S. 898 (1997)
105. United States v. Thompson/Center Arms Co., 504 U.S. 505 (1992) (statutory interpretation case holding that a handgun and rifle kit was not subject to a National Firearms Act tax applicable to short rifles; that a

legislature may deprive a felon "of other civil liberties, and may even deprive a felon of life itself—felons have no fundamental right to keep and bear arms."[106]

As a matter of formal linguistics, Halbrook's reading of *Lewis* is not impermissible. But it is also possible to read the *Lewis* opinion as saying, in effect, "since no-one has a right to have a gun, a law against felons owning guns does not infringe on Constitutional rights."

What of the three Court of Appeals cases cited by Justice Blackmun?

The *Three Winchester 30-30 Caliber Lever Action Carbines* case upholds the forfeiture of guns possessed by a convicted felon. The footnote cited by the Supreme Court states:

Apparently at the district court level the defendant argued that 18 U.S.C. App. § 1202 was invalid as an "infringement of the second amendment's protection of the right to bear arms, the first amendment's prohibition of bills of attainder and ex post facto laws, and the fourteenth amendment's due process clause." These arguments were appropriately rejected. [citations omitted][107]

The *Cody*[108] case upheld the conviction of a felon who falsified a federal gun registration form and falsely claimed that he had no felony conviction. Regarding Cody's Second Amendment claim, the Eighth Circuit stated:

> *It has been settled that the Second Amendment is not an absolute bar to congressional regulation of the use or possession of firearms. The Second Amendment's guarantee extends only to use or possession which "has some reasonable relationship to the preservation or efficiency of a well regulated militia." Id [Miller]. At 178, 59 S. Ct. at 818. See United States v. Synnes, 438 F.2d 764, 772 (8th Cir. 1971), vacated on other grounds, 404 U.S. 1009, 92 S. Ct. 687, 30 L. Ed. 2d 657 (1972); Cases v. United States, 131 F.2d 916, 922 (1st Cir. 1942), cert. denied sub nom., Velazquez v. United States, 319 U.S. 770, 63 S. Ct. 1431, 87 L. Ed. 1718 (1943).[109] We find no evidence that the prohibition of § 922(a)(6) obstructs the maintenance of a well regulated militia.[110]*

In *Johnson*, the Fourth Circuit upheld the Gun Control Act as applied to a convicted felon who transported a firearm in interstate commerce.[111] Regarding Johnson's Second Amendment claim, the Circuit wrote that "The courts have consistently held that the Second Amendment only confers a collective right of keeping and bearing arms which must bear a 'reasonable relationship to the preservation or efficiency of a well regulated militia.'"[112]

Now a "collective right" can be read two ways: it can be like "collective property" in a Communist property; since it belongs to all the people

---

buyer could illegally assemble certain parts to create a short rifle did not bring the lawful sale of rifle and handgun components within the terms of the tax statute).

106. STEPHEN HALBROOK, FIREARMS LAW DESKBOOK 1-11 to 1-12 (1999 ed.)

107. United States v. Three Winchester 30-30 Caliber Lever Action Carbines, 363 F. Supp. 322, 323 (E.D. Wis. 1973).

108. Cody v. United States, 460 F.2d 34 (8th Cir. 1972).

109. As in this quote from *Cody*, the First Circuit's 1943 *Cases* decision is sometimes cited as a lower court following *Miller. See* Cases v. United States, 131 F.2d 916 (1st Cir. 1942). To the contrary, *Cases* limits *Miller* to its facts, and refuses to apply the *Miller* relationship-to-the-militia test. The *Miller* test, explained the *Cases* judges, would allow "private citizens" to possess machine guns and other destructive weapons. *Cases* upholds a federal gun control law while acknowledging that the law limits the exercise of Second Amendment rights.

110. *Cody*, 460 F.2d at 36.

111. Johnson v. Zerbst, 304 U.S. 458, 465 (1938).

112. *See. e.g., Miller*, 307 U.S. at 178.

collectively, it belongs only to the government. Alternatively, a "collective right" to arms can be a right of all the people to have a militia, and for this purpose, each person has a right to possess arms for militia purposes (but not to possess arms for other purposes, such as self-defense).[113] Indeed, this is the approach taken by *Aymette*, the Tennessee Supreme Court case which is the sole citation for the rule of decision in *Miller; Aymette* states that the Second Amendment protects individual possession of militia-type arms, so that those individuals may collectively exercise their rights in a militia.[114]

Neither *Lewis* nor its three cited Court of Appeals cases claim that the Second Amendment right belongs to state governments. And none of them goes so far as to claim that law-abiding American citizens have no Second Amendment right to possess arms. But *Lewis* and its cited cases, especially *Johnson*, certainly come close to that proposition. Although Halbrook's reading of *Lewis* is not formally wrong, the spirit of *Lewis* has little in common with the Standard Model of the Second Amendment.

If *Lewis* were the Supreme Court's last word on the Second Amendment, the Standard Model, no matter how accurate in its assessment of original intent, would seem on shaky ground as a description of contemporary Supreme Court doctrine. But *Lewis*, while not ancient, is no longer contemporary. As discussed above, six subsequent Supreme Court cases have addressed the Second Amendment as an individual right. Only two justices from the *Lewis* majority remain on the Court, and both of those justices (Rehnquist and Stevens) have written 1990s opinions which regard the Second Amendment as an individual right.

The Rehnquist cases suggest that it is unlikely that the current Court would read *Lewis*'s hostile but ambiguous language as negating an individual right.

B. Moore v. East Cleveland

Not only do the Rehnquist cases impede any effort to read *Lewis* as the definitive state's right case, so does a case decided four years before *Lewis*. The *Moore* v. *East Cleveland* litigation arose out of a zoning regulation which made it illegal for extended families to live together.[115] The plurality opinion by Justice Powell found in the Fourteenth Amendment a general protection for families to make their own living arrangements.[116] Thus, the East Cleveland law, which, for example, forbade two minor cousins to live with their grandmother,[117] was unconstitutional.

In discussing the boundaries of the Fourteenth Amendment, the Powell plurality opinion for the Court quoted from Justice Harlan's dissent in *Poe v. Ullman*. This was the same language that was later quoted by Justice O'Connor's majority opinion in *Planned Parenthood* v. *Casey*,[118] and by Justice Stevens' dissent in *Albright v. Oliver*[119]:

---

113. *See, e.g.*, Cockrum v. State, 24 Tex. 394, 397 (1859).

114. Aymette v. State, 21 Tenn. (2 Hum.) 154 (1840) (right to arms is for defense against tyranny, not for "private" defense; while "The citizens have the unqualified right to *keep* the weapon", the legislature can restrict the carrying of firearms) (emphasis in original).

115. Moore v. East Cleveland, 431 U.S. 494, 495-96 (1976).

116. *Id.* at 505-06.

117. *Id.* at 496-97.

118. Planned Parenthood v. Casey, 505 U.S. 833 (1992).

119. Albright v. Oliver, 510 U.S. 266, 306-08 (1994) (Stevens, J., dissenting).

> *But unless we close our eyes to the basic reasons why certain rights associated with the family have been accorded shelter under the Fourteenth Amendment's Due Process Clause, we cannot avoid applying the force and rationale of these precedents to the family choice involved in this case.*
>
> *Understanding those reasons requires careful attention to this Court's function under the Due Process clause. Mr. Justice Harlan described it eloquently:*
>
> Due process cannot be reduced to any formula; its content cannot be determined by reference to any code. . .The balance of which I speak is the balance struck by this country, having regard to what history teaches are the traditions from which it developed as well as the traditions from which it broke. That tradition is a living thing. . . .
>
> [T]he full scope of the liberty guaranteed by the Due Process Clause cannot be found in or limited by the precise terms of the specific guarantees elsewhere provided in the Constitution. This 'liberty" is not a series of isolated points pricked out in terms of the taking of property; the freedom of speech, press, and religion; the right to keep and bear arms; the freedom from unreasonable searches and seizures; and so on. It is a rational continuum which broadly speaking, includes freedom from all substantial arbitrary impositions and purposeless restraints" Poe v. Ullman, *supra*, at 542-543 (dissenting opinion).[120]

In dissent, Justice White also quoted from Justice Harlan's words in *Poe*. While Justice White included the language about the Second Amendment, he did not include the preceding paragraph about tradition.[121]

Since the Fourteenth Amendment belongs exclusively to individuals, and not to state governments, the only possible reading of *Moore* v. *East Cleveland* is that the Second Amendment protects an individual right.

The "tradition" paragraph from Justice Harlan, quoted by Justice Powell, strengthens an argument for incorporating the Second Amendment. The right to arms had roots as one of the "rights of Englishmen" recognized by the English 1689 Bill of Rights,[122] and was adopted in nine of the first fifteen states' constitutions.[123] When the Constitution was proposed, five state ratifying conventions called for a right to arms—more than for any other single right that became part of the Bill of Rights.[124] With the exception of a single concurring opinion by an Arkansas judge in 1842,[125] *every* known judicial opinion and scholarly commentary from the nineteenth century treated the Second Amendment as an individual right.[126]

Justice Harlan's "tradition is a living thing" analysis also looks at whether the right in question is supported by modern "tradition." The right to arms

---

120. *Moore*, 431 U.S. at 502.
121. *Id.* at 542 (White, J., dissenting).
122. 1 Wm. & Mary sess. 2, ch. 2 (1689); see also MALCOLM, *supra* note 9.
123. EUGENE VOLOKH, SOURCES ON THE SECOND AMENDMENT AND RIGHTS TO KEEP AND BEAR ARMS IN STATE CONSTITUTIONS, pt. I <*http://www.law.ucla.edu/faculty/volokh/2amteach/sources.htm#TOC1*>; DAVID YOUNG, THE ORIGIN OF THE SECOND AMENDMENT (1991).
124. SeeYOUNG, *supra* note 123.
125. Buzzard v. State, 20 Ark. 106 (1842).
126. Kopel, *The Second Amendment in the 19th Century*, *supra* note 10.

fares well under this analysis too. Between a third and a half of all American households choose to own firearms,[127] and many others own other types of "arms" (such as edged weapons) which might fall within the scope of protected "arms."[128] Today, forty-four state constitutions guarantee a right to arms[129]; in 15 states in the last three decades, voters have added or strengthened an arms right to their state constitution, always by a very large majority.[130] Twenty years ago, only a few states allowed ordinary citizens to obtain a permit carry a concealed handgun for protection; now twenty-nine states have "shall issue" laws, and two states require no permit at all.[131]

Contrast all the "traditional" support for the right to arms with the absence of such support for the Fifth Amendment's guarantee against the taking of property without due process and just compensation. No state ratifying convention had demanded such a clause, and no such right was recognized in the English Bill of Rights.[132] If the just compensation is "traditional" enough to have been incorporated, as it has been,[133] the argument for incorporating the Second Amendment is all the stronger.

But while the Harlan language quoted in *East Cleveland* has favorable implications for Second Amendment incorporation, *East Cleveland* does not itself perform the incorporation.[134]

And while *East Cleveland*'s implication for the Second Amendment as an individual right seems clear enough under its own terms, Justice Powell's personal views appear to have changed after 1976. After retiring from the Court, in 1988 he gave a speech to the American Bar Association in which he said that the Constitution should not be construed to guarantee a right to own handguns[135]; this speech was not necessarily inconsistent with *East Cleveland,* since a Second Amendment right to arms might exclude some types of arms. But in 1993, Justice Powell went even further, suggesting in a television interview that the Constitution should not be read to as guaranteeing a right to own even sporting guns.[136]

---

127. GARY KLECK, TARGETING GUNS: FIREARMS AND THEIR CONTROL (1997).

128. The dominant line of traditional cases limits the scope of "arms" protected by the Second Amendment to arms which an individual could use in a militia; in the nineteenth century, rifles and swords were the paradigm of such weapons. Kopel, *The Second Amendment in the 19th Century*, *supra* note 10. A minority line of cases goes further, and protects weapons which could be useful for personal defense, even if not useful for militia service. *See, e.g.*, State v. Kessler, 614 P.2d 94 (Or. 1980) (billy club); State v. Delgado, 692 P.2d 610 (Or. 1984) (switchblade knife).

129. In one state, Massachusetts, the highest court has construed the right as belonging to the state government, rather than to individuals. Commonwealth v. Davis, 369 Mass. 886, 343 N.E.2d 847 (1976). But see Commonwealth v. Murphy 166 Mass. 171, 44 N.E. 138 (1896). In Kansas, a 1905 case held that the right in the state constitution belonged to the state government, and not to the people. City of Salinas v. Blaksley, 72 Kan. 230, 83 P. 619 (1905) This holding was implicitly rejected in a later case. Junction City v. Mevis, 226 Kan. 526, 601 P.2d 1145 (1979).

130. JOHN R. LOTT, JR., MORE GUNS, LESS CRIME: UNDERSTANDING CRIME AND GUN-CONTROL LAWS. (Univ. of Chicago Press, 1998).

131. Vermont and Idaho (outside Boise, where a permit is required and readily obtainable).

132. AKHIL AMAR, THE BILL OF RIGHTS 77-78 (1998).

133. Chicago, B. & Q. R.R. v. Chicago, 166 U.S. 226 (1897).

134. *Moore*, 431 U.S. at 502.

135. "With respect to handguns . . . it is not easy to understand why the Second Amendment, or the notion of liberty, should be viewed as creating a right to own and carry a weapon that contributes so directly to the shocking numbers of murders in the United States." American Bar Association Speech, Toronto, Canada, Aug. 7, 1988.

136. The MacNeil/Lehrer NewsHour, Mar.16, 1989, trans. no. #3389, Lexis Transcripts library:
MR. LEHRER: Another issue that was before the court and is still before the nation as we go into a new year is the subject of gun control. You have said that the constitution does not guarantee the right to bear arms. Explain that.
JUSTICE POWELL: Have you read the second amendment?
MR. LEHRER: Well, I think I have but be my guest.

Whatever the evolution of Justice Powell's thoughts about gun rights, the only words he ever put in the United States Reports treat the Second Amendment as an individual right.

C. Adams v. Williams

The only written opinion from a Supreme Court Justice which plainly rejects an individual right came from Justice Douglas, dissenting in the 1972 case of *Adams* v. *Williams*.[137] Acting on a tip, a police officer stopped a motorist for questioning, and then grabbed a revolver hidden in the driver's waistband.[138] The Supreme Court majority upheld the officer's actions as a reasonable effort to protect his safety.[139]

Justice Douglas, a strong defender of the Fourth Amendment right to be free from unreasonable searches, dissented.[140] After discussing Fourth Amendment issues, Justice Douglas then editorialized in favor of handgun control and prohibition, and asserted that the Second Amendment posed no barrier to severe gun laws:

> *The police problem is an acute one not because of the Fourth Amendment, but because of the ease with which anyone can acquire a pistol. A powerful lobby dins into the ears of our citizenry that these gun purchases are constitutional rights protected by the Second Amendment, which reads, "A well regulated Militia, being necessary to the security of a free State, the right of the people to keep and bear Arms, shall not be infringed."*
>
> *There is under our decisions no reason why stiff state laws governing the purchase and possession of pistols may not be enacted. There is no reason why pistols may not be barred from anyone with a police record. There is no reason why a State may not require a purchaser of a pistol to pass a psychiatric test. There is no reason why all pistols should not be barred to everyone except the police.*
>
> *The leading case is United States v. Miller, 307 U.S. 174, upholding a federal law making criminal the shipment in interstate commerce of a sawed-off shotgun. The law was upheld, there being no evidence that a sawed-off shotgun had "some reasonable relationship to the preservation or efficiency of a well regulated militia." Id., at 178. The Second*

JUSTICE POWELL: Well, it talks about militia. In the days that the amendment was adopted in 1791, each state had an organized militia. The states distrusted the national government, didn't believe a national government had the authority or the ability to protect their liberties, so the militia was a very important factor to the states. This court decided a case that I haven't seen decided, I'm not a hundred percent sure, I think it was the United States against Miller decided back in the late 30's, in which the question involved a sawed off shot gun. I won't go into the details of the opinion, but in essence, there's language in that that suggests what I believe, and that is that the second amendment was never intended to apply to hand guns or, indeed to sporting rifles and shot guns. I've had a shot gun since I was 12 years old and I still occasionally like to shoot birds, but hand guns certainly were not even dreamed of in the sense that they now exist at the time the second amendment was adopted.

Actually, handguns had been invented and were well known by 1789. *See* IAN V. HOGG, THE ILLUSTRATED ENCYCLOPEDIA OF FIREARMS (1978). Handguns were common enough in the early sixteenth century so that proposed legislation as early as 1518 addressed them. *Id.* at 16-17. By the latter part of the 1500s, handguns had become standard cavalry weapons. *Id.* at 17. When the Second Amendment was ratified, state militia laws requiring most men to supply their own firearms required officers to supply their own pistols.

137. Adams v. Williams, 407 U.S. 143 (1972).
138. *Id.* at 144-45.
139. *Id.* at 149.
140. *Id.* at 149 (Douglas, J., dissenting).

Amendment, it was held, "must be interpreted and applied" with the view of maintaining a "militia."

"The Militia which the States were expected to maintain and train is set in contrast with Troops which they were forbidden to keep without the consent of Congress. The sentiment of the time strongly disfavored standing armies; the common view was that adequate defense of country and laws could be secured through the Militia - civilians primarily, soldiers on occasion." Id., at 178-179.

Critics say that proposals like this water down the Second Amendment. Our decisions belie that argument, for the Second Amendment, as noted, was designed to keep alive the militia. But if watering-down is the mood of the day, I would prefer to water down the Second rather than the Fourth Amendment. I share with Judge Friendly a concern that the easy extension of Terry v. Ohio, 392 U.S. 1, to "possessory offenses" is a serious intrusion on Fourth Amendment safeguards. "If it is to be extended to the latter at all, this should be only where observation by the officer himself or well authenticated information shows 'that criminal activity may be afoot.'" 436 F.2d, at 39, quoting Terry v. Ohio, supra, at 30.[141]

Justice Douglas's statement is a clear affirmation of the anti-individual interpretation of the Second Amendment which is espoused by the anti-gun lobbies. Since Justice Douglas was writing in dissent, his opinion creates no legal precedent. Nevertheless, the opinion is emblematic of the belief of some civil libertarians that the move to "water down" the Fourth Amendment can be forestalled by watering down the Second Amendment.

Justice Brennan did not join the Douglas dissent, but instead wrote his own. Justice Brennan presciently noted that the Court's loose standard for "stop and frisk" would become a tool for police officers to search people at will, with officer safety often serving as a mere pretext.[142] (*Adams* v. *Williams* is one of the key cases opening the door to the broad variety of warrantless searches which are now allowed.) Justice Brennan also noted the illogic of allowing stop-and-frisk for guns in a state which allows citizens to carry concealed handguns.[143] (Connecticut was one of the first states to adopt "shall issue" laws for concealed handgun permits; now, thirty-one states have such laws.[144])

Justice Marshall's dissent made a similar point, noting that after the officer discovered the gun, he immediately arrested Williams, without asking if Williams had a permit.[145]

141. *Id.* at 150-51. Justice Douglas was a newly-appointed member of the Court that decided *Miller*, but he did not participate in the case, having joined the Court after the case was argued. Justice Black (whose views on the Second Amendment are found *infra* at notes 179-82, 194-96, 221-28) did serve on the Miller Court, and joined in the unanimous decision.

142. *Id.* at 153 (Brennan, J., dissenting).

143. *Id.* at 151-52.

144. See Lott, *supra* note 130.

145. *Adams*, at 153 (Marshall, J., dissenting).

D. Roe v. Wade

The year after Justice Douglas took a clear stand against individual Second Amendment rights in *Adams*, Justice Stewart authored an opinion in the opposite direction.

The majority opinion in *Roe v. Wade*,[146] written by Justice Harry Blackmun, has been justly criticized for having no connection with the text of the Constitution, and only a tenuous connection with the prior precedents of the Supreme Court.[147] Justice Potter Stewart, perhaps recognizing the weakness of the Blackmun opinion, authored a concurring opinion coming to the same result as Justice Blackmun, but attempting to ground the result more firmly in precedent.[148] As part of the analysis arguing that the right to abortion was part of the "liberty" protected by the Fourteenth Amendment, Justice Stewart quoted Justice Harlan's dissenting opinion in *Poe v. Ullman*[149], which had listed the right to keep and bear arms as among the liberties guaranteed by the Fourteenth Amendment:

> *As Mr. Justice Harlan once wrote: "[T]he full scope of the liberty guaranteed by the Due Process Clause cannot be found in or limited by the precise terms of the specific guarantees elsewhere provided in the Constitution. This 'liberty' is not a series of isolated points pricked out in terms of the taking of property; the freedom of speech, press, and religion; the right to keep and bear arms; the freedom from unreasonable searches and seizures; and so on. It is a rational continuum which, broadly speaking, includes a freedom from all substantial arbitrary impositions and purposeless restraints . . . and which also recognizes, what a reasonable and sensitive judgment must, that certain interests require particularly careful scrutiny of the state needs asserted to justify their abridgment." Poe v. Ullman, 367 U.S. 497, 543 (opinion dissenting from dismissal of appeal) (citations omitted). In the words of Mr. Justice Frankfurter, "Great concepts like . . . 'liberty' . . . were purposely left to gather meaning from experience. For they relate to the whole domain of social and economic fact, and the statesmen who founded this Nation knew too well that only a stagnant society remains unchanged." National Mutual Ins. Co. v. Tidewater Transfer Co., 337 U.S. 582, 646 (dissenting opinion).*[150]

Thus, the Harlan dissenting language about the Second Amendment, from *Poe v. Ullman*, has been quoted in one majority opinion (*Planned Parenthood v. Casey*[151]), one plurality opinion (*Moore v. East Cleveland*[152]), two dissents (*Albright v. Oliver* and *Moore v. East*[153]), and one concurrence (*Roe v. Wade*[154]). In contrast, the Douglas dissenting language about the

146. Roe v. Wade, 410 U.S. 113 (1973).

147. *See, e.g.*, William Van Alstyne, *Closing The Circle Of Constitutional Review from* Griswold v. Connecticut *To* Roe v. Wade: *An Outline Of A Decision Merely Overruling* Roe, 1989 DUKE L.J. 1677.

148. Roe, 410 U.S. at 167-68 (Stewart, J., concurring).

149. Poe v. Ullman, 367 U.S. 497, 523 (1961) (Harlan, J., dissenting).

150. *Id.* at 167. Roe, 410 U.S. 113.

151. Planned Parenthood v. Casey, 505 U.S. 833, 848-49 (1992).

152. Moore v. East Cleveland, 431 U.S. 494, 502 (1976).

153. Albright v. Oliver, 510 U.S. 266 (1994); Moore, 410 U.S. at 542.

154. Roe v. Wade, 410 U.S. 113, 169 (1973).

Second Amendment, from *Adams v. Williams,*[155] has never been quoted in an opinion by any Justice.

E. Laird v. Tatum

During the Cold War and the Vietnam War, the United States Army illegally spied on American anti-war critics.[156] When the Army's conduct was to discovered, a group of individuals who had been spied upon brought suit in federal court.[157] In a sharply divided five-four decision, the Supreme Court majority held that the suit was not justiciable.[158] The plaintiffs could not show that they had been harmed by the Army, or that there was a realistic prospect of future harm, and hence there was no genuine controversy for a federal court to hear.[159] Justice Douglas (joined by Justice Marshal) penned a fiery dissent, invoking the long struggle to free civil life from military domination.[160]

Justice Douglas began by examining the power which the Constitution grants Congress over the standing army and over the militia.[161] Since Congress is not granted any power to use the army or militia for domestic surveillance, it necessarily follows that the army has no power on its own to begin a program of domestic surveillance.[162]

Moving onto a broader discussion of the dangers of military dictatorship, Justice Douglas quoted an article which Chief Justice Earl Warren had written in the *New York University Law Review,* which mentioned the Second Amendment as one of the safeguards intended to protect America from rule by a standing army.[163]

> *As Chief Justice Warren has observed, the safeguards in the main body of the Constitution did not satisfy the people on their fear and concern of military dominance:*
>
> "They were reluctant to ratify the Constitution without further assurances, and thus we find in the Bill of Rights Amendments 2 and 3, specifically authorizing a decentralized militia, guaranteeing the right of the people to keep and bear arms, and prohibiting the quartering of troops in any house in time of peace without the consent of the owner. Other Amendments guarantee the right of the people to assemble, to be secure in their homes against unreasonable searches and seizures, and in criminal cases to be accorded a speedy and public trial by an impartial jury after indictment in the district and state wherein the crime was committed. The only exceptions made to these civilian trial procedures are for cases arising in the land and naval forces. Although there is undoubtedly room for argument based on the frequently conflicting sources of history, it is not unreasonable to believe that our Founders' determination to guarantee the preeminence of civil over military power

155. Adams v. Williams, 407 U.S. 143 (1972).
156. Laird v. Tatum, 408 U.S. 1, 2-3 (1972).
157. *Id.* at 3.
158. *Id.* at 15-16.
159. *Id.*
160. *Id.* at 16-17 (Douglas, J., dissenting).
161. *Id.*
162. *Id.* at 17-18.
163. Earl Warren, *The Bill of Rights and the Military*, 37 N.Y.U. L. REV. 181, 185 (1962).

was an important element that prompted adoption of the Constitutional Amendments we call the Bill of Rights."[164]

The Earl Warren law review language is, on its face, consistent with individual rights. He listed the right to arms among other individual rights, and he treated the Second Amendment's subordinate clause (about the importance of well-regulated militia) as protecting something distinct from the Second Amendment's main clause (the right of the people to keep and bear arms).[165]

But based on Justice Douglas's dissent the same year in *Adams*, we cannot ascribe to Justice Douglas the full implication of what Chief Justice Warren wrote in the *N.Y.U. Law Review*. And while Chief Justice Warren's *N.Y.U.* article is interesting, Chief Justice Warren never wrote anything about the Second Amendment in a Supreme Court opinion.

III. The Warren, Vinson, and Hughes Courts

During the tenure of Chief Justices Earl Warren (1953-69) and Fred Vinson (1946-53), opinions in nine cases addressed the Second Amendment. Seven of those opinions (majority opinions by Justices Brennan, Frankfurter, Harlan, and Jackson; a concurrence by Justice Black; and dissents by Justices Black and Harlan) recognized an individual right in the Second Amendment. The eighth case, an "appeal dismissed" contained no explanation, and thus was consistent with both the Standard Model individual right and the Henigan/Bogus state's right. The earliest case in this period was a 1934 decision that used the Second Amendment to support a state's right to control its militia.[166]

A. Burton v. Sills

Burton v. *Sills* involved a challenge to the then-new gun licensing law in New Jersey.[167] The law did not ban any guns, but established a licensing system intended to screen out people with serious criminal convictions, substance abusers, and the like. After the New Jersey Supreme Court rejected a Second Amendment challenge to the law[168], the plaintiffs asked the Supreme Court to review the case; the request came in the form of an "appeal," rather than a petition for a writ of certiorari.[169]

---

164. *Laird*, 408 U.S. at 22-23, *quoting* Earl Warren, *The Bill of Rights and the Military*, *supra* note 163. (emphasis added).

165. For the best analysis of how Madison synthesized two different traditions in the Second Amendment (the republican militia theory in the purpose clause, and the human rights theory in the main clause), *see* Hardy, *Armed Citizens, Citizen Armies: Toward a Jurisprudence of the Second Amendment*, *supra* note 9.

166. Hamilton v. Regents of the Univ. of California, 293 U.S. 245 (1934).

167. Burton v. Sills, 394 U.S. 812 (1969).

168. Burton v. Sills, 248 A.2d 521 (N.J. 1968).

169. *Burton*, 394 U.S. at 812.

The United States Supreme Court declined to hear the case.[170] Since the case had come by appeal, rather than petition for a writ, the Court wrote the standard phrase used at the time in denying an appeal: "The motion to dismiss is granted and the appeal is dismissed for want of a substantial federal question."[171]

The Supreme Court has explained that dismissals such as the one in *Burton* have some value in guiding lower courts:

> *Summary affirmances and dismissals for want of a substantial federal question without doubt reject the specific challenges presented in the statement of jurisdiction and do leave undisturbed the judgment appealed from. They do prevent lower courts from coming to opposite conclusions on the precise issues presented and necessarily decided by those actions. After* Salera, *for example, other courts were not free to conclude that the Pennsylvania provision invalidated was nevertheless constitutional. Summary actions, however, including* Salera, *should not be understood as breaking new ground but as applying principles established by prior decisions to the particular facts involved.*[172]

Thus, following the appeal dismissal in *Burton* v. *Sills*, a lower federal court could not conclude that the New Jersey gun licensing law violated the Second Amendment.

The appeal dismissal does *not* necessarily endorse the reasoning of the state court against which the appeal was taken. (The New Jersey Supreme Court had said that the Second Amendment is not an individual right.[173])

The plaintiffs in *Burton* had conceded that prior Supreme Court cases (particularly the 1886 *Presser* case) had said that the Second Amendment limits only the federal government, and not state governments.[174] The plaintiffs invited the courts to use the *Burton* case as an opportunity to reverse prior precedent.[175] The appeal dismissal in *Burton* may be read as the Court's declining the invitation to re-open the issue decided by *Presser*.

Justice Thomas's concurrence in *Printz*,[176] suggesting that the Brady Act waiting period may violate the Second Amendment, implies he would not read *Burton* as asserting that a New Jersey-style gun licensing system would be constitutional if enacted by the Congress. Reading *Burton* as an authorization for sweeping *federal* gun licensing would be inconsistent with the Supreme Court's teaching that appeal dismissals "should not be understood as breaking new ground."[177]

Given the plaintiffs' requested grounds for Supreme Court review (to overturn *Presser*) it is logical to view *Burton* as a re-affirmance of *Presser*.[178]

---

170. *Id*.
171. *Id.* The decision was per curiam, with Justice Brennan not participating.
172. Mandel v. Bradley, 432 U.S. 173, 176 (1977).
173. The New Jersey court in *Burton* could never be charged with excessive regard for individual rights, for the court wrote, "the common good takes precedence over private rights. . .Our basic freedoms may be curtailed if sufficient reason exists therefor. Only in a very limited sense is a person free to do as he pleases in our modern American society." Burton v. Sills, 240 A.2d 432, 434 (N.J. 1968). In contrast, the New Jersey Supreme Court in 1925 had recognized "The right of a citizen to bear arms," but had explained that the right "is not unrestricted." Hence, a law requiring a license to carry a concealed revolver was not unconstitutional. State v. Angelo, 3 N.J. Misc. 1014 (Sup. Ct. 1925). Since New Jersey is one of the few states without a state constitutional right to arms, the court's reference to the "right of the citizen" must have been a reference to the Second Amendment.
174. For *Presser* see *infra* text at notes 310-20.
175. *Id*.
176. Printz v. United States, 521 U.S. 898, 937 (1997) (Thomas, J., concurring).
177. *Mandel*, 432 U.S. at 176.
178. Presser v. Illinois, 116 U.S. 252 (1886).

On the other hand, since *Burton* contains no explicit reasoning, the case is not directly contradictory to the Henigan/Bogus theory.

B. Duncan v. Louisiana

In this case, the Supreme Court incorporated the Sixth Amendment right to jury trial, as part of the Fourteenth Amendment's "due process" guarantee.[179] Justice Black, joined by Justice Douglas, concurred, and restated his argument from *Adamson v. California*[180] (*infra*) that the Fourteenth Amendment's "privileges and immunities" clause should be read to include everything in the first eight Amendments.[181] He quoted a statement made on the Senate floor by Senator Jacob Howard, one of the lead sponsors of the Fourteenth Amendment:

> *Such is the character of the privileges and immunities spoken of in the second section of the fourth article of the Constitution. . .To these privileges and immunities, whatever they may be—for they are not and cannot be fully defined in their entire extent and precise nature—to these should be added* the personal rights guaranteed and secured by the first eight amendments of the Constitution*; such as the freedom of speech and of the press; the right of the people peaceably to assemble and petition the Government for a redress of grievances, a right appertaining to each and all the people*; the right to keep and bear arms*; the right to be exempted from the quartering of soldiers in a house without consent of the owner. . . .*[182]

Justice Black's use in *Duncan* of the quote describing "the right to keep and bear arms" as one of "the personal rights guaranteed and secured by the first eight amendments" is fully consistent with his writing on the bench and in legal scholarship that the Second Amendment right to arms was one of the individual rights which the Fourteenth Amendment (properly interpreted) makes into a limit on state action.[183]

C. Malloy v. Hogan

This 1964 case used the Fourteenth Amendment's due process clause to incorporate the Fifth Amendment's privilege against self-incrimination.[184] Discussing the history of Fourteenth Amendment jurisprudence, Justice Brennan listed various "Decisions that particular guarantees were not safeguarded against state action by the Privileges and Immunities Clause or other provision of the Fourteenth Amendment."[185] Among these were "Presser v. Illinois, 116 U.S. 252, 265 (Second Amendment),"[186] along with various other cases, almost of which had been, or would be, repudiated by later decisions on incorporation.[187]

---

179. Duncan v. Louisiana, 391 U.S. 145 (1968).
180. Adamson v. California, 332 U.S. 46, 68-78 (1947) (Black, J., dissenting).
181. *Duncan*, 391 U.S. at 164-65 (Black, J., concurring).
182. *Id.* at 166-67 (quoting CONG. GLOBE, 39th Cong., 1st Sess., at 2765-66 (1866)) (emphasis added).
183. *Infra* notes 194-97, 221-28.
184. Malloy v. Hogan, 378 U.S. 1 (1964).
185. *Id.* at 5 n. 2.
186. *Id.*
187. *See* United States v. Cruikshank, 92 U.S. 542, 551 (1875) (right to assemble); Prudential Ins. Co. v. Cheek, 259 U.S. 530, 543 (1922) (First Amendment); Weeks v. United States, 232 U.S. 383, 398 (1914) (Fourth

As discussed above, any discussion of the Second Amendment as something which *could* be incorporated, even if no incorporation has been performed, necessarily presumes that the Second Amendment is an individual right. Justice Brennan's explication of *Presser* as a case which rejects privileges and immunities incorporation is of some significance as a modern interpretation of *Presser*, since, as we shall discuss *infra*, the years after the 1886 *Presser* decision generated a variety of opinions about whether *Presser* actually had rejected incorporation.

D. Konigsberg v. State Bar of California

In *Konigsberg*, the Court majority upheld the state of California's refusal to admit to the practice of law an applicant who refused answer questions about his beliefs regarding communism.[188] In dissent, Justice Black argued that First Amendment rights were absolute and that the inquiry into the prospective lawyer's political beliefs was therefore a violation of the First Amendment.[189]

Justice Harlan's majority opinion rejected Justice Black's standard of constitutional absolutism.[190] The Harlan majority opinion is one of the classic examples of the "balancing" methodology of jurisprudence.[191] Justice Harlan pointed to libel laws as laws which restrict speech, but which do not infringe the First Amendment.[192] Similarly, he pointed to the Supreme Court's ruling in *United States* v. *Miller* as an example of a law which restricted the absolute exercise of rights, but which had been held not to be unconstitutional.[193] Justice Harlan thereby treated the First and Second Amendment as constitutionally identical: guaranteeing an individual right, but not an absolute right.

> *n. 10. That view, which of course cannot be reconciled with the law relating to libel, slander, misrepresentation, obscenity, perjury, false advertising, solicitation of crime, complicity by encouragement, conspiracy, and the like, is said to be compelled by the fact that the commands of the First Amendment are stated in unqualified terms: "Congress shall make no law . . . abridging the freedom speech, or of the press; or the right of the people peaceably to assemble . . . ." But as Mr. Justice Holmes once said: "[T]he provisions of the Constitution are not mathematical formulas having their essence in their form; they are organic living institutions transplanted from English soil. Their significance is vital not formal; it is to be gathered not simply by taking the words and a dictionary, but by considering their origin and the line of their growth." Gompers v. United States, 233 U.S. 604, 610. In this*

Amendment); Hurtado v. California, 110 U.S. 516, 538 (1884) (Fifth Amendment requirement of grand jury indictments); Palko v. Connecticut, 302 U.S. 319, 328 (1937) (Fifth Amendment double jeopardy); Maxwell v. Dow, 176 U.S. 581, 595 (1900) (Sixth Amendment jury trial); Walker v. Sauvinet, 92 U.S. 90, 92 (1875) (Seventh Amendment jury trial); In re Kemmler, 136 U.S. 436 (1890) (Eighth Amendment cruel and unusual punishment, electrocution); McElvaine v. Brush, 142 U.S. 155 (1891); O'Neil v. Vermont, 144 U.S. 323, 332 (1892) (Eighth Amendment prohibition against cruel and unusual punishment). Except for *Hurtardo* and *Walker*, of these cases have been undone by later cases.

188. Konigsberg v. State Bar of California, 366 U.S. 36 (1961)
189. *Id.* at 57-58 (Black, J., dissenting).
190. *Id.* at 44.
191. *See* Frederick Schauer, *Easy Cases*, 58 S. CAL. L. REV. 399, 433 (1985).
192. *Konigsberg*, 366 U.S. at 49-50.
193. *Id.* at 51.

> *connection also* compare the equally unqualified command of the Second Amendment: "the right of the people to keep and bear arms shall not be infringed." *And see United States v. Miller, 307 U.S. 174.*[194]

The year before Justice Black's absolutist interpretative model was rejected by the majority of the Court, Justice Black had detailed the absolutist theory in the first annual James Madison lecture at the New York University School of Law.[195] Discussing each part of the Bill of Rights, Justice Black explained how each guarantee was unequivocal and absolute. For example, under the Sixth Amendment, a defendant had a "definite and absolute" right to confront the witnesses against him.[196] Regarding the Second Amendment, Justice Black explained:

> *Amendment Two provides that:*
>
> *A well regulated Militia being necessary to the security of a free State, the right of the people to keep and bear Arms, shall not be infringed.*
>
> *Although the Supreme Court has held this Amendment to include only arms necessary to a well-regulated militia, as so construed, its prohibition is absolute.*[197]

Did Justice Black mean that individuals have an absolute right to possess militia-type arms, or did Justice Black mean that state governments have an absolute right to arm the state militias as the state governments see fit? His view is particularly important, because he served on the Court that decided *Miller*, and he joined in the Court's unanimous opinion.

Throughout the New York University speech, Justice Black referred exclusively to individual rights, and never to state's rights. For example, he began his speech by explaining "I prefer to think of our Bill of Rights as including all provisions of the original Constitution and Amendments that protect individual liberty. . ."[198] If Justice Black thought that the Second Amendment protected state power, rather than individual liberty, he would not have included the Second Amendment in his litany of "absolute" guarantees in the Bill of Rights. In the discussion of *Adamson* v. *California, infra*, we will see "definite and absolute" proof that Justice Black considered the Second Amendment an individual right.

E. Poe v. Ullman

In the 1961 case *Poe* v. *Ullman*, the Court considered whether married persons had a right to use contraceptives.[199] The majority said "no," but the second Justice Harlan, in a dissent (which gained ascendancy a few years later in *Griswold* v. *Connecticut*), wrote that the Fourteenth Amendment did guarantee a right of privacy. In developing a theory of exactly what the Fourteenth Amendment due process clause did protect, Justice Harlan wrote that the clause was not limited exclusively to "the precise terms of *the specific guarantees elsewhere provided in the Constitution*," such as "the

194. *Id.* at 49-50 (emphasis added).
195. Hugo L. Black, *The Bill of Rights*, 35 N.Y.U. L. REV. 865 (1960).
196. *Id.* at 872.
197. *Id.* at 873.
198. *Id*. at 865.
199. Poe v. Ullman, 367 U.S. 497 (1961).

freedom of speech, press, and religion; *the right to keep and bear arms*; the freedom from unreasonable searches and seizures."[200]

It is impossible to read Justice Harlan's words as anything other than a recognition that the Second Amendment protects the right of individual Americans to possess firearms. The due process clause of the Fourteenth Amendment, obviously, protects a right of individuals *against* governments; it does not protect governments, nor is it some kind of "collective" right. It is also notable that Justice Harlan felt no need to defend or elaborate his position that the Second Amendment guaranteed an individual right. Despite the Henigan claim that the non-individual nature of the Second Amendment is "well-settled," it was unremarkable to Justice Harlan that the Second Amendment guaranteed the right of individual people to keep and bear arms.

Like the Brandeis and Holmes dissents in the early free speech cases, the Harlan dissent in *Poe* today seems to be a correct statement of the law.

Some parts of the Harlan dissent, however, have not been quoted by future courts. For example, even though later opinions have quoted approvingly the Harlan language that the Fourteenth Amendment forbids "all substantial arbitrary impositions,"[201] those quotations omit the list of cases that Justice Harlan cited for the proposition. That list included *Allgeyer* v. *Louisiana*[202] and *Nebbia* v. *New York*,[203] both of which used the Fourteenth Amendment in defense of economic liberty. But Justice Harlan was certainly right that modern use of the Fourteenth Amendment to protect non-enumerated rights has its roots in the liberty of contract due process cases from the turn of the century. Although it is not currently respectable to say so in a Supreme Court opinion, cases such as *Allgeyer* and its progeny have as much a logical claim to be part of the Fourteenth Amendment as do *Griswold*[204] and its progeny; both lines of cases protect personal freedom from "substantial arbitrary impositions."

But the fact that *Allgeyer* and *Nebbia* end up trimmed in later quotations of Justice Harlan's words shows that the Justices who used the quote later (Stevens, O'Connor, Powell, and Stewart) were not just quoting without thought; they knew how to excise parts of Harlan's language that they did not agree with, such as the references to economic liberty. That economic liberty was excised, while the Second Amendment stayed in, may, therefore, be plausibly considered as the writer's decision.

Also unquoted by later Courts has been Justice Harlan's statement, "Again and again this Court has resisted the notion that the Fourteenth Amendment is no more than a shorthand reference to what is explicitly set out elsewhere in the Bill of Rights."[205] In support of this proposition, he cited, *inter alia*, *Presser* v. *Illinois*, a nineteenth century case which will be discussed *infra*.

Interestingly, Justice Douglas wrote his own dissent, in which he stated that the Fourteenth Amendment must protect "all" the Bill of Rights.[206] This

200. *Id.* at 542-43 (Harlan, J., dissenting) (emphasis added).
201. Albright v. Oliver, *supra* note 78; Planned Parenthood v. Casey, *supra* note 83; Moore v. East Cleveland, *supra* notes 120-21.
202. Allgeyer v. Louisiana, 165 U.S. 578 (1897).
203. Nebbia v. New York, 291 U.S. 502 (1934).
204. Griswold v. Connecticut, 381 U.S. 479 (1965).
205. *Poe*, 367 U.S. at 541.
206. *Id.* at 516 (Douglas, J., dissenting):
When the Framers wrote the Bill of Rights they enshrined in the form of constitutional guarantees those rights—in part substantive, in part procedural—which experience indicated were indispensible to a free

implies that the Second Amendment is an individual right, if it can be protected by the Fourteenth Amendment. But Justice Douglas later rejected this view, in his *Adams* v. *Williams* dissent.[207]

F. Knapp v. Schweitzer

Knapp involved the applicability of the Fifth Amendment's self-incrimination clause to the states.[208] Justice Frankfurter's majority opinion refused to enforce the clause against the states. In support of his position, the Justice reeled off a list of nineteenth century cases, including *Cruikshank* (discussed *infra*) which he cited for the proposition that it was well-settled almost all of the individual rights guarantees in the Bill of Rights were not applicable to the states:

> *n.5. By 1900 the applicability of the Bill of Rights to the States had been rejected in cases involving claims based on virtually every provision in the first eight Articles of Amendment. See, e. g., Article I: Permoli v. Municipality No. 1, 3 How. 589, 609 (free exercise of religion); United States v. Cruikshank, 92 U.S. 542, 552 (right to assemble and petition the Government); Article II: United States v. Cruikshank, supra, at 553 (right to keep and bear arms); Article IV: Smith v. Maryland, 18 How. 71, 76 (no warrant except on probable cause); Spies v. Illinois, 123 U.S. 131, 166 (security against unreasonable searches and seizures); Article V: Barron v. Baltimore, note 2, supra, at 247 (taking without just compensation); Fox v. Ohio, 5 How. 410, 434 (former jeopardy); Twitchell v. Pennsylvania, 7 Wall. 321, 325-327 (deprivation of life without due process of law); Spies v. Illinois, supra, at 166 (compulsory self-incrimination); Eilenbecker v. Plymouth County, 134 U.S. 31, 34-35 (presentment or indictment by grand jury); Article VI: Twitchell v. Pennsylvania, supra, at 325-327 (right to be informed of nature and cause of accusation); Spies v. Illinois, supra, at 166 (speedy and public trial by impartial jury); In re Sawyer, 124 U.S. 200, 219 (compulsory process); Eilenbecker v. Plymouth County, supra, at 34-35 (confrontation of witnesses); Article VII: Livingston's Lessee v. Moore, 7 Pet. 469, 551-552 (right of jury trial in civil cases); Justices v. Murray, 9 Wall. 274, 278 (re-examination of facts tried by jury); Article VIII: Pervear v. Massachusetts, 5 Wall. 475, 479-480 (excessive fines, cruel and unusual punishments).*[209]

Here again, the Court majority treated the Second Amendment right to arms as simply one of the many individual rights guarantees contained in the Bill of Rights.

---

society. . . .[T]he constitutional conception of "due process" must, in my view, include them all until and unless there are amendments that remove them. That has indeed been the view of a full court of nine Justices, though the members who make up that court unfortunately did not sit at the same time.

Justice Douglas's list of Justices who favored full incorporation of the Bill of Rights named Bradley, Swayne, Field, Clifford, the first Harlan, Brewer, Black, Murphy, Rutledge, and Douglas. *Id.* at 516 n.8.

207. Adams v. Williams, 407 U.S. 143, 149 (1972) (Douglas, J., dissenting).

208. Knapp v. Schweitzer, 357 U.S. 371 (1958).

209. *Id.* at 378-79.

G. Johnson v. Eisentrager

After the surrender of Germany during World War II, some German soldiers in China aided the Japanese army, in the months that Japan continued to fight alone.[210] The American army captured them, and tried them by court-martial in China as war criminals.[211] The Germans argued that the trial violated their Fifth Amendment rights, and pointed out that the Fifth Amendment is not by its terms limited to American citizens.[212]

Justice Jackson's majority opinion held that Germans had no Fifth Amendment rights.[213] He pointed out that if Germans could invoke the Fifth Amendment, they could invoke the rest of the Bill of Rights.[214] This would lead to the absurd result of American soldiers, in obedience to the Second Amendment, being forbidden to disarm the enemy:

> *If the Fifth Amendment confers its rights on all the world except Americans engaged in defending it,[215] the same must be true of the companion civil-rights Amendments, for none of them is limited by its express terms, territorially or as to persons. Such a construction would mean that during military occupation irreconcilable enemy elements, guerrilla fighters, and "were-wolves" could require the American Judiciary to assure them freedoms of speech, press, and assembly as in the First Amendment,* right to bear arms as in the Second, *security against "unreasonable" searches and seizures as in the Fourth, as well as rights to jury trial as in the Fifth and Sixth Amendments.*[216]

The "irreconcilable enemy elements, guerrilla fighters, and 'were-wolves'" in Justice Jackson's hypothetical are obviously not American state governments. Instead they are individuals and as individuals would have Second Amendment rights, if the Second Amendment were to apply to non-Americans.[217] Interestingly, Justice Jackson's reasoning echoed an argument made in *Ex Parte Milligan* by the Attorney General: the Fifth Amendment must contain implicit exceptions, which allow trial of civilians under martial law; the whole Bill of Rights contains implicit exceptions, for without such exceptions, it would be a violation of the Second Amendment to disarm rebels, and the former slave states' forbidding the slaves to own guns would likewise have been unconstitutional.[218]

---

210. Johnson v. Eisentrager, 339 U.S. 763 (1950).
211. *Id.* at 765-66.
212. *Id.* at 776.
213. *Id.* at 782.
214. *Id.*
215. The Fifth Amendment's prohibition on trial by court martial does not, by its own terms, apply to soldiers in the standing army (or to militiamen engaged in militia duty).
216. *Id.* at 784 (emphasis added).
217. The characters in the hypothetical are not militia members either. A militia is an organized force under government control. In contrast, "guerrilla fighters" or "were-wolves" are small groups or individuals functioning in enemy territory beyond the reach of any friendly government. The legal distinction was of great importance during World War II. Switzerland, for example, made extensive plans for its militia forces (consisting of almost the entire able-bodied adult male population) to resist a German invasion to the last man. But the Swiss government also warned its citizens *not* to engage in guerrilla warfare on their own; the militiamen fighting the Germans would be entitled to the protection of the rules of war and international conventions, but guerrillas would not. *See* STEPHEN HALBROOK, TARGET SWITZERLAND (1998). Having served as a judge of the Nuremburg Trials, Justice Jackson was presumably familiar with the distinctions in the international law of war between guerillas and soldiers/militia.
218. During the Civil War, in 1864, an Indiana man Lambdin P. Milligan was charged with aiding the southern rebellion against the national government. Although Indiana was under full union control, and courts in Indiana

were functioning, Milligan was tried before a military court martial and sentenced to death. In 1866, a unanimous Supreme Court overturned Milligan's conviction, holding that martial law can only be applied in theaters of war, and not in areas where the civil courts were functioning. Ex Parte Milligan, 71 U.S. (4 Wall.) 2 (1866).

The Court did not discuss the Second Amendment, but in argument to the Court, the Attorney General of the United States did. During the argument before the Court, Milligan's lawyers had claimed that Congress could never impose martial law. They pointed out that the Fourth Amendment (no searches without warrants), the Fifth Amendment (no criminal trials without due process), and the Sixth Amendment (criminal defendants always have a right to a jury trial) do not contain any exceptions for wartime.

The Attorney General, who was defending the legality of Milligan's having been sentenced to death by court martial, retorted that under conditions of war, the protections of the Bill of Rights do not apply. Thus, the federal government could disarm a rebel, without violating his Second Amendment right to keep and bear arms. The Attorney General urged the Court to construe the Second, Third, Fourth, Fifth and Sixth Amendments *in pari materia*:

After war is originated, whether by declaration, invasion, or insurrection, the whole power of conducting it, as to manner, and as to all the means and appliances by which war is carried on by civilized nations, is given to the President. He is the sole judge of the exigencies, necessities, and duties of the occasion, their extent and duration. . . . .

Much of the argument on the side of the petitioner will rest, perhaps, upon certain provisions not in the Constitution itself, and as originally made, but now seen in the Amendments made in 1789: the fourth, fifth, and sixth amendments. They may as well be here set out:

4. The right of the people to be secure in their persons, houses, papers, and effects, against unreasonable searches and seizures, shall not be violated, and no warrants shall issue but upon probable cause supported by oath or affirmation, and particularly describing the place to be searched and the persons or things to be seized.

5. No person shall be held to answer for a capital or otherwise infamous crime, unless on a presentment or indictment of a grand jury, except in cases arising in the land or naval forces, or in the militia when in actual service in time of war or public danger; nor shall any person be subject for the same offence to be twice put in jeopardy of life or limb; nor shall be compelled in any criminal case to be a witness against himself, nor be deprived of life, liberty, or property, without due process of law; nor shall private property be taken for public use without just compensation.

6. In all criminal prosecutions the accused shall enjoy the right to a speedy and public trial, by an impartial jury of the State and district wherein the crime shall have been committed, . . . and to be informed of the nature and cause of the accusation; to be confronted with the witnesses against him; to have compulsory process for obtaining witnesses in his favor, and to have the assistance of counsel for his defence.

In addition to these, there are two preceding amendments which we may also mention, to wit: the second and third. They are thus:

2. A well-regulated militia being necessary to the security of a free State, the right of the people to keep and bear arms shall not be infringed.

3. No soldier shall in time of peace be quartered in any house without the consent of the owner, nor in time of war but in a manner to be prescribed by law.

It will be argued that the fourth, fifth, and sixth articles, as above given, are restraints upon the war-making power; but we deny this. All these amendments are in pari materia, and if either is a restraint upon the President in carrying on war, in favor of the citizen, it is difficult to see why all of them are not. Yet will it be argued that the fifth article would be violated in "depriving if life, liberty, or property, without due process of law," armed rebels marching to attack the capital? Or that the fourth would be violated by searching and seizing the papers and houses of persons in open insurrection and war against the government? It cannot properly be so argued, any more than it could be that it was intended by the second article (declaring that "the right of the people to keep and bear arms shall not be infringed") to hinder the President from disarming insurrectionists, rebels, and traitors in arms while he was carrying on war against them.

These, in truth, are all peace provisions of the Constitution and, like all other conventional and legislative laws and enactments, are silent amidst arms, and when the safety of the people becomes the supreme law.

By the Constitution, as originally adopted, no limitations were put upon the war-making and war-conducting powers of Congress and the President; and after discussion, and after the attention of the country was called to the subject, no other limitation by subsequent amendment has been made, except by the Third Article, which prescribes that "no soldier shall be quartered in any house in time of peace without consent of the owner, or in time of war, except in a manner prescribed by law."

This, then, is the only expressed constitutional restraint upon the President as to the manner of carrying on war. There would seem to be no implied one; on the contrary, while carefully providing for the privilege of the writ of habeas corpus in time of peace, the Constitution takes it for granted that it will be suspended "in case of rebellion or invasion (i. e., in time of war), when the public safety requires it."

Id. at 29-33.

Thus, the Attorney General explained, the Second Amendment belongs to individuals, but if a Confederate rebel were disarmed, his Second Amendment right would not be violated, since the Second Amendment would not apply to him—even though the Second Amendment has no explicit exception for wartime. Likewise, if Congress declared martial law in a region, a civilian would be subjected to a court martial, rather than trial by jury, even though the Sixth Amendment (which guarantees jury trials) has no explicit exception for wartime. The Attorney General plainly saw the Second Amendment as guaranteeing an individual right.

The United States government also made another argument showing that the Second Amendment belongs to individuals. On behalf of Milligan, attorney David Dudley Field had presented a passionate and superb argument, explaining that the ultimate issue at bar was the supremacy of the civil power over the military, a principle at the very heart of Anglo-American liberty and republican government.

H. Adamson v. California

In the *Adamson* case, the defendant was convicted after a trial in a California state court; California law allowed the judge to instruct the jury that the jury could draw adverse inferences from a defendant's failure to testify.[219] This jury instruction was plainly inconsistent with established Fifth Amendment doctrine;[220] but did the Fifth Amendment apply in state courts, or only in federal courts?

The *Adamson* majority held that the Fifth Amendment's protection against compelled self-incrimination was *not* made enforceable in state courts by the Fourteenth Amendment's command that states not deprive a person of life, liberty, or property without "due process of law."[221]

In dissent, Justice Black (joined by Justice Douglas) argued that the Fourteenth Amendment made *all* of the Bill of Rights enforceable against the states, via the Amendment's mandate: "No state shall make or enforce any law which shall abridge the privileges or immunities of citizens of the United States."[222] Listing a series of 19th century cases in which the Supreme Court had refused to make certain individual rights from the Bill of Rights enforceable against the states (including *Presser*, involving the right to keep and bear arms), Justice Black argued that the Court's prior cases had not been so explicit as to foreclose the current Court from considering the issue:

Field had made much of the fact that the Fifth Amendment's requirement that persons could only be tried if they had first been indicted by a grand jury had an explicit exception for military circumstances ("except in cases arising in the land or naval forces, or in the militia when in actual service in time of war or public danger"). Field pointed out that Milligan (an Indiana civilian with Confederate sympathies) was obviously not within the terms of the exception.

In response, the Attorney General turned the argument over to Benjamin Franklin Butler. A very successful lawyer, Butler had been one of the most prominent Union Generals during the Civil War; a few months after his Supreme Court argument, Butler would be elected to Congress from Massachusetts, and would become one of the leading Radical Republicans.

Butler told the Supreme Court that the whole Bill of Rights contained implicit exceptions which were not stated in the text. For example, despite the literal language of the Fifth Amendment and the Second Amendment, slaves in antebellum America had been deprived of liberty without due process and had been forbidden to possess arms:

. . .the constitution provides that "no person" shall be deprived of liberty without due process of law. And yet, as we know, whole generations of people in this land—as many as four millions of them at one time—people described in the Constitution by this same word, "persons," have been till lately deprived of liberty ever since the adoption of the Constitution, without any process of law whatever.

The Constitution provides, also, that no "person's" right to bear arms shall be infringed; yet these same people, described elsewhere in the Constitutions as "persons," have been deprived of their arms whenever they had them."

Id. at 178-79.

Butler's point, presented on behalf of the Attorney General, was that the right to arms and the right not to be deprived of liberty without due process were individual rights guaranteed to all "persons." Yet despite the literal guarantee to all "persons," slaves had been deprived of their liberty without a fair trial, and had not been allowed to own or carry guns. Thus, there must an implicit "slavery exception" in the Second Amendment and the Fifth Amendment. And if there could be an unstated "slavery exception," there could also be an unstated "in time of war" exception.

Butler's argument is totally incompatible with the claim that the Second Amendment right does not belong to individuals. According to Henigan and Bogus, the Second Amendment can only be violated when the federal government interferes with state militias. But there were no federal laws forbidding states to enroll slaves in the state militias. (The federal Militia Act of 1792 enrolled whites only, but the Act did not prevent the states from structuring their own militias as they saw fit.) Although there were no federal law interfering with state militias, there were state laws forbidding individual blacks to possess arms. So Butler's argument assumed that the Second Amendment right to arms inhered in individuals (including slaves, if the Amendment were read literally, with no implied exception for slavery).

219. Adamson v. California, 332 U.S. 46, 48 (1947).

220. U.S. CONST. amend. V.

221. *Adamson*, 332 U.S. at 58-59. (*Adamson* was overruled by the Supreme Court in the 1964 decision *Malloy v. Hogan*, *infra* note 183).

222. U.S. CONST. amend. XIV.

Later, but prior to the Twining *case, this Court decided that the following were not "privileges or immunities" of national citizenship, so as to make them immune against state invasion: the Eighth Amendment's prohibition against cruel and unusual punishment, In re Kemmler, 136 U.S. 436; the Seventh Amendment's guarantee of a jury trial in civil cases, Walker v. Sauvinet, 92 U.S. 90; the Second Amendment's 'right of the people to keep and bear arms. . .,' Presser v. Illinois, 116 U.S. 252, 584; the Fifth and Sixth Amendments' requirements for indictment in capital or other infamous crimes, and for trial by jury in criminal prosecutions, Maxwell v. Dow, 176 U.S. 581. While it can be argued that these cases implied that no one of the provisions of the Bill of Rights was made applicable to the states as attributes of national citizenship, no one of them expressly so decided. In fact, the Court in Maxwell v. Dow, supra, 176 U.S. at pages 597, 598, 20 S.Ct. at page 455, concluded no more than that 'the privileges and immunities of citizens of the United States do not necessarily include all the rights protected by the first eight amendments to the Federal Constitution against the powers of the Federal government.' Cf. Palko v. Connecticut, 302 U.S. 319, 329, 153.*[223]

Thus, Justice Black put the Second Amendment in the same boat as Amendments Five, Six, Seven, and Eight: individual rights which prior Courts had declined to enforce against the states, but which the present Court still had the choice to incorporate.

In a lengthy Appendix, Justice Black set forth the history of the creation of the Fourteenth Amendment, quoting at length from congressional proponents of the Amendment, who indicated that the Amendment was intended to make all of the rights in the first eight amendments of the Bill of Rights enforceable against the states.[224] This view, held by Justice Black and many of the backers of the Fourteenth Amendment, is of course inconsistent with the idea that the Second Amendment guarantees only a right of state governments. The point of the Fourteenth Amendment is to make individual rights enforceable against state governments.

First, the Appendix set forth the background to the Fourteenth Amendment. Congress had enacted the Civil Rights Bill in response to problems in states such as Mississippi, where, Senator Trumball (Chairman of the Senate Judiciary Committee) explained, there was a statute to "prohibit any negro or mulatto from having firearms. . ."[225] When the Civil Rights Bill went to the House, Rep. Raymond, who opposed the Bill "conceded that it would guarantee to the negro 'the right of free passage. . .He has a defined status. . . .a right to defend himself. . .to bear arms. . . .to testify in the Federal courts."[226]

Then,

On May 23, 1866, Senator Howard introduced the proposed amendment to the Senate in the absence of Senator Fessenden who was sick. Senator Howard prefaced his remarks by stating:

223. *Adamson*, 332 U.S. at 70-71 (Black, J., dissenting).
224. *Id.* at 92-124.
225. *Id.* at 93 (citing Cong. Globe, 39th Cong., 1st Sess. (1865) 474).
226. *Id.* (citing Cong. Globe, 39th Cong., 1st Sess. (1865) 474).

"I. . .present to the Senate. . .the views and the motives [of the Reconstruction Committee]. . . .One result of their investigation has been the joint resolution for the amendment of the Constitution of the United States now under consideration. . . .

"The first section of the amendment. . .submitted for the consideration of the two Houses, relates to the privileges and immunities of citizens of the several States, and to the rights and privileges of all persons, whether citizens or others, under the laws of the United States. . . .

. . .

"Such is the character of the privileges and immunities spoken of in the second section of the fourth article of the Constitution. To these privileges and immunities, whatever they may be—for they are not and cannot be fully defined in their entire extent and precise nature—to these should be added the personal rights guarantied and secured by the first eight amendments of the Constitution*; such as the freedom of speech and of the press; the right of the people peaceably to assemble and petition the Government for a redress of grievances, a right appertaining to each and all the people;* the right to keep and to bear arms*; the right to be exempted from the quartering of soldiers in a house without the consent of the owner; the right to be exempt from unreasonable searches and seizures, and from any search or seizure except by virtue of a warrant issued upon a formal oath or affidavit; the right of an accused person to be informed of the nature of the accusation against him, and his right to be tried by an impartial jury of the vicinage; and also the right to be secure against excessive bail and against cruel and unusual punishments.*[227]

Later in the Appendix, Justice Black quoted Rep. Dawes' statement that by the Constitution the American citizen

"secured the free exercise of his religious belief, and freedom of speech and of the press. Then again he had secured to him the right to keep and bear arms in his defense. *Then, after that, his home was secured in time of peace from the presence of a soldier. . . ."*[228]

. . . .

"It is all these, Mr. Speaker, which are comprehended in the words 'American citizen,' and it is to protect and to secure him in these rights, privileges, and immunities this bill is before the House. And the question to be settled is, whether by the Constitution, in which these provisions are inserted, there is also power to guard, protect, and enforce these rights of the citizens; whether they are more, indeed, than a mere declaration of rights, carrying with it no power of enforcement. . . ." Cong.Globe, 42d Cong., 1st Sess. Part I (1871) 475, 476.[229]

227. *Id.* at 104-07 (emphasis added).
228. *Id.* at 119 (emphasis added).
229. *Id.* at 120.

Also dissenting, Justice Murphy wrote "that the specific guarantees of the Bill of Rights should be carried over intact into the first Section of the Fourteenth Amendment."[230] The Second Amendment implications of his statement are the same as for Justice Black's longer exposition, although Justice Murphy did not enumerate the Second Amendment, or any other right.

Senator Howard, quoted by Justice Black, listed the individual right to arms in its natural order among the other individual rights listed in the Bill of Rights.[231] The Henigan/Bogus state's right theory, however, requires us to believe that when Congress sent the Bill of Rights to the states, Congress first listed four individual rights (in the First Amendment), then created a state's right (in the Second Amendment), and then reverted to a litany of individual rights (Amendments Three through Eight).[232] Finally, Congress explicitly guaranteed a state's right in the Tenth Amendment.[233] While Congress used "the people" to refer to people in the First, Fourth, and Ninth Amendments, Congress used "the people" to mean "state governments" in the Second Amendment.[234] Finally, even though Congress had used "the people" in the Second Amendment to mean "the states," Congress in the Tenth Amendment explicitly distinguished "the people" from "the states," reserving powers "to the States respectively, or to the people."[235]

Which reading is more sensible: The Black/Howard/Dawes reading, under which "the people" means the same thing throughout the Bill of Rights, and which makes all of the first eight amendments into a straightforward list of individual rights, or the Henigan/Bogus theory, which requires that "the people" change meanings repeatedly, and which inserts a state's right in the middle of a litany of individual rights?

H. Hamilton v. Regents

This case has been almost entirely overlooked by Second Amendment scholarship.[236] *Hamilton's* obscurity is especially surprising, since it is the one Supreme Court case which actually uses the Second Amendment in the way that we would expect the Amendment to be used if it were a state's right: to bolster state authority over the militia.

Two University of California students, the sons of pacifist ministers, sued to obtain an exemption from participation in the University of California's mandatory military training program.[237] The two students did not contest the state of California's authority to force them to participate in state militia exercises, but they argued, in part, that the university's training program was so closely connected with the U.S. War Department as to not really be a militia program.[238] A unanimous Court disagreed, and stated that California's acceptance of federal assistance in militia training did not transform the

230. *Id.* at 124 (Murphy, J., dissenting).
231. *Supra* note 228.
232. *Id.* at 73.
233. *Id.* at 74.
234. *Id.* at 76.
235. *Id.* at 77.
236. Stephen Halbrook cites the case, but for another point. *See* STEPHEN HALBROOK, FIREARMS LAW DESKBOOK, *supra* note 106, at 8-44 n.131.
237. Hamilton v. Regents of the Univ. of California, 293 U.S. 245 (1934).
238. *Id.* at 250-51.

training program into an arm of the standing army. States had the authority to made their own judgements about training:

> *So long as [the state's] action is within retained powers and not inconsistent with any exertion of the authority of the national government, and transgresses no right safeguarded to the citizen by the Federal Constitution, the State is the sole judge of the means to be employed and the amount of training to be exacted for the effective accomplishment of these ends. Second Amendment. Houston v. Moore, 5 Wheat. 1, 16-17, Dunne v. People, (1879) 94 Ill. 120, 129. 1 Kent's Commentaries 265, 389.* Cf. *Presser v. Illinois, 116 U.S. 252.*[239]

Thus, the Court used the Second Amendment to support of a point about a state government's power over its militia.

This usage was not consistent with a meaningful state's right theory. A state's right Second Amendment, to have any legal content, would have to give the state some exemption from the exercise of federal powers.[240] But the Court wrote that the state's discretion in militia training must be "not inconsistent with any exertion of the authority of the national government."[241]

Another way to read *Hamilton*'s Second Amendment citation would be as a reminder of the expectation by all the Founders that states would supervise the militia. This reminder would be consistent with the state's rights theory and with the standard model.

The authorities cited along with "Second Amendment" by the *Hamilton* Court do not support a reading of the Second Amendment as guaranteeing a state's right, but instead support an individual right.

Houston v. Moore (to be discussed in more detail below), involved the state of Pennsylvania's authority to punish a man for evading service in the federal militia, which had been called to fight the war of 1812.[242] The report of the attorneys' arguments, on both sides, shows that the Second Amendment was not raised as an issue.[243] The *Houston* pages which were cited by the *Hamilton* Court contain the statement, spanning the two pages, that "[A]s state militia, the power of the state governments to legislate on the same subjects [organizing, arming, disciplining, training, and officering the militia], having existed prior to the formation of the constitution, and not having been prohibited by that instrument, it remains with the states, subordinate nevertheless to the paramount law of the general government, operating on the same subject."[244] In other words, state militia powers were inherent in the nature of state sovereignty, and continue to exist except to the extent limited by Congress under its Constitutional militia powers.

In *Dunne v. People,* the Illinois Supreme Court affirmed the centrality of state power over the militia, citing the Tenth Amendment and the *Houston v. Moore* precedent.[245] The *Dunne* court also explained how a state's

---

239. *Id.* at 260-61.
240. For a discussion of this point, *see* Glenn Harlan Reynolds & Don B. Kates, *The Second Amendment and States' Rights: A Thought Experiment*, *supra* note 7.
241. Hamilton, 293 U.S. at 260.
242. Houston v. Moore, 18 U.S. (5 Wheat.) 1 (1820). See *infra* text at notes 343-53.
243. *Id.*
244. *Id.* at 16-17.
245. Dunne v. People, 94 Ill. 120 (1879).

constitutional duty to operate a militia was complemented by the right of the state's citizens to have arms:

> *"A well regulated militia being necessary to the security of a free State," the States, by an amendment to the constitution, have imposed a restriction that Congress shall not infringe the right of the "people to keep and bear arms." The chief executive officer of the State is given power by the constitution to call out the militia "to execute the laws, suppress insurrection and repel invasion."*[246] *This would be a mere barren grant of power unless the State had power to organize its own militia for its own purposes. Unorganized, the militia would be of no practical aid to the executive in maintaining order and in protecting life and property within the limits of the State. These are duties that devolve on the State, and unless these rights are secured to the citizen, of what worth is the State government?*[247]

The cited pages of Kent's Commentaries discuss state versus federal powers over the militia. Chancellor Kent uses *Martin v. Mott*[248] to show that a President's decision that there is a need to call out the militia is final. *Houston v. Moore*[249] (state authority to prosecute a person for refusing a federal militia call) is used to show that if the federal government neglects its constitutional duty to organize, arm, and discipline the militia, the states have the inherent authority to do so. The Second Amendment was not used by Kent or by Kent's cited cases to support his propositions.

Presser v. Illinois will be discussed below; the case affirmed a state's authority to make a gun control law (a ban on armed parades in public) which contained an exemption for the state's organized militia.[250]

Later in the opinion, the *Hamilton* Court quoted *United States v. Schwimmer*, a 1929 decision which held that an immigrant pacifist's refusal to bear arms in the army or in the Second Amendment's well-regulated militia proved that the immigrant was not fit for citizenship.[251]

IV. The Taft, Fuller, and Waite Courts

Between the end of Reconstruction and the New Deal, there were eleven opinions (all but one a majority opinion) touching on the Second Amendment. Most involved the scope of the "privileges and immunities" which the Fourteenth Amendment protected from state interference. Nine of the opinions (including the one dissent) treated the Second Amendment as

246. The court was quoting language from Article I, Section 8 of the Constitution, which gives such authority to Congress. This grant is not inconsistent with pre-existent state authority, so long as the state authority is not used in conflict with the federal authority.
247. *Dunne*, 94 Ill. at 132-33.
248. Martin v. Mott, 25 U.S. 19 (1827).
249. *Infra* notes 343-53.
250. *Infra* notes 310-20.
251. *Infra* notes 251-56.

an individual right, while the tenth was ambiguous, and the eleventh refused to address any of a plaintiff's arguments (of which the Second Amendment was one) because of a lack of injury and hence a lack of standing.

A. United States v. Schwimmer

A divided Supreme Court held that a female pacifist who wished to become a United States citizen could be denied citizenship because of her energetic advocacy of pacifism.[252] The Court majority found the promotion of pacifism inconsistent with good citizenship because it dissuaded people from performing their civic duties, including the duty to bear arms in a well regulated militia.[253] Since it is agreed by Standard Modelers and their critics alike that the federal and state governments have the authority to compel citizens to perform militia service, the *Schwimmer* opinion does not help resolve the individual rights controversy:

> *That it is the duty of citizens by force of arms to defend our government against all enemies whenever necessity arises is a fundamental principle of the Constitution.*
>
> *The common defense was one of the purposes for which the people ordained and established the Constitution. It empowers Congress to provide for such defense, to declare war, to raise and support armies, to maintain a navy, to make rules for the government and regulation of the land and naval forces, to provide for organizing, arming, and disciplining the militia, and for calling it forth to execute the laws of the Union, suppress insurrections and repel invasions; it makes the President commander in chief of the army and navy and of the militia of the several states when called into the service of the United States; it declares that, a well-regulated militia being necessary to the security of a free state, the right of the people to keep and bear arms shall not be infringed. We need not refer to the numerous statutes that contemplate defense of the United States, its Constitution and laws, by armed citizens. This court, in the Selective Draft Law Cases,* 245 U.S. 366, *page 378, 38 S. Ct. 159, 161 (62 L. Ed. 349, L. R. A. 1918C, 361, Ann. Cas. 1918B, 856), speaking through Chief Justice White, said that "the very conception of a just government and its duty to the citizen includes the reciprocal obligation of the citizen to render military service in case of need. . . ."*
>
> *Whatever tends to lessen the willingness of citizens to discharge their duty to bear arms in the country's defense detracts from the strength and safety of the Government. . . .The influence of conscientious objectors against the use of military force in defense of the principles of our Government is apt to be more detrimental than their mere refusal to bear arms. . .her objection to military service rests on reasons other than mere inability because of her sex and age personally to bear arms.*[254]

Schwimmer illustrates two points about which the Standard Model authors agree with Bogus and Henigan: first, the phrase "bear arms" in the

252. United States v. Schwimmer, 279 U.S. 644 (1929).
253. *Id.* at 652-53.
254. *Id.* at 650-52.

Second Amendment can have militia service connotations. The Standard Modelers (and Justice Ginsburg)[255], however, disagree with Bogus and Henigan's claim that "bear arms" always has a militia/military meaning, and never any other. Second, *Schwimmer* illustrates that bearing arms can be a duty of citizenship which the government can impose on the citizen. While opponents of the standard model use this fact to argue that the Second Amendment is about a duty, and not about an individual right,[256] the Standard Model professors respond by pointing to jury service, to show that an individual constitutional right (the right to be eligible for jury service[257]) can also be a duty.

B. Stearns v. Wood

This case came to the Court after World War I had broken out in Europe.[258] The U.S. War Department had sent "Circular 8" to the various National Guards, putting restrictions on promotion. Plaintiff Stearns, a Major in the Ohio National Guard, was thereby deprived of any opportunity to win promotion above the rank of Lieutenant Colonel.[259] Stearns argued that Circular 8 violated the Preamble to the Constitution, Article One's specification of Congressional powers over the militia, Article One's grant of army powers to the Congress, Article Two's making the President the Commander in Chief of the militia when called into federal service, the Second Amendment, and the Tenth Amendment.[260]

Writing for a unanimous Court, Justice McReynolds contemptuously dismissed Stearns' claim without reaching the merits.[261] Since Stearns' present rank of Major was undisturbed, there was no genuine controversy for the Court to consider, and the Court would not render advisory opinions.[262]

Even though the Court never reached the merits of the Second Amendment argument, it is possible to draw some inferences simply from the fact that the Second Amendment argument was made in the case. First of all, Major Stearns' argument shows that using the Second Amendment to criticize federal control of the National Guard was not an absurd argument—or at least no more absurd than using the Preamble to the Constitution for the same purpose. And after the 1905 Kansas Supreme Court case *Salina v. Blaksley* ruled that the Kansas constitution's right to arms (and, by analogy, the U.S. Second Amendment) protected the state government, and not the citizen of Kansas,[263] Stearns' attorney's argument did have some foundation in case law.

C. Twining v. New Jersey

In *Twining*, the Supreme Court (with the first Harlan in dissent) refused to make the Fifth Amendment self-incrimination guarantee in the Bill of

255. United States v. Muscarello, 524 U.S. 125 (1998) (Ginsburg, J., dissenting), *supra* text at note 57.
256. *See, e.g.*, sources cited at *supra* note 6.
257. *See, e.g.*, Glenn Harlan Reynolds, *A Critical Guide to the Second Amendment*, *supra* note 8.
258. Stearns v. Wood, 236 U.S. 75 (1915).
259. *Id.* at 76. Colonel would be the next rank up.
260. *Id.* at 78.
261. *Id.*
262. *Id.*
263. Salina v. Blaksley, 83 P. 619 (Kan. 1905).

Rights applicable to state trials, via the Fourteenth Amendment.[264] In support of this result, the majority listed other individual rights which had not been made enforceable against the states, under the Privileges and Immunities clause:

> *The right to trial by jury in civil cases, guaranteed by the Seventh Amendment (Walker v. Sauvinet, 92 U.S. 90), and the right to bear arms guaranteed by the Second Amendment (Presser v. Illinois, 116 U.S. 252) have been distinctly held not to be privileges and immunities of citizens of the United States guaranteed by the Fourteenth Amendment against abridgement by the States, and in effect the same decision was made in respect of the guarantee against prosecution, except by indictment of a grand jury, contained in the Fifth Amendment (Hurtado v. California, 110 U.S. 516), and in respect to the right to be confronted with witnesses, contained in the Sixth Amendment. West v. Louisiana, 194 U.S. 258. In Maxwell v. Dow, supra. . .it was held that indictment, made indispensable by the Fifth Amendment, and the trial by jury guaranteed by the Sixth Amendment, were not privileges and immunities of citizens of the United States.*[265]

The Second Amendment here appears—along with Seventh Amendment civil juries, Sixth Amendment confrontation, and Fifth Amendment grand juries—as a right of individuals, but a right only enforceable against the federal government. As we shall see below, the exact meaning of the 1886 *Presser* case was subject to dispute; some argued that the case simply upheld a particular gun control as not being in violation of the Second Amendment, while others argued that *Presser* held that the Second Amendment was not one of the "Privileges and Immunities" which the Fourteenth Amendment protects against state action. *Twining* clearly takes the latter view.

D. Maxwell v. Dow

Maxwell was the majority's decision (again, over Harlan's dissent) not to make the right to a jury in a criminal case into one of the Privileges or Immunities protected by the Fourteenth Amendment.[266] Regarding the Second Amendment and *Presser*, the Court wrote:

> *In Presser v. Illinois, 116 U.S. 252, it was held that the Second Amendment to the Constitution, in regard to the right of the people to bear arms, is a limitation only on the power of the Congress and the National Government, and not of the States. It was therein said, however, that as all citizens capable of bearing arms constitute the reserved military force of the National Government, the States could not prohibit the people from keeping and bearing arms, so as to deprive the United States of their rightful resource for maintaining the public security, and disable the people from performing their duty to the General Government.*[267]

---

264. Twining v. New Jersey, 211 U.S. 78 (1908)(*overruled by* Malloy v. Hogan, 378 U.S. 1 (1964).
265. *Id.* at 98-99.
266. Maxwell v. Dow, 176 U.S. 581 (1899).
267. *Id.* at 597.

The *Maxwell* description of *Presser* was somewhat narrower than *Twining's* description. *Maxwell* used *Presser* only to show that the Second Amendment does not in itself apply to the states; *Twining* used *Presser* to show that the Fourteenth Amendment privileges and immunities clause did not make the Second Amendment indirectly applicable to the states.

E. Trono v. United States, *and* Kepner v. United States

After the United States won the Spanish-American War, the Philippines were ceded to the United States. American control was successfully imposed only after several years of hard warfare suppressed Filipinos fighting for independence.[268] Congress in 1902 enacted legislation imposing most, but not all of the Bill of Rights on the Territorial Government of the Philippines. The 1905 *Trono*[269] case and the 1904 *Kepner*[270] case both grew out of criminal prosecutions in the Philippines in which the defendant claimed his rights had been violated.

In *Trono,* at the beginning of the Justice Peckham's majority opinion, the Congressional act imposing the Bill of Rights was summarized:

> *The whole language [of the Act] is substantially taken from the Bill of Rights set forth in the amendments to the Constitution of the United States, omitting the provisions in regard to the right of trial by jury and the right of the people to bear arms, and containing the prohibition of the 13th Amendment, and also prohibiting the passage of bills of attainder and ex post facto laws.*[271]

As with other cases, the "right of the people" to arms is listed in a litany of other rights which are universally acknowledged to be individual rights, not state's rights.[272]

It could be argued that the Second Amendment was omitted from the Congressional Act because the Amendment *is* a state's right, and there was no point in putting a state's right item into laws governing a territory. Indeed, the omission of the Tenth Amendment from the Congressional 1902 Act is perfectly explicable on the grounds that the Tenth Amendment protects federalism, but does not control a territorial or state government's dealings with its citizens.[273]

And thus, when the Supreme Court listed the individual rights which were not included in the 1902 Act, the Court did not note the omission of the Tenth Amendment; there was no possibility that Congress could have included the Tenth Amendment, since it would have no application to the territorial government's actions against the Filipino people.[274]

In contrast, the Court did note the omission of "the right of trial by jury and the right of the people to bear arms."[275] The logical implication, then, is that jury trial and the right to arms (unlike the Tenth Amendment) are

268. The war led to the development of the Colt .45 self-loading pistols, since smaller pistol rounds often had insufficient stopping power against the Filipino warriors.
269. Trono v. United States, 199 U.S. 521 (1905).
270. Kepner v. United States, 195 U.S. 100 (1904).
271. *Trono*, 199 U.S. at 528.
272. *Id.*
273. 32 Stat. 691 (1902).
274. Trono, 199 U.S. at 528.
275. *Id.*

individual rights which Congress *could* have required the Territorial Government to respect in the Philippines.[276]

The 1904 *United States v. Kepner* case involved a similar issue.[277] There, the Court described the 1902 Act in more detail. The description of items omitted from the Act was nearly identical to the *Trono* language.[278]

F. Robertson v. Baldwin

In 1897, the Court refused to apply the Thirteenth Amendment to merchant seamen who had jumped ship, been caught, and been impressed back into maritime service without due process.[279] The Court explained that Thirteenth Amendment's ban on involuntary servitude, even though absolute on its face, contained various implicit exceptions.[280] In support of the finding of an exception to the Thirteenth Amendment, the Court argued that the Bill of Rights also contained unstated exceptions:

> *The law is perfectly well settled that the first ten Amendments to the constitution, commonly known as the Bill of Rights, were not intended to lay down any novel principles of government, but simply to embody certain guarantees and immunities which we had inherited from our English ancestors, and which from time immemorial had been subject to certain well-recognized exceptions arising from the necessities of the case. In incorporating these principles into the fundamental law, there was no intention of disregarding the exceptions, which continued to be recognized as if they had been formally expressed. Thus, the freedom of speech and of the press (article 1) does not permit the publication of libels, blasphemous or indecent articles, or other publications injurious to public morals or private reputation; the right of the people to keep and bear arms (article 2) is not infringed by law prohibiting the carrying of concealed weapons; the provision that no person shall be twice put in jeopardy (art. 5) does not prevent a second trial, if upon the first trial the jury failed to agree, or the verdict was set aside upon the defendant's motion. . . .*[281]

Likewise, the self-incrimination clause did not bar a person from being compelled to testify against himself if he were immune from prosecution; and the confrontation clause did not bar the admission of dying declarations.[282]

In 1897, state laws which barred individuals from carrying concealed weapons were common, and usually upheld by state supreme courts[283]; the laws did not forbid state militias from carrying concealed weapons. The prohibitions on concealed carry are the exceptions that prove the rule. Only

276. *See id.*
277. *Kepner*, 195 U.S. at 123-24.
278. *Id.* They are the familiar language of the Bill of Rights, slightly changed in form, but not in substance, as found in the first nine amendments to the Constitution of the United States, with the omission of the provision preserving the right of trial by jury and the right of the people to bear arms, and adding the prohibition of the 13th Amendment against slavery or involuntary servitude except as punishment for crime, and that of Article I, Section 9, to the passage of bills of attainder and ex post facto laws.
279. Robertson v. Baldwin, 165 U.S. 275, 277 (1897).
280. *Id.* at 281.
281. *Id.* at 281-82.
282. *Id.* at 282.
283. *See, e.g.*, State v. Workman, 35 W. Va. 367 (1891). *See generally*, Kopel, *The Second Amendment in the Nineteenth Century*, *supra* note 9; Cramer, For the Defense of Themselves and the State, *supra* note 9.

if the Second Amendment is an individual right does the Court's invocation of a concealed carry exception make any sense.

G. Brown v. Walker

When a witness before an Interstate Commerce Commission investigation invoked the Fifth Amendment to refuse to answer questions under oath, the majority of the Supreme Court ruled against his invocation of the privilege against self-incrimination.[284] The majority pointed out that a Congressional statute protected the witness from any criminal prosecution growing out of the testimony.[285]

Dissenting, Justice Stephen Field (perhaps the strongest civil liberties advocate on the Court during the nineteenth century) contended that the "infamy and disgrace" which might result from the testimony was justification enough not to testify, even if there could be no criminal prosecution.[286] Justice Field's opinion carefully analyzed English and early American precedent, reflecting Field's vivid appreciation of the long Anglo-American struggle for liberty against arbitrary government.[287] Law and order was less important than Constitutional law, he continued, for the claim that "the proof of offenses like those prescribed by the interstate commerce act will be difficult and probably impossible, ought not to have a feather's weight against the abuses which would follow necessarily the enforcement of incriminating testimony."[288] All Constitutional rights ought to be liberally construed, for:

> *As said by counsel for the appellant: "The freedom of thought, of speech, and of the press;* the right to bear arms*; exemption from military dictation; security of the person and of the home; the right to speedy and public trial by jury; protection against oppressive bail and cruel punishment,—are, together with exemption from self-crimination,* the essential and inseparable features of English liberty. *Each one of these features had been involved in the struggle above referred to in England within the century and a half immediately preceding the adoption of the constitution, and the contests were fresh in the memories and traditions of the people at that time."*[289]

This is just the opposite of Dennis Henigan's assertion that the Second Amendment is written so as to be less fundamental than the first.[290] Justice Field's paragraph is not a list of state powers, it is a list of personal rights won at great cost—rights which may never be trumped by the legislature's perceived needs of the moment.

---

284. Brown v. Walker, 161 U.S. 591 (1896).

285. The *Presser* case, discussed *infra* at notes 310-20, appears in the Justice Brown's majority opinion, as part of a string cite for the proposition, "the first eight amendments are limitations only upon the powers of congress and the federal courts, and are not applicable to the several states, except so far as the fourteenth amendment may have made them applicable." *Id.* at 606.

286. *Id.* at 631 (Field, J., dissenting).

287. *Id.* at 632.

288. *Id.* at 635.

289. *Id.* (em phases added).

290. Henigan, Guns and the Constitution, *supra* note 4.

H. Miller v. Texas

Franklin P. Miller was a white man in Dallas who fell in love with a woman whom local newspapers would later call "a greasy negress." In response to a rumor that Miller was carrying a handgun without a license, a gang of Dallas police officers, after some hard drinking at a local tavern, invaded Miller's store with guns drawn. A shoot-out ensued, and the evidence was conflicting as to who fired first, and whether Miller realized that the invaders were police officers. But Miller was stone cold sober, and the police gang was not; thus, Miller killed one of the intruders during the shoot-out, although the gang's superior numbers resulted in Miller's capture.

During Miller's murder trial, the prosecutor asserted to the jury that Miller had been carrying a gun illegally. Upon conviction of murdering the police officer, Miller appealed to various courts, and lost every time.

Appealing to the Supreme Court in 1894, Miller alleged violations of his Second Amendment, Fourth Amendment, Fifth Amendment, and Fourteenth Amendment rights.[291] Regarding the Second Amendment, Miller claimed that it negated the Texas statute against concealed carrying of a weapon.[292]

A unanimous Court rejected Miller's contentions: A "state law forbidding the carrying of dangerous weapons on the person. . . does not abridge the privileges or immunities of citizens of the United States."[293] This statement about concealed weapons laws was consistent with what the Court would say about such laws three years later, in the *Robertson* case.[294]

Moreover, the Second Amendment, like the rest of the Bill of Rights, only operated directly on the federal government, and not on the states: "the restrictions of these amendments [Second, Fourth, and Fifth] operate only upon the Federal power."[295]

But did the Fourteenth Amendment makes the Second, Fourth, and Fifth Amendments applicable to the states? Here, the *Miller* Court was agnostic: "If the Fourteenth Amendment limited the power of the States as to such rights, as pertaining to the citizens of the United States, we think it was fatal to this claim that it was not set up in the trial court."[296]

Just eight years before, in *Presser* the Court had said that the Second Amendment does not apply directly to the states; *Miller* reaffirmed this part of the *Presser*. Another part of *Presser* had implied that the right to arms was not one of the "privileges or immunities" of American citizenship, although the *Presser* Court did not explicitly mention the Fourteenth Amendment.

In *Miller* v. *Texas*, the Court suggested that Miller might have had a Fourteenth Amendment argument, if he had raised the issue properly at trial.[297] If *Presser* foreclosed any possibility that Second Amendment rights could be enforced via the Fourteenth Amendment, then the *Miller* Court's statement would make no sense. Was *Miller* an early hint that the Fourteenth Amendment's due process clause might protect substantive elements of the Bill of Rights? Three years later, the Court used the Fourteenth Amendment's

291. Miller v. Texas, 153 U.S. 535 (1894).
292. *Id.* at 538.
293. *Id.* at 539.
294. *Robertson*, 165 U.S. at 281-82, *supra* text at notes 280-82.
295. *Id.* at 538.
296. *Id.*
297. *Miller*, 153 U.S. at 538.

due process clause for the first time to apply part of the Bill of Rights against a state.[298]

A decade after *Miller, Twining* in 1908 did claim that *Presser* stood for the Second Amendment not being a Fourteenth Amendment privilege or immunity. But between *Presser* in 1886 and *Twining* in 1908, other readings were permissible. Not only does *Miller* in 1894 appear to invite such readings, but so does the 1887 case *Spies* v. *Illinois*, which involved the murder prosecutions arising out of the Haymarket Riot.[299] John Randolph Tucker represented the defendants. Tucker, an eminent Congressman, author of an important treatise on constitutional law, a future President of the American Bar Association, and a leading law professor at Washington and Lee[300]—argued that the whole Bill of Rights was enforceable against the states, including the right to arms.[301]

Tucker argued that all "these ten Amendments" were "privileges and immunities of citizens of the United States, which the Fourteenth Amendment forbids every State to abridge," and cited *Cruikshank* in support.[302] As for *Presser*, that case "did not decide that the right to keep and bear arms was not a privilege of a citizen of the United States which a State might therefore abridge, but that a State could under its police power forbid organizations of armed men, dangerous to the public peace."[303]

Chief Justice Waite's majority opinion in *Spies* cited *Cruikshank* and *Presser* (along with many other cases) only for the proposition that the first ten Amendments do not apply directly to the states.[304] (An 1890 opinion, *Eilenbecker*, again cited *Cruikshank* and *Presser* as holding that the Bill of Rights does not apply directly to the states.[305]) The *Spies'* defendants'

298. Chicago, B. & Q. R.R. v. Chicago, 166 U.S. 226 (1897) (takings clause).

299. Spies v. Illinois, 123 U.S. 131 (1887). *See generally* PAUL AVRICH, THE HAYMARKET TRAGEDY (1986).

300. JOHN RANDOLPH TUCKER, THE CONSTITUTION OF THE UNITED STATES (Fred B. Rothman & Co. 1981) (1899); William G. Bean, *John Randolph Tucker*, in THE DICTIONARY OF AMERICAN BIOGRAPHY (CD-Rom ed. 1997).

301. *I hold the privilege and immunity of a citizen of the United States to be such as have their recognition in or guaranty from the Constitution of the United States. Take then the declared object of the Preamble, "to secure the blessings of liberty to ourselves and our posterity," we ordain this Constitution—that is, we grant powers, declare rights, and create a Union of States. See the provisions as to personal liberty in the States guarded by provision as to ex post facto laws, &c.; as to contract rights—against States' power to impair them, and as to legal tender; the security for habeas corpus; the limits imposed on Federal power in the Amendments and in the original Constitution as to trial by jury, &c.; the Declaration of Rights—the privilege of freedom of speech and press—of peaceable assemblages of the people—of keeping and bearing arms—of immunity from search and seizure—immunity from self-accusation, from second trial—and privilege of trial by due process of law. In these last we find the privileges and immunities secured to the citizen by the Constitution. It may have been that the States did not secure them to all men. It is true that they did not. Being secured by the Constitution of the United States to all, when they were not, and were not required to be, secured by every State, they are, as said in the Slaughter-House Cases, privileges and immunities of citizens of the United States.*
The position I take is this: Though originally the first ten Amendments were adopted as limitations on Federal power, yet in so far as they secure and recognize fundamental rights—common law rights—of the man, they make them privileges and immunities of the man as citizen of the United States, and cannot now be abridged by a State under the Fourteenth Amendment. In other words, while the ten Amendments, as limitations on power, only apply to the Federal government, and not to the States, yet in so far as they declare or recognize rights of persons, these rights are theirs, as citizens of the United States, and the Fourteenth Amendment as to such rights limits state power, as the ten Amendments had limited Federal power.

302. *Id.*

303. *Id.*

304. *Spies*, 123 U.S. at 166.

305. Eilenbecker v. District Court of Plymouth County, 134 U.S. 131 (1890):
The first three of these assignments of error, as we have stated them, being the first and second and fourth of the assignments as numbered in the brief of the plaintiffs in error, are disposed of at once by the principle often decided by this court, that the first eight articles of the amendments to the Constitution have reference to powers exercised by the government of the United States and not to those of the States. Livingston v. Moore, 7 Pet. 469; The Justices v. Murray, 9 Wall. 274; Edwards v. Elliott, 21 Wall. 532; United States v. Cruikshank, 92 U.S.

substantive claims (relating to the criminal procedure and jury portions of the Bill of Rights) were rejected as either incorrect (e.g., the jury was not biased) or as not properly raised at trial, and thus not appropriate for appeal.[306]

Tucker's reading of *Presser* is not the only possible one, but Tucker—one of the most distinguished lawyers of his time—was far too competent to make an argument in a capital case before the Supreme Court that was contrary to Supreme Court precedent from only a year before. It may be permissible to read *Presser* the same way that John Randolph Tucker did (as upholding a particular gun control law), or as *Spies, Maxwell,* and *Eilenbecker* did (as stating that the Second Amendment does not by its own power apply to the states), or as *Twining* and *Malloy v. Hogan* did (as rejecting incorporation of the Second Amendment via the Privileges and Immunities clause). We will get to *Presser* soon, so that the reader can supply her own interpretations.[307]

Whatever *Miller v. Texas* implies about the Fourteenth Amendment, its Second Amendment lessons are easy. First, the Amendment does not directly limit the states. Second, the Amendment protects an individual right. Miller was a private citizen, and never claimed any right as a member of the Texas Militia. But according to the Court, Miller's problem was the Second Amendment was raised against the wrong government (Texas, rather than the federal government), and at the wrong time (on appeal, rather than at trial). If the Henigan/Bogus state's right theory were correct, then the Court should have rejected Miller's Second Amendment claim because Miller was an individual rather than the government of Texas. Instead, the Court treated the Second Amendment exactly like the Fourth and the Fifth, which were also at issue: all three amendments protected individual rights, but only against the federal government; while the Fourteenth Amendment might, arguably, make these rights enforceable against the states, Miller's failure to raise the issue at trial precluded further inquiry.

I. Logan v. United States

This case arose out of a prosecution under the Enforcement Act, a Congressional statute outlawing private conspiracies against the exercise of civil rights.[308] The Enforcement Act was also as issue in *Cruikshank, infra.* In *Logan,* a mob had kidnapped a group of prisoners who were being held in the custody of federal law enforcement.[309] The issue before the Court was whether the prisoners, by action of the mob, had been deprived of any of their federal civil rights.

Logan affirmed *Cruikshank's* position that the First and Second Amendments recognize preexisting fundamental human rights, rather than

---

542; Walker v. Sauvinet, 92 U.S. 90; Fox v. Ohio, 5 How. 410; Holmes v. Jennison, 14 Pet. 540; Presser v. Illinois, 116 U.S. 252.

306. *Spies*, 123 U.S. at 168.

307. During the nineteenth century, the official Supreme Court reports included summaries of counsels' arguments. Besides Tucker's argument in *Spies*, there are two other nineteenth century cases which record use by counsel of the Second Amendment; both uses were by the Attorney General's office, and both regarded the Second Amendment as an individual right. In the argument for *In re Rapier*, Assistant Attorney General Maury defended a federal ban on the mailing of lottery tickets: "Freedom of the press, like freedom of speech, and 'the right to keep and bear arms,' admits of and requires regulation, which is the law of liberty that prevents these rights from running into license." In re Rapier, 143 U.S. 110, 131 (1892). The other argument came from the Attorney General in *Ex Parte Milligan*. Ex Parte Milligan, 71 U.S. (4 Wall.) 2 (1866); *supra* note 217.

308. Logan v. United States, 144 U.S. 263, 281-82 (1892).

309. *Id.* at 285-86.

creating new rights. The First Amendment right of assembly and the Second Amendment right to arms are construed *in pari materia*, suggesting that they both protect individual rights:

> *In U. S. v. Cruikshank,* 92 U.S. 542, *as the same term, in which also the opinion was delivered by the chief justice, the indictment was on section 6 of the enforcement act of 1870, (re-enacted in Rev. St. 5508, under which the present conviction was had,) and the points adjudged on the construction of the constitution and the extent of the powers of congress were as follows:*
>
> *(1) It was held that the first amendment of the constitution, by which it was ordained that congress should make no law abridging the right of the people peaceably to assemble and to petition the government for redress of grievances, did not grant to the people the right peaceably to assemble for lawful purposes, but recognized that right as already existing, and did not guaranty its continuance except as against acts of congress; and therefore the general right was not a right secured by the constitution of the United States. But the court added: "The right of the people peaceably to assemble for the purpose of petitioning congress for a redress of grievances, or for anything else connected with the powers or the duties of the national government, is an attribute of national citizenship, and, as such, under the protection of, and guarantied by, the United States. The very idea of a government, republican in form, implies a right on the part of its citizens to meet peaceably for consultation in respect to public affairs, and to petition for a redress of grievances. If it had been alleged in these counts that the object of the defendants was to prevent a meeting for such a purpose, the cause would have been within the statute, and within the scope of the sovereignty of the United States." 92 U.S. 552, 553.*
>
> *(2) It was held that the second amendment of the constitution, declaring that "the right of the people to keep and bear arms shall not be infringed," was equally limited in its scope. 92 U.S. 553.*
>
> *(3) It was held that a conspiracy of individuals to injure, oppress, and intimidate citizens of the United States, with intent to deprive them of life and liberty without due process of law, did not come within the statute, nor under the power of congress, because the rights of life and liberty were not granted by the constitution, but were natural and inalienable rights of man; and that the fourteenth amendment of the constitution, declaring that no state shall deprive any person of life, liberty, or property, without due process of law, added nothing to the rights of one citizen as against another, but simply furnished an additional guaranty against any encroachment by the states upon the fundamental rights which belong to every citizen as a member of society. It was of these fundamental rights of life and liberty, not created by or dependent on the constitution, that the court said: "Sovereignty, for this purpose, rests alone with the states. It is no more the duty or within the power of the United States to punish for a conspiracy to falsely imprison or murder within a state than it would be to punish for false imprisonment or murder itself." 92 U.S. 553, 554.*

(4) It was held that the provision of the Fourteenth Amendment forbidding any State to deny to any person within its jurisdiction the equal protection of the laws, gave no greater power to Congress. 92 U.S. 555.

(5) It was held, in accordance with United States v. Reese, above cited, that the counts for conspiracy to prevent and hinder citizens of the African race in the free exercise and enjoyment of the right to vote at state elections, or to injure and oppress them for having voted at such election, not alleging that this was on account of their race, or color, or previous condition of servitude, could not be maintained; that court stating: "The right to vote in the States comes from the States; but the right of exemption from prohibited discrimination comes from the United States. The first has not been granted or secured by the Constitution of the United States, but the last has been." 92 U.S. 556

Nothing else was decided in United States v. Cruikshank, except questions of the technical sufficiency of the indictment, having no bearing upon the larger questions.[310]

Thus, to the *Logan* Court, the First Amendment right to assemble and the Second Amendment right to arms are identical: both are individual rights; both pre-exist the Constitution; both are protected by the Constitution, rather than created by the Constitution; both rights are protected only against government interference, not against the interference of private conspirators.

J. Presser v. Illinois

In the late 19th century, many state governments violently suppressed peaceful attempts by workingmen to exercise their economic and collective bargaining rights. In response to the violent state action, some workers created self-defense organizations. In response to the self-defense organizations, some state governments, such as Illinois's, enacted laws against armed public parades.[311]

Defying the Illinois Statue, a self-defense organization composed of German working-class immigrants defied the law, and held a parade in which one of the leaders carried an unloaded rifle. At trial, the leader—Herman Presser—argued that the Illinois law violated the Second Amendment.

The Supreme Court ruled against him unanimously. First, the Court held that the Illinois ban on armed parades "does not infringe the right of the people to keep and bear arms."[312] This holding was consistent with traditional common law boundaries on the right to arms, which prohibited terrifyingly large assemblies of armed men.[313]

310. *Id.* at 286-88.

311. *See* Levinson, *supra* note 9; Stephen Halbrook, *The Right of Workers to Assemble and to Bear Arms: Presser v. Illinois, Last Holdout Against Application of the Bill of Rights to the States*, 76 U. DET. MERCY L. REV. (1999, forthcoming).

312. Presser v. Illinois, 116 U.S. 252, 265 (1886).

313. 1 WILLIAM HAWKINS, A TREATISE OF THE PLEAS OF THE CROWN 126 (Garland Publ. 1978) (1716) (A Justice of the Peace may require surety from persons who "go about with unusual Weapons or Attendants, to the Terror of the People.")

Further, the Second Amendment by its own force "is a limitation only upon the power of Congress and the National Government, and not upon that of the States."[314]

Did some other part of the Constitution make the Second Amendment enforceable against the states? The Court added that the Illinois law did not appear to interfere with any of the "privileges or immunities" of citizens of the United States.[315] Although the Court never actually used the words "Fourteenth Amendment," it is reasonable to read *Presser* as holding that the Fourteenth Amendment's Privileges and Immunities clause does not restrict state interference with keeping and bearing arms. This reading is consistent with all the other Fourteenth Amendment cases from the Supreme Court in the 1870s and 1880s, which consistently reject the proposition that any part of the Bill of Rights is among the "Privileges and Immunities" protected by the Fourteenth Amendment.[316]

As to whether the Second Amendment might be protected by another part of the Fourteenth Amendment—the clause forbidding states to deprive a person of life, liberty, or property without due process of law[317]—the Court had nothing to say. The theory that the Due Process clause of the Fourteenth Amendment might protect substantive constitutional rights had not yet been invented. Most of what the Waite Court had to say about Bill of Rights incorporation has long since been repudiated (although not always formally overruled) by subsequent courts, via the Due Process clause.

It is true that some modern lower courts cling to *Presser* and claim that *Presser* prevents them from addressing a litigant's claim that a state statute violates the Second Amendment.[318] It is hard to take such judicial arguments seriously. An 1886 decision about Privileges and Immunities is hardly binding precedent for 1990s Due Process. The *dicta* from the modern Supreme Court about the Second Amendment as a possible Fourteenth Amendment liberty interest is incompatible with the claim that *Presser* forecloses any possible theory of incorporating the Second Amendment. At most, *Presser* rejects Privileges and Immunities incorporation, but the case cannot be read to address a legal theory (Due Process incorporation) which did not exist at the time the case was decided.

Interestingly, *Presser* does offer another theory on which the United States Constitution might restrict state anti-gun laws. Article I, section 8, clauses 15 and 16 give Congress various powers over the militia.[319] States may not interfere with these Congressional militia powers; so in *dicta*, the *Presser* Court stated that the states could not disarm the public so as to deprive the federal government of its militia:

> *It is undoubtedly true that all citizens capable of bearing arms constitute the reserved military force or reserve militia of the United States, and, in view of this prerogative of the general government. . .the States cannot, even laying the Constitutional provision in question [the Second Amendment] out of view, prohibit the people from keeping and bearing arms, so as to deprive the United States of their rightful resource for*

314. *Presser*, 116 U.S. at 265.
315. *Id.* at 266.
316. *Id*.
317. U.S. Const., amend. XIV, § 1.
318. *E.g.*, Fresno Rifle Club v. Van de Kamp, 965 F.2d 723 (9th Cir. 1992).
319. *Id.* at 265.

> *maintaining the public security, and disable the people from performing their duty to the general government. But, as already stated, we think it clear that the sections under consideration do not have this effect.*[320]

So according to *Presser*, the constitutional militia includes "all citizens capable of bearing arms."[321] But this statement is not directly about the Second Amendment; it is about Congressional powers to use the militia under Article I, section 8, clauses 15 and 16.

V. The Chase, Taney, and Marshall Courts

The majority of the Chase Court was just as hostile to a broad reading of the Fourteenth Amendment as was the Waite Court; unsurprisingly, the Chase Court rejected the idea that Congress could use the Fourteenth Amendment to legislate against private interference with First or Second Amendment rights. At the same time, the Chase Court described the First Amendment assembly right and the Second Amendment arms rights as fundamental human rights which pre-existed the Constitution.

One of the most notable cases of the nineteenth century, *Dred Scott*, used the Second Amendment to support arguments about other subjects; the arguments recognized the Second Amendment right as an individual one.

And the very first Supreme Court opinion to mention the Second Amendment—Justice Story's dissent in *Houston* v. *Moore*—is so obscure that even most Second Amendment specialists are unfamiliar with it. It is analogous to the *Hamilton* case, in that it uses the Second Amendment to underscore state militia powers.

---

320. *Id.* at 265-66.

321. *Id.* For the subsequent interpretation of *Presser*, see Malloy v. Hogan, *supra* note 184 (Second Amendment is not a Fourteenth Amendment Privilege or Immunity); Poe v. Ullman, *supra* note 204 (Harlan, J., dissenting) (Fourteenth Amendment liberty is not co-extensive with Bill of Rights); Adamson v. California, *supra* note 222 (Black, J., dissenting) (Second Amendment not directly applicable against states); Twining v. New Jersey, *supra* note 264 (Second Amendment not a Fourteenth Amendment Privilege or Immunity); Maxwell v. Dow, *supra* note 266 (Second Amendment not directly applicable to states); Brown v. Walker, *supra* note 284 (same); Miller v. Texas, *supra* notes 291-96 (Second Amendment not directly applicable, not a Privilege or Immunity) but enforcement against states via Fourteenth Amendment is an open question; Spies v. Illinois, *supra* note 303 (Second Amendment not directly applicable against states); Eilenbecker, *supra* note 304 (same).

A. United States v. Cruikshank

An important part of Congress's work during Reconstruction was the Enforcement Acts, which criminalized private conspiracies to violate civil rights.[322] Among the civil rights violations which especially concerned Congress was the disarmament of Freedmen by the Ku Klux Klan and similar gangs.[323]

After a rioting band of whites burned down a Louisiana courthouse which was occupied by group of armed blacks (following the disputed 1872 elections), the whites and their leader, Klansman William Cruikshank, were prosecuted under the Enforcement Acts. Cruikshank was convicted of conspiring to deprive the blacks of the rights they had been granted by the Constitution, including the right peaceably to assemble and the right to bear arms.[324]

In *United States* v. *Cruikshank*, the Supreme Court held the Enforcement Acts unconstitutional. The Fourteenth Amendment did give Congress the power to prevent interference with rights granted by the Constitution, said the Court. But the right to assemble and the right to arms were not rights granted or created by the Constitution, because they were fundamental human rights that pre-existed the Constitution:

> *The right of the people peaceably to assemble for lawful purposes* existed long before *the adoption of the Constitution of the United States. In fact, it is, and always has been, one of the attributes of citizenship under a free government. It "derives its source," to use the language of Chief Justice Marshall, in* Gibbons v. Ogden*, 9 Wheat. 211, "from those laws whose authority is acknowledged by civilized man throughout the world." It is found wherever civilization exists. It was not, therefore, a right granted to the people by the Constitution. The government of the United States when established found it in existence, with the obligation on the part of the States to afford it protection.*[325]

A few pages later, the Court made the same point about the right to arms as a fundamental human right:

> *The right. . . of bearing arms for a lawful purpose. . . is not a right granted by the Constitution. Neither is it in any manner dependent on that instrument for its existence. The second amendment declares that it shall not be infringed; but this. . . means no more than it shall not be infringed by Congress. . . leaving the people to look for their protection against any violation by their fellow citizens of the rights it recognizes, to*

322. 16 Stat. 140 § 6 (1870); 18 U.S.C. §§ 241, 242: "That if two or more persons shall band or conspire together, or go in disguise upon the public highway, or upon the premises of another. . .or intimidate any citizen with intent to prevent or hinder his free exercise and enjoyment of any right or privilege secured or granted him by the Constitution or laws of the United States. . . ."

323. STEPHEN HALBROOK, FREEDMEN, FIREARMS, AND THE FOURTEENTH AMENDMENT (1998); ERIC FONER, RECONSTRUCTION 258-59 (1988); Richard L. Aynes, *On Misreading John Bingham and the Fourteenth Amendment*, 103 Yale L.J. 57 (1993).

324. GEORGE C. RABLE, BUT THERE WAS NO PEACE: THE ROLE OF VIOLENCE IN THE POLITICS OF RECONSTRUCTION 125-29 (Athens Univ. of Georgia Pr., 1984).

325. United States v. Cruikshank, 92 U.S. 542, 551 (1875) (emphasis added).

what is called . . .the "powers which relate to merely municipal legislation. . . ."[326]

According to *Cruikshank*, the individual's right to arms is protected by the Second Amendment, but not created by it, because the right derives from natural law. The Court's statement that the freedmen must "look for their protection against any violation by their fellow citizens of the rights" that the Second Amendment recognizes is comprehensible only under the individual rights view. If individuals have a right to own a gun, then individuals can ask local governments to protect them against "fellow citizens" who attempt to disarm them. In contrast, if the Second Amendment right belongs to the state governments as protection against federal interference, then mere "fellow citizens" could not infringe that right by disarming mere individuals.

Cruikshank has occasionally been cited (without explanation) for the proposition that the Second Amendment right belongs only to the state militias, although *Cruikshank* has nothing to say about states or militias.[327]

Cruikshank was also cited in *dicta* in later cases as supporting the theory that the Second Amendment and the rest of Bill of Rights are not enforceable against the states[328] (even though the facts of *Cruikshank* involve private actors, not state actors). That theory, obviously, has long since been abandoned by the Supreme Court. Among the earlier cases to reject non-incorporation was *DeJonge* v. *Oregon*, holding that the right peaceably to assemble (one of the two rights at issue in *Cruikshank*) was guaranteed by the 14th Amendment.[329] And as discussed above, *Cruikshank's* dicta about the Fourteenth Amendment "Privileges and Immunities" is no more binding on modern courts than is *Presser's* statement on the same subject several years later.

B. Scott v. Sandford

Holding that a free black could not be an American citizen,[330] the *Dred Scott* majority opinion listed the unacceptable consequences of black

326. *Id.* at 553 *quoting* New York v. Miln, 36 U.S. (11 Pet.) 125, 139 (1837). *Cf.* Bliss v. Commonwealth, 12 Ky. (2 Litt.) 90, 92, 13 Am. Dec. 251, 253 ("The right [to arms in the Kentucky Constitution] existed at the adoption of the constitution; it had no limits short of the moral power of the citizens to exercise it, and it in fact consisted in nothing else but the liberty of the citizens to bear arms.").

327. "The Second Amendment protects only the right of the states to maintain and equip a militia and does not guarantee individuals the right to bear arms; *United States* v. *Cruikshank* (1875)." C. HERMAN PRITCHETT, THE AMERICAN CONSTITUTION 397 n. 1 (2d ed. McGraw-Hill, 1968).

328. Malloy v. Hogan, *supra* note 186; Knapp v. Schweitzer, *supra* note 208. For different interpretations of *Cruiksbank*, see Spies v. Illinois, *supra* note 303 (Second Amendment not directly applicable to states); Eilenbecker, *supra* note 304 (same); Logon v. United States, *supra* note 309 (First Amendment assembly right and Second Amendment arms right are similar; Bill of Rights protects neither against private interference).

329. DeJonge v. Oregon, 299 U.S. 353 (1937).

330. Scott v. Sandford, 60 U.S. (19 How.) 393 (1856). Among Chief Justice Taney's proofs that free blacks were not citizens was the fact that blacks were often excluded from militia service. The Taney opinion explained that the parties to the original American social compact were only those "who, at that time [American independence], were recognized as the people or citizens of a State, whose rights and liberties had been outraged by the English Government; and who declared their independence, and assumed the powers of Government to defend their rights by force of arms." *Id.* at 407. The new nation's federal militia law of 1792 had enrolled only free white males in the militia of the United States, and blacks had been excluded from the New Hampshire militia. *Id.* at 420. These facts suggested to Chief Justice Taney that free blacks were not recognized as citizens, since they were not in the militia.

Justice Curtis retorted by pointing to the language of the 1792 Militia Act, which enrolled "every free, able-bodied, white male citizen." Justice Curtis pointed out the implication of the language that "citizens" included people who were not able-bodied, were not male, or were not white; otherwise, there would have been no need to limit militia membership of able-bodied white males. *Id.* at 442 (Curtis, J., dissenting). But Justice Curtis's argument had one problem: the use of the word "free" in the Militia Act. It was undisputed that slaves were not citizenship: Black citizens would have the right to enter any state, to stay there as long as they pleased, and within that state they could go where they wanted at any hour of the day or night, unless they committed some act for which a white person could be punished.[331] Further, black citizens would have "the right to. . .full liberty of speech in public and private upon all subjects which [a state's] own citizens might meet; to hold public meetings upon political affairs, and to keep and carry arms wherever they went."[332]

Thus, Chief Justice Taney claimed that the "right to. . .keep and carry arms" (like "the right to. . .full liberty of speech," and like the right to interstate travel without molestation, and like the "the right to. . .hold public meetings on political affairs") was a right of American citizenship. The only logical source of these rights is the United States Constitution. While the right to travel is not textually stated in the Constitution, it has been found there by implication.[333] As for the rest of the rights mentioned by the Taney majority, they appear to be rephrasings of explicit rights contained in the Bill of Rights. Instead of "freedom of speech," Justice Taney discussed "liberty of speech"; instead of the right "peaceably to assemble", he discussed the right "to hold meetings", and instead of the right to "keep and bear arms," he discussed the right to "keep and carry arms."[334]

Although resolution of the citizenship issue was sufficient to end the *Dred Scott* case, the Taney majority decided to address what it considered to be an error in the opinion of the circuit court. Much more than the citizenship holding, the part of *Dred Scott* that created a firestorm of opposition among the northern white population was *Dred Scott's* conclusion that Congress had no power to outlaw slavery in a territory, as Congress had done in the 1820 Missouri Compromise, for the future Territory of Nebraska.[335] Chief Justice Taney's treatment of the question began with the universal assumption that the Bill of Rights constrained Congressional legislation in the territories.

> *No one, we presume, will contend that Congress can make any law in a territory respecting the establishment of religion, or the free exercise thereof, or abridging the freedom of speech or of the press, or the right of*

citizens, since they were deprived of all rights of citizenship. The Militia Act enrolled only "free, able-bodied, white male citizens." If we follow Justice Curtis's logic to conclude that the Militia Act proves that non-whites could be citizens, then the same logic would show that unfree persons could be citizens.

The stronger part of the Curtis dissent was his evidence showing that many of the thirteen original states did recognize blacks as citizens. The Taney majority never directly addressed this part of the Curtis argument, except by listing various disabilities (such as prohibitions on racial intermarriage, or bans on operating schools for blacks) which even anti-slavery states like Massachusetts and Connecticut imposed on free blacks. Thus, in a bizarre way, the Taney majority (despite its pro-slavery taint) pre-figures twentieth century Supreme Court jurisprudence that there can be no second-class citizens in the United States. The Curtis opinion argues that various civil disabilities (including exclusion from the militia) are consistent with citizenship. For the Taney majority, citizenship is all or nothing; exclusion from education, from intermarriage with whites, or from the militia are all incompatible with citizenship. Thus, once a constitutional amendment conclusively declared that blacks are citizens, the logic of the *Dred Scott* majority leads to the results in Brown v. Board, 349 U.S. 294 (1955) (racial discrimination in schooling is incompatible with citizenship rights); Loving v. Virginia, 388 U.S. 1 (1967) (laws against intermarriage are incompatible with citizenship rights); and Bell v. Maryland, 378 U.S. 226, 260 (1964) (segregation in restaurants and lunch counters "is a badge of second-class citizenship."); *Id* at 288 (Douglas, J., concurring) ("The Thirteenth, Fourteenth, and Fifteenth Amendments do not permit Negroes to be considered as second-class citizens in any aspect of our public life."). In contrast, the Curtis dissent (while laudably humane in its anti-slavery sentiments) allows for second-class citizenship on the basis of race.

331. *Id.* at 417.

332. *Id*.

333. *See, e.g.*, Edwards v. California, 314 U.S. 160, 168 (1994) (Douglas, J., concurring); Slaughter-House Cases, 83 U.S. (16 Wall.) 36, 79 (1873).

334. *Scott*, 60 U.S. at 417.

335. Act of Mar. 6, 1820, ch. 22, 8, 3 Stat. 545, 548.

> *the people of the territory peaceably to assemble and to petition the government for redress of grievances.*
>
> *Nor can Congress deny to the people the right to keep and bear arms, nor the right to trial by jury, nor compel anyone to be a witness against itself in a criminal proceeding.*[336]

From the universal assumption that Congress could not infringe the Bill of Rights in the territories, Taney concluded that Congress could not infringe the property rights of slave-owners by abolishing slavery in the territories.[337]

The Taney Court obviously considered the Second Amendment as one of the constitutional rights belonging to individual Americans. The Henigan "state's rights" Second Amendment could have no application in a territory, since a territorial government is by definition not a state government. And since Chief Justice Taney was discussing individual rights which Congress could not infringe, the only reasonable way to read the Chief Justice's reference to the Second Amendment is as a reference to an individual right. Nor can the opinion of Chief Justice Taney (which was shared by six members of the Court on the citizenship issue, and by five on the Territories issue) be dismissed as casual dicta. The Court knew that *Dred Scott* would be one the most momentous cases ever decided, as the Court deliberately thrust itself in the raging national controversy over slavery. The case was argued in two different terms, and the Chief Justice's opinion began by noting that "the questions in controversy are of the highest importance."[338]

And unlike most Supreme Court cases, *Dred Scott* became widely known among the general population. The majority's statement listing the right to arms as one of several individual constitutional rights which Congress could not infringe was widely quoted during antebellum debates regarding Congressional power over slavery.[339]

Dred Scott's holding about black citizenship was overruled by the first sentence of the Fourteenth Amendment, which states that all persons born in the Untied States are citizens of the United States.[340] *Dred Scott*, which had exacerbated rather than cooled the North-South anger which eventually caused the Civil War, became so universally despised that many people forgot the details of what the case actually said. After the Spanish-American War, the United States acquired the new territories of Cuba, Puerto Rico, and the Philippines, and acquired Hawaii after that nation's government was overthrown in a coup orchestrated by American farming interests. Thus, the Supreme Court, in *The Insular Cases*, was forced to determine the constitutional status of the new imperial territories.[341] In *Downes* v. *Bidwell*, the Court majority held that, despite the constitutional requirement that

---

336. *Scott*, 60 U.S. at 450.
337. *Id.* at 450-51.
338. *Id.* at 399.
339. *See, e.g.*, Stephen Douglas, *The Dividing Line Between Federal and Local Authority: Popular Sovereignty in the Territories*, HARPER'S (Sept. 1859) 519, 530.
340. U.S. Const., amend. XIV, § 1 ("All persons born or naturalized in the United States and subject to the jurisdiction thereof, are citizens of the Untied States and of the State wherein they reside.")
341. Dorr v. United States, 195 U.S. 138 (1904); Hawaii v. Mankichi, 190 U.S. 197 (1903) (Sixth Amendment requirement for unanimous jury not applicable in territory of Hawaii; only "fundamental" constitutional rights apply in the territories); De Lima v. Bidwell 182 U.S. 1 (1901) (Puerto Rican goods imported to the states are not subject to the tariff applicable to foreign imports); Dooley v. United States, 182 U.S. 222 (1901) (goods transported from the states to Puerto Rico not subject to tariff applicable to foreign imports to Puerto Rico); Downes v. Bidwell, 182 U.S. 244 (1901) (In taxing imports from Puerto Rico to the states, Congress need not obey the constitutional requirement that taxes imposed by Congress be uniform throughout the United States).

taxes imposed by Congress be uniform throughout the United States, Puerto Rico could be taxed at a different rate; Justice Henry Billings Brown's five-man majority explicitly worried that a contrary result would force the Bill of Rights to be applied in the new territories. Writing to Justice John Harlan to applaud Harlan's dissenting opinion,[342] a New York attorney exclaimed that the majority opinion was "the *Dred Scott* of Imperialism!"[343] But if the *Insular Cases* Court had followed *Dred Scott*, then Justice Harlan and the other three dissenters would have been in the majority; for *Dred Scott* stated that the Bill of Rights did apply in the territories.

Although the citizenship holding in *Dred Scott* was so controversial that it was repudiated by a constitutional amendment, the case's treatment of the Second Amendment as an individual right was not; in each of the six times that the Court addressed the Second Amendment in the rest of the nineteenth century, the Court always treated the Second Amendment as an individual right.

C. Houston v. Moore

The very first case in which a Supreme Court opinion mentioned the Second Amendment was *Houston v. Moore*, an 1821 case so obscure that even modern scholars of the Second Amendment are often unaware of it.[344] Part of the reason is that, thanks to a small error, the case cannot be discovered via a Lexis or Westlaw search for "Second Amendment."

The *Houston* case grew out of a Pennsylvania man's refusal to appear for federal militia duty during the War of 1812. The failure to appear violated a federal statute, as well as a Pennsylvania statute that was a direct copy of the federal statute. When Mr. Houston was prosecuted and convicted in a Pennsylvania court martial for violating the Pennsylvania statute, his attorney argued that only the federal government, not Pennsylvania, had the authority to bring a prosecution; the Pennsylvania statute was alleged to be a state infringement of the federal powers over the militia.

When the case reached the Supreme Court, both sides offered extensive arguments over Article I, section 8, clauses 15 and 16, in the Constitution, which grant Congress certain powers over the militia.[345] Responding to Houston's argument that Congressional power over the national militia is plenary (and therefore Pennsylvania had no authority to punish someone for failing to perform federal militia service), the State of Pennsylvania lawyers retorted that Congressional power over the militia was concurrent with state power, not exclusive.[346] In support of this theory, they pointed to the Tenth Amendment, which reserves to states all powers not granted to the federal government.[347]

342. *Downes*, 182 U.S. at 379 (Harlan, J., dissenting).

343. Richard Warren Barkley, letter of May 28, 1901, to John Marshall Harlan, *quoted in* TINSLEY E. YARBOROUGH, JUDICIAL ENIGMA: THE FIRST JUSTICE HARLAN 197 (1995).

344. Houston v. Moore, 18 U.S. (5 Wheat.) 1 (1820).

345. "To provide for calling forth the Militia to execute the Laws of the Union, suppress Insurrections and repel Invasions." "To provide for organizing, arming, and disciplining, the Militia, and for governing such Part of them as may be employed in the Service of the United States, reserving to the States respectively, the Appointment of the Officers, and the Authority of training the Militia according to the discipline prescribed by Congress."

346. *Houston*, 18 U.S. at 6.

347. U.S. CONST. amend. X.

If, as Henigan, Bogus, and some other modern writers claim, the only purpose of the Second Amendment were to guard state government control over the militia, then the Second Amendment ought to have been the heart of the State of Pennsylvania's argument. But instead, Pennsylvania resorted to the Tenth Amendment to make the "state's right" argument. There are two possibilities to explain the State of Pennsylvania's lawyering. First, the Pennsylvania attorneys committed malpractice, by failing to cite the Constitutional provision that was directly on point (the Second Amendment's supposed guarantee of state government control of the militia). Instead, the Pennsylvania lawyers cited a Constitutional provision which made the state's right argument only in a general sense, rather than in relation to the militia. The other possibility is that the State of Pennsylvania lawyers were competent, and they relied on the Tenth Amendment, rather than the Second, because the Tenth guarantees state's rights, and the Second guarantees an individual right.

Justice Bushrod Washington delivered the opinion of the Court, holding that the Pennsylvania law was constitutional, because Congress had not forbidden the states to enact such laws enforcing the federal militia statute.[348] Moreover, because Houston had never showed up for the militia muster, he had never entered federal service; thus, Houston was still under the jurisdiction of the State of Pennsylvania.[349] Justice William Johnson concurred; he argued that Houston could not be prosecuted for violating the federal law; accordingly, he could be prosecuted for violating the state law.[350]

The Washington and Johnson opinions, therefore, upheld a state's authority over militiaman Houston. Like the attorneys on both sides of the case, neither Justice Washington nor Justice Johnson suggested that the Second Amendment had anything to do with the case.

Justice Joseph Story, a consistent supporter of federal government authority, dissented.[351] He argued that the Congressional legislation punishing militia resisters was exclusive, and left the states no room to act.[352]

Deep in the lengthy dissent, Justice Story raised a hypothetical: What if Congress had not used its militia powers? If Congress were inert, and ignored the militia, could the states act? "Yes," he answered:

> *If, therefore, the present case turned upon the question, whether a state might organize, arm and discipline its own militia, in the absence of, or subordinate to, the regulations of congress, I am certainly not prepared to deny the legitimacy of such an exercise of authority. It does not seem repugnant in its nature to the grant of a like paramount authority to congress; and if not, then it is retained by the states. The fifth [sic] amendment to the constitution, declaring that "a well-regulated militia being necessary to the security of a free state, the right of the people to keep and bear arms shall not be infringed," may not, perhaps, be thought*

348. *Houston*, 18 U.S.at 46-47.
349. *Id.*
350. *Id.*
351. This was the only time that Justice Story dissented from a constitutional decision in which Chief Justice Marshall was in the majority. JAMES MCCLELLAN, JOSEPH STORY AND THE AMERICAN CONSTITUTION 311 n. 161 (2d ed. 1990).
352. *Houston*, 18 U.S. at 46-47.

to have any important bearing on this point. If it have, it confirms and illustrates, rather than impugns, the reasoning already suggested.[353]

After acknowledging that the Second Amendment (mislabeled the "fifth" amendment in a typo) was probably irrelevant, Justice Story suggested that to the extent the Second Amendment did matter, it supported his position.

Justice Story's dissent is inconsistent with the Henigan/Bogus theory that Second Amendment somehow reduces Congress's militia powers. Immediately, after the Second Amendment hypothetical, Justice Story stated that if Congress actually did use its Article I powers over the militia, then Congressional power was exclusive. There could be no state control, "however small."[354] If federal militia powers, when exercised, are absolute, then the Henigan/Bogus theory that the Second Amendment limits federal militia powers is incorrect.

The Story dissent in *Houston* does not address the issue of individual Second Amendment rights. Justice Story laid out a fuller explication of the Second Amendment in his *Commentaries on the Constitution of the United States*, and his *Familiar Exposition of the Constitution of the United States*. The *Familiar Exposition* has the longest analysis of the Second Amendment:

> *The next amendment is, "A well-regulated militia being necessary to the security of a free state, the right of the people to keep and bear arms shall not be infringed." One of the ordinary modes, by which tyrants accomplish their purposes without resistance, is, by disarming the people, and making it an offence to keep arms, and by substituting a regular army in the stead of a resort to the militia. The friends of a free government cannot be too watchful, to overcome the dangerous tendency of the public mind to sacrifice, for the sake of mere private convenience, this powerful check upon the designs of ambitious men.*
>
> *The importance of this article will scarcely be doubted by any persons, who have duly reflected upon the subject. The militia is the natural defence of a free country against sudden foreign invasions, domestic insurrections, and domestic usurpations of power by rulers. It is against sound policy for a free people to keep up large military establishments and standing armies in time of peace, both from the enormous expenses, with which they are attended, and the facile means, which they afford to ambitious and unprincipled rulers, to subvert the government, or trample upon the rights of the people. The right of the citizens to keep and bear arms has justly been considered, as the palladium of the liberties of a republic; since it offers a strong moral check against the usurpation and arbitrary power of rulers; and will generally, even if these are successful in the first instance, enable the people to resist and triumph over them. And yet, though this truth would seem so clear, and the importance of a well regulated militia would seem so undeniable, it cannot be disguised, that among the American people there is a growing indifference to any system of militia discipline, and a strong disposition, from a sense of its burthens, to be rid of all regulations. How it is*

353. *Id.* at 47-48 (Story, J., dissenting)..

354. The Supreme Court decided one other militia case during this period. Writing for a unanimous Court, Justice Story held that the President's determination of the need for a militia call-out was not subject to judicial review. *See* Martin v. Mott, 25 U.S. (12 Wheat.) 19 (1827).

> *practicable to keep the people duly armed without some organization, it is difficult to see. There is certainly no small danger, that indifference may lead to disgust, and disgust to contempt; and thus gradually undermine all the protection intended by this clause of our national bill of rights.*[355]

The Justice's Second Amendment is obviously an individual right, intended to prevent the tyrannical tactic of "making it an offence to keep arms." The purpose of arms possession is to facilitate a militia, and the purpose of the militia is to suppress disorder from below (in the form of riots) and from above (in the form of tyranny). In contrast to some twentieth century commentators,[356] Justice Story shared the conventional wisdom of the nineteenth century[357]: removing a tyrannical government would not be "insurrection" but instead would be the restoration of constitutional law and order.

Conclusion

In addition to the oft-debated case of *United States* v. *Miller,*[358] the Supreme Court has mentioned or quoted the Second Amendment in thirty-seven opinions in thirty-five other cases, almost always in *dicta*. One of the opinions, Justice Douglas's dissent in *Adams v. Williams,* explicitly claims that the Second Amendment is not an individual right.[359] Three majority opinions of the Court (the 1980 *Lewis* case,[360] the 1934 *Hamilton* case,[361] and the 1929 *Schwimmer* case[362]), plus one appeal dismissal (*Burton v. Sills,* 1969[363]), and one dissent (Douglas in *Laird*[364]) are consistent with either the individual rights or the states rights theory, although *Lewis* is better read as not supportive of an individual right, or not supportive of an individual right worthy of any serious protection. (And knowing of Justice Douglas's later dissent in *Adams,* his *Laird* dissent should not be construed as supportive of an individual right.) *Spencer v. Kemna* refers to right to bear arms as an individual right, but the opinion does not specifically mention the Second Amendment, and so the reference could, perhaps, be to the right established by state constitutions.[365]

Two other cases are complicated by off-the-bench statements of the Justices. The 1976 *Moore v. East Cleveland* plurality opinion supports the individual right,[366] but in 1989 the opinion's author, retired Justice Powell, told a television interviewer that there was no right to own a firearm. In an

355. JOSEPH STORY, A FAMILIAR EXPOSITION OF THE CONSTITUTION OF THE UNITED STATES 264-65 (1842) For more on Justice Story's thoughts about the Second Amendment, *see* Kopel, *The Second Amendment in the Nineteenth Century, supra* note 4, at 119-20.
356. *See, e.g.,* Henigan, *Arms, Anarchy, supra* note 5.
357. *See* Kopel, *The Second Amendment in the Nineteenth Century*, *supra* note 7, at 1388-97.
358. United States v. Miller, 307 U.S. 174 (1939), *supra* notes 16-27.
359. Adams v. Williams, 407 U.S. 143, 150-51 (1972) (Douglas, J., dissenting), *supra* note 141.
360. Lewis v. United States, 445 U.S. 55, 65-66 (1980), *supra* note 103.
361. Hamilton v. Regents of the Univ. of California, 293 U.S. 245, 260-61 (1934), *supra* note 238.
362. United States v. Schwimmer, 279 U.S. 644, 650-52 (1929), *supra* note 253.
363. Burton v. Sills, 394 U.S. 812 (1969), *supra* note 170.
364. Laird v. Tatum, 408 U.S. 1, 22-23 (1972), *supra* note 163.
365. Spencer v. Kemna, 523 U.S. 1, 36 (1998) (Stevens, J., dissenting), *supra* note 42.
366. Moore v. East Cleveland, 431 U.S. 494, 502 (1976), *supra* note 120.

1820 dissent, Justice Story pointed to the Second Amendment to make a point about state authority over the militia (although this would not necessarily be to the exclusion of an individual right).[367] Justice Story's later scholarly commentaries on the Second Amendment only addressed the individual right, and did not investigate the Amendment as a basis of state authority.[368]

Concurring in *Printz*, Justice Thomas stated that *United States v. Miller* had not resolved the individual rights question; the tone of the concurrence suggested that Justice Thomas considered the Second Amendment to be an important individual right.[369]

Twenty-eight opinions remain, including nineteen majority opinions. Each of these opinions treats the Second Amendment as a right of individual American citizens. Of these twenty-eight opinions, five come from the present Rehnquist Court, and on the Rehnquist Court there has been no disagreement that the Second Amendment is an individual right.

Of course that fact that a right exists does not mean that every proposed gun control would violate that right; indeed, many of the opinions explicitly or implicitly endorse various controls, and, except for Justice Black, none of the authors of the opinions claim that the right is absolute.[370]

In the face of this Supreme Court record, is it accurate for gun control advocates to claim that the non-individual nature of the Second Amendment is "perhaps the most well-settled" point in all of American constitutional law?[371] The extravagant claim cannot survive a reading of what the Supreme Court has actually said about the Second Amendment. In the written opinions of the Justices of the United States Supreme Court, the Second Amendment does appear to be reasonably well-settled—as an individual right. The argument that a particular Supreme Court opinion's language about the Second Amendment does not reflect what the author "really" thought about the Second Amendment cannot be used to ignore all these written opinions—unless we presume that Supreme Court Justices throughout the Republic's history have written things about the Second Amendment that they did not mean.

While the Warren Court and the Burger Court offered mixed records on the Second Amendment, the opinions from the Rehnquist Court (including from the Court's "liberals" Ginsburg and Stevens) are just as clear as were the opinions from the Supreme Court Justices of the nineteenth century: "the right of the people to keep and bear arms" is a right that belongs to individual American citizens. Although the boundaries of the Second Amendment have only partially been addressed by Supreme Court jurisprudence, the core of the Second Amendment is clear: the Second Amendment—like the First, Third, Fourth, Fifth, Sixth, and Fourteenth Amendments—belongs to "the people," not the government.

---

367. Houston v. Moore, 18 U.S. (5 Wheat.) 1, 47-48 (1820) (Story, J., dissenting), *supra* note 352.
368. *See* STORY, *supra* note 354.
369. Printz v. United States, 521 U.S. 898, 938-39 (1997) (Thomas, J., concurring), *supra* note 64.
370. Justice Black did view the entire Bill of Rights as absolute within it terms. He explicitly so stated with regard to the Second Amendment in his James Madison lecture at New York University. It might be reasonable to read Justice Black's Supreme Court opinions which mention the Second Amendment as reflecting his absolutist view. See *supra* text at notes 179-82, 194-96, 221-34.
371. *Supra* note 3.

Text of the Supreme Court's Gun Cases

by *Alan Korwin and David B. Kopel*

Notes and Cautions
Forty-four decisions presented here are complete and unedited. The rest are excerpted to preserve gun-related portions only. This is noted beneath the title of each case. The complete text of most cases may be obtained on the Internet at www.findlaw.com/casecode/supreme.html and other sites. Online copies, upon which this portion of *Supreme Court Gun Cases* is largely based, are known to have some small differences from the official court decisions, and these will be faithfully reproduced here, such as typos, spellings, or occasionally unusual typesetting styles (ellipses, em dashes, hyphenation, etc.). The only official copy is *U.S. Reports,* which should be used exclusively for any legal matters. See the disclaimer in the front section of this book for other important warnings and information.

Omissions within excerpts are noted by a set of five dots at the left margin.

Editorial comments are in <angle brackets> and are not part of the opinions.

The syllabus is a non-binding abstract prepared by the court, and appears in italics in cases that have one included.

Gists were prepared specifically for this book, precede each case, and are intended to provide an easily readable overview in regular conversational terms for your convenience. The casual reader should be able to enjoy this book by reading the gists and passing over the sometimes complex verbiage of the cases themselves. However, while great care has been taken to produce the gists with a high degree of accuracy, no guarantee of accuracy is expressed or implied, and none of the explanatory sections of this book are to be considered as legal advice or a restatement of law.

Highlighted quotations have been edited for readability and appear right before the paragraph in which they occur verbatim. Highlighted quotations are never drawn from the syllabus. No attempt to sum up or distill the meaning of a case is made or intended by the highlighted quotes. That is the function of the Gist entries.

The highlights serve to showcase the juicier, more dramatic passages of the Court's published decisions **irrespective of the case outcome**, and to aid in navigation, and to help alleviate what some might inexplicably be inclined to criticize in spots as a rather dry text.

Experts can disagree on what the core holding of a case and its effect may be (just consider the 1939 *U.S. v. Miller* decision), and it is certainly not something attempted by the highlighted quotes. Many times, the key judicial phrase has all the charm and lucidity of "reversed and remanded."

In contrast, the Court's history and indeed the nation's is held within the pages of its High Court records. It is this captivating essence the highlights aspire to illuminate. A strong sense emerges of how very gun-conscious the Supreme Court has consistently been over the centuries.

Serious effort was made to highlight quotations evenly on all sides of the gun debate, but the material was simply lopsided. For the collectivist and anti-rights arguments, there isn't very much in here to get excited about. There are several opinions in the last few decades that express a very negative view of guns, or that question where the limits of infringement rest, but that's about it.

You must take special care to note from within context whether a given quotation is part of the decision of the Court, dissenting opinions, concurrences, the facts of the case, the arguments of the parties, pleadings, *dicta* statements by the Court, quotes from other cases, jury instructions, footnotes, reference material quoted in the case, or other language included in the official published decision.

You should also keep an eye out for inconsistent or potentially confusing nomenclature, since the person at the center of a case might be called the plaintiff, respondent, petitioner, appellee, accused, defendant or prisoner.

More difficult still is the resolution of comments that don't agree with each other, and the question of whether a comment is still valid or even meaningful in light of later cases, recent statutes and a new day. Some subjects experience wholesale reversal, like the 14th Amendment's applicability to the states, or the legality of slavery. **If you decide to run off and mouth quotes without carefully checking context you're at great risk of making a fool of yourself.** Always check the *in situ* verbatim language in the paragraph immediately after the highlighted quotes, and other indicators, for context, relevance and meaning.

Although an effort was made initially to highlight gun-specific language, which turned out to be quite revealing if for nothing else than in its copious breadth, all eye-opening passages became candidates for the highlighter as the review process wore on. This being a human endeavor, the reader will no doubt find sections that definitely should or should not be included to personal taste. Permission to use a marker in your own copy of the book is granted.

Complaints regarding the highlighted quotes should be directed solely to Alan Korwin as this element of *Supreme Court Gun Cases*, as well as final responsibility for the Gists, rests upon his desk. He readily admits he could not have done it without invaluable assistance and direct contributions from Dave Kopel, Jerod Tufte and others, duly noted in the acknowledgments, but the buck for the final product stops with him.

HOUSTON v. MOORE

(CASE EXCERPT)
18 U.S. 1; 5 L. Ed. 19; 5 Wheat. 1
FEBRUARY, 1820 Term

GIST: The High Court's first known mention of the 2nd Amendment occurs in a very lengthy decision, as a brief remark in a dissent.

After a man named Houston failed to appear when summoned for militia duty during the War of 1812, he was tried and convicted by the State of Pennsylvania for violating a Pennsylvania statute against failing to perform federal militia service. Houston argued that the Pennsylvania legislature could not enact such a statute, because the statute was inconsistent with federal powers over the militia, since Congress had passed a law providing punishment for people who failed to perform federal militia service. The majority of the Supreme Court disagreed, and ruled that the state and federal statutes could co-exist.

In dissent, Justice Joseph Story (a great advocate of federal power) argued that the federal statute left no room for a state statute on the same subject. In a hypothetical discussion over whether a state statute might be constitutional if there were no federal statute, Justice Story commented that the 2nd Amendment (he says Fifth but quotes the Second, in perhaps the most notable typographical error in all these cases) would probably have no important bearing on the point. The 2nd Amendment played no role in the majority opinions, and was only mentioned in a cursory way in a dissent. The Court's treatment of the 2nd Amendment in this case—it is not present in the lengthy discussion—suggests that the Amendment was not primarily viewed as a guarantee of state government powers to control state militias.

The judgment of the Court was delivered at the present term, by Mr. Justice WASHINGTON, who, after stating the facts of the case, proceeded as follows:

There is but one question in this cause, and it is, whether the act of the legislature of Pennsylvania, under the authority of which the plaintiff in error was tried, and sentenced to pay a fine, is repugnant to the Constitution of the United States, or not?

But before this question can be clearly understood, it will be necessary to inquire, 1. What are the powers granted to the general government, by the Constitution of the United States, over the militia? and, 2. To what extent they have been assumed and exercised?

1. The constitution declares, that Congress shall have power to provide for calling forth the militia in three specified cases: for organizing, arming, and disciplining them; and for governing such part of them as may be employed in the service of the United States; reserving to the States, respectively, the appointment of the officers, and the authority of training the militia according to the discipline prescribed by Congress. It is further provided, that the President of the United States shall be commander of the militia, when called into the actual service of the United States.

The whole ground of Congressional legislation is covered by the laws referred to.

.....

If I am not mistaken in this view of the subject, the way is now open for the examination of the great question in the cause. Is it competent to a Court Martial, deriving its jurisdiction under State authority, to try, and to punish militia men, drafted, detached, and called forth by the President into the service of the United States, who have refused, or neglected to obey the call?

.....

Two of the judges are of opinion, that the law in question is unconstitutional, and that the judgment below ought to be reversed.

The other judges are of opinion, that the judgment ought to be affirmed; but they do not concur in all respects in the reasons which influence my opinion.

Mr. Justice STORY.

.....

If, therefore, the present case turned upon the question, whether a State might organize, arm, and discipline its own militia in the absence of, or subordinate to, the regulations of Congress, I am certainly not prepared to deny the legitimacy of such an exercise of authority. It does not seem repugnant in its nature to the grant of a like paramount authority to Congress; and if not, then it is retained by the States. The fifth amendment to the constitution, declaring that "a well regulated militia being necessary to the security of a free State, the right of the people to keep and bear arms shall not be infringed," may not, perhaps, be thought to have any important bearing on this point. If it have, it confirms and illustrates, rather than impugns the reasoning already suggested.

It is almost too plain for argument, that the power here given to Congress over the militia; is of a limited nature, and confined to the objects specified in these clauses; and that in all other respects, and for all other purposes, the militia are subject to the control and government of the State authorities. Nor can the reservation to the States of the appointment of the officers and authority of the training the militia according to the discipline prescribed by Congress, be justly considered as weakening this conclusion. That reservation constitutes an exception merely from the power given to Congress "to provide for organizing, arming, and disciplining the militia;" and is a limitation upon the authority, which would otherwise have devolved upon it as to the appointment of officers. But the exception from a given power cannot, upon any fair reasoning, he considered as an enumeration of all the powers which belong to the States over the militia. What those powers are must depend upon their own constitutions; and what is not taken away by the Constitution of the United States, must be considered as retained by the States or the people. The exception then ascertains only that Congress have not, and that the States have, the power to appoint the officers of the militia, and to train them according to the discipline prescribed by Congress. Nor does it seem necessary to contend, that the power "to provide for organizing, arming, and disciplining the militia," is exclusively vested in Congress. It is merely an affirmative power, and if not in its own nature incompatible with the existence of a like power in the States, it may well leave a concurrent power in the latter. But when once Congress has carried this power into effect, its laws for the organization, arming, and discipline of the militia, are the supreme law of the land; and all interfering State regulations must necessarily be suspended in their operation. It would certainly seem reasonable, that in the absence of all interfering provisions by Congress on the subject, the States should have authority to organize, arm, and discipline their own militia. The general authority retained by them over the militia would seem to draw after it these, as necessary incidents. If Congress should not have exercised its own power, how, upon any other construction, than that of a concurrent power, could the States sufficiently provide for their own safety against domestic insurrections, or the sudden invasion of a foreign enemy? They are expressly prohibited from keeping troops or ships of war in time of peace; and this, undoubtedly, upon the supposition, that in such cases the militia would be their natural and sufficient defence. Yet what would the militia be without organization, arms, and discipline? It is certainly not compulsory upon Congress to exercise its own authority upon this subject. The time, the mode, and the extent, must rest upon its means and sound discretion. If, therefore, the present case turned upon the question, whether a State might organize, arm, and discipline its own militia in the absence of, or subordinate to, the regulations of Congress, I am certainly not prepared to deny the legitimacy of such an exercise of authority. It does not seem repugnant in its nature to the grant of a like paramount authority to Congress; and if not, then it is retained by the States. The fifth amendment to the constitution, declaring that "a well regulated militia being necessary to the security of a free State, the right of the people to keep and bear arms shall not be infringed," may not, perhaps, be thought to have any important bearing on this point. If it have, it confirms and illustrates, rather than impugns the reasoning already suggested.

.....

Upon the whole, with whatever reluctance, I feel myself bound to declare, that the clauses of the militia act of Pennsylvania now in question, are repugnant to the constitutional laws of Congress on the same subject, and are utterly void; and that, therefore, the judgment of the State Court ought to be reversed. In this opinion I have the concurrence of one of my bretheren.

DRED SCOTT v. SANDFORD

(CASE EXCERPT)
60 U.S. 393; 15 L. Ed. 691; 19 HOW 393
DECEMBER, 1856, Term

GIST: The second gun case in the High Court's history is widely known and extensively studied for its social impact, and as a sobering reflection on our nation's past. It has not, until this time, been thought of by many as a gun case, per se. But a mere few paragraphs within its copious length show a sense of gun rights that is simultaneously abhorrent to modern thought, and as illustrative of the understanding of gun rights at this early point in our history, as any other entry in *Supreme Court Gun Cases.*

This is the infamous case from the pre-Civil War era involving a slave's suit for his freedom. In it, the Court states that if a slave were entitled to the rights and privileges secured by the Constitution, he would have the right to keep and carry arms wherever he went, the same as other citizens, and it certainly "cannot be supposed" that the states "intended to secure to them" such rights.

Later, discussing congressional power over Territories that had not yet become States, the Court said Congress could not deprive Territorial citizens of the protections of the Bill of Rights, including the right to keep and bear arms, or other important rights, such as the right to a jury trial.

It came as quite a surprise to find that *Dred Scott* would turn out to provide a key element in understanding what the 2nd Amendment intended to say, and that blacks, in being denied their rights, helped define what those rights are. After the War Between the States, there were efforts to both secure and to deny the right to keep arms and the right to bear arms for newly freed slaves. This became the focus of local and state activity nationally, and the innards of the 14th Amendment to the U.S. Constitution.

Mr. Chief Justice TANEY delivered the opinion of the court.

The plaintiff in error, who was also the plaintiff in the court below, was, with his wife and children, held as slaves by the defendant, in the State of Missouri; and he brought this action in the Circuit Court of the United States for that district, to assert the title of himself and his family to freedom.

.....

If the question raised by it is legally before us, and the court should be of opinion that the facts stated in it disqualify the plaintiff from becoming a citizen, in the sense in which that word is used in the Constitution of the United States, then the judgment of the Circuit Court is erroneous, and must be reversed.

.....

The question is simply this: Can a negro, whose ancestors were imported into this country, and sold as slaves, become a member of the political community formed and brought into existence by the Constitution of the United States, and as such become entitled to all the rights, and privileges, and immunities, guarantied by that instrument to the citizen? One of which rights is the privilege of suing in a court of the United States in the cases specified in the Constitution.

.....

The words "people of the United States" and "citizens" are synonymous terms, and mean the same thing. They both describe the political body who, according to our republican institutions, form the sovereignty, and who hold the power and conduct the Government through their representatives. They are what we familiarly call the "sovereign people," and every citizen is one of this people, and a constituent member of this sovereignty. The question before us is, whether the class of persons described in the plea in abatement compose a portion of this people, and are constituent members of this sovereignty? We think they are not, and that they are not included, and were not intended to be included, under the word "citizens" in the Constitution, and can therefore claim none of the rights and privileges which that instrument provides for and secures to citizens of the United States. On the contrary, they were at that time considered as a subordinate and inferior class of beings, who had been subjugated by the dominant race, and, whether emancipated or not, yet remained subject to their authority, and had no rights or privileges but such as those who held the power and the Government might choose to grant them.

.....

It would give to persons of the negro race, who were recognized as citizens in any one State of the Union, the right... to keep and carry arms wherever they went.

It cannot be supposed that they <the States> intended to secure to them <"the African race"> rights, and privileges, and rank, in the new political body throughout the Union, which every one of them denied within the limits of its own dominion. More especially, it cannot be believed that the large slaveholding States regarded them as included in the word citizens, or would have consented to a Constitution which might compel them to receive them in that character from another State. For if they were so received, and entitled to the privileges and immunities of citizens, it would exempt them from the operation of the special laws and from the police regulations which they considered to be necessary for their own safety. It would give to persons of the negro race, who were recognized as citizens in any one State of the Union, the right to enter every other State whenever they pleased, singly or in companies, without pass or passport, and without obstruction, to sojourn there as long as they pleased, to go where they pleased at every hour of the day or night without molestation, unless they committed some violation of law for which a white man would be punished; and it would give them the full liberty of speech in public and in private upon all subjects upon which its own citizens might speak; to hold public meetings upon political affairs, and to keep and carry arms wherever they went.

.....

For example, no one, we presume, will contend that Congress can make any law in a Territory respecting that establishment of religion, or the free exercise thereof, or abridging the freedom of speech or of the press, or the right of the people of the Territory peaceably to assemble, and to petition the Government for the redress of grievances.

Nor can Congress deny to the people the right to keep and bear arms

Nor can Congress deny to the people the right to keep and bear arms, nor the right to trial by jury, nor compel any one to be a witness against himself in a criminal proceeding.

These powers, and others, in relation to rights of person, which it is not necessary here to enumerate, are, in express and positive terms, denied to the General Government; and the rights of private property have been guarded with equal care. Thus the rights of property are united with the rights of person, and placed on the same ground by the fifth amendment to the Constitution, which provides that no person shall be deprived of life, liberty, and property, without due process of law. And an act of Congress which deprives a citizen of the United States of his liberty or property, merely because he came himself or brought his property into a particular Territory of the United States, and who had committed no offence against the laws, could hardly be dignified with the name of due process of law.

EX PARTE MILLIGAN

(CASE EXCERPT)

71 U.S. 2; 18 L. Ed. 281; 4 Wall. 2

DECEMBER, 1866, Term

GIST: Milligan, a citizen of Indiana, was sentenced to death by a military court martial during the Civil War because of his sympathies for the Confederate cause. He brought a petition for a writ of habeas corpus, arguing that military tribunals could not displace civil courts in states that were not in rebellion. The Supreme Court unanimously agreed. While the Court's opinion did not discuss the 2nd Amendment, lawyers on both sides of the case used the 2nd

Amendment to argue by analogy, with arguments recognizing the 2nd Amendment as a right belonging to free citizens. As was the norm for 19th century cases, the official report of the case included the attorneys' arguments, preserving their thinking for posterity (and this book). Note how they consistently refer to the various "articles," reminding us that the Bill of Rights was a single amendment with twelve articles, ten of which were ratified.

Milligan also claimed he could not be guilty of violating the laws of war since he was not in the military, or "in the militia in actual service," and the Court again agreed. The distinction between citizens, and citizens called into active militia service, is pronounced in this case. The idea expressed repeatedly is that the militia, when not called into federal service, are just people and hence subject to civil courts, not military tribunals. Milligan's involvement with arms without being an activated militia member is never called into question.

.....

THIS case came before the court upon a certificate of division from the judges of the Circuit Court for Indiana, on a petition for discharge from unlawful imprisonment.

The case was thus:

An act of Congress-the Judiciary Act of 1789, section 14-enacts that the Circuit Courts of the United States

'Shall have power to issue writs of habeas corpus. And that either of the justices of the Supreme Court, as well as judges of the District Court, shall have power to grant writs of habeas corpus for the purpose of an inquiry into the cause of commitment. Provided,' &c.

Another act-that of March 3d, 1863, 'relating to habeas corpus, and regulating judicial proceedings in certain cases'-an act passed in the midst of the Rebellion-makes various provisions in regard to the subject of it.

The first section authorizes the suspension, during the Rebellion, of the writ of habeas corpus, throughout the United States, by the President.

Two following sections limited the authority in certain respects. The second section required that lists of all persons, being citizens of States in which the administration of the laws had continued unimpaired in the Federal courts, who were then held, or might thereafter be held, as prisoners of the United States, under the authority of the President, otherwise than as prisoners of war, should be furnished by the Secretary of State and Secretary of War to the judges of the Circuit and District Courts. These lists were to contain the names of all persons, residing within their respective jurisdictions, charged with violation of national law. And it was required, in cases where the grand jury in attendance upon any of these courts should terminate its session without proceeding by indictment or otherwise against any prisoner named in the list, that the judge of the court should forth-with make an order that such prisoner, desiring a discharge, should be brought before him or the court to be discharged, on entering into recognizance, if required, to keep the peace and for good behavior, or to appear, as the court might direct, to be further dealt with according to law. Every officer of the United States having custody of such prisoners was required to obey and execute the judge's order, under penalty, for refusal or delay, of fine and imprisonment.

The third section enacts, in case lists of persons other than prisoners of war then held in confinement, or thereafter arrested, should not be furnished within twenty days after the passage of the act, or, in cases of subsequent arrest, within twenty days after the time of arrest, that any citizen, after the termination of a session of the grand jury without indictment or presentment, might, by petition alleging the facts and verified by oath, obtain the judge's order of discharge in favor of any person so imprisoned, on the terms and conditions prescribed in the second section.

.....

With both these statutes and this proclamation in force, Lamdin P. Milligan, a citizen of the United States, and a resident and citizen of the State of Indiana, was arrested on the 5th day of October, 1864, at his home in the said State, by the order of Brevet Major-General Hovey, military commandant of the District of Indiana, and by the same authority confined in a military prison, at or near Indianapolis, the capital of the State. On the 21st day of the same month, he was placed on trial before a 'military commission,' convened at Indianapolis, by order of the said General, upon the following charges; preferred by Major Burnett, Judge Advocate of the Northwestern Military Department, namely:

1. 'Conspiracy against the Government of the United States;'
2. 'Affording aid and comfort to rebels against the authority of the United States;'

3. 'Inciting insurrection;'
4. 'Disloyal practices;' and
5. 'Violation of the laws of war.'

a secret society known as the Order of American Knights or Sons of Liberty, for the purpose of overthrowing the Government and duly constituted authorities of the United States

Under each of these charges there were various specifications. The substance of them was, joining and aiding, at different times, between October, 1863, and August, 1864, a secret society known as the Order of American Knights or Sons of Liberty, for the purpose of overthrowing the Government and duly constituted authorities of the United States; holding communication with the enemy; conspiring to seize munitions of war stored in the arsenals; to liberate prisoners of war, &c.; resisting the draft, &c.; . . . 'at a period of war and armed rebellion against the authority of the United States, at or near Indianapolis, [and various other places specified] in Indiana, a State within the military lines of the army of the United States, and the theatre of military operations, and which had been and was constantly threatened to be invaded by the enemy.' These were amplified and stated with various circumstances.

An objection by him to the authority of the commission to try him being overruled, Milligan was found guilty on all the charges, and sentenced to suffer death by hanging; and this sentence, having been approved, he was ordered to be executed on Friday, the 19th of May, 1865.

On the 10th of that same May, 1865, Milligan filed his petition in the Circuit Court of the United States for the District of Indiana, by which, or by the documents appended to which as exhibits, the above facts appeared. These exhibits consisted of the order for the commission; the charges and specifications; the findings and sentence of the court, with a statement of the fact that the sentence was approved by the President of the United States, who directed that it should 'be carried into execution without delay;' all 'by order of the Secretary of War.'

at no time had he been in the military service of the United States, or in any way connected with the land or naval force, or the militia in actual service

it had been 'wholly out of his power to have acquired belligerent rights, or to have placed himself in such relation to the government as to have enabled him to violate the laws of war.'

The petition set forth the additional fact, that while the petitioner was held and detained, as already mentioned, in military custody (and more than twenty days after his arrest), a grand jury of the Circuit Court of the United States for the District of Indiana was convened at Indianapolis, his said place of confinement, and duly empanelled, charged, and sworn for said district, held its sittings, and finally adjourned without having found any bill of indictment, or made any presentment whatever against him. That at no time had he been in the military service of the United States, or in any way connected with the land or naval force, or the militia in actual service; nor within the limits of any State whose citizens were engaged in rebellion against the United States, at any time during the war; but during all the time aforesaid, and for twenty years last past, he had been an inhabitant, resident, and citizen of Indiana. And so, that it had been 'wholly out of his power to have acquired belligerent rights, or to have placed himself in such relation to the government as to have enabled him to violate the laws of war.'

.....

II. THE MERITS OR MAIN QUESTION.

Mr. Speed, A. G., and Mr. Butler: By the settled practice of the courts of the United States, upon application for a writ of habeas corpus, if it appear upon the facts stated by the petitioner, all of which shall be taken to be true, that he could not be discharged upon a return of the writ, then no writ will be issued. Therefore the questions resolve themselves into two:

I. Had the military commission jurisdiction to hear and determine the case submitted to it?

II. The jurisdiction failing, had the military authorities of the United States a right, at the time of filing the petition, to detain the petitioner in custody as a military prisoner, or for trial before a civil court?

.....

As the war progressed, being a civil war, not unlikely, as the facts in this record abundantly show, to break out in any portion of the Union, in any form of insurrection, the President, as commander-in-chief, by this proclamation of September 24th, 1862, ordered:

during the existing insurrection... all persons... resisting militia drafts... shall be subject to martial law

'That during the existing insurrection, and as a necessary means for suppressing the same, all rebels and insurgents, their aiders and abettors, within the United States, and all persons discouraging volunteer enlistments, resisting militia drafts, or guilty of any disloyal practice, affording aid and comfort to rebels, against the authority of the United States, shall be subject to martial law, and liable to trial and punishment by courts martial or military commission.

'Second. That the writ of habeas corpus is suspended in respect to all persons arrested, or who now, or hereafter during the Rebellion shall be, imprisoned in any fort, camp, arsenal, military prison, or other place of confinement, by any military authority, or by the sentence of any court martial or military commission.'

This was an exercise of his sovereignty in carrying on war, which is vested by the Constitution in the President.

This proclamation, which by its terms was to continue during the then existing insurrection, was in full force during the pendency of the proceedings complained of, at the time of the filing of this petition, and is still unrevoked.

While we do not admit that any legislation of Congress was needed to sustain this proclamation of the President, it being clearly within his power, as commander-in-chief, to issue it; yet, if it is asserted that legislative action is necessary to give validity to it, Congress has seen fit to expressly ratify the proclamation by the act of March 3d, 1863, by declaring that the President, whenever in his judgment the public safety may require it, is authorized to suspend the writ of habeas corpus in any case throughout the United States, and in any part thereof.

The offences for which the petitioner for the purpose of this hearing is confessed to be guilty, are the offences enumerated in this proclamation. The prison in which he is confined is a 'military prison' therein mentioned. As to him, his acts and imprisonment, the writ of habeas corpus is expressly suspended.

Apparently admitting by his petition that a military commission might have jurisdiction in certain cases, the petitioner seeks to except himself by alleging that he is a citizen of Indiana, and has never been in the naval or military service of the United States, or since the commencement of the Rebellion a resident of a rebel State, and that, therefore, it had been out of his power to have acquired belligerent rights and to have placed himself in such a relation to the government as to enable him to violate the laws of war.

But neither residence nor propinquity to the field of actual hostilities is the test to determine who is or who is not subject to martial law, even in a time of foreign war, and certainly not in a time of civil insurrection. The commander-in-chief has full power to make an effectual use of his forces. He must, therefore, have power to arrest and punish one who arms men to join the enemy in the field against him; one who holds correspondence with that enemy; one who is an officer of an armed force organized to oppose him; one who is preparing to seize arsenals and release prisoners of war taken in battle and confined within his military lines.

These crimes of the petitioner were committed within the State of Indiana, where his arrest, trial, and imprisonment took place; within a military district of a geographical military department, duly established by the commander-in-chief; within the military lines of the army, and upon the theatre of military operations; in a State which had been and was then threatened with invasion, having arsenals which the petitioner plotted to seize, and prisoners of war whom he plotted to liberate; where citizens were liable to be made soldiers, and were actually ordered into the ranks; and to prevent whose becoming soldiers the petitioner conspired with and armed others.

Thus far the discussion has proceeded without reference to the effect of the Constitution upon war-making powers, duties, and rights, save to that provision which makes the President commander-in-chief of the armies and navies.

Does the Constitution provide restraint upon the exercise of this power?- The people of every sovereign State posses all the rights and powers of government. The people of these States in forming a 'more perfect Union, to insure domestic tranquillity, and to provide for the common defence,' have vested the power of making and carrying on war in the general government, reserving to the States, respectively, only the right to repel invasion and suppress insurrection 'of such imminent danger as will not admit of delay.' This right and power thus granted to the general government is in its nature entirely executive, and in the absence of constitutional limitations would be wholly lodged in the President, as chief executive officer and commander-in-chief of the armies and navies.

Lest this grant of power should be so broad as to tempt its exercise in initiating war, in order to reap the fruits of victory, and, therefore, be unsafe to be vested in a single branch of a republican government, the Constitution has delegated to Congress the power of originating war by declaration, when such declaration is necessary to the commencement of hostilities, and of provoking it by issuing letters of marque and reprisal; consequently, also, the power of raising and supporting armes, maintaining a navy, employing the militia, and of making rules for the government of all armed forces while in the service of the United States.

To keep out of the hands of the Executive the fruits of victory, Congress is also invested with the power to 'make rules for the disposition of captures by land or water.'

After war is originated, whether by declaration, invasion, or insurrection, the whole power of conducting it, as to manner, and as to all the means and appliances by which war is carried on by civilized nations, is given to the President. He is the sole judge of the exigencies, necessities, and duties of the occasion, their extent and duration.

During the war his powers must be without limit, because, if defending, the means of offence may be nearly illimitable; or, if acting offensively, his resources must be proportionate to the end in view,-'to conquer a peace.' New difficulties are constantly arising, and new combinations are at once to be thwarted, which the slow movement of legislative action cannot meet.

These propositions are axiomatic in the absence of all restraining legislation by Congress.

Much of the argument on the side of the petitioner will rest, perhaps, upon certain provisions-not in the Constitution itself, and as originally made, but now seen in the Amendments made in 1789: the fourth, fifth, and sixth amendments. They may as well be here set out:

4. The right of the people to be secure in their persons, houses, papers, and effects, against unreasonable searches and seizures, shall not be violated, and no warrants shall issue but upon probable cause supported by oath or affirmation, and particularly describing the place to be searched and the persons or things to be seized.

5. No person shall be held to answer for a capital or otherwise infamous crime, unless on a presentment or indictment of a grand jury, except in cases arising in the land or naval forces, or in the militia when in actual service in time of war or public danger; nor shall any person be subject for the same offence to be twice put in jeopardy of life or limb; nor shall be compelled in any criminal case to be a witness against himself, nor be deprived of life, liberty, or property, without due process of law; nor shall private property be taken for public use without just compensation.

6. In all criminal prosecutions the accused shall enjoy the right to a speedy and public trial, by an impartial jury of the State and district wherein the crime shall have been committed, . . . and to be informed of the nature and cause of the accusation; to be confronted with the witnesses against him; to have compulsory process for obtaining witnesses in his favor, and to have the assistance of counsel for his defence.

In addition to these, there are two preceding amendments which we may also mention, to wit: the second and third. They are thus:

2. A well-regulated militia being necessary to the security of a free State, the right of the people to keep and bear arms shall not be infringed.

3. No soldier shall in time of peace be quartered in any house without the consent of the owner, nor in time of war but in a manner to be prescribe by law.

It cannot properly be so argued, any more than it could be that it was intended by the second article (declaring that 'the right of the people to keep and bear arms shall not be infringed') to hinder the President from disarming insurrectionists, rebels, and traitors in arms while he was carrying on war against them.

It will be argued that the fourth, fifth, and sixth articles, as above given, are restraints upon the war-making power; but we deny this. All these amendments are in pari materi a, and if either is a restraint upon the President in carrying on war, in favor of the citizen, it is difficult to see why all of them are not. Yet will it be argued that the fifth article would be violated in 'depriving if life, liberty, or property, without due process of law,' armed rebels marching to attack the capital? Or that the fourth would be violated by searching and seizing the papers and houses of persons in open insurrection and war against the government? It cannot properly be so argued, any more than it could be that it was intended by the second article (declaring that 'the right of the people to keep and bear arms shall not be infringed') to hinder the President from disarming insurrectionists, rebels, and traitors in arms while he was carrying on war against them.

These, in truth, are all peace provisions of the Constitution and, like all other conventional and legislative laws and enactments, are silent amidst arms, and when the safety of the people becomes the supreme law.

By the Constitution, as originally adopted, no limitations were put upon the war-making and war-conducting powers of Congress and the President; and after discussion, and after the attention of the country was called to the subject, no other limitation by subsequent amendment has been made, except by the Third Article, which prescribes that 'no soldier shall be quartered in any house in time of peace without consent of the owner, or in time of war, except in a manner prescribed by law.'

This, then, is the only expressed constitutional restraint upon the President as to the manner of carrying on war. There would seem to be no implied one; on the contrary, while carefully providing for the privilege of the writ of habeas corpus in time of peace, the Constitution takes it for granted that it will be suspended 'in case of rebellion or invasion (i.e., in time of war), when the public safety requires it.'

.....

Mr. David Dudley Field:

.....

Certain topics have been brought into this discussion which have no proper place in it, and which I shall endeavor to keep out of it.

This not a question of the discipline of camps; it is not a question of the government of armies in the field; it is not a question respecting the power of a conqueror over conquered armies or conquered states.

It is not a question, how far the legislative department of the government can deal with the question of martial rule. Whatever has been done in these cases, has been done by the executive department alone.

Nor is it a question of the patriotism, or the character, or the services of the late chief magistrate, or of his constitutional advisers.

It is a question of the rights of the citizen in time of war.

Is it true, that the moment a declaration of war is made, the executive department of this government, without an act of Congress, becomes absolute master of our liberties and our lives? Are we, then, subject to martial rule, administered by the President upon his own sense of the exigency, with nobody to control him, and with every magistrate and every authority in the land subject to his will alone? These are the considerations which give to the case its greatest significance.

.....

Then let it be remembered that the petitioners were simple citizens, not belonging to the army or navy; not in any official position; not connected in any manner with the public service.

.....

I submit, therefore, that upon the text of the original Constitution, as it stood when it was ratified, there is no color for the assumption that the President, without act of Congress, could create military commissions for the trial of persons not military, for any cause or under any circumstances whatever.

But, as we well know, the Constitution, in the process of ratification, had to undergo a severe ordeal. To quiet apprehensions, as well as to guard against possible dangers, ten amendments were proposed by the first Congress sitting at New York, in 1789, and were duly ratified by the States. The third and fifth are as follows:

'ART. III. No soldier shall, in time of peace, be quartered in any house, without the consent of the owner, nor in time of war but in a manner to be prescribed by law.'

'ART. V. No person shall be held to answer for a capital or otherwise infamous crime, unless on a presentment or indictment of a grand jury, except in cases arising in the land or naval forces, or in the militia when in actual service, in time of war or public danger; nor shall any person be subject, for the same offence, to be twice put in jeopardy of life or limb, nor shall be compelled in any criminal case to be a witness against himself, nor be deprived of life, liberty, or property, without due process of law, nor shall private property be taken for public use without just compensation.'

If there could have been any doubt whatever, whether military commissions or courts-martial for the trial of persons not 'in the land or naval forces, or the militia' in actual service, could ever be established by the President, or even by Congress, these amendments would have removed the doubt. They were made for a state of war as well as a state of peace; they were aimed at the military authority, as well as the civil; and they were as explicit as our mother tongue could make them.

.....

the person acting under the pressure of necessity, real or supposed, acts at his peril.

Private persons may lawfully tear down a house, if necessary, to prevent the spread of a fire. Indeed, the maxim is not confined in its application to the calamities of war and conflagration. A mutiny, breaking out in a garrison, may make necessary for its suppression, and therefore justify, acts which would otherwise be unjustifiable. In all these cases, however, the person acting under the pressure of necessity, real or supposed, acts at his peril. The correctness of his conclusion must be judged by courts and juries, whenever the acts and the alleged necessity are drawn in question.

.....

though their lives depended on their success in arms, they always asserted and enforced the subordination of the military to the civil arm.

First. As to our own country. The nation began its life in 1776, with a protest against military usurpation. It was one of the grievances set forth in the Declaration of Independence, that the king of Great Britain had 'affected to render the military independent of and superior to the civil power.' The attempts of General Gage, in Boston, and of Lord Dunmore, in Virginia, to enforce martial rule, excited the greatest indignation. Our fathers never forgot their principles; and though the war by which they maintained their independence was a revolutionary one, though their lives depended on their success in arms, they always asserted and enforced the subordination of the military to the civil arm.

The first constitutions of the States were framed with the most jealous care. By the constitution of New Hampshire, it was declared that 'in all cases, and at all times, the military ought to be under strict subordination to, and governed by the civil power;' by the constitution of Massachusetts of 1780, that 'no person can in any case be subjected to law martial, or to any penalties or pains by virtue of that law, except those employed in the army or navy, and except the militia in actual service, but by the authority of the legislature;'

.....

Mr. Garfield, on the same side.

Had the military commission jurisdiction legally to try and sentence the petitioner? This is the main question.

The Constitution establishes the Supreme Court, and empowers Congress--

'To constitute tribunals inferior to the Supreme Court.'

'To make rules for the governments of the land and naval forces, and to provide for governing such part of the militia as may be employed in the service of the United States.'

.....

The main boundary line between the civil and military jurisdictions is the muster into service. In Mills v. Martin, a militiaman, called out by the Governor of the State of New York, and ordered by him to enter the service of the United States, on a requisition of the President for troops, refused to obey the summons, and was tried by a Federal court-martial for disobedience of orders. The Supreme Court of the State of New York decided, that until he had gone to the place of general rendezvous, and had been regularly enrolled, and mustered into the national militia, he was not amenable to the action of a court-martial composed of officers of the United States.

We are apt to regard the military department of the government as an organized despotism, in which all personal rights are merged in the will of the commander-in-chief. But that department has definitely marked boundaries, and all its members are not only controlled, but also sacredly protected by definitely prescribed law. The first law of the Revolutionary Congress, passed September 20th, 1776, touching the organization of the army, provided that no officer or soldier should be kept in arrest more than eight days without being furnished with the written charges and specifications against him; that he should be tried, at as early a day as possible, by a regular military court, whose proceedings were regulated by law, and that no sentence should be carried into execution till the full record of the trial had been submitted to Congress or to the commander-in-chief, and his or their direction be signified thereon. From year to year Congress has added new safeguards to protect the rights of its soldiers, and the rules and articles of war are as really a part of the laws of the land as the Judiciary Act or the act establishing the treasury department. The main boundary line between the civil and military jurisdictions is the muster into service. In Mills v. Martin, a militiaman, called out by the Governor of the State of New York, and ordered by him to enter the service of the United States, on a requisition of the President for troops, refused to obey the summons, and was tried by a Federal court-martial for disobedience of orders. The Supreme Court of the State of New York decided, that until he had gone to the place of general rendezvous, and had been regularly enrolled, and mustered into the national militia, he was not amenable to the action of a court-martial composed of officers of the United States.

.....

ON THE SIDE OF THE UNITED STATES. REPLY.

Mr. Butler:

.....

It has been said that martial law, and its execution by trials by military commission, is fatal to liberty and the pursuit of happiness; but we are only asking for the exercise of military power, when necessity demands and prudence dictates. If the civil law fails to preserve rights, and to insure safety and tranquillity to the country; if there is no intervention of military power to right wrongs and punish crime, an outraged community will improvise come tribunal for themselves, whose execution shall be as swift and whose punishments shall be as terrible as any exhibition of military power; some tribunal wholly unregulated and which is responsible to no one. We are not without such examples on this continent.

.....

And the wisdom of this view appears nowhere more than in the present case. The court, of course, can have no knowledge how extensive was this 'Order of Sons of Liberty;' how extensive was the organization of these American Knights in Indiana. It was a secret Order. Its vast extent was not known generally. But the

Executive might have known; and if I might step out of the record, I could say that I am aware that he did know, that this Order professed to have one hundred thousand men enrolled in it in the States of Indiana, Ohio, and Illinois, so that no jury could be found to pass upon any case, and that any courthouse wherein it had been attempted to try any of the conspirators, would have been destroyed. The President has judged that in this exigency a military tribunal alone could safely act.

.....

There is, in truth, no other way of construing constitutional provisions, than by the maxim, Singula singulis reddenda. Each provision of the Constitution must be taken to refer to the proper time, as to peace or war, in which it operates, as well as to the proper subject of its provisions.

For instance, the Constitution provides that 'no person' shall be deprived of liberty without due process of law. And yet, as we know, whole generations of people in this land-as many as four millions of them at one time-people described in the Constitution by this same word, 'persons,' have been till lately deprived of liberty ever since the adoption of the Constitution, without any process of law whatever.

The Constitution provides, also, that no "person's" right to bear arms shall be infringed; yet these same people <slaves>, described elsewhere in the Constitution as "persons," have been deprived of their arms whenever they had them.

The Constitution provides, also, that no 'person's' right to bear arms shall be infringed; yet these same people, described elsewhere in the Constitution as 'persons,' have been deprived of their arms whenever they had them.

If you are going to stand on that letter of the Constitution which is set up by the opposite side in the matter before us, how are we to explain such features in the Constitution, in various provisions in which slaves are called persons, with nothing in the language used to distinguish them from persons who were free.

.....

We do not ask anything outside of or beyond the Constitution. We insist only that the Constitution be interpreted so as to save the nation, and not to let it perish.

Mr. Black has said, that the very time when a constitutional provision is wanted, is the time of war, and that in time of war, of civil war especially, and the commotions just before and just after it, the constitutional provisions should be most rigidly enforced. We agree to that; but we assert that, in peace, when there is no commotion, the constitutional provisions should be most rigidly enforced as well. Constitutional provisions, within their application, should be always most rigidly enforced. We do not ask anything outside of or beyond the Constitution. We insist only that the Constitution be interpreted so as to save the nation, and not to let it perish.

.....

At the close of the last term the CHIEF JUSTICE announced the order of the court in this and in two other similar cases (those of Bowles and Horsey) as follows:

1. That on the facts stated in said petition and exhibits a writ of habeas corpus ought to be issued, according to the prayer of the said petitioner.

2. That on the facts stated in the said petition and exhibits the said Milligan ought to be discharged from custody as in said petition is prayed, according to the act of Congress passed March 3d, 1863, entitled, "An act relating to habeas corpus and regulating judicial proceedings in certain cases."

3. That on the facts stated in said petition and exhibits, the military commission mentioned therein had no jurisdiction legally to try and sentence said Milligan in the manner and form as in said petition and exhibits are stated.

At the opening of the present term, opinions were delivered.

Mr. Justice DAVIS delivered the opinion of the court.

On the 10th day of May, 1865, Lambdin P. Milligan presented a petition to the Circuit Court of the United States for the District of Indiana, to be discharged from an alleged unlawful imprisonment. The case made by the petition is this: Milligan is a citizen of the United States; has lived for twenty years in Indiana; and, at the time of the grievances complained of, was not, and never had been in the military or naval service of the United States. On the 5th day of October, 1864, while at home, he was arrested by order of General Alvin P. Hovey, commanding the military district of Indiana; and has ever since been kept in close confinement.

.....

It is difficult to see how the safety of the country required martial law in Indiana. If any of her citizens were plotting treason, the power of arrest could secure them, until the government was prepared for their trial, when the courts were open and ready to try them. It was as easy to protect witnesses before a civil as a military tribunal; and as there could be no wish to convict, except on sufficient legal evidence, surely an ordained and established court was better able to judge of this than a military tribunal composed of gentlemen not trained to the profession of the law.

.....

In some parts of the country, during the war of 1812, our officers made arbitrary arrests and, by military tribunals, tried citizens who were not in the military service. These arrests and trials, when brought to the notice of the courts, were uniformly condemned as illegal.

.....

But it is insisted that Milligan was a prisoner of war, and, therefore, excluded from the privileges of the statute. It is not easy to see how he can be treated as a prisoner of war, when he lived in Indiana for the past twenty years, was arrested there, and had not been, during the late troubles, a resident of any of the states in rebellion. If in Indiana he conspired with bad men to assist the enemy, he is punishable for it in the courts of Indiana; but, when tried for the offence, he cannot plead the rights of war; for he was not engaged in legal acts of hostility against the government, and only such persons, when captured, are prisoners of war. If he cannot enjoy the immunities attaching to the character of a prisoner of war, how can he be subject to their pains and penalties?

This case, as well as the kindred cases of Bowles and Horsey, were disposed of at the last term, and the proper orders were entered of record. There is, therefore, no additional entry required.

The CHIEF JUSTICE <CHASE> delivered the following opinion.

Four members of the court, concurring with their brethren in the order heretofore made in this cause, but unable to concur in some important particulars with the opinion which has just been read, think it their duty to make a separate statement of their views of the whole case.

We do not doubt that the Circuit Court for the District of Indiana had jurisdiction of the petition of Milligan for the writ of habeas corpus.

.....

The first question, therefore -- Ought the writ to issue? -- must be answered in the affirmative.

And it is equally clear that he was entitled to the discharge prayed for.

.....

We think that Congress had power, though not exercised, to authorize the military commission which was held in Indiana.

.....

the power of Congress, in the government of the land and naval forces and of the militia, is not at all affected by the fifth or any other amendment.

We think, therefore, that the power of Congress, in the government of the land and naval forces and of the militia, is not at all affected by the fifth or any other amendment. It is not necessary to attempt any precise definition of the boundaries of this power. But may it not be said that government includes protection and defence as well as the regulation of internal administration? And is it impossible to imagine cases in which citizens conspiring or attempting the destruction or great injury of the national forces may be subjected by Congress to military trial and punishment in the just exercise of this undoubted constitutional power? Congress is but the agent of the nation, and does not the security of individuals against the abuse of this, as of every other power, depend on the intelligence and virtue of the people, on their zeal for public and private liberty, upon official responsibility secured by law, and upon the frequency of elections, rather than upon doubtful constructions of legislative powers?

CUMMINGS v. MISSOURI

(CASE EXCERPT)

71 U.S. 277; 18 L. Ed. 356; 4 Wall. 277

DECEMBER, 1866, Term

GIST: This case involved the conviction of a Catholic priest for teaching and preaching without having taken an oath required by the Missouri Constitution. In formulating its opinion, the Court identifies bearing arms as an example of a civil right, and says suspension or deprivation of such rights is punishment.

Mr. Justice FIELD delivered the opinion of the court.

.....

In France, deprivation or suspension of civil rights, or of some of them, and among these of the right of voting, of eligibility to office, of taking part in family councils, of being guardian or trustee, of bearing arms, and of teaching or being employed in a school or seminary of learning, are punishments prescribed by her code.

Any deprivation or suspension of any of these rights for past conduct is punishment, and can be in no otherwise defined.

The theory upon which our political institutions rest is, that all men have certain inalienable rights -- that among these are life, liberty, and the pursuit of happiness; and that in the pursuit of happiness all avocations, all honors, all positions, are alike open to every one, and that in the protection of these rights all are equal before the law. Any deprivation or suspension of any of these rights for past conduct is punishment, and can be in no otherwise defined.

Punishment not being, therefore, restricted, as contended by counsel, to the deprivation of life, liberty, or property, but also embracing deprivation or suspension of political or civil rights, and the disabilities prescribed by the provisions of the Missouri constitution being in effect punishment, we proceed to consider whether there is any inhibition in the Constitution of the United States against their enforcement.

.....

UNITED STATES v. CRUIKSHANK

(FULL CASE)
92 U.S. 542; 23 L. Ed. 588; 2 Otto 542
OCTOBER, 1875 Term

GIST: Often thought of as the first real Supreme Court gun case, we now see that *Cruikshank* is only fifth in line.

William Cruikshank was a Ku Klux Klan leader in the South following the Civil War. He led a band of rioters in Louisiana who burned down a courthouse in which a group of armed blacks had taken refuge, all part of a disputed election. Cruikshank and his white followers were brought to trial—efforts such as theirs to disarm Freedmen were a hot national issue.

The federal Enforcement Act of May, 1870 made it illegal to band together or conspire to deprive people of their rights under the Constitution. It was an expression in statute of principles found in the new 14th Amendment, and created misdemeanor and felony offenses. In order to determine if the defendants were guilty, the Court had to decide if the rights allegedly deprived were actually rights granted by the Constitution.

The Court found that certain basic human rights in that document existed prior to when the Constitution was written, that the rights are fundamental to civilization, and were recognized but not created by the Constitution. All the Constitution did was guarantee against any federal government interference in those extant rights. These rights included free speech, the right to assemble for redress of grievances, and the right to bear arms, among others.

The federal prosecution was for conspiracy to prevent black people from the free exercise and enjoyment of rights and privileges granted and secured to them by the Constitution and laws of the United States. The Court famously stated here that the 2nd Amendment did not create a right to bear arms, but instead recognized and guaranteed a preexisting fundamental human right. Construing the 1st Amendment the same way, the Court held that the indictment against Cruikshank was defective, because the rights of assembly and of bearing arms were not granted or secured by the Constitution; rather, the 1st and 2nd Amendments merely limited the power of Congress to restrict those preexisting rights.

The defendants, charged with 32 counts of oppressing blacks in Louisiana, had been acquitted of murder at the lower court level, and were now exonerated of the remaining charges and released.

1. Citizens are the members of the political community to which they belong. They are the people who compose the community, and who, in their associated capacity, have established or submitted themselves to the dominion of a government for the promotion of their general welfare and the protection of their individual as well as their collective rights. The duty of a government to afford protection is limited always by the power it possesses for that purpose.

2. There is in our political system a government of each of the several States, and a government of the United States. Each is distinct from the others, and has citizens of its own, who owe it allegiance, and whose rights, within its jurisdiction, it must protect. The same person may be at the same time a citizen of the United States and a citizen of a State; but his rights of citizenship under one of these governments will be different from those he has under the other.

3. The government of the United States, although it is, within the scope of its powers, supreme and beyond the States, can neither grant nor secure to its citizens rights or privileges which are not expressly or by implication placed under its jurisdiction. All that cannot be so granted or secured are left to the exclusive protection of the States.

4. The right of the people peaceably to assemble for lawful purposes, with the obligation on the part of the States to afford it protection, existed long before the adoption of the Constitution. The first amendment to the Constitution, prohibiting Congress from abridging the right to assemble and petition, was not intended to limit the action of the State governments in respect to their own citizens, but to operate upon the national government alone. It left the authority of the States unimpaired, added nothing to the already existing powers of the United States, and guaranteed the continuance of the right only against Congressional interference. The people, for their protection in the enjoyment of it, must, therefore, look to the States, where the power for that purpose was originally placed.

5. The right of the people peaceably to assemble, for the purpose of petitioning Congress for a redress of grievances, or for any thing else connected with the powers or duties of the national government, is an attribute of national citizenship, and, as such, under the protection of and guaranteed by the United States. The very idea of a government republican in form implies that right, and an invasion of it presents a case within the sovereignty of the United States.

6. The right to bear arms is not granted by the Constitution; neither is it in any manner dependent upon that instrument for its existence. The second amendment means no more than that it shall not be infringed by Congress, and has no other effect than to restrict the powers of the national government.

7. Sovereignty, for the protection of the rights of life and personal liberty within the respective States, rests alone with the States.

8. The fourteenth amendment prohibits a State from depriving any person of life, liberty, or property, without due process of law, and from denying to any person within its jurisdiction the equal protection of the laws; but it adds nothing to the rights of one citizen as against another. It simply furnishes an additional guaranty against any encroachment by the States upon the fundamental rights which belong to every citizen as a member of society. The duty of protecting all its citizens in the enjoyment of an equality of rights was originally assumed by the States, and it still remains there. The only obligation resting upon the United States is to see that the States do not deny the right. This the amendment guarantees, but no more. The power of the national government is limited to the enforcement of this guaranty.

9. In Minor v. Happersett, 21 Wall. 178, this court decided that the Constitution of the United States has not conferred the right of suffrage upon any one, and that the United States have no voters of their own creation in the States. In United States v. Reese et al., supra, p. 214, it held that the fifteenth amendment has invested the citizens of the United States with a new constitutional right, which is, exemption from discrimination in the exercise of the elective franchise on account of race, color, or previous condition of servitude. The right to vote in the States comes from the States; but the right of exemption from the prohibited discrimination comes from the United States. The first has not been granted or secured by the Constitution of the United States, but the last has been.

10. The counts of an indictment which charge the defendants with having banded and conspired to injure, oppress, threaten, and intimidate citizens of the United States, of African descent, therein named; and which in substance respectively allege that the defendants intended thereby to hinder and prevent such citizens in the free exercise and enjoyment of rights and privileges granted and secured to them in common with other good citizens by the constitution and laws of the United States; to hinder and prevent them in the free exercise of their right peacefully to assemble for lawful purposes; prevent and hinder them from bearing arms for lawful purposes; deprive them of their respective several lives and liberty of person without due process of law; prevent and hinder them in the free exercise and enjoyment of their several right to the full and equal benefit of the law; prevent and hinder them in the free exercise and enjoyment of their several and respective right to vote at any election to be thereafter by law had and held by the people in and of the State of Louisiana, or to put them in great fear of bodily harm, and to injure and oppress them, because, being and having been in all things qualified, they had voted at an election theretofore had and held according to law by the people of said State, -- do not present a case within the sixth section of the Enforcement Act of May 31, 1870 (16 Stat. 141). To bring a case within the operation of that statute, it must appear that the right the enjoyment of which the conspirators intended to hinder or prevent was one granted or secured by the constitution or laws of the United States. If it does not so appear, the alleged offence is not indictable under any act of Congress.

11. The counts of an indictment which, in general language, charge the defendants with an intent to hinder and prevent citizens of the United States, of African descent, therein named, in the free exercise and enjoyment of the rights, privileges, immunities, and protection, granted and secured to them respectively as citizens of the United States, and of the State of Louisiana, because they were persons of African descent, and with the intent to hinder and prevent them in the several and free exercise and enjoyment of every, each, all, and singular the several rights and privileges granted and secured to them by the constitution and laws of the United States, do not specify any particular right the enjoyment of which the conspirators intended to hinder or prevent, are too vague and general, lack the certainty and precision required by the established rules of criminal pleading, and are therefore not good and sufficient in law.

12. In criminal cases, prosecuted under the laws of the United States, the accused has the constitutional right "to be informed of the nature and cause of the accusation." The indictment must set forth the offence with clearness and all necessary certainty, to apprise the accused of the crime with which he stands charged; and every ingredient of which the offence is composed must be accurately and clearly alleged. It is an elementary principle of criminal pleading, that, where the definition of an offence, whether it be at common law or by statute, includes generic terms, it is not sufficient that the indictment shall charge the offence in the same generic terms as in the definition, but it must state the species, -- it must descend to particulars. The object of the indictment is, -- first, to furnish the accused with such a description of the charge against him as will enable him to make his defence, and avail himself of his conviction or acquittal for protection against a further prosecution for the same cause; and, second, to inform the court of the facts alleged, so that it may decide whether they are sufficient in law to support a conviction, if one should be had. For this, facts are to be stated, not conclusions of law alone. A crime is made up of acts and intent; and these must be set forth in the indictment, with reasonable particularity of time, place, and circumstances.

13. By the act under which this indictment was found, the crime is made to consist in the unlawful combination with an intent to prevent the enjoyment of any right granted or secured by the Constitution, &c. All rights are not so granted or secured. Whether one is so or not is a question of law, to be decided by the court. The indictment should, therefore, state the particulars, to inform the court as well as the accused. It must appear from the indictment that the acts charged will, if proved, support a conviction for the offence alleged.

ERROR to the Circuit Court of the United States for the District of Louisiana.

This was an indictment for conspiracy under the sixth section of the act of May 30, 1870, known as the Enforcement Act (16 Stat. 140), and consisted of thirty-two counts.

The first count was for banding together, with intent "unlawfully and feloniously to injure, oppress, threaten, and intimidate" two citizens of the United States, "of African descent and persons of color"

The first count was for banding together, with intent "unlawfully and feloniously to injure, oppress, threaten, and intimidate" two citizens of the United States, "of African descent and persons of color," "with the unlawful and felonious intent thereby" them "to hinder and prevent in their respective free exercise and enjoyment of their lawful right and privilege to peaceably assemble together with each other and with other citizens of the said United States for a peaceable and lawful purpose."

The second avers an intent to hinder and prevent the exercise by the same persons of the "right to keep and bear arms for a lawful purpose."

The second avers an intent to hinder and prevent the exercise by the same persons of the "right to keep and bear arms for a lawful purpose."

The third avers an intent to deprive the same persons "of their respective several lives and liberty of person, without due process of law."

The fourth avers an intent to deprive the same persons of the "free exercise and enjoyment of the right and privilege to the full and equal benefit of all laws and proceedings for the security of persons and property" enjoyed by white citizens.

The fifth avers an intent to hinder and prevent the same persons "in the exercise and enjoyment of the rights, privileges, immunities, and protection granted and secured to them respectively as citizens of the said United States, and as citizens of the said State of Louisiana, by reason of and for and on account of the race and color" of the said persons.

The sixth avers an intent to hinder and prevent the same persons in "the free exercise and enjoyment of the several and respective right and privilege to vote at any election to be thereafter by law had and held by the people in and of the said State of Louisiana."

The seventh avers an intent "to put in great fear of bodily harm, injure, and oppress" the same persons, "because and for the reason" that, having the right to vote, they had voted.

The eighth avers an intent "to prevent and hinder" the same persons "in their several and respective free exercise and enjoyment of every, each, all, and singular the several rights and privileges granted and secured" to them "by the constitution and laws of the United States."

The next eight counts are a repetition of the first eight, except that, instead of the words "band together," the words "combine, conspire, and confederate together" are used. Three of the defendants were found guilty under the first sixteen counts, and not guilty under the remaining counts.

The parties thus convicted moved in arrest of judgment on the following grounds: --

1. Because the matters and things set forth and charged in the several counts, one to sixteen inclusive, do not constitute offences against the laws of the United States, and do not come within the purview, true intent, and meaning of the act of Congress, approved 31st May, 1870, entitled "An Act to enforce the right of citizens of the United States," &c.

2. Because the matters and things in the said indictment set forth and charged do not constitute offences cognizable in the Circuit Court, and do not come within its power and jurisdiction.

3. Because the offences created by the sixth section of the act of Congress referred to, and upon which section the aforesaid sixteen counts are based, are not constitutionally within the jurisdiction of the courts of the United States, and because the matters and things therein referred to are judicially cognizable by State tribunals only, and legislative action thereon is among the constitutionally reserved rights of the several States.

4. Because the said act, in so far as it creates offences and imposes penalties, is in violation of the Constitution of the United States, and an infringement of the rights of the several States and the people.

5. Because the eighth and sixteenth counts of the indictment are too vague, general, insufficient, and uncertain, to afford the accused proper notice to plead and prepare their defence, and set forth no specific offence under the law.

6. Because the verdict of the jury against the defendants is not warranted or supported by law.

On this motion the opinions of the judges were divided, that of the presiding judge being that the several counts in question are not sufficient in law, and do not contain charges of criminal matter indictable under the laws of the United States; and that the motion in arrest of judgment should be granted. The case comes up at the instance of the United States, on certificate of this division of opinion.

Sect. 1 of the Enforcement Act declares, that all citizens of the United States, otherwise qualified, shall be allowed to vote at all elections, without distinction of race, color, or previous servitude.

Sect. 2 provides, that, if by the law of any State or Territory a prerequisite to voting is necessary, equal opportunity for it shall be given to all, without distinction, &c.; and any person charged with the duty of furnishing the prerequisite, who refuses or knowingly omits to give full effect to this section, shall be guilty of misdemeanor.

Sect. 3 provides, that an offer of performance, in respect to the prerequisite, when proved by affidavit of the claimant, shall be equivalent to performance; and any judge or inspector of election who refuses to accept it shall be guilty, &c.

Sect. 4 provides, that any person who, by force, bribery, threats, intimidation, or other unlawful means, hinders, delays, prevents, or obstructs any citizen from qualifying himself to vote, or combines with others to do so, shall be guilty, &c.

Sect. 5 provides, that any person who prevents, hinders, controls, or intimidates any person from exercising the right of suffrage, to whom it is secured by the fifteenth amendment, or attempts to do so, by bribery or threats of violence, or deprivation of property or employment, shall be guilty, &c.

The sixth section is as follows: --

"That if two or more persons shall band or conspire together, or go in disguise upon the public highway, or upon the premises of another, with intent to violate any provisions of this act, or to injure, oppress, threaten, or intimidate any citizen with intent to prevent or hinder his free exercise and enjoyment of any right or privilege granted or secured to him by the constitution or laws of the United States, or because of his having exercised the same, such persons shall be held guilty of felony, and, on conviction thereof, shall be fined or imprisoned, or both, at the discretion of the court, -- the fine not to exceed $5,000, and the imprisonment not to exceed ten years; and shall, moreover, be thereafter ineligible to, and disabled from holding, any office or place of honor, profit, or trust created by the constitution or laws of the United States."

MR. CHIEF JUSTICE WAITE delivered the opinion of the court.

This case comes here with a certificate by the judges of the Circuit Court for the District of Louisiana that they were divided in opinion upon a question which occurred at the hearing. It presents for our consideration an indictment containing sixteen counts, divided into two series of eight counts each, based upon sect. 6 of the Enforcement Act of May 31, 1870. That section is as follows: --

"That if two or more persons shall band or conspire together, or go in disguise upon the public highway, or upon the premises of another, with intent to violate any provision of this act, or to injure, oppress, threaten, or intimidate any citizen, with intent to prevent or hinder his free exercise and enjoyment of any right or privilege granted or secured to him by the constitution or laws of the United States, or because of his having exercised the same, such persons shall be held guilty of felony, and, on conviction thereof, shall be fined or imprisoned, or both, at the discretion of the court, -- the fine not to exceed $5,000, and the imprisonment not to exceed ten years; and shall, moreover, be thereafter ineligible to, and disabled from holding, any office or place of honor, profit, or trust created by the constitution or laws of the United States." 16 Stat. 141.

The question certified arose upon a motion in arrest of judgment after a verdict of guilty generally upon the whole sixteen counts, and is stated to be, whether "the said sixteen counts of said indictment are severally good and sufficient in law, and contain charges of criminal matter indictable under the laws of the United States."

The general charge in the first eight counts is that of "banding," and in the second eight, that of "conspiring" together to injure, oppress, threaten, and intimidate Levi Nelson and Alexander Tillman, citizens of the United States, of African descent and persons of color, with the intent thereby to hinder and prevent them in their free exercise and enjoyment of rights and privileges "granted and secured" to them "in common with all other good citizens of the United States by the constitution and laws of the United States."

The offences provided for by the statute in question do not consist in the mere "banding" or "conspiring" of two or more persons together, but in their banding or conspiring with the intent, or for any of the purposes, specified. To bring this case under the operation of the statute, therefore, it must appear that the right, the enjoyment of which the conspirators intended to hinder or prevent, was one granted or secured by the constitution or laws of the United States. If it does not so appear, the criminal matter charged has not been made indictable by any act of Congress.

We have in our political system a government of the United States and a government of each of the several States. Each one of these governments is distinct from the others, and each has citizens of its own who owe it allegiance, and whose rights, within its jurisdiction, it must protect. The same person may be at the same time a citizen of the United States and a citizen of a State, but his rights of citizenship under one of these governments will be different from those he has under the other. Slaughter-House Cases, 16 Wall. 74.

Citizens are the members of the political community to which they belong. They are the people who compose the community, and who, in their associated capacity, have established or submitted themselves to the dominion of a government for the promotion of their general welfare and the protection of their individual as well as their collective rights.

In the formation of a government, the people may confer upon it such powers as they choose. The government, when so formed, may, and when called upon should, exercise all the powers it has for the protection of the rights of its citizens and the people within its jurisdiction; but it can exercise no other. The duty of a government to afford protection is limited always by the power it possesses for that purpose.

Citizens are the members of the political community to which they belong. They are the people who compose the community, and who, in their associated capacity, have established or submitted themselves to the dominion of a government for the promotion of their general welfare and the protection of their individual as well as their collective rights. In the formation of a government, the people may confer upon it such powers as they choose. The government, when so formed, may, and when called upon should, exercise all the powers it has for the protection of the rights of its citizens and the people within its jurisdiction; but it can exercise no other. The duty of a government to afford protection is limited always by the power it possesses for that purpose.

Experience made the fact known to the people of the United States that they required a national government for national purposes. The separate governments of the separate States, bound together by the articles of confederation alone, were not sufficient for the promotion of the general welfare of the people in respect to foreign nations, or for their complete protection as citizens of the confederated States. For this reason, the people of the United States, "in order to form a more perfect union, establish justice, insure domestic tranquillity, provide for the common defence, promote the general welfare, and secure the blessings of liberty" to themselves and their posterity (Const. Preamble), ordained and established the government of the United States, and defined its powers by a constitution, which they adopted as its fundamental law, and made its rule of action.

The government thus established and defined is to some extent a government of the States in their political capacity. It is also, for certain purposes, a government of the people. Its powers are limited in number, but not in degree. Within the scope of its powers, as enumerated and defined, it is supreme and above the States; but beyond, it has no existence.

The government thus established and defined is to some extent a government of the States in their political capacity. It is also, for certain purposes, a government of the people. Its powers are limited in number, but not in degree. Within the scope of its powers, as enumerated and defined, it is supreme and above the States; but beyond, it has no existence. It was erected for special purposes, and endowed with all the powers necessary for its own preservation and the accomplishment of the ends its people had in view. It can neither grant nor secure to its citizens any right or privilege not expressly or by implication placed under its jurisdiction.

The people of the United States resident within any State are subject to two governments: one State, and the other National; but there need be no conflict between the two. The powers which one possesses, the other does not. They are established for different purposes, and have separate jurisdictions. Together they make one whole, and furnish the people of the United States with a complete government, ample for the protection of all their rights at home and abroad.

The people of the United States resident within any State are subject to two governments: one State, and the other National; but there need be no conflict between the two. The powers which one possesses, the other does not. They are established for different purposes, and have separate jurisdictions. Together they make one whole, and furnish the people of the United States with a complete government, ample for the protection of all their rights at home and abroad. True, it may sometimes happen that a person is amenable to both jurisdictions for one and the same act. Thus, if a marshal of the United States is unlawfully resisted while executing the process of the courts within a State, and the resistance is accompanied by an assault on the officer, the sovereignty of the United States is violated by the resistance, and that of the State by the breach of peace, in the assault. So, too, if one passes counterfeited coin of the United States within a State, it may be an offence against the United States and the State: the United States, because it discredits the coin; and the State, because of the fraud upon him to whom it is passed. This does not, however, necessarily imply that the two governments possess powers in common, or bring them into conflict with each other. It is the natural consequence of a citizenship which owes allegiance to two sovereignties, and claims protection from both. The citizen cannot complain, because he has voluntarily submitted himself to such a form of government. He owes allegiance to the two departments, so to speak, and within their respective spheres must pay the penalties which each exacts for disobedience to its laws. In return, he can demand protection from each within its own jurisdiction.

The government of the United States is one of delegated powers alone. Its authority is defined and limited by the Constitution. All powers not granted to it by that instrument are reserved to the States or the people.

The government of the United States is one of delegated powers alone. Its authority is defined and limited by the Constitution. All powers not granted to it by that instrument are reserved to the States or the people. No rights can be acquired under the constitution or laws of the United States, except such as the government of the United States has the authority to grant or secure. All that cannot be so granted or secured are left under the protection of the States.

We now proceed to an examination of the indictment, to ascertain whether the several rights, which it is alleged the defendants intended to interfere with, are such as had been in law and in fact granted or secured by the constitution or laws of the United States.

The first and ninth counts state the intent of the defendants to have been to hinder and prevent the citizens named in the free exercise and enjoyment of their "lawful right and privilege to peaceably assemble together with each other and with other citizens of the United States for a peaceful and lawful purpose." The right of the people peaceably to assemble for lawful purposes existed long before the adoption of the Constitution of the United States. In fact, it is, and always has been, one of the attributes of citizenship under a free government. It "derives its source," to use the language of Chief Justice Marshall, in Gibbons v. Ogden, 9 Wheat. 211, "from those laws whose authority is acknowledged by civilized man throughout the world." It is found wherever civilization exists. It was not, therefore, a right granted to the people by the Constitution. The government of the United States when established found it in existence, with the obligation on the part of the States to afford it protection. As no direct power over it was granted to Congress, it remains, according to the ruling in Gibbons v. Ogden, id. 203, subject to State jurisdiction. Only such existing rights were committed by the people to the protection of Congress as came within the general scope of the authority granted to the national government.

The first amendment to the Constitution prohibits Congress from abridging "the right of the people to assemble and to petition the government for a redress of grievances." This, like the other amendments proposed and adopted at the same time, was not intended to limit the powers of the State governments in respect to their own citizens, but to operate upon the National government alone. Barron v. The City of Baltimore, 7 Pet. 250; Lessee of Livingston v. Moore, id. 551; Fox v. Ohio, 5 How. 434; Smith v. Maryland, 18 id. 76; Withers v. Buckley, 20 id. 90; Pervear v. The Commonwealth, 5 Wall. 479; Twitchell v. The Commonwealth, 7 id. 321; Edwards v. Elliott, 21 id. 557. It is now too late to question the correctness of this construction. As was said by the late Chief Justice, in Twitchell v. The Commonwealth, 7 Wall. 325, "the scope and application of these amendments are no longer subjects of discussion here." They left the authority of the States just where they found it, and added nothing to the already existing powers of the United States.

The particular amendment now under consideration assumes the existence of the right of the people to assemble for lawful purposes, and protects it against encroachment by Congress. The right was not created by the amendment; neither was its continuance guaranteed, except as against congressional interference. For their protection in its enjoyment, therefore, the people must look to the States. The power for that purpose was originally placed there, and it has never been surrendered to the United States.

The right of the people peaceably to assemble for the purpose of petitioning Congress for a redress of grievances, or for any thing else connected with the powers or the duties of the national government, is an attribute of national citizenship, and, as such, under the protection of, and guaranteed by, the United States. The very idea of a government, republican in form, implies a right on the part of its citizens to meet peaceably for consultation in respect to public affairs and to petition for a redress of grievances. If it had been alleged in these counts that the object of the defendants was to prevent a meeting for such a purpose, the case would have been within the statute, and within the scope of the sovereignty of the United States. Such, however, is not the case. The offence, as stated in the indictment, will be made out, if it be shown that the object of the conspiracy was to prevent a meeting for any lawful purpose whatever.

The right there specified is that of "bearing arms for a lawful purpose." This is not a right granted by the Constitution. Neither is it in any manner dependent upon that instrument for its existence. The second amendment declares that it shall not be infringed; but this, as has been seen, means no more than that it shall not be infringed by Congress. This is one of the amendments that has no other effect than to restrict the powers of the national government

The second and tenth counts are equally defective. The right there specified is that of "bearing arms for a lawful purpose." This is not a right granted by the Constitution. Neither is it in any manner dependent upon that instrument for its existence. The second amendment declares that it shall not be infringed; but this, as has been seen, means no more than that it shall not be infringed by Congress. This is one of the amendments that has no other effect than to restrict the powers of the national government, leaving the people to look for their protection against any violation by their fellow-citizens of the rights it recognizes, to what is called, in The City of New York v. Miln, 11 Pet. 139, the "powers which relate to merely municipal legislation, or what was, perhaps, more properly called internal police," "not surrendered or restrained" by the Constitution of the United States.

The rights of life and personal liberty are natural rights of man. "To secure these rights," says the Declaration of Independence, "governments are instituted among men, deriving their just powers from the consent of the governed." The very highest duty of the States, when they entered into the Union under the Constitution, was to protect all persons within their boundaries in the enjoyment of these "unalienable rights with which they were endowed by their Creator."

The third and eleventh counts are even more objectionable. They charge the intent to have been to deprive the citizens named, they being in Louisiana, "of their respective several lives and liberty of person without due process of law." This is nothing else than alleging a conspiracy to falsely imprison or murder citizens of the United States, being within the territorial jurisdiction of the State of Louisiana. The rights of life and personal liberty are natural rights of man. "To secure these rights," says the Declaration of Independence, "governments are instituted among men, deriving their just powers from the consent of the governed." The very highest duty of the States, when they entered into the Union under the Constitution, was to protect all persons within their boundaries in the enjoyment of these "unalienable rights with which they were endowed by their Creator." Sovereignty, for this purpose, rests alone with the States. It is no more the duty or within the power of the United States to punish for a conspiracy to falsely imprison or murder within a State, than it would be to punish for false imprisonment or murder itself.

The fourteenth amendment prohibits a State from depriving any person of life, liberty, or property, without due process of law; but this adds nothing to the rights of one citizen as against another. It simply furnishes an additional guaranty against any encroachment by the States upon the fundamental rights which belong to every citizen as a member of society.

The fourteenth amendment prohibits a State from depriving any person of life, liberty, or property, without due process of law; but this adds nothing to the rights of one citizen as against another. It simply furnishes an additional guaranty against any encroachment by the States upon the fundamental rights which belong to every citizen as a member of society. As was said by Mr. Justice Johnson, in Bank of Columbia v. Okely, 4 Wheat. 244, it secures "the individual from the arbitrary exercise of the powers of government, unrestrained by the established principles of private rights and distributive justice." These counts in the indictment do not call for the exercise of any of the powers conferred by this provision in the amendment.

The fourth and twelfth counts charge the intent to have been to prevent and hinder the citizens named, who were of African descent and persons of color, in "the free exercise and enjoyment of their several right and privilege to the full and equal benefit of all laws and proceedings, then and there, before that time, enacted or ordained by the said State of Louisiana and by the United States; and then and there, at that time, being in force in the said State and District of Louisiana aforesaid, for the security of their respective persons and property, then and there, at that time enjoyed at and within said State and District of Louisiana by white persons, being citizens of said State of Louisiana and the United States, for the protection of the persons and property of said white citizens." There is no allegation that this was done because of the race or color of the persons conspired against. When stripped of its verbiage, the case as presented amounts to nothing more than that the defendants conspired to prevent certain citizens of the United States, being within the State of Louisiana, from enjoying the equal protection of the laws of the State and of the United States.

The fourteenth amendment prohibits a State from denying to any person within its jurisdiction the equal protection of the laws; but this provision does not, any more than the one which precedes it, and which we have just considered, add any thing to the rights which one citizen has under the Constitution against another. The equality of the rights of citizens is a principle of republicanism. Every republican government is in duty bound to protect all its citizens in the enjoyment of this principle, if within its power. That duty was originally assumed by the States; and it still remains there. The only obligation resting upon the United States is to see that the States do not deny the right. This the amendment guarantees, but no more. The power of the national government is limited to the enforcement of this guaranty.

No question arises under the Civil Rights Act of April 9, 1866 (14 Stat. 27), which is intended for the protection of citizens of the United States in the enjoyment of certain rights, without discrimination on account of race, color, or previous condition of servitude, because, as has already been stated, it is nowhere alleged in these counts that the wrong contemplated against the rights of these citizens was on account of their race or color.

Another objection is made to these counts, that they are too vague and uncertain. This will be considered hereafter, in connection with the same objection to other counts.

The sixth and fourteenth counts state the intent of the defendants to have been to hinder and prevent the citizens named, being of African descent, and colored, "in the free exercise and enjoyment of their several and respective right and privilege to vote at any election to be thereafter by law had and held by the people in and of the said State of Louisiana, or by the people of and in the parish of Grant aforesaid." In Minor v. Happersett, 21 Wall. 178, we decided that the Constitution of the United States has not conferred the right of suffrage upon any one, and that the United States have no voters of their own creation in the States. In United States v. Reese et al., supra, p. 214, we hold that the fifteenth amendment has invested the citizens of the United States with a new constitutional right, which is, exemption from discrimination in the exercise of the elective franchise on account of race, color, or previous condition of servitude. From this it appears that the right of suffrage is not a necessary attribute of national citizenship; but that exemption from discrimination in the exercise of that right on account of race, &c., is. The right to vote in the States comes from the States; but the right of exemption from the prohibited discrimination comes from the United States. The first has not been granted or secured by the Constitution of the United States; but the last has been.

Inasmuch, therefore, as it does not appear in these counts that the intent of the defendants was to prevent these parties from exercising their right to vote on account of their race, &c., it does not appear that it was their intent to interfere with any right granted or secured by the constitution or laws of the United States. We may suspect that race was the cause of the hostility; but it is not so averred. This is material to a description of the substance of the offence, and cannot be supplied by implication. Every thing essential must be charged positively, and not inferentially. The defect here is not in form, but in substance.

The seventh and fifteenth counts are no better than the sixth and fourteenth. The intent here charged is to put the parties named in great fear of bodily harm, and to injure and oppress them, because, being and having been in all things qualified, they had voted "at an election before that time had and held according to law by the people of the said State of Louisiana, in said State, to wit, on the fourth day of November, A.D. 1872, and at divers other elections by the people of the State, also before that time had and held according to law." There is nothing to show that the elections voted at were any other than State elections, or that the conspiracy was formed on account of the race of the parties against whom the conspirators were to act. The charge as made is really of nothing more than a conspiracy to commit a breach of the peace within a State. Certainly it will not be claimed that the United States have the power or are required to do mere police duty in the States. If a State cannot protect itself against domestic violence, the United States may, upon the call of the executive, when the legislature cannot be convened, lend their assistance for that purpose. This is a guaranty of the Constitution (art. 4, sect. 4); but it applies to no case like this.

We are, therefore, of the opinion that the first, second, third, fourth, sixth, seventh, ninth, tenth, eleventh, twelfth, fourteenth, and fifteenth counts do not contain charges of a criminal nature made indictable under the laws of the United States, and that consequently they are not good and sufficient in law. They do not show that it was the intent of the defendants, by their conspiracy, to hinder or prevent the enjoyment of any right granted or secured by the Constitution.

We come now to consider the fifth and thirteenth and the eighth and sixteenth counts, which may be brought together for that purpose. The intent charged in the fifth and thirteenth is "to hinder and prevent the parties in their respective free exercise and enjoyment of the rights, privileges, immunities, and protection granted and secured to them respectively as citizens of the United States, and as citizens of said State of Louisiana," "for the reason that they, . . . being then and there citizens of said State and of the United States, were persons of African descent and race, and persons of color, and not white citizens thereof;" and in the eighth and sixteenth, to hinder and prevent them "in their several and respective free exercise and enjoyment of every, each, all, and singular the several rights and privileges granted and secured to them by the constitution and laws of the United States." The same general statement of the rights to be interfered with is found in the fifth and thirteenth counts.

According to the view we take of these counts, the question is not whether it is enough, in general, to describe a statutory offence in the language of the statute, but whether the offence has here been described at all. The statute provides for the punishment of those who conspire "to injure, oppress, threaten, or intimidate any citizen, with intent to prevent or hinder his free exercise and enjoyment of any right or privilege granted or secured to him by the constitution or laws of the United States." These counts in the indictment charge, in substance, that the intent in this case was to hinder and prevent these citizens in the free exercise and enjoyment of "every, each, all, and singular" the rights granted them by the Constitution, &c. There is no specification of any particular right. The language is broad enough to cover all.

In criminal cases, prosecuted under the laws of the United States, the accused has the constitutional right "to be informed of the nature and cause of the accusation." Amend. VI. In United States v. Mills, 7 Pet. 142, this was construed to mean, that the indictment must set forth the offence "with clearness and all necessary certainty, to apprise the accused of the crime with which he stands charged;" and in United States v. Cook, 17 Wall. 174, that "every ingredient of which the offence is composed must be accurately and clearly alleged." It is an elementary principle of criminal pleading, that where the definition of an offence, whether it be at common law or by statute, "includes generic terms, it is not sufficient that the indictment shall charge the offence in the same generic terms as in the definition; but it must state the species, -- it must descend to particulars. 1 Arch. Cr. Pr. and Pl., 291. The object of the indictment is, first, to furnish the accused with such a description of the charge against him as will enable him to make his defence, and avail himself of his conviction or acquittal for protection against a further prosecution for the same cause; and, second, to inform the court of the facts alleged, so that it may decide whether they are sufficient in law to support a conviction, if one should be had. For this, facts are to be stated, not conclusions of law alone. A crime is made up of acts and intent; and these must be set forth in the indictment, with reasonable particularity of time, place, and circumstances.

It is a crime to steal goods and chattels; but an indictment would be bad that did not specify with some degree of certainty the articles stolen. This, because the accused must be advised of the essential particulars of the charge against him, and the court must be able to decide whether the property taken was such as was the subject of larceny. So, too, it is in some States a crime for two or more persons to conspire to cheat and defraud another out of his property; but it has been held that an indictment for such an offence must contain allegations setting forth the means proposed to be used to accomplish the purpose. This, because, to make such a purpose criminal, the conspiracy must be to cheat and defraud in a mode made criminal by statute; and as all cheating and defrauding has not been made criminal, it is necessary for the indictment to state the means proposed, in order that the court may see that they are in fact illegal. State v. Parker, 43 N.H. 83; State v. Keach, 40 Vt. 118; Alderman v. The People, 4 Mich. 414; State v. Roberts, 34 Me. 32. In Maine, it is an offence for two or more to conspire with the intent unlawfully and wickedly to commit any crime punishable by imprisonment in the State prison (State v. Roberts); but we think it will hardly be claimed that an indictment would be good under this statute, which charges the object of the conspiracy to have been "unlawfully and wickedly to commit each, every, all, and singular the crimes punishable by imprisonment in the State prison." All crimes are not so punishable. Whether a particular crime be such a one or not, is a question of law. The accused has, therefore, the right to have a specification of the charge against him in this respect, in order that he may decide whether he should present his defence by motion to quash, demurrer, or plea; and the court, that it may determine whether the facts will sustain the indictment. So here, the crime is made to consist in the unlawful combination with an intent to prevent the enjoyment of any right granted or secured by the Constitution, &c. All rights are not so granted or secured. Whether one is so or not is a question of law, to be decided by the court, not the prosecutor. Therefore, the indictment should state the particulars, to inform the court as well as the accused. It must be made to appear -- that is to say, appear from the indictment, without going further -- that the acts charged will, if proved, support a conviction for the offence alleged.

But it is needless to pursue the argument further. The conclusion is irresistible, that these counts are too vague and general. They lack the certainty and precision required by the established rules of criminal pleading. It follows that they are not good and sufficient in law. They are so defective that no judgment of conviction should be pronounced upon them.

The order of the Circuit Court arresting the judgment upon the verdict is, therefore, affirmed; and the cause remanded, with instructions to discharge the defendants.

MR. JUSTICE CLIFFORD dissenting.

I concur that the judgment in this case should be arrested, but for reasons quite different from those given by the court.

Power is vested in Congress to enforce by appropriate legislation the prohibition contained in the fourteenth amendment of the Constitution; and the fifth section of the Enforcement Act provides to the effect, that persons who prevent, hinder, control, or intimidate, or who attempt to prevent, hinder, control, or intimidate, any person to whom the right of suffrage is secured or guaranteed by that amendment, from exercising, or in exercising such right, by means of bribery or threats; of depriving such person of employment or occupation; or of ejecting such person from rented house, lands, or other property; or by threats of refusing to renew leases or contracts for labor; or by threats of violence to himself or family, -- such person so offending shall be deemed guilty of a misdemeanor, and, on conviction thereof, shall be fined or imprisoned, or both, as therein provided. 16 Stat. 141.

Provision is also made, by sect. 6 of the same act, that, if two or more persons shall band or conspire together, or go in disguise, upon the public highway, or upon the premises of another, with intent to violate any provision of that act, or to injure, oppress, threaten, or intimidate any citizen with intent to prevent or hinder his free exercise and enjoyment of any right or privilege granted or secured to him by the constitution and laws of the United States, or because of his having exercised the same, such persons shall be deemed guilty of felony, and, on conviction thereof, shall be fined or imprisoned, or both, and be further punished as therein provided.

More than one hundred persons were jointly indicted at the April Term, 1873, of the Circuit Court of the United States for the District of Louisiana, charged with offences in violation of the provisions of the

Enforcement Act. By the record, it appears that the indictment contained thirty-two counts, in two series of sixteen counts each: that the first series were drawn under the fifth and sixth sections of the act; and that the second series were drawn under the seventh section of the same act; and that the latter series charged that the prisoners are guilty of murder committed by them in the act of violating some of the provisions of the two preceding sections of that act.

Eight of the persons named in the indictment appeared on the 10th of June, 1874, and went to trial under the plea of not guilty, previously entered at the time of their arraignment. Three of those who went to trial -- to wit, the three defendants named in the transcript -- were found guilty by the jury on the first series of the counts of the indictment, and not guilty on the second series of the counts in the same indictment.

Subsequently the convicted defendants filed a motion for a new trial, which motion being overruled they filed a motion in arrest of judgment. Hearing was had upon that motion; and the opinions of the judges of the Circuit Court being opposed, the matter in difference was duly certified to this court, the question being whether the motion in arrest of judgment ought to be granted or denied.

Two only of the causes of arrest assigned in the motion will be considered in answering the questions certified: (1.) Because the matters and things set forth and charged in the several counts in question do not constitute offences against the laws of the United States, and do not come within the purview, true intent, and meaning of the Enforcement Act. (2.) Because the several counts of the indictment in question are too vague, insufficient, and uncertain to afford the accused proper notice to plead and prepare their defence, and do not set forth any offence defined by the Enforcement Act.

Four other causes of arrest were assigned; but, in the view taken of the case, it will be sufficient to examine the two causes above set forth.

Since the questions were certified into this court, the parties have been fully heard in respect to all the questions presented for decision in the transcript. Questions not pressed at the argument will not be considered; and, inasmuch as the counsel in behalf of the United States confined their arguments entirely to the thirteenth, fourteenth, and sixteenth counts of the first series in the indictment, the answers may well be limited to these counts, the others being virtually abandoned. Mere introductory allegations will be omitted as unimportant, for the reason that the questions to be answered relate to the allegations of the respective counts describing the offence.

As described in the thirteenth count, the charge is, that the defendants did, at the time and place mentioned, combine, conspire, and confederate together, between and among themselves, for and with the unlawful and felonious intent and purpose one Levi Nelson and one Alexander Tillman, each of whom being then and there a citizen of the United States, of African descent, and a person of color, unlawfully and feloniously to injure, oppress, threaten, and intimidate, with the unlawful and felonious intent thereby the said persons of color, respectively, then and there to hinder and prevent in their respective and several free exercise and enjoyment of the rights, privileges, and immunities, and protection, granted and secured to them respectively as citizens of the United States and citizens of the State, by reason of their race and color; and because that they, the said persons of color, being then and there citizens of the State and of the United States, were then and there persons of African descent and race, and persons of color, and not white citizens thereof; the same being a right or privilege granted or secured to the said persons of color respectively, in common with all other good citizens of the United States, by the Federal Constitution and the laws of Congress.

Matters of law conceded, in the opinion of the court, may be assumed to be correct without argument; and, if so, then discussion is not necessary to show that every ingredient of which an offence is composed must be accurately and clearly alleged in the indictment, or the indictment will be bad, and may be quashed on motion, or the judgment may be arrested before sentence, or be reversed on a writ of error. United States v. Cook, 17 Wall. 174.

Offences created by statute, as well as offences at common law, must be accurately and clearly described in an indictment; and, if the offence cannot be so described without expanding the allegations beyond the mere words of the statute, then it is clear that the allegations of the indictment must be expanded to that extent, as it is universally true that no indictment is sufficient which does not accurately and clearly allege all the ingredients of which the offence is composed, so as to bring the accused within the true intent and meaning of the statute defining the offence. Authorities of great weight, besides those referred to by me, in the dissenting opinion just read, may be found in support of that proposition. 2 East, P.C. 1124; Dord v. People, 9 Barb. 675; Ike v. State, 23 Miss. 525; State v. Eldridge, 7 Eng. 608.

Every offence consists of certain acts done or omitted under certain circumstances; and, in the indictment for the offence, it is not sufficient to charge the accused generally with having committed the offence, but all the circumstances constituting the offence must be specially set forth. Arch. Cr. Pl., 15th ed., 43.

Persons born or naturalized in the United States, and subject to the jurisdiction thereof, are citizens thereof; and the fourteenth amendment also provides, that no State shall make or enforce any law which shall abridge the privileges or immunities of citizens of the United States. Congress may, doubtless, prohibit any violation of that provision, and may provide that any person convicted of violating the same shall be guilty of an offence, and be subject to such reasonable punishment as Congress may prescribe.

Conspiracies of the kind described in the introductory clause of the sixth section of the Enforcement Act are explicitly forbidden by the subsequent clauses of the same section; and it may be that if the indictment was for a conspiracy at common law, and was pending in a tribunal having jurisdiction of common-law offences, the indictment in its present form might be sufficient, even though it contains no definite allegation whatever of any particular overt act committed by the defendants in pursuance of the alleged conspiracy.

Decided cases may doubtless be found in which it is held that an indictment for a conspiracy, at common law, may be sustained where there is an unlawful agreement between two or more persons to do an unlawful act, or to do a lawful act by unlawful means; and authorities may be referred to which support the proposition, that the indictment, if the conspiracy is well pleaded, is sufficient, even though it be not alleged that any overt act had been done in pursuance of the unlawful combination.

Suffice it to say, however, that the authorities to that effect are opposed by another class of authorities equally respectable, and even more numerous, which decide that the indictment is bad unless it is alleged that some overt act was committed in pursuance of the intent and purpose of the alleged conspiracy; and in all the latter class of cases it is held, that the overt act, as well as the unlawful combination, must be clearly and accurately alleged.

Two reasons of a conclusive nature, however, may be assigned which show, beyond all doubt, that it is not necessary to enter into the inquiry which class of those decisions is correct.

1. Because the common law is not a source of jurisdiction in the circuit courts, nor in any other Federal court.

Circuit courts have no common-law jurisdiction of offences of any grade or description; and it is equally clear that the appellate jurisdiction of the Supreme Court does not extend to any case or any question, in a case not within the jurisdiction of the subordinate Federal courts. State v. Wheeling Bridge Co., 13 How. 563; United States v. Hudson et al., 7 Cranch, 32.

2. Because it is conceded that the offence described in the indictment is an offence created and defined by an act of Congress.

Indictments for offences created and defined by statute must in all cases follow the words of the statute: and, where there is no departure from that rule, the indictment is in general sufficient, except in cases where the statute is elliptical, or where, by necessary implication, other constituents are component parts of the offence; as where the words of the statute defining the offence have a compound signification, or are enlarged by what immediately precedes or follows the words describing the offence, and in the same connection. Cases of the kind do arise, as where, in the dissenting opinion in United States v. Reese et al., supra, p. 222, it was held, that the words offer to pay a capitation tax were so expanded by a succeeding clause of the same sentence that the word "offer" necessarily included readiness to perform what was offered, the provision being that the offer should be equivalent to actual performance if the offer failed to be carried into execution by the wrongful act or omission of the party to whom the offer was made.

Two offences are in fact created and defined by the sixth section of the Enforcement Act, both of which consist of a conspiracy with an intent to perpetrate a forbidden act. They are alike in respect to the conspiracy; but differ very widely in respect to the act embraced in the prohibition.

1. Persons, two or more, are forbidden to band or conspire together, or go in disguise upon the public highway, or on the premises of another, with intent to violate any provision of the Enforcement Act, which is an act of twenty-three sections.

Much discussion of that clause is certainly unnecessary, as no one of the counts under consideration is founded on it, or contains any allegations describing such an offence. Such a conspiracy with intent to injure, oppress, threaten, or intimidate any person, is also forbidden by the succeeding clause of that section, if it be done with intent to prevent or hinder his free exercise and enjoyment of any right or privilege granted or secured to him by the constitution or laws of the United States, or because of having exercised the same. Sufficient appears in the thirteenth count to warrant the conclusion, that the grand jury intended to charge the defendants with the second offence created and defined in the sixth section of the Enforcement Act.

Indefinite and vague as the description of the offence there defined is, it is obvious that it is greatly more so as described in the allegations of the thirteenth count. By the act of Congress, the prohibition is extended to any right or privilege granted or secured by the constitution or laws of Congress; leaving it to the pleader to specify the particular right or privilege which had been invaded, in order to give the accusation that certainty which the rules of criminal pleading everywhere require in an indictment; but the pleader in this case, overlooking any necessity for any such specification, and making no attempt to comply with the rules of criminal pleading in that regard, describes the supposed offence in terms much more vague and indefinite than those employed in the act of Congress.

Instead of specifying the particular right or privilege which had been invaded, the pleader proceeds to allege that the defendants, with all the others named in the indictment, did combine, conspire, and confederate together, with the unlawful intent and purpose the said persons of African descent and persons of color then and there to injure, oppress, threaten, and intimidate, and thereby then and there to hinder and prevent them in the free exercise and enjoyment of the rights, privileges, and immunities and protection granted and secured to them as citizens of the United States and citizens of the State, without any other specification of the rights, privileges, immunities, and protection which had been violated or invaded, or which were threatened, except what follows; to wit, the same being a right or privilege granted or secured in common with all other good citizens by the constitution and laws of the United States.

Vague and indefinite allegations of the kind are not sufficient to inform the accused in a criminal prosecution of the nature and cause of the accusation against him, within the meaning of the sixth amendment of the Constitution.

Valuable rights and privileges, almost without number, are granted and secured to citizens by the constitution and laws of Congress; none of which may be, with impunity, invaded in violation of the prohibition contained in that section. Congress intended by that provision to protect citizens in the enjoyment of all such rights and privileges; but in affording such protection in the mode there provided Congress never intended to open the door to the invasion of the rule requiring certainty in criminal pleading, which for ages has been regarded as one of the great safeguards of the citizen against oppressive and groundless prosecutions.

Judge Story says the indictment must charge the time and place and nature and circumstances of the offence with clearness and certainty, so that the party may have full notice of the charge, and be able to make his defence with all reasonable knowledge and ability. 2 Story, Const., sect. 1785.

Nothing need be added to show that the fourteenth count is founded upon the same clause in the sixth section of the Enforcement Act as the thirteenth count, which will supersede the necessity of any extended remarks to explain the nature and character of the offence there created and defined. Enough has already been remarked to show that that particular clause of the section was passed to protect citizens in the free exercise and enjoyment of every right or privilege granted or secured to them by the constitution and laws of Congress, and to provide for the punishment of those who band or conspire together, in the manner described, to injure, oppress, or intimidate any citizen, to prevent or hinder him from the free exercise and enjoyment of all such rights or privileges, or because of his having exercised any such right or privilege so granted or secured.

What is charged in the fourteenth count is, that the defendants did combine, conspire, and confederate the said citizens of African descent and persons of color to injure, oppress, threaten, and intimidate, with intent the said citizens thereby to prevent and hinder in the free exercise and enjoyment of the right and privilege to vote at any election to be thereafter had and held according to law by the people of the State, or by the people of the parish; they, the defendants, well knowing that the said citizens were lawfully qualified to vote at any such election thereafter to be had and held.

Confessedly, some of the defects existing in the preceding count are avoided in the count in question; as, for example, the description of the particular right or privilege of the said citizens which it was the intent of the defendants to invade is clearly alleged: but the difficulty in the count is, that it does not allege for what purpose the election or elections were to be ordered, nor when or where the elections were to be had and held. All that is alleged upon the subject is, that it was the intent of the defendants to prevent and hinder the said citizens of African descent and persons of color in the free exercise and enjoyment of the right and privilege to vote at any election thereafter to be had and held, according to law, by the people of the State, or by the people of the election, or any allegation as to the time and place when and where the election was to be had and held.

Elections thereafter to be held must mean something different from pending elections; but whether the pleader means to charge that the intent and purpose of the alleged conspiracy extended only to the next succeeding elections to be held in the State or parish, or to all future elections to be held in the State or parish during the lifetime of the parties, may admit of a serious question, which cannot be easily solved by any thing contained in the allegations of the count.

Reasonable certainty, all will agree, is required in criminal pleading; and if so it must be conceded, we think, that the allegation in question fails to comply with that requirement. Accused persons, as matter of common justice, ought to have the charge against them set forth in such terms that they may readily understand the nature and character of the accusation, in order that they, when arraigned, may know what answer to make to it, and that they may not be embarrassed in conducting their defence; and the charge ought also to be laid in such terms that, if the party accused is put to trial, the verdict and judgment may be pleaded in bar of a second accusation for the same offence.

Tested by these considerations, it is quite clear that the fourteenth count is not sufficient to warrant the conviction and sentence of the accused.

Defects and imperfections of the same kind as those pointed out in the thirteenth count also exist in the sixteenth count, and of a more decided character in the latter count than in the former; conclusive proof of which will appear by a brief examination of a few of the most material allegations of the charge against the defendants. Suffice it to say, without entering into details, that the introductory allegations of the count are in all respects the same as in the thirteenth and fourteenth counts. None of the introductory allegations allege that any overt act was perpetrated in pursuance of the alleged conspiracy; but the jurors proceed to present that the unlawful and felonious intent and purpose of the defendants were to prevent and hinder the said citizens of African descent and persons of color, by the means therein described, in the free exercise and enjoyment of each, every, all, and singular the several rights and privileges granted and secured to them by the constitution and laws of the United States in common with all other good citizens, without any attempt to describe or designate any particular right or privilege which it was the purpose and intent of the defendants to invade, abridge, or deny.

Descriptive allegations in criminal pleading are required to be reasonably definite and certain, as a necessary safeguard to the accused against surprise, misconception, and error in conducting his defence, and in order that the judgment in the case may be a bar to a second accusation for the same charge. Considerations of the kind are entitled to respect; but it is obvious, that, if such a description of the ingredient of an offence created and defined by an act of Congress is held to be sufficient, the indictment must become a snare to the accused; as it is scarcely possible that an allegation can be framed which would be less certain, or more at variance with the universal rule that every ingredient of the offence must be clearly and accurately described so as to bring the defendant within the true intent and meaning of the provision defining the offence. Such a vague and indefinite description of a material ingredient of the offence is not a compliance with the rules of pleading in framing an indictment. On the contrary, such an indictment is insufficient, and must be held bad on demurrer or in arrest of judgment.

Certain other causes for arresting the judgment are assigned in the record, which deny the constitutionality of the Enforcement Act; but, having come to the conclusion that the indictment is insufficient, it is not necessary to consider that question.

PRESSER v. ILLINOIS

(FULL CASE)

116 U.S. 252; 6 S. Ct. 580; 29 L. Ed. 615

Argued November 23, 24, 1885.

January 4, 1886, Decided

GIST: Herman Presser was indicted and pled guilty to a charge of drilling and parading an armed company of men without permission from the Governor, as required by Illinois law. He marched his company of about 400 men, part of a society called the Lehr und Wehr Verein, through the streets of Chicago, they carrying rifles, and he on horseback with a cavalry sword. In this appeal, Presser argued that the Illinois Military Code, under which he was charged, was in conflict with the United States Constitution.

Presser made constitutional claims against numerous parts of the Code, and the Court sidestepped most, saying it needn't review the entire code to cleanly and legally separate the parts he was charged under. A summary of that code is provided. The contentions made on behalf of Presser by Lyman Trumbull make compelling reading but are not part of the Court's opinion, and in fact the Court found against the plaintiff and his pleadings.

The 2nd Amendment was one basis of Presser's claim. The Court held that the 2nd Amendment is not violated by a ban on armed parades, and that the organizing and drilling of armed units is the prerogative of governments and not of individual citizens. After quoting the Amendment completely for reference, the Court singled out the right of the people to keep and bear arms in its discussions of state vs. federal powers. The Court also said that the 2nd

Amendment (like the rest of the Bill of Rights, under the Court's thinking at the time) limited only the federal government, not state governments.

The doctrine that statutes, constitutional in part only, will be upheld as to what is constitutional, if it can be separated from the unconstitutional provisions, reasserted.

A State statute providing that all able-bodied male citizens of the State between eighteen and forty-five, except those exempted, shall be subject to military duty, and shall be enrolled and designated as the State militia, and prohibiting all bodies of men other than the regularly organized volunteer militia of the State and the troops of the United States from osculating together as military organizations, or drilling or parading with arms in any city of the State without license form the governor, as to these provisions is constitutional and does not infringe the laws of the United States: and it is sustained as to them, although the act contains other provisions, separable from the foregoing, which it was contended infringed upon the powers vested in the United States by the Constitution, or upon laws enacted by Congress in pursuance thereof.

The provision in the Second Amendment to the Constitution, that "the right of the people to keep and bear arms shall not be infringed," is a limitation only on the power of Congress and the national government, and not of the States. But in view of the fact that all citizens capable of bearing arms constitute the reserved military force of the national government as well as in view of its general powers, the States cannot prohibit the people from keeping and bearing arms, so as to deprive the United States of their rightful resource for maintaining the public security.

The provision in the Fourteenth Amendment to the Constitution that "no State shall make or enforce any law which shall abridge the privileges or immunities of citizens of the United States," does not prevent a State from passing such laws to regulate the privileges and immunities of its own citizens as do not abridge their privileges and immunities as citizens of the United States.

Unless restrained by their own Constitutions, State legislatures may enact statutes to control and regulate all organizations, drilling, and parading of military bodies and associations, except those which are authorized by the militia laws of the United States.

Herman Presser, the plaintiff in error, was indicted on September 24, 1879, in the Criminal Court of Cook County, Illinois, for a violation of the following sections of Art. XI. of the Military Code of that State, Act of May 28, 1879, Laws of 1879, 192.

> **It shall not be lawful for any body of men whatever, other than the regular organized volunteer militia of this State, and the troops of the United States, to associate themselves together as a military company or organization, or to drill or parade with arms in any city, or town, of this State, without the license of the Governor**
>
> **students in educational institutions, where military science is a part of the course of instruction, may, with the consent of the Governor, drill and parade with arms in public**
>
> **nothing herein contained shall be construed so as to prevent benevolent or social organizations from wearing swords.**

"§5. It shall not be lawful for any body of men whatever, other than the regular organized volunteer militia of this State, and the troops of the United States, to associate themselves together as a military company or organization, or to drill or parade with arms in any city, or town, of this State, without the license of the Governor thereof, which license may at any time be revoked: And provided, further, that students in educational institutions, where military science is a part of the course of instruction, may, with the consent of the Governor, drill and parade with arms in public, under the superintendence of their instructors, and may take part in any regimental or brigade encampment, under command of their military instructor; and while so encamped shall be governed by the provisions of this act. They shall be entitled only to transportation and subsistence, and shall report and be subject to the commandant of such encampment: Provided, that nothing herein contained shall be construed so as to prevent benevolent or social organizations from wearing swords.

"§6. Whoever offends against the provisions of the preceding section, or belongs to, or parades with, any such unauthorized body of men with arms shall be punished by a fine not exceeding the sum of ten dollars ($10), or by imprisonment in the common jail for a term not exceeding six months, or both."

The indictment charged in substance that Presser, on September 24, 1879, in the county of Cook, in the State of Illinois, "did unlawfully belong to, and did parade and drill in the city of Chicago with an unauthorized body of men with arms, who had associated themselves together as a military company and organization, without having a license from the Governor, and not being a part of, or belonging to, 'the regular organized volunteer militia' of the State of Illinois, or the troops of the United States."

A motion to quash the indictment was overruled. Presser then pleaded not guilty, and both parties having waived a jury the case was tried by the court, which found Presser guilty and sentenced him to pay a fine of $10.

The bill of exceptions taken upon the trial set out all the evidence, from which it appeared that Presser was thirty-one years old, a citizen of the United States and of the State of Illinois, and a voter; that he belonged to a society called the Lehr und Wehr Verein, a corporation organized April 16, 1875, in due form, under chapter 32, Revised Statutes of Illinois, called the General Incorporation Laws of Illinois, "for the purpose," as expressed by its certificate of association, "of improving the mental and bodily condition of its members, so as to qualify them for the duties of citizens of a republic. Its members shall therefore obtain, in the meetings of the association, a knowledge of our laws and political economy, and shall also be instructed in military and gymnastic exercises;" that Presser, in December, 1879, marched at the head of said company, about four hundred in number, in the streets of the city of Chicago, he riding on horseback and in command; that the company was armed with rifles and Presser with a cavalry sword; that the company had no license from the governor of Illinois to drill or parade as a part of the militia of the State, and was not a part of the regular organized militia of the State, nor a part of troops of the United States, and had no organization under the militia law of the United States. The evidence showed no other facts. Exceptions were reserved to the ruling of the court upon the motion to quash the indictment, to the finding of guilty, and to the judgment thereon. The case was taken to the Supreme Court of Illinois, where the judgment was affirmed. Thereupon Presser brought the present writ of error for a review of the judgment of affirmance.

Mr. Allan C. Story for plaintiff in error, argued the following Federal points. -- I. The Illinois act is in conflict with Article I., section 8, subdivisions 12, 14, 15, 16 and 18 of the Constitution of the United States. Houston v. Moore, 5 Wheat. 1, 51, 68; Gibbons v. Ogden, 9 Wheat. 1, 209; Passenger C ses, 7 How. 283; Railroad Co. v. Husen, 95 U.S. 465; McCulloch v. Maryland, 4 Wheat. 315; Sturges v. Crowninshield, 4 Wheat. 122; Opinions of Justices, 14 Gray, 614; United States v. Cruikshank, 92 U.S. 542; Martin v. Mott, 12 Wheat. 19. -- II. It is also in conflict with Article 1, section 18, subdivision 3, of the Constitution. Luther v. Borden, 7 How. 1; Texas v. White, 7 Wall. 700; Green v. Biddle, 8 Wheat. 1; Poole v. Fleeder, 11 Pet. 185; and cases cited above. -- III. It is also in conflict with Article Ii. of the Amendments to the Constitution. See cases cited under Point I. -- IV. It is also in conflict with Amendment XIV. to the Constitution. Slaughter-House Cases, 16 Wall. 36, 74; Ward v. Maryland, 12 Wall. 418, 430; Crandall v. Nevada, 6 Wall. 35, 49; Dred Scott v. Sandford, 19 How. 393, 580; United States v. Cruikshank, cited above. -- V. It is also in conflict with Article I., section 9, subdivision 3 of the Constitution. Fletcher v. Peck, 6 Cranch, 87; Cummings v. Missouri, 4 Wall. 277; Lapeyre v. United States, 17 Wall. 191, 206; Carpenter v. Pennsylvania, 17 How. 456; Ex parte Garland, 4 Wall. 333.

Mr. Lyman Trumbull also filed a supplemental brief for plaintiff in error, contending as follows:

I. The power of organizing, arming and disciplining the militia being confided by the Constitution to Congress, when Congress acts upon the subject and passes a law to carry into effect the constitutional provision, such action excludes the power of legislation by the State on the same subject. This is manifest, not only from the grant of power to Congress to organize, arm and discipline the militia, but from the restriction which the Constitution puts upon the States, limiting them simply to the appointment of the officers, and to the authority to train the militia as Congress shall prescribe. The power of each government in regard to the militia is distinctly stated in the Constitution itself. As well might the Federal government arrogate to itself the appointment of the officers of the militia as for the States to assume to organize and arm them in a different mode from that prescribed by Congress. Congress has exercised its functions, and covered, so far as it deemed expedient, the ground assigned to it by the Constitution, by providing for organizing, arming and disciplining the militia. See. Houston v. Moore, 5 Wheat. 1, especially the language of the court on page 24. Counsel on the other side contend this case was overruled in Sturges v. Crowninshield, 4 Wheat. 122. That is a remarkable statement, as Sturges v. Crowninshield, was decided a year before Houston v. Moore. Moreover there is nothing in the former in conflict with the latter. The Military Code of Illinois differs from the act of Congress not only in details, but in its whole scope and object. Congress aims to arm, organize and discipline all able-bodied male citizens of the specified age. Illinois aims to prevent such arming, organizing and disciplining. Only 8000 are allowed to associate together and drill, and even those are not enrolled and organized as required by Congress.

II. The provisions for organizing, arming and disciplining the Illinois National Guard are in conflict with that clause of the Constitution which declares that no State shall, without the consent of Congress, keep troops in time of peace. Congress has never given its assent to that organization, and it is apparent that the guard are "troops" within the sense of the Constitution. The militia acts of Congress only excepted from their operation certain military organizations then existing, of which the Illinois National Guard was not one. It consists of 8000 men, raised for five years, formed into companies and regiments, with staff officers different in number and rank from those provided for by Congress; is divided into infantry, cavalry and artillery; is required to drill after, to practise at target shooting and rifle practice, and is required to conform to the laws of the United States organizing the militia only in matters not provided for in the act. If these provisions do not constitute the Illinois National Guard "troops," the keeping of which in time of peace by the State is prohibited by the Constitution of the United States, I am at a loss to conceive what kind of troops it is that a State may not keep.

III. The provision of the State statute which prohibits other organizations than that of the "Illinois National Guard," from associating together as military companies, or to parade with arms, without the license of the governor, is in conflict with the act of Congress for the organization &c., of the militia, and also violates Articles Ii. and XIV. of the Amendments to the Constitution. It may be admitted that Article II., securing to the people the right to keep and bear arms, by itself is a prohibition against the power of Congress, and not of the States, to interfere with that right, except when the keeping and bearing of arms is connected with some national purpose. When it is so connected, no State can pass any law abridging the right without a violation of the Second and Fourteenth Amendments.

The citizen of the United States has secured to him the right to keep and bear arms as part of the militia which Congress has the right to organize, and arm, and to drill in companies.

The Fourteenth Amendment makes all persons born or naturalized in the United States, citizens of the United States, and of the State wherein they reside, and then declares that no State shall make any law which shall abridge the privileges and immunities of citizens of the United States. The citizen of the United States has secured to him the right to keep and bear arms as part of the militia which Congress has the right to organize, and arm, and to drill in companies. This is a national right which the national government has the power and which it is its duty to enforce.

This right of the people to keep and bear arms for the purpose of forming a well regulated militia, like "the right of the people peaceably to assemble for the purpose of petitioning Congress for a redress of grievances or for anything else connected with the powers or the duties of the national government, is an attribute of national citizenship, and as such, under the protection of, and guaranteed by the United States." United States v. Cruikshank, 92 U.S. 542, 552.

Whether a State may not prohibit its citizens from keeping or bearing arms for other than militia purposes is a question which need not be considered, as the Illinois statute is aimed against the organizing, arming and drilling of bodies of men as militia

Whether a State may not prohibit its citizens from keeping or bearing arms for other than militia purposes is a question which need not be considered, as the Illinois statute is aimed against the organizing, arming and drilling of bodies of men as militia, except they belong to the Illinois National Guard of eight thousand.

It is contended that the Illinois act does not conflict with the act of Congress until the militia is actually mustered into the service of the United States. This is a mistaken view of the Constitution and of the object and intent of the law of 1792. The power of Congress to organize the militia is not limited to a period of war, or to such time as they may be employed in the service of the United States. It is only the power to govern them that is thus limited. The clause in the Constitution authorizing the President to call out the militia and put it into the service of the United States is separate and distinct from that which authorizes Congress to legislate for its organization, arming, and discipline. The manifest intent of the Constitution is to provide for an organized militia in time of peace, which may be called upon to execute the laws of the Union, and thus dispense with a standing army.

The acts of 1792 and 1795, authorizing the President to use military force to enforce the laws of the Union, suppress insurrections, and repel invasions, limited him to the use of the militia for such purposes. It was not until 1807 that he had authority to employ the land and naval forces of the United States therefor. Act of March 3, 1807, 2 Stat. 443.

The militia acts make definite provisions as to the persons to serve in the militia, the officers of that body, the times of parade and service, the returns to be made to the President, &c. It is absurd to suppose that these have no force till the militia is mustered into the service of the Union. State laws making other provisions are in conflict with it as much before as after such muster.

If it were admitted that State laws for organizing the militia are valid, except in so far as they conflict with the execution and operation of national laws on the same subject, the admission does not help the defendant in error, because it is insisted, and, as I think, shown, that the whole spirit, intent and effect of the Illinois statute is in conflict with the provisions of the act of Congress. If a State law is incompatible with the Constitution of the United States, or any law of Congress in pursuance thereof, it is invalid, whether the conflict arise in the execution and operation of the act of Congress, or in an attempt to put the State law in operation. It is enough if the State law, when sought to be put into execution and operation, conflicts with the national law on the same subject. It may be that a State law in partial execution of the military act of Congress, and conforming to its provisions, would be valid to that extent, upon the principle that power to organize all the militia implies the power to organize a part; but this principle can have no application to the Military Code of Illinois, for the reason that the organization of the Illinois National Guard, provided for by that code, does not, as has been already shown, conform to the act of Congress. It does not constitute any part of the militia upon which the President may call to enforce the laws of the United States, when resisted by combinations too powerful to be overcome by the ordinary course of judicial proceedings. Act of February 28, 1795, 1 Stat. 424; Rev. Stat. §§5298, 5299. It is purely a State force, sworn to serve the State in its military service, subject at all times to the orders of the governor, prohibited from leaving the State without his consent under a penalty, and so far from being part of the militia organized in pursuance of the act of Congress, the Illinois National Guard, in its organization, arming, and the purpose for which it is organized, contravenes the spirit and intent of the national act, and if permitted to stand, it prevents the organizing, arming and disciplining all the male citizens of the State, as Congress has prescribed.

Mr. George Hunt, Attorney-General of Illinois, for defendant in error.

MR. JUSTICE WOODS delivered the opinion of the court.

The position of the plaintiff in error in this court was, that the entire statute under which he was convicted was invalid and void, because its enactment was the exercise of a power by the legislature of Illinois forbidden to the States by the Constitution of the United States.

The clauses of the Constitution of the United States referred to in the assignments of error, were as follows:

Art. I., sec. 8. "The Congress shall have power . . . To raise and support armies. . . . To provide for calling forth the militia to execute the laws of the union, suppress insurrections, and repel invasions. To provide for organizing, arming, and disciplining the militia, and for governing such part of them as may be employed in the service of the United States, reserving to the States, respectively, the appointment of the officers, and the authority of training the militia, according to the discipline prescribed by Congress. . . . To make all laws which shall be necessary and proper, for carrying into execution the foregoing powers," &c.

Art. I., sec. 10. "No State shall, without the consent of Congress, keep troops . . . in time of peace."

Art. II. of Amendments. "A well regulated militia being necessary to the security of a free State, the right of the people to keep and bear arms shall not be infringed."

The plaintiff in error also contended that the enactment of the 5th and 6th sections of Article XI. of the Military Code was forbidden by subdivision 3 of section 9, Art. I., which declares "No bill of attainder or ex post facto law shall be passed," and by Art. XIV. of Amendments, which provides that "No State shall make or enforce any law which shall abridge the privileges or immunities of citizens of the United States, nor shall any State deprive any person of life, liberty, or property without due process of law."

The first contention of counsel for plaintiff in error is that the Congress of the United States having, by virtue of the provisions of Article I., section 8, above quoted, passed the act of May 8, 1792, entitled "An Act more effectually to provide for the National Defence by establishing an Uniform Militia throughout the United States," 1 Stat. 271, the act of February 28, 1795, "to provide for calling forth the militia to execute the laws of the Union, suppress insurrections, and repel invasions," 1 Stat. 424, and the act of July 22, 1861, "to authorize the Employment of Volunteers to aid in enforcing the Laws and protecting Public Property," 12 Stat. 268, and other subsequent acts, now forming "Title XVI., The Militia," of the Revised Statutes of the United States, the legislature of Illinois had no power to pass the act approved May 28, 1879, "to provide for the organization of the State militia, entitled the Military Code of Illinois," under the provisions of which (sections 5 and 6 of Article XI.) the plaintiff in error was indicted.

The argument in support of this contention is, that the power of organizing, arming, and disciplining the militia being confided by the Constitution to Congress, when it acts upon the subject, and passes a law to carry into effect the constitutional provision, such action excludes the power of legislation by the State on the same subject.

It is further argued that the whole scope and object of the Military Code of Illinois is in conflict with that of the law of Congress. It is said that the object of the act of Congress is to provide for organizing, arming, and disciplining all the able-bodied male citizens of the States, respectively, between certain ages, that they may be ready at all times to respond to the call of the nation to enforce its laws, suppress insurrection, and repel invasion, and thereby avoid the necessity for maintaining a large standing army, with which liberty can never be safe, and that on the other hand, the effect if not object of the Illinois statute is to prevent such organizing, arming, and disciplining of the militia.

The plaintiff in error insists that the act of Congress requires absolutely all able-bodied citizens of the State between certain ages, to be enrolled in the militia

The plaintiff in error insists that the act of Congress requires absolutely all able-bodied citizens of the

State between certain ages, to be enrolled in the militia; that the act of Illinois makes the enrolment dependent on the necessity for the use of troops to execute the laws and suppress insurrections, and then leaves it discretionary with the governor by proclamation to require such enrolment; that the act of Congress requires the entire enrolled militia of the State, with a few exemptions made by it and which may be made by State laws, to be formed into companies, battalions, regiments, brigades, and divisions, that every man shall be armed and supplied with ammunition, provides a system of discipline and field exercises for companies, regiments, &c., and subjects the entire militia of the State to the call of the President to enforce the laws, suppress insurrection, or repel invasion, and provides for the punishment of the militia officers and men who refuse obedience to his orders. On the other hand, it is said that the State law makes it unlawful for any of its able-bodied citizens, except eight thousand, called the Illinois National Guard, to associate themselves together as a military company, or to drill or parade with arms without the license of the governor, and declares that no military company shall leave the State with arms and equipments without his consent; that even the eight thousand men, styled the Illinois National Guard, are not enrolled or organized as required by the act of Congress, nor are they subject to the call of the President, but they constitute a military force sworn to serve in the military service of the State, to obey the orders of the governor, and not to leave the State without his consent; and that, if the State act is valid, the national act providing for organizing, arming, and disciplining the militia is of no force in the State of Illinois, for the Illinois act, so far from being in harmony with the act of Congress, is an insurmountable obstacle to its execution.

We have not found it necessary to consider or decide the question thus raised, as to the validity of the entire Military Code of Illinois, for, in our opinion, the sections under which the plaintiff in error was convicted may be valid, even if the other sections of the act were invalid. For it is a settled rule "that statutes that are constitutional in part only will be upheld so far as they are not in conflict with the Constitution, provided the allowed and prohibited parts are separable." Packet Co. v. Keokuk, 95 U.S. 80; Penniman's Case, 103 U.S. 714, 717; Unity v. Burrage, 103 U.S. 459. See also Trade Mark Cases, 100 U.S. 82.

We are of opinion that this rule is applicable in this case. The first two sections of Article I. of the Military Code provide that all able-bodied male citizens of the State between the ages of eighteen and forty-five years, except those exempted, shall be subject to military duty, and be designated the "Illinois State Militia," and declare how they shall be enrolled and under what circumstances. The residue of the Code, except the two sections on which the indictment against the plaintiff in error is based, provides for a volunteer active militia, to consist of not more than eight thousand officers and men, declares how it shall be enlisted and brigaded, and the term of service of its officers and men; provides for brigade generals and their staffs, for the organization of the requisite battalions and companies and the election of company officers; provides for inspections, parades, and encampments, arms and armories, rifle practice, and courts martial; provides for the pay of the officers and men, for medical service, regimental bands, books of instruction and maps; contains provisions for levying and collecting a military fund by taxation, and directs how it shall be expended; and appropriates $25,000 out of the treasury, in advance of the collection of the military fund, to be used for the purposes specified in the Military Code.

It is plain from this statement of the substance of the Military Code, that the two sections upon which the indictment against the plaintiff in error is based may be separated from the residue of the Code, and stand upon their own independent provisions. These sections might have been left out of the Military Code and put in an act by themselves, and the act thus constituted, and the residue of the Military Code, would have been coherent and sensible acts. If it be conceded that the entire Military Code, except these sections, is unconstitutional and invalid, for the reasons stated by the plaintiff in error, these sections are separable, and, put in an act by themselves, could not be considered as forbidden by the clauses of the Constitution having reference to the militia, or to the clause forbidding the States, without the consent of Congress, to keep troops in time of peace. There is no such connection between the sections which prohibit any body of men, other than the organized militia of the State and the troops of the United States, from associating as a military company and drilling with arms in any city or town of the State, and the sections which provide for the enrolment and organization of the State militia, as makes it impossible to declare one, without declaring both, invalid.

This view disposes of the objection to the judgment of the Supreme Court of Illinois, which judgment was in effect that the legislation on which the indictment is based is not invalid by reason of the provisions of the Constitution of the United States, which vest Congress with power to raise and support armies, and to provide for calling out, organizing, arming and disciplining the militia, and governing such part of them as may be employed in the service of the United States, and that provision which declares that "no State shall without the consent of Congress . . . keep troops . . . in time of peace."

We are next to inquire whether the 5th and 6th sections of article XI. of the Military Code are in violation of the other provisions of the Constitution of the United States relied on by the plaintiff in error. The first of these is the Second Amendment, which declares: "A well regulated militia being necessary to the security of a free State, the right of the people to keep and bear arms shall not be infringed."

We think it clear that the sections under consideration, which only forbid bodies of men to associate together as military organizations, or to drill or parade with arms in cities and towns unless authorized by law, do not infringe the right of the people to keep and bear arms.

the amendment is a limitation only upon the power of Congress and the National government, and not upon that of the States.

the right of the people to keep and bear arms "is not a right granted by the Constitution. Neither is it in any manner dependent upon that instrument for its existence. The Second Amendment declares that it shall not be infringed, but this, as has been seen, means no more than that it shall not be infringed by Congress.

We think it clear that the sections under consideration, which only forbid bodies of men to associate together as military organizations, or to drill or parade with arms in cities and towns unless authorized by law, do not infringe the right of the people to keep and bear arms. But a conclusive answer to the contention that this amendment prohibits the legislation in question lies in the fact that the amendment is a limitation only upon the power of Congress and the National government, and not upon that of the States. It was so held by this court in the case of United States v. Cruikshank, 92 U.S. 542, 553, in which the Chief Justice, in delivering the judgment of the court, said, that the right of the people to keep and bear arms "is not a right granted by the Constitution. Neither is it in any manner dependent upon that instrument for its existence. The Second Amendment declares that it shall not be infringed, but this, as has been seen, means no more than that it shall not be infringed by Congress. This is one of the amendments that has no other effect than to restrict the powers of the National government, leaving the people to look for their protection against any violation by their fellow-citizens of the rights it recognizes to what is called in The City of New York v. Miln, 11 Pet. [102] 139, the 'powers which relate to merely municipal legislation, or what was perhaps more properly called internal police,' 'not surrendered or restrained' by the Constitution of the United States." See also Barron v. Baltimore, 7 Pet. 243; Fox v. The State of Ohio, 5 How. 410; Twitchell v. Commonwealth, 7 Wall. 321, 327; Jakson v. Wood, 2 Cowen, 819; Commonwealth v. Purchase, 2 Pick. 521; United States v. Cruikshank, 1 Woods, 308; North Carolina v. Newsom, 5 Iredell, 250; Andrews v. State, 3 Heiskell, 165; Fife v. State, 31 Ark. 455.

It is undoubtedly true that all citizens capable of bearing arms constitute the reserved military force or reserve militia of the United States as well as of the States, and, in view of this prerogative of the general government, as well as of its general powers, the States cannot, even laying the constitutional provision in question out of view, prohibit the people from keeping and bearing arms, so as to deprive the United States of their rightful resource for maintaining the public security, and disable the people from performing their duty to the general government.

It is undoubtedly true that all citizens capable of bearing arms constitute the reserved military force or reserve militia of the United States as well as of the States, and, in view of this prerogative of the general government, as well as of its general powers, the States cannot, even laying the constitutional provision in question out of view, prohibit the people from keeping and bearing arms, so as to deprive the United States of their rightful resource for maintaining the public security, and disable the people from performing their duty to the general government. But, as already stated, we think it clear that the sections under consideration do not have this effect.

The plaintiff in error next insists that the sections of the Military Code of Illinois, under which he was indicted, are an invasion of that clause of the first section of the Fourteenth Amendment to the Constitution of the United States which declares: "No State shall make or enforce any law which shall abridge the privileges or immunities of citizens of the United States."

A State may pass laws to regulate the privileges and immunities of its own citizens, provided that in so doing it does not abridge their privileges and immunities as citizens of the United States.

It is only the privileges and immunities of citizens of the United States that the clause relied on was intended to protect. A State may pass laws to regulate the privileges and immunities of its own citizens, provided that in so doing it does not abridge their privileges and immunities as citizens of the United States. The inquiry is, therefore, pertinent, what privilege or immunity of a citizen of the United States is abridged by sections 5 and 6 of Article XI. of the Military Code of Illinois?

The question is, therefore, had he a right as a citizen of the United States, in disobedience of the State law, to associate with others as a military company, and to drill and parade with arms in the towns and cities of the State?

The plaintiff in error was not a member of the organized volunteer militia of the State of Illinois, nor did he belong to the troops of the United States or to any organization under the militia law of the United States. On the contrary, the fact that he did not belong to the organized militia or the troops of the United States was an ingredient in the offence for which he was convicted and sentenced. The question is, therefore, had he a right as a citizen of the United States, in disobedience of the State law, to associate with others as a military company, and to drill and parade with arms in the towns and cities of the State? If the plaintiff in error has any such privilege he must be able to point to the provision of the Constitutional statutes of the United States by which it is conferred. For as was said by this court in United States v. Cruikshank, 92 U.S. 542, 560, 551, the government of the United States, although it is "within the scope of its powers supreme and above the States," "can neither grant nor secure to its citizens any right or privilege not expressly or by implication placed under its jurisdiction." "All that cannot be so granted or so secured are left to the exclusive protection of the State."

We have not been referred to any statute of the United States which confers upon the plaintiff in error the privilege which he asserts. The only clause in the Constitution which, upon any pretence, could be said to have any relation whatever to his right to associate with others as a military company is found in the First Amendment, which declares that "Congress shall make no law . . . abridging . . . the right of the people peaceably to assemble and to petition the government for a redress of grievances." This is a right which it was held in United States v. Cruikshank, above cited, was an attribute of national citizenship, and, as such, under the protection of, and guaranteed by, the United States. But it was held in the same case that the right peaceably to assemble was not protected by the clause referred to, unless the purpose of the assembly was to petition the government for a redress of grievances.

The right voluntarily to associate together as a military company or organization, or to drill or parade with arms, without, and independent of, an act of Congress or law of the State authorizing the same, is not an attribute of national citizenship. Military organization and military drill and parade under arms are subjects especially under the control of the government of every country. They cannot be claimed as a right independent of law.

The right voluntarily to associate together as a military company or organization, or to drill or parade with arms, without, and independent of, an act of Congress or law of the State authorizing the same, is not an attribute of national citizenship. Military organization and military drill and parade under arms are subjects especially under the control of the government of every country. They cannot be claimed as a right independent of law. Under our political system they are subject to the regulation and control of the State and Federal governments, acting in due regard to their respective prerogatives and powers. The Constitution and laws of the United States will be searched in vain for any support to the view that these rights are privileges and immunities of citizens of the United States independent of some specific legislation on the subject.

The exercise of this power by the States is necessary to the public peace, safety and good order. To deny the power would be to deny the right of the State to disperse assemblages organized for sedition and treason, and the right to suppress armed mobs bent on riot and rapine.

It cannot be successfully questioned that the State governments, unless restrained by their own Constitutions, have the power to regulate or prohibit associations and meetings of the people, except in the case of peaceable assemblies to perform the duties or exercise the privileges of citizens of the United States; and have also the power to control and regulate the organization, drilling, and parading of military bodies and associations, except when such bodies or associations are authorized by the militia laws of the United States. The exercise of this power by the States is necessary to the public peace, safety and good order. To deny the power would be to deny the right of the State to disperse assemblages organized for sedition and treason, and the right to suppress armed mobs bent on riot and rapine.

In the case of New York v. Miln, 11 Pet. 102, 139, this court said: "We choose rather to plant ourselves on what we consider impregnable positions. They are these: that a State has the same undeniable and unlimited jurisdiction over all persons and things within its territorial limits as any foreign nation, where that jurisdiction is not surrendered or restrained by the Constitution of the United States; that by virtue of this, it is not only the right but the bounden and solemn duty of a State to advance the safety, happiness and prosperity of its people, and to provide for its general welfare by any and every act of legislation which it may deem to be conducive to these ends, where the power over the particular subject or the manner of its exercise is not surrendered or restrained in the manner just stated," namely, by the Constitution and laws of the United States. See also Gibbons v. Ogden, 9 Wheat. 1, 203; Gilman v. Philadelphia, 3 Wall. 713; License Tax Cases, 5 Wall. 462; United States v. Dewitt, 9 Wall. 41; United. States v. Cruikshank, 92 U.S. 542. These considerations and authorities sustain the power exercised by the legislature of Illinois in the enactment of sections 5 and 6 of Art. XI. of the Military Code.

The argument of the plaintiff in error that the legislation mentioned deprives him of either life, liberty or property without due process of law, or that it is a bill of attainder or ex post facto law, is so clearly untenable as to require no discussion.

It is clear that their object was to forbid voluntary military associations, unauthorized by law, from organizing or drilling and parading with arms in the cities or towns of the State, and not to interfere with the organization, arming and drilling of the militia under the authority of the acts of Congress.

It is next contended by the plaintiff in error that sections 5 and 6 of Art. XI. of the Military Code, under which he was indicted, are in conflict with the acts of Congress for the organization of the militia. But this position is based on what seems to us to be an unwarranted construction of the sections referred to. It is clear that their object was to forbid voluntary military associations, unauthorized by law, from organizing or drilling and parading with arms in the cities or towns of the State, and not to interfere with the organization, arming and drilling of the militia under the authority of the acts of Congress. If the object and effect of the sections were in irreconcilable conflict with the acts of Congress they would of course be invalid. But it is a rule of construction that a statute must be interpreted so as, if possible, to make it consistent with the Constitution and the paramount law. Parsons v. Bedford, 3 Pet. 433; Grenada County Supervisors v. Brogden, 112 U.S. 261; Marshall v. Grimes, 41 Mississippi, 27. If we yielded to this contention of the plaintiff in error we should render the sections invalid by giving them a strained construction, which would make them antagonistic to the law of Congress. We cannot attribute to the legislature, unless compelled to do so by its plain words, a purpose to pass an act in conflict with an act of Congress on a subject over which Congress is given authority by the Constitution of the United States. We are therefore of opinion that fairly construed the sections of the Military Code referred to do not conflict with the laws of Congress on the subject of the militia.

The plaintiff in error further insists that the organization of the Lehr und Wehr Verein as a corporate body, under the general corporation law of the State of Illinois, was in effect a license from the governor, within the meaning of section 5 of Article XI. of the Military Code, and that such corporate body fell within the Exception of the same section "of students in educational institutions where military science is a part of the course of instruction."

In respect to these points we have to say that they present no Federal question. It is not, therefore, our province to consider or decide them. Murdock v. Memphis, 20 Wall. 590.

All the Federal questions presented by the record were rightly decided by the Supreme Court of Illinois.

Judgment affirmed.

LOGAN v. UNITED STATES

(CASE EXCERPT)

144 U.S. 263; 12 S. Ct. 617; 36 L. Ed. 429

Argued January 26, 27, 1892

April 4, 1892, Decided

GIST: *Logan* marks the beginning of a series of cases in which the Supreme Court sets out the principles of self defense. As was the style at the time, the decisions include graphic depictions of the facts of each case. When it comes to the twelve self-defense cases of the 1890s, these read like good cowboy Westerns. One additional case occurred in 1921, and in 1995, a police use-of-force case (*Tennessee v. Garner*) addressed the tangential self-defense issue of *chase* or stopping a fleeing felon. All 14 self-defense cases are indicated by a

"Δ" marker in the Table of Contents and Descriptive Index. In addition, the introductory essay by Korwin includes a chart assigning the basic principles of self defense to the cases that address them.

The five Marlow brothers were indicted in Texas for larceny in Indian Country. They were out on bail and living at a farm 12 miles from the courthouse. One of the brothers, Boone, was also wanted for murder.

The county sheriff, with a deputy named Collier, rode out one day to serve the murder warrant. As soon as Boone stepped outside, without warning, Collier fired at him. Boone returned fire but missed and ended up killing the sheriff. Boone took off, never to be seen again.

The angry townsfolk, motivated by the killing of their beloved sheriff, went out to the farm and hauled the remaining four brothers off to the local jail. After an angry assault in the jail, repulsed by the Marlows, Collier (who was now the sheriff), arranged with the County Attorney to take the prisoners to an adjacent county jail for safekeeping. Deep in the dark of night, they assembled a three-vehicle convoy, bristling with armed guards, with the prisoners in the lead wagon.

Instead of heading to another jail, the Marlows were driven by their captors into an ambush by a mob a few miles out of town. Though shackled in pairs, they managed to jump out of the hack they were in when the shooting began, grabbed guns from their "guards" and attackers, and drove off the perpetrators in what must have been a scene to rival anything Hollywood has ever produced. The facts of the incident are included in the case below. Two of the Marlows and two of the conspirators were shot dead in the ambush, and people on both sides were wounded.

The two surviving Marlow brothers, wounded and bleeding, managed to unshackle themselves from their dead kin in order to get away, and were eventually taken to federal court in Dallas, by a deputy U.S. Marshal, and tried and acquitted. The Logan case wrestled with their rights while in custody.

A federal statute of the time prohibited conspiracies to injure or threaten a citizen in the exercise of a right secured by the United States Constitution. Similar language can be found in current federal law under 18 USC §§241 and 242. In a rambling decision, the Court states that some rights, such as the right to assemble peacefully, and the right of the people to keep and bear arms, are not guaranteed by the Constitution, they are simply recognized by it as pre-existing rights and in that sense are more fundamentally inherent than those rights granted by the Constitution. These rights are outside of Congress' authority to act, or of any congressional ability to require the states to act. Such rights are part of the "natural and inalienable rights of man," and "the fundamental rights which belong to every citizen as a member of society."

The Court had to decide if the prisoners, even though betrayed by their legal guards, were entitled constitutionally to protection while they were kept defenseless in custody. The Court acknowledged several times that, as prisoners, they were denied the exercise of self defense.

The Justices found that because the United States had the power to punish crimes against the laws of the United States, it necessarily had the power to arrest and safely detain people accused of such crimes while they, as prisoners, are denied the usual means of self defense. This power to detain, they argued, implies a right of the person detained to be protected from unlawful violence.

Where, as here, the right is created by the Constitution, the United States may legislate to protect the right from infringement by individuals and states. Where the right is preexisting and the Constitution merely recognizes it (as with the 1st and 2nd Amendments), the United States is itself barred from infringing the right and is not empowered by the 14th Amendment to legislate to protect it from infringement by states or individuals.

Logan was named as one of the shooters by a wounded Marlow and by others, in testimony that was not without conflicts. It seems that Logan was supposed to be a guard that night, got himself excused by the leaders of the convoy (who were in on the ambush plan), and then tipped off the mob, all of whom were conspirators to deny the prisoners their rights. Along with two other perpetrators, Logan was convicted of the conspiracy charge. No one was found guilty of the murders, and the remaining defendants were acquitted.

STATEMENT BY MR. JUSTICE GRAY.

Four indictments, numbered in the record 33, 34, 35, and 36, on sections 5508 and 5509 of the Revised Statutes, (copied in the margin,1) were returned by the grand jury at January term, 1890, of the district court for the northern district of Texas, sitting at Dallas, in that district, against Eugene Logan, William Williams, Verna Wilkerson, and Clinton Rutherford, for conspiracy to injure and oppress citizens of the United States in the free exercise of a right secured to them by the constitution and laws of the United States, and for murder, committed in the prosecution of the conspiracy; and were forthwith transmitted to the circuit court.

did then and there combine, conspire, and confederate by and between themselves, with force and arms, to injure and oppress them

on January 19, 1889, and in the night-time, went upon the highway in disguise, and waylaid and assaulted the said prisoners, while in the power, custody, and control of said deputy United States marshal, with loaded shotguns, revolvers, and Winchester rifles

Indictment 34 averred, in the first count, that on January 19, 1889, at Graham, in the county of Young, and that district, Charles Marlow, Epp Marlow, Alfred Marlow, George W. Marlow, William D. Burkhardt, and Louis Clift were citizens of the United States, and in the power, custody, and control of Edward W. Johnson, a deputy United States marshal for that district, by virtue of writs of commitment from a commissioner of the circuit court of the United States for the district, in default of bail, to answer to indictments for an offense against the laws of the United States, to-wit, larceny in the Indian country, within the exclusive jurisdiction of the United States; and that, while said Johnson held them in his power, custody, and control, in pursuance of said writs, the defendants, 'together with divers other evil-disposed persons, whose names to the grand jurors aforesaid are unknown, did then and there combine, conspire, and confederate by and between themselves, with force and arms, to injure and oppress them, the said Charles Marlow, Epp Marlow, Alfred Marlow, George W. Marlow, William D. Burkhardt, and Louis Clift, then and there citizens of the United States of America, in the free exercise and enjoyment of a right, and because they were then and there exercising and enjoying said right, then and there secured to them' 'by the constitution and laws of the United States, to-wit, the right to then and there be protected by said deputy United States marshal from the assault of' the defendants and other evil-disposed persons, 'and the right then and there to be held in the power, custody, and control of said deputy United States marshal under and by virtue of said writs heretofore set forth, and the further right, while in said custody, to be secure in their persons from bodily harm and injury and assaults and cruelties until they' 'had been discharged by due process of the laws of the United States;' and that the defendants, in pursuance of such combination and conspiracy, and in the prosecution thereof, on January 19, 1889, and in the night-time, went upon the highway in disguise, and waylaid and assaulted the said prisoners, while in the power, custody, and control of said deputy United States marshal, with loaded shotguns, revolvers, and Winchester rifles, and, in pursuance and prosecution of the conspiracy, feloniously, willfully, and of their malice aforethought, and from a deliberate and premeditated design to effect his death, did with those weapons kill and murder Epp Marlow, then and there in the peace of the United States being (charging the murder in due technical form;) 'contrary to the form of the statute in such case made and provided, and against the peace and dignity of the United States of America.'

The other counts in this indictment were substantially similar, except that some of them alleged the prisoners to have been in the custody of Thomas Collier, sheriff and jailer of Young county, under the writs of commitment from the United States commissioner; or alleged Alfred Marlow to have been the person murdered; or charged one of the defendants as principal and the others as accessories in the murder.

.....

The government introduced evidence tending to prove the following facts:

Shortly before October term, 1888, of the district court of the United States for the northern district of Texas, held at Graham, the four Marlows named in the indictment, and one Boone Marlow, (the five being brothers,) were arrested on warrants issued by a commissioner of the circuit court of the United States on complaints charging them with larceny in the Indian Territory, within the exclusive jurisdiction of the United States; and at that term they were indicted for that offense, and enlarged on bail, and went to live on a farm in Young county, about 12 miles from Graham, known as the 'Denson Farm.'

on December 17, 1888, the sheriff of the county, and his deputy, Collier, went to the farm to arrest Boone Marlow on a capias from a court of the state to answer a charge of murder. Without showing their warrant, Collier fired a pistol at him, and he fired at Collier, and, missing him, killed the sheriff. The killing of the sheriff caused great excitement in Young county, and much resentment on the part of his friends against the Marlows. Boone Marlow escaped, and did not appear again. The four other Marlows were put in the county jail by the citizens

Afterwards, on December 17, 1888, the sheriff of the county, and his deputy, Collier, went to the farm to arrest Boone Marlow on a capias from a court of the state to answer a charge of murder. Without showing their warrant, Collier fired a pistol at him, and he fired at Collier, and, missing him, killed the sheriff. The killing of the sheriff caused great excitement in Young county, and much resentment on the part of his friends against the Marlows. Boone Marlow escaped, and did not appear again. The four other Marlows were put in the county jail by the citizens, and surrendered by their bail, and were again committed to the jail by Edward W. Johnson, a deputy United States marshal, under writs of commitment from the commissioner directing him to do so, to answer the indictments for larceny.

On the night of January 17, 1889, a body of men, armed and partly disguised, entered the jail, surrounded the steel cage in which the four Marlows were confined, and attempted to enter it

On the night of January 17, 1889, a body of men, armed and partly disguised, entered the jail, surrounded the steel cage in which the four Marlows were confined, and attempted to enter it; but, being resisted by the Marlows, and one of the mob knocked down and injured, they finally withdrew, without doing any actual violence to the prisoners.

On January 19, 1889, after dark, Johnson, the deputy-marshal, undertook to remove the Marlows, with Burkhardt and Clift, imprisoned under like commitments, to the jail of an adjoining county.

Johnson, the defendant Wallace, and two other men, all armed, followed in another hack; and the defendant Waggoner and another man, also armed, accompanied them in a buggy.

they were attacked, near a run called 'Dry Creek,' by a large body of men, armed and disguised, who opened fire upon the prisoners. Martin and the guards were in league with the attacking party. The four Marlows, in spite of their shackles, immediately dropped out of the hack, and wrested fire-arms, either from the guards or from their assailants, with which they defended themselves, killed two of the mob, wounded others, and finally put the rest to flight. Johnson was wounded, and he and all the guards also fled. Alfred Marlow and Epp Marlow were killed. The other two Marlows were severely wounded, but succeeded in freeing themselves from their brothers' dead bodies

On January 19, 1889, after dark, Johnson, the deputy-marshal, undertook to remove the Marlows, with Burkhardt and Clift, imprisoned under like commitments, to the jail of an adjoining county. The six prisoners, shackled together, two and two, (Alfred with Charles, Epp with George, and Burkhardt with Clift,) by irons riveted around one leg of each, and connected by a chain, were placed in a hack driven by Martin, who was county attorney. Johnson, the defendant Wallace, and two other men, all armed, followed in another hack; and the defendant Waggoner and another man, also armed, accompanied them in a buggy. When the three vehicles, in close order, had gone along the highway about two miles from Graham, they were attacked, near a run called 'Dry Creek,' by a large body of men, armed and disguised, who opened fire upon the prisoners. Martin and the guards were in league with the attacking party. The four Marlows, in spite of their shackles, immediately dropped out of the hack, and wrested fire- arms, either from the guards or from their assailants, with which they defended themselves, killed two of the mob, wounded others, and finally put the rest to flight. Johnson was wounded, and he and all the guards also fled. Alfred Marlow and Epp Marlow were killed. The other two Marlows were severely wounded, but succeeded in freeing themselves from their brothers' dead bodies, took possession of the hack surviving Marlows. He was there met by with Burkhardt and Clift, made their way to a neighboring village, and thence to the Denson farm.

On the following day Collier, the new sheriff of the county, (one of the defendants in this case, who died before the trial,) went to the Denson farm with a large body of men whom he had collected, for the purpose of recapturing the two surviving Marlows. He was there met by the sheriff of a neighboring county, whose aid he had summoned, but who declined, on learning the facts of the case, to interfere in the matter. The Marlows refused to give themselves up to any one except the United States marshal or one Morton, his deputy; and no violence was offered to them; but Collier, with a body of men, kept guard near the house for some days, until the arrival of Morton, who, against some remonstrance on the part of Collier, took the Marlows into his custody, and removed them to Dallas. They were afterwards tried, and acquitted on the charges against them.

At the trial of the present case, the principal question of fact was of the defendants' connection with the conspiracy charged in the indictment.

There was evidence in the case tending to show that Johnson, while lying wounded at his home after the fight, assented, at the solicitation of some of the defendants, to the publication in a newspaper of a statement that Logan was one of the guards at Dry creek on the night of January 19th. The government, not for the purpose of contradicting Johnson, but as independent evidence that Logan took part in the fight, not as a guard, but as one of the mob, called several witnesses to prove declarations of Johnson made after the fight, some on the same night and others some days after, that Logan was not a guard on that night, had meant to go as a guard, but had been excused from going, and must have been the person who informed the mob of the intended was not a guard on that night, had meant objected to the admission of this evidence, among other grounds, because the declarations were not made in Logan's presence, and were made after the crime had been committed, and the conspirators had separated. The judge overruled the objection, and admitted the evidence, and the defendants excepted to its admission.

The court also admitted, against the like objection and exception of the defendants, testimony to declarations of Collier, of Hollis, and of persons not known to the witnesses, some made on the night of the fight, after the escape of the Marlows, and while Collier, Hollis, and others were in pursuit, and were stopping at houses on their way to get other persons to join them, and some made on the following day, at the funeral of one of the conspirators and elsewhere, that Logan had been present at the fight, and not as a guard, and had been wounded there.

while they, with Burkhardt and Clift, were escaping in the hack after the fight, Charles Marlow told his companions that he believed Logan was the man at whom he shot, and who was shooting at him, during the fight.

The two surviving Marlows were permitted to testify, on behalf of the government, that while they, with Burkhardt and Clift, were escaping in the hack after the fight, Charles Marlow told his companions that he believed Logan was the man at whom he shot, and who was shooting at him, during the fight. The defendants objected to this evidence, as declarations made in their absence, and as hearsay, and excepted to its admission.

When a citizen of the United States is committed to the custody of a United States marshal, or to a state jail... until tried or discharged by due process of law, has the right, under said constitution and laws, to be treated with humanity, and to be protected against all unlawful violence while he is deprived of the ordinary means of defending and protecting himself.

The defendants requested the judge to instruct the jury that the matters alleged in the indictments and the proof made under them constituted no offense under the laws of the United States, and therefore they should return a verdict of not guilty. The judge refused so to instruct the jury, and instructed them as follows: 'When a citizen of the United States is committed to the custody of a United States marshal, or to a state jail, by process issuing from one of the courts of the United States, to be held, in default of bail, to await his trial on a criminal charge within the exclusive jurisdiction of the national courts, such citizen has a right, under the constitution and laws of the United States; to a speedy and public trial by an impartial jury, and, until tried or discharged by due process of law, has the right, under said constitution and laws, to be treated with humanity, and to be protected against all unlawful violence while he is deprived of the ordinary means of defending and protecting himself.' To this instruction, as well as to the refusal to give the instruction requested, the defendants excepted.

The judge further defined the crimes charged,-of conspiracy, and of murder in the prosecution of the conspiracy; and submitted to the jury the questions whether the defendants were guilty of the conspiracy only, and whether they were guilty of the murder also.

Many other rullings and instructions excepted to at the trial are omitted from this statement, because not passed upon by this court. On April 17, 1891, the jury found the defendants Logan, Waggoner, and Wallace guilty of the conspiracy charged in the indictments, and not guilty of murder, and acquitted the other defendants. The court thereupon ordered and adjudged that the other defendants be discharged; and that Logan, Waggoner, and Wallace were guilty of conspiracy as charged in the indictments, and sentenced each of them to pay a fine of $5,000, to be imprisoned for a term of 10 years, and to be ineligible to any office or place of honor, profit, or trust created by the constitution or laws of the United States. On June 23, 1891, they sued out this writ of error under the act of March 3, 1891, c. 517, 5, (26 St. p. 827.)

Mr. Justice GRAY, after stating the facts in the foregoing language, delivered the opinion of the court.

The plaintiffs in error were indicted on sections 5508 and 5509 of the Revised Statutes, for conspiracy, and for murder in the prosecution of the conspiracy; and were convicted, under section 5508, of a conspiracy to injure and oppress citizens of the United States in the free exercise and enjoyment of the right to be secure from assault or bodily harm, and to be protected against unlawful violence, while in the custody of a marshal of the United States under a lawful commitment by a commissioner of the Circuit Court of the United States for trial for an offence against the laws of the United States.

By section 5508 of the Revised Statutes, "if two or more persons conspire to injure, oppress, threaten or intimidate any citizen in the free exercise or enjoyment of any right or privilege secured to him by the Constitution or laws of the United States, or because of his having so exercised the same," "they shall be fined not more than five thousand dollars and imprisoned not more than ten years, and shall, moreover, be thereafter ineligible to any office or place of honor, profit or trust, created by the Constitution or laws of the United States."

1. The principal question in this case is whether the right of a citizen of the United States, in the custody of a United States marshal under a lawful commitment to answer for an offence against the United States, to be protected against lawless violence, is a right secured to him by the Constitution or laws of the United States, or whether it is a right which can be vindicated only under the laws of the several States.

.....

Although the constitution contains no grant, general or specific, to congress of the power to provide for the punishment of crimes, except piracies and felonies on the high seas, offenses against the law of nations, treason, and counterfeiting the securities and current coin of the United States, no one doubts the power of Congress to provide for the punishment of all crimes and offences against the United States, whether committed within one of the States of the Union, or within territory over which Congress has plenary and exclusive jurisdiction.

> **The United States, having the absolute right to hold such prisoners, have an equal duty to protect them, while so held, against assault or injury from any quarter. The existence of that duty on the part of the government necessarily implies a corresponding right of the prisoners to be so protected; and this right of the prisoners is a right secured to them by the Constitution and laws of the United States.**

To accomplish this end, Congress has the right to enact laws for the arrest and commitment of those accused of any such crime or offence, and for holding them in safe custody until indictment and trial; and persons arrested and held pursuant to such laws are in the exclusive custody of the United States, and are not subject to the judicial process or executive warrant of any State. Ableman v. Booth, 21 How. 506; Tarble's Case, 13 Wall. 397; Robb v. Connolly, 111 U.S. 624. The United States, having the absolute right to hold such prisoners, have an equal duty to protect them, while so held, against assault or injury from any quarter. The existence of that duty on the part of the government necessarily implies a corresponding right of the prisoners to be so protected; and this right of the prisoners is a right secured to them by the Constitution and laws of the United States.

The statutes of the United States have provided that any person accused of a crime or offence against the United States may by any United States judge or commissioner of a Circuit Court be arrested and confined, or bailed, as the case may be, for trial before the court of the United States having cognizance of the offence; and, if bailed, may be arrested by his bail, and delivered to the marshal or his deputy, before any judge or other officer having power to commit for the offence, and be thereupon recommitted to the custody of the marshal, to be held until discharged by due course of law. Rev. Stat. §§1014, 1018. They have also provided that all the expenses attendant upon the transportation from place to place, and upon the temporary or permanent confinement, of persons arrested or committed under the laws of the United States, shall be paid out of the Treasury of the United States; and that the marshal, in case of necessity, may provide a convenient place for a temporary jail, and "shall make such other provision as he may deem expedient and necessary for the safe keeping of the prisoners arrested or committed under the authority of the United States, until permanent provision for that purpose is made by law." Rev. Stat. §§5536-5538.

In the case at bar, the indictments alleged, the evidence at the trial tended to prove, and the jury have found by their verdict, that while Charles Marlow and five others, citizens of the United States, were in the custody and control of a deputy marshal of the United States under writs of commitment from a commissioner of the Circuit Court, in default of bail, to answer to indictments for an offence against the laws of the United States, the plaintiffs in error conspired to injure and oppress them in the free exercise and enjoyment of the right, secured to them by the Constitution and laws of the United States, to be protected, while in such custody and control of the deputy marshal, against assault and bodily harm, until they had been discharged by due process of the laws of the United States.

If, as some of the evidence introduced by the government tended to show, the deputy marshal and his assistants made no attempt to protect the prisoners, but were in league and collusion with the conspirators, that does not lessen or impair the right of protection, secured to the prisoners by the Constitution and laws of the United States.

If, as some of the evidence introduced by the government tended to show, the deputy marshal and his assistants made no attempt to protect the prisoners, but were in league and collusion with the conspirators, that does not lessen or impair the right of protection, secured to the prisoners by the Constitution and laws of the United States.

The prisoners were in the exclusive custody and control of the United States, under the protection of the United States, and in the peace of the United States. There was a co-extensive duty on the part of the United States to protect against lawless violence persons so within their custody, control, protection and peace; and a corresponding right of those persons, secured by the Constitution and laws of the United States, to be so protected by the United States. If the officers of the United States, charged with the performance of the duty, in behalf of the United States, of affording that protection and securing that right, neglected or violated their duty, the prisoners were not the less under the shield and panoply of the United States.

.....

In United States v. Reese, 92 U.S. 214, 217, decided at October term, 1875, this court, speaking by Chief Justice Waite, said: "Rights and immunities created by or dependent upon the Constitution of the United States can be protected by Congress. The form and the manner of the protection may be such as Congress, in the legitimate exercise of its legislative discretion, shall provide. These may be varied to meet the necessities of the particular right to be protected." The decision in that case was that the Fifteenth Amendment of the Constitution did not confer on citizens of the United States the right to vote, but only the right of exemption from being denied by a State the right to vote on account of race, color, or previous condition of servitude; and therefore that sections 3 and 4 of the Enforcement Act of May 31, 1870, (16 Stat. 140, 141, reenacted in Rev. Stat. §§2007-2009, 5506,) undertaking to punish the denial or obstruction of the right to vote under the laws of any State or Territory, and not grounded on such discrimination, were unconstitutional.

In United States v. Cruikshank, 92 U.S. 542, at the same term, in which also the opinion was delivered by the Chief Justice, the indictment was on section 6 of the Enforcement Act of 1870, (reenacted in Rev. Stat. §5508, under which the present conviction was had,) and the points adjudged on the construction of the Constitution and the extent of the powers of Congress were as follows:

It was held that the First Amendment of the Constitution... did not grant to the people the right peaceably to assemble for lawful purposes, but recognized that right as already existing, and did not guarantee its continuance except as against acts of Congress; and therefore the general right was not a right secured by the Constitution

of the United States.

1st. It was held that the First Amendment of the Constitution, by which it was ordained that Congress should make no law abridging the right of the people peaceably to assemble and to petition the government for a redress of grievances, did not grant to the people the right peaceably to assemble for lawful purposes, but recognized that right as already existing, and did not guarantee its continuance except as against acts of Congress; and therefore the general right was not a right secured by the Constitution of the United States. But the court added: "The right of the people peaceably to assemble for the purpose of petitioning Congress for a redress of grievances, or for anything else connected with the powers or the duties of the national government, is an attribute of national citizenship, and, as such, under the protection of, and guaranteed by, the United States. The very idea of a government, republican in form, implies a right on the part of its citizens to meet peaceably for consultation in respect to public affairs and to petition for a redress of grievances. If it had been alleged in these counts that the object of the defendants was to prevent a meeting for such a purpose, the case would have been within the statute, and within the scope of the sovereignty of the United States." 92 U.S. 552, 553.

It was held that the Second Amendment of the Constitution, declaring that "the right of the people to keep and bear arms shall not be infringed," was equally limited in its scope.

2d. It was held that the Second Amendment of the Constitution, declaring that "the right of the people to keep and bear arms shall not be infringed," was equally limited in its scope. 92 U.S. 553.

the rights of life and liberty were not granted by the Constitution, but were natural and inalienable rights of man; and that the Fourteenth Amendment of the Constitution, declaring that no State shall deprive any person of life, liberty or property, without due process of law, added nothing to the rights of one citizen as against another, but simply furnished an additional guaranty against any encroachment by the States upon the fundamental rights which belong to every citizen as a member of society.

It was of these fundamental rights of life and liberty, not created by or dependent on the Constitution, that the court said: "Sovereignty, for this purpose, rests alone with the States. It is no more the duty or within the power of the United States to punish for a conspiracy to falsely imprison or murder within a State, than it would be to punish for false imprisonment or murder itself."

3d. It was held that a conspiracy of individuals to injure, oppress and intimidate citizens of the United States, with intent to deprive them of life and liberty without due process of law, did not come within the statute, nor under the power of Congress, because the rights of life and liberty were not granted by the Constitution, but were natural and inalienable rights of man; and that the Fourteenth Amendment of the Constitution, declaring that no State shall deprive any person of life, liberty or property, without due process of law, added nothing to the rights of one citizen as against another, but simply furnished an additional guaranty against any encroachment by the States upon the fundamental rights which belong to every citizen as a member of society. It was of these fundamental rights of life and liberty, not created by or dependent on the Constitution, that the court said: "Sovereignty, for this purpose, rests alone with the States. It is no more the duty or within the power of the United States to punish for a conspiracy to falsely imprison or murder within a State, than it would be to punish for false imprisonment or murder itself." 92 U.S. 553, 554.

4th. It was held that the provision of the Fourteenth Amendment, forbidding any State to deny to any person within its jurisdiction the equal protection of the laws, gave no greater power to Congress. 92 U.S. 555.

5th. It was held, in accordance with United States v. Reese, above cited, that counts for conspiracy to prevent and hinder citizens of the African race in the free exercise and enjoyment of the right to vote at state elections, or to injure and oppress them for having voted at such elections, not alleging that this was on account of their race, or color, or previous condition of servitude, could not be maintained; that court saying: "The right to vote in the States comes from the States; but the right of exemption from the prohibited discrimination comes from the United States. The first has not been granted or secured by the Constitution of the United States, but the last has been." 92 U.S. 556.

Nothing else was decided in United States v. Cruikshank, except questions of the technical sufficiency of the indictment, having no bearing upon the larger questions.

With regard to those acknowledged rights and privileges of the citizen, which form a

part of his political inheritance derived from the mother country, and which were challenged and vindicated by centuries of stubborn resistance to arbitrary power, they belong to him as his birthright, and it is the duty of the particular State of which he is a citizen to protect and enforce them, and to do naught to deprive him of their full enjoyment.

it is at once understood that they are not created or conferred by the Constitution, but that the Constitution only guarantees that they shall not be impaired by the State, or the United States, as the case may be.

The affirmative enforcement of the rights and privileges themselves, unless something more is expressed, does not devolve upon it, but belongs to the state government as a part of its residuary sovereignty.

The main principles on which that decision was based had been clearly summed up by Mr. Justice Bradley when the same case was before the Circuit Court, as follows: "It is undoubtedly a sound proposition, that whenever a right is guaranteed by the Constitution of the United States, Congress has the power to provide for its enforcement, either by implication arising from the correlative duty of government to protect, wherever a right to the citizen is conferred, or under the general power (contained in art. 1, sec. 8, par. 18) 'to make all laws necessary and proper for carrying into execution the foregoing powers, and all other powers vested by this Constitution in the government of the United States, or any department or officer thereof.'" "With regard to those acknowledged rights and privileges of the citizen, which form a part of his political inheritance derived from the mother country, and which were challenged and vindicated by centuries of stubborn resistance to arbitrary power, they belong to him as his birthright, and it is the duty of the particular State of which he is a citizen to protect and enforce them, and to do naught to deprive him of their full enjoyment. When any of these rights and privileges are secured in the Constitution of the United States only by a declaration that the State or the United States shall not violate or abridge them, it is at once understood that they are not created or conferred by the Constitution, but that the Constitution only guarantees that they shall not be impaired by the State, or the United States, as the case may be. The fulfilment of this guaranty by the United States is the only duty with which that government is charged. The affirmative enforcement of the rights and privileges themselves, unless something more is expressed, does not devolve upon it, but belongs to the state government as a part of its residuary sovereignty." 1 Woods, 308, 314-316.

.....

while certain fundamental rights, recognized and declared, but not granted or created, in some of the Amendments to the Constitution, are thereby guaranteed only against violation or abridgment by the United States, or by the States, as the case may be, and cannot therefore be affirmatively enforced by Congress against unlawful acts of individuals

The whole scope and effect of this series of decisions is that, while certain fundamental rights, recognized and declared, but not granted or created, in some of the Amendments to the Constitution, are thereby guaranteed only against violation or abridgment by the United States, or by the States, as the case may be, and cannot therefore be affirmatively enforced by Congress against unlawful acts of individuals; yet that every right, created by, arising under or dependent upon, the Constitution of the United States, may be protected and enforced by Congress by such means and in such manner as Congress, in the exercise of the correlative duty of protection, or of the legislative powers conferred upon it by the Constitution, may in its discretion deem most eligible and best adapted to attain the object.

Among the particular rights which this court, as we have seen, has adjudged to be secured, expressly or by implication, by the Constitution and laws of the United States, and to be within section 5508 of the Revised Statutes, providing for the punishment of conspiracies by individuals to oppress or injure citizens in the free exercise and enjoyment of rights so secured, are the political right of a voter to be protected from violence while exercising his right of suffrage under the laws of the United States; and the private right of a citizen, having made a homestead entry, to be protected from interference while remaining in the possession of the land for the time of occupancy which Congress has enacted shall entitle him to a patent.

In the case at bar, the right in question does not depend upon any of the Amendments to the Constitution, but arises out of the creation and establishment by the Constitution itself of a national government, paramount and supreme within its sphere of action. Any government which has power to indict, try and punish for crime, and to arrest the accused and hold them in safekeeping until trial, must have the power and the duty to protect against unlawful interference its prisoners so held, as well as its executive and judicial officers charged with keeping and trying them.

.....

This duty and the correlative right of protection are not limited to the magistrates and officers charged with expounding and executing the laws, but apply, with at least equal force, to those held in custody on accusation of crime, and deprived of all means of self-defense.

The United States are bound to protect against lawless violence all persons in their service or custody in the course of the administration of justice. This duty and the correlative right of protection are not limited to the magistrates and officers charged with expounding and executing the laws, but apply, with at least equal force, to those held in custody on accusation of crime, and deprived of all means of self-defense.

For these reasons, we are of opinion that the crime of which the plaintiffs in error were indicted and convicted was within the reach of the constitutional powers of Congress, and was covered by section 5508 of the Revised Statutes; and it remains to be considered whether they were denied any legal right by the other rulings and instructions of the Circuit Court.

.....

GOURKO v. UNITED STATES

(FULL CASE)

153 U.S. 183; 14 S. Ct. 806; 38 L. Ed. 680

Submitted November 17, 1893.

April 16, 1894, Decided

GIST: *Gourko* marks the beginning of a string of self-defense cases arising from a single district courthouse. The dreaded "Hanging Judge" Isaac Parker can rightly be seen today as the unintended champion of armed self defense, a right he fought against at that time. Responsible for 88 death sentences and hangings, his hostility toward the idea of self defense afforded the Supreme Court the perfect opportunity to examine and clarify the common law surrounding self defense, in the years from 1893 to 1896. Based in Ft. Smith, Arkansas, where his court is now a National Historic Site, the lawless reaches of Parker's jurisdiction included neighboring Oklahoma, which was then Indian Territory, largely under federal law, and a hotbed of Wild West violence.

As the cases show, Parker consistently misled juries and obtained guilty verdicts. On appeal, the High Court reversed so often that Parker and the Justices were in an open feud. The full story is told in an article by David Kopel in the Summer 2000 edition of the *American Journal of Criminal Law* (posted at davekopel.org). The Supreme Court's cases publicly chastised the court from the Western District of Arkansas and Judge Parker personally, a rare occurrence in Supreme Court decisions.

Civil libertarians of today may find new cause to admire the Court of Chief Justice Fuller, known primarily for its unfortunate racism in *Plessy v. Fergusson.* It was this same Court however, standing against the abuses of Judge Parker, that defended the often poor, uneducated ethnic minorities—American Indians, blacks, immigrants, even people of mixed blood whose jurisdiction itself was in doubt—who carried guns for self defense and had even killed white men in saving their own lives.

John Gourko was a peaceable, frail young Polish immigrant miner who had been repeatedly threatened by Peter Carbo, a physically strong 200-pound "dangerous character." Carbo had loudly and publicly accused Gourko and his brother of stealing some mined coal from him.
After an altercation in which Carbo threatened to "shoot John like a dog," Gourko armed himself with a pistol. Later, Gourko killed Carbo and was convicted of murder. The High Court overturned his conviction and ruled unanimously that if Gourko believed Carbo intended to kill or seriously harm him, he was justified in arming himself. If Gourko later killed Carbo in circumstances where Gourko was not justified on self-defense grounds, the mere fact that Gourko had armed himself defensively did not turn the killing into premeditated murder. The Court takes for granted that personally arming yourself in the face of a serious threat is a normal, understandable, reasonable response to a known danger.

This was an indictment against John Gourko for murder. Defendant was found guilty of murder in the first degree, and brings error.

The plaintiff in error, a white man, and not an Indian, was charged by indictment in the circuit court of the United States for the western district of Arkansas with the crime of having, on the 1st day of November, 1892, at the Choctaw Nation, in the Indian Territory, within the above district, feloniously, willfully, and with malice aforethought killed and murdered one Peter Carbo. A verdict of guilty was returned, and, a motion for a new trial having been overruled, the defendant was adjudged to suffer death. The present writ of error brings up that judgment for review.

Although the Gourko brothers denied this charge, Carbo persisted in repeating it, and, according to the testimony of the younger Gourko, threatened to kill them both, and 'to shoot John like a dog.' Carbo was about 40 or 45 years of age, weighed about 200 pounds, possessed extraordinary physical strength, and was regarded as a dangerous character. The defendant was in delicate health, weighed about 135 pounds, and was deemed a quiet, peaceable boy.

John Gourko and his brother, Mike Gourko, and the deceased, Peter Carbo, all of Polish nativity, were engaged as laborers at certain coal mines in the vicinity of the town of Alderson, Choctaw Nation, Indian Territory. Between Carbo and the Gourko brothers-the two latter being respectively about 19 and 17 years-there was considerable ill feeling, growing out of a charge made by the former that the latter had clandestinely appropriated for their benefit money due for the taking out of several lots of coal that he claimed to have dug, and with the taking of which from the mines they had no connection. Although the Gourko brothers denied this charge, Carbo persisted in repeating it, and, according to the testimony of the younger Gourko, threatened to kill them both, and 'to shoot John like a dog.' Carbo was about 40 or 45 years of age, weighed about 200 pounds, possessed extraordinary physical strength, and was regarded as a dangerous character. The defendant was in delicate health, weighed about 135 pounds, and was deemed a quiet, peaceable boy.

On the morning of November 1, 1892,-that being a holiday for the Polish laborers,-there were quite a number of miners in the town of Alderson. About 9 o'clock Carbo and the defendant were observed to be engaged in an angry conversation near the post office.

The postmistress at Alderson, describing what occurred, testified that Carbo would swear, and call Gourko 'names, and make threats that he would hit him, or something of the kind, and shook his fist right in his face.' Being afraid that Carbo was 'going to hurt the boy,' she spoke to Mr. Anderson, who was working in the store, and said, "Pete is going to kill John, I am afraid.' ... The boy did not show any disposition to want to quarrel with him or want to fight. He would step back as much as two or three steps away, and Pete would follow him up, and shake his fist in his face, and the boy went on; and as he came back I spoke to John, the defendant, and asked him not to have any trouble there by the office, and he said he wasn't going to. He said, 'I have just gone to get a marshal to come and have him arrested,' and he said, 'I will wait until the marshal comes home."

Another witness, John Silluski, also a Polander, gave this account of the meeting between the deceased and the defendant near the post office: 'That day was a holiday, the first of month of November, and on this holiday all Polish stay at home. I stayed at home too. John Gourko was sick. He worked a couple of days, and stay at home three or four. I don't know how many. On that day I stayed at home, and he stayed at home too. He felt bad on that day. About 9 o'clock or half past 9 I go to the post office, and John Gourko too, and Pete Carbo was standing in front of the post office, and three other men were standing there, and he was talking to them, and I passed him, and went inside of the post office. I heard John say, 'Pete, how many cars of coal do you say I stole from you?' and Pete say: 'I don't say you stole. You and your brother together work at that place, and I lost about 6 cars.' John wasn't mad that time. Pete said he stole about six cars. John left home that morning, he did. He wasn't well. He was sick; didn't work. He had chills and faver. Was sick all the time. John said, 'You old sucker, I never stole no six cars of coal." Being asked what next happened, the witness stated that Carbo 'cursed Gourko all the time,' applying to him epithets of the most degrading kind, and which need not be here repeated. The witness further said: 'And Pete said: 'You want to fight this morning. Come on here,' and John said: 'I don't want to fight. I am a sick man. I am going to arrest you. I don't feel well.' And he said, 'Come on and fight, if you want to fight this morning,' and he said, 'I don't want to fight.' John looked behind the store for a policeman or something. He wanted to arrest him, I guess; I don't know.'

> **Gourko drew a small, bright pistol from his pocket, and he shot at Carbo, and he apparently shot almost in that direction, over his head, and he then almost instantly shot the second time, and Carbo dodged to the right and downward, and he shot again, and the third time he shot he dropped his gun further down, and fired, and Carbo fell.'**

It appears from the evidence that the killing occurred about 20 or 30 minutes after the difficulty at the post office, and near a saloon in which a billiard table was kept. The witness who gave the fullest account of the difficulty up to the time of the killing was Mr. Anderson. He testified, in substance, that he saw the beginning of the trouble in front of the post office, in which was the store where he worked. Being asked to state what occurred, he said: 'Well, I was in the store there, and, as usual, around the post office there was a crowd gathered there for the mail, at distributing times, and other times men congregate around in front of the store and in the store; and this morning, which was the morning of the 1st of November, 1892, there was quite a crowd gathered right in front of the window and door of the store or post office, and it was not long until my attention was called to the loud talking out there by the postmistress. ... The man who was doing the loud talking was Peter Carbo, the man who was killed. He appeared at that time to be angry, and was talking pretty loud when I first saw him. I heard him talking there before I got in position where I could see him. I saw him then quarreling with John Gourko; ... and I seen Peter Carbo shake his fist at John, and putting his fist up under his nose, and using considerable bad language. ... I heard him say that frequently, several different times; and John Gourko there, when he would be shaking his fist at him he would be stepping back, backing away. I seen him back as far as from here to you, and pass around the crowd. And it would only be a few moments until Peter would be there. Q. Peter would follow him up? A. Yes, sir. And in the interval he would sometimes have one hand in his bosom and the other hand behind here. Of course, I didn't know whether he was armed or not. I stood in the store where I belonged, and after a little while the disturbance out there ceased, and they separated, and then in few minutes after that,-just a short space of time, I don't know just how long,- Mr. Gourko there came back to the store, and the postmistress spoke to him, called him in, and had a talk with him, and told him she didn't wish any more trouble. And I was speaking to Mr. Gourko there, as I was acquainted with him, and told him that the postmistress didn't want any more trouble in front of here,-in front of her window,-and no more such language as that was, and I told him to keep away from Peter Carbo, and have no more trouble with him. I also asked him if he was armed, and he said he was not. And presently,-just about that time there was a customer come in, and I had to leave him, and go back to my work; and after I went back to my work, waiting on the customers, I can't tell how long that was, but I got through the customers, and I happened to walk to the store door, and I leaned up against the side of the door, and was standing there, and presently I saw Mr. Gourko there coming right to me from behind the billiard hall, that was in front and to the right of me, right across the street or passageway. He was coming around that, and he was coming directly towards me, as though he was coming to the post office, or me and the door, just as though he was coming right over to our store; and as he got up almost opposite the front of the billiard hall I was in the act of calling to him, or saying something to him,-I am pretty noisy sometimes to the boys around there, and call to them or say something,-and just as I was going to speak, Pete Carbo and him got into conversation, and I said nothing. ... When I first saw him he was right in front of the billiard hall, standing out in front, and Gourko was coming right up this way, and when the conversation occurred Gourko stepped out here at the right-hand corner of the billiard hall and Peter Carbo advanced right up towards him, that way, until they were a few paces apart, and they were saying something I could not understand. I don't think it was in our language. If it was, I didn't understand it. Still, I didn't think of any trouble. They were not talking loud at that time, as I understood it. Gourko drew a small, bright pistol from his pocket, and he shot at

Carbo, and he apparently shot almost in that direction, over his head, and he then almost instantly shot the second time, and Carbo dodged to the right and downward, and he shot again, and the third time he shot he dropped his gun further down, and fired, and Carbo fell.' Being asked to describe Carbo's attitude, and what was the position of his hands, the witness said: 'I can't remember just which hand it was. One hand apparently was thrust in his bosom and the other hand was behind him, but which hand it was I cannot call to mind. It wasn't but just a short time from the time he began to advance until the shooting was done.' He further stated, in reply to an inquiry as to when Carbo put his hands behind him: 'I think when he started out in front of the billiard hall-about 10 or 12 feet from the front of the billiard hall is where I saw him start from-advance out to where Gourko stood. Q. I will ask you to state if you know whether he began to talk to the defendant here when you saw him start out of the billiard hall, when he started towards him. A. Yes, sir; but I could not understand what he said. I think that was in the Slavish language,-in some language besides mine. But as he went out there he was talking. I could hear their voices, but I could not understand anything that was said. Q. I believe you say they came around from the front, and Peter came out from the back? A. No, sir. Peter was standing in front, and Gourko, the first I seen of him, he was opposite the rear of the store, coming up the street or passageway, or whatever you call it,-the passway,-and when he got up opposite there, where he could see by the corner of the billiard hall here,-like this was the billiard hall, and Gourko was coming up this way, bearing right across, just as though our store was right over here, and he was bearing over from this, as though he was coming over right direct to where I was standing in the door; and Peter Carbo, the first I seen of him, was right in front of that store, and when they began to talk Peter Carbo advanced right out that way, and when he got up in three or four paces of him Gourko stopped. Q. They met right there? A. Yes, sir. When they got together Peter was talking, and I don't know whether this man was saying anything or not. Q. They were saying something in their own language which you did not understand? A. Yes, sir; that boy was standing still when Peter was advancing, and he was standing still when the first shot was fired. Q. The first shot was fired over his head? A. Yes, sir.'

The third shot fired by defendant took effect, and resulted in the instant death of Carbo. It was clearly proved that he was unarmed at the time he was shot.

There was evidence on behalf of the government tending to show that just before the killing Carbo was in the saloon referred to, watching a game of billiards; that while he was there, Gourko came to the door, and opened a conversation with Carbo, which indicated that he was indignant at the language the latter had previously used towards him, and did not intend to rest quietly under the insults that had been put upon him; that the parties quickly, and as if by mutual agreement, left the saloon to 'settle' the dispute between them; that in a moment or two after they got on the outside the killing occurred; and that Carbo, at the time he was shot, was facing Gourko, with one hand across his bosom, under the lapel of his coat, and the other behind or across his back. There was evidence tending to show that the deceased was often seen, when not quarreling, with his hands in that position. The third shot fired by defendant took effect, and resulted in the instant death of Carbo. It was clearly proved that he was unarmed at the time he was shot.

The evidence disclosed other circumstances, but those above stated are the principal facts, and are sufficient for the purpose of presenting the grounds upon which the defendant seeks a reversal of the judgment.

No appearance, for plaintiff in error.

Asst. Atty. Gen. Conrad, for the United States.

Mr. Justice HARLAN, after stating the facts in the foregoing language, delivered the opinion of the court.

The court below made a long charge in reference to the principles of law which it conceived to be applicable to murder, manslaughter, and self- defense. Among other things, the court said to the jury: 'A man has a deliberate intent to kill in the absence of a right to kill under the law of self-defense, and in the absence of that which would mitigate the offense to manslaughter. He cannot have a deliberate intent to kill and then say that his offense was only manslaughter, because the fact that he had an intent to kill implies that he deliberated over that purpose; that he prepared himself for it; and, as you will learn further on, where deliberation, premeditation upon a purpose to slay, where previous preparation to execute that purpose exists, there is banished from the case that condition known as manslaughter, because that grows into existence upon sudden impulse, without previous preparation to take life. Whenever that exists, we have malice, and nothing else, unless it is a case where a man prepares himself for self-defense, and then, in order to exonerate himself from that killing, he must execute that preparation where the law gives him a right to do it, and in a defensive way. He may prepare himself for self-defense, but if he kills when there is no case of self-defense, such act of previous preparation becomes criminal in its character because of his subsequent act, and it becomes attached to that act. It does not necessarily import especial malevolence toward the individual slain, but also includes the case of a generally depraved, wicked, and malicious spirit, a heart regardless of social duty, and a mind deliberately bent on mischief. It imports premeditation.' To this part of the charge the defendant duly excepted.

The defendant asked the court to instruct the jury 'that preparation in the heat of blood may be followed by manslaughter as well as under a certain state of case it may be followed by murder or self-defense.' The court refused to give this instruction, without modification, and to that action of the court the defendant excepted. The court modified the proposition embodied in this instruction by saying to the jury: 'If a party prepares to defend himself in a case where he could defend himself, he has a right to do that; but if he prepares himself, as I have already told you, and then executes a deadly purpose by killing under circumstances where he would have no right to kill, where there was an absence from the case of the right of self-defense, or an absence of the mitigating conduct that I have given to you that would reduce the grade of the crime to manslaughter, then the fact of his previously preparing himself shows deliberation for a deadly criminal purpose, and there could not be manslaughter under such conditions as that. He may prepare himself, as I have already told you, to defend himself in a proper way; but because he has prepared himself to act upon the defensive, if he afterwards abandons that purpose and kills, if he has no right to kill in the absence of facts that would give him the right to defend, then the fact of previous preparation becomes evidence of deliberation,-evidence of design. As I have already told you, manslaughter cannot spring out of a state of case where a man prepares himself to kill wrongfully, when he prepares himself to take human life when he has no right to do it. That is evidence of malice aforethought, and it is the distinguishing line between manslaughter and malice aforethought.'

We are of opinion that the part of the charge to which the defendant took exception, as well as what the court said in modification of the instruction asked by the defendant, were wanting in the clearness that was requisite in order that the jury might not misapprehend the principles of law by which they were to be controlled.

Assuming, for the purposes of the present inquiry, that the defendant was not entitled to an acquittal as having acted in self-defense, the vital question was as to the effect to be given to the fact that he armed himself with a deadly weapon after the angry meeting with Carbo in the vicinity of the post office.

If he armed himself for the purpose of pursuing his adversary, or with the intention of putting himself in the way of his adversary, so as to obtain an opportunity to kill him, then he was guilty of murder.

the jury were not authorized to find him guilty of murder because of his having deliberately armed himself, provided he rightfully so armed himself for purposes simply of self-defense

If he armed himself for the purpose of pursuing his adversary, or with the intention of putting himself in the way of his adversary, so as to obtain an opportunity to kill him, then he was guilty of murder. But if, in view of that occurred near the post office, the defendant had reasonable grounds to believe, and in fact believed, that the deceased intended to take his life, or to inflict upon him great bodily harm, and, so believing, armed himself solely for necessary self-defense in the event of his being pursued and attacked, and if the circumstances occurring on the occasion of the meeting at or near the saloon were such as, by themselves, made a case of manslaughter, then the defendant's arming himself, after the difficulty near the post office, did not have, in itself, the effect to convert his crime into that of murder. Stated in another form: Although the defendant may not have been justified on the occasion and under the particular circumstances of the difficulty at the billiard saloon in believing that the taking of his adversary's life was then and there necessary to save his own life or to protect himself from serious bodily harm, nevertheless the jury were not authorized to find him guilty of murder because of his having deliberately armed himself, provided he rightfully so armed himself for purposes simply of self-defense, and if, independently of the fact of arming himself, the case tested by what occurred on the occasion of the killing was one of manslaughter only.

If the accused was justified in the eye of the law in arming himself for self-defense, and if, without seeking, but on meeting, his adversary, on a subsequent occasion, he killed him, not in necessary self-defense, then his crime was that of manslaughter or murder, as the circumstances, on the occasion of the killing, made it the one or the other.

The court, in effect, said-or the jury may, not unreasonably, have understood the court as declaring-that preparation by arming, although for self-defense only, could not be followed, in any case, by manslaughter, if the killing, after such arming, was not, in fact, in necessary self- defense. Such we understand to be the meaning of the charge. In our opinion, the court erred in so charging the jury. If the accused was justified in the eye of the law in arming himself for self-defense, and if, without seeking, but on meeting, his adversary, on a subsequent occasion, he killed him, not in necessary self-defense, then his crime was that of manslaughter or murder, as the circumstances, on the occasion of the killing, made it the one or the other. If guilty of manslaughter, looking alone at those circumstances, he could not be found guilty of murder by reason of his having previously armed himself solely for self-defense.

The judgment is reversed, and the cause remanded for a new trial.

MILLER v. STATE OF TEXAS

(FULL CASE)

153 U.S. 535; 14 S. Ct. 874; 38 L. Ed. 812

Submitted April 23, 1894.

May 14, 1894, Decided

GIST: Frank Miller, a convicted murderer from Dallas, appealed his death sentence, arguing in part that the Texas law prohibiting carrying weapons on yourself was in violation of his 2nd Amendment rights, and that this was made enforceable against the states by the 14th Amendment. (Unbeknownst to most people who absorb cultural information from TV, Texas has basically not allowed the carrying of handguns in the state from just after the Civil War until 1995, when a right-to-carry permit-and-fee system was implemented in place of the near-absolute ban.)

Miller also argued that search and seizure of his firearm without a warrant under Texas law was likewise unconstitutional. It's almost a crime that these fundamental constitutional issues—and this one could have been a blockbuster—are so often framed in the context of the worst elements of society, but such is the nature of this business.

The Court closed the door on Miller and rejected his appeal because he had not raised this argument prior to his Supreme Court appeal. Perhaps the Justices recognized it as a desperate last gasp of a doomed man but their hands were tied. The Court delicately sidestepped a landmine of an issue, fell back comfortably on a non-committal procedural way out, and without reading between the lines, simply said he got his paperwork out of order and sent him to his death. The Court appeared to consider the 14th Amendment issue of applying the Bill of Rights to the States to be an unresolved matter of law.

For a discussion of this case in great detail, see the *Journal of Law and Policy* article (Vol. 9, 2001) by Leonardatos, Kopel and Halbrook, on the Internet at davekopel.org.

This court expresses no opinion as to the validity or invalidity of the writ of error in this case.

When the record in a case brought by writ of error from a state court shows nothing of what took place in the state court of original jurisdiction, and in the appellate state court no objection raising a Federal question during the trial and before judgment, but such question is raised for the first time in the appellate court on a motion for a rehearing, the writ of error must be dismissed upon the ground that the Federal question is not properly presented by the record.

MOTION to dismiss. The plaintiff in error was indicted by the grand jury of Dallas County, Texas, for the murder of one Riddle on June 18, 1892. He was convicted July 23, 1892, and sentenced to death. From the judgment of the District Court of Dallas County, before which he was tried, he appealed to the Court of Criminal Appeals of Texas, the court of last resort in criminal cases, where the judgment of the court below was affirmed. A motion for a rehearing was then made and overruled. Defendant thereupon sued out this writ, assigning as error that the statute of the State of Texas prohibiting the carrying of dangerous weapons on the person, by authority of which statute the court charged the jury that, if defendant was on a public street carrying a pistol, he was violating the law, infringed the right of the defendant as a citizen of the United States, and was in conflict with the Second Amendment to the Constitution of the United States, providing that the right of the people to keep and bear arms shall not be infringed; second, that the same statute, which provided that any person carrying arms in violation of the previous section, might be arrested without warrant, under which the court charged the jury that defendant, if he were carrying arms in violation of the statute, was subject to arrest without warrant, was in contravention of the Fourth Amendment of the Constitution, which provides that the right of the people to be secure in their persons against unreasonable searches and seizures shall not be violated; and of the Fifth and Fourteenth Amendments, which provide that no person shall be deprived of life, liberty, or property without due process of law, and that no State shall pass or enforce any law which shall abridge the privileges or immunities of citizens of the United States.

MR. JUSTICE BROWN delivered the opinion of the court.

Motion is made to dismiss the writ of error in this case upon the ground that it was issued and signed by the clerk of the Court of Criminal Appeals of Texas, and was, therefore, insufficient to give this court jurisdiction, and the case of Bondurant v. Watson, 103 U.S. 278, is cited as authority for the position. In that case, however, the writ ran in the name of the Chief Justice of the Supreme Court of the State, to the clerk of that court, was tested in the name of the Chief Justice of the Supreme Court of the State, signed by its clerk, and sealed with the seal of that court. "It had not," said the court, "a single requisite of a writ of this court." Revised Statutes, §999, provides that when a writ of error "is issued by the Supreme Court to a state court, the citation shall be signed by the chief justice, or judge, or chancellor of such court, rendering the judgment or passing the decree complained of, or by a Justice of the Supreme Court of the United States, and the adverse party shall have at least thirty days' notice." And by §1003, "writs of error from the Supreme Court to a state court in cases authorized by law shall be issued in the same manner, and under the same regulations, and shall have the same effect as if the judgment or decree complained of had been rendered or passed in a court of the United States."

In this case the writ runs in the name of the President of the United States, to the judges of the Court of Criminal Appeals, is tested in the name of the Chief Justice of the Supreme Court of the United States, signed by the clerk of the Court of Criminal Appeals, and allowed by its presiding judge. If there was any error, it was in the signature of the writ by the clerk of the Court of Appeals, instead of by the clerk of this court, or of the Circuit Court of the United States for the proper district, Ex parte Ralston, 119 U.S. 613, and such error would be amendable under §1005, which provides that the Supreme Court may allow an amendment of a writ of error in all particulars of form. Texas & Pacific Railway v. Kirk, 111 U.S. 486. Of a similar mistake it was said in McDonogh v. Millaudon, 3 How. 693, 707: "If errors had been assigned by the plaintiff here and joined by the defendant, no motion to dismiss for such a cause could be heard." But the court express no opinion as to whether the error was, in itself, cause for dismissal. As was said in Ex parte Ralston, it has doubtless "been the prevailing custom from the beginning for the clerk of this court, or of the Circuit Court for the proper district, to issue the writ, and for such writ to be lodged with the clerk of the state court," but it has never been held that the signature of the clerk of the state court was fatal to the writ. On the contrary, it was held in Sheppard v. Wilson, 5 How. 210, that the act of 1838, providing that writs of error and appeals from the final decisions of the Supreme Court of a Territory, should be allowed in the same manner and under the same regulations as from the Circuit Courts of the United States, gave to the clerk of the territorial court the power to issue the writ of error, and to a judge of that court the power to sign the citation, and approve the bond.

defendant claimed that the law of the State of Texas forbidding the carrying of weapons, and authorizing the arrest without warrant of any person violating such law, under which certain questions arose upon the trial of the case, was in conflict with the Second and Fourth Amendments to the Constitution of the United States, one of which provides that the right of the people to keep and bear arms shall not be infringed, and the other of which protects the people against unreasonable searches and seizures.

We have examined the record in vain, however, to find where the defendant was denied the benefit of any of these provisions, and even if he were, it is well settled that the restrictions of these amendments operate only upon the Federal power, and have no reference whatever to proceedings in state courts.

Without, however, expressing a decided opinion upon the invalidity of the writ as it now stands, we think there is no Federal question properly presented by the record in this case, and that the writ of error must be dismissed upon that ground. The record exhibits nothing of what took place in the court of original jurisdiction, and begins with the assignment of errors in the Court of Criminal Appeals. In this assignment no claim was made of any ruling of the court below adverse to any constitutional right claimed by the defendant, nor does any such appear in the opinion of the court, which deals only with certain alleged errors relating to the impanelling of the jury, the denial of a continuance, the admission of certain testimony, and certain exceptions taken to the charge of the court. In his motion for a rehearing, however, defendant claimed that the law of the State of Texas forbidding the carrying of weapons, and authorizing the arrest without warrant of any person violating such law, under which certain questions arose upon the trial of the case, was in conflict with the Second and Fourth Amendments to the Constitution of the United States, one of which provides that the right of the people to keep and bear arms shall not be infringed, and the other of which protects the people against unreasonable searches and seizures. We have examined the record in vain, however, to find where the defendant was denied the benefit of any of these provisions, and even if he were, it is well settled that the restrictions of these amendments operate only upon the Federal power, and have no reference whatever to proceedings in state courts. Barron v. Baltimore, 7 Pet. 243; Fox v. Ohio, 5 How. 410; Twitchell v. Commonwealth, 7 Wall. 321; Justices v. Murray, 9 Wall. 274; United States v. Cruikshank, 92 U.S. 542, 552; Spies v. Illinois, 123 U.S. 131.

And if the Fourteenth Amendment limited the power of the States as to such rights, as pertaining to citizens of the United States, we think it was fatal to this claim that it was not set up in the trial court.

And if the Fourteenth Amendment limited the power of the States as to such rights, as pertaining to citizens of the United States, we think it was fatal to this claim that it was not set up in the trial court. In Spies v. Illinois, 123 U.S. 131, 181, objection was made that a certain letter was obtained from the defendant by an unlawful seizure, and the constitutional immunity was set up in the Supreme Court of Illinois, as well as in this court, but it was not made on the trial in the court of original jurisdiction. It was held, both by the Supreme Court of Illinois and by this court, that the defence should have proven that the letter was unlawfully seized by the police, and should then have opposed its admission upon the ground that it was obtained by such unlawful seizure. Said the Chief Justice: "As the Supreme Court of the State was reviewing the decision of the trial court, it must appear that the claim was made in that court, because the Supreme Court was only authorized to review the judgment for errors committed there, and we can do no more. . . . If the right was not set up or claimed in the proper court below, the judgment of the highest court of the State in the action is conclusive, so far as the right of review here is concerned." So in Texas Pacific Railway v. Southern Pacific Co., 137 U.S. 48, it was held directly that a privilege or immunity under the Constitution of the United States cannot be set up here under Revised Statutes, §709, when suggested for the first time in a petition for rehearing after judgment. See also Caldwell v. Texas, 137 U.S. 692, 698.

There was no other question under the Fourteenth Amendment to the Constitution. As the proceedings were conducted under the ordinary forms of criminal prosecutions there certainly was no denial of due process of law, nor did the law of the State, to which reference was made, abridge the privileges or immunities of citizens of the United States, as such privileges and immunities are defined in the Slaughter-house Cases, 16 Wall. 36; and in Crandall v. Nevada, 6 Wall. 35; and Ward v. Maryland, 12 Wall. 163.

The writ of error is, therefore,

Dismissed.

STARR v. UNITED STATES

(CASE EXCERPT)

153 U.S. 614; 14 S. Ct. 919; 38 L. Ed. 841

Submitted March 5, 1894.

May 14, 1894, Decided

GIST: Henry Starr, a teenaged Cherokee Indian, was wanted for stealing horses, and was laying low in the high country, aware the authorities were looking for him. Deputy U.S. Marshall Henry Dickey had summoned Floyd Wilson as his posse to help him serve a warrant on the young man. After a chase on horseback, when they got within talking range of Starr, Wilson whipped out his rifle and started firing. Starr shot back, downing Wilson, who then went for his revolver and fired four shots wildly. Starr rushed forward and fired again at point-blank range, killing Wilson and ending the assault. Witnesses confirmed that Wilson fired first, but Starr was sentenced to hang, in part because it was an officer of the law he had killed. The facts preserved in this case read like a good Western thriller.

Starr appealed his murder conviction on the grounds that, although the deputy and posse were legally serving a warrant, they failed to identify themselves properly and simply opened fire, so Starr had a right of self defense intact. The 2nd Amendment is not directly implicated unless you take into account the Court's complete ease with the fact that people carry guns and use them in natural and lawful personal protection, and there is an extended discussion on the law of self defense.

The Court unanimously reversed the conviction and remanded for a new trial because district Judge Parker's jury instructions too narrowly characterized the defendant's right of self defense against an attack by a person he did not know was an officer lawfully trying to arrest him. Although Starr was a wanted man, his right to defend against an attack did not evaporate. The Supreme Court also scolded the lower court for its handling of the case, and for launching into a tirade in the jury instruction.

A warrant issued by a commissioner of a court of the United States is not void for the want of a seal, the commissioner having no seal, and not being required by statute to affix one to warrants issued by him.

The same result is reached under the laws of Arkansas, which prescribed the form of warrant as attested under hand, but not under seal.

The settled rule that where a person having authority to arrest, and using the proper means for that purpose is resisted, he can repel force with force, and, if the party making the resistance is unavoidably killed, the homicide is justifiable, may be invoked by a person who resists and kills the officer if he was ignorant of the fact that he was an officer; and, when such a defence is set up to an indictment for murder, it is error to charge the jury that, if the threatening or violent conduct of the prisoner prevented the officer from giving notice of his official character, he would not be required to give notice.

The possession of a conscience void of offence towards God and man is not an indispensable prerequisite to justification of action in the face of imminent and deadly peril, nor does the intrinsic rightfulness of the occupation or situation of a party, having in itself no bearing upon or connection with an assault, impose a limitation upon the right to repel it.

The motive of a person, accused of murdering an officer trying to arrest him, in being where he was at the time of the killing, has nothing to do with the question of his right of self-defence in itself, and his previous unlawful conduct should form no element in the solution of that question, except as it throws light on his belief that his arrest was sought by the officer.

While it is well settled in Federal courts that the presiding Judge may sum up the facts to the jury, and express an opinion upon them, he should take care to separate the law from the facts, and leave the latter in unequivocal terms to the judgment of the jury.

The circumstances of this case apparently aroused the indignation of the Judge who presided at the trial of it in an uncommon degree, and that indignation was expressed in terms which were not consistent with due regard to the right and duty of the jury to exercise an independent judgment in the premises, or with the circumspection and caution which should characterize judicial utterances; and this court is constrained to express its disapprobation of this mode of instructing and advising a jury.

HENRY STARR was convicted of the murder of Floyd Wilson, a white man and not an Indian, on December 13, 1892, at the Cherokee Nation in the Indian Territory, and, November 4, 1893, sentenced to be hanged on February 20, 1894, and thereupon sued out this writ of error.

Wilson then sprang from his horse, threw his gun to his shoulder and fired at Starr, who was then standing with his gun in both hands holding it down, but, upon Wilson's shooting, returned the fire and continued to fire rapidly; that Wilson fell, raised himself in a sitting position, jerked his six shooter out and fired four times, when Starr ran up to him and fired point blank into him; Wilson died immediately afterwards.

It appeared on the trial that on November 18, 1892, a warrant was issued by a United States commissioner for the Western District of Arkansas for the arrest of Starr and others on a charge of larceny, which was delivered for execution to Henry E. Dickey, a deputy United States marshal; and that the marshal summoned Floyd Wilson, the deceased, as his posse to aid in the execution of the warrant. The evidence tended to show that they proceeded on horseback to the neighborhood of the place where Starr was to be found, and, after visiting several points, came to the house of one Dodge, where they concealed themselves to await his coming; that Starr passed Dodge's house on horseback, whereupon Wilson mounted his horse and pursued him; that the two jumped from their horses and stood facing each other a short time, apparently talking; that it looked as if Starr "was trying to work off away from Wilson," when Wilson mounted his horse again and rode up to within twenty-five or thirty feet of Starr, who made no effort to flee; that Wilson then sprang from his horse, threw his gun to his shoulder and fired at Starr, who was then standing with his gun in both hands holding it down, but, upon Wilson's shooting, returned the fire and continued to fire rapidly; that Wilson fell, raised himself in a sitting position, jerked his six shooter out and fired four times, when Starr ran up to him and fired point blank into him; Wilson died immediately afterwards. The evidence further tended to show that during the affray Starr fired one shot at the marshal; that he picked up Wilson's gun, found the lever out of order, could not fire it, and turned to go away, and, as he turned, the marshal fired at him; that the marshal's and Starr's horses ran away, but Starr caught Wilson's horse, and, mounting it, rode off. The marshal testified that at the time of this occurrence he had the writ in his possession, and had instructed Wilson as to his duties, and told him, "Now, don't kill this boy if possible to get along without it. We will call on him to surrender."

three or four weeks before the shooting Starr told her that he guessed a marshal named Cowden was hunting for him

One Mrs. Padget testified that she saw the transaction from a distance, called a quarter of a mile, and understood Wilson to say: "Hold up; I have a warrant for you;" and that Starr said: "You hold up." She also, in answer to a question put by the district attorney, stated that three or four weeks before the shooting Starr told her that he guessed a marshal named Cowden was hunting for him, "for jumping his bond." And Dickey said in the course of his testimony that he went up in Starr's neighborhood to see a person "shortly after Henry started, got out and jumped his bond."

The witnesses agreed that Wilson fired the first shot, and also that during the time he was riding up to Starr, Starr did not raise his gun or make any effort to stop Wilson. Starr was a Cherokee Indian, and at that time between eighteen and nineteen years of age.

The witnesses agreed that Wilson fired the first shot, and also that during the time he was riding up to Starr, Starr did not raise his gun or make any effort to stop Wilson. Starr was a Cherokee Indian, and at that time between eighteen and nineteen years of age.

The warrant was signed by Stephen Wheeler, "Commissioner U.S. Court, Western District of Arkansas," and tested as under seal, but no seal was affixed, and counsel for defendant objected to the warrant for the want of a seal, and took exception to its admission on that ground, though in answer to questions by the court they admitted that Wheeler was a United States commissioner for the Western District of Arkansas at the time the writ issued, and that the signature thereto was genuine.

MR. CHIEF JUSTICE FULLER, after stating the case, delivered the opinion of the court.

.....

2. Counsel for defendant asked the court to give to the jury four instructions. Of these, the first does not appear to have been given, but no exception was taken to its refusal, except as involved in an exception to the action of the court in refusing the request as to all. The court modified the last three and gave them, and the defendant excepted to the modifications and the giving of the instructions as modified in each instance. As the case will be sent back for a new trial on other grounds, we will not review the action of the court in respect of these instructions further than to indicate our views as to a particular modification of instruction numbered 3.

That instruction was as follows, the additions and modifications by the court being italicized:

if the defendant, being placed in a position in which his life is imperilled, slay an officer of whose official character he has no notice, or had no reasonable ground to know his character, this is homicide in self-defence, if the killing was apparently necessary to save the defendant's life

if a man stands up and obstructs arrest, prevents arrest, armed with deadly weapons, and using them in a way that is threatening, then the officer has no time, nor is he called upon to make proclamation. The officer can stand on the defensive and

overcome the danger and take his man or overcome him by violence, if necessary.

"The court instructs the jury that if the defendant, being placed in a position in which his life is imperilled, slay an officer of whose official character he has no notice, or had no reasonable ground to know his character, this is homicide in self-defence, if the killing was apparently necessary to save the defendant's life, nor does it matter that the officer was legally seeking to arrest the defendant, the defendant having no notice [of that fact] of the facts or no reason to know what the purpose of the party was: Provided the defendant did not by his threatening and violent conduct prevent the officer from making his character and mission known. This is given in connection with the principle I have given you, that if a man stands up and obstructs arrest, prevents arrest, armed with deadly weapons, and using them in a way that is threatening, then the officer has no time, nor is he called upon to make proclamation. The officer can stand on the defensive and overcome the danger and take his man or overcome him by violence, if necessary.

"If the jury believe from the evidence that the defendant was placed in a position at the time of the killing in which his life was imperilled by the deceased, and he slew him without having any notice of his official character, and the killing was apparently necessary to save his own life, then the killing of the deceased was homicide in self-defence; nor does it matter that the deceased was legally seeking to arrest the defendant, if the defendant had no notice of the fact, or no reasonable grounds to know that he was an officer.

"It is not necessary to know that it is Floyd Wilson, but an officer. But if the defendant prevented Floyd Wilson from giving notice of his character or mission by threatening or violent conduct, then, of course, he would not be required to give notice. He can stand, as upon the other proposition, on the defensive. These propositions are given on the theory that you believe that no proclamation was made. If a proclamation was made, then the defendant had express notice, he had positive notice, of it."

where a person, having authority to arrest and using the proper means for that purpose, is resisted in so doing, he can repel force with force and need not give back; and if the party making the resistance is unavoidably killed in the struggle, the homicide is justifiable.

The doctrine expressed in this instruction, as originally drawn, was taken from section 419 of Wharton's Criminal Law, vol. I, p. 419, where many authorities are cited in its support, and was accepted as correct by the learned trial judge. But he felt called upon to qualify it, not only in the direction whether the defendant had reasonable ground to know that Wilson was an officer, but also to the effect that if the accused prevented Wilson from giving notice that he was acting officially, then the rule invoked would not apply. The text-books lay it down as a general proposition that where a person, having authority to arrest and using the proper means for that purpose, is resisted in so doing, he can repel force with force and need not give back; and if the party making the resistance is unavoidably killed in the struggle, the homicide is justifiable. (1 Russ. on Crimes, 9th Am. ed. 892; Hale, Hawkins, East, and Foster as there cited; 2 Bish. Crim. Law, §647; 1 Whart. Cr. L. §415; and cases referred to.) But the question did not arise here in respect of homicide by the officer, but by the person whom he was trying to arrest, and if defendant had no knowledge, was not informed, and was not chargeable with notice of Wilson's mission or official character, the fact, if there was evidence tending to show it, that defendant prevented the giving of notice, had no such relation to defendant's claim of exemption from liability founded on his ignorance and the appearance of the facts to him as to justify the modification.

His conduct was part of the res gestae and important in other aspects of the case, but the qualification went too far as applied to the instruction under consideration.

First. A man, who, in the lawful pursuit of his business, is attacked by another under circumstances which denote an intention to take away his life, or do him some enormous bodily harm, may lawfully kill the assailant, provided he uses all the means in his power, otherwise, to save his own life or to prevent the intended harm—such as retreating as far as he can, or disabling his adversary without killing him, if it be in his power.

Secondly. When the attack upon him is so sudden, fierce, and violent, that a retreat would not diminish, but increase his danger, he may instantly kill his adversary without retreating at all.

Thirdly. When from the nature of the attack, there is reasonable ground to believe that there is a design to destroy his life, or commit any felony upon his person, the killing

of the assailant will be excusable homicide, although it should afterwards appear that no felony was intended.

3. In the case of Commonwealth v. Selfridge the following propositions were laid down by Mr. Justice Parker, afterwards Chief Justice of Massachusetts: "First. A man, who, in the lawful pursuit of his business, is attacked by another under circumstances which denote an intention to take away his life, or do him some enormous bodily harm, may lawfully kill the assailant, provided he uses all the means in his power, otherwise, to save his own life or to prevent the intended harm -- such as retreating as far as he can, or disabling his adversary without killing him, if it be in his power. Secondly. When the attack upon him is so sudden, fierce, and violent, that a retreat would not diminish, but increase his danger, he may instantly kill his adversary without retreating at all. Thirdly. When from the nature of the attack, there is reasonable ground to believe that there is a design to destroy his life, or commit any felony upon his person, the killing of the assailant will be excusable homicide, although it should afterwards appear that no felony was intended." (Selfridge's Trial, p. 160.)

when we undertake to enter upon the execution of as grave a design as the taking of the life of individuals, we must enter upon it with clean hands and a pure heart. If we have created a condition that leads to a deadly result, the law of self-defence does not apply to it

The learned judge in his charge in the present case, referring to the law as thus declared, said: "Now, what is the first proposition? Before I read it I say to you it contemplates a state of actual danger, real danger, in this case to this defendant at the time of the killing, springing from the hands of Floyd Wilson, and danger that he did not create, or bring into existence by a wrongful act of his, because when we undertake to enter upon the execution of as grave a design as the taking of the life of individuals, we must enter upon it with clean hands and a pure heart. If we have created a condition that leads to a deadly result, the law of self-defence does not apply to it; if we create that condition by doing a wrongful thing upon our part which would naturally or reasonably or probably produce a deadly result, the law says there is no self-defence for us, because we are in the wrong in the first place; and especially does that principle apply to a case when we are doing an act which from its nature and the way we are doing it death would be naturally produced in the conflict that may ensue, because of the act that we do. I say, then, we must enter upon the execution of this grave act upon our part with clean hands and a pure heart, or, as this law expresses it, we must be in the lawful pursuit of our business. It says that a man who is in the lawful pursuit of his business -- that means doing what he had a right to do -- in the right at the time -- is attacked by another under circumstances which denote an intention to take away his life, or, it may be, to do some enormous bodily harm, may lawfully kill the assailant -- when? -- provided he use all the means in his power, otherwise, to save his own life, or prevent the intended harm, such as retreating as far as he can, or disabling his adversary without killing him if it be in his power. Now, that is the first proposition of the law of self-defence. Now, let us see again, by enumerating each condition that must enter into it, what they are. First, we must be in the right; we must be doing what we had a right to do at the time of the killing, and when we are so situated we are attacked by another. How? What sort of attack? . . . Now, in this case, this contemplates as far as this case is concerned, that at the time that Floyd Wilson was killed this defendant was in the right; that he was doing exactly what he had a right to do, and when so situated he was attacked by Wilson in such a way as to indicate a deadly purpose upon his part."

we are of opinion that the language just quoted was open to a different construction and tended fatally to mislead. Whether the right of self-defence is legitimately exercised, depends upon the circumstances of the particular transaction

we take it that the possession of a conscience void of offence toward God and men is not an indispensable prerequisite to justification of action in the face of imminent and deadly peril

We presume that the learned judge intended to express the view that the existence of a state of facts which might render the homicide excusable was subject to the qualification that wrongful action on defendant's part towards Wilson did not occasion the attack. But we are of opinion that the language just quoted was open to a different construction and tended fatally to mislead. Whether the right of self-defence is legitimately exercised, depends upon the circumstances of the particular transaction, and we take it that the possession of a conscience void of offence toward God and men is not an indispensable prerequisite to justification of action in the face of imminent and deadly peril, nor does the intrinsic rightfulness of the occupation or situation of a party, having in itself no bearing upon or connection with an assault, impose a limitation on the right to repel it.

This Cherokee, when riding across the country, was entitled to protect his life, although he may have forfeited a bail bond and been seeking to avoid arrest on that account

This Cherokee, when riding across the country, was entitled to protect his life, although he may have forfeited a bail bond and been seeking to avoid arrest on that account, of which there was some slight evidence incidentally given. But if such were the fact, he could not be considered as doing exactly what he had a right to do, or as having an especially pure heart and clean hands. In a subsequent part of the charge the learned judge said, referring to the defendant: "He was a fugitive from justice if he had jumped the bond he had in this court, as they say; if he had forfeited his bond, and was up in that country hiding out from his usual place of abode to avoid arrest, he was then a fugitive from justice, and you have a right to take that condition into consideration; and in passing upon the question as to what was the probable action of these parties at that time, as to what would be the rights of the officer and of this defendant, you have a right to see this transaction in the condition that surrounded it, and as it was characterized by the position of the parties towards it. You have a right to look at that condition, and see if he was expecting officers to pursue him; if he was hiding away from them, he was then a fugitive from justice, and if that was true it is a fact that becomes pertinent for you to take into consideration, and the question whether he had reasonable ground from what transpired to know that Floyd Wilson was an officer and was seeking to arrest him." This was duly excepted to, but, apart from the exception, and assuming that the circumstance that he may have anticipated arrest for the reason suggested tended to show that he knew or believed that such was the mission of Wilson, these comments put it beyond question that the defendant was not doing what he had a right to do, and if the jury understood that the scope of what had previously been said embraced the rightfulness of his conduct generally, rather than his conduct in respect of the immediate transaction, they could not but have been materially influenced to his prejudice.

In Selfridge's case, the defendant was walking up State Street in Boston on an errand to the bank, and undoubtedly was in the lawful pursuit of his business when he was attacked, and it was in reference to that fact that the first proposition in the charge in that case was laid down; but here the particular words were inapplicable, and their use calculated to create an erroneous impression.

The motive of the accused in being where he was had nothing to do with the question of his right of self-defence in itself, and the unlawfulness of his previous conduct formed in itself no element in the solution of that question

The motive of the accused in being where he was had nothing to do with the question of his right of self-defence in itself, and the unlawfulness of his previous conduct formed in itself no element in the solution of that question, but was to be considered only in so far as it threw light on his belief that his arrest was sought by the officer.

We are not insensible to the consideration that the learned judge probably did not intend that his words should bear so sweeping a signification, but they were used more than once, and were not withdrawn or so qualified that it can be fairly held that they were not substantially prejudicial.

4. We are compelled to add some further observations in relation to the charge before us.

It is true that in the Federal courts the rule that obtains is similar to that in the English courts, and the presiding judge may, if in his discretion he think proper, sum up the facts to the jury; and if no rule of law is incorrectly stated, and the matters of facts are ultimately submitted to the determination of the jury, it has been held that an expression of opinion upon the facts is not reviewable on error. Rucker v. Wheeler, 127 U.S. 85, 93; Lovejoy v. United States, 128 U.S. 171, 173. But he should take care to separate the law from the facts and to leave the latter in unequivocal terms to the judgment of the jury as their true and peculiar province. M'Lanahan v. Universal Insurance Co., 1 Pet. 170, 182. As the jurors are the triers of facts, expressions of opinion by the court should be so guarded as to leave the jury free in the exercise of their own judgments. They should be made distinctly to understand that the instruction is not given as to a point of law by which they are to be governed, but as a mere opinion as to the facts to which they should give no more weight than it was entitled to. Tracy v. Swartwut, 10 Pet. 80, 96; Games v. Stiles, 14 Pet. 322. The same rule prevails in the courts of many of the States, and in the charge in Commonwealth v. Selfridge, referred to by the court below, these views were expressed upon the subject: "As to the evidence, I have no intention to guide or interfere with its just and natural operation upon your minds. I hold it the privilege of the jury to ascertain the facts, and that of the court to declare the law, to be distinct and independent. Should I interfere, with my opinion, with the testimony in order to influence your minds to incline either way, I should certainly step out of the province of the judge into that of an advocate. All that I can see necessary and proper for me to do in this part of the cause, is to call your attention to the points or facts on which the cause may turn, state the prominent testimony in the case which may tend to establish or disprove these points, give you some rules by which you are to weigh the testimony, if a contrariety should have occurred, and leave you to form a decision according to your best judgment, without giving you to understand, if it can be avoided, what my own opinion of the subject is. Where the inquiry is merely into matters of fact, or where the facts and law can be clearly discriminated, I should always wish the jury to leave the stand without being able to ascertain what the opinion of the court as to those facts may be, that their minds may be left entirely unprejudiced to weigh the testimony and settle the merits of the case."

So the Supreme Court of Pennsylvania says: "When there is sufficient evidence upon a given point to go to the jury, it is the duty of the judge to submit it calmly and impartially. And if the expression of an opinion upon such evidence becomes a matter of duty under the circumstances of the particular case, great care should be exercised that such expression should be so given as not to mislead, and especially that it should not be one-sided. The evidence, if stated at all, should be stated accurately, as well that which makes in favor of a party as that which makes against him; deductions and theories not warranted by the evidence should be studiously avoided. They can hardly fail to mislead the jury and work injustice." Burke v. Maxwell, 81 Penn. St. 139, 153. See also 2 Thompson on Trials, §§2293, 2294, and cases cited.

It is obvious that under any system of jury trials the influence of the trial judge on the jury is necessarily and properly of great weight, and that his lightest word or intimation is received with deference, and may prove controlling. Hicks v. United States, 150 U.S. 442, 452. The circumstances of this case apparently aroused the indignation of the learned judge in an uncommon degree, and that indignation was expressed in terms which were not consistent with due regard to the right and duty of the jury to exercise an independent judgment in the premises, or with the circumspection and caution which should characterize judicial utterances.

In addition to what has already been quoted, the following remarks, among others, were made:

"How unjust, how cruel, what a mockery, what a sham, what a bloody crime it would be upon the part of this government to send a man out into that Golgotha to officers, and command them in the solemn name of the President of the United States to execute these processes, and say to them, Men may defy you; men may arm themselves and hold you at bay; they may obstruct your process; they may intimidate your execution of it; they may hinder you in making the arrest; they may delay you in doing it by threats of armed violence upon you, and yet I am unable as chief executive of this government to assure you that you have any protection whatever." . . . "What was this posse to do? What was he commanded to do? To go into the Indian country and hunt up Mr. Starr, and say to him that on a certain day the judge of the Federal court at Fort Smith will want your attendance at a little trial down there wherein you are charged with horse stealing, and you will be kind enough, sir, to put in your attendance on that day; and the judge sends his compliments to you, Mr. Starr. Is that his mission? Is that the message from this court that is to be handed to Mr. Starr upon a silver platter with all the formalities of polite society? Is that what Floyd Wilson was employed or engaged to do? No. This court did not have anything to do with that command; it does not go in the name of this court; it goes in the name of the chief executive officer, the President of the United States. What does he say, of course acting for the people?" . . . "Without these officers what is the use of this court? It takes men who are brave to uphold the law here. I say, because of this, and because there is no protection unless the law is upheld by men of this kind, if it be true that you are satisfied of the fact beyond a reasonable doubt that Floyd Wilson was a man of this kind, that he was properly in the execution of the high duty devolving upon him, and while so properly executing it by the light of these principles of the law I have given you, his life was taken by this defendant, your solemn duty would be to say that he is guilty of the crime of murder, because if the law has been violated it is to be vindicated; you are to stand by the nation; you are to say to all the people that no man can trample upon the law wickedly, violently, and ruthlessly; that it must be upheld if it has been violated."

These expressions are qualified to some extent by other parts of the charge, which we cannot give at length, but we are constrained to express our disapprobation of this mode of instructing and advising a jury.

Whatever special necessity for enforcing the law in all its rigor there may be in a particular quarter of the country, the rules by which and the manner in which the administration of justice should be conducted are the same everywhere, and argumentative matter of this sort should not be thrown into the scales by the judicial officer who holds them.

The judgment is reversed and the cause remanded with a direction to grant a new trial.

THOMPSON v. UNITED STATES

(CASE EXCERPT)
155 U.S. 271; 15 S. Ct. 73; 39 L. Ed. 146
Submitted October 18, 1894.
December 3, 1894, Decided

GIST: The defendant, an Indian boy about 17 years old, was charged with and convicted of murder after killing a man, Charles Hermes, who had previously threatened to "chop his head open." The Arkansas trial court of Judge Parker instructed the jury that, since the boy had deliberately armed himself after an earlier confrontation, a charge of murder would apply.

Thompson had delivered a package for the woman with whom he was boarding, using the only road leading to his destination. On the way, he passed a field where Hermes was working, and was threatened by Hermes directly. Fearing for his safety, Thompson thought it best to arm himself, so he borrowed a Winchester rifle before returning by that same road. Sure enough, a gun fight ensued and Hermes was killed, with the details described in the decision.

The Supreme Court unanimously disagreed with the lower court, holding that deliberately arming yourself after a dispute is not by itself sufficient to make a subsequent homicide into a premeditated murder. They cite related self-defense principles already established under *Gourko*. The Court accepted as routine the concept that firearms are owned by the general public and are used in lawful self defense—lawful firearm possession by individuals is as unremarkable as possession of pens. In understated and ironic judicial style the Court criticized Judge Parker's worst conclusions by repeatedly referring to him as "learned."

IN ERROR TO THE CIRCUIT COURT OF THE UNITED STATES FOR THE WESTERN DISTRICT OF ARKANSAS.

In the District Court of the United States for the Western District of Arkansas, on November 23, 1893, a jury was sworn to try the issue formed between the United States and Thomas Thompson, under an indictment wherein said Thompson was charged with the murder of one Charles Hermes, and to which the accused pleaded not guilty.

.....

Courts of justice are invested with authority to discharge a jury from giving any verdict, whenever in their opinion, taking all the circumstances into consideration, there is a manifest necessity for the act, or the ends of public justice would otherwise be defeated, and to order a trial by another jury; and a defendant is not thereby twice put in jeopardy, within the meaning of the Fifth Amendment to the Constitution of the United States.

Sundry errors in the charge of the court below commented on, and Gourko v. United States, 153 U.S. 183 approved and applied to the issues in this case, viz.:

(1) A person who has an angry altercation with another person, such as to lead him to believe that he may require the means of self defence in case of another encounter, may be justified in the eye of the law, in arming himself for self-defence; and if, on meeting his adversary on a subsequent occasion, he kills him, but not in necessary self-defence, his crime may be that of manslaughter or murder, as the circumstances on the occasion of the killing make it the one or the other:

(2) If, looking alone at those circumstances, his crime be that of manslaughter, it is not converted into murder by reason of his having previously armed himself.

MR. JUSTICE SHIRAS, after stating the case, delivered the opinion of the court.

.....

The evidence in the case substantially disclosed the following facts:

Thompson could not speak or understand the English language, but he had been told by Haynes and another witness that old man Hermes had claimed that he, Thompson, had been abusing and killing his hogs, and that if he "came acting the monkey around him any more he would chop his head open."

The defendant, Thompson, was an Indian boy about seventeen years of age, and lived with Sam Haynes, a Creek Indian, who had a farm near Okmulgee in the Creek Nation. The deceased, Charles Hermes, lived with his father on land rented from Haynes, and distant about half a mile from the house of the latter. There was testimony tending to show ill feeling on the part of Hermes and his sons towards this Indian boy, and that they had threatened to injure him if he came about where they were. Thompson could not speak or understand the English language, but he had been told by Haynes and another witness that old man Hermes had claimed that he, Thompson, had been abusing and killing his hogs, and that if he "came acting the monkey around him any more he would chop his head open."

he got to thinking about what Sam Haynes had told him as to the threats that Hermes had made, and as there was no other road for him to return home by, except the one alongside of the field, he thought it was best for him to arm himself so that he could make a defence in case he was attacked; that he went by Amos Gray's house, and there armed himself with a Winchester rifle belonging to Gray.

the boys called at him and said something about a gun, and the deceased started towards a gun that was standing in the corner of the fence, and that, thinking they intended to kill him, he drew his gun and fired at the deceased, and then ran away on his horse, pursued by the old man, who afterwards shot at him.

In the afternoon of June 8, 1893, Mrs. Haynes directed the boy to take a bundle to Mrs. Checotah's, who lived two or three miles away. The boy caught a horse, got on it without a saddle, took the bundle that Mrs. Haynes gave him, and went off on his errand. Mrs. Haynes testified that he had no arms of any kind when he left her house, and that he appeared in a good humor with everybody at that time. The road to Checotah's ran by a field where the deceased, his father and brother were working, ploughing corn. There was testimony, on the part of Thompson, tending to show that, as he rode along past the field, the old man and the deceased began quarrelling with him; that Thompson saw that they were angry with him, but could not understand much that was said to him, although he could tell that they were talking about hogs. Thompson says that he remembered the threats against him they had made to Haynes and Checotah, and thought they were going to hurt him. He further states that he rode on to Checotah's, where he left the bundle; that he got to thinking about what Sam Haynes had told him as to the threats that Hermes had made, and as there was no other road for him to return home by, except the one alongside of the field, he thought it was best for him to arm himself so that he could make a defence in case he was attacked; that he went by Amos Gray's house, and there armed himself with a Winchester rifle belonging to Gray. The defendant further testified that, after he got the gun, he went back by the road, and, as he got opposite where the men were ploughing the boys were near the fence, and the old man was behind; that the boys called at him and said something about a gun, and the deceased started towards a gun that was standing in the corner of the fence, and that, thinking they intended to kill him, he drew his gun and fired at the deceased, and then ran away on his horse, pursued by the old man, who afterwards shot at him. These particulars of the transaction were principally testified to by Thompson himself, but he was corroborated, to some extent, by William Baxter and James Gregory, who testified that they visited the field where was the body of the deceased, and that Hermes, the father, described the affair to them, and, as so told, the facts differed but little from Thompson's version.

In this state of facts, or, at all events, with evidence tending to show such, the court instructed the jury at great length in respect to the law of the case. Exception was taken to the charge of the court as a whole, because it was "prolix, confusing, abstract, argumentative, and misleading," and this exception is the subject of one of the assignments of error. But we do not need to consider this aspect of the case, as the record discloses errors in vital portions of the charge, and specifically excepted to, which constrain us to reverse the judgment, and direct a new trial.

In instructing the jury as to the right of self-defence, the learned judge said: "It is for you to say whether at the time of the killing of Charles Hermes by this defendant that this defendant was doing what he had a right to do. If he was not, notwithstanding Charles Hermes might have made a violent demonstration that was then and there imminent, then and there impending, then and there hanging over his head, and that he could not avoid it except by killing him; if his conduct wrongfully, illegally, and improperly brought into existence that condition, then he was not in an attitude where, in the language of the law, he was in the lawful pursuit of his business." And again: "Now, in this connection, we have a maxim of the law which says to us that notwithstanding the deceased at the time of the killing may be doing that which indicates an actual, real, and deadly design, if he by his action who seeks to invoke the right of self-defence brought into existence that act upon the part of the deceased at that time by his wrongful act, his wrongful action did it, he is cut off from the law of self-defence, no matter what may have been the conduct of the deceased at that time."

It is not easy to understand what the learned judge meant by those portions of these instructions, in which he leaves it to the jury to say whether the defendant was "doing what he had a right to do," and whether the defendant brought into existence the act of the deceased, in threatening to attack the defendant, "by his, defendant's, wrongful act." Probably what was here adverted to was the conduct of the deceased in returning home by the same route in which he had passed the accused when going to Checotah's, and the implication seems to be that the accused was doing wrong and was guilty of a wrongful act in so doing. The only evidence on that subject was that of the defendant himself, that he had no other mode of returning home except by that road, because of swamps on the other side of the road, and there was no evidence to the contrary.

The learned judge, in these and subsequent instructions, seems to confuse the conduct of the defendant in returning home by the only convenient road, with a supposed return to the scene of a previous quarrel for the purpose of renewing it.

The learned judge, in these and subsequent instructions, seems to confuse the conduct of the defendant in returning home by the only convenient road, with a supposed return to the scene of a previous quarrel for the purpose of renewing it. Thus, he further instructed the jury that "if it be true that Charles Hermes, at the time of the killing, was actually and really, or apparently, in the act or executing a deadly design, or so near in the execution of it that the defendant could not avoid it, and that it was brought into existence by his going to that place where Charles Hermes was, with the purpose of provoking a difficulty, or with the intention of having an affray, he is cut off from the law of self-defence." And again: "You are to look to the evidence to see whether the defendant brought that state of case into existence, to see whether or not in consequence of a conception on his part of a state of grudge, or ill-will, or any hard feelings that existed between the parties, that he went off and armed himself for the purpose of making an attack on Hermes, or any of the party whom the government offered as witnesses, this law of self-defence cannot avail him. Of course, the law of self-defence gives him the right to arm himself for the purpose of defending himself so long as he is in the right, but if he has a conception that deadly danger may come upon him, but he is away from it so he can avoid it, his duty is to stay away from it and avoid it, because he has no right to go to the place where the slain person is, with a deadly weapon for the purpose of provoking a difficulty, or with the intent of having an affray."

These instructions could, and naturally would, be understood by the jury as directing them that the accused lost his right of self-defence by returning home by the road that passed by the place where the accused was, and that they should find that the fact that he had armed himself and returned by that road was evidence from which they should infer that he had gone off and armed himself and returned for the purpose of provoking a difficulty.

Nor did the fact that the defendant, in view of the threats that had been made against him, armed himself, justify the jury in inferring that this was with the purpose of attacking the deceased and not of defending himself, especially in view of the testimony that the purpose of the defendant in arming himself was for self-defence.

These instructions could, and naturally would, be understood by the jury as directing them that the accused lost his right of self-defence by returning home by the road that passed by the place where the accused was, and that they should find that the fact that he had armed himself and returned by that road was evidence from which they should infer that he had gone off and armed himself and returned for the purpose of provoking a difficulty. Certainly the mere fact that the accused used the same road in returning that he had used in going from home would not warrant the inference that his return was with the purpose of provoking an affray, particularly as there was evidence that this road was the proper and convenient one. Nor did the fact that the defendant, in view of the threats that had been made against him, armed himself, justify the jury in inferring that this was with the purpose of attacking the deceased and not of defending himself, especially in view of the testimony that the purpose of the defendant in arming himself was for self-defence.

We had occasion to correct a similar error in the recent case of Gourko v. United States, 153 U.S. 183. That was a case where the deceased had previously uttered threats against the defendant, and there had been a recent rencontre at the post office. The parties then separated, and the defendant armed himself, and subsequently, when the parties again encountered each other, the defendant shot and killed the deceased. The court instructed the jury that, in those circumstances, there was no right of self-defence, and that there was nothing to reduce the offence from that of murder to manslaughter.

In discussing the question this court, by Mr. Justice Harlan, said:

armed himself solely for necessary self-defence in the event of his being pursued and attacked

"Assuming, for the purposes of the present inquiry, that the defendant was not entitled to an acquittal as having acted in self-defence, the vital question was as to the effect to be given to the fact that he armed himself with a deadly weapon after the angry meeting with Carbo in the vicinity of the post office. If he armed himself for the purpose of pursuing his adversary, or with the intention of putting himself in the way of his adversary, so as to obtain an opportunity to kill him, then he was guilty of murder. But, if in view of what had occurred near the post office, the defendant had reasonable grounds to believe, and in fact believed, that the deceased intended to take his life, or to inflict upon him great bodily harm, and so believing armed himself solely for necessary self-defence in the event of his being pursued and attacked, and if the circumstances on the occasion of the meeting at or near the saloon were such as, by themselves, made a case of manslaughter, then the defendant arming himself, after the difficulty near the post office, did not, in itself, have the effect to convert his crime into that of murder.

the jury were not authorized to find him guilty of murder because of his having deliberately armed himself, provided he rightfully armed himself for purposes simply of self-defence

If the accused was justified in the eye of the law in arming himself for self-defence

"Stated in another form: Although the defendant may not have been justified on the occasion and in the particular circumstances of the difficulty at the billiard saloon in believing that the taking of his adversary's life was, then and there, necessary to save his own life or to protect himself from serious bodily harm, nevertheless the jury were not authorized to find him guilty of murder because of his having deliberately armed himself, provided he rightfully armed himself for purposes simply of self-defence, and if, independently of the fact of arming himself, the case, tested by what occurred on the occasion of the killing, was one of manslaughter only. The court, in effect, said, or the jury may not unreasonably have understood the judge as declaring, that preparation by arming, although for self-defence only, could not be followed, in any case, by manslaughter, if the killing, after such arming, was not in fact in necessary self-defence. Such we understand to be the meaning of the charge. In our opinion the court erred in so charging the jury. If the accused was justified in the eye of the law in arming himself for self-defence, and if, without seeking, but on meeting his adversary, on a subsequent occasion, he killed him, not in necessary self-defence, then his crime was that of manslaughter or murder, as the circumstances, on the occasion of the killing, made it the one or the other. If guilty of manslaughter, looking alone at those circumstances, he could not be found guilty of murder by reason of his having previously armed himself solely for self-defence."

We think there was also error in that portion of the charge wherein the court instructed the jury as to the effect which they should give to the evidence on the subject of previous threats, uttered against the defendant by Hermes and his sons. The learned judge seems to have regarded such evidence not merely as not extenuating or excusing the act of the defendant, but as evidence from which the jury might infer special spite, special ill-will, on the part of the defendant. The language of the learned judge was as follows:

"Previous threats fill a certain place in every case where they are brought out in the evidence. If, at the time of the killing, the party is doing nothing which indicates a deadly design, or a design to do a great bodily mischief -- if he is doing nothing, I say, of that kind -- then previous threats cannot be considered by the jury. If they are satisfied from the law and the testimony that the deceased was not doing anything that amounted to a deadly attack, or there is no question in their minds as to what the attitude of the deceased was, previous threats cannot be considered by them; they cannot enter into their consideration of the case by the way of justifying any act that resulted in the death of Charles Hermes from the act of defendant; they cannot be considered, I say, because you cannot kill a man because of previous threats. You cannot weigh in the balance a human life against a threat. There is no right of that kind in law. Threats are only admitted as illustrative of another condition that exists in the case. If the party, at the time of killing, who is killed, is doing that which indicates a purpose to do great bodily harm, to kill, or is about to do it, so near doing it, and goes so far that it can be seen from the nature of the act what his purpose is, then for the purpose of enabling you to more clearly see the situation of the parties you can take into consideration the threats made by him. But if there is an absence in the case of that which indicates a deadly design, a design to do great bodily harm, really or apparently, threats cannot be considered in connection with the asserted right of a defendant that he can avail himself of the right of self-defence. You cannot do that. But if threats are made, and there is an absence from the case of the conditions I have given you where you can use them as evidence, you can only use them and consider them for the purpose of showing the existence of special spite or ill-will or animosity on the part of the defendant."

And again:

"If this defendant killed this party, Charles Hermes, because the old man, the father of Charles Hermes, had threatened him with violence, or threatened to have something done to him because of his belief that he had done something with his hogs or killed them and made threats, that is no defence, that is no mitigation, but that is evidence of malice aforethought; it is evidence of premeditation; it is evidence of deliberation of a deliberately formed design to kill, because of special spite, because of a grudge, because of ill-will, because of animosity that existed upon the part of this defendant towards these people in the field."

While it is no doubt true that previous threats will not, in all circumstances, justify or, perhaps, even extenuate the act of the party threatened in killing the person who uttered the threats, yet it by no means follows that such threats, signifying ill-will and hostility on the part of the deceased, can be used by the jury as indicating a similar state of feeling on the part of the defendant.

While it is no doubt true that previous threats will not, in all circumstances, justify or, perhaps, even extenuate the act of the party threatened in killing the person who uttered the threats, yet it by no means follows that such threats, signifying ill-will and hostility on the part of the deceased, can be used by the jury as indicating a similar state of feeling on the part of the defendant. Such an instruction was not only misleading in itself, but it was erroneous in the present case, for the further reason that it omitted all reference to the alleged conduct of the deceased at the time of the killing, which went to show an intention then and there to carry out the previous threats.

the contention that the defendant acted in self-defence

The instructions which have thus far been the subject of our criticism were mainly applicable to the contention that the defendant acted in self-defence, but they also must have been understood by the jury as extending to the other proposition that the defendant's act constituted the crime of manslaughter and not of murder. The charge shows that the instructions of the learned judge, on these two distinct defences, were so blended as to warrant the jury in believing that such instructions were applicable to both grounds of defence.

Whether this be a just view or not, there were distinct instructions given as to the contention that the act of killing in this case was manslaughter and not murder, which we think cannot be sustained. A portion of such instructions was as follows:

"Now I have been requested to charge you upon the subject of manslaughter. Manslaughter is defined by the law of the United States to be the wrongful killing of a human being, done wilfully, and in the absence of malice aforethought. There must be out of the case that which shows the existence or this distinguishing trait of murder, to find the existence of a state of case that authorizes a mitigation of the offence from murder to manslaughter. It is an unlawful and wilful killing, but a killing in such a way as that the conduct of the deceased Hermes, in this case, at the time he was killed, was not of a character to authorize him to shoot, but that the defendant could so far have the benefit of that conduct provocative in its nature as that he could ask you to mitigate his crime, if crime exists here, from murder to manslaughter. Let us see what is meant by that. It cannot grow out of any base conception of fear. It cannot grow out of a state of case where there is a killing because of threats previously made, because of that which evidences special spite or ill-will, for if the killing is done on that ground, and if it is shown by the threats, and the previous preparation of the defendant, or the fact of his arming himself, and going back to the field where they were at work, and while there he shot Charles Hermes to death, it cannot be evidence of that condition; but at the time of the killing there must have been that in the conduct of Charles Hermes in the shape of acts done by him that were so far provocative as to then and there inflame the mind of the deceased [defendant] to authorize you to say that it was so inflamed; in such an inflamed condition that the defendant did not act with premeditation; that he did not act from a previously formed design to kill, but that the purpose to kill sprang into existence upon the impulse of the moment because of the provocative conduct of Charles Hermes at the time of the killing, that would be a state of manslaughter. . . .The law says that the previous selection, preparation, and subsequent use of a deadly weapon shows that there was a purpose to kill contemplated before that affray existed, and whenever that exists, when it is done unlawfully and improperly so that there is no law of self-defence in it, the fact that they may have been in an actual affray with hands or fists would not reduce the grade of the crime to manslaughter."

The error here is in the assumption that the act of the defendant in arming himself showed a purpose to kill formed before the actual affray.

The error here is in the assumption that the act of the defendant in arming himself showed a purpose to kill formed before the actual affray. This was the same error that we found in the instructions regarding the right of self-defence, and brings the case within the case of Gourko v. United States, previously cited, and the language of which we need not repeat.

These views call for a reversal of the judgment, and it is therefore unnecessary to consider the assignments that allege errors in the selection of the jury.

The judgment is reversed, and the cause remanded for a new trial.

BEARD v. UNITED STATES

(FULL CASE)

158 U.S. 550; 15 S. Ct. 962; 39 L. Ed. 1086

Submitted March 13, 1895.

May 27, 1895, Decided

GIST: This case examines the underpinnings of personal self defense. Presented in colorful detail are the facts of a confrontation between neighbors and relatives over a cow.

Beard used the shotgun he normally carried with him when he was traveling, to defend himself against the three men he encountered on his return, who were trying to take the cow off his property. The men, brothers, had a long-term angry dispute with Beard, and were carrying concealed handguns in their pockets. When the first one made a move as if to draw, Beard hit him over the head with the shotgun, so he wouldn't have to shoot him, according to the testimony. But the blow crushed the skull and proved lethal. Using the shotgun, Beard managed to disarm the other two brothers, without firing a shot.

While it's easy to visualize the sequence of events described in many of the Court's self-defense cases, the descriptions in *Beard* resist visualization— how three armed men, positioned as they were, could be defeated without a hostile shot fired. Taunted by the Jones brothers that his shotgun wasn't loaded, Beard fired a blast into the air. He claimed he had "ten cartridges in the magazine," probably as a boast, since a shotgun with a ten-round magazine didn't exist at the time.

The case touched on numerous aspects of self defense: public threats of harm, reasonable belief of an imminent mortal threat, provocation and mutual combat, equal force, necessity, your rights at home, standing your ground, bad jury instructions, and the differences between murder and manslaughter. Included is some of the longest-winded bombast in this book—extended tracts from Judge Parker's charge to the jury, quoted in the decision. Look for the opening and closing quote marks to avoid the sleep-inducing effect of these lengthy portions.

A strong position is carved out here by the Court, concerning "the ancient doctrine" of a duty to retreat when attacked, saying the "American mind" is very strongly against enforcement of any such rule. The Court found the idea of "retreat to the wall" had medieval English roots, which may have made sense in days of hand-to-hand villainy with clubs and edged weapons, but made no sense in a world of long-distance repeating rifles. The Court determined, with 18 supporting citations, that under the circumstances in this case—a man threatened and attacked on his own property near his home—there was no duty to retreat in acting to save his own life.

A man assailed on his own grounds, without provocation, by a person armed with a deadly weapon and apparently seeking his life, is not obliged to retreat, but may stand his ground and defend himself with such means as are within his control; and so long as there is no intent on his part to kill his antagonist, and no purpose of doing anything beyond what is necessary to save his own life, is not guilty of murder or manslaughter if death results to his antagonist from a blow given him under such circumstances.

MR. JUSTICE HARLAN delivered the opinion of the court.

The plaintiff in error, a white man and not an Indian, was indicted in the Circuit Court of the United States for the Western District of Arkansas for the crime of having killed and murdered in the Indian country, and within that District, one Will Jones, also a white person and not an Indian.

He was found guilty of manslaughter and, a motion for a new trial having been overruled, it was adjudged that he be imprisoned in Kings County Penitentiary, at Brooklyn, New York, for the term of eight years, and pay to the United States a fine of five hundred dollars.

The record contains a bill of exceptions embodying all the evidence, as well as the charge of the court to the jury, and the requests of the accused for instructions. To certain parts of the charge, and to the action of the court in refusing instructions asked by the defendant, exceptions were duly taken.

The principal question in the case arises out of those parts of the charge in which the court instructed the jury as to the principles of the law of self-defence.

The principal question in the case arises out of those parts of the charge in which the court instructed the jury as to the principles of the law of self-defence.

There was evidence before the jury tending to establish the following facts:

An angry dispute arose between Beard and three brothers by the name of Jones -- Will Jones, John Jones, and Edward Jones -- in reference to a cow which a few years before that time, and just after the death of his mother, was set apart to Edward. The children being without any means for their support were distributed among their relatives, Edward being assigned to Beard, whose wife was a sister of Mrs. Jones. Beard took him into his family upon the condition that he should have the right to control him and the cow as if the lad were one of his own children, and the cow his own property. At the time Edward went to live with Beard he was only eight or nine years of age, poorly clad, and not in good physical condition.

After remaining some years with his aunt and uncle, Edward Jones left the Beard house, and determined, with the aid of his older brothers, to take the cow with him, each of them knowing that the accused objected to that being done.

The Jones brothers, one of them taking a shot-gun with him, went upon the premises of the accused for the purpose of taking the cow away, whether Beard consented or not.

The Jones brothers, one of them taking a shot-gun with him, went upon the premises of the accused for the purpose of taking the cow away, whether Beard consented or not. But they were prevented by the accused from accomplishing that object, and he warned them not to come to his place again for such a purpose, informing them that if Edward Jones was entitled to the possession of the cow, he could have it, provided his claim was successfully asserted through legal proceedings instituted by or in his behalf.

Will Jones, the oldest of the brothers, and about 20 or 21 years of age, publicly avowed his intention to get the cow away from the Beard farm or kill Beard, and of that threat the latter was informed on the day preceding that on which the fatal difficulty in question occurred.

In the afternoon of the day on which the Jones brothers were warned by Beard not again to come upon his premises for the cow unless attended by an officer of the law, and in defiance of that warning, they again went to his farm, in his absence -- one of them, the deceased, being armed with a concealed deadly weapon -- and attempted to take the cow away, but were prevented from doing so by Mrs. Beard, who drove it back into the lot from which it was being taken.

Beard returned to his home from a town near by—having with him a shot-gun that he was in the habit of carrying, when absent from home

While the Jones brothers were on the defendant's premises in the afternoon, for the purpose of taking the cow away, Beard returned to his home from a town near by -- having with him a shot-gun that he was in the habit of carrying, when absent from home -- and went at once from his dwelling into the lot, called the orchard lot, a distance of about 50 or 60 yards from his house and near to that part of an adjoining field or lot where the cow was, and in which the Jones brothers and Mrs. Beard were at the time of the difficulty.

the accused asked him what he intended to do, and he replied: "Damn you, I will show you," at the same time making a movement with his left hand as if to draw a pistol from his pocket; whereupon the accused struck him over the head with his gun and knocked him down.

Beard ordered the Jones brothers to leave his premises. They refused to leave. Thereupon Will Jones, who was on the opposite side of the orchard fence, ten or fifteen yards only from Beard, moved towards the latter with an angry manner and in a brisk walk, having his left hand (he being, as Beard knew, left-handed) in the left pocket of his trousers. When he got within five or six steps of Beard, the latter warned him to stop, but he did not do so. As he approached nearer the accused asked him what he intended to do, and he replied: "Damn you, I will show you," at the same time making a movement with his left hand as if to draw a pistol from his pocket, whereupon the accused struck him over the head with his gun and knocked him down.

My purpose in doing this was to disarm him, to prevent him from shooting me

My gun was loaded, having ten cartridges in the magazine. I could have shot him, but did not want to kill him, believing that I could knock him down with the gun and disarm him and protect myself without shooting him.

He said my gun was not loaded; thereupon I shot the gun in the air to show him that it was loaded.

"Believing," the defendant testified, "from his demonstrations just mentioned that he intended to shoot me, I struck him over the head with my gun to prevent him killing me. As soon as I struck him his brother John, who was a few steps behind him, started towards me with his hands in his pocket. Believing that he intended to take part in the difficulty and was also armed, I struck him and he stopped. I then at once jumped over the fence, caught Will Jones by the lapel of the coat, turned him rather to one side, and pulled his left hand out of his pocket. He had a pistol, which I found in his pocket, grasped in his left hand, and I pulled his pistol and his left hand out together. My purpose in doing this was to disarm him, to prevent him from shooting me, as I did not know how badly he was hurt. My gun was loaded, having ten cartridges in the magazine. I could have shot him, but did not want to kill him, believing that I could knock him down with the gun and disarm him and protect myself without shooting him. After getting his pistol, John Jones said something to me about killing him, to which I replied that I had not killed him and did not try to do so, for if I had I could have shot him. He said my gun was not loaded; thereupon I shot the gun in the air to show him that it was loaded."

he died from the effects of a wound given by the defendant; that the wound was across the head, rather on the right side, the skull being crushed by the blow.

he was sorry that it had happened, but that he acted in self-defence and would not go away. Beard seemed a little offended at the suggestion that he should run off, and observed to the witness that the latter could not scare him, for he was perfectly justified in what he did.

Dr. Howard Hunt, a witness on behalf of the government, testified that he called to see Will Jones soon after he was hurt, and found him in a serious condition; that he died from the effects of a wound given by the defendant; that the wound was across the head, rather on the right side, the skull being crushed by the blow. He saw the defendant soon after dressing the wound, and told him that the deceased's condition was serious, and that he, the witness, was sorry the occurrence had happened. The witness suggested to the accused that perhaps he had better get out of the way. The latter replied that he was sorry that it had happened, but that he acted in self-defence and would not go away. Beard seemed a little offended at the suggestion that he should run off, and observed to the witness that the latter could not scare him, for he was perfectly justified in what he did. This witness further testified that he had known the defendant four or five years, was well acquainted in the neighborhood in which he lived, and knew his general reputation, which was that of a peaceable, law-abiding man.

The account we have given of the difficulty is not in harmony, in every particular, with the testimony of some of the witnesses, but it is sustained by what the accused and others testified to at the trial; so that, if the jury had found the facts to be as we have detailed them, it could not have been said that their finding was contrary to the evidence. At any rate, it was the duty of the court to tell the jury by what principles of law they should be guided, in the event they found the facts to be as stated by the accused.

Assuming then that the facts were as we have represented them to be, we are to inquire whether the court erred in its charge to the jury. In the view we take of the case, it will be necessary to refer to those parts only of the charge relating to the law of self-defence.

The court stated at considerable length the general rules that determine whether the killing of a human being is murder or manslaughter, and, among other things, said to the jury: "If these boys, or young men, or whatever you may consider them, went down there, and they were there unlawfully -- if they had no right to go there -- you naturally inquire whether the defendant was placed in such a situation as that he could kill for that reason. Of course, he could not. He could not kill them because they were upon his place. . . . And if these young men were there in the act of attempting the larceny of this cow and calf and the defendant killed because of that, because his mind was inflamed for the reason that they were seeking to do an act of that kind, that is manslaughter; that is all it is; there is nothing else in it; that is considered so far provocative as that it reduces the grade of the crime to manslaughter and no farther. If they had no intent to commit a larceny; if it was a bare, naked trespass; if they were there under a claim of right to get this cow, though they may not have had any right to it, but in good faith they were exercising their claim of that kind, and Will Jones was killed by the defendant for that reason, that would be murder, because you cannot kill a man for bare trespass -- you cannot take his life for a bare trespass -- and say the act is mitigated."

After restating the proposition that a man cannot take life because of mere fear on his part, or in order that he may prevent the commission of a bare trespass, the court proceeded: "Now, a word further upon the proposition that I have already adverted to as to what was his duty at the time. If that danger was real, coming from the hands of Will Jones, or it was apparent as coming from his hands and as affecting this defendant by some overt act at the time, was the defendant called upon to avoid that danger by getting out of the way of it if he could? The court says he was. The court tells you that he was. There is but one place where he need not retreat any further, where he need not go away from the danger, and that is in his dwelling-house. He may be upon his own premises, and if a man, while so situated and upon his own premises, can do that which would reasonably put aside the danger short of taking life, if he can do that, I say, he is called upon to do so by retreating, by getting out of the way if he can, by avoiding a conflict that may be about to come upon him, and the law says that he must do so, and the fact that he is standing upon his own premises away from his own dwelling-house does not take away from him the exercise of the duty of avoiding the danger if he can with a due regard to his own safety by getting away from there or by resorting to some other means of less violence than those resorted to. Now, the rule as applicable to a man of that kind upon his own premises, upon his own property, but outside of his dwelling-house, is as I have just stated." Again: "You are to bear in mind that the first proposition of the law of self-defence was that the defendant in this case was in the lawful pursuit of his business -- that is to say, he was doing what he had a right to do at the time. If he was not he deprives himself of the right of self-defence, and, no matter what his adversary may do, if he by his own conduct creates certain conditions by his own wrongful conduct he cannot take advantage of such conditions created by his own wrongful act or acts. . . . Again, going to the place where the person slain is with a deadly weapon for the purpose of provoking a difficulty or with the intent of having an affray. Now, if a man does that, he is in the wrong, and he is cut off from the right of self-defence, no matter what his adversary may do, because the law says in the very language of these propositions relating to the law of self-defence that he must avoid taking life if he can with due regard to his own safety. Whenever he can do that he must do it; therefore, if he has an adversary and he knows that there is a bitter feeling, that there is a state of feeling that may precipitate a deadly conflict between himself and his adversary, while he has a right to pursue his usual daily avocations that are right and proper, going about his business, to go and do what is necessary to be done in that way, yet if he knows that condition I have named to exist and he goes to the place where the slain person is with a deadly weapon for the purpose of provoking a difficulty or with the intent of having an affray if it comes up, he is there to have it, and he acts for that purpose, the law says there is no self-defence for him. . . . If he went to the place where that young man was, armed with a deadly weapon, even if it was upon his own premises, with the purpose of provoking a difficulty with him, in which he might use that deadly weapon, or of having a deadly affray with him, it does not make any difference what was done by the young man, there is no self-defence for the defendant. The law of self-defence does not apply to a case of that kind, because he cannot be the creator of a wrong, of a wrong state of case, and then act upon it. Now, if either one of these conditions exist, I say, the law of self-defence does not apply in this case."

Later in the charge, the court recurred to the inquiry as to what the law demanded of Beard before striking the deceased with his gun, and said: "If at the time of this killing it be true that the deceased was doing an act of apparent or real deadly violence and that state of case existed, and yet that the defendant at the time could have avoided the necessity of taking his life by the exercise of any other reasonable means and he did not do that, because he did not exercise other reasonable means that would have with equal certainty saved his life, but resorted to this dernier remedy, under those facts and circumstances the law says he is guilty of manslaughter. Now, let us see what that requires. It requires, first, that the proof must show that Will Jones was doing an act of violence or about to do it, or apparently doing it or about to do it, but that it was an act that the defendant could have escaped from by doing something else other than taking the life of Jones, by getting out of the way of that danger, as he was called upon to do, as I have already told you, for he could not stand there as he could stand in his own dwelling-house, and he must have reasonably sought to avoid that danger before he took the life of Jones, and if he did not do that, if you find that to be Jones' position from this testimony, and he could have done so, but did not do it, the defendant would be guilty of manslaughter when he took the life of Jones, because in that kind of a case the law says that the conduct of Jones would be so provocative as to reduce the grade of crime; yet, at the same time, it was a state of case that the defendant could have avoided without taking his life, and because he did not do it he is guilty of the crime of manslaughter." Further: "If it be true that Will Jones at the time he was killed was exercising deadly violence, or about to do so, or apparently exercising it, or apparently about to do so, and the defendant could have paralyzed the effect of that violence without taking the life of Jones, but he did not do it, but resorted to this deadly violence when he could have protected his own life without resorting to that dernier remedy -- if that be the state of case, the law says he is guilty of manslaughter, because he is doing that which he had no right to do. This great law of self-defence commands him at all times to do that which he can do under the circumstances, to wit, exercise reasonable care to avoid the danger by getting out of the way of it, or by exercising less violence than that which will produce death and yet will be equally effective to secure his own life. If either of these propositions exist, and they must exist to the extent I have defined to you, and the defendant took the life of Jones under these circumstances, the defendant would be guilty of manslaughter."

We are of opinion that the charge of the court to the jury was objectionable, in point of law, on several grounds.

There was no evidence tending to show that Beard went from his dwelling-house to the orchard fence for the purpose of provoking a difficulty, or with the intent of having an affray with the Jones brothers or with either of them. On the contrary, from the outset of the dispute, he evinced a purpose to avoid a difficulty or an affray. He expressed his willingness to abide by the law in respect to his right to retain the cow in his possession. He warned the Jones brothers, as he had a legal right to do, against coming upon his premises for the purpose of taking the cow away. They disregarded this warning, and determined to take the law into their own hands, whatever might be the consequences of such a course. Nevertheless, when Beard came to where they were, near the orchard fence, he did nothing to provoke a difficulty, and prior to the moment when he struck Will Jones with his gun he made no demonstration that indicated any desire whatever on his part to engage in an affray or to have an angry controversy. He only commanded them, as he had the legal right to do, to leave his premises. He neither used, nor threatened to use, force against them.

The court several times, in its charge, raised or suggested the inquiry whether Beard was in the lawful pursuit of his business, that is, doing what he had a right to do, when, after returning home in the afternoon, he went from his dwelling-house to a part of his premises near the orchard fence, just outside of which his wife and the Jones brothers were engaged in a dispute -- the former endeavoring to prevent the cow from being taken away, the latter trying to drive it off the premises. Was he not doing what he had the legal right to do, when, keeping within his own premises and near his dwelling, he joined his wife who was in dispute with others, one of whom, as he had been informed, had already threatened to take the cow away or kill him? We have no hesitation in answering this question in the affirmative.

The court also said: "The use of provoking language, or, it seems, resorting to any other device in order to get another to commence an assault so as to have a pretext for taking his life, agreeing with another to fight him with a deadly weapon, either one of these cases, if they exist as the facts in this case, puts the case in such an attitude that there is no self-defence in it." We are at a loss to understand why any such hypothetical cases were put before the jury. The jury must have supposed that, in the opinion of the court, there was evidence showing that Beard sought an opportunity to do physical harm to the Jones boys, or to some one of them. There was not the slightest foundation in the evidence for the intimation that Beard had used provoking language or resorted to any device in order to have a pretext to take the life of either of the brothers. Much less was there any reason to believe that there was an agreement to fight with deadly weapons.

if, without retreating, the accused had taken the life of his assailant, having at the time reasonable grounds to believe, and in good faith believing, that his own life would be taken or great bodily harm done him unless he killed the accused, the case would have been one of justifiable homicide. To that proposition we give our entire assent.

we cannot agree that the accused was under any greater obligation, when on his own

premises, near his dwelling-house, to retreat or run away from his assailant, than he would have been if attacked within his dwelling-house.

they were instructed that the accused could not properly be acquitted on the ground of self-defence if they believed that, by retreating from his adversary, by "getting out of the way," he could have avoided taking life. We cannot give our assent to this doctrine.

But the court below committed an error of a more serious character when it told the jury, as in effect it did by different forms of expression, that if the accused could have saved his own life and avoided taking the life of Will Jones by retreating from and getting out of the way of the latter as he advanced upon him, the law made it his duty to do so; and if he did not, when it was in his power to do so without putting his own life or body in imminent peril, he was guilty of manslaughter. The court seemed to think if the deceased had advanced upon the accused while the latter was in his dwelling-house and under such circumstances as indicated the intention of the former to take life or inflict great bodily injury, and if, without retreating, the accused had taken the life of his assailant, having at the time reasonable grounds to believe, and in good faith believing, that his own life would be taken or great bodily harm done him unless he killed the accused, the case would have been one of justifiable homicide. To that proposition we give our entire assent. But we cannot agree that the accused was under any greater obligation, when on his own premises, near his dwelling-house, to retreat or run away from his assailant, than he would have been if attacked within his dwelling-house. The accused being where he had a right to be, on his own premises, constituting a part of his residence and home, at the time the deceased approached him in a threatening manner, and not having by language or by conduct provoked the deceased to assault him, the question for the jury was whether, without fleeing from his adversary, he had, at the moment he struck the deceased, reasonable grounds to believe, and in good faith believed, that he could not save his life or protect himself from great bodily harm except by doing what he did, namely, strike the deceased with his gun, and thus prevent his further advance upon him. Even if the jury had been prepared to answer this question in the affirmative -- and if it had been so answered the defendant should have been acquitted -- they were instructed that the accused could not properly be acquitted on the ground of self-defence if they believed that, by retreating from his adversary, by "getting out of the way," he could have avoided taking life. We cannot give our assent to this doctrine.

The application of the doctrine of "retreating to the wall" was carefully examined by the Supreme Court of Ohio in Erwin v. State, 29 Ohio St. 186, 193, 199. That was an indictment for murder, the defendant being found guilty. The trial court charged the jury that if the defendant was in the lawful pursuit of his business at the time the fatal shot was fired, and was attacked by the deceased under circumstances denoting an intention to take life or to do great bodily harm, he could lawfully kill his assailant provided he used all means "in his power" otherwise to save his own life or prevent the intended harm, "such as retreating as far as he can, or disabling his adversary, without killing him, if it be in his power;" that if the attack was so sudden, fierce, and violent that a retreat would not diminish but increase the defendant's danger, he might kill his adversary without retreating; and further, that if from the character of the attack there was reasonable ground for defendant to believe, and he did honestly believe, that his life was about to be taken, or he was to suffer great bodily harm, and that he believed honestly that he would be in equal danger by retreating, then, if he took the life of the assailant, he was excused. Of this charge the accused complained.

It is true that all authorities agree that the taking of life in defence of one's person cannot be either justified or excused, except on the ground of necessity; and that such necessity must be imminent at the time; and they also agree that no man can avail himself of such necessity if he brings it upon himself.

a true man who is without fault is not obliged to fly from an assailant, who by violence or surprise maliciously seeks to take his life or do him enormous bodily harm.

Upon a full review of the authorities and looking to the principles of the common law, as expounded by writers and courts of high authority, the Supreme Court of Ohio held that the charge was erroneous, saying: "It is true that all authorities agree that the taking of life in defence of one's person cannot be either justified or excused, except on the ground of necessity; and that such necessity must be imminent at the time; and they also agree that no man can avail himself of such necessity if he brings it upon himself. The question then is simply this: Does the law hold a man who is violently and feloniously assaulted responsible for having brought such necessity upon himself on the sole ground that he failed to fly from his assailant when he might safely have done so? The law, out of tenderness for human life and the frailties of human nature, will not permit the taking of it to repel a mere trespass, or even to save life where the assault is provoked; but a true man who is without fault is not obliged to fly from an assailant, who by violence or surprise maliciously seeks to take his life or do him enormous bodily harm. Now, under the charge below, notwithstanding the defendant may have been without fault, and so assaulted, with the necessity of taking life to save his own upon him; still the jury could not have acquitted if they found he had failed to do all in his power otherwise to save his own life, or prevent the intended harm, as retreating as far as he could, etc. In this case we think the law was not correctly stated."

the ancient doctrine, as to the duty of a person assailed to retreat as far as he can, before he is justified in repelling force by force, has been greatly modified in this country, and has with us a much narrower application than formerly. Indeed, the tendency of the American mind seems to be very strongly against the enforcement of any rule which requires a person to flee when assailed, to avoid chastisement or even to save human life

The weight of modern authority, in our judgment, establishes the doctrine that, when a person, being without fault and in a place where he has a right to be, is violently assaulted, he may, without retreating, repel force by force, and if, in the reasonable exercise of his right of self-defence, his assailant is killed, he is justifiable.

did the defendant have reason to believe, and did he in fact believe, that what he did was necessary for the safety of his own life or to protect him from great bodily harm?

In Runyan v. State, 57 Indiana, 80, 84, which was an indictment for murder, and where the instructions of the trial court involved the present question, the court said: "A very brief examination of the American authorities makes it evident that the ancient doctrine, as to the duty of a person assailed to retreat as far as he can, before he is justified in repelling force by force, has been greatly modified in this country, and has with us a much narrower application than formerly. Indeed, the tendency of the American mind seems to be very strongly against the enforcement of any rule which requires a person to flee when assailed, to avoid chastisement or even to save human life, and that tendency is well illustrated by the recent decisions of our courts, bearing on the general subject of the right of self-defence. The weight of modern authority, in our judgment, establishes the doctrine that, when a person, being without fault and in a place where he has a right to be, is violently assaulted, he may, without retreating, repel force by force, and if, in the reasonable exercise of his right of self-defence, his assailant is killed, he is justifiable. . . . It seems to us that the real question in the case, when it was given to the jury, was, was the defendant, under all the circumstances, justified in the use of a deadly weapon in repelling the assault of the deceased? We mean by this, did the defendant have reason to believe, and did he in fact believe, that what he did was necessary for the safety of his own life or to protect him from great bodily harm? On that question the law is simple and easy of solution, as has been already seen from the authorities cited above."

A man may repel force by force, in defence of his person, habitation or property, against one who manifestly intends or endeavors, by violence or surprise, to commit a known felony, such as murder, rape, robbery, arson, burglary, and the like

In these cases he is not obliged to retreat, but may pursue his adversary until he has secured himself from all danger; and if he kill him in so doing it is called justifiable self-defence

There must be an actual danger at the time.

In East's Pleas of the Crown, the author, considering what sort of an attack it was lawful and justifiable to resist, even by the death of the assailant, says: "A man may repel force by force, in defence of his person, habitation or property, against one who manifestly intends or endeavors, by violence or surprise, to commit a known felony, such as murder, rape, robbery, arson, burglary, and the like, upon either. In these cases he is not obliged to retreat, but may pursue his adversary until he has secured himself from all danger; and if he kill him in so doing it is called justifiable self-defence; as, on the other hand, the killing by such felon of any person so lawfully defending himself will be murder. But a bare fear of any of these offences, however well grounded, as that another lies in wait to take away the party's life, unaccompanied with any overt act indicative of such an intention, will not warrant in killing that other by way of prevention. There must be an actual danger at the time." p. 271. So in Foster's Crown Cases: "In the case of justifiable self-defence, the injured party may repel force with force in defence of his person, habitation, or property, against one who manifestly intendeth and endeavoreth, with violence or surprise, to commit a known felony upon either. In these cases he is not obliged to retreat, but may pursue his adversary till he findeth himself out of danger, and if, in a conflict between them, he happeneth to kill, such killing is justifiable." c. 3, p. 273.

where an attack is made with murderous intent, the person attacked is under no duty to fly; he may stand his ground, and if need be, kill his adversary.

A man may repel force by force in the defence of his person, habitation, or property

In Bishop's New Criminal Law, the author, after observing that cases of mere assault, and of mutual quarrel, where the attacking party has not the purpose of murder in his heart, are those to which is applied the doctrine of the books, that one cannot justify the killing of another, though apparently in self-defence, unless he retreat to the wall or other interposing obstacle before resorting to this extreme right, says that "where an attack is made with murderous intent, the person attacked is under no duty to fly; he may stand his ground, and if need be, kill his adversary. And it is the same where the attack is with a deadly weapon, for in this case the person attacked may well assume that the other intends murder, whether he does in fact or not." Vol. 1, §850. The rule is thus expressed by Wharton: "A man may repel force by force in the defence of his person, habitation, or property, against any one or many who manifestly intend and endeavor by violence or surprise to commit a known felony on either. In such case he is not compelled to retreat, but may pursue his adversary until he finds himself out of danger, and if in the conflict between them he happen to kill him, such killing is justifiable." 2 Wharton on Crim. Law, §1019, 7th rev. ed. Phila. 1874. See also Gallagher v. State, 3 Minnesota, 270, 273; Pond v. People, 8 Michigan, 150, 177; State v. Dixon, 75 N.C. 275, 295; State v. Sherman, 16 R.I. 631; Fields v. State, 32 N.E. Rep. 780; Eversole v. Commonwealth, 26 S.W. Rep. 816; Haynes v. State, 17 Georgia, 465, 483; Long v. State, 52 Mississippi, 23, 35; Tweedy v. State, 5 Iowa, 433; Baker v. Commonwealth, 19 S.W. Rep. 975; Tingle v. Commonwealth, 11 S.W. 812; 3 Rice's Ev. §360.

The defendant was where he had the right to be, when the deceased advanced upon him in a threatening manner, and with a deadly weapon; and if the accused did not provoke the assault and had at the time reasonable grounds to believe and in good faith believed, that the deceased intended to take his life or do him great bodily harm, he was not obliged to retreat, nor to consider whether he could safely retreat, but was entitled to stand his ground and meet any attack made upon him with a deadly weapon, in such way and with such force as, under all the circumstances, he, at the moment, honestly believed, and had reasonable grounds to believe, was necessary to save his own life or to protect himself from great bodily injury.

In our opinion, the court below erred in holding that the accused, while on his premises, outside of his dwelling-house, was under a legal duty to get out of the way, if he could, of his assailant, who, according to one view of the evidence, had threatened to kill the defendant, in execution of that purpose had armed himself with a deadly weapon, with that weapon concealed upon his person went to the defendant's premises, despite the warning of the latter to keep away, and by word and act indicated his purpose to attack the accused. The defendant was where he had the right to be, when the deceased advanced upon him in a threatening manner, and with a deadly weapon; and if the accused did not provoke the assault and had at the time reasonable grounds to believe and in good faith believed, that the deceased intended to take his life or do him great bodily harm, he was not obliged to retreat, nor to consider whether he could safely retreat, but was entitled to stand his ground and meet any attack made upon him with a deadly weapon, in such way and with such force as, under all the circumstances, he, at the moment, honestly believed, and had reasonable grounds to believe, was necessary to save his own life or to protect himself from great bodily injury.

As the proceedings below were not conducted in accordance with these principles, the judgment must be reversed and the cause remanded with directions to grant a new trial.

Other objections to the charge of the court are raised by the assignments of error, but as the questions which they present may not arise upon another trial, they will not be now examined.

Judgment reversed.

ALLISON v. UNITED STATES

(FULL CASE)

160 U.S. 203; 16 S. Ct. 252; 40 L. Ed. 395

Submitted November 20, 1895.

December 16, 1895, Decided

GIST: In this self-defense case, 20-year-old defendant John Allison shot and killed his abusive father William, with a hunting rifle, when it appeared that his father was reaching for the concealed pistol he was known to carry. In the week before the killing, the father had threatened to blow the family's brains out, and he had recently been released from prison for firing a shot at them during an argument.

Trial Judge Isaac Parker, of the Western District of Arkansas, injected all sorts of bias and erroneous interpretation of the law in order to force a conviction. The High Court's decision includes lengthy quotes of the judge's statements and charge to the jury (including Parker's subtle swipe at the High Court for being "technical and hair splitting"). Parker seemed to feel that if a man is threatened, the man then automatically harbors a grudge, and the grudge is a motivation in the homicide. Parker downplayed the character witnesses and prior threats. He said you can't trust the testimony of a person on trial for his life, because anyone in that position will lie. It was a perfect stage for the Supreme Court to set the record straight on armed self defense in America.

The Supreme Court unanimously reversed the murder conviction and called for a new trial. The Justices found that Judge Parker had inappropriately denigrated the right of self defense in his jury instructions, and in other ways misled the jury. The Justices' frustration with Parker was increasing, and they lambasted his actions in their published conclusion. The case hinged on reasonable belief and grounds for that belief, as well as the nature of threats and the character of the adversary, which are jury decisions, not matters of law. As it turned out, the father was not armed as he usually was, when he reached as if to draw and was fatally shot by his son. The son's testimony was the only evidence for key parts of what actually occurred.

ERROR TO THE CIRCUIT COURT OF THE UNITED STATES FOR THE WESTERN DISTRICT OF ARKANSAS.

When a person indicted for the commission of murder, offers himself at the trial as a witness on his own behalf under the provisions of the act of March 16, 1878, c. 37, 20 Stat. 30, the policy of that enactment should not be defeated by hostile intimations of the trial judge. Hicks v. United States, 150 U.S. 442, affirmed.

The defendant in this case having offered himself as a witness in his own behalf, and having testified to circumstances which tended to show that the killing was done in self-defence, the court charged the jury: "You must have something more tangible, more real, more certain, than that which is a simple declaration of the party who slays, made in your presence by him as a witness, when he is confronted with a charge of murder. All men would say that." Held, that this was reversible error.

Other statements made by the court to the jury are held to seriously trench on that untrammelled determination of the facts by a jury to which parties accused of the commission of crime are entitled.

What is or what is not an overt demonstration of violence sufficient to justify a resistance which ends in the death of the party making the demonstration varies with the circumstances; and it is for the jury, and not for the judge, passing upon the weight and effect of the evidence, to determine whether the circumstances justified instant action, because of reasonable apprehension of danger.

Where the charge of the trial judge takes the form of animated argument, the liability is great that the propositions of law may become interrupted by digression, and be so intermingled with inferences springing from forensic ardor, that the jury will be left without proper instructions, their province of dealing with the facts invaded, and errors intervene.

JOHN ALLISON, some twenty years old, was indicted for the murder of his father, William Allison, on the fifth day of January, 1895, at the Cherokee Nation in the Indian country, in the Western District of Arkansas, found guilty by a jury, under the instructions of the court, and sentenced to be hanged, whereupon he sued out this writ of error.

the father had repeatedly threatened the lives of the members of his family, and for an assault upon one of his sons and his son-in-law, by shooting at them with a pistol, had been sent to the penitentiary for a year

The evidence tended to show that the Allisons resided up to the year 1893 in the State of Washington; that the parents had been divorced; that the father had repeatedly threatened the lives of the members of his family, and for an assault upon one of his sons and his son-in-law, by shooting at them with a pistol, had been sent to the penitentiary for a year; and that thereupon the family left the State of Washington and came to the Indian country. In about a year the father appeared, first at Hot Springs, Arkansas, where one daughter had located, and then in the neighborhood of the other members of the family in the Indian country; and at once began threatening the lives of the entire family, and particularly that of his son John. A great variety of vindictive threats by the deceased in Washington, at Hot Springs, and in the Indian country was testified to.

I will go off and get a gun and kill the last damned one of you

he subsequently told his son-in-law to tell John Allison "that he would blow his God damned brains out the first time he seen him

John told the prosecuting attorney that the old man threatened his life, and he thought he was in danger, and asked him if he killed the old man what would be done with him, and he <the prosecutor> replied that "if the old man came to his house and raised a racket and tried to carry out his threats that he told me he had made on him, I told him he would be justified in doing it," but that he must not go "hunting the old man up and trying to kill him," and that John said, "I will not bother him; if he will let me alone, I will let him alone;" and that this was five or six days before the killing.

The evidence further tended to show that the deceased had been in the habit of carrying a pistol; that he stated that he had one; that on New Year's day he threatened one of the witnesses with that weapon, and another witness testified to catching a glimpse of it once when he put his hand around to his hip pocket; but that he had no pistol on him when he was killed.

Evidence was also adduced that on one occasion he came to the house where the mother and her children were living and demanded to see the children, who (except John and one whom he had seen) were not at home, and he then wished to see their mother, who objected to meeting him; that he persisted, whereupon his son John, who had a gun in his hand, told him he must leave, and the father dared John to come out and he would fight him outside, but John answered that he did not want any trouble with him -- only wanted him to stay away from there, and the deceased replied: "God damn you, I will go off and get a gun and kill the last damned one of you;" that he subsequently told his son-in-law to tell John Allison "that he would blow his God damned brains out the first time he seen him; told him to tell him he would kill his mother and the entire family;" that the day after this occurrence John Allison and his mother made an affidavit to get a peace warrant for William Allison, and on that occasion John told the prosecuting attorney that the old man threatened his life, and he thought he was in danger, and asked him if he killed the old man what would be done with him, and he replied that "if the old man came to his house and raised a racket and tried to carry out his threats that he told me he had made on him, I told him he would be justified in doing it," but that he must not go "hunting the old man up and trying to kill him," and that John said, "I will not bother him; if he will let me alone, I will let him alone;" and that this was five or six days before the killing. The evidence further tended to show that the deceased had been in the habit of carrying a pistol; that he stated that he had one; that on New Year's day he threatened one of the witnesses with that weapon, and another witness testified to catching a glimpse of it once when he put his hand around to his hip pocket; but that he had no pistol on him when he was killed. The deceased was staying at the house of one Farris, and a witness testified in rebuttal to conversing with John when he was "warming" on one occasion at the barn --

presumably Farris' barn -- and asking him why he did not go up to the house, and he said he did not want to go up there; that he was afraid he and his father would have some trouble; that he was afraid his father would hurt him; and that he was going to kill him just as quick as he caught him away from the house.

and when he got a few feet from him said: "You have got it, have you?" and threw his hand back as if he was going to get a pistol; "made a demonstration that way," and that this demonstration and the threats he had made led defendant to believe that he was going to draw a pistol, and he <defendant> fired; that he fired three shots, but none after the deceased fell.

contradicted by the government's witnesses in respect of firing after his father was down, they testifying that he fell at the first shot.

As to the circumstances immediately surrounding the homicide, the defendant testified that he and a man by the name of Rucker had killed a deer near Rucker's the day before, and that he had promised Rucker to come back the next day to hunt for others, and was riding by Farris' place, which was on the road to Rucker's, with his gun in his hand, on that errand, on the morning of January 5, when he saw a person whom he took to be his brother Jasper up at Farris' house; that this person turned out to be Farris with his brother's coat on; but he stopped at the stable thinking that his brother would come down that way, as he had learned from his sister that his brother was to be at the place at that time for the purpose of removing some household goods; that he did not go up to the house because he did not want to meet his father; that shortly after he arrived at the barn his father came through the gate, and he stepped to one side to let him go into the barn if he wished to, but deceased did not go towards the door, came straight towards him, and when he got a few feet from him said: "You have got it, have you?" and threw his hand back as if he was going to get a pistol; "made a demonstration that way," and that this demonstration and the threats he had made led defendant to believe that he was going to draw a pistol, and he fired; that he fired three shots, but none after the deceased fell. Defendant was corroborated by Rucker and others in many particulars, but contradicted by the government's witnesses in respect of firing after his father was down, they testifying that he fell at the first shot.

MR. CHIEF JUSTICE FULLER delivered the opinion of the court.

It was claimed on behalf of defendant that the homicide was excusable because committed in self-defence, in that, his life having been repeatedly threatened by deceased, when he saw him on this occasion moving his hand as if to take a pistol from his hip pocket, he believed, and, as a prudent man, might reasonably have believed, at that time and under those circumstances, that he was in imminent and deadly peril which could only be averted by the course he pursued; or that, at the most, he could only be found guilty of manslaughter for acting under an unreasonable access of fear, but without malice.

there was evidence that the deceased was in the habit of carrying a pistol; that he had recently carried one in his hip pocket; that he had sent word to defendant that he should kill him on sight; that defendant had started on a hunting expedition that morning; and that his stopping at Farris' place was accidental; but the facts that he at first stepped away from his father, and that the latter advanced on him and made the threatening demonstration as if to draw a pistol, which the defendant knew he was accustomed to have upon him, apparently depended on defendant's testimony alone. The question for the jury to determine, from all the facts and circumstances adduced in evidence, was the reasonableness of the belief, or fear, of the existence of such peril of death or great bodily harm as would excuse the killing.

The threats were conceded; and there was evidence that the deceased was in the habit of carrying a pistol; that he had recently carried one in his hip pocket; that he had sent word to defendant that he should kill him on sight; that defendant had started on a hunting expedition that morning; and that his stopping at Farris' place was accidental; but the facts that he at first stepped away from his father, and that the latter advanced on him and made the threatening demonstration as if to draw a pistol, which the defendant knew he was accustomed to have upon him, apparently depended on defendant's testimony alone. The question for the jury to determine, from all the facts and circumstances adduced in evidence, was the reasonableness of the belief, or fear, of the existence of such peril of death or great bodily harm as would excuse the killing. And it was for the jury to test the credibility of the defendant as a witness, giving his testimony such weight under all the circumstances as they thought it entitled to, as in the instance of other witnesses, uninfluenced by instructions which might operate to strip him of the competency accorded by the law.

We repeat what was said by Mr. Justice Shiras, speaking for the court, in Hicks v. United States, 150

U.S. 442, 452: "It is not unusual to warn juries that they should be careful in giving effect to the testimony of accomplices, and, perhaps, a judge cannot be considered as going out of his province in giving similar caution as to the testimony of the accused person. Still, it must be remembered, that men may testify truthfully, although their lives hang in the balance, and that the law, in its wisdom, has provided that the accused shall have the right to testify in his own behalf. Such a privilege would be a vain one if the judge, to whose lightest word the jury properly enough give a great weight, should intimate that the dreadful condition in which the accused finds himself should deprive his testimony of probability. The wise and humane provision of the law is, that 'the person charged shall at his own request, and not otherwise, be a competent witness.' The policy of this enactment should not be defeated by hostile intimations of the trial judge, whose duty it is to give reasonable effect and force to the law."

Similar views have been expressed in many cases in the state courts.

In Commonwealth v. Wright, 107 Mass. 403, it was held that there was no presumption either way as to the truthfulness of a defendant's testimony in a criminal case, and that his testimony is to be considered and weighed by the jury, taking all the circumstances of the case and all the other evidence into consideration, and giving such weight to the testimony as in their judgment it ought to have.

"It cannot," observed Scholfield, J., in Chambers v. The People, 105 Illinois, 409, "be true that the evidence given by the defendant charged with crime is not to be treated the same as the evidence of other witnesses. It could not even be true, as a universal proposition, that, as matter of law, it is not to have the same effect as the evidence of other witnesses. Many times it certainly cannot have that effect, but there are times when it can and should, -- and of this the jury are made the judges."

And see Greer v. State, 53 Indiana, 420; Veatch v. State, 56 Indiana, 584; Buckley v. State, 62 Mississippi, 705; State v. Johnson, 16 Nevada, 36.

Among the errors assigned in the present case was one to so much of the charge as is given below in italics, in respect of which a sufficient exception was preserved. The trial judge said:

"You have heard in argument here, incidentally dropped, no doubt, because these things have been repeated here so often in this court that every child knows what the law of self-defence is, that if a man thinks he has a right to slay he can slay. That is a great misapprehension of what this proposition of the law is and what it means. If that was the case how many men, when they were arraigned for the killing of a human being, would not assert that they thought they had a right to kill; they might be mistaken, but they thought so. They perhaps had a misunderstanding of the law, but then they thought they had the right to kill. What a perversion of this protection agency called the law of the land this would be! No, that is not the law. It must be shown by the evidence that the party who was slain was at the time doing something that would satisfy a reasonable man, situated as was the defendant, that the deceased, William Allison, then and there was about to do that which would destroy the life of the defendant, and that he could not prevent it except by doing as he did do. *The question as to whether that is the state of case or not is a question that is to be finally passed upon by the juries of the country, and by you in this case, and you must have something more tangible, more real, more certain, than that which is a simple declaration of the party who slays, made in your presence by him as a witness when he is confronted with a charge of murder. All men would say that. No man created would say otherwise when confronted by such circumstances, and the juries, as a matter of fact, would have nothing to do but to record the finding which was willed or established by the declaration of the party who did the killing.*"

In this there was error. While the trial judge may not have intended to be understood that the defendant could not prove his defence by his own testimony, and had it in his mind simply to warn the jury that they should not rely on the defendant's opinion that his conduct was justifiable, but on the facts, or what reasonably appeared to him to be such, we think these remarks had a much wider scope, and must have been so understood by the jury. The "state of case" put to the jury was whether William Allison was at the time doing something that would satisfy a reasonable man, situated as defendant was, that he was about to do what would destroy defendant's life, and which defendant could not prevent except by doing as he did; and the question as to the existence of that state of case was required by the instruction to be passed on by the jury on something more than defendant's declaration, which, it was stated, would certainly be made by any man created when confronted with a charge of murder.

Defendant had testified to the facts upon which he based his belief that he was in peril, and it was for the jury to say from the evidence whether the facts as he stated them actually or apparently existed, and whether the homicide could, therefore, be excused either wholly or in part.

Defendant had testified to the facts upon which he based his belief that he was in peril, and it was for the jury to say from the evidence whether the facts as he stated them actually or apparently existed, and whether the homicide could, therefore, be excused either wholly or in part. And if the jury regarded the remarks of the court as applicable generally to defendant's testimony, then defendant was practically deprived of its benefit, and the statute enabling him to testify was rendered unavailing. In our opinion the liability of the jury to thus understand these observations was so great that their utterance constitutes reversible error.

As a witness, a defendant is no more to be visited with condemnation than he is to be clothed with sanctity, simply because he is under accusation, and there is no presumption of law in favor of or against his truthfulness.

Nor was this error obviated by what, some time after -- the intervening portion of the charge occupies six closely printed pages -- was said by the trial judge, as follows: "The defendant has gone upon the stand, and he has made his statement. See if it is in harmony with the statements of witnesses you find to be reliable. If they are not, they stand before you as contradicted. If they are, they stand before you as strengthened as you may attach credit to the corroborating facts. In passing upon his evidence you are necessarily to consider his interest in the result of this trial, in the result of this case. He is related to the case more intimately than anybody else, and you are to apply the principle of the law that is laid down everywhere in all civilized countries, commanding you to look at a man's statements in the light of the interest that he has in the case. There is no odor of sanctity thrown around the statements of the defendant as a witness, as is sometimes supposed, because he is charged with crime. You are to view his statements in the light of their consistency, their reasonableness, and their probability, the same as the statements of any other witness, and you are to look at them in the light of the interest he has in the result of the case." If this could be, in any aspect, treated as a modification of the previous assertions of the court, it was too far separated from that connection to permit us to attribute that operation to it, and, moreover, it was in itself erroneous. As a witness, a defendant is no more to be visited with condemnation than he is to be clothed with sanctity, simply because he is under accusation, and there is no presumption of law in favor of or against his truthfulness.

Exception was taken, not with much precision, but, we are disposed to hold, sufficiently to save the point, to the following instruction, given in discussing the question of malice aforethought:

"Now, of course, you are to distinguish (and I have to be particular upon this point; I have my reasons for it, and it is not necessary to name to you what they are) between a case where a man prepares simply to defend himself and keeps himself in the right in that defence, and a state of case where he prepares himself recklessly, wantonly, and without just cause to take the life of another. If he prepares himself in the latter way, and he is on the lookout for the man he has thus prepared himself to kill and he kills him upon sight, that is murder, and it would shock humanity or even the most technical and hair splitting court to decide anything else. That can be nothing else but murder. If he is in the right -- if he is in the right at the time of the killing -- and simply prepared himself to defend his own life, that is preparation not to take the life of another, but preparation to defend himself. That is the distinction, a distinction that is clear and comprehensive."

And also to this in reference to the exercise of the right of self-defence:

If he was hunting up his father for the purpose of getting an opportunity to slay him without just cause and in the absence of legal provocation, he was not in the right, and the consequence would be that he would be deprived of the law of self-defence

"The first proposition is as follows: 'A man, who, in the lawful pursuit of his business' -- I will tell you after a while what is meant by that. I will tell you, in short, in this connection it means that the man is doing at the time just exactly what he had a right to do under the law. When so situated -- 'is attacked by another under circumstances which denote an intention to take away his life, or to do him some enormous bodily harm, may lawfully kill the assailant, provided he uses all the means in his power, otherwise, to save his own life or to prevent the intended harm -- such as retreating as far as he can, or disabling his adversary without killing him, if it be in his power.' Now, that means by its very language that the party was in the right at the time. If he was hunting up his father for the purpose of getting an opportunity to slay him without just cause and in the absence of legal provocation, he was not in the right, and the consequence would be that he would be deprived of the law of self-defence, as you will learn presently, when such a condition as that exists. Now, of course, in this connection -- and I am this particular again for certain reasons -- you are to draw the distinction between a state of case where a man arms himself, where there is ill will, or grudge, or spite, or animosity, existing, and he hunts up his adversary and slays him, and the state of case where he simply arms himself for self-defence. He has a right to do the latter as long as he is in the right, but he has no right to do the former, and if he does the former and slays because of that condition he is guilty of murder."

We are of opinion that defendant's objections to these portions of the charge are well founded. The hypothesis upon which the defence rested on the trial was that John Allison had a gun with him on the morning of the tragedy, in order to hunt deer, and that his stopping at Farris' place, which was on his way to Rucker's, was accidental. His testimony to this effect was corroborated, and was not contradicted.

the evidence tending to show that defendant had not armed himself at all, but had a gun with him for purposes of sport, and that his halt at Farris' had no connection whatever with the deceased

Justice and the law demanded that so far as reference was made to the evidence, that which was favorable to the accused should not be excluded. His guilt or innocence turned on a narrow hinge, and great caution should have been used not to complicate and confuse the issue. But the charge above quoted ignored the evidence tending to show that defendant had not armed himself at all, but had a gun with him for purposes of sport, and that his halt at Farris' had no connection whatever with the deceased; and invited the jury to contemplate the spectacle of a son hunting up his father with the deliberately preconceived intention of murdering him, unrelieved by allusion to defensive matter, which threw a different light on the transaction.

If defendant were "in the right at the time of the killing," the inquiry as to how he came to be armed was immaterial, or, at least, embraced by that expression.

defendant carried his gun that morning for no purpose of offence or defence

If defendant were "in the right at the time of the killing," the inquiry as to how he came to be armed was immaterial, or, at least, embraced by that expression. If there were evidence, and as to this the record permits no doubt, tending to establish that defendant carried his gun that morning for no purpose of offence or defence, then this disquisition of the court was calculated to darken the light cast on the homicide by the attendant circumstances as defendant claimed them to be; and of this he had just cause to complain, even though there were competent evidence indicating that he harbored designs against his father's life, as frequently intimated by the court -- intimations which we fear seriously trenched on that untrammelled determination of the facts by a jury to which parties accused are entitled.

As will have been seen, the theory of the defence was that defendant was in terror of his life by reason of the threats of deceased to take it, and was, therefore, led to interpret the alleged menacing action of deceased as demonstrating an intention then and there to carry those threats into execution. The bearing of the previous threats then was very important, and in relation to them the trial judge admonished the jury as follows:

"Now, then, these mitigating facts which reduce the killing so as to make it manslaughter cannot be previous acts of violence exerted at some other time, and so far in the past as that there was time for the blood to cool, or the party to think or to deliberate -- it cannot be an act of that kind that can be taken into account to mitigate the crime. Nor can they exist in the shape of previous threats, made at some other time than the killing, or, if you please, if the proof had shown that they were made at the time of the killing, because threats of violence, mere threats of that character, cannot be used to justify nor to mitigate a killing, unless they are coupled with some other condition which I will give you in connection with the law given you showing the figure that threats cut in a case. . . . If threats were made previous to the time of the killing, and they were not coupled with the condition that they may be used to illustrate, as I will give it to you presently, and the party kills because of those threats, that is evidence of spite, that is evidence of grudge, that is evidence showing that he kills because of ill will and special animosity existing upon his part against the party who is slain."

After much intervening discussion on other matters, the subject was returned to thus:

"You want to know, of course, what figure threats cut. Evidence has been offered here of threats made by the deceased. You want to know what office they perform in the case, how you are to view them, whether you are to say that the law authorizes you to say that if a man has been threatened at some time previous to the killing and that he kills because of these threats, or he kills when no overt demonstration of violence, really or apparently, is being made by the party slain at the time, whether or not those threats can be taken into consideration by you to excuse that killing or to mitigate it. . . . Now, you see, they do not cut any office at all in favor of a defendant unless at the time, in this case, his father was doing some act, making some actual attempt, to execute the threat, as shown by some act or demonstration at the time of the killing, taken in connection with the threat, that would induce a reasonable belief upon the part of the slayer that it was necessary to deprive his father of life in order to save his own or prevent some felony upon his person. That is the law, stated plainly, as to the office of communicated threats. . . . If he (the deceased) was doing some act or making some demonstration that really or apparently was of a character that indicated a design to take life, then the defendant could couple previous threats made with the act or demonstration. Now, the act or demonstration must have gone sufficiently far to show a reasonable purpose or to induce a reasonable belief, when coupled with threats, under the circumstances, that that was William Allison's purpose at the time. It must have gone to that extent. It must have gone sufficiently far, the overt act done by him, as to induce a reasonable belief, when coupled with threats, that that was his purpose. . . . Now, you see that no matter how many threats William Allison may have made against his family, and no matter to what extent this family broil had gone, this defendant because of threats of that character could not hunt him up and shoot him down because of those threats. If that was the state of case the threats cannot be considered in his favor, but they may be considered to show that he killed him because of malice, because of malice aforethought existing, because of a spirit of spite, or ill will, or grudge, that he was seeking to satisfy by that sort of attack."

Defendant excepted to so much of these instructions as ruled that threats to take his life might be treated as constituting evidence of spite, or ill will, or grudge on his part.

the undisputed proposition that a person's life is not to be taken simply because he has made threats.

In Wiggins v. People, 93 U.S. 465, it was held that, on a trial for a homicide committed in an encounter, where the question as to which of the parties commenced the attack is in doubt, it is competent to prove threats of violence against defendant made by deceased, though not brought to defendant's knowledge, for the evidence, though not relevant to show the quo animo of the defendant, would be relevant, under such circumstances, to show that at the time of the meeting deceased was seeking defendant's life. Wharton Crim. Ev. §757; Stokes v. People, 53 N.Y. 164; Campbell v. People, 16 Illinois, 17; People v. Scoggins, 37 California, 676; Roberts v. State, 68 Alabama, 156. It is from the dissenting opinion in Wiggins' case that the trial judge indulged in quotation in connection with the undisputed proposition that a person's life is not to be taken simply because he has made threats.

Here the threats were recent and were communicated, and were admissible in evidence as relevant to the question whether defendant had reasonable cause to apprehend an attack, fatal to life or fraught with great bodily injury, and hence was justified in acting on a hostile demonstration and one of much less pronounced character than if such threats had not preceded it.

Here the threats were recent and were communicated, and were admissible in evidence as relevant to the question whether defendant had reasonable cause to apprehend an attack, fatal to life or fraught with great bodily injury, and hence was justified in acting on a hostile demonstration and one of much less pronounced character than if such threats had not preceded it. They were relevant because indicating cause for apprehension of danger and reason for promptness to repel attack, but they could not have been admitted on a record such as this, if offered by the prosecution as tending to show spite, ill will, or grudge on the part of the person threatened; nor could they, being admitted on defendant's behalf, if coupled with an actual or apparent hostile demonstration, be turned against him in the absence of evidence justifying such a construction. The logical inference was that these threats excited apprehension, and another and inconsistent inference could not be arbitrarily substituted. If defendant, to use the graphic language of the court, hunted his father up and shot him down merely because he had made the threats, speculation as to his mental processes was uncalled for. If defendant committed the homicide because of the threats, in the sense of acting upon emotions aroused by them, then some basis must be laid by the evidence other than the threats themselves before a particular emotion different from those they would ordinarily inspire under the circumstances, could be imputed as a motive for the fatal shot.

What is or is not an overt demonstration of violence varies with the circumstances. Under some circumstances a slight movement may justify instant action because of reasonable apprehension of danger; under other circumstances this would not be so. And it is for the jury, and not for the judge, passing upon the weight and effect of the evidence, to determine how this may be. In this case it was essential to the defence that the jury should be clearly and distinctly advised as to the bearing of the threats and the appearance of danger, at the moment, from defendant's standpoint, and particularly so as it did not appear that the deceased then had a pistol upon him, though there was evidence that it was his habit to carry one, and that he had had one immediately before.

What is or is not an overt demonstration of violence varies with the circumstances. Under some circumstances a slight movement may justify instant action because of reasonable apprehension of danger; under other circumstances this would not be so. And it is for the jury, and not for the judge, passing upon the weight and effect of the evidence, to determine how this may be. In this case it was essential to the defence that the jury should be clearly and distinctly advised as to the bearing of the threats and the appearance of danger, at the moment, from defendant's standpoint, and particularly so as it did not appear that the deceased then had a pistol upon him, though there was evidence that it was his habit to carry one, and that he had had one immediately before.

While it is no doubt true that previous threats will not, in all circumstances, justify or, perhaps, even extenuate the act of the party threatened in killing the person who uttered the threats, yet it by no means follows that such threats, signifying ill will and hostility on the part of the deceased, can be used by the jury as indicating a similar state of feeling on the part of the defendant.

We think that the language of the court in the particulars named is open to the criticism made in reference to like instructions under consideration in Thompson v. United States, 155 U.S. 271, 281, where we remarked: "While it is no doubt true that previous threats will not, in all circumstances, justify or, perhaps, even extenuate the act of the party threatened in killing the person who uttered the threats, yet it by no means follows that such threats, signifying ill will and hostility on the part of the deceased, can be used by the jury as indicating a similar state of feeling on the part of the defendant. Such an instruction was not only misleading in itself, but it was erroneous in the present case, for the further reason that it omitted all reference to the conduct of the deceased at the time of the killing, which went to show an intention then and there to carry out the previous threats."

Other exceptions to parts of the charge were taken, but, while not to be understood as holding that there was no error in respect thereof, we do not feel called upon to prolong this opinion by their consideration, and they may not arise upon another trial.

Where the charge of the trial judge takes the form of animated argument, the liability is great

Where the charge of the trial judge takes the form of animated argument, the liability is great that the propositions of law may become interrupted by digression, and so intermingled with inferences springing from forensic ardor, that the jury are left without proper instructions; their appropriate province of dealing with the facts invaded; and errors intervene which the pursuit of a different course would have avoided.

Judgment reversed and cause remanded, with a direction to set aside the verdict and grant a new trial.

BROWN v. WALKER

(CASE EXCERPT)

161 U.S. 591; 16 S. Ct. 644; 40 L. Ed. 819

Argued January 23, 1896

March 23, 1896, Decided

GIST: This case involves the 5th Amendment privilege against self incrimination as it applies to a grand jury witness. Brown declined to answer grand jury questions on self incrimination grounds, was held in contempt, and appealed. The Court rejected Brown's claim that he could not be compelled to testify. The majority opinion of Justice Brown referred to the first eight amendments of the Bill of Rights as incorporating "certain principles of natural justice." Justice Field's dissenting opinion refers to the right to bear arms as one of the essential and inseparable features of English liberty.

MR. JUSTICE BROWN delivered the opinion of the court.

.....

As the object of the first eight amendments to the Constitution was to incorporate into the fundamental law of the land certain principles of natural justice which had become permanently fixed in the jurisprudence of the mother country, the construction given to those principles by the English courts is cogent evidence of what they were designed to secure and of the limitations that should be put upon them. This is but another application of the familiar rule that where one State adopts the laws of another, it is also presumed to adopt the known and settled construction of those laws by the courts of the State from which they are taken.

.....

It is argued in this connection that, while the witness is granted immunity from prosecution by the Federal government, he does not obtain such immunity against prosecution in the state courts. We are unable to appreciate the force of this suggestion. It is true that the Constitution does not operate upon a witness testifying in the state courts, since we have held that the first eight amendments are limitations only upon the powers of Congress and the Federal courts, and are not applicable to the several States, except so far as the Fourteenth Amendment may have made them applicable.

.....

MR. JUSTICE FIELD dissenting.

.....

constitutional provisions for the security of person and property should be liberally construed. A close and literal construction deprives them of half their efficacy, and leads to gradual depreciation of the right

"Illegitimate and unconstitutional practices get their first footing in that way, namely, by silent approaches and slight deviations from legal modes of procedure. This can only be obviated by adhering to the rule that constitutional provisions for the security of person and property should be liberally construed. A close and literal construction deprives them of half their efficacy, and leads to gradual depreciation of the right, as if it, consisted more in sound than substance. It is the duty of courts to be watchful for the constitutional rights of the citizens and against any stealthy encroachments thereon. Their motto should be obsta principiis."

freedom of thought, of speech and of the press; the right to bear arms; exemption from military dictation; security of the person and of the home; the right to speedy and public trial by jury; protection against oppressive bail and cruel punishment, are, together with exemption from self-crimination, the essential and inseparable features of English liberty.

And the same great and learned justice adds: "The freedom of thought, of speech and of the press; the right to bear arms; exemption from military dictation; security of the person and of the home; the right to speedy and public trial by jury; protection against oppressive bail and cruel punishment, are, together with exemption from self-crimination, the essential and inseparable features of English liberty. Each one of these features had been involved in the struggle above referred to in England within the century and a half immediately preceding the adoption of the Constitution, and the contests were fresh in the memories and traditions of the people at that time." Boyd v. The United States. 116 U.S. 626

WALLACE v. UNITED STATES

(FULL CASE)

162 U.S. 466; 16 S. Ct. 859; 40 L. Ed. 1039

Submitted March 2, 1896.

April 20, 1896, Decided

GIST: Jerry Wallace lived with his wife Jane on a piece of land she owned in Kansas. Her father Alexander Zane disputed the boundary of her land with his own, and he eventually picked a lethal fight over it. Wallace, described as a quiet, peaceful man with poor eyesight, managed to take down Zane, a known troublemaker, with a single blast. He was charged with and subsequently convicted of murder.

This is a self-defense case—the only one in this time period that is not from Judge Parker in Arkansas. The Court unanimously held that if the defendant started the dispute with the intent of killing the victim, then the killing was murder. If the defendant had no such intent, and the killing was necessary to avoid serious and imminent danger to himself, the fact that the defendant started the dispute did not preclude him from employing deadly force—a double-barreled shotgun in this case—in self defense. The facts involved are a drama of family land ownership, boundary disputes, death threats, getting drunk to build a fence with your buddies on disputed land, a mild mannered defendant, a butcher-knife wielding bully, and a confrontation that soured quickly.

ERROR TO THE DISTRICT COURT OF THE UNITED STATES FOR THE DISTRICT OF KANSAS.

W. lived on a tract of land next to one owned and occupied by his father in law Z., concerning the boundary between which there was a dispute between them. While W. was ploughing his land, Z., being then under the influence of liquor, entered upon the disputed tract and brought a quantity of posts there, for the purpose of erecting a fence on the line which he claimed. W. ordered him off, and continued his ploughing. He did not leave, and W. after reaching his boundary with the plough, unhitched his horses and put them in the barn. In about half an hour he returned with a gun, and an altercation ensued, in the course of which W. was stabbed by a son of Z. and Z. was killed by a shot from W.'s gun. W. was indicted for murder. On the trial evidence was offered in defence, and excluded, of threats of Z. to kill W.; and W. himself was put upon the stand and, after stating that he did not feel safe without some protection against Z., and that Z. had made a hostile demonstration against him, was asked, from that demonstration what he believed Z. was about to do? This question was ruled out. Held, that if W. believed and had reasonable ground for the belief that he was in imminent danger of death or great bodily harm from Z. at the moment he fired, and would not have fired but for such belief, and if that belief, founded on reasonable ground, might in any view the jury could properly take of the circumstances surrounding the killing, have excused his act or reduced the crime from murder to manslaughter, then the evidence in respect of Z.'s threats was relevant and it was error to exclude it; and it was also error to refuse to allow the question to be put to W. as to his belief based on the demonstration on Z.'s part to which he testified.

Where a difficulty is intentionally brought on for the purpose of killing the deceased, the fact of imminent danger to the accused constitutes no defence; but where the accused embarks in a quarrel with no felonious intent, or malice, or premeditated purpose of doing bodily harm or killing, and under reasonable belief of imminent danger he inflicts a fatal wound, it is not murder.

JERRY Wallace was convicted, at the May term, 1895, of the District Court of the United States for the District of Kansas, of the murder of Alexander Zane, on March 7, 1895, at the Wyandotte Indian reservation, and sentenced to be hanged.

he returned with a double barreled shotgun in his hands

The evidence tended to show that Wallace had lived on that reservation, for four years, on a piece of land owned by his wife, Jane, a daughter of Alexander Zane, to whom he was married in 1891. Ill feeling had for a long time existed between Zane and Wallace, growing out of a dispute between them as to the true boundary line of the land owned or claimed by Jane Wallace, and on which she resided, and the land of Julia, a minor daughter of Alexander Zane. Surveys had been made and patents had issued, but the true boundary line, if established by the surveys, had not been accepted by the parties. March 7, 1895, about seven o'clock in the morning, Alexander Zane, accompanied by his son, Noah, who was about fifteen years of age, and three other parties, proceeded with two wagons loaded with posts from his farm to the land on which Wallace resided, and entered the field occupied by Wallace, which he was at that moment engaged in ploughing, through a gap in the fence made by Alexander Zane, and went across it to the fence on the eastern side, and there began to unload the posts and to plant or drive them into the ground along the fence line which they proposed to establish. Wallace and one Denmark were engaged in ploughing the field, being in different parts and moving in opposite directions. As Zane and his party entered the field and were crossing it, Wallace was ploughing towards its eastern side, which he had reached, and was returning when Zane and his party passed about fifty or sixty yards from him, moving in a southeasterly course. Wallace had impaired eyesight and did not see Zane until just before he passed, and then called to him saying, "Alexander Zane, if that is you, take your force and get out of this field," or, as it was put by one or more of the witnesses, "Alexander Zane, I want you to take your mob and get off these premises." There was evidence tending to show that Zane and those who were with him had been drinking, and that they were boisterous, singing and hallooing. Defendant testified: "They were noisy, hollering and singing, and acting as if they were drunk to me, and I guess no doubt was." Zane appears to have made no reply to Wallace, but went on his way. Wallace continued on with his plough until he and reached a ravine that ran north and south through the field, where he halted, unhitched his horses from the plough and took them up to the barn. In about half an hour he returned with a double barreled shotgun in his hands, passed within a few feet of a group of persons consisting of Denmark, his daughter, one Lewis, and Wallace's wife, and in passing said to his wife, "Now Janie, I want you to order these gentlemen out of here." Mrs. Wallace then ordered Alexander Zane and those who were with him to leave, but they paid no attention to her. Thereupon Wallace ordered Zane to leave and said to him, "Are you going?" Zane was standing with his right hand on a post he had driven in the ground and his left arm hanging by his side.

about the time I was struck in the back he made this motion (indicating), and says, 'Damn you, I will kill you;' and then my wife hollers or least she says, 'Look out, Jerry!' and I fired this gun.

Wallace testified: "I asked of him whether he was going or not, and about this time I was struck in the back, and Mr. Zane made a grab like this (indicating), and he was standing with his right hand on the post; about the time I was struck in the back he made this motion (indicating), and says, 'Damn you, I will kill you;' and then my wife hollers or least she says, 'Look out, Jerry!' and I fired this gun."

Lafayette Lewis, another witness, testified: "His wife ordered them out, and Jerry also, and he asked Zane if he was going to go, but I never heard Zane say a word, and then he told him the second time, and he looked up towards him, with his left hand on the post, and threw his hand up this way (indicating) and said, 'Damn you, I am going to kill you!' . . . When Jerry ordered him the second time, he turned and kind of looked at him and threw his hand up this way to his bosom and said, 'Damn you, I will kill you!' and at that moment the boy struck Jerry with the knife and Jerry shot him."

Several other witnesses did not see or hear any word or gesture proceed from Zane, but testified that when Wallace said to Zane, "Are you going?" he immediately raised his gun, aimed it at Zane and fired, shooting Zane in the left breast; that Zane walked off about thirty feet and fell, and when those nearest him reached him he was dead

when Wallace fired his gun at Zane, Noah Zane ran up and stabbed him in the shoulder with a pocket knife, whereupon Wallace turned and pointed his gun at Noah and the gun snapped.

When Zane fell, Noah went to him and took from his person a tomahawk or small hatchet, which was the only thing in the way of a weapon found on him.

Several other witnesses did not see or hear any word or gesture proceed from Zane, but testified that when Wallace said to Zane, "Are you going?" he immediately raised his gun, aimed it at Zane and fired, shooting Zane in the left breast; that Zane walked off about thirty feet and fell, and when those nearest him reached him he was dead; that when Wallace fired his gun at Zane, Noah Zane ran up and stabbed him in the shoulder with a pocket knife, whereupon Wallace turned and pointed his gun at Noah and the gun snapped. When Zane fell, Noah went to him and took from his person a tomahawk or small hatchet, which was the only thing in the way of a weapon found on him.

There was evidence to the effect that the wound thus inflicted on Wallace penetrated about half an inch, bled considerably, was much swollen, and that his stomach was black and blue as though he had been hit with something, as he testified that he was.

Evidence was also adduced that Zane was in the habit of carrying a butcher knife with him in his belt; that he was quarrelsome; and that Wallace had the reputation of being a peaceable and quiet man.

Evidence was also adduced that Zane was in the habit of carrying a butcher knife with him in his belt; that he was quarrelsome; and that Wallace had the reputation of being a peaceable and quiet man. In reference to the survey under which Zane claimed, testimony was given tending to show, as was contended, that Zane caused the disputed line to be so run by the chainmen as to gain four feet, and that Zane said "when he got through with the land he wouldn't leave Jerry Wallace a garden spot; that he could haul it away in a wagon box."

Zane stated that he had got some whiskey "for the purpose of bracing himself up for the purpose of building this fence across the land of this defendant, Jerry Wallace."

Defendant offered to prove by R. C. Patterson that the day before the shooting occurred he had a conversation with Zane, "in which Zane said to him that he was going down there to build a fence across this property of Wallace's the next day, and if Jerry Wallace fooled with him he would kill the blind son of a bitch." This was objected to, the objection sustained and defendant excepted. Also, that in the same conversation Zane stated that he had got some whiskey "for the purpose of bracing himself up for the purpose of building this fence across the land of this defendant, Jerry Wallace." Plaintiff objected, the court sustained the objection and defendant excepted.

"Alex. Zane said to this witness that he was going down to build a fence across Wallace's land, and that if Jerry Wallace interfered with him he would kill him, or shoot the blind son of a bitch," and that all these threats were communicated to Wallace.

Defendant further offered to prove by Charles Luke that he had a conversation with Zane the day before the killing, and "Alex. Zane said to this witness that he was going down to build a fence across Wallace's land, and that if Jerry Wallace interfered with him he would kill him, or shoot the blind son of a bitch," and that all these threats were communicated to Wallace. Plaintiff objected, the objection was sustained and defendant excepted.

Alex. Zane said to this woman and threatened that he would kill Jerry Wallace, and that he had a knife that he was carrying at that time for that purpose, and that these threats were communicated to Jerry Wallace by this witness afterwards.

in that conversation he threatened to kill Jerry Wallace, and that he said to this witness that he at one time made him look down the muzzle of a double barreled shotgun and he wished he had killed him at that time, and that these threats were communicated to the defendant.

Defendant offered to prove by Mrs. Alice Sargent that somewhere near the middle of February, 1895, she had a conversation with Zane, on which occasion "Alex. Zane said to this woman and threatened that he would kill Jerry Wallace, and that he had a knife that he was carrying at that time for that purpose, and that these threats were communicated to Jerry Wallace by this witness afterwards." This was objected to, the objection sustained and defendant excepted. A similar offer of proof by one Taylor was made and a similar exception taken. Defendant also offered to prove by Samuel Collins "that at a time shortly before the 7th of March last he met Alexander Zane and had a conversation with Alexander Zane about Jerry Wallace, and that in that conversation he threatened to kill Jerry Wallace, and that he said to this witness that he at one time made him look down the muzzle of a double barreled shotgun and he wished he had killed him at that time, and that these threats were communicated to the defendant." An offer to prove similar threats prior to the homicide by Mary Crow was made, excluded and exception taken.

When the defendant was on the stand he testified that he took the gun into the field because he was afraid of the party, and especially of Alexander Zane, and did not feel safe without some protection.

When the defendant was on the stand he testified that he took the gun into the field because he was afraid of the party, and especially of Alexander Zane, and did not feel safe without some protection. The following questions were put and ruling made: "Q. You may state, Mr. Wallace, what Zane did at that time, just before you fired the shot. A. He just took his hand something like this (indicating) saying, 'Damn you, I will kill you.' Q. You may state to the jury from that demonstration what you believed Zane was about to do." To this question plaintiff objected, the objection was sustained and defendant excepted.

Various errors were assigned in respect of the jurisdiction of the court; the sufficiency of the indictment; the want of due service of the list of jurors; and instructions given and refused.

MR. CHIEF JUSTICE FULLER, after stating the case, delivered the opinion of the court.

If Jerry Wallace believed and had reasonable ground for the belief that he was in imminent danger of death or great bodily harm from Zane at the moment he fired, and would not have fired but for such belief, and if that belief, founded on reasonable ground, might in any view the jury could properly take of the circumstances surrounding the killing, have excused his act or reduced the crime from murder to manslaughter, then the evidence in respect of Zane's threats was relevant and it was error to exclude it

If Jerry Wallace believed and had reasonable ground for the belief that he was in imminent danger of death or great bodily harm from Zane at the moment he fired, and would not have fired but for such belief, and if that belief, founded on reasonable ground, might in any view the jury could properly take of the circumstances surrounding the killing, have excused his act or reduced the crime from murder to manslaughter, then the evidence in respect of Zane's threats was relevant and it was error to exclude it; and it was also error to refuse to allow the question to be put to Wallace as to his belief based on the demonstration on Zane's part to which he testified.

Where a difficulty is intentionally brought on for the purpose of killing the deceased, the fact of imminent danger to the accused constitutes no defence; but where the accused embarks in a quarrel with no felonious intent, or malice, or premeditated purpose of doing bodily harm or killing, and under reasonable belief of imminent danger he inflicts a fatal wound, it is not murder.

Where a difficulty is intentionally brought on for the purpose of killing the deceased, the fact of imminent danger to the accused constitutes no defence; but where the accused embarks in a quarrel with no felonious intent, or malice, or premeditated purpose of doing bodily harm or killing, and under reasonable belief of imminent danger he inflicts a fatal wound, it is not murder. Whart. Hom. §197; 2 Bish. Cr. L. §§702, 715; 4 Am. and Eng. Ency. Law, 675; State v. Partlow, 90 Missouri 608; Adams v. People, 47 Illinois, 376; State v. Hays, 23 Missouri, 287; State v. McDonnell, 32 Vermont, 491; Reed v. State, 11 Tex. App. 509.

In Adams v. People, it was ruled by the Supreme Court of Illinois, speaking through Mr. Chief Justice Breese, that where the accused sought a difficulty with the deceased for the purpose of killing him, and in the fight did kill him, in pursuance of his malicious intention, he would be guilty of murder, but if the jury found that the accused voluntarily got into the difficulty of fight with the deceased, not intending to kill at the time, but not declining further fighting before the mortal blow was struck by him, and finally drew his knife and with it killed the deceased, the accused would be guilty of manslaughter, although the cutting and killing were done in order to prevent an assault upon him by the deceased or to prevent the deceased from getting the advantage in the fight.

A perfect right of self defence can only obtain and avail where the party pleading it acted from necessity, and was wholly free from wrong or blame in occasioning or producing the necessity which required his action.

In Reed v. State, the Court of Appeals of Texas, in treating of the subject of self defence, said: "It may be divided into two general classes, to wit, perfect and imperfect right of self defence. A perfect right of self defence can only obtain and avail where the party pleading it acted from necessity, and was wholly free from wrong or blame in occasioning or producing the necessity which required his action. If, however, he was in the wrong -- if he was himself violating or in the act of violating the law -- and on account of his own wrong was placed in a situation wherein it became necessary for him to defend himself against an attack made upon himself, which was superinduced or created by his own wrong, then the law justly limits his right of self defence, and regulates it according to the magnitude of his own wrong. Such a state of case may be said to illustrate and determine what in law would be denominated the imperfect right of self defence. Whenever a party by his own wrongful act produces a condition of things wherein it becomes necessary for his own safety that he should take life or do serious bodily harm, then indeed the law wisely imputes to him his own wrong and its consequences, to the extent that they may and should be considered in determining the grade of offence, which but for such acts would never have been occasioned. . . .How far and to what extent he will be excused or excusable in law must depend upon the nature and character of the act he was committing, and which produced the necessity that he should defend himself. When his own original act was in violation of law, then the law takes that fact into consideration in limiting his right of defence and resistance whilst in the perpetration of such unlawful act. If he was engaged in the commission of a felony, and, to prevent its commission, the party seeing it or about to be injured thereby makes a violent assault upon him, calculated to produce death or serious bodily harm, and in resisting such attack he slays his assailant, the law would impute the original wrong to the homicide and make it murder. But if the original wrong was or would have been a misdemeanor, then the homicide growing out of or occasioned by it, though in self defence from any assault made upon him, would be manslaughter under the law."

After quoting from these and other cases, Sherwood, J., delivering the opinion of the Supreme Court of Missouri in State v. Partlow, remarked: "Indeed, the assertion of the doctrine that one who begins a quarrel or brings on a difficulty with the felonious purpose to kill the person assaulted, and accomplishing such purpose, is guilty of murder, and cannot avail himself of the doctrine of self defence, carries with it, in its very bosom, the inevitable corollary, that if the quarrel be begun without a felonious purpose, then the homicidal act will not be murder. To deny this obvious deduction is equivalent to the anomalous assertion that there can be a felony without a felonious intent; that the act done characterizes the intent, and not the intent the act."

But a person cannot repel a mere trespass on his land by the taking of life, or proceed beyond what necessity requires.

In this case it is evident that Wallace was bent as far as practicable on defending his possession against what he regarded and the evidence on his behalf tended to show was an unwarrantable invasion. But a person cannot repel a mere trespass on his land by the taking of life, or proceed beyond what necessity requires. When he uses in the defence of such property a weapon which is not deadly, and death accidentally ensues, the killing will not exceed manslaughter, but when a deadly weapon is employed it may be murder or manslaughter, according to the circumstances. 1 Hale P.C. 473; 1 Hawk. P.C. c. 31, §§34, et seq.; Foster, 291; Davison v. People, 90 Illinois, 221; People v. Payne, 8 California, 341; Carroll v. State, 23 Alabama, 28; 1 Whart. C.L. §462, and cases cited.

Whether the killing with a deadly weapon may be reduced in any case to manslaughter when it is the result of passion excited by a trespass with force to property, we need not consider, as the question, perhaps in view of the interval of time during which Wallace was seeking his gun, does not seem to have been raised. Conceding, though without intimating any opinion on the facts disclosed, that Jerry Wallace committed a crime, still the inquiry arose as to the grade of the offence, and, in respect of that, the threats offered to be proven had an important, and it might be decisive bearing, nor was the mere fact that Wallace procured the gun as stated in itself sufficient ground for their exclusion.

if, under the circumstances on the occasion of the killing, the crime were that of manslaughter, it was not converted into murder by reason of the accused having previously armed himself.

In Gourko v. United States, 153 U.S. 183, this court held that it was error to instruct a jury that preparation by arming, although for self defence only, could not be followed, in any case, by manslaughter, if the killing after such arming was not, in fact, necessarily in self defence; and that if, under the circumstances on the occasion of the killing, the crime were that of manslaughter, it was not converted into murder by reason of the accused having previously armed himself.

if the accused did not provoke the assault and had at the time reasonable grounds to believe, and in good faith believed, that the deceased intended to take his life or to do him great bodily harm, he was not obliged to retreat, nor to consider whether he could safely retreat, but was entitled to stand his ground and meet any attack made upon him with a deadly weapon, in such way and with such force as, under all the circumstances, he, at the moment, honestly believed, and had reasonable grounds to believe, was necessary to save his own life or to protect himself from great bodily injury.

In Beard v. United States, 158 U.S. 550, 563, it was said: "In our opinion, the court below erred in holding that the accused, while on his premises, outside of his dwelling-house, was under a legal duty to get out of the way, if he could, of his assailant, who, according to one view of the evidence, had threatened to kill the defendant, in execution of that purpose had armed himself with a deadly weapon, with, that weapon concealed upon his person went to the defendant's premises, despite the warning of the latter to keep away, and by word and act indicated his purpose to attack the accused. The defendant was where he had a right to be, when the deceased advanced upon him in a threatening manner, and with a deadly weapon; and if the accused did not provoke the assault and had at the time reasonable grounds to believe, and in good faith believed, that the deceased intended to take his life or to do him great bodily harm, he was not obliged to retreat, nor to consider whether he could safely retreat, but was entitled to stand his ground and meet any attack made upon him with a deadly weapon, in such way and with such force as, under all the circumstances, he, at the moment, honestly believed, and had reasonable grounds to believe, was necessary to save his own life or to protect himself from great bodily injury."

in respect of the possession of a deadly weapon by the accused, it was error to ignore evidence indicating that such possession was for an innocent purpose.

In Allison v. United States, 160 U.S. 203, it was held that in charging the jury on a capital trial in respect of the possession of a deadly weapon by the accused, it was error to ignore evidence indicating that such possession was for an innocent purpose. The subject of threats was there somewhat considered and authorities cited.

Necessarily it must frequently happen that particular circumstances qualify the character of the offence, and it is thoroughly settled that it is for the jury to determine what effect shall be given to circumstances having that tendency whenever made to appear in the evidence.

In Stevenson v. United States, 162 U.S. 313, we said:

"The evidence as to manslaughter need not be uncontradicted or in any way conclusive upon the question; so long as there is some evidence upon the subject, the proper weight to be given it is for the jury to determine. If there were any evidence which tended to show such a state of facts as might bring the crime within the grade of manslaughter, it then became a proper question for the jury to say whether the evidence were true and whether it showed that the crime was manslaughter instead of murder. . . . The evidence might appear to the court to be simply overwhelming to show that the killing was in fact murder and not manslaughter, or an act performed in self defence, and yet, so long as there was some evidence relevant to the issue of manslaughter, the credibility and force of such evidence must be for the jury, and cannot be matter of law for the decision of the court.

Malice in connection with the crime of killing is but another name for a certain condition of a man's heart or mind, and as no one can look into the heart or mind of another, the only way to decide upon its condition at the time of a killing is to infer it from the surrounding facts, and that inference is one of fact for a jury. The presence or absence of this malice or mental condition marks the boundary which separates the two crimes of murder and manslaughter.

"By section 1035 of the Revised Statutes of the United States it is enacted that 'in all criminal causes the defendant may be found guilty of any offence, the commission of which is necessarily included in that with which he is charged in the indictment, or may be found guilty of an attempt to commit the offence so charged: Provided, That each attempt be itself a separate offence.' Under this statute a defendant charged in the indictment with the crime of murder may be found guilty of a lower grade of crime, viz., manslaughter. There must, of course, be some evidence which tends to bear upon that issue. The jury would not be justified in finding a verdict of manslaughter if there were no evidence upon which to base such a finding, and in that event the court would have the right to instruct the jury to that effect. Spart v. United States, 156 U.S. 51. . . . Manslaughter at common law was defined to be the unlawful and felonious killing of another without any malice, either express or implied. Whart. Am. Cr. L. (8th ed.) sec. 304. Whether there be what is termed express malice or only implied malice, the proof to show either is of the same nature, viz., the circumstances leading up to and surrounding the killing. The definition of the crime given by section 5341 of the Revised Statutes of the United States is substantially the same. The proof of homicide, as necessarily involving malice, must show the facts under which the killing was effected, and from the whole facts and circumstances surrounding the killing the jury infers malice or its absence. Malice in connection with the crime of killing is but another name for a certain condition of a man's heart or mind, and as no one can look into the heart or mind of another, the only way to decide upon its condition at the time of a killing is to infer it from the surrounding facts, and that inference is one of fact for a jury. The presence or absence of this malice or mental condition marks the boundary which separates the two crimes of murder and manslaughter."

it was for the jury to say whether Wallace's statement that he procured the gun only for self protection was or was not true. And if they believed from the evidence that this was true, and that the killing was under reasonable apprehension of imminent peril, then it was for the jury to determine under all the facts and circumstances whether Wallace had committed the offence of manslaughter, rather than that of murder, if he could not be excused altogether.

Treating the excluded evidence as admitted, and assuming that Wallace would have testified that he believed from Zane's demonstration that Zane intended to kill him, the evidence on defendant's behalf tended to establish bad feeling between Zane and Wallace in reference to the line between Mrs. Wallace's land and that of Julia Zane; an attempt on Zane's part of include a part of Mrs. Wallace's land in the Zane parcel; declarations by Zane the day before the homicide that he was going the next day to run a fence across what Wallace claimed to be his land, and threats, that, if Wallace interfered with him in so doing, Zane would kill him, all communicated to Wallace before the homicide; previous threats also communicated that he would kill Wallace; forcible entrance by Zane, accompanied by several others, into the field claimed by Wallace, in which he was ploughing, and fencing off part of it commenced; boisterous and disorderly manifestations on their part and refusals by Zane to leave when ordered to go; such demonstrations by Zane at the moment as induced Wallace to believe that he was in imminent danger, and action based on that belief. Granting that the jury would have been justified in finding that Wallace's intention in going for the gun and returning with it as he did was to inflict bodily harm on Zane if he did not leave, still the presumption was not an irrebuttable one, and it was for the jury to say whether Wallace's statement that he procured the gun only for self protection was or was not true. And if they believed from the evidence that this was true, and that the killing was under reasonable apprehension of imminent peril, then it was for the jury to determine under all the facts and circumstances whether Wallace had committed the offence of manslaughter, rather than that of murder, if he could not be excused altogether.

We think that the threats were admissible in evidence, and, this being so, that the question as to Wallace's belief should not have been excluded. It has been often decided that where the intent is a material question, the accused may testify in his own behalf as to what his intent was in doing the act. People v. Baker, 96 N.Y. 340; State v. Banks, 73 Missouri, 592; Thurston v. Cornell, 38 N.Y. 281; Over v. Schiffling, 102 Indiana, 191; People v. Quick, 51 Michigan, 547; Fenwick v. Maryland, 63 Maryland, 239. In the latter case it was held that a person on trial for an assault with intent to commit murder is competent to testify as to the purpose for which he procured the instrument with which he committed the assault.

This rule is not controverted, but it is contended that Wallace's belief was immaterial. For the reasons given we cannot concur in that view and are of opinion that the witness should have been allowed to answer.

It is unnecessary to pass upon any of the other points raised on behalf of plaintiff in error.

Judgment reversed and cause remanded with a direction to set aside the verdict and grant a new trial.

ALBERTY v. UNITED STATES

(FULL CASE)

162 U.S. 499; 16 S. Ct. 864; 40 L. Ed. 1051

Submitted March 4, 1896.

April 20, 1896, Decided

GIST: Here you have two young men interested in the same woman. The defendant, Alberty, is her husband. Duncan, the deceased, paid enough attention to her to get her to move to a room of her own at Lipe's, where she worked. One night, from the yard where Alberty worked (also at Lipe's), he saw a man trying to climb into his wife's bedroom window. He approached in the pitch dark, apparently unaware of who the person was, and in an ensuing confrontation, shot Duncan to death while trying to avoid Duncan's apparently drawn knife. Mind reeling, Alberty left the body and ran away.

The case opens with a remarkable discussion of race, in a lengthy effort to determine proper jurisdiction over the parties. If they were both Indians in Indian country, the federal court would have no jurisdiction. The Court concluded that Alberty, a black man born in slavery, was a "member of the Cherokee Nation, but not an Indian," and Duncan, the illegitimate child of a male Choctaw and a black slave, was a "colored citizen of the United States." In the midst of this racially charged decade, the Supreme Court was hearing and defending the rights of the most repressed classes.

Alberty appealed his murder conviction and death sentence, claiming errors were made in the charge to the jury, and in the inference to be drawn from his flight after shooting Duncan to death. The Court discussed in some detail the right of self defense and the duty to retreat. The Court held that, contrary to District Judge Parker's detailed description to the jury, there was no duty to retreat in a case such as this, and that you may stand your ground against such an assault. The Court touched indirectly on the point of matching force with force.

Disagreeing with Judge Parker's jury instruction that Alberty provoked the fight by going over to investigate, the High Court held that it was "perfectly natural" to investigate in such a circumstance, and that responding to any aggression offered was permissible.

Years had passed before Alberty was caught, in St. Louis, turned in by a former prisoner who recognized him. While the lower court insisted that running away after the fact was a pretty sure sign of guilt, the High Court rejected that idea rather eloquently by listing all sorts of reasons why an innocent person might flee after an incident, including among others, the humiliation, annoyance and expense of defense. Granted a new trial, Alberty was acquitted and moved back to St. Louis.

Alberty, the accused, was a negro born in slavery, who became a citizen of the Cherokee Nation under the ninth article of the treaty of 1866 . Duncan, the deceased, and alleged to have been murdered, was the illegitimate child of a Choctaw Indian, by a negro woman who was not his wife, but a slave in the Cherokee Nation. Held, that, for purposes of jurisdiction, Alberty must be treated as a member of the Cherokee Nation, but not an Indian, and Duncan as a colored citizen of the United States, and that, for the purposes of this case, the court below had jurisdiction.

A man who finds another, trying to obtain access to his wife's room in the night time, by opening a window, may not only remonstrate with him, but may employ such force as may be necessary to prevent his doing so; and if the other threatens to kill him, and makes a motion as if so to do, and puts him in fear of his life, or of great bodily harm, he is not bound to retreat, but may use such force as is necessary to repel the assault.

The weight which a jury is entitled to give to the flight of a prisoner, immediately after the commission of a homicide, was carefully considered in Hickory v. United States, 160 U.S. 408; and, without repeating what was there said, it was especially misleading for the court in this case to charge the jury that, from the fact of absconding they might infer the fact of guilt, and that flight is a silent admission by the defendant that he is unable to face the case against him.

ERROR TO THE CIRCUIT COURT OF THE UNITED STATES FOR THE WESTERN DISTRICT OF ARKANSAS.

DEFENDANT, a Cherokee negro, who was known both by his father's name of Burns and that of his former master, Alberty, was convicted of the murder of one Phil Duncan, at the Cherokee Nation, in the Indian Territory. The indictment alleged the crime to have been committed May 15, 1879, but it appeared by the evidence to have been committed in 1880.

Upon judgment of death being pronounced, defendant sued out a writ of error from this court, assigning a want of jurisdiction in the court below and various errors in the charge to the jury connected with the law of homicide, and the inference to be drawn from the flight of the accused.

MR. JUSTICE BROWN delivered the opinion of the court.

Although the prisoner Alberty was not a native Indian, but a negro born in slavery, it was not disputed that he became a citizen of the Cherokee Nation

1. The question of jurisdiction in this case demands a primary consideration. Although the prisoner Alberty was not a native Indian, but a negro born in slavery, it was not disputed that he became a citizen of the Cherokee Nation under the ninth article of the treaty of 1866, 14 Stat. 799, 801, by which the Cherokee Nation agreed to abolish slavery, and further agreed "that all freedmen who have been liberated by voluntary act of their former owners or by law, as well as all free colored persons who were in the country at the commencement of the rebellion and are now residents therein or who may return within six months, and their descendants, shall have all the rights of native Cherokees." While this article of the treaty gave him the rights of a native Cherokee, it did not, standing alone, make him an Indian within the meaning of Rev. Stat. §2146, or absolve him from responsibility to the criminal laws of the United States, as was held in United States v. Rogers, 4 How. 567, 573, and Westmoreland v. United States, 155 U.S. 545.

Duncan, the deceased, was the illegitimate child of a Choctaw Indian, by a colored woman, who was not his wife, but a slave in the Cherokee Nation.

Duncan, the deceased, was the illegitimate child of a Choctaw Indian, by a colored woman, who was not his wife, but a slave in the Cherokee Nation. As his mother was a negro slave, under the rule partus sequitur ventrem, he must be treated as a negro by birth, and not as a Choctaw Indian. There is an additional reason for this in the fact that he was an illegitimate child, and took the status of his mother. Williamson v. Daniel, 12 Wheat. 568; Fowler v. Merrill, 11 How. 375.

He came, however, to the Cherokee Nation when he was about seventeen years of age, and married a freed woman, and a citizen of that Nation. It would seem, however, from such information as we have been able to obtain of the Cherokee laws, that such marriage would not confer upon him the rights and privileges of Cherokee citizenship, beyond that of residing and holding personal property in the Nation; that the courts of the Nation do not claim jurisdiction over such persons, either in criminal or civil suits, and they are not permitted to vote at any elections.

For the purposes of jurisdiction, then, Alberty must be treated as a member of the Cherokee Nation, but not an Indian; and Duncan as a colored citizen of the United States.

For the purposes of jurisdiction, then, Alberty must be treated as a member of the Cherokee Nation, but not an Indian; and Duncan as a colored citizen of the United States.

By Revised Statutes, §2145, except as to certain crimes, "the general laws of the United States as to the punishment of crimes committed within the sole and exclusive jurisdiction of the United States, except the District of Columbia, shall extend to the Indian country;" and by §2146, "the preceding section shall not be construed to extend to crimes committed by one Indian against the person or property of another Indian, nor to any Indian committing any offence in the Indian country who has been punished by the local law of the tribe; or to any case where, by treaty stipulations, the exclusive jurisdiction over such offences is or may be secured to the Indian tribes respectively." Obviously this case is not within the first class, because the crime was not committed by one Indian against the person of another Indian; nor within the second class, because there was no evidence that Alberty had been punished by the local law of the tribe; and the only remaining question is whether, by treaty stipulations, the exclusive jurisdiction over this offence has been secured to the Cherokee tribe.

By article 13 of the Cherokee treaty of July 19, 1866, 14 Stat. 799-803, the establishment of a court of the United States in the Cherokee territory is provided for, "with such jurisdiction and organized in such manner as may be prescribed by law: Provided, That the judicial tribunals of the Nation shall be allowed to retain exclusive jurisdiction in all civil and criminal cases arising within their country in which members of the Nation, by nativity or adoption, shall be the only parties, or where the cause of action shall arise in the Cherokee Nation, except as otherwise provided in this treaty." It is admitted that the present case is not within the last exception.

By the act of May 2, 1890, c. 182, to provide a temporary government for the Territory of Oklahoma and to enlarge the jurisdiction of the United States court in the Indian Territory, 26 Stat. 81, it is provided, §30, "that the judicial tribunals of the Indian Nations shall retain exclusive jurisdiction in all civil and criminal cases arising in the country in which members of the Nation, by nativity or by adoption, shall be the only parties;" and by §31, that "nothing in this act shall be so construed as to deprive any of the courts of the civilized Nations of exclusive jurisdiction over all cases arising wherein members of said Nations, whether by treaty, blood or adoption, are the sole parties; nor so as to interfere with the right and power of said civilized Nations to punish said parties for violation of the statutes and laws enacted by their national councils, where such laws are not contrary to the treaties and laws of the United States."

It will be observed that while this act follows the treaty so far as recognizing the jurisdiction of the Cherokee Nation as to all cases arising in the country, in which members of the Nation, by nativity or by adoption, are the sole or only parties, it omits that portion of the thirteenth article of the treaty, wherein is reserved to the judicial tribunals of the Nation exclusive jurisdiction "where the cause of action shall arise in the Cherokee Nation," and to that extent apparently supersedes the treaty.

The real question as respects the jurisdiction in this case is as to the meaning of the words "sole" or only "parties." These words are obviously susceptible of two interpretations. They may mean a class of actions as to which there is but one party; but as these actions, if they exist at all, are very rare, it can hardly be supposed that Congress intended to legislate with respect to them to the exclusion of the much more numerous actions to which there are two parties. They may mean actions to which members of the Nations are the sole or only parties, to the exclusion of white men, or persons other than members of the Nation; and as respects civil cases at least, this seems the more probable construction.

But the difficulty is with regard to criminal cases, to which the defendant may be said to be the only party; and, if not, as to who is the other party, the sovereignty in whose name the prosecution is conducted -- in this case, the United States, or the prosecuting witness, or, in a homicide case, the person who was killed. Some light is thrown upon this by the seventh article of the same treaty, wherein a special provision is made for the jurisdiction of the United States court to be created in the Indian Territory; and until such court was created therein, the United States District Court, nearest to the Cherokee Nation, was given exclusive original jurisdiction of all cases, civil and criminal, wherein an inhabitant of the district hereinbefore described" (meaning the Canadian district of the Cherokee Nation) "shall be a party, and where an inhabitant outside of said district, in the Cherokee Nation, shall be the other party, as plaintiff or defendant in a civil cause, or shall be defendant or prosecutor in a criminal case." It is true that the homicide in this case was not committed within the Canadian district, and, therefore, that this seventh article has no direct application, but it has an indirect bearing upon the thirteenth section as indicating an intention on the part of Congress to treat the prosecutor in a criminal case as the other party to the cause, and so long as the party injured is alive, it may be proper to speak of him as such; and this we understand to have been the construction generally given. While it is impossible to speak of the deceased in a murder case as a party, in any proper sense, to a criminal prosecution against his assailant, it can scarcely have been the intention of Congress to vest jurisdiction in the Federal courts of cases in which the accused, an indian, was guilty of a felonious assault upon a white man, not resulting in death, and deny it in case of a fatal termination, upon the ground that the accused is the only party to the cause.

In construing these statutes in their application to criminal cases, and in connection with the treaty, there are but three alternative courses.

(1) To treat the defendant as the sole party; in which case the Indian courts would have jurisdiction, whether the victim of the crime were an Indian or a white man. In the Case of Mayfield, 141 U.S. 107, which was a case of adultery, in which the name of the prosecuting witness did not appear, we held that as there was no adverse party, the woman being a consenting party, the defendant was to be regarded as the sole party to the proceeding.

(2) To treat the United States as the other party to the cause; in which case the Federal courts would have jurisdiction of all criminal cases, except as they might be limited by the clause of Rev. Stat. §2146, providing that such jurisdiction "shall not be construed to extend to crimes committed by one Indian against the person or property of another Indian."

(3) To treat the victim of the crime, whose person or property has been invaded, as the other party; in which case the Federal courts would have jurisdiction in all cases in which the victim was a white man, or other than an Indian. Under this construction the word "parties" would really mean parties to the crime and not simply to the prosecution of the crime.

The last proposition harmonizes better with what seems to have been the intention of Congress, as evinced in that clause of Rev. Stat. §2146 which reserves to the courts of the Nation jurisdiction of "crimes committed by one Indian against the person or property of another Indian," and at the same time avoids the anomaly of holding a murdered man to be a party to the prosecution of his slayer. Upon the whole we think it affords the most reasonable solution of the problem. For the purposes of this case, therefore, we hold the court below had jurisdiction.

There were a number of exceptions taken to the charge of the court, only two of which it will be necessary to discuss.

2. The eighth assignment of error is to the following instruction:

"When he" (the defendant) "is in that condition, if he was in that condition in this case, and was then attacked by Duncan, the deceased, in such a way as to denote an intention upon the part of the deceased to take away his, the defendant's, life, or to do him some enormous bodily injury, he could kill Duncan -- when? -- provided he use all the means in his power otherwise to save his own life from the attack of Duncan, or preventing the intending harm, such as retreating as far as he could, or disabling his adversary without killing him. That is still a duty."

a man assailed upon his own premises, without provocation, by a person armed with a deadly weapon, and apparently seeking his life, is not obliged to retreat, but may stand his ground and defend himself with such means as are within his control; and so long as there is no intent on his part to kill his antagonist, and no purpose of doing anything beyond what is necessary to save his own life, is not guilty of murder or manslaughter if death result to his antagonist from the blow given him under such circumstances.

In the case of Beard v. United States, 158 U.S. 550, the doctrine of the necessity of retreating was considered by this court at very considerable length, and it was held, upon a review of the authorities upon the subject, that a man assailed upon his own premises, without provocation, by a person armed with a deadly weapon, and apparently seeking his life, is not obliged to retreat, but may stand his ground and defend himself with such means as are within his control; and so long as there is no intent on his part to kill his antagonist, and no purpose of doing anything beyond what is necessary to save his own life, Is not guilty of murder or manslaughter if death result to his antagonist from the blow given him under such circumstances. In delivering the opinion it was said, p. 559:

we cannot agree that the accused was under any greater obligation, when on his own premises, near his dwelling-house, to retreat or run away from his assailant, than be would have been if attacked within his dwelling-house.

"But we cannot agree that the accused was under any greater obligation, when on his own premises, near his dwelling-house, to retreat or run away from his assailant, than be would have been if attacked within his dwelling-house. The accused being where he had a right to be, on his own premises, constituting a part of his residence and home, at the time the deceased approached him in a threatening manner, and not having by language or by conduct provoked the deceased to assault him, the question for the jury was whether, without fleeing from his adversary, he had, at the moment he struck the deceased, reasonable grounds to believe, and in good faith believed, that he could not save his life or protect himself from great bodily harm except by doing what he did, namely, strike the deceased with his gun, and thus prevent his further advance upon him."

Duncan, the deceased, had been paying such attentions to the defendant's wife that it had caused them to separate, the wife living at a Mr. Lipe's, where the killing occurred, and defendant making his home with some colored people by the name of Graves.

he made at me as if he had something and was going to kill me, and I had this little pistol in my pocket and I run backwards toward the front yard and told him to stand off

and then I moved away—I started to move and this fellow says to me, he says, 'I will kill you, God damn you,' and made for me. He was between me and the house and I was next to the gate, and I broke for the gate to try to get out of his way, and as I broke for the gate he was coming at me, seemed like he was going to cut me with something; I couldn't tell what it was and I threw myself around that way (illustrating) and fired.

In the case under consideration it appeared that Duncan, the deceased, had been paying such attentions to the defendant's wife that it had caused them to separate, the wife living at a Mr. Lipe's, where the killing occurred, and defendant making his home with some colored people by the name of Graves. Defendant himself worked during the day at Lipe's, was frequently with his wife, and upon the evening in question had been to church with her and taken her home to Lipe's after the service. She went into the house and defendant went back into the lot, where the stock was, as it was a part of his duty to look after the stock. His version of the facts was that while he was in the lot he saw a window in the house, which opened into his wife's room, raised, walked out into the yard and found the deceased at the window, and said to him: "Who is that?" To which the deceased replied, with an oath: "You will find out who it is;" "and then made at me at that time. That is the first time I had seen him there. And then I knew his voice, and he made at me as if he had something and was going to kill me, and I had this little pistol in my pocket and I run backwards toward the front yard and told him to stand off, ... and I called Mr. Lipe, who got up and came to the door and asked what was the matter;" to which defendant replied: "This man here was trying to get up in your window where my wife sleeps ... and then I moved away -- I started to move and this fellow says to me, he says, 'I will kill you, God damn you,' and made for me. He was between me and the house and I was next to the gate, and I broke for the gate to try to get out of his way, and as I broke for the gate he was coming at me, seemed like he was going to cut me with something; I couldn't tell what it was and I threw myself around that way (illustrating) and fired."

It was in this connection that the court gave the charge covered by the eighth assignment, adding thereto:

It is our duty, in the first place, to get out of the way of the attack, and that is a duty springing from our own self interest, because if a man can avoid a deadly result with due regard to his own safety, is it not better for him to do it, than to rush rashly into a conflict where he may lose his life?

"If a man attacks us wrongfully, if he is seeking then and there to make an attack upon us in such a way as to jeopardize life, and we can turn aside that attack without destroying his life, it is our duty to do it. It is our duty, in the first place, to get out of the way of the attack, and that is a duty springing from our own self interest, because if a man can avoid a deadly result with due regard to his own safety, is it not better for him to do it, than to rush rashly into a conflict where he may lose his life? He is doing it in the interest of his own life. And then, aside from that, in the interest of the life of the party who attacks him, he is required to do it. Then, under this proposition, to give the defendant the benefit of it, he must have been doing what he had a right to do at the time, and while so situated he must have been attacked by Phil Duncan, the deceased, in such a way as to indicate, from the nature of that attack, and the way he was executing it, a purpose upon the part of Duncan then and there by that conduct to take his life, or to inflict upon him some great violence: and he must have been so situated, so surrounded by danger, that he could not get out of the way of it, or he could not turn it aside by an act of less violence than what he did do. He must have exercised reasonable means, in other words, to avoid the dreadful necessity of taking human life, because the law says that he could kill, provided he use all the means in his power otherwise to save his own life."

if, as he claims, he saw a man in the act of raising a window which led to his wife's room, it was perfectly natural that he should wish to investigate, and to ascertain for

what purpose the man was there.

We think that a man who finds another trying to obtain access to his wife's room in the night time, by opening a window, may not only remonstrate with him, but may employ such force as may be necessary to prevent his doing so; and if the other threatens to kill him, and makes a motion as if to do so, and puts him in fear of his life, or of great bodily harm, he is not bound to retreat, but may use such force as is necessary to repel the assault.

what the facts were was a question for the jury, who had a right to believe the defendant's version, if it seemed probable to them.

We think the charge of the court in this connection is open to the same objection that was made to the charge in the case of Beard v. United States. The only difference suggested is that in that case the attack was made with firearms, and in this case it would appear that the defendant supposed that the deceased was about to attack him with a knife. Defendant, however, was working at Lipe's, where his wife was staying, and if, as he claims, he saw a man in the act of raising a window which led to his wife's room, it was perfectly natural that he should wish to investigate, and to ascertain for what purpose the man was there. It appears to have been so dark at the time that defendant did not recognize deceased except by his voice; that the deceased threatened, with an oath, to kill him, and as he says, "made for him" with a knife. Under such circumstances we think that a charge to the jury that he was bound to retreat as far as he could, or disable his adversary without killing him, was misleading. We think that a man who finds another trying to obtain access to his wife's room in the night time, by opening a window, may not only remonstrate with him, but may employ such force as may be necessary to prevent his doing so; and if the other threatens to kill him, and makes a motion as if to do so, and puts him in fear of his life, or of great bodily harm, he is not bound to retreat, but may use such force as is necessary to repel the assault. Of course it is not intended to intimate that these were the facts, but what the facts were was a question for the jury, who had a right to believe the defendant's version, if it seemed probable to them. Upon the assumption that the jury did believe him, we think the charge imposed upon the defendant a responsibility and duty which he could not justly be called upon to bear.

3. The fourteenth assignment of error was to the following instructions upon the subject of the flight of the accused after the homicide:

"You take into consideration, in other words, the facts and circumstances which led up to the killing, the facts and circumstances that transpired at the time of the killing, and you do not stop there, but you take into consideration the facts and circumstances as affecting the defendant subsequently to the killing. For instance, you take into consideration the defendant's flight from the country -- his going into another part of the country -- as evidence; and you are to pass upon the question as to whether or not he has sufficiently explained away the presumption which the law says arises from flight when a man has taken human life. It is a principle of human nature -- and every man is conscious of it, I apprehend -- that if he does an act which he is conscious is wrong, his conduct will be along a certain line. He will pursue a certain course not in harmony with the conduct of a man who is conscious that he had done an act which is innocent, right and proper. The truth is -- and it is and old scriptural adage -- 'that the wicked flee when no man pursueth, but the righteous are as bold as a lion.' Men who are conscious of right have nothing to fear. They do not hesitate to confront a jury of their country, because that jury will protect them; it will shield them, and the more light there is let in upon their case the better it is for them. We are all conscious of that condition, and it is therefore a proposition of the law that, when a man flees, the fact that he does so may be taken against him, provided he does not explain it away upon some other theory than that of his flight because of his guilt.

"A man accused of crime hides himself, and then absconds. From this fact of absconding we may infer the fact of guilt. This is a presumption of fact, or an argument of a fact from a fact."

Again upon that subject:

... "flight by a defendant is always relevant evidence when offered by the prosecution; and that it is a silent admission by the defendant that he is unwilling or unable to face the case against him. It is in some sense, feeble or strong as the case may be, a confession; and it comes in with the other incidents, the corpus delicti being proved from which guilt may be cumulatively inferred."

"Now, that is the figure that flight cuts in a case. It is a question in this case whether this defendant has sufficiently explained it here to take away the effect of the presumption arising from flight."

In this connection the evidence tended to show that a day or two after the crime the defendant fled from the jurisdiction of the court, went to St. Louis, and there resumed his father's name instead of that of his master, which he had previously borne. Defendant gave his reason for fleeing as follows: "My heart was broke, and I just did not care to stay; I thought I would just go away from the country where I would never hear from my people any more, because my heart was broke, and my children was all young and they had just commenced to love me, and my heart was broke at that time, and that was the reason I went away."

The weight which the jury is entitled to give to the flight of a prisoner immediately after the commission of a homicide was carefully considered by this court in the case of Hickory v. United States, 160 U.S. 408, in which a charge, substantially in the language of the instruction assigned as erroneous in this case, was held to be tantamount to saying to the jury that flight created a legal presumption of guilt so strong and so conclusive that it was the duty of the jury to act on it as axiomatic truth, and as such that it was error.

We do not find it necessary to repeat the argument that was made in that case, but we think it was especially misleading for the court to charge the jury that, from the fact of absconding, they might infer the fact of guilt, and that flight "is a silent admission by the defendant that he is unwilling or unable to face the case against him. It is in some sense, feeble or strong as the case may be, a confession; and it comes in with the other incidents, the corpus delicti being proved from which guilt may be cumulatively inferred." While undoubtedly the flight of the accused is a circumstance proper to be laid before the jury, as having a tendency to prove his guilt; at the same time, as was observed in Ryan v. The People, 79 N.Y. 593, "there are so many reasons for such conduct consistent with innocence, that it scarcely comes up to the standard of evidence tending to establish guilt, but this and similar evidence has been allowed upon the theory that the jury will give it such weight as it descrives, depending upon the surrounding circumstances."

men who are entirely innocent do sometimes fly from the scene of a crime through fear of being apprehended as the guilty parties, or from an unwillingness to appear as witnesses.

Innocent men sometimes hesitate to confront a jury—not necessarily because they fear that the jury will not protect them, but because they do not wish their names to appear in connection with criminal acts, are humiliated at being obliged to incur the popular odium of an arrest and trial, or because they do not wish to be put to the annoyance or expense of defending themselves.

While there is no objection to that part of the charge which permits the jury to take into consideration the defendant's flight form the country as evidence bearing upon the question of his guilt, it is not universally true that a man, who is conscious that he has done a wrong, "will pursue a certain course not in harmony with the conduct of a man who is conscious of having done an act which is innocent, right and proper;" since it is a matter of common knowledge that men who are entirely innocent do sometimes fly from the scene of a crime through fear of being apprehended as the guilty parties, or from an unwillingness to appear as witnesses. Nor is it true as an accepted axiom of criminal law that "the wicked flee when no man pursueth, but the righteous are as bold as a lion." Innocent men sometimes hesitate to confront a jury -- not necessarily because they fear that the jury will not protect them, but because they do not wish their names to appear in connection with criminal acts, are humiliated at being obliged to incur the popular odium of an arrest and trial, or because they do not wish to be put to the annoyance or expense of defending themselves. The criticism to be made upon this charge is, that it lays too much stress upon the fact of flight, and allows the jury to infer that this fact alone is sufficient to create a presumption of guilt. It certainly would not be contended as a universal rule that the fact that a person, who chanced to be present on the scene of a murder, shortly thereafter left the city, would, in the absence of all other testimony, be sufficient in itself to justify his conviction of the murder.

We have found it impossible to reconcile these instructions with the rulings of this court in the two cases above cited, and are therefore compelled to reverse the judgment of the court below, and remand the case with instructions to grant a new trial.

ACERS v. UNITED STATES

(FULL CASE)

164 U.S. 388; 17 S. Ct. 91; 41 L. Ed. 481

Submitted October 22, 1896.

November 30, 1896, Decided

GIST: It's hard to miss the biblical overtones of this self-defense case, in which Acers smashed Owens on the head with a big rock and fractured his skull. The two men had been at odds over their business affairs. Unlike Abel, Owens survived. Acers tried to slide out of the charge of assault-with-intent-to-kill by claiming self defense. Acers said he thought Owens was about to draw a pistol, but there was no corroborating evidence, and no pistol ever turned up. That may be the most tenuous link to guns for a case that has made it into *Supreme Court Gun Cases*, though it is right on target for related self-defense information.

"Hanging Judge" Isaac Parker in Arkansas convicted Acers of murder. The Supreme Court agreed completely, saying you need the elements of self defense present before you can avail yourself of its protections. In doing so the Court described conditions of justifiable self defense, by agreeing with the statements made by Judge Parker. Self defense requires a reasonable perception and belief that there is a present danger of deadly violence. Simple fear is not enough justification.

The Court also said that anything (the rock in this case) can be a deadly weapon depending upon how it is used. Based on the size of this rock (9 by 3 by 2 inches), the force used (enough to crack a skull), and the area attacked (the head), this stone was a deadly weapon. Statutes today often distinguish between a deadly weapon—something designed for lethal use—and a dangerous object, something that could be used lethally but is not so designed. Finally, the Court took yet another slap at the District Court for the Western District of Arkansas, for carelessness in its work.

The exceptions to this charge are taken in the careless way which prevails in the Western District of Arkansas.

In a trial for assault with intent to kill, a charge which distinguishes between the assault and the intent to kill, and charges specifically that each must be proved, that the intent can only be found from the circumstances of the transaction, pointing out things which tend to disclose the real intent, is not objectionable.

There is no error in defining a deadly weapon to be "a weapon with which death may be easily and readily produced; anything, no matter what it is, whether it is made for the purpose of destroying animal life, or whether it was not made by man at all, or whether it was made by him for some other purpose, if it is a weapon, or if it is a thing by which death can be easily and readily produced, the law recognizes it as a deadly weapon."

With reference to the matter of justifying injury done in self-defence by reason of the presence of danger, a charge which says that it must be a present danger, "of great injury to the person injured, that would maim him, or that would be permanent in its character, or that might produce death," is not an incorrect statement.

The same may be said of the instructions in reference to self-defence based on an apparent danger.

MR. JUSTICE BREWER delivered the opinion of the court.

defendant picked up a stone about three inches wide, nine inches long and an inch and a half or two inches thick, and with it struck Owens on the side of the head,

fracturing the skull. The defence was that there was no intent to kill; that defendant acted in self-defence; that, believing Owens was about to draw a pistol, he picked up the stone and pushed him down

the disputed matters were whether Owens had a pistol, and if so, whether he attempted to draw it, or made any motions suggestive of such a purpose.

Plaintiff in error was convicted in the District Court for the Western District of Arkansas of an assault with intent to kill, and sentenced to the penitentiary for the term of two years and six months. The undisputed facts were these: Defendant and one Joseph M. Owens had some dispute about business affairs, and while returning together to the house where they were both stopping, defendant picked up a stone about three inches wide, nine inches long and an inch and a half or two inches thick, and with it struck Owens on the side of the head, fracturing the skull. The defence was that there was no intent to kill; that defendant acted in self-defence; that, believing Owens was about to draw a pistol, he picked up the stone and pushed him down; and the disputed matters were whether Owens had a pistol, and if so, whether he attempted to draw it, or made any motions suggestive of such a purpose. The verdict of the jury was adverse to the contentions of the defendant.

The only questions presented for our consideration arise on the charge of the court, and may be grouped under four heads: First, as to the evidences of intent; second, as to what constitutes a deadly weapon; third, as to real danger; and, fourth, as to apparent danger. It may be premised that the exceptions to this charge are taken in the careless way which prevails in the Western District of Arkansas; but passing this and considering the charge as properly excepted to we find in it no substantial error.

It distinguished between the assault and the intent to kill, and charged specifically that each must be proved

the intent could only be found from the circumstances of the transaction

you take the character of the act done, the manner in which it was executed, the weapon used in executing it, the part of the body upon which it was executed, the very result produced by that act upon that vital part of the body known as the head. These are all circumstances that it is your duty to take into consideration to find whether the party intended to kill him or not.

First. With reference to the charge as to the matter of intent, counsel for plaintiff in error challenge a single sentence, as follows: "But you need not go to a thing of that kind, because the law says you may take the act itself as done, and from it you may find that it was wilfully done." But this sentence is to be taken, not by itself alone, but in connection with many others, in order to determine what the court instructed as to the evidences of intent. It distinguished between the assault and the intent to kill, and charged specifically that each must be proved, that the intent could only be found from the circumstances of the transaction, and, after suggesting that the declarations made by a party at the time of an assault would tend to show the intent with which it was committed, added the sentence which counsel have quoted. Nowhere, not even in the sentence quoted, was it said that the assault of itself necessarily proved the intent, but all through the charge in this respect was the constant declaration that the intent was to be deduced from all the circumstances of the case, the court pointing out many things which tended to disclose the real intent of a party, summing up the matter with these observations: "That is the way you find intent, then, bearing in mind that he is held to have intended whatever consequences might have followed from the act as wilfully done by him with the deadly weapon. You, in other words, to find intent, take the circumstances; you take the character of the act done, the manner in which it was executed, the weapon used in executing it, the part of the body upon which it was executed, the very result produced by that act upon that vital part of the body known as the head. These are all circumstances that it is your duty to take into consideration to find whether the party intended to kill him or not." There is nothing objectionable in this.

With respect to a deadly weapon, the court defined it as "a weapon with which death may be easily and readily produced; anything, no matter what it is, whether it is made for the purpose of destroying animal life, or whether it was not made by man at all, or whether it was made by him for some other purpose, if it is a weapon, or if it is a thing with which death can be easily and readily produced, the law recognizes it as a deadly weapon." We see nothing in this definition to which any reasonable exception can be taken.

We have so little doubt that when one uses a stone of such size and strikes a blow on the skull so severe as to fracture it, a jury ought to find that the stone was a deadly weapon

Second. With respect to a deadly weapon, the court defined it as "a weapon with which death may be easily and readily produced; anything, no matter what it is, whether it is made for the purpose of destroying animal life, or whether it was not made by man at all, or whether it was made by him for some other purpose, if it is a weapon, or if it is a thing with which death can be easily and readily produced, the law recognizes it as a deadly weapon." We see nothing in this definition to which any reasonable exception can be taken. Nor do we find anything in the subsequent language of the court which in any manner qualifies this definition, or can be construed as an instruction to the jury that as matter of law the stone actually used was a deadly weapon. It is true reference was made to the manner in which the stone was used and the part of the body upon which the blow was struck as considerations to aid the jury in determining whether it was properly to be considered a deadly weapon. We have so little doubt that when one uses a stone of such size and strikes a blow on the skull so severe as to fracture it, a jury ought to find that the stone was a deadly weapon, that if the court had expressed a definite opinion to that effect we should have been reluctant on that account alone to have disturbed the judgment. But the court did not so express itself, and in calling attention to the manner of its use and the part of the body upon which the blow was struck it only properly called the attention of the jury to circumstances fairly to be considered in determining the character of the weapon. United States v. Small, 2 Curtis, 241, 243; Commonwealth v. Duncan, 91 Kentucky, 592; State v. Davis, 14 Nevada, 407, 413; People v. Irving, 95 N.Y. 541, 546; Hunt v. State, 6 Tex. App. 663; Melton v. State, 30 Tex. App. 273; Jenkins v. State, 30 Tex. App. 379.

With reference to the matter of self-defence by reason of the presence of a real danger, the court charged that it could not be a past danger, or a danger of a future injury, but a present danger and a danger of "great injury to the person injured that would maim him, or that would be permanent in its character, or that might produce death." In this we think nothing was stated incorrectly

Third. With reference to the matter of self-defence by reason of the presence of a real danger, the court charged that it could not be a past danger, or a danger of a future injury, but a present danger and a danger of "great injury to the person injured that would maim him, or that would be permanent in its character, or that might produce death." In this we think nothing was stated incorrectly, and that there was a fair definition of what is necessary to constitute self defence by reason of the existence of a real danger.

it is not sufficient that the defendant claims that he believed he was in danger, but that it is essential that there were reasonable grounds for such belief

Neither, fourthly, do we find anything to condemn in the instructions in reference to self-defence based on an apparent danger. Several approved authorities are quoted from in which the doctrine is correctly stated that it is not sufficient that the defendant claims that he believed he was in danger, but that it is essential that there were reasonable grounds for such belief, and then the rule was summed up in this way:

there must be some overt act being done by the party which from its character, from its nature, would give a reasonable man, situated as was the defendant, the ground to believe—reasonable ground to believe—that there was danger to his life or of deadly violence to his person

"Now, these cases are along the same line, and they are without limit, going to show that, as far as this proposition of apparent danger is concerned, to rest upon a foundation upon which a conclusion that is reasonable can be erected there must be some overt act being done by the party which from its character, from its nature, would give a reasonable man, situated as was the defendant, the ground to believe -- reasonable ground to believe -- that there was danger to his life or of deadly violence to his person, and unless that condition existed then there is no ground upon which this proposition can stand; there is nothing to which the doctrine of apparent danger could apply."

That implies not that he can act upon a state of case where there is a bare conception of fear, but that there must exist that which is either really or apparently an act of violence, and from that the inference may reasonably be drawn that there was deadly danger hanging over Acers, in this case, at that time.

Counsel criticise the use of the words "deadly violence," as though the court meant thereby to limit the defence to such cases as showed an intention on the part of the person assaulted to take the life of the defendant, but obviously that is not a fair construction of the language, not only because danger to life is expressly named, but also because in other parts of the charge it had indicated that what was meant by those words was simply great violence. This is obvious from this language, found a little preceding the quotation: "'When from the nature of the attack.' You look at the act being done, and you from that draw an inference as to whether there was reasonable ground to believe that there was a design upon the part of Owens in this case to destroy the life of the defendant Acers or to commit any great violence upon his person at the time he was struck by the rock. 'When from the nature of the attack.' That implies not that he can act upon a state of case where there is a bare conception of fear, but that there must exist that which is either really or apparently an act of violence, and from that the inference may reasonably be drawn that there was deadly danger hanging over Acers, in this case, at that time."

These are all the matters complained of. We see no error in the rulings of the court, and, therefore, the judgment is

Affirmed.

MR. JUSTICE SHIRAS dissented.

ALLEN v. UNITED STATES

(FULL CASE)

164 U.S. 492; 17 S. Ct. 154; 41 L. Ed. 528

Submitted October 23, 1896.

December 7, 1896, Decided

GIST: The Court expressed some displeasure with this appeal—the third time it had considered the case—of a murder conviction from Arkansas Judge Parker. Yet while the High Court had easily overturned Parker in the past, here they were confronted not with a justifiable homicide, but with a true murder. They upheld the conviction, and the murderer was sent to prison for life. Alexander Allen, the 14-year-old defendant (they call him the prisoner) had gone through a fence, called out to his adversary, 18-year-old Phillip Henson, punched him in the face, and then shot him twice, once in the back.

The Court described conditions necessary to show premeditation and intent to kill, they defined manslaughter and self defense, and they pointed out that words alone are insufficient to justify an assault. They also indicated that while flight after the fact might suggest guilt it does not prove it. Allen had fled after the incident.

Judge Parker gained a legacy in this case. The High Court approved his instruction to a deadlocked jury, that jurors should each listen to the other side's arguments with a disposition to be convinced. Parker got the language from state courts in Massachusetts and Connecticut. Known as the "Allen charge," *Black's Law Dictionary* notes that it is illegal in some states. It is also known as a dynamite charge, a shotgun instruction, and a third degree instruction.

There is no error in an instruction that evidence recited by the court to the jury leaves them at liberty to infer not only wilfulness, but malice aforethought, if the evidence is as so recited.

There is no error in an instruction on a trial for murder that the intent necessary to constitute malice aforethought need not have existed for any particular time before the act of killing, but that it may spring up at the instant, and may be inferred from the fact of killing.

The language objected to in the sixth assignment of error is nothing more than the statement, in another form, of the familiar proposition that every man is presumed to intend the natural and probable consequences of his own act.

Mere provocative words, however aggravating, are not sufficient to reduce a crime from murder to manslaughter.

To establish a case of justifiable homicide it must appear that the assault made upon the prisoner was such as would lead a reasonable person to believe that his life was in peril.

There was no error in the instruction that the prisoner was bound to retreat as far as he could before slaying his assailant. Beard v. United States, 158 U.S. 550, and Alberty v. United States, 162 U.S. 499, distinguished from this case.

Flight of the accused is competent evidence against him, as having a tendency to establish guilt; and an instruction to that effect in substance is not error, although inaccurate in some other respects which could not have misled the jury.

The refusal to charge that where there is a probability of innocence there is a reasonable doubt of guilt is not error, when the court has already charged that the jury could not find the defendant guilty unless they were satisfied from the testimony that the crime was established beyond a reasonable doubt.

The seventeenth and eighteenth assignments were taken to instructions given to the jury after the main charge was delivered, and when the jury had returned to the court, apparently for further instructions. These instructions were quite lengthy and were, in substance, that in a large proportion of cases absolute certainty could not be expected; that although the verdict must be the verdict of each individual juror, and not a mere acquiescence in the conclusion of his fellows, yet they should examine the question submitted with candor and with a proper regard and deference to the opinions of each other; that it was their duty to decide the case if they could conscientiously do so; that they should listen, with a disposition to be convinced, to each other's arguments; that, if much the larger number were for conviction, a dissenting juror should consider whether his doubt was a reasonable one which made no impression upon the minds of so many men, equally honest, equally intelligent with himself. If, upon the other hand, the majority was for acquittal, the minority ought to ask themselves whether they might not reasonably doubt the correctness of a judgment which was not concurred in by the majority. Held, that there was no error.

THE facts constituting the offence for which Allen was indicted are set forth in Allen v. United States, 150 U.S. 551, and 157 U.S. 675. The rulings passed upon in the present case are stated in the opinion of the court.

MR. JUSTICE BROWN delivered the opinion of the court.

This was a writ of error to a judgment of the Circuit Court of the United States for the Western District of Arkansas sentencing the plaintiff in error to death for the murder of Philip Henson, a white man, in the Cherokee Nation of the Indian Territory. The defendant was tried and convicted in 1893, and upon such conviction being set aside by this court, 150 U.S. 551, was again tried and convicted in 1894. The case was again reversed, 157 U.S. 675, when Allen was tried for the third time and convicted, and this writ of error was sued out.

The facts are so fully set forth in the previous reports of the case that it is unnecessary to repeat them here.

We are somewhat embarrassed in the consideration of this case by the voluminousness of the charge, and of the exceptions taken thereto, as well as by the absence of a brief on the part of the plaintiff in error; but the principal assignments of error, set forth in the record, will be noticed in this opinion.

If you believe the story as narrated by the two Erne boys, who testified as witnesses, is true—that is, that the defendant went up to the fence with his pistol; that he went through the wire fence, and went out in the wheat field where Philip Henson was, and met him, first hollered at him, placed his pistol upon the fence and stopped the boys, and then went through the wire fence and went out to where he was, and struck him first in the mouth with his left fist, and at the same time undertook to fire upon him, and that that firing was prevented by the action of Henson in taking hold of the pistol, and it went off into the ground, and then he fired at him and struck him in the side, and then he fired at him and struck him in the back, you have a state of facts which would authorize you to say that the killing was done wilfully; and, not only that, but to say that it was done with malice aforethought

1. The third assignment of error is taken to certain language in the charge, the material portion of which is as follows:

"If you believe the story as narrated by the two Erne boys, who testified as witnesses, is true -- that is, that the defendant went up to the fence with his pistol; that he went through the wire fence, and went out in the wheat field where Philip Henson was, and met him, first hollered at him, placed his pistol upon the fence and stopped the boys, and then went through the wire fence and went out to where he was, and struck him first in the mouth with his left fist, and at the same time undertook to fire upon him, and that that firing was prevented by the action of Henson in taking hold of the pistol, and it went off into the ground, and then he fired at him and struck him in the side, and then he fired at him and struck him in the back, you have a state of facts which would authorize you to say that the killing was done wilfully; and, not only that, but to say that it was done with malice aforethought, because that state of case, if that be true, would show the doing of a wrongful act, an illegal act, without just cause or excuse, and in the absence of mitigating facts to reduce the grade of the crime."

The learned judge was stating in this connection the theory of the prosecution, and if the facts were as stated by the Ernes, there was no error in saying to the jury, not that they were bound to, but that they were at liberty to, infer not only wilfulness but malice aforethought.

2. The fourth assignment was to the following language:

this age of improved weapons, when a man can discharge a gun in the twinkling of an eye

an act that he could not do in self-defense from the fact that it was done without just cause or excuse, or in the absence of mitigating facts

Malice, says the law, is an intent of the mind and heart.

"How can you find a deliberate intent to kill? Do you have to see whether or not the man had that intent or not in his mind a year or month or day or an hour? Not at all, for in this age of improved weapons, when a man can discharge a gun in the twinkling of an eye, if you see a man draw one of these weapons and fire it, and the man toward whom he presents it falls dead, you have a deliberate intent to kill, as manifested by the way he did that act. You have the existence of a deliberate intent, though it may spring up on the spur of the moment -- as it were, spring up contemporaneous with the doing of it -- evidenced by shooting of the man, if the act was one he could not do under the law and then claim it was manslaughter, or an act that he could not do in self-defense from the fact that it was done without just cause or excuse, or in the absence of mitigating facts, and that is precisely the definition of this characteristic of murder, known as malice aforethought. It does not, as I have already told you, necessarily import any special malevolence towards the individual slain, but also includes the case of a generally depraved, wicked and malicious spirit, a heart regardless of social duty, and a mind deliberately bent on mischief. It imports premeditation. Malice, says the law, is an intent of the mind and heart."

the intent necessary to constitute malice aforethought need not have existed for any particular time before the act of killing, but that it may spring up at the instant and may be inferred from the fact of killing.

in some States, proof of deliberate premeditation is necessary to constitute murder in the first degree.

The substance of this instruction is that the intent necessary to constitute malice aforethought need not have existed for any particular time before the act of killing, but that it may spring up at the instant and may be inferred from the fact of killing. This is within the authorities as applied to the common law crime of murder, though where the crime is classified as in some States, proof of deliberate premeditation is necessary to constitute murder in the first degree. United States v. Cornell, 2 Mason, 91; People v. Clark, 7 N.Y. 385; Whart. on Homicide, §33; Whart. on Crim. Law, 10th ed. §117.

3. The sixth assignment is to the following language:

The law says we have no power to ascertain the certain condition of a man's mind. The best we can do is to infer it more or less satisfactorily from his acts. A person is presumed to intend what he does.

A man who performs an act which it is known will produce a particular result is from our common experience presumed to have anticipated that result and to have intended it.

from the very fact that a fatal bullet was fired, we have the right to infer as a presumption of fact that the blow was intended prior to the striking

"The law says we have no power to ascertain the certain condition of a man's mind. The best we can do is to infer it more or less satisfactorily from his acts. A person is presumed to intend what he does. A man who performs an act which it is known will produce a particular result is from our common experience presumed to have anticipated that result and to have intended it. Therefore we have a right to say, and the law says, that when a homicide is committed by weapons indicating design that it is not necessary to prove that such design existed for any definite period before the fatal blow was fired. From the very fact of a blow being struck, from the very fact that a fatal bullet was fired, we have the right to infer as a presumption of fact that the blow was intended prior to the striking, although at a period of time inappreciably distant."

every man is presumed to intend the natural and probable consequences of his own act.

This is nothing more than a statement of the familiar proposition that every man is presumed to intend the natural and probable consequences of his own act. 1 Greenl. Ev. §18; Regina v. Jones, 9 C. & P. 258; Regina v. Hill, 8 C. & P. 274; Regina v. Beard, 8 C. & P. 143; People v. Herrick, 13 Wend. 87, 91.

4. The eighth assignment is taken to the following definition of manslaughter:

mere words alone do not excuse even a simple assault.

"It is the killing of a man unlawfully and wilfully, but without malice aforethought. Malice aforethought, as I have defined it to you, must be excluded from it; that is, the doing of a wrongful act without just cause or excuse and in the absence of mitigating facts in such a way as to show a heart void of social duty and a mind fatally bent upon mischief must be out of the case. If that is driven out of the case, then if it is a crime at all, it must come under this statute; it must come under this definition of the crime of manslaughter. The common law, which I will read to you, defines it in the same way. It tells you in a little broader terms what kind of conditions it springs out of. Speaking of voluntary manslaughter, it says it is the wilful and unlawful killing of another on sudden quarrel or in the heat of passion. Let us see what is meant by this definition. The party who is killed, at the time of the killing, must offer some provocation to produce a certain condition of mind. Now, what is the character of that provocation that can be recognized by the law as being sufficient to reduce the grade of the crime from murder to manslaughter? He cannot produce it by mere words, because mere words alone do not excuse even a simple assault. Any words offered at the time do not reduce the grade of the killing from murder to manslaughter. He must be doing some act -- that is, the deceased, Philip Henson in this case, the party killed -- which at the time is of a character that would so inflame the mind of the party who does the killing as that the law contemplates he does not act deliberately, but his mind is in a state of passion; in a heat of passion where he is incapable of deliberating."

mere words, however aggravating, are not sufficient to reduce the crime from murder to manslaughter.

There is no error in this instruction. It is well settled by the authorities that mere words, however aggravating, are not sufficient to reduce the crime from murder to manslaughter. Commonwealth v. York, 9 Met. (Mass.) 93, 103; Whart. on Homicide, §393; Whart. on Crim. Law, 10th ed. §455a.

5. The ninth alleged error turned upon the statement made by the court of the circumstances under which the killing would be justifiable:

The law of self-defence is a law of proportions as well as a law of necessity, and it is only danger that is deadly in its character, or that may produce great bodily harm, against which you can exercise a deadly attack. If he is attacked by another in such a way as to denote a purpose to take away his life, or to do him some great bodily harm from which death or permanent injury may follow, in such a case he may lawfully kill the assailant.

"It does not mean that defendant was assaulted in a slight way, or that you can kill a man for a slight attack. The law of self-defence is a law of proportions as well as a law of necessity, and it is only danger that is deadly in its character, or that may produce great bodily harm, against which you can exercise a deadly attack. If he is attacked by another in such a way as to denote a purpose to take away his life, or to do him some great bodily harm from which death or permanent injury may follow, in such a case he may lawfully kill the assailant. When? Provided he use all the means in his power otherwise to save his own life or prevent the intended harm, such as retreating as far as he can, or disabling him without killing him, if it be in his power. The act coming from the assailant must be a deadly act, or an act that would produce great violence to the person, under this proposition. It means an act that is hurled against him, and that he has not created it, or created the necessity for it by his own wrongful, deadly or dangerous conduct -- conduct threatening life. It must be an act where he cannot avoid the consequences. If he can, he must avoid them, if he can reasonably do so with due regard to his own safety."

It is clear that to establish a case of justifiable homicide it must appear that something

more than an ordinary assault was made upon the prisoner; it must also appear that the assault was such as would lead a reasonable person to believe that his life was in peril.

It is clear that to establish a case of justifiable homicide it must appear that something more than an ordinary assault was made upon the prisoner; it must also appear that the assault was such as would lead a reasonable person to believe that his life was in peril. Wallace v. United States, 162 U.S. 466.

Nor is there anything in the instruction of the court that the prisoner was bound to retreat as far as he could before slaying his assailant that conflicts with the ruling of this court in Beard v. United States, 158 U.S. 550. That was the case of an assault upon the defendant upon his own premises, and it was held that the obligation to retreat was no greater than it would have been if he had been assailed in his own house. So, too, in the case of Alberty v. United States, 162 U.S. 499, the defendant found the deceased trying to obtain access to his wife's chamber through a window, in the night time, and it was held that he might repel the attempt by force, and was under no obligation to retreat if the deceased attacked him with a knife. The general duty to retreat instead of killing when attacked was not touched upon in these cases. Whart. on Homicide, §485.

6. The fourteenth assignment is to the following language of the court upon the subject of the flight of the accused after the homicide: "Now, then, you consider his conduct at the time of the killing and his conduct afterwards. If he fled, if he left the country, if he sought to avoid arrest, that is a fact that you are to take into consideration against him, because the law says unless it is satisfactorily explained -- and he may explain it upon some theory, and you are to say whether there is any effort to explain it in this case -- if it is unexplained the law says it is a fact that may be taken into account against the party charged with the crime of murder upon the theory that I have named, upon the existence of this monitor called conscience that teaches us to know whether we have done right or wrong in a given case."

the law is entirely well settled that the flight of the accused is competent evidence against him as having a tendency to establish his guilt.

In the case of Hickory v. United States, 160 U.S. 408, 422, where the same question, as to the weight to be given to flight as evidence of guilt, arose, the court charged the jury that "the law recognizes another proposition as true, and it is that 'the wicked flee, when no man pursueth, but the innocent are as bold as a lion.' That is a self-evident proposition that has been recognized so often by mankind that we can take it as an axiom and apply it to this case." It was held that this was error, and was tantamount to saying to the jury that flight created a legal presumption of guilt, so strong and conclusive, that it was the duty of the jury to act on it as an axiomatic truth. So, also, in the case of Alberty v. United States, 162 U.S. 499, 509, the court used the same language, and added that from the fact of absconding the jury might infer the fact of guilt, and that flight was a silent admission by the defendant that he was unwilling or unable to face the case against him, and was in some sense feeble or strong, as the case might be, a confession. This was also held to be error. But in neither of these cases was it intimated that the flight of the accused was not a circumstance proper to be laid before the jury as having a tendency to prove his guilt. Several authorities were quoted in the Hickory case, (p. 417,) as tending to establish this proposition. Indeed, the law is entirely well settled that the flight of the accused is competent evidence against him as having a tendency to establish his guilt. Whart. on Homicide, §710; People v. Pitcher, 15 Michigan, 397.

This was the substance of the above instruction, and although not accurate in all its parts we do not think it could have misled the jury.

false testimony, knowingly and purposely invoked by defendant, might be used against him, is but another method of stating the principle that the fabrication of testimony raises a presumption against the party guilty of such practice.

7. In the fifteenth assignment exception is taken to the following instruction: "You will understand that your first duty in the case is to reject all evidence that you may find to be false; all evidence that you may find to be fabricated, because it is worthless; and if it is purposely and intentionally invoked by the defendant it is evidence against him; it is the basis for a presumption against him, because the law says that he who resorts to perjury, he who resorts to subornation of perjury to accomplish an end, this is against him, and you may take such action as the basis of a presumption of guilt." There was certainly no error in instructing the jury to disregard evidence that was bound to be false, and the further charge that false testimony, knowingly and purposely invoked by defendant, might be used against him, is but another method of stating the principle that the fabrication of testimony raises a presumption against the party guilty of such practice. 1 Phillips' Evidence, 448; State v. Williams, 27 Vermont, (1 Williams,) 724; 3 Russell on Crimes, 6th ed. 358.

8. The sixteenth assignment was to the refusal of the court to charge the jury that where there is a

probability of innocence there is a reasonable doubt of guilt. In the case of Coffin v. United States, 156 U.S. 432, 452, it was held that a refusal of the court to charge the jury upon the subject of the presumption of innocence was not met by a charge that they could not convict unless the evidence showed guilt beyond a reasonable doubt.

a party starts into a trial, though accused by the grand jury with the crime of murder, or any other crime, with the presumption of innocence in his favor.

Whenever the proof shows, beyond a reasonable doubt, the existence of a crime, then the presumption of innocence disappears from the case.

In the case under consideration, however, the court had already charged the jury that they could not find the defendant guilty unless they were satisfied from the testimony that the crime was established beyond a reasonable doubt. That this meant, "first, that a party starts into a trial, though accused by the grand jury with the crime of murder, or any other crime, with the presumption of innocence in his favor. That stays with him until it is driven out of the case by the testimony. It is driven out of the case when the evidence shows, beyond a reasonable doubt, that the crime as charged has been committed, or, that a crime has been committed. Whenever the proof shows, beyond a reasonable doubt, the existence of a crime, then the presumption of innocence disappears from the case. That exists up to the time that it is driven out in that way by proof to that extent." The court having thus charged upon the subject of the presumption of innocence, could not be required to repeat the charge in a separate instruction at the request of the defendant.

it was their duty to decide the case if they could conscientiously do so; that they should listen, with a disposition to be convinced, to each other's arguments

9. The seventeenth and eighteenth assignments were taken to instructions given to the jury after the main charge was delivered, and when the jury had returned to the court, apparently for further instructions. These instructions were quite lengthy and were, in substance, that in a large proportion of cases absolute certainty could not be expected; that although the verdict must be the verdict of each individual juror, and not a mere acquiescence in the conclusion of his fellows, yet they should examine the question submitted with candor and with a proper regard and deference to the opinions of each other; that it was their duty to decide the case if they could conscientiously do so; that they should listen, with a disposition to be convinced, to each other's arguments; that, if much the larger number were for conviction, a dissenting juror should consider whether his doubt was a reasonable one which made no impression upon the minds of so many men, equally honest, equally intelligent with himself. If, upon the other hand, the majority was for acquittal, the minority ought to ask themselves whether they might not reasonably doubt the correctness of a judgement which was not concurred in by the majority. These instructions were taken literally from a charge in a criminal case which was approved of by the Supreme Court of Massachusetts in Commonwealth v. Tuey, 8 Cush. 1, and by the Supreme Court of Connecticut in State v. Smith, 49 Connecticut, 376, 386.

While, undoubtedly, the verdict of the jury should represent the opinion of each individual juror, it by no means follows that opinions may not be changed by conference in the juryroom. The very object of the jury system is to secure unanimity by a comparison of views, and by arguments among the jurors themselves. It certainly cannot be the law that each juror should not listen with deference to the arguments and with a distrust of his own judgment, if he finds a large majority of the jury taking a different view of the case from what he does himself. It cannot be that each juror should go to the jury-room with a blind determination that the verdict shall represent his opinion of the case at that moment; or, that he should close his ears to the arguments of men who are equally honest and intelligent as himself. There was no error in these instructions.

Several other assignments were made, to which it is unnecessary to call attention.

For the reasons above stated the judgment of the court below will be

Affirmed.

ROWE v. UNITED STATES

(FULL CASE)

164 U.S. 546; 17 S. Ct. 172; 41 L. Ed. 547

Submitted October 22, 1896.

November 30, 1896, Decided

GIST: Here is one of the best Wild West dramas contained in Supreme Court gun-related self-defense cases, and the last one from Judge Isaac Parker, who retired soon after. Rowe traveled 20 horse-drawn miles to town with his wife to go shopping. Later, he met another man, Bozeman, at the dinner table of a hotel and they exchanged some hostile words. Rowe bragged that he was armed.

After dinner they met again in the hotel lobby. Bozeman grossly insulted Rowe, who kicked at him lightly and then stepped back and leaned on a counter. Bozeman then lurched at Rowe and began slicing his face with a knife, so Rowe pulled his pistol and killed his assailant with a single shot. Naturally, the prosecution and defense disagreed on who said what or when. Rowe was convicted of manslaughter, got five years and a $500 fine.

The Justices declared that you can be involved in starting a difficulty, which would normally deny you any claim of self defense, and regain your right to self defense by honestly withdrawing from the conflict you may have begun. They placed great emphasis on determining the sincerity of your withdrawal. The Court also flatly rejected the notion that you should or must shoot to only wound during a deadly struggle, if you are able.

It's interesting to see how the defendant, a Cherokee Indian, kept his gun with him for the long ride to town, but then felt secure enough once in town to leave the gun at the livery stable until before he prepared to journey home again. Also of note, the decision described how the fired shot hit Bozeman near the right elbow and then traveled through his body from right to left. In the conclusion, in addition to having dismissed Parker's shoot-to-wound conjecture, the Court spoke of the folly of trying to wing an assailant's arm to paralyze it and thus hope to stop him, while fighting for your life during mortal combat.

ERROR TO THE CIRCUIT COURT OF THE UNITED STATES FOR THE WESTERN DISTRICT OF ARKANSAS.

On the trial of a person indicted for murder, the defence being that the act was done in self-defence, the evidence on both sides was to the effect that the deceased used language of a character offensive to the accused; that the accused thereupon kicked at or struck at the deceased, hitting him lightly, and then stepped back and leaned against a counter; that the deceased immediately attacked the accused with a knife, cutting his face; and that the accused then shot and killed his assailant. The trial court in its charge pressed upon the jury the proposition that a person who has slain another cannot urge in justification of the killing a necessity produced by his own unlawful acts. Held, that this principle had no application in this case; that the law did not require that the accused should stand still and permit himself to be cut to pieces, under the penalty that, if he met the unlawful attack upon him, and saved his own life by taking that of his assailant, he would be guilty of manslaughter; that under the circumstances the jury might have found that the accused, although in the wrong when he kicked or kicked at the deceased, did not provoke the fierce attack made upon him by the latter with a knife in any sense that would deprive him of the right of self-defence against such attack; and that the accused was entitled, so far as his right to resist the attack was concerned, to remain where he was, and to do whatever was necessary, or what he had grounds to believe at the time was necessary, to save his life, or to protect him from great bodily harm.

If a person, under the provocation of offensive language, assaults the speaker personally, but in such a way as to show that there is no intention to do him serious bodily harm, and then retires under such circumstances as show that he does not intend to do anything more, but in good faith withdraws from further contest, his right of self-defence is restored when the person assaulted, in violation of law pursues him with a deadly weapon and seeks to take his life, or do him great bodily harm.

THIS was an indictment for murder, alleged to have been committed by the plaintiff in error, in the Cherokee Nation, Indian Territory, on the 30th day of March, 1895, -- the person killed, Frank Bozeman, being a white man and not an Indian. The verdict was guilty of manslaughter, and a motion for new trial having been overruled, the accused was sentenced to imprisonment in the penitentiary at Columbus, Ohio, for the term of five years, and to pay to the United States a fine of five hundred dollars.

The following agreed statement as to the evidence is taken from the record:

defendant said that he had his gun, and that he had a right to carry it, as he was a 'traveller'; that he had made a gun play in that town on one occasion and he would make another one; that he said to deceased, 'What do you think of that?

the deceased then said, 'He has got too damn much nigger blood in him to talk anything with any sense'; that defendant then kicked at deceased, hitting him lightly on the lower part of the leg; that immediately deceased sprang at defendant, striking him with a knife and cutting him in two places on the face; that after deceased began cutting defendant the latter drew his pistol and fired, shooting deceased through the body; that at the time the defendant fired the two men were in striking distance of one another. The shot struck deceased in the right arm, near the elbow, and ranged through the body from right to left side; that when shot was fired deceased ran, and when defendant turned round the blood was streaming from his face, where he had been cut by deceased, and he said to the bystanders to go for a doctor, that he was killed

"The testimony on the part of the government tended to show that on the evening of the 30th of March, 1895, the defendant, David Cul Rowe, who is a Cherokee Indian, and the deceased, Frank Bozeman, a white man, a citizen of the United States, and not an Indian, met at a hotel at Pryor's Creek, Indian Territory, at the supper table; that the defendant appeared to be drinking, but was not much intoxicated; that defendant said that he had his gun, and that he had a right to carry it, as he was a 'traveller'; that he had made a gun play in that town on one occasion and he would make another one; that he said to deceased, 'What do you think of that?' The deceased did not reply, and defendant said to him, 'God damn you, I'll make you hide out or I'll make you talk to me'; that in a short time deceased got through his supper and walked out into the office of the hotel, and presently defendant came out of the dining-room; that defendant said something to deceased, which was not understood by the witnesses, but the deceased did not answer; that defendant turned to some other parties present and said, 'He (meaning deceased) will not talk to me'; that one of the parties addressed said to defendant, 'Talk Cherokee to him'; that the deceased then said, 'He has got too damn much nigger blood in him to talk anything with any sense'; that defendant then kicked at deceased, hitting him lightly on the lower part of the leg; that immediately deceased sprang at defendant, striking him with a knife and cutting him in two places on the face; that after deceased began cutting defendant the latter drew his pistol and fired, shooting deceased through the body; that at the time the defendant fired the two men were in striking distance of one another. The shot struck deceased in the right arm, near the elbow, and ranged through the body from right to left side; that when shot was fired deceased ran, and when defendant turned round the blood was streaming from his face, where he had been cut by deceased, and he said to the bystanders to go for a doctor, that he was killed; that a short time after the difficulty the knife used by deceased on defendant was found near the place where the trouble occurred; that a knife was also found on the person of deceased after his death.

on the day of the difficulty defendant came into town from his home, about twenty miles distant, with his wife to do some shopping; that he brought his pistol with him and left it at the livery stable where he put up his team, and at supper time went by the stable and got his pistol, fearing that it might be stolen

when defendant came out in the office deceased used the language indicated in the statement for the government, or words to that effect, and defendant kicked at him and probably struck him lightly; that when defendant kicked he stepped back and leaned up against the counter and deceased sprang at him and began cutting him with a knife; that deceased cut him in the face and kept on striking at him with the knife, and after

he was cut in the face defendant drew his pistol and fired at deceased, who was in the act of striking him again with the knife.

"The testimony on the part of the defence tended to show that on the day of the difficulty defendant came into town from his home, about twenty miles distant, with his wife to do some shopping; that he brought his pistol with him and left it at the livery stable where he put up his team, and at supper time went by the stable and got his pistol, fearing that it might be stolen; that defendant did not have anything to say to deceased in the dining-room, but was talking with the father of the deceased, and that defendant was not intoxicated; that when defendant came out in the office deceased used the language indicated in the statement for the government, or words to that effect, and defendant kicked at him and probably struck him lightly; that when defendant kicked he stepped back and leaned up against the counter and deceased sprang at him and began cutting him with a knife; that deceased cut him in the face and kept on striking at him with the knife, and after he was cut in the face defendant drew his pistol and fired at deceased, who was in the act of striking him again with the knife. The foregoing is in substance the statement of the defendant who testified in his own behalf.

"Proof was also offered tending to show that the reputation of the deceased as a dangerous and lawless man was bad; that the reputation of the defendant as a peaceable and law-abiding man was good, and that the reputation of prosecuting witness Thomas Boseman was bad for truth in the communities where he had resided."

The court delivered an oral charge, occupying twenty-seven pages of the printed record, and embracing a discussion of most of the leading principles in criminal law, as well as many extracts from adjudged cases and elementary treatises.

Referring to the law of self-defence, the court said to the jury:

"A man might be to some extent in the wrong, and yet he might avail himself of the law of self-defence, but what is meant by his being in the lawful pursuit of his business means that he is not himself attempting to kill, or that he is not doing an act which may directly and immediately produce a deadly affray between himself and his adversary. He is not allowed to do either. The only time when he can do an act of that kind is when the condition exists which gives him the right to invoke this law. I say if he is attempting directly to kill, he is not in the lawful pursuit of his business unless it is in his own defence under this law; and when he is doing a wrongful act which immediately contributes to the result -- brings into existence an affray in which violence may be used by the adversary and he may kill because of that violence -- when that is the case, the law says he is so far the author of that violent condition as that he cannot invoke this law of self-defence, and it depends upon the circumstances and conditions of the case whether or not he can invoke the law so far as to have his crime mitigated from murder to manslaughter. Then, when he is in the lawful pursuit of his business -- that is, when he is occupying the relation to the state of case where the killing occurred which I have named -- and then is attacked by another under circumstances which denote an intention to take away his life or to do him some enormous bodily harm, he may lawfully kill the assailant, provided he use all the means in his power otherwise to save his own life or prevent the intended harm, such as retreating as far as he can or disabling his adversary without killing him, if it be in his power. Now, let us go over that again and see what these propositions are. He must be measurably in the right -- and I have defined to you what that means -- and when he is so situated he is attacked, in this case, by Frank Bozeman, the man who was killed, and attacked under circumstances which denoted an intention to take away his life or to do him some enormous bodily harm, he may lawfully kill the assailant, provided he use all the means in his power otherwise to save his own life or prevent the intended harm, such as retreating as far as he can or disabling his adversary without killing him, if it be in his power. This proposition implies that he is measurably in the right. If he is doing any of these things which I will give you after awhile, which deprive him of the law of self-defence because of his own conduct in precipitating a conflict in which he kills, then he is not in the right; he is not doing what he had a right to do, and this proposition of the law of self-defence would not avail him; he could not resort to it, because his own conduct puts him in an attitude where, in the eye of the law, he is by his own wrong the creator of the necessity under which he acts, and he cannot invoke that necessity. The necessity must be one created by the man slain and which was not brought into existence by the direct act of the defendant contributing to that necessity."

After saying that both the accused and the deceased were upon the same plane in respect of the place or house in which they were at the time, each having the right to be there, the court proceeded: "Neither one of them was required to retreat under such circumstances, because the hotel or temporary stopping place of a man may be regarded as his dwelling place, and the law of retreat in a case like that is different from what it would be on the outside. Still, situated as was the defendant and as was the deceased, there was a rule incumbent upon both of them which required that they should use all reasonable means to avoid the condition which led to a deadly conflict, whether that means could have been avoided by keeping out of the affray or by not going into it or by stepping to one side; and this law says again that if a man is in the right, if he stands without being the creator of that condition and that condition is created by the man whom he kills, and the man is doing that in the shape of exercising an act of violence which may destroy his life or inflict great injury upon his person, yet if he could have paralyzed that arm, if he could have turned aside that danger by an act of less deadly character than the one he did exercise, the law says he must do that. If he could have inflicted a less dangerous wound upon the man under the circumstances the law commands him to do that, because when he is doing that he is accomplishing the only purpose the law of self-defence contemplates he has right to accomplish -- that is, to protect himself and not to execute vengeance, not to recklessly, wantonly and wickedly destroy human life, but to protect his own life when he is in the right and the other party is in the wrong."

Mr. Benjamin T. Duval and Mr. William F. Cravens for plaintiff in error.

Mr. Assistant Attorney General Dickinson for defendants in error.

I. The court properly charged that malice must be gathered, as an inference of law, from facts and circumstances proved. It was correct in saying that a man is presumed to intend the natural and probable consequence of his voluntary acts. Clarion Bank v. Jones, 21 Wall. 337; Commonwealth v. York, 9 Met. (Mass.) 93, 103; Commonwealth v. Webster, 5 Cush. 295, 305; People v. Potter, 5 Michigan, 1, 8; People v. Scott, 6 Michigan, 287, 296; United States v. Taintor, 11 Blatchford, 374, 375.

II. The portion of the charge which relates to the right to kill in self-defence when necessary is criticised on two grounds.

(a) It is said that the proof tended to show that defendant had retreated and had declined further contest, and that the above portion of the charge is erroneous because it does not recognize the right of self-defence on the part of one who has begun an affray, has in good faith retired from it, and has thus manifested his purpose, and after that is assailed by his adversary.

This portion of the charge was not upon the particular facts of this case, or upon the theory of either the government or the defence. It was a general declaration of the law of self-defence, confined to a state of facts where the one who does a wrongful act "which immediately contributes to the result" kills his adversary who followed up this act with an attack.

There was no error in what the court said.

Self-defence is no excuse for a homicide if the accused brought on the difficulty and was himself the aggressor. 1 Hale, P.C., 482. Gibson v. State, 89 Alabama, 121; People v. Robertson, 67 California, 646; Kinney v. People, 108 Illinois, 519; State v. Neeley, 20 Iowa, 108; State v. Murdy, 81 Iowa, 603; State v. Scott, 41 Minnesota, 365; Allen v. State, 66 Mississippi, 385; State v. Brittain, 89 N.C. 481; Stewart v. State, 1 Ohio St. 66; Stoffer v. State, 15 Ohio St. 47; State v. Hawkins, 18 Oregon, 476.

This part of the charge had no application to the case of withdrawal from combat assumed in the brief and which is the foundation of the criticism. If the judge did not charge sufficiently, or at all, on that theory, he should have been so requested. No request was preferred.

Therefore, if he charged the law of self-defence correctly as far as he went, the case should not be reversed because he did not extend the charge to a particular theory advanced by defendant. This theory rests on the narrowest of grounds.

There was nothing in the proof for defendant tending to disprove the evidence for the government which tended to show that after they came out of the dining-room defendant accosted deceased. The evidence for the defendant tended to show that immediately after the remark of deceased, which followed this accosting, defendant kicked deceased, and stepped back and leaned up against the counter, and deceased sprang at him, cutting him with a knife, and then defendant shot him. There was no evidence here tending to show a retirement from the affray. The whole tragedy was in one act. There is nothing to indicate any interval.

Even if there be any grounds for saying that this evidence might have indicated such a purpose, it is so slight that the judge ought not to be put in error for not charging upon that aspect of the right of self-defence without a special request. Counsel for defendant were not asleep when the charge was given. They must have been very alert, for they took fifty exceptions.

The record may present sufficient facts to warrant a renewal, if such an instruction had been asked and declined; but the judge should not now be put in error for such cause. The facts which the proof tended to show do not approach what is required to predicate a theory of withdrawal. There must be a withdrawal in good faith, and it must be such as to show the adversary that it is not desired to continue the conflict. The adversary must pursue him. Parker v. State, 88 Alabama, 4; People v. Wong Ah Teak, 63 California, 544; Hittner v. State, 19 Indiana, 48; State v. Dillon, 74 Iowa, 653; Brazzil v. State, 28 Tex. App. 584.

Here there was no retreat, no withdrawal, no pursuit. Can it be that a man can strike another, merely step back and stand his ground, and, when the party assailed strikes back with a deadly weapon, or attempts to shoot, kill him and go free on the plea of self-defence!

(b) That portion of the extract from the charge is assailed which says: "Provided he use all means in his power otherwise to save his own life or prevent the intended harm, such as retreating as far as he can, or disabling his adversary without killing him, if it be in his power." It is said that "defendant could not have retreated farther than he did, and the fierceness of the attack made it impossible to save his life by other means than by slaying his adversary."

What the judge said in this extract about retreating was in the way of a general disquisition. When he came to consider defendant's rights he plainly said that he, being a guest of the hotel, was not bound to retreat at all, as follows: "Upon the question of retreating as far as he can, there is a law which says that if a man is in his dwelling house he need not retreat; and that the hotel where defendant was lodging as a guest or was about to lodge -- was there for his supper anyway -- and where the other man was, put them both upon the same plane. Neither one of them was required to retreat under such circumstances, because the hotel or temporary stopping place of a man may be regarded as his dwelling place, and the law of retreat in a case like that is different from what it would be on the outside."

MR. JUSTICE HARLAN, after stating the case as above reported, delivered the opinion of the court.

> **We think that these portions of the charge (to which the accused duly excepted) were well calculated to mislead the jury. They expressed an erroneous view of the law of self defence.**
>
> **If the jury believed the evidence on behalf of the defence, they might reasonably have inferred from the actions of the accused that he did not intend to make a violent or dangerous personal assault upon the deceased, but only, by kicking at him or kicking him lightly, to express his indignation at the offensive language of the deceased. It should have been submitted to the jury whether the act of the accused in stepping back and leaning against the counter, not in an attitude for personal conflict, was intended to be, and should have been reasonably interpreted as being, a withdrawal by the accused in good faith from further controversy with the deceased.**
>
> **the deceased, despite the efforts of the accused to retire from further contest, sprang at the latter, with knife in hand, for the purpose of taking life, and would most probably have accomplished that object, if the accused had not fired at the moment he did. Under such circumstances, did the law require that the accused should stand still, and permit himself to be cut to pieces, under the penalty that if he met the unlawful attack upon him and saved his own life, by taking that of his assailant, he would be guilty of manslaughter? We think not.**

We think that these portions of the charge (to which the accused duly excepted) were well calculated to mislead the jury. They expressed an erroneous view of the law of self defence. The duty of the jury was to consider the case in the light of all the facts. The evidence on behalf of the government tended to show that the accused sought a difficulty with some one; that on behalf of the accused, would not justify any such conclusion, but rather that he had the reputation of being a peaceable and law-abiding man. But the evidence on both sides was to the effect that the deceased used language of an offensive character for the purpose of provoking a difficulty with the accused, or of subjecting him to the indignity of a personal insult. The offensive words did not, it is true, legally justify the accused in what he did -- the evidence of the government tending to show that "he kicked at deceased, hitting him lightly on the lower part of the leg"; that on the part of the accused tending to show that he "kicked at" the deceased and "probably struck him lightly." According to the evidence of the defence, the accused then "stepped back, and leaned up against the counter," indicating thereby, it may be, that he neither desired nor intended to pursue the matter further. If the jury believed the evidence on behalf of the defence, they might reasonably have inferred from the actions of the accused that he did not intend to make a violent or dangerous personal assault upon the deceased, but only, by kicking at him or kicking him lightly, to express his indignation at the offensive language of the deceased. It should have been submitted to the jury whether the act of the accused in stepping back and leaning against the counter, not in an attitude for personal conflict, was intended to be, and should have been reasonably interpreted as being, a withdrawal by the accused in good faith from further controversy with the deceased. On the contrary, the court, in effect, said that if, because of words used by the deceased, the accused kicked at or kicked the deceased, however lightly, and no matter how offensive those words were, he put himself in a position to make the killing manslaughter, even if the taking of life became, by reason of the suddenness, rapidity and fierceness of the assault of the deceased, absolutely necessary to save his own. By numerous quotations from adjudged cases, the court, by every form of expression, pressed upon the jury the proposition that "a person who has slain another cannot urge in justification of the killing a necessity produced by his own unlawful and wrongful acts." But that abstract principle has no application to this case, if it be true -- as the evidence on behalf of the defence tended to show -- that the first real provocation came from the deceased when he used towards the accused language of an offensive character, and that the accused immediately after kicking at or lightly kicking the deceased, signified by his conduct that he no longer desired controversy with his adversary; whereupon the deceased, despite the efforts of the accused to retire from further contest, sprang at the latter, with knife in hand, for the purpose of taking life, and would most probably have accomplished that object, if the accused had not fired at the moment he did. Under such circumstances, did the law require that the accused should stand still, and permit himself to be cut to pieces, under the penalty that if he met the unlawful attack upon him and saved his own life, by taking that of his assailant, he would be guilty of manslaughter? We think not.

If a person, under the provocation of offensive language, assaults the speaker personally, but in such a way as to show that there is no intention to do him serlous bodily harm, and then retires under such circumstances as show that he does not intend to do anything more, but in good faith withdraws from further contest, his right of self-defence is restored when the person assaulted, in violation of law, pursues him with a deadly weapon and seeks to take his life or do him great bodily harm.

although the defendant originally provoked the conflict, he withdraws from it in good faith, and clearly announces his desire for peace. If he be pursued after this, his right of self-defence, though once lost, revives.

there must be a real and bona fide surrender and withdrawal on his part; for, if there be not, then he will continue to be regarded as the aggressor.

Due caution must be observed by courts and juries in its application, as it involves a principle which is very liable to abuse. The question of the good or bad faith of the retreating party is of the utmost importance

Both parties to a mutual combat are wrong-doers, and the law of self-defence cannot be invoked by either

if one actually and in good faith withdraws from the combat, he ceases to be a wrong-doer

If a person, under the provocation of offensive language, assaults the speaker personally, but in such a way as to show that there is no intention to do him serious bodily harm, and then retires under such circumstances as show that he does not intend to do anything more, but in good faith withdraws from further contest, his right of self-defence is restored when the person assaulted, in violation of law, pursues him with a deadly weapon and seeks to take his life or do him great bodily harm. In Parker v. The State, 88 Alabama, 4, 7, the court, after adverting to the general rule that the aggressor cannot be heard to urge in his justification a necessity for the killing which was produced by his own wrongful act, said: "This rule, however, is not of absolute and universal application. An exception to it exists in cases where, although the defendant originally provoked the conflict, he withdraws from it in good faith, and clearly announces his desire for peace. If he be pursued after this, his right of self-defence, though once lost, revives. 'Of course,' says Mr. Wharton, in referring to this modification of the rule, 'there must be a real and bona fide surrender and withdrawal on his part; for, if there be not, then he will continue to be regarded as the aggressor.' 1 Wharton's Cr. Law, (9th ed.) §486. The meaning of the principle is that the law will always leave the original aggressor an opportunity to repent before he takes the life of his adversary. Bishop's Cr. Law, (7th ed.) §871." Recognizing this exception to be a just one, the court properly said, in addition: "Due caution must be observed by courts and juries in its application, as it involves a principle which is very liable to abuse. The question of the good or bad faith of the retreating party is of the utmost importance, and should generally be submitted to the jury in connection with the fact of retreat itself, especially where there is any room for conflicting inferences on this point from the evidence." Both parties to a mutual combat are wrong-doers, and the law of self-defence cannot be invoked by either, so long as he continues in the combat. But, as said by the Supreme Court of Iowa in State v. Dillon, 74 Iowa, 653, 659, if one "actually and in good faith withdraws from the combat, he ceases to be a wrong-doer; and if his adversary have reasonable ground for holding that he has so withdrawn, it is sufficient, even though the fact is not clearly evinced." See also 1

Bishop's New Crim. Law, §702; People v. Robertson, 67 California, 646, 650; Stoffer's case, 15 Ohio St. 47. In Wharton on Homicide, §483, the author says that "though the defendant may have thus provoked the conflict, yet, if he withdrew from it in good faith and clearly announced his desire for peace, then, if he be pursued, his rights of self defence revive."

It was for the jury to say whether the withdrawal was in good faith, or was a mere device by the accused to obtain some advantage of his adversary.

We do not mean to say that the jury ought to have found that the accused, after kicking the deceased lightly, withdrew in good faith from further contest and that his conduct should have been so interpreted. It was for the jury to say whether the withdrawal was in good faith, or was a mere device by the accused to obtain some advantage of his adversary. But we are of opinion that, under the circumstances, they might have found that the accused, although in the wrong when he kicked or kicked at the deceased, did not provoke the fierce attack made upon him by the latter, with knife in hand, in any sense that would deprive him altogether of the right of self-defence against such attack. If the accused did, in fact, withdraw from the combat, and intended so to do, and if his conduct should have been reasonably so interpreted by the deceased, then the assault of the latter with a deadly weapon, with the intent to take the life of the accused or to do him great bodily harm, entitled the latter to the benefit of the principle announced in Beard v. United States, 158 U.S. 550, 564, in which case it was said: "The defendant was where he had a right to be when the deceased advanced upon him in a threatening manner and with a deadly weapon; and if the accused did not provoke the assault, and had at the time reasonable grounds to believe, and in good faith believed, that the deceased intended to take his life or to do him great bodily harm, he was not obliged to retreat, nor to consider whether he could safely retreat, but was entitled to stand his ground and meet any attack made upon him with a deadly weapon, in such a way and with such force as, under all the circumstances, he, at the moment, honestly believed, and had reasonable grounds to believe, was necessary to save his own life or to protect himself from great bodily injury."

The accused was where he had the right to be, and the law did not require him to step aside when his assailant was rapidly advancing upon him with a deadly weapon. The danger in which the accused was, or believed himself to be, at the moment he fired is to some extent indicated by the fact, proved by the government, that immediately after he disabled his assailant (who had two knives upon his person) he said that he, the accused, was himself mortally wounded and wished a physician to be called.

The accused was entitled, so far as his right to resist the attack was concerned, to remain where he was, and to do whatever was necessary or what he had reasonable grounds to believe at the time was necessary, to save his life or to protect himself from great bodily harm.

under the circumstances, it was error to make the case depend in whole or in part upon the inquiry whether the accused could, by stepping aside, have avoided the attack, or could have so carefully aimed his pistol as to paralyze the arm of his assailant without more seriously wounding him.

The charge, as above quoted, is liable to other objections. The court said that both the accused and the deceased had a right to be in the hotel, and that the law of retreat in a case like that is different from what it would be if they had been on the outside. Still, the court said that, under the circumstances, both parties were under a duty to use all reasonable means to avoid a collision that would lead to a deadly conflict, such as keeping out of the affray, or by not going into it, or "by stepping to one side"; and if the accused could have saved his life, or protected himself against great bodily harm, by inflicting a less dangerous wound than he did upon his assailant, or "if he could have paralyzed that arm," without doing more serious injury, the law commanded him to do so. In other words, according to the theory of the charge, although the deceased sprang at the accused, with knife in hand, for the purpose of cutting him to pieces, yet if the accused could have stepped aside or paralyzed the arm of his assailant, his killing the latter was not in the exercise of the right of self-defence. The accused was where he had the right to be, and the law did not require him to step aside when his assailant was rapidly advancing upon him with a deadly weapon. The danger in which the accused was, or believed himself to be, at the moment he fired is to some extent indicated by the fact, proved by the government, that immediately after he disabled his assailant (who had two knives upon his person) he said that he, the accused, was himself mortally wounded and wished a physician to be called. The accused was entitled, so far as his right to resist the attack was concerned, to remain where he was, and to do whatever was necessary or what he had reasonable grounds to believe at the time was necessary, to save his life or to protect himself from great bodily harm. And under the circumstances, it was error to make the case depend in whole or in part upon the inquiry whether the accused could, by stepping aside, have avoided the attack, or could have so carefully aimed his pistol as to paralyze the arm of his assailant without more seriously wounding him.

Without referring to other errors alleged to have been committed, the judgment below is reversed and the case is remanded for a new trial.

Reversed.

ROBERTSON v. BALDWIN

(CASE EXCERPT)

165 U.S. 275; 17 S. Ct. 326; 41 L. Ed. 715

Argued December 15, 1896. January 25, 1897, Decided

GIST: This is an appeal from dismissal of a petition for writ of habeas corpus. The petitioners were seamen who claimed that their detention, to enforce their service contract, was in violation of the 13th Amendment, which forbids involuntary servitude. The Court affirmed the dismissal of the petition, and explained that all the rights in the Constitution were subject to preexisting common-sense exceptions. In abstractly discussing limits on rights, they said the right of the people to keep and bear arms was not infringed by laws prohibiting concealed carry. In the same sentence they said freedom of speech and of the press did not permit publication of blasphemous or indecent articles, or other publications injurious to public morals. They pointed out that the Bill of Rights didn't invent new rights, it protected existing ones.

MR. JUSTICE BROWN delivered the opinion of the court.

.....

The law is perfectly well settled that the first ten amendments to the Constitution, commonly known as the Bill of Rights, were not intended to lay down any novel principles of government, but simply to embody certain guaranties and immunities which we had inherited from our English ancestors, and which had from time immemorial been subject to certain well-recognized exceptions arising from the necessities of the case.

the right of the people to keep and bear arms (art. 2) is not infringed by laws prohibiting the carrying of concealed weapons

The law is perfectly well settled that the first ten amendments to the Constitution, commonly known as the Bill of Rights, were not intended to lay down any novel principles of government, but simply to embody certain guaranties and immunities which we had inherited from our English ancestors, and which had from time immemorial been subject to certain well-recognized exceptions arising from the necessities of the case. In incorporating these principles into the fundamental law there was no intention of disregarding the exceptions, which continued to be recognized as if they had been formally expressed. Thus, the freedom of speech and of the press (art. 1) does not permit the publication of libels, blasphemous or indecent articles, or other publications injurious to public morals or private reputation; the right of the people to keep and bear arms (art. 2) is not infringed by laws prohibiting the carrying of concealed weapons; the provision that no person shall be twice put in jeopardy (art. 5) does not prevent a second trial, if upon the first trial the jury failed to agree, or if the verdict was set aside upon the defendant's motion, United States v. Ball, 163 U.S. 662, 672; nor does the provision of the same article that no one shall be a witness against himself impair his obligation to testify, if a prosecution against him be barred by the lapse of time, a pardon or by statutory enactment. Brown v. Walker, 161 U.S. 591, and cases cited. Nor does the provision that an accused person shall be confronted with the witnesses against him prevent the admission of dying declarations, or the depositions of witnesses who have died since the former trial.

ANDERSEN v. UNITED STATES

(CASE EXCERPT)
170 U.S. 481; 18 S. Ct. 689; 42 L. Ed. 1116
Argued April 11, 1898
May 9, 1898, Decided

GIST: Andersen, a ship's cook, appealed his conviction for murdering the ship's mate on the high seas. This case reads like a good novel—a small ship in 1879, a cruel captain, a murderous cook running around with three pistols, two bodies dumped overboard, and the ship set ablaze—quite a remarkable tale, and true.

The opening indictment is possibly the worst English in *Supreme Court Gun Cases*. A single 624-word sentence, it is all but indecipherable to a modern reader and was perhaps even worse when written. It uses mind-numbing redundancy and pompous grandiosity of the like, "then and there had and held, then and there piratically, feloniously, wilfully and of his malice aforethought did discharge and shoot off to, against and upon the said William Wallace Saunders, sometimes called William Saunders, with intent him, the said William Wallace Saunders, sometimes called William Saunders, then and there to kill and murder..."

The case itself goes on at length, however, in very readable style, describing the lurid details of the crime and aftermath, with testimony from the shipmates and the defendant. The crew are remarkably uniform in their tale condemning Andersen's actions, who cries out against them for abandoning him, yet on the ship they agreed it was self defense, or so he says.

The fascinating story, taken as a whole, seems to describe Andersen's sure guilt. The Court agreed, rejecting his claims of provocation and self defense. In rejecting Andersen's claims, the Court lays out the precise conditions required for a self-defense claim to win the day, none of which Andersen had. In a bizarre defense tactic, Andersen suggested that since the Mate had been shot and then quickly thrown overboard, the exact cause of death could not be determined. It fell on predictably deaf ears.

Although Anderson apparently committed two murders (the captain and the first mate), he was only tried for the mate's murder. This is because a) there were eye witnesses, b) his self-defense claim in the Captain's quarters, where the first homicide took place, could be an obstacle to the government's case against him, and c) the time between the Captain's murder and the mate's allowed sufficient time to show premeditation at least in the second killing.

The indictment in this case, which is set forth at length in the statement of the case, alleged the murder to have been committed "on the high seas, and within the jurisdiction of this court, and within the admiralty and maritime jurisdiction of the said United States of America, and out of the jurisdiction of any particular State of the said United States of America, in and on board of a certain American vessel." Held, that nothing more was required to show the locality of the offence.

The indictment was claimed to be demurrable because it charged the homicide to have been caused by shooting and drowning, means inconsistent with each other, and not of the same species. Held, that the indictment was sufficient, and was not objectionable on the ground of duplicity or uncertainty.

There was no irregularity in summoning and empaneling the jury.

There was no error in permitting the builder of the vessel on which the crime was alleged to have taken place, to testify as to its general character and situation.

As there was nothing to indicate that antecedent conduct of the captain, an account of which was offered in evidence, was so connected with the killing of the mate as to form part of the res gestae, or that it could have any legitimate tendency to justify, excuse or mitigate the crime for the commission of which he was on trial, there was no error in excluding the evidence relating to it.

After the Government had closed its case in chief, defendant's counsel moved that a verdict of not guilty be directed, because the indictment charged that the mate met his death by drowning, whereas the proof showed that his death resulted from the pistol shots. Held, that there was no error in denying this motion.

While a homicide, committed in actual defence of life or limb, is excusable if it appear that the slayer was acting under a reasonable belief that he was in imminent danger of death or great bodily harm from the deceased, and that his act was necessary in order to avoid death or harm, where there is manifestly no adequate or reasonable ground for such belief, or the slayer brings on the difficulty for the purpose of killing the deceased, or violation of law on his part is the reason of his expectation of an attack, the plea of self-defence cannot avail.

The evidence offered as to the general reputation of the captain was properly excluded.

As the testimony of the accused did not develop the existence of any facts which operated in law to reduce the crime from murder to manslaughter, there was no error in instructing the jury to that effect.

ERROR TO THE CIRCUIT COURT OF THE UNITED STATES FOR THE EASTERN DISTRICT OF VIRGINIA.

ANDERSEN was indicted in the Circuit Court of the United States for the Eastern District of Virginia, for the murder of William Wallace Saunders, on an American vessel, on the high seas, of which vessel Saunders was the mate and Andersen the cook.

The indictment charged that Andersen --

"On the sixth day of August, in the year of our Lord one thousand eight hundred and ninety-seven, with force and arms, on the high seas and within the jurisdiction of this court and within the admiralty and maritime jurisdiction of the said United States of America, and out of the jurisdiction of any particular State of the said United States of America, in and on board of a certain American vessel, the same being then and there a schooner called and named 'Olive Pecker,' then and there belonging to a citizen or citizens of the said United States of America whose name or names is or are to the grand jurors aforesaid unknown, in and upon one William Wallace Saunders, sometimes called William Saunders, then and there being on board said vessel, did piratically, wilfully, feloniously and of his malice aforethought make an assault, and that the said John Andersen, alias John Anderson, a certain pistol then and there charged with gunpowder and leaden bullets, which said pistol he, the said John Andersen, alias John Anderson, in his hand (but which hand is to the said jurors unknown) then and there had and held, then and there piratically, feloniously, wilfully and of his malice aforethought did discharge and shoot off to, against and upon the said William Wallace Saunders, sometimes called William Saunders, with intent him, the said William Wallace Saunders, sometimes called William Saunders, then and there to kill and murder, and that the said John Andersen, alias John Anderson, with the leaden bullets aforesaid out of the pistol by the said John Andersen, alias John Anderson, discharged and shot off as aforesaid, then, to wit: On the said sixth day of August, in the year of our Lord one thousand eight hundred and ninety-seven, and there, to wit: On the high seas as aforesaid, in and on board of the said American vessel, and within the admiralty and maritime jurisdiction of the said United States of America and within the jurisdiction of this court, and out of the jurisdiction of any particular State of the United States of America, piratically, feloniously, wilfully and of his malice aforethought did strike, penetrate and wound the said William Wallace Saunders, sometimes called William Saunders, in and upon the head of him, the said William Wallace Saunders, sometimes called William Saunders, (and in and upon other parts of the body of him, the said William Wallace Saunders, sometimes called William Saunders, to the said jurors unknown,) giving to him, the said William Wallace Saunders, sometimes called William Saunders, then and there, with the leaden bullets aforesaid, so as aforesaid discharged and shot off out of the pistol aforesaid by the said John Andersen, alias John Anderson, with the intent aforesaid, in and upon the head of him, the said William Wallace Saunders, sometimes called William Saunders, (and in and upon other parts of the body of him, the said William Wallace Saunders, sometimes called William Saunders, to the said jurors unknown,) several grievous, dangerous and mortal wounds, and the said John Andersen, alias John Anderson, did then and there, to wit: At the time and place last above mentioned, him, the said William Wallace Saunders, sometimes called William Saunders, piratically, feloniously, wilfully and of his malice aforethought cast and throw from and out of the said vessel into the sea, and plunge, sink and drown him, the said William Wallace Saunders, sometimes called William Saunders, in the sea aforesaid, or which said mortal wounds, casting, throwing, plunging, sinking and drowning the said William Wallace Saunders, sometimes called William

Saunders, in and upon the high seas aforesaid, out of the jurisdiction of any particular State of the United States of America, then and there instantly died.

"And the grand jurors aforesaid, upon their oath aforesaid, do say that by reason of the casting and throwing of the said William Wallace Saunders, sometimes called William Saunders, in the sea as aforesaid, they cannot describe the said mortal wounds with greater particularity."

.....

A jury was thereupon duly empaneled and sworn and the trial proceeded with, and during its progress exceptions to the admission and exclusion of evidence and the giving and refusal of instructions were preserved by defendant. At the close of the Government's case in chief, defendant's counsel moved the court to instruct the jury to bring in a verdict of "not guilty" on the ground that defendant was indicted for the murder of Saunders by drowning, whereas the evidence showed that he met his death by the discharge of a pistol. The court overruled the motion and defendant excepted. A verdict of guilty having been returned, defendant made successive motions for a new trial and in arrest of judgment, which were severally overruled, whereupon he was sentenced to be executed. This writ of error was then sued out, the cause docketed, and duly argued at the bar.

The bill of exceptions contained the following preliminary statement of uncontroverted facts:

"That the American three-masted schooner 'Olive Pecker' sailed from Boston, Massachusetts, on the 20th day of June, 1897, for Buenos Ayres, South America, with a cargo of lumber under and on deck. She had on board a captain, J. W. Whitman; a mate, William Wallace Saunders, sometimes called William Saunders; an engineer of a donkey engine, William Horsburgh; a cook, viz., the defendant, John Andersen, and four seamen, viz., Martin Barstad, a native of Norway; John Lind, a native of Sweden; Juan de Dios Barrial, a native of Spain, and Andrew March, a native of Newfoundland; that the said 'Olive Pecker' was an American vessel, belonging to citizens of the United States; that the said vessel proceeded from Boston on her course to her port of destination until the morning of August 6, 1897, when, on the high seas and about 100 or 150 miles off the Brazilian coast, between nine and ten o'clock on that morning, the captain, Whitman, was shot in his cabin, and shortly thereafter the mate was shot on the left-hand side of the forecastle head and his body immediately thrown into the sea. The body of the captain was also thrown into the sea. Several hours thereafter the said vessel 'Olive Pecker' was burned and the cook, engineer and four seamen took to the sea in an open boat. Twenty-eight or thirty hours thereafter they reached the Brazilian coast, where, having spent the night on shore, they separated the next morning, the accused and John Lind going in a northerly direction and the other four going in a southerly direction. That the accused and Lin, within a few days, reached Bahia, in Brazil. Both shipped, the accused on a vessel called the 'Bernadotte,' bound for Pensacola, in the United States, and Lind on a Brazilian barkentine, bound for some point in Spain. The other four men, having the Spaniard as their spokesman, he being familiar with the language of the country, and not finding an American consul, made known to the Brazilian authorities what had transpired on the 'Olive Pecker,' with the request that telegrams be sent along the coast for the arrest of the accused, John Andersen. These four men, having secured passes on a vessel to Bahia, arrived there several days after the arrest of the accused, and were placed in charge of the American consul at that port. The accused handed to the American consul a statement in his own handwriting, purporting to be an account of the voyage of the 'Olive Pecker,' and also made to the American consul a sworn statement, as did also the other five men, which said statements were duly transmitted to the Department of State at Washington, and upon the call of defendant's counsel were produced for his use at the trial, but were not produced in evidence.

"At the direction of the Government at Washington, the American consul at Bahia kept the accused and the five men in custody at Bahia until the arrival at that port some time in the month of September, 1897, of the United States man-of-war 'Lancaster,' when they were put on board of that vessel and brought into Hampton Roads, Virginia, in the Eastern District of Virginia, that being the first district into which the accused was brought after the commission of the alleged offence; and the said accused, together with the five men, was turned over by the officers of the 'Lancaster' to the United States marshal on the 7th day of November, 1897, and were duly placed in confinement in the city jail at Norfolk, Virginia."

The evidence introduced on the trial was given in full, and included the testimony of the four seamen, Barstad, Lind, Barrial and March, and the engineer Horsburgh, on behalf of the Government, and that of the defendant on his own behalf. A considerable portion is set forth in the margin. n1

n1 Barstad, who was at the wheel when the mate was shot, testified:

I saw him shoot him.

"I last saw William Saunders, the mate of the said vessel, alive on the morning of August the 6th, 1897, on the left side of the forecastle head of that vessel. It was between nine and ten o'clock of that morning. He was shot at that time and place by John Andersen, the cook of the vessel and the prisoner here. I saw him shoot him. I was at the wheel of the vessel in the wheelhouse, just aft of the after-cabin.

the mate started down and said, 'What you got in your hands, cook?' 'I got guns,' he says. 'Where you get them?' says the mate. 'Down in the cabin,' he says.

Then Andersen fired a shot. The mate reeled and faced him, and said, 'For God's sake don't shoot me, cook.' The cook fired another shot, and the mate kept on reeling; and the cook fired another one, and a third one, when the mate fell, and he shot him once after he had fallen.

"I heard a report of a shot in the captain's cabin, which was connected with the wheelhouse by the after companionway. Immediately after I saw John Andersen, the accused, come running up the after companionway and through the wheelhouse, with a pistol in each hand and one in his hip pocket. He ran up to John Lind, who was standing amidships by the rigging of the middle mast. He said something to Lind, but I did not hear what it was. I heard him sing out to the mate, Saunders, who was up on the cross-tree of the foremast, at work in the rigging, and say, 'Come down, Mr. Saunders.' The mate said, 'What do you want, steward?' In a little while the mate finished the job and started down the rigging. When about midway down, and when the cook, Andersen, was standing on top of the forward house, the mate started down and said, 'What you got in your hands, cook?' 'I got guns,' he says. 'Where you get them?' says the mate. 'Down in the cabin,' he says. The mate came down and stepped on the forecastle head, not on the forecastle house. Then Andersen fired a shot. The mate reeled and faced him, and said, 'For God's sake don't shoot me, cook.' The cook fired another shot, and the mate kept on reeling; and the cook fired another one, and a third one, when the mate fell, and he shot him once after he had fallen. Then the cook sung out to the men, who were in the forecastle, 'I am in charge of this vessel; I am next to the mate.' He sung out again, 'Won't you fellows come out?' They came out, and I saw them throw the mate's body overboard. I was at the wheel all the time. Then he marched the whole gang aft and went down in the cabin and brought the captain up and threw him overboard. He then said, 'If any man like he can put me in irons.' He had two or three pistols, one in his hands then. He had said he was in charge of the vessel and had ordered the men to throw the mate and captain overboard. I was at the wheel all the time. Then he says, 'Boys, come down and have a drink.' He went down in the captain's cabin and handed a bottle of whiskey, about two parts full. He gave each a drink and took one himself. Then he marched the whole gang up on deck, just outside the door of the wheelhouse, and said, 'You know all you men is guilty for helping me throw the bodies over the side.'

"The Spaniard told him to keep the vessel off, to clew up the gaff topsails and jibs, the outer jib, and make for port. The cook said, 'Damn; you want me to get hung.' We said, 'No, steward, we don't want you to get hung.' All the time he was armed. After a little he said to the Spaniard, 'You the only sensible man amongst the crowd; I want to speak to you.' Then he called John Lind afterwards and spoke to him. I don't know what he said. He ordered the men to do so and so. I left the wheel and went to the forecastle. The rest of the men came forward to get their clothes. He ordered us to get our best clothes, and no more; he said take no discharges, bank books, nothing. He ordered the men down in the booby hatch to get up a barrel addressed to the American consul at Buenos Ayres. Then he told me to go down in the galley to tap some paraffine oil. I said 'No.' He says, 'You go,' and handed his pistol in my face. 'All right,' I says, 'steward.' I filled three buckets and passed them up, and Andrew March took it and threw it on the deck-load. He was standing there armed all the time. Then he, the cook, ordered me to take the wheel. I went. The first fire commenced at the booby hatch; the next was forward. The boat was lowered and provisions put in it." . . . "It was twelve or one o'clock when we left the 'Olive Pecker.' No vessels were in sight which could have picked up the bodies of the mate and captain."

He then gave the particulars of the sail to the shore; the arrest; etc.

This witness further said that when Andersen called to Saunders to come down --

"The mate asked him, 'What do you want, steward?' He finished his job and hung the marlin spike around his neck and came down the rigging. The marlin spike had a half hitch on the point, which put the point upwards. That is the way sailors do it to keep the point from striking them as they go up and down the rigging.

"There was nothing to keep me from seeing the mate in the rigging and when he came down, and all along the vessel on her port side to where the shooting occurred. The sails were all swinging to starboard. The lumber was so piled on the deck that a man running along on it would run right on top of the forward house. John Andersen was standing on top of the forward house when he shot the mate, and the mate was standing on the forecastle deck. The forecastle deck is about three feet lower than the top of the house where the cook was standing. The body of the mate was lying, when picked up, on the forecastle head, on the left side of the vessel."

I mean to tell the jury that five of us were intimidated by that one man, the cook—the cook with the pistols. He intimidated us so that when he ordered us to burn the ship

we obeyed.

On cross-examination he said: "I mean to tell the jury that five of us were intimidated by that one man, the cook -- the cook with the pistols. He intimidated us so that when he ordered us to burn the ship we obeyed. He was following us up all the time. He ordered one to go there and another to go there, and another one there. We had to follow the man at the point of the pistol or else get killed. We did what we were told to do through his pistol." . . . "When the mate came down out of the rigging, he asked the cook, 'What have you got in your hands, steward?' The steward said, 'I got guns.' The mate came down, stepped on the forecastle head, and John Andersen fired a shot. The marlin spike was not in the mate's hand, but was hanging around his neck, with the point up. I am sure of that, though I was a hundred and fifty feet away. I did not have a glass. the mate was standing with his hands at his side, with the marlin spike around his neck. He did not make any hostile demonstration towards the cook. He did not come at him to strike him. I am positive of that. I do not know the mate had threatened the cook's life."

Lind testified:

I said, 'You better look out because the cook is on deck with revolvers.'

"I last saw Mate William Saunders on the 6th of August of this year; he was killed that morning by John Andersen on the forecastle head, on the left or port side thereof. I saw Andersen just before the shooting of the mate that morning, coming up from the cabin through the after companionway and through the wheelhouse; I was standing amidships; he came up with a revolver in each hand; he cam right up to me and asked me where the mate was, and said, 'I have killed the captain, and now the mate goes too.' The mate was then aloft, in the rigging of the foremast. I went then down on the lee or starboard side of the vessel to the forecastle house; I went and called the watch below in the forecastle house. I said, 'You better look out because the cook is on deck with revolvers.' As I was calling through the window I could not see on the left of the vessel. While I was calling to the men I heard a shot on the port side, on the forecastle head. I heard three or four shots, I don't know exactly how many. I heard the steward call to the men to come out, for all of them to come up there. He was calling the men in the forecastle house. He said he wanted us to throw the body overboard. When I came up, all hands were there except the man at the wheel, Martin Barstad. The mate was lying on the forecastle head with his face downward. He had a marlin spike tied around his neck. A marlin spike is used for splicing ropes, an instrument that all sailors carry aloft when they go up to splice a rope; it is carried around the neck by a long lanyard and a half hitch on the point to keep it from sticking in his legs. We threw the body overboard. Then the cook told us to come aft and get the captain's body overboard. We went in the after cabin and found the captain sitting in his chair; sitting like this, sir, with his hands folded in his lap. He looked as if he was alive. I saw blood on the side of his head, on the left side. We were told to take him up by Andersen; he helped. He was taken up and thrown overboard. Andersen was armed all this time. Before throwing the captain's body overboard, Andersen took hold of the captain's arm and felt his pulse. When the body was thrown overboard, Andersen cursed it. The captain's body was sitting in a chair in the after cabin, near the sofa on the starboard side of the cabin. He was facing forward. I had only been in the cabin once before, when we were in Boston. On American vessels seamen do not go in the captain's cabin unless they are sent or called there. There are doors opening from the forward cabin into the after cabin and from the mate's room into these cabins.

"After the captain's body was thrown overboard, Andersen told us to go down and he would give us a drink. We went down in the cabin, in the forward cabin where the dining-room table was, and got a drink. I don't recollect whether Andersen drank with us or not. There was not much liquor in the bottle, a little over half a bottle I think, not enough to make any one drunk. I didn't see any one drunk. After taking a drink, we went up on deck and talked about making the small sails fast. The Spaniard and myself suggested that the small sails be made fast and to make for land. This was not done. Andersen said, 'No, keep her up to her course,' -- she was off a little. 'Keep her up to her course,' he said; 'you want me to be hanged?' He then said to the Spaniard, 'You are about the sensiblest man; I want to speak to you.' I did not hear what he said to him. He then called me. I went to the lee side of the wheelhouse and he asked me what I thought was best to do with the vessel. I said, 'The only thing we can do now is to try to make for some land.' He said, 'No, nothing is going to be done but to destroy the vessel.' He did not say anything more to me after that. If he spoke to any of the rest, I didn't see or hear it. He then ordered everything to make ready for to leave the ship. The old boat sail was all tore up and I started to patch that. I was engaged about it about an hour I should think. He then gave orders to lower the boat. Me and the Spaniard lowered the boat. It was the big boat you see hanging at the stern in the picture. Me and the Spaniard did lower the boat and Andrew March went down and unhooked the tackle, and we hauled the boat up alongside the vessel and got some provisions down there. Then the cook called Andrew and he went up. After I was through with that I went up on the house again and I saw flames coming out of the after hatch. She was afire then. Then they all went down in the boat and all hands cut the boat adrift, rigged up the mast and started to sail. The cook helped us to rig up the mast and sail. He was armed all that time with pistols. I do not think any other members of the crew had pistols. I did not see any of them have pistols." . . . "There were no vessels sighted after the bodies of the captain and mate were thrown overboard which could possibly have picked up the bodies."

On cross-examination this witness gave an account of a difficulty between the cook and the captain that morning about the captain's dog. About eight o'clock the captain's dog was down by the galley door and the cook threw some water on him. The dog ran up on the deck load "hollering." The captain came up and said to the cook, "Did you throw hot water on that dog?" Andersen replied that he did not throw hot water on him; that it was cold. The captain felt the dog's back and then called the cook a liar, cursed him and struck him. Lind did not see the captain strike the cook but heard the noise in the galley. Shortly after this the cook appealed to the mate, "Won't you protect me until we get to port?" To this the mate replied, "Get to port! You will get killed anyhow," or something like that. "'Go to hell -- you will get killed anyhow,' or something like that."

March testified:

"After the shooting the cook came and called us out of the forecastle. He says, 'Come out here, boys, lower the boat and put me ashore. The captain and mate is dead and I am in charge of this ship.' I got out of the bed and put on my shoes in a hurry, and the cook came back a second time and says, 'Come out here, won't you? Come out here, Manuel,' and he says, 'Yes.' We went out and went on the topgallant forecastle, and he ordered us to throw the mate overboard. The mate was lying on the forecastle head, on the left-hand side. The sails of the vessel were swinging at that time to the starboard, which left the left-hand side of the vessel clear back to the wheelhouse. The cook was armed when he ordered the mate's body to be thrown overboard, and he claimed then to be in charge of the vessel. I do not remember whether he caught hold of the mate's body and helped to throw it overboard or not. The mate had a marlin spike tied around his neck when the body was throw overboard. A marlin spike is a big awl used to stick through the rope in splicing it. When it is used by a man going up and down the rigging a half hitch is taken over the point so it won't stick in his legs or get between the rigging going down. When it is around the man's neck it is tied with a string and with a half hitch on the point. He can't use it without taking the hitch off so as to hurt anybody with it. The top of the forecastle house, where the cook was standing when he shot the mate, is about three feet higher than the forecastle deck, where the mate was standing when he was shot. To get to where Andersen was when he was shot, the mate would have had to step up those three feet on top of the forecastle house." . . . "I couldn't say whether the half hitch was around the point or not.

He swore at it when the body was thrown into the sea, calling it 'a mean bastard.'

"After the mate's body was thrown overboard we were ordered to the cabin to take the captain up and throw him overboard. The cook was armed at that time. When the mate's body was thrown overboard Andersen swore oaths at it. When he swore oaths at the body the Spaniard asked him not to curse the body that way. We all obeyed the cook and went aft and found the captain's body in the after cabin. (Here the witness identified the diagram, showing the inside of the after cabin, and marked number two.) The captain's body was found sitting in his chair, dead, with both arms folded in his lap. He looked as if he was alive, with his head back on one side and a wound in the left part of his head, about an inch above the left ear. The captain was sitting in his chair near the sofa, on the starboard side of the vessel, the point marked on the diagram 'A.' John Andersen ordered the captain's body to be taken up and thrown overboard. Andersen was at that time armed. He assisted in throwing the body overboard. He swore at it when the body was thrown into the sea, calling it 'a mean bastard.' After the body of the captain was thrown overboard the steward ordered us to get ready the boat. He then invited us down into the cabin to get a drink of whiskey. There was about two thirds of a bottle of whiskey. He drank with us. After that was done the boat was got ready. Kerosene oil was thrown over the deck load and the ship was set on fire. Then we made for land in the sail boat. It was about two hours, I think, after the bodies were thrown overboard before we left the 'Olive Pecker.' At the time these bodies were thrown overboard there was no vessel in sight which could possibly have picked them up."

* * *

That morning before the captain was shot and before the mate was shot I heard a difficulty between the cook and the captain about the captain's dog.

"That morning before the captain was shot and before the mate was shot I heard a difficulty between the cook and the captain about the captain's dog. As I was going forward from taking my dishes back from my breakfast, I heard the dog holler. I was standing on the forecastle house. I saw the dog come out and run aft. The captain came out and went to the galley and asked the cook if he had been throwing water on the dog, and he said no. The captain went back and felt the dog. Then I saw the captain go in the galley, but I did not know what he did there. This was about fifteen or twenty minutes, I think, before the captain was shot. I had been at the wheel of the 'Olive Pecker' many times. While standing at the wheel, in the wheelhouse, looking forward, with the sails swinging to the right or starboard side of the vessel, you can see all the way along the left-hand side of the ship, on top the forecastle house, or a man standing on top the forecastle house. The deck load did not interfere with seeing that."

this man intimidated us all at the pistol's point. He ordered us to throw the mate overboard. I obeyed his orders, because I wanted my life a little longer.

We had to throw the body of the captain overboard because the cook ordered us to do it. I took orders from the cook because he gave me to understand he was in charge of the ship. At the time I knew he was, because he had all the guns. It makes a big difference when he had all the arms."

On cross-examination: "I say this man intimidated us all at the pistol's point. He ordered us to throw the mate overboard. I obeyed his orders, because I wanted my life a little longer. After the captain was thrown overboard, we all went into the cabin and took a drink. I can't say that we took a drink at the pistol's point, but he made us throw the mate's body overboard. He did not tell me he would kill me if I did not, but I knew enough to know he would do it. There were four of us altogether. I did not have a knife. I do not know whether I went ahead or who went ahead when we went into the cabin to take a drink. We had to throw the body of the captain overboard because the cook ordered us to do it. I took orders from the cook because he gave me to understand he was in charge of the ship. At the time I knew he was, because he had all the guns. It makes a big difference when he had all the arms."

Barrial testified:

"I last saw Mate Saunders alive on board that vessel on the morning of the 6th of August, 1897, when the vessel was about a hundred or a hundred and fifty miles off the Brazilian coast. On that morning I left the wheel of the vessel about 8 o'clock, being relieved by Martin Barstad, and went after my breakfast; then went to the forecastle and to my cabin. While I was lying down, after that -- I do not know how long -- I heard the captain's dog holler. Andrew March came in the forecastle and says, 'the captain is having a racket with the cook,' and I says, 'What can we do? Let him racket,' says I, and it was a little while before John Lind came and knocked at the window where I was sleeping. When he finished talking to me I heard the report of four shots. I went in the forecastle in a narrow place between the engine room and my bunk. I went in there because I thought the cook wanted to kill us too. The engineer jumped on my bunk and got out, too. I heard the cook sing out in the door, 'Come out here, boys! Come out here quick!' 'Yes, sir,' says I, 'let me finish dressing.' He says, 'Come out here. I am in charge of the vessel.' I went out and the first thing I saw was the mate lying on the top of the forecastle deck on the left-hand side, with his face downwards. The cook says, 'Throw him overboard,' and then I says, 'Don't, cook; don't throw him overboard, he's alive.' He says, 'Throw him overboard; he's dead enough.' We threw him overboard, and after we threw him overboard the cook says, 'Now go aft and pick the captain up.' When he threw the body overboard he cursed at the body. Then he ordered the men aft to throw the captain overboard. All the while he was armed with pistols. We went under his orders and into the captain's cabin. When we got in the cabin we saw the captain sitting in his chair with both hands in his lap, and his head leaning slightly to one side and on his breast. I though he was alive. I saw he had a bullet to go through near the left side of his dead. His body was taken up and thrown overboard. When his body was thrown overboard, the cook cursed it also. After it was thrown over he said, 'Come on, boys, I will give you a drink.' We took a drink, and after we took a drink all came on deck and I said, 'We will make the staysails and the topsails fast and if a squall strikes her we can manage the other sails, and we go right into Rio de Janeiro or Bahia.' I sung out to Martin Barstad at the wheel, 'Keep her off,' and the cook says, 'No, I don't want to go to the land.' He was standing close to the rail. And he said, 'Do you want me to be hung? There is nothing to be done but destroy the vessel,' he said. Then he called me and said to me, 'You are the sensiblest man on board this vessel, and I want to speak to you.' 'All right, cook,' I says. He took me on top the galley and says, 'I am a murderer, and I killed these people to save my life and your lives. Now, you fellows,' he says, 'you are guilty of helping me throw the bodies overboard, and before you leave the vessel you will be as guilty as I am. You ain't got nothing to fear.' Says he, 'Many a vessel leaves port and they don't know where they go, and there's nobody to look after us for a long, long time, and we will have time to run away.' I told him I had nothing to fear with the vessel in port. I says, 'Look here, cook, destroy the vessel, it's a terrible thing, it's worse than what you have done already. Call all hands here and tell us what you want to do and where you want us to sail ashore, and we will help you as much as we can, and let us go into port.' 'No, no,' he says, 'that won't do; the vessel must be burned.' He ordered a small boat to be made ready, and everything was made ready and then he took us down into the cabin and he say, 'I didn't kill these people to rob the vessel. I grant you all fellows clothes out of this large chest,' and we went in and everybody took some clothes, and the cook says, "You fellows can put on your best clothes,' and he gave me a suit of clothes, and he says, 'You don't want to take anything;' so we went forward and put on our best suit of clothes, and the cook had us to pour oil on the deck. The cook called us to hurry up and spread the oil on the deck. I didn't want to do this. I went to the forecastle and the cook came and said, 'What are you doing there? Come and give your hand with this oil.' I says, 'Yes, cook; let me finish shaving and I go.' When I went on deck I could see that the oil was already. It had been spread over the deck. The cook then told us to lower a boat and it was lowered, and Andrew March unhooked the tackle and we took the boat alongside the vessel and I jumped in too. Provisions were then put in the boat and when everything was ready Andersen called to me, 'Come up and light the fire.' 'Well,' I says, 'let me keep the lookout on the boat; it might smash against the vessel.' So he called Andrew March, and the first time he called Andrew he did not come, so he called him again in wild words and March went up."

On cross-examination: "Q. After the cook here had killed the mate, didn't he tell you you might put him in irons? A. You, sir; he came and he says, 'Now you fellows can put me in irons and carry me to port, if you want.' Q. And give me to the American consul? A. No, sir; the same words I told you, sir. 'Now you fellows,' he says, 'can put me in irons and take me in port if you want.' I says, 'No, no, cook, I no put you in irons,' because he looked right in my face; and I says, 'Why don't you throw your revolvers away?' Q. He offered to give himself up to you, holding out his hands, and said: 'Put me in irons?' A. He didn't throw his revolvers away. Q. He didn't? A. No, he didn't. Q. Did he hold out his hands to put him in irons? A. With his revolvers, yes; and I says, 'No, no, cook, I won't put you in irons; no, no.' Q. Do you mean to say he had the revolvers in his hands when he offered you to put him in irons? A. Yes, sir."

Horsburgh was asleep in his berth in the after cabin when the captain was shot. What he supposed was the noise of the shooting of the captain awakened him, and then Andersen came to the companionway and asked him to come on deck, that he had killed the captain. He came on deck and went aft along the starboard side, where he told the crew that the cook had killed the captain. Directly after the shots, the cook came forward, shouting, "Come out, boys: I am in charge of the vessel," and ordered the mate's body to be thrown overboard. The mate was lying with his face down on the port side of the forecastle head, with a marlin spike hanging about his neck. After the mate's body was thrown overboard, the cook ordered them to go aft and throw the captain's body overboard. "We went down in the cabin and found the captain in the chair so we took him up on deck and threw him overboard. Then after that he told us to go down and he would give us a drink; so we went down in the cabin and had a drink." After that the cook ordered them to get the boat ready with provisions, etc. The cook wad armed and witness was frightened. The burning of the vessel and the escape in the open boat as told by this witness corresponded with that of the others. On the cross-examination the difficulty between the captain and the cook about the captain's dog was reiterated.

Defendant Andersen testified in his own behalf:

I was looking around there for some place to run into and hide, as the captain was coming down there into the galley, and I was standing in the middle of the floor of the galley, facing the galley dresser. He struck me in the side here, and that sent me right on top the red-hot stove, on top the pots and pans. He commenced to curse me and threaten me and everything, and I pleaded to him. I says, 'Captain, don't hurt me; don't hurt me, Captain.'

he looked at me; he says, 'You whore's son,' he says, 'I will have the heart out of you.'

I didn't know whether I would live to see the next day or not, so I turned to the mate, with tears rolling down my cheeks, and I said to him, 'Mr. Saunders,' I says, 'won't you protect me until we get into port?' He turned around to me with scorn. He says, 'Go to hell,' he says, 'you will get killed anyhow.' Then I did not know what I was doing.

I commenced sweeping the cabin and started into the mate's room first. I saw the mate's gun lying on the shelf, and I took that down, thinking if worst come to worst, I will have to defend myself.

he took up that bottle like this. He says, 'You whore's son!' Then he took it up like this as if to split my head open, when I pulled my gun out and fired. The bullet struck him in the left temple.

I ran into the captain's room then and got his two guns. He used to keep one gun in under the pillow and one on the shelf.

He got this hitch off the marlin spike and came around to me like this to take the marlin spike off his neck and shove the marlin spike into me. I pulled the gun and shot him.

"It was just after breakfast, and the dog was standing at the galley door. He used to keep himself around there all the time. The captain didn't want him to stay at the galley door, and I took some water I had left in a bucket, some dirty water, to throw it onto the dog, as I always used to throw some water on him, and he used to run and holler. I took the bucket, and there was a little water left at the bottom of it. He was standing right at the door and I had been giving him his breakfast. As the dog turned the bucket slipped in my hand. I had the handle on the edge of it, and it hit him here in the leg, and he ran up on deck and made a noise. I was looking around there for some place to run into and hide, as the captain was coming down there into the galley, and I was standing in the middle of the floor of the galley, facing the galley dresser. He struck me in the side here, and that sent me right on top the red-hot stove, on top the pots and pans. He commenced to curse me and threaten me and everything, and I pleaded to him. I says, 'Captain, don't hurt me; don't hurt me, Captain.' He looked at the axe, and he looked up through the slide. There is a little slide in the galley. He saw John Lind standing on top there, and he looked at me; he says, 'You whore's son,' he says, 'I will have the heart out of you.' And there he left me standing. I had cut them two fingers into my knuckles. The mate came along, and it was my last hopes in that vessel to see maybe another day; I had been sleeping in the galley for a week; I didn't know whether I would live to see the next day or not, so I turned to the mate, with tears rolling down my cheeks, and I said to him, 'Mr. Saunders,' I says, 'won't you protect me until we get into port?' He turned around to me with scorn. He says, 'Go to hell,' he says, 'you will get killed anyhow.' Then I did not know what I was doing. My mind was in that condition I didn't know whether to run overboard or to stay there and go and hide. I didn't know what to do. So I went up in the galley slide and looked around to see if I could see any vessel. Then I made up my mind if I should see any vessel I should take a board and jump overboard. So there I was. My basket of dishes was standing upon the dresser, and dirty, after breakfast, and I was washing them, and I saw at the time it was twenty-five minutes to ten then. I looked around, and I didn't know if I had washed my dishes at all. Of course I was completely out of my head then, so I thought about the cabin. Now, I used to sweep that cabin every morning and dust it and everything before nine o'clock. I used to have my dishes done in the galley before this time, and I had my dinner to have ready before twelve o'clock. So I started into the cabin, thinking that the captain would be on deck, and I came down in the cabin. He was sitting inside of the door in a chair like this, although bigger, and he had a bottle on this here lounge which was alongside of the stool or the chair. He glared at me and he looked fairly black in the face with rage. He blurted out and cursed me when I came into the cabin. Well, I didn't know what to do. If I should run on deck, I would have to run overboard; that was the only way I have to see out of it. I commenced sweeping the cabin and started into the mate's room first. I saw the mate's gun lying on the shelf, and I took that down, thinking if worst come to worst, I will have to defend myself. So I finished the cabin and started into the captain's room. I passed by him in that direction [indicating by gesture], and he took up that bottle like this. He says, 'You whore's son!' Then he took it up like this as if to split my head open, when I pulled my gun out and fired. The bullet struck him in the left temple. He fell into the chair, and I ran into the captain's room. Then I though about the mate. I ran into the captain's room then and got his two guns. He used to keep one gun in under the pillow and one on the shelf. I ran up on deck and I didn't know where the mate was then. I came up to John Lind and he was at the main rigging. I says, 'Where is the mate?' He says, 'He is aloft.' I looked up there, and I think I said something of calling him down, but I don't think I did do that. The mate came down, and before he came down to the -----, piece next to the rail, he says, 'Where in the h--ll did you get them guns?' He says, 'And where is the captain?' I never made no answer to him, but I stayed on top of that house there as the mate came down, and he had this marlin spike around his neck. I will just show you how he had it, if you please. He had this hitch on this marlin spike, as represented to you before. He came down like this and walked up like this [indicating by appropriate gestures] (walking towards the bowsprit) and turned in this direction (to the right) and came towards me in that direction (on the starboard side). He took the half hitch out of the marlin spike like this, and the marlin spike was hanging down when he came towards me. I was standing there and had the guns then. I had three of them and I held them in my hand all the time. I had an apron around my waist, and I had no pockets here in the pants. He got this hitch off the marlin spike and came around to me like this [indicating by proper gesture] to take the marlin spike off his neck and shove the marlin spike into me. I pulled the gun and shot him. The first shot struck him here somewhere (in the side). He was still coming towards me, and I shot twice or three times together, when the man fell dead. In the meantime John Lind has been running into the lee side of the house. Now, he stated here yesterday to you gentlemen that I came up to him and says, 'Now the mate will go, too.' But that belongs on the lee side of the house; to that man. When he came there he told them, 'Now the mate will go, too.'

"Q. You mean by that that you didn't say it at all?

"A. No, sir. That belongs to John Lind and into the lee side of the forecastle; that is where that belongs. So I stood there, and John Lind -- he was the man that came up first, and there was nobody else came up -- so I says, 'Men,' I says, 'ain't you coming up?' I says. In the condition I felt, I felt actually frightened of the men the way I was, because I was completely gone. We throwed the mate overboard. I helped them also, so far as I can remember. And we took the captain out of the cabin and threw him overboard. And now, when this was done, I told them, I says, 'Now, men,' I says, 'you can do as you like with me,' I says; 'you can put me in irons and take into port and give me up. You see I had to defend my own life.' 'Yes,' they says, 'we all know that.' There I was, broke down completely, like a child, and here they are, coming up here yesterday to put everything onto me."

He also gave an account of the burning of the vessel and trip to the shore. On cross-examination he admitted that he was about three feet from the mate when he shot him; that he was standing on the forecastle house and the mate was down on the forecastle head; that the mate asked him not to shoot. As soon as he had killed the captain, what came into his head then was the mate; that he got the captain's pistols; that he ran up on deck through the pilot house where Barstad was and to Lind, who stood amidships, and asked where the mate was; that Lind told him the mate was aloft; that he got on top of the forecastle house, and in the excitement may have called him down. He denied having asked the men to throw the mate's body overboard, but admitted that he asked them to throw the captain's body overboard. He denied asking the crew to take a drink, but admitted that he may have got the whiskey. He denied ordering the vessel to be burned, and said that it was the engineer's suggestion. He admitted that he took the captain's watch and sold it and that the compass was thrown overboard before they reached the beach.

MR. CHIEF JUSTICE FULLER delivered the opinion of the court.

1. The cause assigned in support of the demurrer to the indictment was that it did "not specify the locality on the high seas where the alleged offence occurred." The objection was without merit. The indictment alleged the murder to have been committed "on the high seas and within the jurisdiction of this court, and within the admiralty and maritime jurisdiction of the said United States of America, and out of the jurisdiction of any particular State of the said United States of America, in and on board of a certain American vessel, . . ." Nothing more was required to show the locality of the offence. St. Clair v. United States, 154 U.S. 134, 144. But the point is now made that the indictment was demurrable because it charged the homicide to have been caused by shooting and drowning, which are means contended to be inconsistent in themselves and not of the same species. This ground of demurrer was not brought forward in the Circuit Court, although defendant was admonished that he must state all the grounds on which he relied. But, treating it as open to consideration, we think the indictment was clearly sufficient as ruled in effect in St. Clair's case.

In that case, defendant was charged with the murder of Fitzgerald on board the bark Hesper on the high seas, by striking and beating him with a weapon unknown, and thereby giving him "several grievous, dangerous and mortal wounds," and then and there casting and throwing him from the vessel into the sea, and drowning him, "of which said mortal wounds, casting, throwing, plunging, sinking and drowning," Fitzgerald "then and there instantly died." The language used was much the same as that employed in United States v. Holmes, 5 Wheat. 412. The indictment was sustained though the particular objection under consideration was not commented on. The indictment in this case was evidently drawn from that, and charged that Andersen assaulted Saunders with a pistol with intent to kill him, by the discharge of which he inflicted on him "several grievous, dangerous and mortal wounds," and that he did "cast and throw from and out of the said vessel into the sea and plunge, sink and drown him, the said William Wallace Saunders, sometimes called William Saunders, in the sea aforesaid, of which said mortal wounds, casting, throwing, plunging, sinking and drowning" Saunders "then and there instantly died." And it was further said, as in the indictment against St. Clair, that by reason of the casting and throwing of Saunders into the sea as aforesaid, the grand jurors "could not describe the said mortal wounds with greater particularity."

In Commonwealth v. Webster, 5 Cush. 295, the first count charged an assault and a mortal wound by stabbing with a knife; the second, by a blow on the head with a hammer; and the third, by striking, kicking, beating and throwing on the ground. The fourth count charged that the defendant feloniously, wilfully and of his malice aforethought, deprived the deceased of life "in some way and manner, and by some means, instruments and weapons to the jurors unknown." The Supreme Judicial Court of Massachusetts was unanimously of opinion that the latter was a good count. The court, speaking through Chief Justice Shaw, said: "From the necessity of the case, we think it must be so, because cases may be imagined where the death is proved, and even where remains of the deceased are discovered and identified, and yet they may afford no certain evidence of the form in which the death was occasioned; and then we think it is proper for the jury to say that it is by means to them unknown. . . . The rules of law require the grand jury to state their charge with as much certainty as the circumstances of the case will permit; and, if the circumstances will not permit a fuller and more precise statement of the mode in which the death is occasioned, this count conforms to the rules of law." In explaining the indictment and the setting out of several modes of death, the Chief Justice also said: "Take the instance of a murder at sea; a man is struck down, lies some time on the deck insensible, and in that condition is thrown overboard. The evidence proves the certainty of a homicide by the blow, or by the drowning, but leaves it uncertain by which. That would be a fit case for several counts, charging a death by a blow, and a death by drowning, and perhaps a third alleging a death by the joint result of both causes combined."

Commonwealth v. Desmarteau, 16 Gray, 1, was an indictment for murder, containing three counts. The first charged that the murder was committed by casting, throwing and pushing the deceased into the Connecticut River, and so choking, suffocating and drowning her; the second, that the death was caused by the blows of some weapon or instrument to the jurors unknown; the third, that the death was caused by the blows and drowning both. It was held that all the counts were in proper legal form and related to a single offence, and that as a conviction on any one required the same judgment and the same sentence as a conviction on all, the jury were properly instructed that if they found the prisoner guilty of the murder as set forth in either, they might return a verdict of guilty, generally.

So an indictment which alleged that death was caused by a wounding, an exposure and a starving, was held in Commonwealth v. Macloon, 101 Mass. 1, not to be bad for duplicity, and it was ruled that it was sufficient to allege that the death resulted from all these means, and to prove that it resulted from all or any of them.

And see Joy v. State, 14 Indiana, 139; Woodford v. People, 62 N.Y. 117; State v. Fox, 1 Dutcher, (25 N.J.L.) 566, 601; State v. Johnson, 10 La. Ann. 456; People v. Colt, 3 Hill, 432; Jones v. Georgia, 65 Georgia, 621; Rodgers v. State, 50 Alabama, 102; Gonzales v. State, 5 Tex. App. 584.

In our opinion the indictment was not objectionable on the ground of duplicity or uncertainty.

two lethal means were employed cooperatively by the accused to accomplish his murderous intent, and whether the vital spark had fled before the riddled body struck the water, or lingered until extinguished by the waves, was immaterial.

Granting that death could not occur from shooting and drowning at the same identical instant, yet the charge that it ensued from both involved no repugnancy in the pleading. For the indictment charged the transaction as continuous, and that two lethal means were employed cooperatively by the accused to accomplish his murderous intent, and whether the vital spark had fled before the riddled body struck the water, or lingered until extinguished by the waves, was immaterial.

If the mate had been shot in the rigging and fallen thence into the sea, an indictment alleging death by shooting and drowning would have been sustainable.

The mate was shot and his body immediately thrown overboard, and there was no doubt that, if not then dead, the sea completed what the pistol had begun.

The Government was not required to make the charge in the alternative in separate counts. The mate was shot and his body immediately thrown overboard, and there was no doubt that, if not then dead, the sea completed what the pistol had begun.

.....

4. John Lind had testified, on cross-examination, that Andersen asked the mate: "'Won't you protect me until we get to port?'" and that the mate said: "'Get to port! You will get killed anyhow,' or something like that." The question was then put: "How came he to ask the mate to protect him?" He answered: "The captain was cussing and treating him badly." Objection was made by the District Attorney on the ground that counsel had no right to go into any altercation between the accused and the captain, but counsel for the accused insisted that he might "ask what took place between the captain and Andersen that morning, whether the mate was present or not, and let the jury infer whether Andersen was alluding to that when he asked the mate for protection." The court ruled: "You may ask it. We want all the facts in the case, and if it is not relevant testimony it will be excluded." The witness thereupon gave an account of the quarrel about the captain's dog. He was then asked: "Do you know of any other circumstances? Had this captain been brutal or inhuman to this cook in any other way?" This question was objected to on the ground "that the character of the captain and his treatment of the accused prior to this time was not an issue in this case, which was a trial for the killing of the mate, and was not a part of the res gestae of this case." After argument, the court sustained the objection and excluded the question, and exception was taken. Counsel for plaintiff in error immediately remarked: "I mean by the interrogatories I am going to propound now to confine myself to that morning," and continued the cross-examination. The record makes it plain that all evidence offered as to what occurred that morning was admitted, and that what was excluded in this instance was evidence of the

conduct of the captain prior to the day the mate was killed. And there was nothing to indicate that that antecedent conduct of the captain was so connected with the killing of the mate as to form part of the res gestae, or that it could have any legitimate tendency to justify, excuse or mitigate the crime for the commission of which Andersen was on trial.

5. After the Government had closed its case in chief, defendant's counsel moved that a verdict of not guilty be directed because the indictment charged that the mate met his death by drowning, whereas the proof showed that his death resulted from the pistol shots. There was no error in denying this motion.

We repeat that the indictment charged the death to have resulted from shooting and drowning, and that the fact was uncontroverted that the mate was shot and immediately thrown into the sea. There was no examination to ascertain whether he was then dead or not. He was lying face down and was picked up and thrown overboard as ordered by the accused, according to the testimony for the Government. Lind and March believed he was dead. Horsburgh said he appeared so. Barstad was doubtful, and Barrial testified he told the cook he was alive.

So far as this motion was concerned it was enough that the evidence was not conclusive that he was killed by the pistol shots.

And, as already indicated, the Government was not required to make the charge in the alternative and elect to proceed in respect of one means of death rather than the other, where the murderous action was continuous.

6. Several of the errors assigned relate to the rulings of the court limiting the testimony to the transactions on the day of the homicide. These rulings were made on certain questions propounded to the accused. His counsel asked: "Now, I want to ask this question to the witness: I want you to detail, with truth, to the jury everything that occurred in reference to this business, from the time you shipped on the 16th day of June until you left the vessel on the 6th day of August?"

This was objected to, and after argument the court, through Goff, Circuit Judge, ruled as follows: "I have no objection to your having the accused commence in his own way and detail as to him is best, confining himself to the truth, just what took place there on the morning of that day, and without any assistance from you, but I cannot permit him to detail to the jury the incidents of the voyage from the time they left Boston in June, as I understand your question to indicate." Exception was taken. Counsel then proceeded: "Q. Did you ship on the 'Olive Pecker'? A. Yes, sir. Q. Did you have trouble with the captain?"

This was objected to, and the court said: "I must say, Mr. McIntosh, that I fail to see the pertinency of testimony as to a quarrel with the captain in June or in July. Suppose the mate was a party, the charge is that of killing Saunders in August and the testimony is confined to that time. You can show, if you can, what was the feeling between the accused and the mate, and that it was such growing out of previous quarrels or threats by the mate to take the life of the accused, or anything in that line which would tend to explain the standing of the parties at the time of this occurrence. Now, anything that bears upon what had taken place, so far as the mate is concerned, can go before this jury." Exception was taken.

Counsel continued: "Q. You shipped on board the 'Olive Pecker' some time in June, 1897? A. Yes, sir. Q. Now state to the jury all that occurred between you and the mate during that time, including all the facts and circumstances attending the 6th of August?"

All that part of the question intended to elicit what occurred between the mate and the cook from the time they left Boston was objected to.

The court said: "The trouble, Mr. McIntosh, is this, in the present condition of the testimony of this witness it is hard to see the pertinency of it now, but I do not say that it may not be pertinent. You had better first let the witness detail the transactions of the 6th of August, and if anything is developed thereby which makes it pertinent to bring in previous incidents as tending to explain what took place on the 6th, it can come in." Exception was taken.

The accused was then asked: "Detail to the court and jury all the occurrences which took place on the morning of the 6th of August, 1897." Thereupon the accused gave his account of the transactions of that date, the trip to shore and the subsequent arrest. After he had concluded his counsel put this question: "Now state what trouble, if any, you had had with this mate previous to this occasion?" The question was objected to on the ground that the testimony of the witness should be confined to what occurred on the day of the homicide. After argument, Goff, J., delivered this opinion:

there is no doubt in the world that a party may protect his own life against the party assailing him.

"The reason I suggested to counsel for the accused that the statement as to the occurrences relating to the killing of the mate should be stated as they took place on that day was that the testimony might be confined to a certain limit. Now, there is no doubt in the world that a party may protect his own life against the party assailing him. If he believes that he is about to suffer harm from one who has attacked; if he bases that belief upon a previous threat; if he bases that upon previous personal encounters; if he bases that upon the known brutal character of the party, the law, out of tender consideration for the frailties of human nature, will permit him to act upon that belief and upon that understanding. But can we apply that in this case? Now, we must look at the matter as it is before the jury, as it is presented by this witness. The witness states that he had a controversy with the captain; that the captain was cruel to him; then, in that hour, he turned to the mate and advised with the mate; he asked the protection of the mate. His conduct, at least, does not indicate that there was any feeling between him and the mate at that time. If the testimony is admissible, it is upon the theory that it must tend to explain the situation as it then existed. He had turned to the mate to ask his protection from the captain. Now, if the mate had attacked him, it would be perfectly competent for Andersen to show that the mate, previous to this day, had threatened him or had been cruel to him. We must look at the testimony as the witness has given it himself. It was the witness who sought the mate, and not the mate who sought the witness. I fail to see how a party can, under those circumstances, show, either by himself or by another, that he had had a controversy with the party he is about to attack, the day before or the week before, if he has had time to cool. If there had been a controversy of that kind, even under any circumstances of that kind, it does not authorize the party to take the law into his own hands. I must exclude the testimony and adhere to the intimation I gave some time ago, on another ruling, with reference to threats."

To this ruling exception was taken. Counsel then said:

"Now, in order that this matter may go down right, and in order that I may save the point, but without any disrespect to the court, I want to propound this question to the witness.

"Q. I don't want you to answer this, Andersen, until the court passes upon it. I want it to go down in the record. I want to ask you whether on the day before you had had a difficulty with the mate, and, without provocation on your part, the mate had not attempted to throw you overboard?

"Mr. McIntosh. I understand that your honor rules that I cannot ask that?

"The Court. The question is improper and cannot be answered."

And to this, exception was taken.

The preliminary rulings of the court which required the incidents of August 6 to be given at the outset are not open to criticism. The point to be considered is whether evidence of transactions previous to that day was admissible in the light of the testimony of the accused in respect of what passed on that day. It will be perceived that no specific offer of proof was made. But, assuming that counsel had offered to show by the accused that he had had trouble with the mate previously to August 6, and that the day before he had had a difficulty with him, and the mate, without provocation, had attempted to throw the accused overboard, would such testimony by the accused have been admissible in view of his own detailed account of the homicide and its surrounding circumstances? On what legal principle could it have been held to have a tendency in justification, excuse or mitigation?

Andersen's story was that on the morning of August 6 he had a difficulty with the captain about the dog; that the captain cursed him, struck him and sent him on top the red-hot stove and the pots and pans; that he subsequently appealed to the mate for protection, and he treated the application with scorn and profanity; that some time afterwards he went to the cabin to sweep it, and that the captain glared at him and cursed him. He commenced sweeping the cabin, and started into the mate's room first; saw the mate's gun lying on the shelf and took it down, thinking that if the worst came to the worst he would have to defend himself. He finished the cabin and started into the captain's room; the captain arose and was about to assault him with a bottle and he shot him. "Then I thought about the mate. I ran into the captain's room then and got his two guns." He ran up on deck; asked Lind where the mate was; was told he was aloft; looked up and saw him there, and called him down or waited for him. As the mate came down he asked Andersen where he got the guns and where the captain was, but Andersen made no answer to this, and stayed on top of the forecastle house. Then as he stood on the house with the pistols, and the mate was three feet below on the forecastle head, but coming towards witness as if "to take the marlin spike off his neck and shove the marlin spike into me," witness pulled his gun and shot him. He shot him several times -- the mate begging him not to shoot. Immediately after that he called up the sailors and the body was thrown overboard.

It is true that a homicide committed in actual defence of life or limb is excusable if it appear that the slayer was acting under a reasonable belief that he was in imminent danger of death or great bodily harm from the deceased, and that his act in causing death was necessary in order to avoid the death or great bodily harm which was apparently imminent. But where there is manifestly no adequate or reasonable ground for such belief, or the slayer brings on the difficulty for the purpose of killing the deceased, or violation of law on his part is the reason of his expectation of an attack, the plea of self defence cannot avail.

It is true that a homicide committed in actual defence of life or limb is excusable if it appear that the slayer was acting under a reasonable belief that he was in imminent danger of death or great bodily harm from the deceased, and that his act in causing death was necessary in order to avoid the death or great bodily harm which was apparently imminent. But where there is manifestly no adequate or reasonable ground for such belief, or the slayer brings on the difficulty for the purpose of killing the deceased, or violation of law on his part is the reason of his expectation of an attack, the plea of self defence cannot avail. Wallace v. United States, 162 U.S. 466; Allen v. United States, 164 U.S. 492; Addington v. United States, 165 U.S. 184.

According to his own statement, Andersen, after he had shot the captain, thought about the mate, armed himself with the captain's pistols, went in search of his victim, and finding him aloft on the mainmast at work, called him down, or, seeing him coming down, awaited him, and shot him. He was not only the aggressor but the premeditated aggressor.

The imminent danger which threatened him was the danger of the gallows.

It was, indeed, the duty of the mate to attack Andersen as he stood there with three pistols, fresh from the slaughter of the captain, and in open mutiny. But as the accused told his story he was not repelling violence, and if the mate attempted to make use of the marlin spike, it was simply in self defence.

According to his own statement, Andersen, after he had shot the captain, thought about the mate, armed himself with the captain's pistols, went in search of his victim, and finding him aloft on the mainmast at work, called him down, or, seeing him coming down, awaited him, and shot him. He was not only the aggressor but the premeditated aggressor. The captain being dead, he knew the mate would assume command, and that it would be his duty to arrest him and take him ashore for trial. The imminent danger which threatened him was the danger of the gallows. The inference is irresistible that to avert that danger he killed the mate, cast the bodies into the sea, burned the ship and took to the open boat. There can be no pretence that he was acting under a reasonable belief that he was in imminent danger of death or great bodily harm at the hands of the mate. He testified, to be sure, that when he had armed himself, gone in search of the mate, and stood on the forecastle house ready to receive him, he thought the mate was going to use against him the marlin spike, which he had been using at his work in the rigging, and to protect himself against that marlin spike, swung around the neck of a man standing three feet below him, the accused shot him down while he was asking for his life. It was, indeed, the duty of the mate to attack Andersen as he stood there with three pistols, fresh from the slaughter of the captain, and in open mutiny. But as the accused told his story he was not repelling violence, and if the mate attempted to make use of the marlin spike, it was simply in self defence.

The case as Andersen's testimony made it afforded no basis for the introduction of evidence of prior provocation, or even of injuries previously inflicted, for no overt act on the mate's part provoked the evil intent with which Andersen sought him out on this occasion. Such evidence would not have been relevant, in view of the circumstances, as tending either to make out self defence or to reduce the grade of the crime.

We are not insensible to the suggestion that persons confined to the narrow limits of a small vessel, alone upon the sea, are placed in a situation where brutal conduct on the part of their superiors, from which there is then no possible escape, may possess special circumstances of aggravation. But that does not furnish ground for the particular sufferer from such conduct to take the law into his own hands, nor for the suspension of those general rules intended for the protection of all alike on land or sea.

7. Complaint is made because the court refused to allow a witness to testify as to the general reputation of the captain. If there had been any adequate basis for the contention that Andersen killed the mate in self defence, by reason of a reasonable belief in imminent danger from him, evidence of his character for ferocity, brutality and vindictiveness might have been admissible. Smith v. United States, 161 U.S. 85. But, as the record stood, the character of the captain could have no legal bearing on the issue of the guilt of the accused of the murder of the mate.

8. Various instructions were asked on behalf of the defendant, as well as on behalf of the Government, which were, respectively, refused by the court, except so far as included in the instructions given. But the only ruling in this regard pressed on our attention is the alleged error of the court in instructing the jury as follows: "The other felonious homicide to which I called your attention, manslaughter, is the unlawful killing of a human being without malice, either express or implied. I find it to be my duty, gentlemen of the jury, to say to you that if the defendant has committed a felonious homicide, of which you are the only judges, there is nothing before you that reduces it below the grade of murder."

This instruction was similar to that given by Mr. Justice McKenna, then Circuit Judge, which was reviewed and approved in Sparf v. United States, 156 U.S. 51, 63. That case is decisive of this, for the evidence disclosed no ground whatever upon which the jury could properly have reached the conclusion that the defendant was only guilty of an offence included in the one charged, or of a mere attempt to commit the offence charged. The testimony of the accused did not develop the existence of any facts which operated in law to reduce the crime from murder to manslaughter.

The law, in recognition of the frailty of human nature, regards a homicide committed under the influence of sudden passion, or in hot blood produced by adequate cause, and before a reasonable time has elapsed for the blood to cool, as an offence of a less heinous character than murder. But if there be sufficient time for the passions to subside, and shaken reason to resume its sway, no such distinction can be entertained.

The law, in recognition of the frailty of human nature, regards a homicide committed under the influence of sudden passion, or in hot blood produced by adequate cause, and before a reasonable time has elapsed for the blood to cool, as an offence of a less heinous character than murder. But if there be sufficient time for the passions to subside, and shaken reason to resume its sway, no such distinction can be entertained. And if the circumstances show a killing "with deliberate mind and formed design," -- with comprehension of the act and determination to perform it, the elements of self defence being wanting, -- the act is murder. Nor is the presumption of malice negatived by previous provocation, having no causal connection with the murderous act, or separated from it by such an interval of time as gives reasonable opportunity for the access of fury to moderate. Kerr on Homicide, §68, et seq.; 2 Bishop New Cr. L. §673, et seq.; Whar. Cr. L. §455, et seq.; and cases cited.

There is nothing in Stevenson's case, 162 U.S. 313, to the contrary. The doctrine of Sparf's case is there reaffirmed, that "the jury would not be justified in finding a verdict of manslaughter if there were no evidence upon which to base such a finding, and in that event the court would have the right to instruct the jury to that effect."

No other error assigned requires notice.

Judgment affirmed.

MAXWELL v. DOW

(CASE EXCERPT)

176 U.S. 581; 20 S. Ct. 448; 44 L. Ed. 597

Argued December 4, 1899

February 26, 1900, Decided

GIST: In a state court, Maxwell was charged by information rather than by grand jury indictment, and was later convicted by an eight-person jury on a charge of robbery. The Court rejected Maxwell's contention that he had a right to indictment by a grand jury and trial by a twelve-person jury under the 14th Amendment. Decided in 1900, this case occurred long before the Court, in piecemeal fashion, made most of the Bill of Rights enforceable against the states via the Due Process clause of the 14th Amendment.

Justice Peckham cited several prior cases holding various portions of the Bill of Rights inapplicable to the states. Among the cases was *Presser v. Illinois,* which held that the 2nd Amendment restrained only Congress. Justice Harlan, dissenting, argued that the framers of the 14th Amendment did indeed intend to make the personal rights contained in the Bill of Rights effective against the states. His charming description of the adoption of the Bill of Rights, and his careful reasoning for incorporating the Bill of Rights against the states foreshadowed the Court's later decisions, when concern for state sovereignty would dissolve and federal guarantees for citizens would be mandated more broadly.

While this case, as recently as 1900, flatly says the separate states are unencumbered by the Bill of Rights, today we take it for granted that the protections of the Bill of Rights cannot be abrogated by the states. One of the glaring exceptions of course is in the 2nd Amendment, where incorporation against the states has not been formally addressed under the due-process doctrine.

MR. JUSTICE PECKHAM delivered the opinion of the court.

the first ten amendments to that instrument were proposed to the legislatures of the several States by the first Congress on the 25th of September, 1789. They were intended as restrains and limitations upon the powers of the General Government, and were not intended to and did not have any effect upon the powers of the respective States.

It is conceded that there are certain privileges or immunities possessed by a citizen of the United States, because of his citizenship, and that they cannot be abridged by any action of the States. In order to limit the powers which it was feared might be claimed or exercised by the Federal Government, under the provisions of the Constitution as it was when adopted, the first ten amendments to that instrument were proposed to the legislatures of the several States by the first Congress on the 25th of September, 1789. They were intended as restrains and limitations upon the powers of the General Government, and were not intended to and did not have any effect upon the powers of the respective States. This has been many times decided. The cases herewith cited are to that effect, and they cite many others which decide the same matter. Spies v. Illinois; Holden v. Hardy; Brown v. New Jersey.

they secure and recognize the fundamental rights of the individual as against the exercise of Federal power

It is claimed, however, that since the adoption of the Fourteenth Amendment the effect of the former amendments has been thereby changed and greatly enlarged. It is now urged in substance that all the provisions contained in the first ten amendments, so far as they secure and recognize the fundamental rights of the individual as against the exercise of Federal power, are by virtue of this amendment to be regarded as privileges or immunities of a citizen of the United States, and, therefore, the States cannot provide for any procedure in state courts which could not be followed in a Federal court because of the limitations contained in those amendments. This was also the contention made upon the argument in the Spies case, but in the opinion of the court therein, which was delivered by Mr. Chief Justice Waite, the question was not decided because it was held that the case did not require its decision.

.....

In the same volume as the Slaughter-house cases is that of Bradwell v. The State, where it is held that the right to practice law in the courts of a State is not a privilege or immunity of a citizen of the United States, within the meaning of the Fourteenth Amendment. And in Minor v. Happersett, it was held that the right of suffrage was not necessarily one of the privileges or immunities of citizenship before the adoption of the Fourteenth Amendment, and although a woman was in one sense a citizen of the United States, yet she did not obtain the right of suffrage by the adoption of that amendment. The right to vote is a most important one in our form of government, yet it is not given by the amendment.

.....

That the primary reason for that amendment was to secure the full enjoyment of liberty to the colored race is not denied, yet it is not restricted to that purpose, and it applies to every one, white or black, that comes within its provisions.

But if all these rights are included in the phrase "privileges and immunities" of citizens of the United States, which the States by reason of the Fourteenth Amendment cannot in any manner abridge, then the sovereignty of the State in regard to them has been entirely destroyed

That the primary reason for that amendment was to secure the full enjoyment of liberty to the colored race is not denied, yet it is not restricted to that purpose, and it applies to every one, white or black, that comes within its provisions. But, as said in the Slaughter-house cases, the protection of the citizen in his rights as a citizen of the State still remains with the State. This principle is again announced in the decision in United States v. Cruikshank, wherein it is said that sovereignty, for the protection of the rights of life and personal liberty within the respective States, rests alone with the States. But if all these rights are included in the phrase "privileges and immunities" of citizens of the United States, which the States by reason of the Fourteenth Amendment cannot in any manner abridge, then the sovereignty of the State in regard to them has been entirely destroyed, and the Slaughter-house cases, and United States v. Cruikshank are all wrong, and should be overruled.

It was said in Minor v. Happersett that the amendment did not add to the privileges and immunities of a citizen; it simply furnished an additional guaranty for the protection of such as he already had. And in In re Kemmler, it was stated by the present Chief Justice that --

"The Fourteenth Amendment did not radically change the whole theory of the relations of the state and Federal governments to each other, and of both governments to the people. The same person may be at the same time a citizen of the United States and a citizen of a State. Protection of life, liberty and property rests primarily, with the States, and the amendment furnishes an additional guaranty against any encroachment by the States upon those fundamental rights which belong to citizenship, and which the state governments were created to secure. The privileges and immunities of citizens of the United States, as distinguished from the privileges and immunities of citizens of the States, are indeed protected by it; but those are privileges and immunities arising out of the nature and essential character of the National government, and granted or secured by the Constitution of the United States. United States v. Cruikshank; Slaughter-house cases."

.....

Is any one of the rights secured to the individual by the Fifth or by the Sixth Amendment any more a privilege or immunity of a citizen of the United States than are those secured by the Seventh? In none are they privileges or immunities granted and belonging to the individual as a citizen of the United States, but they are secured to all persons as against the Federal Government, entirely irrespective of such citizenship. As the individual does not enjoy them as a privilege of citizenship of the United States, therefore, when the Fourteenth Amendment prohibits the abridgment by the States of those privileges or immunities which he enjoys as such citizen, it is not correct or reasonable to say that it covers and extends to certain rights which he does not enjoy by reason of his citizenship, but simply because those rights exist in favor of all individuals as against Federal governmental powers. The nature or character of the right of trial by jury is the same in a criminal prosecution as in a civil action, and in neither case does it spring from nor is it founded upon the citizenship of the individual as a citizen of the United States, and if not, then it cannot be said that in either case it is a privilege or immunity which alone belongs to him as such citizen.

.....

In Presser v. Illinois, it was held that the Second Amendment to the Constitution, in regard to the right of the people to bear arms, is a limitation only on the power of Congress and the National Government, and not of the States.

as all citizens capable of bearing arms constitute the reserved military force of the National Government, the States could not prohibit the people from keeping and bearing arms, so as to deprive the United States of their rightful resource for maintaining the public security, and disable the people from performing their duty to the General Government.

In Presser v. Illinois, 116 U.S. 252, it was held that the Second Amendment to the Constitution, in regard to the right of the people to bear arms, is a limitation only on the power of Congress and the National Government, and not of the States. It was therein said, however, that as all citizens capable of bearing arms constitute the reserved military force of the National Government, the States could not prohibit the people from keeping and bearing arms, so as to deprive the United States of their rightful resource for maintaining the public security, and disable the people from performing their duty to the General Government.

.....

We have cited these cases for the purpose of showing that the privileges and immunities of citizens of the United States do not necessarily include all the rights protected by the first eight amendments to the Federal Constitution

We have cited these cases for the purpose of showing that the privileges and immunities of citizens of the United States do not necessarily include all the rights protected by the first eight amendments to the Federal Constitution against the powers of the Federal government. They were decided subsequently to the adoption of the Fourteenth Amendment, and if the particular clause of that amendment, now under consideration, had the effect claimed for it in this case, it is not too much to say that it would have been asserted and the principles applied in some of them.

.....

Counsel for plaintiff in error has cited from the speech of one of the Senators of the United States, made in the Senate when the proposed Fourteenth Amendment was under consideration by that body, wherein he stated that among the privileges and immunities which the committee having the amendment in charge sought to protect against invasion or abridgment by the States, were included those set forth in the first eight amendments to the Constitution, and counsel has argued that this court should, therefore, give that construction to the amendment which was contended for by the Senator in his speech.

What speeches were made by other Senators, and by Representatives in the House, upon this subject is not stated by counsel, nor does he state what construction was given to it, if any, by other members of Congress. It is clear that what is said in Congress upon such an occasion may or may not express the views of the majority of those who favor the adoption of the measure which may be before that body, and the question whether the proposed amendment itself expresses the meaning which those who spoke in its favor may have assumed that it did, is one to be determined by the language actually therein used and not by the speeches made regarding it.

What individual Senators or Representatives may have urged in debate, in regard to the meaning to be given to a proposed constitutional amendment, or bill or resolution, does not furnish a firm ground for its proper construction, nor is it important as explanatory of the grounds upon which the members voted in adopting it. United States v. Trans-Missouri Freight Association; Dunlap v. United States.

In the case of a constitutional amendment it is of less materiality than in that of an ordinary bill or resolution. A constitutional amendment must be agreed to, not only by Senators and Representatives, but it must be ratified by the legislatures, or by conventions, in three fourths of the States before such amendment can take effect. The safe way is to read its language in connection with the known condition of affairs out of which the occasion for its adoption may have arisen, and then to construe it, if there be therein any doubtful expressions, in a way so far as is reasonably possible, to forward the known purpose or object for which the amendment was adopted. This rule could not, of course, be so used as to limit the force and effect of an amendment in a manner which the plain and unambiguous language used therein would not justify or permit.

MR. JUSTICE HARLAN, dissenting.

.....

What are the privileges and immunities of "citizens of the United States"? Without attempting to enumerate them, it ought to be deemed safe to say that such privileges and immunities embrace at least those expressly recognized by the Constitution of the United States and placed beyond the power of Congress to take away or impair.

When the Constitution was adopted by the Convention of 1787 and placed before the people for their acceptance or rejection, many wise statesmen whose patriotism no one then questioned or now questions earnestly objected to its acceptance upon the ground that it did not contain a Bill of Rights guarding the fundamental guarantees of life, liberty and property against the unwarranted exercise of power by the National Government. But the friends of the Constitution, believing that the failure to accept it would destroy all hope for permanent union among the people of the original States, and following the advice of Washington who was the leader of the constitutional forces, met this objection by showing that when the Constitution had been accepted by the requisite number of States and thereby become the supreme law of the land, such amendments could be adopted as would relieve the apprehensions of those who deemed it necessary, by express provisions, to guard against the infringement by the agencies of the General Government of any of the essential rights of American freemen. This view prevailed, and the implied pledge thus given was carried out by the first Congress, which promptly adopted and submitted to the people of the several States the first ten amendments. These amendments have ever since been regarded as the National Bill of Rights.

Let us look at some of those amendments. It is declared by the First, "Congress shall make no law respecting an establishment of religion, or prohibiting the free exercise thereof, or abridging the freedom of speech or of the press, or the right of the people peaceably to assemble and to petition the Government for a redress of grievances;" by the Third, "no soldier shall in time of peace be quartered in any house, without the consent of the owner, nor in time of war, but in a manner to be prescribed by law;" by the Fourth, "the right of the people to be secure in their persons, houses, papers and effects against unreasonable searches and seizures shall not be violated, and no warrants shall issue but upon probable cause, supported by oath or affirmation, and particularly describing the place to be searched, and the persons or things to be seized:" by the Fifth, no person shall "be subject for the same offence to be twice put in jeopardy of life or limb, nor shall he be compelled in any criminal case to be a witness against himself, nor be deprived of life, liberty or property without due process of law, nor shall private property be taken for public use, without just compensation;" by the Sixth, "in all criminal prosecutions the accused shall enjoy the right to a speedy and public trial, by as impartial jury of the State and district wherein the crime shall have been committed, which district shall have been previously ascertained by law, and to be informed of the nature and cause of the accusation, to be confronted with the witnesses against him, to have compulsory process for obtaining witnesses in his favor, and to have the assistance of counsel for his defence;" and by the Eighth, "excessive bail shall not be required nor excessive fines imposed, nor cruel and unusual punishments inflicted."

It seems to me that the privileges and immunities enumerated in these amendments belong to every citizen of the United States. They were universally so regarded prior to the adoption of the Fourteenth Amendment. In order to form a more perfect union, establish justice, insure domestic tranquillity, provide for the common defence, promote the general welfare and secure the blessings of liberty to themselves and their posterity, the political community known as the People of the United States ordained and established the Constitution of the United States; and every member of that political community was a citizen of the United States. It was that community that adopted, in the mode prescribed by the Constitution, the first ten amendments; and what they had in view by so doing was to make it certain that the privileges and immunities therein specified -- the enjoyment of which, the fathers believed, were necessary in order to secure the blessings of liberty -- could never be impaired or destroyed by the National Government.

.....

If the court had not ruled otherwise, I should have thought it indisputable that when by the Fourteenth Amendment it was declared that no State should make or enforce any law abridging the privileges or immunities of citizens of the United States, nor deprive any person of life, liberty or property without due process of law, the people of the United States put upon the States the same restrictions that had been imposed upon the National Government in respect as well of the privileges and immunities of citizens of the United States as of the protection of the fundamental rights of life, liberty and property.

the great men who laid the foundations of our Government regarded the preservation of the privileges and immunities specified in the first ten amendments as vital to the personal security of American citizens. To say of any people that they do not enjoy those privileges and immunities is to say that they do not enjoy real freedom.

Suppose the State of Utah should amend its constitution and make the Mormon religion the established religion of the State, to be supported by taxation on all the people of Utah. Could its right to do so, as far as the Constitution of the United States is concerned, be gainsayed under the principles of the opinion just delivered?

Suppose, again, a State should prescribe as a punishment for crime burning at the stake or putting out the eyes of the accused. Would this court have any alternative under the decision just rendered but to say that the immunity from cruel and unusual punishments recognized in the Eighth Amendment as belonging to every citizen of the United States was not an immunity of a citizen within the meaning of the Fourteenth Amendment and was not protected by that amendment against impairment by the State? The privileges and immunities specified in the first ten amendments as belonging to the people of the United States are equally protected by the Constitution.

And while those amendments originally limited only the powers of the National Government in respect of the privileges and immunities specified therein, since the adoption of the Fourteenth Amendment those privileges and immunities are, in my opinion, also guarded against infringement by the States.

The decision to-day rendered is very far reaching in its consequences. I take it no one doubts that the great men who laid the foundations of our Government regarded the preservation of the privileges and immunities specified in the first ten amendments as vital to the personal security of American citizens. To say of any people that they do not enjoy those privileges and immunities is to say that they do not enjoy real freedom. But suppose a State should prohibit the free exercise of religion; or abridge the freedom of speech or of the press; or forbid its people from peaceably assembling to petition the government for a redress of grievances; or authorize soldiers in time of peace to be quartered in any house without the consent of the owner; or permit the persons, houses, papers and effects of the citizen to be subjected to unreasonable searches and seizures under warrants not issued upon probable cause nor supported by oath or affirmation, nor describing the place to be searched and the persons or things to be seized; or allow a person to be twice put in jeopardy of life or limb; or compel the accused to be a witness against himself; or deny to the accused the right to be informed of the nature and cause of the accusation against him, to be confronted with the witnesses against him, to have compulsory process for obtaining witnesses in his favor, or to have the assistance of counsel; or require excessive bail; or inflict cruel and unusual punishment. These or any of these things being done by a State, this court, according to the reasoning and legal effect of the opinion just delivered, would be bound to say that the privileges and immunities specified were not privileges and immunities of citizens of the United States within the meaning of the Fourteenth Amendment, and that citizens of the United States affected by the action of the State could not invoke the protection of that amendment or of any other provision of the National Constitution. Suppose the State of Utah should amend its constitution and make the Mormon religion the established religion of the State, to be supported by taxation on all the people of Utah. Could its right to do so, as far as the Constitution of the United States is concerned, be gainsayed under the principles of the opinion just delivered? If such an amendment were alleged to be invalid under the National Constitution, could not the opinion herein be cited as showing that the right to the free exercise of religion was not a privilege of a "citizen of the United States" within the meaning of the Fourteenth Amendment? Suppose, again, a State should prescribe as a punishment for crime burning at the stake or putting out the eyes of the accused. Would this court have any alternative under the decision just rendered but to say that the immunity from cruel and unusual punishments recognized in the Eighth Amendment as belonging to every citizen of the United States was not an immunity of a citizen within the meaning of the Fourteenth Amendment and was not protected by that amendment against impairment by the State? The privileges and immunities specified in the first ten amendments as belonging to the people of the United States are equally protected by the Constitution. No judicial tribunal has authority to say that some of them may be abridged by the States while others may not be abridged. If a State can take from the citizen charged with crime the right to be tried by a jury of twelve persons, it can, so far as the Constitution of the United States is concerned, take away the remaining privileges and immunities specified in the National Bill of Rights. There is no middle position, unless it be assumed to be one of the functions of the judiciary by an interpretation of the Constitution to mitigate or defeat what its members may deem the erroneous or unwise action of the people in adopting the Fourteenth Amendment. The court cannot properly say that the Constitution of the United States does not protect the citizen when charged with crime in a state court against trial otherwise than by a jury of twelve persons, but does protect him against cruel and unusual punishment, or against being put twice in jeopardy of life or limb for the same offence, or against being compelled to testify against himself in a criminal prosecution, or in freedom of speech or in the free exercise of religion. The right to be tried when charged with crime by a jury of twelve persons is placed by the Constitution upon the same basis as the other rights specified in the first ten amendments. And while those amendments originally limited only the powers of the National Government in respect of the privileges and immunities specified therein, since the adoption of the Fourteenth Amendment those privileges and immunities are, in my opinion, also guarded against infringement by the States.

KEPNER v. UNITED STATES

(CASE EXCERPT)

195 U.S. 100; 24 S. Ct. 797; 49 L. Ed. 114

Argued April 22, 1904

May 31, 1904

GIST: This case is an appeal from a criminal conviction in the Philippines, at that time a territory of the United States. Kepner was tried without a jury and acquitted in November 1901. The judgment of acquittal was reversed on appeal, and Kepner was retried and convicted. Kepner appealed on the ground that his second trial was in violation of both the territorial law and the U.S. Constitutional provision against twice putting a person in jeopardy for the same offense. At issue was whether the laws of the territory put in place by Congress were intended to adopt the Spanish civil law interpretation of double jeopardy that existed prior to U.S. rule in the Philippines, or the U.S. interpretation of double jeopardy. In making this determination, Justice Day refers to the near-total adoption of the Bill of Rights into the governing law of the Philippines. He notes that the "right of the people to bear arms" is one of two rights omitted (the other was the right to a jury trial).

MR. JUSTICE DAY delivered the opinion of the court.

That it was the intention of the President in the instructions to the Philippine Commission to adopt a well-known part of the fundamental law of the United States, and to give much of the beneficent protection of the bill of rights to the people of the Philippine Islands, is not left to inference, for in his instructions, dated April 7, 1900, (see Public Laws and Resolutions of Philippine Com. 6-9,) he says:

the government which they are establishing is designed not for our satisfaction or for the expression of our theoretical views, but for the happiness, peace and prosperity of the people of the Philippine Islands, and the measures adopted should be made to conform to their customs, their habits, and even their prejudices

"In all the forms of government and administrative provisions which they are authorized to prescribe, the commission should bear in mind that the government which they are establishing is designed not for our satisfaction or for the expression of our theoretical views, but for the happiness, peace and prosperity of the people of the Philippine Islands, and the measures adopted should be made to conform to their customs, their habits, and even their prejudices, to the fullest extent consistent with the accomplishment of the indispensable requisites of just and effective government;"

But he was careful to add:

these principles and these rules of government must be established and maintained in their islands for the sake of their liberty and happiness, however much they may conflict with the customs or laws of procedure with which they are familiar.

"At the same time the commission should bear in mind, and the people of the islands should be made plainly to understand, that there are certain great principles of government which have been made the basis of our governmental system, which we deem essential to the rule of law and maintenance of individual freedom, and of which they have, unfortunately, been denied the experience possessed by us; that there are also certain practical rules of government which we have found to be essential to the preservation of these great principles of liberty and law, and that these principles and these rules of government must be established and maintained in their islands for the sake of their liberty and happiness, however much they may conflict with the customs or laws of procedure with which they are familiar. It is evident that the most enlightened thought of the Philippine Islands fully appreciates the importance of these principles and rules, and they will inevitably within a short time command universal assent. Upon every division and branch of the government of the Philippines, therefore, must be imposed these inviolable rules:

"That no person shall be deprived of life, liberty or property without due process of law; that private property shall not be taken for public use without just compensation; that in all criminal prosecutions the accused shall enjoy the right to a speedy and public trial, to be informed of the nature and cause of the accusation, to be confronted with the witnesses against him, to have compulsory process for obtaining witnesses in his favor, and to have the assistance of counsel for his defence; that excessive bail shall not be required, nor excessive fines imposed, nor cruel and unusual punishment inflicted; that no person shall be put twice in jeopardy for the same offence or be compelled in any criminal case to be a witness against himself; that the right to be secure against unreasonable searches and seizures shall not be violated; that neither slavery nor involuntary servitude shall exist except as a punishment for crime; that no bill of attainer or ex post facto law shall be passed; that no law shall be passed abridging the freedom of speech or of the press or of the rights of the people to peaceably assemble and petition the government for a redress of grievances; that no law shall be made respecting an establishment of religion or prohibiting the free exercise thereof, and that the free exercise and enjoyment of religious profession and worship without discrimination or preference shall forever be allowed."

They are the familiar language of the Bill of Rights, slightly changed in form, but not in substance, as found in the first nine amendments to the Constitution of the United States, with the omission of the provision preserving the right to trial by jury and the right of the people to bear arms

These words are not strange to the American lawyer or student of constitutional history. They are the familiar language of the Bill of Rights, slightly changed in form, but not in substance, as found in the first nine amendments to the Constitution of the United States, with the omission of the provision preserving the right to trial by jury and the right of the people to bear arms, and adding the prohibition of the Thirteenth Amendment against slavery or involuntary servitude except as a punishment for crime, and that of Art. 1, §9, to the passage of bills of attainder and ex post facto laws. These principles were not taken from the Spanish law; they were carefully collated from our own Constitution, and embody almost verbatim the safeguards of that instrument for the protection of life and liberty.

When Congress came to pass the act of July 1, 1902, it enacted, almost in the language of the President's instructions, the Bill of Rights of our Constitution. In view of the expressed declaration of the President, followed by the action of Congress, both adopting, with little alteration, the provisions of the Bill of Rights, there would seem to be no room for argument that in this form it was intended to carry to the Philippine Islands those principles of our Government which the President declared to be established as rules of law for the maintenance of individual freedom, at the same time expressing regret that the inhabitants of the islands had not theretofore enjoyed their benefit.

How can it be successfully maintained that these expressions of fundamental rights, which have been the subject of frequent adjudication in the courts of this country, and the maintenance of which has been ever deemed essential to our Government, could be used by Congress in any other sense than that which has been placed upon them in construing the instrument from which they were taken?

TRONO v. UNITED STATES

(CASE EXCERPT)

199 U.S. 521; 26 S. Ct. 121; 50 L. Ed. 292

Argued October 31, 1905

December 4, 1905 Decided

GIST: This is another double jeopardy case on appeal from the territorial courts of the Philippines. The Court held that there was no constitutional violation when the defendant was acquitted at trial of the highest charge but convicted of a lesser included offense, appealed the conviction, and was subsequently convicted of the highest charge. Discussing the incorporation of most of the Bill of Rights into the law of the Philippines, the Court noted that the right of the people to bear arms was omitted.

MR. JUSTICE PECKHAM, after making the foregoing statement, delivered the opinion of the court.

The plaintiffs in error seek a reversal of the judgment in their case on the ground that the Supreme Court of the Philippine Islands had no power to reverse the judgment of the court of first instance, and then find them guilty of a higher crime than that of which they had been convicted in that court, and of which higher crime that court had acquitted them, and they contend that such conviction by the Supreme Court of the islands was a violation of the act of Congress, passed July 1, 1902, 32 Stat, 691, a portion of the fifth section of the act providing that "no person for the same offense shall be twice put in jeopardy of punishment."

The whole language is substantially taken from the Bill of Rights set forth in the Amendments to the Constitution of the United States, omitting the provisions in regard to the right of trial by jury and the right of the people to bear arms

This language is to be found in connection with other language in the same act, providing for the rights of a person accused of crime in the Philippine Islands. The whole language is substantially taken from the Bill of Rights set forth in the Amendments to the Constitution of the United States, omitting the provisions in regard to the right of trial by jury and the right of the people to bear arms, and containing the prohibition of the Thirteenth Amendment, and also prohibiting the passage of bills of attainder and ex post facto laws.

TWINING v. NEW JERSEY

(CASE EXCERPT)
211 U.S. 78; 29 S. Ct. 14; 53 L. Ed. 97
Argued March 19, 20, 1908
November 9, 1908, Decided

GIST: This appeal asked the Court to require the states to recognize, through the 14th Amendment, the 5th Amendment right against self-incrimination. The Court held the right was neither one of the privileges and immunities of national citizenship, nor was it implicit in the Privileges and Immunities clause of the 14th Amendment. Indicative of the times, the Court draws distinctions between "National citizenship" and associated federal rights, and "citizens of the United States" and rights under the aegis of the individual states. The Court included in its discussion a statement that the right to bear arms guaranteed by the 2nd Amendment, one of the safeguards of personal rights in the first eight Articles of Amendment to the Federal Constitution, is not one of the privileges and immunities secured against state action.

MR. JUSTICE MOODY, after making the foregoing statement, delivered the opinion of the court.

.....

it is recognized by counsel that by a long line of decisions the first ten Amendments are not operative on the States.

The defendants contend, in the first place, that the exemption from self-incrimination is one of the privileges and immunities of citizens of the United States which the Fourteenth Amendment forbids the States to abridge. It is not argued that the defendants are protected by that part of the Fifth Amendment which provides that "no person . . . shall be compelled in any criminal case to be a witness against himself," for it is recognized by counsel that by a long line of decisions the first ten Amendments are not operative on the States. But it is argued that this privilege is one of the fundamental rights of National citizenship, placed under National protection by the Fourteenth Amendment, and it is specifically argued that the "privileges and immunities of citizens of the United States," protected against state action by that Amendment, include those fundamental personal rights which were protected against National action by the first eight Amendments; that this was the intention of the framers of the Fourteenth Amendment, and that this part of it would otherwise have little or no meaning and effect. These arguments are not new to this court and the answer to them is found in its decisions. The meaning of the phrase "privileges and immunities of citizens of the United States," as used in the Fourteenth Amendment, came under early consideration in the Slaughter-House Cases.

.....

On the other hand, if the views of the minority had prevailed it is easy to see how far the authority and independence of the States would have been diminished, by subjecting all their legislative and judicial acts to correction by the legislative and review by the judicial branch of the National Government.

And so it was held that the right of peaceable assembly for a lawful purpose (it not appearing that the purpose had any reference to the National Government) was not a right secured by the Constitution of the United States, although it was said that the right existed before the adoption of the Constitution

There can be no doubt, so far as the decision in the Slaughter-House Cases has determined the question, that the civil rights sometimes described as fundamental and inalienable, which before the war Amendments were enjoyed by state citizenship and protected by state government, were left untouched by this clause of the Fourteenth Amendment. Criticism of this case has never entirely ceased, nor has it ever received universal assent by members of this court. Undoubtedly, it gave much less effect to the Fourteenth Amendment than some of the public men active in framing it intended, and disappointed many others. On the other hand, if the views of the minority had prevailed it is easy to see how far the authority and independence of the States would have been diminished, by subjecting all their legislative and judicial acts to correction by the legislative and review by the judicial branch of the National Government. But we need not now inquire into the merits of the original dispute. This part at least of the Slaughter House Cases has been steadily adhered to by this court, so that it was said of it, in a case where the same clause of the Amendment was under consideration (Maxwell v. Dow), "The opinion upon the matters actually involved and maintained by the judgment in the case has never been doubted or overruled by any judgment of this court." The distinction between National and state citizenship and their respective privileges there drawn has come to be firmly established. And so it was held that the right of peaceable assembly for a lawful purpose (it not appearing that the purpose had any reference to the National Government) was not a right secured by the Constitution of the United States, although it was said that the right existed before the adoption of the Constitution of the United States, and that "it is and always has been one of the attributes of citizenship under a free government." United States v. Cruikshank. In each case the Slaughter-House Cases were cited by the court, and in the latter case the rights described by Mr. Justice Washington were again treated as rights of state citizenship under state protection. If then it be assumed, without deciding the point, that an exemption from compulsory self-incrimination is what is described as a fundamental right belonging to all who live under a free government, and incapable of impairment by legislation or judicial decision, it is, so far as the States are concerned, a fundamental right inherent in state citizenship, and is a privilege or immunity of that citizenship only. Privileges and immunities of citizens of the United States, on the other hand, are only such as arise out of the nature and essential character of the National Government, or are specifically granted or secured to all citizens or persons by the Constitution of the United States.

Thus among the rights and privileges of National citizenship recognized by this court are the right to pass freely from State to State, the right to petition Congress for a redress of grievances, the right to vote for National officers, the right to enter the public lands, the right to be protected against violence while in the lawful custody of a United States marshal, and the right to inform the United States authorities of violation of its laws.

The right of trial by jury in civil cases, guaranteed by the Seventh Amendment, and the right to bear arms guaranteed by the Second Amendment, have been distinctly held not to be privileges and immunities of citizens of the United States guaranteed by the Fourteenth Amendment against abridgment by the States

the decision rested upon the ground that this clause of the Fourteenth Amendment did not forbid the States to abridge the personal rights enumerated in the first eight Amendments, because those rights were not within the meaning of the clause "privileges and immunities of citizens of the United States."

We conclude, therefore, that the exemption from compulsory self-incrimination is not a privilege or immunity of National citizenship guaranteed by this clause of the Fourteenth Amendment against abridgment by the States.

Thus among the rights and privileges of National citizenship recognized by this court are the right to pass freely from State to State, Crandall v. Nevada, the right to petition Congress for a redress of grievances, United States v. Cruikshank, the right to vote for National officers, Ex parte Yarbrough, Wiley v. Sinkler, the right to enter the public lands, United States v. Waddell, the right to be protected against violence while in the lawful custody of a United States marshal, Logan v. United States, and the right to inform the United States authorities of violation of its laws, In re Quarles. Most of these cases were indictments against individuals for conspiracies to deprive persons of rights secured by the Constitution of the United States, and met with a different fate in this court from the indictments in United States v. Cruikshank and Hodges v. United States, because the rights in the latter cases were rights of state and not of National citizenship. But assuming it to be true that the exemption from self-incrimination is not, as a fundamental right of National citizenship, included in the privileges and immunities of citizens of the United States, counsel insist that, as a right specifically granted or secured by the Federal Constitution, it is included in them. This view is based upon the contention which must now be examined, that the safeguards of personal rights which are enumerated in the first eight Articles of amendment to the Federal Constitution, sometimes called the Federal Bill of Rights, though they were by those Amendments originally secured only against National action, are among the privileges and immunities of citizens of the United States, which this clause of the Fourteenth Amendment protects against state action. This view has been, at different times, expressed by justices of this court (Mr. Justice Field in O'Niel v. Vermont, Mr. Justice Harlan in the same case, and in Maxwell v. Dow), and was undoubtedly that entertained by some of those who framed the Amendment. It is, however, not profitable to examine the weighty arguments in its favor, for the question is no longer open in this court. The right of trial by jury in civil cases, guaranteed by the Seventh Amendment (Walker v. Sauvinet), and the right to bear arms guaranteed by the Second Amendment (Presser v. Illinois), have been distinctly held not to be privileges and immunities of citizens of the United States guaranteed by the Fourteenth Amendment against abridgment by the States, and in effect the same decision was made in respect of the guarantee against prosecution, except by indictment of a grand jury, contained in the Fifth Amendment (Hurtado v. California), and in respect of the right to be confronted with witnesses, contained in the Sixth Amendment. West v. Louisiana, In Maxwell v. Dow, where the plaintiff in error had been convicted in a state court of a felony upon an information, and by a jury of eight persons, it was held that the indictment, made indispensable by the Fifth Amendment, and the trial by jury guaranteed by the Sixth Amendment, were not privileges and immunities of citizens of the United States, as those words were used in the Fourteenth Amendment. The discussion in that case ought not to be repeated. All the arguments for the other view were considered and answered, the authorities were examined and analyzed, and the decision rested upon the ground that this clause of the Fourteenth Amendment did not forbid the States to abridge the personal rights enumerated in the first eight Amendments, because those rights were not within the meaning of the clause "privileges and immunities of citizens of the United States." If it be possible to render the principle which governed the decision more clear, it is done so by the dissent of Mr. Justice Harlan. We conclude, therefore, that the exemption from compulsory self-incrimination is not a privilege or immunity of National citizenship guaranteed by this clause of the Fourteenth Amendment against abridgment by the States.

PATSONE v. PENNSYLVANIA

(FULL CASE)

232 U.S. 138; 34 S. Ct. 281; 58 L. Ed. 539

Argued November 4, 1913

January 19, 1914

GIST: This case is a 14th Amendment challenge to a Pennsylvania law prohibiting nonresident aliens from hunting. State law made possession of shotguns and rifles by an alien for hunting unlawful, and subject to a fine and confiscation of the firearms. An Italian was convicted of such an offense, and brought an action on denial of due process since he was singled out as a class. The Court held the law was not in conflict with the United States Constitution because states could classify crimes and were free to properly do so. The Court also noted that wild game in a state belongs to the state, and the state may do with it as they wish.

On the challenge of violating an 1871 treaty with the Kingdom of Italy, the Court noted that weapons such as pistols that may be needed occasionally for self defense were not banned by the state. On the point about affecting trade and commerce under the treaty, the Justices wryly replied that when a case comes up about an Italian possessing a stock of guns for purposes of trade they will deal with that then.

The case begins below (after the syllabus in italics) with the published claims of the plaintiff's attorney, worded to seem quite reasonable, but these were rejected as invalid in the Court's decision.

The act of May 8, 1909, of Pennsylvania, making it unlawful for unnaturalized foreign born residents to kill wild game except in defence of person or property and to that end making the possession of shot guns and rifles unlawful, is not unconstitutional under the due process and equal protection provisions of the Fourteenth Amendment.

A State may protect its wild game and preserve it for its own citizens. Geer v. Connecticut, 161 U.S. 519.

A State may classify with reference to the evil to be prevented.

The determination of the class from which an evil is mainly to be feared and specialized in the legislation is a practical one dependent upon experience; and this court is slow to declare that the state legislature is wrong in its facts. Adams v. Milwaukee, 228 U.S. 572.

A State may direct its police regulations against what it deems the evil as it actually exists without covering the whole field of possible abuse. Central Lumber Co. v. South Dakota, 227 U.S. 157.

The provisions in Article II of the treaty with Italy, giving citizens of Italy the right to carry on trade on the same terms as natives of this country, and provisions in the treaty with Switzerland, applicable to citizens of Italy under the favored nation clause in Article XXIV of the treaty with Italy, relate to trade, and are not applicable to personal use of firearms; and a state statute protecting wild game and prohibiting aliens from owning shot guns and rifles is not incompatible with or violative of such treaty provisions.

Quaere, and not to be decided on this record, whether the statute in this case can be construed as precluding an alien from possessing a stock of guns for purposes of trade and whether in that event it would violate rights under the treaty with Italy of 1871.

Equality of rights assured to citizens of Italy under the treaty of 1871 is that of protection and security for persons and property and nothing in that treaty purports or attempts to prevent a State from exercising its power for preservation of wild game for its own citizens.

THE facts, which involve the constitutionality of the wild game statute of Pennsylvania making it unlawful for any unnaturalized foreign born resident to kill wild birds or animals and the validity of such statute as applied to an Italian citizen in view of the treaty with Italy, are stated in the opinion.

Mr. Marcel Viti for plaintiff in error:

The statute violates the Fourteenth Amendment. It deprives persons of liberty and property without due process of law. Barbier v. Connolly, 113 U.S. 27; Mugler v. Kansas, 123 U.S. 623, 661.

While the legislature may have authority to declare unlawful property which is innocent in itself, yet such power must not be exercised in such a way as to infringe fundamental rights to a greater extent than is absolutely necessary for the accomplishment of the legal purpose in view. Neither Lawton v. Steele, 152 U.S. 133, nor Geer v. Connecticut, control this case.

The cases of People v. West, 106 N.Y. 293, 297; Osborn v. Charlevoix, 114 Michigan, 655; Luck v. Sears, 29 Oregon, 421; State v. Lewis, 134 Indiana, 250; McConnell v. McKillip, 71 Nebraska, 712, can all be distinguished.

A State may forbid absolutely the possession of game within its borders because the individual only acquires therein a qualified right of property; it may also forbid the possession of articles which are not adapted to any but an unlawful use and may confiscate articles actually put to an illegal use or found under circumstances, from which it must necessarily be inferred that such articles had been or were about to be used for an illegal purpose.

Under the terms of the present act the mere possession of property, innocent in itself, and having lawful uses, is made an offence apart from its being used unlawfully and its forfeiture is fixed as part of the penalty.

The legislature cannot provide that implements which are susceptible of beneficial use and which have not been perverted to an unlawful use, be summarily abated or declared forfeited after a hearing, as part of a penalty for the offence of having them in possession.

Shot guns and rifles are articles of property not harmful in themselves, necessary for legitimate uses, and there is no manifest necessity to forbid their possession in order to prevent aliens from hunting game.

Shot guns and rifles are articles of property not harmful in themselves, necessary for legitimate uses, and there is no manifest necessity to forbid their possession in order to prevent aliens from hunting game.

The State has not the right to confiscate such property under such circumstances and without a hearing at which he can offer a defence.

The State has not the right to confiscate such property under such circumstances and without a hearing at which he can offer a defence.

The possession of property harmless in itself and which is necessary for lawful purposes cannot be prohibited and the property itself confiscated merely because it is

also capable of being put to an illegal use.

The possession of property harmless in itself and which is necessary for lawful purposes cannot be prohibited and the property itself confiscated merely because it is also capable of being put to an illegal use.

It forbids the possession of shot guns and rifles by resident aliens alone, thus depriving them of efficient and essential instruments for protection of person and property. It provides for the confiscation of valuable, innocent property when owned by aliens, notwithstanding that it has never been put to any illegal use. It singles out a class for discriminating and hostile legislation.

The equal protection provisions of the Fourteenth Amendment are violated by the act. It forbids the possession of shot guns and rifles by resident aliens alone, thus depriving them of efficient and essential instruments for protection of person and property. It provides for the confiscation of valuable, innocent property when owned by aliens, notwithstanding that it has never been put to any illegal use. It singles out a class for discriminating and hostile legislation. Duncan v. Missouri, 152 U.S. 377, 382; Missouri v. Lewis, 101 U.S. 22, 31.

There is a further discrimination against resident aliens as distinguished from non-resident aliens, as the latter are apparently allowed to possess shot guns and rifles, and use them within the State

There is a further discrimination against resident aliens as distinguished from non-resident aliens, as the latter are apparently allowed to possess shot guns and rifles, and use them within the State for the purpose of hunting game for periods of ten days, subject only to the general game laws of the State. Plessy v. Ferguson, 163 U.S. 530, 537; State v. Montgomery, 94 Maine, 192; Templar v. Barbers' Board, 131 Michigan, 254.

These inequalities cannot be justified on the ground of proper classification; see Railway v. Ellis, 165 U.S. 150, 155; Yick Wo. v. Hopkins, 118 U.S. 356, 369.

By this statute an Italian farmer in Pennsylvania cannot protect his property from birds and dogs even though wild and subject to be killed by citizens.

The statute contravenes the existing treaty between the United States and Italy of 1871; see Arts. II, III, 17 Stat. 845; and under the favored nation clause, Art. XXIV of that treaty, this statute also violates the provisions of the treaty with Switzerland of 1855, 9 Stat. 597, putting citizens on a footing of reciprocal equality. By this statute an Italian farmer in Pennsylvania cannot protect his property from birds and dogs even though wild and subject to be killed by citizens. See In re Marshall, 102 Fed. Rep. 325.

The wording of the treaty is plain and shows that the contracting parties intended that their subjects should at least enjoy in the territory of each other the same liberty of carrying on trade and protection and security of their persons and property as natives under like conditions. Maiorano v. Balt. & Ohio R.R. Co., 213 U.S. 268; Crowley v. Christianson, 137 U.S. 91.

An alien merchant or manufacturer who may have spent most of his life in Pennsylvania, adding to its wealth as well as his own, not only may not shoot game, upon his own land, which has been held a right of property in State v. Mallory, 73 Arkansas, 236, but he is not allowed the possession of a shot gun or rifle upon such property for the protection thereof

The terms of the act are not limited to any class or nationality whatsoever. An alien merchant or manufacturer who may have spent most of his life in Pennsylvania, adding to its wealth as well as his own, not only may not shoot game, upon his own land, which has been held a right of property in State v. Mallory, 73 Arkansas, 236, but he is not allowed the possession of a shot gun or rifle upon such property for the protection thereof or for use in hunting game in other States where he might lawfully shoot under regulations applying to non-resident aliens.

No State may prohibit the possession of any lawful article of trade and commerce to Italian subjects and at the same time allow its possession by natives without violating the quoted treaty provisions.

In addition to violating the Italian treaty the act violates the treaty with Switzerland by imposing upon Italian subjects more burdensome conditions and other conditions in respect to the possession of property and the exercise of commerce than are imposed upon natives.

Treaties are the supreme law of the land and all state authority is subordinate thereto, especially when the treaty, as in this case, is self-executing, Hauenstein v. Lynham, 100 U.S. 484, and relates to a proper subject of treaty negotiation. Jacobson v. Massachusetts, 197 U.S. 11, 24. See also Matter of Heff, 197 U.S. 405, 488.

Mr. John C. Bell, Attorney General of the State of Pennsylvania, and Mr. William M. Hargest, with whom Mr. W. H. Lemon was on the brief, for defendant in error.

MR. JUSTICE HOLMES delivered the opinion of the court.

This statute makes it unlawful for any unnaturalized foreign born resident to kill any wild bird or animal except in defence of person or property, and 'to that end' makes it unlawful for such foreign born person to own or be possessed of a shot gun or rifle; with a penalty of twenty-five dollars and a forfeiture of the gun or guns.

The plaintiff in error was an unnaturalized foreign born resident of Pennsylvania and was complained of for owning or having in his possession a shot gun, contrary to an act of May 8, 1909. Laws, 1909, No. 261, p. 466. This statute makes it unlawful for any unnaturalized foreign born resident to kill any wild bird or animal except in defence of person or property, and 'to that end' makes it unlawful for such foreign born person to own or be possessed of a shot gun or rifle; with a penalty of twenty-five dollars and a forfeiture of the gun or guns. The plaintiff in error was found guilty and was sentenced to pay the above mentioned fine. The judgment was affirmed on successive appeals. 231 Pa. St. 46. He brings the case to this court on the ground that the statute is contrary to the Fourteenth Amendment and also is in contravention of the treaty between the United States and Italy, to which latter country the plaintiff in error belongs.

The possession of rifles and shot guns is not necessary for other purposes not within the statute. It is so peculiarly appropriated to the forbidden use that if such a use may be denied to this class, the possession of the instruments desired chiefly for that end also may be.

The prohibition does not extend to weapons such as pistols that may be supposed to be needed occasionally for self-defence.

Under the Fourteenth Amendment the objection is two-fold; unjustifiably depriving the alien of property and discrimination against such aliens as a class. But the former really depends upon the latter, since it hardly can be disputed that if the lawful object, the protection of wild life (Geer v. Connecticut, 161 U.S. 519), warrants the discrimination, the means adopted for making it effective also might be adopted. The possession of rifles and shot guns is not necessary for other purposes not within the statute. It is so peculiarly appropriated to the forbidden use that if such a use may be denied to this class, the possession of the instruments desired chiefly for that end also may be. The prohibition does not extend to weapons such as pistols that may be supposed to be needed occasionally for self-defence. So far, the case is within the principle of Lawton v. Steele, 152 U.S. 133. See further Silz v. Hesterberg, 211 U.S. 31. Purity Extract Co. v. Lynch, 226 U.S. 192.

The discrimination undoubtedly presents a more difficult question. But we start with the general consideration that a State may classify with reference to the evil to be prevented, and that if the class discriminated against is or reasonably might be considered to define those from whom the evil mainly is to be feared, it properly may be picked out. A lack of abstract symmetry does not matter. The question is a practical one dependent upon experience. The demand for symmetry ignores the specific difference that experience is supposed to have shown to mark the class. It is not enough to invalidate the law that others may do the same thing and go unpunished, if, as a matter of fact, it is found that the danger is characteristic of the class named. Lindsley v. Natural Carbonic Gas Co., 220 U.S. 61, 80, 81. The State 'may direct its law against what it deems the evil as it actually exists without covering the whole field of possible abuses.' Central Lumber Co. v. South Dakota, 226 U.S. 157, 160. Rosenthal v. New York, 226 U.S. 260, 270. L'Hote v. New Orleans, 177 U.S. 587. See further Louisville & Nashville R.R. Co. v. Melton, 218 U.S. 36. The question therefore narrows itself to whether this court can say that the Legislature of Pennsylvania was not warranted in assuming as its premise for the law that resident unnaturalized aliens were the peculiar source of the evil that it desired to prevent. Barrett v. Indiana, 229 U.S. 26, 29.

Obviously the question so stated is one of local experience on which this court ought to be very slow to declare that the state legislature was wrong in its facts. Adams v. Milwaukee, 228 U.S. 572, 583. If we might trust popular speech in some States it was right -- but it is enough that this court has no such knowledge of local conditions as to be able to say that it was manifestly wrong. See Trageser v. Gray, 73 Maryland, 250. Commonwealth v. Hana, 195 Massachusetts, 262.

The defence under the treaty with Italy of February 26, 1871, 17 Stat. 845, appears to us to present less difficulty. The provisions relied upon are those in Article 2, giving to citizens of Italy the right to carry on trade and to do anything incident to it upon the same terms as the natives of this country; in Article 3, assuring them security for persons and property and that they "shall enjoy in this respect the same rights and privileges as are or shall be granted to the natives, on their submitting themselves to the conditions imposed upon the natives" and in Article 24 promising to the Kingdom of Italy the same favors in respect to commerce and navigation that may be granted to other nations. We will say a word about each.

As to Article 2 it will be time enough to consider whether the statute can be construed or upheld as precluding Italians from possessing a stock of guns for purposes of trade when such a case is presented.

It is to be remembered that the subject of this whole discussion is wild game, which the State may preserve for its own citizens if it pleases.

The last article is supposed to make applicable a convention with Switzerland (proclaimed November 9, 1855, 11 Stat. 597) providing against more burdensome conditions being imposed upon the residence of Swiss than upon that of citizens. But Article 24 refers only to commerce and navigation and the case must stand wholly upon Articles 2 and 3. As to Article 2 it will be time enough to consider whether the statute can be construed or upheld as precluding Italians from possessing a stock of guns for purposes of trade when such a case is presented. The act was passed for an object with which possession in the way of trade has nothing to do and well might be interpreted as not extending to it. There remains then only Article 3. With regard to that it was pointed out below that the equality of rights that it assures is equality only in respect of protection and security for persons and property. The prohibition of a particular kind of destruction and of acquiring property in instruments intended for that purpose establishes no inequality in either respect. It is to be remembered that the subject of this whole discussion is wild game, which the State may preserve for its own citizens if it pleases. Geer v. Connecticut, 161 U.S. 519, 529. We see nothing in the treaty that purports or attempts to cut off the exercise of their powers over the matter by the States to the full extent. Compagnie Francaise de Navigation a Vapeur v. State Board of Health, 186 U.S. 380, 394, 395.

Judgment affirmed.

THE CHIEF JUSTICE dissents.

STEARNS v. WOOD

(FULL CASE)

236 U.S. 75; 35 S. Ct. 229; 59 L. Ed. 475

Argued December 18, 1914

January 18, 1915

GIST: Major Stearns, in the Inspector General Dept. of the Ohio National Guard, was facing a ceiling on his career, because the Secretary of War had required all state Adjutants General to limit the attainable rank in such departments to Lieutenant Colonel. Stearns sued his AG, Wood, and in the appeal asked the Supreme Court to assess all sorts of subjects he (and we) would like to see interpreted.

This opinion dismissed Stearns' challenge of the Secretary of War's general order affecting the organization of the Ohio National Guard. Stearns was unable to satisfy the requirement that anyone bringing a case needs constitutional "standing," a sufficiently concrete personal stake in a case or controversy. Accordingly, the Court never addressed Stearns' petition that they interpret the 2nd Amendment, or anything else in the long list he sought opinions on, tersely remarking that they had better things to do with their time.

MR. JUSTICE McREYNOLDS delivered the opinion of the court.

This is a direct appeal from the district court, which held that the original bill states no cause of action. It must be dismissed unless the case involves the construction or application of the Constitution of the United States, or the constitutionality of a Federal statute is fairly drawn in question.

The only serious attempt to show that appellant has a direct personal interest in the subject presented is found in the section of the bill which alleges that he is now serving as a Major in the Inspector General's Department of the Ohio National Guard and is aggrieved because defendant Wood, the Adjutant General of the State, is about to put into full force and effect a general order issued by command of the Secretary of War and known as Circular No. 8, which, without right or authority, directs that the maximum rank of senior officers in complainant's department shall be a Lieutenant Colonel, and if this is done he will be prevented from attaining and serving in the higher rank permitted by the existing laws of Ohio.

on and after January 21, 1910, the organization, armament, and discipline of the organized militia in the several states, territories, and the District of Columbia, shall be the same as that which is now or may hereafter be preseribed for the regular Army of the United States

Sec. 3 of the military law (act of January 21, 1903, chap. 196), 32 Stat. at L. 775, as amended by the act of May 27, 1908, chap. 204, 35 Stat. at L. 399, Comp. Stat. 1913, 3044, provides that on and after January 21, 1910, the organization, armament, and discipline of the organized militia in the several states, territories, and the District of Columbia, shall be the same as that which is now or may hereafter be preseribed for the regular Army of the United States, subject in time of peace to such general exceptions as may be authorized by the Secretary of War. Exercising his discretion, the Secretary of War directed the issuance of circular No. 8, to become effective January 1, 1914. It is comprehensive in terms and prescribes general regulations concerning the members, officers, and organization of the state militia. The validity of the order is denied.

The bill further avers that the adjutant general of Ohio has issued an order with respect to the mobilization of the National Guard of that state, wherein he commands that upon any declaration of war all furloughs shall be revoked and all the officers and soldiers shall assemble and proceed wherever directed by the President, whether within or without the United States. The validity of this is also denied.

The brief in behalf of appellant states that "this action is a test case brought by an officer of the National Guard against the Adjutant General of Ohio, who are nominal complainant and respondent, and involves the construction of certain constitutional provisions, as follows:" Art. I, §8, Par. 16; the Second Amendment; the Tenth Amendment; Art. I, §8, Par. 15; the Preamble to the Constitution; the provision making the President commander in chief of the militia when called into the Federal service; the power granted to Congress to raise and support armies. "The action also seeks a construction with respect to the right of the President and Congress over the National Guard of the several States, and the status and legal relation of the officers thereof to the War Department; and raises the further question whether the National Guard or organized militia may be used without the territorial limits of the United States, as such."

He is not therefore in position to question their validity; and certainly be may not demand that we construe orders, acts of Congress, and the Constitution for the information of himself and others, notwithstanding their laudable feeling of deep interest in the general subject.

The province of courts is to decide real controversies, not to discuss abstract propositions.

The general orders referred to in the bill do not directly violate or threaten interference with the personal rights of appellant -- a Major in the National Guard whose present rank remains undisturbed. He is not therefore in position to question their validity; and certainly be may not demand that we construe orders, acts of Congress, and the Constitution for the information of himself and others, notwithstanding their laudable feeling of deep interest in the general subject. The province of courts is to decide real controversies, not to discuss abstract propositions.

We cannot consider the points suggested and the appeal is

Dismissed.

BROWN v. UNITED STATES

(FULL CASE)
256 U.S. 335; 41 S. Ct. 501; 65 L. Ed. 961
Argued November 19, 1920
May 16, 1921

GIST: Twenty-five years after "Hanging Judge" Parker's self-defense cases occupied the Court's attention, one more self-defense issue arrived, concerning defense at a place of work.

Evidence showed there had been trouble between defendant Brown and Hermes for a long time, and that Hermes had already assaulted Brown twice with a knife. On the day of the incident Brown had brought a handgun to work in his coat pocket—he was doing excavation for a Post Office—fearing recent threats Hermes had made. Sure enough, Hermes showed up with a bad attitude and a blade. Brown ran over to get his coat, retrieved the gun and shot four times as Hermes struck with the knife. He fired his final shot after Hermes was down.

The Court overturned Brown's murder conviction from the lower court, saying, first, if you have a right to be where you are, you have a right to stand your ground against an assailant; there was no automatic duty to retreat. Secondly, the Court remarked that in the heat of mortal combat a late shot does not in and of itself prevent a self-defense claim, and the issue is a point the jury must decide. Finally, the Court indicated that the right to stand your ground was roughly equivalent in your home, on your land or at work discharging your duties. It was in this case Justice Oliver Wendell Holmes made his famous remark:

"Detached reflection cannot be demanded
in the presence of an uplifted knife."

1. The right of a man to stand his ground and defend himself when attacked with a deadly weapon, even to the extent of taking his assailant's life, depends upon whether he reasonably believes that he is in immediate danger of death or grievous bodily harm from his assailant, and not upon the detached test whether a man of reasonable prudence, so situated, might not think it possible to fly with safety or to disable his assailant rather than kill him. P. 343. Beard v. United States, 158 U.S. 550.

2. So held of a homicide committed on a post-office site by one who was there in discharge of his duty. P. 344.

3. In a prosecution for murder, it appeared that the defendant shot the deceased several times and again when the deceased had fallen and was lying on the ground. Held, that evidence of self-defense was for the jury, that, if they disbelieved the defendant's testimony that the last shot was an accident, they might still have acquitted him if, though intentional, it followed close upon the others in the heat of the conflict and while be believed he was fighting for his life. P. 344.

CERTIORARI to review a judgment of the Circuit Court of Appeals affirming a judgment of the District Court upon a conviction of murder in the second degree. The facts are given in the opinion, post, 341.

Mr. James R. Dougherty and Mr. E. C. Brandenburg, with whom Mr. W. E. Pope, Mr. Gordon Boone and Mr. H. S. Bonham were on the brief, for petitioner:

The court below erred in not holding that the indictment upon its face did not charge any offense either against the laws of the United States, or within the territorial jurisdiction of the United States.

It was error to instruct the jury that petitioner, though in a place where he had a right to be and though the deceased was making a felonious assault upon him, with intent to kill him or do him some serious bodily injury, was obliged to retreat, though without fault on his part, before he could exercise his right of self-defense, and slay the deceased.

The duty to retreat did not exist in cases of justifiable homicide or justifiable self-defense at the common law. Russell on Crimes, 3d Amer. ed., pp. 508-521; 1 Bishop's New Criminal Law, §§849, 850, 851; 1 Hale's Pleas of the Crown, 479-481; 4 Blackstone's Comm. 185; 3 Coke's Inst. 55, 56; Foster's Crown Cases, p. 273; 1 East, Pleas of the Crown, p. 271; Hawkins, Pleas of the Crown, 7th ed., vol. 1, p. 172; 2 Wharton, Criminal Law, §1019; Wharton, Homicide, §485; Beard v. United States, 158 U.S. 550; Allen v. United States, 150 U.S. 551, 562; s.c. 164 U.S. 492-497; Rowe v. United States, 164 U.S. 546; Erwin v. State, 29 Oh. St. 186; Runyan v. State, 57 Indiana, 80, 83; United States v. Wiltberger, Fed. Cas. No. 16,738; United States v. Outerbridge, 5 Sawy. 620; Carpenter v. State, 62 Arkansas, 286; State v. Cain, 20 W. Va. 679; State v. Clark, 51 W. Va. 457; Pond v. People, 8 Michigan, 150; State v. Gentry, 125 N. Car. 733.

A man need not retreat from his place of business when feloniously assaulted, but may stand his ground. A servant or employer has the same right as the owner. If petitioner had owned the lot he would not have been obliged to retreat. He was at the place of his business or his master's business. We submit that this gave him the right to stand his ground. Andrews v. State, 159 Alabama, 14; Cary v. State, 76 Alabama, 78; State v. Goodager, 56 Oregon, 198; Haynes v. State, 17 Georgia, 465; Suell v. Derricott, 161 Alabama, 259.

The right to defend one's home, even to the point of slaying a forcible intruder, or one who assaulted the owner therein, does not seem to have depended at the common law entirely upon the fact that the slayer was assaulted feloniously, that is, with an intent to kill him. 1 Bishop's New Criminal Law, §858; 1 Hale's Pleas of the Crown, 458; Aldrich v. Wright, 53 N.H. 398.

Mr. Assistant Attorney General Stewart, with whom Mr. W. C. Herron was on the brief, for the United States:

The question first arises whether any charge as to the law of self-defense was necessary and whether, therefore, the charge as given and complained of by the petitioner may not be disregarded on this writ. Act of February 26, 1919, c. 48, 40 Stat. 1181; Doremus v. United States, 262 Fed. Rep. 849, 853; Battle v. United States, 209 U.S. 36, 38; Addington v. United States, 165 U.S. 184, 187.

The common law never recognized two species of homicide in self-defense, one justifiable and the other excusable; one dispensing with avoidance of, or retreat from, an assault with a deadly weapon, the other requiring it; on the contrary, the common law, in every case where public interests, e.g., aid of justice, were not involved, required the assaulted person to avoid homicide, if he could do so without endangering the life of himself or another. 2 Pollock & Maitland's History of English Law, pp. 476-481; 3 Stephen, History of Criminal Law, pp. 36-41, 47, 49; Beale, Retreat from Murderous Assault, 16 Harv. Law Rev. 567; Bracton (1250), Twiss ed., c. v, bk. 3, ff. 104b, 134, 144b; Britton (1290), c. vi, pp. 34 et seq., 113; Bracton's Note Book Nos. 1084, 1215; Howel's Case (1221), Kenny's Cas. on Crim. Law, pp. 139, 141, 142; Y.B. 30-31, Edw. I, 510, 512 (1302); 6 Edw. I, c. 9; Fitzherbert's Abridgement, Title Corone Nos. 261, 284-287, 305; Compton's Case, 22 Lib. Ass. 97, pl. 55; 24 Henry VIII, c. 5; Cooper's Case (1663), Cro. Car. 544; 3 Coke's Inst., c. 8, p. 55; 1 Hale's Pleas of the Crown, pp. 424, 425, 478 et seq.; Daver's Case (1623), Godbolt, 288; Calfield v. The Keeper, Roll's Reps. 189.

Counsel rely largely upon Foster's view -- that, in case of justifiable self-defense, the assaulted party may repel force with force and is not obliged to retreat -- (Foster's Crown Cases, pp. 255, 267, 273), and upon Beard v. United States, 158 U.S. 550, 564, which sustains their view. But Foster's statement does not represent the common law. 1 Hawkins, Pleas of the Crown, pp. 104-115; Pond v. People, 8 Michigan, 150, 177; Bracton, supra, f. 120b; Morse's Case, 4 Cr. App. Cas. 50; Aldrich v. Wright, 53 N.H. 398, 404, 405. Though repeated as law many times, it has never had any effect on actual cases in the English courts. See Rex v. Smith, 8 C. & P. 160; Rex v. Bull, 9 C. & P. 22; Rex v. Knock, 14 Cox Cr. Cas. 1; Rex v. Rose, 15 Cox Cr. Cas. 540; Rex v. Symondson, 60 J.P. 645. Foster has been often quoted and relied on by the courts of this country, but it is not clear that his view had any effect on the federal courts prior to the Beard Case (1895). See United States v. Wiltberger (1819), 3 Wash. 515, 521; United States v. Outerbridge (1868), 5 Sawy. 620; United States v. Mingo (1854), 2 Curt. 1, 5; United States v. King (1888), 34 Fed. Rep. 302, 307, 308; United States v. Lewis (1901), 111 Fed. Rep. 630, 635. In United States v. Travers (1814), 2 Wheeler Cr. Cas. 490, 497, 498, 507, the law is stated almost in Foster's language, but it is not clear that the point was important in the case or was called to the attention of the judges. In the Beard Case, the defendant was on his own premises, and, in view of the subsequent decisions in Allen v. United States, 164 U.S. 492, 497, 498, and Alberty v. United States, 162 U.S. 499, 507, 508, that decision should be limited to the right not to retreat when assaulted in one's own house. It is not clear whether, in Addington v. United States, 165 U.S. 184, 187, the court meant to reaffirm the general statement of the right to kill without retreating, made in the Beard Case, or not, or to extend it beyond the exact case there presented.

The common law knew nothing of two kinds of homicide in self-defense, mutually destructive. If Foster's statement were correct it would follow that on an assault with manifest intent to commit a known felony on the person assaulted there would be (a) no duty to retreat generally, but (b) a duty to retreat if this manifest assault was part of a "chance medley." Such a distinction is clearly impracticable and impossible of application before a jury.

As it recognized only one species of homicide in self-defense, so the common law applied without question to all such homicides the rule that the person assaulted was under duty to avoid killing his assailant by retreating, if that was practically possible under the circumstances as they appeared to him. Even Foster admits it as to what he calls excusable homicide in self-defense; and when his distinction of two species of such homicides disappears (as it does in so far as the common law is concerned), the rule, since its existence is admitted, must extend as well to his so-called justifiable homicide in self-defense.

Even assuming that Foster's statement can be taken as in any way representing the common law, it should not be extended to cases (like the present) where the assault from which the right to kill is derived is no more than, but, on the contrary, is exactly equivalent to the assault with manifest intent to commit a felony specified in the alleged rule. The doctrine of Foster, if adopted at all, should be limited to cases where the assault is merely a collateral means to carry out an independent intent to commit a felony, as where A lies in wait for B, to murder him, and on his approach attacks him. If the rule be so limited, it does not apply to the case at bar because there is no evidence of any independent intent on the part of Hermes to murder petitioner, but, on the contrary, the evidence of the latter himself shows that Hermes came to the excavation to haul dirt, and that the assault was induced by petitioner's statement in regard to such hauling.

In order to excuse or to justify the taking of human life, it must appear that the killing was reasonably necessary to protect other interests which for good reasons the law regards as more important, under all the circumstances, than the continued existence of the life in question. The difficulty lies in defining such "other interests." In so far as self-defense is concerned, the normal case of another interest is the life of a person other than the one killed. If the protection of that life makes necessary the homicide in question, there can be no doubt that the law must excuse or justify the killing. But one evident method of avoiding a homicide is to avoid a conflict from which it may arise, and hence to retreat if assaulted, provided such a retreat would, under all the circumstances as they present themselves to the person assaulted, accomplish the end desired by the law, viz., to preserve human life if it can be done without seriously endangering other human lives. The rule of the common-law, therefore, that the person assaulted is bound to retreat provided such a retreat would not be dangerous to his personal safety, is clearly founded on a reasonable, sensible principle, and goes as far as such reasonable principle requires, if the only "other interest" had in mind is the life and personal safety of the one assaulted.

The rule laid down by Foster and approved in the Beard Case must be supported by a respect for some interest which the law ought to protect other than human life or personal safety, since the latter are sufficiently protected by the very terms of the common-law rule. The only "other interest" which can be had in mind is the self-respect and honor of the person assaulted. The question therefore is whether such self-respect and honor are in the eye of the law sufficient to weigh down the balance as against human life. We submit that they are not.

MR. JUSTICE HOLMES delivered the opinion of the court.

The petitioner was convicted of murder in the second degree committed upon one Hermes at a place in Texas within the exclusive jurisdiction of the United States, and the judgment was affirmed by the Circuit Court of Appeals. 257 Fed. Rep. 46. A writ of certiorari was granted by this Court. 250 U.S. 637. Two questions are raised. The first is whether the indictment is sufficient, inasmuch as it does not allege that the place of the homicide was acquired by the United States "for the erection of a fort, magazine, arsenal, dock-yard, or other needful building," although it does allege that it was acquired from the State of Texas by the United States for the exclusive use of the United States for its public purposes and was under the exclusive jurisdiction of the same. Penal Code of March 4, 1909, c. 321, §272, Third. 35 Stat. 1088. Constitution, Art. I, §8. In view of our opinion upon the second point we think it unnecessary to do more than to refer to the discussion in the Court below upon this.

There had been trouble between Hermes and the defendant for a long time. There was evidence that Hermes had twice assaulted the defendant with a knife and had made threats communicated to the defendant that the next time, one of them would go off in a black box.

In view of Hermes's threats he had taken a pistol with him and had laid it in his coat upon a dump.

The defendant retreated some twenty or twenty-five feet to where his coat was and got his pistol. Hermes was striking at him and the defendant fired four shots and killed him.

The other question concerns the instructions at the trial. There had been trouble between Hermes and the defendant for a long time. There was evidence that Hermes had twice assaulted the defendant with a knife and had made threats communicated to the defendant that the next time, one of them would go off in a black box. On the day in question the defendant was at the place above mentioned superintending excavation work for a post office. In view of Hermes's threats he had taken a pistol with him and had laid it in his coat upon a dump. Hermes was driven up by a witness, in a cart to be loaded, and the defendant said that certain earth was not to be removed, whereupon Hermes came toward him the defendant says, with a knife. The defendant retreated some twenty or twenty-five feet to where his coat was and got his pistol. Hermes was striking at him and the defendant fired four shots and killed him. The judge instructed the jury among other things that "it is necessary to remember, in considering the question of self-defense, that the party assaulted is always under the obligation to retreat, so long as retreat is open to him, provided he can do so without subjecting himself to the-danger of death or great bodily harm." The instruction was reinforced by the further intimation that unless "retreat would have appeared to a man of reasonable prudence, in the position of the defendant, as involving danger of death or serious bodily harm" the defendant was not entitled to stand his ground. An instruction to the effect that if the defendant had reasonable grounds of apprehension that he was in danger of losing his life or of suffering serious bodily harm from Hermes he was not bound to retreat was refused. So the question is brought out with sufficient clearness whether the formula laid down by the Court and often repeated by the ancient law is adequate to the protection of the defendant's rights.

Rationally the failure to retreat is a circumstance to be considered with all the others in order to determine whether the defendant went farther than he was justified in doing; not a categorical proof of guilt.

if a man reasonably believes that he is in immediate danger of death or grievous bodily harm from his assailant he may stand his ground and that if he kills him he has not exceeded the bounds of lawful self-defense. That has been the decision of this Court.

Detached reflection cannot be demanded in the presence of an uplifted knife.

it is not a condition of immunity that one in that situation should pause to consider whether a reasonable man might not think it possible to fly with safety or to disable his assailant rather than to kill him.

It is useless to go into the developments of the law from the time when a man who had killed another no matter how innocently had to get his pardon, whether of grace or of course. Concrete cases or illustrations stated in the early law in conditions very different from the present, like the reference to retreat in Coke, Third Inst. 55, and elsewhere, have had a tendency to ossify into specific rules without much regard for reason. Other examples may be found in the law as to trespass ab initio, Commonwealth v. Rubin, 165 Massachusetts, 453, and as to fresh complaint after rape. Commonwealth v. Cleary, 172 Massachusetts, 175. Rationally the failure to retreat is a circumstance to be considered with all the others in order to determine whether the defendant went farther than he was justified in doing; not a categorical proof of guilt. The law has grown, and even if historical mistakes have contributed to its growth it has tended in the direction of rules consistent with human nature. Many respectable writers agree that if a man reasonably believes that he is in immediate danger of death or grievous bodily harm from his assailant he may stand his ground and that if he kills him he has not exceeded the bounds of lawful self-defense. That has been the decision of this Court. Beard v. United States, 158 U.S. 550, 559. Detached reflection cannot be demanded in the presence of an uplifted knife. Therefore in this Court, at least, it is not a condition of immunity that one in that situation should pause to consider whether a reasonable man might not think it possible to fly with safety or to disable his assailant rather than to kill him. Rowe v. United States, 164 U.S. 546, 558. The law of Texas very strongly adopts these views as is shown by many cases, of which it is enough to cite two. Cooper v. State, 49 Tex. Crim. Rep. 28, 38. Baltrip v. State, 30 Tex. Ct. App. 545, 549.

in the case of Beard he was upon his own land (not in his house), and in that of Rowe he was in the room of a hotel, but those facts, although mentioned by the Court, would not have bettered the defence by the old common law and were not appreciably more favorable than that the defendant here was at a place where he was called to be, in the discharge of his duty

There was evidence that the last shot was fired after Hermes was down.

if the last shot was intentional and may seem to have been unnecessary when considered in cold blood, the defendant would not necessarily lose his immunity if it followed close upon the others while the heat of the conflict was on, and if the defendant believed that he was fighting for his life.

It is true that in the case of Beard he was upon his own land (not in his house), and in that of Rowe he was in the room of a hotel, but those facts, although mentioned by the Court, would not have bettered the defence by the old common law and were not appreciably more favorable than that the defendant here was at a place where he was called to be, in the discharge of his duty. There was evidence that the last shot was fired after Hermes was down. The jury might not believe the defendant's testimony that it was an accidental discharge, but the suggestion of the Government that this Court may disregard the considerable body of evidence that the shooting was in self-defence is based upon a misunderstanding of what was meant by some language in Battle v. United States, 209 U.S. 36, 38. Moreover if the last shot was intentional and may seem to have been unnecessary when considered in cold blood, the defendant would not necessarily lose his immunity if it followed close upon the others while the heat of the conflict was on, and if the defendant believed that he was fighting for his life.

Of course it was possible for the jury to find that Brown had not sufficient reason to think that his life was in danger at that time, that he exceeded the limits of reasonable self-defence or even that he was the attacking party.

The Government presents a different case. It denies that Hermes had a knife and even that Brown was acting in self-defence. Notwithstanding the repeated threats of Hermes and intimations that one of the two would die at the next encounter, which seem hardly to be denied, of course it was possible for the jury to find that Brown had not sufficient reason to think that his life was in danger at that time, that he exceeded the limits of reasonable self-defence or even that he was the attacking party. But upon the hypothesis to which the evidence gave much color, that Hermes began the attack, the instruction that we have stated was wrong.

Judgment reversed.

UNITED STATES v. SCHWIMMER

(FULL CASE)
279 U.S. 644; 49 S. Ct. 448; 73 L. Ed. 889
April 12, 1929, Argued
May 27, 1929, Decided

GIST: Schwimmer was a Hungarian-born pacifist who sought to become a naturalized citizen of the United States. Her reservations about taking up arms in defense of the United States were held to be sufficient grounds for rejection of her petition, even though, as a 49-year-old female, she would probably never be asked to bear arms for national defense. Among other things, the Court reasoned that, as a pacifist, she might attempt to dissuade other people from performing their duties to bear arms and so she would detract from the country's strength and safety. The Justices state unequivocally that taking up arms when necessary in the nation's defense is a citizen's duty. The Court's quotation of the 2nd Amendment has seven typographical differences from the handwritten parchment version in the rotunda of the National Archives.

Mr. Justice BUTLER delivered the opinion of the Court.

Respondent filed a petition for naturalization in the District Court for the Northern District of Illinois. The court found her unable, without mental reservation, to take the prescribed oath of allegiance, and not attached to the principles of the Constitution of the United States, and not well disposed to the good order and happiness of the same; and it denied her application. The Circuit Court of Appeals reversed the decree, and directed the District Court to grant respondent's petition. Schwimmer v. United States, 27 F.(2d) 742.

The Naturalization Act of June 29, 1906, requires:

'He (the applicant for naturalization) shall, before he is admitted to citizenship, declare on oath in open court ... that he will support and defend the Constitution and laws of the United States against all enemies, foreign and domestic, and bear true faith and allegiance to the same.' U.S.C. tit. 8, 381 (8 USCA 381).

'It shall be made to appear to the satisfaction of the court ... that during that time (at least five years preceding the application) he has behaved as a man of good moral character, attached to the principles of the Constitution of the United States, and well disposed to the good order and happiness of the same. ...' Section 382 (8 USCA 382).

Question 22 was this: 'If necessary, are you willing to take up arms in defense of this country?' She answered: 'I would not take up arms personally.'

Respondent was born in Hungary in 1877 and is a citizen of the country. She came to the United States in August, 1921, to visit and lecture, has resided in Illinois since the latter part of that month, declared her intention to become a citizen the following November, and filed petition for naturalization in September, 1926. On a preliminary form, she stated that she understood the principles of and fully believed in our form of government, and that she had read, and in becoming a citizen was willing to take, the oath of allegiance. Question 22 was this: 'If necessary, are you willing to take up arms in defense of this country?' She answered: 'I would not take up arms personally.'

I cannot see that a woman's refusal to take up arms is a contradiction to the oath of allegiance.

She expressed steadfast opposition to any undemocratic form of government, like proletariat, fascist, white terror, or military dictatorships.

She testified that she did not want to remain subject to Hungary, found the United States nearest her ideals of a democratic republic, and that she could whole-heartedly take the oath of allegiance. She said: 'I cannot see that a woman's refusal to take up arms is a contradiction to the oath of allegiance.' For the fulfillment of the duty to support and defend the Constitution and laws, she had in mind other ways and means. She referred to her interest in civic life, to her wide reading and attendance at lectures and meetings, mentioned her knowledge of foreign languages, and that she occasionally glanced through Hungarian, French, German, Dutch, Scandinavian, and Italian publications, and said that she could imagine finding in meetings and publications attacks on the American form of government, and she would conceive it her duty to uphold it against such attacks. She expressed steadfast opposition to any undemocratic form of government, like proletariat, fascist, white terror, or military dictatorships. 'All my past work proves that I have always served democratic ideals and fought-though not with arms-against undemocratic institutions.' She stated that before coming to this country she had defended American ideals, and had defended America in 1924 during an international pacifist congress in Washington.

If the United States can compel its women citizens to take up arms in the defense of the country—something that no other civilized government has ever attempted—I would not be able to comply with this requirement of American citizenship.

She also testified: 'If ... the United States can compel its women citizens to take up arms in the defense of the country—something that no other civilized government has ever attempted—I would not be able to comply with this requirement of American citizenship. In this case I would recognize the right of the government to deal with me as it is dealing with its male citizens who for conscientious reasons refuse to take up arms.'

The district director of naturalization by letter called her attention to a statement made by her in private correspondence: 'I am an uncompromising pacifist. ... I have no sense of nationalism, only a cosmic consciousness of belonging to the human family.' She answered that the statement in her petition demonstrated that she was an uncompromising pacifist. 'Highly as I prize the privilege of American citizenship, I could not compromise my way into it by giving an untrue answer to question 22, though for all practical purposes I might have done so, as even men of my age-I was 49 years old last September-are not called to take up arms . ... That 'I have no nationalistic feeling' is evident from the fact that I wish to give up the nationality of my birth and to adopt a country which is based on principles and institutions more in harmony with my ideals. My 'cosmic consciousness of belonging to the human family' is shared by all those who believe that all human beings are the children of God.'

I am willing to do everything that an American citizen has to do except fighting. If

American women would be compelled to do that, I would not do that. I am an uncompromising pacifist. ... I do not care how many other women fight, because I consider it a question of conscience. I am not willing to bear arms.

And at the hearing she reiterated her ability and willingness to take the oath of allegiance without reservation and added: 'I am willing to do everything that an American citizen has to do except fighting. If American women would be compelled to do that, I would not do that. I am an uncompromising pacifist. ... I do not care how many other women fight, because I consider it a question of conscience. I am not willing to bear arms. In every other single way I am ready to follow the law and do everything that the law compels American citizens to do. That is why I can take the oath of allegiance, because, as far as I can find out there is nothing that I could be compelled to do that I cannot do. ... With reference to spreading propaganda among the women throughout the country about my being an uncompromising pacifist and not willing to fight, I am always ready to tell any one who wants to hear it that I am an uncompromising pacifist and will not fight. In my writings and in my lectures I take up the question of war and pacifism, if I am asked for that.'

Except for eligibility to the Presidency, naturalized citizens stand on the same footing as do native-born citizens. All alike owe allegiance to the government, and the government owes to them the duty of protection. These are reciprocal obligations, and each is a consideration for the other. Luria v. United States, 231 U.S. 9, 22, 34 S. Ct. 10 (58 L. Ed. 101). But aliens can acquire such equality only by naturalization according to the uniform rules prescribed by the Congress. They have no natural right to become citizens, but only that which is by statute conferred upon them. Because of the great value of the privileges conferred by naturalization, the statutes prescribing qualifications and governing procedure for admission are to be construed with definite purpose to favor and support the government. And, in order to safeguard against admission of those who are unworthy, or who for any reason fail to measure up to required standards, the law puts the burden upon every applicant to show by satisfactory evidence that he has the specified qualifications. Tutun v. United States, 270 U.S. 568, 578, 46 S. Ct. 425 (70 L. Ed. 738). And see United States v. Ginsberg, 243 U.S. 472, 475, 37 S. Ct. 422 (61 L. Ed. 853).

Every alien claiming citizenship is given the right to submit his petition and evidence in support of it. And, if the requisite facts are established, he is entitled as of right to admission. On applications for naturalization, the court's function is 'to receive testimony, to compare it with the law, and to judge on both law and fact.' Spratt v. Spratt, 4 Pet. 393, 408 (7 L. Ed. 897). We quite recently declared that: 'Citizenship is a high privilege, and when doubts exist concerning a grant of it, generally at least, they should be resolved in favor of the United States and against the claimant.' United States v. Manzi, 276 U.S. 463, 467, 48 S. Ct. 328, 329 (72 L. Ed. 654). And when, upon a fair consideration of the evidence adduced upon an application for citizenship, doubt remains in the mind of the court as to any essential matter of fact, the United States is entitled to the benefit of such doubt and the application should be denied.

That it is the duty of citizens by force of arms to defend our government against all enemies whenever necessity arises is a fundamental principle of the Constitution.

That it is the duty of citizens by force of arms to defend our government against all enemies whenever necessity arises is a fundamental principle of the Constitution.

The common defense was one of the purposes for which the people ordained and established the Constitution. It empowers Congress to provide for such defense, to declare war, to raise and support armies, to maintain a navy, to make rules for the government and regulation of the land and naval forces, to provide for organizing, arming, and disciplining the militia, and for calling it forth to execute the laws of the Union, suppress insurrections and repel invasions; it makes the President commander in chief of the army and navy and of the militia of the several states when called into the service of the United States; it declares that, a well-regulated militia being necessary to the security of a free state, the right of the people to keep and bear arms shall not be infringed. We need not refer to the numerous statutes that contemplate defense of the United States, its Constitution and laws, by armed citizens. This court, in the Selective Draft Law Cases, 245 U.S. 366, page 378, 38 S. Ct. 159, 161 (62 L. Ed. 349, L. R. A. 1918C, 361, Ann. Cas. 1918B, 856), speaking through Chief Justice White, said that 'the very conception of a just government and its duty to the citizen includes the reciprocal obligation of the citizen to render military service in case of need. ...'

Whatever tends to lessen the willingness of citizens to discharge their duty to bear arms in the country's defense detracts from the strength and safety of the government.

if all or a large number of citizens oppose such defense the 'good order and happiness' of the United States cannot long endure.

The influence of conscientious objectors against the use of military force in defense of

the principles of our government is apt to be more detrimental than their mere refusal to bear arms.

It is clear from her own statements that the declared opinions of respondent as to armed defense by citizens against enemies of the country were directly pertinent to the investigation of her application.

Whatever tends to lessen the willingness of citizens to discharge their duty to bear arms in the country's defense detracts from the strength and safety of the government. And their opinions and beliefs as well as their behavior indicating a disposition to hinder in the performance of that duty are subjects of inquiry under the statutory provisions governing naturalization and are of vital importance, for if all or a large number of citizens oppose such defense the 'good order and happiness' of the United States cannot long endure. And it is evident that the views of applicants for naturalization in respect of such matters may not be disregarded. The influence of conscientious objectors against the use of military force in defense of the principles of our government is apt to be more detrimental than their mere refusal to bear arms. The fact that, by reason of sex, age or other cause, they may be unfit to serve does not lessen their purpose or power to influence others. It is clear from her own statements that the declared opinions of respondent as to armed defense by citizens against enemies of the country were directly pertinent to the investigation of her application.

Her testimony clearly suggests that she is disposed to exert her power to influence others to such opposition.

The record shows that respondent strongly desires to become a citizen. She is a linguist, lecturer, and writer; she is well educated and accustomed to discuss governments and civic affairs. Her testimony should be considered having regard to her interest and disclosed ability correctly to express herself. Her claim at the hearing that she possessed the required qualifications and was willing to take the oath was much impaired by other parts of her testimony. Taken as a whole, it shows that her objection to military service rests on reasons other than mere inability because of her sex and age personally to bear arms. Her expressed willingness to be treated as the government dealt with conscientious objectors who refused to take up arms in the recent war indicates that she deemed herself to belong to that class. The fact that she is an uncompromising pacifist, with no sense of nationalism, but only a cosmic sense of belonging to the human family, justifies belief that she may be opposed to the use of military force as contemplated by our Constitution and laws. And her testimony clearly suggests that she is disposed to exert her power to influence others to such opposition.

A pacifist, in the general sense of the word, is one who seeks to maintain peace and to abolish war. Such purposes are in harmony with the Constitution and policy of our government. But the word is also used and understood to mean one who refuses or is unwilling for any purpose to bear arms because of conscientious considerations and who is disposed to encourage others in such refusal. And one who is without any sense of nationalism is not well bound or held by the ties of affection to any nation or government. Such persons are liable to be incapable of the attachment for and devotion to the principles of our Constitution that are required of aliens seeking naturalization.

It is shown by official records and everywhere well known that during the recent war there were found among those who described themselves as pacifists and conscientious objectors many citizens-though happily a minute part of all-who were unwilling to bear arms in that crisis and who refused to obey the laws of the United States and the lawful commands of its officers and encouraged such disobedience in others. Local boards found it necessary to issue a great number of noncombatant certificates, and several thousand who were called to camp made claim because of conscience for exemption from any form of military service. Several hundred were convicted and sentenced to imprisonment for offenses involving disobedience, desertion, propaganda and sedition. It is obvious that the acts of such offenders evidence a want of that attachment to the principles of the Constitution of which the applicant is required to give affirmative evidence by the Naturalization Act.

it is a duty of citizenship by force of arms when necessary to defend the country against all enemies.

The language used by respondent to describe her attitude in respect of the principles of the Constitution was vague and ambiguous; the burden was upon her to show what she meant and that her pacifism and lack of nationalistic sense did not oppose the principle that it is a duty of citizenship by force of arms when necessary to defend the country against all enemies, and that her opinions and beliefs would not prevent or impair the true faith and allegiance required by the act. She failed to do so. The District Court was bound by the law to deny her application.

The decree of the Circuit Court of Appeals is reversed.
The decree of the District Court is affirmed.

Mr. Justice HOLMES, dissenting.

So far as the adequacy of her oath is concerned I hardly can see how that is affected by the statement, inasmuch as she is a woman over fifty years of age, and would not be allowed to bear arms if she wanted to.

Surely it cannot show lack of attachment to the principles of the Constitution that she thinks that it can be improved.

The applicant seems to be a woman of superior character and intelligence, obviously more than ordinarily desirable as a citizen of the United States. It is agreed that she is qualified for citizenship except so far as the views set forth in a statement of facts 'may show that the applicant is not attached to the principles of the Constitution of the United States and well disposed to the good order and happiness of the same, and except in so far as the same may show that she cannot take the oath of allegiance without a mental reservation.' The views referred to are an extreme opinion in favor of pacifism and a statement that she would not bear arms to defend the Constitution. So far as the adequacy of her oath is concerned I hardly can see how that is affected by the statement, inasmuch as she is a woman over fifty years of age, and would not be allowed to bear arms if she wanted to. And as to the opinion the whole examination of the applicant shows that she holds none of the now-dreaded creeds but thoroughly believes in organized government and prefers that of the United States to any other in the world. Surely it cannot show lack of attachment to the principles of the Constitution that she thinks that it can be improved. I suppose that most intelligent people think that it might be. Her particular improvement looking to the abolition of war seems to me not materially different in its bearing on this case from a wish to establish cabinet government as in England, or a single house, or one term of seven years for the President. To touch a more burning question, only a judge mad with partisanship would exclude because the applicant thought that the Eighteenth Amendment should be repealed. <Refers to Prohibition, enacted in 1919 and repealed in 1933, four years after this case>

She is an optimist and states in strong and, I do not doubt, sincere words her belief that war will disappear and that the impending destiny of mankind is to unite in peaceful leagues.

If there is any principle of the Constitution that more imperatively calls for attachment than any other it is the principle of free thought—not free thought for those who agree with us but freedom for the thought that we hate.

Of course the fear is that if a war came the applicant would exert activities such as were dealt with in Schenck v. United States, 249 U.S. 47, 39 S. Ct. 247. But that seems to me unfounded. Her position and motives are wholly different from those of Schenck. She is an optimist and states in strong and, I do not doubt, sincere words her belief that war will disappear and that the impending destiny of mankind is to unite in peaceful leagues. I do not share that optimism nor do I think that a philosophic view of the world would regard war as absurd. But most people who have known it regard it with horror, as a last resort, and even if not yet ready for cosmopolitan efforts, would welcome any practicable combinations that would increase the power on the side of peace. The notion that the applicant's optimistic anticipations would make her a worse citizen is sufficiently answered by her examination which seems to me a better argument for her admission than any that I can offer. Some of her answers might excite popular prejudice, but if there is any principle of the Constitution that more imperatively calls for attachment than any other it is the principle of free thought—not free thought for those who agree with us but freedom for the thought that we hate. I think that we should adhere to that principle with regard to admission into, as well as to life within this country. And recurring to the opinion that bars this applicant's way, I would suggest that the Quakers have done their share to make the country what it is, that many citizens agree with the applicant's belief and that I had not supposed hitherto that we regretted our inability to expel them because they believed more than some of us do in the teachings of the Sermon on the Mount.

Mr. Justice BRANDEIS concurs in this opinion.

Mr. Justice SANFORD (dissenting).

I agree, in substance, with the views expressed by the Circuit Court of Appeals, and think its decree should be affirmed.

HAMILTON v. REGENTS OF THE UNIVERSITY OF CALIFORNIA

(CASE EXCERPT)
293 U.S. 245; 55 S. Ct. 197; 79 L. Ed. 343
October 17, 18, 1934, Argued
December 3, 1934, Decided

GIST: This case arises out of a challenge brought by a student who wanted to attend a state university but did not want to attend the required military instruction. Hamilton's argument that the state law was in violation of the 14th Amendment was rejected. The Court cited the 2nd Amendment to support the proposition that states could impose military training on their citizens, so long as the training did not violate federal law or rights.

MR. JUSTICE BUTLER delivered the opinion of the Court.

And the appellees insist that this appeal should be dismissed for the want of a substantial federal question. But that contention cannot be sustained; for we are unable to say that every question that appellants have brought here for decision is so clearly not debatable and utterly lacking in merit as to require dismissal for want of substance.

.....

> **The States are interested in the safety of the United States, the strength of its military forces and its readiness to defend them in war and against every attack of public enemies. Undoubtedly every State has authority to train its able-bodied male citizens of suitable age appropriately to develop fitness, should any such duty be laid upon them, to serve in the United States army or in state militia**
>
> **the State is the sole judge of the means to be employed and the amount of training to be exacted for the effective accomplishment of these ends.**

We take judicial notice of the long-established voluntary cooperation between federal and state authorities in respect of the military instruction given in the land grant colleges. The War Department has not been empowered to determine or in any manner to prescribe the military instruction in these institutions. The furnishing of officers, men and equipment conditioned upon the giving of courses and the imposing of discipline deemed appropriate, recommended or approved by the Department does not support the suggestion that the training is not exclusively prescribed and given under the authority of the State. The States are interested in the safety of the United States, the strength of its military forces and its readiness to defend them in war and against every attack of public enemies. Undoubtedly every State has authority to train its able-bodied male citizens of suitable age appropriately to develop fitness, should any such duty be laid upon them, to serve in the United States army or in state militia (always liable to be called forth by federal authority to execute the laws of the Union, suppress insurrection or repel invasion, Constitution, Art. I, §8, cls. 12, 15 and 16) or as members of local constabulary forces, or as officers needed effectively to police the State. And, when made possible by the national government, the State in order more effectively to teach and train its citizens for these and like purposes, may avail itself of the services of officers and equipment belonging to the military establishment of the United States. So long as its action is within retained powers and not inconsistent with any exertion of the authority of the national government, and transgresses no right safeguarded to the citizen by the Federal Constitution, the State is the sole judge of the means to be employed and the amount of training to be exacted for the effective accomplishment of these ends. Second Amendment. Houston v. Moore, 5 Wheat. 1, 16-17. Cf. Presser v. Illinois, 116 U.S. 252.

.....

United States v. Schwimmer, involved a petition for naturalization by one opposed to bearing arms in defense of country. Holding the applicant not entitled to citizenship, we said (p. 650): "That it is the duty of citizens by force of arms to defend our government against all enemies whenever necessity arises is a fundamental principle of the Constitution. . . . Whatever tends to lessen the willingness of citizens to discharge their duty to bear arms in the country's defense detracts from the strength and safety of the Government."

> **The conscientious objector is relieved from the obligation to bear arms in obedience to no constitutional provision, express or implied; but because, and only because, it has accorded with the policy of Congress thus to relieve him.**

> **this Court [upholding a state compulsory vaccination law] speaking of the liberties guaranteed to the individual by the Fourteenth Amendment, said: '. . . and yet he may be compelled, by force if need be, against his will and without regard to his personal wishes or his pecuniary interests, or even his religious or political convictions, to take his place in the ranks of the army of his country and risk the chance of being shot down in its defense.'"**

In United States v. Macintosh, a later naturalization case, the applicant was unwilling, because of the conscientious objections, to take unqualifiedly the statutory oath of allegiance which contains this statement: "That he will support and defend the Constitution and laws of the United States against all enemies, foreign or domestic, and bear true faith and allegiance to the same." 8 U.S.C., §381. His petition stated that he was willing if necessary to take up arms in defense of this country, "but I should want to be free to judge of the necessity." In amplification he said: "I do not undertake to support 'my country, right or wrong' in any dispute which may arise, and I am not willing to promise beforehand, and without knowing the cause for which my country may go to war, either that I will or that I will not 'take up arms in defense of this country,' however 'necessary' the war may seem to be to the government of the day." The opinion of this Court quotes from petitioner's brief a statement to the effect that it is a "fixed principle of our Constitution, zealously guarded by our laws, that a citizen cannot be forced and need not bear arms in a war if he has conscientious religious scruples against doing so." And, referring to that part of the argument in behalf of the applicant, this Court said (p. 623): " This, if it means what it seems to say, is an astonishing statement. Of course, there is no such principle of the Constitution, fixed or otherwise. The conscientious objector is relieved from the obligation to bear arms in obedience to no constitutional provision, express or implied; but because, and only because, it has accorded with the policy of Congress thus to relieve him. . . . The privilege of the native-born conscientious objector to avoid bearing arms comes not from the Constitution but from the acts of Congress. That body may grant or withhold the exemption as in its wisdom it sees fit; and if it be withheld, the native-born conscientious objector cannot successfully assert the privilege. No other conclusion is compatible with the well-nigh limitless extent of the war powers as above illustrated, which include, by necessary implication, the power, in the last extremity, to compel the armed service of any citizen in the land, without regard to his objections or his views in respect of the justice or morality of the particular war or of war in general. In Jacobson v. Massachusetts, this Court [upholding a state compulsory vaccination law] speaking of the liberties guaranteed to the individual by the Fourteenth Amendment, said: '. . . and yet he may be compelled, by force if need be, against his will and without regard to his personal wishes or his pecuniary interests, or even his religious or political convictions, to take his place in the ranks of the army of his country and risk the chance of being shot down in its defense.'"

SONZINSKY v. UNITED STATES

(FULL CASE)

300 U.S. 506; 57 S. Ct. 554; 81 L. Ed. 772

March 12, 1937, Argued

March 29, 1937, Decided

GIST: Congressional debate surrounding the passage of the National Firearms Act of 1934 showed a marked concern against legislating in the domain of the 2nd Amendment, which was practically nonexistent up until that time (see the "Growth In Federal Gun Law" chart in *Gun Laws of America,* listed at gunlaws.com). Congress had passed a few restrictions on hunting in National Parks in the late 1890s and early 1900s, a ban on mailing concealable guns through the Post Office, and the original militia act in 1792, which required able-bodied citizens to keep arms, but that was pretty much all they had ever done. The NFA was an unprecedented giant leap into the nascent field of federal gun law.

It was only highly publicized gangland rub-outs during the Prohibition Era that prompted Congress to find some way to control the firearms that bootleggers were partial to, like the submachine gun. Fearful that any direct legislation would be unconstitutional, Congress decided to use its taxing authority. The requirements of the NFA, when placed in the statutes, went not into the criminal code, but into the tax code.

Sonzinsky challenged the constitutional authority of the United States government to enforce the National Firearms Act. The Court held that Congress could use its taxing power to impose heavy taxes on certain types of firearms and on firearms dealers, a significant increase in power. The Court explained that it would pay no attention to whether the tax was really designed to raise revenue, or was a subterfuge to impose laws which would otherwise be beyond congressional power.

1. That part of the National Firearms Act which provides that every dealer in firearms shall register and shall pay an annual tax of $200 or be subject to fine and imprisonment, is a valid exercise of the taxing power of Congress.

The term "firearm" is defined by §1 of the Act as meaning a shotgun or rifle having a barrel less than eighteen inches in length, or any other weapon, except a pistol or revolver, from which a shot is discharged by an explosive, if capable of being concealed on the person, or a machine gun, and includes a muffler or silencer for any firearm.

2. Congress may select the subjects of taxation, choosing some and omitting others. It may impose excise taxes on the doing of business.

3. The tax upon dealers, supra, is not in the category of penalties imposed for the enforcement of regulations beyond the scope of congressional power.

4. A tax may have regulatory effects and may burden, restrict or suppress the thing taxed, and still be within the taxing power.

5. Courts may not inquire into the motives of Congress in exercising its powers; they will not undertake, by collateral inquiry as to the measure of the regulatory effect of a tax, to ascribe to Congress an attempt, under the guise of taxation, to exercise another power denied by the Federal Constitution.

6. The Court declines to consider petitioner's contentions not supported by assignment of error.

Mr. Harold J. Bandy, with whom Mr. John M. Karns was on the brief, for petitioner.

Congress is not empowered to tax for those purposes which are within the exclusive province of the States. United States v. Butler, 297 U.S. 1, 64; Gibbons v. Ogden, 9 Wheat. 1, 199.

Beneficent aims can never serve in lieu of constitutional power. Carter v. Carter Coal Co., 298 U.S. 38.

An exaction, called a tax, which is in fact and effect a penalty, is not a tax. While the lawmaker is entirely free to ignore the ordinary meaning of words and make definitions of his own, that device may not be employed so as to change the nature of acts or things to which the words are applied. Carter v. Carter Coal Co., supra; Bailey v. Drexel Furniture Co., 259 U.S. 20; United States v. LaFranca, 282 U.S. 568, 572; United States v. Constantine, 296 U.S. 287, 293; United States v. Butler, supra.

The Constitution made no grant of authority to Congress to legislate substantively for the general welfare, and no such authority exists, save as the general welfare may be promoted by the exercise of the powers which are granted. Cases supra.

The power of taxation which is expressly granted may be adopted as a means to carry into operation another power also expressly granted, but resort to the taxing power to effectuate an end which is not legitimate, not within the scope of the Constitution, is obviously inadmissible. Cases supra.

If the Constitution, in its grant of powers, is to be so construed as to carry into full effect the power granted, it is equally imperative that, where a prohibition or limitation is placed upon the power of Congress, that prohibition or limitation should be enforced in its spirit and to its entirety. Fairbanks v. United States, 181 U.S. 312.

A mere reading of the National Firearms Act <appellant claims> discloses that it was enacted for the purpose of regulating or suppressing traffic in the firearms described in the Act; that it was not enacted for the purpose of collecting any taxes; that it was passed as a police measure, as an aid to local law enforcement, and not as a revenue law.

if the real purpose of the law is disclosed on its face to be a purpose that invades the police powers reserved to the individual States, the courts should not hesitate to declare the Act an unconstitutional usurpation by the Federal Government of powers reserved to the States by the Tenth Amendment.

A mere reading of the National Firearms Act discloses that it was enacted for the purpose of regulating or suppressing traffic in the firearms described in the Act; that it was not enacted for the purpose of collecting any taxes; that it was passed as a police measure, as an aid to local law enforcement, and not as a revenue law. While it is true that, where the law merely imposes the tax without disclosing the indirect purpose of its imposition, the courts might hesitate to declare the law unconstitutional, on the other hand, if the real purpose of the law is disclosed on its face to be a purpose that invades the police powers reserved to the individual States, the courts should not hesitate to declare the Act an unconstitutional usurpation by the Federal Government of powers reserved to the States by the Tenth Amendment. Cooley, Const. L., pp. 56-60; Citizens Savings & Loan Assn. v. Topeka, 20 Wall. 655; Powell v. Pennsylvania, 127 U.S. 678.

Under the American constitutional system, the police power, being an attribute of sovereignty inherent in the original States, and not delegated by the Federal Constitution to the United States, remains with the individual States.

Under the American constitutional system, the police power, being an attribute of sovereignty inherent in the original States, and not delegated by the Federal Constitution to the United States, remains with the individual States. New Orleans Gas Light Co. v. Louisiana Light Co., 115 U.S. 650; Plumley v. Massachusetts, 155 U.S. 461; United States v. L. C. Knight Co., 156 U.S. 1; Connolly v. Union Sewer Pipe Co., 184 U.S. 540.

Whatever may be the motive or pretext of a statute, or in whatever language it may be framed, its real purpose and the question of its validity must be determined by its natural and reasonable effect to be ascertained from its practical operation. Henderson v. New York, 92 U.S. 259; Morgan's Co. v. Board of Health, 118 U.S. 455; Collins v. New Hampshire, 171 U.S. 30; Mugler v. Kansas, 123 U.S. 623; Fairbanks v. United States, 181 U.S. 283; Postal Telegraph Co. v. Adams, 155 U.S. 688.

It is apparent <appellant claims> from reading the National Firearms Act that Congress had no intention of framing a law that would procure any revenue for the Government. In the instant case, the effect of the application of the law to petitioner is to require him to pay a dealer's annual tax of $200.00 and to pay a transfer tax of an additional $200.00 for the privilege of handling and selling a commodity of the value of only

$10.00. The Act further subjects petitioner to the payment of a fine and to imprisonment of not to exceed five years if he should fail to pay the penalties required of him. These facts demonstrate, without the possibility of contradiction, that the purpose was not to tax a business, but to prohibit it.

It is apparent from reading the National Firearms Act that Congress had no intention of framing a law that would procure any revenue for the Government. In the instant case, the effect of the application of the law to petitioner is to require him to pay a dealer's annual tax of $200.00 and to pay a transfer tax of an additional $200.00 for the privilege of handling and selling a commodity of the value of only $10.00. The Act further subjects petitioner to the payment of a fine and to imprisonment of not to exceed five years if he should fail to pay the penalties required of him. These facts demonstrate, without the possibility of contradiction, that the purpose was not not to tax a business, but to prohibit it. It is inconceivable that anyone would anticipate that a dealer within the definition of §2 of the Act could possibly pay the penalty required by the Act. The amount of a levy that a statute makes upon business frequently forms the basis of jurisdictional action and determines the validity of legislation. The courts have found no insuperable difficulty in determining the difference between a tax and a penalty. Bailey v. Drexel Furniture Co., 259 U.S. 20; Atlantic & Pacific Telegraph Co. v. Philadelphia, 190 U.S. 160; Smyth v. Ames, 169 U.S. 466; Linder v. United States, 268 U.S. 5.

The classification made by the Act is arbitrary and unreasonable. It discriminates against one dealer in favor of another, without stating any justification for so doing. Connolly v. Union Sewer Pipe Co., 184 U.S. 540; Oliver v. Washington Mills, 11 Allen 265.

It is the duty of a reviewing court to review the testimony and reverse the conviction if there is no evidence whatever to support it. Miles v. United States, 103 U.S. 304; Degnan v. United States, 271 Fed. 291; Applebaum v. United States, 274 Fed. 43.

Assistant Attorney General McMahon, with whom Solicitor General Reed and Messrs. Gordon Dean and William W. Barron were on the brief, for the United States.

The authority of Congress to enact this statute is found in Art. I, §8, cl. 1 of the Constitution.

It is no objection that the size of the tax tends to burden and discourage the conduct of the occupation of petitioner. Cf. Magnano Co. v. Hamilton, 292 U.S. 40. Nor is it material that Congress may have anticipated and even intended such an effect. Where a tax is laid on a proper subject and discloses a revenue purpose, it is of no consequence that social, or moral, or economic factors may have been considered by Congress in enacting the measure. McCray v. United States, 195 U.S. 27; United States v. Doremus, 249 U.S. 86; Nigro v. United States, 276 U.S. 332; Hampton & Co. v. United States, 276 U.S. 394. The cases relied upon by petitioner are distinguishable. They involve penalties for failure to comply with federal regulations deemed to be beyond the power of Congress.

Petitioner's contention that the statute involves an unreasonable classification is merely an attack on the selection by Congress of the objects of taxation, and is untenable. His further insistence that the evidence does not support the judgment of conviction presses a contention not within the limits of the order granting the writ of certiorari.

MR. JUSTICE STONE delivered the opinion of the Court.

The question for decision is whether §2 of the National Firearms Act, which imposes a $200 annual license tax on dealers in firearms, is a constitutional exercise of the legislative power of Congress.

The question for decision is whether §2 of the National Firearms Act of June 26, 1934, c. 757, 48 Stat. 1236, 26 U.S.C., §§1132 -1132 q, which imposes a $200 annual license tax on dealers in firearms, is a constitutional exercise of the legislative power of Congress.

Petitioner was convicted by the District Court for Eastern Illinois on two counts of an indictment, the first charging him with violation of §2, by dealing in firearms without payment of the tax. On appeal the Court of Appeals set aside the conviction on the second count and affirmed on the first. 86 F.2d 486. On petition of the accused we granted certiorari, limited to the question of the constitutional validity of the statute in its application under the first count in the indictment.

Section 2 of the National Firearms Act requires every dealer in firearms to register with the Collector of Internal Revenue

The term "firearm" is defined by §1 as meaning a shotgun or a rifle having a barrel less than eighteen inches in length, or any other weapon, except a pistol or revolver, from which a shot is discharged by an explosive, if capable of being concealed on the

person, or a machine gun, and includes a muffler or silencer for any firearm.

Section 2 of the National Firearms Act requires every dealer in firearms to register with the Collector of Internal Revenue in the district where he carries on business, and to pay a special excise tax of $200 a year. Importers or manufacturers are taxed $500 a year. Section 3 imposes a tax of $200 on each transfer of a firearm, payable by the transferor, and §4 prescribes regulations for the identification of purchasers. The term "firearm" is defined by §1 as meaning a shotgun or a rifle having a barrel less than eighteen inches in length, or any other weapon, except a pistol or revolver, from which a shot is discharged by an explosive, if capable of being concealed on the person, or a machine gun, and includes a muffler or silencer for any firearm. As the conviction for nonpayment of the tax exacted by §2 has alone been sustained, it is unnecessary to inquire whether the different tax levied by §3 and the regulations pertaining to it are valid. Section 16 declares that the provisions of the Act are separable. Each tax is on a different activity and is collectible independently of the other. Full effect may be given to the license tax standing alone, even though all other provisions are invalid. Weller v. New York, 268 U.S. 319; Field v. Clark, 143 U.S. 649, 697; cf. Champlin Refining Co. v. Commission, 286 U.S. 210, 234.

Petitioner does not deny that Congress may tax his business as a dealer in firearms. He insists that the present levy is not a true tax, but a penalty imposed for the purpose of suppressing traffic in a certain noxious type of firearms, the local regulation of which is reserved to the states because not granted to the national government.

The cumulative effect on the distribution of a limited class of firearms, of relatively small value, by the successive imposition of different taxes, one on the business of the importer or manufacturer, another on that of the dealer, and a third on the transfer to a buyer, is said to be prohibitive in effect and to disclose unmistakably the legislative purpose to regulate rather than to tax.

In the exercise of its constitutional power to lay taxes, Congress may select the subjects of taxation, choosing some and omitting others. See Flint v. Stone Tracy Co., 220 U.S. 107, 158; Nicol v. Ames, 173 U.S. 509, 516; Bromley v. McCaughn, 280 U.S. 124. Its power extends to the imposition of excise taxes upon the doing of business. See License Tax Cases, 5 Wall. 462; Spreckles Sugar Refining Co. v. McClain, 192 U.S. 397, 412; United States v. Doremus, 249 U.S. 86, 94. Petitioner does not deny that Congress may tax his business as a dealer in firearms. He insists that the present levy is not a true tax, but a penalty imposed for the purpose of suppressing traffic in a certain noxious type of firearms, the local regulation of which is reserved to the states because not granted to the national government. To establish its penal and prohibitive character, he relies on the amounts of the tax imposed by §2 on dealers, manufacturers and importers, and of the tax imposed by §3 on each transfer of a "firearm," payable by the transferor. The cumulative effect on the distribution of a limited class of firearms, of relatively small value, by the successive imposition of different taxes, one on the business of the importer or manufacturer, another on that of the dealer, and a third on the transfer to a buyer, is said to be prohibitive in effect and to disclose unmistakably the legislative purpose to regulate rather than to tax.

Here §2 contains no regulation other than the mere registration provisions, which are obviously supportable as in aid of a revenue purpose. On its face it is only a taxing measure

The case is not one where the statute contains regulatory provisions related to a purported tax in such a way as has enabled this Court to say in other cases that the latter is a penalty resorted to as a means of enforcing the regulations. See Child Labor Tax Case, 259 U.S. 20, 35; Hill v. Wallace, 259 U.S. 44; Carter v. Carter Coal Co., 298 U.S. 238. Nor is the subject of the tax described or treated as criminal by the taxing statute. Compare United States v. Constantine, 296 U.S. 287. Here §2 contains no regulation other than the mere registration provisions, which are obviously supportable as in aid of a revenue purpose. On its face it is only a taxing measure, and we are asked to say that the tax, by virtue of its deterrent effect on the activities taxed, operates as a regulation which is beyond the congressional power.

it has long been established that an Act of Congress which on its face purports to be an exercise of the taxing power is not any the less so because the tax is burdensome or tends to restrict or suppress the thing taxed.

Every tax is in some measure regulatory. To some extent it interposes an economic impediment to the activity taxed as compared with others not taxed. But a tax is not any the less a tax because it has a regulatory effect, United States v. Doremus, supra, 93, 94; Nigro v. United States, 276 U.S. 332, 353, 354;

License Tax Cases, supra; see Child Labor Tax Case, supra, 38; and it has long been established that an Act of Congress which on its face purports to be an exercise of the taxing power is not any the less so because the tax is burdensome or tends to restrict or suppress the thing taxed. Veazie Bank v. Fenno, 8 Wall. 533, 548; McCray v. United States, 195 U.S. 27, 60-61; cf. Alaska Fish Co. v. Smith, 255 U.S. 44, 48.

They will not undertake, by collateral inquiry as to the measure of the regulatory effect of a tax, to ascribe to Congress an attempt, under the guise of taxation, to exercise another power denied by the Federal Constitution.

Inquiry into the hidden motives which may move Congress to exercise a power constitutionally conferred upon it is beyond the competency of courts. Veazie Bank v. Fenno, supra; McCray v. United States, supra, 56-59; United States v. Doremus, supra, 93-94; see Magnano Co. v. Hamilton, 292 U.S. 40, 44, 45; cf. Arizona v. California, 283 U.S. 423, 455; Smith v. Kansas City Title Co., 255 U.S. 180, 210; Weber v. Freed, 239 U.S. 325, 329-330; Fletcher v. Peck, 6 Cranch 87, 130. They will not undertake, by collateral inquiry as to the measure of the regulatory effect of a tax, to ascribe to Congress an attempt, under the guise of taxation, to exercise another power denied by the Federal Constitution. McCray v. United States, supra; cf. Magnano Co. v. Hamilton, supra, 45.

We are not free to speculate as to the motives which moved Congress to impose it, or as to the extent to which it may operate to restrict the activities taxed.

Here the annual tax of $200 is productive of some revenue. n1 We are not free to speculate as to the motives which moved Congress to impose it, or as to the extent to which it may operate to restrict the activities taxed. As it is not attended by an offensive regulation, and since it operates as a tax, it is within the national taxing power. Alston v. United States, 274 U.S. 289, 294; Nigro v. United States, supra, 352, 353; Hampton & Co. v. United States, 276 U.S. 394, 411, 413.

n1 The $200 tax was paid by 27 dealers in 1934, and by 22 dealers in 1935. Annual Report of the Commissioner of Internal Revenue, Fiscal Year Ended June 30, 1935, pp. 129-131; id., Fiscal Year ended June 30, 1936, pp. 139-141.

We do not discuss petitioner's contentions which he failed to assign as error below.

Affirmed.

UNITED STATES v. MILLER

(FULL CASE)

307 U.S. 174; 59 S. Ct. 816; 83 L. Ed. 1206

March 30, 1939, Argued

May 15, 1939, Decided

GIST: The most commonly cited gun case in all of the Supreme Court's decisions, the *Miller* case frequently carries a characterization that can now be seen as less than accurate, such as "one of the Court's few pronouncements on the subject." It has been discussed in scores of law review articles without arriving at any consensus. *Miller* is unusual in several ways.

First, the two defendants who were charged with illegal possession of an unregistered short-barreled shotgun ran off before the High Court case and were not heard from in court again (except for a plea agreement described below). Second, no one represented their side before the Supreme Court that day, what the Court refers to as "no appearance for appellees," so only the government's arguments were heard. Third, since the lower court took no evidence concerning the nature or usability of a short shotgun, and the Supreme Court does not take evidence, the case has no record on a central point—the usefulness of this type of firearm. Finally, the short decision can be termed a "wobbler," easily interpreted to support disparate points of view. Anyone who follows these matters knows that the main factions in the gun debate all point to

Miller as supporting their position.

It seems that the Court managed to tiptoe around some crucial elements, upholding the tax law in question. The Justices provided some interesting dicta, historical research about the militia and the 2nd Amendment from the time of the country's founding, and concluded that without better evidence, it could not make a better determination.

The National Firearms Act of 1934 had restricted, among other things, possession of short shotguns unless the guns were federally registered and a hefty tax was paid. The district court easily held the NFA unconstitutional on its face, on 2nd Amendment grounds, and released Miller and his co-defendant Layton. Interestingly, the federal government missed its deadline for filing an appeal, so the district court's decision had effectively invalidated the NFA. Recognizing their oversight later, the government actually re-indicted Miller and Layton, and when the case was dismissed a second time, filed a timely appeal to bring it to the Supreme Court.

After the Supreme Court took the case and the government filed its brief, Miller's lawyer telegraphed the Court that he had no money to file a brief or to come to Washington, D.C., to argue the case, and suggested that the Court rely on the brief of the United States. This would be considered legal malpractice today, in that the defendant's attorney invited the Court to adopt the prosecution's arguments.

The Supreme Court found that it was premature for any court to conclude whether or not the NFA violated the 2nd Amendment, so they remanded the case back to the district court for further proceedings. The Court reasoned that because the case had not presented any evidence of the military usefulness of the weapon, there was no way to say that there was a reasonable relationship between possession of a short-barreled shotgun and "the preservation or efficiency of a well regulated militia."

Meanwhile, Miller (a former bank robber) had been murdered before the decision. After the case was remanded, Layton pled guilty in a plea-bargain agreement with the government. Thus, no evidentiary hearing was ever held on whether a short-barreled shotgun was a militia-type weapon and protected from registration and taxation by the 2nd Amendment.

The National Firearms Act, as applied to one indicted for transporting in interstate commerce a 12-gauge shotgun with a barrel less than 18 inches long, without having registered it and without having in his possession a stamp-affixed written order for it, as required by the Act, held:

1. Not unconstitutional as an invasion of the reserved powers of the States. Citing Sonzinsky v. United States, 300 U.S. 506, and Narcotic Act cases.

2. Not violative of the Second Amendment of the Federal Constitution.

The Court can not take judicial notice that a shotgun having a barrel less than 18 inches long has today any reasonable relation to the preservation or efficiency of a well regulated militia; and therefore can not say that the Second Amendment guarantees to the citizen the right to keep and bear such a weapon.

Mr. Gordon Dean argued the cause, and Solicitor General Jackson, Assistant Attorney General McMahon, and Messrs. William W. Barron, Fred E. Strine, George F. Kneip, W. Marvin Smith, and Clinton R. Barry were on a brief, for the United States.

No appearance for appellees.

MR. JUSTICE McREYNOLDS delivered the opinion of the Court.

An indictment in the District Court Western District Arkansas, charged that Jack Miller and Frank Layton "did unlawfully, knowingly, wilfully, and feloniously transport in interstate commerce from the town of Claremore in the State of Oklahoma to the town of Siloam Springs in the State of Arkansas a certain firearm, to-wit, a double barrel 12-gauge Stevens shotgun having a barrel less than 18 inches in length, bearing identification number 76230, said defendants, at the time of so transporting said firearm in interstate commerce as aforesaid, not having registered said firearm as required by Section 1132d of Title 26, United States Code (Act of June 26, 1934, c. 737, Sec. 4 [§5], 48 Stat. 1237), and not having in their possession a stamp-affixed written order for said firearm as provided by Section 1132c, Title 26, United States Code (June 26, 1934, c. 737, Sec. 4, 48 Stat. 1237) and the regulations issued under authority of the said Act of Congress known as the 'National Firearms Act' approved June 26, 1934, contrary to the form of the statute in such case made and provided, and against the peace and dignity of the United States." n1

n1 Act of June 26, 1934, c. 757, 48 Stat. 1236-1240, 26 U.S.C. §1132.

That for the purposes of this Act --

"(a) The term 'firearm' means a shotgun or rifle having a barrel of less than eighteen inches in length, or any other weapon, except a pistol or revolver, from which a shot is discharged by an explosive if such weapon is capable of being concealed on the person, or a machine gun, and includes a muffler or silencer for any firearm whether or not such firearm is included within the foregoing definition, [The Act of April 10, 1936, c. 169, 49 Stat. 1192 added the words] but does not include any rifle which is within the foregoing provisions solely by reason of the length of its barrel if the caliber of such rifle is .22 or smaller and if its barrel is sixteen inches or more in length.

"Sec. 3. (a) There shall be levied, collected, and paid upon firearms transferred in the continental United States a tax at the rate of $200 for each firearm, such tax to be paid by the transferor, and to be represented by appropriate stamps to be provided by the Commissioner, with the approval of the Secretary; and the stamps herein provided shall be affixed to the order for such firearm, hereinafter provided for. The tax imposed by this section shall be in addition to any import duty imposed on such firearm.

"Sec. 4. (a) It shall be unlawful for any person to transfer a firearm except in pursuance of a written order from the person seeking to obtain such article, on an application form issued in blank in duplicate for that purpose by the Commissioner. Such order shall identify the applicant by such means of identification as may be prescribed by regulations under this Act: Provided, That, if the applicant is an individual, such identification shall include fingerprints and a photograph thereof.

"(c) Every person so transferring a firearm shall set forth in each copy of such order the manufacturer's number or other mark identifying such firearm, and shall forward a copy of such order to the Commissioner. The original thereof with stamps affixed, shall be returned to the applicant.

"(d) No person shall transfer a firearm which has previously been transferred on or after the effective date of this Act, unless such person, in addition to complying with subsection (c), transfers therewith the stamp-affixed order provided for in this section for each such prior transfer, in compliance with such regulations as may be prescribed under this Act for proof of payment of all taxes on such firearms.

"Sec. 5. (a) Within sixty days after the effective date of this Act every person possessing a firearm shall register, with the collector of the district in which he resides, the number or other mark identifying such firearm, together with his name, address, place where such firearm is usually kept, and place of business or employment, and, if such person is other than a natural person, the name and home address of an executive officer thereof: Provided, That no person shall be required to register under this section with respect to any firearm acquired after the effective date of, and in conformity with the provisions of, this Act.

"Sec. 6. It shall be unlawful for any person to receive or possess any firearm which has at any time been transferred in violation of section 3 or 4 of this Act.

"Sec. 11. It shall be unlawful for any person who is required to register as provided in section 5 hereof and who shall not have so registered, or any other person who has not in his possession a stamp-affixed order as provided in section 4 hereof, to ship, carry, or deliver any firearm in interstate commerce.

"Sec. 12. The Commissioner, with the approval of the Secretary, shall prescribe such rules and regulations as may be necessary for carrying the provisions of this Act into effect.

"Sec. 14. Any person who violates or fails to comply with any of the requirements of this Act shall, upon conviction, be fined not more than $2,000 or be imprisoned for not more than five years, or both, in the discretion of the court.

"Sec. 16. If any provision of this Act, or the application thereof to any person or circumstance, is held invalid, the remainder of the Act, and the application of such provision to other persons or circumstances, shall not be affected thereby.

"Sec. 18. This Act may be cited as the 'National Firearms Act.'"

A duly interposed demurrer alleged: The National Firearms Act is not a revenue measure but an attempt to usurp police power reserved to the States, and is therefore

unconstitutional. Also, it offends the inhibition of the Second Amendment to the Constitution

A duly interposed demurrer alleged: The National Firearms Act is not a revenue measure but an attempt to usurp police power reserved to the States, and is therefore unconstitutional. Also, it offends the inhibition of the Second Amendment to the Constitution -- "A well regulated Militia, being necessary to the security of a free State, the right of people to keep and bear Arms, shall not be infringed."

The District Court held that section eleven of the Act violates the Second Amendment. It accordingly sustained the demurrer and quashed the indictment.

The cause is here by direct appeal.

the objection that the Act usurps police power reserved to the States is plainly untenable.

Considering Sonzinsky v. United States (1937), 300 U.S. 506, 513, and what was ruled in sundry causes arising under the Harrison Narcotic Act n2 -- United States v. Jin Fuey Moy (1916), 241 U.S. 394; United States v. Doremus (1919), 249 U.S. 86, 94; Linder v. United States (1925), 268 U.S. 5; Alston v. United States (1927), 274 U.S. 289; Nigro v. United States (1928), 276 U.S. 332 -- the objection that the Act usurps police power reserved to the States is plainly untenable.

n2 Act December 17, 1914, c. 1, 38 Stat. 785; February 24, 1919, c. 18, 40 Stat. 1057.

In the absence of any evidence tending to show that possession or use of a "shotgun having a barrel of less than eighteen inches in length" at this time has some reasonable relationship to the preservation or efficiency of a well regulated militia, we cannot say that the Second Amendment guarantees the right to keep and bear such an instrument. Certainly it is not within judicial notice that this weapon is any part of the ordinary military equipment or that its use could contribute to the common defense.

In the absence of any evidence tending to show that possession or use of a "shotgun having a barrel of less than eighteen inches in length" at this time has some reasonable relationship to the preservation or efficiency of a well regulated militia, we cannot say that the Second Amendment guarantees the right to keep and bear such an instrument. Certainly it is not within judicial notice that this weapon is any part of the ordinary military equipment or that its use could contribute to the common defense. Aymette v. State, 2 Humphreys (Tenn.) 154, 158.

With obvious purpose to assure the continuation and render possible the effectiveness of such forces the declaration and guarantee of the Second Amendment were made. It must be interpreted and applied with that end in view.

The Constitution as originally adopted granted to the Congress power -- "To provide for calling forth the Militia to execute the Laws of the Union, suppress Insurrections and repel Invasions; To provide for organizing, arming, and disciplining, the Militia, and for governing such Part of them as may be employed in the Service of the United States, reserving to the States respectively, the Appointment of the Officers, and the Authority of training the Militia according to the discipline prescribed by Congress." With obvious purpose to assure the continuation and render possible the effectiveness of such forces the declaration and guarantee of the Second Amendment were made. It must be interpreted and applied with that end in view.

The Militia which the States were expected to maintain and train is set in contrast with Troops which they were forbidden to keep without the consent of Congress

the common view was that adequate defense of country and laws could be secured through the Militia—civilians primarily, soldiers on occasion.

The Militia which the States were expected to maintain and train is set in contrast with Troops which they were forbidden to keep without the consent of Congress. The sentiment of the time strongly disfavored standing armies; the common view was that adequate defense of country and laws could be secured through the Militia -- civilians primarily, soldiers on occasion.

the Militia comprised all males physically capable of acting in concert for the common defense. "A body of citizens enrolled for military discipline."

when called for service these men were expected to appear bearing arms supplied by themselves and of the kind in common use at the time.

The signification attributed to the term Militia appears from the debates in the Convention, the history and legislation of Colonies and States, and the writings of approved commentators. These show plainly enough that the Militia comprised all males physically capable of acting in concert for the common defense. "A body of citizens enrolled for military discipline." And further, that ordinarily when called for service these men were expected to appear bearing arms supplied by themselves and of the kind in common use at the time.

Blackstone's Commentaries, Vol. 2, Ch. 13, p. 409 points out "that king Alfred first settled a national militia in this kingdom," and traces the subsequent development and use of such forces.

In a militia, the character of the labourer, artificer, or tradesman, predominates over that of the soldier: in a standing army, that of the soldier predominates over every other character; and in this distinction seems to consist the essential difference between those two different species of military force.

Adam Smith's Wealth of Nations, Book V, Ch. 1, contains an extended account of the Militia. It is there said: "Men of republican principles have been jealous of a standing army as dangerous to liberty." "In a militia, the character of the labourer, artificer, or tradesman, predominates over that of the soldier: in a standing army, that of the soldier predominates over every other character; and in this distinction seems to consist the essential difference between those two different species of military force."

"The American Colonies In The 17th Century," Osgood, Vol. 1, ch. XIII, affirms in reference to the early system of defense in New England --

In all the colonies, as in England, the militia system was based on the principle of the assize of arms. This implied the general obligation of all adult male inhabitants to possess arms, and, with certain exceptions, to cooperate in the work of defence.

"In all the colonies, as in England, the militia system was based on the principle of the assize of arms. This implied the general obligation of all adult male inhabitants to possess arms, and, with certain exceptions, to cooperate in the work of defence." "The possession of arms also implied the possession of ammunition, and the authorities paid quite as much attention to the latter as to the former." "A year later [1632] it was ordered that any single man who had not furnished himself with arms might be put out to service, and this became a permanent part of the legislation of the colony [Massachusetts]."

Clauses intended to insure the possession of arms and ammunition by all who were subject to military service appear in all the important enactments concerning military affairs. Fines were the penalty for delinquency, whether of towns or individuals.

The musketeer should carry a 'good fixed musket,' not under bastard musket bore, not less than three feet, nine inches, nor more than four feet three inches in length, a priming wire, scourer, and mould, a sword, rest, bandoleers, one pound of powder, twenty bullets, and two fathoms of match.

Also "Clauses intended to insure the possession of arms and ammunition by all who were subject to military service appear in all the important enactments concerning military affairs. Fines were the penalty for delinquency, whether of towns or individuals. According to the usage of the times, the infantry of Massachusetts consisted of pikemen and musketeers. The law, as enacted in 1649 and thereafter, provided that each of the former should be armed with a pike, corselet, head-piece, sword, and knapsack. The musketeer should carry a 'good fixed musket,' not under bastard musket bore, not less than three feet, nine inches, nor more than four feet three inches in length, a priming wire, scourer, and mould, a sword, rest, bandoleers, one pound of powder, twenty bullets, and two fathoms of match. The law also required that two-thirds of each company should be musketeers."

The General Court of Massachusetts, January Session 1784, provided for the organization and government of the Militia. It directed that the Train Band should "contain all able bodied men, from sixteen to forty years of age, and the Alarm List, all other men under sixty years of age, . . ." Also, "That every non-commissioned officer and private soldier of the said militia not under the controul of parents, masters or guardians, and being of sufficient ability therefor in the judgment of the Selectmen of the town in which he shall dwell, shall equip himself, and be constantly provided with a good fire arm," &c.

By an Act passed April 4, 1786 the New York Legislature directed: "That every able-bodied Male Person, being a Citizen of this State, or of any of the United States, and residing in this State, (except such Persons as are hereinafter excepted) and who are of the Age of Sixteen, and under the Age of Forty-five Years, shall, by the Captain or commanding Officer of the Beat in which such Citizens shall reside, within four

Months after the passing of this Act, be enrolled in the Company of such Beat. . . . That every Citizen so enrolled and notified, shall, within three Months thereafter, provide himself, at his own Expense, with a good Musket or Firelock, a sufficient Bayonet and Belt, a Pouch with a Box therein to contain not less than Twenty-four Cartridges suited to the Bore of his Musket or Firelock, each Cartridge containing a proper Quantity of Powder and Ball, two spare Flints, a Blanket and Knapsack; . . ."

"The defense and safety of the commonwealth depend upon having its citizens properly armed and taught the knowledge of military duty."

The General Assembly of Virginia, October, 1785, (12 Hening's Statutes) declared, "The defense and safety of the commonwealth depend upon having its citizens properly armed and taught the knowledge of military duty."

It further provided for organization and control of the Militia and directed that "All free male persons between the ages of eighteen and fifty years," with certain exceptions, "shall be inrolled or formed into companies." "There shall be a private muster of every company once in two months."

Also that "Every officer and soldier shall appear at his respective muster-field on the day appointed, by eleven o'clock in the forenoon, armed, equipped, and accoutred, as follows: . . . every non-commissioned officer and private with a good, clean musket carrying an ounce ball, and three feet eight inches long in the barrel, with a good bayonet and iron ramrod well fitted thereto, a cartridge box properly made, to contain and secure twenty cartridges fitted to his musket, a good knapsack and canteen, and moreover, each non-commissioned officer and private shall have at every muster one pound of good powder, and four pounds of lead, including twenty blind cartridges; and each serjeant shall have a pair of moulds fit to cast balls for their respective companies, to be purchased by the commanding officer out of the monies arising on delinquencies. Provided, That the militia of the counties westward of the Blue Ridge, and the counties below adjoining thereto, shall not be obliged to be armed with muskets, but may have good rifles with proper accoutrements, in lieu thereof. And every of the said officers, non-commissioned officers, and privates, shall constantly keep the aforesaid arms, accoutrements, and ammunition, ready to be produced whenever called for by his commanding officer. If any private shall make it appear to the satisfaction of the court hereafter to be appointed for trying delinquencies under this act that he is so poor that he cannot purchase the arms herein required, such court shall cause them to be purchased out of the money arising from delinquents."

Most if not all of the States have adopted provisions touching the right to keep and bear arms. Differences in the language employed in these have naturally led to somewhat variant conclusions concerning the scope of the right guaranteed.

Most if not all of the States have adopted provisions touching the right to keep and bear arms. Differences in the language employed in these have naturally led to somewhat variant conclusions concerning the scope of the right guaranteed. But none of them seem to afford any material support for the challenged ruling of the court below.

In the margin some of the more important opinions and comments by writers are cited. n3

n3 Concerning The Militia -- Presser v. Illinois, 116 U.S. 252; Robertson v. Baldwin, 165 U.S. 275; Fife v. State, 31 Ark. 455; Jeffers v. Fair, 33 Ga. 347; Salina v. Blaksley, 72 Kan. 230; 83 P. 619; People v. Brown, 253 Mich. 537; 235 N. W. 245; Aymette v. State, 2 Humphr. (Tenn.) 154; State v. Duke, 42 Texas 455; State v. Workman, 35 W. Va. 367; 14 S. E. 9; Cooley's Constitutional Limitations, Vol. 1, p. 729; Story on The Constitution, 5th Ed., Vol. 2, p. 646; Encyclopaedia of the Social Sciences, Vol. X, p. 471, 474.

We are unable to accept the conclusion of the court below and the challenged judgment must be reversed. The cause will be remanded for further proceedings.

MR. JUSTICE DOUGLAS took no part in the consideration or decision of this cause.

TOT v. UNITED STATES

(FULL CASE)

319 U.S. 463; 63 S. Ct. 1241; 87 L. Ed. 1519

April 5, 6, 1943, Argued

June 7, 1943, Decided

GIST: The Federal Firearms Act included a clause that said if a person with a prior conviction for a crime of violence, or a fugitive, was found in possession of a firearm, that person was presumed to have obtained the gun in interstate commerce (which would give Congress jurisdiction). The Court decided this was not a rational conclusion, and that this did not provide sufficient facts to establish guilt. In other words, the law cannot presume a gun had just been in interstate commerce just because it was possessed by a felon. The law at the time was seen to affect only receipt of firearms or ammunition as a part of interstate transportation. It did not reach receipt of a gun or ammo in an intrastate transaction, which at some prior time had been transported interstate. That distinction was later addressed in *Bass, Barrett,* and *Scarborough.*

The lower court case (131 F.2d 261) that began the road to this appeal was found by Attorney Stephen Halbrook to be the original source of the "collective rights" conjecture used by anti-rights advocates in modern times. That case purports to be based on the intent of the Framers, but none of the references cited deny that the 2nd Amendment protects an individual right. Subsequent cases that make use of the collectivist argument merely string cite to cases ultimately traceable to *Tot.*

Mr. Justice ROBERTS delivered the opinion of the Court.

These cases involve the construction and validity of 2(f) of the Federal Firearms Act, n1 which is:

n1. c. 850, 52 Stat. 1250, 1251, 15 U.S.C. 902(f), 15 U.S.C.A. 902(f).

'It shall be unlawful for any person who has been convicted of a crime of violence or is a fugutive (fugitive) from justice to receive any firearm or ammunition which has been shipped or transported in interstate or foreign commerce, and the possession of a firearm or ammunition by any such person shall be presumptive evidence that such firearm or ammunition was shipped or transported or received, as the case may be, by such person in violation of this Act.'

In No. 569, Tot, the petitioner, was convicted n2 upon an indictment which charged that he, having been previously convicted of two crimes of violence, a burglary and an assault and battery, with intent to beat, wound, and ill-treat, n3 on or about September 20, 1938, at Newark, New Jersey, knowingly, unlawfully, and feloniously received a described firearm which 'had been shipped and transported in interstate commerce to the said City of Newark.' The Circuit Court of Appeals affirmed the judgment. n4

n2. See 42 F.Supp. 252.

n3. These are crimes of violence according to the definition contained in 1(6) of the Act, 15 U.S.C. 901(6), 15 U.S.C.A. 901(6).

n4. 131 F.2d 261.

The Government's evidence was that Tot had been convicted of assault and battery in 1925, and had pleaded non vult to a charge of burglary in 1932 in state courts, and that, on September 22, 1938, he was found in possession of a loaded automatic pistol. After denial of a motion for a directed verdict, Tot took the stand and testified that he purchased the pistol in 1933 or 1934. He admitted the criminal record charged in the indictment and other convictions. His sister and his wife testified in corroboration of his evidence, but their testimony was shaken on cross-examination. In rebuttal the Government produced a representative of the manufacturer who testified that the pistol had been made in Connecticut in 1919 and shipped by the maker to Chicago, Illinois. At the close of the case petitioner renewed his motion for a directed verdict, which was denied.

The respondent testified that he had, at about the time of his arrest, picked up the revolver when it was dropped by a person who attacked him, but there was testimony which tended to contradict this defense.

In No. 636, Delia, the respondent, was convicted upon two counts. The first alleged that, on September 25, 1941, he was a person previously convicted of a crime of violence-robbery while armed n5 -and that he received and possessed a firearm, described in the indictment, 'which firearm had theretofore been shipped and transported in interstate commerce.' The second repeated the allegation of previous conviction and charged that, on September 25, 1941, he received and possessed certain cartridges which 'had been theretofore shipped and transported in interstate commerce.' The Government's proof was that Delia had been convicted of armed robbery and, on September 25, 1941, had in his possession a loaded revolver which had been manufactured in Massachusetts prior to 1920; that some of the cartridges in the pistol had been manufactured in Ohio and some in Germany, the former after 1934 and the latter at an unknown date. The respondent testified that he had, at about the time of his arrest, picked up the revolver when it was dropped by a person who attacked him, but there was testimony which tended to contradict this defense. The Circuit Court of Appeals reversed the conviction on each count. n6

n5. Armed robbery is a crime of violence as defined in 1(6) of the Act.

n6. 131 F.2d 614.

Both courts below held that the offense created by the Act is confined to the receipt of firearms or ammunition as a part of interstate transportation and does not extend to the receipt, in an intrastate transaction, of such articles which, at some prior time, have been transported interstate. The Government agrees that this construction is correct.

Both courts below held that the offense created by the Act is confined to the receipt of firearms or ammunition as a part of interstate transportation and does not extend to the receipt, in an intrastate transaction, of such articles which, at some prior time, have been transported interstate. The Government agrees that this construction is correct. There remains for decision the question of the power of Congress to create the presumption which 2(f) declares, namely, that, from the prisoner's prior conviction of a crime of violence and his present possession of a firearm or ammunition, it shall be presumed (1) that the article was received by him in interstate or foreign commerce, and (2) that such receipt occurred subsequent to July 30, 1938, the effective date of the statute.

The Government argues that the presumption created by the statute meets the tests of due process heretofore laid down by this court. The defendants assert that it fails to meet them because there is no rational connection between the facts proved and the ultimate fact presumed, that the statute is more than a regulation of the order of proof based upon the relative accessibility of evidence to prosecution and defense, and casts an unfair and practically impossible burden of persuasion upon the defendant.

An indictment charges the defendant with action or failure to act contrary to the law's command. It does not constitute proof of the commission of the offense. Proof of some sort on the part of the prosecutor is requisite to a finding of guilt; it may consist of testimony of those who witnessed the defendant's conduct. Although the Government may be unable to produce testimony of eye witnesses to the conduct on which guilt depends, this does not mean that it cannot produce proof sufficient to support a verdict. The jury is permitted to infer from one fact the existence of another essential to guilt, if reason and experience support the inference. In many circumstances courts hold that proof of the first fact furnishes a basis for inference of the existence of the second. n7

n7. Wilson v. United States, 162 U.S. 613, 619, 16 S.Ct. 895, 898.

The rules of evidence, however, are established not alone by the courts but by the legislature. The Congress has power to prescribe what evidence is to be received in the courts of the United States. n8 The section under consideration is such legislation. But the due process clauses of the Fifth and Fourteenth Amendments set limits upon the power of Congress or that of a state legislature to make the proof of one fact or group of facts evidence of the existence of the ultimate fact on which guilt is predicated. The question is whether, in this instance, the Act transgresses those limits.

n8. Ex parte Fisk, 113 U.S. 713, 721, 5 S.Ct. 724, 727; Adams v. New York 192 U.S. 585, 599, 24 S.Ct. 372, 375; Mobile J. & K.C.R. Co. v. Turnipseed, 219 U.S. 35, 42, 31 S.Ct. 136, 137, 32 L.R.A., N.S. 226, Ann.Cas.1912A, 463; Bailey v. Alabama, 219 U.S. 219, 238, 31 S.Ct. 145, 150; Luria v. United States, 231 U.S. 9, 34 S.Ct. 10; Hawes v. Georgia, 258 U.S. 1, 4, 42 S.Ct. 204, 205.

The Government seems to argue that there are two alternative tests of the validity of a presumption created by statute. The first is that there be a rational connection between the facts proved and the fact presumed; the second that of comparative convenience of producing evidence of the ultimate fact. We are of opinion that these are not independent tests but that the first is controlling and the second but a corollary.

Under our decisions, a statutory presumption cannot be sustained if there be no rational connection between the fact proved and the ultimate fact presumed, if the inference of the one from proof of the other is arbitrary because of lack of connection between the two in common experience. n9 This is not to say that a valid presumption may not be created upon a view of relation broader than that a jury might take in a specific case. n10 But where the inference is so strained as not to have a reasonable relation to the circumstances of life as we know them it is not competent for the legislature to create it as a rule governing the procedure of courts.

n9. Mobile J. & K.C.R. Co. v. Turnipseed, supra, 219 U.S. at page 43, 31 S.Ct. at page 138, 32 L.R.A.,N.S., 226, Ann.Cas.1912A, 463; Bailey v. Alabama, supra, 219 U.S. at page 239, 31 S.Ct. at page 150; Lindsley v. Natural Carbonic Gas Co., 220 U.S. 61, 81, 31 S.Ct. 337, 341, Ann.Cas.1912C, 160; Luria v. United States, supra, 231 U.S. at page 25, 34 S.Ct. at page 14; McFarland v. American Sugar Ref. Co., 241 U.S. 79, 86, 36 S.Ct. 498, 501; Manley v. Georgia, 279 U.S. 1, 49 S.Ct. 215; Western & A.R. Co. v. Henderson, 279 U.S. 639, 642, 49 S.Ct. 445, 447; Morrison v. California, 291 U.S. 82, 90, 54 S.Ct. 281, 284.

n10. Bailey v. Alabama, supra, 219 U.S. at page 235, 31 S.Ct. at page 149.

in most states, laws forbid the acquisition of firearms without a record of the transaction or require registration of ownership.

The Government seeks to support the presumption by a showing that, in most states, laws forbid the acquisition of firearms without a record of the transaction or require registration of ownership. From these circumstances it is argued that mere possession tends strongly to indicate that acquisition must have been in an interstate transaction. But we think the conclusion does not rationally follow. Aside from the fact that a number of states have no such laws, there is no presumption that a firearm must have been lawfully acquired or that it was not transferred interstate prior to the adoption of state regulation. Even less basis exists for the inference from mere possession that acquisition occurred subsequent to the effective date of the statute,-July 30, 1938. And, as no state laws or regulations are cited with respect to the acquisition of ammunition, there seems no reasonable ground for a presumption that its purchase or procurement was in interstate rather than in intrastate commerce.11 It is not too much to say that the presumptions created by the law are violent, and inconsistent with any argument drawn from experience. Nor can the fact that the defendant has the better means of information, standing alone, justify the creation of such a presumption. In every criminal case the defendant has at least an equal familiarity with the facts and in most a greater familiarity with them than the prosecution. It might, therefore, be argued that to place upon all defendants in criminal cases the burden of going forward with the evidence would be proper. But the argument proves too much. If it were sound, the legislature might validly command that the finding of an indictment, or mere proof of the identity of the accused, should create a presumption of the existence of all the facts essential to guilt. This is not permissible.12

n11. Delia was convicted upon an indictment which charged, inter alia, receipt of ammunition.

n12. McFarland v. American Sugar Ref. Co., supra, 241 U.S. at page 86, 36 S.Ct. at page 501.

Whether the statute in question be treated as expressing the normal balance of probability, or as laying down a rule of comparative convenience in the production of evidence, it leaves the jury free to act on the presumption alone once the specified facts are proved, unless the defendant comes forward with opposing evidence. And this we think enough to vitiate the statutory provision.

the defendants in these cases knew better than anyone else whether they acquired the firearms or ammunition in interstate commerce.

it is not permissible thus to shift the burden by arbitrarily making one fact, which has no relevance to guilt of the offense, the occasion of casting on the defendant the obligation of exculpation.

Doubtless the defendants in these cases knew better than anyone else whether they acquired the firearms or ammunition in interstate commerce. It would, therefore, be a convenience to the Government to rely upon the presumption and cast on the defendants the burden of coming forward with evidence to rebut it. But, as we have shown, it is not permissible thus to shift the burden by arbitrarily making one fact, which has no relevance to guilt of the offense, the occasion of casting on the defendant the obligation of exculpation. The argument from convenience is admissible only where the inference is a permissible one, where the defendant has more convenient access to the proof, and where requiring him to go forward with proof will not subject him to unfairness or hardship.13 Even if the presumption in question were in itself reasonable, we think that the nature of the offense, and the elements which go to constitute it, render it impossible to sustain the statute, for the reason that one element of the offense is the prior conviction of a crime of violence. If the presumption warrants conviction unless the defendant comes forward with evidence in explanation and if, as is necessarily true, such evidence must be credited by the jury if the presumption is to be rebutted, the defendant is under the handicap, if he takes the witness stand, of admitting prior convictions of violent crimes. His evidence as to acquisition of the firearm or ammunition is thus discredited in the eyes of the jury before it is given.

n13. Morrison v. California, supra, 291 U.S. at pages 94, 96, 54 S.Ct. at pages 286, 287.

Although the Government recognizes that the authorities cited in Note 9 announce the rule by which the validity of the Act is to be tested, it relies on certain other decisions as supporting the legislation. We think that what was decided in those cases was not a departure from the rule and that they are distinguishable from the instant cases.

In Adams v. New York, 192 U.S. 585, 24 S.Ct. 372, a state statute made it an offense 'knowingly' to possess policy slips and provided that possession should be presumptive evidence 'of possession thereof knowingly'. The statutory presumption was sustained. Accidental and innocent possession of such a paper would be extraordinary and unusual and the statutory presumption was hardly needed to justify a jury in inferring knowledge of the character of the policy slip by one found in possession of it.

In Hawes v. Georgia, 258 U.S. 1, 42 S.Ct. 204, the statutory offense was that of knowingly permitting a still upon the defendant's premises. The statute provided that when distilling apparatus was found on the premises this should be prima facie evidence that the person in actual possession had knowledge of its existence. The defendant's premises were a farm on which a still was found. This court sustained the presumption. The inference so accorded with common experience that a statutory provision scarcely was necessary to shift the burden of proof.

In Fong Yue Ting v. United States, 149 U.S. 698, 13 S.Ct. 1016, an Act of Congress was involved which required every Chinese alien within one year to procure from the Collector of Internal Revenue a certificate of residence and made it the duty of such alien to produce the certificate on request. Any officer was authorized to arrest a Chinese alien failing to produce the certificate on request and to hold him for deportation. The Act placed on the alien the burden of proving at the deportation hearing his residence and of excusing his failure to procure a certificate. Failure to have in his possession the certificate the law required him to have gave rise to a natural inference of intentional failure to procure it or unlawful residence in the country which precluded his procuring it. In such a situation the shifting to the alien of the burden of explanation imposed no unreasonable hardship upon him.

no lawful purchase of smoking opium could occur in this country and that, therefore, possession gave rise to sinister implications.

In Yee Hem v. United States, 268 U.S. 178, 45 S.Ct. 470, it appeared that an Act of Congress prohibited importation of opium except under Treasury regulations and the latter forbade importation of smoking opium. The statute made it an offense knowingly to conceal opium illegally imported and threw upon a defendant found in possession of smoking opium the burden of showing that he had not acquired it through illegal importation. This court sustained the presumption on the ground that no lawful purchase of smoking opium could occur in this country and that, therefore, possession gave rise to sinister implications. It concluded it was not unreasonable to create a presumption of unlawful importation as the source of the commodity the possession of which the defendant concealed. In Casey v. United States, 276 U.S. 413, 48 S.Ct. 373, the offenses created by Act of Congress were the purchase or sale of morphine from packages not stamped with an Internal Revenue tax stamp. The defendant was charged with a purchase from such a package. The evidence showed that he dispensed the drug in clandestine fashion and not from a stamped package. In these circumstances, this court held that the presumption created by the statute that a sale of morphine from an unstamped package should be prima facie evidence of a similar purchase was not unreasonable or beyond the realm of common experience.

The Government seeks to sustain the statute on an alternative ground. It urges that Congress, in view of the interstate commerce in firearms, might, in order to regulate it, have prohibited the possession of all firearms by persons heretofore convicted of crimes of violence; that, as the power of Congress extends so far, the presumption that acquisition was in interstate commerce is the lesser exertion of legislative power and may be upheld.14 Two considerations render the argument inadmissible. First, it will not serve to sustain the presumption of acquisition after the effective date of the Act, and secondly, it is plain that Congress, for whatever reason, did not seek to pronounce general prohibition of possession by certain residents of the various states of firearms in order to protect interstate commerce, but dealt only with their future acquisition in interstate commerce.

n14. See Ferry v. Ramsay, 277 U.S. 88, 48 S.Ct. 443.

The judgment in No. 569 is reversed and that in No. 636 is affirmed.

Reversed in part.

Mr. Justice MURPHY took no part in the consideration or decision of these cases.

Mr. Justice BLACK, with whom Mr. Justice DOUGLAS concurs, concurring.

the mere possession of a pistol coupled with conviction of a prior crime is no evidence at all that the possessor of the pistol has acquired it in interstate commerce or obtained it since the effective date of the Act under consideration.

I agree that the mere possession of a pistol coupled with conviction of a prior crime is no evidence at all that the possessor of the pistol has acquired it in interstate commerce or obtained it since the effective date of the Act under consideration. The Act authorizes, and in effect constrains, juries to convict defendants charged with violation of this statute even though no evidence whatever has been offered which tends to prove an essential ingredient of the offense. The procedural safeguards found in the Constitution and in the Bill of Rights, Chambers v. Florida, 309 U.S. 227, 237, 60 S.Ct. 472, 477, stand as a constitutional barrier against thus obtaining a conviction, ibid., 309 U.S. at pages 235-238, 60 S.Ct. at pages 476, 477. These constitutional provisions contemplate that a jury must determine guilt or innocence in a public trial in which the defendant is confronted with the witnesses against him and in which he enjoys the assistance of counsel; and where guilt is in issue, a verdict against a defendant must be preceded by the introduction of some evidence which tends to prove the elements of the crime charged. Compliance with these constitutional provisions, which of course constitute the supreme law of the land, is essential to due process of law, and a conviction obtained without their observance cannot be sustained.

It is unnecessary to consider whether this statute, which puts the defendant against whom no evidence of guilt has been offered in a procedural situation from which he can escape conviction only by testifying, compels him to give evidence against himself in violation of the Fifth Amendment.

ADAMSON v. CALIFORNIA

(CASE EXCERPT)

332 U.S. 46; 67 S. Ct. 1672; 91 L. Ed. 1903; 171 A.L.R. 1223

January 15-16, 1947, Argued

June 23, 1947, Decided

GIST: This decision reaffirmed earlier cases holding that various provisions of the Bill of Rights, including the 5th Amendment privilege against self incrimination, were not binding on the states through the 14th Amendment. Justice Black, in a dissenting opinion joined by Douglas, quoted the legislative history of the 14th Amendment at length. He argued that it was intended to incorporate the Bill of Rights, including the 2nd Amendment, against the states. Justices Murphy and Rutledge agreed with this view, but would not have limited the content of the 14th Amendment Due Process Clause only to the provisions in the Bill of Rights.

MR. JUSTICE BLACK, dissenting.

.....

Later, but prior to the Twining case, this Court decided that the following were not "privileges or immunities" of national citizenship, so as to make them immune against state invasion: the Eighth Amendment's prohibition against cruel and unusual punishment, In re Kemmler, the Seventh Amendment's guarantee of a jury trial in civil cases, Walker v. Sauvinet, the Second Amendment's "right of the people to keep and bear Arms ... ," Presser v. Illinois, the Fifth and Sixth Amendments' requirements for indictment in capital or other infamous crimes, and for trial by jury in criminal prosecutions, Maxwell v. Dow. While it can be argued that these cases implied that no one of the provisions of the Bill of Rights was made applicable to the states as attributes of national citizenship, no one of them expressly so decided. In fact, the Court in Maxwell v. Dow concluded no more than that "the privileges and immunities of citizens of the United States do not necessarily include all the rights protected by the first eight amendments to the Federal Constitution against the powers of the Federal Government."

.....

I cannot consider the Bill of Rights to be an outworn 18th Century "strait jacket" as the Twining opinion did. Its provisions may be thought outdated abstractions by some. And it is true that they were designed to meet ancient evils. But they are the same kind of human evils that have emerged from century to century wherever excessive power is sought by the few at the expense of the many. In my judgment the people of no nation can lose their liberty so long as a Bill of Rights like ours survives and its basic purposes are conscientiously interpreted, enforced and respected so as to afford continuous protection against old, as well as new, devices and practices which might thwart those purposes. I fear to see the consequences of the Court's practice of substituting its own concepts of decency and fundamental justice for the language of the Bill of Rights as its point of departure in interpreting and enforcing that Bill of Rights. If the choice must be between the selective process of the Palko decision applying some of the Bill of Rights to the States, or the Twining rule applying none of them, I would choose the Palko selective process. But rather than accept either of these choices, I would follow what I believe was the original purpose of the Fourteenth Amendment -- to extend to all the people of the nation the complete protection of the Bill of Rights. To hold that this Court can determine what, if any, provisions of the Bill of Rights will be enforced, and if so to what degree, is to frustrate the great design of a written Constitution.

MR. JUSTICE DOUGLAS joins in this opinion.

APPENDIX. <recounts the legislative history of the Fourteenth Amendment>

.....

"the late slaveholding States" had enacted laws "... depriving persons of African descent of privileges which are essential to freemen ... Statutes of Mississippi ... prohibit any negro or mulatto from having fire-arms

Important events which apparently affected the evolution of the Fourteenth Amendment transpired during the period during which discussion of it was postponed. The Freedman's Bureau Bill which made deprivation of certain civil rights of negroes an offense punishable by military tribunals had been passed. It applied, not to the entire country, but only to the South. On February 19, 1866, President Johnson had vetoed the bill principally on the ground that it was unconstitutional. Cong. Globe, supra, 915. Forthwith, a companion proposal known as the Civil Rights Bill empowering federal courts to punish those who deprived any person anywhere in the country of certain defined civil rights was pressed to passage. Senator Trumbull, Chairman of the Senate Judiciary Committee, who offered the bill in the Senate on behalf of that Committee, had stated that "the late slaveholding States" had enacted laws "... depriving persons of African descent of privileges which are essential to freemen ... Statutes of Mississippi ... provide that ... If any person of African descent residing in that State travels from one county to another without having a pass or a certificate of his freedom, he is liable to be committed to jail and to be dealt with as a person who is in the State without authority. Other provisions of the statute prohibit any negro or mulatto from having fire-arms; and one provision of the statute declares that for 'exercising the functions of a minister of the Gospel free negroes ... on conviction, may be punished by ... lashes ....' Other provisions ... prohibit a free negro ... from keeping a house of entertainment, and subject him to trial before two justices of the peace and five slaveholders for violating ... this law. The statutes of South Carolina make it a highly penal offense for any person, white or colored, to teach slaves; and similar provisions are to be found running through all the statutes of the late slaveholding States. ... The purpose of the bill ... is to destroy all these discriminations ...." Cong. Globe, supra, 474.

And an opponent of the measure, Mr. Raymond, conceded that it would guarantee to the negro "the right of free passage ... He has a defined status ... a right to defend himself ... to bear arms"

In the House, after Mr. Bingham's original proposal for a constitutional amendment had been rejected, the suggestion was also advanced that the bill secured for all "the right of speech, ... transit, ... domicil, ... the right to sue, the writ of habeas corpus, and the right of petition." Cong. Globe, supra, 1263. And an opponent of the measure, Mr. Raymond, conceded that it would guarantee to the negro "the right of free passage ... He has a defined status ... a right to defend himself ... to bear arms ... to testify in the Federal courts ...." Cong. Globe, supra, 1266-1267. But opponents took the position that without a constitutional amendment such as that proposed by Mr. Bingham, the Civil Rights Bill would be unconstitutional. Cong. Globe, supra, 1154-1155, 1263.

.....

"It would be a curious question to solve what are the privileges and immunities of citizens of each of the States in the several States. ... I am not aware that the Supreme Court have ever undertaken to define either the nature or extent of the privileges and immunities thus guarantied. ... But we may gather some intimation of what probably will be the opinion of the judiciary by referring to ... Corfield vs. Coryell [Here

Senator Howard quoted at length from that opinion.]

the personal rights guarantied and secured by the first eight amendments of the Constitution; such as ... the right to keep and to bear arms

"Such is the character of the privileges and immunities spoken of in the second section of the fourth article of the Constitution. To these privileges and immunities, whatever they may be -- for they are not and cannot be fully defined in their entire extent and precise nature -- to these should be added the personal rights guarantied and secured by the first eight amendments of the Constitution; such as the freedom of speech and of the press; the right of the people peaceably to assemble and petition the Government for a redress of grievances, a right appertaining to each and all the people; the right to keep and to bear arms; the right to be exempted from the quartering of soldiers in a house without the consent of the owner; the right to be exempt from unreasonable searches and seizures, and from any search or seizure except by virtue of a warrant issued upon a formal oath or affidavit; the right of an accused person to be informed of the nature of the accusation against him, and his right to be tried by an impartial jury of the vicinage; and also the right to be secure against excessive bail and against cruel and unusual punishments.

.....

VI.

Also just prior to the final votes in both Houses passing the resolution of adoption, the Report of the Joint Committee on Reconstruction, H. R. Rep. No. 30, 39th Cong., 1st Sess. (1866); Sen. Rep. No. 112, 39th Cong., 1st Sess. (1866), was submitted. Cong. Globe, supra, 3038, 3051. This report was apparently not distributed in time to influence the debates in Congress. But a student of the period reports that 150,000 copies of the Report and the testimony which it contained were printed in order that senators and representatives might distribute them among their constituents. Apparently the Report was widely reprinted in the press and used as a campaign document in the election of 1866. Kendrick, Journal of the Joint Committee on Reconstruction (1914) 265. According to Kendrick the Report was "eagerly ... perused" for information concerning "conditions in the South." Kendrick, supra, 265.

The Report of the Committee had said with reference to the necessity of amending the Constitution:

"... The so-called Confederate States are not, at present, entitled to representation in the Congress of the United States; that, before allowing such representation, adequate security for future peace and safety should be required; that this can only be found in such changes of the organic law as shall determine the civil rights and privileges of all citizens in all parts of the republic ...." Report, supra, XXI.

Among the examples recited by the testimony were discrimination against negro churches and preachers by local officials and criminal punishment of those who attended objectionable church services. Report, Part II, 52. Testimony also cited recently enacted Louisiana laws which made it "a highly penal offence for anyone to do anything that might be construed into encouraging the blacks to leave the persons with whom they had made contracts for labor ...." Report, Part III, p. 25. n3

n3 In a widely publicized report to the President which was also submitted to the Congress, Carl Schurz had reviewed similar incidents and emphasized the fact that negroes had been denied the right to bear arms, own property, engage in business, to testify in Court, and that local authorities had arrested them without cause and tried them without juries. Sen. Exec. Doc. No. 2, 39th Cong., 1st Sess. (1865) 23, 24, 26, 36. See also Report of Commissioner of Freedman's Bureau, H. Exec. Doc. No. 70, 39th Cong., 1st Sess. (1866) 41, 47, 48, 233, 236, 265, 376.

And the day after Mr. Garfield's address, Mr. Dawes, also a member of the 39th Congress, stated his understanding of the meaning of the Fourteenth Amendment:

Then again he had secured to him the right to keep and bear arms in his defense.

"Sir, in the progress of constitutional liberty, when, in addition to those privileges and immunities [secured by the original Constitution] ... , there were added from time to time, by amendments, others, and these were augmented, amplified, and secured and fortified in the buttresses of the Constitution itself, he hardly comprehended the full scope and measure of the phrase which appears in this bill. Let me read, one by one, these amendments, and ask the House to tell me when and where and by what chosen phrase has man been able to bring before the Congress of the country a broader sweep of legislation than my friend has in the bill here. In addition to the original rights secured to him in the first article of amendments he had secured the free exercise of his religious belief, and freedom of speech and of the press. Then again he had secured to him the right to keep and bear arms in his defense. Then, after that, his home was secured in time of peace from the presence of a soldier; and, still further, sir, his house, his papers, and his effects were protected against unreasonable seizure. ...

MR. JUSTICE MURPHY, with whom MR. JUSTICE RUTLEDGE concurs, dissenting.

While in substantial agreement with the views of MR. JUSTICE BLACK, I have one reservation and one addition to make.

I agree that the specific guarantees of the Bill of Rights should be carried over intact into the first section of the Fourteenth Amendment. But I am not prepared to say that the latter is entirely and necessarily limited by the Bill of Rights. Occasions may arise where a proceeding falls so far short of conforming to fundamental standards of procedure as to warrant constitutional condemnation in terms of a lack of due process despite the absence of a specific provision in the Bill of Rights.

JOHNSON v. EISENTRAGER

(CASE EXCERPT)

339 U.S. 763; 70 S. Ct. 936; 94 L. Ed. 1255

April 17, 1950, Argued

June 5, 1950, Decided

GIST: German nationals were arrested in China for violations of the laws of war. After Germany's unconditional surrender, these men continued to gather intelligence on U.S. forces and their movements for the Japanese. They were given a military trial in China and then transferred to Germany to serve out their sentences. While confined in Germany, 21 of them petitioned a U.S. district court for a writ of habeas corpus ordering their release.

They argued that their trial and imprisonment was contrary to provisions of the United States Constitution. It's a novel approach—Nazis captured in China and convicted of spying on the U.S. claim their imprisonment violates their constitutional rights. The Supreme Court held that these nonresident enemy aliens were not entitled to access U.S. Courts during wartime, so their petitions for habeas corpus were dismissed. Supporting the argument, Justice Jackson, writing for six Justices, reasoned if constitutional rights extended to nonresident enemy aliens, the absurd result would be that the aliens could require U.S. courts to assure them freedoms of speech, press, and assembly as in the 1st Amendment, and the right to bear arms as in the 2nd Amendment

MR. JUSTICE JACKSON delivered the opinion of the Court.

.....

The alien, to whom the United States has been traditionally hospitable, has been accorded a generous and ascending scale of rights as he increases his identity with our society. Mere lawful presence in the country creates an implied assurance of safe conduct and gives him certain rights; they become more extensive and secure when he makes preliminary declaration of intention to become a citizen, and they expand to those of full citizenship upon naturalization. During his probationary residence, this Court has steadily enlarged his right against Executive deportation except upon full and fair hearing. And, at least since 1886, we have extended to the person and property of resident aliens important constitutional guaranties -- such as the due process of law of the Fourteenth Amendment.

But, in extending constitutional protections beyond the citizenry, the Court has been at pains to point out that it was the alien's presence within its territorial jurisdiction that gave the Judiciary power to act. In the pioneer case of Yick Wo v. Hopkins, the Court said of the Fourteenth Amendment, "These provisions are universal in their application, to all persons within the territorial jurisdiction, without regard to any differences of race, of color, or of nationality; . . . ." And in The Japanese Immigrant Case, the Court held its processes available to "an alien, who has entered the country, and has become subject in all respects to its jurisdiction, and a part of its population, although alleged to be illegally here."

.....

The decision below would extend coverage of our Constitution to nonresident alien enemies denied to resident alien enemies. The latter are entitled only to judicial hearing to determine what the petition of these prisoners admits: that they are really alien enemies. When that appears, those resident here may be deprived of liberty by Executive action without hearing. Ludecke v. Watkins. While this is preventive rather than punitive detention, no reason is apparent why an alien enemy charged with having committed a crime should have greater immunities from Executive action than one who it is only feared might at some future time commit a hostile act.

If the Fifth Amendment confers its rights on all the world except Americans engaged in defending it, the same must be true of the companion civil-rights Amendments, for none of them is limited by its express terms, territorially or as to persons. Such a construction would mean that during military occupation irreconcilable enemy elements, guerrilla fighters, and "werewolves" could require the American Judiciary to assure them freedoms of speech, press, and assembly as in the First Amendment, right to bear arms as in the Second, security against "unreasonable" searches and seizures as in the Fourth, as well as rights to jury trial as in the Fifth and Sixth Amendments.

If the Fifth Amendment confers its rights on all the world except Americans engaged in defending it, the same must be true of the companion civil-rights Amendments, for none of them is limited by its express terms, territorially or as to persons. Such a construction would mean that during military occupation irreconcilable enemy elements, guerrilla fighters, and "werewolves" could require the American Judiciary to assure them freedoms of speech, press, and assembly as in the First Amendment, right to bear arms as in the Second, security against "unreasonable" searches and seizures as in the Fourth, as well as rights to jury trial as in the Fifth and Sixth Amendments.

Such extraterritorial application of organic law would have been so significant an innovation in the practice of governments that, if intended or apprehended, it could scarcely have failed to excite contemporary comment. Not one word can be cited. No decision of this Court supports such a view. None of the learned commentators on our Constitution has even hinted at it. The practice of every modern government is opposed to it.

We hold that the Constitution does not confer a right of personal security or an immunity from military trial and punishment upon an alien enemy engaged in the hostile service of a government at war with the United States.

We hold that the Constitution does not confer a right of personal security or an immunity from military trial and punishment upon an alien enemy engaged in the hostile service of a government at war with the United States.

.....

We are not holding that these prisoners have no right which the military authorities are bound to respect. The United States, by the Geneva Convention of July 27, 1929, 47 Stat. 2021, concluded with forty-six other countries, including the German Reich, an agreement upon the treatment to be accorded captives. These prisoners claim to be and are entitled to its protection. It is, however, the obvious scheme of the Agreement that responsibility for observance and enforcement of these rights is upon political and military authorities. Rights of alien enemies are vindicated under it only through protests and intervention of protecting powers as the rights of our citizens against foreign governments are vindicated only by Presidential intervention.

KNAPP v. SCHWEITZER

(CASE EXCERPT)

357 U.S. 371; 78 S. Ct. 1302; 2 L. Ed. 2d 1393

March 6, 10, 1958, Argued

June 30, 1958, Decided

GIST: The issue in this New York union racketeering case was the scope of the privilege against self-incrimination. A witness had been granted immunity against state prosecution in exchange for his testimony, but, believing he might still be subject to federal prosecution for his testimony, he refused to testify. He was held in contempt of the NY court. Justice Frankfurter, for six members of the Court, held that the 5th Amendment limits only the federal government and not the states. Once the witness has been granted immunity from state prosecution, the state could compel him to testify (which could expose him to separate federal action). In rejecting Knapp's case, the Court pointed to the great historic divide between federal and state law enforcement powers. The Court cited the right to keep and bear arms as one of the rights previously held inapplicable to the states.

.....

MR. JUSTICE FRANKFURTER delivered the opinion of the Court.

.....

Generalities though these observations be, they bear decisively on the issue that has been tendered in this case. To yield to the contention of the petitioner would not only disregard the uniform course of decision by this Court for over a hundred years in recognizing the legal autonomy of state and federal governments. n5 In these days of the extensive sweep of such federal statutes as the income tax law and the criminal sanctions for their evasions, investigation under state law to discover corruption and misconduct, generally, in violation of state law could easily be thwarted if a State were deprived of its power to expose such wrongdoing with a view to remedial legislation or prosecution.

.....

By 1900 the applicability of the Bill of Rights to the States had been rejected in cases involving claims based on virtually every provision in the first eight Articles of Amendment. See, e.g., Article II: United States v. Cruikshank, (right to keep and bear arms)

n5 By 1900 the applicability of the Bill of Rights to the States had been rejected in cases involving claims based on virtually every provision in the first eight Articles of Amendment. See, e.g., Article I: Permoli v. Municipality No. 1, 3 How. 589, 609 (free exercise of religion); United States v. Cruikshank, 92 U.S. 542, 552 (right to assemble and petition the Government); Article II: United States v. Cruikshank, supra, at 553 (right to keep and bear arms); Article IV: Smith v. Maryland, 18 How. 71, 76 (no warrant except on probable cause); Spies v. Illinois, 123 U.S. 131, 166 (security against unreasonable searches and seizures); Article V: Barron v. Baltimore, note 2, supra, at 247 (taking without just compensation); Fox v. Ohio, 5 How. 410, 434 (former jeopardy); Twitchell v. Pennsylvania, 7 Wall. 321, 325-327 (deprivation of life without due process of law); Spies v. Illinois, supra, at 166 (compulsory self-incrimination); Eilenbecker v. Plymouth County, 134 U.S. 31, 34-35 (presentment or indictment by grand jury); Article VI: Twitchell v. Pennsylvania, supra, at 325-327 (right to be informed of nature and cause of accusation); Spies v. Illinois, supra, at 166 (speedy and public trial by impartial jury); In re Sawyer, 124 U.S. 200, 219 (compulsory process); Eilenbecker v. Plymouth County, supra, at 34-35 (confrontation of witnesses); Article VII: Livingston's Lessee v. Moore, 7 Pet. 469, 551-552 (right of jury trial in civil cases); Justices v. Murray, 9 Wall. 274, 278 (re-examination of facts tried by jury); Article VIII: Pervear v. Massachusetts, 5 Wall. 475, 479-480 (excessive fines, cruel and unusual punishments).

KONIGSBERG v. STATE BAR OF CALIFORNIA

(CASE EXCERPT)

366 U.S. 36; 81 S. Ct. 997; 6 L. Ed. 2d 105

December 14, 1960, Argued

April 24, 1961, Decided

GIST: Konigsberg applied for admission to the California Bar. He declined to answer any questions relating to his membership in the Communist Party on the grounds that the questions infringed his right of free association and expression under the 1st Amendment. His application was rejected and this challenge followed. The Court held that his 1st Amendment rights, as incorporated against the states through the 14th Amendment, were not violated. In the course of its discussion, the Court rejected the contention that the seemingly absolute language of the 1st Amendment ("Congress shall make no law...") required an absolute interpretation, and listed many examples of well-established exceptions, such as libel, slander, perjury, false advertising, solicitation of crime and more. The Court then draws a comparison to the "equally unqualified command" of the 2nd Amendment. The dissent argues there can be no such minor tinkering.

MR. JUSTICE HARLAN delivered the opinion of the Court.

At the outset we reject the view that freedom of speech and association (N. A. A. C. P. v. Alabama, 357 U.S. 449, 460), as protected by the First and Fourteenth Amendments, are "absolutes," not only in the undoubted sense that where the constitutional protection exists it must prevail, but also in the sense that the scope of that protection must be gathered solely from a literal reading of the First Amendment. n10 Throughout its history this Court has consistently recognized at least two ways in which constitutionally protected freedom of speech is narrower than an unlimited license to talk. On the one hand, certain forms of speech, or speech in certain contexts, has been considered outside the scope of constitutional protection. On the other hand, general regulatory statutes, not intended to control the content of speech but incidentally limiting its unfettered exercise, have not been regarded as the type of law the First or Fourteenth Amendment forbade Congress or the States to pass, when they have been found justified by subordinating valid governmental interests, a prerequisite to constitutionality which has necessarily involved a weighing of the governmental interest involved.

In this connection also compare the equally unqualified command of the Second Amendment: "the right of the people to keep and bear arms shall not be infringed."

n10 That view, which of course cannot be reconciled with the law relating to libel, slander, misrepresentation, obscenity, perjury, false advertising, solicitation of crime, complicity by encouragement, conspiracy, and the like, is said to be compelled by the fact that the commands of the First Amendment are stated in unqualified terms: "Congress shall make no law . . . abridging the freedom of speech, or of the press; or the right of the people peaceably to assemble . . . ." But as Mr. Justice Holmes once said: "The provisions of the Constitution are not mathematical formulas having their essence in their form; they are organic living institutions transplanted from English soil. Their significance is vital not formal; it is to be gathered not simply by taking the words and a dictionary, but by considering their origin and the line of their growth." Gompers v. United States, 233 U.S. 604, 610. In this connection also compare the equally unqualified command of the Second Amendment: "the right of the people to keep and bear arms shall not be infringed." And see United States v. Miller, 307 U.S. 174.

MR. JUSTICE BLACK, with whom THE CHIEF JUSTICE <WARREN> and MR. JUSTICE DOUGLAS concur, dissenting.

I believe that the First Amendment's unequivocal command that there shall be no abridgment of the rights of free speech and assembly shows that the men who drafted our Bill of Rights did all the "balancing" that was to be done in this field.

it certainly cannot be denied that the very object of adopting the First Amendment, as well as the other provisions of the Bill of Rights, was to put the freedoms protected there completely out of the area of any congressional control that may be attempted through the exercise of precisely those powers that are now being used to "balance" the Bill of Rights out of existence.

The recognition that California has subjected "speech and association to the deterrence of subsequent disclosure" is, under the First Amendment, sufficient in itself to render the action of the State unconstitutional unless one subscribes to the doctrine that permits constitutionally protected rights to be "balanced" away whenever a majority of this Court thinks that a State might have interest sufficient to justify abridgment of those freedoms. As I have indicated many times before, I do not subscribe to that doctrine for I believe that the First Amendment's unequivocal command that there shall be no abridgment of the rights of free speech and assembly shows that the men who drafted our Bill of Rights did all the "balancing" that was to be done in this field. The history of the First Amendment is too well known to require repeating here except to say that it certainly cannot be denied that the very object of adopting the First Amendment, as well as the other provisions of the Bill of Rights, was to put the freedoms protected there completely out of the area of any congressional control that may be attempted through the exercise of precisely those powers that are now being used to "balance" the Bill of Rights out of existence. n11 Of course, the First Amendment originally applied only to the Federal Government and did not apply to the States. But what was originally true only of Congress is now no less true with respect to the governments of the States, unless a majority of this Court wants to overrule a large number of cases in which it has been held unequivocally that the Fourteenth Amendment made the First Amendment's provisions controlling upon the States.

n11 James Madison, for example, indicated clearly that he did not understand the Bill of Rights to permit any encroachments upon the freedoms it was designed to protect. "If they [the first ten Amendments] are incorporated into the Constitution, independent tribunals of justice will consider themselves in a peculiar manner the guardians of those rights; they will be an impenetrable bulwark against every assumption of power in the Legislative or Executive; they will be naturally led to resist every encroachment upon rights expressly stipulated for in the Constitution by the declaration of rights." 1 Annals of Congress 439 (1789). (Emphasis supplied.)

POE v. ULLMAN

(CASE EXCERPT)

367 U.S. 497; 81 S. Ct. 1752; 6 L. Ed. 2d 989

March 1-2, 1961, Argued

June 19, 1961, Decided

GIST: This was a challenge under the 14th Amendment to a Connecticut law banning the use of and the giving of advice for the use of contraceptive devices. Only once since it was enacted in 1879 was anyone charged under the law, but in that case the Connecticut Supreme Court upheld the law. Because there was no apparent risk of prosecution, the Court dismissed the case because there was not a sufficient controversy to merit adjudication. Dissenting, Justice Harlan mentioned the right to keep and bear arms along with other constitutional liberties, in a quote that would be repeatedly used by later Courts, on the breadth of liberty guaranteed by the 14th Amendment.

MR. JUSTICE DOUGLAS, dissenting.

.....

The first eight Amendments to the Constitution have been made applicable to the States only in part. My view has been that when the Fourteenth Amendment was adopted, its Due Process Clause incorporated all of those Amendments.

The Bill of Rights is the primary source of expressed information as to what is meant by constitutional liberty.

The first eight Amendments to the Constitution have been made applicable to the States only in part. My view has been that when the Fourteenth Amendment was adopted, its Due Process Clause incorporated all of those Amendments. Although the history of the Fourteenth Amendment may not be conclusive, the words "due process" acquired specific meaning from Anglo-American experience. As MR. JUSTICE BRENNAN recently stated, "The Bill of Rights is the primary source of expressed information as to what is meant by constitutional liberty. The safeguards enshrined in it are deeply etched in the foundations of America's freedoms." When the Framers wrote the Bill of Rights they enshrined in the form of constitutional guarantees those rights -- in part substantive, in part procedural -- which experience indicated were indispensable to a free society. Some would disagree as to their importance; the debate concerning them did indeed start before their adoption and has continued to this day. Yet the constitutional conception of "due process" must, in my view, include them all until and unless there are amendments that remove them. That has indeed been the view of a full court of nine Justices, though the members who make up that court unfortunately did not sit at the same time.

Though I believe that "due process" as used in the Fourteenth Amendment includes all of the first eight Amendments, I do not think it is restricted and confined to them.

MR. JUSTICE HARLAN, dissenting.

.....

Were due process merely a procedural safeguard it would fail to reach those situations where the deprivation of life, liberty or property was accomplished by legislation which by operating in the future could, given even the fairest possible procedure in application to individuals, nevertheless destroy the enjoyment of all three. Thus the guaranties of due process, though having their roots in Magna Carta's "per legem terrae" and considered as procedural safeguards "against executive usurpation and tyranny," have in this country "become bulwarks also against arbitrary legislation."

it is not the particular enumeration of rights in the first eight Amendments which spells out the reach of Fourteenth Amendment due process

However it is not the particular enumeration of rights in the first eight Amendments which spells out the reach of Fourteenth Amendment due process, but rather, as was suggested in another context long before the adoption of that Amendment, those concepts which are considered to embrace those rights "which are . . . fundamental; which belong . . . to the citizens of all free governments," for "the purposes [of securing] which men enter into society," Again and again this Court has resisted the notion that the Fourteenth Amendment is no more than a shorthand reference to what is explicitly set out elsewhere in the Bill of Rights. Indeed the fact that an identical provision limiting federal action is found among the first eight Amendments, applying to the Federal Government, suggests that due process is a discrete concept which subsists as an independent guaranty of liberty and procedural fairness, more general and inclusive than the specific prohibitions.

Due process has not been reduced to any formula; its content cannot be determined by reference to any code. The best that can be said is that through the course of this Court's decisions it has represented the balance which our Nation, built upon postulates of respect for the liberty of the individual, has struck between that liberty and the demands of organized society. If the supplying of content to this Constitutional concept has of necessity been a rational process, it certainly has not been one where judges have felt free to roam where unguided speculation might take them. The balance of which I speak is the balance struck by this country, having regard to what history teaches are the traditions from which it developed as well as the traditions from which it broke. That tradition is a living thing. A decision of this Court which radically departs from it could not long survive, while a decision which builds on what has survived is likely to be sound. No formula could serve as a substitute, in this area, for judgment and restraint.

As was said in Meyer v. Nebraska, "this Court has not attempted to define with exactness the liberty thus guaranteed . . . . Without doubt, it denotes not merely freedom from bodily restraint . . . ."

This "liberty" is not a series of isolated points pricked out in terms of the taking of property; the freedom of speech, press, and religion; the right to keep and bear arms; the freedom from unreasonable searches and seizures; and so on. It is a rational continuum which, broadly speaking, includes a freedom from all substantial arbitrary impositions and purposeless restraints

It is this outlook which has led the Court continuingly to perceive distinctions in the imperative character of Constitutional provisions, since that character must be discerned from a particular provision's larger context. And inasmuch as this context is one not of words, but of history and purposes, the full scope of the liberty guaranteed by the Due Process Clause cannot be found in or limited by the precise terms of the specific guarantees elsewhere provided in the Constitution. This "liberty" is not a series of isolated points pricked out in terms of the taking of property; the freedom of speech, press, and religion; the right to keep and bear arms; the freedom from unreasonable searches and seizures; and so on. It is a rational continuum which, broadly speaking, includes a freedom from all substantial arbitrary impositions and purposeless restraints and which also recognizes, what a reasonable and sensitive judgment must, that certain interests require particularly careful scrutiny of the state needs asserted to justify their abridgment.

MALLOY v. HOGAN

(CASE EXCERPT)

378 U.S. 1; 84 S. Ct. 1489; 12 L. Ed. 2d 653

March 5, 1964, Argued

June 15, 1964, Decided

GIST: This case touches upon how much of the Bill of Rights applies against the states through the 14th Amendment, which in some measure forbids depriving people of their rights as national citizens. A constant fire has burned on this point since enactment of that Amendment in 1868. Early Courts flatly refused to impose the Bill of Rights rights on the states, as encroachments on state autonomy and sovereignty, and then experienced wholesale turnabouts in more recent years. The Court held, in the context of a gambling prosecution, that the 5th Amendment privilege against self incrimination applies against the states through the 14th Amendment, in the same way the 5th Amendment applies to the federal government.

Recounting the history of "incorporation" of the rights secured by the first eight amendments, the Court cited numerous prior decisions that called for full inclusion, no inclusion, and unpersuasive results. The list of cases holding that the Bill of Rights did not apply to the states includes *Presser,* which found the 2nd Amendment was a federal restriction and did not restrict the states. Today *Presser* stands out as one of the rare cases in which a portion of the Bill of Rights is still not explicitly incorporated under the 14th Amendment, for lack of a case addressing the point since that one in 1886. In this particular regard, the High Court could fairly be characterized as having said little on the subject.

MR. JUSTICE BRENNAN delivered the opinion of the Court.

The extent to which the Fourteenth Amendment prevents state invasion of rights enumerated in the first eight Amendments has been considered in numerous cases

it is possible that some of the personal rights safeguarded by the first eight Amendments against National action may also be safeguarded against state action, because a denial of them would be a denial of due process of law.

The extent to which the Fourteenth Amendment prevents state invasion of rights enumerated in the first eight Amendments has been considered in numerous cases in this Court since the Amendment's adoption in 1868. Although many Justices have deemed the Amendment to incorporate all eight of the Amendments, n2 the view which has thus far prevailed dates from the decision in 1897 in Chicago, B. & Q. R. Co. v. Chicago, which held that the Due Process Clause requires the States to pay just compensation for private property taken for public use. It was on the authority of that decision that the Court said in 1908 in Twining v. New Jersey, that "it is possible that some of the personal rights safeguarded by the first eight Amendments against National action may also be safeguarded against state action, because a denial of them would be a denial of due process of law."

n2 Ten Justices have supported this view. See Gideon v. Wainwright, 372 U.S. 335, 346 (opinion of MR. JUSTICE DOUGLAS). The Court expressed itself as unpersuaded to this view in In re Kemmler, 136 U.S. 436, 448-449; McElvaine v. Brush, 142 U.S. 155, 158-159; Maxwell v. Dow, 176 U.S. 581, 597-598; Twining v. New Jersey, supra, p. 96. See Spies v. Illinois, 123 U.S. 131. Decisions that particular guarantees were not safeguarded against state action by the Privileges and Immunities Clause or other provision of the Fourteenth Amendment are: United States v. Cruikshank, 92 U.S. 542, 551; Prudential Ins. Co. v. Cheek, 259 U.S. 530, 543 (First Amendment); Presser v. Illinois, 116 U.S. 252, 265 (Second Amendment); Weeks v. United States, 232 U.S. 383, 398 (Fourth Amendment); Hurtado v. California, 110 U.S. 516, 538 (Fifth Amendment requirement of grand jury indictments); Palko v. Connecticut, 302 U.S. 319, 328 (Fifth Amendment double jeopardy); Maxwell v. Dow, supra, at 595 (Sixth Amendment jury trial); Walker v. Sauvinet, 92 U.S. 90, 92 (Seventh Amendment jury trial); In re Kemmler, supra; McElvaine v. Brush, supra; O'Neil v. Vermont, 144 U.S. 323, 332 (Eighth Amendment prohibition against cruel and unusual punishment).

The Court has not hesitated to re-examine past decisions according the Fourteenth Amendment a less central role in the preservation of basic liberties than that which was contemplated by its Framers

The Court has not hesitated to re-examine past decisions according the Fourteenth Amendment a less central role in the preservation of basic liberties than that which was contemplated by its Framers when they added the Amendment to our constitutional scheme. Thus, although the Court as late as 1922 said that "neither the Fourteenth Amendment nor any other provision of the Constitution of the United States imposes upon the States any restrictions about 'freedom of speech' . . . ," Prudential Ins. Co. v. Cheek, 259 U.S. 530, 543, three years later Gitlow v. New York, 268 U.S. 652, initiated a series of decisions which today hold immune from state invasion every First Amendment protection for the cherished rights of mind and spirit -- the freedoms of speech, press, religion, assembly, association, and petition for redress of grievances.

MR. JUSTICE HARLAN, whom MR. JUSTICE CLARK joins, dissenting.

.....

"This court has never attempted to define with precision the words 'due process of law' . . . . It is sufficient to say that there are certain immutable principles of justice which inhere in the very idea of free government which no member of the Union may disregard . . . ." Holden v. Hardy, 169 U.S. 366, 389.

It followed from this recognition that due process encompassed the fundamental safeguards of the individual against the abusive exercise of governmental power that some of the restraints on the Federal Government which were specifically enumerated in the Bill of Rights applied also against the States. But, while inclusion of a particular provision in the Bill of Rights might provide historical evidence that the right involved was traditionally regarded as fundamental, inclusion of the right in due process was otherwise entirely independent of the first eight Amendments:

". . . It is possible that some of the personal rights safeguarded by the first eight Amendments against National action may also be safeguarded against state action, because a denial of them would be a denial of due process of law. . . . If this is so, it is not because those rights are enumerated in the first eight Amendments, but because they are of such a nature that they are included in the conception of due process of law." Twining, supra, at 99. (Emphasis supplied.)

MARYLAND v. UNITED STATES

(CASE EXCERPT)

381 U.S. 41; 85 S. Ct. 1293; 14 L. Ed. 2d 205

March 15, 1965, Argued

May 3, 1965, Decided

GIST: Several people died when a Maryland Air National Guard pilot in a jet trainer collided with an airliner. At issue was whether the pilot was in his military or civilian capacity at the time of the accident. The Court held that regardless of whether the pilot was in his civilian or military capacity, he was a state employee, so the federal government was not liable for the accident. Citing the militia clauses of Article I, section 8 of the Constitution, but not citing the 2nd Amendment, the Court wrote "The National Guard is the modern Militia reserved to the States."

MR. JUSTICE HARLAN delivered the opinion of the Court.

The question we decide here is whether a civilian employee and military member of the National Guard is an "employee" of the United States for purposes of the Federal Tort Claims Act when his National Guard unit is not in active federal service.

.....

The National Guard is the modern Militia reserved to the States by the Constitution.

It has only been in recent years that the National Guard has been an organized force

From the days of the Minutemen of Lexington and Concord until just before World War I, the various militias embodied the concept of a citizen army, but lacked the equipment and training necessary for their use as an integral part of the reserve force of the United States Armed Forces.

The passage of the National Defense Act of 1916 materially altered the status of the militias by constituting them as the National Guard.

The National Guard is the modern Militia reserved to the States by Art. I, §8, cl. 15, 16, of the Constitution. n8 It has only been in recent years that the National Guard has been an organized force, capable of being assimilated with ease into the regular military establishment of the United States. From the days of the Minutemen of Lexington and Concord until just before World War I, the various militias embodied the concept of a citizen army, but lacked the equipment and training necessary for their use as an integral part of the reserve force of the United States Armed Forces. The passage of the National Defense Act of 1916 n10 materially altered the status of the militias by constituting them as the National Guard. Pursuant to power vested in Congress by the Constitution (see n.8), the Guard was to be uniformed, equipped, and trained in much the same way as the regular army, subject to federal standards and capable of being "federalized" by units, rather than by drafting individual soldiers. In return, Congress authorized the allocation of federal equipment to the Guard, and provided federal compensation for members of the Guard, supplementing any state emoluments. The Governor, however, remained in charge of the National Guard in each State except when the Guard was called into active federal service; in most instances the Governor administered the Guard through the State Adjutant General, who was required by the Act to report periodically to the National Guard Bureau, a federal organization, on the Guard's reserve status.

n8 "The Congress shall have Power . . .

"To provide for calling forth the Militia to execute the Laws of the Union, suppress Insurrections and repel Invasions;

"To provide for organizing, arming, and disciplining, the Militia, and for governing such Part of them as may be employed in the Service of the United States, reserving to the States respectively, the Appointment of the Officers, and the Authority of training the Militia according to the discipline prescribed by Congress."

It is not argued here that military members of the Guard are federal employees, even though they are paid with federal funds and must conform to strict federal requirements in order to satisfy training and promotion standards. Their appointment by state authorities and the immediate control exercised over them by the States make it apparent that military members of the Guard are employees of the States, and so the courts of appeals have uniformly held.

.....

civilian as well as military personnel of the Guard are to be treated for the purposes of the Tort Claims Act as employees of the States and not of the Federal Government.

In sum, we conclude that the congressional purpose in authorizing the employment by state authorities of civilian caretakers, the administrative practice of the Defense Department in treating caretakers as state employees, the consistent congressional recognition of that status, and the like supervision exercised by the States over both military and civilian personnel of the National Guard, unmistakably lead in combination to the view that civilian as well as military personnel of the Guard are to be treated for the purposes of the Tort Claims Act as employees of the States and not of the Federal Government. This requires a decision that the United States is not liable to petitioners for the negligent conduct of McCoy.

GRISWOLD v. CONNECTICUT

(CASE EXCERPT)

381 U.S. 479; 85 S. Ct. 1678; 14 L. Ed. 2d 510

March 29-30, 1965, Argued

June 7, 1965, Decided

GIST: The Court ruled that a Connecticut statute forbidding the use of contraceptives violates a constitutional right to marital privacy. Although such a right is not specifically mentioned anywhere in the Constitution, the Justices perceived the right in the outer shadows (the "penumbra") of the Bill of Rights, as well as in the 9th Amendment's protection of rights not specifically listed in the document. Though the 2nd Amendment is not specifically named in the case, Justice Goldberg's concurring opinion, in which the Chief Justice and Justice Brennan joined, contains repeated reference to fundamental rights guaranteed to the people in the first eight amendments of the Bill of Rights, which is where the right to keep and bear arms resides.

.....

MR. JUSTICE GOLDBERG, whom THE CHIEF JUSTICE <WARREN> and MR. JUSTICE BRENNAN join, concurring.

Although I have not accepted the view that "due process" as used in the Fourteenth Amendment incorporates all of the first eight Amendments, I do agree that the concept of liberty protects those personal rights that are fundamental, and is not confined to the specific terms of the Bill of Rights.

I agree with the Court that Connecticut's birth-control law unconstitutionally intrudes upon the right of marital privacy, and I join in its opinion and judgment. Although I have not accepted the view that "due process" as used in the Fourteenth Amendment incorporates all of the first eight Amendments (see my concurring opinion in Pointer v. Texas, 380 U.S. 400, 410, and the dissenting opinion of MR. JUSTICE BRENNAN in Cohen v. Hurley, 366 U.S. 117, 154), I do agree that the concept of liberty protects those personal rights that are fundamental, and is not confined to the specific terms of the Bill of Rights. My conclusion that the concept of liberty is not so restricted and that it embraces the right of marital privacy though that right is not mentioned explicitly in the Constitution1 is supported both by numerous decisions of this Court, referred to in the Court's opinion, and by the language and history of the Ninth Amendment. In reaching the conclusion that the right of marital privacy is protected, as being within the protected penumbra of specific guarantees of the Bill of Rights, the Court refers to the Ninth Amendment, ante, at 484. I add these words to emphasize the relevance of that Amendment to the Court's holding.

The Court stated many years ago that the Due Process Clause protects those liberties that are "so rooted in the traditions and conscience of our people as to be ranked as fundamental."

The Court stated many years ago that the Due Process Clause protects those liberties that are "so rooted in the traditions and conscience of our people as to be ranked as fundamental." Snyder v. Massachusetts, 291 U.S. 97, 105. In Gitlow v. New York, 268 U.S. 652, 666, the Court said:

"For present purposes we may and do assume that freedom of speech and of the press - which are protected by the First Amendment from abridgment by Congress - are among the fundamental personal rights and 'liberties' protected by the due process clause of the Fourteenth Amendment from impairment by the States." (Emphasis added.)

And, in Meyer v. Nebraska, 262 U.S. 390, 399, the Court, referring to the Fourteenth Amendment, stated:

"While this Court has not attempted to define with exactness the liberty thus guaranteed, the term has received much consideration and some of the included things have been definitely stated. Without doubt, it denotes not merely freedom from bodily restraint but also [for example,] the right . . . to marry, establish a home and bring up children . . . ."

This Court, in a series of decisions, has held that the Fourteenth Amendment absorbs and applies to the States those specifics of the first eight amendments which express fundamental personal rights. The language and history of the Ninth Amendment reveal that the Framers of the Constitution believed that there are additional fundamental rights, protected from governmental infringement, which exist alongside those fundamental rights specifically mentioned in the first eight constitutional amendments.

This Court, in a series of decisions, has held that the Fourteenth Amendment absorbs and applies to the States those specifics of the first eight amendments which express fundamental personal rights. The language and history of the Ninth Amendment reveal that the Framers of the Constitution believed that there are additional fundamental rights, protected from governmental infringement, which exist alongside those fundamental rights specifically mentioned in the first eight constitutional amendments.

The Ninth Amendment... was proffered to quiet expressed fears that a bill of specifically enumerated rights could not be sufficiently broad to cover all essential rights and that the specific mention of certain rights would be interpreted as a denial that others were protected.

The Ninth Amendment reads, "The enumeration in the Constitution, of certain rights, shall not be construed to deny or disparage others retained by the people." The Amendment is almost entirely the work of James Madison. It was introduced in Congress by him and passed the House and Senate with little or no debate and virtually no change in language. It was proffered to quiet expressed fears that a bill of specifically enumerated rights could not be sufficiently broad to cover all essential rights and that the specific mention of certain rights would be interpreted as a denial that others were protected.

In presenting the proposed Amendment, Madison said:

"It has been objected also against a bill of rights, that, by enumerating particular exceptions to the grant of power, it would disparage those rights which were not placed in that enumeration; and it might follow by implication, that those rights which were not singled out, were intended to be assigned into the hands of the General Government, and were consequently insecure. This is one of the most plausible arguments I have ever heard urged against the admission of a bill of rights into this system; but, I conceive, that it may be guarded against. I have attempted it, as gentlemen may see by turning to the last clause of the fourth resolution [the Ninth Amendment]." I Annals of Congress 439 (Gales and Seaton ed. 1834).

Mr. Justice Story wrote of this argument against a bill of rights and the meaning of the Ninth Amendment:

"In regard to . . . [a] suggestion, that the affirmance of certain rights might disparage others, or might lead to argumentative implications in favor of other powers, it might be sufficient to say that such a course of reasoning could never be sustained upon any solid basis . . . . But a conclusive answer is, that such an attempt may be interdicted (as it has been) by a positive declaration in such a bill of rights that the enumeration of certain rights shall not be construed to deny or disparage others retained by the people." II Story, Commentaries on the Constitution of the United States 626-627 (5th ed. 1891).

He further stated, referring to the Ninth Amendment:

"This clause was manifestly introduced to prevent any perverse or ingenious misapplication of the well-known maxim, that an affirmation in particular cases implies a negation in all others; and, e converso, that a negation in particular cases implies an affirmation in all others." Id., at 651.

the Framers did not intend that the first eight amendments be construed to exhaust the basic and fundamental rights which the Constitution guaranteed to the people.

These statements of Madison and Story make clear that the Framers did not intend that the first eight amendments be construed to exhaust the basic and fundamental rights which the Constitution guaranteed to the people.

While this Court has had little occasion to interpret the Ninth Amendment, "[i]t cannot be presumed that any clause in the constitution is intended to be without effect." Marbury v. Madison, 1 Cranch 137, 174. In interpreting the Constitution, "real effect should be given to all the words it uses." Myers v. United States, 272 U.S. 52, 151. The Ninth Amendment to the Constitution may be regarded by some as a recent discovery and may be forgotten by others, but since 1791 it has been a basic part of the Constitution which we are sworn to uphold. To hold that a right so basic and fundamental and so deep-rooted in our society as the right of privacy in marriage may be infringed because that right is not guaranteed in so many words by the first eight amendments to the Constitution is to ignore the Ninth Amendment and to give it no effect whatsoever. Moreover, a judicial construction that this fundamental right is not protected by the Constitution because it is not mentioned in explicit terms by one of the first eight amendments or elsewhere in the Constitution would violate the Ninth Amendment, which specifically states that "[t]he enumeration in the Constitution, of certain rights, shall not be construed to deny or disparage others retained by the people."

the Ninth Amendment shows a belief of the Constitution's authors that fundamental rights exist that are not expressly enumerated in the first eight amendments and an intent that the list of rights included there not be deemed exhaustive.

The Ninth Amendment simply shows the intent of the Constitution's authors that other fundamental personal rights should not be denied such protection or disparaged in any other way simply because they are not specifically listed in the first eight constitutional amendments.

A dissenting opinion suggests that my interpretation of the Ninth Amendment somehow "broaden[s] the powers of this Court." Post, at 520. With all due respect, I believe that it misses the import of what I am saying. I do not take the position of my Brother BLACK in his dissent in Adamson v. California, 332 U.S. 46, 68, that the entire Bill of Rights is incorporated in the Fourteenth Amendment, and I do not mean to imply that the Ninth Amendment is applied against the States by the Fourteenth. Nor do I mean to state that the Ninth Amendment constitutes an independent source of rights protected from infringement by either the States or the Federal Government. Rather, the Ninth Amendment shows a belief of the Constitution's authors that fundamental rights exist that are not expressly enumerated in the first eight amendments and an intent that the list of rights included there not be deemed exhaustive. As any student of this Court's opinions knows, this Court has held, often unanimously, that the Fifth and Fourteenth Amendments protect certain fundamental personal liberties from abridgment by the Federal Government or the States. See, e. g., Bolling v. Sharpe, 347 U.S. 497 ; Aptheker v. Secretary of State, 378 U.S. 500 ; Kent v. Dulles, 357 U.S. 116 ; Cantwell v. Connecticut, 310 U.S. 296 ; NAACP v. Alabama, 357 U.S. 449 ; Gideon v. Wainwright, 372 U.S. 335 ; New York Times Co. v. Sullivan, 376 U.S. 254. The Ninth Amendment simply shows the intent of the Constitution's authors that other fundamental personal rights should not be denied such protection or disparaged in any other way simply because they are not specifically listed in the first eight constitutional amendments. I do not see how this broadens the authority of the Court; rather it serves to support what this Court has been doing in protecting fundamental rights.

While the Ninth Amendment—and indeed the entire Bill of Rights—originally concerned restrictions upon federal power, the subsequently enacted Fourteenth Amendment prohibits the States as well from abridging fundamental personal liberties.

In sum, the Ninth Amendment simply lends strong support to the view that the "liberty" protected by the Fifth and Fourteenth Amendments from infringement by the Federal Government or the States is not restricted to rights specifically mentioned in the first eight amendments.

Nor am I turning somersaults with history in arguing that the Ninth Amendment is relevant in a case dealing with a State's infringement of a fundamental right. While the Ninth Amendment - and indeed the entire Bill of Rights - originally concerned restrictions upon federal power, the subsequently enacted Fourteenth Amendment prohibits the States as well from abridging fundamental personal liberties. And, the Ninth Amendment, in indicating that not all such liberties are specifically mentioned in the first eight amendments, is surely relevant in showing the existence of other fundamental personal rights, now protected from state, as well as federal, infringement. In sum, the Ninth Amendment simply lends strong support to the view that the "liberty" protected by the Fifth and Fourteenth Amendments from infringement by the Federal Government or the States is not restricted to rights specifically mentioned in the first eight amendments. Cf. United Public Workers v. Mitchell, 330 U.S. 75, 94 -95.

In determining which rights are fundamental, judges are not left at large to decide cases in light of their personal and private notions. Rather, they must look to the "traditions and [collective] conscience of our people" to determine whether a principle is "so rooted [there] . . . as to be ranked as fundamental." Snyder v. Massachusetts, 291 U.S. 97, 105. The inquiry is whether a right involved "is of such a character that it cannot be denied without violating those 'fundamental principles of liberty and justice which lie at the base of all our civil and political institutions' . . . ." Powell v. Alabama, 287 U.S. 45, 67. "Liberty" also "gains content from the emanations of . . . specific [constitutional] guarantees" and "from experience with the requirements of a free society." Poe v. Ullman, 367 U.S. 497, 517 (dissenting opinion of MR. JUSTICE DOUGLAS).7

I agree fully with the Court that, applying these tests, the right of privacy is a fundamental personal right, emanating "from the totality of the constitutional scheme under which we live." Id., at 521. Mr. Justice Brandeis, dissenting in Olmstead v. United States, 277 U.S. 438, 478, comprehensively summarized the principles underlying the Constitution's guarantees of privacy:

"The protection guaranteed by the [Fourth and Fifth] Amendments is much broader in scope. The makers of our Constitution undertook to secure conditions favorable to the pursuit of happiness. They recognized the significance of man's spiritual nature, of his feelings and of his intellect. They knew that only a part of the pain, pleasure and satisfactions of life are to be found in material things. They sought to protect Americans in their beliefs, their thoughts, their emotions and their sensations. They conferred, as against the Government, the right to be let alone - the most comprehensive of rights and the right most valued by civilized men."

MIRANDA v. ARIZONA

(CASE EXCERPT)

384 U.S. 436; 86 S. Ct. 1602; 16 L. Ed. 2d 694

February 28-March 1, 1966, Argued

June 13, 1966, Decided

GIST: This well-known case led to the now familiar verbal warning for criminal suspects, "You have the right to remain silent...". Without that warning, most custodial interrogations would be deemed coercive and thus inadmissible as a violation of the 5th Amendment privilege against self incrimination.

Miranda's basic principles are only tangential to the infringement issues continually arising over the right to keep arms and the right to bear arms, and *Miranda* is by no stretch a gun case itself per se. But it is in a special category of cases that is cited frequently in terms of the general rights involved in firearms rights.

A reader who feels that the inclusion of this case goes too far afield of the *Supreme Court Gun Cases* theme (and case count) will be pleased to note that the following seven cases have not been included for that very reason:

Marbury v. Madison, 5 U.S. 137 1803
"an act of the legislature repugnant to the constitution is void."

Boyd v. United States, 116 U.S. 616 1886
"It is the duty of courts to be watchful for the constitutional rights of the citizen, and against any stealthy encroachments thereon."

Norton v. Shelby County, 118 U.S. 425 1886
"An unconstitutional act is not law; it confers no rights; it imposes no duties; affords no protection; it creates no office; it is in legal contemplation as though it had never been passed."

Olmstead v. United States, 277 U.S. 438 1928
"Experience should teach us to be most on our guard to protect liberty when the government's purposes are beneficent. Men born to freedom are naturally alert to repel invasion of their liberty by evil-minded rulers. The greatest dangers to

liberty lurk in insidious encroachment by men of zeal, well meaning but without understanding." (Note: quoted from dissent.)

Murdock v. Pennsylvania, 319 U.S. 105 1943
"A state may not impose a charge for the enjoyment of a right granted by the Federal Constitution."

"a person cannot be compelled 'to purchase, through a license fee or a license tax, the privilege freely granted by the Constitution.'"

Staub v. Baxley, 355 U.S. 313 1958
"It is settled by a long line of recent decisions of this Court that an ordinance which, like this one, makes the peaceful enjoyment of freedoms which the Constitution guarantees contingent upon the uncontrolled will of an official—as by requiring a permit or license which may be granted or withheld in the discretion of such official—is an unconstitutional censorship or prior restraint upon the enjoyment of those freedoms."

Shuttlesworth v. City of Birmingham Alabama, 394 U.S. 147 1969
"And our decisions have made clear that a person faced with such an unconstitutional licensing law may ignore it and engage with impunity in the exercise of the right of free expression for which the law purports to require a license."

It's probably a good idea to keep in mind that the axiom described in these cases—an unconstitutional law is void—has an important corollary. Even an unconstitutional law is the law, and stays in place with full force and effect, until it is declared unconstitutional by a court of competent jurisdiction, or until removed by the legislature. People are arrested, prosecuted and imprisoned under unconstitutional laws all the time. Some get off later. That can be summed up with a piece of street wisdom: The law means what the officer with the gun in your ear says it means.

MR. CHIEF JUSTICE WARREN delivered the opinion of the Court.

.....

Where rights secured by the Constitution are involved, there can be no rule making or legislation which would abrogate them.

HAYNES v. UNITED STATES

(FULL CASE)

390 U.S. 85; 88 S. Ct. 722; 19 L. Ed. 2d 923

October 11, 1967, Argued

January 29, 1968, Decided

GIST: This case applied the 5th Amendment privilege against self incrimination to the National Firearms Act registration requirements. The Court held the privilege to be a complete defense to a charge of failing to register possession of an NFA firearm or possession of an unregistered NFA firearm. The law in question was written in such a way that you were guilty if you failed to fill out the form, and guilty if you filled it out accurately, a forced self incrimination which the Court could not let stand. The Court stated that Congress' authority to regulate in this area was not at issue, only the 5th Amendment implications of registration of certain NFA weapons. Federal statutes were subsequently amended to address the problem identified in *Haynes,* allowing ongoing registration of NFA weapons. The statutory changes Congress hoped would correct the situation came before the High Court in 1971 in *U.S. v. Freed,* and were upheld.

Petitioner was charged by information with violating 26 U.S.C. §5851 (part of the National Firearms Act, an interrelated statutory system for the taxation of certain classes of firearms used principally by persons engaged in unlawful activities) by knowingly possessing a defined firearm which had not been registered as required by 26 U.S.C. §5841. Section 5841 obligates the possessor of a defined firearm to register the weapon, unless he made it or acquired it by transfer or importation, and the Act's requirements as to transfers, makings and importations "were complied with." Section 5851 declares unlawful the possession of such firearm which has "at any time" been transferred or made in violation of the Act, or which "has not been registered as required by section 5841." Additionally, §5851 provides that "possession shall be deemed sufficient evidence to authorize conviction, unless the defendant explains such possession to the satisfaction of the jury." Petitioner moved before trial to dismiss the charge, sufficiently asserting that §5851 violated his privilege against self-incrimination guaranteed by the Fifth Amendment. The motion was denied, petitioner pleaded guilty, and his conviction was affirmed by the Court of Appeals. Held:

1. Congress, subject to constitutional limitations, has authority to regulate the manufacture, transfer, and possession of firearms, and may tax unlawful activities.

2. Petitioner's conviction under §5851 for possession of an unregistered firearm is not properly distinguishable from a conviction under §5841 for failure to register possession of a firearm, and both offenses must be deemed subject to any constitutional deficiencies arising under the Fifth Amendment from the obligation to register.

3. A proper claim of the privilege against self-incrimination provides a full defense to prosecutions either for failure to register under §5841 or for possession of an unregistered firearm under §5851.

4. Restrictions upon the use by federal and state authorities of information obtained as a consequence of the registration requirement, suggested by the Government, is not appropriate. Marchetti v. United States, ante, p. 39, and Grosso v. United States, ante, p. 62.

5. Since any proceeding in the District Court upon a remand must inevitably result in the reversal of petitioner's conviction, it would be neither just nor appropriate to require such needless action and accordingly the judgment is reversed.

MR. JUSTICE HARLAN delivered the opinion of the Court.

Petitioner was charged by a three-count information filed in the United States District Court for the Northern District of Texas with violations of the National Firearms Act. 48 Stat. 1236. Two of the counts were subsequently dismissed upon motion of the United States Attorney. The remaining count averred that petitioner, in violation of 26 U.S.C. §5851, knowingly possessed a firearm, as defined by 26 U.S.C. §5848 (1), which had not been registered with the Secretary of the Treasury or his delegate, as required by 26 U.S.C. §5841. Petitioner moved before trial to dismiss this count, evidently asserting that §5851 violated his privilege against self-incrimination, as guaranteed by the Fifth Amendment. n1 The motion was denied, and petitioner thereupon entered a plea of guilty. n2 The judgment of conviction was affirmed by the Court of Appeals for the Fifth Circuit. 372 F.2d 651. We granted certiorari to examine the constitutionality under the Fifth Amendment of petitioner's conviction. 388 U.S. 908. For reasons which follow, we reverse.

n1 Petitioner's motion asserted merely that §5851 was "unconstitutional," and the order denying the motion does not indicate more precisely the substance of petitioner's contentions. His subsequent arguments, both in the courts below and here, have, however, consistently asserted a claim of the constitutional privilege. No suggestion is made by the Government that the claim of privilege was not sufficiently made.

n2 Petitioner's plea of guilty did not, of course, waive his previous claim of the constitutional privilege. See, e.g., United States v. Ury, 106 F.2d 28.

I.

These limitations were apparently intended to guarantee that only weapons used principally by persons engaged in unlawful activities would be subjected to taxation.

Section 5851 n3 forms part of the National Firearms Act, an interrelated statutory system for the taxation of certain classes of firearms. The Act's requirements are applicable only to shotguns with barrels less than 18 inches long; rifles with barrels less than 16 inches long; other weapons, made from a rifle or shotgun, with an overall length of less than 26 inches; machine guns and other automatic firearms; mufflers and silencers; and other firearms, except pistols and revolvers, "if such weapon is capable of being concealed on the person . . . ." 26 U.S.C. §5848 (1); Treas. Reg. §179.20, 26 CFR §179.20. These limitations were apparently intended to guarantee that only weapons used principally by persons engaged in unlawful activities would be subjected to taxation. n4

n3 The section provides that "It shall be unlawful for any person to receive or possess any firearm which has at any time been transferred in violation of sections 5811, 5812 (b), 5813, 5814, 5844, or 5846, or which has at any time been made in violation of section 5821, or to possess any firearm which has not been registered as required by section 5841. Whenever on trial for a violation of this section the defendant is shown to have or to have had possession of such firearm, such possession shall be deemed sufficient evidence to authorize conviction, unless the defendant explains such possession to the satisfaction of the jury."

n4 The views of a subsequent Congress of course provide no controlling basis from which to infer the purposes of an earlier Congress. See Rainwater v. United States, 356 U.S. 590, 593; United States v. Price, 361 U.S. 304, 313. Nonetheless, it is pertinent to note that the Committee on Ways and Means of the House of Representatives, while reporting in 1959 on certain proposed amendments to the Act, stated that the "primary purpose of [the Firearms Act] was to make it more difficult for the gangster element to obtain certain types of weapons. The type of weapon with which these provisions are concerned are the types it was thought would be used primarily by the gangster-type element." H. R. Rep. No. 914, 86th Cong., 1st Sess., 2.

Importers, manufacturers, and dealers in such firearms are obliged each year to pay special occupational taxes, and to register with the Secretary of the Treasury or his delegate. 26 U.S.C. §§5801, 5802. Separate taxes are imposed on the making and transfer of such firearms by persons other than those obliged to pay the occupational taxes. 26 U.S.C. §§5811, 5821. For purposes of these additional taxes, the acts of making and transferring firearms are broadly defined. Section 5821 thus imposes a tax on the making of a firearm "whether by manufacture, putting together, alteration, any combination thereof, or otherwise." Similarly, to transfer encompasses "to sell, assign, pledge, lease, loan, give away, or otherwise dispose of" a firearm. 26 U.S.C. §5848 (10).

All these taxes are supplemented by comprehensive requirements calculated to assure their collection. Any individual who wishes to make a weapon, within the meaning of §5821 (a), is obliged, "prior to such making," to declare his intention to the Secretary, and to provide to the Treasury his fingerprints and photograph. 26 U.S.C. §5821 (e); Treas. Reg. §179.78. The declaration must be "supported by a certificate of the local chief of police . . . or such other person whose certificate may . . . be acceptable . . . ." Treas. Reg. §179.78. The certificate must indicate satisfaction that the fingerprints and photograph are those of the declarant, and that the firearm is intended "for lawful purposes." Ibid. Any person who wishes to transfer such a weapon may lawfully do so only if he first obtains a written order from the prospective transferee on an "application form issued . . . for that purpose by the Secretary." 26 U.S.C. §5814 (a). The application, supported by a certificate of the local chief of police, and accompanied by the transferee's fingerprints and photograph, must be approved by the Secretary prior to the transfer. Treas. Reg. §§179.98, 179.99. Finally, every person possessing such a firearm is obliged to register his possession with the Secretary, unless he made the weapon, or acquired it by transfer or importation, and the Act's requirements as to transfers, makings, and importations "were complied with." 26 U.S.C. §5841. n5

n5 The section provides that "Every person possessing a firearm shall register, with the Secretary or his delegate, the number or other mark identifying such firearm, together with his name, address, place where such firearm is usually kept, and place of business or employment, and, if such person is other than a natural person, the name and home address of an executive officer thereof. No person shall be required to register under this section with respect to a firearm which such person acquired by transfer or importation or which such person made, if provisions of this chapter applied to such transfer, importation, or making, as the case may be, and if the provisions which applied thereto were complied with."

Failure to comply with any of the Act's requirements is made punishable by fines and imprisonment. 26 U.S.C. §5861. In addition, §5851 creates a series of supplementary offenses; it declares unlawful the possession of any firearm which has "at any time" been transferred or made in violation of the Act's provisions, or which "has not been registered as required by section 5841." Finally, §5851 provides that in prosecutions conducted under that section "possession shall be deemed sufficient evidence to authorize conviction, unless the defendant explains such possession to the satisfaction of the jury."

II.

we are required to resolve only the narrow issue of whether enforcement of §5851 against petitioner, despite his assertion of the privilege against self-incrimination, is constitutionally permissible.

If, as petitioner urges, his conviction under §5851 is essentially indistinguishable from a conviction premised directly upon a failure to register under §5841, and if a prosecution under §5841 would have punished petitioner for his failure to incriminate himself, it would follow that a proper claim of privilege should have provided a full defense to this prosecution.

At the outset, it must be emphasized that the issue in this case is not whether Congress has authority under the Constitution to regulate the manufacture, transfer, or possession of firearms; nor is it whether Congress may tax activities which are, wholly or in part, unlawful. Rather, we are required to resolve only the narrow issue of whether enforcement of §5851 against petitioner, despite his assertion of the privilege against self-incrimination, is constitutionally permissible. The questions necessary for decision are two: first, whether petitioner's conviction under §5851 is meaningfully distinguishable from a conviction under §5841 for failure to register possession of a firearm; and second, if it is not, whether satisfaction of petitioner's obligation to register under §5841 would have compelled him to provide information incriminating to himself. If, as petitioner urges, his conviction under §5851 is essentially indistinguishable from a conviction premised directly upon a failure to register under §5841, and if a prosecution under §5841 would have punished petitioner for his failure to incriminate himself, it would follow that a proper claim of privilege should have provided a full defense to this prosecution. n6 To these questions we turn.

n6 Indeed, so much is recognized by the Government; it has stated that "we concede that if petitioner's reading of the two provisions were right . . . petitioner's conviction under Section 5851 would not be valid." Brief for the United States 8.

III.

The first issue is whether the elements of the offense under §5851 of possession of a firearm "which has not been registered as required by section 5841" differ in any significant respect from those of the offense under §5841 of failure to register possession of a firearm. The United States contends that the two offenses, despite the similarity of their statutory descriptions, serve entirely different purposes, in that the registration clause of §5851 is intended to punish acceptance of the possession of a firearm which, despite the requirements of §5841, was never registered by any prior possessor, while §5841 punishes only a present possessor who has failed to register the fact of his own possession. If this construction is correct, nothing in a prosecution under §5851 would turn on whether the present possessor had elected to register; his offense would have been complete when he accepted possession of a firearm which no previous possessor had registered. We need not determine whether this construction would be free from constitutional difficulty under the Fifth Amendment, for we have concluded that §5851 cannot properly be construed as the United States has urged. n7

n7 The Government's position is generally supported by several cases in the courts of appeals. See, in addition to the opinion below, Frye v. United States, 315 F.2d 491; Starks v. United States, 316 F.2d 45; Mares v. United States, 319 F.2d 71; Sipes v. United States, 321 F.2d 174; Taylor v. United States, 333 F.2d 721; Castellano v. United States, 350 F.2d 852; Pruitt v. United States, 364 F.2d 826; Decker v. United States, 378 F.2d 245. None of these cases, however, undertook an extended examination of the relationship between §§5851 and 5841. Compare Lovelace v. United States, 357 F.2d 306, 309; and Mansfield, The Albertson Case: Conflict Between the Privilege Against Self-Incrimination and the Government's Need for Information, 1966 Sup. Ct. Rev. 103, 158-159, n. 95.

The United States finds support for its construction of §5851 chiefly in the section's use of the past tense: the act stated to be unlawful is "to possess any firearm which has not been registered as required by section 5841." (Emphasis added.) It is contended that we may infer from this choice of tense that the failure to register must necessarily precede the accused's acquisition of possession. We cannot derive so much from so little. We perceive no more in the draftsman's choice of tense than the obvious fact that the failure to register must precede the moment at which the accused is charged; we find nothing which confines the clause's application to failures to register which have occurred before a present possessor received the firearm. It follows that the phrase fastened upon by the United States is, at the least, equally consistent with the construction advanced by petitioner.

If, however, nothing further were available, it might be incumbent upon us to accept the Government's construction in order to avoid the adjudication of a serious constitutional issue. See, e.g., Ashwander v. Valley Authority, 297 U.S. 288, 348 (concurring opinion); Crowell v. Benson, 285 U.S. 22, 62. But there are persuasive indications at hand which, in our view, preclude adoption of the position urged by the United States. Initially, we must note that each of the other two offenses defined by §5851 indicates very specifically that the violations of the making or transfer provisions, on which the §5851 offenses are ultimately premised, can have occurred "at any time." An analogous phrase in the registration clause would have made plain beyond all question that the construction now urged by the United States should be accepted; if this was indeed Congress' purpose, it is difficult to see why it did not, as it did in the other clauses, insert the few additional words necessary to make clear its wishes. The position suggested by the United States would thus oblige us, at the outset, to assume that Congress has, in this one clause, chosen a remarkably oblique and unrevealing phrasing.

Similarly, it is pertinent to note that the transfer and making clauses of §5851 punish the receipt, as well as the possession, of firearms; the registration clause, in contrast, punishes only possession. Under the construction given §5851 by the United States, Congress might have been expected to declare unlawful, in addition, the receipt of firearms never previously registered; indeed, the receipt of the firearm is, under that construction, the central element of the offense. Congress' preference in the registration clause for "possession," rather than "receipt," is satisfactorily explicable only if petitioner's construction of §5851 is adopted.

Third, and more important, we find it significant that the offense defined by §5851 is the possession of a firearm which has not been registered "as required by section 5841." In the absence of persuasive evidence to the contrary, the clause's final words suggest strongly that the perimeter of the offense which it creates is to be marked by the terms of the registration requirement imposed by §5841. In turn, §5841 indicates quite precisely that "every person possessing a firearm" must, unless excused by the section's exception, register his possession with the Secretary or his delegate. Moreover, the Treasury regulations are entirely unequivocal; they specifically provide that "every person in the United States possessing a firearm (a) not registered to him, . . . must execute an application for the registration of such firearm . . . ." Treas. Reg. §179.120. (Emphasis added.)

The pertinent legislative history offers additional assistance, and points against the Government's construction. The registration clause was inserted into §5851 by the Excise Tax Technical Changes Act of 1958. 72 Stat. 1428. The two committee reports indicate, in identical terms, n8 that the existing section was thought inadequate because, although it defined as an unlawful act the possession of any firearm which had been made or transferred in violation of the Firearms Act, it failed "to so define the possession of an unregistered firearm." H. R. Rep. No. 481, 85th Cong., 1st Sess., 195; S. Rep. No. 2090, 85th Cong., 2d Sess., 212. The section as amended "specifically defines such possession of an unregistered firearm as an unlawful act." Ibid. It is useful to note that the committees did not suggest that the failure to register must have preceded the acquisition of possession. Further, the reports indicate that the proposed amendment was intended to make available in prosecutions for possession of an unregistered firearm the presumption already contained in §5851; they conclude that the "primary purpose of this change is to simplify and clarify the law and to aid in prosecution." H. R. Rep. No. 481, supra, at 196; S. Rep. No. 2090, supra, at 212.

n8 The language in the reports was evidently taken without change or elaboration from the recommendations submitted to the House Committee on Ways and Means by the Treasury. See Hearings before House Committee on Ways and Means on Excise Tax Technical and Administrative Problems, 84th Cong., 1st Sess., 185, 211.

We infer that the amendment was thought to have two purposes. First, it would complete the series of supplementary offenses created by §5851, by adding to those premised on a making or transfer one bottomed on a failure to register. Second, it would facilitate the prosecution of failures to register by permitting the use of the presumption included in §5851. It would thus "aid in prosecution" of conduct also made unlawful by §5841. Both these purposes are fully consistent with the construction of §5851 urged by petitioner; but only the first offers any support to the position suggested by the United States.

We are unable to escape the conclusion that Congress intended the registration clause of §5851 to incorporate the requirements of §5841, by declaring unlawful the possession of any firearm which has not been registered by its possessor, in circumstances in which §5841 imposes an obligation to register. The elements of the offenses created by the two sections are therefore identical. This does not, however, fully resolve the question of whether any hazards of incrimination which stem from the registration requirement imposed by §5841 must be understood also to inhere in prosecutions under §5851. Two additional distinctions between the offenses have been suggested, and we must examine them.

we decline to hold that the performance of an unlawful act, even if there exists a statutory condition that its commission constitutes a waiver of the constitutional privilege, suffices to deprive an accused of the privilege's protection.

First, it has been said that the offenses differ in emphasis, in that §5851 chiefly punishes possession, while §5841 punishes a failure to register. Cf. Frye v. United States, 315 F.2d 491, 494; Castellano v. United States, 350 F.2d 852, 854. We find this supposed distinction entirely unpersuasive, for, as we have found, the possession of a firearm and a failure to register are equally fundamental ingredients of both offenses. Second, it has been suggested that §5841 creates a "status of unlawful possession" which, if assumed by an individual, denies to him the protection of the constitutional privilege. Castellano v. United States, supra, at 854. It has evidently been thought to follow that the privilege may be claimed in prosecutions under §5841, but not in those under §5851. This is no less unpersuasive; for reasons discussed in Marchetti v. United States, decided today, ante, at 51-52, we decline to hold that the performance of an unlawful act, even if there exists a statutory condition that its commission constitutes a waiver of the constitutional privilege, suffices to deprive an accused of the privilege's protection. We hold that petitioner's conviction under the registration clause of §5851 is not properly distinguishable from a conviction under §5841 for failure to register, and that both offenses must be deemed subject to any constitutional deficiencies arising under the Fifth Amendment from the obligation to register.

IV.

We must now consider whether, as petitioner contends, satisfaction of his obligation to register would have compelled him to provide information incriminating to himself.

We must now consider whether, as petitioner contends, satisfaction of his obligation to register would have compelled him to provide information incriminating to himself. n9 We must first mark the terms of the registration requirement. The obligation to register is conditioned simply upon possession of a firearm, within the meaning of §5848 (1). Not every possessor of a firearm must, however, register; one who made the firearm, or acquired it by transfer or importation, need not register if the Act's provisions as to transfers, makings, and importations "were complied with." If those requirements were not met, or if the possessor did not make the firearm, and did not acquire it by transfer or importation, he must furnish the Secretary of the Treasury with his name, address, the place where the firearm is usually kept, and the place of his business or employment. Further, he must indicate his date of birth, social security number, and whether he has ever been convicted of a felony. Finally, he must provide a full description of the firearm. See 26 U.S.C. §5841; Treas. Reg. §179.120; Internal Revenue Service Form 1 (Firearms).

n9 We note that §5841 has several times been held to require incriminating disclosures, in violation of the Fifth Amendment privilege against self-incrimination. See Russell v. United States, 306 F.2d 402; Dugan v. United States, 341 F.2d 85; McCann v. United States, 217 F.Supp. 751; United States v. Fleish, 227 F.Supp. 967. See also Lovelace v. United States, supra, at 309.

a prospective registrant realistically can expect that registration will substantially increase the likelihood of his prosecution. Moreover, he can reasonably fear that the possession established by his registration will facilitate his prosecution under the making and transfer clauses of §5851.

they are compelled, on pain of criminal prosecution, to provide to the Secretary both a formal acknowledgment of their possession of firearms, and supplementary information likely to facilitate their arrest and eventual conviction. The hazards of incrimination created by the registration requirement can thus only be termed "real and appreciable."

The registration requirement is thus directed principally at those persons who have obtained possession of a firearm without complying with the Act's other requirements, and who therefore are immediately threatened by criminal prosecutions under §§5851 and 5861. They are unmistakably persons "inherently suspect of criminal activities." Albertson v. SACB, 382 U.S. 70, 79. It is true, as the United States emphasizes, that registration is not invariably indicative of a violation of the Act's requirements; there are situations, which the United States itself styles "uncommon," n10 in which a possessor who has not violated the Act's other provisions is obliged to register. n11 Nonetheless, the correlation between obligations to register and violations can only be regarded as exceedingly high, and a prospective registrant realistically can expect that registration will substantially increase the likelihood of his prosecution. Moreover, he can reasonably fear that the possession established by his registration will facilitate his prosecution under the making and transfer clauses of §5851. In these circumstances, it can scarcely be said that the risks of criminal prosecution confronted by prospective registrants are "remote possibilities out of the ordinary course of law," Heike v. United States, 227 U.S. 131, 144; yet they are compelled, on pain of criminal prosecution, to provide to the Secretary both a formal acknowledgment of their possession of firearms, and supplementary information likely to facilitate their arrest and eventual conviction. The hazards of incrimination created by the registration requirement can thus only be termed "real and appreciable." Reg. v. Boyes, 1 B. & S. 311, 330; Brown v. Walker, 161 U.S. 591, 599-600.

n10 In particular, the United States emphasizes the position of a finder of a lost or abandoned firearm. Brief for the United States 20.

n11 We must note, however, that certain of these prospective registrants might be threatened by prosecution under state law for possession of firearms, or similar offenses. It is possible that such persons would be obliged, if they registered in compliance with §5841, to provide information incriminating to themselves. Such hazards would, of course, support a proper claim of privilege. See Malloy v. Hogan, 378 U.S. 1. For illustrations of state statutes under which such prosecutions might occur, see Conn. Gen. Stat. Rev. §53-202 (1958); Del. Code Ann., Tit. 11, §465 (1953); Hawaii Rev. Laws §157-8 (1955); Iowa Code §696.1 (1966); Kan. Stat. Ann. §21-2601 (1964); La. Rev. Stat. §40:1752 (1950); Minn. Stat. §609.67 (1965); N. J. Rev. Stat., Tit. 2A, §151-50 (1953). We have discovered no state statute under which the present petitioner might have been subject to prosecution for acts registrable under §5841, and he has not contended that registration would have incriminated him under state law.

nothing we do today will prevent the effective regulation or taxation by Congress of firearms.

We are, however, urged by the United States, for various disparate reasons, to affirm petitioner's conviction. It is first suggested that the registration requirement is a valid exercise of the taxing powers, in that it is calculated merely to assure notice to the Treasury of all taxable firearms. We do not doubt, as we have repeatedly indicated, n12 that this Court must give deference to Congress' taxing powers, and to measures reasonably incidental to their exercise; but we are no less obliged to heed the limitations placed upon those powers by the Constitution's other commands. We are fully cognizant of the Treasury's need for accurate and timely information, but other methods, entirely consistent with constitutional limitations, exist by which such information may be obtained. See generally Counselman v. Hitchcock, 142 U.S. 547, 585. See also Adams v. Maryland, 347 U.S. 179; Murphy v. Waterfront Commission, 378 U.S. 52. Accordingly, nothing we do today will prevent the effective regulation or taxation by Congress of firearms.

n12 See, for example, Sonzinsky v. United States, 300 U.S. 506; Marchetti v. United States, supra.

Nonetheless, these statutory provisions, as now written, cannot be brought within any of the situations in which the Court has held that the constitutional privilege does not prevent the use by the United States of information obtained in connection with regulatory programs of general application. See United States v. Sullivan, 274 U.S. 259; Shapiro v. United States, 335 U.S. 1. For reasons given in Marchetti v. United States, supra, and Grosso v. United States, ante, p. 62, we have concluded that the points of significant dissimilarity between these circumstances and those in Shapiro and Sullivan preclude any proper application of those cases here. The questions propounded by §5841, like those at issue in Albertson, supra, are "directed at a highly selective group inherently suspect of criminal activities"; they concern, not "an essentially non-criminal and regulatory area of inquiry," but "an area permeated with criminal statutes." 382 U.S., at 79. There are, moreover, no records or other documents here to which any "public aspects" might reasonably be said to have attached. Compare Shapiro v. United States, supra, at 34; and Marchetti v. United States, supra.

We recognize that there are a number of apparently uncommon circumstances in which registration is required of one who has not violated the Firearms Act; the United States points chiefly to the situation of a finder of a lost or abandoned firearm.

it appears, from the evidence now before us, that the rights of those subject to the Act will be fully protected if a proper claim of privilege is understood to provide a full defense to any prosecution either for failure to register under §5841 or, under §5851, for possession of a firearm which has not been registered.

The United States next emphasizes that petitioner has consistently contended that §§5841 and 5851 are unconstitutional on their face; it urges that this contention is foreclosed by the inclusion in the registration requirement of situations in which the obligation to register cannot produce incriminating disclosures. We recognize that there are a number of apparently uncommon circumstances in which registration is required of one who has not violated the Firearms Act; the United States points chiefly to the situation of a finder of a lost or abandoned firearm. n13 Compare United States v. Forgett, 349 F.2d 601. We agree that the existence of such situations makes it inappropriate, in the absence of evidence that the exercise of protected rights would otherwise be hampered, to declare these sections impermissible on their face. Instead, it appears, from the evidence now before us, that the rights of those subject to the Act will be fully protected if a proper claim of privilege is understood to provide a full defense to any prosecution either for failure to register under §5841 or, under §5851, for possession of a firearm which has not been registered.

n13 Again, we note that these registrants might be confronted by hazards of prosecution under state law, and that those hazards might support a proper claim of privilege. See supra, n. 11.

Finally, we are asked to avoid the constitutional difficulties which we have found in §§5841 and 5851 by imposing restrictions upon the use by state and federal authorities of information obtained as a consequence of the registration requirement. We note that the provisions of 26 U.S.C. §6107 n14 are applicable to the special occupational taxes imposed by §5801, although not, apparently, to the making and transfer taxes imposed by §§5811 and 5821. In these circumstances, we decline, for reasons indicated in Marchetti, supra, and Grosso, supra, to impose the restrictions urged by the United States.

n14 Section 6107 provides that "In the principal internal revenue office in each internal revenue district there shall be kept, for public inspection, an alphabetical list of the names of all persons who have paid special taxes under subtitle D or E within such district. Such list shall be prepared and kept pursuant to regulations prescribed by the Secretary or his delegate, and shall contain the time, place, and business for which such special taxes have been paid, and upon application of any prosecuting officer of any State, county, or municipality there shall be furnished to him a certified copy thereof, as of a public record, for which a fee of $1 for each 100 words or fraction thereof in the copy or copies so requested may be charged." The special taxes to which the section refers include those imposed by 26 U.S.C. §5801.

We hold that a proper claim of the constitutional privilege against self-incrimination provides a full defense to prosecutions either for failure to register a firearm under §5841 or for possession of an unregistered firearm under §5851.

We hold that a proper claim of the constitutional privilege against self-incrimination provides a full defense to prosecutions either for failure to register a firearm under §5841 or for possession of an unregistered firearm under §5851.

V.

It remains only to determine the appropriate disposition of this case. Petitioner has seasonably and consistently asserted a claim of privilege, but the courts below, believing the privilege inapplicable to prosecutions under §5851, evidently did not assess the claim's merits. It would therefore ordinarily be necessary to remand the cause to the District Court, with instructions to examine the merits of the claim. We note, however, that there can be no suggestion here that petitioner has waived his privilege, and that, moreover, the United States has conceded that petitioner's privilege against self-incrimination must be found to have been impermissibly infringed if his contentions as to the proper construction of §§5851 and 5841 are accepted. Brief for the United States 8. Accordingly, the District Court would be obliged in any additional proceeding to conclude that "there is reasonable ground to apprehend danger to the witness from his being compelled to answer." Reg. v. Boyes, supra, at 330. It follows that any proceeding in the District Court must inevitably result in the reversal of petitioner's conviction. We have plenary authority under 28 U.S.C. §2106 to make such disposition of the case "as may be just under the circumstances." See Yates v. United States, 354 U.S. 298, 327-331; Grosso v. United States, supra. It would be neither just nor appropriate to require the parties and the District Court to commence an entirely needless additional proceeding. Accordingly, the judgment of the Court of Appeals is

Reversed.

MR. JUSTICE MARSHALL took no part in the consideration or decision of this case.

MR. CHIEF JUSTICE WARREN, dissenting.

For reasons stated in my dissent in Marchetti v. United States and Grosso v. United States, ante, p. 77, I cannot agree with the result reached by the Court in this case.

DUNCAN v. LOUISIANA

(CASE EXCERPT)

391 U.S. 145; 88 S. Ct. 1444; 20 L. Ed. 2d 491

January 17, 1968, Argued

May 20, 1968, Decided

GIST: The Court ruled that the 6th Amendment right to a jury trial applied against the states through the 14th Amendment. Justice Black, concurring with Justice Douglas, quoted from the 14th Amendment ratification debates, including a reference to the right to keep and bear arms as one of the "personal rights guarantied and secured by the first eight amendments of the Constitution."

MR. JUSTICE BLACK, with whom MR. JUSTICE DOUGLAS joins, concurring.

.....

What more precious "privilege" of American citizenship could there be than that privilege to claim the protections of our great Bill of Rights?

In addition to the adoption of Professor Fairman's "history," the dissent states that "the great words of the four clauses of the first section of the Fourteenth Amendment would have been an exceedingly peculiar way to say that 'The rights heretofore guaranteed against federal intrusion by the first eight Amendments are henceforth guaranteed against state intrusion as well.'" In response to this I can say only that the words "No State shall make or enforce any law which shall abridge the privileges or immunities of citizens of the United States" seem to me an eminently reasonable way of expressing the idea that henceforth the Bill of Rights shall apply to the States. What more precious "privilege" of American citizenship could there be than that privilege to claim the protections of our great Bill of Rights? I suggest that any reading of "privileges or immunities of citizens of the United States" which excludes the Bill of Rights' safeguards renders the words of this section of the Fourteenth Amendment meaningless. Senator Howard, who introduced the Fourteenth Amendment for passage in the Senate, certainly read the words this way. Although I have cited his speech at length in my Adamson dissent appendix, I believe it would be worthwhile to reproduce a part of it here.

the personal rights guarantied and secured by the first eight amendments of the Constitution; such as... the right to keep and to bear arms

"Such is the character of the privileges and immunities spoken of in the second section of the fourth article of the Constitution [the Senator had just read from the old opinion of Corfield v. Coryell, 6 Fed. Cas. 546 (No. 3,230) (E. D. Pa. 1825)]. To these privileges and immunities, whatever they may be -- for they are not and cannot be fully defined in their entire extent and precise nature -- to these should be added the personal rights guarantied and secured by the first eight amendments of the Constitution; such as the freedom of speech and of the press; the right of the people peaceably to assemble and petition the Government for a redress of grievances, a right appertaining to each and all the people; the right to keep and to bear arms; the right to be exempted from the quartering of soldiers in a house without the consent of the owner; the right to be exempt from unreasonable searches and seizures, and from any search or seizure except by virtue of a warrant issued upon a formal oath or affidavit; the right of an accused person to be informed of the nature of the accusation against him, and his right to be tried by an impartial jury of the vicinage; and also the right to be secure against excessive bail and against cruel and unusual punishments.

TERRY v. OHIO

(CASE EXCERPT)

392 U.S. 1; 88 S. Ct. 1868; 20 L. Ed. 2d 889

December 12, 1967, Argued

June 10, 1968, Decided

GIST: This famous case authorized what has become known as a "Terry frisk," a limited protective non-invasive search for weapons, made by a peace officer under specially defined circumstances.

Terry and his two accomplices were observed apparently casing a jewelry store, by plainclothes Cleveland police detective Martin McFadden, a 39-year police veteran. The suspects walked past the shop and peered in the window a dozen times, after which McFadden approached them, sensing they were up to no good. When they mumbled instead of identifying themselves, after McFadden had identified himself as a policeman, he grabbed Terry, spun him around and patted down the outside of his clothes. He felt a pistol under Terry's overcoat, then found a pistol in the outer pocket of Chilton, one of the accomplices, and nothing on the third man they were with. The officer had a police wagon called to the scene and Terry and Chilton, who hadn't visibly committed any crime in front of him, were subsequently charged with concealed weapons violations based on McFadden's search.

The defendants moved to have the charges against them dropped, claiming the evidence against them had been seized illegally. Officer McFadden, they argued, had no "probable cause" to suspect a crime had been committed when he made the search that found the guns. Without probable cause, they claimed the pat-down violated their protection from unreasonable search and seizure.

In this critically important 4th Amendment case the High Court held that such a "stop and frisk" is a seizure of the person, and a search, conducted without a warrant, but that it could be allowed under the 4th Amendment if it was reasonable. There is an immediate interest of the police officer in taking steps to neutralize a threat of physical harm. Discretion of the officer at the scene, and an evaluation of the facts afterwards by a court determine reasonableness. An arrest would require the higher standard of probable cause, and would justify a full search of the suspect. The more limited Terry frisk, in order to avoid violating the right to be free from unreasonable search and seizure, does not allow a full search, but only a superficial pat down for the safety of the officer and others nearby. The Court recognizes a potential for abuse, especially in populations that complain of police harassment, and that even a frisk of outer clothing for weapons is a severe intrusion upon cherished personal security.

In a lone dissent, Justice Douglas is dismayed at the elimination of the long-held probable-cause requirement that an officer would have to be able to express later, or that a judge would need to issue a warrant. He says such a change, if needed to combat modern forms of lawlessness, is a "long step down the totalitarian path" and should require a choice of the people through an amendment to the Constitution.

In subsequent years, the *Terry* decision has been used to justify a wide variety of frisks, pat-downs and other intermediate searches, often under conditions that have little to do with the officer-safety rationale used here.

MR. CHIEF JUSTICE WARREN delivered the opinion of the Court.

This case presents serious questions concerning the role of the Fourth Amendment in the confrontation on the street between the citizen and the policeman investigating suspicious circumstances.

the prosecution introduced in evidence two revolvers and a number of bullets seized from Terry and a codefendant, Richard Chilton

Petitioner Terry was convicted of carrying a concealed weapon and sentenced to the statutorily prescribed term of one to three years in the penitentiary. Following the denial of a pretrial motion to suppress, the prosecution introduced in evidence two revolvers and a number of bullets seized from Terry and a codefendant, Richard Chilton, by Cleveland Police Detective Martin McFadden. At the hearing on the motion to suppress this evidence, Officer McFadden testified that while he was patrolling in plain clothes in downtown Cleveland at approximately 2:30 in the afternoon of October 31, 1963, his attention was attracted by two men, Chilton and Terry, standing on the corner of Huron Road and Euclid Avenue. He had never seen the two men before, and he was unable to say precisely what first drew his eye to them. However, he testified that he had been a policeman for 39 years and a detective for 35 and that he had been assigned to patrol this vicinity of downtown Cleveland for shoplifters and pickpockets for 30 years. He explained that he had developed routine habits of observation over the years and that he would "stand and watch people or walk and watch people at many intervals of the day." He added: "Now, in this case when I looked over they didn't look right to me at the time."

His interest aroused, Officer McFadden took up a post of observation in the entrance to a store 300 to 400 feet away from the two men. "I get more purpose to watch them when I seen their movements," he testified. He saw one of the men leave the other one and walk southwest on Huron Road, past some stores. The man paused for a moment and looked in a store window, then walked on a short distance, turned around and walked back toward the corner, pausing once again to look in the same store window. He rejoined his companion at the corner, and the two conferred briefly. Then the second man went through the same series of motions, strolling down Huron Road, looking in the same window, walking on a short distance, turning back, peering in the store window again, and returning to confer with the first man at the corner. The two men repeated this ritual alternately between five and six times apiece - in all, roughly a dozen trips. At one point, while the two were standing together on the corner, a third man approached them and engaged them briefly in conversation. This man then left the two others and walked west on Euclid Avenue. Chilton and Terry resumed their measured pacing, peering, and conferring. After this had gone on for 10 to 12 minutes, the two men walked off together, heading west on Euclid Avenue, following the path taken earlier by the third man.

> **he suspected the two men of "casing a job, a stick-up," and that he considered it his duty as a police officer to investigate further.**

> **Officer McFadden grabbed petitioner Terry, spun him around so that they were facing the other two, with Terry between McFadden and the others, and patted down the outside of his clothing.**

> **Officer McFadden proceeded to pat down the outer clothing of Chilton and the third man, Katz.**

By this time Officer McFadden had become thoroughly suspicious. He testified that after observing their elaborately casual and oft-repeated reconnaissance of the store window on Huron Road, he suspected the two men of "casing a job, a stick-up," and that he considered it his duty as a police officer to investigate further. He added that he feared "they may have a gun." Thus, Officer McFadden followed Chilton and Terry and saw them stop in front of Zucker's store to talk to the same man who had conferred with them earlier on the street corner. Deciding that the situation was ripe for direct action, Officer McFadden approached the three men, identified himself as a police officer and asked for their names. At this point his knowledge was confined to what he had observed. He was not acquainted with any of the three men by name or by sight, and he had received no information concerning them from any other source. When the men "mumbled something" in response to his inquiries, Officer McFadden grabbed petitioner Terry, spun him around so that they were facing the other two, with Terry between McFadden and the others, and patted down the outside of his clothing. In the left breast pocket of Terry's overcoat Officer McFadden felt a pistol. He reached inside the overcoat pocket, but was unable to remove the gun. At this point, keeping Terry between himself and the others, the officer ordered all three men to enter Zucker's store. As they went in, he removed Terry's overcoat completely, removed a .38-caliber revolver from the pocket and ordered all three men to face the wall with their hands raised. Officer McFadden proceeded to pat down the outer clothing of Chilton and the third man, Katz. He discovered another revolver in the outer pocket of Chilton's overcoat, but no weapons were found on Katz. The officer testified that he only patted the men down to see whether they had weapons, and that he did not put his hands beneath the outer garments of either Terry or Chilton until he felt their guns. So far as appears from the record, he never placed his hands beneath Katz' outer garments. Officer McFadden seized Chilton's gun, asked the proprietor of the store to call a police wagon, and took all three men to the station, where Chilton and Terry were formally charged with carrying concealed weapons.

On the motion to suppress the guns the prosecution took the position that they had been seized following a search incident to a lawful arrest. The trial court rejected this theory, stating that it "would be stretching the facts beyond reasonable comprehension" to find that Officer McFadden had had probable cause to arrest the men before he patted them down for weapons. However, the court denied the defendants' motion on the ground that Officer McFadden, on the basis of his experience, "had reasonable cause to believe . . . that the defendants were conducting themselves suspiciously, and some interrogation should be made of their action." Purely for his own protection, the court held, the officer had the right to pat down the outer clothing of these men, who he had reasonable cause to believe might be armed. The court distinguished between an investigatory "stop" and an arrest, and between a "frisk" of the outer clothing for weapons and a full-blown search for evidence of crime. The frisk, it held, was essential to the proper performance of the officer's investigatory duties, for without it "the answer to the police officer may be a bullet, and a loaded pistol discovered during the frisk is admissible."

After the court denied their motion to suppress, Chilton and Terry waived jury trial and pleaded not guilty. The court adjudged them guilty, and the Court of Appeals for the Eighth Judicial District, Cuyahoga County, affirmed. State v. Terry, 5 Ohio App. 2d 122, 214 N. E. 2d 114 (1966). The Supreme Court of Ohio dismissed their appeal on the ground that no "substantial constitutional question" was involved. We granted certiorari, 387 U.S. 929 (1967), to determine whether the admission of the revolvers in evidence violated petitioner's rights under the Fourth Amendment, made applicable to the States by the Fourteenth. Mapp v.

Ohio, 367 U.S. 643 (1961). We affirm the conviction.

I.

This inestimable right of personal security belongs as much to the citizen on the streets of our cities as to the homeowner closeted in his study to dispose of his secret affairs.

The Fourth Amendment provides that "the right of the people to be secure in their persons, houses, papers, and effects, against unreasonable searches and seizures, shall not be violated . . . ." This inestimable right of personal security belongs as much to the citizen on the streets of our cities as to the homeowner closeted in his study to dispose of his secret affairs. For, as this Court has always recognized,

"No right is held more sacred, or is more carefully guarded, by the common law, than the right of every individual to the possession and control of his own person, free from all restraint or interference of others, unless by clear and unquestionable authority of law." Union Pac. R. Co. v. Botsford, 141 U.S. 250, 251 (1891).

We have recently held that "the Fourth Amendment protects people, not places," Katz v. United States, 389 U.S. 347, 351 (1967), and wherever an individual may harbor a reasonable "expectation of privacy," id., at 361 (MR. JUSTICE HARLAN, concurring), he is entitled to be free from unreasonable governmental intrusion. Of course, the specific content and incidents of this right must be shaped by the context in which it is asserted. For "what the Constitution forbids is not all searches and seizures, but unreasonable searches and seizures." Elkins v. United States, 364 U.S. 206, 222 (1960). Unquestionably petitioner was entitled to the protection of the Fourth Amendment as he walked down the street in Cleveland. Beck v. Ohio, 379 U.S. 89 (1964); Rios v. United States, 364 U.S. 253 (1960); Henry v. United States, 361 U.S. 98 (1959); United States v. Di Re, 332 U.S. 581 (1948); Carroll v. United States, 267 U.S. 132 (1925). The question is whether in all the circumstances of this on-the-street encounter, his right to personal security was violated by an unreasonable search and seizure.

We would be less than candid if we did not acknowledge that this question thrusts to the fore difficult and troublesome issues regarding a sensitive area of police activity - issues which have never before been squarely presented to this Court. Reflective of the tensions involved are the practical and constitutional arguments pressed with great vigor on both sides of the public debate over the power of the police to "stop and frisk" - as it is sometimes euphemistically termed - suspicious persons.

On the one hand, it is frequently argued that in dealing with the rapidly unfolding and often dangerous situations on city streets the police are in need of an escalating set of flexible responses, graduated in relation to the amount of information they possess. For this purpose it is urged that distinctions should be made between a "stop" and an "arrest" (or a "seizure" of a person), and between a "frisk" and a "search." Thus, it is argued, the police should be allowed to "stop" a person and detain him briefly for questioning upon suspicion that he may be connected with criminal activity. Upon suspicion that the person may be armed, the police should have the power to "frisk" him for weapons. If the "stop" and the "frisk" give rise to probable cause to believe that the suspect has committed a crime, then the police should be empowered to make a formal "arrest," and a full incident "search" of the person. This scheme is justified in part upon the notion that a "stop" and a "frisk" amount to a mere "minor inconvenience and petty indignity," which can properly be imposed upon the citizen in the interest of effective law enforcement on the basis of a police officer's suspicion.

On the other side the argument is made that the authority of the police must be strictly circumscribed by the law of arrest and search as it has developed to date in the traditional jurisprudence of the Fourth Amendment. It is contended with some force that there is not - and cannot be - a variety of police activity which does not depend solely upon the voluntary cooperation of the citizen and yet which stops short of an arrest based upon probable cause to make such an arrest. The heart of the Fourth Amendment, the argument runs, is a severe requirement of specific justification for any intrusion upon protected personal security, coupled with a highly developed system of judicial controls to enforce upon the agents of the State the commands of the Constitution. Acquiescence by the courts in the compulsion inherent in the field interrogation practices at issue here, it is urged, would constitute an abdication of judicial control over, and indeed an encouragement of, substantial interference with liberty and personal security by police officers whose judgment is necessarily colored by their primary involvement in "the often competitive enterprise of ferreting out crime." Johnson v. United States, 333 U.S. 10, 14 (1948). This, it is argued, can only serve to exacerbate police-community tensions in the crowded centers of our Nation's cities.

The State has characterized the issue here as "the right of a police officer . . . to make an on-the-street stop, interrogate and pat down for weapons (known in street vernacular as 'stop and frisk')."

the rule excluding evidence seized in violation of the Fourth Amendment has been recognized as a principal mode of discouraging lawless police conduct.

Courts which sit under our Constitution cannot and will not be made party to lawless invasions of the constitutional rights of citizens by permitting unhindered governmental use of the fruits of such invasions.

In this context we approach the issues in this case mindful of the limitations of the judicial function in controlling the myriad daily situations in which policemen and citizens confront each other on the street. The State has characterized the issue here as "the right of a police officer . . . to make an on-the-street stop, interrogate and pat down for weapons (known in street vernacular as 'stop and frisk')." But this is only partly accurate. For the issue is not the abstract propriety of the police conduct, but the admissibility against petitioner of the evidence uncovered by the search and seizure. Ever since its inception, the rule excluding evidence seized in violation of the Fourth Amendment has been recognized as a principal mode of discouraging lawless police conduct. See Weeks v. United States, 232 U.S. 383, 391 -393 (1914). Thus its major thrust is a deterrent one, see Linkletter v. Walker, 381 U.S. 618, 629 -635 (1965), and experience has taught that it is the only effective deterrent to police misconduct in the criminal context, and that without it the constitutional guarantee against unreasonable searches and seizures would be a mere "form of words." Mapp v. Ohio, 367 U.S. 643, 655 (1961). The rule also serves another vital function - "the imperative of judicial integrity." Elkins v. United States, 364 U.S. 206, 222 (1960). Courts which sit under our Constitution cannot and will not be made party to lawless invasions of the constitutional rights of citizens by permitting unhindered governmental use of the fruits of such invasions. Thus in our system evidentiary rulings provide the context in which the judicial process of inclusion and exclusion approves some conduct as comporting with constitutional guarantees and disapproves other actions by state agents. A ruling admitting evidence in a criminal trial, we recognize, has the necessary effect of legitimizing the conduct which produced the evidence, while an application of the exclusionary rule withholds the constitutional imprimatur.

Street encounters between citizens and police officers are incredibly rich in diversity. They range from wholly friendly exchanges of pleasantries or mutually useful information to hostile confrontations of armed men involving arrests, or injuries, or loss of life.

The exclusionary rule has its limitations, however, as a tool of judicial control. It cannot properly be invoked to exclude the products of legitimate police investigative techniques on the ground that much conduct which is closely similar involves unwarranted intrusions upon constitutional protections. Moreover, in some contexts the rule is ineffective as a deterrent. Street encounters between citizens and police officers are incredibly rich in diversity. They range from wholly friendly exchanges of pleasantries or mutually useful information to hostile confrontations of armed men involving arrests, or injuries, or loss of life. Moreover, hostile confrontations are not all of a piece. Some of them begin in a friendly enough manner, only to take a different turn upon the injection of some unexpected element into the conversation. Encounters are initiated by the police for a wide variety of purposes, some of which are wholly unrelated to a desire to prosecute for crime. Doubtless some police "field interrogation" conduct violates the Fourth Amendment. But a stern refusal by this Court to condone such activity does not necessarily render it responsive to the exclusionary rule. Regardless of how effective the rule may be where obtaining convictions is an important objective of the police, it is powerless to deter invasions of constitutionally guaranteed rights where the police either have no interest in prosecuting or are willing to forgo successful prosecution in the interest of serving some other goal.

The wholesale harassment by certain elements of the police community, of which minority groups, particularly Negroes, frequently complain, will not be stopped by the exclusion of any evidence from any criminal trial.

Proper adjudication of cases in which the exclusionary rule is invoked demands a constant awareness of these limitations. The wholesale harassment by certain elements of the police community, of which minority groups, particularly Negroes, frequently complain, n11 will not be stopped by the exclusion of any evidence from any criminal trial. Yet a rigid and unthinking application of the exclusionary rule, in futile protest against practices which it can never be used effectively to control, may exact a high toll in human injury and frustration of efforts to prevent crime. No judicial opinion can comprehend the protean variety of the street encounter, and we can only judge the facts of the case before us. Nothing we say today is to be taken as indicating approval of police conduct outside the legitimate investigative sphere. Under our decision, courts still retain their traditional responsibility to guard against police conduct which is overbearing or harassing, or which trenches upon personal security without the objective evidentiary justification which the Constitution requires. When such conduct is identified, it must be condemned by the judiciary and its fruits must be excluded from evidence in criminal trials. And, of course, our approval of legitimate and restrained investigative conduct undertaken on the basis of ample factual justification should in no way discourage the employment of other remedies than the exclusionary rule to curtail abuses for which that sanction may prove inappropriate.

n11. The President's Commission on Law Enforcement and Administration of Justice found that "[i]n many communities, field interrogations are a major source of friction between the police and minority groups." President's Commission on Law Enforcement and Administration of Justice, Task Force Report: The Police 183 (1967). It was reported that the friction caused by "[m]isuse of field interrogations" increases "as more police departments adopt `aggressive patrol' in which officers are encouraged routinely to stop and question persons on the street who are unknown to them, who are suspicious, or whose purpose for being abroad is not readily evident." Id., at 184. While the frequency with which "frisking" forms a part of field interrogation practice varies tremendously with the locale, the objective of the interrogation, and the particular officer, see Tiffany, McIntyre & Rotenberg, supra, n. 9, at 47-48, it cannot help but be a severely exacerbating factor in police-community tensions. This is particularly true in situations where the "stop and frisk" of youths or minority group members is "motivated by the officers' perceived need to maintain the power image of the beat officer, an aim sometimes accomplished by humiliating anyone who attempts to undermine police control of the streets." Ibid.

we turn our attention to the quite narrow question posed by the facts before us: whether it is always unreasonable for a policeman to seize a person and subject him to a limited search for weapons unless there is probable cause for an arrest.

Having thus roughly sketched the perimeters of the constitutional debate over the limits on police investigative conduct in general and the background against which this case presents itself, we turn our attention to the quite narrow question posed by the facts before us: whether it is always unreasonable for a policeman to seize a person and subject him to a limited search for weapons unless there is probable cause for an arrest. Given the narrowness of this question, we have no occasion to canvass in detail the constitutional limitations upon the scope of a policeman's power when he confronts a citizen without probable cause to arrest him.

II.

It must be recognized that whenever a police officer accosts an individual and restrains his freedom to walk away, he has "seized" that person. And it is nothing less than sheer torture of the English language to suggest that a careful exploration of the outer surfaces of a person's clothing all over his or her body in an attempt to find weapons is not a "search."

it is simply fantastic to urge that such a procedure performed in public by a policeman while the citizen stands helpless, perhaps facing a wall with his hands raised, is a "petty indignity."

Our first task is to establish at what point in this encounter the Fourth Amendment becomes relevant. That is, we must decide whether and when Officer McFadden "seized" Terry and whether and when he conducted a "search." There is some suggestion in the use of such terms as "stop" and "frisk" that such police conduct is outside the purview of the Fourth Amendment because neither action rises to the level of a "search" or "seizure" within the meaning of the Constitution. We emphatically reject this notion. It is quite plain that the Fourth Amendment governs "seizures" of the person which do not eventuate in a trip to the station house and prosecution for crime - "arrests" in traditional terminology. It must be recognized that whenever a police officer accosts an individual and restrains his freedom to walk away, he has "seized" that person. And it is nothing less than sheer torture of the English language to suggest that a careful exploration of the outer surfaces of a person's clothing all over his or her body in an attempt to find weapons is not a "search." Moreover, it is simply fantastic to urge that such a procedure performed in public by a policeman while the citizen stands helpless, perhaps facing a wall with his hands raised, is a "petty indignity." n13 It is a serious intrusion upon the sanctity of the person, which may inflict great indignity and arouse strong resentment, and it is not to be undertaken lightly.

A thorough search must be made of the prisoner's arms and armpits, waistline and back, the groin and area about the testicles, and entire surface of the legs down to the feet.

n13. Consider the following apt description: "[T]he officer must feel with sensitive fingers every portion of the prisoner's body. A thorough search must be made of the prisoner's arms and armpits, waistline and back, the groin and area about the testicles, and entire surface of the legs down to the feet." Priar & Martin, Searching and Disarming Criminals, 45 J. Crim. L. C. & P. S. 481 (1954).

The danger in the logic which proceeds upon distinctions between a "stop" and an "arrest," or "seizure" of the person, and between a "frisk" and a "search" is two-fold. It seeks to isolate from constitutional scrutiny the initial stages of the contact between the policeman and the citizen. And by suggesting a rigid all-or-nothing model of justification and regulation under the Amendment, it obscures the utility of limitations upon the scope, as well as the initiation, of police action as a means of constitutional regulation. This Court has held in the past that a search which is reasonable at its inception may violate the Fourth Amendment by virtue of its intolerable intensity and scope. Kremen v. United States, 353 U.S. 346 (1957); Go-Bart Importing Co. v. United States, 282 U.S. 344, 356 -358 (1931); see United States v. Di Re, 332 U.S. 581, 586 -587 (1948). The scope of the search must be "strictly tied to and justified by" the circumstances which rendered its initiation permissible. Warden v. Hayden, 387 U.S. 294, 310 (1967) (MR. JUSTICE FORTAS, concurring); see, e. g., Preston v. United States, 376 U.S. 364, 367 -368 (1964); Agnello v. United States, 269 U.S. 20, 30 -31 (1925).

The distinctions of classical "stop-and-frisk" theory thus serve to divert attention from the central inquiry under the Fourth Amendment - the reasonableness in all the circumstances of the particular governmental invasion of a citizen's personal security. "Search" and "seizure" are not talismans. We therefore reject the notions that the Fourth Amendment does not come into play at all as a limitation upon police conduct if the officers stop short of something called a "technical arrest" or a "full-blown search."

In this case there can be no question, then, that Officer McFadden "seized" petitioner and subjected him to a "search" when he took hold of him and patted down the outer surfaces of his clothing. We must decide whether at that point it was reasonable for Officer McFadden to have interfered with petitioner's personal security as he did. n16 And in determining whether the seizure and search were "unreasonable" our inquiry is a dual one - whether the officer's action was justified at its inception, and whether it was reasonably related in scope to the circumstances which justified the interference in the first place.

Obviously, not all personal intercourse between policemen and citizens involves "seizures" of persons. Only when the officer, by means of physical force or show of authority, has in some way restrained the liberty of a citizen may we conclude that a "seizure" has occurred.

n16. We thus decide nothing today concerning the constitutional propriety of an investigative "seizure" upon less than probable cause for purposes of "detention" and/or interrogation. Obviously, not all personal intercourse between policemen and citizens involves "seizures" of persons. Only when the officer, by means of physical force or show of authority, has in some way restrained the liberty of a citizen may we conclude that a "seizure" has occurred. We cannot tell with any certainty upon this record whether any such "seizure" took place here prior to Officer McFadden's initiation of physical contact for purposes of searching Terry for weapons, and we thus may assume that up to that point no intrusion upon constitutionally protected rights had occurred.

.....

there is the more immediate interest of the police officer in taking steps to assure himself that the person with whom he is dealing is not armed with a weapon that could unexpectedly and fatally be used against him.

American criminals have a long tradition of armed violence

The crux of this case, however, is not the propriety of Officer McFadden's taking steps to investigate petitioner's suspicious behavior, but rather, whether there was justification for McFadden's invasion of Terry's personal security by searching him for weapons in the course of that investigation. We are now concerned with more than the governmental interest in investigating crime; in addition, there is the more immediate interest of the police officer in taking steps to assure himself that the person with whom he is dealing is not armed with a weapon that could unexpectedly and fatally be used against him. Certainly it would be unreasonable to require that police officers take unnecessary risks in the performance of their duties. American criminals have a long tradition of armed violence, and every year in this country many law enforcement officers are killed in the line of duty, and thousands more are wounded. Virtually all of these deaths and a substantial portion of the injuries are inflicted with guns and knives. n21

n21. Fifty-seven law enforcement officers were killed in the line of duty in this country in 1966, bringing the total to 335 for the seven-year period beginning with 1960. Also in 1966, there were 23,851 assaults on police officers, 9,113 of which resulted in injuries to the policemen. Fifty-five of the 57 officers killed in 1966 died from gunshot wounds, 41 of them inflicted by handguns easily secreted about the person. The remaining two murders were perpetrated by knives. See Federal Bureau of Investigation, Uniform Crime Reports for the United States - 1966, at 45-48, 152 and Table 51.

The easy availability of firearms to potential criminals in this country is well known and has provoked much debate. See, e.g., President's Commission on Law Enforcement and Administration of Justice, The Challenge of Crime in a Free Society 239-243 (1967). Whatever the merits of gun-control proposals, this fact is relevant to an assessment of the need for some form of self-protective search power.

When an officer is justified in believing that the individual whose suspicious behavior he is investigating at close range is armed and presently dangerous to the officer or to others, it would appear to be clearly unreasonable to deny the officer the power to take necessary measures to determine whether the person is in fact carrying a weapon and to neutralize the threat of physical harm.

In view of these facts, we cannot blind ourselves to the need for law enforcement officers to protect themselves and other prospective victims of violence in situations where they may lack probable cause for an arrest. When an officer is justified in believing that the individual whose suspicious behavior he is investigating at close range is armed and presently dangerous to the officer or to others, it would appear to be clearly unreasonable to deny the officer the power to take necessary measures to determine whether the person is in fact carrying a weapon and to neutralize the threat of physical harm.

We must still consider, however, the nature and quality of the intrusion on individual rights which must be accepted if police officers are to be conceded the right to search for weapons in situations where probable cause to arrest for crime is lacking. Even a limited search of the outer clothing for weapons constitutes a severe, though brief, intrusion upon cherished personal security

We must still consider, however, the nature and quality of the intrusion on individual rights which must be accepted if police officers are to be conceded the right to search for weapons in situations where probable cause to arrest for crime is lacking. Even a limited search of the outer clothing for weapons constitutes a severe, though brief, intrusion upon cherished personal security, and it must surely be an annoying, frightening, and perhaps humiliating experience. Petitioner contends that such an intrusion is permissible only incident to a lawful arrest, either for a crime involving the possession of weapons or for a crime the commission of which led the officer to investigate in the first place. However, this argument must be closely examined.

.....

there must be a narrowly drawn authority to permit a reasonable search for weapons for the protection of the police officer, where he has reason to believe that he is dealing with an armed and dangerous individual, regardless of whether he has probable cause to arrest the individual for a crime.

the issue is whether a reasonably prudent man in the circumstances would be warranted in the belief that his safety or that of others was in danger.

Our evaluation of the proper balance that has to be struck in this type of case leads us to conclude that there must be a narrowly drawn authority to permit a reasonable search for weapons for the protection of the police officer, where he has reason to believe that he is dealing with an armed and dangerous individual, regardless of whether he has probable cause to arrest the individual for a crime. The officer need not be absolutely certain that the individual is armed; the issue is whether a reasonably prudent man in the circumstances would be warranted in the belief that his safety or that of others was in danger. Cf. Beck v. Ohio, 379 U.S. 89, 91 (1964); Brinegar v. United States, 338 U.S. 160, 174 -176 (1949); Stacey v. Emery, 97 U.S. 642, 645 (1878). And in determining whether the officer acted reasonably in such circumstances, due weight must be given, not to his inchoate and unparticularized suspicion or "hunch," but to the specific reasonable inferences which he is entitled to draw from the facts in light of his experience. Cf. Brinegar v. United States supra.

IV.

The actions of Terry and Chilton were consistent with McFadden's hypothesis that

these men were contemplating a daylight robbery—which, it is reasonable to assume, would be likely to involve the use of weapons

We must now examine the conduct of Officer McFadden in this case to determine whether his search and seizure of petitioner were reasonable, both at their inception and as conducted. He had observed Terry, together with Chilton and another man, acting in a manner he took to be preface to a "stick-up." We think on the facts and circumstances Officer McFadden detailed before the trial judge a reasonably prudent man would have been warranted in believing petitioner was armed and thus presented a threat to the officer's safety while he was investigating his suspicious behavior. The actions of Terry and Chilton were consistent with McFadden's hypothesis that these men were contemplating a daylight robbery - which, it is reasonable to assume, would be likely to involve the use of weapons - and nothing in their conduct from the time he first noticed them until the time he confronted them and identified himself as a police officer gave him sufficient reason to negate that hypothesis. Although the trio had departed the original scene, there was nothing to indicate abandonment of an intent to commit a robbery at some point. Thus, when Officer McFadden approached the three men gathered before the display window at Zucker's store he had observed enough to make it quite reasonable to fear that they were armed; and nothing in their response to his hailing them, identifying himself as a police officer, and asking their names served to dispel that reasonable belief. We cannot say his decision at that point to seize Terry and pat his clothing for weapons was the product of a volatile or inventive imagination, or was undertaken simply as an act of harassment; the record evidences the tempered act of a policeman who in the course of an investigation had to make a quick decision as to how to protect himself and others from possible danger, and took limited steps to do so.

.....

The sole justification of the search in the present situation is the protection of the police officer and others nearby, and it must therefore be confined in scope to an intrusion reasonably designed to discover guns, knives, clubs, or other hidden instruments for the assault of the police officer.

We need not develop at length in this case, however, the limitations which the Fourth Amendment places upon a protective seizure and search for weapons. These limitations will have to be developed in the concrete factual circumstances of individual cases. See Sibron v. New York, post, p. 40, decided today. Suffice it to note that such a search, unlike a search without a warrant incident to a lawful arrest, is not justified by any need to prevent the disappearance or destruction of evidence of crime. See Preston v. United States, 376 U.S. 364, 367 (1964). The sole justification of the search in the present situation is the protection of the police officer and others nearby, and it must therefore be confined in scope to an intrusion reasonably designed to discover guns, knives, clubs, or other hidden instruments for the assault of the police officer.

Officer McFadden confined his search strictly to what was minimally necessary to learn whether the men were armed and to disarm them once he discovered the weapons.

The scope of the search in this case presents no serious problem in light of these standards. Officer McFadden patted down the outer clothing of petitioner and his two companions. He did not place his hands in their pockets or under the outer surface of their garments until he had felt weapons, and then he merely reached for and removed the guns. He never did invade Katz' person beyond the outer surfaces of his clothes, since he discovered nothing in his pat-down which might have been a weapon. Officer McFadden confined his search strictly to what was minimally necessary to learn whether the men were armed and to disarm them once he discovered the weapons. He did not conduct a general exploratory search for whatever evidence of criminal activity he might find.

.....

V.

We conclude that the revolver seized from Terry was properly admitted in evidence against him. At the time he seized petitioner and searched him for weapons, Officer McFadden had reasonable grounds to believe that petitioner was armed and dangerous, and it was necessary for the protection of himself and others to take swift measures to discover the true facts and neutralize the threat of harm if it materialized. The policeman carefully restricted his search to what was appropriate to the discovery of the particular items which he sought. Each case of this sort will, of course, have to be decided on its own facts. We merely hold today that where a police officer observes unusual conduct which leads him reasonably to conclude in light of his experience that criminal activity may be afoot and that the persons with whom he is dealing may be armed and presently dangerous, where in the course of investigating this behavior he identifies himself as a policeman and makes reasonable inquiries, and where nothing in the initial stages of the encounter serves to dispel his reasonable fear for his own or others' safety, he is entitled for the protection of himself and others in the area to conduct a carefully limited search of the outer clothing of such persons in an attempt to discover weapons which might be used to assault him. Such a search is a reasonable search under the Fourth Amendment, and any weapons seized may properly be introduced in evidence against the person from whom they were taken.

Affirmed.

.....

MR. JUSTICE HARLAN, concurring.

.....

Since the question in this and most cases is whether evidence produced by a frisk is admissible, the problem is to determine what makes a frisk reasonable.

Concealed weapons create an immediate and severe danger to the public, and though that danger might not warrant routine general weapons checks, it could well warrant action on less than a "probability."

Ohio has not clothed its policemen with routine authority to frisk and disarm on suspicion; in the absence of state authority, policemen have no more right to "pat down" the outer clothing of passers-by, or of persons to whom they address casual questions, than does any other citizen.

Ohio courts did not rest the constitutionality of this frisk upon any general authority in Officer McFadden to take reasonable steps to protect the citizenry, including himself, from dangerous weapons.

If the State of Ohio were to provide that police officers could, on articulable suspicion less than probable cause, forcibly frisk and disarm persons thought to be carrying concealed weapons, I would have little doubt that action taken pursuant to such authority could be constitutionally reasonable. Concealed weapons create an immediate and severe danger to the public, and though that danger might not warrant routine general weapons checks, it could well warrant action on less than a "probability." I mention this line of analysis because I think it vital to point out that it cannot be applied in this case. On the record before us Ohio has not clothed its policemen with routine authority to frisk and disarm on suspicion; in the absence of state authority, policemen have no more right to "pat down" the outer clothing of passers-by, or of persons to whom they address casual questions, than does any other citizen. Consequently, the Ohio courts did not rest the constitutionality of this frisk upon any general authority in Officer McFadden to take reasonable steps to protect the citizenry, including himself, from dangerous weapons.

The state courts held, instead, that when an officer is lawfully confronting a possibly hostile person in the line of duty he has a right, springing only from the necessity of the situation and not from any broader right to disarm, to frisk for his own protection. This holding, with which I agree and with which I think the Court agrees, offers the only satisfactory basis I can think of for affirming this conviction.

.....

The facts of this case are illustrative of a proper stop and an incident frisk. Officer McFadden had no probable cause to arrest Terry for anything, but he had observed circumstances that would reasonably lead an experienced, prudent policeman to suspect that Terry was about to engage in burglary or robbery. His justifiable suspicion afforded a proper constitutional basis for accosting Terry, restraining his liberty of movement briefly, and addressing questions to him, and Officer McFadden did so. When he did, he had no reason whatever to suppose that Terry might be armed, apart from the fact that he suspected him of planning a violent crime. McFadden asked Terry his name, to which Terry "mumbled something." Whereupon McFadden, without asking Terry to speak louder and without giving him any chance to explain his presence or his actions, forcibly frisked him.

I would affirm this conviction for what I believe to be the same reasons the Court relies on. I would, however, make explicit what I think is implicit in affirmance on the present facts. Officer McFadden's right to interrupt Terry's freedom of movement and invade his privacy arose only because circumstances warranted forcing an encounter with Terry in an effort to prevent or investigate a crime. Once that forced encounter was justified, however, the officer's right to take suitable measures for his own safety followed automatically.

.....

MR. JUSTICE DOUGLAS, dissenting.

.....

The opinion of the Court disclaims the existence of "probable cause." If loitering were in issue and that was the offense charged, there would be "probable cause" shown. But the crime here is carrying concealed weapons; and there is no basis for concluding that the officer had "probable cause" for believing that that crime was being committed. Had a warrant been sought, a magistrate would, therefore, have been unauthorized to issue one, for he can act only if there is a showing of "probable cause." We hold today that the police have greater authority to make a "seizure" and conduct a "search" than a judge has to authorize such action. We have said precisely the opposite over and over again.

.....

The infringement on personal liberty of any "seizure" of a person can only be "reasonable" under the Fourth Amendment if we require the police to possess "probable cause" before they seize him. Only that line draws a meaningful distinction between an officer's mere inkling and the presence of facts within the officer's personal knowledge which would convince a reasonable man that the person seized has committed, is committing, or is about to commit a particular crime.

.....

To give the police greater power than a magistrate is to take a long step down the totalitarian path. Perhaps such a step is desirable to cope with modern forms of lawlessness. But if it is taken, it should be the deliberate choice of the people through a constitutional amendment.

To give the police greater power than a magistrate is to take a long step down the totalitarian path. Perhaps such a step is desirable to cope with modern forms of lawlessness. But if it is taken, it should be the deliberate choice of the people through a constitutional amendment.

.....

There have been powerful hydraulic pressures throughout our history that bear heavily on the Court to water down constitutional guarantees and give the police the upper hand. That hydraulic pressure has probably never been greater than it is today.

Yet if the individual is no longer to be sovereign, if the police can pick him up whenever they do not like the cut of his jib, if they can "seize" and "search" him in their discretion, we enter a new regime. The decision to enter it should be made only after a full debate by the people of this country.

.....

BURTON v. SILLS

(FULL CASE)

394 U.S. 812; 89 S. Ct. 1486; 22 L. Ed. 2d 748

April 28, 1969, Decided

GIST: The Supreme Court of New Jersey upheld the constitutionality of a state gun licensing law. This law required a firearm purchaser to have an identification card issued by the local chief of police. Issuance of the identification cards left some discretion in the hands of the police chief. The New Jersey Supreme Court relied on cases holding the 2nd Amendment inapplicable to the states and on selected secondary sources interpreting the 2nd Amendment as not guaranteeing an individual right. The Court dismissed the appeal for want of a substantial federal question.

PER CURIAM.

The motion to dismiss is granted and the appeal is dismissed for want of a substantial federal question. MR. JUSTICE BRENNAN took no part in the consideration or decision of this case.

UNITED STATES v. FREED

(FULL CASE)
401 U.S. 601; 91 S. Ct. 1112; 28 L. Ed. 2d 356
January 11, 1971, Argued
April 5, 1971, Decided

GIST: Although the general public could be compelled to register certain firearms under the National Firearms Act, a felon could not be compelled to do so because it would violate the 5th Amendment guarantee against self incrimination. The Court reached this unexpected result in *Haynes v. U.S.*, and Congress promptly rewrote the law to cure the problem. In *Freed,* under the newly amended statute, the Court rejects a 5th Amendment challenge, establishing the legitimacy of the ingenious new licensing scheme, summarized succinctly in Justice Douglas' third paragraph.

NFA "firearms" aren't guns as most people think of the term, they include a special class of weapons better known as "destructive devices"—bombs, missiles, incendiaries, machine guns, sawed-off rifles and shotguns, and in Freed's case, hand grenades—which the Act refers to collectively (and somewhat confusingly) as "firearms" and regulates under tax law.

In Haynes v. United States, 390 U.S. 85, the Court held invalid under the Self-Incrimination Clause of the Fifth Amendment provisions of the National Firearms Act, which constituted parts of an interrelated statutory scheme for taxing certain classes of firearms primarily used for unlawful purposes, and made the potentially incriminating information available to state and other officials. To eliminate the defects revealed by Haynes, Congress amended the Act so that only a possessor who lawfully makes, manufactures, or imports firearms can and must register them. The transferor must identify himself, describe the firearm, and give the name and address of the transferee, whose application must be supported by fingerprints and a photograph and a law enforcement official's certificate identifying them as those of the transferee and stating that the weapon is intended for lawful uses. Only after the transferor's receipt of the approved application form may the firearm transfer be legally made. A transferee does not and cannot register, though possession of an unregistered firearm is illegal. No information or evidence furnished under the Act can be used as evidence against a registrant or applicant "in a criminal proceeding with respect to a violation of law occurring prior to or concurrently with the filing of the application or registration, or the compiling of the records containing the information or evidence," and no information filed is, as a matter of administration, disclosed to other federal, local, or state agencies. Appellees, who had been indicted under the amended Act for possessing and conspiring to possess unregistered hand grenades, filed motions to dismiss, which the District Court granted on the ground that the amended Act, like its predecessor, compels self-incrimination and that the indictment contravenes due process requirements by failing to allege scienter. Appellees also contend that the provisions relating to fingerprints and photographs will cause future incrimination. Held:

1. The revised statutory scheme of the amended Act, which significantly alters the scheme presented in Haynes, does not involve any violation of the Self-Incrimination Clause of the Fifth Amendment.

2. The amended Act fully protects a person against incrimination for past or present violations, and creates no substantial hazards of future incrimination.

3. The amended Act's prohibition against a person's "receiv[ing] or possess[ing] a firearm which is not registered to him," requires no specific intent and the absence of such a requirement in this essentially regulatory statute in the area of public safety does not violate due process requirements either as respects the substantive count or the conspiracy count.

MR. JUSTICE DOUGLAS delivered the opinion of the Court.

Following our decision in Haynes v. United States, 390 U.S. 85, Congress revised the National Firearms Act with the view of eliminating the defects in it which were revealed in Haynes. n1

n1 See S. Rep. No. 1501, 90th Cong., 2d Sess., 26, 42, 48, 52; H. R. Conf. Rep. No. 1956, 90th Cong., 2d Sess., 35.

At the time of Haynes "only weapons used principally by persons engaged in unlawful activities would be subjected to taxation." Id., at 87. Under the Act, as amended, all possessors of firearms as defined in the Act n2 are covered, except the Federal Government. 26 U.S.C. §5841 (1964 ed., Supp. V).

"grenades" which are involved in the present case.

n2 26 U.S.C. §5845 (f) (1964 ed., Supp. V) defines "destructive device" to include "grenades" which are involved in the present case.

At the time of Haynes any possessor of a weapon included in the Act was compelled to disclose the fact of his possession by registration at any time he had acquired possession, a provision which we held meant that a possessor must furnish potentially incriminating information which the Federal Government made available to state, local, and other federal officials. Id., at 95-100. Under the present Act n3 only possessors who lawfully make, manufacture, or import firearms can and must register them; the transferee does not and cannot register. It is, however, unlawful for any person "to receive or possess a firearm which is not registered to him in the National Firearms Registration and Transfer Record." n4

n3 Title 26 U.S.C. §5812 (a) (1964 ed., Supp. V) provides:

"A firearm shall not be transferred unless (1) the transferor of the firearm has filed with the Secretary or his delegate a written application, in duplicate, for the transfer and registration of the firearm to the transferee on the application form prescribed by the Secretary or his delegate; (2) any tax payable on the transfer is paid as evidenced by the proper stamp affixed to the original application form; (3) the transferee is identified in the application form in such manner as the Secretary or his delegate may by regulations prescribe, except that, if such person is an individual, the identification must include his fingerprints and his photograph; (4) the transferor of the firearm is identified in the application form in such manner as the Secretary or his delegate may by regulations prescribe; (5) the firearm is identified in the application form in such manner as the Secretary or his delegate may by regulations prescribe; and (6) the application form shows that the Secretary or his delegate has approved the transfer and the registration of the firearm to the transferee. Applications shall be denied if the transfer, receipt, or possession of the firearm would place the transferee in violation of law."

Title 26 U.S.C. §5812 (b) (1964 ed., Supp. V) provides:

"The transferee of a firearm shall not take possession of the firearm unless the Secretary or his delegate has approved the transfer and registration of the firearm to the transferee as required by subsection (a) of this section."

Title 26 U.S.C. §5841 (b) (1964 ed., Supp. V) provides:

"Each manufacturer, importer, and maker shall register each firearm he manufactures, imports, or makes. Each firearm transferred shall be registered to the transferee by the transferor."

n4 26 U.S.C. §5861 (d) (1964 ed., Supp. V).

At the time of Haynes, as already noted, there was a provision for sharing the registration and transfer information with other law enforcement officials. Id., at 97-100. The revised statute explicitly states that no information or evidence provided in compliance with the registration or transfer provisions of the Act can be used, directly or indirectly, as evidence against the registrant or applicant "in a criminal proceeding with respect to a violation of law occurring prior to or concurrently with the filing of the application or registration, or the compiling of the records containing the information or evidence." n5 The scope of the privilege extends, of course, to the hazards of prosecution under state law for the same or similar offenses. See Malloy v. Hogan, 378 U.S. 1; Marchetti v. United States, 390 U.S. 39, 54. And the appellees, apparently fearful that the Act as written does not undertake to bar the use of federal filings in state prosecutions, urge that those risks are real in this case. It is said that California statutes n6 punish the possession of grenades and that federal registration will incriminate appellees under that law.

n5 26 U.S.C. §5848 (1964 ed., Supp. V); and see 26 CFR §179.202.

n6 Penal Code §12303 (1970).

The Solicitor General, however, represents to us that no information filed is as a matter of practice disclosed to any law enforcement authority, except as the fact of nonregistration may be necessary to an investigation or prosecution under the present Act.

The District Court nonetheless granted the motion to dismiss on two grounds: (1) the amended Act, like the version in Haynes, violates the Self-Incrimination Clause of the Fifth Amendment; and (2) the conspiracy "to possess destructive devices" and the possession charged do not allege the element of scienter. The case is here on direct appeal. 18 U.S.C. §3731. And see United States v. Spector, 343 U.S. 169; United States v. Nardello, 393 U.S. 286.

I

As noted, a lawful transfer of a firearm may be accomplished only if it is already registered.

The transferor must identify himself, describe the firearm to be transferred, and the name and address of the transferee.

We conclude that the amended Act does not violate the Self-Incrimination Clause of the Fifth Amendment which provides that no person "shall be compelled in any criminal case to be a witness against himself." As noted, a lawful transfer of a firearm may be accomplished only if it is already registered. The transferor -- not the transferee -- does the registering. The transferor pays the transfer tax and receives a stamp n7 denoting payment which he affixes to the application submitted to the Internal Revenue Service. The transferor must identify himself, describe the firearm to be transferred, and the name and address of the transferee. In addition, the application must be supported by the photograph and fingerprints of the transferee and by a certificate of a local or federal law enforcement official that he is satisfied that the photograph and fingerprints are those of the transferee and that the weapon is intended for lawful uses. n8 Only after receipt of the approved application form is it lawful for the transferor to hand the firearm over to the transferee. At that time he is to give the approved application to the transferee. n9 As noted, the Solicitor General advises us that the information in the hands of Internal Revenue Service, as a matter of practice, is not available to state or other federal authorities and, as a matter of law, cannot be used as evidence in a criminal proceeding with respect to a prior or concurrent violation of law. n10

n7 26 U.S.C. §5811 (1964 ed., Supp. V).

n8 26 U.S.C. §5812 (a) (1964 ed., Supp. V); 26 CFR §§179.98-179.99.

n9 26 CFR §179.100.

n10 26 U.S.C. §5848 (1964 ed., Supp. V); 26 CFR §179.202.

the transferee, if he wants the firearm, must cooperate to the extent of supplying fingerprints and photograph. But the information he supplies makes him the lawful, not the unlawful, possessor of the firearm. Indeed, the only transferees who may lawfully receive a firearm are those who have not committed crimes in the past.

The transferor -- not the transferee -- makes any incriminating statements. True, the transferee, if he wants the firearm, must cooperate to the extent of supplying fingerprints and photograph. But the information he supplies makes him the lawful, not the unlawful, possessor of the firearm. Indeed, the only transferees who may lawfully receive a firearm are those who have not committed crimes in the past. The argument, however, is that furnishing the photograph and fingerprints will incriminate the transferee in the future. But the claimant is not confronted by "substantial and 'real'" but merely "trifling or imaginary hazards of incrimination" -- first by reason of the statutory barrier against use in a prosecution for prior or concurrent offenses, and second by reason of the unavailability of the registration data, as a matter of administration, to local, state, and other federal agencies. Marchetti v. United States, supra, at 53-54. Cf. Minor v. United States, 396 U.S. 87, 94. Since the state and other federal agencies never see the information, he is left in the same position as if he had not given it, but "had claimed his privilege in the absence of a . . . grant of immunity." Murphy v. Waterfront Comm'n, 378 U.S. 52, 79. This, combined with the protection against use to prove prior or concurrent offenses, satisfies the Fifth Amendment requirements respecting self-incrimination. n11

n11 We do not reach the question of "use immunity" as opposed to "transactional immunity," cf. Piccirillo v. New York, 400 U.S. 548, but only hold that, under this statutory scheme, the hazards of self-incrimination are not real.

Appellees' argument assumes the existence of a periphery of the Self-Incrimination Clause which protects a person against incrimination not only against past or present transgressions but which supplies insulation for a career of crime about to be launched. We cannot give the Self-Incrimination Clause such an expansive interpretation.

Another argument goes to the question of entrapment. But that is an issue for the trial, not for a motion to dismiss.

II

We also conclude that the District Court erred in dismissing the indictment for absence of an allegation of scienter.

The Act requires no specific intent or knowledge that the hand grenades were unregistered. It makes it unlawful for any person "to receive or possess a firearm

which is not registered to him."

The Act requires no specific intent or knowledge that the hand grenades were unregistered. It makes it unlawful for any person "to receive or possess a firearm which is not registered to him." n12 By the lower court decisions at the time that requirement was written into the Act the only knowledge required to be proved was knowledge that the instrument possessed was a firearm. See Sipes v. United States, 321 F.2d 174, 179, and cases cited.

n12 26 U.S.C. §5861 (d) (1964 ed., Supp. V).

The presence of a "vicious will" or mens rea (Morissette v. United States, 342 U.S. 246, 251) was long a requirement of criminal responsibility. But the list of exceptions grew, especially in the expanding regulatory area involving activities affecting public health, safety, and welfare. Id., at 254. The statutory offense of embezzlement, borrowed from the common law where scienter was historically required, was in a different category. n13 Id., at 260 261.

"Where Congress borrows terms of art in which are accumulated the legal tradition and meaning of centuries of practice, it presumably knows and adopts the cluster of ideas that were attached to each borrowed word in the body of learning from which it was taken and the meaning its use will convey to the judicial mind unless otherwise instructed." Id., at 263.

n13 As respects the Morissette case, J. Marshall, Intention -- In Law and Society 138 (1968), says:

"The defendant wished to take government property from a government bombing range, he had the capacity to take it, he had the opportunity, he tried and succeeded in taking it (his wish was fulfilled, his act accomplished). For recovery in a tort action no more would have to be shown to establish liability, but the court held that to make his action criminal 'a felonious intent,' mens rea, had to be established. This could not be presumed from his actions, which were open, without concealment, and in the belief -- according to his statement -- that the property had been abandoned. In other words, for the happening to be criminal, the wish had to be to accomplish something criminal. So in discussing intent we may have wishes of two different characters: one giving a basis for civil liability (the wish to take property not one's own), and another which would support criminal liability as well as civil (taking property with criminal intent)."

At the other extreme is Lambert v. California, 355 U.S. 225, in which a municipal code made it a crime to remain in Los Angeles for more than five days without registering if a person had been convicted of a felony. Being in Los Angeles is not per se blameworthy. The mere failure to register, we held, was quite "unlike the commission of acts, or the failure to act under circumstances that should alert the doer to the consequences of his deed." Id., at 228. The fact that the ordinance was a convenient law enforcement technique did not save it.

Where a person did not know of the duty to register and where there was no proof of the probability of such knowledge, he may not be convicted consistently with due process.

"Where a person did not know of the duty to register and where there was no proof of the probability of such knowledge, he may not be convicted consistently with due process. Were it otherwise, the evil would be as great as it is when the law is written in print too fine to read or in a language foreign to the community." Id., at 229-230.

In United States v. Dotterweich, 320 U.S. 277, 284, a case dealing with the imposition of a penalty on a corporate officer whose firm shipped adulterated and misbranded drugs in violation of the Food and Drug Act, we approved the penalty "though consciousness of wrongdoing be totally wanting."

This is a regulatory measure in the interest of the public safety, which may well be premised on the theory that one would hardly be surprised to learn that possession of hand grenades is not an innocent act.

The present case is in the category neither of Lambert nor Morissette, but is closer to Dotterweich. This is a regulatory measure in the interest of the public safety, which may well be premised on the theory that one would hardly be surprised to learn that possession of hand grenades is not an innocent act. n14 They are highly dangerous offensive weapons, no less dangerous than the narcotics involved in United States v. Balint, 258 U.S. 250, 254, where a defendant was convicted of sale of narcotics against his claim that he did not know the drugs were covered by a federal act. We say with Chief Justice Taft in that case:

"It is very evident from a reading of it that the emphasis of the section is in securing a close supervision of the business of dealing in these dangerous drugs by the taxing officers of the Government and that it merely uses a criminal penalty to secure recorded evidence of the disposition of such drugs as a means of taxing and restraining the traffic. Its manifest purpose is to require every person dealing in drugs to ascertain at his peril whether that which he sells comes within the inhibition of the statute, and if he sells the inhibited drug in ignorance of its character, to penalize him. Congress weighed the possible injustice of subjecting an innocent seller to a penalty against the evil of exposing innocent purchasers to danger from the drug, and concluded that the latter was the result preferably to be avoided." Id., at 253-254.

n14 We need not decide whether a criminal conspiracy to do an act "innocent in itself" and not known by the alleged conspirators to be prohibited must be actuated by some corrupt motive other than the intention to do the act which is prohibited and which is the object of the conspiracy. An agreement to acquire hand grenades is hardly an agreement innocent in itself. Therefore what we have said of the substantive offense satisfies on these special facts the requirements for a conspiracy. Cf. United States v. Mack, 112 F.2d 290.

Reversed.

MR. JUSTICE BRENNAN, concurring in the judgment of reversal.

I agree that the amendments to the National Firearms Act, 26 U.S.C. §§5841-5872 (1964 ed., Supp. V), do not violate the Fifth Amendment's privilege against self-incrimination, and join Part I of the opinion of the Court. However, I do not join Part II of the opinion; although I reach the same result as the Court on the intent the Government must prove to convict, I do so by another route.

I join Part I on my understanding of the Act's new immunity provision. 26 U.S.C. §5848 (1964 ed., Supp. V). The amended registration provisions of the National Firearms Act do not pose any realistic possibility of self-incrimination of the transferee under federal law. An effective registration of a covered firearm will render the transferee's possession of that firearm legal under federal law. It is only appellees' contention that registration or application for registration will incriminate them under California law that raises the Fifth Amendment issue in this case. Specifically, appellees assert that California law outlaws possession of hand grenades and that registration under federal law would, therefore, incriminate them under state law. Assuming that appellees correctly interpret California law, I think that the Act's immunity provision suffices to supplant the constitutional protection. Section 5848 provides in pertinent part:

"No information or evidence obtained from an application . . . shall . . . be used, directly or indirectly, as evidence against that person in a criminal proceeding with respect to a violation of law occurring prior to or concurrently with the filing of the application . . . ."

In my judgment, this provision would prevent a State from making any use of a federal registration or application, or any fruits thereof, in connection with a prosecution under the State's possession law. n1 This would be true even if the State charged a transferee with possession of the firearm on a date after the date the application was filed, because possession is a continuing violation. n2 Therefore, for purposes of the State's possession law, a transferee's continued possession of a registered firearm would constitute "a violation of law occurring . . . concurrently with the filing of the application."

n1 No question of transactional immunity is raised here since the case involves incrimination under the laws of a jurisdiction different from the one compelling the incriminating information. Piccirillo v. New York, 400 U.S. 548, 552 (BRENNAN, J., dissenting).

n2 The result would be the same if a transferee moved from a State where possession was legal to a State where possession was illegal. The time when the possession became illegal cannot affect the continuing nature of the act of possession.

I agree with the Court that the Self-Incrimination Clause of the Fifth Amendment does not require that immunity be given as to the use of such information in connection with crimes that the transferee might possibly commit in the future with the registered firearm. The only disclosure required under the amended Act is that the transferee has received a firearm and is in possession of it. Thus, in connection with the present general registration scheme, "the relevant class of activities 'permeated with criminal statutes,'" Mackey v. United States, post, at 710 (BRENNAN, J., concurring in judgment), is limited to the class of activities relating to possession of firearms. Id., at 707-711. Since I read the statute's immunity provision to provide immunity co-extensive with the privilege in that regard, I find no Fifth Amendment bar to the enforcement of the federal statute.

To convict appellees of possession of unregistered hand grenades, the Government must prove three material elements: (1) that appellees possessed certain items; (2) that the items possessed were hand grenades; and (3) that the hand grenades were not registered.

The Court's discussion of the intent the Government must prove to convict appellees of violation of 26 U.S.C. §5861 (d) (1964 ed., Supp. V) does not dispel the confusion surrounding a difficult, but vitally important, area of the law. This case does not raise questions of "consciousness of wrongdoing" or "blameworthiness." If the ancient maxim that "ignorance of the law is no excuse" has any residual validity, it indicates that the ordinary intent requirement -- mens rea -- of the criminal law does not require knowledge that an act is illegal, wrong, or blameworthy. Nor is it possible to decide this case by a simple process of classifying the statute involved as a "regulatory" or a "public welfare" measure. To convict appellees of possession of unregistered hand grenades, the Government must prove three material elements: (1) that appellees possessed certain items; (2) that the items possessed were hand grenades; and (3) that the hand grenades were not registered. The Government and the Court agree that the prosecutor must prove knowing possession of the items and also knowledge that the items possessed were hand grenades. Thus, while the Court does hold that no intent at all need be proved in regard to one element of the offense -- the unregistered status of the grenades -- knowledge must still be proved as to the other two elements. Consequently, the National Firearms Act does not create a crime of strict liability as to all its elements. It is no help in deciding what level of intent must be proved as to the third element to declare that the offense falls within the "regulatory" category.

Following the analysis of the Model Penal Code, n3 I think we must recognize, first, that "the existence of a mens rea is the rule of, rather than the exception to, the principles of Anglo-American criminal jurisprudence." Dennis v. United States, 341 U.S. 494, 500 (1951) (Vinson, C. J., announcing judgment); Smith v. California, 361 U.S. 147, 150 (1959); n4 second, that mens rea is not a unitary concept, but may vary as to each element of a crime; and third, that Anglo-American law has developed several identifiable and analytically distinct levels of intent, e.g., negligence, recklessness, knowledge, and purpose. n5 To determine the mental element required for conviction, each material element of the offense must be examined and the determination made what level of intent Congress intended the Government to prove, taking into account constitutional considerations, see Screws v. United States, 325 U.S. 91 (1945), as well as the common-law background, if any, of the crime involved. See Morissette v. United States, 342 U.S. 246 (1952).

n3 ALI Model Penal Code §2.02, Comment 123-132 (Tent. Draft No. 4, 1955).

n4 "Still, it is doubtless competent for the [government] to create strict criminal liabilities by defining criminal offenses without any element of scienter -- though . . . there is precedent in this Court that this power is not without limitations. See Lambert v. California, 355 U.S. 225." Smith v. California, 361 U.S. 147, 150 (1959). The situations in which strict liability may be imposed were stated by Judge, now MR. JUSTICE, BLACKMUN: "Where a federal criminal statute omits mention of intent and where it seems to involve what is basically a matter of policy, where the standard imposed is, under the circumstances, reasonable and adherence thereto properly expected of a person, where the penalty is relatively small, where conviction does not gravely besmirch, where the statutory crime is not one taken over from the common law, and where congressional purpose is supporting, the statute can be construed as one not requiring criminal intent." Holdridge v. United States, 282 F.2d 302, 310 (CA8 1960).

n5 These different levels of intent are defined in the code. ALI Model Penal Code §2.02 (Prop. Official Draft 1962). This Court has relied on the code's definitions. Leary v. United States, 395 U.S. 6, 46 n. 93 (1969); Turner v. United States, 396 U.S. 398, 416 n. 29 (1970).

Although the legislative history of the amendments to the National Firearms Act is silent on the level of intent to be proved in connection with each element of the offense, we are not without some guideposts. I begin with the proposition stated in Morissette v. United States, 342 U.S., at 250, that the requirement of mens rea "is no provincial or transient notion. It is as universal and persistent in mature systems of law as belief in freedom of the human will and a consequent ability and duty of the normal individual to choose between good and evil." In regard to the first two elements of the offense, (1) possession of items that (2) are hand grenades, the general rule in favor of some intent requirement finds confirmation in the case law under the provisions replaced by the present amendments. The cases held that a conviction of an individual of illegal possession of unregistered firearms had to be supported by proof that his possession was "willing and conscious" and that he knew the items possessed were firearms. e.g., Sipes v. United States, 321 F.2d 174, 179 (CA8 1963); United States v. Decker, 292 F.2d 89 (CA6 1961). Congress did not disapprove these cases, and we may therefore properly infer that Congress meant that the Government must prove knowledge with regard to the first two elements of the offense under the amended statute.

The third element -- the unregistered status of the grenades -- presents more difficulty. Proof of intent with regard to this element would require the Government to show that the appellees knew that the grenades were unregistered or negligently or recklessly failed to ascertain whether the weapons were registered. It is true that such a requirement would involve knowledge of law, but it does not involve "consciousness of wrongdoing" in the sense of knowledge that one's actions were prohibited or illegal. n6 Rather, the definition of the crime, as written by Congress, requires proof of circumstances that involve a legal element, namely whether the grenades were registered in accordance with federal law. The knowledge involved is solely knowledge of the circumstances that the law has defined as material to the offense. The Model Penal Code illustrates the distinction:

"It should be noted that the general principle that ignorance or mistake of law is no excuse is usually greatly overstated; it has no application when the circumstances made material by the definition of the offense include a legal element. So, for example, it is immaterial in theft, when claim of right is adduced in defense, that the claim involves a legal judgment as to the right of property. It is a defense because knowledge that the property belongs to someone else is a material element of the crime and such knowledge may involve matter of law as well as fact. . . . The law involved is not the law defining the offense; it is some other legal rule that characterizes the attendant circumstances that are material to the offense." Model Penal Code §2.02, Comment 131 (Tent. Draft No. 4, 1955).

n6 Proof of some crimes may include a requirement of proof of actual knowledge that the act was prohibited by law, or proof of a purpose to bring about the forbidden result. See James v. United States, 366 U.S. 213 (1961); Boyce Motor Lines v. United States, 342 U.S. 337 (1952). United States v. Murdock, 290 U.S. 389 (1933). See generally Note, Counseling Draft Resistance: The Case for a Good Faith Belief Defense, 78 Yale L. J. 1008, 1022-1037 (1969). Cf. Model Penal Code §2.02 (2)(a) (Prop. Official Draft 1962) (definition of "purposely").

the firearms covered by the Act are major weapons such as machineguns and sawed-off shotguns; deceptive weapons such as flashlight guns and fountain pen guns; and major destructive devices such as bombs, grenades, mines, rockets, and large caliber weapons including mortars, antitank guns, and bazookas. Without exception, the likelihood of governmental regulation of the distribution of such weapons is so great that anyone must be presumed to be aware of it.

Therefore, as with the first two elements, the question is solely one of congressional intent. And while the question is not an easy one, two factors persuade me that proof of mens rea as to the unregistered status of the grenades is not required. First, as the Court notes, the case law under the provisions replaced by the current law dispensed with proof of intent in connection with this element. Sipes v. United States, supra. Second, the firearms covered by the Act are major weapons such as machineguns and sawed-off shotguns; deceptive weapons such as flashlight guns and fountain pen guns; and major destructive devices such as bombs, grenades, mines, rockets, and large caliber weapons including mortars, antitank guns, and bazookas. Without exception, the likelihood of governmental regulation of the distribution of such weapons is so great that anyone must be presumed to be aware of it. In the context of a taxing and registration scheme, I therefore think it reasonable to conclude that Congress dispensed with the requirement of intent in regard to the unregistered status of the weapon, as necessary to effective administration of the statute.

UNITED STATES v. BASS

(FULL CASE)

404 U.S. 336; 92 S. Ct. 515; 30 L. Ed. 2d 488

October 18, 1971, Argued

December 20, 1971, Decided

GIST: Bass was convicted of violating the federal ban on possession of a firearm by a convicted felon. The felon-in-possession ban, like the rest of the Gun Control Act of 1968, was enacted on the basis of Congress' power to regulate interstate commerce. On appeal, Bass argued that the government failed to show that his firearms possession had a nexus with interstate commerce. Interpreting the language Congress used, the Court held that an interstate commerce nexus must be shown for all three offenses: receiving, possessing, and transporting firearms by a felon. The Court went on to say that proof that the firearm in question had previously traveled in interstate commerce, which would be true of most firearms, would be sufficient to satisfy the nexus for possession.

Government prosecutors had not attempted to show this connection at trial, thinking it unnecessary, based on the omission of a single comma in the law (they made other arguments too, but the comma became key, see the discussion at Roman numeral "I"). That cost them the case, freed the defendant, and put the onus on the government to prove this in all future cases (it's not a tremendously difficult proof to make).

The government's arguments here seek easier convictions. On one hand that would be desirable to help take criminals out of circulation, but on the other hand, it is undesirable to the extent it could more easily lead to convictions of the innocent, or be abused by the authorities. The Court actually rebukes Congress mildly for not making the statute more clear.

Respondent was convicted of possessing firearms in violation of §1202 (a)(1) of the Omnibus Crime Control and Safe Streets Act, which provides that a person convicted of a felony "who receives, possesses, or transports in commerce or affecting commerce . . . any firearm . . ." shall be punished as prescribed therein. The indictment did not allege and no attempt was made to show that the firearms involved had been possessed "in commerce or affecting commerce," the Government contending that the statute does not require proof of a connection with interstate commerce in individual cases involving possession or receipt. Doubting its constitutionality if the statute were thus construed, the Court of Appeals reversed. Held: It is not clear from the language and legislative history of §1202 (a)(1) whether or not receipt or possession of a firearm by a convicted felon has to be shown in an individual prosecution to have been connected with interstate commerce. The ambiguity of this provision (which is not only a criminal statute but one whose broad construction would define as a federal offense conduct readily proscribed by the States), must therefore be resolved in favor of the narrower reading that a nexus with interstate commerce must be shown with respect to all three offenses embraced by the provision.

MR. JUSTICE MARSHALL delivered the opinion of the Court.

Respondent was convicted in the Southern District of New York of possessing firearms in violation of Title VII of the Omnibus Crime Control and Safe Streets Act of 1968, 18 U.S.C. App. §1202 (a). In pertinent part, that statute reads:

"Any person who --

"(1) has been convicted by a court of the United States or of a State or any political subdivision thereof of a felony . . . and who receives, possesses, or transports in commerce or affecting commerce . . . any firearm shall be fined not more than $10,000 or imprisoned for not more than two years, or both." n1

n1 Section 1202 (a) reads in full:

"Any person who --

"(1) has been convicted by a court of the United States or of a State or any political subdivision thereof of a felony, or

"(2) has been discharged from the Armed Forces under dishonorable conditions, or

"(3) has been adjudged by a court of the United States or of a State or any political subdivision thereof of being mentally incompetent, or

"(4) having been a citizen of the United States has renounced his citizenship, or

"(5) being an alien is illegally or unlawfully in the United States, and who receives, possesses, or transports in commerce or affecting commerce, after the date of enactment of this Act, any firearm shall be fined not more than $10,000 or imprisoned for not more than two years, or both."

The evidence showed that respondent, who had previously been convicted of a felony in New York State, possessed on separate occasions a pistol and then a shotgun. There was no allegation in the indictment and no attempt by the prosecution to show that either firearm had been possessed "in commerce or affecting commerce." The Government proceeded on the assumption that §1202 (a)(1) banned all possessions and receipts of firearms by convicted felons, and that no connection with interstate commerce had to be demonstrated in individual cases.

After his conviction, n2 respondent unsuccessfully moved for arrest of judgment on two primary grounds: that the statute did not reach possession of a firearm not shown to have been "in commerce or affecting commerce," and that, if it did, Congress had overstepped its constitutional powers under the Commerce Clause. 308 F.Supp. 1385. The Court of Appeals reversed the conviction, being of the view that if the Government's construction of the statute were accepted, there would be substantial doubt about the statute's constitutionality. 434 F.2d 1296. We granted certiorari to resolve a conflict among lower courts over the proper reach of the statute. n3 We affirm the judgment of the court below, but for substantially different reasons. n4 We conclude that §1202 is ambiguous in the critical respect. Because its sanctions are criminal and because, under the Government's broader reading, the statute would mark a major inroad into a domain traditionally left to the States, we refuse to adopt the broad reading in the absence of a clearer direction from Congress.

n2 Respondent was acquitted on another count charging him with carrying a firearm during the commission of a felony (the sale of a narcotic drug), a federal offense under 18 U.S.C. §924 (c)(2).

n3 At this date, six circuits and numerous district courts have decided the issue. The Government's view was adopted in United States v. Cabbler, 429 F.2d 577 (CA4 1970), cert. denied, 400 U.S. 901; United States v. Donofrio, 450 F.2d 1054 (CA5 1971); Stevens v. United States, 440 F.2d 144 (CA6 1971) (one judge dissenting); United States v. Synnes, 438 F.2d 764 (CA8 1971); United States v. Daniels, 431 F.2d 697 (CA9 1970). The result reached by the Second Circuit in this case has also been reached in United States v. Harbin, 313 F.Supp. 50 (ND Ind. 1970); United States v. Steed, No. CR 70-57 (WD Tenn., May 11, 1970); United States v. Phelps, No. CR 14,465 (MD Tenn., Feb. 10, 1970); United States v. Francis, No. CR 12,684 (ED Tenn., Dec. 12, 1969).

we do not reach the question whether, upon appropriate findings, Congress can constitutionally punish the "mere possession" of firearms

n4 In light of our disposition of the case, we do not reach the question whether, upon appropriate findings, Congress can constitutionally punish the "mere possession" of firearms; thus, we need not consider the relevance, in that connection, of our recent decision in Perez v. United States, 402 U.S. 146 (1971). The question whether the definition of "felony" in §1202 (c)(2) creates a classification violating the Fifth Amendment was not raised in the Government's Petition for Certiorari, and is also not considered here.

I

the quip that only when legislative history is doubtful do you go to the statute

Not wishing "to give point to the quip that only when legislative history is doubtful do you go to the statute," n5 we begin by looking to the text itself. The critical textual question is whether the statutory phrase "in commerce or affecting commerce" applies to "possesses" and "receives" as well as to "transports." If it does, then the Government must prove as an essential element of the offense that a possession, receipt, or transportation was "in commerce or affecting commerce" -- a burden not undertaken in this prosecution for possession.

n5 Frankfurter, Some Reflections on the Reading of Statutes, 47 Col. L. Rev. 527, 543 (1947).

While the statute does not read well under either view, "the natural construction of the language" suggests that the clause "in commerce or affecting commerce" qualifies all three antecedents in the list. Porto Rico Railway, Light & Power Co. v. Mor, 253 U.S. 345, 348 (1920). Since "in commerce or affecting commerce" undeniably applies to at least one antecedent, and since it makes sense with all three, the more plausible construction here is that it in fact applies to all three. But although this is a beginning, the argument is certainly neither overwhelming nor decisive. n6

n6 Compare United States v. Standard Brewery, Inc., 251 U.S. 210, 218 (1920), with FTC v. Mandel Brothers, Inc., 359 U.S. 385, 389-390 (1959); see also 2 J. Sutherland, Statutory Construction §4921 (3d ed. 1943); K. Llewellyn, The Common Law Tradition 527 (1960).

But many leading grammarians, while sometimes noting that commas at the end of series can avoid ambiguity, concede that use of such commas is discretionary.

The Government, noting that there is no comma after "transports," argues that the punctuation indicates a congressional intent to limit the qualifying phrase to the last antecedent. But many leading grammarians, while sometimes noting that commas at the end of series can avoid ambiguity, concede that use of such commas is discretionary. See, e.g., B. Evans & C. Evans, A Dictionary of Contemporary American Usage 103 (1957); M. Nicholson, A Dictionary of American-English Usage 94 (1957); R. Copperud, A Dictionary of Usage and Style 94-95 (1964); cf. W. Strunk & E. White, The Elements of Style 1-2 (1959). When grammarians are divided, and surely where they are cheerfully tolerant, we will not attach significance to an omitted comma. It is enough to say that the statute's punctuation is fully consistent with the respondent's interpretation, and that in this case grammatical expertise will not help to clarify the statute's meaning.

In a more significant respect, however, the language of the statute does provide support for respondent's reading. Undeniably, the phrase "in commerce or affecting commerce" is part of the "transports" offense. But if that phrase applies only to "transports," the statute would have a curious reach. While permitting transportation of a firearm unless it is transported "in commerce or affecting commerce," the statute would prohibit all possessions of firearms, and both interstate and intrastate receipts. Since virtually all transportations, whether interstate or intrastate, involve an accompanying possession or receipt, it is odd indeed to argue that on the one hand the statute reaches all possessions and receipts, and on the other hand outlaws only interstate transportations. Even assuming that a person can "transport" a firearm under the statute without possessing or receiving it, there is no reason consistent with any discernible purpose of the statute to apply an interstate commerce requirement to the "transports" offense alone. n7 In short, the Government has no convincing explanation for the inclusion of the clause "in commerce or affecting commerce" if that phrase only applies to the word "transports." It is far more likely that the phrase was meant to apply to "possesses" and "receives" as well as "transports." As the court below noted, the inclusion of such a phrase "mirror[s] the approach to federal criminal jurisdiction reflected in many other federal statutes." n8

n7 The Government urges that "transports" includes the act of "causing a firearm to be transported," and therefore would connote an offense separate in some cases from "receives" or "possesses." From this, the Government argues that "Congress might have felt that the broader scope of the term 'transports,' as compared to the terms 'receives' or 'possesses,' justified its qualification by the interstate commerce requirement." Brief for the United States 14-15. The Government's view about the comparative breadth of the various offenses certainly does not follow from its definition of "transports." But beyond that, its argument about what Congress "might have felt" is purely speculative, and finds no support in any arguable purpose of the statute. There is certainly no basis for concluding that Congress was less concerned about the transporting and supplying of guns than their acquisition.

n8 434 F.2d, at 1298. See, e.g., 18 U.S.C. §2421 (prostitution); 18 U.S.C. §1952 (Travel Act); 18 U.S.C. §1951 (robbery and extortion); 18 U.S.C. §1231 (strikebreaking); 18 U.S.C. §1201 (kidnaping); 18 U.S.C. §1084 (gambling); 18 U.S.C. §842 (i) (explosives); 15 U.S.C. §1 et seq. (antitrust); 15 U.S.C. §77e (securities fraud).

Nevertheless, the Government argues that its reading is to be preferred because the defendant's narrower interpretation would make Title VII redundant with Title IV of the same Act. Title IV, inter alia, makes it a crime for four categories of people -- including those convicted of a crime punishable for a term exceeding one year -- "to ship or transport any firearm or ammunition in interstate or foreign commerce . . . [or] to receive any firearm or ammunition which has been shipped or transported in interstate or foreign commerce." 18 U.S.C. §§922 (g) and (h). As Senator Long, the sponsor of Title VII, represented to Senator Dodd, the sponsor of Title IV, Title VII indeed does complement Title IV. 114 Cong. Rec. 14774; see also 114 Cong. Rec. 16286. Respondent's reading of Title VII is fully consistent with this view. First, although subsections of the two Titles do address their prohibitions to some of the same people, each statute also reaches substantial groups of people not reached by the other. n9 Secondly, Title VII complements Title IV by punishing a broader class of behavior. Even under respondent's view, a Title VII offense is made out if the firearm was possessed or received "in commerce or affecting commerce"; however, Title IV apparently does not reach possessions or intrastate transactions at all, even those with an interstate commerce nexus, but is limited to the sending or receiving of firearms as part of an interstate transportation. n10

n9 Title VII limits the firearm-related activity of convicted felons, dishonorable dischargees from the Armed Services, persons adjudged "mentally incompetent," aliens illegally in the country, and former citizens who have renounced their citizenship. See n. 1, supra. A felony is defined as "any offense punishable by imprisonment for a term exceeding one year, but does not include any offense (other than one involving a firearm or explosive) classified as a misdemeanor under the laws of a State and punishable by a term of imprisonment of two years or less . . . ." 18 U.S.C. App. §1202 (c)(2).

Title IV reaches persons "under indictment for, or . . . convicted in any court of, a crime punishable by imprisonment for a term exceeding one year"; fugitives from justice; users or addicts of various drugs; persons adjudicated as "mental defective[s] or . . . committed" to a mental institution. 18 U.S.C. §§922 (g) and (h).

Each amendment enlarged the group of people coming within the Act's substantive prohibitions against transportation or receipt of firearms in interstate commerce.

n10 Title IV, 18 U.S.C. §§922 (g) and (h), is a modified and recodified version of 15 U.S.C. §§902 (e) and (f) (1964 ed.), 75 Stat. 757, which in turn amended the original statute passed in 1938, 52 Stat. 1250, 1251. Each amendment enlarged the group of people coming within the Act's substantive prohibitions against transportation or receipt of firearms in interstate commerce. The wording of the substantive offense has remained identical, although the original Act had a provision that possession of a firearm "shall be presumptive evidence that such firearm or ammunition was shipped or transported or received [in interstate or foreign commerce]." That presumption was struck down in Tot v. United States, 319 U.S. 463 (1943), and the Court there noted:

"The Act is confined to the receipt of firearms or ammunition as a part of interstate transportation and does not extend to the receipt, in an intrastate transaction, of such articles which, at some prior time, have been transported interstate." Id., at 466.

While the reach of Title IV itself is a question to be decided finally some other day, the Government has presented here no learning or other evidence indicating that the 1968 Act changed the prior approach to the "receipt" offense. See, e.g., S. Rep. No. 1097, 90th Cong., 2d Sess., 115 (1968).

In addition, whatever reading is adopted, Title VII and Title IV are, in part, redundant. The interstate commerce requirement in Title VII minimally applies to transportation. Since Title IV also prohibits convicted criminals from transporting firearms in interstate commerce, the two Titles overlap under both readings. The Government's broader reading of Title VII does not eliminate the redundancy, but simply creates a larger area in which there is no overlap. While the Government would be on stronger ground if its reading were necessary to give Title VII some unique and independent thrust, this is not the case here. In any event, circumstances surrounding the passage of Title VII make plain that Title VII was not carefully molded to complement Title IV. Title VII was a last-minute Senate amendment to the Omnibus Crime Control and Safe Streets Act. The Amendment was hastily passed, with little discussion, no hearings, and no report. n11 The notion that it was enacted to dovetail neatly with Title IV rests perhaps on a conception of the model legislative process; but we cannot pretend that all statutes are model statutes. While courts should interpret a statute with an eye to the surrounding statutory landscape and an ear for harmonizing potentially discordant provisions, these guiding principles are not substitutes for congressional lawmaking. In our view, no conclusion can be drawn from Title IV concerning the correct interpretation of Title VII.

n11 The Omnibus Crime Control and Safe Streets Act of 1968 started its life as a measure designed to aid state and local governments in law enforcement by means of financial and administrative assistance. See H. R. Rep. No. 488, 90th Cong., 1st Sess. (1967). The bill passed the House on August 8, 1967, and went to the Senate. A similar bill was introduced in the Senate (S. 917) and went to the Committee on the Judiciary, which rewrote it completely. See S. Rep. No. 1097, 90th Cong., 2d Sess., supra. The amendments included the much-debated provisions regarding the admissibility of confessions, wiretapping, and state firearms control.

On May 17, 1968, Senator Long introduced on the floor his amendment to S. 917, which he designated Title VII. His introductory remarks set forth the purpose of the amendment. 114 Cong. Rec. 13867-13869. About a week later he explained his amendment once again. There was a brief debate; the reaction was favorable but cautious, with "further thought" and "study" being suggested by several favorably inclined Senators who observed some problems with the bill as drafted. Unexpectedly, however, there was a call for a vote and Title VII passed without modification. See 114 Cong. Rec. 14772-14775. The amendment received only passing mention in the House discussion of the bill, 114 Cong. Rec. 16286, 16298, and never received committee consideration or study in the House either.

Other aspects of the meager legislative history, however, do provide some significant support for the Government's interpretation. On the Senate floor, Senator Long, who introduced §1202, described various evils that prompted his statute. These evils included assassinations of public figures and threats to the operation of businesses significant enough in the aggregate to affect commerce. n12 Such evils, we note, would be most thoroughly mitigated by forbidding every possession of any firearm by specified classes of especially risky people, regardless of whether the gun was possessed, received, or transported "in commerce or affecting commerce." In addition, specific remarks of the Senator can be read to state that the amendment reaches the mere possession of guns without any showing of an interstate commerce nexus. n13 But Senator Long never specifically says that no connection with commerce need be shown in the individual case. And nothing in his statements explains why, if an interstate commerce nexus is irrelevant in individual cases, the phrase "in commerce or affecting commerce" is in the statute at all. n14 But even if Senator Long's remarks were crystal clear to us, they were apparently not crystal clear to his congressional colleagues. Meager as the discussion of Title VII was, one of the few Congressmen who discussed the amendment summarized Title VII as "mak[ing] it a Federal crime to take, possess, or receive a firearm across State lines . . . ." 114 Cong. Rec. 16298 (statement of Rep. Pollock).

n12 See 114 Cong. Rec. 13868-13871, 14772-14775.

n13 For example, Senator Long began his floor statement by announcing:

"I have prepared an amendment which I will offer at an appropriate time, simply setting forth the fact that anybody who has been convicted of a felony [or comes within certain other categories] . . . is not permitted to possess a firearm . . . ." 114 Cong. Rec. 13868.

n14 For the same, and additional, reasons, §1201, which contains the congressional "findings" applicable to §1202 (a), is not decisive support for the Government. That section reports that:

"The Congress hereby finds and declares that the receipt, possession, or transportation of a firearm by felons, veterans who are discharged under dishonorable conditions, mental incompetents, aliens who are illegally in the country, and former citizens who have renounced their citizenship, constitutes --

"(1) a burden on commerce or threat affecting the free flow of commerce,

"(2) a threat to the safety of the President of the United States and Vice President of the United States,

"(3) an impediment or a threat to the exercise of free speech and the free exercise of a religion guaranteed by the first amendment to the Constitution of the United States, and

"(4) a threat to the continued and effective operation of the Government of the United States and of the government of each State guaranteed by article IV of the Constitution."

The Government argues that these findings would have been "wholly unnecessary" unless Congress intended to prohibit all receipts and possessions of firearms by felons. But these findings of "burdens" and "threats" simply state Congress' view of the constitutional basis for its power to act; the findings do not tell us how much of Congress' perceived power was in fact invoked. That the findings in fact support a statute broader than the one actually passed is suggested by the fact that "in commerce or affecting commerce" does not appear at all in the introductory clause to the "findings," even though §1202 (a) contains the phrase and concededly reaches only transportation "in commerce or affecting commerce."

In short, "the legislative history of [the] Act hardly speaks with that clarity of purpose which Congress supposedly furnishes courts in order to enable them to enforce its true will." Universal Camera Corp. v. NLRB, 340 U.S. 474, 483 (1951). Here, as in other cases, the various remarks by legislators "are sufficiently ambiguous insofar as this narrow issue is concerned . . . to invite mutually destructive dialectic," and not much more. FCC v. Columbia Broadcasting System, 311 U.S. 132, 136 (1940). Taken together, the statutory materials are inconclusive on the central issue of whether or not the statutory phrase "in commerce or affecting commerce" applies to "possesses" and "receives" as well as "transports." While standing alone, the legislative history might tip in the Government's favor, the respondent explains far better the presence of critical language in the statute. The Government concedes that "the statute is not a model of logic or clarity." Pet. for Cert. 5. After "seiz[ing] every thing from which aid can be derived," United States v. Fisher, 2 Cranch 358, 386 (1805) (Marshall, C. J.), we are left with an ambiguous statute.

II

Given this ambiguity, we adopt the narrower reading: the phrase "in commerce or affecting commerce" is part of all three offenses, and the present conviction must be set aside because the Government has failed to show the requisite nexus with interstate commerce. This result is dictated by two wise principles this Court has long followed.

a fair warning should be given to the world in language that the common world will understand, of what the law intends to do if a certain line is passed. To make the warning fair, so far as possible the line should be clear.

where there is ambiguity in a criminal statute, doubts are resolved in favor of the defendant.

we conclude that Congress has not "plainly and unmistakably," made it a federal crime for a convicted felon simply to possess a gun absent some demonstrated nexus with interstate commerce.

First, as we have recently reaffirmed, "ambiguity concerning the ambit of criminal statutes should be resolved in favor of lenity." Rewis v. United States, 401 U.S. 808, 812 (1971). See also Ladner v. United States, 358 U.S. 169, 177 (1958); Bell v. United States, 349 U.S. 81 (1955); United States v. Five Gambling Devices, 346 U.S. 441 (1953) (plurality opinion for affirmance). In various ways over the years, we have stated that "when choice has to be made between two readings of what conduct Congress has made a crime, it is appropriate, before we choose the harsher alternative, to require that Congress should have spoken in language that is clear and definite." United States v. Universal C. I. T. Credit Corp., 344 U.S. 218, 221-222 (1952). This principle is founded on two policies that have long been part of our tradition. First, "a fair warning should be given to the world in language that the common world will understand, of what the law intends to do if a certain line is passed. To make the warning fair, so far as possible the line should be clear." McBoyle v. United States, 283 U.S. 25, 27 (1931) (Holmes, J.). n15 See also United States v. Cardiff, 344 U.S. 174 (1952). Second, because of the seriousness of criminal penalties, and because criminal punishment usually represents the moral condemnation of the community, legislatures and not courts should define criminal activity. This policy embodies "the instinctive distaste against men languishing in prison unless the lawmaker has clearly said they should." H. Friendly, Mr. Justice Frankfurter and the Reading of Statutes, in Benchmarks 196, 209 (1967). Thus, where there is ambiguity in a criminal statute, doubts are resolved in favor of the defendant. Here, we conclude that Congress has not "plainly and unmistakably," United States v. Gradwell, 243 U.S. 476, 485 (1917), made it a federal crime for a convicted felon simply to possess a gun absent some demonstrated nexus with interstate commerce.

it is not likely that a criminal will carefully consider the text of the law before he murders or steals

in the case of gun acquisition and possession it is not unreasonable to imagine a citizen attempting to "[steer] a careful course between violation of the statute [and lawful conduct]

There are many States, however, that do not have their own laws prohibiting felons from possessing firearms.

n15 Holmes prefaced his much-quoted statement with the observation that "it is not likely that a criminal will carefully consider the text of the law before he murders or steals . . . ." But in the case of gun acquisition and possession it is not unreasonable to imagine a citizen attempting to "[steer] a careful course between violation of the statute [and lawful conduct]," United States v. Hood, 343 U.S. 148, 151 (1952). Of course, where there is a state law prohibiting felons from possessing firearms, as in New York State, N. Y. Penal Law §265.05 (Supp. 1971-1972), it may be unreal to argue that there are notice problems under the federal law. There are many States, however, that do not have their own laws prohibiting felons from possessing firearms. See Geisel, Roll, & Wettick, The Effectiveness of State and Local Regulation of Handguns: A Statistical Analysis, 1969 Duke L. J. 647, 652-653. Since ex-offenders in these States are limited only by the federal gun control laws, the notice problem of that law may be quite real.

Congress has traditionally been reluctant to define as a federal crime conduct readily denounced as criminal by the States.

the broad construction urged by the Government renders traditionally local criminal conduct a matter for federal enforcement and would also involve a substantial extension of federal police resources. Absent proof of some interstate commerce nexus in each case, §1202 (a) dramatically intrudes upon traditional state criminal jurisdiction.

Absent a clearer statement of intention from Congress than is present here, we do not interpret §1202 (a) to reach the "mere possession" of firearms.

There is a second principle supporting today's result: unless Congress conveys its purpose clearly, it will not be deemed to have significantly changed the federal-state balance. n16 Congress has traditionally been reluctant to define as a federal crime conduct readily denounced as criminal by the States. n17 This congressional policy is rooted in the same concepts of American federalism that have provided the basis for judge-made doctrines. See, e.g., Younger v. Harris, 401 U.S. 37 (1971). As this Court emphasized only last Term in Rewis v. United States, supra, we will not be quick to assume that Congress has meant to effect a significant change in the sensitive relation between federal and state criminal jurisdiction. In traditionally sensitive areas, such as legislation affecting the federal balance, the requirement of clear statement assures that the legislature has in fact faced, and intended to bring into issue, the critical matters involved in the judicial decision. In Rewis, we declined to accept an expansive interpretation of the Travel Act. To do so, we said then, "would alter sensitive federal-state relationships [and] could overextend limited federal police resources." While we noted there that "it is not for us to weigh the merits of these factors," we went on to conclude that "the fact that they are not even discussed in the legislative history . . . strongly suggests that Congress did not intend that [the statute have the broad reach]." 401 U.S., at 812. In the instant case, the broad construction urged by the Government renders traditionally local criminal conduct a matter for federal enforcement and would also involve a substantial extension of federal police resources. Absent proof of some interstate commerce nexus in each case, §1202 (a) dramatically intrudes upon traditional state criminal jurisdiction. As in Rewis, the legislative history provides scanty basis for concluding that Congress faced these serious questions and meant to affect the federal-state balance in the way now claimed by the Government. Absent a clearer statement of intention from Congress than is present here, we do not interpret §1202 (a) to reach the "mere possession" of firearms.

n16 Apex Hosiery Co. v. Leader, 310 U.S. 469, 513 (1940); United States v. Five Gambling Devices, 346 U.S. 441, 449-450 (1953) (plurality opinion); FTC v. Bunte Bros., Inc., 312 U.S. 349, 351, 354-355 (1941); Frankfurter, Some Reflections on the Reading of Statutes, 47 Col. L. Rev. 527, 539-540 (1947). Cf. Auto Workers v. Wisconsin Board, 351 U.S. 266, 274-275 (1956); Palmer v. Massachusetts, 308 U.S. 79, 83-84 (1939); Leiter Minerals, Inc. v. United States, 352 U.S. 220, 225-226 (1957).

n17 H. Hart & A. Sacks, The Legal Process: Basic Problems in the Making and Application of Law 1241 (tent. ed. 1958).

III

we conclude that the Government meets its burden here if it demonstrates that the firearm received has previously traveled in interstate commerce.

Having concluded that the commerce requirement in §1202 (a) must be read as part of the "possesses" and "receives" offenses, we add a final word about the nexus with interstate commerce that must be shown in individual cases. The Government can obviously meet its burden in a variety of ways. We note only some of these. For example, a person "possesses . . . in commerce or affecting commerce" if at the time of the offense the gun was moving interstate or on an interstate facility, or if the possession affects commerce. Significantly broader in reach, however, is the offense of "receiv[ing] . . . in commerce or affecting commerce," for we conclude that the Government meets its burden here if it demonstrates that the firearm received has previously traveled in interstate commerce. n18 This is not the narrowest possible reading of the statute, but canons of clear statement and strict construction do "not mean that every criminal statute must be given the narrowest possible meaning in complete disregard of the purpose of the legislature." United States v. Bramblett, 348 U.S. 503, 510 (1955). We have resolved the basic uncertainty about the statute in favor of the narrow reading, concluding that "in commerce or affecting commerce" is part of the offense of possessing or receiving a firearm. But, given the evils that prompted the statute and the basic legislative purpose of restricting the firearm-related activity of convicted felons, the readings we give to the commerce requirement, although not all narrow, are appropriate. And consistent with our regard for the sensitive relation between federal and state criminal jurisdiction, our reading preserves as an element of all the offenses a requirement suited to federal criminal jurisdiction alone.

n18 This reading preserves a significant difference between the "receipt" offenses under Title IV and Title VII. See supra, at 342-343.

The judgment is
Affirmed.

MR. JUSTICE BLACKMUN, with whom THE CHIEF JUSTICE <BURGER> joins, dissenting.

I cannot join the Court's opinion and judgment. Five of the six United States courts of appeals that have passed upon the issue presented by this case have decided it adversely to the position urged by the respondent here. United States v. Cabbler, 429 F.2d 577 (CA4 1970). cert. denied, 400 U.S. 901; United States v. Mullins, [404 U.S. 336, 352] 432 F.2d 1003 (CA4 1970); United States v. Donofrio, 450 F.2d 1054 (CA5 1971); Stevens v. United States, 440 F.2d 144 (CA6 1971) (one judge dissenting); United States v. Synnes, 438 F.2d 764 (CA8 1971); United States v. Wiley, 438 F.2d 773 (CA8 1971); United States v. Taylor, 438 F.2d 774 (CA8 1971); United States v. Daniels, 431 F.2d 697 (CA9 1970); United States v. Crow, 439 F.2d 1193 (CA9 1971). Only the Second Circuit stands opposed.1

1. The statute, 18 U.S.C. App. §1202 (a), when it speaks of one "who receives, possesses, or transports in commerce or affecting commerce," although arguably ambiguous and, as the Government concedes, "not a model of logic or clarity," is clear enough. The structure of the vital language and its punctuation make it refer to one who receives, to one who possesses, and to one who transports in commerce. If one wished to say that he would welcome a cat, would welcome a dog, or would welcome a cow that jumps over the moon, he would likely say "I would like to have a cat, a dog, or a cow that jumps over the moon." So it is here.

2. The meaning the Court implants on the statute is justified only by the addition and interposition of a comma after the word "transports." I perceive no warrant for this judicial transfiguration.

3. In the very same statute the phrase "after the date of enactment of this Act" is separated by commas and undeniably modifies each of the preceding words, "receives," "possesses," and "transports." Obviously, then, the draftsman -- and the Congress -- knew the use of commas for phrase modification. We should give effect to the only meaning attendant upon that use.

Congress was attempting to reach and prohibit every possession of a firearm by a felon

Congress found that such possession, whether interstate or intrastate, affected interstate commerce

Congress did not conclude that intrastate possession was a matter of less concern to it than interstate possession.

4. The specific finding in 18 U.S.C. App. §1201 n3 clearly demonstrates that Congress was attempting to reach and prohibit every possession of a firearm by a felon; that Congress found that such possession, whether interstate or intrastate, affected interstate commerce; and that Congress did not conclude that

intrastate possession was a matter of less concern to it than interstate possession. That finding was unnecessary if Congress also required proof that each receipt or possession of a firearm was in or affected interstate or foreign commerce.

n3 "§1201. Congressional findings and declaration.

"The Congress hereby finds and declares that the receipt, possession, or transportation of a firearm by felons . . . constitutes --

"(1) a burden on commerce or threat affecting the free flow of commerce . . . ."

5. Senator Long's explanatory comments reveal clearly the purpose, the intent, and the extent of the legislation:

"I have prepared an amendment which I will offer at an appropriate time, simply setting forth the fact that anybody who has been convicted of a felony . . . is not permitted to possess a firearm . . . .

When a man has been convicted of a felony, unless—as this bill sets forth—he has been expressly pardoned by the President and the pardon states that the person is to be permitted to possess firearms in the future, that man would have no right to possess firearms. He would be punished criminally if he is found in possession of them.

"It might be well to analyze, for a moment, the logic involved. When a man has been convicted of a felony, unless -- as this bill sets forth -- he has been expressly pardoned by the President and the pardon states that the person is to be permitted to possess firearms in the future, that man would have no right to possess firearms. He would be punished criminally if he is found in possession of them." 114 Cong. Rec. 13868 (emphasis supplied).

So Congress simply finds that the possession of these weapons by the wrong kind of people is either a burden on commerce or a threat that affects the free flow of commerce.

"So Congress simply finds that the possession of these weapons by the wrong kind of people is either a burden on commerce or a threat that affects the free flow of commerce.

You cannot do business in an area, and you certainly cannot do as much of it and do it as well as you would like, if in order to do business you have to go through a street where there are burglars, murderers, and arsonists armed to the teeth against innocent citizens. So the threat certainly affects the free flow of commerce.

"You cannot do business in an area, and you certainly cannot do as much of it and do it as well as you would like, if in order to do business you have to go through a street where there are burglars, murderers, and arsonists armed to the teeth against innocent citizens. So the threat certainly affects the free flow of commerce." 114 Cong. Rec. 13869 (emphasis supplied).

What the amendment seeks to do is to make it unlawful for a firearm—be it a handgun, a machinegun, a long-range rifle, or any kind of firearm—to be in the possession of a convicted felon who has not been pardoned and who has therefore lost his right to possess firearms. . . . It also relates to the transportation of firearms.

"What the amendment seeks to do is to make it unlawful for a firearm -- be it a handgun, a machinegun, a long-range rifle, or any kind of firearm -- to be in the possession of a convicted felon who has not been pardoned and who has therefore lost his right to possess firearms. . . . It also relates to the transportation of firearms. <The following centered dots appear in the original.>

. . . . . .

Stated simply, they may not be trusted to possess a firearm without becoming a threat to society.

"Clauses 1-5 describe persons who, by their actions, have demonstrated that they are dangerous, or that they may become dangerous. Stated simply, they may not be trusted to possess a firearm without becoming a threat to society. This title would apply both to hand guns and to long guns.

. . . . . .

All of these murderers had shown violent tendencies before they committed the crime for which they are most infamous. They should not have been permitted to possess a gun. Yet, there is no Federal law which would deny possession to these undesirables.

"All of these murderers had shown violent tendencies before they committed the crime for which they are most infamous. They should not have been permitted to possess a gun. Yet, there is no Federal law which would deny possession to these undesirables.

"The killer of Medgar Evers, the murderer of the three civil rights workers in Mississippi, the defendants who shot Captain Lemuel Penn (on a highway while he was driving back to Washington after completion of reserve Military duty) would all be free under present Federal law to acquire another gun and repeat those same sorts of crimes in the future.

. . . . . .

every citizen could possess a gun until the commission of his first felony. Upon his conviction, however, Title VII would deny every assassin, murderer, thief and burglar of the right to possess a firearm in the future

"So, under Title VII, every citizen could possess a gun until the commission of his first felony. Upon his conviction, however, Title VII would deny every assassin, murderer, thief and burglar of the right to possess a firearm in the future except where he has been pardoned by the President or a State Governor and has been expressly authorized by his pardon to possess a firearm.

It has been said that Congress lacks the power to outlaw mere possession of weapons.

"It has been said that Congress lacks the power to outlaw mere possession of weapons....

possession of a deadly weapon by the wrong people can be controlled by Congress, without regard to where the police power resides under the Constitution.

". . . The important point is that this legislation demonstrates that possession of a deadly weapon by the wrong people can be controlled by Congress, without regard to where the police power resides under the Constitution.

Without question, the Federal Government does have power to control possession of weapons where such possession could become a threat to interstate commerce

"Without question, the Federal Government does have power to control possession of weapons where such possession could become a threat to interstate commerce . . . .

State gun control laws where they exist have proven inadequate to bar possession of firearms from those most likely to use them for unlawful purposes.

"State gun control laws where they exist have proven inadequate to bar possession of firearms from those most likely to use them for unlawful purposes.

. . . . . .

Nor would Title VII impinge upon the rights of citizens generally to possess firearms for legitimate and lawful purposes. It deals solely with those who have demonstrated that they cannot be trusted to possess a firearm—those whose prior acts—mostly voluntary—have placed them outside of our society.

"Nor would Title VII impinge upon the rights of citizens generally to possess firearms for legitimate and lawful purposes. It deals solely with those who have demonstrated that they cannot be trusted to possess a firearm -- those whose prior acts -- mostly voluntary -- have placed them outside of our society.

. . . . . .

I am convinced that we have enough constitutional power to prohibit these categories of people from possessing, receiving, or transporting a firearm.

". . . I am convinced that we have enough constitutional power to prohibit these categories of people from possessing, receiving, or transporting a firearm. . . .

. . . . . .

"This amendment would provide that a convicted felon who participates in one of these marches and is carrying a firearm would be violating the law. . . ." 114 Cong. Rec. 14773-14774 (emphasis supplied).

One cannot detect in these remarks any purpose to restrict or limit the type of possession that was being considered for proscription.

6. The Court's construction of §1202 (a), limiting its application to interstate possession and receipt, shrinks the statute into something little more than a duplication of 18 U.S.C. §§922 (g) and (h). I cannot ascribe to Congress such a gesture of nonaccomplishment.

I thus conclude that §1202 (a) was intended to and does reach all possessions and receipts of firearms by convicted felons, and that the Court should move on and decide the constitutional issue present in this case.

UNITED STATES v. BISWELL

(CASE EXCERPT)
406 U.S. 311; 92 S. Ct. 1593; 32 L. Ed. 2d 87
March 28, 1972, Argued
May 15, 1972, Decided

GIST: Biswell was a pawn shop owner and federally licensed firearms dealer. He got a visit one day from a local police officer and a federal agent from the Treasury Dept. After identifying themselves, they asked to look in his locked gun storeroom. He asked if they had a warrant. They said no, but showed him instead the statute authorizing unannounced searches for licensed dealers. Biswell replied, "Well, that's what it says so I guess it's okay." Inside, they found two sawed-off rifles, and he was arrested and convicted for dealing in National Firearms Act firearms without paying the required special occupational tax.

This is a 4th Amendment case in which the Court held that no warrant is required for the government to conduct an unannounced search of a federal firearms licensee's business, under 18 U.S.C. §923 (g), and to confiscate illegally possessed weapons. A dealer who "chooses to engage in this pervasively regulated business" knows the requirement, and effective inspection is a necessary deterrent to criminal activity. This is also the first case in which the word "sporting" appears in connection with firearms, in an inaccurate reference to the defendant being "federally licensed to deal in sporting weapons," since a dealer license makes no such distinction.

Warrantless search of locked storeroom during business hours as part of inspection procedure authorized by §923 (g) of the Gun Control Act of 1968, which resulted in the seizure of unlicensed firearms from a dealer federally licensed to deal in sporting weapons held not violative of Fourth Amendment.

MR. JUSTICE WHITE delivered the opinion of the Court.

He was indicted and convicted for dealing in firearms without having paid the required special occupational tax.

The Court of Appeals concluded that the sawed-off rifles, having been illegally seized, were inadmissible in evidence. We granted certiorari and now reverse the judgment of the Court of Appeals.

The Gun Control Act of 1968, 82 Stat. 1213, 18 U.S.C. §921 et seq., authorizes official entry during business hours into "the premises (including places of storage) of any firearms or ammunition . . . dealer . . . for the purpose of inspecting or examining (1) any records or documents required to be kept . . . and (2) any firearms or ammunition kept or stored by such . . . dealer . . . at such premises." n1 18 U.S.C. §923 (g). Respondent, a pawn shop operator who was federally licensed to deal in sporting weapons, was visited one afternoon by a city policeman and a Federal Treasury agent who identified himself, inspected respondent's books, and requested entry into a locked gun storeroom. Respondent asked whether the agent had a search warrant, and the investigator told him that he did not, but that §923 (g) authorized such inspections. Respondent was given a copy of the section to read and he replied, "Well, that's what it says so I guess it's okay." Respondent unlocked the storeroom, and the agent found and seized two sawed-off rifles which respondent was not licensed to possess. He was indicted and convicted for dealing in firearms without having paid the required special occupational tax. n2 The Court of Appeals reversed, however, holding that §923 (g) was unconstitutional under the Fourth Amendment because it authorized warrantless searches of business premises and that respondent's ostensible consent to the search was invalid under Bumper v. North Carolina (1968). The Court of Appeals concluded that the sawed-off rifles, having been illegally seized, were inadmissible in evidence. We granted certiorari and now reverse the judgment of the Court of Appeals.

n1 "Each licensed importer, licensed manufacturer, licensed dealer, and licensed collector shall maintain such records of importation, production, shipment, receipt, sale, or other disposition, of firearms and ammunition at such place, for such period, and in such form as the Secretary [of the Treasury] may by regulations prescribe. Such importers, manufacturers, dealers, and collectors shall make such records available for inspection at all reasonable times, and shall submit to the Secretary such reports and information with respect to such records and the contents thereof as he shall by regulations prescribe. The Secretary may enter during business hours the premises (including places of storage) of any firearms or ammunition importer, manufacturer, dealer, or collector for the purpose of inspecting or examining (1) any records or documents required to be kept by such importer, manufacturer, dealer, or collector under the provisions of this chapter or regulations issued under this chapter, and (2) any firearms or ammunition kept or stored by such importer, manufacturer, dealer, or collector at such premises. Upon the request of any State or any political subdivision thereof, the Secretary may make available to such State or any political subdivision thereof, any information which he may obtain by reason of the provisions of this chapter with respect to the identification of persons within such State or political subdivision thereof, who have purchased or received firearms or ammunition, together with a description of such firearms or ammunition." 18 U.S.C. §923 (g).

n2 Respondent was licensed under 18 U.S.C. §923 to sell certain sporting weapons as defined in 18 U.S.C. §921. The sawed-off rifles, however, fell under 26 U.S.C. §5845's technical definition of "firearms," and every dealer in such firearms was required by 26 U.S.C. §5801 to pay a special occupational tax of $200 a year. Such firearms are also required to be registered to a dealer in the National Firearms Registration and Transfer Record. 26 U.S.C. §5841. Respondent was indicted on six counts. Count I, on which he was convicted, charged that he had "wilfully and knowingly engaged in business as a dealer in firearms, as defined by 26 U.S.C. 5845 . . . without having paid the special (occupational) tax required by 26 U.S.C. 5801 for his business." Counts II-V, on which he was acquitted, charged that he had possessed certain firearms that were not identified by serial number, as required by 26 U.S.C. §5842, and that were not registered in the National Firearms Registration and Transfer Record, as required by 26 U.S.C. §5841. Count VI, which charged respondent with failing to maintain properly the records required under 18 U.S.C. §923, was severed and is awaiting trial.

.....

inspection is a crucial part of the regulatory scheme, since it assures that weapons are distributed through regular channels and in a traceable manner

Federal regulation of the interstate traffic in firearms is not as deeply rooted in history as is governmental control of the liquor industry, but close scrutiny of this traffic is undeniably of central importance to federal efforts to prevent violent crime and to assist the States in regulating the firearms traffic within their borders. See Congressional Findings and Declaration, Note preceding 18 U.S.C. 922. Large interests are at stake, and inspection is a crucial part of the regulatory scheme, since it assures that weapons are distributed through regular channels and in a traceable manner and makes possible the prevention of sales to undesirable customers and the detection of the origin of particular firearms.

if inspection is to be effective and serve as a credible deterrent, unannounced, even frequent, inspections are essential. In this context, the prerequisite of a warrant could easily frustrate inspection

It is also apparent that if the law is to be properly enforced and inspection made effective, inspections without warrant must be deemed reasonable official conduct under the Fourth Amendment. In See v. City of Seattle (1967), the mission of the inspection system was to discover and correct violations of the building code, conditions that were relatively difficult to conceal or to correct in a short time. Periodic inspection sufficed, and inspection warrants could be required and privacy given a measure of protection with little if any threat to the effectiveness of the inspection system there at issue. We expressly refrained in that case from questioning a warrantless regulatory search such as that authorized by §923 of the Gun Control Act. Here, if inspection is to be effective and serve as a credible deterrent, unannounced, even frequent, inspections are essential. In this context, the prerequisite of a warrant could easily frustrate inspection; and if the necessary flexibility as to time, scope, and frequency is to be preserved, the protections afforded by a warrant would be negligible.

When a dealer chooses to engage in this pervasively regulated business and to accept a federal license, he does so with the knowledge that his business records, firearms, and ammunition will be subject to effective inspection.

It is also plain that inspections for compliance with the Gun Control Act pose only limited threats to the dealer's justifiable expectations of privacy. When a dealer chooses to engage in this pervasively regulated business and to accept a federal license, he does so with the knowledge that his business records, firearms, and ammunition will be subject to effective inspection. Each licensee is annually furnished with a revised compilation of ordinances that describe his obligations and define the inspector's authority. 18 U.S.C. §921 (a)(19). The dealer is not left to wonder about the purposes of the inspector or the limits of his task.

The seizure of respondent's sawed-off rifles was not unreasonable under the Fourth Amendment

We have little difficulty in concluding that where, as here, regulatory inspections further urgent federal interest, and the possibilities of abuse and the threat to privacy are not of impressive dimensions, the inspection may proceed without a warrant where specifically authorized by statute. The seizure of respondent's sawed-off rifles was not unreasonable under the Fourth Amendment, and the judgment of the Court of Appeals is reversed, and the case is remanded to that court for further proceedings consistent with this opinion.

So ordered.

.....

ADAMS v. WILLIAMS

(CASE EXCERPT)
407 U.S. 143; 92 S. Ct. 1921; 32 L. Ed. 2d 612
April 10, 1972, Argued
June 12, 1972, Decided

GIST: This is a 4th Amendment case with a discussion of carrying guns and the justification needed for a police officer to frisk someone for weapons. At 2:15 a.m. in a high-crime area, a police officer received a tip from an informant he knew that a man was sitting in a nearby car with drugs and a gun at his waist. The officer tapped on the car window, asking Williams to open the door. When Williams rolled down the window, the officer reached in and pulled a revolver from Williams' waistband. After Williams was arrested for unlawful possession of the gun, drugs were found on Williams and in the car. Williams challenged the sufficiency of the justification for the stop and frisk.

The Court held that Williams' 4th Amendment rights were not violated. Compare this case with *J.L. v. Florida,* where a similar tip made anonymously was found insufficient to support a stop and frisk. In dissent, Justice Douglas, joined by Justice Marshall, called for sweeping gun control, psychological tests for gun owners, and a ban on pistols for everyone but the police. He would prefer, he says, to "water down" the 2nd Amendment.

MR. JUSTICE REHNQUIST delivered the opinion of the Court.

"When an officer is justified in believing that the individual whose suspicious behavior he is investigating at close range is armed and presently dangerous to the officer or to others," he may conduct a limited protective search for concealed weapons.

The Court recognized in Terry that the policeman making a reasonable investigatory stop should not be denied the opportunity to protect himself from attack by a hostile suspect. "When an officer is justified in believing that the individual whose suspicious behavior he is investigating at close range is armed and presently dangerous to the officer or to others," he may conduct a limited protective search for concealed weapons. The purpose of this limited search is not to discover evidence of crime, but to allow the officer to pursue his investigation without fear of violence, and thus the frisk for weapons might be equally necessary and reasonable, whether or not carrying a concealed weapon violated any applicable state law. So long as the officer is entitled to make a forcible stop, and has reason to believe that the suspect is armed and dangerous, he may conduct a weapons search limited in scope to this protective purpose.

Applying these principles to the present case, we believe that Sgt. Connolly acted justifiably in responding to his informant's tip. The informant was known to him personally and had provided him with information in the past. This is a stronger case than obtains in the case of an anonymous telephone tip. The informant here came forward personally to give information that was immediately verifiable at the scene. Indeed, under Connecticut law, the informant might have been subject to immediate arrest for making a false complaint had Sgt. Connolly's investigation proved the tip incorrect. Thus, while the Court's decisions indicate that this informant's unverified tip may have been insufficient for a narcotics arrest or search warrant, the information carried enough indicia of reliability to justify the officer's forcible stop of Williams.

.....

the policeman's action in reaching to the spot where the gun was thought to be hidden constituted a limited intrusion designed to insure his safety, and we conclude that it was reasonable. The loaded gun seized as a result of this intrusion was therefore admissible at Williams' trial.

While properly investigating the activity of a person who was reported to be carrying narcotics and a concealed weapon and who was sitting alone in a car in a high-crime area at 2:15 in the morning, Sgt. Connolly had ample reason to fear for his safety. n3 When Williams rolled down his window, rather than complying with the policeman's request to step out of the car so that his movements could more easily be seen, the revolver allegedly at Williams' waist became an even greater threat. Under these circumstances the policeman's action in reaching to the spot where the gun was thought to be hidden constituted a limited intrusion designed to insure his safety, and we conclude that it was reasonable. The loaded gun seized as a result of this intrusion was therefore admissible at Williams' trial.

n3 Figures reported by the Federal Bureau of Investigation indicate that 125 policemen were murdered in 1971, with all but five of them having been killed by gunshot wounds. Federal Bureau of Investigation Law Enforcement Bulletin, Feb. 1972, p. 33. According to one study, approximately 30% of police shootings occurred when a police officer approached a suspect seated in an automobile. Bristow, Police Officer Shootings -- A Tactical Evaluation, 54 J. Crim. L. C. & P. S. 93 (1963).

MR. JUSTICE DOUGLAS, with whom MR. JUSTICE MARSHALL concurs, dissenting.

My views have been stated in substance by Judge Friendly, dissenting, in the Court of Appeals. Connecticut allows its citizens to carry weapons, concealed or otherwise, at will, provided they have a permit. Connecticut law gives its police no authority to frisk a person for a permit. Yet the arrest was for illegal possession of a gun. The only basis for that arrest was the informer's tip on the narcotics. Can it be said that a man in possession of narcotics will not have a permit for his gun? Is that why the arrest for possession of a gun in the free-and-easy State of Connecticut becomes constitutional?

A powerful lobby dins into the ears of our citizenry that these gun purchases are constitutional rights protected by the Second Amendment

The police problem is an acute one not because of the Fourth Amendment, but because of the ease with which anyone can acquire a pistol. A powerful lobby dins into the ears of our citizenry that these gun purchases are constitutional rights protected by the Second Amendment, which reads, "A well regulated Militia, being necessary to the security of a free State, the right of the people to keep and bear Arms, shall not be infringed."

There is under our decisions no reason why stiff state laws governing the purchase and possession of pistols may not be enacted. There is no reason why pistols may not be barred from anyone with a police record. There is no reason why a State may not require a purchaser of a pistol to pass a psychiatric test. There is no reason why all pistols should not be barred to everyone except the police.

There is under our decisions no reason why stiff state laws governing the purchase and possession of pistols may not be enacted. There is no reason why pistols may not be barred from anyone with a police record. There is no reason why a State may not require a purchaser of a pistol to pass a psychiatric test. There is no reason why all pistols should not be barred to everyone except the police.

The leading case is United States v. Miller, upholding a federal law making criminal the shipment in interstate commerce of a sawed-off shotgun.

The Second Amendment, it was held, "must be interpreted and applied" with the view of maintaining a "militia."

The leading case is United States v. Miller, upholding a federal law making criminal the shipment in interstate commerce of a sawed-off shotgun. The law was upheld, there being no evidence that a sawed-off shotgun had "some reasonable relationship to the preservation or efficiency of a well regulated militia." The Second Amendment, it was held, "must be interpreted and applied" with the view of maintaining a "militia."

the common view was that adequate defense of country and laws could be secured through the Militia—civilians primarily, soldiers on occasion."

"The Militia which the States were expected to maintain and train is set in contrast with Troops which they were forbidden to keep without the consent of Congress. The sentiment of the time strongly disfavored standing armies; the common view was that adequate defense of country and laws could be secured through the Militia -- civilians primarily, soldiers on occasion."

Critics say that proposals like this water down the Second Amendment. Our decisions belie that argument, for the Second Amendment, as noted, was designed to keep alive the militia. But if watering-down is the mood of the day, I would prefer to water down the Second rather than the Fourth Amendment.

Critics say that proposals like this water down the Second Amendment. Our decisions belie that argument, for the Second Amendment, as noted, was designed to keep alive the militia. But if watering-down is the mood of the day, I would prefer to water down the Second rather than the Fourth Amendment. I share with Judge Friendly a concern that the easy extension of Terry v. Ohio, 392 U.S. 1, to "possessory offenses" is a serious intrusion on Fourth Amendment safeguards. "If it is to be extended to the latter at all, this should be only where observation by the officer himself or well authenticated information shows 'that criminal activity may be afoot.'" 436 F.2d, at 39, quoting Terry v. Ohio, supra, at 30.

MR. JUSTICE BRENNAN, dissenting.

I would affirm, believing, for the following reasons stated by Judge, now Chief Judge, Friendly, dissenting, 436 F.2d 30, 38-39, that the State did not make that showing:

"To begin, I have the gravest hesitancy in extending [Terry v. Ohio, 392 U.S. 1 (1968)] to crimes like the possession of narcotics .... There is too much danger that, instead of the stop being the object and the protective frisk an incident thereto, the reverse will be true. Against that we have here the added fact of the report that Williams had a gun on his person. ... [But] Connecticut allows its citizens to carry weapons, concealed or otherwise, at will, provided only they have a permit, Conn. Gen. Stat. §§29-35 and 29-38, and gives its police officers no special authority to stop for the purpose of determining whether the citizen has one. ...

"If I am wrong in thinking that Terry should not be applied at all to mere possessory offenses, ... I would not find the combination of Officer Connolly's almost meaningless observation and the tip in this case to be sufficient justification for the intrusion. The tip suffered from a threefold defect, with each fold compounding the others. The informer was unnamed, he was not shown to have been reliable with respect to guns or narcotics, and he gave no information which demonstrated personal knowledge or -- what is worse -- could not readily have been manufactured by the officer after the event. To my mind, it has not been sufficiently recognized that the difference between this sort of tip and the accurate prediction of an unusual event is as important on the latter score as on the former. [In Draper v. United States, 358 U.S. 307 (1959),] Narcotics Agent Marsh would hardly have been at the Denver Station at the exact moment of the arrival of the train Draper had taken from Chicago unless someone had told him something important, although the agent might later have embroidered the details to fit the observed facts. ... There is no such guarantee of a patrolling officer's veracity when he testifies to a 'tip' from an unnamed informer saying no more than that the officer will find a gun and narcotics on a man across the street, as he later does. If the state wishes to rely on a tip of that nature to validate a stop and frisk, revelation of the name of the informer or demonstration that his name is unknown and could not reasonably have been ascertained should be the price.

"Terry v. Ohio was intended to free a police officer from the rigidity of a rule that would prevent his doing anything to a man reasonably suspected of being about to commit or having just committed a crime of violence, no matter how grave the problem or impelling the need for swift action, unless the officer had what a court would later determine to be probable cause for arrest. It was meant for the serious cases of imminent danger or of harm recently perpetrated to persons or property, not the conventional ones of possessory offenses. If it is to be extended to the latter at all, this should be only where observation by the officer himself or well authenticated information shows 'that criminal activity may be afoot.' 392 U.S., at 30. ... I greatly fear that if the [contrary view] should be followed, Terry will have opened the sluicegates for serious and unintended erosion of the protection of the Fourth Amendment."

MR. JUSTICE MARSHALL, with whom MR. JUSTICE DOUGLAS joins, dissenting.

Four years have passed since we decided Terry v. Ohio. They were the first cases in which this Court explicitly recognized the concept of "stop and frisk" and squarely held that police officers may, under appropriate circumstances, stop and frisk persons suspected of criminal activity even though there is less than probable cause for an arrest.

.....

police officers have a "narrowly drawn authority to ... search for weapons" without a warrant.

Hence, Terry stands only for the proposition that police officers have a "narrowly drawn authority to ... search for weapons" without a warrant.

.....

Respondent was sitting on the passenger side of the front seat of a car parked on the street in a "high crime area" in Bridgeport, Connecticut, at 2:15 a.m. when a police officer approached his car. During a conversation that had just taken place nearby, the officer was told by an informant that respondent had narcotics on his person and that he had a gun in his waistband. The officer saw that the motor was not running, that respondent was seated peacefully in the car, and that there was no indication that he was about to leave the scene. After the officer asked respondent to open the door, respondent rolled down his window instead and the officer reached into the car and pulled a gun from respondent's waistband. The officer immediately placed respondent under arrest for carrying the weapon and searched him, finding heroin in his coat. More heroin was found in a later search of the automobile. Respondent moved to suppress both the gun and the heroin prior to trial. His motion was denied and he was convicted of possessing both items.

B. The Court erroneously attempts to describe the search for the gun as a protective search incident to a reasonable investigatory stop. But, as in Terry, Sibron and Peters, supra, there is no occasion in this case to determine whether or not police officers have a right to seize and to restrain a citizen in order to interrogate him. The facts are clear that the officer intended to make the search as soon as he approached the respondent. He asked no questions; he made no investigation; he simply searched. There was nothing apart from the information supplied by the informant to cause the officer to search. Our inquiry must focus, therefore, as it did in Terry on whether the officer had sufficient facts from which he could reasonably infer that respondent was not only engaging in illegal activity, but also that he was armed and dangerous. The focus falls on the informant.

The only information that the informant had previously given the officer involved homosexual conduct in the local railroad station. The following colloquy took place between respondent's counsel and the officer at the hearing on respondent's motion to suppress the evidence that had been seized from him.

"Q. Now, with respect to the information that was given you about homosexuals in the Bridgeport Police Station [sic], did that lead to an arrest? A. No.

"Q. An arrest was not made. A. No. There was no substantiating evidence.

.... "Q. There was no substantiating evidence? A. No.

"Q. And what do you mean by that? A. I didn't have occasion to witness these individuals committing any crime of any nature.

"Q. In other words, after this person gave you the information, you checked for corroboration before you made an arrest. Is that right? A. Well, I checked to determine the possibility of homosexual activity.

"Q. And since an arrest was made, I take it you didn't find any substantiating information. A. I'm sorry counselor, you say since an arrest was made.

"Q. Was not made. Since an arrest was not made, I presume you didn't find any substantiating information. A. No.

"Q. So that, you don't recall any other specific information given you about the commission of crimes by this informant. A. No.

"Q. And you still thought this person was reliable. A. Yes."

Were we asked to determine whether the information supplied by the informant was sufficient to provide probable cause for an arrest and search, rather than a stop and frisk, there can be no doubt that we would hold that it was insufficient. This Court has squarely held that a search and seizure cannot be justified on the basis of conclusory allegations of an unnamed informant who is allegedly credible. Aguilar v. Texas, 378 U.S. 108 (1964). In the recent case of Spinelli v. United States, 393 U.S. 410 (1969), Mr. Justice Harlan made it plain beyond any doubt that where police rely on an informant to make a search and seizure, they must know that the informant is generally trustworthy and that he has obtained his information in a reliable way. Id., at 417. Since the testimony of the arresting officer in the instant case patently fails to demonstrate that the informant was known to be trustworthy and since it is also clear that the officer had no idea of the source of the informant's "knowledge," a search and seizure would have been illegal.

Assuming, arguendo, that this case truly involves, not an arrest and a search incident thereto, but a stop and frisk, we must decide whether or not the information possessed by the officer justified this interference with respondent's liberty. Terry, our only case to actually uphold a stop and frisk, is not directly in point, because the police officer in that case acted on the basis of his own personal observations. No informant was involved. But the rationale of Terry is still controlling, and it requires that we condemn the conduct of the police officer in encountering the respondent.

.....

Terry did not hold that whenever a policeman has a hunch that a citizen is engaging in criminal activity, he may engage in a stop and frisk. It held that if police officers want to stop and frisk, they must have specific facts from which they can reasonably infer that an individual is engaged in criminal activity and is armed and dangerous. n4 It was central to our decision in Terry that the police officer acted on the basis of his own personal observations and that he carefully scrutinized the conduct of his suspects before interfering with them in any way. When we legitimated the conduct of the officer in Terry we did so because of the substantial reliability of the information on which the officer based his decision to act.

With respect to the gun, the officer did not know if or when the informant had ever seen the gun, or whether the gun was carried legally, as Connecticut law permitted, or illegally.

If the Court does not ignore the care with which we examined the knowledge possessed by the officer in Terry when he acted, then I cannot see how the actions of the officer in this case can be upheld. The Court explains what the officer knew about respondent before accosting him. But what is more significant is what he did not know. With respect to the scene generally, the officer had no idea how long respondent had been in the car, how long the car had been parked, or to whom the car belonged. With respect to the gun, n5 the officer did not know if or when the informant had ever seen the gun, or whether the gun was carried legally, as Connecticut law permitted, or illegally. And with respect to the narcotics, the officer did not know what kind of narcotics respondent allegedly had, whether they were legally or illegally possessed, what the basis of the informant's knowledge was, or even whether the informant was capable of distinguishing narcotics from other substances.

The fact that the respondent carried his gun in a high-crime area is irrelevant. In such areas it is more probable than not that citizens would be more likely to carry weapons authorized by the State to protect themselves.

n5 The fact that the respondent carried his gun in a high-crime area is irrelevant. In such areas it is more probable than not that citizens would be more likely to carry weapons authorized by the State to protect themselves.

.....

Since Connecticut has not made it illegal for private citizens to carry guns, there is nothing in the facts of this case to warrant a man "of prudence and caution" to believe that any offense had been committed merely because respondent had a gun on his person. Any implication that respondent's silence was some sort of a tacit admission of guilt would be utterly absurd.

Once the officer seized the gun from respondent, it is uncontradicted that he did not ask whether respondent had a license to carry it, or whether respondent carried it for any other legal reason under Connecticut law. Rather, the officer placed him under arrest immediately and hastened to search his person. Since Connecticut has not made it illegal for private citizens to carry guns, there is nothing in the facts of this case to warrant a man "of prudence and caution" to believe that any offense had been committed merely because respondent had a gun on his person. n9 Any implication that respondent's silence was some sort of a tacit admission of guilt would be utterly absurd.

n9 The Court appears to rely on the fact that the existence of the gun corroborated the information supplied to the officer by the informant. It cannot be disputed that there is minimal corroboration here, but the fact remains that the officer still lacked any knowledge that respondent had done anything illegal. Since carrying a gun is not per se illegal in Connecticut, the fact that respondent carried a gun is no more relevant to probable cause than the fact that his shirt may have been blue, or that he was wearing a jacket. Moreover, the fact that the informant can identify a gun on sight does not indicate an ability to do the same with narcotics. The corroboration of this one fact is a far cry from the corroboration that the Court found sufficient to sustain an arrest in Draper v. United States, 358 U.S. 307 (1959).

It is simply not reasonable to expect someone to protest that he is not acting illegally before he is told that he is suspected of criminal activity. It would have been a simple matter for the officer to ask whether respondent had a permit, but he chose not to do so. In making this choice, he clearly violated the Fourth Amendment.

LAIRD v. TATUM

(CASE EXCERPT)

408 U.S. 1; 92 S. Ct. 2318; 33 L. Ed. 2d 154

March 27, 1972, Argued

June 26, 1972, Decided

GIST: This case arose out of a challenge to domestic surveillance conducted by Army Intelligence, in assisting local authorities in Detroit, immediately following riots in 1967. Five members of the Court held that the 1st Amendment claims did not present a sufficient controversy for adjudication, as there was no showing of present or future harm. Dissenting, Justices Douglas and Marshall emphasized the importance of civilian control over the military. In support of this argument, they pointed to the role of the 2nd Amendment "specifically authorizing a decentralized militia, guaranteeing the right of the people to keep and bear arms."

.....

MR. JUSTICE DOUGLAS, with whom MR. JUSTICE MARSHALL concurs, dissenting.

As Chief Justice Warren has observed, the safeguards in the main body of the Constitution did not satisfy the people on their fear and concern of military dominance:

> **"They were reluctant to ratify the Constitution without further assurances, and thus we find in the Bill of Rights Amendments 2 and 3, specifically authorizing a decentralized militia, guaranteeing the right of the people to keep and bear arms, and prohibiting the quartering of troops in any house in time of peace without the consent of the owner.**

"They were reluctant to ratify the Constitution without further assurances, and thus we find in the Bill of Rights Amendments 2 and 3, specifically authorizing a decentralized militia, guaranteeing the right of the people to keep and bear arms, and prohibiting the quartering of troops in any house in time of peace without the consent of the owner. Other Amendments guarantee the right of the people to assemble, to be secure in their homes against unreasonable searches and seizures, and in criminal cases to be accorded a speedy and public trial by an impartial jury after indictment in the district and state wherein the crime was committed. The only exceptions made to these civilian trial procedures are for cases arising in the land and naval forces. Although there is undoubtedly room for argument based on the frequently conflicting sources of history, it is not unreasonable to believe that our Founders' determination to guarantee the preeminence of civil over military power was an important element that prompted adoption of the Constitutional Amendments we call the Bill of Rights."

ROE v. WADE

(CASE EXCERPT)
410 U.S. 113; 93 S. Ct. 705; 35 L. Ed. 2d 147
December 13, 1971, Argued
January 22, 1973, Decided

GIST: This is the well-known abortion case striking down a Texas abortion law, because it infringed rights protected by the 9th and 14th Amendments. Concurring, Justice Stewart quoted Justice Harlan's list of liberties protected by the Bill of Rights, including the right to keep and bear arms, from *Poe v. Ullman.*

MR. JUSTICE STEWART, concurring.

.....

This 'liberty' is not a series of isolated points pricked out in terms of the taking of property; the freedom of speech, press, and religion; the right to keep and bear arms; the freedom from unreasonable searches and seizures; and so on.

As Mr. Justice Harlan once wrote: "The full scope of the liberty guaranteed by the Due Process Clause cannot be found in or limited by the precise terms of the specific guarantees elsewhere provided in the Constitution. This 'liberty' is not a series of isolated points pricked out in terms of the taking of property; the freedom of speech, press, and religion; the right to keep and bear arms; the freedom from unreasonable searches and seizures; and so on. It is a rational continuum which, broadly speaking, includes a freedom from all substantial arbitrary impositions and purposeless restraints . . . and which also recognizes, what a reasonable and sensitive judgment must, that certain interests require particularly careful scrutiny of the state needs asserted to justify their abridgment."

HUDDLESTON v. UNITED STATES

(FULL CASE)
415 U.S. 814; 94 S. Ct. 1262; 39 L. Ed. 2d 782
November 7, 1973, Argued
March 26, 1974, Decided

GIST: William Huddleston pawned his wife's Winchester 30-30 for $25 at a pawnshop in Oxnard, California. He later hocked her Russian 7.62 and a Remington .22, and then redeemed them a few months later. He filled out and signed the 4473 federal firearms transfer form inaccurately. His story is told in this case rather well, and you get a glimpse of how a defendant moves through the system.

This is a case interpreting the Gun Control Act of 1968 as it applies to redemption of guns from a pawn shop by a felon who had pawned them. Huddleston argued that the GCA wasn't intended to apply to pawn transactions, that he retained title in the pawn and didn't "acquire" the guns when they were redeemed. The Court disagreed, holding that the Act applied to pawn the same as sales from dealers, to fulfill Congress' intent to keep guns out of the hands of felons, fugitives, juveniles and the mentally defective. The Court recognized a congressional intent to prohibit firearms to individuals whose possession would be contrary to the public interest.

Petitioner, a previously convicted felon, was convicted of violating 18 U.S.C. §922 (a)(6), a part of the Gun Control Act of 1968, by falsely stating, in connection with the redemption from a pawnbroker of three guns petitioner had pawned, that he had not been convicted of a crime punishable by imprisonment for more than a year. The pawnbroker was a federally licensed firearms dealer. The Court of Appeals affirmed. Section 922 (a)(6) makes it an offense knowingly to make a false statement "in connection with the acquisition . . . of any firearm . . . from a . . . licensed dealer" and "intended or likely to deceive such . . . dealer . . . with respect to any fact material to the lawfulness of the sale or other disposition of such firearm . . . ." Held: Section 922 (a)(6) applies to the redemption of a firearm from a pawnshop.

(a) Petitioner's contention that the statute covers only a salelike transaction is without merit, since "acquisition" as used in §922 (a)(6) clearly includes any person, by definition, who "comes into possession, control, or power of disposal" of a firearm. Moreover, the statutory terms "acquisition" and "sale or other disposition" are correlatives. It is reasonable to conclude that a pawnbroker might "dispose" of a firearm through a redemptive transaction. Finally, Congress explicitly included pawnbrokers in the Gun Control Act, specifically mentioned pledge and pawn transactions involving firearms, and did not include them in the statutory exemptions.

(b) That pawnshop firearms redemptions are covered by the challenged provision comports with the legislative history of Title IV of the Omnibus Crime Control and Safe Streets Act of 1968 and the Gun Control Act of 1968, which are aimed at controlling access to weapons by those whose possession thereof is contrary to the public interest, through a regulatory scheme focusing on the federally licensed firearms dealer.

(c) Section 922 (a)(6) contains no ambiguity warranting a narrow construction in petitioner's favor, and application of the statute to the pawn redemptions here raises no issue of constitutional dimension.

MR. JUSTICE BLACKMUN delivered the opinion of the Court.

This case presents the issue whether 18 U.S.C. §922 (a)(6), n1 declaring that it is unlawful knowingly to make a false statement "in connection with the acquisition . . . of any firearm . . . from a . . . licensed dealer," covers the redemption of a firearm from a pawnshop.

n1 "§922. Unlawful acts.

"(a) It shall be unlawful --

. . . .

"(6) for any person in connection with the acquisition . . . of any firearm . . . from a . . . licensed dealer . . . knowingly to make any false or fictitious oral or written statement . . . intended or likely to deceive such . . . dealer . . . with respect to any fact material to the lawfulness of the sale or other disposition of such firearm . . . under the provisions of this chapter."

I

On October 6, 1971, petitioner, William C. Huddleston, Jr., pawned his wife's Winchester 30-30-caliber rifle for $25 at a pawnshop in Oxnard, California. On the following October 15 and on December 28, he pawned at the same shop two other firearms, a Russian 7.62-caliber rifle and a Remington .22-caliber rifle, belonging to his wife. For these he received loans of $10 and $15, respectively. The owner of the pawnshop was a federally licensed firearms dealer.

Some weeks later, on February 1, 1972, and on March 10, Huddleston redeemed the weapons. In connection with each of the redemptions, the pawnbroker required petitioner to complete Treasury Form 4473, entitled "Firearms Transaction Record." This is a form used in the enforcement of the gun control provision of Title IV of the Omnibus Crime Control and Safe Streets Act of 1968, Pub. L. 90-351, 82 Stat. 225, as amended by the Gun Control Act of 1968, Pub. L. 90-618, 82 Stat. 1213, of which the above-cited 18 U.S.C. §922 (a)(6) is a part. Question 8b of the form is: "Have you been convicted in any court of a crime punishable by imprisonment for a term exceeding one year? (Note: The actual sentence given by the judge does not matter -- a yes answer is necessary if the judge could have given a sentence of more than one year.)"

The question is derived from the statutory prohibition against a dealer's selling or otherwise disposing of a firearm to any person who "has been convicted in any court of . . . a crime punishable by imprisonment for a term exceeding one year." 18 U.S.C. §922 (d)(1). n2 Petitioner answered "no" to Question 8b on each of the three Forms 4473. He then affixed his signature to each form's certification that the answers were true and correct, that he understood that a person who answers any of the questions in the affirmative is prohibited by federal law from "purchasing and/or possessing a firearm," and that he also understood that the making of any false statement with respect to the transaction is a crime punishable as a felony.

n2 "§922. Unlawful acts.

. . . .

"(d) It shall be unlawful for any . . . licensed dealer . . . to sell or otherwise dispose of any firearm . . . to any person knowing or having reasonable cause to believe that such person --

"(1) is under indictment for, or has been convicted in any court of, a crime punishable by imprisonment for a term exceeding one year."

In fact, Huddleston, six years earlier, had been convicted in a California state court for writing checks without sufficient funds, an offense punishable under California law by a maximum term of 14 years. n3 This fact, if revealed to the pawnshop proprietor, would have precluded the proprietor from selling or otherwise disposing of any of the rifles to the petitioner because of the proscription in 18 U.S.C. §922 (d)(1).

n3 Cal. Penal Code §476a (1970). The California complaint against Huddleston was in six counts and contained an allegation that he had been convicted previously in the State of Iowa of an offense which, if committed in California, would have been a violation of §476 of the California Penal Code. He was eventually sentenced on the check charge to 30 days in jail.

Huddleston was charged in a three-count indictment with violating 18 U.S.C. §§922 (a)(6) and 924 (a). n4 He moved to dismiss the indictment, in part on the ground that §922 (a)(6) was never intended to apply, and should not apply, to a pawnor's redemption of a weapon he had pawned. This motion was denied. Petitioner then pleaded not guilty and waived a jury trial.

n4 "§924. Penalties.

"(a) Whoever violates any provision of this chapter or knowingly makes any false statement or representation with respect to the information required by the provisions of this chapter to be kept in the records of a person licensed under this chapter, . . . shall be fined not more than $5,000, or imprisoned not more than five years, or both, and shall become eligible for parole as the Board of Parole shall determine."

The Government's evidence consisted primarily of the three Treasury Forms 4473 Huddleston had signed; the record of his earlier California felony conviction; and the pawnbroker's federal license. A Government agent also testified that petitioner, after being arrested and advised of his rights, made statements admitting that he had known, when filling out the forms, that he was a felon and that he had lied each time when he answered Question 8b in the negative.

He stated that he did not knowingly make a false statement; that he did not read the form and simply answered "no" upon prompting from the pawnbroker

Huddleston testified in his own defense. He stated that he did not knowingly make a false statement; that he did not read the form and simply answered "no" upon prompting from the pawnbroker; and that he was unaware that his California conviction was punishable by a term exceeding one year. n5

n5 Huddleston at first testified that his California attorney and his probation officer there told him that when he completed his probation period and made restitution, "it would go on record as a misdemeanor," and that the attorney had told him he "couldn't get over a year." App. 37, 39. Upon inquiry by the court, he testified that when he was arraigned he thought he "could get more than one year," and was so informed. Id., at 41.

The United States Court of Appeals for the Ninth Circuit, by a divided vote, affirmed the conviction. The dissenting judge agreed that the statute was constitutional as applied, but concluded that what Huddleston did was to "reacquire" the rifles, and that "reacquire" is not necessarily included within the statute's term "acquire." We granted certiorari, to resolve an existing conflict among the circuits on the issue whether the prohibition against making false statements in connection with the acquisition of a firearm covers a firearm's redemption from a pawnshop

The District Judge found the petitioner guilty on all counts. He sentenced Huddleston to three concurrent three-year terms. The sentences were suspended, however, except for 20 days to be served on weekends. The United States Court of Appeals for the Ninth Circuit, by a divided vote, affirmed the conviction. 472 F.2d 592 (1973). The dissenting judge agreed that the statute was constitutional as applied, but concluded that what Huddleston did was to "reacquire" the rifles, and that "reacquire" is not necessarily included within the statute's term "acquire." Id., at 593. We granted certiorari, 411 U.S. 930 (1973), to resolve an existing conflict among the circuits on the issue whether the prohibition against making false statements in connection with the acquisition of a firearm covers a firearm's redemption from a pawnshop. n6

n6 In agreement with the Ninth Circuit's decision is United States v. Beebe, 467 F.2d 222 (CA10 1972). To the contrary is United States v. Laisure, 460 F.2d 709 (CA5 1972).

II

Petitioner's assault on the statute under which he was convicted is two pronged. First, it is argued that both the statute's language and its legislative history indicate that Congress did not intend a pawnshop redemption of a firearm to be an "acquisition" covered by the statute. Second, it is said that even if Congress did intend a pawnshop redemption to be a covered "acquisition," the statute is so ambiguous that its construction is controlled by the maxim that ambiguity in a criminal statute is to be resolved in favor of the defendant.

We turn first to the language and structure of the Act. Reduced to a minimum, §922 (a)(6) relates to any false statement made "in connection with the acquisition . . . of any firearm" from a licensed dealer and intended or likely to deceive the dealer "with respect to any fact material to the lawfulness of the sale or other disposition of such firearm."

Petitioner attaches great significance to the word "acquisition." He urges that it suggests only a sale-like transaction. Since Congress in §922 (a)(6) did not use words of transfer or delivery, as it did in other sections of the Act, he argues that "acquisition" must have a narrower meaning than those terms. Moreover, since a pawn transaction is only a temporary bailment of personal property, with the pawnshop having merely a security interest in the pledged property, title or ownership is constant in the pawnor, and the pawn-plus-redemption transaction is no more than an interruption in the pawnor's possession. The pawnor simply repossesses his own property, and he does not "acquire" any new title or interest in the object pawned. At most, he "reacquires" the object, and reacquisition, as the dissenting judge in the Court of Appeals noted, is not necessarily included in the statutory term "acquisition."

On its face, this argument might be said to have some force. A careful look at the statutory language and at complementary provisions of the Act, however, convinces us that the asserted ambiguity is contrived. Petitioner is mistaken in focusing solely on the term "acquisition" and in enshrouding it with an extra-statutory "legal title" or "ownership" analysis. The word "acquire" is defined to mean simply "to come into possession, control, or power of disposal of." Webster's New International Dictionary (3d ed., 1966, unabridged); United States v. Laisure, 460 F.2d 709, 712 n. 3 (CA5 1972). There is no intimation here that title or ownership would be necessary for possession, or control, or disposal power, and there is nothing else in the statute that justifies the imposition of that gloss. Moreover, a full reading of §922 (a)(6) clearly demonstrates that the false statements that are prohibited are those made with respect to the lawfulness of the sale "or other disposition" of a firearm by a licensed dealer. The word "acquisition," therefore, cannot be considered apart from the phrase "sale or other disposition." As the Government suggests, and indeed as the petitioner implicitly reasoned at oral argument, Tr. of Oral Arg. 11, if the pawnbroker "sells" or "disposes" under §922 (a)(6), the transferee necessarily "acquires." These words, as used in the statute, are correlatives. The focus of our inquiry, therefore, should be to determine whether a "sale or other disposition" of a firearm by a pawnbroker encompasses the redemption of the firearm by a pawnor.

Clearly, a redemption is not a "sale" for the simple reason that a sale has definite connotations of ownership and title. Some "other disposition" of a firearm, however, could easily encompass a pawnshop redemption. We believe that it does.

It is the dealer who sells or disposes of the firearm. The statute defines the dealer to be:

"(A) any person engaged in the business of selling firearms or ammunition at wholesale or retail, (B) any person engaged in the business of repairing firearms or of making or fitting special barrels, stocks, or trigger mechanisms to firearms, or (C) any person who is a pawnbroker." 18 U.S.C. §921 (a)(11) (emphasis supplied).

It defines a "pawnbroker" as "any person whose business or occupation includes the taking or receiving, by way of pledge or pawn, of any firearm or ammunition as security for the payment or repayment of money." 18 U.S.C. §921 (a)(12) (emphasis supplied).

These definitions surely suggest that a "sale or other disposition" of a firearm in a pawnshop is covered by the statute. This, of course, does not of itself resolve the question as to exactly what "other disposition" by a pawnbroker is included. It should be apparent, however, that if Congress had intended to include only a pawnbroker's default sales of pledged or pawned goods, or his wholesale and retail sales of nonpawned goods, and to exclude the redemption of pawned articles, then the explicit inclusion of the pawnbroker in the definition of "dealer" would serve no purpose, since part (A) of the definition, covering wholesale and retail sales, would otherwise reach all such sales. United States v. Rosen, 352 F.Supp. 727, 729 (Idaho 1973). At oral argument counsel suggested that the specific reference to a pawnbroker might have been intended to include "disposition" by barter, swap, trade, or gift. Tr. of Oral Arg. 5-7. This interpretation strains belief. Trades or gifts are not peculiar to pawnbrokers. Wholesalers and retailers may indulge in such dispositions. There is nothing in the legislative history to indicate that this interpretation prompted the specific mention of a pawnbroker in part (C) of the definition. To the contrary, the committee reports indicate that part (C) "specifically provides that a pawnbroker dealing in firearms shall be considered a dealer." H. R. Rep. No. 1577, 90th Cong., 2d Sess., 11 (1968) (emphasis supplied). See also S. Rep. No.

1501, 90th Cong., 2d Sess., 30 (1968).

We also cannot ignore the explicit reference to a firearm transaction "by way of pledge or pawn" in the statutory definition of "pawnbroker" in §921 (a)(12). Had Congress' desire been to exempt a transaction of this kind, it would have artfully worded the definition so as to exclude it. We are equally impressed by Congress' failure to exempt redemptive transactions from the prohibitions of the Act when it so carefully carved out exceptions for a dealer "returning a firearm" and for an individual mailing a firearm to a dealer "for the sole purpose of repair or customizing." §922 (a)(2)(A). Petitioner contends that a redemptive transaction is no different from the return of a gun left for repair. His argument is that the pawned weapon is simply "returned" to the individual who left it and represents a mere restoration to its original status. We believe, however, that it was not unreasonable for Congress to choose to view the pawn transaction as something more than the mere interruption in possession typical of repair. The fact that Congress thought it necessary specifically to exempt the repair transaction indicates that it otherwise would have been covered and, if this were so, clearly a pawn transaction likewise would be covered.

Other provisions of the Act also make it clear that the statute generally covers all transfers of firearms by dealers to recipients. Section 922 (a)(1) makes it unlawful for any person, except a licensed importer, manufacturer, or dealer, to engage in the business of "dealing" in firearms, or in the course of such business "to ship, transport, or receive any firearm." Section 922 (b)(1) makes it unlawful for a dealer "to sell or deliver" firearms of specified types to persons under 18 or 21 years of age. Section 922 (b)(2) makes it unlawful for a dealer to "sell or deliver" a weapon to a person in any State where "at the place of sale, delivery or other disposition," the transfer would violate local law. Section 922 (d) makes it unlawful for a dealer "to sell or otherwise dispose of" a firearm to a person under a felony indictment, a felon, a fugitive, a narcotic addict, or a mental defective. Section 923 (g) requires that each licensed dealer maintain "records of importation, production, shipment, receipt, sale, or other disposition, of firearms."

In sum, the word "acquisition," as used in §922 (a)(6), is not ambiguous, but clearly includes any person, by definition, who "come[s] into possession, control, or power of disposal" of a firearm. As noted above, "acquisition" and "sale or other disposition" are correlatives. It is reasonable to conclude that a pawnbroker might "dispose" of a firearm through a redemptive transaction. And because Congress explicitly included pawnbrokers in the Act, explicitly mentioned pledge and pawn transactions involving firearms, and clearly failed to include them among the statutory exceptions, we are not at liberty to tamper with the obvious reach of the statute in proscribing the conduct in which the petitioner engaged.

III

The legislative history, too, supports this reading of the statute. This is apparent from the aims and purposes of the Act and from the method Congress adopted to achieve those objectives. When Congress enacted the provisions under which petitioner was convicted, it was concerned with the widespread traffic in firearms and with their general availability to those whose possession thereof was contrary to the public interest. Pub. L. 90-351, §1201, 82 Stat. 236, as amended by Pub. L. 90-618, §301 (a)(1), 82 Stat. 1236, 18 U.S.C. App. §1201. Congress determined that the ease with which firearms could be obtained contributed significantly to the prevalence of lawlessness and violent crime in the United States. S. Rep. No. 1097, 90th Cong., 2d Sess., 108 (1968). The principal purpose of the federal gun control legislation, therefore, was to curb crime by keeping "firearms out of the hands of those not legally entitled to possess them because of age, criminal background, or incompetency. " S. Rep. No. 1501, 90th Cong., 2d Sess., 22 (1968).

The principal agent of federal enforcement is the dealer.

Title IV of the Omnibus Crime Control and Safe Streets Act of 1968 and the Gun Control Act of 1968 are thus aimed at restricting public access to firearms. Commerce in firearms is channeled through federally licensed importers, manufacturers, and dealers in an attempt to halt mail-order and interstate consumer traffic in these weapons. The principal agent of federal enforcement is the dealer. He is licensed, §§922 (a)(1) and 923 (a); he is required to keep records of "sale . . . or other disposition," §923 (g); and he is subject to a criminal penalty for disposing of a weapon contrary to the provisions of the Act, §924.

Information drawn from records kept by dealers was a prime guarantee of the Act's effectiveness in keeping "these lethal weapons out of the hands of criminals, drug addicts, mentally disordered persons, juveniles, and other persons whose possession of them is too high a price in danger to us all to allow."

Section 922 (a)(6), the provision under which petitioner was convicted, was enacted as a means of providing adequate and truthful information about firearms transactions. Information drawn from records kept by dealers was a prime guarantee of the Act's effectiveness in keeping "these lethal weapons out of the hands of criminals, drug addicts, mentally disordered persons, juveniles, and other persons whose possession of them is too high a price in danger to us all to allow." 114 Cong. Rec. 13219 (1968) (remarks of

Sen. Tydings). Thus, any false statement with respect to the eligibility of a person to obtain a firearm from a licensed dealer was made subject to a criminal penalty.

Firearms are channeled through dealers to eliminate the mail order and the generally widespread commerce in them, and to insure that, in the course of sales or other dispositions by these dealers, weapons could not be obtained by individuals whose possession of them would be contrary to the public interest.

From this outline of the Act, it is apparent that the focus of the federal scheme is the federally licensed firearms dealer, at least insofar as the Act directly controls access to weapons by users. Firearms are channeled through dealers to eliminate the mail order and the generally widespread commerce in them, and to insure that, in the course of sales or other dispositions by these dealers, weapons could not be obtained by individuals whose possession of them would be contrary to the public interest. Thus, the conclusion we reached above with respect to the language and structure of the Act, that firearms redemptions in pawnshops are covered, is entirely consonant with the achievement of this congressional objective and method of enforcing the Act.

Moreover, as was said in United States v. Bramblett, 348 U.S. 503, 507 (1955), "There is no indication in either the committee reports or in the congressional debates that the scope of the statute was to be in any way restricted" (footnotes omitted). Indeed, the committee reports indicate that the proscription under §922 (d) on the sale or other disposition of a firearm to a felon "goes to all types of sales or dispositions -- over-the-counter as well as mail order." n7 S. Rep. No. 1097, 90th Cong., 2d Sess., 115 (1968). See S. Rep. No. 1501, 90th Cong., 2d Sess., 34 (1968). As far as the parties have informed us, and as far as our independent research has revealed, there is no discussion of the actual meaning of "acquisition" or of "sale or other disposition" in the legislative history. Previous legislation relating to the particular term "other disposition" sheds some light, however, and prudence calls on us to look to it in ascertaining the legislative purpose. United States v. Katz, 271 U.S. 354, 357 (1926). The term apparently had its origin in §1 (k) of the National Firearms Act, Pub. L. 474, 48 Stat. 1236 (1934). That Act set certain conditions on the "transfer" of machine guns and other dangerous weapons. As defined by the Act, "transfer" meant "to sell, assign, pledge, lease, loan, give away, or otherwise dispose of." The term "otherwise dispose of" in that context was aimed at providing maximum coverage. The interpretation we adopt here accomplishes the same objective. n8

n7 James V. Bennett, then Director of the Federal Bureau of Prisons, in Senate testimony offered a "case study" vividly illustrating nonsale situations that would qualify as a firearms "disposition" or "acquisition." One of his illustrations was the following:

"On September 26, 1958, a 20-year-old youth shot and seriously wounded a teller during the course of a bank robbery in St. Paul; only a week previously he had bought the revolver, a .357 Smith & Wesson, in a Minneapolis sporting goods store, pawned it the same day, and on the day of the robbery redeemed it with money obtained from check forgeries."

Mr. Bennett concluded his testimony with the observation, "No responsible and thoughtful citizen can, in my opinion, seriously object to measures which would discourage youngsters, the mentally ill, and criminals from coming into possession of handguns." Hearings before the Subcommittee to Investigate Juvenile Delinquency of the Senate Committee on the Judiciary, 88th Cong., 1st Sess., pt. 14, pp. 3369, 3377 (1963).

n8 Testimony by then Attorney General Ramsey Clark also supports the rejection of petitioner's suggestion that the language of the statute be given a restrictive meaning:

"Mr. Donohue. Do you not think, Mr. Attorney General, to attain the real objective and purpose of this bill, it should not only deal with the sale, but whoever sells or delivers?

"Mr. Clark: It covers delivery, too.

"Mr. Donohue. Where?

"Mr. Clark. Well, generally, through the bill when you talk about -- well, it would be unlawful for any licensed importer to sell or deliver. Any licensed dealer to sell or deliver.

"Mr. Donohue. It is not restricted to just sale for consideration?

"Mr. Clark. No. The delivery, too."

Hearings on an Anti-Crime Program before Subcommittee No. 5 of the House Committee on the Judiciary, 90th Cong., 1st Sess., 260 (1967).

There also can be no doubt of Congress' intention to deprive the juvenile, the mentally incompetent, the criminal, and the fugitive of the use of firearms.

There also can be no doubt of Congress' intention to deprive the juvenile, the mentally incompetent, the criminal, and the fugitive of the use of firearms. Senator Tydings stated:

"Title IV, the concealed weapons amendment, is a very limited, stripped-down, bare-minimum gun-traffic control bill, primarily designed to reduce access to handguns for criminals, juveniles, and fugitives. . . . I can fairly say that this concealed weapons amendment does not significantly inconvenience hunters and sportsmen in any way. The people it does frustrate are the juveniles, felons, and fugitives who today can, with total anonymity and impunity, obtain guns by mail or by crossing into neighboring States with lax or no gun laws at all, regardless of the law of their own State." 114 Cong. Rec. 13647 (1968).

Congressman Celler, the House Manager, stated:

"Mr. Chairman, none of us who support Federal firearms controls believe that any bill or any system of control can guarantee that society will be safe from firearms misuse. But we are convinced that a strengthened system can significantly contribute to reducing the danger of crime in the United States. No one can dispute the need to prevent drug addicts, mental incompetents, persons with a history of mental disturbances, and persons convicted of certain offenses, from buying, owning, or possessing firearms. This bill seeks to maximize the possibility of keeping firearms out of the hands of such persons." Id., at 21784.

Congressman McCulloch, a senior member of the House Committee on the Judiciary, in referring specifically to §922 (a)(6), stated, "[The bill] makes it unlawful . . . for any person, in connection with obtaining a firearm or ammunition from a licensee, to make a false representation material to such acquisition." Id., at 21789. n9 Given these statements of congressional purpose, it would be unwarranted to except pawnshop redemptions when, by virtue of the statutory language itself, such redemptions would be covered. Otherwise every evil Congress hoped to cure would continue unabated. n10

It should be apparent from these statements that Congress was not so much concerned with guaranteeing no interference with the ownership of weapons as it was in distinguishing between law-abiding citizens and those whose possession of weapons would be contrary to the public interest. Hunting, target practice, gun collecting, and the legitimate use of guns for individual protection are not proscribed by the Act.

The Act itself thus contemplates interference with the ownership of weapons when those weapons fall into the hands of juveniles, criminals, drug addicts, and mental incompetents.

n9 It should be apparent from these statements that Congress was not so much concerned with guaranteeing no interference with the ownership of weapons as it was in distinguishing between law-abiding citizens and those whose possession of weapons would be contrary to the public interest. Hunting, target practice, gun collecting, and the legitimate use of guns for individual protection are not proscribed by the Act. Ownership of a weapon, however, may be interfered with by seizure and forfeiture under the Act for any violation of its provisions. Section 924 (d) incorporates the seizure and forfeiture provisions of the Internal Revenue Code when there is any violation of the provisions of the chapter or any rule or regulation thereunder. The Act itself thus contemplates interference with the ownership of weapons when those weapons fall into the hands of juveniles, criminals, drug addicts, and mental incompetents.

n10 What few references there are to pawnbrokers in the debates indicate that Congress was definitely interested in curbing firearms traffic between pawnbrokers and convicted felons. Senator Tydings, a strong proponent of the bill which became the Act, expressed his concern when he compared the bill to a proposal that was offered as an alternative:

We all have seen the virtual arsenals displayed in the windows of pawnshop dealers in all of the major cities of the country.

"One reading through the amendment for the first time would assume that pawnbrokers are covered by the critically important provisions of the affidavit-waiting period procedure. But, if a pawnbroker only receives secondhand weapons as security for the repayment of a loan and does not deal in new firearms, he is not transporting, shipping, or receiving a firearm in interstate or foreign commerce. Used weapons presumably will have come to rest in the hands of the borrower, and the transaction will be wholly intrastate. Such a pawnbroker would not need a Federal firearms license to conduct over-the-counter transactions in firearms. And, accordingly, he would not be a 'licensed dealer' required to comply with the affidavit-waiting period procedure for his over-the-counter sales in handguns. Now, if this analysis is correct, and I believe it is, this is no small omission. Surely the great bulk of criminally irresponsible purchasers of pistols and revolvers buy their weapons secondhand, and many of them from pawnshops. We all have seen the virtual arsenals displayed in the windows of pawnshop dealers in all of the major cities of the country. To say that we have effectively regulated traffic in firearms when we will not have touched the great bulk of these pawnbroker operations is a complete and utter hypocrisy." 114 Cong. Rec. 13222 (1968).

See also Memorandum placed in the record by Senator Dodd. Id., at 13320. Senator Tydings made this further comparison:

"It is obvious that many persons with criminal records purchase from pawnbrokers, and there are many occasions when the pawnbroker knows the criminal background of the client.

"It is obvious that many persons with criminal records purchase from pawnbrokers, and there are many occasions when the pawnbroker knows the criminal background of the client. Under Amendment No. 708, many of these pawnbrokers will not be required to be licensed. They would not need to comply with the affidavit procedure. And even if they were licensed, there would be no prohibition on their selling firearms to known criminals. Under title IV, on the other hand, all of these pawnbrokers would be required to be licensed -- because all dealers and manufacturers must be licensed whether or not they ship, receive, or transport in commerce -- and all of them would be under direct Federal sanction not to sell firearms to known criminals. I ask you, which bill is likely to be more effective?" Id., at 13223.

It must be conceded that these remarks refer to "selling" firearms, but we do not credit this fact as significant for purposes of determining whether a pawnshop redemption is covered by the Act. The plain language of the statute as enacted prohibits a dealer from "selling or disposing of" firearms to felons, and petitioner's counsel at oral argument intimated that a pawnbroker, under this language, could dispose of a firearm other than by sale and be covered by the Act. Tr. of Oral Arg. 4-5. References in the legislative debate, moreover, are replete with shorthand language and this is merely an instance of its use. Had the legislators been engaged in a colloquy on the actual meaning of "sale or other disposition of," we might be more receptive to the interpretation proffered by the petitioner.

the President of the Pawnbrokers' Association of the City of New York testified during congressional hearings that almost all firearm transactions by pawnshops are by pledge and redemption

We also note that the President of the Pawnbrokers' Association of the City of New York testified during congressional hearings that almost all firearm transactions by pawnshops are by pledge and redemption, and contended, therefore, that pawnbrokers should not be included as dealers under the Act. Hearings on a Federal Firearms Act before the Subcommittee to Investigate Juvenile Delinquency of the Senate Committee on the Judiciary, 90th Cong., 1st Sess., 1062-1065 (1967). Thus, informed of the fact that almost all firearms transactions by pawnbrokers were through pledge and redemption, and faced with the argument that pawnbrokers should not be considered as "dealers," Congress clearly chose to retain pawnbrokers as firearms dealers.

Finally, the language of the committee reports indicates that a "sale or disposition" includes "all types of sales or dispositions." S. Rep. No. 1097, 90th Cong., 2d Sess., 115 (1968).

IV

This rule of narrow construction is rooted in the concern of the law for individual rights, and in the belief that fair warning should be accorded as to what conduct is criminal and punishable by deprivation of liberty or property.

The rule is also the product of an awareness that legislators and not the courts should define criminal activity.

sound rules of statutory interpretation exist to discover and not to direct the Congressional will

Although penal laws are to be construed strictly, they "ought not to be construed so strictly as to defeat the obvious intention of the legislature."

Petitioner urges that the intention to include pawn redemptions is so ambiguous and uncertain that the statute should be narrowly construed in his favor. Reliance is placed upon the maxim that an "ambiguity concerning the ambit of criminal statutes should be resolved in favor of lenity." Rewis v. United States, 401 U.S. 808, 812 (1971); United States v. Bass, 404 U.S. 336, 347 (1971). This rule of narrow construction is rooted in the concern of the law for individual rights, and in the belief that fair warning should be accorded as to what conduct is criminal and punishable by deprivation of liberty or property. United States v. Wiltberger, 5 Wheat. 76, 95 (1820); United States v. Bass, 404 U.S., at 348. The rule is also the product of an awareness that legislators and not the courts should define criminal activity. Zeal in forwarding these laudable policies, however, must not be permitted to shadow the understanding that "sound rules of statutory interpretation exist to discover and not to direct the Congressional will." United States ex rel. Marcus v. Hess, 317 U.S. 537, 542 (1943). Although penal laws are to be construed strictly, they "ought not to be construed so strictly as to defeat the obvious intention of the legislature." American Fur Co. v. United States, 2 Pet. 358, 367 (1829); United States v. Wiltberger, supra; United States v. Morris, 14 Pet. 464, 475 (1840); United States v. Lacher, 134 U.S. 624 (1890); United States v. Bramblett, 348 U.S., at 510; United States v. Bass, 404 U.S., at 351.

We perceive no grievous ambiguity or uncertainty in the language and structure of the Act. The statute in question clearly proscribes petitioner's conduct and accorded him fair warning of the sanctions the law placed on that conduct. Huddleston was not short of notice that his actions were unlawful. The question he answered untruthfully was preceded by a warning in boldface type that "an untruthful answer may subject you to criminal prosecution." The question itself was forthright and direct, stating that it was concerned with conviction of a crime punishable by imprisonment for a term exceeding one year and that this meant the term which could have been imposed and not the sentence actually given. Finally, petitioner was required to certify by his signature that his answers were true and correct and that he understood that "the making of any false oral or written statement . . . with respect to this transaction is a crime punishable as a felony." This warning also was in boldface type. Clearly, petitioner had adequate notice and warning of the consequences of his action.

Our reading of the statute cannot be viewed as judicial usurpation of the legislative function. The statute's language reveals an unmistakable attempt to include pawnshop transactions, by pledge or pawn, among the transactions covered by the Act. And Congress unquestionably made it unlawful for dealers, including pawnbrokers, "to sell or otherwise dispose of any firearm" to a convicted felon, a juvenile, a drug addict, or a mental defective. §922 (d). Under these circumstances we will not blindly incant the rule of lenity to "destroy the spirit and force of the law which the legislature intended to [and did] enact." American Tobacco Co. v. Werckmeister, 207 U.S. 284, 293 (1907); United States v. Katz, 271 U.S., at 357. n11

n11 The decision today does not ignore the admonition of the Court in United States v. Bass, 404 U.S. 336, 349 (1971), that "in traditionally sensitive areas, such as legislation affecting the federal balance, the requirement of clear statement assures that the legislature has in fact faced, and intended to bring into issue, the critical matters involved in the judicial decision." This statute did affect the federal balance and it did so intentionally. As Senator Tydings explained:

"This concealed weapons amendment does not violate any State's right to make its own gun laws. Quite the contrary, title IV provides the controls on interstate gun traffic which only the Federal Government can apply, and without which no State gun law is worth the paper it is written on. . . . Without such Federal assistance, any State gun law can be subverted by any child, fugitive, or felon who orders a gun by mail or buys one in a neighboring State which has lax gun laws." 114 Cong. Rec. 13647 (1968).

V

The petitioner suggests, lastly, that the application of §922 (a)(6) to a pawn redemption would raise constitutional questions of some moment, and that these would not arise if the statute were narrowly construed. We fail to see the presence of issues of that import. There was no taking of Huddleston's property without just compensation. The rifles, in fact, were not his but his wife's. Moreover, Congress has determined that a convicted felon may not lawfully obtain weapons of that kind. Nor were petitioner's false answers in any way coerced. United States v. Knox, 396 U.S. 77, 79 (1969); Bryson v. United States, 396 U.S. 64, 72 (1969). Finally, no interstate commerce nexus need be demonstrated. Congress intended, and properly so, that §§922 (a)(6) and (d)(1), in contrast to 18 U.S.C. App. §1202 (a)(1), see United States v. Bass, supra, were to reach transactions that are wholly intrastate, as the Court of Appeals correctly reasoned, "on the theory that such transactions affect interstate commerce." 472 F.2d, at 593. See also United States v. Menna, 451 F.2d 982, 984 (CA9 1971), cert. denied, 405 U.S. 963 (1972), and United States v. O'Neill, 467 F.2d 1372, 1373-1374 (CA2 1972).

We affirm the judgment of the Court of Appeals.

It is so ordered.

MR. JUSTICE DOUGLAS, dissenting.

This case presents a minor version of the problem confronting the Court in Rosenberg v. United States, 346 U.S. 273. That case involved an ambiguity in a criminal law, an ambiguity that normally would be resolved in favor of life. A split Court in a tense period of American history unhappily resolved the ambiguity against life -- a break with history which the conscience of our people will sometime rectify.

A person who took his gun to a pawnshop for a loan undoubtedly had "acquired" the gun prior to that time. It is therefore odd to think of the "acquisition" occurring when he redeemed his own gun from the pawnshop.

The present case is a minor species of the same genus. A person who took his gun to a pawnshop for a loan undoubtedly had "acquired" the gun prior to that time. It is therefore odd to think of the "acquisition" occurring when he redeemed his own gun from the pawnshop. I agree with the Court of Appeals for the Fifth Circuit, United States v. Laisure, 460 F.2d 709, that the ambiguity should be resolved in favor of the accused. That is what we have quite consistently done, except in Rosenberg, in the past. See United States v. Bass, 404 U.S. 336, 347-348, and cases cited. *

For application of a law that sends people to prison for years where Congress has not made it clear they should be there, is only another device as lacking in due process as Caligula's practice of printing the laws in small print and placing them so high on a wall that the ordinary man did not receive fair warning.

* Civil cases cited by the Court, e.g. American Tobacco Co. v. Werckmeister, 207 U.S. 284, 293, are wide of the mark. For application of a law that sends people to prison for years where Congress has not made it clear they should be there, United States v. Bass, supra, at 346, is only another device as lacking in due process as Caligula's practice of printing the laws in small print and placing them so high on a wall that the ordinary man did not receive fair warning.

"When taxes of this kind had been proclaimed, but not published in writing, inasmuch as many offenses were committed through ignorance of the letter of the law, he at last, on the urgent demand of the people, had the law posted up, but in a very narrow place and in excessively small letters, to prevent the making of a copy." Suetonius, The Lives of the Twelve Caesars 192 (Modern Lib. ed. 1931).

UNITED STATES v. POWELL

(FULL CASE)

423 U.S. 87; 96 S. Ct. 316; 46 L. Ed. 2d 228

Argued October 6, 1975

December 2, 1975

GIST: This is an appeal from a conviction for mailing a firearm capable of being concealed on the person. Based on one of the oldest federal gun laws, enacted in 1927, the statute outlawed such mail in order to remove the U.S. Post Office as a vehicle for criminals to arm themselves. Powell advanced both a statutory construction argument and an argument that the statute was unconstitutionally vague. In particular, she claimed the law did not ban mailing a 10-inch barrel, 22-inch overall sawed off shotgun. The Court rejected her arguments, holding that the statute did not apply only to handguns, and that the statute gave adequate notice of the prohibited conduct.

Respondent was convicted of violating 18 U.S.C. §1715, which proscribes mailing pistols, revolvers, and "other firearms capable of being concealed on the person," by having sent a 22-inch sawed-off shotgun through the mails. There was evidence at the trial that the gun could be concealed on an average person. The Court of Appeals reversed, holding that the quoted portion of §1715 was so vague as to violate due process. In addition to the constitutional claim respondent contends that as a matter of statutory construction, particularly in light of the ejusdem generis doctrine, the quoted portion does not embrace sawed-off shotguns. Held:

1. The narrow reading of the statute urged by respondent does not comport with the legislative purpose of making it more difficult for criminals to obtain concealable weapons, and the rule of ejusdem generis may not be used to defeat that purpose. Here a properly instructed jury could have found the shotgun mailed by respondent to have been a "firearm capable of being concealed on the person" within the meaning of §1715.

2. Section 1715 intelligibly forbids a definite course of conduct (mailing concealable firearms) and gave respondent adequate warning that mailing the gun was a criminal offense. That Congress might have chosen [c]learer and more precise language" equally capable of achieving its objective does not mean that the statute is unconstitutionally vague. United States v. Petrillo, 332 U.S. 1, 7.

MR. JUSTICE REHNQUIST delivered the opinion for the Court.

Mrs. Theresa Bailey received by mail an unsolicited package from Spokane, Wash., addressed to her at her home in Tacoma, Wash. The package contained two shotguns, shotgun shells, and 20 or 30 hacksaw blades.

The Court of Appeals in a brief per curiam opinion held that portion of an Act of Congress prohibiting the mailing of firearms "capable of being concealed on the person," 18 U.S.C. §1715, to be unconstitutionally vague, and we granted certiorari to review this determination. 420 U.S. 971 (1975). Respondent was found guilty of having violated the statute by a jury in the United States District Court for the Eastern District of Washington, and was sentenced by that court to a term of two years' imprisonment. The testimony adduced at trial showed that a Mrs. Theresa Bailey received by mail an unsolicited package from Spokane, Wash., addressed to her at her home in Tacoma, Wash. The package contained two shotguns, shotgun shells, and 20 or 30 hacksaw blades.

Mrs. Bailey turned the package over to federal officials, and subsequent investigation disclosed that both of the shotguns had been purchased on the same date. One had been purchased by respondent, and another by an unidentified woman.

While the source of this package was unknown to Mrs. Bailey, its receipt by her not unnaturally turned her thoughts to her husband George, an inmate at nearby McNeil Island Federal Penitentiary.

While the source of this package was unknown to Mrs. Bailey, its receipt by her not unnaturally turned her thoughts to her husband George, an inmate at nearby McNeil Island Federal Penitentiary. Her husband, however, disclaimed any knowledge of the package or its contents. n1 Mrs. Bailey turned the package over to federal officials, and subsequent investigation disclosed that both of the shotguns had been purchased on the same date. One had been purchased by respondent, and another by an unidentified woman.

n1 Respondent's husband, Travis Powell, also was an inmate at McNeil Island.

Ten days after having received the first package, Mrs. Bailey received a telephone call from an unknown woman who advised her that a second package was coming but that "it was a mistake." The caller advised her to give the package to "Sally." When Mrs. Bailey replied that she "did not have the address or any way of giving it to Sally," the caller said she would call back. n2

n2 Mrs. Bailey testified at trial that she did not know "Sally."

Several days later, the second package arrived, and Mrs. Bailey gave it unopened to the investigating agents.

This package contained a sawed-off shotgun with a barrel length of 10 inches and an overall length of 22 1/8 inches, together with two boxes of shotgun shells.

Several days later, the second package arrived, and Mrs. Bailey gave it unopened to the investigating agents. The return address was that of respondent, and it was later determined that the package bore respondent's handwriting. This package contained a sawed-off shotgun with a barrel length of 10 inches and an overall length of 22 1/8 inches, together with two boxes of shotgun shells.

Respondent was indicted on a single count of mailing a firearm capable of being concealed on the person (the sawed-off shotgun contained in the second package), in violation of 18 U.S.C. §1715. At trial there was evidence that the weapon could be concealed on an average person.

Respondent was indicted on a single count of mailing a firearm capable of being concealed on the person (the sawed-off shotgun contained in the second package), in violation of 18 U.S.C. §1715. n3 At trial there was evidence that the weapon could be concealed on an average person. Respondent was convicted by a jury which was instructed that in order to return a guilty verdict it must find that she "knowingly caused to be delivered by mail a firearm capable of being concealed on the person."

n3 Title 18 U.S.C. §1715 provides in pertinent part:

"Pistols, revolvers, and other firearms capable of being concealed on the person are nonmailable....

"Whoever knowingly deposits for mailing or delivery, or knowingly causes to be delivered by mail according to the direction thereon... any pistol, revolver, or firearm declared nonmailable by this section, shall be fined not more than $1,000 or imprisoned not more than two years, or both."

She appealed her judgment of conviction to the Court of Appeals, and that court held that the portion of

§1715 proscribing the mailing of "other firearms capable of being concealed on the person" was so vague that it violated the Due Process Clause of the Fifth Amendment to the United States Constitution. 501 F. 2d 1136 (CA9 1974). Citing Lanzetta v. New Jersey, 306 U.S. 451 (1939), the court held that, although it was clear that a pistol could be concealed on the person, "the statutory prohibition as it might relate to sawed-off shotguns is not so readily recognizable to persons of common experience and intelligence." 501 F. 2d, at 1137.

While the Court of Appeals considered only the constitutional claim, respondent in this Court makes a statutory argument which may fairly be described as an alternative basis for affirming the judgment of that court. She contends that as a matter of statutory construction, particularly in light of the doctrine of ejusdem generis, the language "other firearms capable of being concealed on the person" simply does not extend to sawed-off shotguns. We must decide this threshold question of statutory interpretation first, since if we found the statute inapplicable to respondent, it would be unnecessary to reach the constitutional question, Dandridge v. Williams, 397 U.S. 471, 475-476 (1970).

The thrust of respondent's argument is that the more general language of the statute ("firearms") should be limited by the more specific language ("pistols and revolvers") so that the phrase "other firearms capable of being concealed on the person" would be limited to "concealable weapons such as pistols and revolvers."

We reject this contention. The statute by its terms bans the mailing of "firearms capable of being concealed on the person," and we would be justified in narrowing the statute only if such a narrow reading was supported by evidence of congressional intent over and above the language of the statute.

In Gooch v. United States, 297 U.S. 124, 128 (1936), the Court said:

"The rule of ejusdem generis, while firmly established, is only an instrumentality for ascertaining the correct meaning of words when there is uncertainty. Ordinarily, it limits general terms which follow specific ones to matters similar to those specified; but it may not be used to defeat the obvious purpose of legislation. And, while penal statutes are narrowly construed, this does not require rejection of that sense of the words which best harmonizes with the context and the end in view."

I

It would seem that sawed-off shotguns would be even more likely to be prohibited by local laws than would pistols and revolvers.

The legislative history of this particular provision is sparse, but the House report indicates that the purpose of the bill upon which §1715 is based was to avoid having the Post Office serve as an instrumentality for the violation of local laws which prohibited the purchase and possession of weapons. H. R. Rep. No. 610, 69th Cong., 1st Sess. (1926). It would seem that sawed-off shotguns would be even more likely to be prohibited by local laws than would pistols and revolvers. A statement by the author of the bill, Representative Miller of Washington, on the floor of the House indicates that the purpose of the bill was to make it more difficult for criminals to obtain concealable weapons. 66 Cong. Rec. 726 (1924). To narrow the meaning of the language Congress used so as to limit it to only those weapons which could be concealed as readily as pistols or revolvers would not comport with that purpose. Cf. United States v. Alpers, 338 U.S. 680, 682 (1950).

a properly instructed jury could have found the 22-inch sawed-off shotgun mailed by respondent to have been a "firearm capable of being concealed on the person"

We therefore hold that a properly instructed jury could have found the 22-inch sawed-off shotgun mailed by respondent to have been a "firearm capable of being concealed on the person" within the meaning of 18 U.S.C. §1715. Having done so, we turn to the Court of Appeals' holding that this portion of the statute was unconstitutionally vague.

We said last Term that "[i]t is well established that vagueness challenges to statutes which do not involve First Amendment freedoms must be examined in the light of the facts of the case at hand." United States v. Mazurie, 419 U.S. 544, 550 (1975). The Court of Appeals dealt with the statute generally, rather than as applied to respondent in this case. It must necessarily have concluded, therefore, that the prohibition against mailing "firearms capable of being concealed on the person" proscribed no comprehensible course of conduct at all. It is well settled, of course, that such a statute may not constitutionally be applied to any set of facts. Lanzetta v. New Jersey, 306 U.S., at 453; Connally v. General Constr. Co., 269 U.S. 385, 391 (1926).

An example of such a vague statute is found in United States v. Cohen Grocery Co., 255 U.S. 81, 89 (1921). The statute there prohibited any person from "willfully... mak[ing] any unjust or unreasonable rate or charge in... dealing in or with any necessaries...." So worded it "forbids no specific or definite act" and "leaves open... the widest conceivable inquiry, the scope of which no one can foresee and the result of which no one can foreshadow or adequately guard against." Ibid.

On the other hand, a statute which provides that certain oversized or heavy loads must be transported by the "shortest practicable route" is not unconstitutionally vague. Sproles v. Binford, 286 U.S. 374, 393 (1932). The carrier has been given clear notice that a reasonably ascertainable standard of conduct is mandated; it is for him to insure that his actions do not fall outside the legal limits. The sugar dealer in Cohen, to the contrary, could have had no idea in advance what an "unreasonable rate" would be because that would have been determined by the vagaries of supply and demand, factors over which he had no control. Engaged in a lawful business which Congress had in no way sought to proscribe, he could not have charged any price with the confidence that it would not be later found unreasonable.

we think that the statute gave respondent adequate warning that her mailing of a 22-inch-long sawed-off shotgun was a criminal offense.

But the challenged language of 18 U.S.C. §1715 is quite different from that of the statute involved in Cohen. It intelligibly forbids a definite course of conduct: the mailing of concealable firearms. While doubts as to the applicability of the language in marginal fact situations may be conceived, we think that the statute gave respondent adequate warning that her mailing of a 22-inch-long sawed-off shotgun was a criminal offense. Even as to more doubtful cases than that of respondent, we have said that "the law is full of instances where a man's fate depends on his estimating rightly, that is, as the jury subsequently estimates it, some matter of degree." Nash v. United States, 229 U.S. 373, 377 (1913).

The Court of Appeals questioned whether the "person" referred to in the statute to measure capability of concealment was to be "the person mailing the firearm, the person receiving the firearm, or, perhaps, an average person, male or female, wearing whatever garb might be reasonably appropriate, wherever the place and whatever the season." 501 F. 2d, at 1137. But we think it fair to attribute to Congress the commonsense meaning that such a person would be an average person garbed in a manner to aid, rather than hinder, concealment of the weapons. Such straining to inject doubt as to the meaning of words where no doubt would be felt by the normal reader is not required by the "void for vagueness" doctrine, and we will not indulge in it.

The Court of Appeals also observed that "[t]o require Congress to delimit the size of the firearms (other than pistols and revolvers) that it intends to declare unmailable is certainly to impose no insurmountable burden upon it...." Ibid. Had Congress chosen to delimit the size of the firearms intended to be declared unmailable, it would have written a different statute and in some respects a narrower one than it actually wrote. To the extent that it was intended to proscribe the mailing of all weapons capable of being concealed on the person, a statute so limited would have been less inclusive than the one Congress actually wrote.

But the more important disagreement we have with this observation of the Court of Appeals is that it seriously misconceives the "void for vagueness" doctrine. The fact that Congress might, without difficulty, have chosen "[c]learer and more precise language" equally capable of achieving the end which it sought does not mean that the statute which it in fact drafted is unconstitutionally vague. United States v. Petrillo, 332 U.S. 1, 7 (1947).

The judgment of the Court of Appeals is
Reversed.

MR. JUSTICE STEWART, concurring in part and dissenting in part.

I agree with the Court that the statutory provision before us is not unconstitutionally vague, because I think the provision has an objectively measurable meaning under established principles of statutory construction. Specifically, I think the rule of ejusdem generis is applicable here, and that 18 U.S.C. §1715 must thus be read specifically to make criminal the mailing of a pistol or revolver, or of any firearm as "capable of being concealed on the person" as a pistol or revolver.

The rule of ejusdem generis is applicable in a setting such as this unless its application would defeat the intention of Congress or render the general statutory language meaningless. See United States v. Alpers, 338 U.S. 680, 682; United States v. Salen, 235 U.S. 237, 249-251; United States v. Stever, 222 U.S. 167, 174-175. Application of the rule in the present situation entails neither of those results. Instead of draining meaning from the general language of the statute, an ejusdem generis construction gives to that language an ascertainable and intelligible content. And, instead of defeating the intention of Congress, an ejusdem generis construction coincides with the legislative intent.

The legislative history of the bill on which §1715 was based contains persuasive indications that it was not intended to apply to firearms larger than the largest pistols or revolvers.

Is there anything in this bill that will prevent the citizens of Oklahoma from buying sawed-off shotguns to defend themselves against these bank-robbing bandits?

That may come next.

The legislative history of the bill on which §1715 was based contains persuasive indications that it was not intended to apply to firearms larger than the largest pistols or revolvers. Representative Miller, the bill's author, made it clear that the legislative concern was not with the "shotgun, the rifle, or any firearm used in hunting or by the sportsman." 66 Cong. Rec. 727. As a supporter of the legislation stated: "The purpose... is to prevent the shipment of pistols and revolvers through the mails." 67 Cong. Rec. 12041. The only reference to sawed-off shotguns came in a question posed by Representative McKeown: "Is there anything in this bill that will prevent the citizens of Oklahoma from buying sawed-off shotguns to defend themselves against these bank-robbing bandits?" Representative Blanton, an opponent of the bill, responded: "That may come next. Sometimes a revolver is more necessary than a sawed-off shotgun." 66 Cong. Rec. 729. In the absence of more concrete indicia of legislative intent, the pregnant silence that followed Representative Blanton's response can surely be taken as an indication that Congress intended the law to reach only weapons of the same general size as pistols and revolvers.

I would vacate the judgment of the Court of Appeals and remand the case to that court for further proceedings consistent with these views.

BARRETT v. UNITED STATES

(FULL CASE)

423 U.S. 212; 96 S. Ct. 498; 46 L. Ed. 2d 450

Argued November 4, 1975

January 13, 1976

GIST: Pearl Barrett was caught and convicted of housebreaking, a felony in Kentucky, and received a two-year sentence. Five years later, he walked into an auto parts store, owned by the local dentist in Booneville, Ky., his home town, and bought a .32 caliber Smith and Wesson revolver. The dentist knew him, and skipped filling out the required 4473 form. Within an hour, Barrett had gotten himself liquored up and arrested for driving while intoxicated; the county sheriff who made the arrest found Barrett's fully loaded gun lying on the floorboard on the driver's side.

This time, Barrett was convicted of receiving a firearm that had been shipped in interstate commerce. Barrett tried to wiggle out of his conviction by claiming he was outside the scope of the law because he bought the gun at a local dealer in his state of residence. He suggested that Congress had only meant to reach felons who were acting in some interstate way, not merely intrastate transactions with a gun that might have, at some time in the past, traveled across state lines. The gun had been made in Massachusetts, shipped to a distributor in North Carolina, and then to the Kentucky dentist.

The Court had little difficulty rejecting it. The Court held that the government need not prove the defendant had participated in the interstate shipment of the firearm. Rather, the government need only prove that at some point the firearm had crossed state lines. Because Barrett had not filled out a 4473 form, he faced no issues related to making false statements.

The provision of the Gun Control Act of 1968, 18 U.S.C. §922(h), making it unlawful for a convicted felon, inter alia, "to receive any firearm or ammunition which has been shipped or transported in interstate or foreign commerce," held to apply to a convicted felon's intrastate purchase from a retail dealer of a firearm that previously, but independently of the felon's receipt, had been transported in interstate commerce from the manufacturer to a distributor and then from the distributor to the dealer.

MR. JUSTICE BLACKMUN delivered the opinion of the Court.

Petitioner Pearl Barrett has been convicted by a jury in the United States District Court for the Eastern District of Kentucky of a violation of 18 U.S.C.§922 (h), n1 a part of the Gun Control Act of 1968, Pub. L. 90-618, 82 Stat. 1213, amending the Omnibus Crime Control and Safe Streets Act of 1968, Pub. L. 90-351, 82 Stat. 197, enacted earlier the same year. The issue before us is whether §922 (h) has application to a purchaser's intrastate acquisition of a firearm that previously, but independently of the purchaser's receipt, had been transported in interstate commerce from the manufacturer to a distributor and then from the distributor to the dealer.

n1 " §922. Unlawful acts.

. . . . .

"(h) It shall be unlawful for any person -

"(1) who is under indictment for, or who has been convicted in any court of, a crime punishable by imprisonment for a term exceeding one year;

"(2) who is a fugitive from justice;

"(3) who is an unlawful user of or addicted to marihuana or any depressant or stimulant drug (as defined in section 201 (v) of the Federal Food, Drug, and Cosmetic Act) or narcotic drug (as defined in section 4731 (a) of the Internal Revenue Code of 1954); or

"(4) who has been adjudicated as a mental defective or who has been committed to any mental institution;

"to receive any firearm or ammunition which has been shipped or transported in interstate or foreign commerce."

I

On April 1, 1972, he purchased a .32-caliber Smith & Wesson revolver over the counter from a Western Auto Store in Booneville, Ky.

In January 1967, petitioner was convicted in a Kentucky state court of housebreaking. He received a two year sentence. On April 1, 1972, he purchased a .32-caliber Smith & Wesson revolver over the counter from a Western Auto Store in Booneville, Ky., where petitioner resided. n2 The vendor, who was a local dentist as well as the owner of the store, and who was acquainted with petitioner, was a federally licensed firearms dealer. The weapon petitioner purchased had been manufactured in Massachusetts, shipped by the manufacturer to a distributor in North Carolina, and then received by the Kentucky dealer from the distributor in March 1972, a little less than a month prior to petitioner's purchase. The sale to Barrett was the firearm's first retail transaction. It was the only handgun then in the dealer's stock. Tr. 36-47.

n2 Petitioner at the time of the purchase was not asked to complete Treasury Form 4473, designed for use in the enforcement of the gun control provisions of the statute. Tr. 45-47. Accordingly, there is no issue here as to the making of any false statement, in violation of §922(a)(6). See Huddleston v. United States, 415 U.S. 814 (1974)

Within an hour after the purchase petitioner was arrested by a county sheriff for driving while intoxicated. The firearm, fully loaded, was on the floorboard of the car on the driver's side.

Within an hour after the purchase petitioner was arrested by a county sheriff for driving while intoxicated. The firearm, fully loaded, was on the floorboard of the car on the driver's side.

Petitioner was charged with a violation of §922 (h). He pleaded not guilty. At the trial no evidence was presented to show that Barrett personally had participated in any way in the previous interstate movement of the firearm. The evidence was merely to the effect that he had purchased the revolver out of the local dealer's stock, and that the gun, having been manufactured and then warehoused in other States, had reached the dealer through interstate channels. At the close of the prosecution's case, Barrett moved for a directed verdict of acquittal on the ground that §922 (h) was not applicable to his receipt of the firearm. n3 The motion was denied. The court instructed the jury that the statute's interstate requirement was satisfied if the firearm at some time in its past had traveled in interstate commerce. n4 A verdict of guilty was returned. Petitioner received a sentence of three years, subject to the immediate parole eligibility provisions of 18 U.S.C. §4208 (a)(2).

n3 The defense also moved to quash the indictment on the ground that on June 20, 1969, the Governor of Kentucky, by executive order in the nature of a pardon, had granted petitioner "all the rights of citizenship denied him in consequence of said judgment of conviction." It was suggested that this served to wipe out petitioner's state felony conviction of January 1967. The motion to quash was denied. The same argument was made in the Court of Appeals, but that court unanimously rejected it for reasons stated in the court's respective majority and dissenting opinions. 504 F. 2d 629, 632-634 (CA6 1974). The issue is not presented here.

n4 "Now, interstate commerce, ladies and gentlemen, is the movement of something of value from one political subdivision, which we call a state, to another political subdivision, which we call a state. Interstate commerce occurs when something of value crosses a state boundary line. Now, if you believe that from this evidence... the firearm in question was manufactured in a state other than Kentucky, then you are entitled to make the permissible inference that in order for that firearm to be physically located in Kentucky,... it had to be engaged in interstate transportation at some point or another, but this is a permissible inference. You are not required to make that inference unless you believe from the evidence that that is a logical, reasonable determination to make from the facts." Tr. 99-100.

On appeal, the Court of Appeals affirmed by a divided vote on the question before us. 504 F. 2d 629 (CA6 1974). Because of the importance of the issue and because the Sixth Circuit's decision appeared to have overtones of conflict with the opinion and decision of the United States Court of Appeals for the Eighth Circuit in United States v. Ruffin, 490 F. 2d 557 (1974), we granted certiorari limited to the §922 (h) issue. 420 U.S. 923 (1975).

II

Petitioner concedes that Congress, under the Commerce Clause of the Constitution, has the power to regulate interstate trafficking in firearms.

Petitioner concedes that Congress, under the Commerce Clause of the Constitution, has the power to regulate interstate trafficking in firearms. Brief for Petitioner 7. He states, however, that the issue before us concerns the scope of Congress' exercise of that power in this statute. He argues that, in its enactment of §922 (h), Congress was interested in "the business of gun traffic," Brief for Petitioner 11; that the Act was meant "to deal with businesses, not individuals per se" (emphasis in original), id., at 14, that is, with mail-order houses, out-of-state sources, and the like; and that the Act was not intended to, and does not, reach an isolated intrastate receipt, such as Barrett's transaction, where the handgun was sold within Kentucky by a local merchant to a local resident with whom the merchant was acquainted, and where the transaction "has no apparent connection with interstate commerce," despite the weapon's manufacture and original distribution in States other than Kentucky. Id., at 6.

We feel, however, that the language of §922 (h), the structure of the Act of which §922 (h) is a part, and the manifest purpose of Congress are all adverse to petitioner's position.

A. Section 922 (h) pointedly and simply provides that it is unlawful for four categories of persons, including a convicted felon, "to receive any firearm or ammunition which has been shipped or transported in interstate or foreign commerce." The quoted language is without ambiguity. It is directed unrestrictedly at the felon's receipt of any firearm that "has been" shipped in interstate commerce. It contains no limitation to a receipt which itself is part of the interstate movement. We therefore have no reason to differ with the Court of Appeals' majority's conclusion that the language "means exactly what it says." 504 F. 2d, at 632.

It is to be noted, furthermore, that while the proscribed act, "to receive any firearm," is in the present tense, the interstate commerce reference is in the present perfect tense, denoting an act that has been completed. Thus, there is no warping or stretching of language when the statute is applied to a firearm that already has completed its interstate journey and has come to rest in the dealer's showcase at the time of its purchase and receipt by the felon. Congress knew the significance and meaning of the language it employed. It used the present perfect tense elsewhere in the same section, namely, in §922(h)(1) (a person who "has been convicted"), and in §922 (h)(4) (a person who "has been adjudicated" or who "has been committed"), in contrast to its use of the present tense ("who is") in §§922 (h)(1), (2), and (3). The statute's pattern is consistent and no unintended misuse of language or of tense is apparent.

Had Congress intended to confine §922 (h) to direct interstate receipt, it would have so provided, just as it did in other sections of the Gun Control Act. See §922 (a)(3) (declaring it unlawful for a nonlicensee to receive in the State where he resides a firearm purchased or obtained "by such person outside that State"); §922(j) (prohibiting the receipt of a stolen firearm "moving as... interstate... commerce"); and §922 (k)(prohibiting the receipt "in interstate... commerce" of a firearm the serial number of which has been removed). Statutes other than the Gun Control Act similarly utilize restrictive language when only direct interstate commerce is to be reached. See, e.g., 18 U.S.C. §§659, 1084, 1201, 1231, 1951, 1952, 2313, 2315, and 2421, and 15 U.S.C. §77e. As we have said, there is no ambiguity in the words of §922 (h), and there is no justification for indulging in uneasy statutory construction. United States v. Wiltberger, 5 Wheat. 76, 95-96 (1820); Yates v. United States, 354 U.S. 298, 305 (1957); Huddleston v. United States, 415 U.S. 814, 831 (1974). See United States v. Sullivan, 332 U.S. 689, 696 (1948). There is no occasion here to resort to a rule of lenity, see Rewis v. United States, 401 U.S. 808, 812 (1971); United States v. Bass, 404 U.S. 336,

347 (1971), for there is no ambiguity that calls for a resolution in favor of lenity. A criminal statute, to be sure, is to be strictly construed, but it is "not to be construed so strictly as to defeat the obvious intention of the legislature." American Fur Co. v. United States, 2 Pet. 358, 367 (1829); Huddleston v. United States, 415 U.S., at 831.

The very structure of the Gun Control Act demonstrates that Congress did not intend merely to restrict interstate sales but sought broadly to keep firearms away from the persons Congress classified as potentially irresponsible and dangerous. These persons are comprehensively barred by the Act from acquiring firearms by any means.

B. The very structure of the Gun Control Act demonstrates that Congress did not intend merely to restrict interstate sales but sought broadly to keep firearms away from the persons Congress classified as potentially irresponsible and dangerous. These persons are comprehensively barred by the Act from acquiring firearms by any means. Thus, §922 (d) prohibits a licensee from knowingly selling or otherwise disposing of any firearm (whether in an interstate or intrastate transaction, see Huddleston v. United States, 415 U.S., at 833) to the same categories of potentially irresponsible persons. If §922 (h) were to be construed as petitioner suggests, it would not complement §922 (d), and a gap in the statute's coverage would be created, for then, although the licensee is prohibited from selling either interstate or intrastate to the designated person, the vendee is not prohibited from receiving unless the transaction is itself interstate.

Similarly, §922 (g) prohibits the same categories of potentially irresponsible persons from shipping or transporting any firearm in interstate commerce or, see 18 U.S.C. §2 (b), causing it to be shipped interstate. Petitioner's proposed narrow construction of §922 (h) would reduce that section to a near redundancy with §922 (g), since almost every interstate shipment is likely to have been solicited or otherwise caused by the direct recipient. That proposed narrow construction would also create another anomaly: if a prohibited person seeks to buy from his local dealer a firearm that is not currently in the dealer's stock, and the dealer then orders it interstate, that person violates §922(h), but under the suggested construction, he would not violate §922(h) if the firearm were already on the dealer's shelf.

We note, too, that other sections of the Act clearly apply to and regulate intrastate sales of a gun that has moved in intrastate commerce. For example, the licensing provisions, §§922(a)(1) and 923(a), apply to exclusively intrastate, as well as interstate, activity. Under §922 (d), as noted above, a licensee may not knowingly sell a firearm to any prohibited person, even if the sale is intrastate. Huddleston v. United States, 415 U.S., at 833. Sections 922 (c) and (a)(6), relating, respectively, to a physical presence at the place of purchase and to the giving of false information, apply to intrastate as well as to interstate transactions. So, too, do §§922 (b)(2) and (5).

Construing §922 (h) as applicable to an intrastate retail sale that has been preceded by movement of the firearm in interstate commerce is thus consistent with the entire pattern of the Act. To confine §922 (h) to direct interstate receipts would result in having the Gun Control Act cover every aspect of intrastate transactions in firearms except receipt. This, however, and obviously, is the most crucial of all. Congress surely did not intend to except from the direct prohibitions of the statute the very act it went to such pains to prevent indirectly, through complex provisions, in the other sections of the Act.

The new Act also added many prophylactic provisions

the 1938 Act, it was said, was designed "to prevent the crook and gangster, racketeer and fugitive from justice from being able to purchase or in any way come in contact with firearms of any kind."

C. The legislative history is fully supportive of our construction of §922 (h). The Gun Control Act of 1968 was an amended and, for present purposes, a substantially identical version of Title IV of the Omnibus Crime Control and Safe Streets Act of 1968. Each of the statutes enlarged and extended the Federal Firearms Act, 52 Stat. 1250 (1938). Section 922 (h), although identical in its operative phrase with §2 (f) of the Federal Firearms Act, expanded the categories of persons prohibited from receiving firearms. n5 The new Act also added many prophylactic provisions, hereinabove referred to, governing intrastate as well as interstate transactions. See Zimring, Firearms and Federal Law: The Gun Control Act of 1968, 4 J. Legal Studies 133 (1975). But the 1938 Act, it was said, was designed "to prevent the crook and gangster, racketeer and fugitive from justice from being able to purchase or in any way come in contact with firearms of any kind." S. Rep. No. 1189, 75th Cong., 1st Sess., 33 (1937). Nothing we have found in the committee reports or hearings on the 1938 legislation indicates any intention on the part of Congress to confine §2 (f) to direct interstate receipt of firearms.

n5 Section 2 (f) provided:

"It shall be unlawful for any person who has been convicted of a crime of violence or is a fugitive [sic] from justice to receive any firearm or ammunition which has been shipped or transported in interstate or foreign commerce...." 52 Stat. 1251.

The history of the 1968 Act reflects a similar concern with keeping firearms out of the hands of categories of potentially irresponsible persons, including convicted felons. Its broadly stated principal purpose was "to make it possible to keep firearms out of the hands of those not legally entitled to possess them because of age, criminal background, or incompetency."

The history of the 1968 Act reflects a similar concern with keeping firearms out of the hands of categories of potentially irresponsible persons, including convicted felons. Its broadly stated principal purpose was "to make it possible to keep firearms out of the hands of those not legally entitled to possess them because of age, criminal background, or incompetency." S. Rep. No. 1501, 90th Cong., 2d Sess., 22 (1968). See also 114 Cong. Rec. 13219 (1968) (remarks by Sen. Tydings); Huddleston v. United States, 415 U.S., at 824-825. Congressman Celler, the House Manager, expressed the same concern: "This bill seeks to maximize the possibility of keeping firearms out of the hands of such persons." 114 Cong. Rec. 21784 (1968); Huddleston v. United States, 415 U.S., at 828. In the light of this principal purpose, Congress could not have intended that the broad and unambiguous language of §922 (h) was to be confined, as petitioner suggests, to direct interstate receipts. That suggestion would remove from the statute the most usual transaction, namely, the felon's purchase or receipt from his local dealer.

III

Two statements of this Court in past cases, naturally relied upon by petitioner, deserve mention. The first is an observation made over 30 years ago in reference to the 1938 Act's §2 (f), the predecessor of §922(h):

"Both courts below held that the offense created by the Act is confined to the receipt of firearms or ammunition as a part of interstate transportation and does not extend to the receipt, in an intrastate transaction, of such articles which, at some prior time, have been transported interstate. The Government agrees that this construction is correct." Tot v. United States, 319 U.S. 463, 466 (1943).

In that case, the Court held that the presumption contained in §2(f), to the effect that "the possession of a firearm or ammunition by any such person [one convicted of a crime of violence or a fugitive from justice] shall be presumptive evidence that such firearm or ammunition was shipped or transported or received, as the case may be, by such person in violation of this Act," was violative of due process.

The quoted observation, of course, is merely a recital as to what the District Court and the Court of Appeals in that case had held and a further statement that the Government had agreed that the construction by the lower courts was correct. Having made this observation, the Court then understandably moved on to the only issue in Tot, namely, the validity of the statutory presumption. The fact that the Government long ago took a narrow position on the reach of the 1938 Act may not serve to help its posture here, when it seemingly argues to the contrary, but it does not prevent the Government from arguing that the current gun control statute is broadly based and reaches a purchase such as that made by Barrett. n6

There is, of course, no rule of law to the effect that the Government must be consistent in its stance in litigation over the years.

n6 There is, of course, no rule of law to the effect that the Government must be consistent in its stance in litigation over the years. It has changed positions before. See, e.g., Automobile Club of Michigan v. Commissioner, 353 U.S. 180, 183 (1957).

The second statement is more recent and appears in United States v. Bass, supra. n7 The Bass comment, of course, is dictum, for Bass had to do with a prosecution under 18 U.S.C. §1202(a), a provision which was part of Title VII, not of Title IV, of the Omnibus Crime Control and Safe Streets Act of 1968, as amended. Section 1202(a) concerned any member of stated categories of persons "who receives, possesses, or transports in commerce or affecting commerce... any firearm." The Government contended that the statute did not require proof of a connection with interstate commerce. The Court held, however, that the statute was ambiguous and that, therefore, it must be read to require such a nexus. In so holding, the Court noted the connection between Title VII and Title IV, and observed that although subsections of the two Titles addressed their prohibitions to some of the same people, each also reached groups not reached by the other. Then followed the dictum in question. The Court went on to state:

"While the reach of Title IV itself is a question to be decided finally some other day, the Government has presented here no learning or other evidence indicating that the 1968 Act changed the prior approach to the 'receipt' offense." 404 U.S., at 343 n. 10.

n7 "Even under respondent's view, a Title VII offense is made out if the firearm was possessed or received 'in commerce or affecting commerce'; however, Title IV apparently does not reach possessions or intrastate transactions at all, even those with an interstate commerce nexus, but is limited to the sending or receiving of firearms as part of an interstate transportation." 404 U.S. 336, 342-343 (1971).

The Bass dictum was just another observation made in passing as the Court proceeded to consider §1202 (a). The observation went so far as to intimate that Title IV was to be limited even with respect to a transaction possessing an interstate commerce nexus, a situation that Barrett here concedes is covered by §922 (h). In any event, the Court, by its statement in n.10 of the Bass opinion, reserved the question of the reach of Title IV for "some other day." That day is now at hand, with Barrett's case before us. And it is at hand with the benefit of full briefing and an awareness of the plain language of §922 (h), of the statute's position in the structure of the entire Act, and of the legislative aims and purpose.

Furthermore, we are not willing to decide the present case on the assumption that Congress, in passing the Gun Control Act 25 years after Tot was decided, had the Court's casual recital in Tot in mind when it used language identical to that in the 1938 Act. n8 There is one mention of Tot in the debates, 114 Cong. Rec. 21807 (1968), and one mention in the reports, S. Rep. No. 1097, 90th Cong., 2d Sess., 272 (1968) (additional views of Sens. Dirksen, Hruska, Thurmond, and Burdick). These reflect a concern with the fact that Tot eliminated the presumption of interstate movement, thus increasing the burden of proof on the Government. They do not focus on what showing was necessary to carry that burden of proof. Similarly, the few references to Tot in the hearings reflect objections to the elimination of the presumption, but mention only in passing the type of proof that the witness believed was necessary to satisfy §2 (f). See, e.g., Hearings on S. 1, Amendment 90 to S. 1, S. 1853, and S. 1854 before Subcommittee to Investigate Juvenile Delinquency of the Senate Committee on the Judiciary, 90th Cong., 1st Sess., 46 (1967); Hearings on H. R. 5037, H. R. 5038, H. R. 5384, H. R. 5385, and H. R. 5386 before Subcommittee No. 5 of the House Committee on the Judiciary, 90th Cong., 1st Sess., 561-562, 564, 677-678. Nothing in this legislative history persuades us that Congress intended to adopt Tot's limited interpretation. If we were to conclude otherwise, we would fly in the face of, and ignore, obvious congressional intent at the price of a passing recital. See Girouard v. United States, 328 U.S. 61, 69-70 (1946). To hold, as the Court did in Bass, 404 U.S., at 350, that Title VII, directed to a receipt of any firearm "in commerce or affecting commerce," requires only a showing that the firearm received previously traveled in interstate commerce, but that Title IV, relating to a receipt of any firearm "which has been shipped or transported in interstate... commerce," is limited to the receipt of the firearm as part of an interstate movement, would be inconsistent construction of sections of the same Act and, indeed, would be downgrading the stronger language and upgrading the weaker.

Congressional inaction frequently betokens unawareness, preoccupation, or paralysis.

n8 "The verdict of quiescent years cannot be invoked to baptize a statutory gloss that is otherwise impermissible. This Court has many times reconsidered statutory constructions that have been passively abided by Congress. Congressional inaction frequently betokens unawareness, preoccupation, or paralysis." Zuber v. Allen, 396 U.S. 168, 185-186, n. 21 (1969).

We conclude that §922(h) covers the intrastate receipt, such as petitioner's purchase here, of a firearm that previously had moved in interstate commerce. The judgment of the Court of Appeals, accordingly, is affirmed.

It is so ordered.

MR. JUSTICE STEVENS took no part in the consideration or decision of this case.

MR. JUSTICE WHITE, concurring.

In meeting petitioner's contention that Tot v. United States, 319 U.S. 463 (1943), necessarily confines the offense created by 18 U.S.C. §922(h) to the receipt of a firearm in the course of an interstate shipment, the Court reads the Tot opinion as reciting but not adopting the lower courts' holdings that §2(f) of the Federal Firearms Act of 1938 did not cover the intrastate receipt of a firearm that previously had moved in interstate commerce. Ante, at 221-222. I join the Court in this respect. Also, I find its construction of §922(h) to be correct even if it is assumed, as MR. JUSTICE STEWART concludes, post, at 228-230, and n. 3, that the Tot decision did adopt the more limited construction of §2(f).

Section 2(f) of the Federal Firearms Act of 1938, 52 Stat. 1251, at issue in Tot, read as follows:

"It shall be unlawful for any person who has been convicted of a crime of violence or is a fug[i]tive from justice to receive any firearm or ammunition which has been shipped or transported in interstate or foreign commerce, and the possession of a firearm or ammunition by any such person shall be presumptive evidence that such firearm or ammunition was shipped or transported or received, as the case may be, by such person in violation of this Act."

The opening words of the section broadly describing the statutory violation as receiving a firearm which "has been shipped or transported" in interstate commerce were immediately followed by a provision that it could be presumed from possession alone that the defendant possessor had personally participated in the interstate movement of the possessed firearm. Had Congress intended to proscribe the mere intrastate receipt by a defendant of a gun which had previously moved in interstate commerce without any involvement by the defendant in that movement, there would have been little or no reason to provide that his personal participation in the interstate movement could be inferred from his possession alone. Proof of personal possession and previous interstate movement independent of any act of the defendant, which would be sufficient to make out intrastate receipt of a firearm which had previously moved in interstate commerce, requires no such presumptive assistance.

In this light it is not surprising that the otherwise broad language of the statute, which was not limited to receipts that were themselves part of the interstate movement, was nonetheless understood to reach only receipts directly involved in interstate commerce. Tot v. United States, supra, it is argued, so understood the statute. Striking down the presumption did not remove this gloss from the language defining the violation. Thus after Tot, and as long as Congress left §2(f) intact, to establish a violation of §2(f) it was necessary to prove that a convicted felon found in possession of a firearm actually participated in an interstate shipment.

When §922(h) was enacted, however, Congress omitted the presumptive language of the prior statute and removed any basis for reading the plain language of the statute to reach only receipts of firearms which have moved in interstate commerce with the aid or participation of the defendant. That the plain language of §922(h) contains no limitation to receipts which are themselves part of an interstate movement is not disputed. Instead the argument is that by reenacting the initial language of §2(f) Congress intended to maintain the restricted meaning even though it dropped the presumption which had provided the gloss and added nothing in its stead.

It is noted that Congress was aware that after Tot, "in order to establish a violation of this statute, it is necessary to prove that a convicted felon found in possession of a firearm actually received it in the course of an interstate shipment." * From this it is inferred that in enacting §922(h) Congress adopted Tot's interpretation of the glossed language of §2(f). But the quoted statement simply describes the continuing effect of the gloss provided by the language of the invalidated presumption in §2(f). Congressional awareness of the effect of Tot does not overcome the concededly plain language of §922(h) or the force of the Court's analysis of the statutory scheme of which it is a part. Ante, at 216-219. Indeed I find that congressional understanding of the history of §2(f), first with and then without its presumption, supports the Court's determination that §922(h) "covers the intrastate receipt... of a firearm that previously had moved in interstate commerce." Ante, at 225.

* Hearings on S. 1, Amendment 90 to S. 1, S. 1853, and S. 1854 before Subcommittee to Investigate Juvenile Delinquency of the Senate Committee on the Judiciary, 90th Cong., 1st Sess., 46 (1967). See also Hearings on H.R. 5037, H.R. 5038, H.R. 5384, H.R. 5385, and H.R. 5386 before Subcommittee No. 5 of the House Committee on the Judiciary, 90th Cong., 1st Sess., 561 (1967).

MR. JUSTICE STEWART, with whom MR. JUSTICE REHNQUIST joins, dissenting.

The petitioner in this case, a former convict, was arrested for driving while intoxicated. A revolver, fully loaded, was found on the floorboard of his car. These circumstances are offensive to those who believe in law and order. They are particularly offensive to those concerned with the need to control handguns.

The petitioner in this case, a former convict, was arrested for driving while intoxicated. A revolver, fully loaded, was found on the floorboard of his car. These circumstances are offensive to those who believe in law and order. They are particularly offensive to those concerned with the need to control handguns. While I understand these concerns, I cannot join the Court in its rush to judgment, because I believe that as a matter of law the petitioner was simply not guilty of the federal statutory offense of which he stands convicted.

The petitioner bought a revolver from the Western Auto Store in Booneville, Ky., in an over-the-counter retail sale. Within an hour, he was arrested for driving while intoxicated and the revolver was found on the floorboard of his car. The revolver had been manufactured in Massachusetts and shipped to the Booneville retailer from a North Carolina distributor. The prosecution submitted no evidence of any kind that the petitioner had participated in any interstate activity involving the revolver, either before or after its purchase. On these facts, he was convicted of violating 18 U.S.C. §922(h), which makes it unlawful for a former criminal offender like the petitioner, "to receive any firearm or ammunition which has been shipped or transported in interstate or foreign commerce."

This clause first appeared in the predecessor of §922(h), §2(f) of the Federal Firearms Act of 1938, 52 Stat. 1250, 1251. n1 In Tot v. United States, 319 U.S. 463 (1943), the Court interpreted this statutory language to prohibit only receipt of firearms or ammunition as part of an interstate transaction:

"Both courts below held that the offense created by the Act is confined to the receipt of firearms or ammunition as a part of interstate transportation and does not extend to the receipt, in an intrastate transaction, of such articles which, at some prior time, have been transported interstate. The Government agrees that this construction is correct." Id., at 466.

n1 Section 2(f) of the Federal Firearms Act provided:

"It shall be unlawful for any person who has been convicted of a crime of violence or is a fug[i]tive from justice to receive any firearm or ammunition which has been shipped or transported in interstate or foreign commerce, and the possession of a firearm or ammunition by any such person shall be presumptive evidence that such firearm or ammunition was shipped or transported or received, as the case may be, by such person in violation of this Act."

Although the Tot Court was principally concerned with the constitutionality of the presumption established by the last clause of §2(f), n2 its interpretation of the first clause of the statute was essential to its holding. n3 The statutory presumption was that possession of a firearm or ammunition by any person in the class specified in §2(f) established receipt in violation of the statute. The Court in Tot held the presumption unconstitutional for lack of a rational connection between the fact proved and the facts presumed. 319 U.S., at 467-468. The Court could not have reached that decision without first determining what set of facts needed to exist in order to constitute a violation of the statute.

n2 See n. 1, supra.

n3 The Court today reads the Tot opinion as only attributing this interpretation to the courts below and to the Government, and not as adopting it. Ante, at 221-222. This reading is mistaken, for in rejecting an argument premised on the power of Congress to prohibit all possession of firearms by felons, the Tot opinion stated:

"[I]t is plain that Congress, for whatever reason, did not seek to pronounce general prohibition of possession by certain residents of the various states of firearms in order to protect interstate commerce, but dealt only with their future acquisition in interstate commerce." 319 U.S., at 472 (emphasis added).

The Tot case did not go unnoticed when 18 U.S.C. §922(h) was enacted in its present form in 1968, as the legislative history clearly reveals. Subcommittees of both the Senate and House Judiciary Committees in 1967 conducted hearings on bills to amend the Federal Firearms Act. At both hearings, the Commissioner of Internal Revenue explained the decision in Tot:

"The Supreme Court declared [the presumption in §2(f)] unconstitutional in a 1943 case, Tot v. United States, 319 U.S. 463. Consequently, in order to establish a violation of this statute, it is necessary to prove that a convicted felon found in possession of a firearm actually received it in the course of an interstate shipment." Hearings on S. 1, Amendment 90 to S. 1, S. 1853, and S. 1854 before Subcommittee to Investigate Juvenile Delinquency of the Senate Committee on the Judiciary, 90th Cong., 1st Sess., 46 (1967).

"The Supreme Court has declared [the presumption in §2(f)] unconstitutional. In order to establish the violation of the statute it is necessary to find that the felon found in possession of the firearm actually received it in the course of interstate commerce or transportation." Hearings on H.R. 5037, H.R. 5038, H.R. 5384, H.R. 5385, and H.R. 5386 before Subcommittee No. 5 of the House Committee on the Judiciary, 90th Cong., 1st Sess., 561 (1967). n4l

n4 See also these at Hearings 575 (1967) (statement of Commissioner of Internal Revenue) 629-630, 677-678 (statements of other witnesses).

In both hearings, the Commissioner was speaking in support of bills that omitted the presumption held unconstitutional in Tot, but that otherwise retained the same language there construed. See Hearings on S. 1, Amendment 90 to S. 1, S. 1853, and S. 1854, supra, at 16, 43-44; Hearings on H. R. 5037, H. R. 5038, H. R. 5384, H. R. 5385, and H. R. 5386, supra, at 13, 555. That is precisely the form in which the statute now before us, §922(h), was enacted in 1968. It is thus evident that Congress was aware of Tot and adopted its interpretation of the statutory language in enacting the present law. See Francis v. Southern Pacific Co., 333 U.S. 445, 449-450 (1948); Apex Hosiery Co. v. Leader, 310 U.S. 469, 488-489 (1940); Commissioner v. Estate of Church, 335 U.S. 632, 682, 690 (1949) (Frankfurter, J., dissenting). n5

n5 The cases relied upon by the Court, ante, at 223 n. 8 and 224, stand for the quite different proposition that where it cannot be shown that Congress was aware of a decision of this Court interpreting a statute, such awareness cannot be presumed: Zuber v. Allen, 396 U.S. 168, 185-186, n. 21 (1969); Girouard v. United States, 328 U.S. 61, 69-70 (1946).

Just four years ago, in United States v. Bass, 404 U.S. 336 (1971), the Court expressly stated that it found nothing to indicate "that the 1968 Act changed the prior approach to the 'receipt' offense." Id., at 343 n. 10. I would adhere to the Court's settled interpretation of the statutory language here involved and reverse the judgment of the Court of Appeals.

MOORE v. CITY OF EAST CLEVELAND

(CASE EXCERPT)

431 U.S. 494; 97 S. Ct. 1932; 52 L. Ed. 2d 531

Argued November 2, 1976

May 31, 1977

GIST: This case is a substantive due process case challenging a zoning regulation that prohibited certain family members from living together. In discussing the scope of the 14th Amendment Due Process Clause, both the majority and the dissent quote Justice Harlan's dissent in *Poe v. Ullman* listing the right to keep and bear arms among other constitutional liberties.

MR. JUSTICE POWELL announced the judgment of the Court, and delivered an opinion in which MR. JUSTICE BRENNAN, MR. JUSTICE MARSHALL, and MR. JUSTICE BLACKMUN joined.

.....

"Due process has not been reduced to any formula; its content cannot be determined by reference to any code. The best that can be said is that through the course of this Court's decisions it has represented the balance which our Nation, built upon postulates of respect for the liberty of the individual, has struck between that liberty and the demands of organized society. If the supplying of content to this Constitutional concept has of necessity been a rational process, it certainly has not been one where judges have felt free to roam where unguided speculation might take them. The balance of which I speak is the balance struck by this country, having regard to what history teaches are the traditions from which it developed as well as the traditions from which it broke. That tradition is a living thing. A decision of this Court which radically departs from it could not long survive, while a decision which builds on what has survived is likely to be sound. No formula could serve as a substitute, in this area, for judgment and restraint.

This 'liberty' is not a series of isolated points pricked out in terms of the taking of property; the freedom of speech, press, and religion; the right to keep and bear arms; the freedom from unreasonable searches and seizures; and so on.

"The full scope of the liberty guaranteed by the Due Process Clause cannot be found in or limited by the precise terms of the specific guarantees elsewhere provided in the Constitution. This 'liberty' is not a series of isolated points pricked out in terms of the taking of property; the freedom of speech, press, and religion; the right to keep and bear arms; the freedom from unreasonable searches and seizures; and so on. It is a rational continuum which, broadly speaking, includes a freedom from all substantial arbitrary impositions and purposeless restraints,... and which also recognizes, what a reasonable and sensitive judgment must, that certain interests require particularly careful scrutiny of the state needs asserted to justify their abridgment." Poe v. Ullman (dissenting opinion).

MR. JUSTICE WHITE, dissenting.

.....

The emphasis of the Due Process Clause is on "process." As Mr. Justice Harlan once observed, it has been "ably and insistently argued in response to what were felt to be abuses by this Court of its reviewing power," that the Due Process Clause should be limited "to a guarantee of procedural fairness." These arguments had seemed "persuasive" to Justices Brandeis and Holmes, but they recognized that the Due Process Clause, by virtue of case-to-case "judicial inclusion and exclusion," had been construed to proscribe matters of substance, as well as inadequate procedures, and to protect from invasion by the States "all fundamental rights comprised within the term liberty."

Mr. Justice Black also recognized that the Fourteenth Amendment had substantive as well as procedural content. But believing that its reach should not extend beyond the specific provisions of the Bill of Rights, he never embraced the idea that the Due Process Clause empowered the courts to strike down merely unreasonable or arbitrary legislation, nor did he accept Mr. Justice Harlan's consistent view. Writing at length in dissent in Poe v. Ullman, Mr. Justice Harlan stated the essence of his position as follows:

"This 'liberty' is not a series of isolated points pricked out in terms of the taking of property; the freedom of speech, press, and religion; the right to keep and bear arms; the freedom from unreasonable searches and seizures; and so on. It is a rational continuum which, broadly speaking, includes a freedom from all substantial arbitrary impositions and purposeless restraints and which also recognizes, what a reasonable and sensitive judgment must, that certain interests require particularly careful scrutiny of the state needs asserted to justify their abridgment.

SCARBOROUGH v. UNITED STATES

(FULL CASE)

431 U.S. 563; 97 S. Ct. 1963; 52 L. Ed. 2d 582

Argued March 2, 1977

June 6, 1977; as amended

GIST: This case involves the interpretation of the Gun Control Act's prohibition of firearms possession "in commerce or affecting commerce" by a convicted felon. The Court held that if the firearm had once traveled in interstate commerce, no matter how long ago, that was sufficient to make a case against a violator. The defendant, a convicted drug dealer, also argued that the gun moved in commerce before he was convicted. The Court rejected this argument as any sort of defense, taking a very broad view of the needed nexus between commerce and any gun in question. As with previous Gun Control Act cases, the case was about statutory construction, not whether the Gun Control Act was a constitutionally proper exercise of the interstate commerce power.

In dissent by himself, Justice Stewart wrestles with a problem the Court's decision creates. A person who legally possesses firearms becomes guilty automatically of a serious crime if ever convicted of any felony, as a felon in possession of firearms. The government argues it would be reasonable about this, and that "prosecutorial discretion" would take care of the problem. Proper construction of a criminal statute though, Stewart says, cannot depend upon the good will of those who must enforce it.

In a prosecution for possession of a firearm in violation of the provision of Title VII of the Omnibus Crime Control and Safe Streets Act of 1968, 18 U.S.C. App. §1202(a), making it a crime for a convicted felon to possess "in commerce or affecting commerce" any firearm, proof that the possessed firearm previously traveled at some time in interstate commerce held sufficient to satisfy the statutorily required nexus between possession and commerce. This is so, where, as in this case, the firearm in question traveled in interstate commerce before the accused became a convicted felon; the nexus need not be "contemporaneous" with the possession. Both the text and legislative history of the statute show a congressional intent to require no more than the minimal nexus that the firearm have been, at some time, in interstate commerce and to outlaw possession broadly, with little concern for when the nexus with commerce occurred.

MR. JUSTICE MARSHALL delivered the opinion of the Court.

Petitioner was convicted of possessing a firearm in violation of Title VII of the Omnibus Crime Control and Safe Streets Act of 1968 (Omnibus Crime Control Act), 18 U.S.C. App.§§1201-1203. The statute provides, in pertinent part:

"Any person who -

"(1) has been convicted by a court of the United States or of a State or any political subdivision thereof of a felony...

. . .

"and who receives, possesses, or transports in commerce or affecting commerce... any firearm shall be fined not more than $10,000 or imprisoned for not more than two years, or both." 18 U.S.C. App. §1202(a). n1

n1 Section 1202(a) reads in full:

"(a) Any person who -

"(1) has been convicted by a court of the United States or of a State or any political subdivision thereof of a felony, or

"(2) has been discharged from the Armed Forces under dishonorable conditions, or

"(3) has been adjudged by a court of the United States or of a State or any political subdivision thereof of being mentally incompetent, or

"(4) having been a citizen of the United States has renounced his citizenship, or

"(5) being an alien is illegally or unlawfully in the United States, "who receives, possesses, or transports in commerce or affecting commerce, after the date of enactment of this Act, any firearm shall be fined not more than $10,000 or imprisoned for not more than two years, or both."

The issue in this case is whether proof that the possessed firearm previously traveled in interstate commerce is sufficient to satisfy the statutorily required nexus between the possession of a firearm by a convicted felon and commerce.

I

In 1972 petitioner pleaded guilty in the Circuit Court of Fairfax County, Va., to the felony of possession of narcotics with intent to distribute. A year later, in August 1973, law enforcement officials, in the execution of a search warrant for narcotics, seized four firearms from petitioner's bedroom. Petitioner was subsequently charged with both receipt and possession of the four firearms in violation of 18 U.S.C. App. §1202(a)(1).

In a jury trial in the Eastern District of Virginia, the Government offered evidence to show that all of the seized weapons had traveled in interstate commerce. All the dates established for such interstate travel were prior to the date petitioner became a convicted felon. n2 The Government made no attempt to prove that the petitioner acquired these weapons after his conviction. n3 Holding such proof necessary for a receipt conviction, the judge, at the close of the Government's case, granted petitioner's motion for a judgment of acquittal on that part of the indictment charging receipt.

The Government's evidence showed that the Colt revolver was shipped from Connecticut to North Carolina in 1969 and entered Virginia by unknown means

the Universal Enforcer came from Florida to Virginia in 1969 and was purchased by petitioner in 1970

the M-1 carbine rifle was sent to Maryland from Illinois in 1966, coming to Virginia by unknown means

the St. Etienne Ordinance revolver was manufactured in France in the 19th century and was somehow later brought into Virginia

n2 The Government's evidence showed that the Colt revolver was shipped from Connecticut to North Carolina in 1969 and entered Virginia by unknown means, App. 6-7; that the Universal Enforcer came from Florida to Virginia in 1969 and was purchased by petitioner in 1970, id., at 7-8; that the M-1 carbine rifle was sent to Maryland from Illinois in 1966, coming to Virginia by unknown means, id., at 8-9; and that the St. Etienne Ordinance revolver was manufactured in France in the 19th century and was somehow later brought into Virginia, id., at 9-10.

n3 The Government showed that petitioner bought the Enforcer in 1970. The only evidence regarding acquisition of the other weapons came from petitioner. He claimed he purchased the Colt revolver in 1970, Tr. 88, and the M-1 rifle in 1968, id., at 108. The French revolver, he claimed, was left in his house shortly before the state conviction but he was not sure by whom. Id., at 88, 105.

As a matter of fact, he contended that by the time of his conviction he no longer possessed the firearms. His claim was that, to avoid violating this statute, he had transferred these guns to his wife prior to pleading guilty to the narcotics felony.

Petitioner's defense to the possession charge was twofold. As a matter of fact, he contended that by the time of his conviction he no longer possessed the firearms. His claim was that, to avoid violating this statute, he had transferred these guns to his wife prior to pleading guilty to the narcotics felony. Secondly, he argued that, as a matter of law, proof that the guns had at some time traveled in interstate commerce did not provide an adequate nexus between the possession and commerce. In furtherance of this defense, petitioner requested that the jury be instructed as follows:

"In order for the defendant to be found guilty of the crime with which he is charged, it is incumbent upon the Government to demonstrate a nexus between the 'possession' of the firearms and interstate commerce. For example, a person 'possesses' in commerce or affecting commerce if at the time of the offense the firearms were moving interstate or on an interstate facility, or if the 'possession' affected commerce. It is not enough that the Government merely show that the firearms at some time had travelled in interstate commerce...." App. 12-13.

The judge rejected this instruction. Instead he informed the jury:

"The government may meet its burden of proving a connection between commerce and the possession of a firearm by a convicted felon if it is demonstrated that the firearm possessed by a convicted felon had previously travelled in interstate commerce.

. . .

"It is not necessary that the government prove that the defendant purchased the gun in some state other than that where he was found with it or that he carried it across the state line, nor must the government prove who did purchase the gun." Id., at 14.

Petitioner was found guilty and he appealed. The Court of Appeals for the Fourth Circuit affirmed. 539 F. 2d 331. It held that the interstate commerce nexus requirement of the possession offense was satisfied by proof that the firearm petitioner possessed had previously traveled in interstate commerce. In view of the split among the Circuits on this issue, n4 we granted certiorari. 429 U.S. 815 (1976). n5 We affirm.

n4 Agreeing with the Fourth Circuit that proof of previous interstate movement of the firearm provides a sufficient commerce nexus for the possession offense are the Sixth Circuit, United States v. Jones, 533 F. 2d 1387 (1976), and the Tenth Circuit, United States v. Bumphus, 508 F. 2d 1405 (1975) (dictum).Three other Circuits have indicated that such proof is adequate for a receipt offense but that the possession offense requires that the possession have a contemporaneous nexus with commerce. United States v. Ressler, 536 F. 2d 208 (CA7 1976); United States v. Bell, 524 F. 2d 202 (CA2 1975); United States v. Steeves, 525 F. 2d 33 (CA8 1975) (dictum). The Ninth Circuit apparently has an intra-Circuit conflict. Compare United States v. Malone, 538 F. 2d 250 (1976), and United States v. Cassity, 509 F. 2d 682 (1974), with United States v. Burns, 529 F. 2d 114 (1975).

n5 The grant of the petition was limited to the question "[whether] the Court erred in holding that a conviction under 18 U.S.C. App. §1202(a) for possession of a firearm in commerce or affecting commerce by a convicted felon is sustainable merely upon a showing that the possessed firearm has previously at any time however remote travelled in interstate commerce." Petitioner's Fourth Amendment claim was excluded.

II

Our first encounter with Title VII of the Omnibus Crime Control Act came in United States v. Bass, 404 U.S. 336 (1971). There we had to decide whether the statutory phrase "in commerce or affecting commerce" in §1202(a) applied to "possesses" and "receives" as well as to "transports." We noted that the statute was not a model of clarity. On the one hand, we found "significant support" in the legislative history for the contention that the statute "reaches the mere possession of guns without any showing of an interstate commerce nexus" in individual cases. 404 U.S., at 345-346. On the other hand, we could not ignore Congress' inserting the phrase "in commerce or affecting commerce" in the statute. Id., at 345. The phrase clearly modified "transport" and we could find no sensible explanation for requiring a nexus only for transport. Id., at 340. Faced with this ambiguity, n6 the Court adopted the narrower reading that the phrase modified all three offenses. We found this result dictated by two principles of statutory interpretation: First, that "ambiguity concerning the ambit of criminal statutes should be resolved in favor of lenity," Rewis v. United States, 401 U.S. 808, 812 (1971), and second, that "unless Congress conveys its purpose clearly, it will not be deemed to have significantly changed the federal-state balance," Bass, supra, at 349. Since "[absent] proof of some interstate commerce nexus in each case §1202(a) dramatically intrudes upon traditional state criminal jurisdiction," 404 U.S., at 350, we were unwilling to conclude, without a "clearer statement of intention," ibid., that Congress meant to dispense entirely with a nexus requirement in individual cases.

n6 As one commentator described our dilemma: "[The] legislative history looked one way and the logic and structure of the statute another, while the language was not clear." Stern, The Commerce Clause Revisited - The Federalization of Intrastate Crime, 15 Ariz. L. Rev. 271, 281 (1973).

It was unnecessary in Bass for us to decide what would constitute an adequate nexus with commerce as the Government had made no attempt to show any nexus at all. While we did suggest some possibilities, n7 the present case presents the first opportunity to focus on the question with the benefit of full briefing and argument.

n7 See n. 11, infra.

The Government's position is that to establish a nexus with interstate commerce it need prove only that the firearm possessed by the convicted felon traveled at some time in interstate commerce. The petitioner contends, however, that the nexus must be "contemporaneous" with the possession, that the statute proscribes "only crimes with a present connection to commerce." Brief for Petitioner 9. He suggests that at the time of the offense the possessor must be engaging in commerce or must be carrying the gun at an interstate facility. Tr. of Oral Arg. 11. At oral argument he suggested an alternative theory - that one can be convicted for possession without any proof of a present connection with commerce so long as the firearm was acquired after conviction. Id., at 15.

In our effort to resolve the dispute, we turn first to the text of the statute. Petitioner contends that the meaning can be readily determined from the face of the statute, at least when it is contrasted with Title IV of the Omnibus Crime Control Act, another title dealing with gun control. n8 He points to one section of Title IV, 18 U.S.C. §922(h), arguing, in reliance on our decision in Barrett v. United States, 423 U.S. 212 (1976), that this section shows how Congress can, if it chooses, specify an offense based on firearms that have previously traveled in commerce. In §922(h), Congress employed the present perfect tense, as it prohibited a convicted felon from receiving a firearm "which has been shipped or transported in interstate or foreign commerce." This choice of tense led us to conclude in Barrett that Congress clearly "[denoted] an act that has been completed." 423 U.S., at 216. Thus, petitioner argues, since Congress knows how to specify completed transactions, its failure to use that language in the present statute must mean that it wanted to reach only ongoing transactions.

n8 The provisions of Title IV of the Omnibus Crime Control Act were re-enacted later that year without relevant change in the Gun Control Act of 1968, 82 Stat. 1213. For convenience, those provisions are referred to here collectively as Title IV.

The essential difficulty with this argument is that it is not very meaningful to compare Title VII with Title IV. See Bass, 404 U.S., at 344. Title VII was a last-minute amendment to the Omnibus Crime Control Act enacted hastily with little discussion and no hearings.n9 The statute, as we noted in Bass, is not the product of model legislative deliberation or draftsmanship. Id., at 339, 344. Title IV, on the other hand, is a carefully constructed package of gun control legislation. It is obvious that the tenses used throughout Title IV were chosen with care. For example, in addition to the prohibition in §922(h) on receipt by convicted felons, Congress also made it illegal in §922(g) for such person to "ship or transport any firearm or ammunition in interstate or foreign commerce." In §922(j), Congress made it unlawful for "any person to receive, conceal, store, barter, sell or dispose of any stolen firearm..., which is moving as, which is part of, or which constitutes, interstate or foreign commerce." And §922(k) makes it illegal for "any person knowingly to transport, ship, or receive, in interstate or foreign commerce, any firearm which has had [its] serial number removed, obliterated or altered." In view of such fine nuances in the tenses employed in the statute, the Court could easily conclude in Barrett that "Congress knew the significance and meaning of the language it employed." 423 U.S., at 217. The language it chose was "without ambiguity." Id., at 216. "Had Congress intended to confine §922(h) to direct interstate receipts, it would have so provided, just as it did in other sections of [Title IV]." Id., at 217.

n9 Senator Long introduced it on the floor of the Senate on May 17, 1968. About a week later he explained his amendment again; there was brief debate; a vote was called; and the amendment was agreed to without having been referred to any committee. Accordingly, there were no legislative hearings and no committee reports. The amendment received only passing mention in the House discussion of the bill and never received committee consideration there either.

In the present case, by contrast, Congress' choice of language was ambiguous at best. While it is true that Congress did not choose the precise language used in §922(h) to indicate that a present nexus with commerce is not required, neither did it use the language of §922(j) to indicate that the gun must have a contemporaneous connection with commerce at the time of the offense. Thus, while petitioner is correct in noting that Congress has the skills to be precise, the fact that it did not employ those skills here helps us not at all.

we see no basis for contending that a weapon acquired after a conviction affects commerce differently from one acquired before and retained.

While Congress' choice of tenses is not very revealing, its findings and its inclusion of the phrase "affecting commerce" are somewhat more helpful. In the findings at the beginning of Title VII, Congress expressly declared that "the receipt, possession, or transportation of a firearm by felons... constitutes... a burden on commerce or threat affecting the free flow of commerce," 18 U.S.C. App. §1201 (1). n10 It then implemented those findings by prohibiting possessions "in commerce and affecting commerce." As we have previously observed, Congress is aware of the "distinction between legislation limited to activities 'in commerce' and an assertion of its full Commerce Clause power so as to cover all activity substantially affecting interstate commerce." United States v. American Bldg. Maintenance Industries, 422 U.S. 271, 280

(1975); see also NLRB v. Reliance Fuel Corp., 371 U.S. 224, 226 (1963). Indeed, that awareness was explicitly demonstrated here. In arguing that Congress could, consistent with the Constitution, "outlaw the mere possession of weapons," Senator Long, in introducing Title VII, pointed to the fact that "many of the items and transactions reached by the broad swath of the Civil Rights Act of 1964 were reached by virtue of the power of Congress to regulate matters affecting commerce, not just to regulate interstate commerce itself." 114 Cong. Rec. 13868 (1968). He advised a similar reliance on the power to regulate matters affecting commerce and urged that "Congress simply [find] that the possession of these weapons by the wrong kind of people is either a burden on commerce or a threat that affects the free flow of commerce." Id., at 13869. While in Bass we noted that we could not be sure that Congress meant to do away entirely with a nexus requirement, it does seem apparent that in implementing these findings by prohibiting both possessions in commerce and those affecting commerce, Congress must have meant more than to outlaw simply those possessions that occur in commerce or in interstate facilities. And we see no basis for contending that a weapon acquired after a conviction affects commerce differently from one acquired before and retained.

n10 Title 18 U.S.C. App. §1201 reads in its entirety:

"Congressional findings and declaration.

"The Congress hereby finds and declares that the receipt, possession, or transportation of a firearm by felons, veterans who are discharged under dishonorable conditions, mental incompetents, aliens who are illegally in the country, and former citizens who have renounced their citizenship, constitutes -

"(1) a burden on commerce or threat affecting the free flow of commerce,

"(2) a threat to the safety of the President of the United States and Vice President of the United States,

"(3) an impediment or a threat to the exercise of free speech and the free exercise of a religion guaranteed by the first amendment to the Constitution of the United States, and

"(4) a threat to the continued and effective operation of the Government of the United States and of the government of each State guaranteed by article IV of the Constitution."

The legislative history in its entirety, while brief, further supports the view that Congress sought to rule broadly—to keep guns out of the hands of those who have demonstrated that "they may not be trusted to possess a firearm without becoming a threat to society."

The legislative history in its entirety, while brief, further supports the view that Congress sought to rule broadly - to keep guns out of the hands of those who have demonstrated that "they may not be trusted to possess a firearm without becoming a threat to society." Id., at 14773. There is simply no indication of any concern with either the movement of the gun or the possessor or with the time of acquisition.

In introducing the amendment, Senator Long stated:

"I have prepared an amendment which I will offer at an appropriate time, simply setting forth the fact that anybody who has been convicted of a felony... is not permitted to possess a firearm....

When a man has been convicted of a felony, unless—as this bill sets forth—he has been expressly pardoned by the President and the pardon states that the person is to be permitted to possess firearms in the future, that man would have no right to possess firearms.

"It might be well to analyze, for a moment, the logic involved. When a man has been convicted of a felony, unless - as this bill sets forth - he has been expressly pardoned by the President and the pardon states that the person is to be permitted to possess firearms in the future, that man would have no right to possess firearms. He would be punished criminally if he is found in possession of them.

. . .

"It seems to me that this simply strikes at the possession of firearms by the wrong kind of people. It avoids the problem of imposing on an honest hardware store owner the burden of keeping a lot of records and trying to keep up with the ultimate disposition of weapons sold. It places the burden and the punishment on the kind of people who have no business possessing firearms in the event they come into possession of them." Id., at 13868-13869.

The purpose of the amendment was to complement Title IV. Id., at 14774; see also id., at 16286. Senator Long noted:

"Of all the gun bills that have been suggested, debated, discussed and considered, none except this Title VII attempts to bar possession of a firearm from persons whose prior behaviors have established their violent tendencies....

Under Title VII, every citizen could possess a gun until the commission of his first felony. Upon his conviction, however, Title VII would deny every assassin, murderer, thief and burglar of the right to possess a firearm in the future

"... Under Title VII, every citizen could possess a gun until the commission of his first felony. Upon his conviction, however, Title VII would deny every assassin, murderer, thief and burglar of [sic] the right to possess a firearm in the future....

. . .

"Despite all that has been said about the need for controlling firearms in this Country, no other amendment heretofore offered would get at the Oswalds or the Galts. They are the types of people at which Title VII is aimed." Id., at 14773-14774.

He proposed this amendment to remedy what he thought was an erroneous conception of the drafters of Title IV that there was "a constitutional doubt that the Federal Government could outlaw the mere possession of weapons." Id., at 13868.

The intent to outlaw possession without regard to movement and to apply it to a case such as petitioner's could not have been more clearly revealed than in a colloquy between Senators Long and McLellan:

"Mr. McClellan. I have not had an opportunity to study the amendment.... The thought that occurred to me, as the Senator explained it, is that if a man had been in the penitentiary, had been a felon, and had been pardoned, without any condition in his pardon to which the able Senator referred, granting him the right to bear arms, could that man own a shotgun for the purpose of hunting?

"Mr. Long of Louisiana. No, he could not. He could own it, but he could not possess it.

"Mr. McClellan. I beg the Senator's pardon?

"Mr. Long of Louisiana. This amendment does not seek to do anything about who owns a firearm. He could not carry it around; he could not have it.

"Mr. McClellan. Could he have it in his home?

"Mr. Long of Louisiana. No, he could not." Id., at 14774 (emphasis added).

It was after this colloquy that Senator McClellan suggested that the amendment be taken to conference for "further thought." Ibid. While that appeared to be its destination, the House, after Senate passage of the bill, defeated a motion to go to conference and adopted the entire Senate bill, including Title VII, without alteration. Id., at 16077-16078, 16299-16300. Title VII thus became law without modification.

It seems apparent from the foregoing that the purpose of Title VII was to proscribe mere possession but that there was some concern about the constitutionality of such a statute. It was that observed ambivalence that made us unwilling in Bass to find the clear intent necessary to conclude that Congress meant to dispense with a nexus requirement entirely. However, we see no indication that Congress intended to require any more than the minimal nexus that the firearm have been, at some time, in interstate commerce. n11 In particular, we find no support for petitioner's theories.

Congress was not particularly concerned with the impact on commerce except as a means to insure the constitutionality of Title VII. State gun control laws were found "inadequate to bar possession of firearms from those most likely to use them for unlawful purposes" and Congress sought to buttress the States' efforts.

n11 In Bass, the Court suggested that there might be a distinction between receipt and possession and that possession might require a stricter nexus with commerce. While such a requirement would make sense, see United States v. Bell, 524 F. 2d, at 209, further consideration has persuaded us that that was not the choice Congress made. Congress was not particularly concerned with the impact on commerce except as a means to insure the constitutionality of Title VII. State gun control laws were found "inadequate to bar possession of firearms from those most likely to use them for unlawful purposes" and Congress sought to buttress the States' efforts. 114 Cong. Rec. 14774 (1968). All indications are that Congress meant to reach possessions broadly.

Initially, we note our difficulty in fully comprehending petitioner's conception of a nexus with commerce. In his view, if an individual purchases a gun before his conviction, the fact that the gun once traveled in commerce does not provide an adequate nexus. It is necessary, in addition, that the person also carry it in an interstate facility. If, however, one purchases the same gun from the same dealer one day after the conviction as opposed to one day before, somehow the nexus magically appears, regardless of whether the purchaser carries the gun in any particular place. Such an interpretation strains credulity. We find no evidence in either the language or the legislative history for such a construction. n12

n12 The argument sounds more like an effort to define possession, but the only issue before us is the nexus requirement. Petitioner has raised no objections to the trial court's definition of possession. Even as a proposed definition of possession, however, there is no support for it in the history or text. While Senator Long used the word "acquire" a few times in discussing the amendment, it is clear his concern was with the dangers of certain people having guns, not with when they obtained them. Furthermore, his use of the term "acquire" is better explained as a synonym for "receive" than for "possess." See United States v. Kelly, 519 F. 2d 251, 253 n. 3 (CA8 1975).

More significantly, these theories create serious loopholes in the congressional plan to "make it unlawful for a firearm... to be in the possession of a convicted felon." 114 Cong. Rec. 14773 (1968). A person who obtained a firearm prior to his conviction can retain it forever so long as he is not caught with it in an interstate facility. Indeed, petitioner's interpretation allows an individual to go out in the period between his arrest and conviction and purchase and stockpile weapons with impunity. In addition, petitioner's theories would significantly impede enforcement efforts. Those who do acquire guns after their conviction obviously do so surreptitiously and, as petitioner concedes, Tr. of Oral Arg. 19, it is very difficult as a practical matter to prove that such possession began after the possessor's felony conviction.

Petitioner responds that the Government's reading of the statute fails to give effect to all three terms of the statute - receive, possess, transport. He argues that someone guilty of receipt or transport will necessarily be guilty of possession and that, therefore, there was no need to include the other two offenses in the statute. While this contention is not frivolous, n13 the fact is that petitioner's theory is similarly vulnerable. By his proposed definitions, there are essentially only two crimes - receipt and transport. The possessor who acquires the weapon after his conviction is guilty of receipt and the one who is carrying the gun in commerce or at an interstate facility presumably is guilty of transporting. n14 Thus, the definitions offered by both sides fail to give real substance to all three terms. The difference, however, is that the Government's definition captures the essence of Congress' intent, striking at the possession of weapons by people "who have no business possessing [them]." 114 Cong. Rec. 13869 (1968). Petitioner's version, on the other hand, fails completely to fulfill the congressional purpose. It virtually eliminates the one offense on which Congress focused in enacting the law.

n13 We note, however, that it is also arguable that one could receive and perhaps transport a weapon without necessarily exercising dominion and control over it.

n14 Petitioner suggests that a possessor's simply waiting in an interstate facility is not transporting. Even if that is true, we find it inconceivable, in view of the legislative history, that Congress intended the possession offense to have so limited a scope.

Finally, petitioner seeks to invoke the two principles of statutory construction relied on in Bass - lenity in construing criminal statutes and caution where the federal-state balance is implicated. Petitioner, however, overlooks the fact that we did not turn to these guides in Bass until we had concluded that "[after] 'seizing every thing from which aid can be derived,'... we are left with an ambiguous statute." 404 U.S., at 347. The principles are applicable only when we are uncertain about the statute's meaning and are not to be used "in complete disregard of the purpose of the legislature." United States v. Bramblett, 348 U.S. 503, 510 (1955). Here, the intent of Congress is clear. We do not face the conflicting pull between the text and the history that confronted us in Bass. In this case, the history is unambiguous and the text consistent with it. Congress sought to reach possessions broadly, with little concern for when the nexus with commerce occurred. Indeed, it was a close question in Bass whether §1202(a) even required proof of any nexus at all in individual cases. The only reason we concluded it did was because it was not "plainly and unmistakably" clear that it did not. 404 U.S., at 348. But there is no question that Congress intended no more than a minimal nexus requirement.

Since the District Court and the Court of Appeals employed the proper standard, we affirm the conviction of petitioner.

It is so ordered.

MR. JUSTICE REHNQUIST took no part in the consideration or decision of this case.

MR. JUSTICE STEWART, dissenting.

So far as the record reflects, the petitioner in this case acquired the four weapons in question before he was convicted of a felony in August 1972. Until that time, his possession of the guns was entirely legal under federal law. Under the Court's construction of 18 U.S.C. App. §1202(a)(1), however, the petitioner was automatically guilty of a serious federal criminal offense at the moment he was convicted in the state felony case. This result is in my view inconsistent with the time-honored rule of lenity in construing federal criminal statutes. See, e.g., Rewis v. United States, 401 U.S. 808, 812; Ladner v. United States, 358 U.S. 169, 177-178; Bell v. United States, 349 U.S. 81, 83; United States v. Universal C.I.T. Credit Corp., 344 U.S. 218, 221-222. I would hold that §1202(a)(1) does not come into play unless and until a person first comes into possession of a firearm after he is convicted of a felony.

The language of §1202(a)(1) does not compel the construction that the Court adopts. The statute covers "[any] person who... has been convicted... of a felony... and who receives, possesses, or transports... any firearm...." Plainly the acts of receiving and transporting are prohibited only if they occur after the defendant's conviction. The language does not indicate, however, whether the illegal possession must also first begin after conviction, or whether a prior possession becomes illegal at the moment the possessor is adjudged guilty of a felony. And, as the Court observes, ante, at 576-577, any reading of the statute makes one or another part of it redundant. If §1202(a) makes criminal any postconviction possession of a gun by a convicted felon, then there will almost never be a situation where the Government would need to rely on the prohibition against receipt of the gun, for in most cases receipt would result in possession, and the latter is generally easier to prove. On the other hand, if the prohibition against possession refers to a possession that begins only after a felony conviction, the Government presumably could proceed on a receipt charge in such cases, without relying on the possession offense (or vice versa).

The legislative history does not provide much help. There are statements suggesting that Congress meant to proscribe any possession of a firearm by a convicted felon. Other statements, however, intimate that the statute's purpose was to prevent a convicted felon from coming into possession of a weapon after his conviction. For instance, Senator Long, the drafter and sponsor of §1202, stated that the statute "places the burden and the punishment on the kind of people who have no business possessing firearms in the event they come into possession of them." 114 Cong. Rec. 13869 (1968). Later he added that §1202(a) "would deny every assassin, murderer, thief and burglar... the right to possess a firearm in the future...." 114 Cong. Rec., 14773.

In my view, we are under no mandate to construe this statute so that a person in lawful possession of a firearm, and presumed to be innocent of a felony until proved guilty, must upon his conviction of a felony also be automatically and instantly guilty of a wholly different serious criminal offense.

In short, I disagree with the Court that the scope of §1202(a) is so crystal clear that there is no room for the operation of the rule of lenity. In my view, we are under no mandate to construe this statute so that a person in lawful possession of a firearm, and presumed to be innocent of a felony until proved guilty, must upon his conviction of a felony also be automatically and instantly guilty of a wholly different serious criminal offense. n1 The statute could equally be read to apply only when a person first comes into possession of a firearm after his felony conviction.n2 That being so, I would choose the latter alternative, for "it is appropriate, before we choose the harsher alternative, to require that Congress should have spoken in language that is clear and definite. We should not derive criminal outlawry from some ambiguous implication." United States v. Universal C.I.T. Credit Corp., supra, at 222.

Under this construction, for example, a bookkeeper who owns a hunting rifle and who later commits embezzlement will, immediately upon his embezzlement conviction, also be guilty of violating §1202(a). At oral argument the Government agreed that such a person should have a reasonable time to relinquish possession without being automatically in violation of the statute, and suggested that prosecutorial discretion would take care of the problem. Proper construction of a criminal statute, however, cannot depend upon the good will of those who must enforce it.

n1 Under this construction, for example, a bookkeeper who owns a hunting rifle and who later commits embezzlement will, immediately upon his embezzlement conviction, also be guilty of violating §1202(a). At oral argument the Government agreed that such a person should have a reasonable time to relinquish possession without being automatically in violation of the statute, and suggested that prosecutorial discretion would take care of the problem. Proper construction of a criminal statute, however, cannot depend upon the good will of those who must enforce it.

n2 Contrary to the Court's suggestion, this reading would not allow a person "to go out in the period between his arrest and conviction and purchase and stockpile weapons with impunity." Ante, at 576. Title 18 U.S.C. §922(h) makes it unlawful for any person who is under indictment for a crime punishable by imprisonment for a term exceeding one year to receive any firearm or ammunition that has been shipped or transported in interstate or foreign commerce.

Since the petitioner in this case came into possession of the firearms before he was convicted of any felony, I would hold that he did not violate §1202(a)(1). Accordingly, I respectfully dissent from the opinion and judgment of the Court.

SIMPSON v. UNITED STATES

(CASE EXCERPT)

435 U.S. 6; 98 S. Ct. 909; 55 L. Ed. 2d 70

November 1, 1977, Argued

February 28, 1978, Decided

GIST: Armed bank robbers got away with $40,000 from a bank in Kentucky, and then two months later hit a branch of the same bank on the other side of town for about the same amount. They were caught, tried and convicted of both crimes, and received lengthy sentences. Their sentences were increased for using guns in the commission of the crimes, under both the federal bank robbery statute (18 USC §2113) and the federal felony-with-a-firearm statute (18 USC §924). Wrestling with the question of double jeopardy, the Court applied the "Blockburger test," which they describe below, and other reasoning, to decide that the sentences cannot be enhanced under both statutes for the same crime.

MR. JUSTICE BRENNAN delivered the opinion of the Court.

.....

Petitioners were convicted of two separate bank robberies committed with firearms. The question for decision is whether 2113 (d) and 924 (c) should be construed as intended by Congress to authorize, in the case of a bank robbery committed with firearms, not only the imposition of the increased penalty under 2113 (d), but also the imposition of an additional consecutive penalty under 924 (c).

I

petitioners, using handguns to intimidate the bank's employees, robbed some $40,000

On September 8, 1975, petitioners, using handguns to intimidate the bank's employees, robbed some $40,000 from the East End Branch of the Commercial Bank of Middlesboro, Ky. App. 20. Less than two months later, on November 4, 1975, petitioners returned to Middlesboro and this time, again using handguns, robbed the West End Branch of the Commercial Bank of about the same amount.

.....

II

Quite clearly, 924 (c) and 2113 (d) are addressed to the same concern and designed to combat the same problem: the use of dangerous weapons - most particularly firearms - to commit federal felonies. n4 Although we agree with the Court of Appeals that 924 (c) creates an offense distinct from the underlying federal felony, United States v. Ramirez, 482 F.2d 807 (CA2 1973); United States v. Sudduth, 457 F.2d 1198 (CA1 1972), we believe that this is the beginning and not the end of the analysis necessary to answer the question presented for decision.

the legislation was directed at the rash of "gangsterism" by which roving bandits in the Southwest and Northwest would rob banks and then elude capture by state authorities by crossing state lines.

the provision would not reach the conduct of a bank robber who walked into a bank with a bottle of nitroglycerin and threatened to blow it up unless his demands were met.

n4. Both the Senate and House Reports on the 1934 Bank Robbery Act, which first made bank robbery a federal offense and which included the provisions of 2113 (d), state that the legislation was directed at the rash of "gangsterism" by which roving bandits in the Southwest and Northwest would rob banks and then elude capture by state authorities by crossing state lines. S. Rep. No. 537, 73d Cong., 2d Sess., 1 (1934); H. R. Rep. No. 1461, 73d Cong., 2d Sess., 2 (1934). The vast majority of such bank robberies were undoubtedly accomplished by the use of guns of various sorts. Indeed, as originally proposed, the provision that became 2113 (d) covered only the use of "dangerous weapons." The "or device" language was added in response to concern expressed on the

House floor that the provision would not reach the conduct of a bank robber who walked into a bank with a bottle of nitroglycerin and threatened to blow it up unless his demands were met. 78 Cong. Rec. 8132-8133 (1934). Thus, although 2113 (d) undoubtedly covers bank robberies with weapons and devices other than firearms, the use of guns to commit bank robbery was the primary evil 2113 (d) was designed to deter. On the other hand, although the overriding purpose of 924 (c) was to combat the increasing use of guns to commit federal felonies, the ambit of that provision is broader. The section imposes increased penalties when a "firearm" is used to commit, or is unlawfully carried during the commission of any federal felony. Title 18 U.S.C. 921 (a) (3) (D) defines "firearm" to include "any destructive device." A "destructive device," in turn, is defined by 921 (a) (4) (A) to include "any explosive, incendiary, or poison gas - (i) bomb, (ii) grenade, (iii) rocket . . ., (iv) missile . . ., (v) mine, or (vi) device similar to any of the devices described in the preceding clauses." See United States v. Melville, 309 F. Supp. 774 (SDNY 1970).

the test to be applied to determine whether there are two offenses or only one, is whether each provision requires proof of a fact which the other does not."

In Blockburger v. United States, 284 U.S. 299 (1932), this Court set out the test for determining "whether two offenses are sufficiently distinguishable to permit the imposition of cumulative punishment." Brown v. Ohio, 432 U.S. 161, 166 (1977). We held that "[t]he applicable rule is that where the same act or transaction constitutes a violation of two distinct statutory provisions, the test to be applied to determine whether there are two offenses or only one, is whether each provision requires proof of a fact which the other does not." Blockburger v. United States, supra, at 304. See also Brown v. Ohio, supra, at 166; Ianelli î v. United States, 420 U.S. 770 (1975); Gore v. United States, 357 U.S. 386 (1958). The Blockburger test has its primary relevance in the double jeopardy context, where it is a guide for determining when two separately defined crimes constitute the "same offense" for double jeopardy purposes. Brown v. Ohio, supra.

.....

Before an examination is made to determine whether cumulative punishments for the two offenses are constitutionally permissible, it is necessary, following our practice of avoiding constitutional decisions where possible, to determine whether Congress intended to subject the defendant to multiple penalties for the single criminal transaction in which he engaged.

.....

We believe that several tools of statutory construction applied to the statutes "in a case like the present one" - where the Government relied on the same proofs to support the convictions under both statutes - require the conclusion that Congress cannot be said to have authorized the imposition of the additional penalty of 924 (c) for commission of bank robbery with firearms already subject to enhanced punishment under 2113 (d).

.....

Indeed, at one time, the Government was not insensitive to these concerns respecting the availability of the additional penalty under 924 (c). In 1971, the Department of Justice found the interpretive preference for specific criminal statutes over general criminal statutes of itself sufficient reason to advise all United States Attorneys not to prosecute a defendant under 924 (c) (1) where the substantive statute the defendant was charged with violating already "provid[ed] for increased penalties where a firearm is used in the commission of the offense." 19 U.S. Attys. Bull. 63 (U.S. Dept. of Justice, 1971).

we hold that in a prosecution growing out of a single transaction of bank robbery with firearms, a defendant may not be sentenced under both 2113 (d) and 924 (c).

Obviously, the Government has since changed its view of the relationship between 924 (c) and 2113 (d). We think its original view was the better view of the congressional understanding as to the proper interaction between the two statutes. Accordingly, we hold that in a prosecution growing out of a single transaction of bank robbery with firearms, a defendant may not be sentenced under both 2113 (d) and 924 (c). The cases are therefore reversed and remanded to the Court of Appeals for proceedings consistent with this opinion.

It is so ordered.

MR. JUSTICE REHNQUIST, dissenting.

I am unable to agree with the Court's conclusion in this litigation that petitioners, upon being convicted and sentenced under 18 U.S.C. 2113 (d) for armed robbery, could not have their sentence enhanced pursuant to the provisions of 18 U.S.C. 924 (c), which provides that when a defendant uses a firearm in the commission of a felony, he "shall, in addition to the punishment provided for the commission of such felony, be sentenced to a term of imprisonment for not less than one year nor more than ten years." The plain language of the statutes involved certainly confers this sentencing authority upon the District Court. The Court chooses to avoid this plain meaning by resort to a canon of construction with which no one disagrees, "our practice of avoiding constitutional decisions where possible," ante, at 12.

.....

Several different bills dealing with firearms control, which had been bottled up in various stages of the legislative process prior to June 1968, were brought to the floor and enacted with dramatic swiftness following the assassination of Senator Robert F. Kennedy

the similar killing of Reverend Martin Luther King, obviously focused the attention of Congress on the problem of firearms control.

The Court's disregard of this plain meaning is inappropriate in this litigation both because of the circumstances under which the Gun Control Act was passed in June 1968, and because of the gauzy nature of the constitutional concerns which apparently underlie its reluctance to read the statutes as they are written. Several different bills dealing with firearms control, which had been bottled up in various stages of the legislative process prior to June 1968, were brought to the floor and enacted with dramatic swiftness following the assassination of Senator Robert F. Kennedy in the early part of that month. Senator Kennedy's assassination, following by less than three months the similar killing of Reverend Martin Luther King, obviously focused the attention of Congress on the problem of firearms control. It seems to me not only permissible but irresistible, in reading the language of the two statutes, to conclude that Congress intended when it enacted 924 (c) to authorize the enhancement of the sentence already imposed by virtue of 18 U.S.C. 2113 (d).

.....

To speak of a congressional provision for enhanced punishment for an offense, as 924 (c) clearly is, as raising constitutional doubts under the "Blockburger test" is to use the language of metaphysics, rather than of constitutional law.

LEWIS v. UNITED STATES

(FULL CASE)

445 U.S. 55; 100 S. Ct. 915; 63 L. Ed. 2d 198

January 7, 1980, Argued

February 27, 1980, Decided

GIST: George Lewis appealed his conviction for "possession of a firearm by a convicted felon" on the grounds that his prior conviction was unconstitutional under the 6th Amendment. He had been found guilty of a Florida breaking-and-entering felony 16 years earlier without being represented by a lawyer, before this arrest for gun possession in 1977. The Court held that a defendant may not contest the validity of a prior felony conviction at his trial for unlawful possession of a firearm. A felony conviction, even one apparently unconstitutional, was found to be a sufficient basis for a conviction of possession of a firearm by a convicted felon.

The Court repeatedly notes Congress' intent to ban gun possession by people deemed specifically dangerous, and Congress' expressed intent to leave the rights of the innocent untouched. The Court says the "fact of conviction must deprive the person of a right to a firearm," implying the right must exist in the first place, since it can be removed. In a footnote, Justice Blackmun's majority opinion comes close to endorsing the anti-individual interpretation of the 2nd Amendment.

Held: Even though petitioner's extant prior state-court felony conviction may be subject to collateral attack under Gideon v. Wainwright, 372 U.S. 335, it could properly be used as a predicate for his subsequent conviction for possession of a firearm in violation of §1202 (a)(1) of Title VII of the Omnibus Crime Control and Safe Streets Act of 1968.

(a) The plain meaning of §1202 (a)(1)'s sweeping language proscribing the possession of firearms by any person who "has been convicted by a court of the United States or of a State . . . of a felony," is that the fact of a felony conviction imposes firearm disability until the conviction is vacated or the felon is relieved of his disability by some affirmative action. Other provisions of the statute demonstrate and reinforce its broad sweep, and there is nothing in §1202 (a)(1)'s legislative history to suggest that Congress was willing to allow a defendant to question the validity of his prior conviction as a defense to a charge under §1202 (a)(1). Moreover, the fact that there are remedies available to a convicted felon -- removal of the firearm disability by a qualifying pardon or the Secretary of the Treasury's consent, as specified in the Act, or a challenge to the prior conviction in an appropriate court proceeding -- suggests that Congress intended that the defendant clear his status before obtaining a firearm, thereby fulfilling Congress' purpose to keep firearms away from persons classified as potentially irresponsible and dangerous.

(b) The firearm regulatory scheme at issue here is consonant with the concept of equal protection embodied in the Due Process Clause of the Fifth Amendment, since Congress could rationally conclude that any felony conviction, even an allegedly invalid one, is a sufficient basis on which to prohibit the possession of a firearm. And use of an uncounseled felony conviction as the basis for imposing a civil firearms disability, enforceable by criminal sanction, is not inconsistent with Burgett v. Texas, 389 U.S. 109; United States v. Tucker, 404 U.S. 443; and Loper v. Beto, 405 U.S. 473.

MR. JUSTICE BLACKMUN delivered the opinion of the Court.

This case presents the question whether a defendant's extant prior conviction, flawed because he was without counsel, as required by Gideon v. Wainwright, 372 U.S. 335 (1963), may constitute the predicate for a subsequent conviction under §1202 (a)(1), as amended, of Title VII of the Omnibus Crime Control and Safe Streets Act of 1968, 18 U.S.C. App. §1202 (a)(1). n1

n1 Section 1202 (a) reads in full:

"Any person who --

"(1) has been convicted by a court of the United States or of a State or any political subdivision thereof of a felony, or

"(2) has been discharged from the Armed Forces under dishonorable conditions, or

"(3) has been adjudged by a court of the United States or of a State or any political subdivision thereof of being mentally incompetent, or

"(4) having been a citizen of the United States has renounced his citizenship, or

"(5) being an alien is illegally or unlawfully in the United States,

"and who receives, possesses, or transports in commerce or affecting commerce, after the date of enactment of this Act, any firearm shall be fined not more than $10,000 or imprisoned for not more than two years, or both."

I

In 1961, petitioner George Calvin Lewis, Jr., upon his plea of guilty, was convicted in a Florida state court of a felony for breaking and entering with intent to commit a misdemeanor. See Fla. Stat. §810.05 (1961). He served a term of imprisonment. That conviction has never been overturned, nor has petitioner ever received a qualifying pardon or permission from the Secretary of the Treasury to possess a firearm. See 18 U.S.C. App. §1203 (2) and 18 U.S.C. §925 (c).

In January 1977, Lewis, on probable cause, was arrested in Virginia, and later was charged by indictment with having knowingly received and possessed at that time a specified firearm, in violation of 18 U.S.C. App. §1202 (a)(1). n2 He waived a jury and was given a bench trial. It was stipulated that the weapon in question had been shipped in interstate commerce. The Government introduced in evidence an exemplified copy of the judgment and sentence in the 1961 Florida felony proceeding. App. 10.

n2 The indictment also charged petitioner with a violation of 18 U.S.C. §922 (h)(1). That statute reads in pertinent part:

"It shall be unlawful for any person --

"(1) who is under indictment for, or who has been convicted in any court of, a crime punishable by imprisonment for a term exceeding one year;

. . . .

"to receive any firearm . . . which has been shipped or transported in interstate . . . commerce."

Petitioner was acquitted on the §922 (h)(1) charge and it is not before us here.

Shortly before the trial, petitioner's counsel informed the court that he had been advised that Lewis was not represented by counsel in the 1961 Florida proceeding. n3 He claimed that under Gideon v.

Wainwright, supra, a violation of §1202 (a)(1) could not be predicated on a prior conviction obtained in violation of petitioner's Sixth and Fourteenth Amendment rights. The court rejected that claim, ruling that the constitutionality of the outstanding Florida conviction was immaterial with respect to petitioner's status under §1202 (a)(1) as a previously convicted felon at the time of his arrest. Petitioner, accordingly, offered no evidence as to whether in fact he had been convicted in 1961 without the aid of counsel. We therefore assume, for present purposes, that he was without counsel at that time.

n3 Petitioner's counsel stated that a Florida attorney had advised him that the court records in that State showed affirmatively that Lewis had no lawyer. He noted also that Lewis had been charged with the same offense as had the defendant in Gideon v. Wainwright, 372 U.S. 335 (1963), and that petitioner had been tried in the same State about six months before Gideon was tried. App. 2-3.

On appeal, the United States Court of Appeals for the Fourth Circuit, by a divided vote, affirmed. 591 F.2d 978 (1979). It held that a defendant, purely as a defense to a prosecution under §1202 (a)(1), could not attack collaterally an outstanding prior felony conviction, and that the statutory prohibition applied irrespective of whether that prior conviction was subject to collateral attack. The Court of Appeals also rejected Lewis' constitutional argument to the effect that the use of the prior conviction as a predicate for his prosecution under §1202 (a)(1) violated his rights under the Fifth and Sixth Amendments.

Because of conflict among the Courts of Appeals, n4 we granted certiorari. 442 U.S. 939 (1979).

n4 Compare United States v. Lufman, 457 F.2d 165 (CA7 1972) (use of an underlying felony conviction unconstitutionally obtained to support a conviction under §1202 (a)(1) is reversible error), with the Fourth Circuit's ruling in the present case, and with United States v. Maggard, 573 F.2d 926 (CA6 1978); and United States v. Graves, 554 F.2d 65 (CA3 1977) (en banc) (claim of constitutional error in the underlying conviction may not be raised). The Ninth Circuit has distinguished between a claim of constitutional invalidity in the underlying conviction, which it has held may be raised, and a claim that the underlying conviction has been, or should be, reversed on other grounds. Compare United States v. O'Neal, 545 F.2d 85 (1976), and United States v. Pricepaul, 540 F.2d 417 (1976), with United States v. Liles, 432 F.2d 18 (1970). See also United States v. Herrell, 588 F.2d 711 (CA9 1978), cert. denied, 440 U.S. 964 (1979) (underlying conviction in a prosecution under 18 U.S.C. §922 (h)(1) may not be challenged on nonconstitutional grounds).

The identical issue that is presented in this case has also arisen in the context of challenges to convictions under 18 U.S.C. §922 (g)(1) (proscribing shipping or transport of a firearm in interstate or foreign commerce by a person under indictment for, or convicted of, a felony) and §922 (h)(1) (proscribing receipt of a firearm shipped in interstate or foreign commerce by such a person). Compare United States v. Scales, 599 F.2d 78 (CA5 1979); Dameron v. United States, 488 F.2d 724 (CA5 1974); Pasterchik v. United States, 466 F.2d 1367 (CA9 1972); and United States v. DuShane, 435 F.2d 187 (CA2 1970) (underlying conviction may be attacked as unconstitutional), with Barker v. United States, 579 F.2d 1219, 1226 (CA10 1978) (underlying conviction may not be so challenged in prosecution under §922 (h)(1)).

The Courts of Appeals have treated the issue somewhat differently in prosecutions under 18 U.S.C. §922 (a)(6) (prohibiting the falsification of one's status as a convicted felon in purchasing a firearm). Nonuniformity has prevailed nonetheless on the question whether a defendant charged with violating that statute may challenge the constitutionality of the underlying felony conviction. Compare United States v. O'Neal, supra, and United States v. Pricepaul, supra (permitting the challenge), with United States v. Allen, 556 F.2d 720 (CA4 1977); United States v. Graves, supra; and Cassity v. United States, 521 F.2d 1320 (CA6 1975) (holding that the challenge may not be made). The Eighth Circuit has stated that it will not permit a challenge to the constitutionality of the underlying conviction where the defendant is charged under §922 (a)(6), while reserving the question under §1202 (a)(1) and §§922 (g)(1) and (h)(1). United States v. Edwards, 568 F.2d 68, 70-72, and n. 3 (1977). See also United States v. Graves, 554 F.2d, at 83-88 (Garth, J., and Seitz, C. J., concurring in part and dissenting in part) (the Government need not prove the validity of the underlying conviction in a prosecution brought under §922 (a)(6), but it must do so in a prosecution under §1202 (a)(1)).

II

Four cases decided by this Court provide the focus for petitioner's attack upon his conviction. The first, and pivotal one, is Gideon v. Wainwright, supra, where the Court held that a state felony conviction without counsel, and without a valid waiver of counsel, was unconstitutional under the Sixth and Fourteenth Amendments. That ruling is fully retroactive. Kitchens v. Smith, 401 U.S. 847 (1971).

The second case is Burgett v. Texas, 389 U.S. 109 (1967). There the Court held that a conviction invalid under Gideon could not be used for enhancement of punishment under a State's recidivist statute. The third is United States v. Tucker, 404 U.S. 443 (1972), where it was held that such a conviction could not be considered by a court in sentencing a defendant after a subsequent conviction. And the fourth is Loper v.

Beto, 405 U.S. 473 (1972), where the Court disallowed the use of the conviction to impeach the general credibility of the defendant. The prior conviction, the plurality opinion said, "lacked reliability." Id., at 484, quoting Linkletter v. Walker, 381 U.S. 618, 639, and n. 20 (1965).

We, of course, accept these rulings for purposes of the present case. Petitioner's position, however, is that the four cases require a reversal of his conviction under §1202 (a)(1) on both statutory and constitutional grounds.

III

The obvious breadth of the language may well reflect the expansive legislative approach revealed by Congress' express findings and declarations, concerning the problem of firearm abuse by felons and certain specifically described persons.

The Court has stated repeatedly of late that in any case concerning the interpretation of a statute the "starting point" must be the language of the statute itself. Reiter v. Sonotone Corp., 442 U.S. 330, 337 (1979). See also Touche Ross & Co. v. Redington, 442 U.S. 560, 568 (1979); Southeastern Community College v. Davis, 442 U.S. 397, 405 (1979). An examination of §1202 (a)(1) reveals that its proscription is directed unambiguously at any person who "has been convicted by a court of the United States or of a State . . . of a felony." No modifier is present, and nothing suggests any restriction on the scope of the term "convicted." "Nothing on the face of the statute suggests a congressional intent to limit its coverage to persons [whose convictions are not subject to collateral attack]." United States v. Culbert, 435 U.S. 371, 373 (1978); see United States v. Naftalin, 441 U.S. 768, 772 (1979). The statutory language is sweeping, and its plain meaning is that the fact of a felony conviction imposes a firearm disability until the conviction is vacated or the felon is relieved of his disability by some affirmative action, such as a qualifying pardon or a consent from the Secretary of the Treasury. n5 The obvious breadth of the language may well reflect the expansive legislative approach revealed by Congress' express findings and declarations, in 18 U.S.C. App. §1201, n6 concerning the problem of firearm abuse by felons and certain specifically described persons.

we view the language Congress chose as consistent with the common-sense notion that a disability based upon one's status as a convicted felon should cease only when the conviction upon which that status depends has been vacated.

n5 One might argue, of course, that the language is so sweeping that it includes in its proscription even a person whose predicate conviction in the interim had been finally reversed on appeal and thus no longer was outstanding. The Government, however, does not go so far, Tr. of Oral Arg. 29-30, 37-40, and though we have no need to pursue that extreme argument in this case, we reject it. We are not persuaded that the mere possibility of making that argument renders the statute, as petitioner suggests, unconstitutionally vague. And unlike the dissent, post, at 69, we view the language Congress chose as consistent with the common-sense notion that a disability based upon one's status as a convicted felon should cease only when the conviction upon which that status depends has been vacated.

We note, nonetheless, that the disability effected by §1202 (a)(1) would apply while a felony conviction was pending on appeal. See Note, Prior Convictions and the Gun Control Act of 1968, 76 Colum. L. Rev. 326, 334, and n. 42 (1976).

n6 "The Congress hereby finds and declares that the receipt, possession, or transportation of a firearm by felons, veterans who are discharged under dishonorable conditions, mental incompetents, aliens who are illegally in the country, and former citizens who have renounced their citizenship, constitutes --

"(1) a burden on commerce or threat affecting the free flow of commerce,

"(2) a threat to the safety of the President of the United States and Vice President of the United States,

"(3) an impediment or a threat to the exercise of free speech and the free exercise of a religion guaranteed by the first amendment to the Constitution of the United States, and

"(4) a threat to the continued and effective operation of the Government of the United States and of the government of each State guaranteed by article IV of the Constitution."

Other provisions of the statute demonstrate and reinforce its broad sweep. Section 1203 enumerates exceptions to §1202 (a)(1) (a prison inmate who by reason of his duties has expressly been entrusted with a firearm by prison authority; a person who has been pardoned and who has expressly been authorized to receive, possess, or transport a firearm). In addition, §1202 (c)(2) defines "felony" to exclude certain state crimes punishable by no more than two years' imprisonment. No exception, however, is made for a person whose outstanding felony conviction ultimately might turn out to be invalid for any reason. On its face, therefore, §1202 (a)(1) contains nothing by way of restrictive language. It thus stands in contrast with other federal statutes that explicitly permit a defendant to challenge, by way of defense, the validity or constitutionality of the predicate felony. See, e.g., 18 U.S.C. §3575 (e) (dangerous special offender) and 21 U.S.C. §851 (c)(2) (recidivism under the Comprehensive Drug Abuse Prevention and Control Act of 1970).

What little legislative history there is that is relevant reflects an intent to impose a firearms disability on any felon based on the fact of conviction.

For example, the Senator observed: "So, under Title VII, every citizen could possess a gun until the commission of his first felony. Upon his conviction, however, Title VII would deny every assassin, murderer, thief and burglar of the right to possess a firearm in the future except where he has been pardoned by the President or a State Governor and had been expressedly authorized by his pardon to possess a firearm." Inasmuch as Senator Long was the sponsor and floor manager of the bill, his statements are entitled to weight.

When we turn to the legislative history of §1202 (a)(1), we find nothing to suggest that Congress was willing to allow a defendant to question the validity of his prior conviction as a defense to a charge under §1202 (a)(1). The section was enacted as part of Title VII of the Omnibus Crime Control and Safe Streets Acts of 1968, 82 Stat. 236. It was added by way of a floor amendment to the Act and thus was not a subject of discussion in the legislative reports. See United States v. Batchelder, 442 U.S. 114, 120 (1979); Scarborough v. United States, 431 U.S. 563, 569-570 (1977); United States v. Bass, 404 U.S. 336, 344, and n. 11 (1971). What little legislative history there is that is relevant reflects an intent to impose a firearms disability on any felon based on the fact of conviction. Senator Long, who introduced and directed the passage of Title VII, repeatedly stressed conviction, not a "valid" conviction, and not a conviction not subject to constitutional challenge, as the criterion. For example, the Senator observed: "So, under Title VII, every citizen could possess a gun until the commission of his first felony. Upon his conviction, however, Title VII would deny every assassin, murderer, thief and burglar of the right to possess a firearm in the future except where he has been pardoned by the President or a State Governor and had been expressedly authorized by his pardon to possess a firearm." 114 Cong. Rec. 14773 (1968). See also id., at 13868, 14774. Inasmuch as Senator Long was the sponsor and floor manager of the bill, his statements are entitled to weight. Simpson v. United States, 435 U.S. 6, 13 (1978).

It is not without significance, furthermore, that Title VII, as well as Title IV of the Omnibus Act, was enacted in response to the precipitous rise in political assassinations, riots, and other violent crimes involving firearms, that occurred in this country in the 1960's. See, e.g., S. Rep. No. 1097, 90th Cong., 2d Sess., 76-78 (1968); H. R. Rep. No. 1577, 90th Cong., 2d Sess., 7 (1968); S. Rep. No. 1501, 90th Cong., 2d Sess., 22-23 (1968). This Court, accordingly, has observed:

The legislative history [of Title VII] in its entirety, while brief, further supports the view that Congress sought to rule broadly—to keep guns out of the hands of those who have demonstrated that 'they may not be trusted to possess a firearm without becoming a threat to society.'

"The legislative history [of Title VII] in its entirety, while brief, further supports the view that Congress sought to rule broadly -- to keep guns out of the hands of those who have demonstrated that 'they may not be trusted to possess a firearm without becoming a threat to society.'" Scarborough v. United States, 431 U.S., at 572.

Section 1202 (a) was a sweeping prophylaxis, in simple terms, against misuse of firearms.

The legislative history, therefore, affords no basis for a loophole, by way of a collateral constitutional challenge, to the broad statutory scheme enacted by Congress. Section 1202 (a) was a sweeping prophylaxis, in simple terms, against misuse of firearms. There is no indication of any intent to require the Government to prove the validity of the predicate conviction.

Those sections impose a disability not only on a convicted felon but also on a person under a felony indictment, even if that person subsequently is acquitted of the felony charge. Since the fact of mere indictment is a disabling circumstance, a fortiori the much more significant fact of conviction must deprive the person of a right to a firearm.

The very structure of the Omnibus Act's Title IV, enacted simultaneously with Title VII, reinforces this conclusion. Each Title prohibits categories of presumptively dangerous persons from transporting or receiving firearms. See 18 U.S.C. §§922 (g) and (h). Actually, with regard to the statutory question at issue here, we detect little significant difference between Title IV and Title VII. Each seeks to keep a firearm away from "any person . . . who has been convicted" of a felony, although the definition of "felony" differs somewhat in the respective statutes. But to limit the scope of §§922 (g)(1) and (h)(1) to a validly convicted felon would be at odds with the statutory scheme as a whole. Those sections impose a disability not only on a convicted felon but also on a person under a felony indictment, even if that person subsequently is acquitted of the felony charge. Since the fact of mere indictment is a disabling circumstance, a fortiori the much more significant fact of conviction must deprive the person of a right to a firearm.

it is important to note that a convicted felon is not without relief.

Finally, it is important to note that a convicted felon is not without relief. As has been observed above, the Omnibus Act, in §§1203 (2) and 925 (c), states that the disability may be removed by a qualifying pardon or the Secretary's consent. Also, petitioner, before obtaining his firearm, could have challenged his prior conviction in an appropriate proceeding in the Florida state courts. See Fla. Const., Art. 5, §5 (3); L'Hommedieu v. State, 362 So. 2d 72 (Fla. App. 1978); Weir v. State, 319 So. 2d 80 (Fla. App. 1975). See also United States v. Morgan, 346 U.S. 502 (1954). n7

n7 This being so, §1202 (a)(1) does not attach "what may amount to lifelong sanctions to a mere finding of probable cause," as has been argued by one commentator. See Comment, 92 Harv. L. Rev. 1790, 1795 (1979).

It seems fully apparent to us that the existence of these remedies, two of which are expressly contained in the Omnibus Act itself, suggests that Congress clearly intended that the defendant clear his status before obtaining a firearm, thereby fulfilling Congress' purpose "broadly to keep firearms away from the persons Congress classified as potentially irresponsible and dangerous." Barrett v. United States, 423 U.S. 212, 218 (1976).

With the face of the statute and the legislative history so clear, petitioner's argument that the statute nevertheless should be construed so as to avoid a constitutional issue is inapposite. That course is appropriate only when the statute provides a fair alternative construction. This statute could not be more plain. Swain v. Pressley, 430 U.S. 372, 378, and n. 11 (1977); United States v. Batchelder, 442 U.S., at 122-123. Similarly, any principle of lenity, see Rewis v. United States, 401 U.S. 808, 812 (1971), has no application. The touchstone of that principle is statutory ambiguity. Huddleston v. United States, 415 U.S. 814, 832 (1974); United States v. Batchelder, 442 U.S., at 121-122. There is no ambiguity here.

We therefore hold that §1202 (a)(1) prohibits a felon from possessing a firearm despite the fact that the predicate felony may be subject to collateral attack on constitutional grounds.

We therefore hold that §1202 (a)(1) prohibits a felon from possessing a firearm despite the fact that the predicate felony may be subject to collateral attack on constitutional grounds.

IV

The firearm regulatory scheme at issue here is consonant with the concept of equal protection embodied in the Due Process Clause of the Fifth Amendment if there is "some 'rational basis' for the statutory distinctions made . . . or . . . they 'have some relevance to the purpose for which the classification is made.'" Marshall v. United States, 414 U.S. 417, 422 (1974), quoting from McGinnis v. Royster, 410 U.S. 263, 270 (1973), and Baxstrom v. Herold, 383 U.S. 107, 111 (1966). See Vance v. Bradley, 440 U.S. 93, 97 (1979). n8

These legislative restrictions on the use of firearms are neither based upon constitutionally suspect criteria, nor do they trench upon any constitutionally protected liberties. See... United States v. Miller, (the Second Amendment guarantees no right to keep and bear a firearm that does not have "some reasonable relationship to the preservation or efficiency of a well regulated militia")

n8 These legislative restrictions on the use of firearms are neither based upon constitutionally suspect criteria, nor do they trench upon any constitutionally protected liberties. See United States v. Miller, 307 U.S. 174, 178 (1939) (the Second Amendment guarantees no right to keep and bear a firearm that does not have "some reasonable relationship to the preservation or efficiency of a well regulated militia"); United States v. Three Winchester 30-30 Caliber Lever Action Carbines, 504 F.2d 1288, 1290, n. 5 (CA7 1974); United States v. Johnson, 497 F.2d 548 (CA4 1974); Cody v. United States, 460 F.2d 34 (CA8), cert. denied, 409 U.S. 1010 (1972) (the latter three cases holding, respectively, that §1202 (a)(1), §922 (g), and §922 (a)(6) do not violate the Second Amendment).

Congress, as its expressed purpose in enacting Title VII reveals, 18 U.S.C. App. §1201, was concerned that the receipt and possession of a firearm by a felon constitutes a threat, among other things, to the continued and effective operation of the Government of the United States. The legislative history of the gun control laws discloses Congress' worry about the easy availability of firearms, especially to those persons who pose a threat to community peace. And Congress focused on the nexus between violent crime and the possession of a firearm by any person with a criminal record.

This Court has recognized repeatedly that a legislature constitutionally may prohibit a convicted felon from engaging in activities far more fundamental than the possession of a firearm.

Section 1202 (a)(1) clearly meets that test. Congress, as its expressed purpose in enacting Title VII reveals, 18 U.S.C. App. §1201, was concerned that the receipt and possession of a firearm by a felon constitutes a threat, among other things, to the continued and effective operation of the Government of the United States. The legislative history of the gun control laws discloses Congress' worry about the easy availability of firearms, especially to those persons who pose a threat to community peace. And Congress focused on the nexus between violent crime and the possession of a firearm by any person with a criminal record. 114 Cong. Rec. 13220 (1968) (remarks of Sen. Tydings); id., at 16298 (remarks of Rep. Pollock). Congress could rationally conclude that any felony conviction, even an allegedly invalid one, is a sufficient basis on which to prohibit the possession of a firearm. See, e.g., United States v. Ransom, 515 F.2d 885, 891-892 (CA5 1975), cert. denied, 424 U.S. 944 (1976). This Court has recognized repeatedly that a legislature constitutionally may prohibit a convicted felon from engaging in activities far more fundamental than the possession of a firearm. See Richardson v. Ramirez, 418 U.S. 24 (1974) (disenfranchisement); De Veau v. Braisted, 363 U.S. 144 (1960) (proscription against holding office in a waterfront labor organization); Hawker v. New York, 170 U.S. 189 (1898) (prohibition against the practice of medicine).

We recognize, of course, that under the Sixth Amendment an uncounseled felony conviction cannot be used for certain purposes. See Burgett, Tucker, and Loper, all supra. The Court, however, has never suggested that an uncounseled conviction is invalid for all purposes. See Scott v. Illinois, 440 U.S. 367 (1979); Loper v. Beto, 405 U.S., at 482, n. 11 (plurality opinion).

Use of an uncounseled felony conviction as the basis for imposing a civil firearms disability, enforceable by a criminal sanction, is not inconsistent with Burgett, Tucker, and Loper. In each of those cases, this Court found that the subsequent conviction or sentence violated the Sixth Amendment because it depended upon the reliability of a past uncounseled conviction. The federal gun laws, however, focus not on reliability, but on the mere fact of conviction, or even indictment, in order to keep firearms away from potentially dangerous persons. Congress' judgment that a convicted felon, even one whose conviction was allegedly uncounseled, is among the class of persons who should be disabled from dealing in or possessing firearms because of potential dangerousness is rational. n9 Enforcement of that essentially civil disability through a criminal sanction does not "support guilt or enhance punishment," see Burgett, 389 U.S., at 115, on the basis of a conviction that is unreliable when one considers Congress' broad purpose. Moreover, unlike the situation in Burgett, the sanction imposed by §1202 (a)(1) attaches immediately upon the defendant's first conviction.

n9 The dissent's assertion that Congress' judgment in this regard cannot rationally be supported, post, at 72, is one we do not share. Moreover, such an assertion seems plainly inconsistent with the deference that a reviewing court should give to a legislative determination that, in essence, predicts a potential for future criminal behavior.

it is important to note that a convicted felon may challenge the validity of a prior conviction, or otherwise remove his disability, before obtaining a firearm.

Again, it is important to note that a convicted felon may challenge the validity of a prior conviction, or otherwise remove his disability, before obtaining a firearm. We simply hold today that the firearms prosecution does not open the predicate conviction to a new form of collateral attack. See Note, Prior Convictions and the Gun Control Act of 1968, 76 Colum. L. Rev. 326, 338-339 (1976). Cf. Walker v. City of Birmingham, 388 U.S. 307 (1967).

The judgment of the Court of Appeals is affirmed.

It is so ordered.

MR. JUSTICE BRENNAN, with whom MR. JUSTICE MARSHALL and MR. JUSTICE POWELL join, dissenting.

In disagreement with every other Court of Appeals that has addressed the issue, n1 the Court of Appeals for the Fourth Circuit, held, by a divided vote, that an uncounseled and hence unconstitutional felony conviction may form the predicate for conviction under §1202 (a)(1) of the Omnibus Crime Control and Safe Streets Act of 1968. Today the Court affirms that judgment, but by an analysis that cannot be squared with either the literal language of the statute or controlling decisions of this Court. I respectfully dissent.

n1 See, e.g., Dameron v. United States, 488 F.2d 724 (CA5 1974); United States v. Lufman, 457 F.2d 165 (CA7 1972); United States v. DuShane, 435 F.2d 187 (CA2 1970); United States v. Thoresen, 428 F.2d 654 (CA9 1970). See generally Comment, 92 Harv. L. Rev. 1790 (1979).

I

Two longstanding principles of statutory construction independently mandate reversal of petitioner's conviction. The first is the precept that "when choice has to be made between two readings of what conduct Congress has made a crime, it is appropriate, before we choose the harsher alternative, to require that Congress should have spoken in language that is clear and definite." United States v. Universal C.I.T. Credit Corp., 344 U.S. 218, 221-222 (1952). The Court has repeatedly reaffirmed this "rule of lenity." See, e.g., Simpson v. United States, 435 U.S. 6, 14 (1978); United States v. Bass, 404 U.S. 336, 347-349 (1971); Rewis v. United States, 401 U.S. 808, 812 (1971); Ladner v. United States, 358 U.S. 169, 177 (1958); Bell v. United States, 349 U.S. 81 (1955). Indeed, the principle that "ambiguity concerning the ambit of criminal statutes should be resolved in favor of lenity" has previously been invoked in interpreting the very provision at issue in this case. See United States v. Bass, supra.

The Court declines to apply this established rule of construction in this case because, in its view, "[there] is no ambiguity here." Ante, at 65. In light of the gloss the Court places on the literal language of the statute, I find this to be a curious conclusion. By its own terms, §1202 (a)(1) reaches "[any] person who has been convicted . . . of a felony." The provision on its face admits of no exception to its sweeping proscription. Yet despite the absence of any qualifying phrase, the Court concedes -- as it must -- that the statute cannot be interpreted so as to include those persons whose predicate convictions have been vacated or reversed on appeal. Ante, at 60-61, and n. 5.

It thus appears that the plain words of §1202 (a)(1) are not so clear after all, and we therefore must determine the section's reach. Two alternative constructions are offered: The first is the Government's -- that §1202 (a)(1) may be read to permit only outstanding felony convictions to serve as the basis for prosecution. Tr. of Oral Arg. 29-30. The second is petitioner's -- that the predicate conviction must be not only outstanding, but also constitutionally valid. Because either interpretation fairly comports with the statutory language, surely the principle of lenity requires us to resolve any doubts against the harsher alternative and to read the statute to prohibit the possession of firearms only by those who have been constitutionally convicted of a felony.

> **however expansive §1202 was meant to be, we are not faithful to "our duty to protect the rights of the individual," when we are so quick to ascribe to Congress the intent to punish the possession of a firearm by a person whose predicate felony conviction was obtained in violation of the right to the assistance of counsel**

The Court nevertheless adopts the Government's construction, relying on a supposed legislative resolve to enact a sweeping measure against the misuse of firearms. But however expansive §1202 was meant to be, we are not faithful to "our duty to protect the rights of the individual," Dalia v. United States, 441 U.S. 238, 263 (1979) (STEVENS, J., dissenting), when we are so quick to ascribe to Congress the intent to punish the possession of a firearm by a person whose predicate felony conviction was obtained in violation of the right to the assistance of counsel, "one of the safeguards of the Sixth Amendment deemed necessary to insure fundamental human rights of life and liberty." Johnson v. Zerbst, 304 U.S. 458, 462 (1938). Petitioner has once already been imprisoned in violation of the Constitution. In the absence of any clear congressional expression of its intent, I cannot accept a construction of §1202 (a)(1) that reflects such an indifference to petitioner's plight and such a derogation of the principles of Gideon v. Wainwright, 372 U.S. 335 (1963). n2

n2 As the Court has previously observed, §1202 "was hastily passed, with little discussion, no hearings, and no report." United States v. Bass, 404 U.S. 336, 344 (1971). "In short, 'the legislative history of [the] Act hardly speaks with that clarity of purpose which Congress supposedly furnishes courts in order to enable them to enforce its true will.'" Id., at 346 (quoting Universal Camera Corp. v. NLRB, 340 U.S. 474, 483 (1951)). It is thus little wonder that the Court finds no explicit support in the statute's legislative history for petitioner's construction.

Nor do the few signposts that do exist in the history and structure of Title VII point unambiguously to the Court's conclusion. That Congress included provisions within the Omnibus Act whereby a convicted felon could have his disability removed by a qualifying pardon or the

Secretary's consent, see §§1203 (2) and 925 (c), does not mean that Congress intended them to be exclusive remedies. Indeed, these provisions were clearly designed only to provide a mechanism for those persons with valid felony convictions to seek relief from the prohibitions of §1202.

Similarly, a comparison between the scope of Title IV and Title VII is unenlightening on the question before us. Simply because the former Title imposes a disability on any person under a felony indictment, it by no means follows, a fortiori or otherwise, that Congress intended by the latter Title to impose a somewhat harsher disability on those persons with unconstitutional felony convictions. Cf. ante, at 64. Significantly, the restrictions attaching to an individual under indictment are necessarily temporary, while those imposed on the basis of a previous conviction are indefinite in duration. Moreover, Congress' failure to include persons "under indictment" within the proscriptions of §1202 more plausibly signals its desire to demand a greater indication of potential dangerousness than would be provided by the mere fact of indictment -- or, for that matter, by an uncounseled felony conviction. In fact, in a slightly different context, Congress has expressly rejected the proposition that an invalid prior conviction is a reliable indicator of "dangerousness." See 18 U.S.C. §3575 (e) (dangerous special offender).

II

The second maxim of statutory construction that compels a narrow reading of §1202 (a)(1) is the "cardinal principle" that "if a serious doubt of constitutionality is raised, . . . this Court will first ascertain whether a construction of the statute is fairly possible by which the question may be avoided." Crowell v. Benson, 285 U.S. 22, 62 (1932). Accord, Schneider v. Smith, 390 U.S. 17, 26 (1968); United States v. Rumely, 345 U.S. 41, 45 (1953); United States v. CIO, 335 U.S. 106, 120-121, and n. 20 (1948). And doubts as to the constitutionality of a statute that could predicate criminal liability solely on the existence of a previous uncounseled felony conviction are indeed serious, for a trilogy of this Court's decisions would seem to prohibit precisely such a result.

Burgett v. Texas, 389 U.S. 109 (1967), held that a prior uncounseled felony conviction was void and thus inadmissible in a prosecution under a Texas recidivist statute. Burgett stated: "To permit a conviction obtained in violation of Gideon v. Wainwright to be used against a person either to support guilt or enhance punishment for another offense . . . is to erode the principle of that case. Worse yet, since the defect in the prior conviction was denial of the right to counsel, the accused in effect suffers anew from the deprivation of that Sixth Amendment right." Id., at 115 (citation omitted). United States v. Tucker, 404 U.S. 443 (1972), and Loper v. Beto, 405 U.S. 473 (1972), respectively prohibited the use of uncounseled felony convictions as a factor to be considered in sentencing, and to impeach the defendant's credibility.

Burgett and its progeny appear to control the result in this case. The clear teaching of those decisions is that an uncounseled felony conviction can never be used "to support guilt or enhance punishment for another offense." Here, petitioner could not have been tried and convicted for violating §1202 (a)(1) in the absence of his previous felony conviction. It could not be plainer that his constitutionally void conviction was therefore used "to support guilt" for the current offense. The Court's bald assertion to the contrary is simply inexplicable.

The Court's attempt to distinguish Burgett, Tucker, and Loper on the ground that the validity of the subsequent convictions or sentences in those cases depended on the reliability of the prior uncounseled felony convictions, while in the present case the law focuses on the mere fact of the prior conviction, is unconvincing. The fundamental rationale behind those decisions was the concern that according any credibility to an uncounseled felony conviction would seriously erode the protections of the Sixth Amendment. Congress' decision to include convicted felons within the class of persons prohibited from possessing firearms can rationally be supported only if the historical fact of conviction is indeed a reliable indicator of potential dangerousness. As we have so often said, denial of the right to counsel impeaches "the very integrity of the fact-finding process." Linkletter v. Walker, 381 U.S. 618, 639 (1965). Accord, Lakeside v. Oregon, 435 U.S. 333, 341 (1978); Argersinger v. Hamlin, 407 U.S. 25, 31 (1972). And the absence of counsel impairs the reliability of a felony conviction just as much when used to prove potential dangerousness as when used as direct proof of guilt. Cf. Loper v. Beto, supra, at 483 (opinion of STEWART, J.).

III

Finally, it is simply irrelevant that petitioner could have challenged the validity of his prior conviction in appropriate proceedings in the state courts. Nor can the existence of such a remedy prohibit him from raising the unconstitutionality of that conviction as a defense to the present charge. In the first place, neither Burgett nor Loper imposed any requirement that a defendant collaterally attack his uncounseled conviction before he faces prosecution under §1202 (a)(1); in both cases the Court held the use of the prior invalid convictions impermissible even though the defendants had taken no affirmative steps to have them overturned. More to the point, however, where the very defect in the initial proceedings was that the accused did not have the assistance of counsel in defending the felony charges against him, it simply defies reason and sensibility to suggest that the defendant must be regarded as having waived his defense to the §1202 (a)(1) prosecution because he failed first to retain counsel to seek an extraordinary writ of coram nobis.

BUSIC v. UNITED STATES

(CASE EXCERPT)

446 U.S. 398; 100 S. Ct. 1747; 64 L. Ed. 2d 381

February 27, 1980, Argued

May 19, 1980, Decided

GIST: Michael Busic and Anthony LaRocca, Jr., arranged to sell $30,000 of narcotics to a man they didn't realize was a DEA undercover agent. When the agent showed up with the money, they tried to rob him instead. The agent called in his backup, LaRocca fired a few shots but hit no one, and the pair were taken into custody and disarmed (Busic had a gun tucked under his belt). The pair were convicted and received stiff prison terms, part of which came from a sentence enhancement under 18 USC §111 for armed assault of a federal officer, and also from 18 USC §924, for committing a federal felony with a firearm. For reasons similar to the *Simpson* decision, the Court held that the sentences could be increased only under the provision of the armed assault law.

MR. JUSTICE BRENNAN delivered the opinion of the Court.

Title 18 U.S.C. 924 (c) authorizes the imposition of enhanced penalties on a defendant who uses or carries a firearm while committing a federal felony. The question for decision in these cases is whether that section may be applied to a defendant who uses a firearm in the course of a felony that is proscribed by a statute which itself authorizes enhancement if a dangerous weapon is used. We hold that the sentence received by such a defendant may be enhanced only under the enhancement provision in the statute defining the felony he committed and that 924 (c) does not apply in such a case.

I

The evidence showed that in May 1976 the two arranged a drug buy with an agent of the Drug Enforcement Administration who was to supply $30,000 in cash. When the agent arrived with the money, LaRocca attempted to rob him at gunpoint.

Petitioners Anthony LaRocca, Jr., and Michael Busic were tried together on a multicount indictment charging drug, firearms, and assault offenses flowing from a narcotics conspiracy and an attempt to rob an undercover agent. The evidence showed that in May 1976 the two arranged a drug buy with an agent of the Drug Enforcement Administration who was to supply $30,000 in cash. When the agent arrived with the money, LaRocca attempted to rob him at gunpoint. The agent signalled for reinforcements, and as other officers began to close in LaRocca fired several shots at them. No one was hit and the agents succeeded in disarming and arresting LaRocca. Busic was also arrested and the officers seized a gun he was carrying in his belt but had not drawn. Additional weapons were found in the pair's automobile.

LaRocca as the actual triggerman and Busic as an aider and abettor

A jury in the United States District Court for the Western District of Pennsylvania convicted petitioners of narcotics and possession-of-firearms counts, and of two counts of armed assault on federal officers in violation of 18 U.S.C. 111 - LaRocca as the actual triggerman and Busic as an aider and abettor, and thus derivatively a principal under 18 U.S.C. 2. In addition, LaRocca was convicted of using a firearm in the commission of a federal felony in violation of 18 U.S.C. 924 (c) (1), and Busic was convicted of carrying a firearm in the commission of a federal felony in violation of 18 U.S.C. 924 (c) (2). Each petitioner was sentenced to a total of 30 years, of which 5 resulted from concurrent sentences on the narcotics charges, 5 were a product of concurrent terms on the firearms and assault charges, and 20 were imposed for the 924 (c) violations.

.....

Relying upon the legislative history and applicable canons of statutory construction, Simpson held that the Congress cannot be understood to have intended that a defendant who has been convicted of robbing a bank with a firearm may be sentenced under both 924 (c) and 2113 (d).

.....

In our view, Simpson's language and reasoning support one conclusion alone - that prosecution and enhanced sentencing under 924 (c) is simply not permissible where the predicate felony statute contains its own enhancement provision. This result is supported not only by the general principles underlying the doctrine of stare decisis - principles particularly apposite in cases of statutory construction - but also by the legislative history and relevant canons of statutory construction. The Government has not persuaded us that this result is irrational or depends upon implausible inferences as to congressional intent.

.....

What we have said thus far disposes of LaRocca's case by making it clear that he may not be sentenced under 924 (c) for using his gun to assault the federal officers. This holding also applies in Busic's case. But in that case the Government has a fallback position. Even if a person who uses a gun to violate 111 may not be sentenced for doing so under 924 (c) (1), the argument goes, a person who carries a gun in the commission of a 111 violation may be sentenced under 924 (c) (2) because the enhancement provision of 111 does not apply to those who carry but do not use their weapons. Thus, the Government urges, whatever our holding with regard to LaRocca, Busic may be sentenced under 924 (c) (2) for carrying his gun while committing the crime of aiding and abetting LaRocca's violation of 111.

this argument would suggest, Busic might be punished for carrying a gun in his belt and also for shooting that same gun. Yet such results are wholly implausible.

create a situation in which aiders and abettors would often be more culpable and more severely punished than those whom they aid and abet. We decline to read the statutes to produce such an ungainly result.

The central flaw in this argument as applied here is that Busic is being punished for using a weapon. Through the combination of 111 and 18 U.S.C. 2, he was found guilty as a principal of using a firearm to assault the undercover agents. LaRocca's gun, in other words, became Busic's as a matter of law. And the Government's argument thus amounts to the contention that had Busic shot one gun at the officers and carried another in his belt he could have been punished under 111 for the one he fired and under 924 (c) (2) for the one he did not fire. Similarly, this argument would suggest, Busic might be punished for carrying a gun in his belt and also for shooting that same gun. Yet such results are wholly implausible. They would stand both Simpson and our holding in Part II, supra, on their heads, impute to Congress the unlikely intention to punish each weapon as a separate offense, and create a situation in which aiders and abettors would often be more culpable and more severely punished than those whom they aid and abet. We decline to read the statutes to produce such an ungainly result. It seems to us that our holding of Part II is equally applicable here - Busic's vicarious assault and use of a dangerous weapon are subject to prosecution and punishment under 111 and he has been duly prosecuted and punished pursuant to that provision. In such a case, Simpson, the legislative history, and applicable canons of statutory construction make it clear that neither subsection of 924 (c) is available.

These cases are reversed and remanded to the Court of Appeals for proceedings consistent with this opinion.

So ordered.

DICKERSON v. NEW BANNER INSTITUTE

(FULL CASE)

460 U.S. 103; 103 S. Ct. 986; 74 L. Ed. 2d 845

November 29, 1982, Argued

February 23, 1983, Decided

GIST: This case involves the interpretation of the federal prohibition on possession of firearms by anyone who has been convicted of a crime punishable by more than a year in prison. The Court held that a person who pled guilty to such a crime, was given probation and a deferred judgment, and later had the record of the deferred judgment expunged was still "convicted" for the purpose of applying the federal statute and keeping the prohibition in place.

Title IV of the Gun Control Act of 1968, 18 U.S.C. §§922(g)(1) and (h)(1), makes it unlawful for any person "who has been convicted . . . of . . . a crime punishable by imprisonment for a term exceeding one year" to ship, transport, or receive any firearm or ammunition in interstate commerce. Title IV also makes it unlawful to engage in the business of importing, manufacturing, or dealing in firearms without a license from the Secretary of the Treasury. One ground for denial of a license is where the applicant is under the prohibitions imposed by §§922(g)(1) and (h)(1), and if the applicant is a corporation, a license will be denied if a person with power to direct the management of the corporation is under such prohibitions. One Kennison, the chairman of the board and a shareholder of respondent corporation, after plea negotiations, pleaded guilty in an Iowa state court to the state crime of carrying a concealed handgun. This crime was punishable by a fine or imprisonment for not more than five years, or both. The state court, however, pursuant to an Iowa statute, "deferred" entry of a formal judgment and placed Kennison on probation. At the completion of his probation term he was discharged, also pursuant to a state statute, and his record with respect to the deferred judgment was expunged. Subsequently, respondent applied to the Treasury Department's Bureau of Alcohol, Tobacco and Firearms (Bureau) for licenses as a firearms and ammunition dealer and manufacturer, but did not disclose Kennison's plea of guilty to the Iowa concealed weapon charge. The licenses were issued but were later revoked when the Bureau learned of the Iowa charge. The District Court upheld the revocation, but the Court of Appeals reversed, holding that although Kennison had been "convicted" of an offense that triggered firearms disabilities, that fact could not serve as a predicate for a Gun Control Act violation or license revocation because the conviction had been expunged under the Iowa deferred judgment procedure.

Held: The firearms disabilities imposed by §§922(g)(1) and (h)(1) apply to Kennison and were not removed by the expunction of the record of his guilty plea to the concealed weapon charge.

(a) For purposes of the federal gun control laws, a plea of guilty to a disqualifying crime and its notation by a state court, followed by a sentence of probation, is equivalent to being "convicted" within the language of §§922(g)(1) and (h)(1).

(b) Iowa's expunction provisions, as carried out in Kennison's case prior to respondent's license applications, did not nullify his conviction for purposes of the federal statute. Expunction under state law does not alter the legality of the previous conviction, does not open the way to a license despite the conviction, and does not signify that the defendant was innocent of the crime to which he pleaded guilty. Expunction in Iowa means no more than that the State has provided a means for the trial court not to accord a conviction certain continuing effects under state law.

(c) Provisions of the federal gun control laws other than the provisions in question, as well as related federal statutes, support the conclusion that Congress did not intend expunction of a state conviction automatically to remove the firearms disabilities imposed by §§922(g)(1) and (h)(1).

(d) There is nothing in the legislative history of Title IV or related federal statutes to suggest an opposite intent. Title IV's purpose to curb crime by keeping firearms out of the hands of those not legally entitled to possess them because of age, criminal background, or incompetency, would be frustrated by a ruling that gave effect to state expunctions. In the absence of a plain indication to the contrary, it is assumed that Congress did not intend to make the application of Title IV dependent on state law. Title IV is carefully constructed gun control legislation. Congress knew the significance and meaning of the language it employed.

(e) A rule that would give effect to expunction under varying state statutes would seriously hamper effective enforcement of Title IV.

JUSTICE BLACKMUN delivered the opinion of the Court.

This case presents the issue whether firearms disabilities imposed by 18 U.S.C. §§922(g) and (h) apply with respect to a person who pleads guilty to a state offense punishable by imprisonment for more than one year, when the record of the proceeding subsequently is expunged under state procedure following a successfully served term of probation.

I

Title IV of the Omnibus Crime Control and Safe Streets Act of 1968, 82 Stat. 226, was amended by the Gun Control Act of 1968, 82 Stat. 1214, and now appears as 18 U.S.C. §921 et seq. (1976 ed. and Supp. V). Title IV makes it unlawful for any person "who is under indictment for, or who has been convicted in any court of, a crime punishable by imprisonment for a term exceeding one year" n1 to ship, transport, or receive any firearm or ammunition in interstate commerce. §§922(g) and (h). Title IV also makes it unlawful to engage in the business of importing, manufacturing, or dealing in firearms without a license from the Secretary of the Treasury. §§922(a) and 923(a). One ground, specified by the statute, for denial of a license is the fact that the applicant is barred by §§922(g) and (h) from transporting, shipping, or receiving firearms or ammunition. §923(d)(1)(B). The same statute provides that where the applicant is a corporation, partnership, or association, a license will be denied if an individual possessing, directly or indirectly, the power to direct the management and policies of the entity is under the prohibitions imposed by §§922(g) and (h). Title IV also makes it a crime to violate any of its provisions or to make a willful misrepresentation with respect to information required to be furnished. §924(a).

n1 The Act provides exemptions from its proscriptions for certain business and commercial crimes, such as antitrust violations, punishable by imprisonment for more than one year, and for nonfirearms and nonexplosives state offenses classified by the State as misdemeanors and punishable by imprisonment for two years or less. 18 U.S.C. §921(a)(20). These exemptions are of no relevance here.

Although, as noted above, Title IV imposes disabilities upon any "person who has been convicted . . . of a crime punishable by imprisonment for a term exceeding one year," it does permit certain persons in that category to apply to the Secretary for relief from those disabilities. Under §925(c), the Secretary may grant relief "if it is established to his satisfaction that the circumstances regarding the conviction, and the applicant's record and reputation, are such that the applicant will not be likely to act in a manner dangerous to public safety and that the granting of the relief would not be contrary to the public interest." When the Secretary grants relief, he must publish notice of his action promptly in the Federal Register, together with a statement of reasons. Ibid.

II

David F. Kennison, a resident of Columbia, S. C., is a director, chairman of the board, and a shareholder of respondent New Banner Institute, Inc., a corporation. In September 1974, when Kennison was in Iowa, he was arrested and charged with kidnaping his estranged wife. After plea negotiation, see Tr. of Oral Arg. 40-41, he pleaded guilty to the state crime of carrying a concealed handgun, and the kidnaping charge was dismissed. The concealed weapon offense, under then Iowa law, see Iowa Code §§695.2 and .3 (1977), was punishable by a fine of not more than $1,000 or by imprisonment for not more than five years, or both. n2 In accord with the provisions of Iowa Code §789A.1 (1977), then in effect, n3 the state court entered an order reciting that Kennison had "entered a plea of guilty to the charge of carrying a concealed weapon," that "the defendant has consented to a deferment of sentence in this matter," that "he has stable employment," and that there were "unusual circumstances" in the case. The order then stated that the court "deferred" entry of a formal judgment and placed Kennison on probation.

n2 The court, however, in its discretion, in the case of a first offense, could reduce that punishment. See Iowa Code §695.3 (1977). Sections 695.2 and .3 were repealed effective January 1, 1978, and are now replaced by Iowa Code §§724.4 and 903.1 (1981).

n3 Section 789A.1 then read in pertinent part:

"The trial court may, upon a plea of guilty, verdict of guilty, or a special verdict upon which a judgment of conviction may be rendered, exercise either of the options contained in subsections 1 and 2. However, this section shall not apply to the crimes of treason, murder, or violation of [other specified statutes].

"1. With the consent of the defendant, the court may defer judgment and place the defendant on probation upon such terms and conditions as it may require. Upon fulfillment of the terms of probation the defendant shall be discharged without entry of judgment. Upon violation of the terms, the court may enter an adjudication of guilt and proceed as otherwise provided.

"However, this subsection shall not be available if any of the following is true:

"[Here are recited specific exceptions to the availability of the procedure outlined in subsection 1.]

"2. By record entry at time of or after sentencing, the court may suspend the sentence and place the defendant on probation upon such terms and conditions as it may require.

"Before exercising either of the options contained in subsections 1 and 2, the court shall first determine which of them will provide maximum opportunity for the rehabilitation of the defendant and protection of the community from further offenses by the defendant and others. In making this determination the court shall consider the age of the defendant, his prior record of convictions, if any, his employment circumstances, his family circumstances, the nature of the offense committed, whether a dangerous weapon or force was used in the commission of such offense, and such other factors as shall be appropriate. The court shall file a specific written statement of its reasons for and the facts supporting its decision to defer judgment or to suspend sentence and its decision on the length of probation."

Section 789A.1 was enacted by 1973 Iowa Acts, ch. 295, §1. It was repealed by 1976 Iowa Acts, ch. 1245, §526, effective January 1, 1978. The current replacement statutes are Iowa Code

§§907.3, .4, and .5 (1981).

Kennison returned to South Carolina where he completed his probation term. When that term expired in February 1976, he was discharged pursuant to Iowa Code §789A.6 (1977), then in effect, n4 and the Iowa court's record with reference to the deferred judgment was expunged.

n4 Section 789A.6 then read in pertinent part:

"At any time that the court determines that the purposes of probation have been fulfilled, the court may order the discharge of any person from probation. . . . A person who has been discharged from probation shall no longer be held to answer for his offense. Upon discharge from probation, if judgment has been deferred under section 789A.1, the court's criminal record with reference to the deferred judgment shall be expunged. The record maintained by the supreme court administrator required by section 789A.1 shall not be expunged. . . ."

Section 789A.6 was also enacted in 1973 and was repealed, effective January 1, 1978, by the same Iowa statutes cited in the last paragraph of n. 3, supra. The current statute replacing §789A.6 is Iowa Code §907.9 (1981).

In May 1976, respondent filed three applications with the Treasury Department's Bureau of Alcohol, Tobacco and Firearms (Bureau), for licenses as a dealer in firearms and ammunition, as a manufacturer of ammunition, and as a collector of curios and relics.

In May 1976, respondent filed three applications with the Treasury Department's Bureau of Alcohol, Tobacco and Firearms (Bureau), for licenses as a dealer in firearms and ammunition, as a manufacturer of ammunition, and as a collector of curios and relics. On the application forms, respondent listed Kennison as a "responsible person," that is, an individual possessing direct or indirect power to control the management and policies of respondent. See 18 U.S.C. §923(d)(1)(B). In answering an inquiry on the forms as to whether such person had been convicted of a crime punishable by a prison term exceeding one year, respondent did not disclose the Iowa events or Kennison's plea of guilty in that State. The requested licenses were issued.

The Bureau, however, subsequently learned of the Iowa concealed weapon charge and the plea of guilty. In conformity with the provisions of §§923(e) and (f)(1) and of 27 CFR §178.75 (1982), it mailed respondent Notices of Contemplated Revocation of Licenses. After an informal hearing, the Bureau's Regional Regulatory Administrator issued the revocation notices. Respondent, pursuant to §923(f)(2), then requested and received a formal hearing before an Administrative Law Judge. At that hearing, the Bureau contended that respondent's licenses should be revoked because respondent had failed to reveal that Kennison had been convicted of a felony and also because respondent had not been entitled to the licenses in the first place.

The Administrative Law Judge recommended against revocation. App to Pet. for Cert. 41a. Although he concluded that Kennison's plea of guilty "represented a conviction . . . within the meaning of Section 922(g) and (h)," id., at 47a, he also concluded that respondent's statements in the applications did not justify revocation because its representatives had a good-faith belief that Kennison had not been convicted within the meaning of the federal statute.

On review, the Director of the Bureau, petitioner here, ruled that willful misrepresentation had not been shown; that Kennison, however, possessed the power to direct respondent's management and policies; that Kennison had been convicted in Iowa of an offense that brought him within the prohibitions of §§922(g) and (h); and that the licenses should be revoked because respondent was ineligible for them under §923(d)(1)(B). App. to Pet. for Cert. 23a. The Director ordered the issuance of Final Notices of Revocation. Id., at 40a.

Court of Appeals for the Fourth Circuit reversed. It concluded that although Kennison indeed had been "convicted" of an offense that triggered firearms disabilities, that fact could not serve as a predicate for a Gun Control Act violation or license revocation because the conviction had been expunged under the Iowa deferred judgment procedure. The court acknowledged that other Courts of Appeals entertained contrary views. Because of the importance of the issue and the obvious need for its resolution, we granted certiorari.

Respondent then filed a timely petition for review in the United States District Court for the District of South Carolina. See §923(f)(3). On cross-motions for summary judgment, the Director's motion was granted. On respondent's appeal, however, the United States Court of Appeals for the Fourth Circuit reversed. 649 F.2d 216 (1981). It concluded, id., at 219, that although Kennison indeed had been "convicted" of an offense that triggered firearms disabilities, that fact could not serve as a predicate for a Gun Control Act violation or license revocation because the conviction had been expunged under the Iowa deferred judgment procedure. The court acknowledged, id., at 220, that other Courts of Appeals entertained contrary views. n5 Because of the importance of the issue and the obvious need for its resolution, we granted certiorari. 455 U.S. 1015 (1982).

n5 See United States v. Bergeman, 592 F.2d 533 (CA9 1979); United States v. Mostad, 485 F.2d 199 (CA8 1973), cert. denied, 415 U.S. 947 (1974); United States v. Lehmann, 613 F.2d 130 (CA5 1980). See also, e.g., United States v. Padia, 584 F.2d 85 (CA5 1978); United States v. Gray, 692 F.2d 352 (CA5 1982); United States v. Nord, 586 F.2d 1288 (CA8 1978); United States v. Kelly, 519 F.2d 794 (CA8), cert. denied, 423 U.S. 926 (1975).

III

This is not the first time the Court has examined firearms provisions of the Omnibus Crime Control and Safe Streets Act and of the Gun Control Act.

This is not the first time the Court has examined firearms provisions of the Omnibus Crime Control and Safe Streets Act and of the Gun Control Act. See Lewis v. United States, 445 U.S. 55 (1980); Scarborough v. United States, 431 U.S. 563 (1977); Barrett v. United States, 423 U.S. 212 (1976); Huddleston v. United States, 415 U.S. 814 (1974); United States v. Bass, 404 U.S. 336 (1971).

Despite the fact that the slate on which we write is thus not a clean one, we state once again the obvious when we note that, in determining the scope of a statute, one is to look first at its language. Lewis v. United States, 445 U.S., at 60; United States v. Turkette, 452 U.S. 576, 580 (1981). If the language is unambiguous, ordinarily it is to be regarded as conclusive unless there is "'a clearly expressed legislative intent to the contrary.'" Ibid., quoting Consumer Product Safety Comm'n v. GTE Sylvania, Inc., 447 U.S. 102, 108 (1980). It would seem, therefore, from the clear words of the statute ("any person . . . who has been convicted"), that, for respondent to be deprived of its licenses, Kennison must have been "convicted" of the type of crime specified by the statute, and the Iowa deferred judgment procedure and "expunction" must not have operated to nullify that conviction. If Kennison was not "convicted" in the first place, or if he was and that conviction somehow was rendered a nullity, respondent should not be ineligible for licenses on the grounds asserted by the Bureau.

A

We turn first to the issue of conviction. The salient fact is Kennison's plea of guilty to a state charge punishable by more than a year's imprisonment. The usual entry of a formal judgment upon a jury verdict or upon a court's specific finding of guilt after a bench trial is absent. Present, however, are (a) the charge of a crime of the disqualifying type, (b) the plea of guilty to that charge, and (c) the court's placing Kennison upon probation.

In Lewis v. United States, supra, we had under consideration §1202(a)(1) of Title VII of the 1968 Act, 18 U.S.C. App. §1202(a)(1), a gun control statute similar to and partially overlapping §§922(g) and (h). The language of §1202(a)(1) that is pertinent for present purposes is familiar, for it concerns any person who "has been convicted . . . of a felony." The Court there characterized the language of the statute as "sweeping." 445 U.S., at 60. Despite the fact that Lewis' conviction was subject to collateral attack on constitutional grounds, the Court held that conviction to be disabling. What was important to the Court was the presence or fact of the conviction. In speaking of Title VII, we said: "No modifier is present, and nothing suggests any restriction on the scope of the term 'convicted.'" Ibid. Still further: "'Nothing on the face of the statute suggests a congressional intent to limit its coverage . . . .'" Ibid., quoting United States v. Culbert, 435 U.S. 371, 373 (1978). And, finally: "Actually, . . . we detect little significant difference between Title IV and Title VII." 445 U.S., at 64.

Whether one has been "convicted" within the language of the gun control statutes is necessarily, as the Court of Appeals in the present case correctly recognized, a question of federal, not state, law, despite the fact that the predicate offense and its punishment are defined by the law of the State.

This makes for desirable national uniformity unaffected by varying state laws, procedures, and definitions of "conviction."

Whether one has been "convicted" within the language of the gun control statutes is necessarily, as the Court of Appeals in the present case correctly recognized, 649 F.2d, at 219, a question of federal, not state, law, despite the fact that the predicate offense and its punishment are defined by the law of the State. United States v. Benson, 605 F.2d 1093, 1094 (CA9 1979). This makes for desirable national uniformity unaffected by varying state laws, procedures, and definitions of "conviction."

Congress sought to rule broadly—to keep guns out of the hands of those who have demonstrated that "they may not be trusted to possess a firearm without becoming a

threat to society."

He voluntarily, in negotiation, entered a plea of guilty to a disqualifying crime.

In Lewis, the possible, and indeed probable, vulnerability of the predicate conviction to collateral attack on constitutional grounds did not affect the disqualification. This followed from the statute's plain language and from a legislative history that, as we have repeatedly observed, makes clear that "'Congress sought to rule broadly -- to keep guns out of the hands of those who have demonstrated that they may not be trusted to possess a firearm without becoming a threat to society."'" 445 U.S., at 63, quoting Scarborough v. United States, 431 U.S., at 572. Like considerations apply here with respect to whether Kennison was one who was "convicted" within the meaning of the federal statute. n6 He voluntarily, in negotiation, entered a plea of guilty to a disqualifying crime. In some circumstances, we have considered a guilty plea alone enough to constitute a "conviction": "A plea of guilty differs in purpose and effect from a mere admission or an extrajudicial confession; it is itself a conviction. Like a verdict of a jury it is conclusive. More is not required; the court has nothing to do but give judgment and sentence." Kercheval v. United States, 274 U.S. 220, 223 (1927). Accord, Boykin v. Alabama, 395 U.S. 238, 242 (1969). n7

To be sure, the terms "convicted" or "conviction" do not have the same meaning in every federal statute.

n6 To be sure, the terms "convicted" or "conviction" do not have the same meaning in every federal statute. In some statutes those terms specifically are made to apply to one whose guilty plea has been accepted whether or not a final judgment has been entered. See, e.g., 15 U.S.C. §§80a-2(10) and 80b-2(6). In other federal statutes, however, the term "convicted" is clearly limited to persons against whom a formal judgment has been entered. See, e.g., 18 U.S.C. §4251(e) and 28 U.S.C. §2901(f).

Congress' intent in enacting §§922(g) and (h) and §1202 was to keep firearms out of the hands of presumptively risky people.

The term "convicted" in §§922(g) and (h) is not there defined, but we have no reason whatsoever to suppose that Congress meant that term to apply only to one against whom a formal judgment has been entered. Congress' intent in enacting §§922(g) and (h) and §1202 was to keep firearms out of the hands of presumptively risky people. See United States v. Bass, 404 U.S. 336, 345 (1971). In this connection, it is significant that §§922(g) and (h) apply not only to a person convicted of a disqualifying offense but also to one who is merely under indictment for such a crime.

n7 As noted in n. 6, supra, the meaning of the terms "convicted" and "conviction" vary from statute to statute. In Lott v. United States, 367 U.S. 421 (1961), for example, the Court had under consideration Federal Rule of Criminal Procedure 34 and a plea of nolo contendere, rather than a plea of guilty. The question was whether the time within which certain motions could be made began to run at the time the nolo plea was entered or at the time judgment was pronounced and sentence imposed. The Court spoke of the possibility of the plea's being withdrawn before sentence was imposed and therefore said that "it is the judgment of the court -- not the plea -- that constitutes the 'determination of guilt.'" Id., at 427. In construing Rule 34, of course, the Court had before it no evidence of a congressional intent to rule broadly to protect the public comparable to that animating Title IV. Moreover, in Lott the Court did not deal with the situation where probation is imposed on the basis of the plea. Under the Iowa expunction statute, one who has pleaded guilty is treated identically to one who has been found guilty by a jury. See n. 3, supra. There is no suggestion in the Iowa statutes, and respondent has not suggested, that once the plea was noted and probation imposed Kennison could withdraw his plea. Indeed, it was a negotiated plea accompanied by the dismissal of the kidnapping charge.

for purposes of the federal gun control laws, we equate a plea of guilty and its notation by the state court, followed by a sentence of probation, with being "convicted" within the language of §§922(g) and (h).

Here, we do have more. The state judge who noted Kennison's plea placed him on probation. To be sure, there was no written adjudication of guilt and there was no formal pronouncement of a sentence of imprisonment for a specified term. But that was due to special provisions of Iowa statutory law and procedure. It was plainly irrelevant to Congress whether the individual in question actually receives a prison term; the statute imposes disabilities on one convicted of "a crime punishable by imprisonment for a term exceeding one year." §922(g) (emphasis supplied). It is also plain that one cannot be placed on probation if the court does not deem him to be guilty of a crime n8 -- in this case a crime that Congress considered demonstrative of unreliability with firearms. Thus, for purposes of the federal gun control laws, we equate a plea of guilty and its notation by the state court, followed by a sentence of probation, with being "convicted" within the language of §§922(g) and (h). See United States v. Woods, 696 F.2d 566, 570 (CA8 1982) ("once guilt has been established whether by plea or by verdict and nothing remains to be done except pass sentence, the defendant has been convicted within the intendment of Congress").

n8 Counsel acknowledged that during the period of Kennison's probation, respondent was disqualified for a license. Tr. of Oral Arg. 36-37.

B

That, however, is not an end to the matter. We still must determine whether Iowa's expunction provisions, as carried out in Kennison's case prior to respondent's license applications, nullified his conviction for purposes of the federal statute. n9

n9 For purposes of Iowa's own gun control statute, Iowa Code §724.26 (1981), it might be argued that the conviction was nullified. See State v. Walton, 311 N. W. 2d 110, 112 (Iowa 1981). Nevertheless, the Supreme Court of Iowa has observed that the "word 'conviction' is of equivocal meaning, and its use in a statute presents a question of legislative intent." State v. Hanna, 179 N. W. 2d 503, 507 (1970). Presumably, therefore, if the Supreme Court of Iowa were called upon to construe the term "convicted" in a statute like §§922(g) and (h), that court would look to "legislative intent."

In any event, Iowa's law is not federal law, and it does not control our decision here. We therefore look to federal considerations in resolving the present case.

Clearly, firearms disabilities may be attached constitutionally to an expunged conviction

We recognized in Lewis that a qualifying pardon, see 27 CFR §178.142 (1982), or a consent from the Secretary of the Treasury would operate to relieve the disability. 445 U.S., at 60-61. n10 So far as the face of the statute is concerned, however, expunction under state law does not alter the historical fact of the conviction, and does not open the way to a license despite the conviction, as does positive or "affirmative action," ibid., by way of the Secretary's consent on the conditions specified by §925(c). In Lewis, it is true, we recognized an obvious exception to the literal language of the statute for one whose predicate conviction had been vacated or reversed on direct appeal. 445 U.S., at 61, n. 5; see Note, Prior Convictions and the Gun Control Act of 1968, 76 Colum. L. Rev. 326, 334, n. 42 (1976). But, in contrast, expunction does not alter the legality of the previous conviction and does not signify that the defendant was innocent of the crime to which he pleaded guilty. Expunction in Iowa means no more than that the State has provided a means for the trial court not to accord a conviction certain continuing effects under state law. Clearly, firearms disabilities may be attached constitutionally to an expunged conviction, see Lewis v. United States, 445 U.S., at 65-68, and an exception for such a conviction, unlike one reversed or vacated due to trial error, is far from obvious. In Lewis we held that the exception for convictions reversed or vacated on direct appeal did not make ambiguous the statute's clear application to convictions arguably vulnerable to collateral attack. We perceive no more ambiguity in the statute here than we did in Lewis.

pardons granted by the President of the United States or a state governor, specifying that the recipient is authorized to receive, possess, or transport firearms, lift the disabilities

n10 Title VII, which we construed in Lewis, explicitly provides that pardons granted by the President of the United States or a state governor, specifying that the recipient is authorized to receive, possess, or transport firearms, lift the disabilities imposed by that Title. 18 U.S.C. App. §1203(2). Except §925(c), permitting the Secretary to remove the disabilities in specified circumstances, there is no comparable provision in Title IV. By regulation, the Secretary has given Presidential pardons, but not gubernatorial pardons, automatic enabling effect under Title IV. 27 CFR §178.142 (1982).

IV

Other provisions of the federal gun control laws and related federal statutes fortify our conclusion that expunction of a state conviction was not intended by Congress automatically to remove the federal firearms disability.

Other provisions of the federal gun control laws and related federal statutes fortify our conclusion that expunction of a state conviction was not intended by Congress automatically to remove the federal firearms disability.

Even conviction is not necessary for disqualification. The mere existence of an outstanding indictment is sufficient under §§922(g) and (h). Congress was reaching

far and was doing so intentionally.

1. Even conviction is not necessary for disqualification. The mere existence of an outstanding indictment is sufficient under §§922(g) and (h). Congress was reaching far and was doing so intentionally.

2. Sections 922(g) and (h) impose the same disabilities upon a person who "is under indictment" for certain crimes, or who "is a fugitive from justice," or who "is" a drug addict or an unlawful user of certain drugs, or who "has been convicted in any court" of certain crimes, or who "has been adjudicated as a mental defective," or who "has been committed to a mental institution" (emphasis supplied). This use of the respective tenses is significant and demonstrates that Congress carefully distinguished between present status and a past event. We have noted this distinction in tenses in §922, and its significance, before: "Congress knew the significance and meaning of the language it employed. It used the present perfect tense elsewhere in the same section . . . , in contrast to its use of the present tense ('who is') in §§922(h)(1), (2), and (3). The statute's pattern is consistent and no unintended misuse of language or of tense is apparent." Barrett v. United States, 423 U.S., at 217. And in Scarborough v. United States, 431 U.S., at 570, we observed: "It is obvious that the tenses used throughout Title IV were chosen with care."

A person adjudicated as a mental defective may later be adjudged competent, and a person committed to a mental institution later may be deemed cured and released. Yet Congress made no exception for subsequent curative events. The past adjudication or commitment disqualifies. Congress obviously felt that such a person, though unfortunate, was too much of a risk to be allowed firearms privileges.

In the face of this fact, we cannot believe that Congress intended to have a person convicted of a firearms felony under state law become eligible for firearms automatically because of a state expunction for whatever reason.

3. The imposition, by §§922(g)(4) and (h)(4), of continuing disability on a person who "has been" adjudicated a mental defective or committed to a mental institution is particularly instructive. A person adjudicated as a mental defective may later be adjudged competent, and a person committed to a mental institution later may be deemed cured and released. Yet Congress made no exception for subsequent curative events. The past adjudication or commitment disqualifies. Congress obviously felt that such a person, though unfortunate, was too much of a risk to be allowed firearms privileges. See United States v. Bass, 404 U.S., at 344-345. In the face of this fact, we cannot believe that Congress intended to have a person convicted of a firearms felony under state law become eligible for firearms automatically because of a state expunction for whatever reason.

4. Section 925(c) empowers the Secretary to grant relief from these disabilities in certain cases. The Secretary may not grant such relief, however, to one convicted of a crime involving the use of a firearm or of a federal firearms offense, and may not grant relief in any event unless specific conditions are met to his satisfaction. Again, it is highly unlikely that Congress intended to permit its own circumscription of the ability of the Secretary to grant relief to be overcome by the vagaries of state law. That would be too easy a route to follow in order to circumvent the federal statute. See S. Rep. No. 666, 89th Cong., 1st Sess., 2 (1965).

even a pardon is not sufficient to remove the firearms disabilities unless there is express authorization to have the firearm. It is inconceivable that Congress could have so provided and yet have intended, as the Court of Appeals concluded, to give a state expunction a contrary and unconditional effect.

5. Provisions of Title VII, enacted simultaneously with Title IV, are helpful to our analysis. We have treated Titles VII and IV as in pari materia in construing statutory language identical to that at issue here. Lewis v. United States, 445 U.S., at 61-62. Title 18 U.S.C. App. §1203(2) exempts from Title VII "any person who has been pardoned by the President of the United States or the chief executive of a State and has expressly been authorized by the President or such chief executive, as the case may be, to receive, possess, or transport in commerce a firearm." Thus, in that statute, even a pardon is not sufficient to remove the firearms disabilities unless there is express authorization to have the firearm. It is inconceivable that Congress could have so provided and yet have intended, as the Court of Appeals concluded, 649 F.2d, at 220-221, to give a state expunction a contrary and unconditional effect. After all, expunction devices were not unknown or unusual when Title IV came into being in 1968. See Comment, Expungement in California: Legislative Neglect and Judicial Abuse of the Statutory Mitigation of Felony Convictions, 12 U. San Fran. L. Rev. 155, 161 (1977); 1909 Cal. Stats., ch. 232, §1. And the Federal Youth Corrections Act, in which Congress itself provided for expunction in certain circumstances, see 18 U.S.C. §5021, was enacted as far back as 1950. See 64 Stat. 1089.

6. Title 21 U.S.C. §844(b) is a federal expunction statute providing that a first offender found guilty of simple possession of a controlled substance may be placed on probation without entry of judgment, and that, upon successful completion of the probation, the court shall discharge the defendant and dismiss the proceeding against him. But Congress also specifically provided in §844(b)(1) that such discharge or dismissal "shall not be deemed a conviction for purposes of disqualifications or disabilities imposed by law upon conviction of a crime . . . or for any other purpose." This provision would be superfluous if Congress had believed that expunction automatically removes the disqualification. Congress obviously knew the plain meaning of the terms it employed in statutes of this kind, and when it wished to create an exception for an expunged conviction, it did so expressly.

V

The principal purpose of federal gun control legislation, therefore, was to curb crime by keeping 'firearms out of the hands of those not legally entitled to possess them because of age, criminal background, or incompetency.'

"As in all cases of statutory construction, our task is to interpret the words of [the statute] in light of the purposes Congress sought to serve." Chapman v. Houston Welfare Rights Organization, 441 U.S. 600, 608 (1979). In our previous cases we have recognized and given weight to the Act's broad prophylactic purpose: "When Congress enacted [18 U.S.C. §921 et seq.] it was concerned with the widespread traffic in firearms and with their general availability to those whose possession thereof was contrary to the public interest. . . . The principal purpose of federal gun control legislation, therefore, was to curb crime by keeping 'firearms out of the hands of those not legally entitled to possess them because of age, criminal background, or incompetency.'" Huddleston v. United States, 415 U.S., at 824, quoting S. Rep. No. 1501, 90th Cong., 2d Sess., 22 (1968). See also Barrett v. United States, 423 U.S., at 220-221.

In order to accomplish this goal, Congress obviously determined that firearms must be kept away from persons, such as those convicted of serious crimes, who might be expected to misuse them. Such persons are also barred from obtaining licenses to deal in firearms or ammunition.

federal gun laws generally funnel access to firearms almost exclusively through dealers.

The principal agent of federal enforcement is the dealer.

In order to accomplish this goal, Congress obviously determined that firearms must be kept away from persons, such as those convicted of serious crimes, who might be expected to misuse them. Such persons are also barred from obtaining licenses to deal in firearms or ammunition. This latter provision is particularly important because Title IV and federal gun laws generally funnel access to firearms almost exclusively through dealers. See Huddleston v. United States, 415 U.S., at 825. "The principal agent of federal enforcement is the dealer." Id., at 824.

Although we have searched diligently, we have found nothing in the legislative history of Title IV or related federal firearms statutes that suggests, even remotely, that a state expunction was intended automatically to remove the disabilities imposed by §§922(g)(1) and (h)(1). See, e.g., S. Rep. No. 1501, 90th Cong., 2d Sess. (1968); S. Rep. No. 1097, 90th Cong., 2d Sess. (1968); H. R. Rep. No. 1577, 90th Cong., 2d Sess. (1968); H. R. Conf. Rep. No. 1956, 90th Cong., 2d Sess. (1968); H. R. Rep. No. 488, 90th Cong., 1st Sess. (1967). This lack of evidence is significant for several reasons. First, the purpose of the statute would be frustrated by a ruling that gave effect to state expunctions; a state expunction typically does not focus upon the question with which Title IV is concerned, namely, whether the convicted person is fit to engage in the firearms business or to possess a firearm. Second, "'[in] the absence of a plain indication to the contrary, . . . it is to be assumed when Congress enacts a statute that it does not intend to make its application dependent on state law.'" NLRB v. Natural Gas Utility Dist., 402 U.S. 600, 603 (1971), quoting NLRB v. Randolph Electric Membership Corp., 343 F.2d 60, 62-63 (CA4 1965). This is because the application of federal legislation is nationwide and at times the federal program would be impaired if state law were to control. Jerome v. United States, 318 U.S. 101, 104 (1943). The legislative history reveals that Congress believed a uniform national program was necessary to assist in curbing the illegal use of firearms. See S. Rep. No. 1097, 90th Cong., 2d Sess., 28, 76-77 (1968). Third, Title IV "is a carefully constructed package of gun control legislation. . . . 'Congress knew the significance and meaning of the language it employed.' " Scarborough v. United States, 431 U.S., at 570, quoting Barrett v. United States, 423 U.S., at 217. And Congress carefully crafted a procedure for removing those disabilities in appropriate cases. §925(c).

such convictions provide a convenient, although somewhat inexact, way of identifying "especially risky people."

There is no inconsistency in the refusal of Congress to be bound by postconviction state actions, such as expunctions, that vary widely from State to State and that provide less than positive assurance that the person in question no longer poses an unacceptable risk of dangerousness. Any potential harshness of the federal rule is alleviated by the power given the Secretary to grant relief where relief is appropriate based on uniform federal standards.

Congress, of course, did use state convictions to trigger Title IV's disabilities in the first instance. This, however, was not because Congress wanted to tie those disabilities to the intricacies of state law, but because such convictions provide a convenient, although somewhat inexact, way of identifying "especially risky people." United States v. Bass, 404 U.S., at 345. There is no inconsistency in the refusal of Congress to be bound by postconviction state actions, such as expunctions, that vary widely from State to State and that provide less than positive assurance that the person in question no longer poses an unacceptable risk of dangerousness. Any potential harshness of the federal rule is alleviated by the power given the Secretary to grant relief where relief is appropriate based on uniform federal standards.

The facts of the present case are illustrative. Because Kennison had "stable employment" at home in South Carolina and no previous conviction, he was placed on probation and allowed to go home. App. to Pet. for Cert. 45a-46a. Although he had no previous conviction, Kennison did have prior arrests for "assault and battery of a high and aggravated nature" and for "child abuse." Record, Govt. Exh. 13. According to him, his supervision during probation consisted of "occasionally [reporting] that [he] had not been arrested." App. to Brief in Opposition 157a. In short, the circumstances surrounding the expunction of his conviction provide little, if any, assurance that Kennison is a person who can be trusted with a dangerous weapon.

VI

Finally, a rule that would give effect to expunctions under varying state statutes would seriously hamper effective enforcement of Title IV. Over half the States have enacted one or more statutes that may be classified as expunction provisions that attempt to conceal prior convictions or to remove some of their collateral or residual effects. These statutes differ, however, in almost every particular. Some are applicable only to young offenders, e.g., Mich. Comp. Laws §§780.621 and .622 (1982). Some are available only to persons convicted of certain offenses, e.g., N. J. Stat. Ann. §2C:52-2(b) (West 1982); others, however, permit expunction of a conviction for any crime including murder, e.g., Mass. Gen. Laws Ann., ch. 276, §100A (West Supp. 1982-1983). Some are confined to first offenders, e.g., Okla. Stat., Tit. 22, §991c (Supp. 1982-1983). Some are discretionary, e.g., Minn. Stat. §638.02(2) (Supp. 1982), while others provide for automatic expunction under certain circumstances, e.g., Ariz. Rev. Stat. Ann. §13-912 (1978). The statutes vary in the language employed to describe what they do. Some speak of expunging the conviction, others of "sealing" the file or of causing the dismissal of the charge. The statutes also differ in their actual effect. Some are absolute; others are limited. Only a minority address questions such as whether the expunged conviction may be considered in sentencing for a subsequent offense or in setting bail on a later charge, or whether the expunged conviction may be used for impeachment purposes, or whether the convict may deny the fact of his conviction. Some statutes, too, clearly were not meant to prevent use of the conviction in a subsequent prosecution. See, e.g., Ariz. Rev. Stat. §13-907 (1978); United States v. Herrell, 588 F.2d 711 (CA9 1978), cert. denied, 440 U.S. 964 (1979). These and other differences provide nothing less than a national patchwork.

In this case, for example, although the Court of Appeals referred to Iowa's deferred judgment statute as "unconditional and absolute," 649 F.2d, at 221, it is obvious from the face of the statute that that description is not entirely accurate. At the time of expunction, a separate record is maintained, not destroyed, by the Supreme Court administrator. Iowa Code §907.4 (1981). See Tr. of Oral Arg. 44. In addition, all "criminal history data" may be released to "criminal justice agencies." Iowa Code §§692.1(5) and 692.2 (1981). In short, the record of a conviction expunged under Iowa law is not expunged completely.

Congress used unambiguous language in attaching gun control disabilities to any person "who has been convicted" of a qualifying offense. We give full effect to that language.

Under the decision below, perplexing problems would confront those required to enforce federal gun control laws as well as those bound by their provisions. Because, as we have noted, Title IV "is a carefully constructed package of gun control legislation," Scarborough v. United States, 431 U.S., at 570, Congress, in framing it, took pains to avoid the very problems that the Court of Appeals' decision inevitably would create, such as individualized federal treatment of every expunction law. Congress used unambiguous language in attaching gun control disabilities to any person "who has been convicted" of a qualifying offense. We give full effect to that language.

The judgment of the Court of Appeals is reversed.

It is so ordered.

JUSTICE REHNQUIST, with whom JUSTICE BRENNAN, JUSTICE STEVENS, and JUSTICE O'CONNOR join, dissenting.

Contrary to the conclusion reached by the Court, I do not believe that Kennison was "convicted." Accordingly, I dissent.

The Gun Control Act provides that any person "who has been convicted in any court of a crime punishable by imprisonment for a term exceeding one year" is ineligible for a federal license to ship, transport, or receive any firearm or ammunition in interstate commerce. 18 U.S.C. §§922(g) and (h). Thus, as the Court points out, "[if] Kennison was not 'convicted' in the first place . . . respondent should not be ineligible for licenses on the grounds asserted by the Bureau." Ante, at 111. Contrary to the conclusion reached by the Court, I do not believe that Kennison was "convicted." Accordingly, I dissent.

I agree with the Court that whether one has been convicted within the meaning of the Gun Control Act is a question of federal, rather than state, law. Ante, at 111-112. Congress did not, however, expressly define the term "conviction" in the Act. Where Congress has defined the term, the Court recognizes that it has given the term different meanings in different statutes. Ante, at 112, n. 6. In the Investment Company Act of 1940, Congress expressly provided that the term "convicted" includes "a verdict, judgment, or plea of guilty, or a finding of guilt on a plea of nolo contendere, if such verdict, judgment, plea, or finding has not been reversed, set aside, or withdrawn, whether or not sentence has been imposed." 15 U.S.C. §80a-2(a)(10). The same definition was used in the Investment Advisers Act of 1940. 15 U.S.C. §80b-2(a)(6). Congress used a more narrow definition in two sections of the Narcotic Addict Rehabilitation Act of 1966, providing that "'[conviction]' and 'convicted' mean the final judgment on a verdict or finding of guilty, a plea of guilty, or a plea of nolo contendere, and do not include a final judgment which has been expunged by pardon, reversed, set aside, or otherwise rendered nugatory." 18 U.S.C. §4251(e); 28 U.S.C. §2901(f). Finally, in the Federal Youth Corrections Act, Congress has provided that the term "'conviction' means the judgment on a verdict or finding of guilty, a plea of guilty, or a plea of nolo contendere." 18 U.S.C. §5006(g).

Thus at the most, Congress has required the entry of a formal judgment as the signpost of a "conviction." At the least, Congress has required the acceptance of a plea. In this case, we have neither. The Court relies on Kercheval v. United States, 274 U.S. 220 (1927), and Boykin v. Alabama, 395 U.S. 238 (1969), for the proposition that "[in] some circumstances, we have considered a guilty plea alone enough to constitute a 'conviction.' " Ante, at 112. The Court concludes that in this case "we . . . have more," because the state trial judge "noted" the plea and placed Kennison on probation. Ante, at 113. I cannot agree.

Even if Kercheval and Boykin would otherwise be relevant to our interpretation of the Gun Control Act, both cases spoke of an accepted guilty plea. Whatever a trial court does when it "notes" a plea, it is less, instead of more, than an acceptance of the plea which is preceded by an examination of the defendant to insure that the plea is voluntary.

Where the Iowa deferred judgment statute can be used, "[the] trial court may, upon a plea of guilty [and] [with] the consent of the defendant . . . defer judgment and place the defendant on probation." Iowa Code §789A.1 (1977) (emphasis added) (current version at Iowa Code §907.3 (1981)). Congress has never before considered such circumstances sufficient for a finding of a "conviction"; there is nothing in the Gun Control Act to infer that Congress has adopted such a standard now. It is likely that at the most Congress intended that a "conviction" be represented by a formal entry of judgment, or at the least an acceptance of a guilty plea. But in either case, such criteria are absent where, following a guilty plea, the Iowa deferred judgment statute is invoked. *

* The Court points out that respondent acknowledged in oral argument that during the period of Kennison's probation, respondent was disqualified for a license. Ante, at 114, n. 8. This disqualification, if it existed, however, would be based on the provision of the Gun Control Act applying to any person "who is under indictment," 18 U.S.C. §§922(g) and (h), rather than on a "conviction."

UNITED STATES v. ONE ASSORTMENT OF 89 FIREARMS

(FULL CASE)

465 U.S. 354; 104 S. Ct. 1099; 79 L. Ed. 2d 361

November 30, 1983, Argued

February 22, 1984, Decided

GIST: Patrick Mulcahey was charged with dealing in firearms without a federal license, a serious crime. When brought to trial, he claimed he had been entrapped into making the illegal transactions, and the jury acquitted him. Despite being found not guilty, the government moved to confiscate his firearms, suing the guns, not Mulcahey, in an *in rem* civil procedure.

Mulcahey argued the matter was settled with his acquittal, and that the 5th Amendment protection against being charged twice for the same crime prevented the government from taking his property. The issues decided by the Court do not involve the right to bear arms, as Mulcahey did not raise the 2nd Amendment in his defense.

The Court upheld the forfeiture, deciding that acquittal of criminal charges does not automatically bar a subsequent civil proceeding. The forfeiture was remedial in nature, not criminal, and thus not a violation of double jeopardy. The lower threshold of evidence needed to win in a civil proceeding allowed the government to make its case and confiscate the firearms. Although the defendant was not found guilty of dealing without a license, the guns were destined to be sold in violation of law and therefore could be seized. In making their decision, they overturned *Coffey v. U.S.* which, since 1886, had suggested a civil forfeiture could not constitutionally proceed after acquittal on related criminal charges. This weakening of the protections against double jeopardy contributes to the risk citizens now face of federal, state, criminal and civil trials for the same offense.

This turned out to be a major case setting the stage for massive use of civil forfeiture of people's property in subsequent decades. Congress limited the government's firearms forfeitures abuses somewhat by enacting the Firearms Owners' Protection Act soon afterwards in 1986. However, *One Assortment* remains a major pro-forfeiture precedent in many other judicial contexts.

Upon trial in Federal District Court, defendant Mulcahey, who asserted the defense of entrapment, was acquitted of charges of knowingly engaging in the business of dealing in firearms without a license, in violation of 18 U.S.C. §922(a)(1). The Government then instituted this in rem action for forfeiture of the firearms involved, pursuant to 18 U.S.C. §924(d), which authorizes forfeitures of any firearms "involved in or used or intended to be used in, any violation of the provisions of this chapter." Ordering forfeiture, the District Court rejected Mulcahey's defenses of res judicata and collateral estoppel based on his earlier acquittal. The Court of Appeals reversed, concluding that because the §924(d) forfeiture proceeding was criminal and punitive in nature, it was barred by double jeopardy principles in view of Mulcahey's prior acquittal. Relying on Coffey v. United States, 116 U.S. 436, the Court of Appeals also held that the forfeiture action was barred by collateral estoppel, because it was based upon the same facts as the earlier criminal action.

Held: A gun owner's acquittal on criminal charges involving firearms does not preclude a subsequent in rem forfeiture proceeding against those firearms under §924(d).

(a) To the extent that Coffey v. United States, supra, suggests that collateral estoppel or double jeopardy automatically bars a civil, remedial forfeiture proceeding following an acquittal on related criminal charges, it is disapproved. Cf. Helvering v. Mitchell, 303 U.S. 391; One Lot Emerald Cut Stones v. United States, 409 U.S. 232.

(b) The difference in the relative burdens of proof in the criminal and civil actions precludes the application of the doctrine of collateral estoppel. Acquittal on a criminal charge merely reflects the existence of a reasonable doubt as to Mulcahey's guilt, not innocence. Nor did the acquittal negate the possibility that a preponderance of the evidence in the forfeiture proceeding could show that Mulcahey was engaged in an unlicensed firearms business.

(c) The Double Jeopardy Clause does not apply to civil proceedings and is not applicable here. Under the procedural mechanisms established for enforcing forfeitures under §924(d), Congress intended such forfeitures to be civil and remedial, rather than criminal and punitive. Moreover, the differences in the language of §924(d), which subjects to forfeiture firearms used or "intended to be used" in substantive offenses, and §922(a)(1), which does not render unlawful mere intention to deal in firearms without a license, shows that the forfeiture provisions were meant to be broader in scope than the criminal sanctions. The forfeiture provision also furthers broad remedial aims of controlling the indiscriminate flow of firearms. Nor is the statutory scheme so punitive either in purpose or effect as to negate Congress' intention to establish a civil remedial mechanism.

CHIEF JUSTICE BURGER delivered the opinion of the Court.

We granted certiorari to decide whether a gun owner's acquittal on criminal charges involving firearms precludes a subsequent in rem forfeiture proceeding against those same firearms.

I

A

His defense was that he had been entrapped into making the illegal firearms transactions. The jury returned a verdict of not guilty.

On January 20, 1977, the Bureau of Alcohol, Tobacco, and Firearms seized a cache of firearms from the home of Patrick Mulcahey. Mulcahey was subsequently indicted on charges that he had knowingly engaged in the business of dealing in firearms without a license, in violation of 18 U.S.C. §922(a)(1). n1 At his criminal trial, Mulcahey admitted that he had no license to deal in firearms and that he had bought and sold firearms during the period set forth in the indictment. His defense was that he had been entrapped into making the illegal firearms transactions. The jury returned a verdict of not guilty.

n1 Title 18 U.S.C. §922(a)(1) provides:

"It shall be unlawful . . . for any person, except a licensed importer, licensed manufacturer, or licensed dealer, to engage in the business of importing, manufacturing, or dealing in firearms or ammunition, or in the course of such business to ship, transport, or receive any firearm or ammunition in interstate or foreign commerce."

Following Mulcahey's acquittal of the criminal charges, the United States, pursuant to its authority under 18 U.S.C. §924(d), n2 instituted this in rem action for forfeiture of the seized firearms. n3 On the basis of his earlier acquittal, Mulcahey asserted the defenses of res judicata and collateral estoppel. The United States District Court for the District of South Carolina struck Mulcahey's defenses, reasoning that an in rem forfeiture proceeding under 18 U.S.C. §924(d) is remedial in nature and is therefore properly characterized as a civil proceeding. The District Court then concluded that "the firearms here in question were involved in, used or intended to be used in violation of 18 U.S.C. §922(a)(1). Such firearms are rendered subject to forfeiture under 18 U.S.C. §924(d), which forfeiture is hereby ordered."

n2 Title 18 U.S.C. §924(d) provides:

"Any firearm or ammunition involved in or used or intended to be used in, any violation of the provisions of this chapter or any rule or regulation promulgated thereunder, or any violation of any other criminal law of the United States, shall be subject to seizure and forfeiture and all provisions of the Internal Revenue Code of 1954 relating to the seizure, forfeiture, and disposition of firearms, as defined in section 5845(a) of that Code, shall, so far as applicable, extend to seizures and forfeitures under the provisions of this chapter."

The number of firearms involved in this action has varied somewhat with time. Federal agents originally seized 105 firearms from Mulcahey, but later learned that 13 of them had been stolen. The stolen items were returned to their rightful owners, and the forfeiture action proceeded against the remaining 92 items. Later an additional automatic pistol was found, bringing the total to 93. Still later, for reasons not relevant

here, 4 of the seized firearms were returned to Mulcahey's wife, leaving 89 firearms as the subject of the forfeiture proceeding.

n3 The number of firearms involved in this action has varied somewhat with time. Federal agents originally seized 105 firearms from Mulcahey, but later learned that 13 of them had been stolen. The stolen items were returned to their rightful owners, and the forfeiture action proceeded against the remaining 92 items. Later an additional automatic pistol was found, bringing the total to 93. Still later, for reasons not relevant here, 4 of the seized firearms were returned to Mulcahey's wife, leaving 89 firearms as the subject of the forfeiture proceeding.

B

A divided United States Court of Appeals for the Fourth Circuit, sitting en banc, reversed. n4 The en banc majority relied upon two theories for its conclusion that the forfeiture proceeding against these firearms was barred by Mulcahey's prior acquittal, although it did not sharply distinguish between the two. Because the majority considered the §924(d) forfeiture proceeding to be criminal and punitive in nature, the Court of Appeals concluded that it was barred by double jeopardy principles. Looking to Coffey v. United States (1886), as authority, the Court of Appeals also determined that the forfeiture action was barred by collateral estoppel, because it was based upon the same facts as the earlier criminal action. In dissent, four judges argued that neither collateral estoppel nor double jeopardy should preclude forfeiture proceedings brought under §924(d). We granted certiorari and we reverse.

n4 A divided panel of the Fourth Circuit had previously reversed the District Court's forfeiture order.

I

In Coffey v. United States, this Court held that a forfeiture action brought against certain distilling equipment was barred by the owner's prior acquittal on charges of removing and concealing distilled spirits with the intent to defraud the revenue. The Court stated:

"[Where] an issue raised as to the existence of the act or fact denounced has been tried in a criminal proceeding, instituted by the United States, and a judgment of acquittal has been rendered in favor of a particular person, that judgment is conclusive in favor of such person, on the subsequent trial of a suit in rem by the United States, where, as against him, the existence of the same act or fact is the matter in issue, as a cause for the forfeiture of the property prosecuted in such suit in rem. It is urged as a reason for not allowing such effect to the judgment, that the acquittal in the criminal case may have taken place because of the rule requiring guilt to be proved beyond a reasonable doubt, and that, on the same evidence, on the question of preponderance of proof, there might be a verdict for the United States, in the suit in rem. Nevertheless, the fact or act has been put in issue and determined against the United States; and all that is imposed by the statute, as a consequence of guilt, is a punishment therefor. There could be no new trial of the criminal prosecution after the acquittal in it; and a subsequent trial of the civil suit amounts to substantially the same thing, with a difference only in the consequences following a judgment adverse to the claimant." Id., at 443.

Although the language quoted above incorporates notions of both collateral estoppel and double jeopardy, the Coffey Court did not identify the precise legal foundation for the rule of preclusion it announced. Perhaps for this reason, later decisions of this Court have reflected uncertainty as to the exact scope of the Coffey holding.

In Helvering v. Mitchell, 303 U.S. 391 (1938), the Court considered the preclusive effect of a prior criminal acquittal on a subsequent action for a monetary penalty. The defendant taxpayer in Mitchell was acquitted of charges that he willfully attempted to evade and defeat the income tax by fraudulently misstating certain items on his income tax return. When the Commissioner of Internal Revenue then brought an action to recover a substantial monetary penalty for fraudulent avoidance of income tax, the taxpayer argued that the subsequent penalty action was barred by res judicata, collateral estoppel, and the Coffey rule of preclusion.

This Court, speaking through Justice Brandeis, disagreed. Although the taxpayer argued and the Government conceded that the factual matters at issue in the penalty proceeding had been litigated and determined in the prior criminal action, the Court concluded that "[the] difference in degree of the burden of proof in criminal and civil cases precludes application of the doctrine of res judicata." 303 U.S., at 397. The Mitchell Court viewed the criminal acquittal as nothing more than a determination that the evidence in the criminal setting was not sufficient to overcome all reasonable doubt that the accused was guilty. See Lewis v. Frick, 233 U.S. 291, 302 (1914). The Court went on to state:

"That acquittal on a criminal charge is not a bar to a civil action by the Government, remedial in its nature, arising out of the same facts on which the criminal proceeding was based has long been settled. Stone v. United States, 167 U.S. 178, 188; Murphy v. United States, 272 U.S. 630, 631, 632. Compare Chantangco v. Abaroa, 218 U.S. 476, 481, 482. " 303 U.S., at 397-398 (footnote omitted).

Turning to the taxpayer's argument that double jeopardy barred the assessment of a monetary penalty following his acquittal on related criminal charges, the Court noted:

"Congress may impose both a criminal and a civil sanction in respect to the same act or omission; for the double jeopardy clause prohibits merely punishing twice, or attempting a second time to punish criminally, for the same offense. The question for decision is thus whether [the monetary penalty] imposes a criminal sanction. That question is one of statutory interpretation." Id., at 399.

In concluding that the monetary penalty was merely a remedial civil sanction authorized by Congress to be assessed at the discretion of those administering the tax law, the Court observed that forfeiture of goods or their value and the payment of fixed or variable sums of money are sanctions that have long been recognized as enforceable by civil proceedings. Id., at 400.

Finally, the Mitchell Court considered the effect of the holding in Coffey upon the facts before it. The Court distinguished Coffey on the ground that the Coffey rule did not apply where an acquittal on a criminal charge was followed by a civil action requiring a different degree of proof. The Mitchell Court concluded that the monetary penalty imposed by the revenue laws was a civil administrative sanction; it therefore found Coffey no obstacle to the recovery of the penalty from the taxpayer. 303 U.S., at 405-406.

Most recently, in One Lot Emerald Cut Stones v. United States, 409 U.S. 232 (1972) (per curiam), the Court held that a civil action for forfeiture of a ring and stones was not barred by the owner's prior acquittal on charges of willfully and knowingly, with intent to defraud the United States, smuggling articles into the United States without complying with customs procedures. Reaffirming the principles articulated in Helvering v. Mitchell, supra, the Court reasoned that the difference between the burdens of proof in the criminal and civil cases precluded the application of the doctrine of collateral estoppel. Double jeopardy was equally inapposite, the Court continued, because the forfeiture asserted against the ring and stones was a civil, not a criminal, sanction. The Court distinguished Coffey on the ground that acquittal on the criminal charges in One Lot Emerald Cut Stones did not necessarily resolve the issues in the later forfeiture action. 409 U.S., at 235, n. 5.

an acquittal of a criminal charge does not automatically bar an action to enforce sanctions by way of forfeiture of goods or other civil penalties.

an acquittal in a criminal trial does not bar a civil action for forfeiture even though based on the identical facts.

The time has come to clarify that neither collateral estoppel nor double jeopardy bars a civil, remedial forfeiture proceeding initiated following an acquittal on related criminal charges.

In focusing on Coffey v. United States, the Court of Appeals appears to have overlooked the significance of Mitchell and One Lot Emerald Cut Stones. At the very least, Mitchell signaled that an acquittal of a criminal charge does not automatically bar an action to enforce sanctions by way of forfeiture of goods or other civil penalties. Whatever the validity of Coffey on its facts, its ambiguous reasoning seems to have been a source of confusion for some time. As long ago as Mitchell, this Court was urged to disapprove Coffey so as to make clear that an acquittal in a criminal trial does not bar a civil action for forfeiture even though based on the identical facts. Indeed, for nearly a century, the analytical underpinnings of Coffey have been recognized as less than adequate. n5 The time has come to clarify that neither collateral estoppel nor double jeopardy bars a civil, remedial forfeiture proceeding initiated following an acquittal on related criminal charges. To the extent that Coffey v. United States suggests otherwise, it is hereby disapproved.

n5 See, e.g., United States v. Burch, 294 F.2d 1, 3, n. 2 (CA5 1961); United States v. One Dodge Sedan, 113 F.2d 552, 553, and n. 1 (CA3 1940) (collecting cases and law review articles); 1B J. Moore, J. Lucas, & T. Currier, Moore's Federal Practice para. 0.418[3], pp. 587-589, and n. 12 (1983) (collecting cases).

III

A

an acquittal on criminal charges does not prove that the defendant is innocent; it merely proves the existence of a reasonable doubt as to his guilt.

the jury verdict in the criminal action did not negate the possibility that a preponderance of the evidence could show that Mulcahey was engaged in an unlicensed firearms business.

The disposition of the instant case follows readily from the principles articulated in Mitchell and One Lot Emerald Cut Stones. Mulcahey first argues that, because of his earlier criminal acquittal, the doctrine of collateral estoppel operates to preclude the §924(d) forfeiture action. But an acquittal on criminal charges does not prove that the defendant is innocent; it merely proves the existence of a reasonable doubt as to his guilt. We need not be concerned whether the jury decided to acquit Mulcahey because he was entrapped into making an illegal sale or whether the jurors were not convinced of his guilt beyond a reasonable doubt for other reasons. In either case, the jury verdict in the criminal action did not negate the possibility that a preponderance of the evidence could show that Mulcahey was engaged in an unlicensed firearms business. Mulcahey's acquittal on charges brought under §922(a)(1) therefore does not estop the Government from proving in a civil proceeding that the firearms should be forfeited pursuant to §924(d). It is clear that the difference in the relative burdens of proof in the criminal and civil actions precludes the application of the doctrine of collateral estoppel. Helvering v. Mitchell, 303 U.S., at 397; One Lot Emerald Cut Stones v. United States, supra, at 235.

B

Mulcahey next contends that a forfeiture proceeding under §924(d) is barred by the Double Jeopardy Clause of the Fifth Amendment. Unless the forfeiture sanction was intended as punishment, so that the proceeding is essentially criminal in character, the Double Jeopardy Clause is not applicable. Helvering v. Mitchell, 303 U.S., at 398-399. The question, then, is whether a §924(d) forfeiture proceeding is intended to be, or by its nature necessarily is, criminal and punitive, or civil and remedial. Resolution of this question begins as a matter of statutory interpretation. Id., at 399. As the Court noted in United States v. Ward, 448 U.S. 242, 248 (1980):

"Our inquiry in this regard has traditionally proceeded on two levels. First, we have set out to determine whether Congress, in establishing the penalizing mechanism, indicated either expressly or impliedly a preference for one label or the other. See One Lot Emerald Cut Stones v. United States, supra, at 236-237. Second, where Congress has indicated an intention to establish a civil penalty, we have inquired further whether the statutory scheme was so punitive either in purpose or effect as to negate that intention. See Flemming v. Nestor, 363 U.S. 603, 617-621 (1960)."

Applying the first prong of the Ward test to the facts of the instant case, we conclude that Congress designed forfeiture under §924(d) as a remedial civil sanction. Congress' intent in this regard is most clearly demonstrated by the procedural mechanisms it established for enforcing forfeitures under the statute. Section 924(d) does not prescribe the steps to be followed in effectuating a forfeiture, but rather incorporates by reference the procedures of the Internal Revenue Code of 1954 (Code), 26 U.S.C. §§7321-7328. The Code in turn provides that an action to enforce a forfeiture "shall be in the nature of a proceeding in rem in the United States District Court for the district where such seizure is made." 26 U.S.C. §7323. In contrast to the in personam nature of criminal actions, actions in rem have traditionally been viewed as civil proceedings, with jurisdiction dependent upon seizure of a physical object. See Calero-Toledo v. Pearson Yacht Leasing Co., 416 U.S. 663, 684 (1974). In addition to establishing the in rem nature of the action, the Code authorizes a summary administrative proceeding for forfeiture of items valued at $2,500 or less, for which notice of a seizure may be by publication. See 26 U.S.C. §7325. By creating such distinctly civil procedures for forfeitures under §924(d), Congress has "[indicated] clearly that it intended a civil, not a criminal, sanction." Helvering v. Mitchell, supra, at 402.

Moreover, §924(d) is somewhat broader in scope than the criminal provisions of 18 U.S.C. §922. Section 924(d) subjects to forfeiture "[any] firearm or ammunition involved in or used or intended to be used in, any violation of the provisions of this chapter." (Emphasis added.) But §922(a)(1), the substantive criminal provision under which Mulcahey was prosecuted, does not render unlawful an intention to engage in the business of dealing in firearms without a license; only the completed act of engaging in the prohibited business is made a crime. See n. 1, supra. Whatever the actual scope of the conduct embraced by §924(d), it is apparent from the differences in the language of these two statutes that the forfeiture provisions of §924(d) were meant to be broader in scope than the criminal sanctions of §922(a)(1).

Congress sought to "control the indiscriminate flow" of firearms and to "assist and encourage States and local communities to adopt and enforce stricter gun control laws."

Keeping potentially dangerous weapons out of the hands of unlicensed dealers is a goal plainly more remedial than punitive. Accordingly, we hold that Congress viewed §924(d) forfeiture as a remedial civil sanction rather than a criminal punishment.

Finally, the forfeiture provision of §924(d) furthers broad remedial aims. Section 924(d) was enacted as part of the Omnibus Crime Control and Safe Streets Act of 1968, Pub. L. 90-351, 82 Stat. 233, and later retained without alteration in the Gun Control Act of 1968, Pub. L. 90-618, 82 Stat. 1224. In enacting the 1968 gun control legislation, Congress "was concerned with the widespread traffic in firearms and with their general availability to those whose possession thereof was contrary to the public interest." Huddleston v. United States, 415 U.S. 814, 824 (1974). Accordingly, Congress sought to "control the indiscriminate flow" of firearms and to "assist and encourage States and local communities to adopt and enforce stricter gun control laws." H. R. Rep. No. 1577, 90th Cong., 2d Sess., 8 (1968). Section 924(d) plays an important role in furthering the prophylactic purposes of the 1968 gun control legislation by discouraging unregulated commerce in firearms and by removing from circulation firearms that have been used or intended for use outside regulated channels of commerce. Keeping potentially dangerous weapons out of the hands of unlicensed dealers is a goal plainly more remedial than punitive. Accordingly, we hold that Congress viewed §924(d) forfeiture as a remedial civil sanction rather than a criminal punishment. n6

n6 Mulcahey relies heavily upon Congress' labeling of §924 with the appellation "Penalties," arguing that inclusion of the forfeiture provision in that section demonstrates Congress' intention to create an additional criminal sanction. This argument is unavailing; both criminal and civil sanctions may be labeled "penalties." Moreover, the congressional Reports accompanying §924 describe it as "[containing] the penalty and forfeiture provisions," H. R. Rep. No. 1577, 90th Cong., 2d Sess., 17 (1968); S. Rep. No. 1097, 90th Cong., 2d Sess., 117 (1968), indicating that Congress was cognizant of the important differences between criminal punishment and in rem forfeiture.

We now turn to the second aspect of our inquiry: "whether the statutory scheme [is] so punitive either in purpose or effect as to negate" Congress' intention to establish a civil remedial mechanism. United States v. Ward, 448 U.S., at 248-249. "'Only the clearest proof'" that the purpose and effect of the forfeiture are punitive will suffice to override Congress' manifest preference for a civil sanction. Id., at 249 (quoting Flemming v. Nestor, 363 U.S. 603, 617 (1960)). In Kennedy v. Mendoza-Martinez, 372 U.S. 144, 168-169 (1963), we set forth a list of considerations that has proved helpful in the past in making such determinations. n7 See, e.g., United States v. Ward, supra, at 249-251; Bell v. Wolfish, 441 U.S. 520, 537-538 (1979).

n7 In Kennedy v. Mendoza-Martinez, the Court enumerated "the tests traditionally applied to determine whether an Act of Congress is penal or regulatory in character." 372 U.S., at 168.

"Whether the sanction involves an affirmative disability or restraint, whether it has historically been regarded as a punishment, whether it comes into play only on a finding of scienter, whether its operation will promote the traditional aims of punishment -- retribution and deterrence, whether the behavior to which it applies is already a crime, whether an alternative purpose to which it may rationally be connected is assignable for it, and whether it appears excessive in relation to the alternative purpose assigned are all relevant to the inquiry, and may often point in differing directions." Id., at 168-169 (footnotes omitted).

This list of considerations is, however, "neither exhaustive nor dispositive." United States v. Ward, 448 U.S. 242, 249 (1980).

Only one of the Mendoza-Martinez factors -- whether or not the proscribed behavior is already a crime -- lends any support to Mulcahey's position that §924(d) imposes a criminal penalty. The fact that actions giving rise to forfeiture proceedings under §924(d) may also entail the criminal penalties of §922(a)(1) admittedly suggests that §924(d) is criminal in nature. But that indication is not as strong as it might seem at first blush. United States v. Ward, supra, at 250. Clearly "Congress may impose both a criminal and a civil sanction in respect to the same act or omission," Helvering v. Mitchell, 303 U.S., at 399; indeed, it has done so on other occasions. Moreover, Congress in fact drafted §924(d) to cover a broader range of conduct than is proscribed by the criminal provisions of §922(a)(1). See supra, at 363-364. Because the sanction embodied in §924(d) is not limited to criminal misconduct, the forfeiture remedy cannot be said to be coextensive with the criminal penalty. What overlap there is between the two sanctions is not sufficient to persuade us that the forfeiture proceeding may not legitimately be viewed as civil in nature.

In short, an analysis of the Mendoza-Martinez factors in no way undermines Congress' classification of the §924(d) forfeiture action as a civil sanction. Mulcahey has failed to establish by the "clearest proof" that Congress has provided a sanction so punitive as to "[transform] what was clearly intended as a civil remedy into a criminal penalty." Rex Trailer Co. v. United States, 350 U.S. 148, 154 (1956). We accordingly conclude that the forfeiture mechanism set forth in §924(d) is not an additional penalty for the commission of a criminal act, but rather is a separate civil sanction, remedial in nature. Because the §924(d) forfeiture proceeding brought against Mulcahey's firearms is not a criminal proceeding, it is not barred by the Double Jeopardy Clause.

IV

We hold that a gun owner's acquittal on criminal charges involving firearms does not preclude a subsequent in rem forfeiture proceeding against those firearms under §924(d).

We hold that a gun owner's acquittal on criminal charges involving firearms does not preclude a subsequent in rem forfeiture proceeding against those firearms under §924(d). Neither collateral estoppel nor the Double Jeopardy Clause affords a doctrinal basis for such a rule of preclusion, and we reject today the contrary rationale of Coffey v. United States, 116 U.S. 436 (1886). The judgment of the United States Court of Appeals for the Fourth Circuit is accordingly reversed, and the case is remanded for proceedings consistent with this opinion.

It is so ordered.

TENNESSEE v. GARNER

(CASE EXCERPT)

471 U.S. 1; 105 S. Ct. 1694; 85 L. Ed. 2d 1

October 30, 1984, Argued

March 27, 1985, Decided

GIST: Common law in existence from before the Bill of Rights, explicit statutes of nearly half the states, and the law in Tennessee at the time of this case allowed police officers to shoot a fleeing felony suspect if it was the only way to prevent the person from escaping. Many arguments exist for and against such a long-standing and widely held policy, and they are examined in this case. The Court decided that such open-ended authorization of the use of deadly force is an unreasonable form of seizure under the 4th Amendment.

This is the only High Court case touching upon the fringe self-defense issue of pursuit. While deadly force is recognized as legitimate in responding to a potentially deadly attack, its use to stop a suspect from getting away is much less reliable justification.

Typically viewed in legal circles as a deadly force case, or a 4th Amendment case, to many police officers *Garner* is the quintessential gun case because it illuminates the question of when you can draw and use your sidearm. Additional conditions must be present now before deadly force is permissible for officers dealing with a fleeing suspect. Conditions include whether the suspect poses a threat to the community, or threatens the officer with a weapon, or if there is probable cause to believe the suspect has committed a crime involving the infliction or threatened infliction of serious physical harm. An officer must also give some warning if feasible.

Memphis police officer Elton Hymon, responding to a residential burglary call, found a jimmied window and then heard the back door slam. In the junk-strewn backyard he saw a figure crouching near a fence. He shouted a police warning and ordered the individual to freeze. The shadowy figure jumped up on the fence and was one leap from escape when the officer took him into custody and prevented his escape, with a revolver shot to the back of the head. The officer acted under authority of Tennessee law written to prevent such escapes, and fifteen-year-old Edward Garner, unarmed, died on the way to the hospital.

The High Court decided that Tennessee's law was unconstitutional and rewrote the requirements for use of deadly force by the police. It is important to keep in mind that the conditions discussed in here apply to the authorities, or a person called to assist the authorities, but not to the general public, who are not addressed in this regard at the Supreme Court level. Common wisdom holds that its better for a criminal to get away than to have a lien on your home from legal bills after shooting someone running away with your TV or the family jewels. State laws vary widely about citizen use of deadly force against fleeing felons, and of course, a person is only determined to be a felon after a conviction.

Justice Sandra Day O'Conner, writing in dissent for a minority of three, agrees that shooting a fleeing suspect is a "seizure" for constitutional purposes, but the dissenters characterize the majority's decision as a new right for burglary suspects to blithely leave the scene of a crime, and argue that the 4th Amendment contains no such right. The dissent takes the position that using deadly force to apprehend a fleeing burglar under the circumstances of this case is not unreasonable.

A Tennessee statute provides that if, after a police officer has given notice of an intent to arrest a criminal suspect, the suspect flees or forcibly resists, "the officer may use all the necessary means to effect the arrest." Acting under the authority of this statute, a Memphis police officer shot and killed appellee-respondent Garner's son as, after being told to halt, the son fled over a fence at night in the backyard of a house he was suspected of burglarizing. The officer used deadly force despite being "reasonably sure" the suspect was unarmed and thinking that he was 17 or 18 years old and of slight build. The father subsequently brought an action in Federal District Court, seeking damages under 42 U.S.C. 1983 for asserted violations of his son's constitutional rights. The District Court held that the statute and the officer's actions were constitutional. The Court of Appeals reversed.

Held:

The Tennessee statute is unconstitutional insofar as it authorizes the use of deadly force against, as in this case, an apparently unarmed, nondangerous fleeing suspect; such force may not be used unless necessary to prevent the escape and the officer has probable cause to believe that the suspect poses a significant threat of death or serious physical injury to the officer or others. Pp. 7-22.

(a) Apprehension by the use of deadly force is a seizure subject to the Fourth Amendment's reasonableness requirement. To determine whether such a seizure is reasonable, the extent of the intrusion on the suspect's rights under that Amendment must be balanced against the governmental interests in effective law enforcement. This balancing process demonstrates that, notwithstanding probable cause to seize a suspect, an officer may not always do so by killing him. The use of deadly force to prevent the escape of all felony suspects, whatever the circumstances, is constitutionally unreasonable. Pp. 7-12.

(b) The Fourth Amendment, for purposes of this case, should not be construed in light of the common-law rule allowing the use of whatever force is necessary to effect the arrest of a fleeing felon. Changes in the legal and technological context mean that that rule is distorted almost beyond recognition when literally applied. Whereas felonies were formerly capital crimes, few are now, or can be, and many crimes classified as misdemeanors, or nonexistent, at common law are now felonies. Also, the common-law rule developed at a time when weapons were rudimentary. And, in light of the varied rules adopted in the States indicating a long-term movement away from the common-law rule, particularly in the police departments themselves, that rule is a dubious indicium of the constitutionality of the Tennessee statute. There is no indication that holding a police practice such as that authorized by the statute unreasonable will severely hamper effective law enforcement. Pp. 12-20.

(c) While burglary is a serious crime, the officer in this case could not reasonably have believed that the suspect - young, slight, and unarmed - posed any threat. Nor does the fact that an unarmed suspect has broken into a dwelling at night automatically mean he is dangerous. Pp. 20-22.

710 F.2d 240, affirmed and remanded.

WHITE, J., delivered the opinion of the Court, in which BRENNAN, MARSHALL, BLACKMUN, POWELL, and STEVENS, JJ., joined. O'CONNOR, J., filed a dissenting opinion, in which BURGER, C. J., and REHNQUIST, J., joined, post, p. 22.

JUSTICE WHITE delivered the opinion of the Court.

This case requires us to determine the constitutionality of the use of deadly force to prevent the escape of an apparently unarmed suspected felon.

such force may not be used unless it is necessary to prevent the escape and the officer has probable cause to believe that the suspect poses a significant threat of death or serious physical injury to the officer or others.

This case requires us to determine the constitutionality of the use of deadly force to prevent the escape of an apparently unarmed suspected felon. We conclude that such force may not be used unless it is necessary to prevent the escape and the officer has probable cause to believe that the suspect poses a significant threat of death or serious physical injury to the officer or others.

I

Convinced that if Garner made it over the fence he would elude capture, Hymon shot him. The bullet hit Garner in the back of the head.

At about 10:45 p.m. on October 3, 1974, Memphis Police Officers Elton Hymon and Leslie Wright were dispatched to answer a "prowler inside call." Upon arriving at the scene they saw a woman standing on her porch and gesturing toward the adjacent house. She told them she had heard glass breaking and that "they" or "someone" was breaking in next door. While Wright radioed the dispatcher to say that they were on the scene, Hymon went behind the house. He heard a door slam and saw someone run across the backyard. The fleeing suspect, who was appellee-respondent's decedent, Edward Garner, stopped at a 6-feet-high chain link fence at the edge of the yard. With the aid of a flashlight, Hymon was able to see Garner's face and hands. He saw no sign of a weapon, and, though not certain, was "reasonably sure" and "figured" that Garner was unarmed. App. 41, 56; Record 219. He thought Garner was 17 or 18 years old and about 5' 5" or 5' 7" tall. While Garner was crouched at the base of the fence, Hymon called out "police, halt" and took a few steps toward him. Garner then began to climb over the fence. Convinced that if Garner made it over the fence he would elude capture, Hymon shot him. The bullet hit Garner in the back of the head. Garner was taken by ambulance to a hospital, where he died on the operating table. Ten dollars and a purse taken from the house were found on his body.

In using deadly force to prevent the escape, Hymon was acting under the authority of a Tennessee statute and pursuant to Police Department policy.

In using deadly force to prevent the escape, Hymon was acting under the authority of a Tennessee statute and pursuant to Police Department policy. The statute provides that "[i]f, after notice of the intention to arrest the defendant, he either flee or forcibly resist, the officer may use all the necessary means to effect the arrest." Tenn. Code Ann. 40-7-108 (1982). The Department policy was slightly more restrictive than the statute, but still allowed the use of deadly force in cases of burglary. App. 140-144. The incident was reviewed by the Memphis Police Firearm's Review Board and presented to a grand jury. Neither took any action. Id., at 57.

Garner had "recklessly and heedlessly attempted to vault over the fence to escape, thereby assuming the risk of being fired upon."

Garner's father then brought this action in the Federal District Court for the Western District of Tennessee, seeking damages under 42 U.S.C. 1983 for asserted violations of Garner's constitutional rights. The complaint alleged that the shooting violated the Fourth, Fifth, Sixth, Eighth, and Fourteenth Amendments of the United States Constitution. It named as defendants Officer Hymon, the Police Department, its Director, and the Mayor and city of Memphis. After a 3-day bench trial, the District Court entered judgment for all defendants. It dismissed the claims against the Mayor and the Director for lack of evidence. It then concluded that Hymon's actions were authorized by the Tennessee statute, which in turn was constitutional. Hymon had employed the only reasonable and practicable means of preventing Garner's escape. Garner had "recklessly and heedlessly attempted to vault over the fence to escape, thereby assuming the risk of being fired upon." App. to Pet. for Cert. A10.

The District Court was directed to consider whether a city enjoyed a qualified immunity, whether the use of deadly force and hollow point bullets in these circumstances was constitutional

The Court of Appeals for the Sixth Circuit affirmed with regard to Hymon, finding that he had acted in good-faith reliance on the Tennessee statute and was therefore within the scope of his qualified immunity. 600 F.2d 52 (1979). It remanded for reconsideration of the possible liability of the city, however, in light of Monell v. New York City Dept. of Social Services, 436 U.S. 658 (1978), which had come down after the District Court's decision. The District Court was directed to consider whether a city enjoyed a qualified immunity, whether the use of deadly force and hollow point bullets in these circumstances was constitutional, and whether any unconstitutional municipal conduct flowed from a "policy or custom" as required for liability under Monell. 600 F.2d, at 54-55.

The District Court concluded that Monell did not affect its decision. While acknowledging some doubt as to the possible immunity of the city, it found that the statute, and Hymon's actions, were constitutional. Given this conclusion, it declined to consider the "policy or custom" question. App. to Pet. for Cert. A37-A39.

The Court of Appeals reversed and remanded. 710 F.2d 240 (1983). It reasoned that the killing of a fleeing suspect is a "seizure" under the Fourth Amendment, and is therefore constitutional only if "reasonable." The Tennessee statute failed as applied to this case because it did not adequately limit the use of deadly force by distinguishing between felonies of different magnitudes - "the facts, as found, did not justify the use of deadly force under the Fourth Amendment." Id., at 246. Officers cannot resort to deadly force unless they "have probable cause . . . to believe that the suspect [has committed a felony and] poses a threat to the safety of the officers or a danger to the community if left at large." Ibid.

The State of Tennessee, which had intervened to defend the statute, see 28 U.S.C. 2403(b), appealed to this Court. The city filed a petition for certiorari. We noted probable jurisdiction in the appeal and granted the petition. 465 U.S. 1098 (1984).

II

Whenever an officer restrains the freedom of a person to walk away, he has seized that person.

there can be no question that apprehension by the use of deadly force is a seizure subject to the reasonableness requirement of the Fourth Amendment.

Whenever an officer restrains the freedom of a person to walk away, he has seized that person. United States v. Brignoni-Ponce, 422 U.S. 873, 878 (1975). While it is not always clear just when minimal police interference becomes a seizure, see United States v. Mendenhall, 446 U.S. 544 (1980), there can be no question that apprehension by the use of deadly force is a seizure subject to the reasonableness requirement of the Fourth Amendment.

A

A police officer may arrest a person if he has probable cause to believe that person committed a crime. E. g., United States v. Watson, 423 U.S. 411 (1976). Petitioners and appellant argue that if this requirement is satisfied the Fourth Amendment has nothing to say about how that seizure is made. This submission ignores the many cases in which this Court, by balancing the extent of the intrusion against the need for it, has examined the reasonableness of the manner in which a search or seizure is conducted. To determine the constitutionality of a seizure "[w]e must balance the nature and quality of the intrusion on the individual's Fourth Amendment interests against the importance of the governmental interests alleged to justify the intrusion." United States v. Place, 462 U.S. 696, 703 (1983); see Delaware v. Prouse, 440 U.S. 648, 654 (1979); United States v. Martinez-Fuerte, 428 U.S. 543, 555 (1976). We have described "the balancing of competing interests" as "the key principle of the Fourth Amendment." Michigan v. Summers, 452 U.S. 692, 700, n. 12 (1981). See also Camara v. Municipal Court, 387 U.S. 523, 536 -537 (1967). Because one of the factors is the extent of the intrusion, it is plain that reasonableness depends on not only when a seizure is made, but also how it is carried out. United States v. Ortiz, 422 U.S. 891, 895 (1975); Terry v. Ohio, 392 U.S. 1, 28 -29 (1968).

.....

B

The same balancing process applied in the cases cited above demonstrates that, notwithstanding probable cause to seize a suspect, an officer may not always do so by killing him.

The use of deadly force also frustrates the interest of the individual, and of society, in judicial determination of guilt and punishment.

It is argued that overall violence will be reduced by encouraging the peaceful submission of suspects who know that they may be shot if they flee. Effectiveness in making arrests requires the resort to deadly force, or at least the meaningful threat thereof.

The same balancing process applied in the cases cited above demonstrates that, notwithstanding probable cause to seize a suspect, an officer may not always do so by killing him. The intrusiveness of a seizure by means of deadly force is unmatched. The suspect's fundamental interest in his own life need not be elaborated upon. The use of deadly force also frustrates the interest of the individual, and of society, in judicial determination of guilt and punishment. Against these interests are ranged governmental interests in effective law enforcement. It is argued that overall violence will be reduced by encouraging the peaceful submission of suspects who know that they may be shot if they flee. Effectiveness in making arrests requires the resort to deadly force, or at least the meaningful threat thereof. "Being able to arrest such individuals is a condition precedent to the state's entire system of law enforcement." Brief for Petitioners 14.

Without in any way disparaging the importance of these goals, we are not convinced that the use of deadly force is a sufficiently productive means of accomplishing them to justify the killing of nonviolent suspects.

while the meaningful threat of deadly force might be thought to lead to the arrest of more live suspects by discouraging escape attempts, the presently available evidence does not support this thesis.

The fact is that a majority of police departments in this country have forbidden the use of deadly force against nonviolent suspects.

Petitioners and appellant have not persuaded us that shooting nondangerous fleeing suspects is so vital as to outweigh the suspect's interest in his own life.

Without in any way disparaging the importance of these goals, we are not convinced that the use of deadly force is a sufficiently productive means of accomplishing them to justify the killing of nonviolent suspects. Cf. Delaware v. Prouse, supra, at 659. The use of deadly force is a self-defeating way of apprehending a suspect and so setting the criminal justice mechanism in motion. If successful, it guarantees that that mechanism will not be set in motion. And while the meaningful threat of deadly force might be thought to lead to the arrest of more live suspects by discouraging escape attempts, the presently available evidence does not support this thesis. The fact is that a majority of police departments in this country have forbidden the use of deadly force against nonviolent suspects. See infra, at 18-19. If those charged with the enforcement of the criminal law have abjured the use of deadly force in arresting nondangerous felons, there is a substantial basis for doubting that the use of such force is an essential attribute of the arrest power in all felony cases. See Schumann v. McGinn, 307 Minn. 446, 472, 240 N. W. 2d 525, 540 (1976) (Rogosheske, J., dissenting in part). Petitioners and appellant have not persuaded us that shooting nondangerous fleeing suspects is so vital as to outweigh the suspect's interest in his own life.

The use of deadly force to prevent the escape of all felony suspects, whatever the circumstances, is constitutionally unreasonable. It is not better that all felony suspects die than that they escape.

Where the suspect poses no immediate threat to the officer and no threat to others, the harm resulting from failing to apprehend him does not justify the use of deadly force to do so.

It is no doubt unfortunate when a suspect who is in sight escapes, but the fact that the police arrive a little late or are a little slower afoot does not always justify killing the suspect.

A police officer may not seize an unarmed, nondangerous suspect by shooting him dead. The Tennessee statute is unconstitutional insofar as it authorizes the use of deadly force against such fleeing suspects.

The use of deadly force to prevent the escape of all felony suspects, whatever the circumstances, is constitutionally unreasonable. It is not better that all felony suspects die than that they escape. Where the suspect poses no immediate threat to the officer and no threat to others, the harm resulting from failing to apprehend him does not justify the use of deadly force to do so. It is no doubt unfortunate when a suspect who is in sight escapes, but the fact that the police arrive a little late or are a little slower afoot does not always justify killing the suspect. A police officer may not seize an unarmed, nondangerous suspect by shooting him dead. The Tennessee statute is unconstitutional insofar as it authorizes the use of deadly force against such fleeing suspects.

Where the officer has probable cause to believe that the suspect poses a threat of serious physical harm, either to the officer or to others, it is not constitutionally unreasonable to prevent escape by using deadly force.

if the suspect threatens the officer with a weapon or there is probable cause to believe that he has committed a crime involving the infliction or threatened infliction of serious

physical harm, deadly force may be used if necessary to prevent escape, and if, where feasible, some warning has been given.

It is not, however, unconstitutional on its face. Where the officer has probable cause to believe that the suspect poses a threat of serious physical harm, either to the officer or to others, it is not constitutionally unreasonable to prevent escape by using deadly force. Thus, if the suspect threatens the officer with a weapon or there is probable cause to believe that he has committed a crime involving the infliction or threatened infliction of serious physical harm, deadly force may be used if necessary to prevent escape, and if, where feasible, some warning has been given. As applied in such circumstances, the Tennessee statute would pass constitutional muster.

III

A

the common-law rule, which allowed the use of whatever force was necessary to effect the arrest of a fleeing felon, though not a misdemeanant.

It is insisted that the Fourth Amendment must be construed in light of the common-law rule, which allowed the use of whatever force was necessary to effect the arrest of a fleeing felon, though not a misdemeanant. As stated in Hale's posthumously published Pleas of the Crown:

"[I]f persons that are pursued by these officers for felony or the just suspicion thereof . . . shall not yield themselves to these officers, but shall either resist or fly before they are apprehended or being apprehended shall rescue themselves and resist or fly, so that they cannot be otherwise apprehended, and are upon necessity slain therein, because they cannot be otherwise taken, it is no felony." 2 M. Hale, Historia Placitorum Coronae 85 (1736).

Most American jurisdictions also imposed a flat prohibition against the use of deadly force to stop a fleeing misdemeanant, coupled with a general privilege to use such force to stop a fleeing felon.

See also 4 W. Blackstone, Commentaries *289. Most American jurisdictions also imposed a flat prohibition against the use of deadly force to stop a fleeing misdemeanant, coupled with a general privilege to use such force to stop a fleeing felon. E. g., Holloway v. Moser, 193 N.C. 185, 136 S. E. 375 (1927); State v. Smith, 127 Iowa 534, 535, 103 N. W. 944, 945 (1905); Reneau v. State, 70 Tenn. 720 (1879); Brooks v. Commonwealth, 61 Pa. 352 (1869); Roberts v. State, 14 Mo. 138 (1851); see generally R. Perkins & R. Boyce, Criminal Law 1098-1102 (3d ed. 1982); Day, Shooting the Fleeing Felon: State of the Law, 14 Crim. L. Bull. 285, 286-287 (1978); Wilgus, Arrest Without a Warrant, 22 Mich. L. Rev. 798, 807-816 (1924). But see Storey v. State, 71 Ala. 329 (1882); State v. Bryant, 65 N.C. 327, 328 (1871); Caldwell v. State, 41 Tex. 86 (1874).

The State and city argue that because this was the prevailing rule at the time of the adoption of the Fourth Amendment and for some time thereafter, and is still in force in some States, use of deadly force against a fleeing felon must be "reasonable."

The State and city argue that because this was the prevailing rule at the time of the adoption of the Fourth Amendment and for some time thereafter, and is still in force in some States, use of deadly force against a fleeing felon must be "reasonable." It is true that this Court has often looked to the common law in evaluating the reasonableness, for Fourth Amendment purposes, of police activity. See, e. g., United States v. Watson, 423 U.S. 411, 418 -419 (1976); Gerstein v. Pugh, 420 U.S. 103, 111, 114 (1975); Carroll v. United States, 267 U.S. 132, 149 -153 (1925). On the other hand, it "has not simply frozen into constitutional law those law enforcement practices that existed at the time of the Fourth Amendment's passage." Payton v. New York, 445 U.S. 573, 591, n. 33 (1980). Because of sweeping change in the legal and technological context, reliance on the common-law rule in this case would be a mistaken literalism that ignores the purposes of a historical inquiry.

B

the common-law rule is best understood in light of the fact that it arose at a time when virtually all felonies were punishable by death.

It has been pointed out many times that the common-law rule is best understood in light of the fact that it arose at a time when virtually all felonies were punishable by death. "Though effected without the protections and formalities of an orderly trial and conviction, the killing of a resisting or fleeing felon resulted in no greater consequences than those authorized for punishment of the felony of which the individual was charged or suspected." American Law Institute, Model Penal Code 3.07, Comment 3, p. 56 (Tentative Draft

No. 8, 1958) (hereinafter Model Penal Code Comment). Courts have also justified the common-law rule by emphasizing the relative dangerousness of felons. See, e. g., Schumann v. McGinn, 307 Minn., at 458, 240 N. W. 2d, at 533; Holloway v. Moser, supra, at 187, 136 S. E., at 376 (1927).

the concept, which was questionable to begin with, that use of deadly force against a fleeing felon is merely a speedier execution of someone who has already forfeited his life.

Neither of these justifications makes sense today. Almost all crimes formerly punishable by death no longer are or can be. See, e. g., Enmund v. Florida, 458 U.S. 782 (1982); Coker v. Georgia, 433 U.S. 584 (1977). And while in earlier times "the gulf between the felonies and the minor offences was broad and deep," 2 Pollock & Maitland 467, n. 3; Carroll v. United States, supra, at 158, today the distinction is minor and often arbitrary. Many crimes classified as misdemeanors, or nonexistent, at common law are now felonies. Wilgus, 22 Mich. L. Rev., at 572-573. These changes have undermined the concept, which was questionable to begin with, that use of deadly force against a fleeing felon is merely a speedier execution of someone who has already forfeited his life. They have also made the assumption that a "felon" is more dangerous than a misdemeanant untenable. Indeed, numerous misdemeanors involve conduct more dangerous than many felonies.

The common-law rule developed at a time when weapons were rudimentary.

Handguns were not carried by police officers until the latter half of the last century. Only then did it become possible to use deadly force from a distance as a means of apprehension.

There is an additional reason why the common-law rule cannot be directly translated to the present day. The common-law rule developed at a time when weapons were rudimentary. Deadly force could be inflicted almost solely in a hand-to-hand struggle during which, necessarily, the safety of the arresting officer was at risk. Handguns were not carried by police officers until the latter half of the last century. L. Kennett & J. Anderson, The Gun in America 150-151 (1975). Only then did it become possible to use deadly force from a distance as a means of apprehension. As a practical matter, the use of deadly force under the standard articulation of the common-law rule has an altogether different meaning - and harsher consequences - now than in past centuries. See Wechsler & Michael, A Rationale for the Law of Homicide: I, 37 Colum. L. Rev. 701, 741 (1937).

One other aspect of the common-law rule bears emphasis. It forbids the use of deadly force to apprehend a misdemeanant, condemning such action as disproportionately severe. See Holloway v. Moser, 193 N.C., at 187, 136 S. E., at 376; State v. Smith, 127 Iowa, at 535, 103 N. W., at 945. See generally Annot., 83 A. L. R. 3d 238 (1978).

In short, though the common-law pedigree of Tennessee's rule is pure on its face, changes in the legal and technological context mean the rule is distorted almost beyond recognition when literally applied.

C

In evaluating the reasonableness of police procedures under the Fourth Amendment, we have also looked to prevailing rules in individual jurisdictions. See, e. g., United States v. Watson, 423 U.S., at 421 - 422. The rules in the States are varied. See generally Comment, 18 Ga. L. Rev. 137, 140-144 (1983). Some 19 States have codified the common-law rule, though in two of these the courts have significantly limited the statute. Four States, though without a relevant statute, apparently retain the common-law rule. Two States have adopted the Model Penal Code's provision verbatim. Eighteen others allow, in slightly varying language, the use of deadly force only if the suspect has committed a felony involving the use or threat of physical or deadly force, or is escaping with a deadly weapon, or is likely to endanger life or inflict serious physical injury if not arrested. Louisiana and Vermont, though without statutes or case law on point, do forbid the use of deadly force to prevent any but violent felonies. The remaining States either have no relevant statute or case law, or have positions that are unclear.

It cannot be said that there is a constant or overwhelming trend away from the common-law rule. In recent years, some States have reviewed their laws and expressly rejected abandonment of the common-law rule. Nonetheless, the long-term movement has been away from the rule that deadly force may be used against any fleeing felon, and that remains the rule in less than half the States.

The Federal Bureau of Investigation and the New York City Police Department, for example, both forbid the use of firearms except when necessary to prevent death or grievous bodily harm.

This trend is more evident and impressive when viewed in light of the policies adopted by the police departments themselves. Overwhelmingly, these are more restrictive than the common-law rule. C. Milton, J. Halleck, J. Lardner, & G. Abrecht, Police Use of Deadly Force 45-46 (1977). The Federal Bureau of Investigation and the New York City Police Department, for example, both forbid the use of firearms except when necessary to prevent death or grievous bodily harm. Id., at 40-41; App. 83. For accreditation by the Commission on Accreditation for Law Enforcement Agencies, a department must restrict the use of deadly force to situations where "the officer reasonably believes that the action is in defense of human life . . . or in defense of any person in immediate danger of serious physical injury." Commission on Accreditation for Law Enforcement Agencies, Inc., Standards for Law Enforcement Agencies 1-2 (1983) (italics deleted). A 1974 study reported that the police department regulations in a majority of the large cities of the United States allowed the firing of a weapon only when a felon presented a threat of death or serious bodily harm. Boston Police Department, Planning & Research Division, The Use of Deadly Force by Boston Police Personnel (1974), cited in Mattis v. Schnarr, 547 F.2d 1007, 1016, n. 19 (CA8 1976), vacated as moot sub nom. Ashcroft v. Mattis, 431 U.S. 171 (1977). Overall, only 7.5% of departmental and municipal policies explicitly permit the use of deadly force against any felon; 86.8% explicitly do not. K. Matulia, A Balance of Forces: A Report of the International Association of Chiefs of Police 161 (1982) (table). See also Record 1108-1368 (written policies of 44 departments). See generally W. Geller & K. Karales, Split-Second Decisions 33-42 (1981); Brief for Police Foundation et al. as Amici Curiae. In light of the rules adopted by those who must actually administer them, the older and fading common-law view is a dubious indicium of the constitutionality of the Tennessee statute now before us.

D

Actual departmental policies are important for an additional reason. We would hesitate to declare a police practice of long standing "unreasonable" if doing so would severely hamper effective law enforcement. But the indications are to the contrary. There has been no suggestion that crime has worsened in any way in jurisdictions that have adopted, by legislation or departmental policy, rules similar to that announced today. Amici note that "[a]fter extensive research and consideration, [they] have concluded that laws permitting police officers to use deadly force to apprehend unarmed, non-violent fleeing felony suspects actually do not protect citizens or law enforcement officers, do not deter crime or alleviate problems caused by crime, and do not improve the crime-fighting ability of law enforcement agencies." Id., at 11. The submission is that the obvious state interests in apprehension are not sufficiently served to warrant the use of lethal weapons against all fleeing felons. See supra, at 10-11, and n. 10.

Nor do we agree with petitioners and appellant that the rule we have adopted requires the police to make impossible, split-second evaluations of unknowable facts. See Brief for Petitioners 25; Brief for Appellant 11. We do not deny the practical difficulties of attempting to assess the suspect's dangerousness. However, similarly difficult judgments must be made by the police in equally uncertain circumstances. See, e. g., Terry v. Ohio, 392 U.S., at 20, 27. Nor is there any indication that in States that allow the use of deadly force only against dangerous suspects, see nn. 15, 17-19, supra, the standard has been difficult to apply or has led to a rash of litigation involving inappropriate second-guessing of police officers' split-second decisions. Moreover, the highly technical felony/misdemeanor distinction is equally, if not more, difficult to apply in the field. An officer is in no position to know, for example, the precise value of property stolen, or whether the crime was a first or second offense. Finally, as noted above, this claim must be viewed with suspicion in light of the similar self-imposed limitations of so many police departments.

IV

The District Court concluded that Hymon was justified in shooting Garner because state law allows, and the Federal Constitution does not forbid, the use of deadly force to prevent the escape of a fleeing felony suspect if no alternative means of apprehension is available. See App. to Pet. for Cert. A9-A11, A38. This conclusion made a determination of Garner's apparent dangerousness unnecessary. The court did find, however, that Garner appeared to be unarmed, though Hymon could not be certain that was the case. Id., at A4, A23. See also App. 41, 56; Record 219. Restated in Fourth Amendment terms, this means Hymon had no articulable basis to think Garner was armed.

the fact that Garner was a suspected burglar could not, without regard to the other circumstances, automatically justify the use of deadly force.

In reversing, the Court of Appeals accepted the District Court's factual conclusions and held that "the facts, as found, did not justify the use of deadly force." 710 F.2d, at 246. We agree. Officer Hymon could not reasonably have believed that Garner - young, slight, and unarmed - posed any threat. Indeed, Hymon never attempted to justify his actions on any basis other than the need to prevent an escape. The District Court stated in passing that "[t]he facts of this case did not indicate to Officer Hymon that Garner was `nondangerous.'" App. to Pet. for Cert. A34. This conclusion is not explained, and seems to be based solely on the fact that Garner had broken into a house at night. However, the fact that Garner was a suspected burglar could not, without regard to the other circumstances, automatically justify the use of deadly force.

Hymon did not have probable cause to believe that Garner, whom he correctly believed to be unarmed, posed any physical danger to himself or others.

The dissent argues that the shooting was justified by the fact that Officer Hymon had probable cause to believe that Garner had committed a nighttime burglary. While we agree that burglary is a serious crime, we cannot agree that it is so dangerous as automatically to justify the use of deadly force.

Although the armed burglar would present a different situation, the fact that an unarmed suspect has broken into a dwelling at night does not automatically mean he is physically dangerous.

In fact, the available statistics demonstrate that burglaries only rarely involve physical violence. During the 10-year period from 1973-1982, only 3.8% of all burglaries involved violent crime.

The dissent argues that the shooting was justified by the fact that Officer Hymon had probable cause to believe that Garner had committed a nighttime burglary. Post, at 29, 32. While we agree that burglary is a serious crime, we cannot agree that it is so dangerous as automatically to justify the use of deadly force. The FBI classifies burglary as a "property" rather than a "violent" crime. See Federal Bureau of Investigation, Uniform Crime Reports, Crime in the United States 1 (1984). Although the armed burglar would present a different situation, the fact that an unarmed suspect has broken into a dwelling at night does not automatically mean he is physically dangerous. This case demonstrates as much. See also Solem v. Helm, 463 U.S. 277, 296 -297, and nn. 22-23 (1983). In fact, the available statistics demonstrate that burglaries only rarely involve physical violence. During the 10-year period from 1973-1982, only 3.8% of all burglaries involved violent crime. Bureau of Justice Statistics, Household Burglary 4 (1985). See also T. Reppetto, Residential Crime 17, 105 (1974); Conklin & Bittner, Burglary in a Suburb, 11 Criminology 208, 214 (1973).

V

We wish to make clear what our holding means in the context of this case. The complaint has been dismissed as to all the individual defendants. The State is a party only by virtue of 28 U.S.C. 2403(b) and is not subject to liability. The possible liability of the remaining defendants - the Police Department and the city of Memphis - hinges on Monell v. New York City Dept. of Social Services, 436 U.S. 658 (1978), and is left for remand. We hold that the statute is invalid insofar as it purported to give Hymon the authority to act as he did. As for the policy of the Police Department, the absence of any discussion of this issue by the courts below, and the uncertain state of the record, preclude any consideration of its validity.

The judgment of the Court of Appeals is affirmed, and the case is remanded for further proceedings consistent with this opinion.

So ordered.

.....

JUSTICE O'CONNOR, with whom THE CHIEF JUSTICE and JUSTICE REHNQUIST join, dissenting.

By disregarding the serious and dangerous nature of residential burglaries and the longstanding practice of many States, the Court effectively creates a Fourth Amendment right allowing a burglary suspect to flee unimpeded from a police officer who has probable cause to arrest, who has ordered the suspect to halt, and who has no means short of firing his weapon to prevent escape. I do not believe that the Fourth Amendment supports such a right, and I accordingly dissent.

The Court today holds that the Fourth Amendment prohibits a police officer from using deadly force as a last resort to apprehend a criminal suspect who refuses to halt when fleeing the scene of a nighttime burglary. This conclusion rests on the majority's balancing of the interests of the suspect and the public interest in effective law enforcement. Ante, at 8. Notwithstanding the venerable common-law rule authorizing the use of deadly force if necessary to apprehend a fleeing felon, and continued acceptance of this rule by nearly half the States, ante, at 14, 16-17, the majority concludes that Tennessee's statute is unconstitutional inasmuch as it allows the use of such force to apprehend a burglary suspect who is not obviously armed or otherwise dangerous. Although the circumstances of this case are unquestionably tragic and unfortunate, our constitutional holdings must be sensitive both to the history of the Fourth Amendment and to the general implications of the Court's reasoning. By disregarding the serious and dangerous nature of residential burglaries and the longstanding practice of many States, the Court effectively creates a Fourth Amendment right allowing a burglary suspect to flee unimpeded from a police officer who has probable cause to arrest, who has ordered the suspect to halt, and who has no means short of firing his weapon to prevent escape. I do not believe that the Fourth Amendment supports such a right, and I accordingly dissent.

.....

II

For purposes of Fourth Amendment analysis, I agree with the Court that Officer Hymon "seized" Garner by shooting him.

The clarity of hindsight cannot provide the standard for judging the reasonableness of police decisions made in uncertain and often dangerous circumstances.

I am far more reluctant than is the Court to conclude that the Fourth Amendment proscribes a police practice that was accepted at the time of the adoption of the Bill of Rights and has continued to receive the support of many state legislatures.

For purposes of Fourth Amendment analysis, I agree with the Court that Officer Hymon "seized" Garner by shooting him. Whether that seizure was reasonable and therefore permitted by the Fourth Amendment requires a careful balancing of the important public interest in crime prevention and detection and the nature and quality of the intrusion upon legitimate interests of the individual. United States v. Place, 462 U.S. 696, 703 (1983). In striking this balance here, it is crucial to acknowledge that police use of deadly force to apprehend a fleeing criminal suspect falls within the "rubric of police conduct . . . necessarily [involving] swift action predicated upon the on-the-spot observations of the officer on the beat." Terry v. Ohio, 392 U.S. 1, 20 (1968). The clarity of hindsight cannot provide the standard for judging the reasonableness of police decisions made in uncertain and often dangerous circumstances. Moreover, I am far more reluctant than is the Court to conclude that the Fourth Amendment proscribes a police practice that was accepted at the time of the adoption of the Bill of Rights and has continued to receive the support of many state legislatures. Although the Court has recognized that the requirements of the Fourth Amendment must respond to the reality of social and technological change, fidelity to the notion of constitutional - as opposed to purely judicial - limits on governmental action requires us to impose a heavy burden on those who claim that practices accepted when the Fourth Amendment was adopted are now constitutionally impermissible. See, e. g., United States v. Watson, 423 U.S. 411, 416 -421 (1976); Carroll v. United States, 267 U.S. 132, 149 -153 (1925). Cf. United States v. Villamonte-Marquez, 462 U.S. 579, 585 (1983) (noting "impressive historical pedigree" of statute challenged under Fourth Amendment).

three-fifths of all rapes in the home, three-fifths of all home robberies, and about a third of home aggravated and simple assaults are committed by burglars.

Victims of a forcible intrusion into their home by a nighttime prowler will find little consolation in the majority's confident assertion that "burglaries only rarely involve physical violence."

The public interest involved in the use of deadly force as a last resort to apprehend a fleeing burglary suspect relates primarily to the serious nature of the crime. Household burglaries not only represent the illegal entry into a person's home, but also "pos[e] real risk of serious harm to others." Solem v. Helm, 463 U.S. 277, 315 -316 (1983) (BURGER, C. J., dissenting). According to recent Department of Justice statistics, "[t]hree-fifths of all rapes in the home, three-fifths of all home robberies, and about a third of home aggravated and simple assaults are committed by burglars." Bureau of Justice Statistics Bulletin, Household Burglary 1 (January 1985). During the period 1973-1982, 2.8 million such violent crimes were committed in the course of burglaries. Ibid. Victims of a forcible intrusion into their home by a nighttime prowler will find little consolation in the majority's confident assertion that "burglaries only rarely involve physical violence." Ante, at 21. Moreover, even if a particular burglary, when viewed in retrospect, does not involve physical harm to others, the "harsh potentialities for violence" inherent in the forced entry into a home preclude characterization of the crime as "innocuous, inconsequential, minor, or `nonviolent.'" Solem v. Helm, supra, at 316 (BURGER, C. J., dissenting). See also Restatement of Torts 131, Comment g (1934) (burglary is among felonies that normally cause or threaten death or serious bodily harm); R. Perkins & R. Boyce, Criminal Law 1110 (3d ed. 1982) (burglary is dangerous felony that creates unreasonable risk of great personal harm).

Because burglary is a serious and dangerous felony, the public interest in the prevention and detection of the crime is of compelling importance. Where a police officer has probable cause to arrest a suspected burglar, the use of deadly force as a last resort might well be the only means of apprehending the suspect.

the Captain of the Memphis Police Department testified that in his city, if apprehension is not immediate, it is likely that the suspect will not be caught.

Although some law enforcement agencies may choose to assume the risk that a criminal will remain at large, the Tennessee statute reflects a legislative determination that the use of deadly force in prescribed circumstances will serve generally to protect the public.

Such statutes assist the police in apprehending suspected perpetrators of serious crimes and provide notice that a lawful police order to stop and submit to arrest may not be ignored with impunity.

Because burglary is a serious and dangerous felony, the public interest in the prevention and detection of the crime is of compelling importance. Where a police officer has probable cause to arrest a suspected burglar, the use of deadly force as a last resort might well be the only means of apprehending the suspect. With respect to a particular burglary, subsequent investigation simply cannot represent a substitute for immediate apprehension of the criminal suspect at the scene. See President's Commission on Law Enforcement and Administration of Justice, Task Force Report: The Challenge of Crime in a Free Society 97 (1967). Indeed, the Captain of the Memphis Police Department testified that in his city, if apprehension is not immediate, it is likely that the suspect will not be caught. App. in No. 81-5605 (CA6), p. 334. Although some law enforcement agencies may choose to assume the risk that a criminal will remain at large, the Tennessee statute reflects a legislative determination that the use of deadly force in prescribed circumstances will serve generally to protect the public. Such statutes assist the police in apprehending suspected perpetrators of serious crimes and provide notice that a lawful police order to stop and submit to arrest may not be ignored with impunity. See, e. g., Wiley v. Memphis Police Department, 548 F.2d 1247, 1252-1253 (CA6), cert. denied, 434 U.S. 822 (1977); Jones v. Marshall, 528 F.2d 132, 142 (CA2 1975).

.....

Without questioning the importance of a person's interest in his life, I do not think this interest encompasses a right to flee unimpeded from the scene of a burglary.

.....

The legitimate interests of the suspect in these circumstances are adequately accommodated by the Tennessee statute: to avoid the use of deadly force and the consequent risk to his life, the suspect need merely obey the valid order to halt.

.....

A proper balancing of the interests involved suggests that use of deadly force as a last resort to apprehend a criminal suspect fleeing from the scene of a nighttime burglary is not unreasonable within the meaning of the Fourth Amendment.

.....

He ordered the suspect to halt, and when the suspect refused to obey and attempted to flee into the night, the officer fired his weapon to prevent escape. The reasonableness of this action for purposes of the Fourth Amendment is not determined by the unfortunate nature of this particular case; instead, the question is whether it is constitutionally impermissible for police officers, as a last resort, to shoot a burglary suspect fleeing the scene of the crime.

.....

Nor do I believe that a criminal suspect who is shot while trying to avoid apprehension has a cognizable claim of a deprivation of his Sixth Amendment right to trial by jury.

.....

By declining to limit its holding to the use of firearms, the Court unnecessarily implies that the Fourth Amendment constrains the use of any police practice that is potentially lethal, no matter how remote the risk.

.....

The Court's silence on critical factors in the decision to use deadly force simply invites second-guessing of difficult police decisions that must be made quickly in the most trying of circumstances. Cf. Payton v. New York, 445 U.S., at 619 (WHITE, J., dissenting). Police are given no guidance for determining which objects, among an array of potentially lethal weapons ranging from guns to knives to baseball bats to rope, will justify the use of deadly force.

.....

We can expect an escalating volume of litigation as the lower courts struggle to determine if a police officer's split-second decision to shoot was justified by the danger posed by a particular object and other facts related to the crime.

.....

The Court's opinion sweeps broadly to adopt an entirely new standard for the constitutionality of the use of deadly force to apprehend fleeing felons. Thus, the Court "lightly brushe[s] aside," Payton v. New York, supra, at 600, a longstanding police practice that predates the Fourth Amendment and continues to receive the approval of nearly half of the state legislatures. I cannot accept the majority's creation of a constitutional right to flight for burglary suspects seeking to avoid capture at the scene of the crime. Whatever the constitutional limits on police use of deadly force in order to apprehend a fleeing felon, I do not believe they are exceeded in a case in which a police officer has probable cause to arrest a suspect at the scene of a residential burglary, orders the suspect to halt, and then fires his weapon as a last resort to prevent the suspect's escape into the night. I respectfully dissent.

UNITED STATES v. GALIOTO

(FULL CASE)

477 U.S. 556; 106 S. Ct. 2683; 91 L. Ed. 2d 459

March 26, 1986, Argued

June 27, 1986, Decided

GIST: Galioto brought an equal protection challenge to the federal prohibition on selling a firearm to a person who had been adjudicated mentally defective or involuntarily committed. He argued there was no rational basis for distinguishing felons, who could have their civil rights restored and regain the legal ability to buy firearms, from former mental patients, who had no provision for restoring their legal ability to buy firearms. Between the time the district court of New Jersey ruled in Galioto's favor, finding the arrangement in violation of the Constitution, and when the Supreme Court heard the case, Congress amended the law to create a remedy for former mental patients. Thus, the Court dismissed the equal protection challenge as moot.

Appellee, who had been involuntarily committed to a mental hospital for a period of several days in 1971, was unable to purchase a firearm from a store in 1982 because of the provisions of 18 U.S.C. §922(d) prohibiting sales of firearms to such persons. Section 922(d) and other federal statutes prohibiting persons who have been committed to mental institutions from possessing, receiving, or transporting firearms also apply to felons. However, under 18 U.S.C. §925(c), certain felons could apply to the Bureau of Alcohol, Tobacco and Firearms for administrative relief from the disabilities imposed by federal firearms laws, but no such relief was permitted for former mental patients. After unsuccessfully seeking a special exemption from the Bureau, appellee brought suit in Federal District Court, challenging the constitutionality of the firearms legislation. The court held that the statutory scheme was unconstitutional as violating equal protection principles because there was no rational basis for singling out mental patients for permanent disabled status, particularly as compared to convicts. The court also concluded that the statutory scheme unconstitutionally created an "irrebuttable presumption" that one who has been committed, no matter what the circumstances, is forever mentally ill and dangerous.

Held: The equal protection and "irrebuttable presumption" issues are now moot because, after this Court noted probable jurisdiction over this appeal and heard arguments, Congress amended §925(c) to afford the administrative remedy contained therein to former mental patients ineligible to purchase firearms. Since appellee's complaint appears to raise other issues best addressed in the first instance by the District Court, the case is remanded for further proceedings.

CHIEF JUSTICE BURGER delivered the opinion of the Court.

We noted probable jurisdiction to decide whether Congress may, consistent with the Fifth Amendment, forbid all involuntarily committed former mental patients to purchase firearms while permitting some felons to do so.

In 1982 appellee attempted to purchase a firearm at Ray's Sport Shop in North Plainfield, New Jersey. The Sport Shop gave appellee a standard questionnaire, which asked, inter alia: "Have you ever been adjudicated mentally defective or have you ever been committed to a mental institution?" Appellee had been involuntarily committed to a mental hospital for a period of several days in 1971, and accordingly answered "yes" to this question. The store then refused to sell him a gun by reason of 18 U.S.C. §922(d)(4), which makes it unlawful for a licensed dealer in firearms "to sell . . . any firearm . . . to any person knowing or having reasonable cause to believe that such person . . . has been adjudicated as a mental defective or had been committed to any mental institution." Federal firearms laws also forbid "any person . . . who has been adjudicated as a mental defective or who has been committed to a mental institution . . . to ship or transport any firearm or ammunition in interstate or foreign commerce," 18 U.S.C. §922(g), or to "receive any firearm or ammunition which has been shipped or transported in interstate or foreign commerce," §922(h). Partially overlapping provisions of 18 U.S.C. App. §§1202(a)(1) and (3) prohibit any person who has "been adjudged by a court . . . of being mentally incompetent" from receiving, possessing, or transporting firearms.

After unsuccessfully seeking a special exemption from the Bureau of Alcohol, Tobacco and Firearms, appellee brought suit in the United States District Court for the District of New Jersey, challenging the constitutionality of the firearms legislation. The District Court concluded that those portions of the federal firearms statutes that deprived appellee of his ability to purchase a firearm were constitutionally infirm. 602 F.Supp. 682, 683 (1985). Both felons and persons who have been committed to mental institutions, inter alia, are subject to the firearms disabilities contained in 18 U.S.C. §922(d). Under 18 U.S.C. §925(c), however, felons who have committed crimes not involving firearms may apply to the Bureau for administrative relief from these disabilities. No such relief is permitted for former mental patients.

Section 925(c) provides in relevant part:

"A person who has been convicted for a crime punishable by imprisonment for a term exceeding one year (other than a crime involving the use of a firearm or other weapon or a violation of this chapter or of the National Firearms Act) may make application to the Secretary for relief from the disabilities imposed by Federal laws with respect to the acquisition, receipt, transfer, shipment, or possession of firearms and incurred by reason of such conviction, and the Secretary may grant such relief if it is established to his satisfaction that the circumstances regarding the conviction, and the applicant's record and reputation, are such that the applicant will not be likely to act in a manner dangerous to public safety and that the granting of the relief would not be contrary to the public interest."

The District Court held that this scheme violated equal protection principles because, in its view, "[there] is no rational basis for thus singling out mental patients for permanent disabled status, particularly as compared to convicts." 602 F.Supp., at 689. The court also concluded that the statutory scheme was unconstitutional because it "in effect creates an irrebuttable presumption that one who has been committed, no matter the circumstances, is forever mentally ill and dangerous." Id., at 690. We noted probable jurisdiction over the Government's appeal, 474 U.S. 943 (1985), and the case was argued on March 26, 1986.

any person who "is prohibited from possessing, shipping, transporting, or receiving firearms or ammunition" may apply to the Secretary of the Treasury for relief.

Meanwhile, Congress came to the conclusion, as a matter of legislative policy, that the firearms statutes should be redrafted. On May 19, 1986, while this case was under consideration here, the President signed into law Pub. L. 99-308, 100 Stat. 449. Section 105 of the statute amends the provision providing for administrative relief from firearms disabilities, 18 U.S.C. §925(c), by striking out the language limiting the provision to certain felons and changing the statute to read that any person who "is prohibited from possessing, shipping, transporting, or receiving firearms or ammunition" may apply to the Secretary of the Treasury for relief. Section 110 of the statute provides that the amendment made by §105 "shall be applicable to any action, petition, or appellate proceeding pending on the date of the enactment of this Act."

no "irrebuttable presumption" now exists since a hearing is afforded to anyone subject to firearms disabilities.

This enactment significantly alters the posture of this case. The new statutory scheme permits the Secretary to grant relief in some circumstances to former involuntarily committed mental patients such as appellee. The new approach affords an administrative remedy to former mental patients like that Congress provided for others prima facie ineligible to purchase firearms. Thus, it can no longer be contended that such persons have been "singled out." Also, no "irrebuttable presumption" now exists since a hearing is afforded to anyone subject to firearms disabilities. Accordingly, the equal protection and "irrebuttable presumption" issues discussed by the District Court are now moot. See United Building and Construction Trades Council of Camden County and Vicinity v. Mayor and Council of Camden, 465 U.S. 208, 213 (1984).

In such circumstances, "it is the duty of the appellate court to set aside the decree below . . . ." Duke Power Co. v. Greenwood County, 299 U.S. 259, 267 (1936); see also United States v. Munsingwear, Inc., 340 U.S. 36, 39-40 (1950). We therefore vacate the judgment of the District Court. However, since appellee's complaint appears to raise other issues best addressed in the first instance by the District Court, we also remand the case for further proceedings consistent with this opinion.

Vacated and remanded.

DeSHANEY v. WINNEBAGO COUNTY DEPARTMENT OF SOCIAL SERVICES

(CASE EXCERPT)

489 U.S. 189; 109 S. Ct. 998; 103 L. Ed. 2d 249

November 2, 1988, Argued

February 22, 1989, Decided

GIST: At the center of the gun issue is the question of whether the state is ultimately responsible for providing you personally with security and safety, especially when those in government know you are under a specific threat. In *DeShaney* the Court affirms the state is not responsible for your safety, concluding, among other things, that the 14th Amendment was intended "to protect the people from the State, not to ensure that the State protected them from each other."

The case hinges on a claim that Winnebago County violated a young boy's civil rights by failing to protect him from a father the Department of Social Services knew was abusive. Young Joshua was beaten nearly to death and will have to be institutionalized for life. The Court rejected his claim that his constitutional rights were violated, holding that the substantive component of the 14th Amendment Due Process Clause is a limitation on undue government action against life, liberty or property, not a guarantee that the state will protect its citizens from private violations of life, liberty or property. In a dissent, three Justices chastise the government for providing protective services and displacing private sources of protection, and then, at the critical moment, abandoning the victims and shrugging their shoulders.

CHIEF JUSTICE REHNQUIST delivered the opinion of the Court.

Petitioner is a boy who was beaten and permanently injured by his father, with whom he lived. Respondents are social workers and other local officials who received complaints that petitioner was being abused by his father and had reason to believe that this was the case, but nonetheless did not act to remove petitioner from his father's custody. Petitioner sued respondents claiming that their failure to act deprived him of his liberty in violation of the Due Process Clause of the Fourteenth Amendment to the United States Constitution. We hold that it did not.

.....

In March 1984, Randy DeShaney beat 4-year-old Joshua so severely that he fell into a life-threatening coma. Emergency brain surgery revealed a series of hemorrhages caused by traumatic injuries to the head inflicted over a long period of time. Joshua did not die, but he suffered brain damage so severe that he is expected to spend the rest of his life confined to an institution for the profoundly retarded. Randy DeShaney was subsequently tried and convicted of child abuse.

The complaint alleged that respondents had deprived Joshua of his liberty without due process of law, in violation of his rights under the Fourteenth Amendment, by failing to intervene to protect him against a risk of violence at his father's hands of which they knew or should have known.

Joshua and his mother brought this action under 42 U.S.C. §1983 in the United States District Court for the Eastern District of Wisconsin against respondents Winnebago County, DSS, and various individual employees of DSS. The complaint alleged that respondents had deprived Joshua of his liberty without due process of law, in violation of his rights under the Fourteenth Amendment, by failing to intervene to protect him against a risk of violence at his father's hands of which they knew or should have known.

.....

The Due Process Clause of the Fourteenth Amendment provides that "[n]o State shall . . . deprive any person of life, liberty, or property, without due process of law." Petitioners contend that the State deprived Joshua of his liberty interest in "free[dom] from . . . unjustified intrusions on personal security," see Ingraham v. Wright, 430 U.S. 651, 673 (1977), by failing to provide him with adequate protection against his father's violence. The claim is one invoking the substantive rather than the procedural component of the Due Process Clause; petitioners do not claim that the State denied Joshua protection without according him appropriate procedural safeguards, see Morrissey v. Brewer, 408 U.S. 471, 481 (1972), but that it was categorically obligated to protect him in these circumstances, see Youngberg v. Romeo, 457 U.S. 307, 309 (1982).

nothing in the language of the Due Process Clause itself requires the State to protect the life, liberty, and property of its citizens against invasion by private actors. The Clause is phrased as a limitation on the State's power to act, not as a guarantee of certain minimal levels of safety and security.

Its purpose was to protect the people from the State, not to ensure that the State protected them from each other.

But nothing in the language of the Due Process Clause itself requires the State to protect the life, liberty, and property of its citizens against invasion by private actors. The Clause is phrased as a limitation on the State's power to act, not as a guarantee of certain minimal levels of safety and security. It forbids the State itself to deprive individuals of life, liberty, or property without "due process of law," but its language cannot fairly be extended to impose an affirmative obligation on the State to ensure that those interests do not come to harm through other means. Nor does history support such an expansive reading of the constitutional text. Like its counterpart in the Fifth Amendment, the Due Process Clause of the Fourteenth Amendment was intended to prevent government "from abusing [its] power, or employing it as an instrument of oppression." Its purpose was to protect the people from the State, not to ensure that the State protected them from each other. The Framers were content to leave the extent of governmental obligation in the latter area to the democratic political processes.

We conclude that a State's failure to protect an individual against private violence simply does not constitute a violation of the Due Process Clause.

the Due Process Clauses generally confer no affirmative right to governmental aid, even where such aid may be necessary to secure life, liberty, or property interests of which the government itself may not deprive the individual.

the Due Process Clause does not require the State to provide its citizens with particular protective services, it follows that the State cannot be held liable under the Clause for injuries that could have been averted had it chosen to provide them.

Consistent with these principles, our cases have recognized that the Due Process Clauses generally confer no affirmative right to governmental aid, even where such aid may be necessary to secure life, liberty, or property interests of which the government itself may not deprive the individual. As we said in Harris v. McRae: "Although the liberty protected by the Due Process Clause affords protection against unwarranted government interference . . ., it does not confer an entitlement to such [governmental aid] as may be necessary to realize all the advantages of that freedom." If the Due Process Clause does not require the State to provide its citizens with particular protective services, it follows that the State cannot be held liable under the Clause for injuries that could have been averted had it chosen to provide them. n3 As a general matter, then, we conclude that a State's failure to protect an individual against private violence simply does not constitute a violation of the Due Process Clause.

n3 The State may not, of course, selectively deny its protective services to certain disfavored minorities without violating the Equal Protection Clause. See Yick Wo v. Hopkins, 118 U.S. 356 (1886). But no such argument has been made here.

.....

While the State may have been aware of the dangers that Joshua faced in the free world, it played no part in their creation, nor did it do anything to render him any more vulnerable to them.

the State does not become the permanent guarantor of an individual's safety by having once offered him shelter.

The Estelle-Youngberg analysis simply has no applicability in the present case. Petitioners concede that the harms Joshua suffered occurred not while he was in the State's custody, but while he was in the custody of his natural father, who was in no sense a state actor. n9 While the State may have been aware of the dangers that Joshua faced in the free world, it played no part in their creation, nor did it do anything to render him any more vulnerable to them. That the State once took temporary custody of Joshua does not alter the analysis, for when it returned him to his father's custody, it placed him in no worse position than that in which he would have been had it not acted at all; the State does not become the permanent guarantor of an individual's safety by having once offered him shelter. Under these circumstances, the State had no constitutional duty to protect Joshua.

.....

It may well be that, by voluntarily undertaking to protect Joshua against a danger it concededly played no part in creating, the State acquired a duty under state tort law to provide him with adequate protection against that danger. See Restatement (Second) of Torts §323 (1965) (one who undertakes to render services to another may in some circumstances be held liable for doing so in a negligent fashion); see generally W. Keeton, D. Dobbs, R. Keeton, & D. Owen, Prosser and Keeton on the Law of Torts §56 (5th ed. 1984) (discussing "special relationships" which may give rise to affirmative duties to act under the common law of tort). But the claim here is based on the Due Process Clause of the Fourteenth Amendment, which, as we have said many times, does not transform every tort committed by a state actor into a constitutional violation. See Daniels v. Williams, 474 U.S., at 335-336; Parratt v. Taylor, 451 U.S., at 544; Martinez v. California, 444 U.S. 277, 285 (1980); Baker v. McCollan, 443 U.S. 137, 146 (1979); Paul v. Davis, 424 U.S. 693, 701 (1976). A State may, through its courts and legislatures, impose such affirmative duties of care and protection upon its agents as it wishes. But not "all common-law duties owed by government actors were . . . constitutionalized by the Fourteenth Amendment." Daniels v. Williams, supra, at 335. Because, as explained above, the State had no constitutional duty to protect Joshua against his father's violence, its failure to do so -- though calamitous in hindsight -- simply does not constitute a violation of the Due Process Clause.

.....

Judges and lawyers, like other humans, are moved by natural sympathy in a case like this to find a way for Joshua and his mother to receive adequate compensation for the grievous harm inflicted upon them. But before yielding to that impulse, it is well to remember once again that the harm was inflicted not by the State of Wisconsin, but by Joshua's father. The most that can be said of the state functionaries in this case is that they stood by and did nothing when suspicious circumstances dictated a more active role for them. In defense of them it must also be said that had they moved too soon to take custody of the son away from the father, they would likely have been met with charges of improperly intruding into the parent-child relationship, charges based on the same Due Process Clause that forms the basis for the present charge of failure to provide adequate protection.

The people of Wisconsin may well prefer a system of liability which would place upon the State and its officials the responsibility for failure to act in situations such as the present one. They may create such a system, if they do not have it already, by changing the tort law of the State in accordance with the regular lawmaking process. But they should not have it thrust upon them by this Court's expansion of the Due Process Clause of the Fourteenth Amendment.

Affirmed.

JUSTICE BRENNAN, with whom JUSTICE MARSHALL and JUSTICE BLACKMUN join, dissenting.

.....

Today's opinion construes the Due Process Clause to permit a State to displace private sources of protection and then, at the critical moment, to shrug its shoulders and turn away from the harm that it has promised to try to prevent.

As the Court today reminds us, "the Due Process Clause of the Fourteenth Amendment was intended to prevent government 'from abusing [its] power, or employing it as an instrument of oppression.'" Ante, at 196, quoting Davidson, supra, U.S., at 348. My disagreement with the Court arises from its failure to see that inaction can be every bit as abusive of power as action, that oppression can result when a State undertakes a vital duty and then ignores it. Today's opinion construes the Due Process Clause to permit a State to displace private sources of protection and then, at the critical moment, to shrug its shoulders and turn away from the harm that it has promised to try to prevent. Because I cannot agree that our Constitution is indifferent to such indifference, I respectfully dissent.

UNITED STATES v. VERDUGO-URQUIDEZ

(CASE EXCERPT)

494 U.S. 259; 110 S. Ct. 1056; 108 L. Ed. 2d 222

November 7, 1989, Argued

February 28, 1990, Decided

GIST: Rene Martin Verdugo-Urquidez was the kind of drug lord who makes the newspapers. A resident and citizen of Mexico, the suspect had been captured in Mexico and brought to the United States. Some evidence against him was obtained by searching his Mexican residence after arrest, all with the cooperation of the two nations' authorities. He tried to get off by claiming the evidence was the result of an illegal search and seizure, and hence inadmissible. Upon this ignoble specimen rests an important 4th Amendment decision in which the Court held that a suspected drug lord of Mexican citizenship did not have 4th Amendment rights against unreasonable search and seizure with respect to his property in a foreign country. (This man was subsequently convicted, in a separate prosecution, of the highly publicized torture-murder of DEA Special Agent Enrique Camarena Salazar.)

In reaching its decision, the Court wrestled with the meaning of the phrase, "the people," and decided it is a term of art in the Constitution, referring to a class of persons who are part of the national community. In this light Verdugo-Urquidez had insufficient ties to the United States to be one of "the people." The Court compared the words and phrases chosen by the Framers for various clauses in the Constitution, noting that "the people" which the 2nd Amendment "protects" are the same class of persons mentioned in the Constitution's Preamble, and protected by the 1st, 4th, 9th and 10th Amendments, as well as Article 1, §2, cl.1, which specifies that Representatives are to be chosen by "the people."

CHIEF JUSTICE REHNQUIST delivered the opinion of the Court.

.....

The Fourth Amendment provides:

"The right of the people to be secure in their persons, houses, papers, and effects, against unreasonable searches and seizures, shall not be violated, and no Warrants shall issue, but upon probable cause, supported by Oath or affirmation, and particularly describing the place to be searched, and the persons or things to be seized."

The Preamble declares that the Constitution is ordained and established by "the People of the United States." The Second Amendment protects "the right of the people to keep and bear Arms," and the Ninth and Tenth Amendments provide that certain rights and powers are retained by and reserved to "the people."

"the people" protected by the Fourth Amendment, and by the First and Second Amendments, and to whom rights and powers are reserved in the Ninth and Tenth Amendments, refers to a class of persons who are part of a national community or who

have otherwise developed sufficient connection with this country to be considered part of that community.

That text, by contrast with the Fifth and Sixth Amendments, extends its reach only to "the people." Contrary to the suggestion of amici curiae that the Framers used this phrase "simply to avoid [an] awkward rhetorical redundancy," "the people" seems to have been a term of art employed in select parts of the Constitution. The Preamble declares that the Constitution is ordained and established by "the People of the United States." The Second Amendment protects "the right of the people to keep and bear Arms," and the Ninth and Tenth Amendments provide that certain rights and powers are retained by and reserved to "the people." See also U.S. Const., Amdt. 1 ("Congress shall make no law . . . abridging . . . the right of the people peaceably to assemble") (emphasis added); Art. I, §2, cl. 1 ("The House of Representatives shall be composed of Members chosen every second Year by the People of the several States") (emphasis added). While this textual exegesis is by no means conclusive, it suggests that "the people" protected by the Fourth Amendment, and by the First and Second Amendments, and to whom rights and powers are reserved in the Ninth and Tenth Amendments, refers to a class of persons who are part of a national community or who have otherwise developed sufficient connection with this country to be considered part of that community. See United States ex rel. Turner v. Williams (1904) (Excludable alien is not entitled to First Amendment rights, because "he does not become one of the people to whom these things are secured by our Constitution by an attempt to enter forbidden by law"). The language of these Amendments contrasts with the words "person" and "accused" used in the Fifth and Sixth Amendments regulating procedure in criminal cases.

.....

We think that the text of the Fourth Amendment, its history, and our cases discussing the application of the Constitution to aliens and extraterritorially require rejection of respondent's claim. At the time of the search, he was a citizen and resident of Mexico with no voluntary attachment to the United States, and the place searched was located in Mexico. Under these circumstances, the Fourth Amendment has no application.

JUSTICE BRENNAN, with whom JUSTICE MARSHALL joins, dissenting.

.....

the term "the people" is better understood as a rhetorical counterpoint to "the Government," such that rights that were reserved to the "the people" were to protect all those subject to "the Government."

The majority looks to various constitutional provisions and suggests that "'the people' seems to have been a term of art." Ante, at 265. But the majority admits that its "textual exegesis is by no means conclusive." n9 One member of the majority even states that he "cannot place any weight on the reference to 'the people' in the Fourth Amendment as a source of restricting its protections." The majority suggests a restrictive interpretation of those with "sufficient connection" to this country to be considered among "the people," but the term "the people" is better understood as a rhetorical counterpoint to "the Government," such that rights that were reserved to the "the people" were to protect all those subject to "the Government." Cf. New Jersey v. T.L.O. (1985) ("[T]he Court has long spoken of the Fourth Amendment's strictures as restraints imposed upon 'governmental action'"). "The people" are "the governed."

n9 The majority places an unsupportable reliance on the fact that the drafters used "the people" in the Fourth Amendment while using "person" and "accused" in the Fifth and Sixth Amendments respectively. The drafters purposely did not use the term "accused." As the majority recognizes, the Fourth Amendment is violated at the time of an unreasonable governmental intrusion, even if the victim of unreasonable governmental action is never formally "accused" of any wrongdoing. The majority's suggestion that the drafters could have used "person" ignores the fact that the Fourth Amendment then would have begun quite awkwardly: "The right of persons to be secure in their persons. . . ."

Americans vehemently attacked the notion that rights were matters of "'favor and grace,'" given to the people from the Government.

In drafting both the Constitution and the Bill of Rights, the Framers strove to create a form of Government decidedly different from their British heritage. Whereas the British Parliament was unconstrained, the Framers intended to create a Government of limited powers. See B. Bailyn, The Ideological Origins of the American Revolution 182 (1967); 1 The Complete Anti-Federalist 65 (H. Storing ed. 1981). The colonists considered the British government dangerously omnipotent. After all, the British declaration of rights in 1688 had been enacted not by the people, but by Parliament. The Federalist No. 84, p. 439(M. Beloff ed. 1987). Americans vehemently attacked the notion that rights were matters of "'favor and grace,'" given to the people from the Government. B. Bailyn, supra, at 187 (quoting John Dickinson).

Thus, the Framers of the Bill of Rights did not purport to "create" rights. Rather, they designed the Bill of Rights to prohibit our Government from infringing rights and liberties presumed to be pre-existing.

The Fourth Amendment, for example, does not create a new right of security against unreasonable searches and seizures. It states that "[t]he right of the people to be secure in their persons, houses, papers, and effects, against unreasonable searches and seizures, shall not be violated. . . ." The focus of the Fourth Amendment is on what the Government can and cannot do, and how it may act, not on against whom these actions may be taken.

Thus, the Framers of the Bill of Rights did not purport to "create" rights. Rather, they designed the Bill of Rights to prohibit our Government from infringing rights and liberties presumed to be pre-existing. See, e.g., U.S. Const., Amdt. 9 ("The enumeration in the Constitution of certain rights, shall not be construed to deny or disparage others retained by the people"). The Fourth Amendment, for example, does not create a new right of security against unreasonable searches and seizures. It states that "[t]he right of the people to be secure in their persons, houses, papers, and effects, against unreasonable searches and seizures, shall not be violated. . . ." The focus of the Fourth Amendment is on what the Government can and cannot do, and how it may act, not on against whom these actions may be taken. Bestowing rights and delineating protected groups would have been inconsistent with the drafters' fundamental conception of a Bill of Rights as a limitation on the Government's conduct with respect to all whom it seeks to govern. It is thus extremely unlikely that the Framers intended the narrow construction of the term "the people" presented today by the majority.

PERPICH v. DEPARTMENT OF DEFENSE

(FULL CASE)

496 U.S. 334; 110 S. Ct. 2418; 110 L. Ed. 2d 312

March 27, 1990, Argued

June 11, 1990, Decided

GIST: This was a challenge brought by the Governor of Minnesota to a change in federal law that allowed the federal government to call up members of the National Guard for duty or training overseas without the Governor's consent.

The Court unanimously ruled that the militia clauses in Article I did not require consent of the state governor, as the federal power is supreme over military affairs. Despite intense deliberation on the nature of and the state's power over its own militia, the arguments center entirely on Article 1 clauses of the Constitution and related statutes, and fail to include any reference to the 2nd Amendment. It is difficult to reconcile the absence of the 2nd Amendment in this case if, as proposed by recent commentators, that amendment conveys power to the states to organize their militias. In that regard, it seems impossible to reconcile this new "collectivist" view of the right to keep and bear arms with the Court's entire history.

The case provides a detailed historical view of the development of the militia, from its humble beginnings with quotations from Alexander Hamilton and from the first militia law, through the various separate and distinct elements it contains today. President Teddy Roosevelt is credited with declaring in 1901 that the 1792 militia law was worthless, and thus began the process of distinguishing between an unorganized militia composed of the citizenry at large, and a highly organized militia known today as the National Guard. It was the Dick Act of 1903 that created this separation and distinction, and of course a statute is incapable of rewriting the Constitution.

The Court also expresses comfort with the dual enlistment system, which since 1933 has required state National Guard members to simultaneously enroll in the National Guard of the United States, which is the national armed forces reserves. State members of the Guard lose their status as members of the State militia during any period of active federal duty and regain it when they muster out of federal duty. The relationship of the various parts of our armed strength is the heart of the discussion in this case.

Since 1933, federal law has provided that persons enlisting in a state National Guard unit simultaneously enlist in the National Guard of the United States, a part of the Army. The enlistees retain their status as state Guard members unless and until ordered to active federal duty and revert to state status upon being relieved from federal services. The authority to order the Guard to federal duty was limited to periods of national emergency until 1952, when Congress broadly authorized orders "to active duty or active duty for training" without any emergency requirement, but provided that such orders could not be issued without the consent of the governor of the State concerned. After two State Governors refused to consent to federal training missions abroad for their Guard units, the gubernatorial consent requirement was partially repealed in 1986 by the "Montgomery Amendment," which provides that a governor cannot withhold consent with regard to active duty outside the United States because of any objection to the location, purpose, type, or schedule of such duty. Petitioner Governor of Minnesota filed a complaint for injunctive relief, alleging, inter alia, that the Montgomery Amendment had prevented him from withholding his consent to a 1987 federal training mission in Central America for certain members of the state Guard, and that the Amendment violates the Militia Clauses of Article I, §8, of the Constitution, which authorize Congress to provide for (1) calling forth the militia to execute federal law, suppress insurrections, and repel invasions, and (2) organizing, arming, disciplining, and governing such part of the militia as may be employed in the federal service, reserving to the States the appointment of officers and the power to train the militia according to the discipline prescribed by Congress. The District Court rejected the Governor's challenge, holding that the federal Guard was created pursuant to Congress' Article I, §8, power to raise and support armies; that the fact that Guard units also have an identity as part of the state militia does not limit Congress' plenary authority to train the units as it sees fit when the Guard is called to active federal service; and that, accordingly, the Constitution neither required the gubernatorial veto nor prohibited its withdrawal. The Court of Appeals affirmed.

Held: Article I's plain language, read as a whole, establishes that Congress may authorize members of the National Guard of the United States to be ordered to active federal duty for purposes of training outside the United States without either the consent of a state governor or the declaration of a national emergency.

(a) The unchallenged validity of the dual enlistment system means that Guard members lose their status when called to active federal duty, and, if that duty is a training mission, the training is performed by the Army. During such periods, the second Militia Clause is no longer applicable.

(b) This view of the constitutional issue was presupposed by the Selective Draft Law Cases, 245 U.S. 366, 375, 377, 381-384, which held that the Militia Clauses do not constrain Congress' Article I, §8, powers to provide for the common defense, raise and support armies, make rules for the governance of the Armed Forces, and enact necessary and proper laws for such purposes, but in fact provide additional grants of power to Congress.

(c) This interpretation merely recognizes the supremacy of federal power in the military affairs area and does not significantly affect either the State's basic training responsibility or its ability to rely on its own Guard in state emergency situations.

(d) In light of the exclusivity of federal power over many aspects of military affairs, see Tarble's Case, 13 Wall. 397, the powers allowed to the States by existing statutes are significant.

(e) Thus, the Montgomery Amendment is not inconsistent with the Militia Clauses. Since the original veto was not constitutionally compelled, its partial repeal by the Amendment is constitutionally valid.

Stevens, J., delivered the opinion of a unanimous Court.

The question presented is whether the Congress may authorize the President to order members of the National Guard to active duty for purposes of training outside the United States during peace time without either the consent of a state governor or the declaration of a national emergency.

The question presented is whether the Congress may authorize the President to order members of the National Guard to active duty for purposes of training outside the United States during peace time without either the consent of a state governor or the declaration of a national emergency.

A gubernatorial consent requirement that had been enacted in 1952 n1 was partially repealed in 1986 by the "Montgomery Amendment," which provides:

"The consent of a Governor described in subsections (b) and (d) may not be withheld (in whole or in part) with regard to active duty outside the United States, its territories, and its possessions, because of any objection to the location, purpose, type, or schedule of such active duty." n2

In this litigation the Governor of Minnesota challenges the constitutionality of that Amendment. He contends that it violates the Militia Clauses of the Constitution. n3

n1 The Armed Forces Reserve Act of 1952, provided in part:

"Sec. 101. When used in this Act --

"(c) 'Active duty for training' means full-time duty in the active military service of the United States for training purposes.'" 66 Stat. 481.

"[Section 233] (c) At any time, any unit and the members thereof, or any member not assigned to a unit organized for the purpose of serving as such, in an active status in any reserve component may, by competent authority, be ordered to and required to perform active duty or active duty for training, without his consent, for not to exceed fifteen days annually: Provided, That units and members of the National Guard of the United States or the Air National Guard of the United States shall not be ordered to or required to serve on active duty in the service of the United States pursuant to this subsection without the consent of the Governor of the State or Territory concerned, or the Commanding General of the District of Columbia National Guard.

"(d) A member of a reserve component may, by competent authority, be ordered to active duty or active duty for training at any time with his consent: Provided, That no member of the National Guard of the United States or Air National Guard of the United States shall be so ordered without the consent of the Governor or other appropriate authority of the State, Territory, or District of Columbia concerned." Id., at 490

These provisions, as amended, are now codified at 10 U.S.C. §§672(b) and 672(d).

n2 The Montgomery Amendment was enacted as §522 of the National Defense Authorization Act for Fiscal Year 1987, Pub. L. 99-661, §522, 100 Stat. 3871.

n3 Two clauses of Article I -- clauses 15 and 16 of §8 -- are commonly described as "the Militia Clause" or "the Militia Clauses." They provide:

"The Congress shall have Power . . .

. . . . .

"To provide for calling forth the Militia to execute the Laws of the Union, suppress Insurrections and repel Invasions;

"To provide for organizing, arming, and disciplining, the Militia, and for governing such Part of them as may be employed in the Service of the United States, reserving to the States respectively, the Appointment of the Officers, and the Authority of training the Militia according to the discipline prescribed by Congress; . . . ." U.S. Const., Art. I, §8, cl. 15, 16.

the Governor alleged that pursuant to a state statute the Minnesota National Guard is the organized militia of the State of Minnesota

In his complaint the Governor alleged that pursuant to a state statute the Minnesota National Guard is the organized militia of the State of Minnesota and that pursuant to a federal statute members of that militia "are also members of either the Minnesota unit of the Air National Guard of the United States of the Minnesota unit of the Army National Guard of the United States (hereinafter collectively referred to as the 'National Guard of the United States')." App. 5 The complaint further alleged that the Montgomery Amendment had prevented the Governor from withholding his consent to a training mission in Central America for certain members of the Minnesota National Guard in January 1987, and prayed for an injunction against the implementation of any similar orders without his consent.

The District Judge rejected the Governor's challenge. He explained that the National Guard consists of "two overlapping, but legally distinct, organizations. Congress, under its constitutional authority to 'raise and support armies' has created the National Guard of the United States, a federal organization comprised of state national guard units and their members." 666 F. Supp. 1319, 1320 (Minn. 1987). n4 The fact that these units also maintain an identity as State National Guards, part of the militia described in Art. I, §8, of the Constitution, does not limit Congress' plenary authority to train the Guard "as it sees fit when the Guard is called to active federal service." Id., at 1324. He therefore concluded that "the gubernatorial veto found in §§672(b) and 672(d) is not constitutionally required. Having created the gubernatorial veto as an accommodation to the states, rather than pursuant to a constitutional mandate, the Congress may withdraw the veto without violating the Constitution." Ibid.

n4 In addition to the powers granted by the Militia Clauses, supra, n. 3, Congress possesses the following powers conferred by Art. I, §8:

"The Congress shall have Power . . . to pay the Debts and provide for the common Defense and general Welfare of the United States; . . .

. . . . .

"To declare War, grant Letters of Marque and Reprisal, and make Rules concerning Captures on Land and Water;

"To raise and support Armies, but no Appropriation of Money to that Use shall be for a longer Term than two Years;

"To provide and maintain a Navy;

"To make Rules for the Government and Regulation of the land and naval Forces; . . .

. . . . .

"To make all Laws which shall be necessary and proper for carrying into Execution the foregoing Powers, and all other Powers vested by this Constitution in the Government of the United States, or in any Department or Officer thereof."

Moreover, Art. IV, §4, provides:

"The United States shall guarantee to every State in this Union a Republican Form of Government, and shall protect each of them against Invasion; and on Application of the Legislature, or of the Executive (when the Legislature cannot be convened) against domestic Violence."

A divided panel of the Court of Appeals for the Eighth Circuit reached a contrary conclusion. It read the Militia Clause as preserving state authority over the training of the National Guard and its membership unless and until Congress "determined that there was some sort of exigency or extraordinary need to exert federal power."

A divided panel of the Court of Appeals for the Eighth Circuit reached a contrary conclusion. It read the Militia Clause as preserving state authority over the training of the National Guard and its membership unless and until Congress "determined that there was some sort of exigency or extraordinary need to exert federal power." App. to Pet. for Cert. A92. Only in that event could the Army Power dissipate the authority reserved to the States under the Militia Clauses.

"Congress' army power is plenary and exclusive" and that the State's authority to train the militia did not conflict with congressional power to raise armies for the common defense and to control the training of federal reserve forces.

In response to a petition for rehearing en banc, the Court of Appeals vacated the panel decision and affirmed the judgment of the District Court. Over the dissent of two judges, the en banc court agreed with the District Court's conclusion that "Congress' army power is plenary and exclusive" and that the State's authority to train the militia did not conflict with congressional power to raise armies for the common defense and to control the training of federal reserve forces. 880 F.2d 11, 17-18 (1989).

Because of the manifest importance of the issue, we granted the Governor's petition for certiorari. In the end, we conclude that the plain language of Article I of the Constitution, read as whole, requires affirmance of the Court of Appeals' judgment. We believe, however, that a brief description of the evolution of the present statutory scheme will help to explain that holding.

I

On the one hand, there was a widespread fear that a national standing Army posed an intolerable threat to individual liberty and to the sovereignty of the separate States, while, on the other hand, there was a recognition of the danger of relying on inadequately trained soldiers as the primary means of providing for the common defense. Thus, Congress was authorized both to raise and support a national army and also to organize "the Militia."

Two conflicting themes, developed at the Constitutional Convention and repeated in debates over military policy during the next century, led to a compromise in the text of the Constitution and in later statutory enactments. On the one hand, there was a widespread fear that a national standing Army posed an intolerable threat to individual liberty and to the sovereignty of the separate States, n5 while, on the other hand, there was a recognition of the danger of relying on inadequately trained soldiers as the primary means of providing for the common defense. n6 Thus, Congress was authorized both to raise and support a national army and also to organize "the Militia."

n5 At the Virginia ratification convention, Edmund Randolph stated that "there was not a member in the federal Convention, who did not feel indignation" at the idea of a standing Army. 3 J. Elliot, Debates on the Federal Constitution 401 (1863).

n6 As Alexander Hamilton argued in the Federalist Papers:

Here I expect we shall be told that the militia of the country is its natural bulwark, and would be at all times equal to the national defence. This doctrine, in substance, had like to have lost us our independence.

The steady operations of war against a regular disciplined army can only be successfully conducted by a force of the same kind.

The American militia, in the course of the late war, have, by their valor on numerous occasions, erected eternal monuments to their fame; but the bravest of them feel and know that the liberty of their county could not have been established by their efforts alone, however great and valuable they were.

"Here I expect we shall be told that the militia of the country is its natural bulwark, and would be at all times equal to the national defence. This doctrine, in substance, had like to have lost us our independence. It cost millions to the United States that might have been saved. The facts which, from our own experience, forbid a reliance of this kind, are too recent to permit us to be the dupes of such a suggestion. The steady operations of war against a regular disciplined army can only be successfully conducted by a force of the same kind. Considerations of economy, not less than of stability and vigor, confirm this position. The American militia, in the course of the late war, have, by their valor on numerous occasions, erected eternal monuments to their fame; but the bravest of them feel and know that the liberty of their county could not have been established by their efforts alone, however great and valuable they were. War, like most other things, is a science to be acquired and perfected by diligence, by perseverance, by time, and by practice." The Federalist No. 25, pp. 156-157 (E. Earle ed. 1938).

In 1792, it <Congress> did pass a statute that purported to establish "an Uniform Militia throughout the United States," but its detailed command that every able-bodied male citizen between the ages of 18 and 45 be enrolled therein and equip himself with appropriate weaponry was virtually ignored for more than a century, during which time the militia proved to be a decidedly unreliable fighting force.

President Theodore Roosevelt declared, "Our militia law is obsolete and worthless." The process of transforming "the National Guard of the several States" into an effective fighting force then began.

In the early years of the Republic, Congress did neither. In 1792, it did pass a statute that purported to establish "an Uniform Militia throughout the United States," but its detailed command that every able-bodied male citizen between the ages of 18 and 45 be enrolled therein and equip himself with appropriate weaponry n7 was virtually ignored for more than a century, during which time the militia proved to be a decidedly unreliable fighting force. n8 The statute was finally repealed in 1901. n9 it was in that year that President Theodore Roosevelt declared, "Our militia law is obsolete and worthless." n10 The process of transforming "the National Guard of the several States" into an effective fighting force then began.

every citizen so enrolled and notified, shall, within six months thereafter, provide himself with a good musket or firelock, sufficient bayonet and belt, two spare flints, and a knapsack, a pouch with a box therein to contain not less than twenty-four cartridges, suited to the bore of his musket or firelock, each cartridge to contain a proper quantity of powder and ball

or with a good rifle, knapsack, shot-pouch and powder-horn, twenty balls suited to the bore of his rifle, and a quarter of a pound of powder

n7 "That every citizen so enrolled and notified, shall, within six months thereafter, provide himself with a good musket or firelock, sufficient bayonet and belt, two spare flints, and a knapsack, a pouch with a box therein to contain not less than twenty-four cartridges, suited to the bore of his musket or firelock, each cartridge to contain a proper quantity of powder and ball: or with a good rifle, knapsack, shot-pouch and powder-horn, twenty balls suited to the bore of his rifle, and a quarter of a pound of powder, and shall appear, so armed, accountred and provided, when called out to exercise, or into service, except, that when called out on company days to exercise only, he may appear without a knapsack." 1 Stat. 271.

n8 Weiner, The Militia Clause of the Constitution, 54 Harv. L. Rev. 181, 187-194 (1940).

n9 See 31 Stat. 748, 758

Action should be taken in reference to the militia and to the raising of volunteer forces. Our militia law is obsolete and worthless. The organization and armament of the National Guard of the several States, which are treated as militia in the appropriations by the Congress, should be made identical with those provided for the regular forces.

n10 "Action should be taken in reference to the militia and to the raising of volunteer forces. Our militia law is obsolete and worthless. The organization and armament of the National Guard of the several States, which are treated as militia in the appropriations by the Congress, should be made identical with those provided for the regular forces. The obligations and duties of the Guard in time of war should be carefully defined, and a system established by law under which the method of procedure of raising volunteer forces should be prescribed in advance. It is utterly impossible in the excitement and haste of impending war to do this satisfactorily if the arrangements have not been made long beforehand. Provision should be made for utilizing in the first volunteer organizations called out the training of those citizens who have already had experience under arms, and especially for the selection in advance of the officers of any force which may be raised; for careful selection of the kind necessary is impossible after the outbreak of war." First Annual Message to Congress, Dec. 3, 1901, 14 Messages and Papers of the Presidents 6672.

The Dick Act divided the class of able-bodied male citizens between 18 and 45 years of age into an "organized militia" to be known as the National Guard of the several States, and the remainder of which was then described as the "reserve militia," and which later statutes have termed the "unorganized militia."

It is undisputed that Congress was acting pursuant to the Militia Clauses of the Constitution in passing the Dick Act.

The Dick Act divided the class of able-bodied male citizens between 18 and 45 years of age into an "organized militia" to be known as the National Guard of the several States, and the remainder of which was then described as the "reserve militia," and which later statutes have termed the "unorganized militia." The statute created a table of organization for the National Guard conforming to that of the Regular Army, and provided that federal funds and Regular Army instructors should be used to train its members. n11 It is undisputed that Congress was acting pursuant to the Militia Clauses of the Constitution in passing the Dick Act. Moreover, the legislative history of that Act indicates that Congress contemplated that the services of the organized militia would "be rendered only upon the soil of the United States or of its Territories." H. R. Rep. No. 1094, 57th Cong., 1st Sess., 22 (1902). In 1908, however, the statute was amended to provide expressly that the Organized Militia should be available for service "either within or without the territory of the United States." n12

n11 The Act of January 21, 1903, 32 Stat. 775, provided in part:

the militia shall consist of every able-bodied male citizen of the respective States

"That the militia shall consist of every able-bodied male citizen of the respective States, Territories, and the District of Columbia, and every able-bodied male of foreign birth who has declared his intention to become a citizen, who is more than eighteen and less than forty-five years of age, and shall be divided into two classes -- the organized militia, to be known as the National Guard of the State, Territory, or District of Columbia, or by such other designations as may be given them by the laws of the respective States or Territories, and the remainder to be known as the Reserve Militia."

Section 3 provided, in part:

"That the regularly enlisted, organized, and uniformed active militia in the several States and Territories and the District of Columbia who have heretofore participated or shall hereafter participate in the apportionment of the annual appropriation provided by section sixteen hundred and sixty-one of the Revised Statutes of the United States, as amended, whether known and designated as National Guard, militia, or otherwise, shall constitute the organized militia." Ibid.

Section 4 of the 1903 Act authorized the President to call forth the militia for a period of not exceeding nine months. Id., at 776.

n12 §4, 35 Stat. 400.

in 1916 Congress decided to "federalize" the National Guard. In addition to providing for greater federal control and federal funding of the Guard, the statute required every guardsman to take a dual oath—to support the Nation as well as the States and to obey the President as well as the Governor

when drafted into federal service by the President, members of the Guard so drafted should "from the date of their draft, stand discharged from the militia, and shall from said date be subject to" the rules and regulations governing the Regular Army.

When the Army made plans to invoke that authority by using National Guard units south of the Mexican border, Attorney General Wickersham expressed the opinion that the Militia Clauses precluded such use outside the Nation's borders. n13 In response to that opinion and to the widening conflict in Europe, in 1916 Congress decided to "federalize" the National Guard. n14 In addition to providing for greater federal control and federal funding of the Guard, the statute required every guardsman to take a dual oath -- to support the Nation as well as the States and to obey the President as well as the Governor -- and authorized the President to draft members of the Guard into federal service. The statute expressly provided that the Army of the United States should include not only "the Regular Army," but also "the National Guard while in the service of the United States," n15 and that when drafted into federal service by the President, members of the Guard so drafted should "from the date of their draft, stand discharged from the militia, and shall from said date be subject to" the rules and regulations governing the Regular Army. §111, 39 Stat. 211.

n13 "It is certain that it is only upon one or more of these three occasions -- when it is necessary to suppress insurrections, repeal invasions, or to execute the laws of the United States -- that even Congress can call this militia into the service of the United States, or authorize it to be done." 29 Op. Atty. Gen. 322, 323-324 (1912).

"The plain and certain meaning and effect of this constitutional provision is to confer upon Congress the power to call out the militia 'to execute the laws of the Union' within our own borders where, and where only, they exist, have any force, or can be executed by any one. This confers no power to send the militia into a foreign country to execute our laws which have no existence or force there and can not be there executed." Id., at 327.

Under Attorney General Wickersham's analysis, it would apparently be unconstitutional to call forth the militia for training duty outside the United States, even with the consent of the appropriate Governor. Of course, his opinion assumed that the militia units so called forth would retain their separate status in the state militia during their period of federal service.

n14 See Weiner, 54 Harv. L. Rev., at 199-203.

n15 The National Defense Act of June 3, 1916, 39 Stat. 166, provided in part:

"That the Army of the United States shall consist of the Regular Army, the Volunteer Army, the Officers' Reserve Corps, the Enlisted Reserve Corps, the National Guard while in the service of the United States, and such other land forces as are now or may hereafter be authorized by law."

During World War I, the President exercised the power to draft members of the National Guard into the Regular Army. That power, as well as the power to compel civilians to render military service, was upheld in the Selective Draft Law Cases, 245 U.S. 366 (1918). n16 Specifically, in that case, and in Cox v. Wood, 247 U.S. 3 (1918), the Court held that the plenary power to raise armies was "not qualified or restricted by the provisions of the militia clause." n17

n16 "The possession of authority to enact the statute must be found in the clauses of the constitution giving Congress power 'to declare war, . . . to raise and support armies, but no appropriation of money to that use shall be for a longer term than two years; . . . to make rules for the government and regulation of the land and naval forces.' Article I, §8. And of course the powers conferred by these provisions like all other powers given carry with them as provided by the Constitution the authority 'to make all laws which shall be necessary and proper for carrying into execution the foregoing powers.' Article I, §8." 245 U.S., at 377.

the power to call for military duty under the authority to declare war and raise armies and the duty of the citizen to serve when called

n17 "This result is apparent since on the face of the opinion delivered in those cases the constitutional power of Congress to compel the military service which the assailed law commanded was based on the following propositions: (a) That the power of Congress to compel military service and the duty of the citizen to render it when called for were derived from the authority given to Congress by the Constitution to declare war and to raise armies. (b) That those powers were not qualified or restricted by the provisions of the militia clause, and hence the authority in the exercise of the war power to raise armies and use them when raised was not subject to limitations as to use of the militia, if any, deducted from the militia clause. And (c) that from these principles it also follows that the power to call for military duty under the authority to declare war and raise armies and the duty of the citizen to serve when called were coterminous with the constitutional grant from which the authority was derived and knew no limit deduced from a separate, and for the purpose of the war power, wholly incidental, if not irrelevant and subordiante, provision concerning the militia, found in the Constitution. Our duty to affirm is therefore made clear." 247 U.S., at 6.

The draft of the individual members of the National Guard into the Army during World War I virtually destroyed the Guard as an effective organization. The draft terminated the members' status as militiamen, and the statue did not provide for a restoration of their prewar status as members of the Guard when they were mustered out of the Army. This problem was ultimately remedied by the 1933 amendments to the 1916 Act. Those amendments created the "two overlapping but distinct organizations" described by the District Court -- the National Guard of the various States and the National Guard of the United States.

Since 1933 all persons who have enlisted in a state National Guard unit have simultaneously enlisted in the National Guard of the United States. In the latter capacity they became a part of the Enlisted Reserve Corps of the Army, but unless and until ordered to active duty in the Army, they retained their status as members of a separate state Guard unit. Under the 1933 Act, they could be ordered into active service whenever Congress declared a national emergency and authorized the use of troops in excess of those in the Regular Army. The statute plainly described the effect of such an order.

"All persons so ordered into the active military service of the United States shall from the date of such order stand relieved from duty in the National Guard of their respective States, Territories, and the District of Columbia so long as they shall remain in the active military service of the United States, and during such time shall be subject to such laws and regulations for the government of the Army of the United States as may be applicable to members of the Army whose permanent retention in active military service is not contemplated by law. The organization of said units existing at the date of the order into active Federal service shall be maintained intact insofar as practicable." §18, 48 Stat. 160-161.

"Upon being relieved from active duty in the military service of the United States all individuals and units shall thereupon revert to their National Guard status.'" Id., at 161.

Thus, under the "dual enlistment" provisions of the statute that have been in effect since 1933, a member of the Guard who is ordered to active duty in the federal service is thereby relieved of his or her status in the state Guard for the entire period of federal service.

The National Guard units have under this plan become a sizeable portion of the Nation's military forces

gubernatorial consents to training missions were routinely obtained until 1985, when the Governor of California refused to consent to a training mission for 450 members of the California National Guard in Honduras

Until 1952 the statutory authority to order National Guard units to active duty was limited to periods of national emergency. In that year, Congress broadly authorized orders to "active duty or active duty for training" without any emergency requirement, but provided that such orders could not be issued without gubernatorial consent. The National Guard units have under this plan become a sizeable portion of the Nation's military forces; for example, "the Army National Guard provides 46 percent of the combat units and 28 percent of the support forces of the Total Army." n18 Apparently gubernatorial consents to training missions were routinely obtained until 1985, when the Governor of California refused to consent to a training mission for 450 members of the California National Guard in Honduras, and the Governor of Maine shortly thereafter refused to consent to a similar mission. Those incidents led to the enactment of the Montgomery Amendment and this litigation ensued.

n18 App. 12 (Testimony of James H. Webb, Assistant Secretary of Defense for Reserve Affairs, before a subcommittee of the Senate Armed Services Committee on July 15, 1986).

II

The Governor's attack on the Montgomery Amendment relies in part on the traditional understanding that "the Militia" can only be called forth for three limited purposes that do not encompass either foreign service or nonemergency conditions, and in part on the express language in the Militia Clause reserving to the States "the Authority of training the Militia." The Governor does not, however, challenge the authority of Congress to create a dual enlistment program. n19 Nor does the Governor claim that membership in a state Guard unit -- or any type of state militia -- creates any sort of constitutional immunity from being drafted into the federal armed forces. Indeed, it would be ironic to claim such immunity when every member of the Minnesota National Guard has voluntarily enlisted, or accepted a commission as an officer, in the National Guard of the United States and thereby become a member of the reserve corps of the Army.

n19 "The dual enlistment system requires state National Guard members to simultaneously enroll in the National Guard of the United States (NGUS), a reserve component of the national armed forces. 10 U.S.C. §§101(11) and (13), 591(a), 3261, 8261; 32 U.S.C. §101(5) and (7). It is an essential aspect of traditional military policy of the United States. 32 U.S.C. §102. The State of Minnesota fully supports dual enlistment and has not challenged the concept in any respect." Reply Brief for Petitioner 9 (footnote omitted).

the dual enlistment system means that the members of the National Guard of Minnesota who are ordered into federal service with the National Guard of the United States lose their status as members of the State militia during their period of active duty.

The unchallenged validity of the dual enlistment system means that the members of the National Guard of Minnesota who are ordered into federal service with the National Guard of the United States lose their status as members of the State militia during their period of active duty. If that duty is a training mission, the training is performed by the Army in which the trainee is serving, not by the militia from which the member has been temporarily disassociated. "Each member of the Army National Guard of the United States or the Air National Guard of the United States who is ordered to active duty is relieved from duty in the National Guard of his State or Territory, or of Puerto Rico or the District of Columbia, as the case may be, from the effective date of his order to active duty until he is relieved from that duty." 32 U.S.C. §325(a).

the traditional understanding of the militia as a part-time, nonprofessional fighting force.

This change in status is unremarkable in light of the traditional understanding of the militia as a part-time, nonprofessional fighting force. In Dunne v. People, 94 Ill. 120 (1879), the Illinois Supreme Court expressed its understanding of the term "militia" as follows:

"Lexicographers and others define militia, and so the common understanding is, to be 'a body of armed citizens trained to military duty, who may be called out in certain cases, but may not be kept on service like standing armies, in time of peace.' That is the case as to the active militia of this State. The men comprising it come from the body of the militia, and when not engaged at stated periods in drilling and other exercises, they return to their usual avocations, as is usual with militia, and are subject to call when the public exigencies demand it." Id., at 138.

Notwithstanding the brief periods of federal service, the members of the state Guard unit continue to satisfy this description of a militia. In a sense, all of them now must keep three hats in their closets -- a civilian hat, a state militia hat, and an army hat -- only one of which is worn at any particular time. When the state militia hat is being worn, the "drilling and other exercises" referred to by the Illinois Supreme Court are performed pursuant to "the Authority of training of Militia according to the discipline prescribed by Congress," but when that hat is replaced by the federal hat, the Militia Clause is no longer applicable.

This conclusion is unaffected by the fact that prior to 1952 Guard members were traditionally not ordered into active service in peace time or for duty abroad. That tradition is at least partially the product of political debate and political compromise, but even if the tradition were compelled by the text of the Constitution, its constitutional aspect is related only to service by state Guard personnel who retain their state affiliation during their periods of service. There now exists a wholly different situation, in which the state affiliation is suspended in favor of an entirely federal affiliation during the period of active duty.

the Militia Clauses are—as the constitutional text plainly indicates—additional grants of power to Congress.

This view of the constitutional issue was presupposed by our decision in the Selective Draft Law Cases, 245 U.S. 366 (1918). Although the Governor is correct in pointing out that those cases were decided in the context of an actual war, the reasoning is our opinion was not so limited. After expressly noting that the 1916 Act had incorporated members of the National Guard into the National Army, the Court held that the Militia Clauses do not constrain the powers of Congress "to provide for the common Defence," to "raise and support Armies," to "make Rules for the Government and Regulation of the land and naval Forces," or to enact such laws as "shall be necessary and proper" for executing those powers. 245 U.S., at 375, 377, 381-384. The Court instead held that, far from being a limitation on those powers, the Militia Clauses are -- as the constitutional text plainly indicates -- additional grants of power to Congress.

The congressional power to call forth the militia may in appropriate cases supplement its broader power to raise armies and provide for the common defense and general welfare, but it does not limit those powers.

The first empowers Congress to call forth the militia "to execute the Laws of the Union, suppress Insurrections and repel Invasions." We may assume that Attorney General Wickersham was entirely correct in reasoning that when a National Guard unit retains its status as a state militia, Congress could not "impress" the entire unit for any other purpose. Congress did, however, authorize the President to call forth the entire membership of the Guard into federal service during World War I, even though the soldiers who fought in France were not engaged in any of the three specified purposes. Membership in the Militia did not exempt them from a valid order to perform federal service, whether that service took the form of combat duty or training for such duty. n20 The congressional power to call forth the militia may in appropriate cases supplement its broader power to raise armies and provide for the common defense and general welfare, but it does not limit those powers. n21

n20 See Selective Draft Law Cases, 245 U.S., at 382-389; Cox v. Wood, 247 U.S. 3, 6 (1918).

n21 Congress has by distinct statutes provided for activating the National Guard of the United States and for calling forth the militia, including the National Guards of the various States. See 10 U.S.C. §§672-675 (authorizing executive officials to order reserve forces, including the National Guard of the United States and the Air National Guard of the United States, to active duty); 10 U.S.C. §§331-333 (authorizing executive officials to call forth the militia of the States); 10 U.S.C. §§3500, 8500 (authorizing executive officials to call forth the National Guards of the various States). When the National Guard units of the States are called forth, the orders "shall be issued through the governors of the States." 10 U.S.C. §3500.

It is by congressional choice that the available pool of citizens has been formed into organized units. Over the years, Congress has exercised this power in various ways, but its current choice of a dual enlistment system is just as permissible as the 1792 choice to have the members of the militia arm themselves.

The second Militia Clause enhances federal power in three additional ways. First, it authorizes Congress to provide for "organizing, arming and disciplining the Militia." It is by congressional choice that the available pool of citizens has been formed into organized units. Over the years, Congress has exercised this power in various ways, but its current choice of a dual enlistment system is just as permissible as the 1792 choice to have the members of the militia arm themselves. Second, the Clause authorizes Congress to provide for governing such part of the militia as may be employed in the service of the United States. Surely this authority encompasses continued training while on active duty. Finally, although the appointment of officers "and the Authority of training of Militia" is reversed to the States respectively, that limitation is, in turn, limited by the words "according to the discipline prescribed by the Congress." If the discipline required for effective service in the Armed Forces of a global power requires training in distant lands, or distant skies, Congress has the authority to provide it. The subordinate authority to perform the actual training prior to active duty in the federal service does not include the right to edit the discipline that Congress may prescribe for Guard members after they are ordered into federal service.

The Governor argues that this interpretation of the Militia Clause has the practical effect of nullifying an important State power that is expressly reserved in the Constitution. We disagree. It merely recognizes the supremacy of federal power in the area of military affairs. The Federal Government provides virtually all of the funding, the material, and the leadership for the state Guard units.

Indeed, if the federal training mission were to interfere with the State Guard's capacity to respond to local emergencies, the Montgomery Amendment would permit the Governor to veto the proposed mission.

in addition to its National Guard, a State may provide and maintain at its own expense a defense force that is exempt from being drafted into the Armed Forces of the United States.

The Governor argues that this interpretation of the Militia Clause has the practical effect of nullifying an important State power that is expressly reserved in the Constitution. We disagree. It merely recognizes the supremacy of federal power in the area of military affairs. n22 The Federal Government provides virtually all of the funding, the material, and the leadership for the state Guard units. The Minnesota unit, which includes about 13,000 members is affected only slightly when a few dozen, or at most a few hundred, soldiers are ordered into active service for brief periods of time. n23 Neither the State's basic training responsibility, nor its ability to rely on its own Guard in state emergency situations, is significantly affected. Indeed, if the federal training mission were to interfere with the State Guard's capacity to respond to local emergencies, the

Montgomery Amendment would permit the Governor to veto the proposed mission. n24 Moreover, Congress has provided by statute that in addition to its National Guard, a State may provide and maintain at its own expense a defense force that is exempt from being drafted into the Armed Forces of the United States. See 32 U.S.C. §109(c). As long as that provision remains in effect, there is no basis for an argument that the federal statutory scheme deprives Minnesota of any constitutional entitlement to a separate militia of its own. n25

n22 This supremacy is evidenced by several constitutional provisions, especially the prohibition in Art. I, §10, of the Constitution, which states:

"No State shall, without the Consent of Congress, lay any duty of Tonnage, keep Troops, or Ships of War in time of Peace, enter into any Agreement or Compact with another State, or with a foreign Power, or engage in War, unless actually invaded, or in such imminent Danger as will not admit of delay."

n23 According to the Governor, at most "only several hundred" of Minnesota's National Guard members "will be in federal training at any one time." Brief for Petitioner 41.

n24 The Montgomery Amendment deprives the Governors of the power to veto participation in a National Guard of the United States training mission on the basis of any objection to "the location, purpose, type, or schedule of such active duty." 10 U.S.C. §672(f). Governors may withhold their consent on other grounds. The Governor and the United States agree that if the federalization of the Guard would interfere with the State Guard's ability to address a local emergency, that circumstance would be a valid basis for a gubernatorial veto. Brief for Petitioner 41; Brief for Respondents 9.

The Governor contends that the residual veto power is of little use. He predicates this argument, however, on a claim that the federal training program has so minimal an impact upon the State Guard that the veto is never necessary:

"Minnesota has approximately 13,000 members of the National Guard. At most, only several hundred will be in federal training at any one time. To suggest that a governor will ever be able to withhold consent under the Montgomery Amendment assumes (1) local emergencies can be adequately predicted in advance, and (2) a governor can persuade federal authorities that National Guard members designated for training are needed for state purposes when the overwhelming majority of the National Guard remains at home." Brief for Petitioner 41.

Under the interpretation of the Montgomery Amendment advanced by the United States, it seems that a governor might also properly withhold consent to an active duty order if the order were so intrusive that it deprived the State of the power to train its forces effectively for local service:

"Under the current statutory scheme, the States are assured of the use of their National Guard units for any legitimate state purpose. They are simply forbidden to use their control over the state National Guard to thwart federal use of the NGUS for national security and foreign policy objectives with which they disagree." Brief for Respondents 13.

n25 The Governor contends that the state defense forces are irrelevant to this case because they are not subject to being called forth by the National Government, and therefore cannot be militia within the meaning of the Constitution. We are not, however, satisfied that this argument is persuasive. First, the immunity of those forces from impressment into the national services appears -- if indeed they have any such immunity -- to be the consequence of a purely statutory choice, and it is not obvious why that choice should alter the constitutional status of the forces allowed the States. Second, although we do not believe it necessary to resolve the issue, the Governor's construction of the relevant statute is subject to question. It is true that the state defense forces "may not be called, ordered, or drafted into the armed forces." 32 U.S.C. §109(c). It is nonetheless possible that they are subject to call under 10 U.S.C. §§331-333, which distinguish the "militia" from the "armed forces," and which appear to subject all portions of the "militia" -- organized or not -- to call if needed for the purposes specified in the Militia Clauses. See n. 21, supra.

In light of the Constitution's more general plan for providing for the common defense, the powers allowed to the States by existing statutes are significant. As has already been mentioned, several constitutional provisions commit matters of foreign policy and military affairs to the exclusive control of the National Government. n26 This Court in Tarble's Case, 13 Wall 397 (1871), had occasion to observe that the constitutional allocation of powers in this realm gave rise to a presumption that federal control over the armed forces was exclusive. n27 Were it not for the Militia Clauses, it might be possible to argue on like grounds that the constitutional allocation of powers precluded the formation of organized state militia. n28 The Militia Clauses, however, subordinate any such structural inferences to an express permission while also subjecting State militia to express federal limitations. n29

n26 See, e.g., Art. I, §8, cl. 11 (Congress's power to declare war); Art. I, §10, cl. 1 (States forbidden to enter into treaties); Art. I, §10, cl. 3 (States forbidden to keep troops in time of peace, enter into agreements with foreign powers, or engage in War absent imminent invasion); Art. II, §3 (President shall receive ambassadors).

n27 In the course of holding that a Wisconsin court had no jurisdiction to issue a writ of habeas corpus to inquire into the validity of a soldier's enlistment in the United States Army, we observed:

"Now, among the powers assigned to the National government, is the power 'to raise and support armies,' and the power 'to provide for the government and regulation of the land and naval forces.' The execution of these powers falls within the line of its control over the subject is plenary and exclusive. It can determine, without question from any State authority, how the armies shall be raised, whether by voluntary enlistment or forced draft, the age at which the soldier shall be received, and the period for which he shall be taken, the compensation he shall be allowed, and the service to which he shall be assigned. And it can provide the rules for the government and regulation of the forces after they are raised, define what shall constitute military offences, and prescribe their punishment. No interference with the execution of this power to the National government in the formation, organization, and government of its armies by any State officials could be permitted without greatly impairing the efficiency, if it did not utterly destroy, this branch of the public service." 13 Wall., at 408.

n28 See United States v. Curtiss-Wright Export Corp., 299 U.S. 304, 318 (1936) ("The powers to declare and wage war, to conclude peace, to make treaties, to maintain diplomatic relations with other sovereignties, if they had never been mentioned in the Constitution, would have vested in the federal government as necessary concomitants of nationality"); The Federalist No. 23, p. 143 (E. Earle ed. 1938) ("It must be admitted . . . that there can be no limitation of that authority which is to provide for the defense and protection of the community, in any matter essential to its efficacy -- that is, in any matter essential to the formation, direction, or support of the NATIONAL FORCES"); L. Henkin, Foreign Affairs and the Constitution 234-244 (1972) (discussing implied constitutional restrictions upon State policies related to foreign affairs); Comment, The Legality of Nuclear Free Zones, 55 U. Chi. L. Rev. 965, 991-997 (1988) (discussing implied constitutional restrictions upon State policies related to foreign affairs or military).

n29 The powers allowed by statute to the States make it unnecessary for us to examine that portion of the Selective Draft Law Cases, 245 U.S. 366 (1918), in which we stated:

"[The Constitution left] under the sway of the States undelegated the control of the militia to the extent that such control was not taken away by the exercise by Congress of its power to raise armies. This did not diminish the military power or curb the full potentiality of the right to exert it but left an area of authority requiring to be provided for (military area) unless and until by the exertion of the military power of Congress that area had been circumscribed or totally disappeared." Id., at 383.

we of course do not pass upon the relative virtues of the various political choices that have frequently altered the relationship between the Federal Government and the States in the field of military affairs.

We thus conclude that the Montgomery Amendment is not inconsistent with the Militia Clauses. In so doing, we of course do not pass upon the relative virtues of the various political choices that have frequently altered the relationship between the Federal Government and the States in the field of military affairs. This case does not raise any question concerning the wisdom of the gubernatorial veto established in 1952, or of its partial repeal in 1986. We merely hold that since the former was not constitutionally compelled, the Montgomery Amendment is constitutionally valid.

The judgment of the Court of Appeals is affirmed.

UNITED STATES v. THOMPSON/CENTER ARMS COMPANY

(FULL CASE)

504 U.S. 505; 112 S. Ct. 2102; 119 L. Ed. 2d 308

January 13, 1992, Argued

June 8, 1992, Decided

GIST: Thompson/Center challenged the government's assessment that its Contender pistol fell under the scope of the National Firearms Act of 1934 if it was possessed along with a kit that could be used to convert the Contender into a rifle. With the kit, a person could turn the Contender pistol into an ordinary rifle (entirely legal) or could put a rifle stock on the gun, while leaving the pistol barrel in place. Under federal law, this would create a short-barreled rifle, which would be illegal unless the gun were registered and the special National Firearms Act tax were paid.

The question in the case is whether a regulated firearm (the short rifle) has been "made" merely by possessing a Contender pistol and the conversion kit which could be used for legal or illegal conversions. The Court held that the statutory language was ambiguous, and because the NFA is a tax statute carrying criminal sanctions with no additional requirement of willfulness, the disputed term should be resolved in favor of the respondent, Thompson/Center, under the well-established principle of lenity.

The Court discussed that in many instances, having a collection of parts that assembles into an NFA "firearm" constitutes having one (silencers, machine guns, a gun and a machine-gun-conversion kit for it, etc.). In an interesting use of language, part of this decision relies upon the word "gun" to mean a regular firearm, such as any store might carry, and "firearm," to refer to an NFA weapon, which includes short-barreled long guns, disguised firearms like pen guns, cane guns and wallet guns, and heavier armament like explosives, bombs, rockets, mortars, incendiaries and more.

Attorney Stephen Halbrook was the lead attorney on this case and made the winning oral arguments before the Justices.

Respondent manufactures the "Contender" pistol and, for a short time, also manufactured a kit that could be used to convert the Contender into a rifle with either a 21-inch or a 10-inch barrel. The Bureau of Alcohol, Tobacco and Firearms advised respondent that when the kit was possessed or distributed with the Contender, the unit constituted a "firearm" under the National Firearms Act (NFA or Act), 26 U.S.C. §5845(a)(3), which defines that term to include a rifle with a barrel less than 16 inches long, known as a short-barreled rifle, but not a pistol or a rifle having a barrel 16 inches or more in length. Respondent paid the $200 tax levied by §5821 upon anyone "making" a "firearm" and filed a claim for a refund. When its refund claim proved fruitless, respondent brought this suit under the Tucker Act. The Claims Court entered summary judgment for the Government, but the Court of Appeals reversed, holding that a short-barreled rifle "actually must be assembled" in order to be "made" within the NFA's meaning.

Held: The judgment is affirmed.

JUSTICE SOUTER, joined by THE CHIEF JUSTICE and JUSTICE O'CONNOR, concluded that the Contender and conversion kit when packaged together have not been "made" into a short-barreled rifle for NFA purposes.

(a) The language of §5845(i) -- which provides that "the term 'make', and [its] various derivatives . . ., shall include manufacturing . . ., putting together . . ., or otherwise producing a firearm" -- clearly demonstrates that the aggregation of separate parts that can be assembled only into a firearm, and the aggregation of a gun other than a firearm and parts that would have no use in association with the gun except to convert it into a firearm, constitute the "making" of a firearm. If, as the Court of Appeals held, a firearm were only made at the time of final assembly (the moment the firearm was "put together"), the statutory "manufacturing . . . or otherwise producing" language would be redundant. Thus, Congress must have understood "making" to cover more than final assembly, and some disassembled aggregation of parts must be included.

(b) However, application of the ordinary rules of statutory construction shows that the Act is ambiguous as to whether, given the fact that the Contender can be converted into either an NFA-regulated firearm or an unregulated rifle, the mere possibility of its use with the kit to assemble the former renders their combined packaging "making."

(c) The statutory ambiguity is properly resolved by applying the rule of lenity in respondent's favor. See, e.g., Crandon v. United States, 494 U.S. 152, 168, 108 L. Ed. 2d 132, 110 S. Ct. 997. Although it is a tax statute that is here construed in a civil setting, the NFA has criminal applications that carry no additional requirement of willfulness. Making a firearm without approval may be subject to criminal sanction, as is possession of, or failure to pay the tax on, an unregistered firearm.

JUSTICE SCALIA, joined by JUSTICE THOMAS, agreed that the rule of lenity prevents respondent's pistol and conversion kit from being covered by the NFA, but on the basis of different ambiguities: whether a firearm includes unassembled parts, and whether the requisite "intent to be fired from the shoulder" existed as to the short-barrel component.

JUSTICE SOUTER announced the judgment of the Court and delivered an opinion, in which THE CHIEF JUSTICE and JUSTICE O'CONNOR join.

Section 5821 of the National Firearms Act (NFA or Act), see 26 U.S.C. §5849, levies a tax of $200 per unit upon anyone "making" a "firearm" as that term is defined in the Act. Neither pistols nor rifles with barrels 16 inches long or longer are firearms within the NFA definition, but rifles with barrels less than 16 inches long, known as short-barreled rifles, are. §5845(a)(3). This case presents the question whether a gun manufacturer "makes" a short-barreled rifle when it packages as a unit a pistol together with a kit containing a shoulder stock and a 21-inch barrel, permitting the pistol's conversion into an unregulated long-barreled rifle, n1 or, if the pistol's barrel is left on the gun, a short-barreled rifle that is regulated. We hold that the statutory language may not be construed to require payment of the tax under these facts.

n1 Unregulated, that is, under the NFA.

I

The word "firearm" is used as a term of art in the NFA. It means, among other things, "a rifle having a barrel or barrels of less than 16 inches in length.

The word "firearm" is used as a term of art in the NFA. It means, among other things, "a rifle having a barrel or barrels of less than 16 inches in length . . . ." §5845(a)(3). "The term 'rifle' means a weapon designed or redesigned, made or remade, and intended to be fired from the shoulder and designed or redesigned and made or remade to use the energy of the explosive in a fixed cartridge to fire only a single projectile through a rifled bore for each single pull of the trigger, and shall include any such weapon which may be readily restored to fire a fixed cartridge." §5845(c).

The consequence of being the maker of a firearm are serious.

The consequence of being the maker of a firearm are serious. Section 5821(a) imposes a tax of $200 "for each firearm made," which "shall be paid by the person making the firearm," §5821(b). Before one may make a firearm, one must obtain the approval of the Secretary of the Treasury, §5822, and §5841 requires that the "manufacturer, importer, and maker . . . register each firearm he manufactures, imports, or makes" in a central registry maintained by the Secretary of the Treasury. A maker who fails to comply with the NFA's provisions is subject to criminal penalties of up to 10 years' imprisonment and a fine of up to $10,000, or both, which may be imposed without proof of willfulness or knowledge. §5871.

Respondent Thompson/Center Arms Company manufactures a single-shot pistol called the "Contender," designed so that its handle and barrel can be removed from its "receiver," the metal frame housing the trigger, hammer, and firing mechanism.

The entire conversion, from pistol to long-barreled rifle takes only a few minutes; conversion to a short-barreled rifle takes even less time.

Respondent Thompson/Center Arms Company manufactures a single-shot pistol called the "Contender," designed so that its handle and barrel can be removed from its "receiver," the metal frame housing the trigger, hammer, and firing mechanism. See 27 CFR §179.11 (1991) (definition of frame or receiver). For a short time in 1985, Thompson/Center also manufactured a carbine-conversion kit consisting of a 21-inch barrel, a rifle stock, and a wooden fore-end. If one joins the receiver with the conversion kit's rifle stock, the 21-inch barrel, and the rifle fore-end, the product is a carbine rifle with a 21-inch barrel. If, however, the shorter, pistol length barrel is not removed from the receiver when the rifle stock is added, one is left with a 10-inch or "short-barreled" carbine rifle. The entire conversion, from pistol to long-barreled rifle takes only a few minutes; conversion to a short-barreled rifle takes even less time.

In 1985, the Bureau of Alcohol, Tobacco and Firearms advised Thompson/Center that when its conversion kit was possessed or distributed together with the Contender pistol, the unit constituted a firearm subject to the NFA. Thompson/Center responded by paying the $200 tax for a single such firearm, and submitting an application for permission under 26 U.S.C. §5822 "to make, use, and segregate as a single unit" a package consisting of a serially numbered pistol, together with an attachable shoulder stock and a 21-inch barrel. Thompson/Center then filed a refund claim. After more than six months had elapsed without action on it, the company brought this suit in the United States Claims Court under the Tucker Act, 28 U.S.C. §1491, arguing that the unit registered was not a firearm within the meaning of the NFA because Thompson/Center had not assembled a short-barreled rifle from its components. The Claims Court entered summary judgment for the Government, concluding that the Contender pistol together with its conversion kit is a firearm within the meaning of the NFA. 19 Cl. Ct. 725 (1990).

The Court of Appeals for the Federal Circuit reversed, holding that a short-barreled rifle "actually must be assembled" in order to be "made" within the meaning of the NFA. 924 F.2d 1041, 1043 (1991). The Court of Appeals expressly declined to follow the decision of the Court of Appeals for the Seventh Circuit in United States v. Drasen, 845 F.2d 731, cert. denied, 488 U.S. 909, 102 L. Ed. 2d 250, 109 S. Ct. 262 (1988), which had held that an unassembled "complete parts kit" for a short-barreled rifle was in fact a short-barreled rifle for purposes of the NFA. We granted certiorari to resolve this conflict. 502 U.S. 807 (1991).

II

the provision does not expressly address the question whether a short-barreled rifle can be "made" by the aggregation of finished parts that can readily be assembled into one. The Government contends that assembly is not necessary; Thompson/Center argues that it is.

The NFA provides that "the term 'make', and the various derivatives of such word, shall include manufacturing (other than by one qualified to engage in such business under this chapter), putting together, altering, any combination of these, or otherwise producing a firearm." 26 U.S.C. §5845(i). n2 But the provision does not expressly address the question whether a short-barreled rifle can be "made" by the aggregation of finished parts that can readily be assembled into one. The Government contends that assembly is not necessary; Thompson/Center argues that it is.

n2 The phrase "other than by one qualified to engage in such business under this chapter" apparently refers to those manufacturers who have sought and obtained qualification as a firearms manufacturer under 26 U.S.C. §5801(a)(1), which requires payment of a $1,000 occupational tax. Rather than seek such qualification, Thompson/Center applied for permission to make a firearm as a nonqualified manufacturer under §5822, which requires payment of the $200 per firearm "making tax" under §5821(a).

A

The Government urges us to view the shipment of the pistol with the kit just as we would the shipment of a bicycle that requires some home assembly. "The fact that a short-barrel rifle, or any other 'firearm,' is possessed or sold in a partially unassembled state does not remove it from regulation under the Act." Brief for United States 6.

The Government's analogy of the partially assembled bicycle to the packaged pistol and conversion kit is not, of course, exact.

The Government's analogy of the partially assembled bicycle to the packaged pistol and conversion kit is not, of course, exact. While each example includes some unassembled parts, the crated bicycle parts can be assembled into nothing but a bicycle, whereas the contents of Thompson/Center's package can constitute a pistol, a long-barreled rifle, or a short-barreled version. These distinctions, however, do define the issues raised by the Government's argument, the first of which is whether the aggregation and segregation of separate parts that can be assembled only into a short-barreled rifle and are sufficient for that purpose amount to "making" that firearm, or whether the firearm is not "made" until the moment of final assembly. This is the issue on which the Federal and Seventh Circuits are divided.

We think the language of the statute provides a clear answer on this point. The definition of "make" includes not only "putting together," but also "manufacturing . . . or otherwise producing a firearm." If as Thompson/Center submits, a firearm were only made at the time of final assembly (the moment the firearm was "put together"), the additional language would be redundant. Congress must, then, have understood "making" to cover more than final assembly, and some disassembled aggregation of parts must be included. Since the narrowest example of a combination of parts that might be included is a set of parts that could be used to make nothing but a short-barreled rifle, the aggregation of such a set of parts, at the very least, must fall within the definition of "making" such a rifle.

unassembled silencer is a silencer

unassembled machineguns are machineguns

This is consistent with the holdings of every Court of Appeals, except the court below, to consider a combination of parts that could only be assembled into an NFA-regulated firearm, either under the definition of rifle at issue here or under similar statutory language. See United States v. Drasen, supra; United States v. Endicott, 803 F.2d 506, 508-509 (CA9 1986) (unassembled silencer is a silencer); United States v. Luce, 726 F.2d 47, 48-49 (CA1 1984) (same); United States v. Lauchli, 371 F.2d 303, 311-313 (CA7 1966) (unassembled machineguns are machineguns). n3 We thus reject the broad language of the Court of Appeals for the Federal Circuit to the extent that it would mean that a disassembled complete short-barreled rifle kit must be assembled before it has been "made" into a short-barreled rifle. The fact that the statute would serve almost no purpose if this were the rule only confirms the reading we have given it. n4

n3 In Drasen, a complete-parts kit was sold with a flash suppressor, which, if affixed to the rifle barrel, would have extended it beyond the regulated length. See Drasen, 845 F.2d at 737. Because the Drasen court concluded that such a flash suppressor was not a part of the rifle's barrel, see ibid., its holding is consistent with ours.

In our system, avoidance of a tax by remaining outside the ambit of the law that imposes it is every person's right. "Over and over again courts have said that there is nothing sinister in so arranging one's affairs as to keep taxes as low as possible. Everybody does so, rich or poor; and all do right, for nobody owes any public duty to pay more than the law demands: taxes are enforced exactions, not voluntary contributions.

n4 We do not accept the Government's suggestion, however, that complete-parts kits must be taxable because otherwise manufacturers will be able to "avoid the tax." Brief for United States 11. Rather, we conclude that such kits are within the definition of the taxable item. Failure to pay the tax on such a kit thus would amount to evasion, not avoidance. In our system, avoidance of a tax by remaining outside the ambit of the law that imposes it is every person's right. "Over and over again courts have said that there is nothing sinister in so arranging one's affairs as to keep taxes as low as possible. Everybody does so, rich or poor; and all do right, for nobody owes any public duty to pay more than the law demands: taxes are enforced exactions, not voluntary contributions. To demand more in the name of morals is mere cant." Commissioner v. Newman, 159 F.2d 848, 850-851 (CA2) (L. Hand, J., dissenting), cert. denied, 331 U.S. 859, 91 L. Ed. 1866, 67 S. Ct. 1755 (1947).

carbine together with all parts necessary to convert it into a machinegun is a machinegun

pistol and attachable shoulder stock found "in different drawers of the same dresser" constitute a short-barreled rifle

We also think that a firearm is "made" on facts one step removed from the paradigm of the aggregated parts that can be used for nothing except assembling a firearm. Two courts to our knowledge have dealt in some way with claims that when a gun other than a firearm was placed together with a further part or parts that would have had no use in association with the gun except to convert it into a firearm, a firearm was produced. See United States v. Kokin, 365 F.2d 595, 596 (CA3) (carbine together with all parts necessary to convert it into a machinegun is a machinegun), cert. denied, 385 U.S. 987, 17 L. Ed. 2d 448, 87 S. Ct. 597 (1966); see also United States v. Zeidman, 444 F.2d 1051, 1053 (CA7 1971) (pistol and attachable shoulder stock found "in different drawers of the same dresser" constitute a short-barreled rifle). Here it is true, of course, that some of the parts could be used without ever assembling a firearm, but the likelihood of that is belied by the utter uselessness of placing the converting parts with the others except for just such a conversion. Where the evidence in a given case supports a finding of such uselessness, the case falls within the fair intendment of "otherwise producing a firearm." See 26 U.S.C. §5845(i). n5

n5 Contrary to JUSTICE SCALIA's suggestion, see post, at 522, our understanding of these aggregations of parts, shared by a majority of the Court (those who join this opinion and the four Members of the Court in dissent, see post, p. 523 (WHITE, J., joined by BLACKMUN, STEVENS, and KENNEDY, JJ., dissenting) (any aggregation of parts necessary to assemble a firearm is a firearm)), applies to all the provisions of the Act, whether they regulate the "making" of a firearm, e.g., 26 U.S.C. §5821(a), or not, see, e.g., §5842(b) (possession of a firearm that has no serial number); §5844 (importation of a firearm); §5811 (transfer of a firearm). Since, as we conclude, such a combination of parts, or of a complete gun and an additional part or parts, is "made" into a firearm, it follows, in the absence of some reason to the contrary, that all portions of the Act that apply to "firearms" apply to such a combination. JUSTICE SCALIA does not explain how we would be free to construe "firearm" in a different way for purposes of those provisions that do not contain the verb "to make." Our normal canons of construction caution us to read the statute as a whole, and, unless there is a good reason, to adopt a consistent interpretation of a term used in more than one place within a statute.

B

The packaging of pistol and kit has an obvious utility for those who want both a pistol and a regular rifle

Here, however, we are not dealing with an aggregation of parts that can serve no useful purpose except the assembly of a firearm, or with an aggregation having no ostensible utility except to convert a gun into such a weapon. There is, to be sure, one resemblance to the latter example in the sale of the Contender with the converter kit, for packaging the two has no apparent object except to convert the pistol into something else at some point. But the resemblance ends with the fact that the unregulated Contender pistol can be converted not only into a short-barreled rifle, which is a regulated firearm, but also into a long-barreled rifle, which is not. The packaging of pistol and kit has an obvious utility for those who want both a pistol and a regular rifle, and the question is whether the mere possibility of their use to assemble a regulated firearm is enough to place their combined packaging within the scope of "making" one. n6

Surely Justice Scalia's argument would take us over the line between lenity and credulity when he suggests that one who makes what would otherwise be a short-barreled rifle could escape liability by carving a warning into the shoulder stock.

n6 Thompson/Center suggests that further enquiry could be avoided when it contends that the Contender and carbine kit do not amount to a "rifle" of any kind because, until assembled into a rifle, they are not "'made' and 'intended to be fired from the shoulder.'" Brief for Respondent 8. From what we have said thus far, however, it is apparent that, though disassembled, the parts included when the Contender and its carbine kit are packaged together have been "made" into a rifle. The inclusion of the rifle stock in the package brings the Contender and carbine kit within the "intended to be fired from the shoulder" language contained in the definition of rifle in the statute. See 26 U.S.C. §5845(c). The only question is whether this combination of parts constitutes a short-barreled rifle. Surely JUSTICE SCALIA's argument would take us over the line between lenity and credulity when he suggests that one who makes what would otherwise be a short-barreled rifle could escape liability by carving a warning into the shoulder stock. See post, at 523 (SCALIA, J., concurring in judgment).

1

Neither the statute's language nor its structure provides any definitive guidance. Thompson/Center suggests guidance may be found in some subsections of the statute governing other types of weapons by language that expressly covers combinations of parts. The definition of "machinegun," for example, was amended by the Gun Control Act of 1968 to read that "the term shall also include . . . any combination of parts from which a machinegun can be assembled if such parts are in the possession or under the control of a person." 26 U.S.C. §5845(b). n7 In 1986, the definition of "silencer" was amended by the Firearms Owners' Protection Act to "include any combination of parts, designed or redesigned, and intended for use in assembling or fabricating a firearm silencer . . . ." See 26 U.S.C. §5845(a)(7); 18 U.S.C. §921(a)(24).

n7 At the same time, the definition of "destructive device" was amended to include "any combination of parts either designed or intended for use in converting any device into a destructive device . . . and from which a destructive device may readily be assembled." 26 U.S.C. §5845(f). This appears to envision by its terms only combinations of parts for converting something into a destructive device.

Thompson/Center stresses the contrast between these references to "any combination of parts" and the silence about parts in the definition of rifle in arguing that no aggregation of parts can suffice to make the regulated rifle. This argument is subject to a number of answers, however. First, it sweeps so broadly as to conflict with the statutory definition of "make," applicable to all firearms, which implies that a firearm may be "made" even where not fully "put together." If this were all, of course, the conflict might well be resolved in Thompson/Center's favor. We do not, however, read the machinegun and silencer definitions as contrasting with the definition of rifle in such a way as to raise a conflict with the broad concept of "making."

The definition of "silencer" is now included in the NFA only by reference, see 26 U.S.C. §5845(a)(7), whereas its text appears only at 18 U.S.C. §921(a)(24), in a statute that itself contains no definition of "make." Prior to 1986 the definition of "firearm" in the NFA included "a muffler or a silencer for any firearm whether or not such firearm is included within this definition." 26 U.S.C. §5845 (a)(7) (1982 ed.). Two Courts of Appeals held this language to include unassembled silencers that could be readily and easily assembled. See United States v. Endicott, 803 F.2d at 508-509; United States v. Luce, 726 F.2d at 48-49.

In 1986, Congress replaced that language with "any silencer (as defined in section 921 of title 18, United States Code)." Pub. L. 99-308, §109(b), 100 Stat. 460. The language defining silencer that was added to 18 U.S.C. §921 at that same time reads: "The terms 'firearm silencer' and 'firearm muffler' mean any device for silencing, muffling, or diminishing the report of a portable firearm, including any combination of parts, designed or redesigned, and intended for use in assembling or fabricating a firearm silencer or firearm muffler, and any part intended only for use in such assembly or fabrication." Pub. L. 99-308, §101, 100 Stat. 451.

Thompson/Center argues that if, even before the amendment, a combination of parts was already "made" into a firearm, the "any combination of parts" language would be redundant. While such a conclusion of redundancy could suggest that Congress assumed that "make" in the NFA did not cover unassembled parts, the suggestion (and the implied conflict with our reading of "make") is proven false by evidence that Congress actually understood redundancy to result from its new silencer definition. Congress apparently assumed that the statute reached complete-parts kits even without the "combination" language and understood the net effect of the new definition as expanding the coverage of the Act beyond complete-parts kits. "The definition of silencer is amended to include any part designed or redesigned and intended to be used as a silencer for a firearm. This will help to control the sale of incomplete silencer kits that now circumvent the prohibition on selling complete kits." H. R. Rep. No. 99-495, p. 21 (1986). Because the addition of the "combination of parts" language to the definition of silencer does not, therefore, bear the implication Thompson/Center would put on it, that definition cannot give us much guidance in answering the question before us. n8

A statute, like other living organisms, derives significance and sustenance from its environment, from which it cannot be severed without being mutilated. Especially is this true where the statute, like the one before us, is part of a legislative process having a history and a purpose. The meaning of such a statute cannot be gained by confining inquiry within its four corners. Only the historic process of which such legislation is an incomplete fragment—that to which it gave rise as well as that which gave rise to it—can yield its true meaning.

n8 JUSTICE SCALIA upbraids us for reliance on legislative history, his "St. Jude of the hagiology of statutory construction." Post, at 521. The shrine, however, is well peopled (though it has room for one more) and its congregation has included such noted elders as Justice Frankfurter: "A statute, like other living organisms, derives significance and sustenance from its environment, from which it cannot be severed without being mutilated. Especially is this true where the statute, like the one before us, is part of a legislative process having a history and a purpose. The meaning of such a statute cannot be gained by confining inquiry within its four corners. Only the historic process of which such legislation is an incomplete fragment -- that to which it gave rise as well as that which gave rise to it -- can yield its true meaning." United States v. Monia, 317 U.S. 424, 432, 87 L. Ed. 376, 63 S. Ct. 409 (1943) (dissenting opinion).

We get no more help from analyzing the machinegun definition's reference to parts. It speaks of "any combination" of them in the possession or control of any one person. Here the definition sweeps broader than the aggregation of parts clearly covered by "making" a rifle. The machinegun parts need not even be in any particular proximity to each other. There is thus no conflict between definitions, but neither is much light shed on the limits of "making" a short-barreled rifle. We can only say that the notion of an unassembled machinegun is probably broader than that of an unassembled rifle. But just where the line is to be drawn on short-barreled rifles is not demonstrated by textual considerations.

2

the congressional purpose behind the NFA, of regulating weapons useful for criminal purposes

the clearly indicated congressional intent to cover under the National Firearms Act only such modern and lethal weapons, except pistols and revolvers, as could be used readily and efficiently by criminals or gangsters

Thompson/Center also looks for the answer in the purpose and history of the NFA, arguing that the congressional purpose behind the NFA, of regulating weapons useful for criminal purposes, should caution against drawing the line in such a way as to apply the Act to the Contender pistol and carbine kit. See H. R. Rep. No. 1337, 83d Cong., 2d Sess., A395 (1954) (the adoption of the original definition of rifle was intended to preclude coverage of antique guns held by collectors, "in pursuance of the clearly indicated congressional intent to cover under the National Firearms Act only such modern and lethal weapons, except pistols and revolvers, as could be used readily and efficiently by criminals or gangsters").

the regulation of short-barreled rifles, for example, addresses a concealable weapon likely to be so used.

It is of course clear from the face of the Act that the NFA's object was to regulate certain weapons likely to be used for criminal purposes, just as the regulation of short-barreled rifles, for example, addresses a concealable weapon likely to be so used. But when Thompson/Center urges us to recognize that "the Contender pistol and carbine kit is not a criminal-type weapon," Brief for Respondent 20, it does not really address the issue of where the line should be drawn in deciding what combinations of parts are "made" into short-barreled rifles. Its argument goes to the quite different issue whether the single-shot Contender should be treated as a firearm within the meaning of the Act even when assembled with a rifle stock.

Since Thompson/Center's observations on this extraneous issue shed no light on the limits of unassembled "making" under the Act, we will say no more about congressional purpose. Nor are we helped by the NFA's legislative history, in which we find nothing to support a conclusion one way or the other about the narrow issue presented here.

III

After applying the ordinary rules of statutory construction, then, we are left with an ambiguous statute.

Making a firearm without approval may be subject to criminal sanction, as is possession of an unregistered firearm and failure to pay the tax on one. It is proper, therefore, to apply the rule of lenity and resolve the ambiguity in Thompson/Center's favor. Accordingly, we conclude that the Contender pistol and carbine kit when packaged together by Thompson/Center have not been "made" into a short-barreled rifle for purposes of the NFA.

After applying the ordinary rules of statutory construction, then, we are left with an ambiguous statute. The key to resolving the ambiguity lies in recognizing that although it is a tax statute that we construe now in a civil setting, the NFA has criminal applications that carry no additional requirement of willfulness. Cf. Cheek v. United States, 498 U.S. 192, 200, 112 L. Ed. 2d 617, 111 S. Ct. 604 (1991) ("Congress has . . . softened the impact of the common-law presumption [that ignorance of the law is no defense to criminal prosecution] by making specific intent to violate the law an element of certain federal criminal tax offenses"); 26 U.S.C. §§7201, 7203 (criminalizing willful evasion of taxes and willful failure to file a return). Making a firearm without approval may be subject to criminal sanction, as is possession of an unregistered firearm and failure to pay the tax on one, 26 U.S.C. §§5861, 5871. It is proper, therefore, to apply the rule of lenity and resolve the ambiguity in Thompson/Center's favor. See Crandon v. United States, 494 U.S. 152, 168, 108 L. Ed. 2d 132, 110 S. Ct. 997 (1990) (applying lenity in interpreting a criminal statute invoked in a civil action); Commissioner v. Acker, 361 U.S. 87, 91, 4 L. Ed. 2d 127, 80 S. Ct. 144 (1959). n9 Accordingly, we conclude that the Contender pistol and carbine kit when packaged together by Thompson/Center have not been "made" into a short-barreled rifle for purposes of the NFA. n10 The judgment of the Court of Appeals is therefore

Affirmed.

n9 The Government has urged us to defer to an agency interpretation contained in two longstanding Revenue Rulings. Even if they were entitled to deference, neither of the rulings, Rev.

Rul. 61-45, 1961-1 Cum. Bull. 663, and Rev. Rul. 61-203, 1961-2 Cum. Bull. 224 (same), goes to the narrow question presented here, addressing rather the question whether pistols with short barrels and attachable shoulder stocks are short-barreled rifles. We do not read the Government to be relying upon Rev. Rul. 54-606, 1954-2 Cum. Bull. 33, which was repealed as obsolete in 1972, Rev. Rul. 72-178, 1972-1 Cum. Bull. 423, and which contained broader language that "possession or control of sufficient parts to assemble an operative firearm . . . constitutes the possession of a firearm." Reply Brief for United States 10.

n10 JUSTICE STEVENS contends that lenity should not be applied because this is a "'tax statute,'" post, at 526, rather than a "criminal statute," see post, at 525, n. 1, quoting Crandon v. United States, 494 U.S. 152, 168, 108 L. Ed. 2d 132, 110 S. Ct. 997 (1990). But this tax statute has criminal applications, and we know of no other basis for determining when the essential nature of a statute is "criminal." Surely, JUSTICE STEVENS cannot mean to suggest that in order for the rule of lenity to apply, the statute must be contained in the Criminal Code. See, e.g., United States v. Universal C. I. T. Credit Corp., 344 U.S. 218, 221-222, 97 L. Ed. 260, 73 S. Ct. 227 (1952) (construing the criminal provisions of the Fair Labor Standards Act, 29 U.S.C. §§215, 216(a)). JUSTICE STEVENS further suggests that lenity is inappropriate because we construe the statute today "'in a civil setting,'" rather than a "criminal prosecution." Post, at 526. The rule of lenity, however, is a rule of statutory construction whose purpose is to help give authoritative meaning to statutory language. It is not a rule of administration calling for courts to refrain in criminal cases from applying statutory language that would have been held to apply if challenged in civil litigation.

JUSTICE SCALIA, with whom JUSTICE THOMAS joins, concurring in the judgment.

I think the ambiguity pertains to the much more fundamental point of whether the making of a regulated firearm includes the manufacture, without assembly, of component parts where the definition of the particular firearm does not so indicate.

I agree with the plurality that the application of the National Firearms Act (NFA) to Thompson/Center's pistol and conversion kit is sufficiently ambiguous to trigger the rule of lenity, leading to the conclusion that the kit is not covered. I disagree with the plurality, however, over where the ambiguity lies -- a point that makes no difference to the outcome here, but will make considerable difference in future cases. The plurality thinks the ambiguity pertains to whether the making of a regulated firearm includes (i) the manufacture of parts kits that can possibly be used to assemble a regulated firearm, or rather includes only (ii) the manufacture of parts kits that serve no useful purpose except assembly of a regulated firearm. Ante, at 512-513, 517. I think the ambiguity pertains to the much more fundamental point of whether the making of a regulated firearm includes the manufacture, without assembly, of component parts where the definition of the particular firearm does not so indicate.

As JUSTICE WHITE points out, the choice the plurality worries about is nowhere suggested by the language of the statute: §5845 simply makes no reference to the "'utility'" of aggregable parts. Post, at 524 (dissenting opinion). It does, however, conspicuously combine references to "combination of parts" in the definitions of regulated silencers, machineguns, and destructive devices with the absence of any such reference in the definition of regulated rifles. This, rather than the utility or not of a given part in a given parts assemblage, convinces me that the provision does not encompass Thompson/Center's pistol and conversion kit, or at least does not do so unambiguously.

The plurality reaches its textually uncharted destination by determining that the statutory definition of "make," the derivative of which appears as an operative word in 26 U.S.C. §5821 ("There shall be levied, collected, and paid upon the making of a firearm a tax at the rate of $200 for each firearm made"), covers the making of parts that, assembled, are firearms. Noting that the "definition of 'make' includes not only 'putting together,' but also 'manufacturing . . . or otherwise producing a firearm,'" the plurality reasons that if "a firearm were only made at the time of final assembly (the moment the firearm was 'put together'), the additional language would be redundant." Ante, at 510.

an inflexible rule of avoiding redundancy will produce disaster.

This reasoning seems to me mistaken. I do not think that if "making" requires "putting together," other language of the definition section ("manufacturing" and "otherwise producing") becomes redundant. "Manufacturing" is qualified by the parenthetical phrase "(other than by one qualified to engage in such business under this chapter)," whereas "putting together" is not. Thus, one who assembles a firearm and also engages in the prior activity of producing the component parts can be immunized from being considered to be making firearms by demonstrating the relevant qualification, whereas one who merely assembles parts manufactured by others cannot. Recognition of this distinction is alone enough to explain the separate inclusion of "putting together," even though "manufacturing" itself includes assembly. As for the phrase "otherwise producing," that may well be redundant, but such residual provisions often are. They are often meant for insurance, to cover anything the draftsman might inadvertently have omitted in the antecedent catalog; and if the draftsman is good enough, he will have omitted nothing at all. They are a prime example of provisions in which "iteration is obviously afoot," Moskal v. United States, 498 U.S. 103, 120, 112 L. Ed. 2d 449, 111 S. Ct. 461 (1990) (SCALIA, J., dissenting), and for which an inflexible rule of avoiding redundancy will produce disaster. In any event, the plurality's own interpretation (whereby "manufacturing" a firearm does not require assembling it, and "putting together" is an entirely separate category of "making") renders it not a bit easier to conceive of a nonredundant application for "otherwise producing."

The plurality struggles to explain why its interpretation ("making" does not require assembly of component parts) does not itself render redundant the "combination of parts" language found elsewhere in 26 U.S.C. §5845, in the definitions of machinegun and destructive device, §§5845(b) and (f), and in the incorporated-by-reference definition of silencer, §5845(a)(7) (referring to 18 U.S.C. §(21). See ante, at 513-516. I do not find its explanations persuasive, particularly that with respect to silencer, which resorts to that last hope of lost interpretive causes, that St. Jude of the hagiology of statutory construction, legislative history. As I have said before, reliance on that source is particularly inappropriate in determining the meaning of a statute with criminal application. United States v. R. L. C., 503 U.S. 291, 307, 112 S. Ct. 1329, 117 L. Ed. 2d 559 (1992) (opinion concurring in part and concurring in judgment).

There is another reason why the plurality's interpretation is incorrect: It determines what constitutes a regulated "firearm" via an operative provision of the NFA (here §5821, the making tax) rather than by way of §5845, which defines firearms covered by the chapter. With respect to the definitions of machineguns, destructive devices, and silencers, for instance, the reference to "combination of parts" causes parts aggregations to be firearms whenever those nouns are used, and not just when they are used in conjunction with the verb "make" and its derivatives. Thus, the restrictions of §5844, which regulate the importation of "firearm[s]" (a term defined to include "machinegun[s]," see §5845(a)(6)), apply to a "combination of parts from which a machinegun can be assembled" (because that is part of the definition of machinegun) even though the word "make" and its derivatives do not appear in §5844. This demonstrates, I say, the error of the plurality's interpretation, because it makes no sense to have the firearms regulated by the NFA bear one identity (which includes components of rifles and shotguns) when they are the object of the verb "make," and a different identity (excluding such components) when they are not. Section 5842(a), for example, requires anyone "making" a firearm to identify it with a serial number that may not be readily removed; §5842(b) requires any person who "possesses" a firearm lacking the requisite serial number to identify it with one assigned by the Secretary of the Treasury. Under the plurality's interpretation, all the firearms covered by (a) are not covered by (b), since a person who "possesses" the components for a rifle or shotgun does not possess a firearm, even though a person who "makes" the components for a rifle or shotgun makes a firearm. For similar reasons, the tax imposed on "the making of a firearm" by §5821 would apply to the making of components for rifles and shotguns, but the tax imposed on "firearms transferred" by §5811 would not apply to the transfer of such components. This cannot possibly be right. *

* The plurality, as I read its opinion, relies on the derivative of "make" that appears in §5821, not that appearing (in a quite different context) in the definition of "rifle." See 26 U.S.C. §5845(c) ("The term 'rifle' means a weapon designed or redesigned, made or remade . . ."). I think it would not be possible to rely upon the use of "made" in §5845(c), where the context is obviously suggestive of assembled rather than unassembled rifles. But even if the plurality means to apply its interpretation of "make" to §5845(c), it still does not entirely avoid the problem I have identified. The definition of "any other weapon," another in §5845's arsenal of defined firearms, does not contain relevant uses of the verb "make" or any derivative thereof. See 26 U.S.C. §5845(e). It necessarily follows that "any other weapon" will mean one thing when a making tax is at hand but something else when a transfer tax is.

The kit's instructions emphasized that legal sanctions attached to the unauthorized making of a short-barreled rifle, and there was even carved into the shoulder stock itself the following: "WARNING. FEDERAL LAW PROHIBITS USE WITH BARREL LESS THAN 16 INCHES."

Finally, even if it were the case that unassembled parts could constitute a rifle, I do not think it was established in this case that respondent manufactured (assembled or not) a rifle "having a barrel or barrels of less than 16 inches in length," which is what the definition of "firearm" requires, §5845(a)(3). For the definition of "rifle" requires that it be "intended to be fired from the shoulder," §5845(c), and the only combination of parts so intended, as far as respondent is concerned (and the record contains no indication of anyone else's intent), is the combination that forms a rifle with a 21-inch barrel. The kit's instructions emphasized that legal sanctions attached to the unauthorized making of a short-barreled rifle, and there was even carved into the shoulder stock itself the following: "WARNING. FEDERAL LAW PROHIBITS USE WITH BARREL LESS THAN 16 INCHES."

Since I agree (for a different reason) that the rule of lenity prevents these kits from being considered firearms within the meaning of the NFA, I concur in the judgment of the Court.

JUSTICE WHITE, with whom JUSTICE BLACKMUN, JUSTICE STEVENS, and JUSTICE KENNEDY join, dissenting.

Because one "makes" a firearm not only in the actual "putting together" of the parts, but also by "manufacturing . . . or otherwise producing a firearm," Congress clearly intended that the "making" include a "disassembled aggregation of parts"

The Court of Appeals for the Federal Circuit concluded that, to meet the definition of "firearm" under the National Firearms Act (NFA), 26 U.S.C. §5845(a)(3), "a short-barreled rifle actually must be assembled." 924 F.2d 1041, 1043 (1991) (footnote omitted). I agree with the plurality that this pinched interpretation of the statute would fail to accord the term "make" its full meaning as that term is defined, §5845(i), and used in the definition of the term "rifle," §5845(c). Because one "makes" a firearm not only in the actual "putting together" of the parts, but also by "manufacturing . . . or otherwise producing a firearm," Congress clearly intended that the "making" include a "disassembled aggregation of parts," ante, at 510, where the assemblage of such parts results in a firearm. In short, when the components necessary to assemble a rifle are produced and held in conjunction with one another, a "rifle" is, not surprisingly, the result.

This was the difficult issue presented by this case, and its resolution, for me, is dispositive, as respondent Thompson/Center concedes that it manufactures and distributes together a collection of parts that may be readily assembled into a short-barreled rifle. Indeed, Thompson/Center's argument concerning statutory construction, as well as its appeal to the rule of lenity, does not suggest, nor does any case brought to our attention, that one may escape the tax and registration requirements the NFA imposes on those who "make" regulated rifles simply by distributing as part of the package other interchangeable pieces of sufficient design to avoid the regulated definition. The plurality nevertheless draws an artificial line between, on the one hand, those parts that "can serve no useful purpose except the assembly of a firearm" or that have "no ostensible utility except to convert a gun into such a weapon," and, on the other hand, those parts that have "an obvious utility for those who want both a pistol and a regular rifle." Ante, at 512-513.

I cannot agree. Certainly the statute makes no distinction based on the "utility" of the extra parts. While the plurality prefers to view this silence as creating ambiguity, I find it only to signal that such distinctions are irrelevant. To conclude otherwise is to resort to "'ingenuity to create ambiguity'" that simply does not exist in this statute. United States v. James, 478 U.S. 597, 604, 92 L. Ed. 2d 483, 106 S. Ct. 3116 (1986), quoting Rothschild v. United States, 179 U.S. 463, 465, 45 L. Ed. 277, 21 S. Ct. 197 (1900). As noted by the Government, when a weapon comes within the scope of the "firearm" definition, the fact that it may also have a nonregulated form provides no basis for failing to comply with the requirements of the NFA. Brief for United States 13-14.

The Court today thus closes one loophole—one cannot circumvent the NFA simply by offering an unassembled collection of parts—only to open another of equal dimension—one can circumvent the NFA by offering a collection of parts that can be made either into a "firearm" or an unregulated rifle.

The Court today thus closes one loophole -- one cannot circumvent the NFA simply by offering an unassembled collection of parts -- only to open another of equal dimension -- one can circumvent the NFA by offering a collection of parts that can be made either into a "firearm" or an unregulated rifle. I respectfully dissent.

JUSTICE STEVENS, dissenting.

If this were a criminal case in which the defendant did not have adequate notice of the Government's interpretation of an ambiguous statute, then it would be entirely appropriate to apply the rule of lenity. n1 I am persuaded, however, that the Court has misapplied that rule to this quite different case.

n1 See, e.g., Crandon v. United States, 494 U.S. 152, 168, 108 L. Ed. 2d 132, 110 S. Ct. 997 (1990) ("Finally, as we have already observed, we are construing a criminal statute and are therefore bound to consider application of the rule of lenity. To the extent that any ambiguity over the temporal scope of [18 U.S.C.] §209(a) remains, it should be resolved in petitioners' favor unless and until Congress plainly states that we have misconstrued its intent"); Commissioner v. Acker, 361 U.S. 87, 91, 4 L. Ed. 2d 127, 80 S. Ct. 144 (1959) ("The law is settled that 'penal statutes are to be construed strictly,' . . . and that one 'is not to be subjected to a penalty unless the words of the statute plainly impose it'") (citations omitted).

I agree with JUSTICE WHITE, see ante, at 523-524, and also with the plurality, see ante, at 511, that respondent has made a firearm even though it has not assembled its constituent parts. I also agree with JUSTICE WHITE that that should be the end of the case, see ante, at 524, and therefore, I join his opinion. I add this comment, however, because I am persuaded that the Government should prevail even if the statute were ambiguous.

The main function of the rule of lenity is to protect citizens from the unfair application of ambiguous punitive statutes. Obviously, citizens should not be subject to punishment without fair notice that their conduct is prohibited by law. n2 The risk that this respondent would be the victim of such unfairness, is, however, extremely remote. In 1985, the Government properly advised respondent of its reading of the statute and gave it ample opportunity to challenge that reading in litigation in which nothing more than tax liability of $200 was at stake. See 924 F.2d 1041, 1042-1043 (CA Fed. 1991). Moreover, a proper construction of the statute in this case would entirely remove the risk of criminal liability in the future.

a fair warning should be given to the world in language that the common world will understand, of what the law intends to do if a certain line is passed

n2 Ambiguity in a criminal statute is resolved in favor of the defendant because "'a fair warning should be given to the world in language that the common world will understand, of what the law intends to do if a certain line is passed'" and because "of the seriousness of criminal penalties, and because criminal punishment usually represents the moral condemnation of the community, [and therefore] legislatures and not courts should define criminal activity." United States v. Bass, 404 U.S. 336, 348, 30 L. Ed. 2d 488, 92 S. Ct. 515 (1971).

This statute serves the critical objective of regulating the manufacture and distribution of concealable firearms—dangerous weapons that are a leading cause of countless crimes that occur every day throughout the Nation. This is a field that has long been subject to pervasive governmental regulation because of the dangerous nature of the product and the public interest in having that danger controlled.

The plurality, after acknowledging that this case involves "a tax statute" and its construction "in a civil setting," ante, at 517, nevertheless proceeds to treat the case as though it were a criminal prosecution. In my view, the Court should approach this case like any other civil case testing the Government's interpretation of an important regulatory statute. This statute serves the critical objective of regulating the manufacture and distribution of concealable firearms -- dangerous weapons that are a leading cause of countless crimes that occur every day throughout the Nation. This is a field that has long been subject to pervasive governmental regulation because of the dangerous nature of the product and the public interest in having that danger controlled. n3 The public interest in carrying out the purposes that motivated the enactment of this statute is, in my judgment and on this record, far more compelling than a mechanical application of the rule of lenity.

n3 See, e.g., Gun Control Act of 1968, 18 U.S.C. §921 et seq.; Arms Export Control Act, as amended Pub. L. 94-329, 90 Stat. 744, 22 U.S.C. §2778; United States v. Biswell, 406 U.S. 311, 316, 32 L. Ed. 2d 87, 92 S. Ct. 1593 (1972) (acknowledging that the sale of firearms is a "pervasively regulated business").

Accordingly, for this reason, as well as for the reasons stated by JUSTICE WHITE, I respectfully dissent.

PLANNED PARENTHOOD v. CASEY

(CASE EXCERPT)

505 U.S. 833; 112 S. Ct. 2791; 120 L. Ed. 2d 674

April 22, 1992, Argued

June 29, 1992, Decided

GIST: This important case upholds certain abortion restrictions, while affirming abortion as a constitutional right. The Court's opinion—jointly written by O'Connor, Kennedy, and Souter—quotes a Supreme Court precedent from *Poe v. Ullman,* on the full scope of liberties guaranteed by the 14th Amendment, including language about the right to keep and bear arms along with other constitutional rights and liberties.

JUSTICE O'CONNOR, JUSTICE KENNEDY, and JUSTICE SOUTER announced the judgment of the Court and delivered the opinion of the Court.

.....

Neither the Bill of Rights nor the specific practices of States at the time of the adoption of the Fourteenth Amendment marks the outer limits of the substantive sphere of liberty which the Fourteenth Amendment protects. See U.S. Const., Amdt. 9. As the second Justice Harlan recognized:

This 'liberty' is not a series of isolated points pricked out in terms of the taking of property; the freedom of speech, press, and religion; the right to keep and bear arms; the freedom from unreasonable searches and seizures; and so on.

It is a rational continuum which, broadly speaking, includes a freedom from all substantial arbitrary impositions and purposeless restraints

"The full scope of the liberty guaranteed by the Due Process Clause cannot be found in or limited by the precise terms of the specific guarantees elsewhere provided in the Constitution. This 'liberty' is not a series of isolated points pricked out in terms of the taking of property; the freedom of speech, press, and religion; the right to keep and bear arms; the freedom from unreasonable searches and seizures; and so on. It is a rational continuum which, broadly speaking, includes a freedom from all substantial arbitrary impositions and purposeless restraints, . . . and which also recognizes, what a reasonable and sensitive judgment must, that certain interests require particularly careful scrutiny of the state needs asserted to justify their abridgment." Poe v. Ullman.

DEAL v. UNITED STATES

(CASE EXCERPT)

508 U.S. 129; 113 S. Ct. 1993; 124 L. Ed. 2d 44

March 1, 1993, Argued

May 17, 1993, Decided

GIST: This case involves interpretation of a federal statute prescribing a 5-year prison sentence for using a gun in a crime during a crime of violence and a 20-year sentence for a second or subsequent offense. The Court held that the second conviction may occur at the same trial as the first conviction. Deal, convicted at trial of six separate armed bank robberies, was sentenced to five years for the first and 20 years for robberies two through five.

JUSTICE SCALIA delivered the opinion of the Court.

petitioner committed six bank robberies on six different dates in the Houston, Texas, area. In each robbery, he used a gun.

Between January and April 1990, petitioner committed six bank robberies on six different dates in the Houston, Texas, area. In each robbery, he used a gun. Petitioner was convicted of six counts of bank robbery, 18 U.S.C. §§2113(a) and (d), six counts of carrying and using a firearm during and in relation to a crime of violence, §924(c), and one count of being a felon in possession of firearms, §922(g). Title 18 U.S.C. §924(c)(1) (1988 ed., Supp. III) provides:

"Whoever, during and in relation to any crime of violence . . . uses or carries a firearm, shall, in addition to the punishment provided for such crime of violence . . . , be sentenced to imprisonment for five years . . . . In the case of his second or subsequent conviction under this subsection, such person shall be sentenced to imprisonment for twenty years...."

The United States District Court for the Southern District of Texas sentenced petitioner to 5 years' imprisonment on the first §924(c)(1) count and to 20 years on each of the other five §924(c)(1) counts, the terms to run consecutively. The United States Court of Appeals for the Fifth Circuit affirmed the convictions and sentence. We granted certiorari on the question whether petitioner's second through sixth convictions under §924(c)(1) in this single proceeding arose "in the case of his second or subsequent conviction" within the meaning of §924(c)(1).

.....

We are also confirmed in our conclusion by the recognition that petitioner's reading would give a prosecutor unreviewable discretion either to impose or to waive the enhanced sentencing provisions of §924(c)(1) by opting to charge and try the defendant either in separate prosecutions or under a multicount indictment. Although the present prosecution would not have permitted enhanced sentencing, if the same charges had been divided into six separate prosecutions for the six separate bank robberies, enhanced sentencing would clearly have been required. We are not disposed to give the statute a meaning that produces such strange consequences.

SMITH v. UNITED STATES

(FULL CASE)

508 U.S. 223; 113 S. Ct. 2050; 124 L. Ed. 2d 138

March 23, 1993, Argued

June 1, 1993, Decided

GIST: The Court was called upon to interpret a federal statute prescribing a mandatory sentence for "using" a firearm during and in relation to a drug-trafficking crime. Smith offered to trade his MAC-10, converted to full auto, to an undercover agent for drugs. The Court held that using a weapon, within the meaning of the drug statute, did not require using the firearm as a weapon. Any manner of facilitating the crime, including barter, was sufficient to trigger the mandatory sentence—30 years in Smith's case. The Court made an exception for a firearm that in no way furthered the crime, such as one used to scratch your head. Many colorful and unusual hypotheticals such as that are strewn throughout this case and in the dissent by three of the Justices.

JUSTICE O'CONNOR delivered the opinion of the Court.

We decide today whether the exchange of a gun for narcotics constitutes "use" of a firearm "during and in relation to . . . [a] drug trafficking crime" within the meaning of 18 U.S.C. §924(c)(1). We hold that it does.

The MAC-10 apparently is a favorite among criminals. It is small and compact, lightweight, and can be equipped with a silencer. Most important of all, it can be devastating: a fully automatic MAC-10 can fire more than 1,000 rounds per minute.

I

Petitioner John Angus Smith and his companion went from Tennessee to Florida to buy cocaine; they hoped to resell it at a profit. While in Florida, they met petitioner's acquaintance, Deborah Hoag. Hoag agreed to, and in fact did, purchase cocaine for petitioner. She then accompanied petitioner and his friend to her motel room, where they were joined by a drug dealer. While Hoag listened, petitioner and the dealer discussed petitioner's MAC-10 firearm, which had been modified to operate as an automatic. The MAC-10 apparently is a favorite among criminals. It is small and compact, lightweight, and can be equipped with a silencer. Most important of all, it can be devastating: A fully automatic MAC-10 can fire more than 1,000 rounds per minute. The dealer expressed his interest in becoming the owner of a MAC-10, and petitioner promised that he would discuss selling the gun if his arrangement with another potential buyer fell through.

He was willing to trade his MAC-10, he said, for two ounces of cocaine.

Unfortunately for petitioner, Hoag had contacts not only with narcotics traffickers but also with law enforcement officials. In fact, she was a confidential informant. Consistent with her post, she informed the Broward County Sheriff's Office of petitioner's activities. The Sheriff's Office responded quickly, sending an undercover officer to Hoag's motel room. Several others were assigned to keep the motel under surveillance. Upon arriving at Hoag's motel room, the undercover officer presented himself to petitioner as a pawnshop dealer. Petitioner, in turn, presented the officer with a proposition: He had an automatic MAC-10 and silencer with which he might be willing to part. Petitioner then pulled the MAC-10 out of a black canvas bag and showed it to the officer. The officer examined the gun and asked petitioner what he wanted for it. Rather than asking for money, however, petitioner asked for drugs. He was willing to trade his MAC-10, he said, for two ounces of cocaine. The officer told petitioner that he was just a pawnshop dealer and did not distribute narcotics. Nonetheless, he indicated that he wanted the MAC-10 and would try to get the cocaine. The officer then left, promising to return within an hour.

Rather than seeking out cocaine as he had promised, the officer returned to the Sheriff's Office to arrange for petitioner's arrest. But petitioner was not content to wait. The officers who were conducting surveillance saw him leave the motel room carrying a gun bag; he then climbed into his van and drove away. The officers reported petitioner's departure and began following him. When law enforcement authorities tried to stop petitioner, he led them on a high-speed chase. Petitioner eventually was apprehended.

Petitioner, it turns out, was well armed. A search of his van revealed the MAC-10 weapon, a silencer, ammunition, and a "fast-feed" mechanism. In addition, the police found a MAC-11 machine gun, a loaded .45 caliber pistol, and a .22 caliber pistol with a scope and homemade silencer.

Petitioner, it turns out, was well armed. A search of his van revealed the MAC-10 weapon, a silencer, ammunition, and a "fast-feed" mechanism. In addition, the police found a MAC-11 machine gun, a loaded .45 caliber pistol, and a .22 caliber pistol with a scope and homemade silencer. Petitioner also had a loaded 9 millimeter handgun in his waistband.

A grand jury sitting in the District Court for the Southern District of Florida returned an indictment charging petitioner with, among other offenses, two drug trafficking crimes -- conspiracy to possess cocaine with intent to distribute and attempt to possess cocaine with intent to distribute in violation of 21 U.S.C. §§841(a)(1), 846, and 18 U.S.C. §2. App. 3-9. Most important here, the indictment alleged that petitioner knowingly used the MAC-10 and its silencer during and in relation to a drug trafficking crime. Id., at 4-5. Under 18 U.S.C. §924(c)(1), a defendant who so uses a firearm must be sentenced to five years' incarceration. And where, as here, the firearm is a "machinegun" or is fitted with a silencer, the sentence is 30 years. See §924(c)(1) ("If the firearm is a machinegun, or is equipped with a firearm silencer," the sentence is "thirty years"); §921(a)(23), 26 U.S.C. §5845(b) (term "machinegun" includes automatic weapons). The jury convicted petitioner on all counts.

petitioner argued that §924(c)(1)'s penalty for using a firearm during and in relation to a drug trafficking offense covers only situations in which the firearm is used as a weapon. According to petitioner, the provision does not extend to defendants who use a firearm solely as a medium of exchange or for barter. The Court of Appeals for the Eleventh Circuit disagreed.

On appeal, petitioner argued that §924(c)(1)'s penalty for using a firearm during and in relation to a drug trafficking offense covers only situations in which the firearm is used as a weapon. According to petitioner, the provision does not extend to defendants who use a firearm solely as a medium of exchange or for barter. The Court of Appeals for the Eleventh Circuit disagreed. 957 F.2d 835 (1992). The plain language of the statute, the court explained, imposes no requirement that the firearm be used as a weapon. Instead, any use of "the weapon to facilitate in any manner the commission of the offense" suffices. Id., at 837 (internal quotation marks omitted).

the Court of Appeals for the Ninth Circuit held that trading a gun in a drug-related transaction could not constitute use of a firearm during and in relation to a drug trafficking offense within the meaning of §924(c)(1). We granted certiorari to resolve the conflict among the Circuits.

Shortly before the Eleventh Circuit decided this case, the Court of Appeals for the District of Columbia Circuit arrived at the same conclusion. United States v. Harris, 294 U.S. App. D.C. 300, 315-316, 959 F.2d 246, 261-262 (per curiam), cert. denied, 506 U.S. 932 (1992). In United States v. Phelps, 877 F.2d 28 (1989), however, the Court of Appeals for the Ninth Circuit held that trading a gun in a drug-related transaction could not constitute use of a firearm during and in relation to a drug trafficking offense within the meaning of §924(c)(1). We granted certiorari to resolve the conflict among the Circuits. 506 U.S. 814 (1992). We now affirm.

II

Section 924(c)(1) requires the imposition of specified penalties if the defendant, "during and in relation to any crime of violence or drug trafficking crime[,] uses or carries a firearm." By its terms, the statute requires the prosecution to make two showings. First, the prosecution must demonstrate that the defendant "use[d] or carrie[d] a firearm." Second, it must prove that the use or carrying was "during and in relation to" a "crime of violence or drug trafficking crime."

A

nothing in the record indicates that he fired the MAC-10, threatened anyone with it, or employed it for self-protection.

Petitioner argues that exchanging a firearm for drugs does not constitute "use" of the firearm within the meaning of the statute. He points out that nothing in the record indicates that he fired the MAC-10, threatened anyone with it, or employed it for self-protection. In essence, petitioner argues that he cannot be said to have "use[d]" a firearm unless he used it as a weapon, since that is how firearms most often are used. See 957 F.2d at 837 (firearm often facilitates drug offenses by protecting drugs or protecting or emboldening the defendant). Of course, §924(c)(1) is not limited to those cases in which a gun is used; it applies with equal force whenever a gun is "carrie[d]." In this case, however, the indictment alleged only that petitioner "use[d]" the MAC-10. App. 4. Accordingly, we do not consider whether the evidence might support the conclusion that petitioner carried the MAC-10 within the meaning of §924(c)(1). Instead we confine our discussion to what the parties view as the dispositive issue in this case: whether trading a firearm for drugs can constitute "use" of the firearm within the meaning of §924(c)(1).

Surely petitioner's treatment of his MAC-10 can be described as "use" within the everyday meaning of that term. Petitioner "used" his MAC-10 in an attempt to obtain drugs by offering to trade it for cocaine.

When a word is not defined by statute, we normally construe it in accord with its ordinary or natural meaning. See Perrin v. United States, 444 U.S. 37, 42, 62 L. Ed. 2d 199, 100 S. Ct. 311 (1979) (words not defined in statute should be given ordinary or common meaning). Accord, post, at 242 ("In the search for statutory meaning, we give nontechnical words and phrases their ordinary meaning"). Surely petitioner's treatment of his MAC-10 can be described as "use" within the everyday meaning of that term. Petitioner "used" his MAC-10 in an attempt to obtain drugs by offering to trade it for cocaine. Webster's defines "to use" as "to convert to one's service" or "to employ." Webster's New International Dictionary 2806 (2d ed. 1950). Black's Law Dictionary contains a similar definition: "to make use of; to convert to one's service; to employ; to avail oneself of; to utilize; to carry out a purpose or action by means of." Black's Law Dictionary 1541 (6th ed. 1990). Indeed, over 100 years ago we gave the word "use" the same gloss, indicating that it means "'to employ'" or "'to derive service from.'" Astor v. Merritt, 111 U.S. 202, 213, 28 L. Ed. 401, 4 S. Ct. 413 (1884). Petitioner's handling of the MAC-10 in this case falls squarely within those definitions. By attempting to trade his MAC-10 for the drugs, he "used" or "employed" it as an item of barter to obtain cocaine; he "derived service" from it because it was going to bring him the very drugs he sought.

In petitioner's view, §924(c)(1) should require proof not only that the defendant used the firearm, but also that he used it as a weapon. But the words "as a weapon" appear nowhere in the statute. Rather, §924(c)(1)'s language sweeps broadly, punishing any "use" of a firearm, so long as the use is "during and in relation to" a drug trafficking offense. See United States v. Long, 284 U.S. App. D.C. 405, 409-410, 905 F.2d 1572, 1576-1577 (Thomas, J.) (although not without limits, the word "use" is "expansive" and extends even to situations where the gun is not actively employed), cert. denied, 498 U.S. 948, 112 L. Ed. 2d 328, 111 S. Ct. 365 (1990). Had Congress intended the narrow construction petitioner urges, it could have so indicated. It did not, and we decline to introduce that additional requirement on our own.

an image of the most familiar use to which a firearm is put—use as a weapon.

Language, of course, cannot be interpreted apart from context. The meaning of a word that appears ambiguous if viewed in isolation may become clear when the word is analyzed in light of the terms that surround it. Recognizing this, petitioner and the dissent argue that the word "uses" has a somewhat reduced scope in §924(c)(1) because it appears alongside the word "firearm." Specifically, they contend that the average person on the street would not think immediately of a guns-for-drugs trade as an example of "us[ing] a firearm." Rather, that phrase normally evokes an image of the most familiar use to which a firearm is put -- use as a weapon. Petitioner and the dissent therefore argue that the statute excludes uses where the weapon is not fired or otherwise employed for its destructive capacity. See post, at 242-244. Indeed, relying on that argument -- and without citation to authority -- the dissent announces its own, restrictive definition of "use." "To use an instrumentality," the dissent argues, "ordinarily means to use it for its intended purpose." Post, at 242.

It is one thing to say that the ordinary meaning of "uses a firearm" includes using a firearm as a weapon, since that is the intended purpose of a firearm and the example of "use" that most immediately comes to mind. But it is quite another to conclude that, as

a result, the phrase also excludes any other use.

In this case, it is both reasonable and normal to say that petitioner "used" his MAC-10 in his drug trafficking offense by trading it for cocaine

There is a significant flaw to this argument. It is one thing to say that the ordinary meaning of "uses a firearm" includes using a firearm as a weapon, since that is the intended purpose of a firearm and the example of "use" that most immediately comes to mind. But it is quite another to conclude that, as a result, the phrase also excludes any other use. Certainly that conclusion does not follow from the phrase "uses . . . a firearm" itself. As the dictionary definitions and experience make clear, one can use a firearm in a number of ways. That one example of "use" is the first to come to mind when the phrase "uses . . . a firearm" is uttered does not preclude us from recognizing that there are other "uses" that qualify as well. In this case, it is both reasonable and normal to say that petitioner "used" his MAC-10 in his drug trafficking offense by trading it for cocaine; the dissent does not contend otherwise. Ibid.

The dissent's example of how one might "use" a cane, ibid., suffers from a similar flaw. To be sure, "use" as an adornment in a hallway is not the first "use" of a cane that comes to mind. But certainly it does not follow that the only "use" to which a cane might be put is assisting one's grandfather in walking. Quite the opposite: The most infamous use of a cane in American history had nothing to do with walking at all, see J. McPherson, Battle Cry of Freedom 150 (1988) (describing the caning of Senator Sumner in the United States Senate in 1856); and the use of a cane as an instrument of punishment was once so common that "to cane" has become a verb meaning "to beat with a cane." Webster's New International Dictionary, supra, at 390. In any event, the only question in this case is whether the phrase "uses . . . a firearm" in §924(c)(1) is most reasonably read as excluding the use of a firearm in a gun-for-drugs trade. The fact that the phrase clearly includes using a firearm to shoot someone, as the dissent contends, does not answer it.

it is perfectly reasonable to construe §2B3.1(b)(2)(B) as including uses, such as trading and bludgeoning, that do not constitute use for the firearm's "intended purpose."

The dissent relies on one authority, the United States Sentencing Commission, Guidelines Manual (Nov. 1992), as "reflect[ing]" its interpretation of the phrase "uses . . . a firearm." See post, at 243. But the Guidelines do not define "using a firearm" as using it for its intended purposes, which the dissent apparently assumes are limited to firing, brandishing, displaying, and possessing. In fact, if we entertain for the moment the dubious assumption that the Sentencing Guidelines are relevant in the present context, they support the opposite view. Section 2B3.1(b)(2), upon which the dissent relies, ibid., provides for increases in a defendant's offense level, and therefore his sentence, if the offense involved a firearm. The extent of the adjustment varies according to the nature of the gun's involvement. There is a seven-point upward adjustment if the firearm "was discharged," §2B3.1(b)(2)(A); a six-point enhancement if a gun was "otherwise used," §2B3.1(b)(2)(B) (emphasis added); and a five-point adjustment if the firearm was brandished, displayed, or possessed, §2B3.1(b)(2)(C). Unless the six-point enhancement for "other use[s]" is mere surplusage, there must be "uses" for a firearm other than its "intended purposes" of firing, brandishing, displaying, or possessing. The dissent points out that there may be some uses that are not firing or brandishing but constitute use as a weapon nonetheless. See post, at 243-244, n.2. But nothing in §2B3.1(b)(2)(B) suggests that the phrase "other use[s]" must be so limited. On the contrary, it is perfectly reasonable to construe §2B3.1(b)(2)(B) as including uses, such as trading and bludgeoning, that do not constitute use for the firearm's "intended purpose."

It is true that the Guidelines commentary defines "'otherwise used'" as conduct that falls short of "'discharg[ing] a firearm but [is] more than brandishing, displaying, or possessing [it].'" Post, at 243 (quoting USSG §1B1.1, comment., n.1(g)). That definition, however, simply reflects the peculiar hierarchy of culpability established in USSG §2B3.1(b)(2). It clarifies that between the most culpable conduct of discharging the firearm and less culpable actions such as "brandishing, displaying, or possessing" lies a category of "other use[s]" for which the Guidelines impose intermediate punishment. It does not by its terms exclude from its scope trading, bludgeoning, or any other use beyond the firearm's "intended purpose."

As we already have noted, and will explain in greater detail later, §924(c)(1) requires not only that the defendant "use" the firearm, but also that he use it "during and in relation to" the drug trafficking crime. As a result, the defendant who "uses" a firearm to scratch his head, or for some other innocuous purpose, would avoid punishment for that conduct altogether: Although scratching one's head with a gun might constitute "use," that action cannot support punishment under §924(c)(1) unless it facilitates or furthers the drug crime; that the firearm served to relieve an itch is not enough.

We are not persuaded that our construction of the phrase "uses . . . a firearm" will produce anomalous applications. See post, at 242 (example of using a gun to scratch one's head). As we already have noted, see supra, at 227-228, and will explain in greater detail later, infra, at 237-239, §924(c)(1) requires not only that the defendant "use" the firearm, but also that he use it "during and in relation to" the drug trafficking crime. As a result, the defendant who "uses" a firearm to scratch his head, see post, at 242, or for some other innocuous purpose, would avoid punishment for that conduct altogether: Although scratching one's head with a gun might constitute "use," that action cannot support punishment under §924(c)(1) unless it facilitates or furthers the drug crime; that the firearm served to relieve an itch is not enough. See infra, at 238 (phrase "in relation to" requires, at a minimum, that the use facilitate the crime). Such a defendant would escape the six-point enhancement provided in USSG §2B3.1(b)(2)(B) as well. As the Guidelines definition of "otherwise use[d]" makes clear, see USSG §1B1.1, comment., n.1(g), the six-point enhancement does not apply unless the use is "more than" brandishing. While pistol-whipping a victim with a firearm might be "more than" brandishing, scratching one's head is not.

No court of appeals ever has held that using a gun to pistol-whip a victim is anything but the "use" of a firearm

In any event, the "intended purpose" of a firearm is not that it be used in any offensive manner whatever, but rather that it be used in a particular fashion -- by firing it. The dissent's contention therefore cannot be that the defendant must use the firearm "as a weapon," but rather that he must fire it or threaten to fire it, "as a gun." Under the dissent's approach, then, even the criminal who pistol-whips his victim has not used a firearm within the meaning of §924(c)(1), for firearms are intended to be fired or brandished, not used as bludgeons. It appears that the dissent similarly would limit the scope of the "other use[s]" covered by USSG §2B3.1(b) (2)(B). The universal view of the courts of appeals, however, is directly to the contrary. No court of appeals ever has held that using a gun to pistol-whip a victim is anything but the "use" of a firearm; nor has any court ever held that trading a firearm for drugs falls short of being the "use" thereof. But cf. Phelps, 877 F.2d at 30 (holding that trading a gun for drugs is not use "in relation to" a drug trafficking offense).

To the extent there is uncertainty about the scope of the phrase "uses . . . a firearm" in §924(c)(1), we believe the remainder of §924 appropriately sets it to rest. Just as a single word cannot be read in isolation, nor can a single provision of a statute. As we have recognized: "Statutory construction . . . is a holistic endeavor. A provision that may seem ambiguous in isolation is often clarified by the remainder of the statutory scheme -- because the same terminology is used elsewhere in a context that makes its meaning clear, or because only one of the permissible meanings produces a substantive effect that is compatible with the rest of the law." United Savings Assn. of Texas v. Timbers of Inwood Forest Associates, Ltd., 484 U.S. 365, 371, 98 L. Ed. 2d 740, 108 S. Ct. 626 (1988) (citations omitted).

Here, Congress employed the words "use" and "firearm" together not only in §924(c)(1), but also in §924(d)(1), which deals with forfeiture of firearms. See United States v. One Assortment of 89 Firearms, 465 U.S. 354 (1984) (discussing earlier version of the statute). Under §924(d)(1), any "firearm or ammunition intended to be used" in the various offenses listed in §924(d)(3) is subject to seizure and forfeiture. Consistent with petitioner's interpretation, §924(d)(3) lists offenses in which guns might be used as offensive weapons. See §§924(d)(3)(A), (B) (weapons used in a crime of violence or drug trafficking offense). But it also lists offenses in which the firearm is not used as a weapon but instead as an item of barter or commerce. For example, any gun intended to be "used" in an interstate "transfer, sale, trade, gift, transport, or delivery" of a firearm prohibited under §922(a)(5) where there is a pattern of such activity, see §924(d)(3)(C), or in a federal offense involving "the exportation of firearms," §924(d)(3)(F), is subject to forfeiture. In fact, none of the offenses listed in four of the six subsections of §924(d)(3) involves the bellicose use of a firearm; each offense involves use as an item in commerce. * Thus, it is clear from §924(d)(3) that one who transports, exports, sells, or trades a firearm "uses" it within the meaning of §924(d)(1) -- even though those actions do not involve using the firearm as a weapon. Unless we are to hold that using a firearm has a different meaning in §924(c)(1) than it does in §924(d) -- and clearly we should not, United Savings Assn., supra, at 371 -- we must reject petitioner's narrow interpretation.

* Section 924(d)(3)(C) lists four offenses: unlicensed manufacture of or commerce in firearms, in violation of §922(a)(1); unlicensed receipt of a weapon from outside the State, in violation of §922(a)(3); unlicensed transfer of a firearm to a resident of a different State, in violation of §922(a)(5); and delivery of a gun by a licensed entity to a resident of a State that is not the licensee's, in violation of §922(b)(3). Section 924(d)(3)(D) mentions only one offense, the transfer or sale of a weapon to disqualified persons, such as fugitives from justice and felons, in violation of §922(d). Under §924(d)(3)(E), firearms are subject to forfeiture if they are intended to be used in any of five listed offenses: shipping stolen firearms, in violation of §922(i); receipt of stolen firearms, in violation of §922(j); importation of firearms, in violation of §922(l); shipment of a firearm by a

felon, in violation of §922(n); and shipment or receipt of a firearm with intent to commit a felony, in violation of §924(b). Finally, §924(d)(3)(F) subjects to forfeiture any firearm intended to be used in any offense that may be prosecuted in federal court if it involves the exportation of firearms.

The evident care with which Congress chose the language of §924(d)(1) reinforces our conclusion in this regard. Although §924(d)(1) lists numerous firearm-related offenses that render guns subject to forfeiture, Congress did not lump all of those offenses together and require forfeiture solely of guns "used" in a prohibited activity. Instead, it carefully varied the statutory language in accordance with the guns' relation to the offense. For example, with respect to some crimes, the firearm is subject to forfeiture not only if it is "used," but also if it is "involved in" the offense. §924(d)(1). Examination of the offenses to which the "involved in" language applies reveals why Congress believed it necessary to include such an expansive term. One of the listed offenses, violation of §922(a)(6), is the making of a false statement material to the lawfulness of a gun's transfer. Because making a material misstatement in order to acquire or sell a gun is not "use" of the gun even under the broadest definition of the word "use," Congress carefully expanded the statutory language. As a result, a gun with respect to which a material misstatement is made is subject to forfeiture because, even though the gun is not "used" in the offense, it is "involved in" it. Congress, however, did not so expand the language for offenses in which firearms were "intended to be used," even though the firearms in many of those offenses function as items of commerce rather than as weapons. Instead, Congress apparently was of the view that one could use a gun by trading it. In light of the common meaning of the word "use" and the structure and language of the statute, we are not in any position to disagree.

Just as a defendant may "use" a firearm within the meaning of §924(c)(1) by trading it for drugs or using it to shoot someone, so too would a defendant "carry" the firearm by keeping it on his person whether he intends to exchange it for cocaine or fire it in self-defense.

The dissent suggests that our interpretation produces a "strange dichotomy" between "using" a firearm and "carrying" one. Post, at 246. We do not see why that is so. Just as a defendant may "use" a firearm within the meaning of §924(c)(1) by trading it for drugs or using it to shoot someone, so too would a defendant "carry" the firearm by keeping it on his person whether he intends to exchange it for cocaine or fire it in self-defense. The dichotomy arises, if at all, only when one tries to extend the phrase "'uses . . . a firearm'" to any use "'for any purpose whatever.'" Ibid. For our purposes, it is sufficient to recognize that, because §924(d)(1) includes both using a firearm for trade and using a firearm as a weapon as "us[ing] a firearm," it is most reasonable to construe §924(c)(1) as encompassing both of those "uses" as well.

Finally, it is argued that §924(c)(1) originally dealt with use of a firearm during crimes of violence; the provision concerning use of a firearm during and in relation to drug trafficking offenses was added later. Ibid. From this, the dissent infers that "use" originally was limited to use of a gun "as a weapon." That the statute in its current form employs the term "use" more broadly is unimportant, the dissent contends, because the addition of the words "'drug trafficking crime' would have been a peculiar way to expand its meaning." Ibid. Even if we assume that Congress had intended the term "use" to have a more limited scope when it passed the original version of §924(c) in 1968, but see supra, at 229-231, we believe it clear from the face of the statute that the Congress that amended §924(c) in 1986 did not. Rather, the 1986 Congress employed the term "use" expansively, covering both use as a weapon, as the dissent admits, and use as an item of trade or barter, as an examination of §924(d) demonstrates. Because the phrase "uses . . . a firearm" is broad enough in ordinary usage to cover use of a firearm as an item of barter or commerce, Congress was free in 1986 so to employ it. The language and structure of §924 indicate that Congress did just that. Accordingly, we conclude that using a firearm in a guns-for-drugs trade may constitute "us[ing] a firearm" within the meaning of §924(c)(1).

B

Using a firearm, however, is not enough to subject the defendant to the punishment required by §924(c)(1). Instead, the firearm must be used "during and in relation to" a "crime of violence or drug trafficking crime." 18 U.S.C. §924(c)(1). Petitioner does not deny that the alleged use occurred "during" a drug trafficking crime. Nor could he. The indictment charged that petitioner and his companion conspired to possess cocaine with intent to distribute. App. 3-4. There can be no doubt that the gun-for-drugs trade was proposed during and in furtherance of that interstate drug conspiracy. Nor can it be contended that the alleged use did not occur during the "attempt" to possess cocaine with which petitioner also was charged, id., at 4; the MAC-10 served as an inducement to convince the undercover officer to provide petitioner with the drugs that petitioner sought.

As one court has observed, the "in relation to" language "allay[s] explicitly the concern that a person could be" punished under §924(c)(1) for committing a drug trafficking offense "while in possession of a firearm" even though the firearm's

presence is coincidental or entirely "unrelated" to the crime.

Petitioner, however, does dispute whether his use of the firearm was "in relation to" the drug trafficking offense. The phrase "in relation to" is expansive, cf. District of Columbia v. Greater Washington Board of Trade, 506 U.S. 125, 129, 121 L. Ed. 2d 513, 113 S. Ct. 580 (1992) (the phrase "relate to" is "deliberately expansive" (internal quotation marks omitted)), as the Courts of Appeals construing §924(c)(1) have recognized, United States v. Phelps, 877 F.2d at 30 ("the phrase 'in relation to' is broad"); United States v. Harris, 294 U.S. App. D.C. at 315, 959 F.2d at 261 (per curiam) (firearm is used "in relation to" the crime if it "facilitate[s] the predicate offense in some way"). Nonetheless, the phrase does illuminate §924(c)(1)'s boundaries. According to Webster's, "in relation to" means "with reference to" or "as regards." Webster's New International Dictionary, at 2102. The phrase "in relation to" thus, at a minimum, clarifies that the firearm must have some purpose or effect with respect to the drug trafficking crime; its presence or involvement cannot be the result of accident or coincidence. As one court has observed, the "in relation to" language "allay[s] explicitly the concern that a person could be" punished under §924(c)(1) for committing a drug trafficking offense "while in possession of a firearm" even though the firearm's presence is coincidental or entirely "unrelated" to the crime. United States v. Stewart, 779 F.2d 538, 539 (CA9 1985) (Kennedy, J.). Instead, the gun at least must "facilitate, or have the potential of facilitating," the drug trafficking offense. Id., at 540. Accord, United States v. Ocampo, 890 F.2d 1363, 1371-1372 (CA7 1989); 957 F.2d at 837.

The undercover officer posing as a pawnshop dealer expressly told petitioner that he was not in the narcotics business and that he did not get involved with drugs. For a MAC-10, however, he was willing to see if he could track down some cocaine.

We need not determine the precise contours of the "in relation to" requirement here, however, as petitioner's use of his MAC-10 meets any reasonable construction of it. The MAC-10's presence in this case was not the product of happenstance. On the contrary, "far more than [in] the ordinary case" under §924(c)(1), in which the gun merely facilitates the offense by providing a means of protection or intimidation, here "the gun . . . was an integral part of the transaction." United States v. Phelps, 895 F.2d 1281, 1283 (CA9 1990) (Kozinski, J., dissenting from denial of rehearing en banc). Without it, the deal would not have been possible. The undercover officer posing as a pawnshop dealer expressly told petitioner that he was not in the narcotics business and that he did not get involved with drugs. For a MAC-10, however, he was willing to see if he could track down some cocaine.

Relying on the decision of the Court of Appeals for the Ninth Circuit in Phelps and on the legislative record, petitioner insists that the relationship between the gun and the drug offense in this case is not the type of connection Congress contemplated when it drafted §924(c)(1). With respect to that argument, we agree with the District of Columbia Circuit's observation:

Whether guns are used as the medium of exchange for drugs sold illegally or as a means to protect the transaction or dealers, their introduction into the scene of drug transactions dramatically heightens the danger to society.

"It may well be that Congress, when it drafted the language of [§] 924(c), had in mind a more obvious use of guns in connection with a drug crime, but the language [of the statute] is not so limited[;] nor can we imagine any reason why Congress would not have wished its language to cover this situation. Whether guns are used as the medium of exchange for drugs sold illegally or as a means to protect the transaction or dealers, their introduction into the scene of drug transactions dramatically heightens the danger to society." Harris, supra, at 316, 959 F.2d at 262.

One need look no further than the pages of the Federal Reporter to verify the truth of that observation. In Phelps, supra, the defendant arranged to trade his MAC-10 for chemicals necessary to make methamphetamine. The Ninth Circuit held that the gun was not used or carried "in relation to" the drug trafficking offense because it was used as an item of barter and not as a weapon. The defendant, however, did not believe his MAC-10's capabilities were so limited. When he was stopped for a traffic violation, "the MAC 10, suddenly transmogrified [from an item of commerce] into an offensive weapon, was still in [the defendant's] possession[.] [He] opened fire and shot a deputy sheriff." Id., at 1288, n.4 (Kozinski, J., dissenting from denial of rehearing en banc).

C

Finally, the dissent and petitioner invoke the rule of lenity. Post, at 246-247. The mere possibility of articulating a narrower construction, however, does not by itself make the rule of lenity applicable. Instead, that venerable rule is reserved for cases where, "after 'seiz[ing] every thing from which aid can be derived,'" the Court is "left with an ambiguous statute." United States v. Bass, 404 U.S. 336, 347, 30 L. Ed. 2d 488, 92 S. Ct. 515 (1971) (quoting United States v. Fisher, 6 U.S. 358, 386, 2 L. Ed. 304 (1805)). Accord, Moskal v. United States, 498 U.S. 103, 108, 112 L. Ed. 2d 449, 111 S. Ct. 461 (1990). This is not such a case. Not only does petitioner's use of his MAC-10 fall squarely within the common usage and dictionary definitions of the terms "uses . . . a firearm," but Congress affirmatively demonstrated that it meant to include transactions like petitioner's as "us[ing] a firearm" by so employing those terms in §924(d).

The fact that a gun is treated momentarily as an item of commerce does not render it inert or deprive it of destructive capacity. Rather, as experience demonstrates, it can be converted instantaneously from currency to cannon.

Imposing a more restrictive reading of the phrase "uses . . . a firearm" does violence not only to the structure and language of the statute, but to its purpose as well. When Congress enacted the current version of §924(c)(1), it was no doubt aware that drugs and guns are a dangerous combination. In 1989, 56 percent of all murders in New York City were drug related; during the same period, the figure for the Nation's Capital was as high as 80 percent. The American Enterprise 100 (Jan.-Feb. 1991). The fact that a gun is treated momentarily as an item of commerce does not render it inert or deprive it of destructive capacity. Rather, as experience demonstrates, it can be converted instantaneously from currency to cannon. See supra, at 239. We therefore see no reason why Congress would have intended courts and juries applying §924(c)(1) to draw a fine metaphysical distinction between a gun's role in a drug offense as a weapon and its role as an item of barter; it creates a grave possibility of violence and death in either capacity.

We therefore hold that a criminal who trades his firearm for drugs "uses" it during and in relation to a drug trafficking offense within the meaning of §924(c)(1).

We have observed that the rule of lenity "cannot dictate an implausible interpretation of a statute, nor one at odds with the generally accepted contemporary meaning of a term." Taylor v. United States, 495 U.S. 575, 596, 109 L. Ed. 2d 607, 110 S. Ct. 2143 (1990). That observation controls this case. Both a firearm's use as a weapon and its use as an item of barter fall within the plain language of §924(c)(1), so long as the use occurs during and in relation to a drug trafficking offense; both must constitute "uses" of a firearm for §924(d)(1) to make any sense at all; and both create the very dangers and risks that Congress meant §924(c)(1) to address. We therefore hold that a criminal who trades his firearm for drugs "uses" it during and in relation to a drug trafficking offense within the meaning of §924(c)(1). Because the evidence in this case showed that petitioner "used" his MAC-10 machine gun and silencer in precisely such a manner, proposing to trade them for cocaine, petitioner properly was subjected to §924(c)(1)'s 30-year mandatory minimum sentence. The judgment of the Court of Appeals, accordingly, is affirmed.

It is so ordered.

JUSTICE BLACKMUN, concurring.

I join the Court's opinion in full because I understand the discussion in Part II-B not to foreclose the possibility that the "in relation to" language of 18 U.S.C. §924(c)(1) requires more than mere furtherance or facilitation of a crime of violence or drug-trafficking crime. I agree with the Court that because petitioner's use of his MAC-10 meets any reasonable construction of the phrase, it is unnecessary to determine in this case the precise contours of "in relation to" as it appears in §924(c)(1). See ante, at 238.

JUSTICE SCALIA, with whom JUSTICE STEVENS and JUSTICE SOUTER join, dissenting.

Section 924(c)(1) mandates a sentence enhancement for any defendant who "during and in relation to any crime of violence or drug trafficking crime . . . uses . . . a firearm." 18 U.S.C. §924(c)(1). The Court begins its analysis by focusing upon the word "use" in this passage, and explaining that the dictionary definitions of that word are very broad. See ante, at 228-229. It is, however, a "fundamental principle of statutory construction (and, indeed, of language itself) that the meaning of a word cannot be determined in isolation, but must be drawn from the context in which it is used." Deal v. United States, ante, at 132. That is particularly true of a word as elastic as "use," whose meanings range all the way from "to partake of" (as in "he uses tobacco") to "to be wont or accustomed" (as in "he used to smoke tobacco"). See Webster's New International Dictionary 2806 (2d ed. 1950).

It is unquestionably not reasonable and normal, I think, to say simply "do not use firearms" when one means to prohibit selling or scratching with them.

In the search for statutory meaning, we give nontechnical words and phrases their ordinary meaning. See Chapman v. United States, 500 U.S. 453, 462, 114 L. Ed. 2d 524, 111 S. Ct. 1919 (1991); Perrin v. United States, 444 U.S. 37, 42, 62 L. Ed. 2d 199, 100 S. Ct. 311 (1979); Minor v. Mechanics Bank of Alexandria, 26 U.S. 46, 7 L. Ed. 47 (1 Pet.) 46, 64, 7 L. Ed. 47 (1828). To use an instrumentality ordinarily means to use it for its intended purpose. When someone asks, "Do you use a cane?," he is not inquiring whether you have your grandfather's silver-handled walking stick on display in the hall; he wants to know whether you walk with a cane. Similarly, to speak of "using a firearm" is to speak of using it for its distinctive purpose, i.e., as a weapon. To be sure, "one can use a firearm in a number of ways," ante, at 230, including as an article of exchange, just as one can "use" a cane as a hall decoration -- but that is not the ordinary meaning of "using" the one or the other. n1 The Court does not appear to grasp the distinction between how a word can be used and how it ordinarily is used. It would, indeed, be "both reasonable and normal to say that petitioner 'used' his MAC-10 in his drug trafficking offense by trading it for cocaine." Ibid. It would also be reasonable and normal to say that he "used" it to scratch his head. When one wishes to describe the action of employing the instrument of a firearm for such unusual purposes, "use" is assuredly a verb one could select. But that says nothing about whether the ordinary meaning of the phrase "uses a firearm" embraces such extraordinary employments. It is unquestionably not reasonable and normal, I think, to say simply "do not use firearms" when one means to prohibit selling or scratching with them.

The ordinary meaning of "uses a firearm" does not include using it as an article of commerce. I think it perfectly obvious, for example, that the objective falsity requirement for a perjury conviction would not be satisfied if a witness answered "no" to a prosecutor's inquiry whether he had ever "used a firearm," even though he had once sold his grandfather's Enfield rifle to a collector.

n1 The Court asserts that the "significant flaw" in this argument is that "to say that the ordinary meaning of 'uses a firearm' includes using a firearm as a weapon" is quite different from saying that the ordinary meaning "also excludes any other use." Ante, at 230 (emphases in original). The two are indeed different -- but it is precisely the latter that I assert to be true: The ordinary meaning of "uses a firearm" does not include using it as an article of commerce. I think it perfectly obvious, for example, that the objective falsity requirement for a perjury conviction would not be satisfied if a witness answered "no" to a prosecutor's inquiry whether he had ever "used a firearm," even though he had once sold his grandfather's Enfield rifle to a collector.

The normal usage is reflected, for example, in the United States Sentencing Guidelines, which provide for enhanced sentences when firearms are "discharged," "brandished, displayed, or possessed," or "otherwise used." See, e.g., United States Sentencing Commission, Guidelines Manual §2B3.1(b)(2) (Nov. 1992). As to the latter term, the Guidelines say: "'Otherwise used' with reference to a dangerous weapon (including a firearm) means that the conduct did not amount to the discharge of a firearm but was more than brandishing, displaying, or possessing a firearm or other dangerous weapon." USSG §1B1.1, comment., n.1(g) (definitions). "Otherwise used" in this provision obviously means "otherwise used as a weapon." n2

Though it excludes an enhanced penalty for the burglar who scratches his head with the barrel of a gun, it requires one for the burglar who happens to use a gun handle, rather than a rock, to break the window affording him entrance—hardly a distinction that ought to make a sentencing difference if the gun has no other connection to the crime.

n2 The Court says that it is "not persuaded that [its] construction of the phrase 'uses . . . a firearm' will produce anomalous applications." Ante, at 232. But as proof it points only to the fact that §924(c)(1) fortuitously contains other language -- the requirement that the use be "during and in relation to any crime of violence or drug trafficking crime" -- that happens to prevent untoward results. Ibid. That language does not, in fact, prevent all untoward results: Though it excludes an enhanced penalty for the burglar who scratches his head with the barrel of a gun, it requires one for the burglar who happens to use a gun handle, rather than a rock, to break the window affording him entrance -- hardly a distinction that ought to make a sentencing difference if the gun has no other connection to the crime. But in any event, an excuse that turns upon the language of §924(c)(1) is good only for that particular statute. The Court cannot avoid "anomalous applications" when it applies its anomalous meaning of "use a firearm" in other contexts -- for example, the Guidelines provision just described in text.

Reading the Guidelines as they are written... and interpreting "use a firearm" In the strange fashion the Court does, produces a full seven-point upward sentence adjustment for firing a gun at a storekeeper during a robbery; a mere five-point adjustment for pointing the gun at the storekeeper (which falls within the Guidelines' definition of "brandished,"); but an intermediate six-point adjustment for using the gun to pry open the cash register or prop open the door. Quite obviously ridiculous. When the Guidelines speak of "otherwise us[ing]" a firearm, they mean, in accordance with normal usage, otherwise "using" it as a weapon—for example, placing the gun barrel in the mouth of the storekeeper to intimidate him.

In a vain attempt to show the contrary, it asserts that the phrase "otherwise used" in the

Guidelines means used for any other purpose at all (the Court's preferred meaning of "use a firearm"), so long as it is more "culpable" than brandishing. See ante, at 232. But whence does it derive that convenient limitation? It appears nowhere in the text -- as well it should not, since the whole purpose of the Guidelines is to take out of the hands of individual judges determinations as to what is "more culpable" and "less culpable." The definition of "otherwise used" in the Guidelines merely says that it means "more than" brandishing and less than firing. The Court is confident that "scratching one's head" with a firearm is not "more than" brandishing it. See ante, at 233. I certainly agree -- but only because the "more" use referred to is more use as a weapon. Reading the Guidelines as they are written (rather than importing the Court's deus ex machina of a culpability scale), and interpreting "use a firearm" in the strange fashion the Court does, produces, see ante, at 232, a full seven-point upward sentence adjustment for firing a gun at a storekeeper during a robbery; a mere five-point adjustment for pointing the gun at the storekeeper (which falls within the Guidelines' definition of "brandished," see USSG §1B1.1, comment., n.1(c)); but an intermediate six-point adjustment for using the gun to pry open the cash register or prop open the door. Quite obviously ridiculous. When the Guidelines speak of "otherwise us[ing]" a firearm, they mean, in accordance with normal usage, otherwise "using" it as a weapon -- for example, placing the gun barrel in the mouth of the storekeeper to intimidate him.

Given our rule that ordinary meaning governs, and given the ordinary meaning of "uses a firearm," it seems to me inconsequential that "the words 'as a weapon' appear nowhere in the statute," ante, at 229; they are reasonably implicit. Petitioner is not, I think, seeking to introduce an "additional requirement" into the text, ibid., but is simply construing the text according to its normal import.

the statute provides that its prohibition on certain transactions in firearms "shall not apply to the loan or rental of a firearm to any person for temporary use for lawful sporting purposes," I have no doubt that the "use" referred to is only use as a sporting weapon, and not the use of pawning the firearm to pay for a ski trip.

The Court seeks to avoid this conclusion by referring to the next subsection of the statute, §924(d), which does not employ the phrase "uses a firearm," but provides for the confiscation of firearms that are "used in" referenced offenses which include the crimes of transferring, selling, or transporting firearms in interstate commerce. The Court concludes from this that whenever the term appears in this statute, "use" of a firearm must include nonweapon use. See ante, at 233-236. I do not agree. We are dealing here not with a technical word or an "artfully defined" legal term, cf. Dewsnup v. Timm, 502 U.S. 410, 423, 116 L. Ed. 2d 903, 112 S. Ct. 773 (1992) (SCALIA, J., dissenting), but with common words that are, as I have suggested, inordinately sensitive to context. Just as adding the direct object "a firearm" to the verb "use" narrows the meaning of that verb (it can no longer mean "partake of"), so also adding the modifier "in the offense of transferring, selling, or transporting firearms" to the phrase "use a firearm" expands the meaning of that phrase (it then includes, as it previously would not, nonweapon use). But neither the narrowing nor the expansion should logically be thought to apply to all appearances of the affected word or phrase. Just as every appearance of the word "use" in the statute need not be given the narrow meaning that word acquires in the phrase "use a firearm," so also every appearance of the phrase "use a firearm" need not be given the expansive connotation that phrase acquires in the broader context "use a firearm in crimes such as unlawful sale of firearms." When, for example, the statute provides that its prohibition on certain transactions in firearms "shall not apply to the loan or rental of a firearm to any person for temporary use for lawful sporting purposes," 18 U.S.C. §§922(a)(5)(B), (b)(3)(B), I have no doubt that the "use" referred to is only use as a sporting weapon, and not the use of pawning the firearm to pay for a ski trip. Likewise when, in §924(c)(1), the phrase "uses . . . a firearm" is not employed in a context that necessarily envisions the unusual "use" of a firearm as a commodity, the normally understood meaning of the phrase should prevail.

Another consideration leads to the same conclusion: §924(c)(1) provides increased penalties not only for one who "uses" a firearm during and in relation to any crime of violence or drug trafficking crime, but also for one who "carries" a firearm in those circumstances. The interpretation I would give the language produces an eminently reasonable dichotomy between "using a firearm" (as a weapon) and "carrying a firearm" (which in the context "uses or carries a firearm" means carrying it in such manner as to be ready for use as a weapon). The Court's interpretation, by contrast, produces a strange dichotomy between "using a firearm for any purpose whatever, including barter," and "carrying a firearm." n3

n3 The Court responds to this argument by abandoning all pretense of giving the phrase "uses a firearm" even a permissible meaning, much less its ordinary one. There is no problem, the Court says, because it is not contending that "uses a firearm" means "uses for any purpose," only that it means "uses as a weapon or for trade." See ante, at 236. Unfortunately, that is not one of the options that our mother tongue makes available. "Uses a firearm" can be given a broad meaning ("uses for any purpose") or its more ordinary narrow meaning ("uses as a weapon"); but it can not possibly mean "uses as a weapon or for trade."

Finally, although the present prosecution was brought under the portion of §924(c)(1) pertaining to use of a firearm "during and in relation to any . . . drug trafficking crime," I think it significant that that portion is affiliated with the preexisting provision pertaining to use of a firearm "during and in relation to any crime of violence," rather than with the firearm trafficking offenses defined in §922 and referenced in §924(d). The word "use" in the "crime of violence" context has the unmistakable import of use as a weapon, and that import carries over, in my view, to the subsequently added phrase "or drug trafficking crime." Surely the word "use" means the same thing as to both, and surely the 1986 addition of "drug trafficking crime" would have been a peculiar way to expand its meaning (beyond "use as a weapon") for crimes of violence.

Even if the reader does not consider the issue to be as clear as I do, he must at least acknowledge, I think, that it is eminently debatable—and that is enough, under the rule of lenity, to require finding for the petitioner here.

Even if the reader does not consider the issue to be as clear as I do, he must at least acknowledge, I think, that it is eminently debatable -- and that is enough, under the rule of lenity, to require finding for the petitioner here. "At the very least, it may be said that the issue is subject to some doubt. Under these circumstances, we adhere to the familiar rule that, 'where there is ambiguity in a criminal statute, doubts are resolved in favor of the defendant.'" Adamo Wrecking Co. v. United States, 434 U.S. 275, 284-285, 54 L. Ed. 2d 538, 98 S. Ct. 566 (1978), quoting United States v. Bass, 404 U.S. 336, 348, 30 L. Ed. 2d 488, 92 S. Ct. 515 (1971). n4

Stretching language in order to write a more effective statute than Congress devised is not an exercise we should indulge in.

n4 The Court contends that giving the language its ordinary meaning would frustrate the purpose of the statute, since a gun "can be converted instantaneously from currency to cannon," ante, at 240. Stretching language in order to write a more effective statute than Congress devised is not an exercise we should indulge in. But in any case, the ready ability to use a gun that is at hand as a weapon is perhaps one of the reasons the statute sanctions not only using a firearm, but carrying one. Here, however, the Government chose not to indict under that provision. See ante, at 228.

For the foregoing reasons, I respectfully dissent.

STINSON v. UNITED STATES

(CASE EXCERPT)

508 U.S. 36; 113 S. Ct. 1913; 123 L. Ed. 2d 598

March 24, 1993, Argued

May 3, 1993, Decided

GIST: At trial, three-time loser Terry Stinson was convicted as a career offender on the basis of a court decision that possession of a firearm by a convicted felon was a crime of violence. The issue in the case was whether the commentary to the U.S. Sentencing Guidelines is binding on the federal courts. The Court held that the commentary is indeed binding on federal courts, and thus an amendment to the Guidelines that specifically excluded firearms possession by a felon from the definition of "crime of violence" should have been applied.

JUSTICE KENNEDY delivered the opinion of the Court.

In this case we review a decision of the Court of Appeals for the Eleventh Circuit holding that the commentary to the Sentencing Guidelines is not binding on the federal courts. We decide that commentary in the Guidelines Manual that interprets or explains a guideline is authoritative unless it violates the Constitution or a federal statute, or is inconsistent with, or a plainly erroneous reading of, that guideline.

Petitioner Terry Lynn Stinson entered a plea of guilty to a five-count indictment resulting from his robbery of a Florida bank. The presentence report recommended that petitioner be sentenced as a career offender under the Sentencing Guidelines. See United States Sentencing Commission, Guidelines Manual §4B1.1 (Nov. 1989). Section 4B1.1 provided that a defendant is a career offender if: "(1) the defendant was at least eighteen years old at the time of the instant offense, (2) the instant offense of conviction is a felony that is either a crime of violence or a controlled substance offense, and (3) the defendant has at least two prior felony convictions of either a crime of violence or a controlled substance offense."

The District Court found that petitioner's conviction for the offense of possession of a firearm by a convicted felon was a crime of violence, satisfying the second element of the career offender definition.

All concede that petitioner was at least 18 years old when the events leading to the indictment occurred and that he then had at least two prior felony convictions for crimes of violence, thereby satisfying the first and third elements in the definition of career offender. It is the second element in this definition, the requirement that the predicate offense be a crime of violence, that gave rise to the ultimate problem in this case. At the time of his sentencing, the Guidelines defined "crime of violence" as, among other things, "any offense under federal or state law punishable by imprisonment for a term exceeding one year that . . . involves conduct that presents a serious potential risk of physical injury to another." §4B1.2(1). The United States District Court for the Middle District of Florida found that petitioner's conviction for the offense of possession of a firearm by a convicted felon, 18 U.S.C. §922(g), was a crime of violence, satisfying the second element of the career offender definition. Although the indictment contained other counts, the District Court relied only upon the felon-in-possession offense in applying the career offender provision of the Guidelines. In accord with its conclusions, the District Court sentenced petitioner as a career offender.

The Court of Appeals affirmed, holding that possession of a firearm by a felon was, as a categorical matter, a crime of violence. After its decision, however, Amendment 433 to the Guidelines Manual, which added a sentence to the commentary to §4B1.2, became effective. The new sentence stated that "the term 'crime of violence' does not include the offense of unlawful possession of a firearm by a felon."

On appeal, petitioner maintained his position that the offense relied upon by the District Court was not a crime of violence under USSG §§4B1.1 and 4B1.2(1). The Court of Appeals affirmed, holding that possession of a firearm by a felon was, as a categorical matter, a crime of violence. After its decision, however, Amendment 433 to the Guidelines Manual, which added a sentence to the commentary to §4B1.2, became effective. The new sentence stated that "the term 'crime of violence' does not include the offense of unlawful possession of a firearm by a felon." n1 USSG App. C, p. 253 (Nov. 1992). See §4B1.2, comment., n.2. Petitioner sought rehearing, arguing that Amendment 433 should be given retroactive effect, but the Court of Appeals adhered to its earlier interpretation of "crime of violence" and denied the petition for rehearing in an opinion.

.....

Amended commentary is binding on the federal courts even though it is not reviewed by Congress, and prior judicial constructions of a particular guideline cannot prevent the Commission from adopting a conflicting interpretation that satisfies the standard we set forth today.

ALBRIGHT v. OLIVER

(CASE EXCERPT)
510 U.S. 266; 114 S. Ct. 807; 127 L. Ed. 2d 114
October 12, 1993, Argued
January 24, 1994, Decided

GIST: This case rejected Albright's argument that the 14th Amendment Due Process Clause protects a right to be free of malicious prosecution. In dissent, Justices Stevens and Blackmun argued for a more expansive reading of the Due Process Clause, listing the right to keep and bear arms as a liberty guaranteed by the Constitution, by quoting the decision in *Poe v. Ullman*.

JUSTICE STEVENS, with whom JUSTICE BLACKMUN joins, dissenting.

At bottom, the plurality opinion seems to rest on one fundamental misunderstanding: that the incorporation cases have somehow "substituted" the specific provisions of the Bill of Rights for the "more generalized language contained in the earlier cases construing the Fourteenth Amendment." In fact, the incorporation cases themselves rely on the very "generalized language" THE CHIEF JUSTICE would have them displacing. Those cases add to the liberty protected by the Due Process Clause most of the specific guarantees of the first eight Amendments, but they do not purport to take anything away; that a liberty interest is not the subject of an incorporated provision of the Bill of Rights does not remove it from the ambit of the Due Process Clause. I cannot improve on Justice Harlan's statement of this settled proposition:

The full scope of the liberty guaranteed by the Due Process Clause cannot be found in or limited by the precise terms of the specific guarantees elsewhere provided in the Constitution. This 'liberty' is not a series of isolated points pricked out in terms of the taking of property; the freedom of speech, press, and religion; the right to keep and bear arms; the freedom from unreasonable searches and seizures; and so on.

"The full scope of the liberty guaranteed by the Due Process Clause cannot be found in or limited by the precise terms of the specific guarantees elsewhere provided in the Constitution. This 'liberty' is not a series of isolated points pricked out in terms of the taking of property; the freedom of speech, press, and religion; the right to keep and bear arms; the freedom from unreasonable searches and seizures; and so on. It is a rational continuum which, broadly speaking, includes a freedom from all substantial arbitrary impositions and purposeless restraints . . . and which also recognizes, what a reasonable and sensitive judgment must, that certain interests require particularly careful scrutiny of the state needs asserted to justify their abridgment." Poe v. Ullman (1961).

BEECHAM v. UNITED STATES

(FULL CASE)

511 U.S. 368; 114 S. Ct. 1669; 128 L. Ed. 2d 383

March 23, 1993, Argued

May 16, 1994, Decided

GIST: Federal law makes it illegal for a convicted felon to possess a firearm, but a felon who has had civil rights restored is no longer under that disability. The Court held that a state restoration of civil rights does not eliminate the federal disability; the jurisdiction that convicted the person must be the one that restores the civil rights. The Court notes that a person cannot restore those rights currently at the federal level, but that this leaves the person no worse off than in states (it names eleven) that also have no current provision for restoring these lost rights.

Petitioners Beecham and Jones were each convicted of violating 18 U.S.C. §922(g), which makes it unlawful for a convicted felon to possess a firearm. Title 18 U.S.C. §921(a)(20) qualifies the definition of "conviction": "What constitutes a conviction [is] determined in accordance with the law of the jurisdiction in which the proceedings were held," ibid. (choice-of-law clause), and "any conviction which has been expunged, or set aside or for which a person has been pardoned or has had civil rights restored shall not be considered a conviction . . .," ibid. (exemption clause). The respective District Courts decided that Beecham's and Jones' prior federal convictions could not be counted because petitioners' civil rights had been restored under state law. The Court of Appeals reversed, holding that state restoration of civil rights could not undo the federal disability flowing from a federal conviction.

Held: Petitioners can take advantage of §921(a)(20) only if their civil rights have been restored under federal law, the law of the jurisdiction where the earlier proceedings were held. The choice-of-law clause is logically read to apply to the exemption clause. The inquiry throughout the statutory scheme is whether the person has a qualifying conviction on his record. The choice-of-law clause defines the rule for determining what constitutes a conviction. Asking, under the exemption clause, whether a person's civil rights have been restored is just one step in determining whether something should "be considered a conviction," a determination that, by the terms of the choice-of-law clause, is governed by the law of the convicting jurisdiction. That the other three items listed in the exemption clause are either always or almost always done by the jurisdiction of conviction also counsels in favor of interpreting civil rights restoration as possessing the same attribute. This statutory structure rebuts the arguments used by other Circuits to support their conclusion that the two clauses should be read separately. Moreover, even if there is no federal law procedure for restoring civil rights to federal felons, nothing in §921(a)(20) supports the assumption that Congress intended all felons to have access to all the procedures specified in the exemption clause, especially because there are many States that do not restore civil rights, either. Because the statutory language is unambiguous, the rule of lenity is inapplicable. See Chapman v. United States, 500 U.S. 453, 463-464. Pp. 370-374, 114 L. Ed. 2d 524, 111 S. Ct. 1919.

JUSTICE O'CONNOR delivered the opinion of the Court.

Today we construe three provisions of the federal fire-arms statutes:

"It shall be unlawful for any person who has been convicted . . . [of] a crime punishable by imprisonment for a term exceeding one year . . . [to possess] any firearm . . . ." 18 U.S.C. §922(g).

"What constitutes a conviction . . . shall be determined in accordance with the law of the jurisdiction in which the proceedings were held." §921(a)(20) (the choice-of-law clause).

"Any conviction which has been expunged, or set aside or for which a person has been pardoned or has had civil rights restored shall not be considered a conviction . . . ." Ibid. (the exemption clause).

The question before us is which jurisdiction's law is to be considered in determining whether a felon "has had civil rights restored" for a prior federal conviction.

I

Each of the petitioners was convicted of violating §922(g). Beecham was convicted in Federal District Court in North Carolina, Jones in Federal District Court in West Virginia. Beecham's relevant prior conviction was a 1979 federal conviction in Tennessee, for violating 18 U.S.C. §922(h). App. 11. Jones' prior convictions were two West Virginia state convictions, for breaking and entering and for forgery, and one 1971 federal conviction in Ohio for interstate transportation of a stolen automobile. Id., at 19-20.

The question presented to the District Courts was whether these restorations of civil rights by States could remove the disabilities imposed as a result of Beecham's and Jones' federal convictions.

Jones had gotten his civil rights restored by West Virginia, so his two West Virginia state convictions were not considered. Beecham claimed his civil rights had been restored by Tennessee, the State in which he had been convicted of his federal offense. The question presented to the District Courts was whether these restorations of civil rights by States could remove the disabilities imposed as a result of Beecham's and Jones' federal convictions.

In both cases, the District Courts concluded the answer was "yes," though for different reasons: In Beecham's case the court looked to the law of the State in which the earlier federal crime was committed (Tennessee); in Jones' case the court looked to the law of the State in which Jones lived when he committed the §922(g) offense (West Virginia). The Fourth Circuit reversed both rulings, reasoning that state restoration of civil rights could not undo the federal disability flowing from a federal conviction. See 993 F.2d 1131 (1993) (Jones' case) and 993 F.2d 1539 (1993) (judgt. order in Beecham's case). We granted certiorari to resolve the conflict this decision created with United States v. Edwards, 946 F.2d 1347 (CA8 1991), and United States v. Geyler, 932 F.2d 1330 (CA9 1991). 510 U.S. 975 (1993).

II

The question in these cases is how the choice-of-law clause and the exemption clause of §921(a)(20) are related. If, as the Fourth Circuit held, the choice-of-law clause applies to the exemption clause, then we must look to whether Beecham's and Jones' civil rights were restored under federal law (the law of the jurisdiction in which the earlier proceedings were held). On the other hand, if, as the Eighth and Ninth Circuits concluded, the two clauses ought to be read separately, see Geyler, supra, 932 F.2d at 1334-1335; Edwards, supra, 946 F.2d at 1349-1350, then we would have to come up with a special choice-of-law principle for the exemption clause.

We think the Fourth Circuit's reading is the better one. Throughout the statutory scheme, the inquiry is: Does the person have a qualifying conviction on his record? Section 922(g) imposes a disability on people who "have been convicted." The choice-of-law clause defines the rule for determining "what constitutes a conviction." The exemption clause says that a conviction for which a person has had civil rights restored "shall not be considered a conviction." Asking whether a person has had civil rights restored is thus just one step in determining whether something should "be considered a conviction." By the terms of the choice-of-law clause, this determination is governed by the law of the convicting jurisdiction.

This interpretation is supported by the fact that the other three procedures listed in the exemption clause -- pardons, expungements, and set-asides -- are either always or almost always (depending on whether one considers a federal grant of habeas corpus to be a "set-aside," a question we do not now decide) done by the jurisdiction of conviction. That several items in a list share an attribute counsels in favor of interpreting the other items as possessing that attribute as well. Dole v. Steelworkers, 494 U.S. 26, 36,

108 L. Ed. 2d 23, 110 S. Ct. 929 (1990); Third Nat. Bank in Nashville v. Impac Limited, Inc., 432 U.S. 312, 322, 53 L. Ed. 2d 368, 97 S. Ct. 2307 (1977); Jarecki v. G. D. Searle & Co., 367 U.S. 303, 307, 6 L. Ed. 2d 859, 81 S. Ct. 1579 (1961). Though this canon of construction is by no means a hard and fast rule, it is a factor pointing toward the Fourth Circuit's construction of the statute.

The exemption clause does not simply say that a person whose civil rights have been restored is exempted from §922(g)'s firearms disqualification. It says that the person's conviction "shall not be considered a conviction."

In light of the statutory structure, the fact that both clauses speak of "conviction[s]" rebuts the Eighth and Ninth Circuits' argument that the two clauses "pertain to two entirely different sets of circumstances" -- "the question of what constitutes a conviction" and "the effect of post-conviction events." Geyler, supra, 932 F.2d at 1334-1335; see also Edwards, supra, at 1349. The exemption clause does not simply say that a person whose civil rights have been restored is exempted from §922(g)'s firearms disqualification. It says that the person's conviction "shall not be considered a conviction." The effect of postconviction events is therefore, under the statutory scheme, just one element of the question of what constitutes a conviction.

Likewise, the presence of the choice-of-law clause rebuts the Eighth and Ninth Circuits' argument that the "plain, unlimited language," Edwards, supra, at 1349; see also Geyler, supra, at 1334, of the exemption clause -- with its reference to "any conviction . . . for which a person has . . . had civil rights restored" (emphasis added) -- refers to all civil rights restorations, even those by a jurisdiction other than the one in which the conviction was entered. Regardless of what the quoted phrase might mean standing alone, in conjunction with the choice-of-law clause it must refer only to restorations of civil rights by the convicting jurisdiction. The plain meaning that we seek to discern is the plain meaning of the whole statute, not of isolated sentences. See King v. St. Vincent's Hospital, 502 U.S. 215, 221, 116 L. Ed. 2d 578, 112 S. Ct. 570 (1991); Massachusetts v. Morash, 490 U.S. 107, 115, 104 L. Ed. 2d 98, 109 S. Ct. 1668 (1989); Shell Oil Co. v. Iowa Dept. of Revenue, 488 U.S. 19, 26, 109 S. Ct. 278, 102 L. Ed. 2d 186 (1988).

We are also unpersuaded by the Ninth Circuit's argument that "because there is no federal procedure for restoring civil rights to a federal felon, Congress could not have expected that the federal government would perform this function," and that therefore "the reference in §921(a)(20) to the restoration of civil rights must be to the state procedure."

Many jurisdictions have no procedure for restoring civil rights.

at least 11 States—Arkansas, Indiana, Kentucky, Maryland, Missouri, New Jersey, Oklahoma, Pennsylvania, Texas, Vermont, and Virginia suspend felons' civil rights but provide no procedure for restoring them

Under our reading of the statute, a person convicted in federal court is no worse off than a person convicted in a court of a State that does not restore civil rights.

We are also unpersuaded by the Ninth Circuit's argument that "because there is no federal procedure for restoring civil rights to a federal felon, Congress could not have expected that the federal government would perform this function," and that therefore "the reference in §921(a)(20) to the restoration of civil rights must be to the state procedure." Geyler, 932 F.2d at 1333.* This reasoning assumes that Congress intended felons convicted by all jurisdictions to have access to all the procedures (pardon, expungement, set-aside, and civil rights restoration) specified in the exemption clause; but nothing in §921(a)(20) supports the assumption on which this reasoning is based. Many jurisdictions have no procedure for restoring civil rights. See Apps. A and B to Brief for Petitioners (indicating that at least 11 States -- Arkansas, Indiana, Kentucky, Maryland, Missouri, New Jersey, Oklahoma, Pennsylvania, Texas, Vermont, and Virginia suspend felons' civil rights but provide no procedure for restoring them); see, e.g., Mo. Rev. Stat. §561.026 (1979 and Supp. 1994); United States v. Thomas, 991 F.2d 206, 213-214 (CA5) (Texas law), cert. denied, 510 U.S. 1014, 126 L. Ed. 2d 572, 114 S. Ct. 607 (1993). However one reads the statutory scheme -- as looking to the law of the convicting jurisdiction, or to the law of the State in which the prior conduct took place, or to the law of the State in which the felon now lives or has at one time lived -- people in some jurisdictions would have options open to them that people in other jurisdictions may lack. Under our reading of the statute, a person convicted in federal court is no worse off than a person convicted in a court of a State that does not restore civil rights.

* We express no opinion on whether a federal felon cannot have his civil rights restored under federal law. This is a complicated question, one which involves the interpretation of the federal law relating to federal civil rights, see U.S. Const., Art. I, §2, cl. 1 (right to vote for Representatives);

U.S. Const., Amdt. XVII (right to vote for Senators); 28 U.S.C. §1865 (right to serve on a jury); consideration of the possible relevance of 18 U.S.C. §925(c) (1988 ed., Supp. IV), which allows the Secretary of the Treasury to grant relief from the disability imposed by §922(g); and the determination whether civil rights must be restored by an affirmative act of a Government official, see United States v. Ramos, 961 F.2d 1003, 1008 (CA1), cert. denied, 506 U.S. 934, 121 L. Ed. 2d 277, 113 S. Ct. 364 (1992), or whether they may be restored automatically by operation of law, see United States v. Hall, 20 F.3d 1066 (CA10 1994). We do not address these matters today.

Because the statutory language is unambiguous, the rule of lenity, which petitioners urge us to employ here, is inapplicable. See Chapman v. United States, 500 U.S. 453, 463-464, 114 L. Ed. 2d 524, 111 S. Ct. 1919 (1991). Of course, by denying the existence of an ambiguity, we do not claim to be perfectly certain that we have divined Congress' intentions as to this particular situation. It is possible that the phrases on which our reading of the statute turns -- "what constitutes a conviction" and "shall not be considered a conviction" -- were accidents of statutory drafting; it is possible that some legislators thought the two sentences of §921(a)(20) should be read separately, or, more likely, that they never considered the matter at all. And we recognize that in enacting the choice-of-law clause, legislators may have been simply responding to our decision in Dickerson v. New Banner Institute, Inc., 460 U.S. 103, 74 L. Ed. 2d 845, 103 S. Ct. 986 (1983), which held that federal law rather than state law controls the definition of what constitutes a conviction, not setting forth a choice-of-law principle for the restoration of civil rights following a conviction.

But our task is not the hopeless one of ascertaining what the legislators who passed the law would have decided had they reconvened to consider petitioners' particular cases. Rather, it is to determine whether the language the legislators actually enacted has a plain, unambiguous meaning. In this instance, we believe it does.

III

We therefore conclude that petitioners can take advantage of §921(a)(20) only if they have had their civil rights restored under federal law

We therefore conclude that petitioners can take advantage of §921(a)(20) only if they have had their civil rights restored under federal law, and accordingly affirm the judgment of the Court of Appeals.

So ordered.

CUSTIS v. UNITED STATES

(CASE EXCERPT)

511 U.S. 485; 114 S. Ct. 1732; 128 L. Ed. 2d 517

February 28, 1994, Argued

May 23, 1994, Decided

GIST: Custis was convicted at trial of possession of a firearm by a felon. The government used two state convictions to enhance his sentence under the Armed Career Criminal Act of 1984. Custis challenged the use of the state convictions on the grounds that his constitutional rights were violated during those trials. The Court held that a defendant may not challenge the validity of a prior conviction in a federal sentencing hearing.

CHIEF JUSTICE REHNQUIST delivered the opinion of the Court.

The Armed Career Criminal Act of 1984, 18 U.S.C. §924(e) (ACCA), raises the penalty for possession of a firearm by a felon from a maximum of 10 years in prison to a mandatory minimum sentence of 15 years and a maximum of life in prison without parole if the defendant "has three previous convictions . . . for a violent felony or a serious drug offense." We granted certiorari to determine whether a defendant in a federal sentencing proceeding may collaterally attack the validity of previous state convictions that are used to enhance his sentence under the ACCA. We hold that a defendant has no such right (with the sole exception of convictions obtained in violation of the right to counsel) to collaterally attack prior convictions.

STAPLES v. UNITED STATES

(FULL CASE)

511 U.S. 600; 114 S. Ct. 1793; 128 L. Ed. 2d 608

November 30, 1993, Argued

May 23, 1994, Decided

GIST: Possession of an unregistered machine gun is illegal under the National Firearms Act of 1934. Staples was charged under this law when officers discovered his semiautomatic AR-15 rifle, that had been modified to enable automatic fire. The Court held that a conviction under this law requires proof that the defendant knew that the rifle was capable of automatic fire. The Court expresses discomfort several times with the government's zeal in prosecuting gun owners who have no guilty state of mind, or *mens rea,* just possession of a weapon they either do not know the characteristics of, or do not recognize as a specially regulated type of device. The Court takes the stance that, because guns are so commonly owned in this country, and so widely held historically to be legal at state and federal levels, that people would not automatically equate a gun with wrongdoing, as the government suggests. They reject the argument that dangerousness automatically implies regulatory control.

In concurrence, Justice Ginsburg, joined by O'Connor, implies that widespread legal gun ownership exists because Congress and the states have allowed it to persist. In dissent, Justices Stevens and Blackmun take some of the most anti-rights positions in all these cases, and condone the possibility of some injustice in protecting the public safety.

The case has particular significance in the number of times and certainty with which the Court states that gun ownership is and has always been widespread and lawful in the United States.

The National Firearms Act criminalizes possession of an unregistered "firearm," 26 U.S.C. §5861(d), including a "machinegun," §5845(a)(6), which is defined as a weapon that automatically fires more than one shot with a single pull of the trigger, §5845(b). Petitioner Staples was charged with possessing an unregistered machinegun in violation of §5861(d) after officers searching his home seized a semiautomatic rifle -- i.e., a weapon that normally fires only one shot with each trigger pull -- that had apparently been modified for fully automatic fire. At trial, Staples testified that the rifle had never fired automatically while he possessed it and that he had been ignorant of any automatic firing capability. He was convicted after the District Court rejected his proposed jury instruction under which, to establish a §5861(d) violation, the Government would have been required to prove beyond a reasonable doubt that Staples knew that the gun would fire fully automatically. The Court of Appeals affirmed, concluding that the Government need not prove a defendant's knowledge of a weapon's physical properties to obtain a conviction under §5861(d).

Held: To obtain a §5861(d) conviction, the Government should have been required to prove beyond a reasonable doubt that Staples knew that his rifle had the characteristics that brought it within the statutory definition of a machinegun.

(a) The common-law rule requiring mens rea as an element of a crime informs interpretation of §5861(d) in this case. Because some indication of congressional intent, express or implied, is required to dispense with mens rea, §5861(d)'s silence on the element of knowledge required for a conviction does not suggest that Congress intended to dispense with a conventional mens rea requirement, which would require that the defendant know the facts making his conduct illegal.

(b) The Court rejects the Government's argument that the Act fits within the Court's line of precedent concerning "public welfare" or "regulatory" offenses and thus that the presumption favoring mens rea does not apply in this case. In cases concerning public welfare offenses, the Court has inferred from silence a congressional intent to dispense with conventional mens rea requirements in statutes that regulate

potentially harmful or injurious items. In such cases, the Court has reasoned that as long as a defendant knows that he is dealing with a dangerous device of a character that places him in responsible relation to a public danger, he should be alerted to the probability of strict regulation, and is placed on notice that he must determine at his peril whether his conduct comes within the statute's inhibition. See, e.g., United States v. Balint, 258 U.S. 250, 66 L. Ed. 604, 42 S. Ct. 301; United States v. Freed, 401 U.S. 601, 28 L. Ed. 2d 356, 91 S. Ct. 1112. Guns, however, do not fall within the category of dangerous devices as it has been developed in public welfare offense cases. In contrast to the selling of dangerous drugs at issue in Balint or the possession of hand grenades considered in Freed, private ownership of guns in this country has enjoyed a long tradition of being entirely lawful conduct. Thus, the destructive potential of guns in general cannot be said to put gun owners sufficiently on notice of the likelihood of regulation to justify interpreting §5861(d) as dispensing with proof of knowledge of the characteristics that make a weapon a "firearm" under the statute. The Government's interpretation potentially would impose criminal sanctions on a class of persons whose mental state -- ignorance of the characteristics of weapons in their possession -- makes their actions entirely innocent. Had Congress intended to make outlaws of such citizens, it would have spoken more clearly to that effect.

(c) The potentially harsh penalty attached to violation of §5861(d) -- up to 10 years' imprisonment -- confirms the foregoing reading of the Act. Where, as here, dispensing with mens rea would require the defendant to have knowledge only of traditionally lawful conduct, a severe penalty is a further factor tending to suggest that Congress did not intend to eliminate a mens rea requirement.

(d) The holding here is a narrow one that depends on a commonsense evaluation of the nature of the particular device Congress has subjected to regulation, the expectations that individuals may legitimately have in dealing with that device, and the penalty attached to a violation. It does not set forth comprehensive criteria for distinguishing between crimes that require a mental element and crimes that do not.

JUSTICE THOMAS delivered the opinion of the Court.

Petitioner contends that, to convict him under the Act, the Government should have been required to prove beyond a reasonable doubt that he knew the weapon he possessed had the characteristics that brought it within the statutory definition of a machinegun. We agree and accordingly reverse the judgment of the Court of Appeals.

The National Firearms Act makes it unlawful for any person to possess a machinegun that is not properly registered with the Federal Government. Petitioner contends that, to convict him under the Act, the Government should have been required to prove beyond a reasonable doubt that he knew the weapon he possessed had the characteristics that brought it within the statutory definition of a machinegun. We agree and accordingly reverse the judgment of the Court of Appeals.

I

The National Firearms Act (Act), 26 U.S.C. §§5801-5872, imposes strict registration requirements on statutorily defined "firearms." The Act includes within the term "firearm" a machinegun, §5845(a)(6), and further defines a machinegun as "any weapon which shoots, . . . or can be readily restored to shoot, automatically more than one shot, without manual reloading, by a single function of the trigger," §5845(b). Thus, any fully automatic weapon is a "firearm" within the meaning of the Act. n1 Under the Act, all firearms must be registered in the National Firearms Registration and Transfer Record maintained by the Secretary of the Treasury. §5841. Section 5861(d) makes it a crime, punishable by up to 10 years in prison, see §5871, for any person to possess a firearm that is not properly registered.

n1 As used here, the terms "automatic" and "fully automatic" refer to a weapon that fires repeatedly with a single pull of the trigger. That is, once its trigger is depressed, the weapon will automatically continue to fire until its trigger is released or the ammunition is exhausted. Such weapons are "machineguns" within the meaning of the Act. We use the term "semiautomatic" to designate a weapon that fires only one shot with each pull of the trigger, and which requires no manual manipulation by the operator to place another round in the chamber after each round is fired.

the AR-15 is manufactured with a metal stop on its receiver that will prevent an M-16 selector switch, if installed, from rotating to the fully automatic position. The metal stop on petitioner's rifle, however, had been filed away, and the rifle had been assembled with an M-16 selector switch and several other M-16 internal parts, including a hammer, disconnector, and trigger.

Upon executing a search warrant at petitioner's home, local police and agents of the Bureau of Alcohol, Tobacco and Firearms (BATF) recovered, among other things, an AR-15 rifle. The AR-15 is the civilian version of the military's M-16 rifle, and is, unless modified, a semiautomatic weapon. The M-16, in contrast, is a selective fire rifle that allows the operator, by rotating a selector switch, to choose semiautomatic or automatic fire. Many M-16 parts are interchangeable with those in the AR-15 and can be used to convert the AR-15 into an automatic weapon. No doubt to inhibit such conversions, the AR-15 is manufactured with a metal stop on its receiver that will prevent an M-16 selector switch, if installed, from rotating to the fully automatic position. The metal stop on petitioner's rifle, however, had been filed away, and the rifle had been assembled with an M-16 selector switch and several other M-16 internal parts, including a hammer, disconnector, and trigger. Suspecting that the AR-15 had been modified to be capable of fully automatic fire, BATF agents seized the weapon. Petitioner subsequently was indicted for unlawful possession of an unregistered machinegun in violation of §5861(d).

BATF agents testified that when the AR-15 was tested, it fired more than one shot with a single pull of the trigger.

Petitioner testified that the rifle had never fired automatically when it was in his possession.

According to petitioner, his alleged ignorance of any automatic firing capability should have shielded him from criminal liability for his failure to register the weapon.

At trial, BATF agents testified that when the AR-15 was tested, it fired more than one shot with a single pull of the trigger. It was undisputed that the weapon was not registered as required by §5861(d). Petitioner testified that the rifle had never fired automatically when it was in his possession. He insisted that the AR-15 had operated only semiautomatically, and even then imperfectly, often requiring manual ejection of the spent casing and chambering of the next round. According to petitioner, his alleged ignorance of any automatic firing capability should have shielded him from criminal liability for his failure to register the weapon. He requested the District Court to instruct the jury that, to establish a violation of §5861(d), the Government must prove beyond a reasonable doubt that the defendant "knew that the gun would fire fully automatically." 1 App. to Brief for Appellant in No. 91-5033 (CA10), p. 42.

The District Court rejected petitioner's proposed instruction and instead charged the jury as follows:

"The Government need not prove the defendant knows he's dealing with a weapon possessing every last characteristic [which subjects it] n2 to the regulation. It would be enough to prove he knows that he is dealing with a dangerous device of a type as would alert one to the likelihood of regulation." Tr. 465.

Petitioner was convicted and sentenced to five years' probation and a $5,000 fine.

n2 In what the parties regard as a mistranscription, the transcript contains the word "suggested" instead of "which subjects it."

The Court of Appeals affirmed. Relying on its decision in United States v. Mittleider, 835 F.2d 769 (CA10 1987), cert. denied, 485 U.S. 980, 99 L. Ed. 2d 490, 108 S. Ct. 1279 (1988), the court concluded that the Government need not prove a defendant's knowledge of a weapon's physical properties to obtain a conviction under §5861(d). 971 F.2d 608, 612-613 (CA10 1992). We granted certiorari, 508 U.S. 939 (1993), to resolve a conflict in the Courts of Appeals concerning the mens rea required under §5861(d).

II

A

Whether or not §5861(d) requires proof that a defendant knew of the characteristics of his weapon that made it a "firearm" under the Act is a question of statutory construction. As we observed in Liparota v. United States, 471 U.S. 419, 85 L. Ed. 2d 434, 105 S. Ct. 2084 (1985), "the definition of the elements of a criminal offense is entrusted to the legislature, particularly in the case of federal crimes, which are solely creatures of statute." Id., at 424 (citing United States v. Hudson, 11 U.S. 32, 7 Cranch 32, 3 L. Ed. 259 (1812)). Thus, we have long recognized that determining the mental state required for commission of a federal crime requires "construction of the statute and . . . inference of the intent of Congress." United States v. Balint, 258 U.S. 250, 253, 66 L. Ed. 604, 42 S. Ct. 301 (1922). See also Liparota, supra, at 423.

The language of the statute, the starting place in our inquiry, see Connecticut Nat. Bank v. Germain, 503 U.S. 249, 253-254, 117 L. Ed. 2d 391, 112 S. Ct. 1146 (1992), provides little explicit guidance in this case. Section 5861(d) is silent concerning the mens rea required for a violation. It states simply that "it shall be unlawful for any person . . . to receive or possess a firearm which is not registered to him in the National Firearms Registration and Transfer Record." 26 U.S.C. §5861(d). Nevertheless, silence on this point by itself does not necessarily suggest that Congress intended to dispense with a conventional mens rea element, which would require that the defendant know the facts that make his conduct illegal. See Balint, supra, at 251 (stating that traditionally, "scienter" was a necessary element in every crime). See also n. 3, infra. On the contrary, we must construe the statute in light of the background rules of the common law, see United States v. United States Gypsum Co., 438 U.S. 422, 436-437, 57 L. Ed. 2d 854, 98 S. Ct. 2864 (1978), in which the requirement of some mens rea for a crime is firmly embedded. As we have observed, "the existence of a mens rea is the rule of, rather than the exception to, the principles of Anglo-American criminal jurisprudence." Id., at 436 (internal quotation marks omitted). See also Morissette v. United States, 342 U.S. 246, 250, 96 L. Ed. 288, 72 S. Ct. 240 (1952) ("The contention that an injury can amount to a crime only when inflicted by intention is no provincial or transient notion. It is as universal and persistent in mature systems of law as belief in freedom of the human will and a consequent ability and duty of the normal individual to choose between good and evil").

There can be no doubt that this established concept has influenced our interpretation of criminal statutes. Indeed, we have noted that the common-law rule requiring mens rea has been "followed in regard to statutory crimes even where the statutory definition did not in terms include it." Balint, supra, 258 U.S. at 251-252. Relying on the strength of the traditional rule, we have stated that offenses that require no mens rea generally are disfavored, Liparota, supra, at 426, and have suggested that some indication of congressional intent, express or implied, is required to dispense with mens rea as an element of a crime. Cf. United States Gypsum, supra, at 438; Morissette, supra, at 263.

According to the Government, however, the nature and purpose of the Act suggest that the presumption favoring mens rea does not apply to this case. The Government argues that Congress intended the Act to regulate and restrict the circulation of dangerous weapons. Consequently, in the Government's view, this case fits in a line of precedent concerning what we have termed "public welfare" or "regulatory" offenses, in which we have understood Congress to impose a form of strict criminal liability through statutes that do not require the defendant to know the facts that make his conduct illegal. In construing such statutes, we have inferred from silence that Congress did not intend to require proof of mens rea to establish an offense.

For example, in Balint, we concluded that the Narcotic Act of 1914, which was intended in part to minimize the spread of addictive drugs by criminalizing undocumented sales of certain narcotics, required proof only that the defendant knew that he was selling drugs, not that he knew the specific items he had sold were "narcotics" within the ambit of the statute. See Balint, supra, at 254. Cf. United States v. Dotterweich, 320 U.S. 277, 281, 88 L. Ed. 48, 64 S. Ct. 134 (1943) (stating in dicta that a statute criminalizing the shipment of adulterated or misbranded drugs did not require knowledge that the items were misbranded or adulterated). As we explained in Dotterweich, Balint dealt with "a now familiar type of legislation whereby penalties serve as effective means of regulation. Such legislation dispenses with the conventional requirement for criminal conduct -- awareness of some wrongdoing." 320 U.S. at 280-281. See also Morissette, supra, 342 U.S. at 252-256.

Such public welfare offenses have been created by Congress, and recognized by this Court, in "limited circumstances." United States Gypsum, supra, at 437. Typically, our cases recognizing such offenses involve statutes that regulate potentially harmful or injurious items. Cf. United States v. International Minerals & Chemical Corp., 402 U.S. 558, 564-565, 29 L. Ed. 2d 178, 91 S. Ct. 1697 (1971) (characterizing Balint and similar cases as involving statutes regulating "dangerous or deleterious devices or products or obnoxious waste materials"). In such situations, we have reasoned that as long as a defendant knows that he is dealing with a dangerous device of a character that places him "in responsible relation to a public danger," Dotterweich, supra, at 281, he should be alerted to the probability of strict regulation, and we have assumed that in such cases Congress intended to place the burden on the defendant to "ascertain at his peril whether [his conduct] comes within the inhibition of the statute." Balint, supra, at 254. Thus, we essentially have relied on the nature of the statute and the particular character of the items regulated to determine whether congressional silence concerning the mental element of the offense should be interpreted as dispensing with conventional mens rea requirements. See generally Morissette, supra, 342 U.S. at 252-260. n3

n3 By interpreting such public welfare offenses to require at least that the defendant know that he is dealing with some dangerous or deleterious substance, we have avoided construing criminal statutes to impose a rigorous form of strict liability. See, e.g., United States v. International Minerals & Chemical Corp., 402 U.S. 558, 563-564, 29 L. Ed. 2d 178, 91 S. Ct. 1697 (1971) (suggesting that if a person shipping acid mistakenly thought that he was shipping distilled water, he would not violate a statute criminalizing undocumented shipping of acids). True strict liability might suggest that the defendant need not know even that he was dealing with a dangerous item. Nevertheless, we have referred to public welfare offenses as "dispensing with" or "eliminating" a mens rea requirement or "mental element," see, e.g., Morissette, 342 U.S. at 250, 263; United States v. Dotterweich, 320 U.S. 277, 281, 88 L. Ed. 48, 64 S. Ct. 134 (1943), and have described them as strict liability crimes, United States v. United States Gypsum Co., 438 U.S. 422, 437, 57 L. Ed. 2d 854, 98 S. Ct. 2864 (1978). While use of the term "strict liability" is really a misnomer, we have interpreted statutes defining public welfare offenses to eliminate the requirement of mens rea; that is, the requirement of a "guilty mind" with respect to an element of a crime. Under such statutes we have not required that the defendant know the facts that make his conduct fit the definition of the offense. Generally speaking, such knowledge is necessary to establish mens rea, as is reflected in the maxim ignorantia facti excusat. See generally J. Hawley & M. McGregor, Criminal Law 26-30

(1899); R. Perkins, Criminal Law 785-786 (2d ed. 1969); G. Williams, Criminal Law: The General Part 113-174 (1953). Cf. Queen v. Tolson, 23 Q. B. 168, 187 (1889) (Stephen, J.) ("It may, I think, be maintained that in every case knowledge of fact [when not appearing in the statute] is to some extent an element of criminality as much as competent age and sanity").

B

The Government argues that §5861(d) defines precisely the sort of regulatory offense described in Balint. In this view, all guns, whether or not they are statutory "firearms," are dangerous devices that put gun owners on notice that they must determine at their hazard whether their weapons come within the scope of the Act. On this understanding, the District Court's instruction in this case was correct, because a conviction can rest simply on proof that a defendant knew he possessed a "firearm" in the ordinary sense of the term.

one would hardly be surprised to learn that possession of hand grenades is not an innocent act.

Grenades, we explained, "are highly dangerous offensive weapons, no less dangerous than the narcotics

The Government seeks support for its position from our decision in United States v. Freed, 401 U.S. 601, 28 L. Ed. 2d 356, 91 S. Ct. 1112 (1971), which involved a prosecution for possession of unregistered grenades under §5861(d). n4 The defendant knew that the items in his possession were grenades, and we concluded that §5861(d) did not require the Government to prove the defendant also knew that the grenades were unregistered. Id., at 609. To be sure, in deciding that mens rea was not required with respect to that element of the offense, we suggested that the Act "is a regulatory measure in the interest of the public safety, which may well be premised on the theory that one would hardly be surprised to learn that possession of hand grenades is not an innocent act." Ibid. Grenades, we explained, "are highly dangerous offensive weapons, no less dangerous than the narcotics involved in United States v. Balint." Ibid. But that reasoning provides little support for dispensing with mens rea in this case.

A grenade is a "firearm" under the Act.

n4 A grenade is a "firearm" under the Act. 26 U.S.C. §§5845(a)(8), 5845(f)(1)(B).

As the Government concedes, Freed did not address the issue presented here. In Freed, we decided only that §5861(d) does not require proof of knowledge that a firearm is unregistered. The question presented by a defendant who possesses a weapon that is a "firearm" for purposes of the Act, but who knows only that he has a "firearm" in the general sense of the term, was not raised or considered. And our determination that a defendant need not know that his weapon is unregistered suggests no conclusion concerning whether §5861(d) requires the defendant to know of the features that make his weapon a statutory "firearm"; different elements of the same offense can require different mental states. See Liparota, 471 U.S. at 423, n. 5; United States v. Bailey, 444 U.S. 394, 405-406, 62 L. Ed. 2d 575, 100 S. Ct. 624 (1980). See also W. La-Fave & A. Scott, Handbook on Criminal Law 194-195 (1972). Moreover, our analysis in Freed likening the Act to the public welfare statute in Balint rested entirely on the assumption that the defendant knew that he was dealing with hand grenades -- that is, that he knew he possessed a particularly dangerous type of weapon (one within the statutory definition of a "firearm"), possession of which was not entirely "innocent" in and of itself. 401 U.S. at 609. The predicate for that analysis is eliminated when, as in this case, the very question to be decided is whether the defendant must know of the particular characteristics that make his weapon a statutory firearm.

the Government urges that Freed's logic applies because guns, no less than grenades, are highly dangerous devices that should alert their owners to the probability of regulation. But the gap between Freed and this case is too wide to bridge. In glossing over the distinction between grenades and guns, the Government ignores the particular care we have taken to avoid construing a statute to dispense with mens rea where doing so would "criminalize a broad range of apparently innocent conduct."

Notwithstanding these distinctions, the Government urges that Freed's logic applies because guns, no less than grenades, are highly dangerous devices that should alert their owners to the probability of regulation. But the gap between Freed and this case is too wide to bridge. In glossing over the distinction between grenades and guns, the Government ignores the particular care we have taken to avoid construing a statute to dispense with mens rea where doing so would "criminalize a broad range of apparently innocent conduct." Liparota, 471 U.S. at 426. In Liparota, we considered a statute that made unlawful the unauthorized acquisition or possession of food stamps. We determined that the statute required proof that the defendant knew his possession of food stamps was unauthorized, largely because dispensing with such a mens rea requirement would have resulted in reading the statute to outlaw a number of apparently innocent acts. Ibid. Our conclusion that the statute should not be treated as defining a public welfare offense rested on the commonsense distinction that a "food stamp can hardly be compared to a hand grenade." Id., at 433.

Neither, in our view, can all guns be compared to hand grenades

the fact remains that there is a long tradition of widespread lawful gun ownership by private individuals in this country.

Here, the Government essentially suggests that we should interpret the section under the altogether different assumption that "one would hardly be surprised to learn that owning a gun is not an innocent act." That proposition is simply not supported by common experience. Guns in general are not "deleterious devices or products or obnoxious waste materials" that put their owners on notice that they stand "in responsible relation to a public danger."

Neither, in our view, can all guns be compared to hand grenades. Although the contrast is certainly not as stark as that presented in Liparota, the fact remains that there is a long tradition of widespread lawful gun ownership by private individuals in this country. Such a tradition did not apply to the possession of hand grenades in Freed or to the selling of dangerous drugs that we considered in Balint. See also International Minerals, 402 U.S. at 563-565; Balint, 258 U.S. at 254. In fact, in Freed we construed §5861(d) under the assumption that "one would hardly be surprised to learn that possession of hand grenades is not an innocent act." Freed, supra, at 609. Here, the Government essentially suggests that we should interpret the section under the altogether different assumption that "one would hardly be surprised to learn that owning a gun is not an innocent act." That proposition is simply not supported by common experience. Guns in general are not "deleterious devices or products or obnoxious waste materials," International Minerals, supra, 402 U.S. at 565, that put their owners on notice that they stand "in responsible relation to a public danger," Dotterweich, 320 U.S. at 281.

that an item is "dangerous," in some general sense, does not necessarily suggest, as the Government seems to assume, that it is not also entirely innocent.

As suggested above, despite their potential for harm, guns generally can be owned in perfect innocence.

we might surely classify certain categories of guns—no doubt including the machineguns, sawed-off shotguns, and artillery pieces that Congress has subjected to regulation—as items the ownership of which would have the same quasi-suspect character we attributed to owning hand grenades in Freed.

guns falling outside those categories traditionally have been widely accepted as lawful possessions

The Government protests that guns, unlike food stamps, but like grenades and narcotics, are potentially harmful devices. n5 Under this view, it seems that Liparota's concern for criminalizing ostensibly innocuous conduct is inapplicable whenever an item is sufficiently dangerous -- that is, dangerousness alone should alert an individual to probable regulation and justify treating a statute that regulates the dangerous device as dispensing with mens rea. But that an item is "dangerous," in some general sense, does not necessarily suggest, as the Government seems to assume, that it is not also entirely innocent. Even dangerous items can, in some cases, be so commonplace and generally available that we would not consider them to alert individuals to the likelihood of strict regulation. As suggested above, despite their potential for harm, guns generally can be owned in perfect innocence. Of course, we might surely classify certain categories of guns -- no doubt including the machineguns, sawed-off shotguns, and artillery pieces that Congress has subjected to regulation -- as items the ownership of which would have the same quasi-suspect character we attributed to owning hand grenades in Freed. But precisely because guns falling outside those categories traditionally have been widely accepted as lawful possessions, their destructive potential, while perhaps even greater than that of some items we would classify along with narcotics and hand grenades, cannot be said to put gun owners sufficiently on notice of the likelihood of regulation to justify interpreting §5861(d) as not requiring proof of knowledge of a weapon's characteristics. n6

n5 The dissent's assertions to the contrary notwithstanding, the Government's position, "accurately identified," post, at 632, is precisely that "guns in general" are dangerous items. The Government, like the dissent, cites Sipes v. United States, 321 F.2d 174, 179 (CA8), cert. denied, 375 U.S. 913, 11 L. Ed. 2d 150, 84 S. Ct. 208 (1963), for the proposition that a defendant's knowledge that the item he possessed "was a gun" is sufficient for a conviction under §5861(d). Brief for United States 21. Indeed, the Government argues that "guns" should be placed in the same category as the misbranded drugs in Dotterweich and the narcotics in Balint because "'one would hardly be surprised to learn' (Freed, 401 U.S. at 609) that there are laws that affect one's rights of gun ownership." Brief for United States 22. The dissent relies upon the Government's repeated contention that the statute requires knowledge that "the item at issue was highly dangerous and of a type likely to be subject to regulation." Id., at 9. But that assertion merely patterns the general language we have used to describe the mens rea requirement in public welfare offenses and amounts to no more than an assertion that the statute should be treated as defining a public welfare offense.

The dissent asserts that the question is not whether all guns are deleterious devices, but whether a gun "such as the one possessed by petitioner," is such a device. If the dissent intends to suggest that the category of readily convertible semiautomatics provides the benchmark for defining the knowledge requirement for §5861(d), it is difficult to see how it derives that class of weapons as a standard.

The parties assume that virtually all semiautomatics may be converted into automatics, and limiting the class to those "readily" convertible provides no real guidance

n6 The dissent asserts that the question is not whether all guns are deleterious devices, but whether a gun "such as the one possessed by petitioner," post, at 632 (which the dissent characterizes as a "semiautomatic weapon that [is] readily convertible into a machinegun," post, at 624, 633, 640), is such a device. If the dissent intends to suggest that the category of readily convertible semiautomatics provides the benchmark for defining the knowledge requirement for §5861(d), it is difficult to see how it derives that class of weapons as a standard. As explained above, see n. 5, supra, the Government's argument has nothing to do with this ad hoc category of weapons. And the statute certainly does not suggest that any significance should attach to readily convertible semiautomatics, for that class bears no relation to the definitions in the Act. Indeed, in the absence of any definition, it is not at all clear what the contours of this category would be. The parties assume that virtually all semiautomatics may be converted into automatics, and limiting the class to those "readily" convertible provides no real guidance concerning the required mens rea. In short, every owner of a semiautomatic rifle or handgun would potentially meet such a mens rea test.

But the dissent apparently does not conceive of the mens rea requirement in terms of specific categories of weapons at all, and rather views it as a more fluid concept that does not require delineation of any concrete elements of knowledge that will apply consistently from case to case. The dissent sees no need to define a class of items the knowing possession of which satisfies the mens rea element of the offense, for in the dissent's view the exact content of the knowledge requirement can be left to the jury in each case. As long as the jury concludes that the item in a given case is "sufficiently dangerous to alert [the defendant] to the likelihood of regulation," post, at 637, the knowledge requirement is satisfied. See also post, at 624, 639, 640. But the mens rea requirement under a criminal statute is a question of law, to be determined by the court. Our decisions suggesting that public welfare offenses require that the defendant know that he stands in "responsible relation to a public danger," Dotterweich, 320 U.S. at 281, in no way suggest that what constitutes a public danger is a jury question. It is for courts, through interpretation of the statute, to define the mens rea required for a conviction. That task cannot be reduced to setting a general "standard," post, at 637, that leaves it to the jury to determine, based presumably on the jurors' personal opinions, whether the items involved in a particular prosecution are sufficiently dangerous to place a person on notice of regulation.

Moreover, as our discussion above should make clear, to determine as a threshold matter whether a particular statute defines a public welfare offense, a court must have in view some category of dangerous and deleterious devices that will be assumed to alert an individual that he stands in "responsible relation to a public danger." Dotterweich, supra, at 281. The truncated mens rea requirement we have described applies precisely because the court has determined that the statute regulates in a field where knowing possession of some general class of items should alert individuals to probable regulation. Under the dissent's approach, however, it seems that every regulatory statute potentially could be treated as a public welfare offense as long as the jury -- not the court -- ultimately determines that the specific items involved in a prosecution were sufficiently dangerous.

the Government suggests that guns are subject to an array of regulations at the federal, state, and local levels that put gun owners on notice that they must determine the characteristics of their weapons and comply with all legal requirements.

despite the overlay of legal restrictions on gun ownership, we question whether regulations on guns are sufficiently intrusive that they impinge upon the common experience that owning a gun is usually licit and blameless conduct.

Roughly 50 percent of American homes contain at least one firearm of some sort, and in the vast majority of States, buying a shotgun or rifle is a simple transaction that would not alert a person to regulation any more than would buying a car.

On a slightly different tack, the Government suggests that guns are subject to an array of regulations at the federal, state, and local levels that put gun owners on notice that they must determine the characteristics of their weapons and comply with all legal requirements. n7 But regulation in itself is not sufficient to place gun ownership in the category of the sale of narcotics in Balint. The food stamps at issue in Liparota were subject to comprehensive regulations, yet we did not understand the statute there to dispense with a mens rea requirement. Moreover, despite the overlay of legal restrictions on gun ownership, we question whether regulations on guns are sufficiently intrusive that they impinge upon the common experience that owning a gun is usually licit and blameless conduct. Roughly 50 percent of American homes contain at least one firearm of some sort, n8 and in the vast majority of States, buying a shotgun or rifle is a simple transaction that would not alert a person to regulation any more than would buying a car. n9

n7 See, e.g., 18 U.S.C. §§921-928 (1988 ed. and Supp. IV) (requiring licensing of manufacturers, importers, and dealers of guns and regulating the sale, possession, and interstate transportation of certain guns).

n8 See U.S. Dept. of Justice, Bureau of Justice Statistics, Sourcebook of Criminal Justice Statistics 209 (1992) (Table 2.58).

For example, as of 1990, 39 States allowed adult residents, who are not felons or mentally infirm, to purchase a rifle or shotgun simply with proof of identification (and in some cases a simultaneous application for a permit).

n9 For example, as of 1990, 39 States allowed adult residents, who are not felons or mentally infirm, to purchase a rifle or shotgun simply with proof of identification (and in some cases a simultaneous application for a permit). See U.S. Dept. of Justice, Bureau of Justice Statistics, Identifying Persons, Other Than Felons, Ineligible to Purchase Firearms 114, Exh. B.4 (1990); U.S. Congress, Office of Technology Assessment, Automated Record Checks of Firearm Purchasers 27 (July 1991). See also M. Cooper, Reassessing the Nation's Gun Laws, Editorial Research Reports 158, 160 (Jan.-Mar. 1991) (table) (suggesting the total is 41 States); Dept. of Treasury, Bureau of Alcohol, Tobacco and Firearms, State Laws and Published Ordinances -- Firearms (19th ed. 1989).

If we were to accept as a general rule the Government's suggestion that dangerous and regulated items place their owners under an obligation to inquire at their peril into compliance with regulations, we would undoubtedly reach some untoward results. Automobiles, for example, might also be termed "dangerous" devices and are highly regulated at both the state and federal levels. Congress might see fit to criminalize the violation of certain regulations concerning automobiles, and thus might make it a crime to operate a vehicle without a properly functioning emission control system. But we probably would hesitate to conclude on the basis of silence that Congress intended a prison term to apply to a car owner whose vehicle's emissions levels, wholly unbeknownst to him, began to exceed legal limits between regular inspection dates.

the Government's construction of the statute potentially would impose criminal sanctions on a class of persons whose mental state—ignorance of the characteristics of weapons in their possession—makes their actions entirely innocent.

The Government does not dispute the contention that virtually any semiautomatic weapon may be converted, either by internal modification or, in some cases, simply by wear and tear, into a machinegun within the meaning of the Act. Such a gun may give no externally visible indication that it is fully automatic.

in the Government's view, any person who has purchased what he believes to be a semiautomatic rifle or handgun, or who simply has inherited a gun from a relative and left it untouched in an attic or basement, can be subject to imprisonment, despite absolute ignorance of the gun's firing capabilities, if the gun turns out to be an automatic.

Here, there can be little doubt that, as in Liparota, the Government's construction of the statute potentially would impose criminal sanctions on a class of persons whose mental state -- ignorance of the characteristics of weapons in their possession -- makes their actions entirely innocent. n10 The Government does not dispute the contention that virtually any semiautomatic weapon may be converted, either by internal modification or, in some cases, simply by wear and tear, into a machinegun within the meaning of the Act. Cf. United States v. Anderson, 885 F.2d 1248, 1251, 1253-1254 (CA5 1989) (en banc). Such a gun may give no externally visible indication that it is fully automatic. See United States v. Herbert, 698 F.2d 981, 986 (CA9), cert. denied, 464 U.S. 821, 78 L. Ed. 2d 95, 104 S. Ct. 87 (1983). But in the Government's view, any person who has purchased what he believes to be a semiautomatic rifle or handgun, or who simply has inherited a gun from a relative and left it untouched in an attic or basement, can be subject to imprisonment, despite absolute ignorance of the gun's firing capabilities, if the gun turns out to be an automatic.

n10 We, of course, express no view concerning the inferences a jury may have drawn regarding petitioner's knowledge from the evidence in this case.

It is unthinkable to us that Congress intended to subject such law-abiding, well-intentioned citizens to a possible ten-year term of imprisonment if . . . what they genuinely and reasonably believed was a conventional semi-automatic [weapon] turns out to have worn down into or been secretly modified to be a fully automatic weapon.

the "purpose and obvious effect of doing away with the requirement of a guilty intent is to ease the prosecution's path to conviction."

We concur in the Fifth Circuit's conclusion on this point: "It is unthinkable to us that Congress intended to subject such law-abiding, well-intentioned citizens to a possible ten-year term of imprisonment if . . . what they genuinely and reasonably believed was a conventional semi-automatic [weapon] turns out to have worn down into or been secretly modified to be a fully automatic weapon." Anderson, supra, at 1254. As we noted in Morissette, the "purpose and obvious effect of doing away with the requirement of a guilty intent is to ease the prosecution's path to conviction." 342 U.S. at 263. n11 We are reluctant to impute that purpose to Congress where, as here, it would mean easing the path to convicting persons whose conduct would not even alert them to the probability of strict regulation in the form of a statute such as §5861(d).

The Government contends that Congress intended precisely such an aid to obtaining convictions, because requiring proof of knowledge would place too heavy a burden on the Government

firing a fully automatic weapon would make the regulated characteristics of the weapon immediately apparent to its owner.

we are confident that when the defendant knows of the characteristics of his weapon that bring it within the scope of the Act, the Government will not face great difficulty in proving that knowledge. Of course, if Congress thinks it necessary to reduce the Government's burden at trial to ensure proper enforcement of the Act, it remains free to amend §5861(d) by explicitly eliminating a mens rea requirement.

n11 The Government contends that Congress intended precisely such an aid to obtaining convictions, because requiring proof of knowledge would place too heavy a burden on the Government and obstruct the proper functioning of §5861(d). Cf. United States v. Balint, 258 U.S. 250, 254, 66 L. Ed. 604, 42 S. Ct. 301 (1922) (difficulty of proving knowledge suggests Congress did not intend to require mens rea). But knowledge can be inferred from circumstantial evidence, including any external indications signaling the nature of the weapon. And firing a fully automatic weapon would make the regulated characteristics of the weapon immediately apparent to its owner. In short, we are confident that when the defendant knows of the characteristics of his weapon that bring it within the scope of the Act, the Government will not face great difficulty in proving that knowledge. Of course, if Congress thinks it necessary to reduce the Government's burden at trial to ensure proper enforcement of the Act, it remains free to amend §5861(d) by explicitly eliminating a mens rea requirement.

C

The potentially harsh penalty attached to violation of §5861(d) -- up to 10 years' imprisonment -- confirms our reading of the Act. Historically, the penalty imposed under a statute has been a significant consideration in determining whether the statute should be construed as dispensing with mens rea. Certainly, the cases that first defined the concept of the public welfare offense almost uniformly involved statutes that provided for only light penalties such as fines or short jail sentences, not imprisonment in the state penitentiary. See, e.g., Commonwealth v. Raymond, 97 Mass. 567 (1867) (fine of up to $200 or six months in jail, or both); Commonwealth v. Farren, 91 Mass. 489 (1864) (fine); People v. Snowburger, 113 Mich. 86, 71 N.W. 497 (1897) (fine of up to $500 or incarceration in county jail). n12

n12 Leading English cases developing a parallel theory of regulatory offenses similarly involved violations punishable only by fine or short-term incarceration. See, e.g., Queen v. Woodrow, 15 M. & W. 404, 153 Eng. Rep. 907 (Ex. 1846) (fine of # 200 for adulterated tobacco); Hobbs v. Winchester Corp., [1910] 2 K. B. 471 (maximum penalty of three months' imprisonment for sale of unwholesome meat).

As commentators have pointed out, the small penalties attached to such offenses logically complemented the absence of a mens rea requirement: In a system that generally requires a "vicious will" to establish a crime, 4 W. Blackstone, Commentaries * 21, imposing severe punishments for offenses that require no mens rea would seem incongruous. See Sayre, Public Welfare Offenses, 33 Colum. L. Rev. 55, 70 (1933). Indeed, some courts justified the absence of mens rea in part on the basis that the offenses did not bear the same punishments as "infamous crimes," Tenement House Dept. v. McDevitt, 215 N.Y. 160, 168, 109 N.E. 88, 90 (1915) (Cardozo, J.), and questioned whether imprisonment was compatible with the reduced culpability required for such regulatory offenses. See, e.g., People ex rel. Price v. Sheffield Farms-Slawson-Decker Co., 225 N.Y. 25, 32-33, 121 N.E. 474, 477 (1918) (Cardozo, J.); id., at 35, 121 N.E. at 478 (Crane, J., concurring) (arguing that imprisonment for a crime that requires no mens rea would stretch the law regarding acts mala prohibita beyond its limitations). n13 Similarly, commentators collecting the early cases have argued that offenses punishable by imprisonment cannot be understood to be public welfare offenses, but must require mens rea. See R. Perkins, Criminal Law 793-798 (2d ed. 1969) (suggesting that the penalty should be the starting point in determining whether a statute describes a public welfare offense); Sayre, supra, at 72 ("Crimes punishable with prison sentences . . . ordinarily require proof of a guilty intent"). n14

n13 Cf. Queen v. Tolson, 23 QB at 177 (Wills, J.) (In determining whether a criminal statute dispenses with mens rea, "the nature and extent of the penalty attached to the offence may reasonably be considered. There is nothing that need shock any mind in the payment of a small pecuniary penalty by a person who has unwittingly done something detrimental to the public interest").

n14 But see, e.g., State v. Lindberg, 125 Wash. 51, 215 P. 41 (1923) (applying the public welfare offense rationale to a felony).

In rehearsing the characteristics of the public welfare offense, we, too, have included in our consideration the punishments imposed and have noted that "penalties commonly are relatively small, and conviction does no grave damage to an offender's reputation." Morissette, 342 U.S. at 256. n15 We have even recognized that it was "under such considerations" that courts have construed statutes to dispense with mens rea. Ibid.

n15 See also United States Gypsum, 438 U.S. at 442, n. 18 (noting that an individual violation of the Sherman Antitrust Act is a felony punishable by three years in prison or a fine not exceeding $100,000 and stating that "the severity of these sanctions provides further support for our conclusion that the [Act] should not be construed as creating strict-liability crimes"). Cf. Holdridge v. United States, 282 F.2d 302, 310 (CA8 1960) (Blackmun, J.) ("Where a federal criminal statute omits mention of intent and . . . where the penalty is relatively small, where conviction does not gravely besmirch, [and] where the statutory crime is not one taken over from the common law, . . . the statute can be construed as one not requiring criminal intent").

Our characterization of the public welfare offense in Morissette hardly seems apt, however, for a crime that is a felony, as is violation of §5861(d). n16 After all, "felony" is, as we noted in distinguishing certain common-law crimes from public welfare offenses, "'as bad a word as you can give to man or thing.'" Id., 342 U.S. at 260 (quoting 2 F. Pollock & F. Maitland, History of English Law 465 (2d ed. 1899)). Close adherence to the early cases described above might suggest that punishing a violation as a felony is simply incompatible with the theory of the public welfare offense. In this view, absent a clear statement from Congress that mens rea is not required, we should not apply the public welfare offense rationale to interpret any statute defining a felony offense as dispensing with mens rea. But see United States v. Balint, 258 U.S. 250, 66 L. Ed. 604, 42 S. Ct. 301 (1922).

n16 Title 18 U.S.C. §3559 makes any crime punishable by more than one year in prison a felony.

We need not adopt such a definitive rule of construction to decide this case, however. Instead, we note only that where, as here, dispensing with mens rea would require the defendant to have knowledge only of traditionally lawful conduct, a severe penalty is a further factor tending to suggest that Congress did not intend to eliminate a mens rea requirement. In such a case, the usual presumption that a defendant must know the facts that make his conduct illegal should apply.

III

the Government should have been required to prove that petitioner knew of the features of his AR-15 that brought it within the scope of the Act.

In short, we conclude that the background rule of the common law favoring mens rea should govern interpretation of §5861(d) in this case. Silence does not suggest that Congress dispensed with mens rea for the element of §5861(d) at issue here. Thus, to obtain a conviction, the Government should have been required to prove that petitioner knew of the features of his AR-15 that brought it within the scope of the Act. n17

n17 In reaching our conclusion, we find it unnecessary to rely on the rule of lenity, under which an ambiguous criminal statute is to be construed in favor of the accused. That maxim of construction "is reserved for cases where, 'after "seizing every thing from which aid can be derived,"' the Court is 'left with an ambiguous statute.'" Smith v. United States, 508 U.S. 223, 239, 124 L. Ed. 2d 138, 113 S. Ct. 2050 (1993) (quoting United States v. Bass, 404 U.S. 336, 347, 30 L. Ed. 2d 488, 92 S. Ct. 515 (1971), in turn quoting United States v. Fisher, 6 U.S. 358, 2 Cranch 358, 386, 2 L. Ed. 304 (1805)). See also United States v. R. L. C., 503 U.S. 291, 311, 112 S. Ct. 1329, 117 L. Ed. 2d 559 (1992) (THOMAS, J., concurring in part and concurring in judgment); Chapman v. United States, 500 U.S. 453, 463, 114 L. Ed. 2d 524, 111 S. Ct. 1919 (1991) (rule of lenity inapplicable unless there is a "'grievous ambiguity or uncertainty'" in the statute). Here, the background rule of the common law favoring mens rea and the substantial body of precedent we have developed construing statutes that do not specify a mental element provide considerable interpretive tools from which we can "seize aid," and they do not leave us with the ultimate impression that §5861(d) is "grievously" ambiguous. Certainly, we have not concluded in the past that statutes silent with respect to mens rea are ambiguous. See, e.g., United States v. Balint, 258 U.S. 250, 66 L. Ed. 604, 42 S. Ct. 301 (1922).

if Congress had intended to make outlaws of gun owners who were wholly ignorant of the offending characteristics of their weapons, and to subject them to lengthy prison terms, it would have spoken more clearly to that effect.

We emphasize that our holding is a narrow one. As in our prior cases, our reasoning depends upon a commonsense evaluation of the nature of the particular device or substance Congress has subjected to regulation and the expectations that individuals may legitimately have in dealing with the regulated items. In addition, we think that the penalty attached to §5861(d) suggests that Congress did not intend to eliminate a mens rea requirement for violation of the section. As we noted in Morissette: "Neither this Court nor, so far as we are aware, any other has undertaken to delineate a precise line or set forth comprehensive criteria for distinguishing between crimes that require a mental element and crimes that do not." 342 U.S. at 260. We attempt no definition here, either. We note only that our holding depends critically on our view that if Congress had intended to make outlaws of gun owners who were wholly ignorant of the offending characteristics of their weapons, and to subject them to lengthy prison terms, it would have spoken more clearly to that effect. Cf. United States v. Harris, 294 U.S. App. D.C. 300, 959 F.2d 246, 261 (CADC), cert. denied, 506 U.S. 932 (1992).

For the foregoing reasons, the judgment of the Court of Appeals is reversed, and the case is remanded for further proceedings consistent with this opinion.

So ordered.

JUSTICE GINSBURG, with whom JUSTICE O'CONNOR joins, concurring in the judgment.

The statute petitioner Harold E. Staples is charged with violating, 26 U.S.C. §5861(d), makes it a crime for any person to "receive or possess a firearm which is not registered to him." Although the word "knowingly" does not appear in the statute's text, courts generally assume that Congress, absent a contrary indication, means to retain a mens rea requirement. Ante, at 606; see Liparota v. United States, 471 U.S. 419, 426, 85 L. Ed. 2d 434, 105 S. Ct. 2084 (1985); United States v. United States Gypsum Co., 438 U.S. 422, 437-438, 57 L. Ed. 2d 854, 98 S. Ct. 2864 (1978). n1 Thus, our holding in United States v. Freed, 401 U.S. 601, 28 L. Ed. 2d 356, 91 S. Ct. 1112 (1971), that §5861(d) does not require proof of knowledge that the firearm is unregistered, rested on the premise that the defendant indeed knew the items he possessed were hand grenades. Id., at 607; id., at 612 (Brennan, J., concurring in judgment) ("The Government and the Court agree that the prosecutor must prove knowing possession of the items and also knowledge that the items possessed were hand grenades.").

n1 Contrary to the dissent's suggestion, we have not confined the presumption of mens rea to statutes codifying traditional common-law offenses, but have also applied the presumption to offenses that are "entirely a creature of statute," post, at 625, such as those at issue in Liparota, Gypsum, and, most recently, Posters 'N' Things, Ltd. v. United States, ante, at 522-523.

Conviction under §5861(d), the Government accordingly concedes, requires proof that Staples "knowingly" possessed the machinegun. Brief for United States 23. The question before us is not whether knowledge of possession is required, but what level of knowledge suffices: (1) knowledge simply of possession of the object; (2) knowledge, in addition, that the object is a dangerous weapon; (3) knowledge, beyond dangerousness, of the characteristics that render the object subject to regulation, for example, awareness that the weapon is a machinegun. n2

n2 Some Courts of Appeals have adopted a variant of the third reading, holding that the Government must show that the defendant knew the gun was a machinegun, but allowing inference of the requisite knowledge where a visual inspection of the gun would reveal that it has been converted into an automatic weapon. See United States v. O'Mara, 963 F.2d 1288, 1291 (CA9 1992); United States v. Anderson, 885 F.2d 1248, 1251 (CA5 1989) (en banc).

The Government, however, does not take adequate account of the "widespread lawful gun ownership" Congress and the States have allowed to persist in this country.

Recognizing that the first reading effectively dispenses with mens rea, the Government adopts the second, contending that it avoids criminalizing "apparently innocent conduct," Liparota, supra, at 426, because under the second reading, "a defendant who possessed what he thought was a toy or a violin case, but which in fact was a machinegun, could not be convicted." Brief for United States 23. The Government, however, does not take adequate account of the "widespread lawful gun ownership" Congress and the States have allowed to persist in this country. See United States v. Harris, 294 U.S. App. D.C. 300, 959 F.2d 246, 261 (CADC) (per curiam), cert. denied, 506 U.S. 932 (1992). Given the notable lack of comprehensive regulation, "mere unregistered possession of certain types of [regulated weapons] -- often [difficult to distinguish] from other, [nonregulated] types," has been held inadequate to establish the requisite knowledge. See 959 F.2d at 261.

The Nation's legislators chose to place under a registration requirement only a very limited class of firearms, those they considered especially dangerous.

The Nation's legislators chose to place under a registration requirement only a very limited class of firearms, those they considered especially dangerous. The generally "dangerous" character of all guns, the Court therefore observes, ante, at 611-612, did not suffice to give individuals in Staples' situation cause to inquire about the need for registration. Cf. United States v. Balint, 258 U.S. 250, 66 L. Ed. 604, 42 S. Ct. 301 (1922) (requiring reporting of sale of strictly regulated narcotics, opium and cocaine). Only the third reading, then, suits the purpose of the mens rea requirement -- to shield people against punishment for apparently innocent activity. n3

n3 The mens rea presumption requires knowledge only of the facts that make the defendant's conduct illegal, lest it conflict with the related presumption, "deeply rooted in the American legal system," that, ordinarily, "ignorance of the law or a mistake of law is no defense to criminal prosecution." Cheek v. United States, 498 U.S. 192, 199, 112 L. Ed. 2d 617, 111 S. Ct. 604 (1991). Cf. United States v. Freed, 401 U.S. 601, 612, 28 L. Ed. 2d 356, 91 S. Ct. 1112 (1971) (Brennan, J., concurring in judgment) ("If the ancient maxim that 'ignorance of the law is no excuse' has any residual validity, it indicates that the ordinary intent requirement -- mens rea -- of the criminal law does not require knowledge that an act is illegal, wrong, or blameworthy."). The maxim explains why some "innocent" actors -- for example, a defendant who knows he possesses a weapon with all of the characteristics that subject it to registration, but was unaware of the registration requirement, or thought the gun was registered -- may be convicted under §5861(d), see post, at 638. Knowledge of whether the gun was registered is so closely related to knowledge of the registration requirement that requiring the Government to prove the former would in effect require it to prove knowledge of the law. Cf. Freed, supra, 401 U.S. at 612-614 (Brennan, J., concurring in judgment).

The Government can reconcile the jury instruction with the indictment only on the implausible assumption that the term "firearm" has two different meanings when used once in the same charge—simply "gun" when referring to what petitioner knew, and "machinegun" when referring to what he possessed.

The indictment in Staples' case charges that he "knowingly received and possessed firearms." 1 App. to Brief for Appellant in No. 91-5033 (CA10), p. 1. n4 "Firearms" has a circumscribed statutory definition. See 26 U.S.C. §5845(a). The "firearm" the Government contends Staples possessed in violation of §5861(d) is a machinegun. See §5845(a)(6). The indictment thus effectively charged that Staples knowingly possessed a machinegun. "Knowingly possessed" logically means "possessed and knew that he possessed." The Government can reconcile the jury instruction n5 with the indictment only on the implausible assumption that the term "firearm" has two different meanings when used once in the same charge -- simply "gun" when referring to what petitioner knew, and "machinegun" when referring to what he possessed. See Cunningham, Levi, Green, & Kaplan, Plain Meaning and Hard Cases, 103 Yale L. J. 1561, 1576-1577 (1994); cf. Ratzlaf v. United States, 510 U.S. 135, 143, 126 L. Ed. 2d 615, 114 S. Ct. 655 (1994) (construing statutory term to bear same meaning "each time it is called into play").

The indictment charged Staples with possession of two unregistered machineguns, but the jury found him guilty of knowingly possessing only one of them.

n4 The indictment charged Staples with possession of two unregistered machineguns, but the jury found him guilty of knowingly possessing only one of them. Tr. 477.

n5 The trial court instructed the jury:

"[A] person is knowingly in possession of a thing if his possession occurred voluntarily and intentionally and not because of mistake or accident or other innocent reason. The purpose of adding the word 'knowingly' is to insure that no one can be convicted of possession of a firearm he did not intend to possess. The Government need not prove the defendant knows he's dealing with a weapon possessing every last characteristic [which subjects it] to the regulation. It would be enough to prove he knows that he is dealing with a dangerous device of a type as would alert one to the likelihood of regulation. If he has such knowledge and if the particular item is, in fact, regulated, then that person acts at his peril. Mere possession of an unregistered firearm is a violation of the law of the United States, and it is not necessary for the Government to prove that the defendant knew that the weapon in his possession was a firearm within the meaning of the statute, only that he knowingly possessed the firearm." Id., at 465.

For these reasons, I conclude that conviction under §5861(d) requires proof that the defendant knew he possessed not simply a gun, but a machinegun. The indictment in this case, but not the jury instruction, properly described this knowledge requirement. I therefore concur in the Court's judgment.

JUSTICE STEVENS, with whom JUSTICE BLACKMUN joins, dissenting.

To avoid a slight possibility of injustice to unsophisticated owners of machineguns and sawed-off shotguns, the Court has substituted its views of sound policy for the judgment Congress made when it enacted the National Firearms Act

To avoid a slight possibility of injustice to unsophisticated owners of machineguns and sawed-off shotguns, the Court has substituted its views of sound policy for the judgment Congress made when it enacted the National Firearms Act (or Act). Because the Court's addition to the text of 26 U.S.C. §5861(d) is foreclosed by both the statute and our precedent, I respectfully dissent.

The Court is preoccupied with guns that "generally can be owned in perfect innocence."

These are not guns "of some sort" that can be found in almost "50 percent of American homes." Ante, at 613-614. n1 They are particularly dangerous—indeed, a substantial percentage of the unregistered machineguns now in circulation are converted semiautomatic weapons.

The Court is preoccupied with guns that "generally can be owned in perfect innocence." Ante, at 611. This case, however, involves a semiautomatic weapon that was readily convertible into a machinegun -- a weapon that the jury found to be "'a dangerous device of a type as would alert one to the likelihood of regulation.'" Ante, at 604. These are not guns "of some sort" that can be found in almost "50 percent of American homes." Ante, at 613-614. n1 They are particularly dangerous -- indeed, a substantial percentage of the unregistered machineguns now in circulation are converted semiautomatic weapons. n2

only about 15 percent of all the guns in the United States are semiautomatic.

n1 Indeed, only about 15 percent of all the guns in the United States are semiautomatic. See National Rifle Association, Fact Sheet, Semi-Automatic Firearms 1 (Feb. 1, 1994). Although it is not known how many of those weapons are readily convertible into machineguns, it is obviously a lesser share of the total.

over 20 percent of the machineguns seized or purchased by the Bureau of Alcohol, Tobacco and Firearms had been converted from semiautomatic weapons by "simple tool work or the addition of readily available parts"

n2 See U.S. Dept. of Justice, Attorney General's Task Force on Violent Crime: Final Report 29, 32 (Aug. 17, 1981) (stating that over an 18-month period over 20 percent of the machineguns seized or purchased by the Bureau of Alcohol, Tobacco and Firearms had been converted from semiautomatic weapons by "simple tool work or the addition of readily available parts") (citing U.S. Dept. of Treasury, Bureau of Alcohol, Tobacco and Firearms, Firearms Case Summary (Washington: U.S. Govt. Printing Office 1981)).

The question presented is whether the National Firearms Act imposed on the Government the burden of proving beyond a reasonable doubt not only that the defendant knew he possessed a dangerous device sufficient to alert him to regulation, but also that he knew it had all the characteristics of a "firearm" as defined in the statute. Three unambiguous guideposts direct us to the correct answer to that question: the text and structure of the Act, our cases construing both this Act and similar regulatory legislation, and the Act's history and interpretation.

I

Contrary to the assertion by the Court, the text of the statute does provide "explicit guidance in this case." Cf. ante, at 605. The relevant section of the Act makes it "unlawful for any person . . . to receive or possess a firearm which is not registered to him in the National Firearms Registration and Transfer Record." 26 U.S.C. §5861(d). Significantly, the section contains no knowledge requirement, nor does it describe a common-law crime.

The common law generally did not condemn acts as criminal unless the actor had "an evil purpose or mental culpability," Morissette v. United States, 342 U.S. 246, 252, 96 L. Ed. 288, 72 S. Ct. 240 (1952), and was aware of all the facts that made the conduct unlawful, United States v. Balint, 258 U.S. 250, 251-252, 66 L. Ed. 604, 42 S. Ct. 301 (1922). In interpreting statutes that codified traditional common-law offenses, courts usually followed this rule, even when the text of the statute contained no such requirement. Ibid. Because the offense involved in this case is entirely a creature of statute, however, "the background rules of the common law," cf. ante, at 605, do not require a particular construction, and critically different rules of construction apply. See Morissette v. United States, 342 U.S. at 252-260.

In Morissette, Justice Jackson outlined one such interpretive rule:

"Congressional silence as to mental elements in an Act merely adopting into federal statutory law a concept of crime already . . . well defined in common law and statutory interpretation by the states may warrant quite contrary inferences than the same silence in creating an offense new to general law, for whose definition the courts have no guidance except the Act." Id., at 262.

Although the lack of an express knowledge requirement in §5861(d) is not dispositive, see United States v. United States Gypsum Co., 438 U.S. 422, 438, 57 L. Ed. 2d 854, 98 S. Ct. 2864 (1978), its absence suggests that Congress did not intend to require proof that the defendant knew all of the facts that made his conduct illegal. n3

The crime is possessing an unregistered firearm -- not 'knowingly' possessing an unregistered firearm, or possessing a weapon knowing it to be a firearm, or possessing a firearm knowing it to be unregistered. . . . [Petitioner's] proposal is not that we interpret a knowledge or intent requirement in §5861(d); it is that we invent one.

n3 The Seventh Circuit's comment in a similar case is equally apt here: "The crime is possessing an unregistered firearm -- not 'knowingly' possessing an unregistered firearm, or possessing a weapon knowing it to be a firearm, or possessing a firearm knowing it to be unregistered. . . . [Petitioner's] proposal is not that we interpret a knowledge or intent requirement in §5861(d); it is that we invent one." United States v. Ross, 917 F.2d 997, 1000 (1990) (per curiam) (emphasis in original), cert. denied, 498 U.S. 1122, 112 L. Ed. 2d 1183, 111 S. Ct. 1078 (1991).

In 1934, when Congress originally enacted the statute, it limited the coverage of the 1934 Act to a relatively narrow category of weapons such as submachineguns and sawed-off shotguns—weapons characteristically used only by professional gangsters like Al Capone, Pretty Boy Floyd, and their henchmen. At the time, the Act would have had little application to guns used by hunters or guns kept at home as protection against unwelcome intruders. Congress therefore could reasonably presume that a person found in possession of an unregistered machinegun or sawed-off shotgun intended to use it for criminal purposes.

The provision's place in the overall statutory scheme, see Crandon v. United States, 494 U.S. 152, 158, 108 L. Ed. 2d 132, 110 S. Ct. 997 (1990), confirms this intention. In 1934, when Congress originally enacted the statute, it limited the coverage of the 1934 Act to a relatively narrow category of weapons such as submachineguns and sawed-off shotguns -- weapons characteristically used only by professional gangsters like Al Capone, Pretty Boy Floyd, and their henchmen. n4 At the time, the Act would have had little application to guns used by hunters or guns kept at home as protection against unwelcome intruders. n5 Congress therefore could reasonably presume that a person found in possession of an unregistered machinegun or sawed-off shotgun intended to use it for criminal purposes. The statute as a whole, and particularly the decision to criminalize mere possession, reflected a legislative judgment that the likelihood of innocent possession of such an unregistered weapon was remote, and far less significant than the interest in depriving gangsters of their use.

The late 1920s and early 1930s brought . . . a growing perception of crime both as a major problem and as a national one. . . . Criminal gangs found the submachinegun (a fully automatic, shoulder-fired weapon utilizing automatic pistol cartridges) and sawed-off shotgun deadly for close-range fighting.

n4 "The late 1920s and early 1930s brought . . . a growing perception of crime both as a major problem and as a national one. . . . Criminal gangs found the submachinegun (a fully automatic, shoulder-fired weapon utilizing automatic pistol cartridges) and sawed-off shotgun deadly for close-range fighting." Hardy, The Firearms Owners' Protection Act: A Historical and Legal Perspective, 17 Cumb. L. Rev. 585, 590 (1987).

The gangster as a law violator must be deprived of his most dangerous weapon, the machinegun. Your committee is of the opinion that limiting the bill to the taxing of sawed-off guns and machineguns is sufficient at this time. It is not thought necessary to go so far as to include pistols and revolvers and sporting arms. But while there is justification for permitting the citizen to keep a pistol or revolver for his own protection without any restriction, there is no reason why anyone except a law officer should have a machinegun or sawed-off shotgun.

n5 The Senate Report on the bill explained: "The gangster as a law violator must be deprived of his most dangerous weapon, the machinegun. Your committee is of the opinion that limiting the bill to the taxing of sawed-off guns and machineguns is sufficient at this time. It is not thought necessary to go so far as to include pistols and revolvers and sporting arms. But while there is justification for permitting the citizen to keep a pistol or revolver for his own protection without any restriction, there is no reason why anyone except a law officer should have a machinegun or sawed-off shotgun." S. Rep. No. 1444, 73d Cong., 2d Sess., 1-2 (1934).

In addition, at the time of enactment, this Court had already construed comparable provisions of the Harrison Anti-Narcotic Act not to require proof of knowledge of all the facts that constitute the proscribed offense. United States v. Balint, 258 U.S. 250, 66 L. Ed. 604, 42 S. Ct. 301 (1922). n6 Indeed, Attorney General Cummings expressly advised Congress that the text of the gun control legislation deliberately followed the language of the Anti-Narcotic Act to reap the benefit of cases construing it. n7 Given the reasoning of Balint, we properly may infer that Congress did not intend the Court to read a stricter knowledge requirement into the gun control legislation than we read into the Anti-Narcotic Act. Cannon v. University of Chicago, 441 U.S. 677, 698-699, 60 L. Ed. 2d 560, 99 S. Ct. 1946 (1979).

n6 In the Balint case, after acknowledging the general common-law rule that made knowledge of the facts an element of every crime, we held that as to statutory crimes the question is one of legislative intent, and that the Anti-Narcotic Act should be construed to authorize "punishment of a person for an act in violation of law[,] [even] when ignorant of the facts making it so." Balint, 258 U.S. at 251-252. The "policy of the law may, in order to stimulate proper care, require the punishment of the negligent person though he be ignorant of the noxious character of what he sells." Id., at 253.

n7 See National Firearms Act: Hearings on H. R. 9066 before the House Committee on Ways and Means, 73d Cong., 2d Sess., 6 (1934).

The Secretary of the Treasury must maintain a central registry that includes the names and addresses of persons in possession of all firearms not controlled by the Government. §5841. Congress also prohibited certain acts and omissions, including the possession of an unregistered firearm.

Like the 1934 Act, the current National Firearms Act is primarily a regulatory measure. The statute establishes taxation, registration, reporting, and recordkeeping requirements for businesses and transactions involving statutorily defined firearms, and requires that each firearm be identified by a serial number. 26

U.S.C. §§5801-5802, 5811-5812, 5821-5822, 5842-5843. The Secretary of the Treasury must maintain a central registry that includes the names and addresses of persons in possession of all firearms not controlled by the Government. §5841. Congress also prohibited certain acts and omissions, including the possession of an unregistered firearm. n8 §5861.

n8 "Omission of a mental element is the norm for statutes designed to deal with inaction. Not registering your gun, not cleaning up your warehouse, United States v. Park, 421 U.S. 658, 44 L. Ed. 2d 489, 95 S. Ct. 1903 . . . (1975), and like 'acts' are done without thinking. Often the omission occurs because of lack of attention. . . . Yet Congress may have sound reasons for requiring people to investigate and act, objectives that cannot be achieved if the courts add mental elements to the statutes." Ross, 917 F.2d at 1000.

As the Court acknowledges, ante, at 607, to interpret statutory offenses such as §5861(d), we look to "the nature of the statute and the particular character of the items regulated" to determine the level of knowledge required for conviction. An examination of §5861(d) in light of our precedent dictates that the crime of possession of an unregistered machinegun is in a category of offenses described as "public welfare" crimes. n9 Our decisions interpreting such offenses clearly require affirmance of petitioner's conviction.

n9 These statutes are sometimes referred to as "strict liability" offenses. As the Court notes, because the defendant must know that he is engaged in the type of dangerous conduct that is likely to be regulated, the use of the term "strict liability" to describe these offenses is inaccurate. Ante, at 607-608, n. 3. I therefore use the term "public welfare offense" to describe this type of statute.

II

"Public welfare" offenses share certain characteristics: (1) they regulate "dangerous or deleterious devices or products or obnoxious waste materials," see United States v. International Minerals & Chemical Corp., 402 U.S. 558, 565, 29 L. Ed. 2d 178, 91 S. Ct. 1697 (1971); (2) they "heighten the duties of those in control of particular industries, trades, properties or activities that affect public health, safety or welfare," Morissette, 342 U.S. at 254; and (3) they "depend on no mental element but consist only of forbidden acts or omissions," id., at 252-253. Examples of such offenses include Congress' exertion of its power to keep dangerous narcotics, n10 hazardous substances, n11 and impure and adulterated foods and drugs n12 out of the channels of commerce. n13

n10 See United States v. Balint, 258 U.S. 250, 66 L. Ed. 604, 42 S. Ct. 301 (1922).

n11 See United States v. International Minerals & Chemical Corp., 402 U.S. 558, 29 L. Ed. 2d 178, 91 S. Ct. 1697 (1971).

n12 See United States v. Dotterweich, 320 U.S. 277, 88 L. Ed. 48, 64 S. Ct. 134 (1943).

n13 The Court in Morissette v. United States, 342 U.S. 246, 96 L. Ed. 288, 72 S. Ct. 240 (1952), expressing approval of our public welfare offense cases, stated:

"Neither this Court nor, so far as we are aware, any other has undertaken to delineate a precise line or set forth comprehensive criteria for distinguishing between crimes that require a mental element and crimes that do not. We attempt no closed definition, for the law on the subject is neither settled nor static." Id., at 260 (footnotes omitted).

Public welfare statutes render criminal "a type of conduct that a reasonable person should know is subject to stringent public regulation and may seriously threaten the community's health or safety." Liparota v. United States, 471 U.S. 419, 433, 85 L. Ed. 2d 434, 105 S. Ct. 2084 (1985). Thus, under such statutes, "a defendant can be convicted even though he was unaware of the circumstances of his conduct that made it illegal." Id., at 443, n. 7 (White, J., dissenting). Referring to the strict criminal sanctions for unintended violations of the food and drug laws, Justice Frankfurter wrote:

"The purposes of this legislation thus touch phases of the lives and health of people which, in the circumstances of modern industrialism, are largely beyond self-protection. Regard for these purposes should infuse construction of the legislation if it is to be treated as a working instrument of government and not merely as a collection of English words. The prosecution . . . is based on a now familiar type of legislation whereby penalties serve as effective means of regulation. Such legislation dispenses with the conventional requirement for criminal conduct -- awareness of some wrongdoing. In the interest of the larger good it puts the burden of acting at hazard upon a person otherwise innocent but standing in responsible relation to a public danger." United States v. Dotterweich, 320 U.S. 277, 280-281, 88 L. Ed. 48, 64 S. Ct. 134 (1943) (citing United States v. Balint, 258 U.S. 250, 66 L. Ed. 604, 42 S. Ct. 301 (1922); other citations omitted).

Congress fashioned a legislative scheme to regulate the commerce and possession of certain types of dangerous devices, including specific kinds of weapons, to protect the health and welfare of the citizenry.

The National Firearms Act unquestionably is a public welfare statute. United States v. Freed, 401 U.S. 601, 609, 28 L. Ed. 2d 356, 91 S. Ct. 1112 (1971) (holding that this statute "is a regulatory measure in the interest of the public safety"). Congress fashioned a legislative scheme to regulate the commerce and possession of certain types of dangerous devices, including specific kinds of weapons, to protect the health and welfare of the citizenry. To enforce this scheme, Congress created criminal penalties for certain acts and omissions. The text of some of these offenses -- including the one at issue here -- contains no knowledge requirement.

The Court recognizes:

"We have reasoned that as long as a defendant knows that he is dealing with a dangerous device of a character that places him 'in responsible relation to a public danger,' Dotterweich, supra, at 281, he should be alerted to the probability of strict regulation, and we have assumed that in such cases Congress intended to place the burden on the defendant to 'ascertain at his peril whether [his conduct] comes within the inhibition of the statute.' Balint, 258 U.S. at 254." Ante, at 607.

We thus have read a knowledge requirement into public welfare crimes, but not a requirement that the defendant know all the facts that make his conduct illegal. Although the Court acknowledges this standard, it nevertheless concludes that a gun is not the type of dangerous device that would alert one to the possibility of regulation.

the Court instead reaches the rather surprising conclusion that guns are more analogous to food stamps than to hand grenades.

Both the Court and JUSTICE GINSBURG erroneously rely upon the "tradition[al]" innocence of gun ownership to find that Congress must have intended the Government to prove knowledge of all the characteristics that make a weapon a statutory "firearm." Ante, at 610-612; ante, at 621-622 (GINSBURG, J., concurring in judgment). We held in Freed, however, that a §5861(d) offense may be committed by one with no awareness of either wrongdoing or of all the facts that constitute the offense. n14 401 U.S. at 607-610. Nevertheless, the Court, asserting that the Government "gloss[es] over the distinction between grenades and guns," determines that "the gap between Freed and this case is too wide to bridge." Ante, at 610. As such, the Court instead reaches the rather surprising conclusion that guns are more analogous to food stamps than to hand grenades. n15 Even if one accepts that dubious proposition, the Court founds it upon a faulty premise: its mischaracterization of the Government's submission as one contending that "all guns . . . are dangerous devices that put gun owners on notice . . . ." Ante, at 608 (emphasis added). n16 Accurately identified, the Government's position presents the question whether guns such as the one possessed by petitioner "'are highly dangerous offensive weapons, no less dangerous than the narcotics'" in Balint or the hand grenades in Freed, see ante, at 609 (quoting Freed, 401 U.S. at 609). n17

n14 Freed, 401 U.S. at 607 (holding that a violation of §5861(d) may be established without proof that the defendant was aware of the fact that the firearm he possessed was unregistered). Our holding in Freed is thus squarely at odds with the Court's conclusion that the "defendant must know the facts that make his conduct illegal," ante, at 619.

n15 The Court's and JUSTICE GINSBURG's reliance upon Liparota v. United States, 471 U.S. 419, 85 L. Ed. 2d 434, 105 S. Ct. 2084 (1985), is misplaced. Ante, at 610-612; ante, at 621-622. Although the Court is usually concerned with fine nuances of statutory text, its discussion of Liparota simply ignores the fact that the food stamp fraud provision, unlike §5861(d), contained the word "knowingly." The Members of the Court in Liparota disagreed on the proper interpretation. The dissenters accepted the Government's view that the term merely required proof that the defendant had knowledge of the facts that constituted the crime. See Liparota, 471 U.S. at 442-443 (White, J., dissenting) ("I would read §2024(b)(1) . . . to require awareness of only the relevant aspects of one's conduct rendering it illegal, not the fact of illegality"). The majority, however, concluded that "knowingly" also connoted knowledge of illegality. Id., at 424-425. Because neither "knowingly" nor any comparable term appears in §5861(d), the statute before us today requires even less proof of knowledge than the dissenters would have demanded in Liparota.

n16 JUSTICE GINSBURG similarly assumes that the character of "all guns" cannot be said to place upon defendants an obligation "to inquire about the need for registration." Ante, at 622 (emphasis added).

n17 The Government does note that some Courts of Appeals have required proof of knowledge only that "the weapon was 'a firearm, within the general meaning of that term,'" Brief for United States 24-25 (citing cases). Contrary to the assertion by the Court, ante, at 632, n. 5, however, the Government does not advance this test as the appropriate knowledge requirement, but instead supports the one used by other Courts of Appeals. Compare the Court's description of the Government's position, ibid., with the following statements in the Government's brief:

"A defendant may be convicted of such offenses so long as the government proves that he knew the item at issue was highly dangerous and of a type likely to be subject to regulation." Brief for United States 9.

"The court of appeals correctly required the government to prove only that petitioner knew that he possessed a dangerous weapon likely to be subject to regulation." Id., at 13.

"B. The intent requirement applicable to Section 5861(d) is knowledge that one is dealing with a dangerous item of a type likely to be subject to regulation." Id., at 16.

"But where a criminal statute involves regulation of a highly hazardous substance -- and especially where it penalizes a failure to act or to comply with a registration scheme -- the defendant's knowledge that he was dealing with such a substance and that it was likely to be subject to regulation provides sufficient intent to support a conviction." Id., at 17-18.

"Rather, absent contrary congressional direction, knowledge of the highly dangerous nature of the articles involved and the likelihood that they are subject to regulation takes the place of the more rigorous knowledge requirement applicable where apparently innocent and harmless devices are subject to regulation." Id., at 20.

"But the instruction did not require the government to prove that petitioner knew his weapon 'possessed every last characteristic [which subjects it] to regulation'; he need only have 'known that he [was] dealing with a dangerous device of a type as would alert one to the likelihood of regulation.' Tr. 465.

"That instruction accurately describes the mental state necessary for a violation of Section 5861(d)." Id., at 23.

"Proof that a defendant was on fair notice that the item he possessed was highly dangerous and likely to be regulated is sufficient to support a conviction." Id., at 24.

Thus, even assuming that the Court is correct that the mere possession of an ordinary rifle or pistol does not entail sufficient danger to alert one to the possibility of regulation, that conclusion does not resolve this case. Petitioner knowingly possessed a semiautomatic weapon that was readily convertible into a machinegun. The "'character and nature'" of such a weapon is sufficiently hazardous to place the possessor on notice of the possibility of regulation. See Posters 'N' Things, Ltd. v. United States, ante, at 525 (citation omitted). n18 No significant difference exists between imposing upon the possessor a duty to determine whether such a weapon is registered, Freed, 401 U.S. at 607-610, and imposing a duty to determine whether that weapon has been converted into a machinegun.

The owner of a semiautomatic weapon that is readily convertible into a machinegun can certainly be aware of its dangerous nature and the consequent probability of regulation even if he does not know whether the weapon is actually a machinegun.

n18 The Court and JUSTICE GINSBURG apparently assume that the outer limits of any such notice can be no broader than the category of dangerous objects that Congress delineated as "firearms." Ante, at 611-612; ante, at 621-622. Our holding in Posters 'N' Things, illustrates the error in that assumption. A retailer who may not know whether certain merchandise is actually drug paraphernalia, as that term is defined in the relevant federal statute, may nevertheless violate the law if "aware that customers in general are likely to use the merchandise with drugs." Ante, at 524. The owner of a semiautomatic weapon that is readily convertible into a machinegun can certainly be aware of its dangerous nature and the consequent probability of regulation even if he does not know whether the weapon is actually a machinegun. If ignorance of the precise characteristics that render an item forbidden should be a defense, items that are likely to be "drug paraphernalia" are no more obviously dangerous, and thus regulated, than items that are likely to be "firearms."

Cases arise, of course, in which a defendant would not know that a device was dangerous unless he knew that it was a "firearm" as defined in the Act. Freed was such a case; unless the defendant knew that the device in question was a hand grenade, he would not necessarily have known that it was dangerous. But given the text and nature of the statute, it would be utterly implausible to suggest that Congress intended the owner of a sawed-off shotgun to be criminally liable if he knew its barrel was 17.5 inches long but not if he mistakenly believed the same gun had an 18-inch barrel. Yet the Court's holding today assumes that Congress intended that bizarre result.

The enforcement of public welfare offenses always entails some possibility of injustice. Congress nevertheless has repeatedly decided that an overriding public interest in health or safety may outweigh that risk

The enforcement of public welfare offenses always entails some possibility of injustice. Congress nevertheless has repeatedly decided that an overriding public interest in health or safety may outweigh that risk when a person is dealing with products that are sufficiently dangerous or deleterious to make it reasonable to presume that he either knows, or should know, whether those products conform to special regulatory requirements. The dangerous character of the product is reasonably presumed to provide sufficient notice of the probability of regulation to justify strict enforcement against those who are merely guilty of negligent, rather than willful, misconduct.

The National Firearms Act is within the category of public welfare statutes enacted by Congress to regulate highly dangerous items.

The National Firearms Act is within the category of public welfare statutes enacted by Congress to regulate highly dangerous items. The Government submits that a conviction under such a statute may be supported by proof that the defendant "knew the item at issue was highly dangerous and of a type likely to be subject to regulation." Brief for United States 9. n19 It is undisputed that the evidence in this case met that standard. Nevertheless, neither JUSTICE THOMAS for the Court nor JUSTICE GINSBURG has explained why such a knowledge requirement is unfaithful to our cases or to the text of the Act. n20 Instead, following the approach of their decision in United States v. Harris, 294 U.S. App. D.C. 300, 959 F.2d 246, 260-261 (CADC) (per curiam), cert. denied sub nom. Smith v. United States, 506 U.S. 932 (1992), they have simply explained why, in their judgment, it would be unfair to punish the possessor of this machinegun.

n19 As a matter of law, this is the level of knowledge required by the statute. Therefore, contrary to the Court's suggestion, ante, at 612, n. 6, I have not left the determination of the "exact content of the knowledge requirement" to the jury. I only leave to the jury its usual function: the application of this legal standard to the facts. In performing this function, juries are frequently required to determine if a law has been violated by application of just such a "general 'standard.'" See, e.g., Posters 'N' Things, ante, at 523-525; Miller v. California, 413 U.S. 15, 24, 37 L. Ed. 2d 419, 93 S. Ct. 2607 (1973).

n20 The Court also supports its conclusion on the basis of the purported disparity between the penalty provided by this statute and those of other regulatory offenses. Although a modest penalty may indicate that a crime is a public welfare offense, such a penalty is not a requisite characteristic of public welfare offenses. For example, the crime involved in Balint involved punishment of up to five years' imprisonment. See Dotterweich, 320 U.S. at 285; see also Morissette, 342 U.S. at 251, n. 8 (noting that rape of one too young to consent is an offense "in which the victim's actual age was determinative despite defendant's reasonable belief that the girl had reached age of consent"). Moreover, congressional authorization of a range of penalties in some cases -- petitioner, for instance, is on probation -- demonstrates a recognition that relatively innocent conduct should be punished less severely.

III

The history and interpretation of the National Firearms Act supports the conclusion that Congress did not intend to require knowledge of all the facts that constitute the offense of possession of an unregistered weapon. During the first 30 years of enforcement of the 1934 Act, consistent with the absence of a knowledge requirement and with the reasoning in Balint, courts uniformly construed it not to require knowledge of all the characteristics of the weapon that brought it within the statute. In a case decided in 1963, then-Judge Blackmun reviewed the earlier cases and concluded that the defendant's knowledge that he possessed a gun was "all the scienter which the statute requires." Sipes v. United States, 321 F.2d 174, 179 (CA8), cert. denied, 375 U.S. 913, 11 L. Ed. 2d 150, 84 S. Ct. 208 (1963).

Congress subsequently amended the statute twice, once in 1968 and again in 1986. Both amendments added knowledge requirements to other portions of the Act, n21 but neither the text nor the history of either amendment discloses an intent to add any other knowledge requirement to the possession of an unregistered firearm offense. Given that, with only one partial exception, n22 every federal tribunal to address the question had concluded that proof of knowledge of all the facts constituting a violation was not required for a conviction under §5861(d), n23 we may infer that Congress intended that interpretation to survive. See Lorillard v. Pons, 434 U.S. 575, 580, 55 L. Ed. 2d 40, 98 S. Ct. 866 (1978).

n21 Significantly, in 1968, Congress included a knowledge requirement in §5861(l). 26 U.S.C. §5861(l) (making it unlawful "to make, or cause the making of, a false entry on any application, return, or record required by this chapter, knowing such entry to be false") (emphasis added). "Where Congress includes particular language in one section of a statute but omits it in another section of the same Act, it is generally presumed that Congress acts intentionally and purposely in the disparate inclusion or exclusion." Rodriguez v. United States, 480 U.S. 522, 525, 94 L. Ed. 2d 533, 107 S. Ct. 1391 (1987) (internal quotation marks and citations omitted); see also Lawrence County v. Lead-Deadwood School Dist. No. 40-1, 469 U.S. 256, 267-268, 105 S. Ct. 695, 83 L. Ed. 2d 635 (1985).

n22 United States v. Herbert, 698 F.2d 981, 986-987 (CA9), cert. denied, 464 U.S. 821, 78 L. Ed. 2d 95, 104 S. Ct. 87 (1983) (requiring the Government to prove knowledge of all the characteristics of a weapon only when no external signs indicated that the weapon was a "firearm"). Not until 1989 did a Court of Appeals adopt the view of the majority today. See United States v. Williams, 872 F.2d 773 (CA6).

n23 See, e.g., United States v. Gonzalez, 719 F.2d 1516, 1522 (CA11 1983), cert. denied, 465 U.S. 1037, 79 L. Ed. 2d 710, 104 S. Ct. 1312 (1984); Morgan v. United States, 564 F.2d 803, 805-806 (CA8 1977); United States v. Cowper, 503 F.2d 130, 132-133 (CA6 1974), cert. denied, 420

U.S. 930, 43 L. Ed. 2d 403, 95 S. Ct. 1133 (1975); United States v. DeBartolo, 482 F.2d 312, 316 (CA1 1973); United States v. Vasquez, 476 F.2d 730, 732 (CA5), cert. denied, 414 U.S. 836, 38 L. Ed. 2d 72, 94 S. Ct. 181 (1973), overruled by United States v. Anderson, 885 F.2d 1248 (CA5 1989) (en banc).

And, as I have already noted, United States v. Freed, 401 U.S. 601, 28 L. Ed. 2d 356, 91 S. Ct. 1112 (1971), was consistent with the Government's position here. Although the Government accepted the burden of proving that Freed knew that the item he possessed was a hand grenade, the possessor of an unfamiliar object such as a hand grenade would not know that it was "a dangerous item of a type likely to be subject to regulation," Brief for United States 16; see also id., at 20, 23, 24, unless he knew what it was.

In short, petitioner's knowledge that he possessed an item that was sufficiently dangerous to alert him to the likelihood of regulation would have supported a conviction during the first half century of enforcement of this statute. Unless application of that standard to a particular case violates the Due Process Clause, n24 it is the responsibility of Congress, not this Court, to amend the statute if Congress deems it unfair or unduly strict.

n24 Petitioner makes no such claim in this Court.

IV

On the premise that the purpose of the mens rea requirement is to avoid punishing people "for apparently innocent activity," JUSTICE GINSBURG concludes that proof of knowledge that a weapon is "'a dangerous device of a type as would alert one to the likelihood of regulation'" is not an adequate mens rea requirement, but that proof of knowledge that the weapon possesses "'every last characteristic'" that subjects it to regulation is. Ante, at 622-623, and n. 5 (GINSBURG, J., concurring in judgment) (quoting the trial court's jury instruction).

Assuming that "innocent activity" describes conduct without any consciousness of wrongdoing, the risk of punishing such activity can be avoided only by reading into the statute the common-law concept of mens rea: "an evil purpose or mental culpability." Morissette, 342 U.S. at 252. n25 But even petitioner does not contend that the Government must prove guilty intent or intentional wrongdoing. Instead, the "mens rea" issue in this case is simply what knowledge requirement, if any, Congress implicitly included in this offense. There are at least five such possible knowledge requirements, four of which entail the risk that a completely innocent mistake will subject a defendant to punishment.

Our use of the term mens rea has not been consistent. In Morissette, we used the term as if it always connoted a form of wrongful intent. In other cases, we employ it simply to mean whatever level of knowledge is required for any particular crime.

n25 Our use of the term mens rea has not been consistent. In Morissette, we used the term as if it always connoted a form of wrongful intent. In other cases, we employ it simply to mean whatever level of knowledge is required for any particular crime. See, e.g., United States v. Bailey, 444 U.S. 394, 403, 62 L. Ed. 2d 575, 100 S. Ct. 624 (1980). In this sense, every crime except a true strict-liability offense contains a mens rea requirement. For instance, the Court defined mens rea in Liparota v. United States, 471 U.S. at 426, as "knowledge of illegality." In dissent, however, Justice White equated the term with knowledge of the facts that make the conduct illegal. Id., at 442-443. Today, the Court assigns the term the latter definition, ante, at 605, but in fact requires proof of knowledge of only some of the facts that constitute the violation, ante, at 609 (not requiring proof of knowledge of the fact that the gun is unregistered).

First, a defendant may know that he possesses a weapon with all of the characteristics that make it a "firearm" within the meaning of the statute and also know that it has never been registered, but be ignorant of the federal registration requirement. In such a case, we presume knowledge of the law even if we know the defendant is "innocent" in the sense that JUSTICE GINSBURG uses the word. Second, a defendant may know that he possesses a weapon with all of the characteristics of a statutory firearm and also know that the law requires that it be registered, but mistakenly believe that it is in fact registered. Freed squarely holds that this defendant's "innocence" is not a defense. Third, a defendant may know only that he possesses a weapon with all of the characteristics of a statutory firearm. Neither ignorance of the registration requirement nor ignorance of the fact that the weapon is unregistered protects this "innocent" defendant. Fourth, a defendant may know that he possesses a weapon that is sufficiently dangerous to likely be regulated, but not know that it has all the characteristics of a statutory firearm. Petitioner asserts that he is an example of this "innocent" defendant. Fifth, a defendant may know that he possesses an ordinary gun and, being aware of the widespread lawful gun ownership in the country, reasonably assume that there is no need "to inquire about the need for registration." Ante, at 622 (GINSBURG, J., concurring in judgment). That, of course, is not this case. See supra, 511 U.S. at 624, and n. 1. n26

I disagree with the assumption that "widespread lawful gun ownership" provides a sufficient reason for believing that there is no need to register guns (there is also widespread lawful automobile ownership)

n26 Although I disagree with the assumption that "widespread lawful gun ownership" provides a sufficient reason for believing that there is no need to register guns (there is also widespread lawful automobile ownership), acceptance of that assumption neither justifies the majority's holding nor contradicts my conclusion on the facts of this case.

JUSTICE GINSBURG treats the first, second, and third alternatives differently from the fourth and fifth. Her acceptance of knowledge of the characteristics of a statutory "firearm" as a sufficient predicate for criminal liability -- despite ignorance of either the duty to register or the fact of nonregistration, or both -- must rest on the premise that such knowledge would alert the owner to the likelihood of regulation, thereby depriving the conduct of its "apparent innocen[ce]." Yet in the fourth alternative, a jury determines just such knowledge: that the characteristics of the weapon known to the defendant would alert the owner to the likelihood of regulation.

In short, JUSTICE GINSBURG's reliance on "the purpose of the mens rea requirement -- to shield people against punishment for apparently innocent activity," ante, at 622, neither explains why ignorance of certain facts is a defense although ignorance of others is not, nor justifies her disagreement with the jury's finding that this defendant knew facts that should have caused him to inquire about the need for registration. n27

n27 In addition, contrary to JUSTICE GINSBURG's assumption, if one reads the term "firearm" from the quoted section of the indictment to mean "gun," the indictment still charges an offense under §5861(d) and does not differ from the critical jury instruction. See ante, at 622-623. Even if JUSTICE GINSBURG is correct that there is a technical variance, petitioner makes no claim that any such variance prejudiced him. The wording of the indictment, of course, sheds no light on the proper interpretation of the underlying statutory text. Although the repeated use of a term in a statute may shed light on the statute's construction, see Ratzlaf v. United States, 510 U.S. 135, 143, 126 L. Ed. 2d 615, 114 S. Ct. 655 (1994), such use in an indictment is irrelevant to that question.

V

This case presents no dispute about the dangerous character of machine guns and sawed-off shotguns. Anyone in possession of such a weapon is "standing in responsible relation to a public danger."

Semiautomatic weapons that are readily convertible into machine guns are sufficiently dangerous to alert persons who knowingly possess them to the probability of stringent public regulation.

This case presents no dispute about the dangerous character of machine guns and sawed-off shotguns. Anyone in possession of such a weapon is "standing in responsible relation to a public danger." See Dotterweich, 320 U.S. at 281 (citation omitted). In the National Firearms Act, Congress determined that the serious threat to health and safety posed by the private ownership of such firearms warranted the imposition of a duty on the owners of dangerous weapons to determine whether their possession is lawful. Semiautomatic weapons that are readily convertible into machine guns are sufficiently dangerous to alert persons who knowingly possess them to the probability of stringent public regulation. The jury's finding that petitioner knowingly possessed "a dangerous device of a type as would alert one to the likelihood of regulation" adequately supports the conviction.

Accordingly, I would affirm the judgment of the Court of Appeals.

UNITED STATES v. LOPEZ

(FULL CASE)

514 U.S. 549; 115 S. Ct. 1624; 131 L. Ed. 2d 626

November 8, 1994, Argued

April 26, 1995, Decided

GIST: To exert control over increasingly broad swaths of activity, Congress has used its constitutional power to regulate commerce between the states. The

Congressional commerce power has been the primary tool used for implementing federal gun law in recent history. In the early Republic, Congress did comparatively little with this power, and was challenged infrequently. In more recent times, the interstate Commerce Clause has been held to control everything from growing and eating your own wheat, to possession of a firearm on or near any local school—which is the kernel of this case of a Texas 12th grader who brought a .38 caliber revolver and ammo to school.

The Supreme Court used this challenge of a gun-ban law—The Gun-Free School Zones Act of 1990—to draw in the reins of an increasingly powerful Congress, and to partially reestablish boundaries for Congress' enumerated power over interstate commerce. It was the first significant attenuation of congressional commerce power in decades.

The Court chides the federal government for proposing standards so broad that they could basically use the Commerce Clause to remove any limitation on federal power over the states and the public, right down to a direct national police force, and even in areas where states historically have enjoyed sovereignty. When asked at oral argument what limits the government's interpretation of the Commerce Clause would provide, the government's attorneys were speechless. The dissenting opinion also could not find a single example of where federal power would end if the notion was allowed to stand that everything, basically, has some connection to interstate commerce, as the four Justices in the minority argued to establish.

In this five-to-four decision the Court found the Gun-Free School Zone law to be a criminal statute that had nothing to do with "commerce" or any sort of economic enterprise, however broadly one might define those terms. The majority put the brakes on a potentially huge increase in federal power. The dissent makes a good case though that schools are indeed an economic enterprise and are directly connected in myriad ways to interstate commerce, and that violence in general and guns in particular interfere with the educational process. They posit that guns have no place in a school environment (without limiting that sentiment to illegally possessed guns), and that Congress should have the power to ban guns outright, at least in this setting.

There is a good examination in this case of what Congress can and cannot do, as a function of federalism and the Commerce Clause, and the history leading us to present conditions.

Although the commerce power is where the federal government hangs its hat in these arguments, it is police power at the local level that it would have obtained if it had been successful. The net effect, if the Court would have decided the other way, would be to empower federal authorities to make and enforce law at every level, in the name of influencing commerce. Justice Thomas suggests that a review of the Court's recent doctrine behind commerce-clause power is in need of review due to the unintended consequences of changes made in the last 60 years.

As soon as the law was invalidated as an unconstitutional exercise of authority, Congress waltzed around the decision by reenacting the law, adding brief verbiage about interstate commerce in an effort to surmount the Supreme Court's objections, and placed it back on the books where the old law had just been removed (18 USC §922(q)). The Gun-Free School Zone law thus stands unless challenged again at some future time.

Questions came up about including this lengthy case unedited, since large sections of it are not directly related to guns per se. Seeing, however, that Congress has relied almost exclusively on this broad grant of power to implement its firearm (and other) controls across the country in recent decades, the enormous significance of *Lopez* argued for its full inclusion. The case is discussed in detail in an article in the *Connecticut Law Review* (Volume 30, 1997), available on davekopel.org, and in the book *Gun Laws of America*, available at gunlaws.com.

After respondent, then a 12th-grade student, carried a concealed handgun into his high school, he was charged with violating the Gun-Free School Zones Act of 1990, which forbids "any individual knowingly to possess a firearm at a place that [he] knows . . . is a school zone," 18 U.S.C. §922(q)(1)(A). The District Court denied his motion to dismiss the indictment, concluding that §922(q) is a constitutional exercise of Congress' power to regulate activities in and affecting commerce. In reversing, the Court of Appeals held that, in light of what it characterized as insufficient congressional findings and legislative history, §922(q) is invalid as beyond Congress' power under the Commerce Clause.

Held: The Act exceeds Congress' Commerce Clause authority. First, although this Court has upheld a wide variety of congressional Acts regulating intrastate economic activity that substantially affected interstate commerce, the possession of a gun in a local school zone is in no sense an economic activity that might, through repetition elsewhere, have such a substantial effect on interstate commerce. Section 922(q) is a criminal statute that by its terms has nothing to do with "commerce" or any sort of economic enterprise, however broadly those terms are defined. Nor is it an essential part of a larger regulation of economic activity, in which the regulatory scheme could be undercut unless the intrastate activity were regulated. It cannot, therefore, be sustained under the Court's cases upholding regulations of activities that arise out of or are connected with a commercial transaction, which, viewed in the aggregate, substantially affects interstate commerce. Second, §922(q) contains no jurisdictional element that would ensure, through case-by-case inquiry, that the firearms possession in question has the requisite nexus with interstate commerce. Respondent was a local student at a local school; there is no indication that he had recently moved in interstate commerce, and there is no requirement that his possession of the firearm have any concrete tie to interstate commerce. To uphold the Government's contention that §922(q) is justified because firearms possession in a local school zone does indeed substantially affect interstate commerce would require this Court to pile inference upon inference in a manner that would bid fair to convert congressional Commerce Clause authority to a general police power of the sort held only by the States.

CHIEF JUSTICE REHNQUIST delivered the opinion of the Court.

In the Gun-Free School Zones Act of 1990, Congress made it a federal offense "for any individual knowingly to possess a firearm at a place that the individual knows, or has reasonable cause to believe, is a school zone." 18 U.S.C. §922 (q)(1)(A) (1988 ed., Supp. V). The Act neither regulates a commercial activity nor contains a requirement that the possession be connected in any way to interstate commerce. We hold that the Act exceeds the authority of Congress "to regulate Commerce . . . among the several States . . . ." U.S. Const., Art. I, §8, cl. 3.

a 12th-grade student arrived at Edison High School in San Antonio, Texas, carrying a concealed .38 caliber handgun and five bullets.

On March 10, 1992, respondent, who was then a 12th-grade student, arrived at Edison High School in San Antonio, Texas, carrying a concealed .38 caliber handgun and five bullets. Acting upon an anonymous tip, school authorities confronted respondent, who admitted that he was carrying the weapon. He was arrested and charged under Texas law with firearm possession on school premises. See Tex. Penal Code Ann. §46.03(a)(1) (Supp. 1994). The next day, the state charges were dismissed after federal agents charged respondent by complaint with violating the Gun-Free School Zones Act of 1990. 18 U.S.C. §922(q)(1)(A) (1988 ed., Supp. V). n1

n1 The term "school zone" is defined as "in, or on the grounds of, a public, parochial or private school" or "within a distance of 1,000 feet from the grounds of a public, parochial or private school." §921(a)(25).

A federal grand jury indicted respondent on one count of knowing possession of a firearm at a school zone, in violation of §922(q). Respondent moved to dismiss his federal indictment on the ground that §922(q) "is unconstitutional as it is beyond the power of Congress to legislate control over our public schools." The

District Court denied the motion, concluding that §922(q) "is a constitutional exercise of Congress' well-defined power to regulate activities in and affecting commerce, and the 'business' of elementary, middle and high schools . . . affects interstate commerce." App. to Pet. for Cert. 55a. Respondent waived his right to a jury trial. The District Court conducted a bench trial, found him guilty of violating §922(q), and sentenced him to six months' imprisonment and two years' supervised release.

On appeal, respondent challenged his conviction based on his claim that §922(q) exceeded Congress' power to legislate under the Commerce Clause. The Court of Appeals for the Fifth Circuit agreed and reversed respondent's conviction. It held that, in light of what it characterized as insufficient congressional findings and legislative history, "section 922(q), in the full reach of its terms, is invalid as beyond the power of Congress under the Commerce Clause." 2 F.3d 1342, 1367-1368 (1993). Because of the importance of the issue, we granted certiorari, 511 U.S. 1029 (1994), and we now affirm.

We start with first principles. The Constitution creates a Federal Government of enumerated powers. See Art. I, §8. As James Madison wrote, "the powers delegated by the proposed Constitution to the federal government are few and defined. Those which are to remain in the State governments are numerous and indefinite." The Federalist No. 45, pp. 292-293 (C. Rossiter ed. 1961). This constitutionally mandated division of authority "was adopted by the Framers to ensure protection of our fundamental liberties." Gregory v. Ashcroft, 501 U.S. 452, 458, 115 L. Ed. 2d 410, 111 S. Ct. 2395 (1991) (internal quotation marks omitted). "Just as the separation and independence of the coordinate branches of the Federal Government serve to prevent the accumulation of excessive power in any one branch, a healthy balance of power between the States and the Federal Government will reduce the risk of tyranny and abuse from either front." Ibid.

The Constitution delegates to Congress the power "to regulate Commerce with foreign Nations, and among the several States, and with the Indian Tribes." Art. I, §8, cl. 3. The Court, through Chief Justice Marshall, first defined the nature of Congress' commerce power in Gibbons v. Ogden, 22 U.S. 1, 9 Wheat. 1, 189-190, 6 L. Ed. 23 (1824): "Commerce, undoubtedly, is traffic, but it is something more: it is intercourse. It describes the commercial intercourse between nations, and parts of nations, in all its branches, and is regulated by prescribing rules for carrying on that intercourse."

The commerce power "is the power to regulate; that is, to prescribe the rule by which commerce is to be governed. This power, like all others vested in congress, is complete in itself, may be exercised to its utmost extent, and acknowledges no limitations, other than are prescribed in the constitution." Id., at 196. The Gibbons Court, however, acknowledged that limitations on the commerce power are inherent in the very language of the Commerce Clause.

"It is not intended to say that these words comprehend that commerce, which is completely internal, which is carried on between man and man in a State, or between different parts of the same State, and which does not extend to or affect other States. Such a power would be inconvenient, and is certainly unnecessary.

"Comprehensive as the word 'among' is, it may very properly be restricted to that commerce which concerns more States than one. . . . The enumeration presupposes something not enumerated; and that something, if we regard the language, or the subject of the sentence, must be the exclusively internal commerce of a State." Id., at 194-195.

For nearly a century thereafter, the Court's Commerce Clause decisions dealt but rarely with the extent of Congress' power, and almost entirely with the Commerce Clause as a limit on state legislation that discriminated against interstate commerce. See, e.g., Veazie v. Moor, 55 U.S. 568, 14 How. 568, 573-575, 14 L. Ed. 545 (1853) (upholding a state-created steamboat monopoly because it involved regulation of wholly internal commerce); Kidd v. Pearson, 128 U.S. 1, 17, 20-22, 32 L. Ed. 346, 9 S. Ct. 6 (1888) (upholding a state prohibition on the manufacture of intoxicating liquor because the commerce power "does not comprehend the purely internal domestic commerce of a State which is carried on between man and man within a State or between different parts of the same State"); see also L. Tribe, American Constitutional Law 306 (2d ed. 1988). Under this line of precedent, the Court held that certain categories of activity such as "production," "manufacturing," and "mining" were within the province of state governments, and thus were beyond the power of Congress under the Commerce Clause. See Wickard v. Filburn, 317 U.S. 111, 121, 87 L. Ed. 122, 63 S. Ct. 82 (1942) (describing development of Commerce Clause jurisprudence).

In 1887, Congress enacted the Interstate Commerce Act, 24 Stat. 379, and in 1890, Congress enacted the Sherman Antitrust Act, 26 Stat. 209, as amended, 15 U.S.C. §1 et seq. These laws ushered in a new era of federal regulation under the commerce power. When cases involving these laws first reached this Court, we imported from our negative Commerce Clause cases the approach that Congress could not regulate activities such as "production," "manufacturing," and "mining." See, e.g., United States v. E. C. Knight Co., 156 U.S. 1, 12, 39 L. Ed. 325, 15 S. Ct. 249 (1895) ("Commerce succeeds to manufacture, and is not part of it"); Carter v. Carter Coal Co., 298 U.S. 238, 304, 80 L. Ed. 1160, 56 S. Ct. 855 (1936) ("Mining brings the subject matter of commerce into existence. Commerce disposes of it"). Simultaneously, however, the Court held that, where the interstate and intrastate aspects of commerce were so mingled together that full regulation of interstate commerce required incidental regulation of intrastate commerce, the Commerce Clause authorized such regulation. See, e.g., Shreveport Rate Cases, 234 U.S. 342, 58 L. Ed. 1341, 34 S. Ct. 833 (1914).

In A. L. A. Schechter Poultry Corp. v. United States, 295 U.S. 495, 550, 79 L. Ed. 1570, 55 S. Ct. 837 (1935), the Court struck down regulations that fixed the hours and wages of individuals employed by an intrastate business because the activity being regulated related to interstate commerce only indirectly. In doing so, the Court characterized the distinction between direct and indirect effects of intrastate transactions upon interstate commerce as "a fundamental one, essential to the maintenance of our constitutional system." Id., at 548. Activities that affected interstate commerce directly were within Congress' power; activities that affected interstate commerce indirectly were beyond Congress' reach. Id., at 546. The justification for this formal distinction was rooted in the fear that otherwise "there would be virtually no limit to the federal power and for all practical purposes we should have a completely centralized government." Id., at 548.

Two years later, in the watershed case of NLRB v. Jones & Laughlin Steel Corp., 301 U.S. 1, 81 L. Ed. 893, 57 S. Ct. 615 (1937), the Court upheld the National Labor Relations Act against a Commerce Clause challenge, and in the process, departed from the distinction between "direct" and "indirect" effects on interstate commerce. Id., at 36-38 ("The question [of the scope of Congress' power] is necessarily one of degree"). The Court held that intrastate activities that "have such a close and substantial relation to interstate commerce that their control is essential or appropriate to protect that commerce from burdens and obstructions" are within Congress' power to regulate. Id., at 37.

In United States v. Darby, 312 U.S. 100, 85 L. Ed. 609, 61 S. Ct. 451 (1941), the Court upheld the Fair Labor Standards Act, stating:

"The power of Congress over interstate commerce is not confined to the regulation of commerce among the states. It extends to those activities intrastate which so affect interstate commerce or the exercise of the power of Congress over it as to make regulation of them appropriate means to the attainment of a legitimate end, the exercise of the granted power of Congress to regulate interstate commerce." Id., at 118.

See also United States v. Wrightwood Dairy Co., 315 U.S. 110, 119, 86 L. Ed. 726, 62 S. Ct. 523 (1942) (the commerce power "extends to those intrastate activities which in a substantial way interfere with or obstruct the exercise of the granted power").

In Wickard v. Filburn, the Court upheld the application of amendments to the Agricultural Adjustment Act of 1938 to the production and consumption of homegrown wheat. 317 U.S. at 128-129. The Wickard Court explicitly rejected earlier distinctions between direct and indirect effects on interstate commerce, stating:

"Even if appellee's activity be local and though it may not be regarded as commerce, it may still, whatever its nature, be reached by Congress if it exerts a substantial economic effect on interstate commerce, and this irrespective of whether such effect is what might at some earlier time have been defined as 'direct' or 'indirect.'" Id., at 125.

The Wickard Court emphasized that although Filburn's own contribution to the demand for wheat may have been trivial by itself, that was not "enough to remove him from the scope of federal regulation where, as here, his contribution, taken together with that of many others similarly situated, is far from trivial." Id., at 127-128.

Jones & Laughlin Steel, Darby, and Wickard ushered in an era of Commerce Clause jurisprudence that greatly expanded the previously defined authority of Congress under that Clause. In part, this was a recognition of the great changes that had occurred in the way business was carried on in this country. Enterprises that had once been local or at most regional in nature had become national in scope. But the doctrinal change also reflected a view that earlier Commerce Clause cases artificially had constrained the authority of Congress to regulate interstate commerce.

But even these modern-era precedents which have expanded congressional power under the Commerce Clause confirm that this power is subject to outer limits. In Jones & Laughlin Steel, the Court warned that the scope of the interstate commerce power "must be considered in the light of our dual system of government and may not be extended so as to embrace effects upon interstate commerce so indirect and remote that to embrace them, in view of our complex society, would effectually obliterate the distinction between what is national and what is local and create a completely centralized government." 301 U.S. at 37; see also Darby, supra, at 119-120 (Congress may regulate intrastate activity that has a "substantial effect" on interstate commerce); Wickard, supra, at 125 (Congress may regulate activity that "exerts a substantial economic effect on interstate commerce"). Since that time, the Court has heeded that warning and undertaken to decide whether a rational basis existed for concluding that a regulated activity sufficiently affected interstate commerce. See, e.g., Hodel v. Virginia Surface Mining & Reclamation Assn., Inc., 452 U.S. 264, 276-280, 69 L. Ed. 2d 1, 101 S. Ct. 2352 (1981); Perez v. United States, 402 U.S. 146, 155-156, 28 L. Ed. 2d 686, 91 S. Ct. 1357 (1971); Katzenbach v. McClung, 379 U.S. 294, 299-301, 13 L. Ed. 2d 290, 85 S.

Ct. 377 (1964); Heart of Atlanta Motel, Inc. v. United States, 379 U.S. 241, 252-253, 13 L. Ed. 2d 258, 85 S. Ct. 348 (1964). n2

n2 See also Hodel, 452 U.S. at 311 ("Simply because Congress may conclude that a particular activity substantially affects interstate commerce does not necessarily make it so") (REHNQUIST, J., concurring in judgment); Heart of Atlanta Motel, 379 U.S. at 273 ("Whether particular operations affect interstate commerce sufficiently to come under the constitutional power of Congress to regulate them is ultimately a judicial rather than a legislative question, and can be settled finally only by this Court") (Black, J., concurring).

Similarly, in Maryland v. Wirtz, 392 U.S. 183, 20 L. Ed. 2d 1020, 88 S. Ct. 2017 (1968), the Court reaffirmed that "the power to regulate commerce, though broad indeed, has limits" that "the Court has ample power" to enforce. Id., at 196, overruled on other grounds, National League of Çities v. Usery, 426 U.S. 833, 49 L. Ed. 2d 245, 96 S. Ct. 2465 (1976), overruled by Garcia v. San Antonio Metropolitan Transit Authority, 469 U.S. 528, 83 L. Ed. 2d 1016, 105 S. Ct. 1005 (1985). In response to the dissent's warnings that the Court was powerless to enforce the limitations on Congress' commerce powers because "all activities affecting commerce, even in the minutest degree, [Wickard], may be regulated and controlled by Congress," 392 U.S. at 204 (Douglas, J., dissenting), the Wirtz Court replied that the dissent had misread precedent as "neither here nor in Wickard has the Court declared that Congress may use a relatively trivial impact on commerce as an excuse for broad general regulation of state or private activities," id., at 197, n. 27. Rather, "the Court has said only that where a general regulatory statute bears a substantial relation to commerce, the de minimis character of individual instances arising under that statute is of no consequence." Ibid. (first emphasis added).

Consistent with this structure, we have identified three broad categories of activity that Congress may regulate under its commerce power. Perez, supra, at 150; see also Hodel, supra, at 276-277. First, Congress may regulate the use of the channels of interstate commerce. See, e.g., Darby, 312 U.S. at 114; Heart of Atlanta Motel, supra, at 256 ("'The authority of Congress to keep the channels of interstate commerce free from immoral and injurious uses has been frequently sustained, and is no longer open to question'" (quoting Caminetti v. United States, 242 U.S. 470, 491, 61 L. Ed. 442, 37 S. Ct. 192 (1917))). Second, Congress is empowered to regulate and protect the instrumentalities of interstate commerce, or persons or things in interstate commerce, even though the threat may come only from intrastate activities. See, e.g., Shreveport Rate Cases, 234 U.S. 342, 34 S. Ct. 833, 58 L. Ed. 1341 (1914); Southern R. Co. v. United States, 222 U.S. 20, 56 L. Ed. 72, 32 S. Ct. 2 (1911) (upholding amendments to Safety Appliance Act as applied to vehicles used in intrastate commerce); Perez, supra, at 150 ("For example, the destruction of an aircraft (18 U.S.C. §32), or . . . thefts from interstate shipments (18 U.S.C. §659)"). Finally, Congress' commerce authority includes the power to regulate those activities having a substantial relation to interstate commerce, Jones & Laughlin Steel, 301 U.S. at 37, i.e., those activities that substantially affect interstate commerce, Wirtz, supra, at 196, n. 27.

Within this final category, admittedly, our case law has not been clear whether an activity must "affect" or "substantially affect" interstate commerce in order to be within Congress' power to regulate it under the Commerce Clause. Compare Preseault v. ICC, 494 U.S. 1, 17, 108 L. Ed. 2d 1, 110 S. Ct. 914 (1990), with Wirtz, supra, at 196, n. 27 (the Court has never declared that "Congress may use a relatively trivial impact on commerce as an excuse for broad general regulation of state or private activities"). We conclude, consistent with the great weight of our case law, that the proper test requires an analysis of whether the regulated activity "substantially affects" interstate commerce.

We now turn to consider the power of Congress, in the light of this framework, to enact §922(q). The first two categories of authority may be quickly disposed of: §922(q) is not a regulation of the use of the channels of interstate commerce, nor is it an attempt to prohibit the interstate transportation of a commodity through the channels of commerce; nor can §922(q) be justified as a regulation by which Congress has sought to protect an instrumentality of interstate commerce or a thing in interstate commerce. Thus, if §922(q) is to be sustained, it must be under the third category as a regulation of an activity that substantially affects interstate commerce.

First, we have upheld a wide variety of congressional Acts regulating intrastate economic activity where we have concluded that the activity substantially affected interstate commerce. Examples include the regulation of intrastate coal mining; Hodel, supra, intrastate extortionate credit transactions, Perez, supra, restaurants utilizing substantial interstate supplies, McClung, supra, inns and hotels catering to interstate guests, Heart of Atlanta Motel, supra, and production and consumption of homegrown wheat, Wickard v. Filburn, 317 U.S. 111, 87 L. Ed. 122, 63 S. Ct. 82 (1942). These examples are by no means exhaustive, but the pattern is clear. Where economic activity substantially affects interstate commerce, legislation regulating that activity will be sustained.

Even Wickard, which is perhaps the most far reaching example of Commerce Clause authority over intrastate activity, involved economic activity in a way that the possession of a gun in a school zone does not.

Even Wickard, which is perhaps the most far reaching example of Commerce Clause authority over intrastate activity, involved economic activity in a way that the possession of a gun in a school zone does not. Roscoe Filburn operated a small farm in Ohio, on which, in the year involved, he raised 23 acres of wheat. It was his practice to sow winter wheat in the fall, and after harvesting it in July to sell a portion of the crop, to feed part of it to poultry and livestock on the farm, to use some in making flour for home consumption, and to keep the remainder for seeding future crops. The Secretary of Agriculture assessed a penalty against him under the Agricultural Adjustment Act of 1938 because he harvested about 12 acres more wheat than his allotment under the Act permitted. The Act was designed to regulate the volume of wheat moving in interstate and foreign commerce in order to avoid surpluses and shortages, and concomitant fluctuation in wheat prices, which had previously obtained. The Court said, in an opinion sustaining the application of the Act to Filburn's activity:

"One of the primary purposes of the Act in question was to increase the market price of wheat and to that end to limit the volume thereof that could affect the market. It can hardly be denied that a factor of such volume and variability as home-consumed wheat would have a substantial influence on price and market conditions. This may arise because being in marketable condition such wheat overhangs the market and, if induced by rising prices, tends to flow into the market and check price increases. But if we assume that it is never marketed, it supplies a need of the man who grew it which would otherwise be reflected by purchases in the open market. Home-grown wheat in this sense competes with wheat in commerce." 317 U.S. at 128.

Section 922(q) is a criminal statute that by its terms has nothing to do with "commerce" or any sort of economic enterprise, however broadly one might define those terms. n3 Section 922(q) is not an essential part of a larger regulation of economic activity, in which the regulatory scheme could be undercut unless the intrastate activity were regulated. It cannot, therefore, be sustained under our cases upholding regulations of activities that arise out of or are connected with a commercial transaction, which viewed in the aggregate, substantially affects interstate commerce.

Under our federal system, the States possess primary authority for defining and enforcing the criminal law.

When Congress criminalizes conduct already denounced as criminal by the States, it effects a change in the sensitive relation between federal and state criminal jurisdiction.

President George Bush on Signing the Crime Control Act of 1990, "Most egregiously, section 922(q) inappropriately overrides legitimate State firearms laws with a new and unnecessary Federal law. The policies reflected in these provisions could legitimately be adopted by the States, but they should not be imposed upon the States by the Congress."

n3 Under our federal system, the "'States possess primary authority for defining and enforcing the criminal law.'" Brecht v. Abrahamson, 507 U.S. 619, 635, 123 L. Ed. 2d 353, 113 S. Ct. 1710 (1993) (quoting Engle v. Isaac, 456 U.S. 107, 128, 71 L. Ed. 2d 783, 102 S. Ct. 1558 (1982)); see also Screws v. United States, 325 U.S. 91, 109, 89 L. Ed. 1495, 65 S. Ct. 1031 (1945) (plurality opinion) ("Our national government is one of delegated powers alone. Under our federal system the administration of criminal justice rests with the States except as Congress, acting within the scope of those delegated powers, has created offenses against the United States"). When Congress criminalizes conduct already denounced as criminal by the States, it effects a "'change in the sensitive relation between federal and state criminal jurisdiction.'" United States v. Enmons, 410 U.S. 396, 411-412, 35 L. Ed. 2d 379, 93 S. Ct. 1007 (1973) (quoting United States v. Bass, 404 U.S. 336, 349, 30 L. Ed. 2d 488, 92 S. Ct. 515 (1971)). The Government acknowledges that §922(q) "displace[s] state policy choices in . . . that its prohibitions apply even in States that have chosen not to outlaw the conduct in question." Brief for United States 29, n. 18; see also Statement of President George Bush on Signing the Crime Control Act of 1990, 26 Weekly Comp. of Pres. Doc. 1944, 1945 (Nov. 29, 1990) ("Most egregiously, section [922(q)] inappropriately overrides legitimate State firearms laws with a new and unnecessary Federal law. The policies reflected in these provisions could legitimately be adopted by the States, but they should not be imposed upon the States by the Congress").

§922(q) contains no jurisdictional element which would ensure, through case-by-case inquiry, that the firearm possession in question affects interstate commerce.

The Bass Court set aside the conviction because although the Government had demonstrated that Bass had possessed a firearm, it had failed "to show the requisite nexus with interstate commerce." The Court thus interpreted the statute to reserve the constitutional question whether Congress could regulate, without more, the "mere possession" of firearms.

Second, §922(q) contains no jurisdictional element which would ensure, through case-by-case inquiry, that the firearm possession in question affects interstate commerce. For example, in United States v. Bass, 404 U.S. 336, 30 L. Ed. 2d 488, 92 S. Ct. 515 (1971), the Court interpreted former 18 U.S.C. §1202(a), which made it a crime for a felon to "receive, posses[s], or transport in commerce or affecting commerce . . . any firearm." 404 U.S. at 337. The Court interpreted the possession component of §1202(a) to require an additional nexus to interstate commerce both because the statute was ambiguous and because "unless Congress conveys its purpose clearly, it will not be deemed to have significantly changed the federal-state balance." Id., at 349. The Bass Court set aside the conviction because although the Government had demonstrated that Bass had possessed a firearm, it had failed "to show the requisite nexus with interstate commerce." Id., at 347. The Court thus interpreted the statute to reserve the constitutional question whether Congress could regulate, without more, the "mere possession" of firearms. See id., at 339, n. 4; see also United States v. Five Gambling Devices, 346 U.S. 441, 448, 98 L. Ed. 179, 74 S. Ct. 190 (1953) (plurality opinion) ("The principle is old and deeply imbedded in our jurisprudence that this Court will construe a statute in a manner that requires decision of serious constitutional questions only if the statutory language leaves no reasonable alternative"). Unlike the statute in Bass, §922(q) has no express jurisdictional element which might limit its reach to a discrete set of firearm possessions that additionally have an explicit connection with or effect on interstate commerce.

neither the statute nor its legislative history contains express congressional findings regarding the effects upon interstate commerce of gun possession in a school zone.

Although as part of our independent evaluation of constitutionality under the Commerce Clause we of course consider legislative findings, and indeed even congressional committee findings, regarding effect on interstate commerce, see, e.g., Preseault v. ICC, 494 U.S. at 17, the Government concedes that "neither the statute nor its legislative history contain[s] express congressional findings regarding the effects upon interstate commerce of gun possession in a school zone." Brief for United States 5-6. We agree with the Government that Congress normally is not required to make formal findings as to the substantial burdens that an activity has on interstate commerce. See McClung, 379 U.S. at 304; see also Perez, 402 U.S. at 156 ("Congress need [not] make particularized findings in order to legislate"). But to the extent that congressional findings would enable us to evaluate the legislative judgment that the activity in question substantially affected interstate commerce, even though no such substantial effect was visible to the naked eye, they are lacking here. n4

President Clinton signed into law the Violent Crime Control and Law Enforcement Act of 1994. Section 320904 of that Act amends §922(q) to include congressional findings regarding the effects of firearm possession in and around schools upon interstate and foreign commerce.

n4 We note that on September 13, 1994, President Clinton signed into law the Violent Crime Control and Law Enforcement Act of 1994, Pub. L. 103-322, 108 Stat. 1796. Section 320904 of that Act, id., at 2125, amends §922(q) to include congressional findings regarding the effects of firearm possession in and around schools upon interstate and foreign commerce. The Government does not rely upon these subsequent findings as a substitute for the absence of findings in the first instance. Tr. of Oral Arg. 25 ("We're not relying on them in the strict sense of the word, but we think that at a very minimum they indicate that reasons can be identified for why Congress wanted to regulate this particular activity").

section 922(q) plows thoroughly new ground and represents a sharp break with the long-standing pattern of federal firearms legislation.

The Government argues that Congress has accumulated institutional expertise regarding the regulation of firearms through previous enactments. Cf. Fullilove v. Klutznick, 448 U.S. 448, 503, 65 L. Ed. 2d 902, 100 S. Ct. 2758 (1980) (Powell, J., concurring). We agree, however, with the Fifth Circuit that importation of previous findings to justify §922(q) is especially inappropriate here because the "prior federal enactments or Congressional findings [do not] speak to the subject matter of section 922(q) or its relationship to interstate commerce. Indeed, section 922(q) plows thoroughly new ground and represents a sharp break with the long-standing pattern of federal firearms legislation." 2 F.3d at 1366.

The Government's essential contention, in fine, is that we may determine here that §922(q) is valid because possession of a firearm in a local school zone does indeed substantially affect interstate commerce.

The Government argues that possession of a firearm in a school zone may result in violent crime and that violent crime can be expected to affect the functioning of the national economy in two ways.

First, the costs of violent crime are substantial, and, through the mechanism of insurance, those costs are spread throughout the population. Second, violent crime reduces the willingness of individuals to travel to areas within the country that are perceived to be unsafe. The Government also argues that the presence of guns in schools poses a substantial threat to the educational process by threatening the learning environment. A handicapped educational process, in turn, will result in a less productive citizenry. That, in turn, would have an adverse effect on the Nation's economic well-being. As a result, the Government argues that Congress could rationally have concluded that §922(q) substantially affects interstate commerce.

The Government's essential contention, in fine, is that we may determine here that §922(q) is valid because possession of a firearm in a local school zone does indeed substantially affect interstate commerce. Brief for United States 17. The Government argues that possession of a firearm in a school zone may result in violent crime and that violent crime can be expected to affect the functioning of the national economy in two ways. First, the costs of violent crime are substantial, and, through the mechanism of insurance, those costs are spread throughout the population. See United States v. Evans, 928 F.2d 858, 862 (CA9 1991). Second, violent crime reduces the willingness of individuals to travel to areas within the country that are perceived to be unsafe. Cf. Heart of Atlanta Motel, 379 U.S. at 253. The Government also argues that the presence of guns in schools poses a substantial threat to the educational process by threatening the learning environment. A handicapped educational process, in turn, will result in a less productive citizenry. That, in turn, would have an adverse effect on the Nation's economic well-being. As a result, the Government argues that Congress could rationally have concluded that §922(q) substantially affects interstate commerce.

Under the theories that the Government presents in support of §922(q), it is difficult to perceive any limitation on federal power, even in areas such as criminal law enforcement or education where States historically have been sovereign.

if we were to accept the Government's arguments, we are hard pressed to posit any activity by an individual that Congress is without power to regulate.

We pause to consider the implications of the Government's arguments. The Government admits, under its "costs of crime" reasoning, that Congress could regulate not only all violent crime, but all activities that might lead to violent crime, regardless of how tenuously they relate to interstate commerce. See Tr. of Oral Arg. 8-9. Similarly, under the Government's "national productivity" reasoning, Congress could regulate any activity that it found was related to the economic productivity of individual citizens: family law (including marriage, divorce, and child custody), for example. Under the theories that the Government presents in support of §922(q), it is difficult to perceive any limitation on federal power, even in areas such as criminal law enforcement or education where States historically have been sovereign. Thus, if we were to accept the Government's arguments, we are hard pressed to posit any activity by an individual that Congress is without power to regulate.

Although Justice Breyer argues that acceptance of the Government's rationales would not authorize a general federal police power, he is unable to identify any activity that the States may regulate but Congress may not.

Although JUSTICE BREYER argues that acceptance of the Government's rationales would not authorize a general federal police power, he is unable to identify any activity that the States may regulate but Congress may not. JUSTICE BREYER posits that there might be some limitations on Congress' commerce power, such as family law or certain aspects of education. Post, at 624. These suggested limitations, when viewed in light of the dissent's expansive analysis, are devoid of substance.

Justice Breyer focuses, for the most part, on the threat that firearm possession in and near schools poses to the educational process and the potential economic consequences flowing from that threat. Specifically, the dissent reasons that (1) gun-related violence is a serious problem; (2) that problem, in turn, has an adverse effect on classroom learning; and (3) that adverse effect on classroom learning, in turn, represents a substantial threat to trade and commerce.

JUSTICE BREYER focuses, for the most part, on the threat that firearm possession in and near schools poses to the educational process and the potential economic consequences flowing from that threat. Post, at 619-624. Specifically, the dissent reasons that (1) gun-related violence is a serious problem; (2) that problem, in turn, has an adverse effect on classroom learning; and (3) that adverse effect on classroom learning, in turn, represents a substantial threat to trade and commerce. Post, at 623. This analysis would be equally applicable, if not more so, to subjects such as family law and direct regulation of education.

For instance, if Congress can, pursuant to its Commerce Clause power, regulate activities that adversely affect the learning environment, then, a fortiori, it also can regulate the educational process directly. Congress could determine that a school's curriculum has a "significant" effect on the extent of classroom learning. As a result, Congress could mandate a federal curriculum for local elementary and secondary schools because what is taught in local schools has a significant "effect on classroom learning," cf. ibid., and that, in turn, has a substantial effect on interstate commerce.

JUSTICE BREYER rejects our reading of precedent and argues that "Congress . . . could rationally conclude that schools fall on the commercial side of the line." Post, at 629. Again, JUSTICE BREYER's rationale lacks any real limits because, depending on the level of generality, any activity can be looked upon as commercial. Under the dissent's rationale, Congress could just as easily look at child rearing as "falling on the commercial side of the line" because it provides a "valuable service -- namely, to equip [children] with the skills they need to survive in life and, more specifically, in the workplace." Ibid. We do not doubt that Congress has authority under the Commerce Clause to regulate numerous commercial activities that substantially affect interstate commerce and also affect the educational process. That authority, though broad, does not include the authority to regulate each and every aspect of local schools.

Admittedly, a determination whether an intrastate activity is commercial or noncommercial may in some cases result in legal uncertainty. But, so long as Congress' authority is limited to those powers enumerated in the Constitution, and so long as those enumerated powers are interpreted as having judicially enforceable outer limits, congressional legislation under the Commerce Clause always will engender "legal uncertainty." Post, at 630. As Chief Justice Marshall stated in McCulloch v. Maryland, 17 U.S. 316, 4 Wheat. 316, 4 L. Ed. 579 (1819): "The [federal] government is acknowledged by all to be one of enumerated powers. The principle, that it can exercise only the powers granted to it . . . is now universally admitted. But the question respecting the extent of the powers actually granted, is perpetually arising, and will probably continue to arise, as long as our system shall exist." Id., at 405. See also Gibbons v. Ogden, 9 Wheat., at 195 ("The enumeration presupposes something not enumerated"). The Constitution mandates this uncertainty by withholding from Congress a plenary police power that would authorize enactment of every type of legislation. See Art. I, §8. Congress has operated within this framework of legal uncertainty ever since this Court determined that it was the Judiciary's duty "to say what the law is." Marbury v. Madison, 5 U.S. 137, 1 Cranch 137, 177, 2 L. Ed. 60 (1803) (Marshall, C. J.). Any possible benefit from eliminating this "legal uncertainty" would be at the expense of the Constitution's system of enumerated powers.

In Jones & Laughlin Steel, 301 U.S. at 37, we held that the question of congressional power under the Commerce Clause "is necessarily one of degree." To the same effect is the concurring opinion of Justice Cardozo in Schechter Poultry:

"There is a view of causation that would obliterate the distinction between what is national and what is local in the activities of commerce. Motion at the outer rim is communicated perceptibly, though minutely, to recording instruments at the center. A society such as ours 'is an elastic medium which transmits all tremors throughout its territory; the only question is of their size.'" 295 U.S. at 554 (quoting United States v. A. L. A. Schechter Poultry Corp., 76 F.2d 617, 624 (CA2 1935) (L. Hand, J., concurring)).

The possession of a gun in a local school zone is in no sense an economic activity that might, through repetition elsewhere, substantially affect any sort of interstate commerce.

These are not precise formulations, and in the nature of things they cannot be. But we think they point the way to a correct decision of this case. The possession of a gun in a local school zone is in no sense an economic activity that might, through repetition elsewhere, substantially affect any sort of interstate commerce. Respondent was a local student at a local school; there is no indication that he had recently moved in interstate commerce, and there is no requirement that his possession of the firearm have any concrete tie to interstate commerce.

To uphold the Government's contentions here, we would have to pile inference upon inference in a manner that would bid fair to convert congressional authority under the Commerce Clause to a general police power of the sort retained by the States. Admittedly, some of our prior cases have taken long steps down that road

To uphold the Government's contentions here, we would have to pile inference upon inference in a manner that would bid fair to convert congressional authority under the Commerce Clause to a general police power of the sort retained by the States. Admittedly, some of our prior cases have taken long steps down that road, giving great deference to congressional action. See supra, at 556-558. The broad language in these opinions has suggested the possibility of additional expansion, but we decline here to proceed any further. To do so would require us to conclude that the Constitution's enumeration of powers does not presuppose something not enumerated, cf. Gibbons v. Ogden, supra, at 195, and that there never will be a distinction between what is truly national and what is truly local, cf. Jones & Laughlin Steel, supra, at 30. This we are unwilling to do.

For the foregoing reasons the judgment of the Court of Appeals is

Affirmed.

JUSTICE KENNEDY, with whom JUSTICE O'CONNOR joins, concurring.

The history of the judicial struggle to interpret the Commerce Clause during the transition from the economic system the Founders knew to the single, national market still emergent in our own era counsels great restraint before the Court determines that the Clause is insufficient to support an exercise of the national power. That history gives me some pause about today's decision, but I join the Court's opinion with these observations on what I conceive to be its necessary though limited holding.

Chief Justice Marshall announced that the national authority reaches "that commerce which concerns more States than one" and that the commerce power "is complete in itself, may be exercised to its utmost extent, and acknowledges no limitations, other than are prescribed in the constitution." Gibbons v. Ogden, 22 U.S. 1, 9 Wheat. 1, 194, 196, 6 L. Ed. 23 (1824). His statements can be understood now as an early and authoritative recognition that the Commerce Clause grants Congress extensive power and ample discretion to determine its appropriate exercise. The progression of our Commerce Clause cases from Gibbons to the present was not marked, however, by a coherent or consistent course of interpretation; for neither the course of technological advance nor the foundational principles for the jurisprudence itself were self-evident to the courts that sought to resolve contemporary disputes by enduring principles.

Furthermore, for almost a century after the adoption of the Constitution, the Court's Commerce Clause decisions did not concern the authority of Congress to legislate. Rather, the Court faced the related but quite distinct question of the authority of the States to regulate matters that would be within the commerce power had Congress chosen to act. The simple fact was that in the early years of the Republic, Congress seldom perceived the necessity to exercise its power in circumstances where its authority would be called into question. The Court's initial task, therefore, was to elaborate the theories that would permit the States to act where Congress had not done so. Not the least part of the problem was the unresolved question whether the congressional power was exclusive, a question reserved by Chief Justice Marshall in Gibbons v. Ogden, supra, at 209-210.

At the midpoint of the 19th century, the Court embraced the principle that the States and the National Government both have authority to regulate certain matters absent the congressional determination to displace local law or the necessity for the Court to invalidate local law because of the dormant national power. Cooley v. Board of Wardens of Port of Philadelphia ex rel. Soc. for Relief of Distressed Pilots, 53 U.S. 299, 12 HOW 299, 318-321, 13 L. Ed. 996 (1852). But the utility of that solution was not at once apparent, see generally F. Frankfurter, The Commerce Clause under Marshall, Taney and Waite (1937) (hereinafter Frankfurter), and difficulties of application persisted, see Leisy v. Hardin, 135 U.S. 100, 122-125, 34 L. Ed. 128, 10 S. Ct. 681 (1890).

One approach the Court used to inquire into the lawfulness of state authority was to draw content-based or subject-matter distinctions, thus defining by semantic or formalistic categories those activities that were commerce and those that were not. For instance, in deciding that a State could prohibit the in-state manufacture of liquor intended for out-of-state shipment, it distinguished between manufacture and commerce. "No distinction is more popular to the common mind, or more clearly expressed in economic and political literature, than that between manufacture and commerce. Manufacture is transformation -- the fashioning of raw materials into a change of form for use. The functions of commerce are different." Kidd v. Pearson, 128 U.S. 1, 20, 32 L. Ed. 346, 9 S. Ct. 6 (1888). Though that approach likely would not have survived even if confined to the question of a State's authority to enact legislation, it was not at all propitious when applied to the quite different question of what subjects were within the reach of the national power when Congress chose to exercise it.

This became evident when the Court began to confront federal economic regulation enacted in response to the rapid industrial development in the late 19th century. Thus, it relied upon the manufacture-commerce dichotomy in United States v. E. C. Knight Co., 156 U.S. 1, 39 L. Ed. 325, 15 S. Ct. 249 (1895), where a manufacturers' combination controlling some 98% of the Nation's domestic sugar refining capacity was held to be outside the reach of the Sherman Act. Conspiracies to control manufacture, agriculture, mining, production, wages, or prices, the Court explained, had too "indirect" an effect on interstate commerce. Id., at 16. And in Adair v. United States, 208 U.S. 161, 52 L. Ed. 436, 28 S. Ct. 277 (1908), the Court rejected the view that the commerce power might extend to activities that, although local in the sense of having originated within a single State, nevertheless had a practical effect on interstate commercial activity. The Court concluded that there was not a "legal or logical connection . . . between an employe's membership in a labor organization and the carrying on of interstate commerce," id., at 178, and struck down a federal statute forbidding the discharge of an employee because of his membership in a labor organization. See also The Employers' Liability Cases, 207 U.S. 463, 497, 52 L. Ed. 297, 28 S. Ct. 141 (1908) (invalidating statute creating negligence action against common carriers for personal injuries of employees sustained in the course of employment, because the statute "regulates the persons because they engage in interstate commerce and does not alone regulate the business of interstate commerce").

Even before the Court committed itself to sustaining federal legislation on broad principles of economic practicality, it found it necessary to depart from these decisions. The Court disavowed E. C. Knight's reliance on the manufacturing-commerce distinction in Standard Oil Co. of N. J. v. United States, 221 U.S. 1, 68-69, 55 L. Ed. 619, 31 S. Ct. 502 (1911), declaring that approach "unsound." The Court likewise rejected the rationale of Adair when it decided, in Texas & New Orleans R. Co. v. Railway Clerks, 281 U.S. 548, 570-571, 50 S. Ct. 427, 74 L. Ed. 1034 (1930), that Congress had the power to regulate matters pertaining to the organization of railroad workers.

In another line of cases, the Court addressed Congress' efforts to impede local activities it considered undesirable by prohibiting the interstate movement of some essential element. In the Lottery Case, 188 U.S. 321, 47 L. Ed. 492, 23 S. Ct. 321 (1903), the Court rejected the argument that Congress lacked power to prohibit the interstate movement of lottery tickets because it had power only to regulate, not to prohibit. See also Hipolite Egg Co. v. United States, 220 U.S. 45, 55 L. Ed. 364, 31 S. Ct. 364 (1911); Hoke v. United States, 227 U.S. 308, 57 L. Ed. 523, 33 S. Ct. 281 (1913). In Hammer v. Dagenhart, 247 U.S. 251, 62 L. Ed. 1101, 38 S. Ct. 529 (1918), however, the Court insisted that the power to regulate commerce "is directly the contrary of the assumed right to forbid commerce from moving," id., at 269-270, and struck down a prohibition on the interstate transportation of goods manufactured in violation of child labor laws.

Even while it was experiencing difficulties in finding satisfactory principles in these cases, the Court was pursuing a more sustainable and practical approach in other lines of decisions, particularly those involving the regulation of railroad rates. In the Minnesota Rate Cases, 230 U.S. 352, 57 L. Ed. 1511, 33 S. Ct. 729 (1913), the Court upheld a state rate order, but observed that Congress might be empowered to regulate in this area if "by reason of the interblending of the interstate and intrastate operations of interstate carriers" the regulation of interstate rates could not be maintained without restrictions on "intrastate rates which substantially affect the former." Id., at 432-433. And in the Shreveport Rate Cases, 234 U.S. 342, 34 S. Ct. 833, 58 L. Ed. 1341 (1914), the Court upheld an Interstate Commerce Commission order fixing railroad rates with the explanation that congressional authority, "extending to these interstate carriers as instruments of interstate commerce, necessarily embraces the right to control their operations in all matters having such a close and substantial relation to interstate traffic that the control is essential or appropriate to the security of that traffic, to the efficiency of the interstate service, and to the maintenance of conditions under which interstate commerce may be conducted upon fair terms and without molestation or hindrance." Id., at 351.

Even the most confined interpretation of "commerce" would embrace transportation between the States, so the rate cases posed much less difficulty for the Court than cases involving manufacture or production. Nevertheless, the Court's recognition of the importance of a practical conception of the commerce power was not altogether confined to the rate cases. In Swift & Co. v. United States, 196 U.S. 375, 49 L. Ed. 518, 25 S. Ct. 276 (1905), the Court upheld the application of federal antitrust law to a combination of meat dealers that occurred in one State but that restrained trade in cattle "sent for sale from a place in one State, with the expectation that they will end their transit . . . in another." Id., at 398. The Court explained that "commerce among the States is not a technical legal conception, but a practical one, drawn from the course of business." Ibid. Chief Justice Taft followed the same approach in upholding federal regulation of stockyards in Stafford v. Wallace, 258 U.S. 495, 66 L. Ed. 735, 42 S. Ct. 397 (1922). Speaking for the Court, he rejected a "nice and technical inquiry," id., at 519, when the local transactions at issue could not "be separated from the movement to which they contribute," id., at 516.

Reluctance of the Court to adopt that approach in all of its cases caused inconsistencies in doctrine to persist, however. In addressing New Deal legislation the Court resuscitated the abandoned abstract distinction between direct and indirect effects on interstate commerce. See Carter v. Carter Coal Co., 298 U.S. 238, 309, 80 L. Ed. 1160, 56 S. Ct. 855 (1936) (Act regulating price of coal and wages and hours for miners held to have only "secondary and indirect" effect on interstate commerce); Railroad Retirement Bd. v. Alton R. Co., 295 U.S. 330, 368, 79 L. Ed. 1468, 55 S. Ct. 758 (1935) (compulsory retirement and pension plan for railroad carrier employees too "remote from any regulation of commerce as such"); A. L. A. Schechter Poultry Corp. v. United States, 295 U.S. 495, 548, 79 L. Ed. 1570, 55 S. Ct. 837 (1935) (wage and hour law provision of National Industrial Recovery Act had "no direct relation to interstate commerce").

The case that seems to mark the Court's definitive commitment to the practical conception of the commerce power is NLRB v. Jones & Laughlin Steel Corp., 301 U.S. 1, 81 L. Ed. 893, 57 S. Ct. 615 (1937), where the Court sustained labor laws that applied to manufacturing facilities, making no real attempt to distinguish Carter, supra, and Schechter, supra. 301 U.S. at 40-41. The deference given to Congress has since been confirmed. United States v. Darby, 312 U.S. 100, 116-117, 85 L. Ed. 609, 61 S. Ct. 451 (1941), overruled Hammer v. Dagenhart, supra. And in Wickard v. Filburn, 317 U.S. 111, 87 L. Ed. 122, 63 S. Ct. 82 (1942), the Court disapproved E. C. Knight and the entire line of direct-indirect and manufacture-production cases, explaining that "broader interpretations of the Commerce Clause [were] destined to supersede the earlier ones," 317 U.S. at 122, and "whatever terminology is used, the criterion is necessarily one of degree and must be so defined. This does not satisfy those who seek mathematical or rigid formulas. But such formulas are not provided by the great concepts of the Constitution," id., at 123, n. 24. Later examples of the exercise of federal power where commercial transactions were the subject of regulation include Heart of Atlanta Motel, Inc. v. United States, 379 U.S. 241, 13 L. Ed. 2d 258, 85 S. Ct. 348 (1964), Katzenbach v. McClung, 379 U.S. 294, 13 L. Ed. 2d 290, 85 S. Ct. 377 (1964), and Perez v. United States, 402 U.S. 146, 28 L. Ed. 2d 686, 91 S. Ct. 1357 (1971). These and like authorities are within the fair ambit of the Court's practical conception of commercial regulation and are not called in question by our decision today.

The history of our Commerce Clause decisions contains at least two lessons of relevance to this case. The first, as stated at the outset, is the imprecision of content-based boundaries used without more to define the limits of the Commerce Clause. The second, related to the first but of even greater consequence, is that the Court as an institution and the legal system as a whole have an immense stake in the stability of our Commerce Clause jurisprudence as it has evolved to this point. Stare decisis operates with great force in counseling us not to call in question the essential principles now in place respecting the congressional power to regulate transactions of a commercial nature. That fundamental restraint on our power forecloses us from reverting to an understanding of commerce that would serve only an 18th-century economy, dependent then upon production and trading practices that had changed but little over the preceding centuries; it also mandates against returning to the time when congressional authority to regulate undoubted commercial activities was limited by a judicial determination that those matters had an insufficient connection to an interstate system. Congress can regulate in the commercial sphere on the assumption that we have a single market and a unified purpose to build a stable national economy.

In referring to the whole subject of the federal and state balance, we said this just three Terms ago:

"This framework has been sufficiently flexible over the past two centuries to allow for enormous changes in the nature of government. The Federal Government undertakes activities today that would have been unimaginable to the Framers in two senses: first, because the Framers would not have conceived that any government would conduct such activities; and second, because the Framers would not have believed that the Federal Government, rather than the States, would assume such responsibilities. Yet the powers conferred upon the Federal Government by the Constitution were phrased in language broad enough to allow for the expansion of the Federal Government's role." New York v. United States, 505 U.S. 144, 157, 120 L. Ed. 2d 120, 112 S. Ct. 2408 (1992) (emphasis deleted).

It does not follow, however, that in every instance the Court lacks the authority and responsibility to review congressional attempts to alter the federal balance. This case requires us to consider our place in the design of the Government and to appreciate the significance of federalism in the whole structure of the Constitution.

Of the various structural elements in the Constitution, separation of powers, checks and balances, judicial review, and federalism, only concerning the last does there seem to be much uncertainty respecting the existence, and the content, of standards that allow the Judiciary to play a significant role in maintaining the design contemplated by the Framers. Although the resolution of specific cases has proved difficult, we have derived from the Constitution workable standards to assist in preserving separation of powers and checks and balances. See, e.g., Prize Cases, 67 U.S. 635, 2 Black 635, 17 L. Ed. 459 (1863); Youngstown Sheet & Tube Co. v. Sawyer, 343 U.S. 579, 96 L. Ed. 1153, 72 S. Ct. 863 (1952); United States v. Nixon, 418

U.S. 683, 41 L. Ed. 2d 1039, 94 S. Ct. 3090 (1974); Buckley v. Valeo, 424 U.S. 1, 46 L. Ed. 2d 659, 96 S. Ct. 612 (1976); INS v. Chadha, 462 U.S. 919, 77 L. Ed. 2d 317, 103 S. Ct. 2764 (1983); Bowsher v. Synar, 478 U.S. 714, 92 L. Ed. 2d 583, 106 S. Ct. 3181 (1986); Plaut v. Spendthrift Farm, Inc., ante, p. 211. These standards are by now well accepted. Judicial review is also established beyond question, Marbury v. Madison, 5 U.S. 137, 1 Cranch 137, 2 L. Ed. 60 (1803), and though we may differ when applying its principles, see, e.g., Planned Parenthood of Southeastern Pa. v. Casey, 505 U.S. 833, 120 L. Ed. 2d 674, 112 S. Ct. 2791 (1992), its legitimacy is undoubted. Our role in preserving the federal balance seems more tenuous.

> **of the four structural elements in the Constitution just mentioned <separation of powers, checks and balances, judicial review, and federalism>, federalism was the unique contribution of the Framers to political science and political theory. Though on the surface the idea may seem counter-intuitive, it was the insight of the Framers that freedom was enhanced by the creation of two governments, not one.**
>
> **Just as the separation and independence of the coordinate branches of the Federal Government serve to prevent the accumulation of excessive power in any one branch, a healthy balance of power between the States and the Federal Government will reduce the risk of tyranny and abuse from either front ... In the tension between federal and state power lies the promise of liberty**
>
> **The Constitution divides authority between federal and state governments for the protection of individuals. State sovereignty is not just an end in itself: Rather, federalism secures to citizens the liberties that derive from the diffusion of sovereign power.**

There is irony in this, because of the four structural elements in the Constitution just mentioned, federalism was the unique contribution of the Framers to political science and political theory. See Friendly, Federalism: A Foreword, 86 Yale L. J. 1019 (1977); G. Wood, The Creation of the American Republic, 1776-1787, pp. 524-532, 564 (1969). Though on the surface the idea may seem counter-intuitive, it was the insight of the Framers that freedom was enhanced by the creation of two governments, not one. "In the compound republic of America, the power surrendered by the people is first divided between two distinct governments, and then the portion allotted to each subdivided among distinct and separate departments. Hence a double security arises to the rights of the people. The different governments will control each other, at the same time that each will be controlled by itself." The Federalist No. 51, p. 323 (C. Rossiter ed. 1961) (J. Madison). See also Gregory v. Ashcroft, 501 U.S. 452, 458-459, 115 L. Ed. 2d 410, 111 S. Ct. 2395 (1991) ("Just as the separation and independence of the coordinate branches of the Federal Government serve to prevent the accumulation of excessive power in any one branch, a healthy balance of power between the States and the Federal Government will reduce the risk of tyranny and abuse from either front. . . . In the tension between federal and state power lies the promise of liberty"); New York v. United States, supra, at 181 ("The Constitution divides authority between federal and state governments for the protection of individuals. State sovereignty is not just an end in itself: 'Rather, federalism secures to citizens the liberties that derive from the diffusion of sovereign power'") (quoting Coleman v. Thompson, 501 U.S. 722, 759, 115 L. Ed. 2d 640, 111 S. Ct. 2546 (1991) (Blackmun, J., dissenting)).

The theory that two governments accord more liberty than one requires for its realization two distinct and discernable lines of political accountability: one between the citizens and the Federal Government; the second between the citizens and the States. If, as Madison expected, the Federal and State Governments are to control each other, see The Federalist No. 51, and hold each other in check by competing for the affections of the people, see The Federalist No. 46, those citizens must have some means of knowing which of the two governments to hold accountable for the failure to perform a given function. "Federalism serves to assign political responsibility, not to obscure it." FTC v. Ticor Title Ins. Co., 504 U.S. 621, 636, 119 L. Ed. 2d 410, 112 S. Ct. 2169 (1992). Were the Federal Government to take over the regulation of entire areas of traditional state concern, areas having nothing to do with the regulation of commercial activities, the boundaries between the spheres of federal and state authority would blur and political responsibility would become illusory. Cf. New York v. United States, supra, at 155-169; FERC v. Mississippi, 456 U.S. 742, 787, 72 L. Ed. 2d 532, 102 S. Ct. 2126 (1982) (O'CONNOR, J., concurring in judgment in part and dissenting in part). The resultant inability to hold either branch of the government answerable to the citizens is more dangerous even than devolving too much authority to the remote central power.

To be sure, one conclusion that could be drawn from The Federalist Papers is that the balance between national and state power is entrusted in its entirety to the political process. Madison's observation that "the people ought not surely to be precluded from giving most of their confidence where they may discover it to be most due," The Federalist No. 46, p. 295 (C. Rossiter ed. 1961), can be interpreted to say that the essence of responsibility for a shift in power from the State to the Federal Government rests upon a political judgment, though he added assurance that "the State governments could have little to apprehend, because it is only within a certain sphere that the federal power can, in the nature of things, be advantageously administered, " ibid. Whatever the judicial role, it is axiomatic that Congress does have substantial discretion and control over the federal balance.

For these reasons, it would be mistaken and mischievous for the political branches to forget that the sworn obligation to preserve and protect the Constitution in maintaining the federal balance is their own in the first and primary instance. In the Webster-Hayne Debates, see The Great Speeches and Orations of Daniel Webster 227-272 (E. Whipple ed. 1879), and the debates over the Civil Rights Acts, see Hearings on S. 1732 before the Senate Committee on Commerce, 88th Cong., 1st Sess., pts. 1-3 (1963), some Congresses have accepted responsibility to confront the great questions of the proper federal balance in terms of lasting consequences for the constitutional design. The political branches of the Government must fulfill this grave constitutional obligation if democratic liberty and the federalism that secures it are to endure.

At the same time, the absence of structural mechanisms to require those officials to undertake this principled task, and the momentary political convenience often attendant upon their failure to do so, argue against a complete renunciation of the judicial role. Although it is the obligation of all officers of the Government to respect the constitutional design, see Public Citizen v. Department of Justice, 491 U.S. 440, 466, 105 L. Ed. 2d 377, 109 S. Ct. 2558 (1989); Rostker v. Goldberg, 453 U.S. 57, 64, 69 L. Ed. 2d 478, 101 S. Ct. 2646 (1981), the federal balance is too essential a part of our constitutional structure and plays too vital a role in securing freedom for us to admit inability to intervene when one or the other level of Government has tipped the scales too far.

In the past this Court has participated in maintaining the federal balance through judicial exposition of doctrines such as abstention, see, e.g., Younger v. Harris, 401 U.S. 37, 27 L. Ed. 2d 669, 91 S. Ct. 746 (1971); Railroad Comm'n of Tex. v. Pullman Co., 312 U.S. 496, 85 L. Ed. 971, 61 S. Ct. 643 (1941); Burford v. Sun Oil Co., 319 U.S. 315, 87 L. Ed. 1424, 63 S. Ct. 1098 (1943), the rules for determining the primacy of state law, see, e.g., Erie R. Co. v. Tompkins, 304 U.S. 64, 82 L. Ed. 1188, 58 S. Ct. 817 (1938), the doctrine of adequate and independent state grounds, see, e.g., Murdock v. Memphis, 87 U.S. 590, 20 Wall. 590, 22 L. Ed. 429 (1875); Michigan v. Long, 463 U.S. 1032, 77 L. Ed. 2d 1201, 103 S. Ct. 3469 (1983), the whole jurisprudence of pre-emption, see, e.g., Rice v. Santa Fe Elevator Corp., 331 U.S. 218, 91 L. Ed. 1447, 67 S. Ct. 1146 (1947); Cipollone v. Liggett Group, Inc., 505 U.S. 504, 120 L. Ed. 2d 407, 112 S. Ct. 2608 (1992), and many of the rules governing our habeas jurisprudence, see, e.g., Coleman v. Thompson, 501 U.S. 722, 115 L. Ed. 2d 640, 111 S. Ct. 2546 (1991); McCleskey v. Zant, 499 U.S. 467, 113 L. Ed. 2d 517, 111 S. Ct. 1454 (1991); Teague v. Lane, 489 U.S. 288, 103 L. Ed. 2d 334, 109 S. Ct. 1060 (1989); Rose v. Lundy, 455 U.S. 509, 71 L. Ed. 2d 379, 102 S. Ct. 1198 (1982); Wainwright v. Sykes, 433 U.S. 72, 53 L. Ed. 2d 594, 97 S. Ct. 2497 (1977).

Our ability to preserve this principle under the Commerce Clause has presented a much greater challenge. See supra, at 568-574. "This clause has throughout the Court's history been the chief source of its adjudications regarding federalism," and "no other body of opinions affords a fairer or more revealing test of judicial qualities." Frankfurter 66-67. But as the branch whose distinctive duty it is to declare "what the law is," Marbury v. Madison, 1 Cranch, at 177, we are often called upon to resolve questions of constitutional law not susceptible to the mechanical application of bright and clear lines. The substantial element of political judgment in Commerce Clause matters leaves our institutional capacity to intervene more in doubt than when we decide cases, for instance, under the Bill of Rights even though clear and bright lines are often absent in the latter class of disputes. See County of Allegheny v. American Civil Liberties Union, Greater Pittsburgh Chapter, 492 U.S. 573, 630, 106 L. Ed. 2d 472, 109 S. Ct. 3086 (1989) (O'CONNOR, J., concurring in part and concurring in judgment) ("We cannot avoid the obligation to draw lines, often close and difficult lines" in adjudicating constitutional rights). But our cases do not teach that we have no role at all in determining the meaning of the Commerce Clause.

Our position in enforcing the dormant Commerce Clause is instructive. The Court's doctrinal approach in that area has likewise "taken some turns." Oklahoma Tax Comm'n v. Jefferson Lines, Inc., ante, at 180. Yet in contrast to the prevailing skepticism that surrounds our ability to give meaning to the explicit text of the Commerce Clause, there is widespread acceptance of our authority to enforce the dormant Commerce Clause, which we have but inferred from the constitutional structure as a limitation on the power of the States. One element of our dormant Commerce Clause jurisprudence has been the principle that the States may not impose regulations that place an undue burden on interstate commerce, even where those regulations do not discriminate between in-state and out-of-state businesses. See Brown-Forman Distillers Corp. v. New York State Liquor Authority, 476 U.S. 573, 579, 90 L. Ed. 2d 552, 106 S. Ct. 2080 (1986) (citing

Pike v. Bruce Church, Inc., 397 U.S. 137, 142, 25 L. Ed. 2d 174, 90 S. Ct. 844 (1970)). Distinguishing between regulations that do place an undue burden on interstate commerce and regulations that do not depends upon delicate judgments. True, if we invalidate a state law, Congress can in effect overturn our judgment, whereas in a case announcing that Congress has transgressed its authority, the decision is more consequential, for it stands unless Congress can revise its law to demonstrate its commercial character. This difference no doubt informs the circumspection with which we invalidate an Act of Congress, but it does not mitigate our duty to recognize meaningful limits on the commerce power of Congress.

The statute before us upsets the federal balance to a degree that renders it an unconstitutional assertion of the commerce power, and our intervention is required. As THE CHIEF JUSTICE explains, unlike the earlier cases to come before the Court here neither the actors nor their conduct have a commercial character, and neither the purposes nor the design of the statute have an evident commercial nexus. See ante, at 559-561. The statute makes the simple possession of a gun within 1,000 feet of the grounds of the school a criminal offense. In a sense any conduct in this interdependent world of ours has an ultimate commercial origin or consequence, but we have not yet said the commerce power may reach so far. If Congress attempts that extension, then at the least we must inquire whether the exercise of national power seeks to intrude upon an area of traditional state concern.

An interference of these dimensions occurs here, for it is well established that education is a traditional concern of the States. Milliken v. Bradley, 418 U.S. 717, 741-742, 41 L. Ed. 2d 1069, 94 S. Ct. 3112 (1974); Epperson v. Arkansas, 393 U.S. 97, 104, 21 L. Ed. 2d 228, 89 S. Ct. 266 (1968). The proximity to schools, including of course schools owned and operated by the States or their subdivisions, is the very premise for making the conduct criminal. In these circumstances, we have a particular duty to ensure that the federal-state balance is not destroyed. Cf. Rice, supra, at 230 ("We start with the assumption that the historic police powers of the States" are not displaced by a federal statute "unless that was the clear and manifest purpose of Congress"); Florida Lime & Avocado Growers, Inc. v. Paul, 373 U.S. 132, 146, 10 L. Ed. 2d 248, 83 S. Ct. 1210 (1963).

While it is doubtful that any State, or indeed any reasonable person, would argue that it is wise policy to allow students to carry guns on school premises, considerable disagreement exists about how best to accomplish that goal.

While it is doubtful that any State, or indeed any reasonable person, would argue that it is wise policy to allow students to carry guns on school premises, considerable disagreement exists about how best to accomplish that goal. In this circumstance, the theory and utility of our federalism are revealed, for the States may perform their role as laboratories for experimentation to devise various solutions where the best solution is far from clear. See San Antonio Independent School Dist. v. Rodriguez, 411 U.S. 1, 49-50, 36 L. Ed. 2d 16, 93 S. Ct. 1278 (1973); New State Ice Co. v. Liebmann, 285 U.S. 262, 311, 76 L. Ed. 747, 52 S. Ct. 371 (1932) (Brandeis, J., dissenting).

If a State or municipality determines that harsh criminal sanctions are necessary and wise to deter students from carrying guns on school premises, the reserved powers of the States are sufficient to enact those measures. Indeed, over 40 States already have criminal laws outlawing the possession of firearms on or near school grounds.

If a State or municipality determines that harsh criminal sanctions are necessary and wise to deter students from carrying guns on school premises, the reserved powers of the States are sufficient to enact those measures. Indeed, over 40 States already have criminal laws outlawing the possession of firearms on or near school grounds. See, e.g., Alaska Stat. Ann. §§11.61.195(a)(2)(A), 11.61.220(a)(4)(A) (Supp. 1994); Cal. Penal Code Ann. §626.9 (West Supp. 1994); Mass. Gen. Laws §269:10(j) (1992); N. J. Stat. Ann. §2C:39-5(e) (West Supp. 1994); Va. Code Ann. §18.2-308.1 (1988); Wis. Stat. §948.605 (1991-1992).

Other, more practicable means to rid the schools of guns may be thought by the citizens of some States to be preferable for the safety and welfare of the schools

These might include inducements to inform on violators where the information leads to arrests or confiscation of the guns; programs to encourage the voluntary surrender of guns with some provision for amnesty; penalties imposed on parents or guardians for failure to supervise the child; fining parents who allow students to possess firearm at school; misdemeanor for parents to allow student to possess firearm at school; laws providing for suspension or expulsion of gun-toting students; expulsion with assignment to special facilities; automatic year-long expulsion for students with guns and intense semester-long reentry program.

Other, more practicable means to rid the schools of guns may be thought by the citizens of some States to be preferable for the safety and welfare of the schools those States are charged with maintaining. See Brief for National Conference of State Legislatures et al. as Amici Curiae 26-30 (injection of federal officials into local problems causes friction and diminishes political accountability of state and local governments). These might include inducements to inform on violators where the information leads to arrests or confiscation of the guns, see Lima, Schools May Launch Weapons Hot Line, Los Angeles Times, Ventura Cty. East ed., Jan. 13, 1995, p. B1, col. 5; Reward for Tips on Guns in Tucson Schools, The Arizona Republic, Jan. 7, 1995, p. B2; programs to encourage the voluntary surrender of guns with some provision for amnesty, see Zaidan, Akron Rallies to Save Youths, The Plain Dealer, Mar. 2, 1995, p. 1B; Swift, Legislators Consider Plan to Get Guns Off Streets, Hartford Courant, Apr. 29, 1992, p. A4; penalties imposed on parents or guardians for failure to supervise the child, see, e.g., Okla. Stat., Tit. 21, §858 (Supp. 1995) (fining parents who allow students to possess firearm at school); Tenn. Code Ann. §39-17-1312 (Supp. 1992) (misdemeanor for parents to allow student to possess firearm at school); Straight Shooter: Gov. Casey's Reasonable Plan to Control Assault Weapons, Pittsburgh Post-Gazette, Mar. 14, 1994, p. B2 (proposed bill); Bailey, Anti-Crime Measures Top Legislators' Agenda, Los Angeles Times, Orange Cty. ed., Mar. 7, 1994, p. B1, col. 2 (same); Krupa, New Gun-Control Plans Could Tighten Local Law, The Boston Globe, June 20, 1993, p. 29; laws providing for suspension or expulsion of gun-toting students, see, e.g., Ala. Code §16-1-24.1 (Supp. 1994); Ind. Code §20-8.1-5-4(b)(1)(D) (1993); Ky. Rev. Stat. Ann. §158.150(1)(a) (Michie 1992); Wash. Rev. Code §9.41.280 (1994), or programs for expulsion with assignment to special facilities, see Martin, Legislators Poised to Take Harsher Stand on Guns in Schools, The Seattle Times, Feb. 1, 1995, p. B1 (automatic year-long expulsion for students with guns and intense semester-long reentry program).

The statute now before us forecloses the States from experimenting and exercising their own judgment in an area to which States lay claim by right of history and expertise

an invisible federal zone extending 1,000 feet beyond the (often irregular) boundaries of the school property

school officials would find their own programs for the prohibition of guns in danger of displacement by the federal authority

The statute now before us forecloses the States from experimenting and exercising their own judgment in an area to which States lay claim by right of history and expertise, and it does so by regulating an activity beyond the realm of commerce in the ordinary and usual sense of that term. The tendency of this statute to displace state regulation in areas of traditional state concern is evident from its territorial operation. There are over 100,000 elementary and secondary schools in the United States. See U.S. Dept. of Education, National Center for Education Statistics, Digest of Education Statistics 73, 104 (NCES 94-115, 1994) (Tables 63, 94). Each of these now has an invisible federal zone extending 1,000 feet beyond the (often irregular) boundaries of the school property. In some communities no doubt it would be difficult to navigate without infringing on those zones. Yet throughout these areas, school officials would find their own programs for the prohibition of guns in danger of displacement by the federal authority unless the State chooses to enact a parallel rule.

This is not a case where the etiquette of federalism has been violated by a formal command from the National Government directing the State to enact a certain policy, cf. New York v. United States, 505 U.S. 144, 120 L. Ed. 2d 120, 112 S. Ct. 2408 (1992), or to organize its governmental functions in a certain way, cf. FERC v. Mississippi, 456 U.S. at 781 (O'CONNOR, J., concurring in judgment in part and dissenting in part). While the intrusion on state sovereignty may not be as severe in this instance as in some of our recent Tenth Amendment cases, the intrusion is nonetheless significant. Absent a stronger connection or identification with commercial concerns that are central to the Commerce Clause, that interference contradicts the federal balance the Framers designed and that this Court is obliged to enforce.

For these reasons, I join in the opinion and judgment of the Court.

JUSTICE THOMAS, concurring.

The Court today properly concludes that the Commerce Clause does not grant Congress the authority to prohibit gun possession within 1,000 feet of a school, as it attempted to do in the Gun-Free School Zones Act of 1990, Pub. L. 101-647, 104 Stat. 4844. Although I join the majority, I write separately to observe that our case law has drifted far from the original understanding of the Commerce Clause. In a future case, we ought to temper our Commerce Clause jurisprudence in a manner that both makes sense of our more recent case law and is more faithful to the original understanding of that Clause.

We have said that Congress may regulate not only "Commerce . . . among the several States," U.S. Const., Art. I, §8, cl. 3, but also anything that has a "substantial effect" on such commerce. This test, if taken to its logical extreme, would give Congress a "police power" over all aspects of American life. Unfortunately, we have never come to grips with this implication of our substantial effects formula. Although we have supposedly applied the substantial effects test for the past 60 years, we always have rejected readings of the Commerce Clause and the scope of federal power that would permit Congress to exercise a police power; our cases are quite clear that there are real limits to federal power. See New York v. United States, 505 U.S. 144, 155, 120 L. Ed. 2d 120, 112 S. Ct. 2408 (1992) ("No one disputes the proposition that 'the Constitution created a Federal Government of limited powers'") (quoting Gregory v. Ashcroft, 501 U.S. 452, 457, 115 L. Ed. 2d 410, 111 S. Ct. 2395 (1991); Maryland v. Wirtz, 392 U.S. 183, 196, 20 L. Ed. 2d 1020, 88 S. Ct. 2017 (1968); NLRB v. Jones & Laughlin Steel Corp., 301 U.S. 1, 37, 81 L. Ed. 893, 57 S. Ct. 615 (1937). Cf. Chisholm v. Georgia, 2 U.S. 419, 2 Dall. 419, 435, 1 L. Ed. 440 (1793) (Iredell, J.) ("Each State in the Union is sovereign as to all the powers reserved. It must necessarily be so, because the United States have no claim to any authority but such as the States have surrendered to them") (emphasis deleted). Indeed, on this crucial point, the majority and JUSTICE BREYER agree in principle: The Federal Government has nothing approaching a police power. Compare ante, at 556-558, with post, at 624.

> **the sweeping nature of our current test enables the dissent to argue that Congress can regulate gun possession. But it seems to me that the power to regulate "commerce" can by no means encompass authority over mere gun possession, any more than it empowers the Federal Government to regulate marriage, littering, or cruelty to animals, throughout the 50 States.**

While the principal dissent concedes that there are limits to federal power, the sweeping nature of our current test enables the dissent to argue that Congress can regulate gun possession. But it seems to me that the power to regulate "commerce" can by no means encompass authority over mere gun possession, any more than it empowers the Federal Government to regulate marriage, littering, or cruelty to animals, throughout the 50 States. Our Constitution quite properly leaves such matters to the individual States, notwithstanding these activities' effects on interstate commerce. Any interpretation of the Commerce Clause that even suggests that Congress could regulate such matters is in need of reexamination.

In an appropriate case, I believe that we must further reconsider our "substantial effects" test with an eye toward constructing a standard that reflects the text and history of the Commerce Clause without totally rejecting our more recent Commerce Clause jurisprudence.

Today, however, I merely support the Court's conclusion with a discussion of the text, structure, and history of the Commerce Clause and an analysis of our early case law. My goal is simply to show how far we have departed from the original understanding and to demonstrate that the result we reach today is by no means "radical," see post, at 602 (STEVENS, J., dissenting). I also want to point out the necessity of refashioning a coherent test that does not tend to "obliterate the distinction between what is national and what is local and create a completely centralized government." Jones & Laughlin Steel Corp., supra, at 37.

I

At the time the original Constitution was ratified, "commerce" consisted of selling, buying, and bartering, as well as transporting for these purposes. See 1 S. Johnson, A Dictionary of the English Language 361 (4th ed. 1773) (defining commerce as "Intercour[s]e; exchange of one thing for another; interchange of any thing; trade; traffick"); N. Bailey, An Universal Etymological English Dictionary (26th ed. 1789) ("trade or traffic"); T. Sheridan, A Complete Dictionary of the English Language (6th ed. 1796) ("Exchange of one thing for another; trade, traffick"). This understanding finds support in the etymology of the word, which literally means "with merchandise." See 3 Oxford English Dictionary 552 (2d ed. 1989) (com -- "with"; merci -- "merchandise "). In fact, when Federalists and Anti-Federalists discussed the Commerce Clause during the ratification period, they often used trade (in its selling/bartering sense) and commerce interchangeably. See The Federalist No. 4, p. 22 (J. Jay) (asserting that countries will cultivate our friendship when our "trade" is prudently regulated by Federal Government); n1 id., No. 7, at 39-40 (A. Hamilton) (discussing "competitions of commerce" between States resulting from state "regulations of trade"); id., No. 40, at 262 (J. Madison) (asserting that it was an "acknowledged object of the Convention . . . that the regulation of trade should be submitted to the general government"); Lee, Letters of a Federal Farmer No. 5, in Pamphlets on the Constitution of the United States 319 (P. Ford ed. 1888); Smith, An Address to the People of the State of New-York, in id., at 107.

n1 All references to The Federalist are to the Jacob E. Cooke 1961 edition.

As one would expect, the term "commerce" was used in contradistinction to productive activities such as manufacturing and agriculture. Alexander Hamilton, for example, repeatedly treated commerce, agriculture, and manufacturing as three separate endeavors. See, e.g., The Federalist No. 36, at 224 (referring to "agriculture, commerce, manufactures"); id., No. 21, at 133 (distinguishing commerce, arts, and industry); id., No. 12, at 74 (asserting that commerce and agriculture have shared interests). The same distinctions were made in the state ratification conventions. See, e.g., 2 Debates in the Several State Conventions on the Adoption of the Federal Constitution 57 (J. Elliot ed. 1836) (hereinafter Debates) (T. Dawes at Massachusetts convention); id., at 336 (M. Smith at New York convention).

Moreover, interjecting a modern sense of commerce into the Constitution generates significant textual and structural problems. For example, one cannot replace "commerce" with a different type of enterprise, such as manufacturing. When a manufacturer produces a car, assembly cannot take place "with a foreign nation" or "with the Indian Tribes." Parts may come from different States or other nations and hence may have been in the flow of commerce at one time, but manufacturing takes place at a discrete site. Agriculture and manufacturing involve the production of goods; commerce encompasses traffic in such articles.

The Port Preference Clause also suggests that the term "commerce" denoted sale and/or transport rather than business generally. According to that Clause, "no Preference shall be given by any Regulation of Commerce or Revenue to the Ports of one State over those of another." U.S. Const., Art. I, §9, cl. 6. Although it is possible to conceive of regulations of manufacturing or farming that prefer one port over another, the more natural reading is that the Clause prohibits Congress from using its commerce power to channel commerce through certain favored ports.

The Constitution not only uses the word "commerce" in a narrower sense than our case law might suggest, it also does not support the proposition that Congress has authority over all activities that "substantially affect" interstate commerce. The Commerce Clause n2 does not state that Congress may "regulate matters that substantially affect commerce with foreign Nations, and among the several States, and with the Indian Tribes." In contrast, the Constitution itself temporarily prohibited amendments that would "affect" Congress' lack of authority to prohibit or restrict the slave trade or to enact unproportioned direct taxation. Art. V. Clearly, the Framers could have drafted a Constitution that contained a "substantially affects interstate commerce" Clause had that been their objective.

n2 Even to speak of "the Commerce Clause" perhaps obscures the actual scope of that Clause. As an original matter, Congress did not have authority to regulate all commerce; Congress could only "regulate Commerce with foreign Nations, and among the several States, and with the Indian Tribes." U.S. Const., Art. I, §8, cl. 3. Although the precise line between interstate/foreign commerce and purely intrastate commerce was hard to draw, the Court attempted to adhere to such a line for the first 150 years of our Nation. See infra, at 593-599.

In addition to its powers under the Commerce Clause, Congress has the authority to enact such laws as are "necessary and proper" to carry into execution its power to regulate commerce among the several States. U.S. Const., Art. I, §8, cl. 18. But on this Court's understanding of congressional power under these two Clauses, many of Congress' other enumerated powers under Art. I, §8, are wholly superfluous. After all, if Congress may regulate all matters that substantially affect commerce, there is no need for the Constitution to specify that Congress may enact bankruptcy laws, cl. 4, or coin money and fix the standard of weights and measures, cl. 5, or punish counterfeiters of United States coin and securities, cl. 6. Likewise, Congress would not need the separate authority to establish post offices and post roads, cl. 7, or to grant patents and copyrights, cl. 8, or to "punish Piracies and Felonies committed on the high Seas," cl. 10. It might not even need the power to raise and support an Army and Navy, cls. 12 and 13, for fewer people would engage in commercial shipping if they thought that a foreign power could expropriate their property with ease. Indeed, if Congress could regulate matters that substantially affect interstate commerce, there would have been no need to specify that Congress can regulate international trade and commerce with the Indians. As the Framers surely understood, these other branches of trade substantially affect interstate commerce.

Put simply, much if not all of Art. I, §8 (including portions of the Commerce Clause itself), would be surplusage if Congress had been given authority over matters that substantially affect interstate commerce. An interpretation of cl. 3 that makes the rest of §8 superfluous simply cannot be correct. Yet this Court's Commerce Clause jurisprudence has endorsed just such an interpretation: The power we have accorded Congress has swallowed Art. I, §8. n3

n3 There are other powers granted to Congress outside of Art. I, §8, that may become wholly superfluous as well due to our distortion of the Commerce Clause. For instance, Congress has plenary power over the District of Columbia and the territories. See U.S. Const., Art. I, §8, cl. 17, and Art. IV, §3, cl. 2. The grant of comprehensive legislative power over certain areas of the Nation, when read in conjunction with the rest of the Constitution, further confirms that Congress was not ceded plenary authority over the whole Nation.

Indeed, if a "substantial effects" test can be appended to the Commerce Clause, why not to every other power of the Federal Government? There is no reason for singling out the Commerce Clause for special treatment. Accordingly, Congress could regulate all matters that "substantially affect" the Army and Navy, bankruptcies, tax collection, expenditures, and so on. In that case, the Clauses of §8 all mutually overlap, something we can assume the Founding Fathers never intended.

Our construction of the scope of congressional authority has the additional problem of coming close to turning the Tenth Amendment on its head. Our case law could be read to reserve to the United States all powers not expressly prohibited by the Constitution. Taken together, these fundamental textual problems should, at the very least, convince us that the "substantial effects" test should be reexamined.

II

The exchanges during the ratification campaign reveal the relatively limited reach of the Commerce Clause and of federal power generally. The Founding Fathers confirmed that most areas of life (even many matters that would have substantial effects on commerce) would remain outside the reach of the Federal Government. Such affairs would continue to be under the exclusive control of the States.

Early Americans understood that commerce, manufacturing, and agriculture, while distinct activities, were intimately related and dependent on each other -- that each "substantially affected" the others. After all, items produced by farmers and manufacturers were the primary articles of commerce at the time. If commerce was more robust as a result of federal superintendence, farmers and manufacturers could benefit. Thus, Oliver Ellsworth of Connecticut attempted to convince farmers of the benefits of regulating commerce. "Your property and riches depend on a ready demand and generous price for the produce you can annually spare," he wrote, and these conditions exist "where trade flourishes and when the merchant can freely export the produce of the country" to nations that will pay the highest price. A Landholder No. 1, Connecticut Courant, Nov. 5, 1787, in 3 Documentary History of the Ratification of the Constitution 399 (M. Jensen ed. 1978) (hereinafter Documentary History). See also The Federalist No. 35, at 219 (A. Hamilton) ("Discerning citizens are well aware that the mechanic and manufacturing arts furnish the materials of mercantile enterprise and industry. Many of them indeed are immediately connected with the operations of commerce. They know that the merchant is their natural patron and friend"); id., at 221 ("Will not the merchant . . . be disposed to cultivate . . . the interests of the mechanic and manufacturing arts to which his commerce is so nearly allied?"); A Jerseyman: To the Citizens of New Jersey, Trenton Mercury, Nov. 6, 1787, in 3 Documentary History 147 (noting that agriculture will serve as a "source of commerce"); Marcus, The New Jersey Journal, Nov. 14, 1787, id., at 152 (both the mechanic and the farmer benefit from the prosperity of commerce). William Davie, a delegate to the North Carolina Convention, illustrated the close link best: "Commerce, sir, is the nurse of [agriculture and manufacturing]. The merchant furnishes the planter with such articles as he cannot manufacture himself, and finds him a market for his produce. Agriculture cannot flourish if commerce languishes; they are mutually dependent on each other." 4 Debates 20.

Yet, despite being well aware that agriculture, manufacturing, and other matters substantially affected commerce, the founding generation did not cede authority over all these activities to Congress. Hamilton, for instance, acknowledged that the Federal Government could not regulate agriculture and like concerns: "The administration of private justice between the citizens of the same State, the supervision of agriculture and of other concerns of a similar nature, all those things in short which are proper to be provided for by local legislation, can never be desirable cares of a general jurisdiction." The Federalist No. 17, at 106.

In the unlikely event that the Federal Government would attempt to exercise authority over such matters, its effort "would be as troublesome as it would be nugatory." Ibid. n4

n4 Cf. 3 Debates 40 (E. Pendleton at the Virginia convention) (The proposed Federal Government "does not intermeddle with the local, particular affairs of the states. Can Congress legislate for the state of Virginia? Can [it] make a law altering the form of transferring property, or the rule of descents, in Virginia?"); id., at 553 (J. Marshall at the Virginia convention) (denying that Congress could make "laws affecting the mode of transferring property, or contracts, or claims, between citizens of the same state"); The Federalist No. 33, at 206 (A. Hamilton) (denying that Congress could change laws of descent or could pre-empt a land tax); A Native of Virginia: Observations upon the Proposed Plan of Federal Government, Apr. 2, 1788, in 9 Documentary History 692 (States have sole authority over "rules of property").

The comments of Hamilton and others about federal power reflected the well-known truth that the new Government would have only the limited and enumerated powers found in the Constitution. See, e.g., 2 Debates 267-268 (A. Hamilton at New York convention) (noting that there would be just cause for rejecting the Constitution if it would enable the Federal Government to "alter, or abrogate . . . [a State's] civil and criminal institutions [or] penetrate the recesses of domestic life, and control, in all respects, the private conduct of individuals"); The Federalist No. 45, at 313 (J. Madison); 3 Debates 259 (J. Madison) (Virginia convention); R. Sherman & O. Ellsworth, Letter to Governor Huntington, Sept. 26, 1787, in 3 Documentary History 352; J. Wilson, Speech in the State House Yard, Oct. 6, 1787, in 2 id., at 167-168. Agriculture and manufacture, since they were not surrendered to the Federal Government, were state concerns. See The Federalist No. 34, at 212-213 (A. Hamilton) (observing that the " internal encouragement of agriculture and manufactures" was an object of state expenditure). Even before the passage of the Tenth Amendment, it was apparent that Congress would possess only those powers "herein granted" by the rest of the Constitution. Art. I, §1.

Where the Constitution was meant to grant federal authority over an activity substantially affecting interstate commerce, the Constitution contains an enumerated power over that particular activity. Indeed, the Framers knew that many of the other enumerated powers in §8 dealt with matters that substantially affected interstate commerce. Madison, for instance, spoke of the bankruptcy power as being "intimately connected with the regulation of commerce." The Federalist No. 42, at 287. Likewise, Hamilton urged that "if we mean to be a commercial people or even to be secure on our Atlantic side, we must endeavour as soon as possible to have a navy." Id., No. 24, at 157.

In short, the Founding Fathers were well aware of what the principal dissent calls "'economic . . . realities.'" See post, at 625 (BREYER, J.) (quoting North American Co. v. SEC, 327 U.S. 686, 705, 90 L. Ed. 945, 66 S. Ct. 785 (1946)). Even though the boundary between commerce and other matters may ignore "economic reality" and thus seem arbitrary or artificial to some, we must nevertheless respect a constitutional line that does not grant Congress power over all that substantially affects interstate commerce.

III

If the principal dissent's understanding of our early case law were correct, there might be some reason to doubt this view of the original understanding of the Constitution. According to that dissent, Chief Justice Marshall's opinion in Gibbons v. Ogden, 22 U.S. 1, 9 Wheat. 1, 6 L. Ed. 23 (1824), established that Congress may control all local activities that "significantly affect interstate commerce," post, at 615. And, "with the exception of one wrong turn subsequently corrected," this has been the "traditional" method of interpreting the Commerce Clause. Post, at 631 (citing Gibbons and United States v. Darby, 312 U.S. 100, 116-117, 85 L. Ed. 609, 61 S. Ct. 451 (1941)).

In my view, the dissent is wrong about the holding and reasoning of Gibbons. Because this error leads the dissent to characterize the first 150 years of this Court's case law as a "wrong turn," I feel compelled to put the last 50 years in proper perspective.

A

In Gibbons, the Court examined whether a federal law that licensed ships to engage in the "coasting trade" pre-empted a New York law granting a 30-year monopoly to Robert Livingston and Robert Fulton to navigate the State's waterways by steamship. In concluding that it did, the Court noted that Congress could regulate "navigation" because "all America . . . has uniformly understood, the word 'commerce,' to comprehend navigation. It was so understood, and must have been so understood, when the constitution was framed." 9 Wheat., at 190. The Court also observed that federal power over commerce "among the several States" meant that Congress could regulate commerce conducted partly within a State. Because a portion of interstate commerce and foreign commerce would almost always take place within one or more States, federal power over interstate and foreign commerce necessarily would extend into the States. Id., at 194-196.

At the same time, the Court took great pains to make clear that Congress could not regulate commerce "which is completely internal, which is carried on between man and man in a State, or between different parts of the same State, and which does not extend to or affect other States." Id., at 194. Moreover, while suggesting that the Constitution might not permit States to regulate interstate or foreign commerce, the Court observed that "inspection laws, quarantine laws, health laws of every description, as well as laws for regulating the internal commerce of a State" were but a small part "of that immense mass of legislation . . . not surrendered to a general government." Id., at 203. >From an early moment, the Court rejected the notion that Congress can regulate everything that affects interstate commerce. That the internal commerce of the States and the numerous state inspection, quarantine, and health laws had substantial effects on interstate commerce cannot be doubted. Nevertheless, they were not "surrendered to the general government."

Of course, the principal dissent is not the first to misconstrue Gibbons. For instance, the Court has stated that Gibbons "described the federal commerce power with a breadth never yet exceeded." Wickard v. Filburn, 317 U.S. 111, 120, 87 L. Ed. 122, 63 S. Ct. 82 (1942). See also Perez v. United States, 402 U.S. 146, 151, 28 L. Ed. 2d 686, 91 S. Ct. 1357 (1971) (claiming that with Darby and Wickard, "the broader view of the Commerce Clause announced by Chief Justice Marshall had been restored"). I believe that this misreading stems from two statements in Gibbons.

First, the Court made the uncontroversial claim that federal power does not encompass "commerce" that "does not extend to or affect other States." 9 Wheat., at 194 (emphasis added). From this statement, the principal dissent infers that whenever an activity affects interstate commerce, it necessarily follows that Congress can regulate such activities. Of course, Chief Justice Marshall said no such thing and the inference the dissent makes cannot be drawn.

There is a much better interpretation of the "affect[s]" language: Because the Court had earlier noted that the commerce power did not extend to wholly intrastate commerce, the Court was acknowledging that although the line between intrastate and interstate/foreign commerce would be difficult to draw, federal authority could not be construed to cover purely intrastate commerce. Commerce that did not affect another State could never be said to be commerce "among the several States."

But even if one were to adopt the dissent's reading, the "affect[s]" language, at most, permits

Congress to regulate only intrastate commerce that substantially affects interstate and foreign commerce. There is no reason to believe that Chief Justice Marshall was asserting that Congress could regulate all activities that affect interstate commerce. See ibid.

The second source of confusion stems from the Court's praise for the Constitution's division of power between the States and the Federal Government:

"The genius and character of the whole government seem to be, that its action is to be applied to all the external concerns of the nation, and to those internal concerns which affect the States generally; but not to those which are completely within a particular State, which do not affect other States, and with which it is not necessary to interfere, for the purpose of executing some of the general powers of the government." Id., at 195.

In this passage, the Court merely was making the well understood point that the Constitution commits matters of "national" concern to Congress and leaves "local" matters to the States. The Court was not saying that whatever Congress believes is a national matter becomes an object of federal control. The matters of national concern are enumerated in the Constitution: war, taxes, patents, and copyrights, uniform rules of naturalization and bankruptcy, types of commerce, and so on. See generally Art. I, §8. Gibbons' emphatic statements that Congress could not regulate many matters that affect commerce confirm that the Court did not read the Commerce Clause as granting Congress control over matters that "affect the States generally." n5 Gibbons simply cannot be construed as the principal dissent would have it.

n5 None of the other Commerce Clause opinions during Chief Justice Marshall's tenure, which concerned the "dormant" Commerce Clause, even suggested that Congress had authority over all matters substantially affecting commerce. See Brown v. Maryland, 25 U.S. 419, 12 Wheat. 419, 6 L. Ed. 678 (1827); Willson v. Black Bird Creek Marsh Co., 2 Pet. 245 (1829).

B

I am aware of no cases prior to the New Deal that characterized the power flowing from the Commerce Clause as sweepingly as does our substantial effects test. My review of the case law indicates that the substantial effects test is but an innovation of the 20th century.

I am aware of no cases prior to the New Deal that characterized the power flowing from the Commerce Clause as sweepingly as does our substantial effects test. My review of the case law indicates that the substantial effects test is but an innovation of the 20th century.

Even before Gibbons, Chief Justice Marshall, writing for the Court in Cohens v. Virginia, 19 U.S. 264, 6 Wheat. 264, 5 L. Ed. 257 (1821), noted that Congress had "no general right to punish murder committed within any of the States," id., at 426, and that it was "clear that congress cannot punish felonies generally," id., at 428. The Court's only qualification was that Congress could enact such laws for places where it enjoyed plenary powers -- for instance, over the District of Columbia. Id., at 426. Thus, whatever effect ordinary murders, or robbery, or gun possession might have on interstate commerce (or on any other subject of federal concern) was irrelevant to the question of congressional power. n6

n6 It is worth noting that Congress, in the first federal criminal Act, did not establish nationwide prohibitions against murder and the like. See Act of Apr. 30, 1790, ch. 9, 1 Stat. 112. To be sure, Congress outlawed murder, manslaughter, maiming, and larceny, but only when those acts were either committed on United States territory not part of a State or on the high seas. Ibid. See U.S. Const., Art. I, §8, cl. 10 (authorizing Congress to outlaw piracy and felonies on high seas); Art. IV, §3, cl. 2 (plenary authority over United States territory and property). When Congress did enact nationwide criminal laws, it acted pursuant to direct grants of authority found in the Constitution. Compare Act of Apr. 30, 1790, supra, §§1 and 14 (prohibitions against treason and the counterfeiting of U.S. securities), with U.S. Const., Art. I, §8, cl. 6 (counterfeiting); Art. III, §3, cl. 2 (treason). Notwithstanding any substantial effects that murder, kidnaping, or gun possession might have had on interstate commerce, Congress understood that it could not establish nationwide prohibitions.

Likewise, there were no laws in the early Congresses that regulated manufacturing and agriculture. Nor was there any statute that purported to regulate activities with "substantial effects" on interstate commerce.

United States v. Dewitt, 76 U.S. 41, 9 Wall. 41, 19 L. Ed. 593 (1870), marked the first time the Court struck down a federal law as exceeding the power conveyed by the Commerce Clause. In a two-page opinion, the Court invalidated a nationwide law prohibiting all sales of naphtha and illuminating oils. In so doing, the Court remarked that the Commerce Clause "has always been understood as limited by its terms; and as a virtual denial of any power to interfere with the internal trade and business of the separate States." Id., at 44. The law in question was "plainly a regulation of police," which could have constitutional application only where Congress had exclusive authority, such as the territories. Id., at 44-45. See also License Tax

Cases, 72 U.S. 462, 5 Wall. 462, 470-471, 18 L. Ed. 497 (1867) (Congress cannot interfere with the internal commerce and business of a State); Trade-Mark Cases, 100 U.S. 82, 25 L. Ed. 550 (1879) (Congress cannot regulate internal commerce and thus may not establish national trademark registration).

In United States v. E. C. Knight Co., 156 U.S. 1, 39 L. Ed. 325, 15 S. Ct. 249 (1895), this Court held that mere attempts to monopolize the manufacture of sugar could not be regulated pursuant to the Commerce Clause. Raising echoes of the discussions of the Framers regarding the intimate relationship between commerce and manufacturing, the Court declared that "commerce succeeds to manufacture, and is not a part of it." Id., at 12. The Court also approvingly quoted from Kidd v. Pearson, 128 U.S. 1, 20, 32 L. Ed. 346, 9 S. Ct. 6 (1888):

"'No distinction is more popular to the common mind, or more clearly expressed in economic and political literature, than that between manufacture and commerce . . . . If it be held that the term [commerce] includes the regulation of all such manufactures as are intended to be the subject of commercial transactions in the future, it is impossible to deny that it would also include all productive industries that contemplate the same thing. The result would be that Congress would be invested . . . with the power to regulate, not only manufactures, but also agriculture, horticulture, stock raising, domestic fisheries, mining -- in short, every branch of human industry.'" E. C. Knight, supra, at 14.

If federal power extended to these types of production "comparatively little of business operations and affairs would be left for state control." Id., at 16. See also Newberry v. United States, 256 U.S. 232, 257, 65 L. Ed. 913, 41 S. Ct. 469 (1921) ("It is settled . . . that the power to regulate interstate and foreign commerce does not reach whatever is essential thereto. Without agriculture, manufacturing, mining, etc., commerce could not exist, but this fact does not suffice to subject them to the control of Congress "). Whether or not manufacturing, agriculture, or other matters substantially affected interstate commerce was irrelevant.

As recently as 1936, the Court continued to insist that the Commerce Clause did not reach the wholly internal business of the States. See Carter v. Carter Coal Co., 298 U.S. 238, 308, 80 L. Ed. 1160, 56 S. Ct. 855 (1936) (Congress may not regulate mine labor because "the relation of employer and employee is a local relation"); see also A. L. A. Schechter Poultry Corp. v. United States, 295 U.S. 495, 543-550, 79 L. Ed. 1570, 55 S. Ct. 837 (1935) (holding that Congress may not regulate intrastate sales of sick chickens or the labor of employees involved in intrastate poultry sales). The Federal Government simply could not reach such subjects regardless of their effects on interstate commerce.

These cases all establish a simple point: From the time of the ratification of the Constitution to the mid-1930's, it was widely understood that the Constitution granted Congress only limited powers, notwithstanding the Commerce Clause. n7 Moreover, there was no question that activities wholly separated from business, such as gun possession, were beyond the reach of the commerce power. If anything, the "wrong turn" was the Court's dramatic departure in the 1930's from a century and a half of precedent.

n7 To be sure, congressional power pursuant to the Commerce Clause was alternatively described less narrowly or more narrowly during this 150-year period. Compare United States v. Coombs, 12 Pet. 72, 78 (1838) (commerce power "extends to such acts, done on land, which interfere with, obstruct, or prevent the due exercise of the power to regulate [interstate and international] commerce" such as stealing goods from a beached ship), with United States v. E. C. Knight Co., 156 U.S. 1, 13, 39 L. Ed. 325, 15 S. Ct. 249 (1895) ("Contracts to buy, sell, or exchange goods to be transported among the several States, the transportation and its instrumentalities . . . may be regulated, but this is because they form part of interstate trade or commerce"). During this period, however, this Court never held that Congress could regulate everything that substantially affects commerce.

IV

the substantial effects test suffers from the further flaw that it appears to grant Congress a police power over the Nation. When asked at oral argument if there were any limits to the Commerce Clause, the Government was at a loss for words. Likewise, the principal dissent insists that there are limits, but it cannot muster even one example.

Apart from its recent vintage and its corresponding lack of any grounding in the original understanding of the Constitution, the substantial effects test suffers from the further flaw that it appears to grant Congress a police power over the Nation. When asked at oral argument if there were any limits to the Commerce Clause, the Government was at a loss for words. Tr. of Oral Arg. 5. Likewise, the principal dissent insists that there are limits, but it cannot muster even one example. Post, at 624. Indeed, the dissent implicitly concedes that its reading has no limits when it criticizes the Court for "threatening legal uncertainty in an area of law that . . . seemed reasonably well settled." Post, at 630. The one advantage of the dissent's standard is certainty: It is certain that under its analysis everything may be regulated under the guise of the Commerce Clause.

The substantial effects test suffers from this flaw, in part, because of its "aggregation principle." Under so-called "class of activities" statutes, Congress can regulate whole categories of activities that are not themselves either "interstate" or "commerce." In applying the effects test, we ask whether the class of activities as a whole substantially affects interstate commerce, not whether any specific activity within the class has such effects when considered in isolation. See Maryland v. Wirtz, 392 U.S. at 192-193 (if class of activities is "'within the reach of federal power,'" courts may not excise individual applications as trivial) (quoting Darby, 312 U.S. at 120-121).

The aggregation principle is clever, but has no stopping point. Suppose all would agree that gun possession within 1,000 feet of a school does not substantially affect commerce, but that possession of weapons generally (knives, brass knuckles, nunchakus, etc.) does. Under our substantial effects doctrine, even though Congress cannot single out gun possession, it can prohibit weapon possession generally. But one always can draw the circle broadly enough to cover an activity that, when taken in isolation, would not have substantial effects on commerce. Under our jurisprudence, if Congress passed an omnibus "substantially affects interstate commerce" statute, purporting to regulate every aspect of human existence, the Act apparently would be constitutional. Even though particular sections may govern only trivial activities, the statute in the aggregate regulates matters that substantially affect commerce.

V

This extended discussion of the original understanding and our first century and a half of case law does not necessarily require a wholesale abandonment of our more recent opinions. n8 It simply reveals that our substantial effects test is far removed from both the Constitution and from our early case law and that the Court's opinion should not be viewed as "radical" or another "wrong turn" that must be corrected in the future. n9 The analysis also suggests that we ought to temper our Commerce Clause jurisprudence.

n8 Although I might be willing to return to the original understanding, I recognize that many believe that it is too late in the day to undertake a fundamental reexamination of the past 60 years. Consideration of stare decisis and reliance interests may convince us that we cannot wipe the slate clean.

Our invalidation of the Gun-Free School Zones Act therefore falls comfortably within our proper role in reviewing federal legislation to determine if it exceeds congressional authority as defined by the Constitution itself.

n9 Nor can the majority's opinion fairly be compared to Lochner v. New York, 198 U.S. 45, 49 L. Ed. 937, 25 S. Ct. 539 (1905). See post, at 604-609 (SOUTER, J., dissenting). Unlike Lochner and our more recent "substantive due process" cases, to-day's decision enforces only the Constitution and not "judicial policy judgments." See post, at 607. Notwithstanding JUSTICE SOUTER's discussion, "'commercial' character" is not only a natural but an inevitable "ground of Commerce Clause distinction." See post, at 608 (emphasis added). Our invalidation of the Gun-Free School Zones Act therefore falls comfortably within our proper role in reviewing federal legislation to determine if it exceeds congressional authority as defined by the Constitution itself. As John Marshall put it: "If [Congress] were to make a law not warranted by any of the powers enumerated, it would be considered by the judges as an infringement of the Constitution which they are to guard . . . . They would declare it void." 3 Debates 553 (before the Virginia ratifying convention); see also The Federalist No. 44, at 305 (J. Madison) (asserting that if Congress exercises powers "not warranted by [the Constitution's] true meaning" the judiciary will defend the Constitution); id., No. 78, at 526 (A. Hamilton) (asserting that the "courts of justice are to be considered as the bulwarks of a limited constitution against legislative encroachments"). Where, as here, there is a case or controversy, there can be no "misstep," post, at 614, in enforcing the Constitution.

If we wish to be true to a Constitution that does not cede a police power to the Federal Government, our Commerce Clause's boundaries simply cannot be "defined" as being "'commensurate with the national needs'" or self-consciously intended to let the Federal Government "'defend itself against economic forces that Congress decrees inimical or destructive of the national economy.'" Such a formulation of federal power is no test at all: It is a blank check.

Unless the dissenting Justices are willing to repudiate our long-held understanding of the limited nature of federal power, I would think that they, too, must be willing to reconsider the substantial effects test in a future case. If we wish to be true to a Constitution that does not cede a police power to the Federal Government, our Commerce Clause's boundaries simply cannot be "defined" as being "'commensurate with the national needs'" or self-consciously intended to let the Federal Government "'defend itself against economic forces that Congress decrees inimical or destructive of the national economy.'" See post, at 625 (BREYER, J., dissenting) (quoting North American Co. v. SEC, 327 U.S. at 705). Such a formulation of federal power is no test at all: It is a blank check.

At an appropriate juncture, I think we must modify our Commerce Clause jurisprudence. Today, it is easy enough to say that the Clause certainly does not empower Congress to ban gun possession within 1,000 feet of a school.

JUSTICE STEVENS, dissenting.

The welfare of our future "Commerce with foreign Nations, and among the several States," is vitally dependent on the character of the education of our children. I therefore agree entirely with Justice Breyer's explanation of why Congress has ample power to prohibit the possession of firearms in or near schools—just as it may protect the school environment from harms posed by controlled substances such as asbestos or alcohol.

The welfare of our future "Commerce with foreign Nations, and among the several States, " U.S. Const., Art. I, §8, cl. 3, is vitally dependent on the character of the education of our children. I therefore agree entirely with JUSTICE BREYER's explanation of why Congress has ample power to prohibit the possession of firearms in or near schools -- just as it may protect the school environment from harms posed by controlled substances such as asbestos or alcohol. I also agree with JUSTICE SOUTER's exposition of the radical character of the Court's holding and its kinship with the discredited, pre-Depression version of substantive due process. Cf. Dolan v. City of Tigard, 512 U.S. 374, 405-411, 129 L. Ed. 2d 304, 114 S. Ct. 2309 (1994) (STEVENS, J., dissenting). I believe, however, that the Court's extraordinary decision merits this additional comment.

Guns are both articles of commerce and articles that can be used to restrain commerce. Their possession is the consequence, either directly or indirectly, of commercial activity. In my judgment, Congress' power to regulate commerce in firearms includes the power to prohibit possession of guns at any location because of their potentially harmful use; it necessarily follows that Congress may also prohibit their possession in particular markets. The market for the possession of handguns by school-age children is, distressingly, substantial.

Guns are both articles of commerce and articles that can be used to restrain commerce. Their possession is the consequence, either directly or indirectly, of commercial activity. In my judgment, Congress' power to regulate commerce in firearms includes the power to prohibit possession of guns at any location because of their potentially harmful use; it necessarily follows that Congress may also prohibit their possession in particular markets. The market for the possession of handguns by school-age children is, distressingly, substantial.* Whether or not the national interest in eliminating that market would have justified federal legislation in 1789, it surely does today.

there is evidence that firearm manufacturers—aided by a federal grant—are specifically targeting schoolchildren as consumers by distributing, at schools, hunting-related videos styled "educational materials for grades four through 12

* Indeed, there is evidence that firearm manufacturers -- aided by a federal grant -- are specifically targeting schoolchildren as consumers by distributing, at schools, hunting-related videos styled "educational materials for grades four through 12," Herbert, Reading, Writing, Reloading, N. Y. Times, Dec. 14, 1994, p. A23, col. 1.

JUSTICE SOUTER, dissenting.

In reviewing congressional legislation under the Commerce Clause, we defer to what is often a merely implicit congressional judgment that its regulation addresses a subject substantially affecting interstate commerce "if there is any rational basis for such a finding." Hodel v. Virginia Surface Mining & Reclamation Assn., Inc., 452 U.S. 264, 276, 69 L. Ed. 2d 1, 101 S. Ct. 2352 (1981); Preseault v. ICC, 494 U.S. 1, 17, 108 L. Ed. 2d 1, 110 S. Ct. 914 (1990); see Maryland v. Wirtz, 392 U.S. 183, 190, 20 L. Ed. 2d 1020, 88 S. Ct. 2017 (1968), quoting Katzenbach v. McClung, 379 U.S. 294, 303-304, 13 L. Ed. 2d 290, 85 S. Ct. 377 (1964). If that congressional determination is within the realm of reason, "the only remaining question for judicial inquiry is whether 'the means chosen by Congress [are] reasonably adapted to the end permitted by the Constitution.'" Hodel v. Virginia Surface Mining & Reclamation Assn., Inc., supra, at 276, quoting Heart of Atlanta Motel, Inc. v. United States, 379 U.S. 241, 262, 13 L. Ed. 2d 258, 85 S. Ct. 348 (1964); see also Preseault v. ICC, supra, at 17. n1

n1 In this case, no question has been raised about means and ends; the only issue is about the effect of school zone guns on commerce.

The practice of deferring to rationally based legislative judgments "is a paradigm of judicial restraint." FCC v. Beach Communications, Inc., 508 U.S. 307, 314, 124 L. Ed. 2d 211, 113 S. Ct. 2096 (1993). In judicial review under the Commerce Clause, it reflects our respect for the institutional competence of the Congress on a subject expressly assigned to it by the Constitution and our appreciation of the legitimacy that comes from Congress's political accountability in dealing with matters open to a wide range of possible choices. See id., at 313-316; Hodel v. Virginia Surface Mining & Reclamation Assn., Inc., supra, at 276; United States v. Carolene Products Co., 304 U.S. 144, 147, 151-154, 82 L. Ed. 1234, 58 S. Ct. 778 (1938); cf. Williamson v. Lee Optical of Okla., Inc., 348 U.S. 483, 488, 99 L. Ed. 563, 75 S. Ct. 461 (1955).

It was not ever thus, however, as even a brief overview of Commerce Clause history during the past century reminds us. The modern respect for the competence and primacy of Congress in matters affecting commerce developed only after one of this Court's most chastening experiences, when it perforce repudiated an earlier and untenably expansive conception of judicial review in derogation of congressional commerce power. A look at history's sequence will serve to show how today's decision tugs the Court off course, leading it to suggest opportunities for further developments that would be at odds with the rule of restraint to which the Court still wisely states adherence.

I

Notwithstanding the Court's recognition of a broad commerce power in Gibbons v. Ogden, 22 U.S. 1, 9 Wheat. 1, 196-197, 6 L. Ed. 23 (1824) (Marshall, C. J.), Congress saw few occasions to exercise that power prior to Reconstruction, see generally 2 C. Warren, The Supreme Court in United States History 729-739 (rev. ed. 1935), and it was really the passage of the Interstate Commerce Act of 1887 that opened a new age of congressional reliance on the Commerce Clause for authority to exercise general police powers at the national level, see id., at 729-730. Although the Court upheld a fair amount of the ensuing legislation as being within the commerce power, see, e.g., Stafford v. Wallace, 258 U.S. 495, 66 L. Ed. 735, 42 S. Ct. 397 (1922) (upholding an Act regulating trade practices in the meat packing industry); Shreveport Rate Cases, 234 U.S. 342, 34 S. Ct. 833, 58 L. Ed. 1341 (1914) (upholding Interstate Commerce Commission order to equalize interstate and intrastate rail rates); see generally Warren, supra, at 729-739, the period from the turn of the century to 1937 is better noted for a series of cases applying highly formalistic notions of "commerce" to invalidate federal social and economic legislation, see, e.g., Carter v. Carter Coal Co., 298 U.S. 238, 303-304, 80 L. Ed. 1160, 56 S. Ct. 855 (1936) (striking Act prohibiting unfair labor practices in coal industry as regulation of "mining" and "production," not "commerce"); A. L. A. Schechter Poultry Corp. v. United States, 295 U.S. 495, 545-548, 79 L. Ed. 1570, 55 S. Ct. 837 (1935) (striking congressional regulation of activities affecting interstate commerce only "indirectly"); Hammer v. Dagenhart, 247 U.S. 251, 62 L. Ed. 1101, 38 S. Ct. 529 (1918) (striking Act prohibiting shipment in interstate commerce of goods manufactured at factories using child labor because the Act regulated "manufacturing," not "commerce"); Adair v. United States, 208 U.S. 161, 52 L. Ed. 436, 28 S. Ct. 277 (1908) (striking protection of labor union membership as outside "commerce").

These restrictive views of commerce subject to congressional power complemented the Court's activism in limiting the enforceable scope of state economic regulation. It is most familiar history that during this same period the Court routinely invalidated state social and economic legislation under an expansive conception of Fourteenth Amendment substantive due process. See, e.g., Louis K. Liggett Co. v. Baldridge, 278 U.S. 105, 73 L. Ed. 204, 49 S. Ct. 57 (1928) (striking state law requiring pharmacy owners to be licensed as pharmacists); Coppage v. Kansas, 236 U.S. 1, 59 L. Ed. 441, 35 S. Ct. 240 (1915) (striking state law prohibiting employers from requiring their employees to agree not to join labor organizations); Lochner v. New York, 198 U.S. 45, 49 L. Ed. 937, 25 S. Ct. 539 (1905) (striking state law establishing maximum working hours for bakers). See generally L. Tribe, American Constitutional Law 568-574 (2d ed. 1988). The fulcrums of judicial review in these cases were the notions of liberty and property characteristic of laissez-faire economics, whereas the Commerce Clause cases turned on what was ostensibly a structural limit of federal power, but under each conception of judicial review the Court's character for the first third of the century showed itself in exacting judicial scrutiny of a legislature's choice of economic ends and of the legislative means selected to reach them.

It was not merely coincidental, then, that sea changes in the Court's conceptions of its authority under the Due Process and Commerce Clauses occurred virtually together, in 1937, with West Coast Hotel Co. v. Parrish, 300 U.S. 379, 81 L. Ed. 703, 57 S. Ct. 578, and NLRB v. Jones & Laughlin Steel Corp., 301 U.S. 1, 81 L. Ed. 893, 57 S. Ct. 615. See Stern, The Commerce Clause and the National Economy, 1933-1946, 59 Harv. L. Rev. 645, 674-682 (1946). In West Coast Hotel, the Court's rejection of a due process challenge to a state law fixing minimum wages for women and children marked the abandonment of its expansive protection of contractual freedom. Two weeks later, Jones & Laughlin affirmed congressional commerce power to authorize NLRB injunctions against unfair labor practices. The Court's finding that the regulated activity had a direct enough effect on commerce has since been seen as beginning the abandonment, for practical purposes, of the formalistic distinction between direct and indirect effects.

In the years following these decisions, deference to legislative policy judgments on commercial regulation became the powerful theme under both the Due Process and Commerce Clauses, see United States v. Carolene Products Co., 304 U.S. at 147-148, 152; United States v. Darby, 312 U.S. 100, 119-121, 85 L. Ed. 609, 61 S. Ct. 451 (1941); United States v. Wrightwood Dairy Co., 315 U.S. 110, 118-119, 86 L. Ed. 726, 62 S. Ct. 523 (1942), and in due course that deference became articulate in the standard of rationality review. In due process litigation, the Court's statement of a rational basis test came quickly. See United States v. Carolene Products Co., supra, at 152; see also Williamson v. Lee Optical Co., supra, at 489-490. The parallel formulation of the Commerce Clause test came later, only because complete elimination of the direct/indirect effects dichotomy and acceptance of the cumulative effects doctrine, Wickard v. Filburn, 317 U.S. 111, 125, 127-129, 87 L. Ed. 122, 63 S. Ct. 82 (1942); United States v. Wrightwood Dairy Co., supra, at 124-126, so far settled the pressing issues of congressional power over commerce as to leave the Court for years without any need to phrase a test explicitly deferring to rational legislative judgments. The moment came, however, with the challenge to congressional Commerce Clause authority to prohibit racial discrimination in places of public accommodation, when the Court simply made explicit what the earlier cases had implied: "where we find that the legislators, in light of the facts and testimony before them, have a rational basis for finding a chosen regulatory scheme necessary to the protection of commerce, our investigation is at an end." Katzenbach v. McClung, 379 U.S. at 303-304, discussing United States v. Darby, supra; see Heart of Atlanta Motel, Inc. v. United States, 379 U.S. at 258-259. Thus, under commerce, as under due process, adoption of rational basis review expressed the recognition that the Court had no sustainable basis for subjecting economic regulation as such to judicial policy judgments, and for the past half century the Court has no more turned back in the direction of formalistic Commerce Clause review (as in deciding whether regulation of commerce was sufficiently direct) than it has inclined toward reasserting the substantive authority of Lochner due process (as in the inflated protection of contractual autonomy). See, e.g., Maryland v. Wirtz, 392 U.S. at 190, 198; Perez v. United States, 402 U.S. 146, 151-157, 28 L. Ed. 2d 686, 91 S. Ct. 1357 (1971); Hodel v. Virginia Surface Mining & Reclamation Assn., Inc., 452 U.S. at 276, 277.

II

There is today, however, a backward glance at both the old pitfalls, as the Court treats deference under the rationality rule as subject to gradation according to the commercial or noncommercial nature of the immediate subject of the challenged regulation. See ante, at 558-561. The distinction between what is patently commercial and what is not looks much like the old distinction between what directly affects commerce and what touches it only indirectly. And the act of calibrating the level of deference by drawing a line between what is patently commercial and what is less purely so will probably resemble the process of deciding how much interference with contractual freedom was fatal. Thus, it seems fair to ask whether the step taken by the Court today does anything but portend a return to the untenable jurisprudence from which the Court extricated itself almost 60 years ago. The answer is not reassuring. To be sure, the occasion for today's decision reflects the century's end, not its beginning. But if it seems anomalous that the Congress of the United States has taken to regulating school yards, the Act in question is still probably no more remarkable than state regulation of bake shops 90 years ago. In any event, there is no reason to hope that the Court's qualification of rational basis review will be any more successful than the efforts at substantive economic review made by our predecessors as the century began. Taking the Court's opinion on its own terms, JUSTICE BREYER has explained both the hopeless porosity of "commercial" character as a ground of Commerce Clause distinction in America's highly connected economy, and the inconsistency of this categorization with our rational basis precedents from the last 50 years.

Further glosses on rationality review, moreover, may be in the offing. Although this case turns on commercial character, the Court gestures toward two other considerations that it might sometime entertain in applying rational basis scrutiny (apart from a statutory obligation to supply independent proof of a jurisdictional element): does the congressional statute deal with subjects of traditional state regulation, and does the statute contain explicit factual findings supporting the otherwise implicit determination that the regulated activity substantially affects interstate commerce? Once again, any appeal these considerations may have depends on ignoring the painful lesson learned in 1937, for neither of the Court's suggestions would square with rational basis scrutiny.

A

The Court observes that the Gun-Free School Zones Act operates in two areas traditionally subject to legislation by the States, education and enforcement of criminal law. The suggestion is either that a connection between commerce and these subjects is remote, or that the commerce power is simply weaker when it touches subjects on which the States have historically been the primary legislators. Neither suggestion is tenable. As for remoteness, it may or may not be wise for the National Government to deal with education, but JUSTICE BREYER has surely demonstrated that the commercial prospects of an illiterate State or Nation are not rosy, and no argument should be needed to show that hijacking interstate shipments of cigarettes can affect commerce substantially, even though the States have traditionally prosecuted robbery.

And as for the notion that the commerce power diminishes the closer it gets to customary state concerns, that idea has been flatly rejected, and not long ago. The commerce power, we have often observed, is plenary. Hodel v. Virginia Surface Mining & Reclamation Assn., Inc., supra, at 276; United States v. Darby, 312 U.S. at 114; see Garcia v. San Antonio Metropolitan Transit Authority, 469 U.S. 528, 549-550, 83 L. Ed. 2d 1016, 105 S. Ct. 1005 (1985); Gibbons v. Ogden, 9 Wheat., at 196-197. Justice Harlan put it this way in speaking for the Court in Maryland v. Wirtz:

"There is no general doctrine implied in the Federal Constitution that the two governments, national and state, are each to exercise its powers so as not to interfere with the free and full exercise of the powers of the other. . . . It is clear that the Federal Government, when acting within a delegated power, may override countervailing state interests . . . . As long ago as [1925], the Court put to rest the contention that state concerns might constitutionally 'outweigh' the importance of an otherwise valid federal statute regulating commerce." 392 U.S. at 195-196 (citations and internal quotation marks omitted).

See also United States v. Darby, supra, at 114; Gregory v. Ashcroft, 501 U.S. 452, 460, 115 L. Ed. 2d 410, 111 S. Ct. 2395 (1991); United States v. Carolene Products Co., 304 U.S. at 147.

Nor is there any contrary authority in the reasoning of our cases imposing clear statement rules in some instances of legislation that would significantly alter the state-national balance. In the absence of a clear statement of congressional design, for example, we have refused to interpret ambiguous federal statutes to limit fundamental state legislative prerogatives, Gregory v. Ashcroft, supra, at 460-464, our understanding being that such prerogatives, through which "a State defines itself as a sovereign," are "powers with which Congress does not readily interfere," 501 U.S. at 460, 461. Likewise, when faced with two plausible interpretations of a federal criminal statute, we generally will take the alternative that does not force us to impute an intention to Congress to use its full commerce power to regulate conduct traditionally and ably regulated by the States. See United States v. Enmons, 410 U.S. 396, 411-412, 35 L. Ed. 2d 379, 93 S. Ct. 1007 (1973); United States v. Bass, 404 U.S. 336, 349-350, 30 L. Ed. 2d 488, 92 S. Ct. 515 (1971); Rewis v. United States, 401 U.S. 808, 812, 28 L. Ed. 2d 493, 91 S. Ct. 1056 (1971).

These clear statement rules, however, are merely rules of statutory interpretation, to be relied upon only when the terms of a statute allow, United States v. Culbert, 435 U.S. 371, 379-380, 55 L. Ed. 2d 349, 98 S. Ct. 1112 (1978); see Gregory v. Ashcroft, supra, at 470; United States v. Bass, supra, at 346-347, and in cases implicating Congress's historical reluctance to trench on state legislative prerogatives or to enter into spheres already occupied by the States, Gregory v. Ashcroft, supra, at 461; United States v. Bass, supra, at 349; see Rewis v. United States, supra, at 811-812. They are rules for determining intent when legislation leaves intent subject to question. But our hesitance to presume that Congress has acted to alter the state-federal status quo (when presented with a plausible alternative) has no relevance whatever to the enquiry whether it has the commerce power to do so or to the standard of judicial review when Congress has definitely meant to exercise that power. Indeed, to allow our hesitance to affect the standard of review would inevitably degenerate into the sort of substantive policy review that the Court found indefensible 60 years ago. The Court does not assert (and could not plausibly maintain) that the commerce power is wholly devoid of congressional authority to speak on any subject of traditional state concern; but if congressional action is not forbidden absolutely when it touches such a subject, it will stand or fall depending on the Court's view of the strength of the legislation's commercial justification. And here once again history raises its objections that the Court's previous essays in overriding congressional policy choices under the Commerce Clause were ultimately seen to suffer two fatal weaknesses: when dealing with Acts of Congress (as distinct from state legislation subject to review under the theory of dormant commerce power) nothing in the Clause compelled the judicial activism, and nothing about the judiciary as an institution made it a superior source of policy on the subject Congress dealt with. There is no reason to expect the lesson would be different another time.

B

this case might well have been different if Congress had made explicit findings that guns in schools have a substantial effect on interstate commerce, and the Court today does not repudiate that position

There remain questions about legislative findings. The Court of Appeals expressed the view, 2 F.3d 1342, 1363-1368 (CA5 1993), that the result in this case might well have been different if Congress had made explicit findings that guns in schools have a substantial effect on interstate commerce, and the Court today does not repudiate that position, see ante, at 562-563. Might a court aided by such findings have subjected this legislation to less exacting scrutiny (or, put another way, should a court have deferred to such findings if Congress had made them)? n2 The answer to either question must be no, although as a general matter findings are important and to be hoped for in the difficult cases.

n2 Unlike the Court, (perhaps), I would see no reason not to consider Congress's findings, insofar as they might be helpful in reviewing the challenge to this statute, even though adopted in later legislation. See the Violent Crime Control and Law Enforcement Act of 1994, Pub. L. 103-322,

§320904, 108 Stat. 2125 ("The occurrence of violent crime in school zones has resulted in a decline in the quality of education in our country; . . . this decline . . . has an adverse impact on interstate commerce and the foreign commerce of the United States; . . . Congress has power, under the interstate commerce clause and other provisions of the Constitution, to enact measures to ensure the integrity and safety of the Nation's schools by enactment of this subsection"). The findings, however, go no further than expressing what is obviously implicit in the substantive legislation, at such a conclusory level of generality as to add virtually nothing to the record. The Solicitor General certainly exercised sound judgment in placing no significant reliance on these particular afterthoughts. Tr. of Oral Arg. 24-25.

It is only natural to look for help with a hard job, and reviewing a claim that Congress has exceeded the commerce power is much harder in some cases than in others. A challenge to congressional regulation of interstate garbage hauling would be easy to resolve; review of congressional regulation of gun possession in school yards is more difficult, both because the link to interstate commerce is less obvious and because of our initial ignorance of the relevant facts. In a case comparable to this one, we may have to dig hard to make a responsible judgment about what Congress could reasonably find, because the case may be close, and because judges tend not to be familiar with the facts that may or may not make it close. But while the ease of review may vary from case to case, it does not follow that the standard of review should vary, much less that explicit findings of fact would even directly address the standard.

The question for the courts, as all agree, is not whether as a predicate to legislation Congress in fact found that a particular activity substantially affects interstate commerce. The legislation implies such a finding, and there is no reason to entertain claims that Congress acted ultra vires intentionally. Nor is the question whether Congress was correct in so finding. The only question is whether the legislative judgment is within the realm of reason. See Hodel v. Virginia Surface Mining & Reclamation Assn., Inc., 452 U.S. at 276-277; Katzenbach v. McClung, 379 U.S. at 303-304; Railroad Retirement Bd. v. Alton R. Co., 295 U.S. 330, 391-392, 79 L. Ed. 1468, 55 S. Ct. 758 (1935) (Hughes, C. J., dissenting); cf. FCC v. Beach Communications, Inc., 508 U.S. at 315 (in the equal protection context, "those attacking the rationality of the legislative classification have the burden to negate every conceivable basis which might support it[;] . . . it is entirely irrelevant for constitutional purposes whether the conceived reason for the challenged distinction actually motivated the legislature") (citations and internal quotation marks omitted); Ferguson v. Skrupa, 372 U.S. 726, 731-733, 10 L. Ed. 2d 93, 83 S. Ct. 1028 (1963); Williamson v. Lee Optical Co., 348 U.S. at 487. Congressional findings do not, however, directly address the question of reasonableness; they tell us what Congress actually has found, not what it could rationally find. If, indeed, the Court were to make the existence of explicit congressional findings dispositive in some close or difficult cases something other than rationality review would be afoot. The resulting congressional obligation to justify its policy choices on the merits would imply either a judicial authority to review the justification (and, hence, the wisdom) of those choices, or authority to require Congress to act with some high degree of deliberateness, of which express findings would be evidence. But review for congressional wisdom would just be the old judicial pretension discredited and abandoned in 1937, and review for deliberateness would be as patently unconstitutional as an Act of Congress mandating long opinions from this Court. Such a legislative process requirement would function merely as an excuse for covert review of the merits of legislation under standards never expressed and more or less arbitrarily applied. Under such a regime, in any case, the rationality standard of review would be a thing of the past.

On the other hand, to say that courts applying the rationality standard may not defer to findings is not, of course, to say that findings are pointless. They may, in fact, have great value in telling courts what to look for, in establishing at least one frame of reference for review, and in citing to factual authority. The research underlying JUSTICE BREYER's dissent was necessarily a major undertaking; help is welcome, and it not incidentally shrinks the risk that judicial research will miss material scattered across the public domain or buried under pounds of legislative record. Congressional findings on a more particular plane than this record illustrates would accordingly have earned judicial thanks. But thanks do not carry the day as long as rational possibility is the touchstone, and I would not allow for the possibility, as the Court's opinion may, ante, at 563, that the addition of congressional findings could in principle have affected the fate of the statute here.

III

Because JUSTICE BREYER's opinion demonstrates beyond any doubt that the Act in question passes the rationality review that the Court continues to espouse, today's decision may be seen as only a misstep, its reasoning and its suggestions not quite in gear with the prevailing standard, but hardly an epochal case. I would not argue otherwise, but I would raise a caveat. Not every epochal case has come in epochal trappings. Jones & Laughlin did not reject the direct-indirect standard in so many words; it just said the relation of the regulated subject matter to commerce was direct enough. 301 U.S. at 41-43. But we know what happened.

I respectfully dissent.

JUSTICE BREYER, with whom JUSTICE STEVENS, JUSTICE SOUTER, and JUSTICE GINSBURG join, dissenting.

The issue in this case is whether the Commerce Clause authorizes Congress to enact a statute that makes it a crime to possess a gun in, or near, a school. 18 U.S.C. §922(q)(1)(A) (1988 ed., Supp. V). In my view, the statute falls well within the scope of the commerce power as this Court has understood that power over the last half century.

I

In reaching this conclusion, I apply three basic principles of Commerce Clause interpretation. First, the power to "regulate Commerce . . . among the several States," U.S. Const., Art. I, §8, cl. 3, encompasses the power to regulate local activities insofar as they significantly affect interstate commerce. See, e.g., Gibbons v. Ogden, 22 U.S. 1, 9 Wheat. 1, 194-195, 6 L. Ed. 23 (1824) (Marshall, C. J.); Wickard v. Filburn, 317 U.S. 111, 125, 87 L. Ed. 122, 63 S. Ct. 82 (1942). As the majority points out, ante, at 559, the Court, in describing how much of an effect the Clause requires, sometimes has used the word "substantial" and sometimes has not. Compare, e.g., Wickard, supra, at 125 ("substantial economic effect"), with Hodel v. Virginia Surface Mining & Reclamation Assn., Inc., 452 U.S. 264, 276, 69 L. Ed. 2d 1, 101 S. Ct. 2352 (1981) ("affects interstate commerce"); see also Maryland v. Wirtz, 392 U.S. 183, 196, n. 27, 20 L. Ed. 2d 1020, 88 S. Ct. 2017 (1968) (cumulative effect must not be "trivial"); NLRB v. Jones & Laughlin Steel Corp., 301 U.S. 1, 37, 81 L. Ed. 893, 57 S. Ct. 615 (1937) (speaking of "close and substantial relation" between activity and commerce, not of "substantial effect") (emphasis added); Gibbons, supra, at 194 (words of Commerce Clause do not "comprehend . . . commerce, which is completely internal . . . and which does not . . . affect other States"). And, as the majority also recognizes in quoting Justice Cardozo, the question of degree (how much effect) requires an estimate of the "size" of the effect that no verbal formulation can capture with precision. See ante, at 567. I use the word "significant" because the word "substantial" implies a somewhat narrower power than recent precedent suggests. See, e.g., Perez v. United States, 402 U.S. 146, 154, 28 L. Ed. 2d 686, 91 S. Ct. 1357 (1971); Daniel v. Paul, 395 U.S. 298, 308, 23 L. Ed. 2d 318, 89 S. Ct. 1697 (1969). But to speak of "substantial effect" rather than "significant effect" would make no difference in this case.

a court must consider, not the effect of an individual act (a single instance of gun possession), but rather the cumulative effect of all similar instances (i.e., the effect of all guns possessed in or near schools).

Second, in determining whether a local activity will likely have a significant effect upon interstate commerce, a court must consider, not the effect of an individual act (a single instance of gun possession), but rather the cumulative effect of all similar instances (i.e., the effect of all guns possessed in or near schools). See, e.g., Wickard, supra, at 127-128. As this Court put the matter almost 50 years ago:

"It is enough that the individual activity when multiplied into a general practice . . . contains a threat to the interstate economy that requires preventative regulation." Mandeville Island Farms, Inc. v. American Crystal Sugar Co., 334 U.S. 219, 236, 92 L. Ed. 1328, 68 S. Ct. 996 (1948) (citations omitted).

Third, the Constitution requires us to judge the connection between a regulated activity and interstate commerce, not directly, but at one remove. Courts must give Congress a degree of leeway in determining the existence of a significant factual connection between the regulated activity and interstate commerce -- both because the Constitution delegates the commerce power directly to Congress and because the determination requires an empirical judgment of a kind that a legislature is more likely than a court to make with accuracy. The traditional words "rational basis" capture this leeway. See Hodel, supra, at 276-277. Thus, the specific question before us, as the Court recognizes, is not whether the "regulated activity sufficiently affected interstate commerce," but, rather, whether Congress could have had "a rational basis" for so concluding. Ante, at 557 (emphasis added).

I recognize that we must judge this matter independently. "Simply because Congress may conclude that a particular activity substantially affects interstate commerce does not necessarily make it so." Hodel, supra, at 311 (REHNQUIST, J., concurring in judgment). And, I also recognize that Congress did not write specific "interstate commerce" findings into the law under which Lopez was convicted. Nonetheless, as I have already noted, the matter that we review independently (i.e., whether there is a "rational basis") already has considerable leeway built into it. And, the absence of findings, at most, deprives a statute of the benefit of some extra leeway. This extra deference, in principle, might change the result in a close case, though, in practice, it has not made a critical legal difference. See, e.g., Katzenbach v. McClung, 379 U.S. 294, 299, 13 L. Ed. 2d 290, 85 S. Ct. 377 (1964) (noting that "no formal findings were made, which of course are not necessary"); Perez, supra, at 156-157; cf. Turner Broadcasting System, Inc. v. FCC, 512 U.S. 622, 666, 129 L. Ed. 2d 497, 114 S. Ct. 2445 (1994) (opinion of KENNEDY, J.) ("Congress is not obligated, when enacting its statutes, to make a record of the type that an administrative agency or court does to accommodate judicial review"); Fullilove v. Klutznick, 448 U.S. 448, 503, 65 L. Ed. 2d 902, 100 S. Ct. 2758 (1980) (Powell, J., concurring) ("After Congress has legislated repeatedly in an area of national concern, its Members gain experience that may reduce the need for fresh hearings or prolonged debate . . ."). It would seem particularly unfortunate to make the validity of the statute at hand turn on the presence or absence of findings. Because Congress did make findings (though not until after Lopez was prosecuted), doing so would appear to elevate form over substance. See Pub. L. 103-322, §§320904 (2)(F), (G), 108 Stat. 2125, 18 U.S.C. §§922(q)(1)(F), (G).

In addition, despite the Court of Appeals' suggestion to the contrary, see 2 F.3d 1342, 1365 (CA5 1993), there is no special need here for a clear indication of Congress' rationale. The statute does not interfere with the exercise of state or local authority. Cf., e.g., Dellmuth v. Muth, 491 U.S. 223, 227-228, 105 L. Ed. 2d 181, 109 S. Ct. 2397 (1989) (requiring clear statement for abrogation of Eleventh Amendment immunity). Moreover, any clear statement rule would apply only to determine Congress' intended result, not to clarify the source of its authority or measure the level of consideration that went into its decision, and here there is no doubt as to which activities Congress intended to regulate. See Ibid.; Id., at 233 (SCALIA, J., concurring) (to subject States to suits for money damages, Congress need only make that intent clear, and need not refer explicitly to the Eleventh Amendment); EEOC v. Wyoming, 460 U.S. 226, 243, n. 18, 75 L. Ed. 2d 18, 103 S. Ct. 1054 (1983) (Congress need not recite the constitutional provision that authorizes its action).

II

we must ask whether Congress could have had a rational basis for finding a significant (or substantial) connection between gun-related school violence and interstate commerce.

Applying these principles to the case at hand, we must ask whether Congress could have had a rational basis for finding a significant (or substantial) connection between gun-related school violence and interstate commerce. Or, to put the question in the language of the explicit finding that Congress made when it amended this law in 1994: Could Congress rationally have found that "violent crime in school zones," through its effect on the "quality of education," significantly (or substantially) affects "interstate" or "foreign commerce"? 18 U.S.C. §§922(q)(1)(F), (G). As long as one views the commerce connection, not as a "technical legal conception," but as "a practical one," Swift & Co. v. United States, 196 U.S. 375, 398, 49 L. Ed. 518, 25 S. Ct. 276 (1905) (Holmes, J.), the answer to this question must be yes. Numerous reports and studies -- generated both inside and outside government -- make clear that Congress could reasonably have found the empirical connection that its law, implicitly or explicitly, asserts. (See Appendix, infra, at 631, for a sample of the documentation, as well as for complete citations to the sources referenced below.)

reports, hearings, and other readily available literature make clear that the problem of guns in and around schools is widespread and extremely serious.

four percent of American high school students (and six percent of inner-city high school students) carry a gun to school at least occasionally

12 percent of urban high school students have had guns fired at them; that 20 percent of those students have been threatened with guns; and that, in any 6-month period, several hundred thousand schoolchildren are victims of violent crimes in or near their schools

this widespread violence in schools throughout the Nation significantly interferes with the quality of education in those schools.

For one thing, reports, hearings, and other readily available literature make clear that the problem of guns in and around schools is widespread and extremely serious. These materials report, for example, that four percent of American high school students (and six percent of inner-city high school students) carry a gun to school at least occasionally, Centers for Disease Control 2342; Sheley, McGee, & Wright 679; that 12 percent of urban high school students have had guns fired at them, ibid.; that 20 percent of those students have been threatened with guns, ibid.; and that, in any 6-month period, several hundred thousand schoolchildren are victims of violent crimes in or near their schools, U.S. Dept. of Justice 1 (1989); House Select Committee Hearing 15 (1989). And, they report that this widespread violence in schools throughout the Nation significantly interferes with the quality of education in those schools. See, e.g., House Judiciary Committee Hearing 44 (1990) (linking school violence to dropout rate); U.S. Dept. of Health 118-119 (1978) (school-violence victims suffer academically); compare U.S. Dept. of Justice 1 (1991) (gun violence worst in inner-city schools), with National Center 47 (dropout rates highest in inner cities). Based on reports such as these, Congress obviously could have thought that guns and learning are mutually exclusive. Senate Labor and Human Resources Committee Hearing 39 (1993); U.S. Dept. of Health 118, 123-124 (1978). Congress could therefore have found a substantial educational problem -- teachers unable to teach, students unable to learn -- and concluded that guns near schools contribute substantially to the size and scope of that problem.

Having found that guns in schools significantly undermine the quality of education in our Nation's classrooms, Congress could also have found, given the effect of education upon interstate and foreign commerce, that gun-related violence in and around schools is a commercial, as well as a human, problem.

Having found that guns in schools significantly undermine the quality of education in our Nation's classrooms, Congress could also have found, given the effect of education upon interstate and foreign commerce, that gun-related violence in and around schools is a commercial, as well as a human, problem. Education, although far more than a matter of economics, has long been inextricably intertwined with the Nation's economy. When this Nation began, most workers received their education in the workplace, typically (like Benjamin Franklin) as apprentices. See generally Seybolt; Rorabaugh; U.S. Dept. of Labor (1950). As late as the 1920's, many workers still received general education directly from their employers -- from large corporations, such as General Electric, Ford, and Goodyear, which created schools within their firms to help both the worker and the firm. See Bolino 15-25. (Throughout most of the 19th century fewer than one percent of all Americans received secondary education through attending a high school. See id., at 11.) As public school enrollment grew in the early 20th century, see Becker 218 (1993), the need for industry to teach basic educational skills diminished. But, the direct economic link between basic education and industrial productivity remained. Scholars estimate that nearly a quarter of America's economic growth in the early years of this century is traceable directly to increased schooling, see Denison 243; that investment in "human capital" (through spending on education) exceeded investment in "physical capital" by a ratio of almost two to one, see Schultz 26 (1961); and that the economic returns to this investment in education exceeded the returns to conventional capital investment, see, e.g., Davis & Morrall 48-49.

In recent years the link between secondary education and business has strengthened, becoming both more direct and more important. Scholars on the subject report that technological changes and innovations in management techniques have altered the nature of the workplace so that more jobs now demand greater educational skills. See, e.g., MIT 32 (only about one-third of handtool company's 1,000 workers were qualified to work with a new process that requires high-school-level reading and mathematical skills); Cyert & Mowery 68 (gap between wages of high school dropouts and better trained workers increasing); U.S. Dept. of Labor 41 (1981) (job openings for dropouts declining over time). There is evidence that "service, manufacturing or construction jobs are being displaced by technology that requires a better-educated worker or, more likely, are being exported overseas," Gordon, Ponticell, & Morgan 26; that "workers with truly few skills by the year 2000 will find that only one job out of ten will remain," ibid.; and that "over the long haul the best way to encourage the growth of high-wage jobs is to upgrade the skills of the work force. . . . Better-trained workers become more productive workers, enabling a company to become more competitive and expand." Henkoff 60.

Increasing global competition also has made primary and secondary education economically more important. The portion of the American economy attributable to international trade nearly tripled between 1950 and 1980, and more than 70 percent of American-made goods now compete with imports. Marshall 205; Marshall & Tucker 33. Yet, lagging worker productivity has contributed to negative trade balances and to real hourly compensation that has fallen below wages in 10 other industrialized nations. See National Center 57; Handbook of Labor Statistics 561, 576 (1989); Neef & Kask 28, 31. At least some significant part of this serious productivity problem is attributable to students who emerge from classrooms without the reading or mathematical skills necessary to compete with their European or Asian counterparts, see, e.g., MIT 28, and, presumably, to high school dropout rates of 20 to 25 percent (up to 50 percent in inner cities), see, e.g., National Center 47; Chubb & Hanushek 215. Indeed, Congress has said, when writing other statutes, that "functionally or technologically illiterate" Americans in the work force "erode" our economic "standing in the international marketplace," Pub. L. 100-418, §6002(a)(3), 102 Stat. 1469, and that "our Nation is . . . paying the price of scientific and technological illiteracy, with our productivity declining, our industrial base ailing, and our global competitiveness dwindling," H. R. Rep. No. 98-6, pt. 1, p. 19 (1983).

Finally, there is evidence that, today more than ever, many firms base their location decisions upon the presence, or absence, of a work force with a basic education. See MacCormack, Newman, & Rosenfield 73; Coffee 296. Scholars on the subject report, for example, that today, "high speed communication and transportation make it possible to produce most products and services anywhere in the world," National Center 38; that "modern machinery and production methods can therefore be combined with low wage workers to drive costs down," ibid.; that managers can perform "'back office functions anywhere in the world now,'" and say that if they "'can't get enough skilled workers here'" they will "'move the skilled jobs out of the country,'" id., at 41; with the consequence that "rich countries need better education and retraining, to reduce the supply of unskilled workers and to equip them with the skills they require for tomorrow's jobs," Survey of Global Economy 37. In light of this increased importance of education to individual firms, it is no surprise that half of the Nation's manufacturers have become involved with setting standards and shaping curricula for local schools, Maturi 65-68, that 88 percent think this kind of involvement is important, id., at 68, that more than 20 States have recently passed educational reforms to attract new business, Overman 61-62, and that business magazines have begun to rank cities according to the quality of their schools, see Boyle 24.

guns in the hands of six percent of inner-city high school students and gun-related violence throughout a city's schools must threaten the trade and commerce that those schools support.

The economic links I have just sketched seem fairly obvious. Why then is it not equally obvious, in light of those links, that a widespread, serious, and substantial physical threat to teaching and learning also substantially threatens the commerce to which that teaching and learning is inextricably tied? That is to say, guns in the hands of six percent of inner-city high school students and gun-related violence throughout a city's schools must threaten the trade and commerce that those schools support. The only question, then, is whether the latter threat is (to use the majority's terminology) "substantial." The evidence of (1) the extent of the gun-related violence problem, see supra, at 619, (2) the extent of the resulting negative effect on classroom learning, see ibid., and (3) the extent of the consequent negative commercial effects, see supra, at 620-622, when taken together, indicate a threat to trade and commerce that is "substantial." At the very least, Congress could rationally have concluded that the links are "substantial."

Congress could have found that gun-related violence near the classroom poses a serious economic threat

Congress has written that "the occurrence of violent crime in school zones" has brought about a "decline in the quality of education" that "has an adverse impact on interstate commerce and the foreign commerce of the United States."

Specifically, Congress could have found that gun-related violence near the classroom poses a serious economic threat (1) to consequently inadequately educated workers who must endure low paying jobs, see, e.g., National Center 29, and (2) to communities and businesses that might (in today's "information society") otherwise gain, from a well-educated work force, an important commercial advantage, see, e.g., Becker 10 (1992), of a kind that location near a railhead or harbor provided in the past. Congress might also have found these threats to be no different in kind from other threats that this Court has found within the commerce power, such as the threat that loan sharking poses to the "funds" of "numerous localities," Perez v. United States, 402 U.S. at 157, and that unfair labor practices pose to instrumentalities of commerce, see Consolidated Edison Co. v. NLRB, 305 U.S. 197, 221-222, 83 L. Ed. 126, 59 S. Ct. 206 (1938). As I have pointed out, supra, at 618, Congress has written that "the occurrence of violent crime in school zones" has brought about a "decline in the quality of education" that "has an adverse impact on interstate commerce and the foreign commerce of the United States." 18 U.S.C. §§922 (q)(1)(F), (G). The violence-related facts, the educational facts, and the economic facts, taken together, make this conclusion rational. And, because under our case law, see supra, at 615-617; infra, at 627-628, the sufficiency of the constitutionally necessary Commerce Clause link between a crime of violence and interstate commerce turns simply upon size or degree, those same facts make the statute constitutional.

this statute is aimed at curbing a particularly acute threat to the educational process—the possession (and use) of life-threatening firearms in, or near, the classroom. The empirical evidence that I have discussed above unmistakably documents the special way in which guns and education are incompatible.

To hold this statute constitutional is not to "obliterate" the "distinction between what is national and what is local," ante, at 567 (citation omitted; internal quotation marks omitted); nor is it to hold that the Commerce Clause permits the Federal Government to "regulate any activity that it found was related to the economic productivity of individual citizens," to regulate "marriage, divorce, and child custody," or to regulate any and all aspects of education. Ante, at 564. First, this statute is aimed at curbing a particularly acute threat to the educational process -- the possession (and use) of life-threatening firearms in, or near, the classroom. The empirical evidence that I have discussed above unmistakably documents the special way in which guns and education are incompatible. See supra, at 619. This Court has previously recognized the singularly disruptive potential on interstate commerce that acts of violence may have. See Perez, supra, at 156-157. Second, the immediacy of the connection between education and the national economic well-being is documented by scholars and accepted by society at large in a way and to a degree that may not hold true for other social institutions. It must surely be the rare case, then, that a statute strikes at conduct that (when considered in the abstract) seems so removed from commerce, but which (practically speaking) has so significant an impact upon commerce.

in today's economic world, gun-related violence near the classroom makes a significant difference to our economic, as well as our social, well-being.

In sum, a holding that the particular statute before us falls within the commerce power would not expand the scope of that Clause. Rather, it simply would apply pre-existing law to changing economic circumstances. See Heart of Atlanta Motel, Inc. v. United States, 379 U.S. 241, 251, 13 L. Ed. 2d 258, 85 S. Ct. 348 (1964). It would recognize that, in today's economic world, gun-related violence near the classroom makes a significant difference to our economic, as well as our social, well-being. In accordance with well-accepted precedent, such a holding would permit Congress "to act in terms of economic . . . realities," would interpret the commerce power as "an affirmative power commensurate with the national needs," and would acknowledge that the "commerce clause does not operate so as to render the nation powerless to defend itself against economic forces that Congress decrees inimical or destructive of the national economy." North American Co. v. SEC, 327 U.S. 686, 705, 90 L. Ed. 945, 66 S. Ct. 785 (1946) (citing Swift & Co. v. United States, 196 U.S. at 398 (Holmes, J.)).

III

Presumably, Congress reasoned that threatening or using force, say with a gun on a street corner, to collect a debt occurs sufficiently often so that the activity (by helping organized crime) affects commerce among the States. But, why then cannot Congress also reason that the threat or use of force—the frequent consequence of possessing a gun—in or near a school occurs sufficiently often so that such activity (by inhibiting basic education) affects commerce among the States?

The majority's holding -- that §922 falls outside the scope of the Commerce Clause -- creates three serious legal problems. First, the majority's holding runs contrary to modern Supreme Court cases that have upheld congressional actions despite connections to interstate or foreign commerce that are less significant than the effect of school violence. In Perez v. United States, supra, the Court held that the Commerce Clause authorized a federal statute that makes it a crime to engage in loan sharking ("extortionate credit transactions") at a local level. The Court said that Congress may judge that such transactions, "though purely intrastate, . . . affect interstate commerce." 402 U.S. at 154 (emphasis added). Presumably, Congress reasoned that threatening or using force, say with a gun on a street corner, to collect a debt occurs sufficiently often so that the activity (by helping organized crime) affects commerce among the States. But, why then cannot Congress also reason that the threat or use of force -- the frequent consequence of possessing a gun -- in or near a school occurs sufficiently often so that such activity (by inhibiting basic education) affects commerce among the States? The negative impact upon the national economy of an inability to teach basic skills seems no smaller (nor less significant) than that of organized crime.

Businesses are less likely to locate in communities where violence plagues the classroom. Families will hesitate to move to neighborhoods where students carry guns instead of books. (Congress expressly found in 1994 that "parents may decline to send their children to school" in certain areas "due to concern about violent crime and gun violence."

In Katzenbach v. McClung, 379 U.S. 294, 13 L. Ed. 2d 290, 85 S. Ct. 377 (1964), this Court upheld, as within the commerce power, a statute prohibiting racial discrimination at local restaurants, in part because that discrimination discouraged travel by African Americans and in part because that discrimination affected purchases of food and restaurant supplies from other States. See id., at 300; Heart of Atlanta Motel, supra, at 274 (Black, J., concurring in McClung and in Heart of Atlanta). In Daniel v. Paul, 395 U.S. 298, 23 L. Ed. 2d 318, 89 S. Ct. 1697 (1969), this Court found an effect on commerce caused by an amusement park located several miles down a country road in the middle of Alabama -- because some customers (the Court assumed), some food, 15 paddleboats, and a juke box had come from out of state. See id., at 304-305, 308. In both of these cases, the Court understood that the specific instance of discrimination (at a local place of accommodation) was part of a general practice that, considered as a whole, caused not only the most serious human and social harm, but had nationally significant economic dimensions as well. See McClung, supra, at

301; Daniel, supra, at 307, n. 10. It is difficult to distinguish the case before us, for the same critical elements are present. Businesses are less likely to locate in communities where violence plagues the classroom. Families will hesitate to move to neighborhoods where students carry guns instead of books. (Congress expressly found in 1994 that "parents may decline to send their children to school" in certain areas "due to concern about violent crime and gun violence." 18 U.S.C. §922(q)(1)(E).) And (to look at the matter in the most narrowly commercial manner), interstate publishers therefore will sell fewer books and other firms will sell fewer school supplies where the threat of violence disrupts learning. Most importantly, like the local racial discrimination at issue in McClung and Daniel, the local instances here, taken together and considered as a whole, create a problem that causes serious human and social harm, but also has nationally significant economic dimensions.

In Wickard v. Filburn, 317 U.S. 111, 87 L. Ed. 122, 63 S. Ct. 82 (1942), this Court sustained the application of the Agricultural Adjustment Act of 1938 to wheat that Filburn grew and consumed on his own local farm because, considered in its totality, (1) homegrown wheat may be "induced by rising prices" to "flow into the market and check price increases, " and (2) even if it never actually enters the market, homegrown wheat nonetheless "supplies a need of the man who grew it which would otherwise be reflected by purchases in the open market" and, in that sense, "competes with wheat in commerce." Id., at 128. To find both of these effects on commerce significant in amount, the Court had to give Congress the benefit of the doubt. Why would the Court, to find a significant (or "substantial") effect here, have to give Congress any greater leeway? See also United States v. Women's Sportswear Mfrs. Assn., 336 U.S. 460, 464, 93 L. Ed. 805, 69 S. Ct. 714 (1949) ("If it is interstate commerce that feels the pinch, it does not matter how local the operation which applies the squeeze"); Mandeville Island Farms, Inc. v. American Crystal Sugar Co., 334 U.S. at 236 ("It is enough that the individual activity when multiplied into a general practice . . . contains a threat to the interstate economy that requires preventive regulation").

The second legal problem the Court creates comes from its apparent belief that it can reconcile its holding with earlier cases by making a critical distinction between "commercial" and noncommercial "transaction[s]." Ante, at 561. That is to say, the Court believes the Constitution would distinguish between two local activities, each of which has an identical effect upon interstate commerce, if one, but not the other, is "commercial" in nature. As a general matter, this approach fails to heed this Court's earlier warning not to turn "questions of the power of Congress" upon "formula[s]" that would give "controlling force to nomenclature such as 'production' and 'indirect' and foreclose consideration of the actual effects of the activity in question upon interstate commerce." Wickard, supra, at 120.

See also United States v. Darby, 312 U.S. 100, 116-117, 85 L. Ed. 609, 61 S. Ct. 451 (1941) (overturning the Court's distinction between "production" and "commerce" in the child labor case, Hammer v. Dagenhart, 247 U.S. 251, 271-272, 62 L. Ed. 1101, 38 S. Ct. 529 (1918)); Swift & Co. v. United States, 196 U.S. at 398 (Holmes, J.) ("Commerce among the States is not a technical legal conception, but a practical one, drawn from the course of business"). Moreover, the majority's test is not consistent with what the Court saw as the point of the cases that the majority now characterizes. Although the majority today attempts to categorize Perez, McClung, and Wickard as involving intrastate "economic activity," ante, at 559, the Courts that decided each of those cases did not focus upon the economic nature of the activity regulated. Rather, they focused upon whether that activity affected interstate or foreign commerce. In fact, the Wickard Court expressly held that Filburn's consumption of homegrown wheat, "though it may not be regarded as commerce," could nevertheless be regulated -- "whatever its nature" -- so long as "it exerts a substantial economic effect on interstate commerce." Wickard, supra, at 125 (emphasis added).

if a distinction between commercial and noncommercial activities is to be made, this is not the case in which to make it. The majority clearly cannot intend such a distinction to focus narrowly on an act of gun possession standing by itself

More importantly, if a distinction between commercial and noncommercial activities is to be made, this is not the case in which to make it. The majority clearly cannot intend such a distinction to focus narrowly on an act of gun possession standing by itself, for such a reading could not be reconciled with either the civil rights cases (McClung and Daniel) or Perez -- in each of those cases the specific transaction (the race-based exclusion, the use of force) was not itself "commercial." And, if the majority instead means to distinguish generally among broad categories of activities, differentiating what is educational from what is commercial, then, as a practical matter, the line becomes almost impossible to draw. Schools that teach reading, writing, mathematics, and related basic skills serve both social and commercial purposes, and one cannot easily separate the one from the other. American industry itself has been, and is again, involved in teaching. See supra, at 620, 622. When, and to what extent, does its involvement make education commercial? Does the number of vocational classes that train students directly for jobs make a difference? Does it matter if the school is public or private, nonprofit or profit seeking? Does it matter if a city or State adopts a voucher plan that pays private firms to run a school? Even if one were to ignore these practical questions, why should there be a theoretical distinction between education, when it significantly benefits commerce, and environmental pollution, when it causes economic harm? See Hodel v. Virginia Surface Mining & Reclamation Assn., Inc., 452 U.S. 264, 69 L. Ed. 2d 1, 101 S. Ct. 2352 (1981).

Regardless, if there is a principled distinction that could work both here and in future cases, Congress (even in the absence of vocational classes, industry involvement, and private management) could rationally conclude that schools fall on the commercial side of the line. In 1990, the year Congress enacted the statute before us, primary and secondary schools spent $230 billion -- that is, nearly a quarter of a trillion dollars -- which accounts for a significant portion of our $5.5 trillion gross domestic product for that year. See Statistical Abstract 147, 442 (1993). The business of schooling requires expenditure of these funds on student transportation, food and custodial services, books, and teachers' salaries. See U.S. Dept. of Education 4, 7 (1993). These expenditures enable schools to provide a valuable service -- namely, to equip students with the skills they need to survive in life and, more specifically, in the workplace. Certainly, Congress has often analyzed school expenditure as if it were a commercial investment, closely analyzing whether schools are efficient, whether they justify the significant resources they spend, and whether they can be restructured to achieve greater returns. See, e.g., S. Rep. No. 100-222, p. 2 (1987) (federal school assistance is "a prudent investment"); Senate Appropriations Committee Hearing (1994) (private sector management of public schools); cf. Chubb & Moe 185-229 (school choice); Hanushek 85-122 (performance based incentives for educators); Gibbs (decision in Hartford, Conn., to contract out public school system). Why could Congress, for Commerce Clause purposes, not consider schools as roughly analogous to commercial investments from which the Nation derives the benefit of an educated work force?

The third legal problem created by the Court's holding is that it threatens legal uncertainty in an area of law that, until this case, seemed reasonably well settled. Congress has enacted many statutes (more than 100 sections of the United States Code), including criminal statutes (at least 25 sections), that use the words "affecting commerce" to define their scope, see, e.g., 18 U.S.C. §844(i) (destruction of buildings used in activity affecting interstate commerce), and other statutes that contain no jurisdictional language at all, see, e.g., 18 U.S.C. §922 (o)(1) (possession of machineguns). Do these, or similar, statutes regulate noncommercial activities? If so, would that alter the meaning of "affecting commerce" in a jurisdictional element? Cf. United States v. Staszcuk, 517 F.2d 53, 57-58 (CA7 1975) (en banc) (Stevens, J.) (evaluation of Congress' intent "requires more than a consideration of the consequences of the particular transaction"). More importantly, in the absence of a jurisdictional element, are the courts nevertheless to take Wickard, 317 U.S. at 127-128, (and later similar cases) as inapplicable, and to judge the effect of a single noncommercial activity on interstate commerce without considering similar instances of the forbidden conduct? However these questions are eventually resolved, the legal uncertainty now created will restrict Congress' ability to enact criminal laws aimed at criminal behavior that, considered problem by problem rather than instance by instance, seriously threatens the economic, as well as social, well-being of Americans.

IV

Upholding this legislation would do no more than simply recognize that Congress had a "rational basis" for finding a significant connection between guns in or near schools and (through their effect on education) the interstate and foreign commerce they threaten.

In sum, to find this legislation within the scope of the Commerce Clause would permit "Congress . . . to act in terms of economic . . . realities." North American Co. v. SEC, 327 U.S. at 705 (citing Swift & Co. v. United States, 196 U.S. at 398 (Holmes, J.)). It would interpret the Clause as this Court has traditionally interpreted it, with the exception of one wrong turn subsequently corrected. See Gibbons v. Ogden, 9 Wheat., at 195 (holding that the commerce power extends "to all the external concerns of the nation, and to those internal concerns which affect the States generally"); United States v. Darby, 312 U.S. at 116-117 ("The conclusion is inescapable that Hammer v. Dagenhart [the child labor case] was a departure from the principles which have prevailed in the interpretation of the Commerce Clause both before and since the decision . . . . It should be and now is overruled"). Upholding this legislation would do no more than simply recognize that Congress had a "rational basis" for finding a significant connection between guns in or near schools and (through their effect on education) the interstate and foreign commerce they threaten. For these reasons, I would reverse the judgment of the Court of Appeals. Respectfully, I dissent.

APPENDIX TO OPINION OF BREYER, J. <List of references, omitted>

BAILEY v. UNITED STATES

(FULL CASE)

516 U.S. 137; 116 S. Ct. 501; 133 L. Ed. 2d 472

October 30, 1995, Argued

December 6, 1995, Decided

GIST: The Court interprets a federal statute that imposes an additional five-year prison term on anyone who uses or carries a firearm during and in relation to a drug-trafficking crime. Cases of this sort have long been thought of as really a statutory interpretation case, or a drug case, or a sentencing case, or an instruction on police procedure case. The Court's deep examination of what precisely constitutes use of a firearm makes it relevant to the theme of *Supreme Court Gun Cases.*

Two drug dealers' cases are consolidated in this decision. Bailey and Robinson were caught red-handed with cocaine and arrested, and in the subsequent searches, each was found to have a gun. The government argued that the presence of the gun constituted "use" for the purpose of enhancing the sentence. The only problem with the government's argument was that Bailey's loaded pistol was in a bag locked in his trunk, and Robinson's unloaded .22 caliber Derringer was holstered in a locked trunk in her bedroom closet. The defendants argued that this did not amount to "use" under the law.

The Court agreed with them, and held that to be convicted for using a gun in a drug-trafficking crime, you must in some way actively employ the gun, not merely possess it somewhere. Congress later amended the law to reach anyone who, "in furtherance of any such crime, possesses a firearm," described as a higher standard than possession "during and in relation to" the crime.

The concept "use a firearm" is described here only in relation to a specific penalty enhancement for a type of drug offense. If ever a question comes up concerning "use" of a firearm in another context, this case will become an obvious reference point.

Petitioners Bailey and Robinson were each convicted of federal drug offenses and of violating 18 U.S.C. §924(c)(1), which, in relevant part, imposes a prison term upon a person who "during and in relation to any . . . drug trafficking crime . . . uses or carries a firearm." Bailey's §924(c)(1) conviction was based on a loaded pistol that the police found inside a bag in his locked car trunk after they arrested him for possession of cocaine revealed by a search of the car's passenger compartment. The unloaded, holstered firearm that provided the basis for Robinson's §924(c)(1) conviction was found locked in a trunk in her bedroom closet after she was arrested for a number of drug-related offenses. There was no evidence in either case that the defendant actively employed the firearm in any way. In consolidating the cases and affirming the convictions, the Court of Appeals sitting en banc applied an "accessibility and proximity" test to determine "use" within §924(c)(1)'s meaning, holding, in both cases, that the gun was sufficiently accessible and proximate to the drugs or drug proceeds that the jury could properly infer that the defendant had placed the gun in order to further the drug offenses or to protect the possession of the drugs.

Held:

1. Section 924(c)(1) requires evidence sufficient to show an active employment of the firearm by the defendant, a use that makes the firearm an operative factor in relation to the predicate offense. Evidence of the proximity and accessibility of the firearm to drugs or drug proceeds is not alone sufficient to support a conviction for "use" under the statute. Pp. 142-151.

(a) Although the Court of Appeals correctly ruled that "use" must connote more than mere possession of a firearm by a person who commits a drug offense, the court's accessibility and proximity standard

renders "use" virtually synonymous with "possession" and makes any role for the statutory word "carries" superfluous. Section §924(c)(1)'s language instead indicates that Congress intended "use" in the active sense of "to avail oneself of." Smith v. United States, 508 U.S. 223, 228-229, 124 L. Ed. 2d 138, 113 S. Ct. 2050. This reading receives further support from §924(c)(1)'s context within the statutory scheme, and neither the section's amendment history nor Smith, supra, at 236, is to the contrary. Thus, to sustain a conviction under the "use" prong of §924(c)(1), the Government must show that the defendant actively employed the firearm during and in relation to the predicate crime. Under this reading, "use" includes the acts of brandishing, displaying, bartering, striking with, and firing or attempting to fire a firearm, as well as the making of a reference to a firearm in a defendant's possession. It does not include mere placement of a firearm for protection at or near the site of a drug crime or its proceeds or paraphernalia, nor the nearby concealment of a gun to be at the ready for an imminent confrontation. Pp. 142-150.

(b) The evidence was insufficient to support either Bailey's or Robinson's §924(c)(1) conviction for "use" under the active-employment reading of that word. Pp. 150-151.

2. However, because the Court of Appeals did not consider liability under the "carry" prong of §924(c)(1) as a basis for upholding these convictions, the cases must be remanded. P. 151.

JUSTICE O'CONNOR delivered the opinion of the Court.

We are asked to decide whether evidence of the proximity and accessibility of a firearm to drugs or drug proceeds is alone sufficient to support a conviction for "use" of a firearm during and in relation to a drug trafficking offense

These consolidated petitions each challenge a conviction under 18 U.S.C. §924(c)(1). In relevant part, that section imposes a 5-year minimum term of imprisonment upon a person who "during and in relation to any crime of violence or drug trafficking crime . . . uses or carries a firearm." We are asked to decide whether evidence of the proximity and accessibility of a firearm to drugs or drug proceeds is alone sufficient to support a conviction for "use" of a firearm during and in relation to a drug trafficking offense under 18 U.S.C. §924(c)(1).

I

A search of the passenger compartment revealed one round of ammunition and 27 plastic bags containing a total of 30 grams of cocaine.

In May 1989, petitioner Roland Bailey was stopped by police officers after they noticed that his car lacked a front license plate and an inspection sticker. When Bailey failed to produce a driver's license, the officers ordered him out of the car. As he stepped out, the officers saw Bailey push something between the seat and the front console. A search of the passenger compartment revealed one round of ammunition and 27 plastic bags containing a total of 30 grams of cocaine. After arresting Bailey, the officers searched the trunk of his car where they found, among a number of items, a large amount of cash and a bag containing a loaded 9-mm. pistol.

Bailey was charged on several counts, including using and carrying a firearm in violation of 18 U.S.C. §924(c)(1). A prosecution expert testified at trial that drug dealers frequently carry a firearm to protect their drugs and money as well as themselves. Bailey was convicted by the jury on all charges, and his sentence included a consecutive 60-month term of imprisonment on the §924(c)(1) conviction.

The Court of Appeals for the District of Columbia Circuit rejected Bailey's claim that the evidence was insufficient to support his conviction under §924(c)(1). United States v. Bailey, 302 U.S. App. D.C. 45, 995 F.2d 1113 (CADC 1993). The court held that Bailey could be convicted for "using" a firearm during and in relation to a drug trafficking crime if the jury could reasonably infer that the gun facilitated Bailey's commission of a drug offense. 995 F.2d at 1119. In Bailey's case, the court explained, the trier of fact could reasonably infer that Bailey had used the gun in the trunk to protect his drugs and drug proceeds and to facilitate sales. Judge Douglas H. Ginsburg, dissenting in part, argued that prior Circuit precedent required reversal of Bailey's conviction.

the police found, among other things, an unloaded, holstered .22-caliber Derringer, papers and a tax return belonging to Robinson, 10.88 grams of crack cocaine, and a marked $20 bill from the first controlled buy.

In June 1991, an undercover officer made a controlled buy of crack cocaine from petitioner Candisha Robinson. The officer observed Robinson retrieve the drugs from the bedroom of her one-bedroom apartment. After a second controlled buy, the police executed a search warrant of the apartment. Inside a locked trunk in the bedroom closet, the police found, among other things, an unloaded, holstered .22-caliber Derringer, papers and a tax return belonging to Robinson, 10.88 grams of crack cocaine, and a marked $20 bill from the first controlled buy.

A prosecution expert testified that the Derringer was a "second gun," i.e., a type of gun a drug dealer might hide on his or her person for use until reaching a "real gun."

Robinson was indicted on a number of counts, including using or carrying a firearm in violation of §924(c)(1). A prosecution expert testified that the Derringer was a "second gun," i.e., a type of gun a drug dealer might hide on his or her person for use until reaching a "real gun." The expert also testified that drug dealers generally use guns to protect themselves from other dealers, the police, and their own employees. Robinson was convicted on all counts, including the §924(c)(1) count, for which she received a 60-month term of imprisonment. The District Court denied Robinson's motion for a judgment of acquittal with respect to the "using or carrying" conviction and ruled that the evidence was sufficient to establish a violation of §924(c)(1).

The court held that Robinson's possession of an unloaded .22-caliber Derringer in a locked trunk in a bedroom closet fell significantly short of the type of evidence the court had previously held necessary to establish actual use

A divided panel of the Court of Appeals reversed Robinson's conviction on the §924(c)(1) count. United States v. Robinson, 302 U.S. App. D.C. 194, 997 F.2d 884 (CADC 1993). The court determined, "given the way section 924(c)(1) is drafted, even if an individual intends to use a firearm in connection with a drug trafficking offense, the conduct of that individual is not reached by the statute unless the individual actually uses the firearm for that purpose." 997 F.2d at 887. The court held that Robinson's possession of an unloaded .22-caliber Derringer in a locked trunk in a bedroom closet fell significantly short of the type of evidence the court had previously held necessary to establish actual use under §924(c)(1). The mere proximity of the gun to the drugs was held insufficient to support the conviction. Judge Henderson dissented, arguing, among other things, that the firearm facilitated Robinson's distribution of drugs because it protected Robinson and the drugs during sales.

In order to resolve the apparent inconsistencies in its decisions applying §924(c)(1), the Court of Appeals for the District of Columbia Circuit consolidated the two cases and reheard them en banc. In a divided opinion, a majority of the court held that the evidence was sufficient to establish that each defendant had used a firearm in relation to a drug trafficking offense and affirmed the §924(c)(1) conviction in each case. 36 F.3d 106 (CADC 1994) (en banc).

The District of Columbia Circuit had previously applied a nonexclusive set of factors, including: accessibility of the gun, its proximity to drugs, whether or not it was loaded, what type of weapon was involved, and whether expert testimony supported the government's theory of "use."

The majority rejected a multifactor weighing approach to determine sufficiency of the evidence to support a §924(c)(1) conviction. The District of Columbia Circuit had previously applied a nonexclusive set of factors, including: accessibility of the gun, its proximity to drugs, whether or not it was loaded, what type of weapon was involved, and whether expert testimony supported the government's theory of "use." The majority explained that this approach invited the reviewing court to reweigh the evidence and make its own finding with respect to an ultimate fact, a function properly left to the jury; had produced widely divergent and contradictory results; and was out of step with the broader definition of "use" employed by other Circuits.

The court replaced the multifactor test with an "accessibility and proximity" test. "We hold that one uses a gun, i.e., avails oneself of a gun, and therefore violates [§924(c)(1)], whenever one puts or keeps the gun in a particular place from which one (or one's agent) can gain access to it if and when needed to facilitate a drug crime." Id., at 115. The court applied this new standard and affirmed the convictions of both Bailey and Robinson. In both cases, the court determined that the gun was sufficiently accessible and proximate to the drugs or drug proceeds that the jury could properly infer that the defendant had placed the gun in order to further the drug offenses or to protect the possession of the drugs.

Judge Wald, in dissent, argued that the court's previous multifactor test provided a better standard for appellate review of §924(c)(1) convictions. Judge Williams, joined by Judges Silberman and Buckley, also dissented. He explained his understanding that "use" under §924(c)(1) denoted active employment of the firearm "rather than possession with a contingent intent to use." Id., at 121. "By articulating a 'proximity' plus 'accessibility' test, however, the court has in effect diluted 'use' to mean simply possession with a floating intent to use." Ibid.

As the debate within the District of Columbia Circuit illustrates, §924(c)(1) has been the source of much perplexity in the courts. The Circuits are in conflict both in the standards they have articulated, compare United States v. Torres-Rodriguez, 930 F.2d 1375, 1385 (CA9 1991) (mere possession sufficient to satisfy §924(c)), with United States v. Castro-Lara, 970 F.2d 976, 983 (CA1 1992), cert. denied sub nom. Sarraff v.

United States, 508 U.S. 962, 124 L. Ed. 2d 684, 113 S. Ct. 2935 (1993) (mere possession insufficient); and in the results they have reached, compare United States v. Feliz-Cordero, 859 F.2d 250, 254 (CA2 1988) (presence of gun in dresser drawer in apartment with drugs, drug proceeds, and paraphernalia insufficient to meet §924(c)(1)), with United States v. McFadden, 13 F.3d 463, 465 (CA1 1994) (evidence of gun hidden under mattress with money, near drugs, was sufficient to show "use"), and United States v. Hager, 969 F.2d 883, 889 (CA10), cert. denied, 506 U.S. 964, 121 L. Ed. 2d 357, 113 S. Ct. 437 (1992) (gun in boots in living room near drugs was "used"). We granted certiorari to clarify the meaning of "use" under §924(c)(1). 514 U.S. 1062 (1995).

II

Petitioners argue that "use" signifies active employment of a firearm. The Government opposes that definition and defends the proximity and accessibility test adopted by the Court of Appeals. We agree with petitioners, and hold that §924(c)(1) requires evidence sufficient to show an active employment of the firearm by the defendant, a use that makes the firearm an operative factor in relation to the predicate offense.

Section 924(c)(1) requires the imposition of specified penalties if the defendant, "during and in relation to any crime of violence or drug trafficking crime . . ., uses or carries a firearm." Petitioners argue that "use" signifies active employment of a firearm. The Government opposes that definition and defends the proximity and accessibility test adopted by the Court of Appeals. We agree with petitioners, and hold that §924(c)(1) requires evidence sufficient to show an active employment of the firearm by the defendant, a use that makes the firearm an operative factor in relation to the predicate offense.

Consider the paradoxical statement: "I use a gun to protect my house, but I've never had to use it."

This action is not the first one in which the Court has grappled with the proper understanding of "use" in §924(c)(1). In Smith, we faced the question whether the barter of a gun for drugs was a "use," and concluded that it was. Smith v. United States, 508 U.S. 223, 124 L. Ed. 2d 138, 113 S. Ct. 2050 (1993). As the debate in Smith illustrated, the word "use" poses some interpretational difficulties because of the different meanings attributable to it. Consider the paradoxical statement: "I use a gun to protect my house, but I've never had to use it." "Use" draws meaning from its context, and we will look not only to the word itself, but also to the statute and the sentencing scheme, to determine the meaning Congress intended.

Had Congress intended possession alone to trigger liability under §924(c)(1), it easily could have so provided. This obvious conclusion is supported by the frequent use of the term "possess" in the gun-crime statutes to describe prohibited gun-related conduct.

We agree with the majority below that "use" must connote more than mere possession of a firearm by a person who commits a drug offense. See 36 F.3d at 109; accord, United States v. Castro-Lara, supra, at 983; United States v. Theodoropoulos, 866 F.2d 587, 597-598 (CA3 1989); United States v. Wilson, 884 F.2d 174, 177 (CA5 1989). Had Congress intended possession alone to trigger liability under §924(c)(1), it easily could have so provided. This obvious conclusion is supported by the frequent use of the term "possess" in the gun-crime statutes to describe prohibited gun-related conduct. See, e.g., §§922(g), 922(j), 922(k), 922(o)(1), 930(a), 930(b).

Where the Court of Appeals erred was not in its conclusion that "use" means more than mere possession, but in its standard for evaluating whether the involvement of a firearm amounted to something more than mere possession. Its proximity and accessibility standard provides almost no limitation on the kind of possession that would be criminalized; in practice, nearly every possession of a firearm by a person engaged in drug trafficking would satisfy the standard, "thereby erasing the line that the statutes, and the courts, have tried to draw." United States v. McFadden, supra, at 469 (Breyer, C. J., dissenting). Rather than requiring actual use, the District of Columbia Circuit would criminalize "simple possession with a floating intent to use." 36 F.3d at 121 (Williams, J., dissenting). The shortcomings of this test are succinctly explained in Judge Williams' dissent:

"While the majority attempts to fine-tune the concept of facilitation (and thereby, use) through its twin guide-posts of proximity and accessibility, the ultimate result is that possession amounts to 'use' because possession enhances the defendant's confidence. Had Congress intended that, all it need have mentioned is possession. In this regard, the majority's test is either so broad as to assure automatic affirmance of any jury conviction or, if not so broad, is unlikely to produce a clear guideline." Id., at 124-125 (citations omitted).

An evidentiary standard for finding "use" that is satisfied in almost every case by evidence of mere possession does not adhere to the obvious congressional intent to require more than possession to trigger the statute's application.

What must the Government show, beyond mere possession, to establish "use" for the purposes of the statute? We conclude that the language, context, and history of §924(c)(1) indicate that the Government must show active employment of the firearm.

This conclusion -- that a conviction for "use" of a firearm under §924(c)(1) requires more than a showing of mere possession -- requires us to answer a more difficult question. What must the Government show, beyond mere possession, to establish "use" for the purposes of the statute? We conclude that the language, context, and history of §924(c)(1) indicate that the Government must show active employment of the firearm.

We start, as we must, with the language of the statute. See United States v. Ron Pair Enterprises, Inc., 489 U.S. 235, 241, 103 L. Ed. 2d 290, 109 S. Ct. 1026 (1989). The word "use" in the statute must be given its "ordinary or natural" meaning, a meaning variously defined as "to convert to one's service," "to employ," "to avail oneself of," and "to carry out a purpose or action by means of." Smith, supra, 508 U.S. at 228-229 (internal quotation marks omitted) (citing Webster's New International Dictionary of English Language 2806 (2d ed. 1949) and Black's Law Dictionary 1541 (6th ed. 1990)). These various definitions of "use" imply action and implementation. See also McFadden, 13 F.3d at 467 (Breyer, C. J., dissenting) ("The ordinary meanings of the words 'use and 'carry' . . . connote activity beyond simple possession").

We consider not only the bare meaning of the word but also its placement and purpose in the statutory scheme. "'The meaning of statutory language, plain or not, depends on context.'" Brown v. Gardner, 513 U.S. 115, 118, 130 L. Ed. 2d 462, 115 S. Ct. 552 (1994) (citing King v. St. Vincent's Hospital, 502 U.S. 215, 221, 116 L. Ed. 2d 578, 112 S. Ct. 570 (1991)). Looking past the word "use" itself, we read §924(c)(1) with the assumption that Congress intended each of its terms to have meaning. "Judges should hesitate . . . to treat [as surplusage] statutory terms in any setting, and resistance should be heightened when the words describe an element of a criminal offense." Ratzlaf v. United States, 510 U.S. 135, 140-141, 126 L. Ed. 2d 615, 114 S. Ct. 655 (1994). Here, Congress has specified two types of conduct with a firearm: "uses" or "carries."

Under the Government's reading of §924(c)(1), "use" includes even the action of a defendant who puts a gun into place to protect drugs or to embolden himself. This reading is of such breadth that no role remains for "carry." The Government admits that the meanings of "use" and "carry" converge under its interpretation, but maintains that this overlap is a product of the particular history of §924(c)(1). Therefore, the Government argues, the canon of construction that instructs that "a legislature is presumed to have used no superfluous words," Platt v. Union Pacific R. Co., 99 U.S. 48, 58, 25 L. Ed. 424 (1879), is inapplicable. Brief for United States 24-25. We disagree. Nothing here indicates that Congress, when it provided these two terms, intended that they be understood to be redundant.

Under the interpretation we enunciate today, a firearm can be used without being carried, e.g., when an offender has a gun on display during a transaction, or barters with a firearm without handling it; and a firearm can be carried without being used, e.g., when an offender keeps a gun hidden in his clothing throughout a drug transaction.

We assume that Congress used two terms because it intended each term to have a particular, nonsuperfluous meaning. While a broad reading of "use" undermines virtually any function for "carry," a more limited, active interpretation of "use" preserves a meaningful role for "carries" as an alternative basis for a charge. Under the interpretation we enunciate today, a firearm can be used without being carried, e.g., when an offender has a gun on display during a transaction, or barters with a firearm without handling it; and a firearm can be carried without being used, e.g., when an offender keeps a gun hidden in his clothing throughout a drug transaction.

Congress recognized a distinction between firearms "used" in commission of a crime and those "intended to be used," and provided for forfeiture of a weapon even before it had been "used."

This reading receives further support from the context of §924(c)(1). As we observed in Smith, "using a firearm" should not have a "different meaning in §924(c)(1) than it does in §924(d)." 508 U.S. at 235. See also United Sav. Assn. of Tex. v. Timbers of Inwood Forest Associates, Ltd., 484 U.S. 365, 371, 98 L. Ed. 2d 740, 108 S. Ct. 626 (1988) ("A provision that may seem ambiguous in isolation is often clarified by the remainder of the statutory scheme"). Section 924(d)(1) provides for the forfeiture of any firearm that is "used" or "intended to be used" in certain crimes. In that provision, Congress recognized a distinction between firearms "used" in commission of a crime and those "intended to be used," and provided for forfeiture of a weapon even before it had been "used." In §924(c)(1), however, liability attaches only to cases of actual use, not intended use, as when an offender places a firearm with the intent to use it later if necessary. The difference between the two provisions demonstrates that, had Congress meant to broaden application of the statute beyond actual "use," Congress could and would have so specified, as it did in §924(d)(1).

The amendment history of §924(c) casts further light on Congress' intended meaning. The original version, passed in 1968, read:

"(c) Whoever --

"(1) uses a firearm to commit any felony which may be prosecuted in a court of the United States, or

"(2) carries a firearm unlawfully during the commission of any felony which may be prosecuted in a court of the United States,

"shall be sentenced to a term of imprisonment for not less than one year nor more than 10 years." §102, 82 Stat. 1224.

The phrase "uses to commit" indicates that Congress originally intended to reach the situation where the firearm was actively employed during commission of the crime. This original language would not have stretched so far as to cover a firearm that played no detectable role in the crime's commission. For example, a defendant who stored a gun in a nearby closet for retrieval in case the deal went sour would not have "used a firearm to commit" a crime. This version also shows that "use" and "carry" were employed with distinctly different meanings.

Congress' 1984 amendment to §924(c) altered the scope of predicate offenses from "any felony" to "any crime of violence," removed the "unlawfully" requirement, merged the "uses" and "carries" prongs, substituted "during and in relation to" the predicate crimes for the earlier provisions linking the firearm to the predicate crimes, and raised the minimum sentence to five years. §1005(a), 98 Stat. 2138-2139. The Government argues that this amendment stripped "uses" and "carries" of the qualifications ("to commit" and "unlawfully during") that originally gave them distinct meanings, so that the terms should now be understood to overlap. Of course, in Smith we recognized that Congress' subsequent amendments to §924(c) employed "use" expansively, to cover both use as a weapon and use as an item of barter. See Smith, supra, 508 U.S. at 236. But there is no evidence to indicate that Congress intended to expand the meaning of "use" so far as to swallow up any significance for "carry." If Congress had intended to deprive "use" of its active connotations, it could have simply substituted a more appropriate term -- "possession" -- to cover the conduct it wished to reach.

The Government nonetheless argues that our observation in Smith that "§924(c)(1)'s language sweeps broadly," 508 U.S. at 229, precludes limiting "use" to active employment. But our decision today is not inconsistent with Smith. Although there we declined to limit "use" to the meaning "use as a weapon," our interpretation of §924(c)(1) nonetheless adhered to an active meaning of the term. In Smith, it was clear that the defendant had "used" the gun; the question was whether that particular use (bartering) came within the meaning of §924(c)(1). Smith did not address the question we face today of what evidence is required to permit a jury to find that a firearm had been used at all.

To illustrate the activities that fall within the definition of "use" provided here, we briefly describe some of the activities that fall within "active employment" of a firearm, and those that do not.

The active-employment understanding of "use" certainly includes brandishing, displaying, bartering, striking with, and, most obviously, firing or attempting to fire a firearm.

The active-employment understanding of "use" certainly includes brandishing, displaying, bartering, striking with, and, most obviously, firing or attempting to fire a firearm. We note that this reading compels the conclusion that even an offender's reference to a firearm in his possession could satisfy §924(c)(1). Thus, a reference to a firearm calculated to bring about a change in the circumstances of the predicate offense is a "use," just as the silent but obvious and forceful presence of a gun on a table can be a "use."

according to this argument, that a gun placed in a closet is "used," because its mere presence emboldens or protects its owner. We disagree.

inert presence of a firearm, without more, is not enough to trigger §924(c)(1).

A defendant cannot be charged under §924(c)(1) merely for storing a weapon near drugs or drug proceeds.

The example given above -- "I use a gun to protect my house, but I've never had to use it" -- shows that "use" takes on different meanings depending on context. In the first phrase of the example, "use" refers to an ongoing, inactive function fulfilled by a firearm. It is this sense of "use" that underlies the Government's contention that "placement for protection" -- i.e., placement of a firearm to provide a sense of security or to embolden -- constitutes a "use." It follows, according to this argument, that a gun placed in a closet is "used," because its mere presence emboldens or protects its owner. We disagree. Under this reading, mere possession of a firearm by a drug offender, at or near the site of a drug crime or its proceeds or paraphernalia, is a "use" by the offender, because its availability for intimidation, attack, or defense would always, presumably, embolden or comfort the offender. But the inert presence of a firearm, without more, is not enough to trigger §924(c)(1). Perhaps the nonactive nature of this asserted "use" is clearer if a synonym is used: storage. A defendant cannot be charged under §924(c)(1) merely for storing a weapon near drugs or drug proceeds. Storage of a firearm, without its more active employment, is not reasonably distinguishable from possession.

A possibly more difficult question arises where an offender conceals a gun nearby to be at the ready for an imminent confrontation.

Some might argue that the offender has "actively employed" the gun by hiding it where he can grab and use it if necessary. In our view, "use" cannot extend to encompass this action. If the gun is not disclosed or mentioned by the offender, it is not actively employed, and it is not "used."

Placement for later active use does not constitute "use."

A possibly more difficult question arises where an offender conceals a gun nearby to be at the ready for an imminent confrontation. Cf. 36 F.3d at 119 (Wald, J., dissenting) (discussing distinction between firearm's accessibility to drugs or drug proceeds and its accessibility to defendant). Some might argue that the offender has "actively employed" the gun by hiding it where he can grab and use it if necessary. In our view, "use" cannot extend to encompass this action. If the gun is not disclosed or mentioned by the offender, it is not actively employed, and it is not "used." To conclude otherwise would distort the language of the statute as well as create an impossible line-drawing problem. How "at the ready" was the firearm? Within arm's reach? In the room? In the house? How long before the confrontation did he place it there? Five minutes or 24 hours? Placement for later active use does not constitute "use." An alternative rationale for why "placement at the ready" is a "use" -- that such placement is made with the intent to put the firearm to a future active use -- also fails. As discussed above, §924(d)(1) demonstrates that Congress knew how to draft a statute to reach a firearm that was "intended to be used." In §924(c)(1), it chose not to include that term, but instead established the 5-year mandatory minimum only for those defendants who actually "use" the firearm.

the word "use" in §924(c)(1) cannot support the extended applications that prosecutors have sometimes placed on it, in order to penalize drug-trafficking offenders for firearms possession.

While it is undeniable that the active-employment reading of "use" restricts the scope of §924(c)(1), the Government often has other means available to charge offenders who mix guns and drugs. The "carry" prong of §924(c)(1), for example, brings some offenders who would not satisfy the "use" prong within the reach of the statute. And Sentencing Guidelines §2D1.1(b)(1) provides an enhancement for a person convicted of certain drug-trafficking offenses if a firearm was possessed during the offense. United States Sentencing Commission, Guidelines Manual §2D1.1(b)(1) (Nov. 1994). But the word "use" in §924(c)(1) cannot support the extended applications that prosecutors have sometimes placed on it, in order to penalize drug-trafficking offenders for firearms possession.

The test set forth by the Court of Appeals renders "use" virtually synonymous with "possession" and makes any role for "carry" superfluous. The language of §924(c)(1), supported by its history and context, compels the conclusion that Congress intended "use" in the active sense of "to avail oneself of." To sustain a conviction under the "use" prong of §924(c)(1), the Government must show that the defendant actively employed the firearm during and in relation to the predicate crime.

III

Having determined that "use" denotes active employment, we must conclude that the evidence was insufficient to support either Bailey's or Robinson's conviction for "use" under §924(c)(1).

The police stopped Bailey for a traffic offense and arrested him after finding cocaine in the driver's compartment of his car. The police then found a firearm inside a bag in the locked car trunk. There was no evidence that Bailey actively employed the firearm in any way. In Robinson's case, the unloaded, holstered firearm that provided the basis for her §924(c)(1) conviction was found locked in a footlocker in a bedroom closet. No evidence showed that Robinson had actively employed the firearm. We reverse both judgments.

Bailey and Robinson were each charged under both the "use" and "carry" prongs of §924(c)(1). Because the Court of Appeals did not consider liability under the "carry" prong of §924(c)(1) for Bailey or Robinson, we remand for consideration of that basis for upholding the convictions.

It is so ordered.

UNITED STATES v. URSERY

(CASE EXCERPT)

518 U.S. 267; 116 S. Ct. 2135; 135 L. Ed. 2d 549

April 17, 1996, Argued

June 24, 1996, Decided

GIST: Guy Ursery was caught growing marijuana for personal use in and around his house in a heavily wooded area in Michigan. In addition to convicting him on drug charges, the government moved to confiscate his home, alleging it had been used to facilitate illegal drug transactions. The lengthy case addresses complex issues concerning the Constitution's double jeopardy clause, and civil asset forfeiture law. The Court holds that the taking of this man's house by the government is a civil forfeiture, not an additional penalty for committing a crime, and is remedial in nature. If the forfeiture had been found instead to be punitive, double jeopardy would prohibit it after a criminal conviction on the same set of facts. They describe a history of treating *in rem* cases (which are taken against a thing instead of a person), as being remedial.

In rem cases have a certain awkwardness to them, first evident by their very names, because they resort to a legal fiction invented to find property guilty "as though it were conscious instead of inanimate and insentient."

Some key precedents relied upon in *Ursery* were set by the *in rem* case of *U.S. v. One Assortment of 89 Firearms,* which established a two-stage test for allowable forfeitures. There's nothing uniquely important about guns per se in *Ursery*, and indeed, the other two precedent-setting cases concerned smuggled emeralds in 1972, and a liquor still in 1931 during Prohibition. So while this is "only" a drug case, and a double jeopardy case, and an asset forfeiture case, and a congressional intent case, it mentions firearms 54 times and could hardly be excluded. In delivering its opinion, the Court discusses what it did in *89 Firearms* in concise terms, a case that took away a man's inventory of firearms, after he was acquitted on the same set of facts, for the alleged commission of a separate crime.

The Court came to the conclusion that civil actions against property are not punishment in a criminal sense, and so they do not violate the double jeopardy clause of the 5th Amendment, and a person can effectively be tried twice for the same event. In a lone dissent, Justice Stevens says what he finds obvious—that of course confiscating Ursery's house was punishment, that the historical record speaks frequently of forfeiture as punishment, and that the logic the Court uses here implies that the federal government could have, during Prohibition, confiscated the homes of everyone who drank alcohol during those interesting times, called it remedial, and cut deeply into guarantees our Founders found fundamental.

Chief Justice Rehnquist delivered the opinion of the Court.

.....

In our most recent decision considering whether a civil forfeiture constitutes punishment under the Double Jeopardy Clause, we again affirmed the rule of Various Items. In United States v. One Assortment of 89 Firearms, 465 U.S. 354 (1984), the owner of the defendant weapons was acquitted of charges of dealing firearms without a license. The Government then brought a forfeiture action against the firearms under 18 U.S.C. Section(s) 924(d), alleging that they were used or were intended to be used in violation of federal law.

In another unanimous decision, we held that the forfeiture was not barred by the prior criminal proceeding. We began our analysis by stating the rule for our decision:

"Unless the forfeiture sanction was intended as punishment, so that the proceeding is essentially criminal in character, the Double Jeopardy Clause is not applicable. The question, then, is whether a Section(s) 924(d) forfeiture proceeding is intended to be, or by its nature necessarily is, criminal and punitive, or civil and remedial." 89 Firearms, supra, at 362 (citations omitted).

Third, we concluded that the civil forfeiture "further[ed] broad remedial aims," including both "discouraging unregulated commerce in firearms," and "removing from circulation firearms that have been used or intended for use outside regulated channels of commerce."

Our inquiry proceeded in two stages. In the first stage, we looked to Congress' intent, and concluded that "Congress designed forfeiture under Section(s) 924(d) as a remedial civil sanction." 465 U.S., at 363. This conclusion was based upon several findings. First, noting that the forfeiture proceeding was in rem, we found it significant that "actions in rem have traditionally been viewed as civil proceedings, with jurisdiction dependent upon the seizure of a physical object." 89 Firearms, id., at 363, citing, Calero-Toledo v. Pearson Yacht Leasing Co., 416 U.S., at 684. Second, we found that the forfeiture provision, because it reached both weapons used in violation of federal law and those "intended to be used" in such a manner, reached a broader range of conduct than its criminal analogue. Third, we concluded that the civil forfeiture "further[ed] broad remedial aims," including both "discouraging unregulated commerce in firearms," and "removing from circulation firearms that have been used or intended for use outside regulated channels of commerce." 89 Firearms, supra, at 364.

civil forfeiture is "not an additional penalty for the commission of a criminal act, but rather is a separate civil sanction, remedial in nature."

In the second stage of our analysis, we looked to "'whether the statutory scheme was so punitive either in purpose or effect as to negate' Congress' intention to establish a civil remedial mechanism," 465 U.S., at 365, quoting United States v. Ward, 448 U.S. 242, 248-249 (1980). Considering several factors that we had used previously in order to determine whether a civil proceeding was so punitive as to require application of the full panoply of constitutional protections required in a criminal trial, see id., at 248, we found only one of those factors to be present in the Section(s) 924(d) forfeiture. By itself, however, the fact that the behavior proscribed by the forfeiture was already a crime proved insufficient to turn the forfeiture into a punishment subject to the Double Jeopardy Clause. Hence, we found that the petitioner had "failed to establish by the 'clearest proof' that Congress has provided a sanction so punitive as to 'transfor[m] what was clearly intended as a civil remedy into a criminal penalty.'" 89 Firearms, supra, at 366, quoting Rex Trailer Co. v. United States, 350 U.S. 148, 154 (1956). We concluded our decision by restating that civil forfeiture is "not an additional penalty for the commission of a criminal act, but rather is a separate civil sanction, remedial in nature." 89 Firearms, supra, at 366.

B

the two-part analytical construct employed in 89 Firearms was more refined, perhaps, than that we had used over 50 years earlier in Various Items, the conclusion was the same in each case: in rem civil forfeiture is a remedial civil sanction

Our cases reviewing civil forfeitures under the Double Jeopardy Clause adhere to a remarkably consistent theme. Though the two-part analytical construct employed in 89 Firearms was more refined, perhaps, than that we had used over 50 years earlier in Various Items, the conclusion was the same in each case: in rem civil forfeiture is a remedial civil sanction, distinct from potentially punitive in personam civil penalties such as fines, and does not constitute a punishment under the Double Jeopardy Clause. See Gore v. United States, 357 U.S. 386, 392 (1958) ("In applying a provision like that of double jeopardy, which is rooted in history and is not an evolving concept . . . a long course of adjudication in this Court carries impressive authority").

In the case that we currently review, the Court of Appeals for the Ninth Circuit recognized as much, concluding that after 89 Firearms, "the law was clear that civil forfeitures did not constitute 'punishment' for double jeopardy purposes." 33 F. 3d, at 1218. Nevertheless, that court read three of our decisions to have "abandoned" 89 Firearms and the oft-affirmed rule of Various Items. According to the Court of Appeals for the Ninth Circuit, through our decisions in United States v. Halper, 490 U.S. 435 (1989), Austin v. United States, 509 U.S. 602 (1993), and Department of Revenue of Mont. v. Kurth Ranch, 511 U. S. ___ (1994), we "changed [our] collective mind," and "adopted a new test for determining whether a nominally civil sanction constitutes 'punishment' for double jeopardy purposes." 33 F. 3d, at 1218-1219. The Court of Appeals for the Sixth Circuit shared the view of the Ninth Circuit, though it did not directly rely upon Kurth Ranch. We turn now to consider whether Halper, Austin, and Kurth Ranch accomplished the radical jurisprudential shift perceived by the Courts of Appeals.

.....

In sum, nothing in Halper, Kurth Ranch, or Austin, purported to replace our traditional understanding that civil forfeiture does not constitute punishment for the purpose of the Double Jeopardy Clause. Congress long has authorized the Government to bring parallel criminal proceedings and civil forfeiture proceedings, and this Court consistently has found civil forfeitures not to constitute punishment under the Double Jeopardy Clause. It would have been quite remarkable for this Court both to have held unconstitutional a well-established practice, and to have overruled a long line of precedent, without having even suggested that it was doing so. Halper dealt with in personam civil penalties under the Double Jeopardy Clause; Kurth Ranch with a tax proceeding under the Double Jeopardy Clause; and Austin with civil forfeitures under the Excessive Fines Clause. None of those cases dealt with the subject of this case: in rem civil forfeitures for purposes of the Double Jeopardy Clause.

.....

We hold that these in rem civil forfeitures are neither "punishment" nor criminal for purposes of the Double Jeopardy Clause.

.....

Justice Stevens, concurring in the judgment in part and dissenting in part.

.....

In 89 Firearms, the Court explored in even greater detail the character of a federal statute that forfeited unregistered firearms. It reasoned that the sanction "further[ed] broad remedial aims" in preventing commerce in such weapons, and also covered a broader range of conduct than simply criminal behavior. 465 U.S., at 364. For those reasons, it was not properly characterized as a punitive sanction.

The majority, surprisingly, claims that Austin v. United States, 509 U.S. 602 (1993), "expressly recognized and approved" those decisions. Ante, at 18. But the Court creates the appearance that we endorsed its interpretation of 89 Firearms and Emerald Cut Stones by quoting selectively from Austin. We actually stated the following:

"The Double Jeopardy Clause has been held not to apply in civil forfeiture proceedings, but only in cases where the forfeiture could properly be characterized as remedial. See United States v. One Assortment of 89 Firearms, 465 U.S. 354, 364 (1984); One Lot Emerald Cut Stones v. United States, 409 U.S. 232, 237 (1972); see generally United States v. Halper, 490 U.S. 435, 446-449 (1989) (Double Jeopardy Clause prohibits second sanction that may not be fairly characterized as remedial)." 509 U.S., at 608, n. 4 (emphasis added).

In reality, both cases rejected the monolithic view that all in rem civil forfeitures should be treated the same, and recognized the possibility that other types of forfeitures that could not "properly be characterized as remedial" might constitute "an additional penalty for the commission of a criminal act." 465 U.S., at 366.

.....

In reaching the conclusion that the civil forfeiture at issue yielded punishment, the Austin Court surveyed the history of civil forfeitures at some length. That history is replete with expressions of the idea that forfeitures constitute punishment.

.....

There is simply no rational basis for characterizing the seizure of this respondent's home as anything other than punishment for his crime. The house was neither proceeds nor contraband and its value had no relation to the Government's authority to seize it.

formalistic distinctions that obscure the obvious practical consequences of governmental action disserve the "humane interests" protected by the Double Jeopardy Clause.

Even if the point had not been settled by prior decisions, common sense would dictate the result in this case. There is simply no rational basis for characterizing the seizure of this respondent's home as anything other than punishment for his crime. The house was neither proceeds nor contraband and its value had no relation to the Government's authority to seize it. Under the controlling statute an essential predicate for the forfeiture was proof that respondent had used the property in connection with the commission of a crime. The forfeiture of this property was unquestionably "a penalty that had absolutely no correlation to any damages sustained by society or to the cost of enforcing the law." United States v. Ward, 448 U.S., at 254. As we unanimously recognized in Halper, formalistic distinctions that obscure the obvious practical consequences of governmental action disserve the "'humane interests'" protected by the Double Jeopardy Clause. 490 U.S., at 447, quoting United States ex rel. Marcus v. Hess, 317 U.S. 537, 554 (1943) (Frankfurter, J., concurring). Fidelity to both reason and precedent dictates the conclusion that this forfeiture was "punishment" for purposes of the Double Jeopardy Clause.

.....

the Court's treatment of our cases has cut deeply into a guarantee deemed fundamental by the Founders.

Consider how drastic the remedy would have been if Congress in 1931 had authorized the forfeiture of every home in which alcoholic beverages were consumed.

One final example may illustrate the depth of my concern that the Court's treatment of our cases has cut deeply into a guarantee deemed fundamental by the Founders. The Court relies heavily on a few early decisions that involved the forfeiture of vessels whose entire mission was unlawful and on the Prohibition-era precedent sustaining the forfeiture of a distillery-a property that served no purpose other than the manufacture of illegal spirits. Notably none of those early cases involved the forfeiture of a home as a form of punishment for misconduct that occurred therein. Consider how drastic the remedy would have been if Congress in 1931 had authorized the forfeiture of every home in which alcoholic beverages were consumed. Under the Court's reasoning, I fear that the label "civil," or perhaps "in rem," would have been sufficient to avoid characterizing such forfeitures as "punitive" for purposes of the Double Jeopardy Clause. Our recent decisions in Halper, Austin, and Kurth Ranch, dictate a far different conclusion. I remain persuaded that those cases were correctly decided and should be followed today.

Accordingly, I respectfully dissent from the judgment in No. 95-345.

UNITED STATES v. GONZALES

(CASE EXCERPT)

520 U.S. 1; 117 S. Ct. 1032; 137 L. Ed. 2d 132

December 11, 1996, Argued

March 3, 1997, Decided

GIST: The drug bust started to sour when two of the perps pulled guns on undercover police during a sting operation. The suspects wound up convicted in New Mexico courts and were serving their sentences when the federal government tried and convicted them of similar charges based on the same set of facts from the same sting. This case involves interpretation of a federal statute that requires a mandatory five-year sentence for using or carrying a gun during and in relation to a drug-trafficking offense. The statute says the prison sentence must run consecutively with any other sentence, so that it adds to the total time served. The Court ruled that the law means what it says, and that a federal judge may not order that this sentence run concurrently with a state-imposed sentence. Being tried twice for the same criminal act, by both state and federal authorities, and the seemingly apparent 5th Amendment violation this implies against double jeopardy, was not at issue.

JUSTICE O'CONNOR delivered the opinion of the Court.

We are asked to decide whether a federal court may direct that a prison sentence under 18 U.S.C. § 924(c) run concurrently with a state imposed sentence, even though §924(c) provides that a sentence imposed under that statute "shall [not] . . . run concurrently with any other term of imprisonment." We hold that it may not.

Respondents were arrested in a drug sting operation during which two of them pulled guns on undercover police officers.

60 months reflected the mandatory sentence required for their firearms convictions.

Respondents were arrested in a drug sting operation during which two of them pulled guns on undercover police officers. All three were convicted in New Mexico courts on charges arising from the hold up. The state courts sentenced them to prison terms ranging from 13 to 17 years. After they began to serve their state sentences, respondents were convicted in federal court of committing various drug offenses connected to the sting operation, and conspiring to do so, in violation of 21 U.S.C. §§ 841 and 846. They were also convicted of using firearms during and in relation to those drug trafficking crimes, in violation of 18 U.S.C. § 924(c). Respondents received sentences ranging from 120 to 147 months in prison, of which 60 months reflected the mandatory sentence required for their firearms convictions. Pursuant to §924(c), the District Court ordered that the portion of respondents' federal sentences attributable to the drug convictions run concurrently with their state sentences, with the remaining 60 months due to the firearms offenses to run consecutively to both.

The Court of Appeals for the Tenth Circuit vacated respondents' sentences for the firearms violations, on the ground that the §924(c) sentences should have run concurrently with the state prison terms. 65 F. 3d 814 (1995). (The court also vacated the respondents' substantive drug convictions and dealt with various other sentencing issues not before us.) Although the Court of Appeals recognized that other circuits had uniformly "held that §924(c)'s plain language prohibits sentences imposed under that statute from running concurrently with state sentences," it nevertheless thought that "a literal reading of the statutory language would produce an absurd result." Id., at 819. Feeling obliged to "venture into the thicket of legislative history," id., at 820 (citations and internal quotation marks omitted), the court found a line in a Senate Committee Report indicating that " `the mandatory sentence under the revised subsection 924(c) [should] be served prior to the start of the sentence for the underlying or any other offense,' " ibid. (quoting S. Rep. No. 98-225, pp. 313-314 (1983) (hereinafter S. Rep.)) (emphasis deleted). If this statement were applied literally, respondents would have to serve first their state sentences, then their 5 year federal firearm sentences, and finally the sentences for their narcotics convictions--even though the narcotics sentences normally would have run concurrently with the state sentences, since they all arose out of the same criminal activity. 65 F. 3d, at 821. To avoid this irrational result, the court held that "§924(c)'s mandatory five year sentence may run concurrently with a previously imposed state sentence that a defendant has already begun to serve." Id., at 819.

We granted certiorari, 518 U. S. ___, and now reverse.

Our analysis begins, as always, with the statutory text. Section 924(c)(1) provides:

"Whoever, during and in relation to any . . . drug trafficking crime . . . for which he may be prosecuted in a court of the United States, uses or carries a firearm, shall, in addition to the punishment provided for such crime . . . , be sentenced to imprisonment for five years . . . . Notwithstanding any other provision of law, the court shall not place on probation or suspend the sentence of any person convicted of a violation of this subsection, nor shall the term of imprisonment imposed under this subsection run concurrently with any other term of imprisonment including that imposed for the . . . drug trafficking crime in which the firearm was used or carried." 18 U.S.C. § 924(c)(1) (emphasis added).

The question we face is whether the phrase "any other term of imprisonment" "means what it says, or whether it should be limited to some subset" of prison sentences, Maine v. Thiboutot, 448 U.S. 1, 4 (1980)--namely, only federal sentences. Read naturally, the word "any" has an expansive meaning, that is, "one or some indiscriminately of whatever kind." Webster's Third New International Dictionary 97 (1976). Congress did not add any language limiting the breadth of that word, and so we must read §924(c) as referring to all "term[s] of imprisonment," including those imposed by state courts. Cf. United States v. Alvarez Sanchez, 511 U.S. 350, 358 (1994) (noting that statute referring to "any law enforcement officer" includes "federal, state, or local" officers); Collector v. Hubbard, 12 Wall. 1, 15 (1871) (stating "it is quite clear" that a statute prohibiting the filing of suit "in any court" "includes the State courts as well as the Federal courts," because "there is not a word in the[statute] tending to show that the words `in any court' are not used in their ordinary sense"). There is no basis in the text for limiting §924(c) to federal sentences.

In his dissenting opinion, Justice Stevens suggests that the word "any" as used in the first sentence of §924(c) "unquestionably has the meaning `any federal.' " Post, at 3. In that first sentence, however, Congress explicitly limited the scope of the phrase "any crime of violence or drug trafficking crime" to those "for which [a defendant] may be prosecuted in a court of the United States." Given that Congress expressly limited the phrase "any crime" to only federal crimes, we find it significant that no similar restriction modifies the phrase "any other term of imprisonment," which appears only two sentences later and is at issue in this case. See Russello v. United States, 464 U.S. 16, 23 (1983) (" 'Where Congress includes particular language in one section of a statute but omits it in another section of the same Act, it is generally presumed that Congress acts intentionally and purposely in the disparate inclusion or exclusion' ").

The Court of Appeals also found ambiguity in Congress' decision, in drafting §924(c), to prohibit concur rent sentences instead of simply mandating consecutive sentences. 65 F. 3d, at 820. Unlike the lower court, however, we see nothing remarkable (much less ambiguous) about Congress' choice of words. Because consecutive and concurrent sentences are exact opposites, Congress implicitly required one when it prohibited the other. This "ambiguity" is, in any event, beside the point because this phraseology has no bearing on whether Congress meant §924(c) sentences to run consecutively only to other federal terms of imprisonment.

Given the straightforward statutory command, there is no reason to resort to legislative history. Connecticut Nat. Bank v. Germain, 503 U.S. 249, 254 (1992). Indeed, far from clarifying the statute, the legislative history only muddies the waters. The excerpt from the Senate Report accompanying the 1984 amendment to §924(c), relied upon by the Court of Appeals, reads:

"[T]he Committee intends that the mandatory sentence under the revised subsection 924(c) be served prior to the start of the sentence for the underlying or any other offense." S. Rep., at 313-314.

This snippet of legislative history injects into §924(c) an entirely new idea—that a defendant must serve the five year prison term for his firearms conviction before any other sentences. This added requirement, however, is "in no way anchored in the text of the statute."

This snippet of legislative history injects into §924(c) an entirely new idea--that a defendant must serve the five year prison term for his firearms conviction before any other sentences. This added requirement, however, is "in no way anchored in the text of the statute." Shannon v. United States, 512 U.S. 573, 583 (1994).

The Court of Appeals was troubled that this rule might lead to irrational results. Normally, a district court has authority to decide whether federal prison terms should run concurrently with or consecutively to other prison sentences. 18 U.S.C. § 3584(a) (vesting power in district court to run most prison terms either concurrently or consecutively); United States Sentencing Commission, Guidelines Manual §5G1.3 (Nov. 1995) (USSG) (guiding court's discretion under §3584(a)). If the prison terms for respondents' other federal sentences could not begin until after their §924(c) terms were completed, however, the district court would effectively be stripped of its statutory power to decide whether the sentences for the underlying narcotics offenses should run concurrently with respondents' state terms of imprisonment. 65 F. 3d, at 822. The court observed that such a rule could lead to dramatically higher sentences, particularly for the respondents in this case. Perez, for example, is already serving a 17 year state prison term for his role in the hold up. Normally, his 7.25 year federal sentence for narcotics possession would run concurrently with that state term under USSG §5G1.3(b); his 5 year firearm sentence under §924(c) would follow both, for a total of 22 years in prison. If he must serve his federal narcotics sentence after his 5-year firearms sentence, however, he would face a total of 29.25 years in prison. 65 F. 3d, at 821.

Seeking to avoid this conflict between §924(c) (as reinterpreted in light of its legislative history) and §3584(a), the Court of Appeals held that §924(c) only prohibited running federal terms of imprisonment concurrently. Ibid. It also reasoned that such a narrow reading was necessary because "there is no way in which a later sentencing federal court can cause the mandatory 5 year §924(c) sentence to be served before a state sentence that is already being served." Ibid.

The statutes clash only if we engraft onto §924(c) a requirement found only in a single sentence buried in the legislative history: that the firearms sentence must run first. We therefore follow the text, rather than the legislative history, of §924(c).

We see three flaws in this reasoning. First, the statutory texts of §§924(c) and 3584(a), unvarnished by legislative history, are entirely consistent. Section 924(c) specifies only that a court must not run a firearms sentence concurrently with other prison terms. It leaves plenty of room for a court to run other sentences--whether for state or federal offenses--concurrently with one another pursuant to §3584(a) and USSG §5G1.3. The statutes clash only if we engraft onto §924(c) a requirement found only in a single sentence buried in the legislative history: that the firearms sentence must run first. We therefore follow the text, rather than the legislative history, of §924(c). By disregarding the suggestion that a district court must specify that a sentence for a firearms conviction be served before other sentences, we give full meaning to the texts of both §§924(c) and 3584(a). See United States v. Wiltberger, 5 Wheat. 76, 95-96 (1820) (Marshall, C. J.) ("Where there is no ambiguity in the words, there is no room for construction. The case must be a strong one indeed, which would justify a court in departing from the plain meaning of words . . . in search of an intention which the words themselves did not suggest").

Second, even if we ignored the plain language of §924(c) and required courts to list the order in which a defendant must serve the sentences for different convictions, we would thereby create a rule that is superfluous in light of 18 U.S.C. § 3584(c). That statute instructs the Bureau of Prisons to treat multiple terms of imprisonment, whether imposed concurrently or consecutively, "for administrative purposes as a single, aggregate term of imprisonment." Ibid. As a practical matter, then, it makes no difference whether a court specifies the sequence in which each portion of an aggregate sentence must be served. We will not impose on sentencing courts new duties that, in view of other statutory commands, will be effectively meaningless.

Third, the Court of Appeals' solution--to allow §924(c) prison terms to run concurrently with state sentences-- does not eliminate any anomaly that arises when a firearms sentence must run "first." Although it is clear that a prison term under §924(c) cannot possibly run before an earlier imposed state prison term, the same holds true when a prisoner is already serving a federal sentence. See §3585(a) (providing that a federal prison term commences when the defendant is received into custody or voluntarily arrives to begin serving the sentence). Because it is impossible to start a §924(c) sentence before any prison term that the prisoner is already serving, whether imposed by a state or federal court, limiting the phrase "any other term of imprisonment" to state sentences does not get rid of the problem. Thus, we think that the Court of Appeals both invented the problem and devised the wrong solution.

Justice Breyer questions, in dissent, whether Congress wanted to impose a §924(c) sentence on a defendant who is already serving a prison term pursuant to a virtually identical state sentencing enhancement statute. Post, at 2. A federal court could not (for double jeopardy reasons) sentence a person to two consecutive federal prison terms for a single violation of a federal criminal statute, such as §924(c). If Congress cannot impose two consecutive federal §924(c) sentences, the dissent argues, it is unlikely that Congress would have wanted to stack a §924(c) sentence onto a prison term under a virtually identical state firearms enhancement. Post, at 2.

As we have already observed, however, the straightforward language of §924(c) leaves no room to speculate about congressional intent. See supra, at 3-4. The statute speaks of "any term of imprisonment" without limitation, and there is no intimation that Congress meant §924(c) sentences to run consecutively only to certain types of prison terms. District courts have some discretion under the Sentencing Guidelines, of course, in cases where related offenses are prosecuted in multiple proceedings, to establish sentences "with an eye toward having such punishments approximate the total penalty that would have been imposed had the sentences for the different offenses been imposed at the same time . . . ." Witte v. United States, 515 U. S. ___, ___ (1995) (slip op., at 15) (discussing USSG §5G1.3). See post, at 1-2 (Breyer, J., dissenting). When Congress enacted §924(c)'s consecutive sentencing provision, however, it cabined the sentencing discretion of district courts in a single circumstance: when a defendant violates §924(c), his sentencing enhancement under that statute must run consecutively to all other prison terms. Given this clear legislative directive, it is not for the courts to carve out statutory exceptions based on judicial perceptions of good sentencing policy.

At that point, Congress made clear its desire to run §924(c) enhancements consecutively to all other prison terms, regardless of whether they were imposed under firearms enhancement statutes similar to §924(c).

Other language in §924(c) reinforces our conclusion. In 1984, Congress amended §924(c) so that its sentencing enhancement would apply regardless of whether the underlying felony statute "provides for an enhanced punishment if committed by the use of a deadly or dangerous weapon or device." Comprehensive Crime Control Act of 1984, Pub. L. 98-473, §1005(a), 98 Stat. 2138-2139. Congress thus repudiated the result we reached in Busic v. United States, 446 U.S. 398 (1980), in which we held that "prosecution and enhanced sentencing under §924(c) is simply not permissible where the predicate felony statute contains its own enhancement provision," irrespective of whether the Government had actually sought an enhancement under that predicate statute. Id., at 404; see also Simpson v. United States, 435 U.S. 6, 15 (1978) (holding that a federal court may not impose sentences under both §924(c) and the weapon enhancement under the armed bank robbery statute, 18 U.S.C. § 2113 based on a single criminal transaction). Our holdings in these cases were based on our conclusion that the unamended text of §924(c) left us with little "more than a guess" as to how Congress meant to mesh that statute with the sentencing enhancement provisions scattered throughout the federal criminal code. Simpson, supra, at 15; Busic, supra, at 405. The 1984 amendment, however, eliminated these ambiguities. At that point, Congress made clear its desire to run §924(c) enhancements consecutively to all other prison terms, regardless of whether they were imposed under firearms enhancement statutes similar to §924(c). We therefore cannot agree with Justice Breyer's contention that our interpretation of §924(c) distinguishes between "those subject to undischarged state, and those subject to undischarged federal, sentences." Post, at 2. Both sorts of defendants face sentences for their other convictions that run concurrently with or consecutively to each other according to normal sentencing principles, plus an enhancement under §924(c). In short, in light of the 1984 amendment, we think that Congress has foreclosed the dissent's argument that §924(c) covers only federal sentences.

Finally, we pause to comment on Justice Stevens' concern over how today's decision might affect other cases where "the state trial follows the federal trial and the state judge imposes a concurrent sentence" that might be viewed as inconsistent with §924(c). Post, at 2. That, of course, was not the sequence in which the respondents were sentenced in this case, and so we have no occasion to decide whether a later sentencing state court is bound to order its sentence to run consecutively to the §924(c) term of imprisonment. See ibid. All that is before us today is the authority of a later sentencing federal court to impose a consecutive sentence under §924(c). We are hesitant to reach beyond the facts of this case to decide a question that is not squarely presented for our review.

In sum, we hold that the plain language of 18 U.S.C. § 924(c) forbids a federal district court to direct that a term of imprisonment under that statute run concurrently with any other term of imprisonment, whether state or federal. The statute does not, however, limit the court's authority to order that other federal sentences run concurrently with or consecutively to other prison terms--state or federal--under §3584.

The judgment of the Court of Appeals is vacated, and the case is remanded for further proceedings consistent with this opinion.

It is so ordered.

PRINTZ/MACK v. UNITED STATES

(FULL CASE)

521 U.S. 898; 117 S. Ct. 2365; 138 L. Ed. 2d 914

December 3, 1996, Argued

June 27, 1997, Decided

GIST: The Sheriffs of two counties, first Mack in Arizona, and then Printz in Montana, challenged the portion of the Brady law that commanded the chief law enforcement officer of the region to conduct a background check before approving the sale of a handgun. The Court held on 10th Amendment grounds that the federal government may not command state officers to implement a federal regulatory scheme. A concurring opinion by Justice Thomas suggested that the Brady law might violate the 2nd Amendment.

Sometimes called the Brady-law case, and therefore a gun case, this is actually a detailed study of the balance of power between the states and the central government. The Court used its review of this federal law to protect state authorities from federal incursions on a state's sovereignty. The sweeping limitations the Court describes for federal mandates were in response to a temporary provision in the Brady law, a provision that expired in 1998, five years after enactment.

The federal government, seeking a "highly attractive power," claims that the nation's earliest cases support direct federal use of state resources. The Court, acknowledging this as critically important in the operation of the country, concludes that, although impositions have been made on state courts in the past and are in limited ways permissible, the same is not generally true for the executive power in a state, which is responsible for enforcing the laws. Thus, the Brady requirement that local officials conduct background checks for the federal government's gun control plan was unconstitutional. The majority opinion says nothing about whether subjecting gun buyers themselves to the Brady scheme is constitutional.

The Court comes close to rebuking the federal government for pushing the envelope so far, referring to nearly two centuries of Congressional avoidance of compelling states to act. Justice Thomas' concurrence makes bold statements about the 2nd Amendment's relevance as an individual right, and cites an impressive list of scholarly publications that provide historical evidence.

The dissent in this case is among the most strident of all the gun cases. A single vote separates the Court in this 5 to 4 decision, between diametrically opposed positions, and an ideological schism of epic proportion. If the Court's four dissenting liberal Justices had the extra vote, the federal government would be empowered to use local officials for implementing federal regulatory programs, without federal cost, and with a significant shift in the historic character of federalism—the balance between state and central authority. The dissenters vigorously support their position, deriding the majority repeatedly.

Both sides accuse the other of inventing new law, ignoring or misreading precedent, taking quotes deceptively out of context and more. The dissent hinges much of its position on Congress' presumed power to act for the benefit of the public, especially during emergencies, or at other times if the action is temporary, and when the impact on traditional separations of powers are only, as the dissenters characterize this case: a modest obligation, minimal requirement, minimal request, trivial burden, modest burden, minor burden, and a minimal temporary imposition. They give examples of prior federal mandates they see as roughly equivalent, such as: enlisting air-raid wardens during WWII, inoculations to prevent epidemics, a military draft, and international terrorist threats. The two sides hurl Madison and Hamilton quotes at each other, and come to opposite conclusions drawn from the same historical record.

The problem, sometimes referred to as *unfunded mandates,* was resolved (sort of) according to the Court, with the passage of a law that allowed the feds to simply use state resources as long as the cost of each program was under a $50 million threshold.

The dissent accuses the majority of activism, though the majority points to more than two centuries of precedent. Justice Souter argues separately that if Congress cannot force local sheriffs to implement federal programs because it is just too great an affront to state sovereignty, the federal government will instead have to grow to implement its program, and the net affront to state sovereignty is worse.

Attorney Stephen Halbrook represented Sheriff Printz, and successfully argued the case before the Supreme Court. Attorney David Kopel assisted in the amicus brief filed by Colorado Attorney General Gale Norton on behalf of states seeking to uphold their 10th Amendment powers. For further details on this case, see the *George Mason University Civil Rights Law Journal* (Volume 7, 1999), posted at davekopel.org.

Brady Handgun Violence Prevention Act provisions require the Attorney General to establish a national system for instantly checking prospective handgun purchasers' backgrounds, note following 18 U.S.C. §922, and command the "chief law enforcement officer" (CLEO) of each local jurisdiction to conduct such checks and perform related tasks on an interim basis until the national system becomes operative, §922(s). Petitioners, the CLEOs for counties in Montana and Arizona, filed separate actions challenging the interim provisions' constitutionality. In each case, the District Court held that the background-check provision was unconstitutional, but concluded that it was severable from the remainder of the Act, effectively leaving a

voluntary background-check system in place. The Ninth Circuit reversed, finding none of the interim provisions unconstitutional.

Held:

1. The Brady Act's interim provision commanding CLEOs to conduct background checks, §922(s)(2), is unconstitutional. Extinguished with it is the duty implicit in the background-check requirement that the CLEO accept completed handgun-applicant statements (Brady Forms) from firearms dealers, §§922(s)(1)(A)(i)(III) and (IV).

(a) Because there is no constitutional text speaking to the precise question whether congressional action compelling state officers to execute federal laws is unconstitutional, the answer to the CLEOs' challenge must be sought in historical understanding and practice, in the Constitution's structure, and in this Court's jurisprudence.

(b) Relevant constitutional practice tends to negate the existence of the congressional power asserted here, but is not conclusive. Enactments of the early Congresses seem to contain no evidence of an assumption that the Federal Government may command the States' executive power in the absence of a particularized constitutional authorization. The early enactments establish, at most, that the Constitution was originally understood to permit imposition of an obligation on state judges to enforce federal prescriptions related to matters appropriate for the judicial power. The Government misplaces its reliance on portions of The Federalist suggesting that federal responsibilities could be imposed on state officers. None of these statements necessarily implies--what is the critical point here--that Congress could impose these responsibilities without the States' consent. They appear to rest on the natural assumption that the States would consent, see FERC v. Mississippi, 456 U.S. 742, 796, n.35, 72 L. Ed. 2d 532, 102 S. Ct. 2126 (O'CONNOR, J., concurring in judgment and dissenting in part). Finally, there is an absence of executive-commandeering federal statutes in the country's later history, at least until very recent years. Even assuming that newer laws represent an assertion of the congressional power challenged here, they are of such recent vintage that they are not probative of a constitutional tradition.

(c) The Constitution's structure reveals a principle that controls these cases: the system of "dual sovereignty." See, e.g., Gregory v. Ashcroft, 501 U.S. 452, 457, 115 L. Ed. 2d 410, 111 S. Ct. 2395. Although the States surrendered many of their powers to the new Federal Government, they retained a residuary and inviolable sovereignty that is reflected throughout the Constitution's text. See, e.g., Lane County v. Oregon, 74 U.S. 71, 7 Wall. 71, 76, 19 L. Ed. 101. The Framers rejected the concept of a central government that would act upon and through the States, and instead designed a system in which the State and Federal Governments would exercise concurrent authority over the people. The Federal Government's power would be augmented immeasurably and impermissibly if it were able to impress into its service--and at no cost to itself--the police officers of the 50 States.

(d) Federal control of state officers would also have an effect upon the separation and equilibration of powers between the three branches of the Federal Government itself. The Brady Act effectively transfers the President's responsibility to administer the laws enacted by Congress, Art. II, §§2 and 3, to thousands of CLEOs in the 50 States, who are left to implement the program without meaningful Presidential control. The Federal Executive's unity would be shattered, and the power of the President would be subject to reduction, if Congress could simply require state officers to execute its laws.

(e) Contrary to the dissent's contention, the Brady Act's direction of the actions of state executive officials is not constitutionally valid under Art. I, §8, as a law "necessary and proper" to the execution of Congress's Commerce Clause power to regulate handgun sales. Where, as here, a law violates the state sovereignty principle, it is not a law "proper for carrying into Execution" delegated powers within the Necessary and Proper Clause's meaning. Cf. New York v. United States, 505 U.S. 144, 166, 120 L. Ed. 2d 120, 112 S. Ct. 2408. The Supremacy Clause does not help the dissent, since it makes "Law of the Land" only "Laws of the United States which shall be made in Pursuance [of the Constitution.]" Art. VI, cl. 2.

(f) Finally, and most conclusively in these cases, the Court's jurisprudence makes clear that the Federal Government may not compel the States to enact or administer a federal regulatory program. See, e.g., New York, supra, at 188. The attempts of the Government and the dissent to distinguish New York--on grounds that the Brady Act's background-check provision does not require state legislative or executive officials to make policy; that requiring state officers to perform discrete, ministerial federal tasks does not diminish the state or federal officials' accountability; and that the Brady Act is addressed to individual CLEOs while the provisions invalidated in New York were directed to the State itself--are not persuasive. A "balancing" analysis is inappropriate here, since the whole object of the law is to direct the functioning of the state executive, and hence to compromise the structural framework of dual sovereignty; it is the very principle of separate state sovereignty that such a law offends. See e.g., New York, supra, at 187.

2. With the Act's background-check and implicit receipt-of-forms requirements invalidated, the Brady Act requirements that CLEOs destroy all Brady Forms and related records, §922(s)(6)(B)(i), and give would-be purchasers written statements of the reasons for determining their ineligibility to receive handguns,

§922(s)(6)(C), require no action whatsoever on the part of CLEOs such as petitioners, who are not voluntary participants in administration of the federal scheme. As to them, these provisions are not unconstitutional, but simply inoperative.

3. The Court declines to address the severability question briefed and argued by the parties: whether firearms dealers remain obliged to forward Brady Forms to CLEOs, §§922(s)(1)(A)(i)(III) and (IV), and to wait five business days thereafter before consummating a firearms sale, §922(s)(1)(A)(ii). These provisions burden only dealers and firearms purchasers, and no plaintiff in either of those categories is before the Court.

JUSTICE SCALIA delivered the opinion of the Court.

The question presented in these cases is whether certain interim provisions of the Brady Handgun Violence Prevention Act, Pub. L. 103-159, 107 Stat. 1536, commanding state and local law enforcement officers to conduct background checks on prospective handgun purchasers and to perform certain related tasks, violate the Constitution.

I

The Gun Control Act of 1968 (GCA), 18 U.S.C. §921 et seq., establishes a detailed federal scheme governing the distribution of firearms. It prohibits firearms dealers from transferring handguns to any person under 21, not resident in the dealer's State, or prohibited by state or local law from purchasing or possessing firearms, §922(b). It also forbids possession of a firearm by, and transfer of a firearm to, convicted felons, fugitives from justice, unlawful users of controlled substances, persons adjudicated as mentally defective or committed to mental institutions, aliens unlawfully present in the United States, persons dishonorably discharged from the Armed Forces, persons who have renounced their citizenship, and persons who have been subjected to certain restraining orders or been convicted of a misdemeanor offense involving domestic violence. §§922(d) and (g).

In 1993, Congress amended the GCA by enacting the Brady Act. The Act requires the Attorney General to establish a national instant background check system by November 30, 1998, Pub. L. 103-159, as amended, Pub. L. 103-322, 103 Stat. 2074, note following 18 U.S.C. §922, and immediately puts in place certain interim provisions until that system becomes operative. Under the interim provisions, a firearms dealer who proposes to transfer a handgun must first: (1) receive from the transferee a statement (the Brady Form), §922(s)(1)(A) (i)(I), containing the name, address and date of birth of the proposed transferee along with a sworn statement that the transferee is not among any of the classes of prohibited purchasers, §922(s)(3); (2) verify the identity of the transferee by examining an identification document, §922(s)(1)(A)(i)(II); and (3) provide the "chief law enforcement officer" (CLEO) of the transferee's residence with notice of the contents (and a copy) of the Brady Form, §§922(s)(1)(A)(i)(III) and (IV). With some exceptions, the dealer must then wait five business days before consummating the sale, unless the CLEO earlier notifies the dealer that he has no reason to believe the transfer would be illegal. §922(s)(1)(A)(ii).

The Brady Act creates two significant alternatives to the foregoing scheme. A dealer may sell a handgun immediately if the purchaser possesses a state handgun permit issued after a background check, §922(s)(1)(C), or if state law provides for an instant background check, §922(s)(1)(D). In States that have not rendered one of these alternatives applicable to all gun purchasers, CLEOs are required to perform certain duties. When a CLEO receives the required notice of a proposed transfer from the firearms dealer, the CLEO must "make a reasonable effort to ascertain within 5 business days whether receipt or possession would be in violation of the law, including research in whatever State and local recordkeeping systems are available and in a national system designated by the Attorney General." §922(s)(2). The Act does not require the CLEO to take any particular action if he determines that a pending transaction would be unlawful; he may notify the firearms dealer to that effect, but is not required to do so. If, however, the CLEO notifies a gun dealer that a prospective purchaser is ineligible to receive a handgun, he must, upon request, provide the would-be purchaser with a written statement of the reasons for that determination. §922(s)(6)(C). Moreover, if the CLEO does not discover any basis for objecting to the sale, he must destroy any records in his possession relating to the transfer, including his copy of the Brady Form. §922(s)(6)(B)(i). Under a separate provision of the GCA, any person who "knowingly violates [the section of the GCA amended by the Brady Act] shall be fined under this title, imprisoned for no more than 1 year, or both." §924(a)(5).

Petitioners Jay Printz and Richard Mack, the CLEOs for Ravalli County, Montana, and Graham County, Arizona, respectively, filed separate actions challenging the constitutionality of the Brady Act's interim provisions. In each case, the District Court held that the provision requiring CLEOs to perform background checks was unconstitutional, but concluded that that provision was severable from the remainder of the Act, effectively leaving a voluntary background-check system in place. 856 F. Supp. 1372 (Ariz. 1994); 854 F. Supp. 1503 (Mont. 1994). A divided panel of the Court of Appeals for the Ninth Circuit reversed, finding none of the Brady Act's interim provisions to be unconstitutional. 66 F.3d 1025 (1995). We granted certiorari. 135 L. Ed. 2d 1046, 116 S. Ct. 2521. (1996).

II

From the description set forth above, it is apparent that the Brady Act purports to direct state law enforcement officers to participate, albeit only temporarily, in the administration of a federally enacted regulatory scheme. Regulated firearms dealers are required to forward Brady Forms not to a federal officer or employee, but to the CLEOs, whose obligation to accept those forms is implicit in the duty imposed upon them to make "reasonable efforts" within five days to determine whether the sales reflected in the forms are lawful. While the CLEOs are subjected to no federal requirement that they prevent the sales determined to be unlawful (it is perhaps assumed that their state-law duties will require prevention or apprehension), they are empowered to grant, in effect, waivers of the federally prescribed 5-day waiting period for handgun purchases by notifying the gun dealers that they have no reason to believe the transactions would be illegal.

The petitioners here object to being pressed into federal service, and contend that congressional action compelling state officers to execute federal laws is unconstitutional.

Because there is no constitutional text speaking to this precise question, the answer to the CLEOs' challenge must be sought in historical understanding and practice, in the structure of the Constitution, and in the jurisprudence of this Court. We treat those three sources, in that order, in this and the next two sections of this opinion.

Petitioners contend that compelled enlistment of state executive officers for the administration of federal programs is, until very recent years at least, unprecedented. The Government contends, to the contrary, that "the earliest Congresses enacted statutes that required the participation of state officials in the implementation of federal laws," Brief for United States 28. The Government's contention demands our careful consideration, since early congressional enactments "provide 'contemporaneous and weighty evidence' of the Constitution's meaning," Bowsher v. Synar, 478 U.S. 714, 723-724, 92 L. Ed. 2d 583, 106 S. Ct. 3181 (1986) (quoting Marsh v. Chambers, 463 U.S. 783, 790, 77 L. Ed. 2d 1019, 103 S. Ct. 3330 (1983)). Indeed, such "contemporaneous legislative exposition of the Constitution . . ., acquiesced in for a long term of years, fixes the construction to be given its provisions." Myers v. United States, 272 U.S. 52, 175, 71 L. Ed. 160, 47 S. Ct. 21 (1926) (citing numerous cases). Conversely if, as petitioners contend, earlier Congresses avoided use of this highly attractive power, we would have reason to believe that the power was thought not to exist.

The Government observes that statutes enacted by the first Congresses required state courts to record applications for citizenship, Act of Mar. 26, 1790, ch. 3, §1, 1 Stat. 103, to transmit abstracts of citizenship applications and other naturalization records to the Secretary of State, Act of June 18, 1798, ch. 54, §2, 1 Stat. 567, and to register aliens seeking naturalization and issue certificates of registry, Act of Apr. 14, 1802, ch. 28, §2, 2 Stat. 154-155. It may well be, however, that these requirements applied only in States that authorized their courts to conduct naturalization proceedings. See Act of Mar. 26, 1790, ch. 3, §1, 1 Stat. 103; Holmgren v. United States, 217 U.S. 509, 516-517, 54 L. Ed. 861, 30 S. Ct. 588 (1910) (explaining that the Act of March 26, 1790 "conferred authority upon state courts to admit aliens to citizenship" and refraining from addressing the question "whether the States can be required to enforce such naturalization laws against their consent"); United States v. Jones, 109 U.S. 513, 519-520, 27 L. Ed. 1015, 3 S. Ct. 346 (1883) (stating that these obligations were imposed "with the consent of the States" and "could not be enforced against the consent of the States"). n1 Other statutes of that era apparently or at least arguably required state courts to perform functions unrelated to naturalization, such as resolving controversies between a captain and the crew of his ship concerning the seaworthiness of the vessel, Act of July 20, 1790, ch. 29, §3, 1 Stat. 132, hearing the claims of slave owners who had apprehended fugitive slaves and issuing certificates authorizing the slave's forced removal to the State from which he had fled, Act of Feb. 12, 1793, ch. 7, §3, 1 Stat. 302-305, taking proof of the claims of Canadian refugees who had assisted the United States during the Revolutionary War, Act of Apr. 7, 1798, ch. 26, §3, 1 Stat. 548, and ordering the deportation of alien enemies in times of war, Act of July 6, 1798, ch. 66, §2, 1 Stat. 577-578.

n1 The dissent is wrong in suggesting, post, at 13, n.9, that the Second Employers' Liability Cases, 223 U.S. 1, 56 L. Ed. 327, 32 S. Ct. 169 (1912), eliminate the possibility that the duties imposed on state courts and their clerks in connection with naturalization proceedings were contingent on the State's voluntary assumption of the task of adjudicating citizenship applications. The Second Employers' Liability Cases stand for the proposition that a state court must entertain a claim arising under federal law "when its ordinary jurisdiction as prescribed by local law is appropriate to the occasion and is invoked in conformity with those laws." 223 U.S. 1 at 56-57, 56 L. Ed. 327; 32 S. Ct. 169. This does not necessarily conflict with Holmgren and Jones, as the States obviously regulate the "ordinary jurisdiction" of their courts. (Our references throughout this opinion to "the dissent" are to the dissenting opinion of JUSTICE STEVENS, joined by JUSTICE GINSBURG and JUSTICE BREYER. The separate dissenting opinions of JUSTICE BREYER and JUSTICE SOUTER will be referred to as such.)

These early laws establish, at most, that the Constitution was originally understood to permit imposition of an obligation on state judges to enforce federal prescriptions, insofar as those prescriptions related to matters appropriate for the judicial power. That assumption was perhaps implicit in one of the provisions of the Constitution, and was explicit in another. In accord with the so-called Madisonian Compromise, Article III, §1, established only a Supreme Court, and made the creation of lower federal courts optional with the Congress--even though it was obvious that the Supreme Court alone could not hear all federal cases throughout the United States. See C. Warren, The Making of the Constitution 325-327 (1928). And the Supremacy Clause, Art. VI, cl. 2, announced that "the Laws of the United States . . . shall be the supreme Law of the Land; and the Judges in every State shall be bound thereby." It is understandable why courts should have been viewed distinctively in this regard; unlike legislatures and executives, they applied the law of other sovereigns all the time. The principle underlying so-called "transitory" causes of action was that laws which operated elsewhere created obligations in justice that courts of the forum state would enforce. See, e.g., McKenna v. Fisk, 42 U.S. 241, 1 HOW 241, 247-249, 11 L. Ed. 117 (1843). The Constitution itself, in the Full Faith and Credit Clause, Art. IV, §1, generally required such enforcement with respect to obligations arising in other States. See Hughes v. Fetter, 341 U.S. 609, 95 L. Ed. 1212, 71 S. Ct. 980 (1951).

we do not think the early statutes imposing obligations on state courts imply a power of Congress to impress the state executive into its service.

For these reasons, we do not think the early statutes imposing obligations on state courts imply a power of Congress to impress the state executive into its service. Indeed, it can be argued that the numerousness of these statutes, contrasted with the utter lack of statutes imposing obligations on the States' executive (notwithstanding the attractiveness of that course to Congress), suggests an assumed absence of such power. n2 The only early federal law the Government has brought to our attention that imposed duties on state executive officers is the Extradition Act of 1793, which required the "executive authority" of a State to cause the arrest and delivery of a fugitive from justice upon the request of the executive authority of the State from which the fugitive had fled. See Act of Feb. 12, 1793, ch. 7, §1, 1 Stat. 302. That was in direct implementation, however, of the Extradition Clause of the Constitution itself, see Art. IV, §2. n3

Bereft of even a single early, or indeed even pre-20th-century, statute compelling state executive officers to administer federal laws

n2 Bereft of even a single early, or indeed even pre-20th-century, statute compelling state executive officers to administer federal laws, the dissent is driven to claim that early federal statutes compelled state judges to perform executive functions, which implies a power to compel state executive officers to do so as well. Assuming that this implication would follow (which is doubtful), the premise of the argument is in any case wrong. None of the early statutes directed to state judges or court clerks required the performance of functions more appropriately characterized as executive than judicial (bearing in mind that the line between the two for present purposes is not necessarily identical with the line established by the Constitution for federal separation-of-powers purposes, see Sweezy v. New Hampshire, 354 U.S. 234, 255, 1 L. Ed. 2d 1311, 77 S. Ct. 1203 (1957)). Given that state courts were entrusted with the quintessentially adjudicative task of determining whether applicants for citizenship met the requisite qualifications, see Act of Mar. 26, 1790, ch. 3, §1, 1 Stat. 103, it is unreasonable to maintain that the ancillary functions of recording, registering, and certifying the citizenship applications were unalterably executive rather than judicial in nature.

The dissent's assertion that the Act of July 20, 1790, ch. 29, §3, 1 Stat. 132-133, which required state courts to resolve controversies between captain and crew regarding seaworthiness of a vessel, caused state courts to act "like contemporary regulatory agencies," post, at 14, is cleverly true--because contemporary regulatory agencies have been allowed to perform adjudicative ("quasi-judicial") functions. See 5 U.S.C. §554; Humphrey's Executor v. United States, 295 U.S. 602, 79 L. Ed. 1611, 55 S. Ct. 869 (1935). It is foolish, however, to mistake the copy for the original, and to believe that 18th-century courts were imitating agencies, rather than 20th-century agencies imitating courts. The Act's requirement that the court appoint "three persons in the neighborhood . . . most skilful in maritime affairs" to examine the ship and report on its condition certainly does not change the proceeding into one "supervised by a judge but otherwise more characteristic of executive activity," post, at 14; that requirement is not significantly different from the contemporary judicial practice of appointing expert witnesses, see e.g., Fed. Rule Evid. 706. The ultimate function of the judge under the Act was purely adjudicative; he was, after receiving the report, to "adjudge and determine . . . whether said ship or vessel is fit to proceed on the intended voyage . . . ." 1 Stat. 132.

n3 Article IV, §2, cl. 2 provides:

"A Person charged in any State with Treason, Felony, or other Crime, who shall flee from Justice, and be found in another State, shall on Demand of the executive Authority of the State from which he fled, be delivered up, to be removed to the State having Jurisdiction of the Crime."

To the extent the legislation went beyond the substantive requirement of this provision and specified procedures to be followed in complying with the constitutional obligation, we have found that that was an exercise of the congressional power to "prescribe the Manner in which such Acts, Records and Proceedings, shall be proved, and the Effect thereof," Art. IV, §1. See California v. Superior Court of Cal., San Bernardino Cty., 482 U.S. 400, 407, 96 L. Ed. 2d 332, 107 S. Ct. 2433 (1987).

the early Congresses, as far as we are aware, contain no evidence of an assumption that the Federal Government may command the States' executive power in the absence of a particularized constitutional authorization

Not only do the enactments of the early Congresses, as far as we are aware, contain no evidence of an assumption that the Federal Government may command the States' executive power in the absence of a particularized constitutional authorization, they contain some indication of precisely the opposite assumption. On September 23, 1789--the day before its proposal of the Bill of Rights, see 1 Annals of Congress 912-913--the First Congress enacted a law aimed at obtaining state assistance of the most rudimentary and necessary sort for the enforcement of the new Government's laws: the holding of federal prisoners in state jails at federal expense. Significantly, the law issued not a command to the States' executive, but a recommendation to their legislatures. Congress "recommended to the legislatures of the several States to pass laws, making it expressly the duty of the keepers of their gaols, to receive and safe keep therein all prisoners committed under the authority of the United States," and offered to pay 50 cents per month for each prisoner. Act of Sept. 23, 1789, 1 Stat. 96. Moreover, when Georgia refused to comply with the request, see L. White, The Federalists 402 (1948), Congress's only reaction was a law authorizing the marshal in any State that failed to comply with the Recommendation of September 23, 1789, to rent a temporary jail until provision for a permanent one could be made, see Resolution of Mar. 3, 1791, 1 Stat. 225.

the Constitution "opens a door to the appointment of a swarm of revenue and excise officers to prey upon the honest and industrious part of the community, eat up their substance, and riot on the spoils of the country,"

In addition to early legislation, the Government also appeals to other sources we have usually regarded as indicative of the original understanding of the Constitution. It points to portions of The Federalist which reply to criticisms that Congress's power to tax will produce two sets of revenue officers--for example, "Brutus's" assertion in his letter to the New York Journal of December 13, 1787, that the Constitution "opens a door to the appointment of a swarm of revenue and excise officers to prey upon the honest and industrious part of the community, eat up their substance, and riot on the spoils of the country," reprinted in 1 Debate on the Constitution 502 (B. Bailyn ed. 1993). "Publius" responded that Congress will probably "make use of the State officers and State regulations, for collecting" federal taxes, The Federalist No. 36, p. 221 (C. Rossiter ed. 1961) (A. Hamilton) (hereinafter The Federalist), and predicted that "the eventual collection [of internal revenue] under the immediate authority of the Union, will generally be made by the officers, and according to the rules, appointed by the several States," id., No. 45, at 292 (J. Madison). The Government also invokes the Federalist's more general observations that the Constitution would "enable the [national] government to employ the ordinary magistracy of each [State] in the execution of its laws," id., No. 27, at 176 (A. Hamilton), and that it was "extremely probable that in other instances, particularly in the organization of the judicial power, the officers of the States will be clothed in the correspondent authority of the Union," id., No. 45, at 292 (J. Madison). But none of these statements necessarily implies--what is the critical point here--that Congress could impose these responsibilities without the consent of the States. They appear to rest on the natural assumption that the States would consent to allowing their officials to assist the Federal Government, see FERC v. Mississippi, 456 U.S. 742, 796, n.35, 72 L. Ed. 2d 532, 102 S. Ct. 2126 (1982) (O'CONNOR, J., concurring in judgment in part and dissenting in part), an assumption proved correct by the extensive mutual assistance the States and Federal Government voluntarily provided one another in the early days of the Republic, see generally White, supra, at 401-404, including voluntary federal implementation of state law, see, e.g., Act of Apr. 2, 1790, ch. 5, §1, 1 Stat. 106 (directing federal tax collectors and customs officers to assist in enforcing state inspection laws).

Another passage of The Federalist reads as follows:

"It merits particular attention . . ., that the laws of the Confederacy as to the enumerated and legitimate objects of its jurisdiction will become the SUPREME LAW of the land; to the observance of which all officers, legislative, executive, and judicial in each State will be bound by the sanctity of an oath. Thus, the legislatures, courts, and magistrates, of the respective members will be incorporated into the operations of the national government as far as its just and constitutional authority extends; and will be rendered auxiliary to the enforcement of its laws." The Federalist No. 27, at 177 (A. Hamilton) (emphasis in original).

The Government does not rely upon this passage, but JUSTICE SOUTER (with whose conclusions on this point the dissent is in agreement, see post, at 11) makes it the very foundation of his position; so we pause to examine it in some detail. JUSTICE SOUTER finds "the natural reading" of the phrases "will be incorporated into the operations of the national government" and "will be rendered auxiliary to the enforcement of its laws" to be that the National Government will have "authority . . ., when exercising an otherwise legitimate power (the commerce power, say), to require state 'auxiliaries' to take appropriate action." Post, at 2. There are several obstacles to such an interpretation. First, the consequences in question ("incorporated into the operations of the national government" and "rendered auxiliary to the enforcement of its laws") are said in the quoted passage to flow automatically from the officers' oath to observe the "the laws of the Confederacy as to the enumerated and legitimate objects of its jurisdiction." n4 Thus, if the passage means that state officers must take an active role in the implementation of federal law, it means that they must do so without the necessity for a congressional directive that they implement it. But no one has ever thought, and no one asserts in the present litigation, that that is the law. The second problem with JUSTICE SOUTER's reading is that it makes state legislatures subject to federal direction. (The passage in question, after all, does not include legislatures merely incidentally, as by referring to "all state officers"; it refers to legislatures specifically and first of all.) We have held, however, that state legislatures are not subject to federal direction. New York v. United States, 505 U.S. 144, 120 L. Ed. 2d 120, 112 S. Ct. 2408 (1992). n5

n4 Both the dissent and JUSTICE SOUTER dispute that the consequences are said to flow automatically. They are wrong. The passage says that (1) federal laws will be supreme, and (2) all state officers will be oath-bound to observe those laws, and thus (3) state officers will be "incorporated" and "rendered auxiliary." The reason the progression is automatic is that there is not included between (2) and (3): "(2a) those laws will include laws compelling action by state officers." It is the mere existence of all federal laws that is said to make state officers "incorporated" and "auxiliary."

n5 JUSTICE SOUTER seeks to avoid incompatibility with New York (a decision which he joined and purports to adhere to), by saying, post, at 3-4, that the passage does not mean "any conceivable requirement may be imposed on any state official," and that "the essence of legislative power . . . is a discretion not subject to command," so that legislatures, at least, cannot be commanded. But then why were legislatures mentioned in the passage? It seems to us assuredly not a "natural reading" that being "rendered auxiliary to the enforcement of [the national government's] laws" means impressibility into federal service for "courts and magistrates" but something quite different for "legislatures." Moreover, the novel principle of political science that JUSTICE SOUTER invokes in order to bring forth disparity of outcome from parity of language--namely, that "the essence of legislative power . . . is a discretion not subject to command"--seems to us untrue. Perhaps legislatures are inherently uncommandable as to the outcome of their legislation, but they are commanded all the time as to what subjects they shall legislate upon--commanded, that is, by the people, in constitutional provisions that require, for example, the enactment of annual budgets or forbid the enactment of laws permitting gambling. We do not think that state legislatures would be betraying their very "essence" as legislatures (as opposed to their nature as sovereigns, a nature they share with the other two branches of government) if they obeyed a federal command to enact laws, for example, criminalizing the sale of marijuana.

These problems are avoided, of course, if the calculatedly vague consequences the passage recites--"incorporated into the operations of the national government" and "rendered auxiliary to the enforcement of its laws"--are taken to refer to nothing more (or less) than the duty owed to the National Government, on the part of all state officials, to enact, enforce, and interpret state law in such fashion as not to obstruct the operation of federal law, and the attendant reality that all state actions constituting such obstruction, even legislative acts, are ipso facto invalid. n6 See Silkwood v. Kerr-McGee Corp., 464 U.S. 238, 248, 78 L. Ed. 2d 443, 104 S. Ct. 615 (1984) (federal pre-emption of conflicting state law). This meaning accords well with the context of the passage, which seeks to explain why the new system of federal law directed to individual citizens, unlike the old one of federal law directed to the States, will "bid much fairer to avoid the necessity of using force" against the States, The Federalist No. 27, at 176. It also reconciles the passage with Hamilton's statement in Federalist No. 36, at 222, that the Federal Government would in some circumstances do well "to employ the state officers as much as possible, and to attach them to the Union by an accumulation of their emoluments"--which surely suggests inducing state officers to come aboard by paying them, rather than merely commandeering their official services. n7

n6 If JUSTICE SOUTER finds these obligations too insignificant, see post, at 3, n.1, then perhaps he should subscribe to the interpretations of "essential agency" given by Madison, see infra, at 15 and n.8, or by Story, see infra, n.9. The point is that there is no necessity to give the phrase the problematic meaning which alone enables him to use it as a basis for deciding this case.

n7 JUSTICE SOUTER deduces from this passage in No. 36 that although the Federal Government may commandeer state officers, it must compensate them for their services. This is a mighty leap, which would create a constitutional jurisprudence (for determining when the compensation was adequate) that would make takings cases appear clear and simple.

JUSTICE SOUTER contends that his interpretation of Federalist No. 27 is "supported by No. 44," written by Madison, wherefore he claims that "Madison and Hamilton" together stand opposed to our view. Post, at 4. In fact, Federalist No. 44 quite clearly contradicts JUSTICE SOUTER's reading. In that Number, Madison justifies the requirement that state officials take an oath to support the Federal Constitution on the ground that they "will have an essential agency in giving effect to the federal Constitution." If the dissent's reading of Federalist No. 27 were correct (and if Madison agreed with it), one would surely have expected that "essential agency" of state executive officers (if described further) to be described as their responsibility to execute the laws enacted under the Constitution. Instead, however, Federalist No. 44 continues with the following description:

"The election of the President and Senate will depend, in all cases, on the legislatures of the several States. And the election of the House of Representatives will equally depend on the same authority in the first instance; and will, probably, forever be conducted by the officers and according to the laws of the States." Id., at 287 (emphasis added).

It is most implausible that the person who labored for that example of state executive officers' assisting the Federal Government believed, but neglected to mention, that they had a responsibility to execute federal laws. n8 If it was indeed Hamilton's view that the Federal Government could direct the officers of the States, that view has no clear support in Madison's writings, or as far as we are aware, in text, history, or early commentary elsewhere. n9

n8 JUSTICE SOUTER's discussion of this passage omits to mention that it contains an example of state executives' "essential agency"--and indeed implies the opposite by observing that "other numbers of the Federalist give examples" of the "essential agency" of state executive officers. Post, at 4 (emphasis added). In seeking to explain the curiousness of Madison's not mentioning the state executives' obligation to administer federal law, JUSTICE SOUTER says that in speaking of "an essential agency in giving effect to the Federal Constitution," Federalist No. 44, Madison "was not talking about executing congressional statutes; he was talking about putting the National Constitution into effect," post, at 4, n.2. Quite so, which is our very point.

It is interesting to observe that Story's Commentaries on the Constitution, commenting upon the same issue of why state officials are required by oath to support the Constitution, uses the same "essential agency" language as Madison did in Federalist No. 44, and goes on to give more numerous examples of state executive agency than Madison did; all of them, however, involve not state administration of federal law, but merely the implementation of duties imposed on state officers by the Constitution itself: "The executive authority of the several states may be often called upon to exert Powers or allow Rights given by the Constitution, as in filling vacancies in the senate during the recess of the legislature; in issuing writs of election to fill vacancies in the house of representatives; in officering the militia, and giving effect to laws for calling them; and in the surrender of fugitives from justice." 2 Story, Commentaries on the Constitution of the United States 577 (1851).

The Federalist reads with a split personality on matters of federalism.

To choose Hamilton's view, as Justice Souter would, is to turn a blind eye to the fact that it was Madison's—not Hamilton's—that prevailed

n9 Even if we agreed with JUSTICE SOUTER's reading of the Federalist No. 27, it would still seem to us most peculiar to give the view expressed in that one piece, not clearly confirmed by any other writer, the determinative weight he does. That would be crediting the most expansive view of federal authority ever expressed, and from the pen of the most expansive expositor of federal power. Hamilton was "from first to last the most nationalistic of all nationalists in his interpretation of the clauses of our federal Constitution." C. Rossiter, Alexander Hamilton and the Constitution 199 (1964). More specifically, it is widely recognized that "The Federalist reads with a split personality" on matters of federalism. See D. Braveman, W. Banks, & R. Smolla, Constitutional Law: Structure and Rights in Our Federal System 198-199 (3d ed. 1996). While overall The Federalist reflects a "large area of agreement between Hamilton and Madison," Rossiter, supra, at 58, that is not the case with respect to the subject at hand, see Braveman, supra, at 198-199. To choose Hamilton's view, as JUSTICE SOUTER would, is to turn a blind eye to the fact that it was Madison's--not Hamilton's--that prevailed, not only at the Constitutional Convention and in popular sentiment, see Rossiter, supra, at 44-47, 194, 196; 1 Records of the Federal Convention (M. Farrand ed. 1911) 366, but in the subsequent struggle to fix the meaning of the Constitution by early congressional practice, see supra, at 5-10.

To complete the historical record, we must note that there is not only an absence of executive-commandeering statutes in the early Congresses, but there is an absence of them in our later history as well, at least until very recent years. The Government points to the Act of August 3, 1882, ch. 376, §§2, 4, 22 Stat. 214, which enlisted state officials "to take charge of the local affairs of immigration in the ports within such

State, and to provide for the support and relief of such immigrants therein landing as may fall into distress or need of public aid"; to inspect arriving immigrants and exclude any person found to be a "convict, lunatic, idiot," or indigent; and to send convicts back to their country of origin "without compensation." The statute did not, however, mandate those duties, but merely empowered the Secretary of the Treasury "to enter into contracts with such State . . . officers as may be designated for that purpose by the governor of any State." (Emphasis added.)

it is far from clear that the authorization "to utilize the service" of state officers was an authorization to compel the service of state officers

The Government cites the World War I selective draft law that authorized the President "to utilize the service of any or all departments and any or all officers or agents of the United States and of the several States, Territories, and the District of Columbia, and subdivisions thereof, in the execution of this Act," and made any person who refused to comply with the President's directions guilty of a misdemeanor. Act of May 18, 1917, ch. 15, §6, 40 Stat. 80-81 (emphasis added). However, it is far from clear that the authorization "to utilize the service" of state officers was an authorization to compel the service of state officers; and the misdemeanor provision surely applied only to refusal to comply with the President's authorized directions, which might not have included directions to officers of States whose governors had not volunteered their services. It is interesting that in implementing the Act President Wilson did not commandeer the services of state officers, but instead requested the assistance of the States' governors, see Proclamation of May 18, 1917, 40 Stat. 1665 ("calling upon the Governor of each of the several States . . . and all officers and agents of the several States . . . to perform certain duties"); Registration Regulations Prescribed by the President Under the Act of Congress Approved May 18, 1917, Part I, §7 ("the governor [of each State] is requested to act under the regulations and rules prescribed by the President or under his direction") (emphasis added), obtained the consent of each of the governors, see Note, The President, the Senate, the Constitution, and the Executive Order of May 8, 1926, 21 Ill. L. Rev. 142, 144 (1926), and left it to the governors to issue orders to their subordinate state officers, see Selective Service Regulations Prescribed by the President Under the Act of May 18, 1917, §27 (1918); J. Clark, The Rise of a New Federalism 91 (1965). See generally Note, 21 Ill. L. Rev., at 144. It is impressive that even with respect to a wartime measure the President should have been so solicitous of state independence.

the precise issue before us here, which is the forced participation of the States' executive in the actual administration of a federal program.

The Government points to a number of federal statutes enacted within the past few decades that require the participation of state or local officials in implementing federal regulatory schemes. Some of these are connected to federal funding measures, and can perhaps be more accurately described as conditions upon the grant of federal funding than as mandates to the States; others, which require only the provision of information to the Federal Government, do not involve the precise issue before us here, which is the forced participation of the States' executive in the actual administration of a federal program. We of course do not address these or other currently operative enactments that are not before us; it will be time enough to do so if and when their validity is challenged in a proper case. For deciding the issue before us here, they are of little relevance. Even assuming they represent assertion of the very same congressional power challenged here, they are of such recent vintage that they are no more probative than the statute before us of a constitutional tradition that lends meaning to the text. Their persuasive force is far outweighed by almost two centuries of apparent congressional avoidance of the practice. Compare INS v. Chadha, 462 U.S. 919, 77 L. Ed. 2d 317, 103 S. Ct. 2764 (1983), in which the legislative veto, though enshrined in perhaps hundreds of federal statutes, most of which were enacted in the 1970's and the earliest of which was enacted in 1932, see id., at 967-975 (White, J., dissenting), was nonetheless held unconstitutional.

III

The constitutional practice we have examined above tends to negate the existence of the congressional power asserted here, but is not conclusive. We turn next to consideration of the structure of the Constitution, to see if we can discern among its "essential postulates," Principality of Monaco v. Mississippi, 292 U.S. 313, 322, 78 L. Ed. 1282, 54 S. Ct. 745 (1934), a principle that controls the present cases.

A

It is incontestible that the Constitution established a system of "dual sovereignty." Although the States surrendered many of their powers to the new Federal Government, they retained "a residuary and inviolable sovereignty"

It is incontestible that the Constitution established a system of "dual sovereignty." Gregory v. Ashcroft, 501 U.S. 452, 457, 115 L. Ed. 2d 410, 111 S. Ct. 2395 (1991); Tafflin v. Levitt, 493 U.S. 455, 458, 107 L. Ed.

2d 887, 110 S. Ct. 792 (1990). Although the States surrendered many of their powers to the new Federal Government, they retained "a residuary and inviolable sovereignty," The Federalist No. 39, at 245 (J. Madison). This is reflected throughout the Constitution's text, Lane County v. Oregon, 74 U.S. 71, 7 Wall. 71, 76, 19 L. Ed. 101 (1869); Texas v. White, 74 U.S. 700, 7 Wall. 700, 725, 19 L. Ed. 227 (1869), including (to mention only a few examples) the prohibition on any involuntary reduction or combination of a State's territory, Art. IV, §3; the Judicial Power Clause, Art. III, §2, and the Privileges and Immunities Clause, Art. IV, §2, which speak of the "Citizens" of the States; the amendment provision, Article V, which requires the votes of three-fourths of the States to amend the Constitution; and the Guarantee Clause, Art. IV, §4, which "presupposes the continued existence of the states and . . . those means and instrumentalities which are the creation of their sovereign and reserved rights," Helvering v. Gerhardt, 304 U.S. 405, 414-415, 82 L. Ed. 1427, 58 S. Ct. 969 (1938). Residual state sovereignty was also implicit, of course, in the Constitution's conferral upon Congress of not all governmental powers, but only discrete, enumerated ones, Art. I, §8, which implication was rendered express by the Tenth Amendment's assertion that "the powers not delegated to the United States by the Constitution, nor prohibited by it to the States, are reserved to the States respectively, or to the people."

The Framers explicitly chose a Constitution that confers upon Congress the power to regulate individuals, not States.

As Madison expressed it: "The local or municipal authorities form distinct and independent portions of the supremacy, no more subject, within their respective spheres, to the general authority than the general authority is subject to them, within its own sphere."

The Framers' experience under the Articles of Confederation had persuaded them that using the States as the instruments of federal governance was both ineffectual and provocative of federal-state conflict. See The Federalist No. 15. Preservation of the States as independent political entities being the price of union, and "the practicality of making laws, with coercive sanctions, for the States as political bodies" having been, in Madison's words, "exploded on all hands," 2 Records of the Federal Convention of 1787, p. 9 (M. Farrand ed. 1911), the Framers rejected the concept of a central government that would act upon and through the States, and instead designed a system in which the state and federal governments would exercise concurrent authority over the people--who were, in Hamilton's words, "the only proper objects of government," The Federalist No. 15, at 109. We have set forth the historical record in more detail elsewhere, see New York v. United States, 505 U.S. at 161-166, and need not repeat it here. It suffices to repeat the conclusion: "The Framers explicitly chose a Constitution that confers upon Congress the power to regulate individuals, not States." Id., at 166. n10 The great innovation of this design was that "our citizens would have two political capacities, one state and one federal, each protected from incursion by the other"--"a legal system unprecedented in form and design, establishing two orders of government, each with its own direct relationship, its own privity, its own set of mutual rights and obligations to the people who sustain it and are governed by it." U.S. Term Limits, Inc. v. Thornton, 514 U.S. 779, 838, 131 L. Ed. 2d 881, 115 S. Ct. 1842 (1995) (Kennedy, J., concurring). The Constitution thus contemplates that a State's government will represent and remain accountable to its own citizens. See New York, supra, at 168-169; United States v. Lopez, 514 U.S. 549, 576-577, 131 L. Ed. 2d 626, 115 S. Ct. 1624 (1995) (Kennedy, J., concurring). Cf. Edgar v. MITE Corp., 457 U.S. 624, 644, 73 L. Ed. 2d 269, 102 S. Ct. 2629 (1982) ("the State has no legitimate interest in protecting nonresidents"). As Madison expressed it: "The local or municipal authorities form distinct and independent portions of the supremacy, no more subject, within their respective spheres, to the general authority than the general authority is subject to them, within its own sphere." The Federalist No. 39, at 245. n11

n10 The dissent, reiterating JUSTICE STEVENS' dissent in New York, 505 U.S. at 210-213, maintains that the Constitution merely augmented the pre-existing power under the Articles to issue commands to the States with the additional power to make demands directly on individuals. See post, at 7-8. That argument, however, was squarely rejected by the Court in New York, supra, at 161-166, and with good reason. Many of Congress's powers under Art. I, §8, were copied almost verbatim from the Articles of Confederation, indicating quite clearly that "where the Constitution intends that our Congress enjoy a power once vested in the Continental Congress, it specifically grants it." Prakash, Field Office Federalism, 79 Va. L. Rev. 1957, 1972 (1993).

n11 JUSTICE BREYER'S dissent would have us consider the benefits that other countries, and the European Union, believe they have derived from federal systems that are different from ours. We think such comparative analysis inappropriate to the task of interpreting a constitution, though it was of course quite relevant to the task of writing one. The Framers were familiar with many federal systems, from classical antiquity down to their own time; they are discussed in Nos. 18-20 of The

Federalist. Some were (for the purpose here under discussion) quite similar to the modern "federal" systems that JUSTICE BREYER favors. Madison's and Hamilton's opinion of such systems could not be clearer. Federalist No. 20, after an extended critique of the system of government established by the Union of Utrecht for the United Netherlands, concludes:

"I make no apology for having dwelt so long on the contemplation of these federal precedents. Experience is the oracle of truth; and where its responses are unequivocal, they ought to be conclusive and sacred. The important truth, which it unequivocally pronounces in the present case, is that a sovereignty over sovereigns, a government over governments, a legislation for communities, as contradistinguished from individuals, as it is a solecism in theory, so in practice it is subversive of the order and ends of civil polity . . . ." Id., at 138.

Antifederalists, on the other hand, pointed specifically to Switzerland--and its then-400 years of success as a "confederate republic"--as proof that the proposed Constitution and its federal structure was unnecessary. See Patrick Henry, Speeches given before the Virginia Ratifying Convention, 4 and 5 June, 1788, reprinted in The Essential Antifederalist 123, 135-136 (W. Allen & G. Lloyd ed. 1985). The fact is that our federalism is not Europe's. It is "the unique contribution of the Framers to political science and political theory." United States v. Lopez, 514 U.S. 549, 575, 131 L. Ed. 2d 626, 115 S. Ct. 1624 (1995) (Kennedy, J., concurring) (citing Friendly, Federalism: A Forward, 86 Yale L. J. 1019 (1977)).

This separation of the two spheres is one of the Constitution's structural protections of liberty. "Just as the separation and independence of the coordinate branches of the Federal Government serve to prevent the accumulation of excessive power in any one branch, a healthy balance of power between the States and the Federal Government will reduce the risk of tyranny and abuse from either front." Gregory, supra, at 458. To quote Madison once again:

"In the compound republic of America, the power surrendered by the people is first divided between two distinct governments, and then the portion allotted to each subdivided among distinct and separate departments. Hence a double security arises to the rights of the people. The different governments will control each other, at the same time that each will be controlled by itself." The Federalist No. 51, at 323.

The power of the Federal Government would be augmented immeasurably if it were able to impress into its service—and at no cost to itself—the police officers of the 50 States.

See also The Federalist No. 28, at 180-181 (A. Hamilton). The power of the Federal Government would be augmented immeasurably if it were able to impress into its service--and at no cost to itself--the police officers of the 50 States.

B

The Constitution does not leave to speculation who is to administer the laws enacted by Congress; the President, it says, "shall take Care that the Laws be faithfully executed,"

The Brady Act effectively transfers this responsibility to thousands of CLEOs in the 50 States, who are left to implement the program without meaningful Presidential control (if indeed meaningful Presidential control is possible without the power to appoint and remove).

the power of the President would be subject to reduction, if Congress could act as effectively without the President as with him, by simply requiring state officers to execute its laws.

We have thus far discussed the effect that federal control of state officers would have upon the first element of the "double security" alluded to by Madison: the division of power between State and Federal Governments. It would also have an effect upon the second element: the separation and equilibration of powers between the three branches of the Federal Government itself. The Constitution does not leave to speculation who is to administer the laws enacted by Congress; the President, it says, "shall take Care that the Laws be faithfully executed," Art. II, §3, personally and through officers whom he appoints (save for such inferior officers as Congress may authorize to be appointed by the "Courts of Law" or by "the Heads of Departments" who are themselves presidential appointees), Art. II, §2. The Brady Act effectively transfers this responsibility to thousands of CLEOs in the 50 States, who are left to implement the program without meaningful Presidential control (if indeed meaningful Presidential control is possible without the power to appoint and remove). The insistence of the Framers upon unity in the Federal Executive--to insure both vigor and accountability--is well known. See The Federalist No. 70 (A. Hamilton); 2 Documentary History of the Ratification of the Constitution 495 (M. Jensen ed. 1976) (statement of James Wilson); see also Calabresi & Prakash, The President's Power to Execute the Laws, 104 Yale L. J. 541 (1994). That unity would be shattered, and the power of the President would be subject to reduction, if Congress could act as effectively without the President as with him, by simply requiring state officers to execute its laws. n12

n12 There is not, as the dissent believes, post, at 23, "tension" between the proposition that impressing state police officers into federal service will massively augment federal power, and the proposition that it will also sap the power of the Federal Presidency. It is quite possible to have a more powerful Federal Government that is, by reason of the destruction of its Executive unity, a less efficient one. The dissent is correct, post, at 24, that control by the unitary Federal Executive is also sacrificed when States voluntarily administer federal programs, but the condition of voluntary state participation significantly reduces the ability of Congress to use this device as a means of reducing the power of the Presidency

C

Even where Congress has the authority under the Constitution to pass laws requiring or prohibiting certain acts, it lacks the power directly to compel the States to require or prohibit those acts.

The dissent of course resorts to the last, best hope of those who defend ultra vires congressional action, the Necessary and Proper Clause. It reasons, post, at 3-5, that the power to regulate the sale of handguns under the Commerce Clause, coupled with the power to "make all Laws which shall be necessary and proper for carrying into Execution the foregoing Powers," Art. I, §8, conclusively establishes the Brady Act's constitutional validity, because the Tenth Amendment imposes no limitations on the exercise of delegated powers but merely prohibits the exercise of powers "not delegated to the United States." What destroys the dissent's Necessary and Proper Clause argument, however, is not the Tenth Amendment but the Necessary and Proper Clause itself. n13 When a "Law... for carrying into Execution" the Commerce Clause violates the principle of state sovereignty reflected in the various constitutional provisions we mentioned earlier, supra, at 19-20, it is not a "Law . . . proper for carrying into Execution the Commerce Clause," and is thus, in the words of The Federalist, "merely [an] act of usurpation" which "deserves to be treated as such." The Federalist No. 33, at 204 (A. Hamilton). See Lawson & Granger, The "Proper" Scope of Federal Power: A Jurisdictional Interpretation of the Sweeping Clause, 43 Duke L. J. 267, 297-326, 330-333 (1993). We in fact answered the dissent's Necessary and Proper Clause argument in New York: "Even where Congress has the authority under the Constitution to pass laws requiring or prohibiting certain acts, it lacks the power directly to compel the States to require or prohibit those acts. . . . The Commerce Clause, for example, authorizes Congress to regulate interstate commerce directly; it does not authorize Congress to regulate state governments' regulation of interstate commerce." 505 U.S. at 166.

n13 This argument also falsely presumes that the Tenth Amendment is the exclusive textual source of protection for principles of federalism. Our system of dual sovereignty is reflected in numerous constitutional provisions, see supra, at 19-20, and not only those, like the Tenth Amendment, that speak to the point explicitly. It is not at all unusual for our resolution of a significant constitutional question to rest upon reasonable implications. See, e.g., Myers v. United States, 272 U.S. 52, 71 L. Ed. 160, 47 S. Ct. 21 (1926) (finding by implication from Art. II, §§1, 2, that the President has the exclusive power to remove executive officers); Plaut v. Spendthrift Farm, Inc., 514 U.S. 211, 131 L. Ed. 2d 328, 115 S. Ct. 1447 (1995) (finding that Article III implies a lack of congressional power to set aside final judgments).

The dissent perceives a simple answer in that portion of Article VI which requires that "all executive and judicial Officers, both of the United States and of the several States, shall be bound by Oath or Affirmation, to support this Constitution," arguing that by virtue of the Supremacy Clause this makes "not only the Constitution, but every law enacted by Congress as well," binding on state officers, including laws requiring state-officer enforcement. Post, at 6. The Supremacy Clause, however, makes "Law of the Land" only "Laws of the United States which shall be made in Pursuance [of the Constitution]"; so the Supremacy Clause merely brings us back to the question discussed earlier, whether laws conscripting state officers violate state sovereignty and are thus not in accord with the Constitution.

IV

Federal commandeering of state governments is such a novel phenomenon that this Court's first experience with it did not occur until the 1970's, when the Environmental Protection Agency promulgated regulations requiring States to prescribe auto emissions testing, monitoring and retrofit programs, and to designate preferential bus and carpool lanes.

After we granted certiorari to review the statutory and constitutional validity of the regulations, the Government declined even to defend them

Finally, and most conclusively in the present litigation, we turn to the prior jurisprudence of this Court. Federal commandeering of state governments is such a novel phenomenon that this Court's first experience with it did not occur until the 1970's, when the Environmental Protection Agency promulgated regulations requiring States to prescribe auto emissions testing, monitoring and retrofit programs, and to designate preferential bus and carpool lanes. The Courts of Appeals for the Fourth and Ninth Circuits invalidated the regulations on statutory grounds in order to avoid what they perceived to be grave constitutional issues, see Maryland v. EPA, 530 F.2d 215, 226 (CA4 1975); Brown v. EPA, 521 F.2d 827, 838-842 (CA9 1975); and the District of Columbia Circuit invalidated the regulations on both constitutional and statutory grounds, see District of Columbia v. Train, 172 U.S. App. D.C. 311, 521 F.2d 971, 994 (CADC 1975). After we granted certiorari to review the statutory and constitutional validity of the regulations, the Government declined even to defend them, and instead rescinded some and conceded the invalidity of those that remained, leading us to vacate the opinions below and remand for consideration of mootness. EPA v. Brown, 431 U.S. 99, 97 S. Ct. 1635, 52 L. Ed. 2d 166 (1977).

the Federal Government may not compel the States to implement, by legislation or executive action, federal regulatory programs.

Although we had no occasion to pass upon the subject in Brown, later opinions of ours have made clear that the Federal Government may not compel the States to implement, by legislation or executive action, federal regulatory programs. In Hodel v. Virginia Surface Mining & Reclamation Assn., Inc., 452 U.S. 264, 69 L. Ed. 2d 1, 101 S. Ct. 2352 (1981), and FERC v. Mississippi, 456 U.S. 742, 72 L. Ed. 2d 532, 102 S. Ct. 2126 (1982), we sustained statutes against constitutional challenge only after assuring ourselves that they did not require the States to enforce federal law. In Hodel we cited the lower court cases in EPA v. Brown, supra, but concluded that the Surface Mining Control and Reclamation Act did not present the problem they raised because it merely made compliance with federal standards a precondition to continued state regulation in an otherwise pre-empted field, Hodel, supra, at 288. In FERC, we construed the most troubling provisions of the Public Utility Regulatory Policies Act of 1978, to contain only the "command" that state agencies "consider" federal standards, and again only as a precondition to continued state regulation of an otherwise pre-empted field. 456 U.S. at 764-765. We warned that "this Court never has sanctioned explicitly a federal command to the States to promulgate and enforce laws and regulations," id., at 761-762.

When we were at last confronted squarely with a federal statute that unambiguously required the States to enact or administer a federal regulatory program, our decision should have come as no surprise. At issue in New York v. United States, 505 U.S. 144, 120 L. Ed. 2d 120, 112 S. Ct. 2408 (1992), were the so-called "take title" provisions of the Low-Level Radioactive Waste Policy Amendments Act of 1985, which required States either to enact legislation providing for the disposal of radioactive waste generated within their borders, or to take title to, and possession of the waste--effectively requiring the States either to legislate pursuant to Congress's directions, or to implement an administrative solution. 505 U.S. 144 at 175-176, 112 S. Ct. 2408, 120 L. Ed. 2d 120. We concluded that Congress could constitutionally require the States to do neither. Id., at 176. "The Federal Government," we held, "may not compel the States to enact or administer a federal regulatory program." Id., at 188.

The Government contends that New York is distinguishable on the following ground: unlike the "take title" provisions invalidated there, the background-check provision of the Brady Act does not require state legislative or executive officials to make policy, but instead issues a final directive to state CLEOs. It is permissible, the Government asserts, for Congress to command state or local officials to assist in the implementation of federal law so long as "Congress itself devises a clear legislative solution that regulates private conduct" and requires state or local officers to provide only "limited, non-policymaking help in enforcing that law." "The constitutional line is crossed only when Congress compels the States to make law in their sovereign capacities." Brief for United States 16.

The Government's distinction between "making" law and merely "enforcing" it, between "policymaking" and mere "implementation," is an interesting one. It is perhaps not meant to be the same as, but it is surely reminiscent of, the line that separates proper congressional conferral of Executive power from unconstitutional delegation of legislative authority for federal separation-of-powers purposes. See A. L. A. Schechter Poultry Corp. v. United States, 295 U.S. 495, 530, 79 L. Ed. 1570, 55 S. Ct. 837 (1935); Panama Refining Co. v. Ryan, 293 U.S. 388, 428-429, 79 L. Ed. 446, 55 S. Ct. 241 (1935). This Court has not been notably successful in describing the latter line; indeed, some think we have abandoned the effort to do so. See FPC v. New England Power Co., 415 U.S. 345, 352-353, 39 L. Ed. 2d 383, 94 S. Ct. 1151 (1974) (Marshall, J., concurring in result); Schoenbrod, The Delegation Doctrine: Could the Court Give it Substance? 83 Mich. L. Rev. 1223, 1233 (1985). We are doubtful that the new line the Government proposes would be any more distinct. Executive action that has utterly no policymaking component is rare, particularly at an executive level as high as a jurisdiction's chief law-enforcement officer. Is it really true that there is no policymaking involved in deciding, for example, what "reasonable efforts" shall be expended to conduct a background check? It may well satisfy the Act for a CLEO to direct that (a) no background checks will be conducted that divert personnel time from pending felony investigations, and (b) no background check will be permitted to consume more than one-half hour of an officer's time. But nothing in the Act requires a CLEO to be so parsimonious; diverting at least some felony-investigation time, and permitting at least some background checks beyond one-half hour would certainly not be unreasonable. Is this decision whether to devote maximum "reasonable efforts" or minimum "reasonable efforts" not preeminently a matter of policy? It is quite impossible, in short, to draw the Government's proposed line at "no policymaking," and we would have to fall back upon a line of "not too much policymaking." How much is too much is not likely to be answered precisely; and an imprecise barrier against federal intrusion upon state authority is not likely to be an effective one.

Even assuming, moreover, that the Brady Act leaves no "policymaking" discretion with the States, we fail to see how that improves rather than worsens the intrusion upon state sovereignty. Preservation of the States as independent and autonomous political entities is arguably less undermined by requiring them to make policy in certain fields than (as Judge Sneed aptly described it over two decades ago) by "reducing [them] to puppets of a ventriloquist Congress," Brown v. EPA, 521 F.2d at 839. It is an essential attribute of the States' retained sovereignty that they remain independent and autonomous within their proper sphere of authority. See Texas v. White, 7 Wall. at 725. It is no more compatible with this independence and autonomy that their officers be "dragooned" (as Judge Fernandez put it in his dissent below, 66 F.3d at 1035) into administering federal law, than it would be compatible with the independence and autonomy of the United States that its officers be impressed into service for the execution of state laws.

The Government purports to find support for its proffered distinction of New York in our decisions in Testa v. Katt, 330 U.S. 386, 91 L. Ed. 967, 67 S. Ct. 810 (1947), and FERC v. Mississippi, 456 U.S. 742, 72 L. Ed. 2d 532, 102 S. Ct. 2126 (1982). We find neither case relevant. Testa stands for the proposition that state courts cannot refuse to apply federal law--a conclusion mandated by the terms of the Supremacy Clause ("the Judges in every State shall be bound [by federal law]"). As we have suggested earlier, supra, at 6-7, that says nothing about whether state executive officers must administer federal law. Accord New York, 505 U.S. at 178-179. As for FERC, it stated (as we have described earlier) that "this Court never has sanctioned explicitly a federal command to the States to promulgate and enforce laws and regulations," 456 U.S. at 761-762, and upheld the statutory provisions at issue precisely because they did not commandeer state government, but merely imposed preconditions to continued state regulation of an otherwise pre-empted field, in accord with Hodel, 452 U.S. at 288, and required state administrative agencies to apply federal law while acting in a judicial capacity, in accord with Testa, See FERC, supra, at 759-771, and n.24. n14

n14 The dissent points out that FERC cannot be construed as merely following the principle recognized in Testa that state courts must apply relevant federal law because "although the commission was serving an adjudicative function, the commissioners were unquestionably not 'judges' within the meaning of [the Supremacy Clause]." Post, at 33. That is true enough. But the answer to the question of which state officers must apply federal law (only "'judges' within the meaning of [the Supremacy Clause]") is different from the answer to the question of which state officers may be required by statute to apply federal law (officers who conduct adjudications similar to those traditionally performed by judges). It is within the power of the States, as it is within the power of the Federal Government, see Crowell v. Benson, 285 U.S. 22, 76 L. Ed. 598, 52 S. Ct. 285 (1932), to transfer some adjudicatory functions to administrative agencies, with opportunity for subsequent judicial review. But it is also within the power of Congress to prescribe, explicitly or by implication (as in the legislation at issue in FERC), that those adjudications must take account of federal law. The existence of this latter power should not be unacceptable to a dissent that believes distinguishing among officers on the basis of their title rather than the function they perform is "empty formalistic reasoning of the highest order," post, at 15. We have no doubt that FERC would not have been decided the way it was if nonadjudicative responsibilities of the state agency were at issue.

By forcing state governments to absorb the financial burden of implementing a federal regulatory program, Members of Congress can take credit for "solving" problems without having to ask their constituents to pay for the solutions with higher federal taxes.

And even when the States are not forced to absorb the costs of implementing a federal program, they are still put in the position of taking the blame for its burdensomeness and for its defects.

Under the present law, for example, it will be the CLEO and not some federal official who stands between the gun purchaser and immediate possession of his gun. And it will likely be the CLEO, not some federal official, who will be blamed for any error (even one in the designated federal database) that causes a purchaser to be mistakenly rejected.

The Government also maintains that requiring state officers to perform discrete, ministerial tasks specified by Congress does not violate the principle of New York because it does not diminish the accountability of state or federal officials. This argument fails even on its own terms. By forcing state governments to absorb the financial burden of implementing a federal regulatory program, Members of Congress can take credit for "solving" problems without having to ask their constituents to pay for the solutions with higher federal taxes. And even when the States are not forced to absorb the costs of implementing a federal program, they are still put in the position of taking the blame for its burdensomeness and for its defects. See Merritt, Three Faces of Federalism: Finding a Formula for the Future, 47 Vand. L. Rev. 1563, 1580, n.65 (1994). Under the present law, for example, it will be the CLEO and not some federal official who stands between the gun purchaser and immediate possession of his gun. And it will likely be the CLEO, not some federal official, who will be blamed for any error (even one in the designated federal database) that causes a purchaser to be mistakenly rejected.

To say that the Federal Government cannot control the State, but can control all of its officers, is to say nothing of significance.

The dissent makes no attempt to defend the Government's basis for distinguishing New York, but instead advances what seems to us an even more implausible theory. The Brady Act, the dissent asserts, is different from the "take title" provisions invalidated in New York because the former is addressed to individuals--namely CLEOs--while the latter were directed to the State itself. That is certainly a difference, but it cannot be a constitutionally significant one. While the Brady Act is directed to "individuals," it is directed to them in their official capacities as state officers; it controls their actions, not as private citizens, but as the agents of the State. The distinction between judicial writs and other government action directed against individuals in their personal capacity, on the one hand, and in their official capacity, on the other hand, is an ancient one, principally because it is dictated by common sense. We have observed that "a suit against a state official in his or her official capacity is not a suit against the official but rather is a suit against the official's office. . . . As such, it is no different from a suit against the State itself." Will v. Michigan Dept. of State Police, 491 U.S. 58, 71, 105 L. Ed. 2d 45, 109 S. Ct. 2304 (1989). And the same must be said of a directive to an official in his or her official capacity. To say that the Federal Government cannot control the State, but can control all of its officers, is to say nothing of significance. n15 Indeed, it merits the description "empty formalistic reasoning of the highest order," post, at 15. By resorting to this, the dissent not so much distinguishes New York as disembowels it. n16

n15 Contrary to the dissent's suggestion, post, at 18-19, n.16, and 29, the distinction in our Eleventh Amendment jurisprudence between States and municipalities is of no relevance here. We long ago made clear that the distinction is peculiar to the question of whether a governmental entity is entitled to Eleventh Amendment sovereign immunity, see Monell v. New York City Dept. of Social Servs., 436 U.S. 658, 690, n.55, 56 L. Ed. 2d 611, 98 S. Ct. 2018 (1978); we have refused to apply it to the question of whether a governmental entity is protected by the Constitution's guarantees of federalism, including the Tenth Amendment, see National League of Cities v. Usery, 426 U.S. 833, 855-856, n.20, 49 L. Ed. 2d 245, 96 S. Ct. 2465 (1976) (overruled on other grounds by Garcia v. San Antonio Metropolitan Transit Authority, 469 U.S. 528, 83 L. Ed. 2d 1016, 105 S. Ct. 1005 (1985)); see also Garcia, supra (resolving Tenth Amendment issues in suit brought by local transit authority).

n16 The dissent's suggestion, post, at 28-29, n.27, that New York v. United States, 505 U.S. 144, 120 L. Ed. 2d 120, 112 S. Ct. 2408 (1992), itself embraced the distinction between congressional control of States (impermissible) and congressional control of state officers (permissible) is based upon the most egregious wrenching of statements out of context. It would take too much to reconstruct the context here, but by examining the entire passage cited, 505 U.S. 144 at 178-179, 112 S. Ct. 2408, 120 L. Ed. 2d 120, the reader will readily perceive the distortion. The passage includes, for example, the following:

"Additional cases cited by the United States discuss the power of federal courts to order state officials to comply with federal law. . . . Again, however, the text of the Constitution plainly confers this authority on the federal courts . . . . The Constitution contains no analogous grant of authority to Congress." Id., at 179.

Finally, the Government puts forward a cluster of arguments that can be grouped under the heading: "The Brady Act serves very important purposes, is most efficiently administered by CLEOs during the interim period, and places a minimal and only temporary burden upon state officers." There is considerable disagreement over the extent of the burden, but we need not pause over that detail. Assuming all the mentioned factors were true, they might be relevant if we were evaluating whether the incidental application to the States of a federal law of general applicability excessively interfered with the functioning of state governments. See, e.g., Fry v. United States, 421 U.S. 542, 548, 44 L. Ed. 2d 363, 95 S. Ct. 1792 (1975); National League of Cities v. Usery, 426 U.S. 833, 853, 49 L. Ed. 2d 245, 96 S. Ct. 2465 (1976) (overruled by Garcia v. San Antonio Metropolitan Transit Authority, 469 U.S. 528, 83 L. Ed. 2d 1016, 105 S. Ct. 1005 (1985)); South Carolina v. Baker, 485 U.S. 505, 529, 99 L. Ed. 2d 592, 108 S. Ct. 1355 (1988) (REHNQUIST, C. J., concurring in judgment). But where, as here, it is the whole object of the law to direct the functioning of the state executive, and hence to compromise the structural framework of dual sovereignty, such a "balancing" analysis is inappropriate.n17 It is the very principle of separate state sovereignty that such a law offends, and no comparative assessment of the various interests can overcome that fundamental defect. Cf. Bowsher, 478 U.S., at 736 (declining to subject principle of separation of powers to a balancing test); Chadha, 462 U.S. at 944-946 (same); Plaut v. Spendthrift Farm, Inc., 514 U.S. 211, 239-240, 131 L. Ed. 2d 328, 115 S. Ct. 1447 (1995) (holding legislated invalidation of final judgments to be categorically unconstitutional). We expressly rejected such an approach in New York, and what we said bears repeating:

the Constitution protects us from our own best intentions: It divides power among sovereigns and among branches of government precisely so that we may resist the temptation to concentrate power in one location as an expedient solution to the crisis of the day.

"Much of the Constitution is concerned with setting forth the form of our government, and the courts have traditionally invalidated measures deviating from that form. The result may appear 'formalistic' in a given case to partisans of the measure at issue, because such measures are typically the product of the era's perceived necessity. But the Constitution protects us from our own best intentions: It divides power among sovereigns and among branches of government precisely so that we may resist the temptation to concentrate power in one location as an expedient solution to the crisis of the day." 505 U.S. 144 at 187, 112 S. Ct. 2408, 120 L. Ed. 2d 120.

The Federal Government may not compel the States to enact or administer a federal regulatory program. The mandatory obligation imposed on CLEOs to perform background checks on prospective handgun purchasers plainly runs afoul of that rule.

We adhere to that principle today, and conclude categorically, as we concluded categorically in New York: "The Federal Government may not compel the States to enact or administer a federal regulatory program." Id., at 188. The mandatory obligation imposed on CLEOs to perform background checks on prospective handgun purchasers plainly runs afoul of that rule.

Congress could require private persons, such as hospital executives or school administrators, to provide arms merchants with relevant information about a prospective purchaser's fitness to own a weapon

n17 The dissent observes that "Congress could require private persons, such as hospital executives or school administrators, to provide arms merchants with relevant information about a prospective purchaser's fitness to own a weapon," and that "the burden on police officers [imposed by the Brady Act] would be permissible if a similar burden were also imposed on private parties with access to relevant data." Post, at 25. That is undoubtedly true, but it does not advance the dissent's case. The Brady Act does not merely require CLEOs to report information in their private possession. It requires them to provide information that belongs to the State and is available to them only in their official capacity; and to conduct investigation in their official capacity, by examining databases and records that only state officials have access to. In other words, the suggestion that extension of this statute to private citizens would eliminate the constitutional problem posits the impossible.

V

What we have said makes it clear enough that the central obligation imposed upon CLEOs by the interim provisions of the Brady Act--the obligation to "make a reasonable effort to ascertain within 5 business days whether receipt or possession [of a handgun] would be in violation of the law, including research in whatever State and local recordkeeping systems are available and in a national system designated by the Attorney General," 18 U.S.C. §922(s)(2)--is unconstitutional. Extinguished with it, of course, is the duty implicit in the background-check requirement that the CLEO accept notice of the contents of, and a copy of, the completed Brady Form, which the firearms dealer is required to provide to him, §§922(s)(1)(A)(i)(III) and (IV).

Petitioners also challenge, however, two other provisions of the Act: (1) the requirement that any CLEO "to whom a [Brady Form] is transmitted" destroy the form and any record containing information derived from it, §922(s)(6)(B)(i), and (2) the requirement that any CLEO who "determines that an individual is ineligible to receive a handgun" provide the would-be purchaser, upon request, a written statement of the reasons for that determination, §922(s)(6)(C). With the background-check and implicit receipt-of-forms requirements invalidated, however, these provisions require no action whatsoever on the part of the CLEO. Quite obviously, the obligation to destroy all Brady Forms that he has received when he has received none, and the obligation to give reasons for a determination of ineligibility when he never makes a determination of ineligibility, are no obligations at all. These two provisions have conceivable application to a CLEO, in other words, only if he has chosen, voluntarily, to participate in administration of the federal scheme. The present petitioners are not in that position. n18 As to them, these last two challenged provisions are not unconstitutional, but simply inoperative.

it is at least clear that Montana and Arizona do not require their CLEOs to implement the Brady Act, and CLEOs Printz and Mack have chosen not to do so.

n18 We note, in this regard, that both CLEOs before us here assert that they are prohibited from taking on these federal responsibilities under state law. That assertion is clearly correct with regard to Montana law, which expressly enjoins any "county . . . or other local government unit" from "prohibiting . . . or regulating the purchase, sale or other transfer (including delay in purchase, sale, or other transfer), ownership, [or] possession . . . of any . . . handgun," Mont. Code §45-8-351(1) (1995). It is arguably correct with regard to Arizona law as well, which states that "[a] political subdivision of this state shall not . . . prohibit the ownership, purchase, sale or transfer of firearms," Ariz. Rev. Stat. §13-3108(B) (1989). We need not resolve that question today; it is at least clear that Montana and Arizona do not require their CLEOs to implement the Brady Act, and CLEOs Printz and Mack have chosen not to do so.

There is involved in this Brady Act conundrum a severability question, which the parties have briefed and argued: whether firearms dealers in the jurisdictions at issue here, and in other jurisdictions, remain obliged to forward to the CLEO (even if he will not accept it) the requisite notice of the contents (and a copy) of the Brady Form, §§922(s)(1)(A)(i)(III) and (IV); and to wait five business days before consummating the sale, §922(s)(1)(A)(ii). These are important questions, but we have no business answering them in these cases. These provisions burden only firearms dealers and purchasers, and no plaintiff in either of those categories is before us here. We decline to speculate regarding the rights and obligations of parties not before the Court. Cf., e.g., New York, supra, at 186-187 (addressing severability where remaining provisions at issue affected the plaintiffs).

* * *

Congress cannot compel the States to enact or enforce a federal regulatory program. Today we hold that Congress cannot circumvent that prohibition by conscripting the State's officers directly.

The Federal Government may neither issue directives requiring the States to address particular problems, nor command the States' officers, or those of their political subdivisions, to administer or enforce a federal regulatory program.

no case-by-case weighing of the burdens or benefits is necessary; such commands are fundamentally incompatible with our constitutional system of dual sovereignty.

We held in New York that Congress cannot compel the States to enact or enforce a federal regulatory program. Today we hold that Congress cannot circumvent that prohibition by conscripting the State's officers directly. The Federal Government may neither issue directives requiring the States to address particular problems, nor command the States' officers, or those of their political subdivisions, to administer or enforce a federal regulatory program. It matters not whether policymaking is involved, and no case-by-case weighing of the burdens or benefits is necessary; such commands are fundamentally incompatible with our constitutional system of dual sovereignty. Accordingly, the judgment of the Court of Appeals for the Ninth Circuit is reversed.

It is so ordered.

JUSTICE O'CONNOR, concurring.

The Brady Act violates the Tenth Amendment to the extent it forces States and local law enforcement officers to perform background checks on prospective handgun owners and to accept Brady Forms from firearms dealers.

States and chief law enforcement officers may voluntarily continue to participate in the federal program.

Congress is also free to amend the interim program to provide for its continuance on a contractual basis with the States if it wishes, as it does with a number of other federal programs.

Our precedent and our Nation's historical practices support the Court's holding today. The Brady Act violates the Tenth Amendment to the extent it forces States and local law enforcement officers to perform background checks on prospective handgun owners and to accept Brady Forms from firearms dealers. See ante, at 23. Our holding, of course, does not spell the end of the objectives of the Brady Act. States and chief law enforcement officers may voluntarily continue to participate in the federal program. Moreover, the directives to the States are merely interim provisions scheduled to terminate November 30, 1998. Note following 18 U.S.C. §922. Congress is also free to amend the interim program to provide for its continuance on a contractual basis with the States if it wishes, as it does with a number of other federal programs. See, e.g., 23 U.S.C. §402 (conditioning States' receipt of federal funds for highway safety program on compliance with federal requirements).

In addition, the Court appropriately refrains from deciding whether other purely ministerial reporting requirements imposed by Congress on state and local authorities pursuant to its Commerce Clause powers are similarly invalid. See, e.g., 42 U.S.C. §5779(a) (requiring state and local law enforcement agencies to report cases of missing children to the Department of Justice). The provisions invalidated here, however, which directly compel state officials to administer a federal regulatory program, utterly fail to adhere to the design and structure of our constitutional scheme.

JUSTICE THOMAS, concurring.

Although I join the Court's opinion in full, I write separately to emphasize that the Tenth Amendment affirms the undeniable notion that under our Constitution, the Federal Government is one of enumerated, hence limited, powers.

the Federal Government may act only where the Constitution authorizes it to do so.

The Court today properly holds that the Brady Act violates the Tenth Amendment in that it compels state law enforcement officers to "administer or enforce a federal regulatory program." See ante, at 25. Although I join the Court's opinion in full, I write separately to emphasize that the Tenth Amendment affirms the undeniable notion that under our Constitution, the Federal Government is one of enumerated, hence limited, powers. See, e.g., McCulloch v. Maryland, 17 U.S. 316, 4 Wheat. 316, 405, 4 L. Ed. 579 (1819) ("This government is acknowledged by all to be one of enumerated powers"). "That those limits may not be mistaken, or forgotten, the constitution is written." Marbury v. Madison, 5 U.S. 137, 1 Cranch 137, 176, 2 L. Ed. 60 (1803). Accordingly, the Federal Government may act only where the Constitution authorizes it to do so. Cf. New York v. United States, 505 U.S. 144, 120 L. Ed. 2d 120, 112 S. Ct. 2408 (1992).

Absent the underlying authority to regulate the intrastate transfer of firearms, Congress surely lacks the corollary power to impress state law enforcement officers into administering and enforcing such regulations.

In my "revisionist" view, see post, at 3, the Federal Government's authority under the Commerce Clause, which merely allocates to Congress the power "to regulate Commerce . . . among the several states," does not extend to the regulation of wholly intrastate, point-of-sale transactions. See United States v. Lopez, 514 U.S. 549, 584, 131 L. Ed. 2d 626, 115 S. Ct. 1624 (1995) (concurring opinion). Absent the underlying authority to regulate the intrastate transfer of firearms, Congress surely lacks the corollary power to impress state law enforcement officers into administering and enforcing such regulations. Although this Court has long interpreted the Constitution as ceding Congress extensive authority to regulate commerce (interstate or otherwise), I continue to believe that we must "temper our Commerce Clause jurisprudence" and return to an interpretation better rooted in the Clause's original understanding. Id., at 601; (concurring opinion); see also Camps Newfound/Owatonna, Inc. v. Town of Harrison, 117 S. Ct. 1590, 137 L. Ed. 2d 852 (1997) (THOMAS, J., dissenting).

The Constitution, in addition to delegating certain enumerated powers to Congress, places whole areas outside the reach of Congress' regulatory authority.

The Second Amendment similarly appears to contain an express limitation on the government's authority.

This Court has not had recent occasion to consider the nature of the substantive right safeguarded by the Second Amendment. If, however, the Second Amendment is read to confer a personal right to "keep and bear arms," a colorable argument exists that the Federal Government's regulatory scheme, at least as it pertains to the purely intrastate sale or possession of firearms, runs afoul of that Amendment's protections. As the parties did not raise this argument, however, we need not consider it here. Perhaps, at some future date, this Court will have the opportunity to determine whether Justice Story was correct when he wrote that the right to bear arms "has justly been considered, as the palladium of the liberties of a republic."

Even if we construe Congress' authority to regulate interstate commerce to encompass those intrastate transactions that "substantially affect" interstate commerce, I question whether Congress can regulate the particular transactions at issue here. The Constitution, in addition to delegating certain enumerated powers to Congress, places whole areas outside the reach of Congress' regulatory authority. The First Amendment, for example, is fittingly celebrated for preventing Congress from "prohibiting the free exercise" of religion or "abridging the freedom of speech." The Second Amendment similarly appears to contain an express limitation on the government's authority. That Amendment provides: "[a] well regulated Militia, being necessary to the security of a free State, the right of the people to keep and bear arms, shall not be infringed." This Court has not had recent occasion to consider the nature of the substantive right safeguarded by the Second Amendment. n1 If, however, the Second Amendment is read to confer a personal right to "keep and bear arms," a colorable argument exists that the Federal Government's regulatory scheme, at least as it pertains to the purely intrastate sale or possession of firearms, runs afoul of that Amendment's protections. n2 As the parties did not raise this argument, however, we need not consider it here. Perhaps, at some future date, this Court will have the opportunity to determine whether Justice Story was correct when he wrote that the right to bear arms "has justly been considered, as the palladium of the liberties of a republic." 3 J. Story, Commentaries §1890, p. 746 (1833). In the meantime, I join the Court's opinion striking down the challenged provisions of the Brady Act as inconsistent with the Tenth Amendment.

Our most recent treatment of the Second Amendment occurred in United States v. Miller

In Miller, we determined that the Second Amendment did not guarantee a citizen's right to possess a sawed-off shotgun because that weapon had not been shown to be "ordinary military equipment" that could "contribute to the common defense."

The Court did not, however, attempt to define, or otherwise construe, the substantive right protected by the Second Amendment.

n1 Our most recent treatment of the Second Amendment occurred in United States v. Miller, 307 U.S. 174, 83 L. Ed. 1206, 59 S. Ct. 816 (1939), in which we reversed the District Court's invalidation of the National Firearms Act, enacted in 1934. In Miller, we determined that the Second Amendment did not guarantee a citizen's right to possess a sawed-off shotgun because that weapon had not been shown to be "ordinary military equipment" that could "contribute to the common defense." Id., at 178. The Court did not, however, attempt to define, or otherwise construe, the substantive right protected by the Second Amendment.

Marshaling an impressive array of historical evidence, a growing body of scholarly commentary indicates that the "right to keep and bear arms" is, as the Amendment's text suggests, a personal right.

Although somewhat overlooked in our jurisprudence, the Amendment has certainly engendered considerable academic, as well as public, debate.

n2 Marshaling an impressive array of historical evidence, a growing body of scholarly commentary indicates that the "right to keep and bear arms" is, as the Amendment's text suggests, a personal right. See, e.g., J. Malcolm, To Keep and Bear Arms: The Origins of an Anglo-American Right 162 (1994); S. Halbrook, That Every Man Be Armed, The Evolution of a Constitutional Right

(1984); Van Alstyne, The Second Amendment and the Personal Right to Arms, 43 Duke L. J. 1236 (1994); Amar, The Bill of Rights and the Fourteenth Amendment, 101 Yale L. J. 1193 (1992); Cottrol & Diamond, The Second Amendment: Toward an Afro-Americanist Reconsideration, 80 Geo. L. J. 309 (1991); Levinson, The Embarrassing Second Amendment, 99 Yale L. J. 637 (1989); Kates, Handgun Prohibition and the Original Meaning of the Second Amendment, 82 Mich. L. Rev. 204 (1983). Other scholars, however, argue that the Second Amendment does not secure a personal right to keep or to bear arms. See, e.g., Bogus, Race, Riots, and Guns, 66 S. Cal. L. Rev. 1365 (1993); Williams, Civic Republicanism and the Citizen Militia: The Terrifying Second Amendment, 101 Yale L. J. 551 (1991); Brown, Guns, Cowboys, Philadelphia Mayors, and Civic Republicanism: On Sanford Levinson's The Embarrassing Second Amendment, 99 Yale L. J. 661 (1989); Cress, An Armed Community: The Origins and Meaning of the Right to Bear Arms, 71 J. Am. Hist. 22 (1984). Although somewhat overlooked in our jurisprudence, the Amendment has certainly engendered considerable academic, as well as public, debate.

JUSTICE STEVENS, with whom JUSTICE SOUTER, JUSTICE GINSBURG, and JUSTICE BREYER join, dissenting.

When Congress exercises the powers delegated to it by the Constitution, it may impose affirmative obligations on executive and judicial officers of state and local governments as well as ordinary citizens. This conclusion is firmly supported by the text of the Constitution, the early history of the Nation, decisions of this Court, and a correct understanding of the basic structure of the Federal Government.

The question is whether Congress, acting on behalf of the people of the entire Nation, may require local law enforcement officers to perform certain duties during the interim needed for the development of a federal gun control program.

These cases do not implicate the more difficult questions associated with congressional coercion of state legislatures addressed in New York v. United States, 505 U.S. 144, 120 L. Ed. 2d 120, 112 S. Ct. 2408 (1992). Nor need we consider the wisdom of relying on local officials rather than federal agents to carry out aspects of a federal program, or even the question whether such officials may be required to perform a federal function on a permanent basis. The question is whether Congress, acting on behalf of the people of the entire Nation, may require local law enforcement officers to perform certain duties during the interim needed for the development of a federal gun control program. It is remarkably similar to the question, heavily debated by the Framers of the Constitution, whether the Congress could require state agents to collect federal taxes. Or the question whether Congress could impress state judges into federal service to entertain and decide cases that they would prefer to ignore.

the ultimate issue is one of power

Indeed, since the ultimate issue is one of power, we must consider its implications in times of national emergency. Matters such as the enlistment of air raid wardens, the administration of a military draft, the mass inoculation of children to forestall an epidemic, or perhaps the threat of an international terrorist, may require a national response before federal personnel can be made available to respond. If the Constitution empowers Congress and the President to make an appropriate response, is there anything in the Tenth Amendment, "in historical understanding and practice, in the structure of the Constitution, [or] in the jurisprudence of this Court," ante, at 4, that forbids the enlistment of state officers to make that response effective? More narrowly, what basis is there in any of those sources for concluding that it is the Members of this Court, rather than the elected representatives of the people, who should determine whether the Constitution contains the unwritten rule that the Court announces today?

Perhaps today's majority would suggest that no such emergency is presented by the facts of these cases. But such a suggestion is itself an expression of a policy judgment. And Congress' view of the matter is quite different from that implied by the Court today.

The Brady Act was passed in response to what Congress described as an "epidemic of gun violence."

The Act's legislative history notes that 15,377 Americans were murdered with firearms in 1992, and that 12,489 of these deaths were caused by handguns.

Congress expressed special concern that "the level of firearm violence in this country is, by far, the highest among developed nations."

The partial solution contained in the Brady Act, a mandatory background check before a handgun may be purchased, has met with remarkable success. Between 1994 and

1996, approximately 6,600 firearm sales each month to potentially dangerous persons were prevented by Brady Act checks; over 70% of the rejected purchasers were convicted or indicted felons.

The Brady Act was passed in response to what Congress described as an "epidemic of gun violence." H. R. Rep. No. 103-344, p. 8 (1993). The Act's legislative history notes that 15,377 Americans were murdered with firearms in 1992, and that 12,489 of these deaths were caused by handguns. Ibid. Congress expressed special concern that "the level of firearm violence in this country is, by far, the highest among developed nations." Ibid. The partial solution contained in the Brady Act, a mandatory background check before a handgun may be purchased, has met with remarkable success. Between 1994 and 1996, approximately 6,600 firearm sales each month to potentially dangerous persons were prevented by Brady Act checks; over 70% of the rejected purchasers were convicted or indicted felons. See U.S. Dept. of Justice, Bureau of Justice Statistics Bulletin, A National Estimate: Presale Firearm Checks 1 (Feb. 1997). Whether or not the evaluation reflected in the enactment of the Brady Act is correct as to the extent of the danger and the efficacy of the legislation, the congressional decision surely warrants more respect than it is accorded in today's unprecedented decision.

I

The text of the Constitution provides a sufficient basis for a correct disposition of this case.

the additional grant of authority in that section of the Constitution "to make all Laws which shall be necessary and proper for carrying into Execution the foregoing Powers" is surely adequate to support the temporary enlistment of local police officers in the process of identifying persons who should not be entrusted with the possession of handguns.

Article I, §8, grants the Congress the power to regulate commerce among the States. Putting to one side the revisionist views expressed by JUSTICE THOMAS in his concurring opinion in United States v. Lopez, 514 U.S. 549, 584, 131 L. Ed. 2d 626, 115 S. Ct. 1624 (1995), there can be no question that that provision adequately supports the regulation of commerce in handguns effected by the Brady Act. Moreover, the additional grant of authority in that section of the Constitution "to make all Laws which shall be necessary and proper for carrying into Execution the foregoing Powers" is surely adequate to support the temporary enlistment of local police officers in the process of identifying persons who should not be entrusted with the possession of handguns. In short, the affirmative delegation of power in Article I provides ample authority for the congressional enactment.

Unlike the First Amendment, which prohibits the enactment of a category of laws that would otherwise be authorized by Article I, the Tenth Amendment imposes no restriction on the exercise of delegated powers. Using language that plainly refers only to powers that are "not" delegated to Congress, it provides:

"The powers not delegated to the United States by the Constitution, nor prohibited by it to the States, are reserved to the States respectively, or to the people." U.S. Const., Amdt. 10.

The Amendment confirms the principle that the powers of the Federal Government are limited to those affirmatively granted by the Constitution, but it does not purport to limit the scope or the effectiveness of the exercise of powers that are delegated to Congress. n1 See New York v. United States, 505 U.S. 144, 156, 120 L. Ed. 2d 120, 112 S. Ct. 2408 (1992) ("in a case . . . involving the division of authority between federal and state governments, the two inquiries are mirror images of each other"). Thus, the Amendment provides no support for a rule that immunizes local officials from obligations that might be imposed on ordinary citizens. n2 Indeed, it would be more reasonable to infer that federal law may impose greater duties on state officials than on private citizens because another provision of the Constitution requires that "all executive and judicial Officers, both of the United States and of the several States, shall be bound by Oath or Affirmation, to support this Constitution." U.S. Const., Art. VI, cl. 3.

n1 Indeed, the Framers repeatedly rejected proposed changes to the Tenth Amendment that would have altered the text to refer to "powers not expressly delegated to the United States." 3 W. Crosskey & W. Jeffrey, Politics and the Constitution in the History of the United States 36 (1980). This was done, as Madison explained, because "it was impossible to confine a Government to the exercise of express powers; there must necessarily be admitted powers by implication, unless the constitution descended to recount every minutia." 1 Annals of Cong. 790 (Aug. 18, 1789); see McCulloch v. Maryland, 17 U.S. 316, 4 Wheat. 316, 406-407, 4 L. Ed. 579 (1819).

n2 Recognizing the force of the argument, the Court suggests that this reasoning is in error because--even if it is responsive to the submission that the Tenth Amendment roots the principle set forth by the majority today--it does not answer the possibility that the Court's holding can be rooted in a "principle of state sovereignty" mentioned nowhere in the constitutional text. See ante, at 24. As a ground for invalidating important federal legislation, this argument is remarkably weak. The majority's further claim that, while the Brady Act may be legislation "necessary" to Congress' execution of its undisputed Commerce Clause authority to regulate firearms sales, it is nevertheless not "proper" because it violates state sovereignty, see ibid., is wholly circular and provides no traction for its argument. Moreover, this reading of the term "proper" gives it a meaning directly contradicted by Chief Justice Marshall in McCulloch v. Maryland, 17 U.S. 316, 4 Wheat. 316, 4 L. Ed. 579 (1819). As the Chief Justice explained, the Necessary and Proper Clause by "its terms purports to enlarge, not to diminish the powers vested in the government. It purports to be an additional power, not a restriction on those already granted." Id., at 420; see also id., at 418-419 (explaining that "the only possible effect" of the use of the term "proper" was "to present to the mind the idea of some choice of means of legislation not straitened and compressed within . . . narrow limits").

Our ruling in New York that the Commerce Clause does not provide Congress the authority to require States to enact legislation--a power that affects States far closer to the core of their sovereign authority--does nothing to support the majority's unwarranted extension of that reasoning today.

It is appropriate for state officials to make an oath or affirmation to support the Federal Constitution because, as explained in The Federalist, they "have an essential agency in giving effect to the federal Constitution." n3 The Federalist No. 44, p. 312 (E. Bourne ed. 1947) (J. Madison). There can be no conflict between their duties to the State and those owed to the Federal Government because Article VI unambiguously provides that federal law "shall be the supreme Law of the Land," binding in every State. U.S. Const., Art. VI, cl. 2. Thus, not only the Constitution, but every law enacted by Congress as well, establishes policy for the States just as firmly as do laws enacted by state legislatures.

n3 "It has been asked why it was thought necessary, that the State magistracy should be bound to support the federal Constitution, and unnecessary that a like oath should be imposed on the officers of the United States, in favor of the State constitutions.

"Several reasons might be assigned for the distinction. I content myself with one, which is obvious and conclusive. The members of the federal government will have no agency in carrying the State constitutions into effect. The members and officers of the State governments, on the contrary, will have an essential agency in giving effect to the federal Constitution." The Federalist No. 44, at 312 (J. Madison).

The reasoning in our unanimous opinion explaining why state tribunals with ordinary jurisdiction over tort litigation can be required to hear cases arising under the Federal Employers' Liability Act applies equally to local law enforcement officers whose ordinary duties parallel the modest obligations imposed by the Brady Act:

"The suggestion that the act of Congress is not in harmony with the policy of the State, and therefore that the courts of the State are free to decline jurisdiction, is quite inadmissible, because it presupposes what in legal contemplation does not exist. When Congress, in the exertion of the power confided to it by the Constitution, adopted that act, it spoke for all the people and all the States, and thereby established a policy for all. That policy is as much the policy of Connecticut as if the act had emanated from its own legislature, and should be respected accordingly in the courts of the State. As was said by this court in Claflin v. Houseman, 93 U.S. 130, 136, 137, 23 L. Ed. 833:

'The laws of the United States are laws in the several States, and just as much binding on the citizens and courts thereof as the State laws are. The United States is not a foreign sovereignty as regards the several States, but is a concurrent, and, within its jurisdiction, paramount sovereignty.'" Second Employers' Liability Cases, 223 U.S. 1, 57, 56 L. Ed. 327, 32 S. Ct. 169 (1912).

See also Testa v. Katt, 330 U.S. 386, 392, 91 L. Ed. 967, 67 S. Ct. 810 (1947).

There is not a clause, sentence, or paragraph in the entire text of the Constitution of the United States that supports the proposition that a local police officer can ignore a command contained in a statute enacted by Congress pursuant to an express delegation of power enumerated in Article I.

There is not a clause, sentence, or paragraph in the entire text of the Constitution of the United States that supports the proposition that a local police officer can ignore a command contained in a statute enacted by Congress pursuant to an express delegation of power enumerated in Article I.

II

Under the Articles of Confederation the National Government had the power to issue commands to the several sovereign states, but it had no authority to govern individuals directly. Thus, it raised an army and financed its operations by issuing requisitions to the constituent members of the Confederacy, rather than by creating federal agencies to draft soldiers or to impose taxes.

That method of governing proved to be unacceptable, not because it demeaned the sovereign character of the several States, but rather because it was cumbersome and inefficient. Indeed, a confederation that allows each of its members to determine the ways and means of complying with an overriding requisition is obviously more deferential to state sovereignty concerns than a national government that uses its own agents to impose its will directly on the citizenry. The basic change in the character of the government that the Framers conceived was designed to enhance the power of the national government, not to provide some new, unmentioned immunity for state officers. Because indirect control over individual citizens ("the only proper objects of government") was ineffective under the Articles of Confederation, Alexander Hamilton explained that "we must extend the authority of the Union to the persons of the citizens." The Federalist No. 15, at 101 (emphasis added).

Hamilton's meaning was unambiguous; the federal government was to have the power to demand that local officials implement national policy programs.

Indeed, the historical materials strongly suggest that the Founders intended to enhance the capacity of the federal government by empowering it--as a part of the new authority to make demands directly on individual citizens--to act through local officials. Hamilton made clear that the new Constitution, "by extending the authority of the federal head to the individual citizens of the several States, will enable the government to employ the ordinary magistracy of each, in the execution of its laws." The Federalist No. 27, at 180. Hamilton's meaning was unambiguous; the federal government was to have the power to demand that local officials implement national policy programs. As he went on to explain: "It is easy to perceive that this will tend to destroy, in the common apprehension, all distinction between the sources from which [the state and federal governments] might proceed; and will give the federal government the same advantage for securing a due obedience to its authority which is enjoyed by the government of each State." Ibid. n4

n4 The notion that central government would rule by directing the actions of local magistrates was scarcely a novel conception at the time of the founding. Indeed, as an eminent scholar recently observed: "At the time the Constitution was being framed . . . Massachusetts had virtually no administrative apparatus of its own but used the towns for such purposes as tax gathering. In the 1830s Tocqueville observed this feature of government in New England and praised it for its ideal combination of centralized legislation and decentralized administration." S. Beer, To Make a Nation: The Rediscovery of American Federalism 252 (1993). This may have provided a model for the expectation of "Madison himself . . . [that] the new federal government [would] govern through the state governments, rather in the manner of the New England states in relation to their local governments." Ibid.

More specifically, during the debates concerning the ratification of the Constitution, it was assumed that state agents would act as tax collectors for the federal government. Opponents of the Constitution had repeatedly expressed fears that the new federal government's ability to impose taxes directly on the citizenry would result in an overbearing presence of federal tax collectors in the States. n5 Federalists rejoined that this problem would not arise because, as Hamilton explained, "the United States . . . will make use of the State officers and State regulations for collecting" certain taxes. Id., No. 36, at 235. Similarly, Madison made clear that the new central government's power to raise taxes directly from the citizenry would "not be resorted to, except for supplemental purposes of revenue . . . and that the eventual collection, under the immediate authority of the Union, will generally be made by the officers . . . appointed by the several States." Id., No. 45, at 318. n6

statement of Patrick Henry at the Virginia Convention that "the salaries and fees of the swarm of officers and dependants on the Government will cost this Continent immense sums" and noting that "double sets of tax collectors will double the expense"

n5 See, e.g., 1 Debate on the Constitution 502 (B. Bailyn ed. 1993) (statement of "Brutus" that the new Constitution would "open a door to the appointment of a swarm of revenue and excise officers to prey upon the honest and industrious part of the community"); 2 id., at 633 (statement of Patrick Henry at the Virginia Convention that "the salaries and fees of the swarm of officers and dependants on the Government will cost this Continent immense sums" and noting that "double sets of [tax] collectors will double the expense").

n6 Antifederalists acknowledged this response, and recognized the likelihood that the federal government would rely on state officials to collect its taxes. See, e.g., 3 J. Elliot, Debates on the Federal Constitution 167-168 (2d ed. 1891) (statement of Patrick Henry). The wide acceptance of this point by all participants in the framing casts serious doubt on the majority's efforts, see ante, at 16, n.9, to suggest that the view that state officials could be called upon to implement federal programs was somehow an unusual or peculiar position.

The Court's response to this powerful historical evidence is weak. The majority suggests that "none of these statements necessarily implies . . . Congress could impose these responsibilities without the consent of the States." Ante, at 10-11 (emphasis omitted). No fair reading of these materials can justify such an interpretation. As Hamilton explained, the power of the government to act on "individual citizens"--including "employing the ordinary magistracy" of the States--was an answer to the problems faced by a central government that could act only directly "upon the States in their political or collective capacities." The Federalist, No. 27, at 179-180. The new Constitution would avoid this problem, resulting in "a regular and peaceable execution of the law of the Union." Ibid.

This point is made especially clear in Hamilton's statement that "the legislatures, courts, and magistrates, of the respective members, will be incorporated into the operations of the national government as far as its just and constitutional authority extends; and will be rendered auxiliary to the enforcement of its laws." Ibid. (second emphasis added). It is hard to imagine a more unequivocal statement that state judicial and executive branch officials may be required to implement federal law where the National Government acts within the scope of its affirmative powers. n7

n7 Hamilton recognized the force of his comments, acknowledging but rejecting opponents' "sophistic" arguments to the effect that this position would "tend to the destruction of the State governments." The Federalist No. 27, at 180, *.

The Court makes two unpersuasive attempts to discount the force of this statement. First, according to the majority, because Hamilton mentioned the Supremacy Clause without specifically referring to any "congressional directive," the statement does not mean what it plainly says. Ante, at 12. But the mere fact that the Supremacy Clause is the source of the obligation of state officials to implement congressional directives does not remotely suggest that they might be "'incorporated into the operations of the national government'" before their obligations have been defined by Congress. Federal law establishes policy for the States just as firmly as laws enacted by state legislatures, but that does not mean that state or federal officials must implement directives that have not been specified in any law. n8 Second, the majority suggests that interpreting this passage to mean what it says would conflict with our decision in New York v. United States. Ante, at 12. But since the New York opinion did not mention Federalist No. 27, it does not affect either the relevance or the weight of the historical evidence provided by No. 27 insofar as it relates to state courts and magistrates.

n8 Indeed, the majority's suggestion that this consequence flows "automatically" from the officers' oath, ante, at 12 (emphasis omitted), is entirely without foundation in the quoted text. Although the fact that the Court has italicized the word "automatically" may give the reader the impression that it is a word Hamilton used, that is not so.

Bereft of support in the history of the founding, the Court rests its conclusion on the claim that there is little evidence the National Government actually exercised such a power in the early years of the Republic. See ante, at 5. This reasoning is misguided in principle and in fact. While we have indicated that the express consideration and resolution of difficult constitutional issues by the First Congress in particular "provides 'contemporaneous and weighty evidence' of the Constitution's meaning since many of [its] Members . . . 'had taken part in framing that instrument,'" Bowsher v. Synar, 478 U.S. 714, 723-724, 92 L. Ed. 2d 583, 106 S. Ct. 3181 (1986) (quoting Marsh v. Chambers, 463 U.S. 783, 790, 77 L. Ed. 2d 1019, 103 S. Ct. 3330 (1983)), we have never suggested that the failure of the early Congresses to address the scope of federal power in a particular area or to exercise a particular authority was an argument against its existence. That position, if correct, would undermine most of our post-New Deal Commerce Clause jurisprudence. As JUSTICE O'CONNOR quite properly noted in New York, "the Federal Government undertakes activities today that would have been unimaginable to the Framers." 505 U.S. at 157.

the fact that Congress did elect to rely on state judges and the clerks of state courts to perform a variety of executive functions, see ante, at 5-6, is surely evidence of a contemporary understanding that their status as state officials did not immunize them from federal service.

More importantly, the fact that Congress did elect to rely on state judges and the clerks of state courts to perform a variety of executive functions, see ante, at 5-6, is surely evidence of a contemporary understanding that their status as state officials did not immunize them from federal service. The majority's description of these early statutes is both incomplete and at times misleading.

the early Congresses required in mandatory terms that state judges and their clerks perform various executive duties with respect to applications for citizenship.

For example, statutes of the early Congresses required in mandatory terms that state judges and their clerks perform various executive duties with respect to applications for citizenship. The First Congress enacted a statute requiring that the state courts consider such applications, specifying that the state courts "shall administer" an oath of loyalty to the United States, and that "the clerk of such court shall record such application." Act of Mar. 26, 1790, ch. 3, §1, 1 Stat. 103 (emphasis added).

Early legislation passed by the Fifth Congress also imposed reporting requirements relating to naturalization on court clerks, specifying that failure to perform those duties would result in a fine. Act of June 18, 1798, ch. 54, §2, 1 Stat. 567 (specifying that these obligations "shall be the duty of the clerk" (emphasis added)). Not long thereafter, the Seventh Congress mandated that state courts maintain a registry of aliens seeking naturalization. Court clerks were required to receive certain information from aliens, record that data, and provide certificates to the aliens; the statute specified fees to be received by local officials in compensation. Act of Apr. 14, 1802, ch. 28, §2, 2 Stat. 154-155 (specifying that these burdens "shall be the duty of such clerk" including clerks "of a . . . state" (emphasis added)). n9

n9 The majority asserts that these statutes relating to the administration of the federal naturalization scheme are not proper evidence of the original understanding because over a century later, in Holmgren v. United States, 217 U.S. 509, 54 L. Ed. 861, 30 S. Ct. 588 (1910), this Court observed that that case did not present the question whether the States can be required to enforce federal laws "against their consent," id., at 517. The majority points to similar comments in United States v. Jones, 109 U.S. 513, 519-520, 27 L. Ed. 1015, 3 S. Ct. 346 (1883). See ante, at 5-6.

Those cases are unpersuasive authority. First, whatever their statements in dicta, the naturalization statutes at issue here, as made clear in the text, were framed in quite mandatory terms. Even the majority only goes so far as to say that "it may well be" that these facially mandatory statutes in fact rested on voluntary state participation. Ante, at 5. Any suggestion to the contrary is belied by the language of the statutes themselves.

Second, both of the cases relied upon by the majority rest on now-rejected doctrine. In Jones, the Court indicated that various duties, including the requirement that state courts of appropriate jurisdiction hear federal questions, "could not be enforced against the consent of the States." 109 U.S. at 520. That view was unanimously resolved to the contrary thereafter in the Second Employers' Liability Cases, 223 U.S. 1, 57, 56 L. Ed. 327, 32 S. Ct. 169 (1912), and in Testa v. Katt, 330 U.S. 386, 91 L. Ed. 967, 67 S. Ct. 810 (1947).

Finally, the Court suggests that the obligation set forth in the latter two cases that state courts hear federal claims is "voluntary" in that States need not create courts of ordinary jurisdiction. That is true, but unhelpful to the majority. If a State chooses to have no local law enforcement officials it may avoid the Brady Act's requirements, and if it chooses to have no courts it may avoid Testa. But neither seems likely.

Similarly, the First Congress enacted legislation requiring state courts to serve, functionally, like contemporary regulatory agencies in certifying the seaworthiness of vessels. Act of July 20, 1790, ch. 29, §3, 1 Stat. 132-133. The majority casts this as an adjudicative duty, ante, at 6, but that characterization is misleading. The law provided that upon a complaint raised by a ship's crew members, the state courts were (if no federal court was proximately located) to appoint an investigative committee of three persons "most skilful in maritime affairs" to report back. On this basis, the judge was to determine whether the ship was fit for its intended voyage. The statute sets forth, in essence, procedures for an expert inquisitorial proceeding, supervised by a judge but otherwise more characteristic of executive activity. n10

n10 Other statutes mentioned by the majority are also wrongly miscategorized as involving essentially judicial matters. For example, the Fifth Congress enacted legislation requiring state courts to serve as repositories for reporting what amounted to administrative claims against the United States Government, under a statute providing compensation in land to Canadian refugees who had supported the United States during the Revolutionary War. Contrary to the majority's suggestion, that statute did not amount to a requirement that state courts adjudicate claims, see ante, at 8, n.2; final decisions as to appropriate compensation were made by federal authorities, see Act of Apr. 7, 1798, ch. 26, §3, 1 Stat. 548.

The Court assumes that the imposition of such essentially executive duties on state judges and their clerks sheds no light on the question whether executive officials might have an immunity from federal obligations. Ante, at 6. Even assuming that the enlistment of state judges in their judicial role for federal purposes is irrelevant to the question whether executive officials may be asked to perform the same function--a claim disputed below, see infra, at 32--the majority's analysis is badly mistaken.

We are far truer to the historical record by applying a functional approach in assessing the role played by these early state officials. The use of state judges and their clerks to perform executive functions was, in historical context, hardly unusual.

We are far truer to the historical record by applying a functional approach in assessing the role played by these early state officials. The use of state judges and their clerks to perform executive functions was, in historical context, hardly unusual. As one scholar has noted, "two centuries ago, state and local judges and associated judicial personnel performed many of the functions today performed by executive officers, including such varied tasks as laying city streets and ensuring the seaworthiness of vessels." Caminker,

State Sovereignty and Subordinacy: May Congress Commandeer State Officers to Implement Federal Law?, 95 Colum. L. Rev. 1001, 1045, n.176 (1995). And, of course, judges today continue to perform a variety of functions that may more properly be described as executive. See, e.g., Forrester v. White, 484 U.S. 219, 227, 98 L. Ed. 2d 555, 108 S. Ct. 538 (1988) (noting "intelligible distinction between judicial acts and the administrative, legislative, or executive functions that judges may on occasion be assigned to perform"). The majority's insistence that this evidence of federal enlistment of state officials to serve executive functions is irrelevant simply because the assistance of "judges" was at issue rests on empty formalistic reasoning of the highest order. n11

considerable tension with the Court's holding that the minor burden imposed by the Brady Act violates the Constitution.

n11 Able to muster little response other than the bald claim that this argument strikes the majority as "doubtful," ante, at 8, n.2, the Court proceeds to attack the basic point that the statutes discussed above called state judges to serve what were substantially executive functions. The argument has little force. The majority's view that none of the statutes referred to in the text required judges to perform anything other than "quintessentially adjudicative tasks," ibid., is quite wrong. The evaluation of applications for citizenship and the acceptance of Revolutionary War claims for example, both discussed above, are hard to characterize as the sort of adversarial proceedings to which common-law courts are accustomed. As for the majority's suggestion that the substantial administrative requirements imposed on state court clerks under the naturalization statutes are merely "ancillary" and therefore irrelevant, this conclusion is in considerable tension with the Court's holding that the minor burden imposed by the Brady Act violates the Constitution. Finally, the majority's suggestion that the early statute requiring federal courts to assess the seaworthiness of vessels is essentially adjudicative in nature is not compelling. Activities of this sort, although they may bear some resemblance to traditional common-law adjudication, are far afield from the classical model of adversarial litigation.

the decision by Congress to give President Wilson the authority to utilize the services of state officers in implementing the World War I draft, surely indicates that the national legislature saw no constitutional impediment to the enlistment of state assistance during a federal emergency.

The Court's evaluation of the historical evidence, furthermore, fails to acknowledge the important difference between policy decisions that may have been influenced by respect for state sovereignty concerns, and decisions that are compelled by the Constitution. n12 Thus, for example, the decision by Congress to give President Wilson the authority to utilize the services of state officers in implementing the World War I draft, see Act of May 18, 1917, ch. 15, §6, 40 Stat. 80-81, surely indicates that the national legislature saw no constitutional impediment to the enlistment of state assistance during a federal emergency. The fact that the President was able to implement the program by respectfully "requesting" state action, rather than bluntly commanding it, is evidence that he was an effective statesman, but surely does not indicate that he doubted either his or Congress' power to use mandatory language if necessary. n13 If there were merit to the Court's appraisal of this incident, one would assume that there would have been some contemporary comment on the supposed constitutional concern that hypothetically might have motivated the President's choice of language. n14

n12 Indeed, an entirely appropriate concern for the prerogatives of state government readily explains Congress' sparing use of this otherwise "highly attractive," ante, at 5, 7, power. Congress' discretion, contrary to the majority's suggestion, indicates not that the power does not exist, but rather that the interests of the States are more than sufficiently protected by their participation in the National Government. See infra, at 19-20.

n13 Indeed, the very commentator upon whom the majority relies noted that the "President might, under the act, have issued orders directly to every state officer, and this would have been, for war purposes, a justifiable Congressional grant of all state powers into the President's hands." Note, The President, The Senate, The Constitution, and the Executive Order of May 8, 1926, 21 U. Ill. L. Rev. 142, 144 (1926).

n14 Even less probative is the Court's reliance on the decision by Congress to authorize federal marshalls to rent temporary jail facilities instead of insisting that state jailkeepers house federal prisoners at federal expense. See ante, at 9. The majority finds constitutional significance in the fact that the First Congress (apparently following practice appropriate under the Articles of Confederation) had issued a request to state legislatures rather than a command to state jailkeepers, see Resolution of Sept. 29, 1789, 1 Stat. 96, and the further fact that it chose not to change that request to a command 18 months later, see Resolution of Mar. 3, 1791, 1 Stat. 225. The Court does not point us to a single comment by any Member of Congress suggesting that either decision was motivated in the slightest by constitutional doubts. If this sort of unexplained congressional action provides sufficient historical evidence to support the fashioning of judge-made rules of constitutional law, the doctrine of judicial restraint has a brief, though probably colorful, life expectancy.

The Court concludes its review of the historical materials with a reference to the fact that our decision in INS v. Chadha, 462 U.S. 919, 77 L. Ed. 2d 317, 103 S. Ct. 2764 (1983), invalidated a large number of statutes enacted in the 1970's, implying that recent enactments by Congress that are similar to the Brady Act are not entitled to any presumption of validity. But in Chadha, unlike this case, our decision rested on the Constitution's express bicameralism and presentment requirements, id., at 946, not on judicial inferences drawn from a silent text and a historical record that surely favors the congressional understanding. Indeed, the majority's opinion consists almost entirely of arguments against the substantial evidence weighing in opposition to its view; the Court's ruling is strikingly lacking in affirmative support. Absent even a modicum of textual foundation for its judicially crafted constitutional rule, there should be a presumption that if the Framers had actually intended such a rule, at least one of them would have mentioned it. n15

n15 Indeed, despite the exhaustive character of the Court's response to this dissent, it has failed to find even an iota of evidence that any of the Framers of the Constitution or any Member of Congress who supported or opposed the statutes discussed in the text ever expressed doubt as to the power of Congress to impose federal responsibilities on local judges or police officers. Even plausible rebuttals of evidence consistently pointing in the other direction are no substitute for affirmative evidence. In short, a neutral historian would have to conclude that the Court's discussion of history does not even begin to establish a prima facie case.

III

The Court's "structural" arguments are not sufficient to rebut that presumption. The fact that the Framers intended to preserve the sovereignty of the several States simply does not speak to the question whether individual state employees may be required to perform federal obligations, such as registering young adults for the draft, 40 Stat. 80-81, creating state emergency response commissions designed to manage the release of hazardous substances, 42 U.S.C. §§11001, 11003, collecting and reporting data on underground storage tanks that may pose an environmental hazard, §6991a, and reporting traffic fatalities, 23 U.S.C. §402(a), and missing children, 42 U.S.C. §5779(a), to a federal agency. n16

The majority's argument is particularly peculiar because these cases do not involve the enlistment of state officials at all, but only an effort to have federal policy implemented by officials of local government. Both Sheriffs Printz and Mack are county officials.

n16 The majority's argument is particularly peculiar because these cases do not involve the enlistment of state officials at all, but only an effort to have federal policy implemented by officials of local government. Both Sheriffs Printz and Mack are county officials. Given that the Brady Act places its interim obligations on Chief law enforcement officers (CLEOs), who are defined as "the chief of police, the sheriff, or an equivalent officer," 18 U.S.C. §922(s)(8), it seems likely that most cases would similarly involve local government officials.

If the federal judicial power may be exercised over local government officials, it is hard to see why they are not subject to the legislative power as well.

This Court has not had cause in its recent federalism jurisprudence to address the constitutional implications of enlisting non-state officials for federal purposes. (We did pass briefly on the issue in a footnote in National League of Cities v. Usery, 426 U.S. 833, 855, n.20, 49 L. Ed. 2d 245, 96 S. Ct. 2465 (1976), but that case was overruled in its entirety by Garcia v. San Antonio Metropolitan Transit Authority, 469 U.S. 528, 83 L. Ed. 2d 1016, 105 S. Ct. 1005 (1985). The question was not called to our attention in Garcia itself.) It is therefore worth noting that the majority's decision is in considerable tension with our Eleventh Amendment sovereign immunity cases. Those decisions were designed to "accord the States the respect owed them as members of the federation." Puerto Rico Aqueduct and Sewer Authority v. Metcalf & Eddy, Inc., 506 U.S. 139, 146, 121 L. Ed. 2d 605, 113 S. Ct. 684 (1993). But despite the fact that "political subdivisions exist solely at the whim and behest of their State," Port Authority Trans-Hudson Corp. v. Feeney, 495 U.S. 299, 313, 109 L. Ed. 2d 264, 110 S. Ct. 1868 (1990) (Brennan, J., concurring in part and concurring in judgment), we have "consistently refused to construe the Amendment to afford protection to political subdivisions such as counties and municipalities." Lake Country Estates, Inc. v. Tahoe Regional Planning Agency, 440 U.S. 391, 401, 59 L. Ed. 2d 401, 99 S. Ct. 1171 (1979); see also Hess v. Port Authority Trans-Hudson Corporation, 513 U.S. 30, 47, 130 L. Ed. 2d 245, 115 S. Ct. 394 (1994). Even if the protections that the majority describes as rooted in the Tenth Amendment ought to benefit state officials, it is difficult to reconcile the decision to extend these principles to local officials with our refusal to do so in the Eleventh Amendment context. If the federal judicial power may be exercised over local government officials, it is hard to see why they are not subject to the legislative power as well.

It is far more reasonable to presume that their decisions to impose modest burdens on state officials from time to time reflect a considered judgment that the people in each of the States will benefit therefrom.

As we explained in Garcia v. San Antonio Metropolitan Transit Authority, 469 U.S. 528, 83 L. Ed. 2d 1016, 105 S. Ct. 1005 (1985):"The principal means chosen by the Framers to ensure the role of the States in the federal system lies in the structure of the Federal Government itself. It is no novelty to observe that the composition of the Federal Government was designed in large part to protect the States from overreaching by Congress." Id., at 550-551. Given the fact that the Members of Congress are elected by the people of the several States, with each State receiving an equivalent number of Senators in order to ensure that even the smallest States have a powerful voice in the legislature, it is quite unrealistic to assume that they will ignore the sovereignty concerns of their constituents. It is far more reasonable to presume that their decisions to impose modest burdens on state officials from time to time reflect a considered judgment that the people in each of the States will benefit therefrom.

Indeed, the presumption of validity that supports all congressional enactments n17 has added force with respect to policy judgments concerning the impact of a federal statute upon the respective States. The majority points to nothing suggesting that the political safeguards of federalism identified in Garcia need be supplemented by a rule, grounded in neither constitutional history nor text, flatly prohibiting the National Government from enlisting state and local officials in the implementation of federal law.

n17 "Whenever called upon to judge the constitutionality of an Act of Congress--'the gravest and most delicate duty that this Court is called upon to perform,' Blodgett v. Holden, 275 U.S. 142, 148, 72 L. Ed. 206, 48 S. Ct. 105 (1927) (Holmes, J.)--the Court accords 'great weight to the decisions of Congress.' Columbia Broadcasting System, Inc. v. Democratic National Committee, 412 U.S. 94, 102, 36 L. Ed. 2d 772, 93 S. Ct. 2080 (1973). The Congress is a coequal branch of government whose Members take the same oath we do to uphold the Constitution of the United States. As Justice Frankfurter noted in Joint Anti-Fascist Refugee Committee v. McGrath, 341 U.S. 123, 164, 95 L. Ed. 817, 71 S. Ct. 624 (1951) (concurring opinion), we must have 'due regard to the fact that this Court is not exercising a primary judgment but is sitting in judgment upon those who also have taken the oath to observe the Constitution and who have the responsibility for carrying on government.'" Rostker v. Goldberg, 453 U.S. 57, 64, 69 L. Ed. 2d 478, 101 S. Ct. 2646 (1981).

Recent developments demonstrate that the political safeguards protecting Our Federalism are effective. The majority expresses special concern that were its rule not adopted the Federal Government would be able to avail itself of the services of state government officials "at no cost to itself." Ante, at 23; see also ante, at 31 (arguing that "Members of Congress can take credit for 'solving' problems without having to ask their constituents to pay for the solutions with higher federal taxes"). But this specific problem of federal actions that have the effect of imposing so-called "unfunded mandates" on the States has been identified and meaningfully addressed by Congress in recent legislation. n18 See Unfunded Mandates Reform Act of 1995, Pub. L. 104-4, 109 Stat. 48.

n18 The majority also makes the more general claim that requiring state officials to carry out federal policy causes states to "take the blame" for failed programs. Ante, at 31. The Court cites no empirical authority to support the proposition, relying entirely on the speculations of a law review article. This concern is vastly overstated.

Unlike state legislators, local government executive officials routinely take action in response to a variety of sources of authority: local ordinance, state law, and federal law.

Unlike state legislators, local government executive officials routinely take action in response to a variety of sources of authority: local ordinance, state law, and federal law. It doubtless may therefore require some sophistication to discern under which authority an executive official is acting, just as it may not always be immediately obvious what legal source of authority underlies a judicial decision. In both cases, affected citizens must look past the official before them to find the true cause of their grievance. See FERC v. Mississippi, 456 U.S. 742, 785, 72 L. Ed. 2d 532, 102 S. Ct. 2126 (1982) (O'CONNOR, J., concurring in part and dissenting in part) (legislators differ from judges because legislators have "the power to choose subjects for legislation"). But the majority's rule neither creates nor alters this basic truth.

Sheriffs Printz and Mack have made public statements, including their decisions to serve as plaintiffs in these actions, denouncing the Brady Act.

Indeed, Sheriff Mack has written a book discussing his views on the issue. See R. Mack & T. Walters, From My Cold Dead Fingers: Why America Needs Guns (1994).

we can be sure that CLEOs will inform disgruntled constituents who have been denied permission to purchase a handgun about the origins of the Brady Act requirements. The Court's suggestion that voters will be confused over who is to "blame" for the statute reflects a gross lack of confidence in the electorate that is at war with the basic assumptions underlying any democratic government.

The problem is of little real consequence in any event, because to the extent that a particular action proves politically unpopular, we may be confident that elected officials charged with implementing it will be quite clear to their constituents where the source of the misfortune lies. These cases demonstrate the point. Sheriffs Printz and Mack have made public statements, including their decisions to serve as plaintiffs in these actions, denouncing the Brady Act. See, e.g., Shaffer, Gun Suit Shoots Sheriff into Spotlight, Arizona Republic, July 5, 1994, p. B1; Downs, Most Gun Dealers Shrug off Proposal to Raise License Fee, Missoulian, Jan. 5, 1994. Indeed, Sheriff Mack has written a book discussing his views on the issue. See R. Mack & T. Walters, From My Cold Dead Fingers: Why America Needs Guns (1994). Moreover, we can be sure that CLEOs will inform disgruntled constituents who have been denied permission to purchase a handgun about the origins of the Brady Act requirements. The Court's suggestion that voters will be confused over who is to "blame" for the statute reflects a gross lack of confidence in the electorate that is at war with the basic assumptions underlying any democratic government.

The statute was designed "to end the imposition, in the absence of full consideration by Congress, of Federal mandates on State . . . governments without adequate Federal funding, in a manner that may displace other essential State . . . governmental priorities." 2 U.S.C. A. §1501(2) (Supp. 1997). It functions, inter alia, by permitting Members of Congress to raise an objection by point of order to a pending bill that contains an "unfunded mandate," as defined by the statute, of over $50 million. n19 The mandate may not then be enacted unless the Members make an explicit decision to proceed anyway. See Recent Legislation, Unfunded Mandates Reform Act of 1995, 109 Harv. L. Rev. 1469 (1996) (describing functioning of statute). Whatever the ultimate impact of the new legislation, its passage demonstrates that unelected judges are better off leaving the protection of federalism to the political process in all but the most extraordinary circumstances. n20

n19 Unlike the majority's judicially crafted rule, the statute excludes from its coverage bills in certain subject areas, such as emergency matters, legislation prohibiting discrimination, and national security measures. See 2 U.S.C. A. §1503 (Supp. 1997).

n20 The initial signs are that the Act will play an important role in curbing the behavior about which the majority expresses concern. In the law's first year, the Congressional Budget Office identified only five bills containing unfunded mandates over the statutory threshold. Of these, one was not enacted into law, and three were modified to limit their effect on the States. The fifth, which was enacted, was scarcely a program of the sort described by the majority at all; it was a generally applicable increase in the minimum wage. See Congressional Budget Office, The Experience of the Congressional Budget Office During the First Year of the Unfunded Mandates Reform Act 13-15 (Jan. 1997).

By limiting the ability of the Federal Government to enlist state officials in the implementation of its programs, the Court creates incentives for the National Government to aggrandize itself. In the name of State's rights, the majority would have the Federal Government create vast national bureaucracies to implement its policies.

Perversely, the majority's rule seems more likely to damage than to preserve the safeguards against tyranny provided by the existence of vital state governments. By limiting the ability of the Federal Government to enlist state officials in the implementation of its programs, the Court creates incentives for the National Government to aggrandize itself. In the name of State's rights, the majority would have the Federal Government create vast national bureaucracies to implement its policies. This is exactly the sort of thing that the early Federalists promised would not occur, in part as a result of the National Government's ability to rely on the magistracy of the states. See, e.g., The Federalist No. 36, at 234-235 (Hamilton); id., No. 45, at 318(Madison). n21

it is difficult to see how state sovereignty and individual liberty are more seriously threatened by federal reliance on state police officers to fulfill this minimal request than by the aggrandizement of a national police force. The Court's alarmist

hypothetical is no more persuasive than the likelihood that Congress would actually enact any such program.

n21 The Court raises the specter that the National Government seeks the authority "to impress into its service . . . the police officers of the 50 States." Ante, at 23. But it is difficult to see how state sovereignty and individual liberty are more seriously threatened by federal reliance on state police officers to fulfill this minimal request than by the aggrandizement of a national police force. The Court's alarmist hypothetical is no more persuasive than the likelihood that Congress would actually enact any such program.

With colorful hyperbole, the Court suggests that the unity in the Executive Branch of the Federal Government "would be shattered, and the power of the President would be subject to reduction, if Congress could . . . require . . . state officers to execute its laws." Ante, at 23-24. Putting to one side the obvious tension between the majority's claim that impressing state police officers will unduly tip the balance of power in favor of the federal sovereign and this suggestion that it will emasculate the Presidency, the Court's reasoning contradicts New York v. United States. n22

The enactment of statutes that merely involve the gathering of information, or the use of state officials on an interim basis, do not raise even arguable separation-of-powers concerns.

n22 Moreover, with respect to programs that directly enlist the local government officials, the majority's position rests on nothing more than a fanciful hypothetical. The enactment of statutes that merely involve the gathering of information, or the use of state officials on an interim basis, do not raise even arguable separation-of-powers concerns.

That decision squarely approved of cooperative federalism programs, designed at the national level but implemented principally by state governments. New York disapproved of a particular method of putting such programs into place, not the existence of federal programs implemented locally. See New York, 505 U.S. at 166 ("Our cases have identified a variety of methods . . . by which Congress may urge a State to adopt a legislative program consistent with federal interests"). Indeed, nothing in the majority's holding calls into question the three mechanisms for constructing such programs that New York expressly approved. Congress may require the States to implement its programs as a condition of federal spending, n23 in order to avoid the threat of unilateral federal action in the area, n24 or as a part of a program that affects States and private parties alike. n25 The majority's suggestion in response to this dissent that Congress' ability to create such programs is limited, ante, at 24, n.12, is belied by the importance and sweep of the federal statutes that meet this description, some of which we described in New York. See id., at 167-168 (mentioning, inter alia, the Clean Water Act, the Occupational Safety and Health Act of 1970, and the Resource Conservation and Recovery Act of 1976).

n23 See New York, 505 U.S. at 167; see, e.g., South Dakota v. Dole, 483 U.S. 203, 97 L. Ed. 2d 171, 107 S. Ct. 2793 (1987); see also ante, at 1-2 (O'CONNOR, J., concurring).

n24 New York, 505 U.S. at 167; see, e.g., Hodel v. Virginia Surface Mining & Reclamation Assn., Inc., 452 U.S. 264, 69 L. Ed. 2d 1, 101 S. Ct. 2352 (1981).

n25 New York, 505 U.S. at 160; see, e.g., Garcia v. San Antonio Metropolitan Transit Authority, 469 U.S. 528, 83 L. Ed. 2d 1016, 105 S. Ct. 1005 (1985).

Nor is there force to the assumption undergirding the Court's entire opinion that if this trivial burden on state sovereignty is permissible, the entire structure of federalism will soon collapse.

The Court seems to accept the fact that Congress could require private persons, such as hospital executives or school administrators, to provide arms merchants with relevant information about a prospective purchaser's fitness to own a weapon

Nor is there force to the assumption undergirding the Court's entire opinion that if this trivial burden on state sovereignty is permissible, the entire structure of federalism will soon collapse. These cases do not involve any mandate to state legislatures to enact new rules. When legislative action, or even administrative rule-making, is at issue, it may be appropriate for Congress either to pre-empt the State's lawmaking power and fashion the federal rule itself, or to respect the State's power to fashion its own rules. But this case, unlike any precedent in which the Court has held that Congress exceeded its powers, merely involves the imposition of modest duties on individual officers. The Court seems to accept the fact that Congress could require private persons, such as hospital executives or school administrators, to provide arms merchants with relevant information about a prospective purchaser's fitness to own a weapon; indeed, the Court does not disturb the conclusion that flows directly from our prior holdings that the burden on police officers would be permissible if a similar burden were also imposed on private parties with access to relevant data. See New York, 505 U.S. at 160; Garcia v. San Antonio Metropolitan Transit Authority, 469 U.S. 528, 83 L. Ed. 2d 1016, 105 S. Ct. 1005 (1985). A structural problem that vanishes when the statute affects private individuals as well as public officials is not much of a structural problem.

Neither explicitly nor implicitly did the Framers issue any command that forbids Congress from imposing federal duties on private citizens or on local officials.

Justice Holmes' reminder that "the machinery of government would not work if it were not allowed a little play in its joints."

Far more important than the concerns that the Court musters in support of its new rule is the fact that the Framers entrusted Congress with the task of creating a working structure of intergovernmental relationships around the framework that the Constitution authorized. Neither explicitly nor implicitly did the Framers issue any command that forbids Congress from imposing federal duties on private citizens or on local officials. As a general matter, Congress has followed the sound policy of authorizing federal agencies and federal agents to administer federal programs. That general practice, however, does not negate the existence of power to rely on state officials in occasional situations in which such reliance is in the national interest. Rather, the occasional exceptions confirm the wisdom of Justice Holmes' reminder that "the machinery of government would not work if it were not allowed a little play in its joints." Bain Peanut Co. of Tex. v. Pinson, 282 U.S. 499, 501, 75 L. Ed. 482, 51 S. Ct. 228 (1931).

IV

Finally, the Court advises us that the "prior jurisprudence of this Court" is the most conclusive support for its position. Ante, at 26. That "prior jurisprudence" is New York v. United States. n26 The case involved the validity of a federal statute that provided the States with three types of incentives to encourage them to dispose of radioactive wastes generated within their borders. The Court held that the first two sets of incentives were authorized by affirmative grants of power to Congress, and therefore "not inconsistent with the Tenth Amendment." 505 U.S. at 173, 174. That holding, of course, sheds no doubt on the validity of the Brady Act.

n26 The majority also cites to FERC v. Mississippi, 456 U.S. 742, 72 L. Ed. 2d 532, 102 S. Ct. 2126 (1982), and Hodel v. Virginia Surface Mining & Reclamation Assn., Inc., 452 U.S. 264, 69 L. Ed. 2d 1, 101 S. Ct. 2352 (1981). See ante, at 26-27. Neither case addressed the issue presented here. Hodel simply reserved the question. See 452 U.S. at 288. The Court's subsequent opinion in FERC did the same, see 456 U.S. at 764-765; and, both its holding and reasoning cut against the majority's view in this case.

The third so-called "incentive" gave the States the option either of adopting regulations dictated by Congress or of taking title to and possession of the low level radioactive waste. The Court concluded that, because Congress had no power to compel the state governments to take title to the waste, the "option" really amounted to a simple command to the States to enact and enforce a federal regulatory program. 505 U.S. at 176. The Court explained:

A choice between two unconstitutionally coercive regulatory techniques is no choice at all.

"A choice between two unconstitutionally coercive regulatory techniques is no choice at all. Either way, 'the Act commandeers the legislative processes of the States by directly compelling them to enact and enforce a federal regulatory program,' Hodel v. Virginia Surface Mining & Reclamation Assn., Inc., supra, at 288, an outcome that has never been understood to lie within the authority conferred upon Congress by the Constitution." Ibid.

After noting that the "take title provision appears to be unique" because no other federal statute had offered "a state government no option other than that of implementing legislation enacted by Congress," the Court concluded that the provision was "inconsistent with the federal structure of our Government established by the Constitution." Id., at 177.

Our statements, taken in context, clearly did not decide the question presented here, whether state executive officials--as opposed to state legislators--may in appropriate circumstances be enlisted to implement federal policy. The "take title" provision at issue in New York was beyond Congress' authority to enact because it was "in principle . . . no different than a congressionally compelled subsidy from state governments to radioactive waste producers," 505 U.S. at 175, almost certainly a legislative act.

it is hard to characterize the minimal requirement that CLEOs perform background checks as one involving the exercise of substantial policymaking discretion

The majority relies upon dictum in New York to the effect that "the Federal Government may not compel the States to enact or administer a federal regulatory program." Id., at 188 (emphasis added); see ante, at 35. But that language was wholly unnecessary to the decision of the case. It is, of course, beyond dispute that we are not bound by the dicta of our prior opinions. See, e.g., U.S. Bancorp Mortgage Co. v. Bonner Mall Partnership, 513 U.S. 18, 24, 130 L. Ed. 2d 233, 115 S. Ct. 386 (1994) (SCALIA, J.) ("invoking our customary refusal to be bound by dicta"). To the extent that it has any substance at all, New York's administration language may have referred to the possibility that the State might have been able to take title to and devise an elaborate scheme for the management of the radioactive waste through purely executive policymaking. But despite the majority's effort to suggest that similar activities are required by the Brady Act, see ante, at 28-29, it is hard to characterize the minimal requirement that CLEOs perform background checks as one involving the exercise of substantial policymaking discretion on that essentially legislative scale. n27

n27 Indeed, this distinction is made in the New York opinion itself. In that case, the Court rejected the Government's argument that earlier decisions supported the proposition that "the Constitution does, in some circumstances, permit federal directives to state governments." New York, 505 U.S. at 178. But in doing so, it distinguished those cases on a ground that applies to the federal directive in the Brady Act:

"All involve congressional regulation of individuals, not congressional requirements that States regulate.

. . . . .

"The cases relied upon by the United States hold only that federal law is enforceable in state courts and that federal courts may in proper circumstances order state officials to comply with federal law, propositions that by no means imply any authority on the part of Congress to mandate state regulation." Id., at 178-179.

The Brady Act contains no command directed to a sovereign State or to a state legislature. It does not require any state entity to promulgate any federal rule. In this case, the federal statute is not even being applied to any state official. It is a "congressional regulation of individuals," including gun retailers and local police officials. Those officials, like the judges referred to in the New York opinion, are bound by the Supremacy Clause to comply with federal law.

The Brady Act contains no command directed to a sovereign State or to a state legislature. It does not require any state entity to promulgate any federal rule. In this case, the federal statute is not even being applied to any state official. See n.16, supra. It is a "congressional regulation of individuals," New York, 505 U.S. at 178, including gun retailers and local police officials. Those officials, like the judges referred to in the New York opinion, are bound by the Supremacy Clause to comply with federal law. Thus if we accept the distinction identified in the New York opinion itself, that decision does not control the disposition of these cases.

Indeed, JUSTICE KENNEDY's recent comment about another case that was distinguishable from New York applies to these cases as well:

"This is not a case where the etiquette of federalism has been violated by a formal command from the National Government directing the State to enact a certain policy, cf. New York v. United States, 505 U.S. 144, 120 L. Ed. 2d 120, 112 S. Ct. 2408 (1992), or to organize its governmental functions in a certain way, cf. FERC v. Mississippi, 456 U.S. at 781, (O'CONNOR, J., concurring in judgment in part and dissenting in part)." Lopez, 514 U.S. at 583 (KENNEDY, J., concurring).

there is abundant authority in our Eleventh Amendment jurisprudence recognizing a constitutional distinction between local government officials, such as the CLEO's who brought this action, and State entities that are entitled to sovereign immunity.

In response to this dissent, the majority asserts that the difference between a federal command addressed to individuals and one addressed to the State itself "cannot be a constitutionally significant one." Ante, at 32. But as I have already noted, n.16, supra, there is abundant authority in our Eleventh Amendment jurisprudence recognizing a constitutional distinction between local government officials, such as the CLEO's who brought this action, and State entities that are entitled to sovereign immunity. To my knowledge, no one has previously thought that the distinction "disembowels," ante, at 32-33, the Eleventh Amendment. n28

n28 Ironically, the distinction that the Court now finds so preposterous can be traced to the majority opinion in National League of Cities. See 426 U.S. at 854 ("the States as States stand on a quite different footing from an individual or a corporation when challenging the exercise of Congress' power to regulate commerce"). The fact that the distinction did not provide an adequate basis for curtailing the power of Congress to extend the coverage of the Fair Labor Standards Act to state employees does not speak to the question whether it may identify a legitimate difference between a directive to local officers to provide information or assistance to the Federal Government and a directive to a State to enact legislation.

Importantly, the majority either misconstrues or ignores three cases that are more directly on point. In FERC, we upheld a federal statute requiring state utilities commissions, inter alia, to take the affirmative step of considering federal energy standards in a manner complying with federally specified notice and comment procedures, and to report back to Congress periodically. The state commissions could avoid this obligation only by ceasing regulation in the field, a "choice" that we recognized was realistically foreclosed, since Congress had put forward no alternative regulatory scheme to govern this very important area. 456 U.S. at 764, 766, 770. The burden on state officials that we approved in FERC was far more extensive than the minimal, temporary imposition posed by the Brady Act. n29

n29 The majority correctly notes the opinion's statement that "this Court never has sanctioned explicitly a federal command to the States to promulgate and enforce laws and regulations . . . ." FERC, 456 U.S. at 761-762. But the Court truncates this quotation in a grossly misleading fashion. We continued by noting in that very sentence that "there are instances where the Court has upheld federal statutory structures that in effect directed state decisionmakers to take or to refrain from taking certain actions." Ibid. Indeed, the Court expressly rejected as "rigid and isolated," id., at 761, our suggestion long ago in Kentucky v. Dennison, 65 U.S. 66, 24 HOW 66, 107, 16 L. Ed. 717 (1861), that Congress "has no power to impose on a State officer, as such, any duty whatever."

Similarly, in Puerto Rico v. Branstad, 483 U.S. 219, 97 L. Ed. 2d 187, 107 S. Ct. 2802 (1987), we overruled our earlier decision in Kentucky v. Dennison, 65 U.S. 66, 24 HOW 66, 16 L. Ed. 717 (1861), and held that the Extradition Act of 1793 permitted the Commonwealth of Puerto Rico to seek extradition of a fugitive from its laws without constitutional barrier. The Extradition Act, as the majority properly concedes, plainly imposes duties on state executive officers. See ante, at 8. The majority suggests that this statute is nevertheless of little importance because it simply constitutes an implementation of the authority granted the National Government by the Constitution's Extradition Clause, Art. IV, §2. But in Branstad we noted ambiguity as to whether Puerto Rico benefits from that Clause, which applies on its face only to "States." Avoiding the question of the Clause's applicability, we held simply that under the Extradition Act Puerto Rico had the power to request that the State of Iowa deliver up the fugitive the Commonwealth sought. 483 U.S. at 229-230. Although Branstad relied on the authority of the Act alone, without the benefit of the Extradition Clause, we noted no barrier to our decision in the principles of federalism--despite the fact that one Member of the Court brought the issue to our attention, see id., at 231(SCALIA, J., concurring in part and concurring in judgment). n30

n30 Moreover, Branstad unequivocally rejected an important premise that resonates throughout the majority opinion: namely, that because the States retain their sovereignty in areas that are unregulated by federal law, notions of comity rather than constitutional power govern any direction by the National Government to state executive or judicial officers. That construct was the product of the ill-starred opinion of Chief Justice Taney in Kentucky v. Dennison, 65 U.S. 66, 24 HOW 66, 16 L. Ed. 717 (1861), announced at a time when "the practical power of the Federal Government [was] at its lowest ebb," Branstad, 483 U.S. at 225. As we explained:

"If it seemed clear to the Court in 1861, facing the looming shadow of a Civil War, that 'the Federal Government, under the Constitution, has no power to impose on a State officer, as such, any duty whatever, and compel him to perform it,' 24 How., at 107, basic constitutional principles now point as clearly the other way." 483 U.S. at 227.

"Kentucky v. Dennison is the product of another time. The conception of the relation between the States and the Federal Government there announced is fundamentally incompatible with more than a century of constitutional development. Yet this decision has stood while the world of which it was a part has passed away. We conclude that it may stand no longer." Id., at 230.

Finally, the majority provides an incomplete explanation of our decision in Testa v. Katt, 330 U.S. 386, 91 L. Ed. 967, 67 S. Ct. 810 (1947), and demeans its importance. In that case the Court unanimously held that state courts of appropriate jurisdiction must occupy themselves adjudicating claims brought by private litigants under the federal Emergency Price Control Act of 1942, regardless of how otherwise crowded their dockets might be with state law matters. That is a much greater imposition on state sovereignty than the Court's characterization of the case as merely holding that "state courts cannot refuse to apply federal law," ante, at 30. That characterization describes only the narrower duty to apply federal law in cases that the state courts have consented to entertain.

The language drawn from the Supremacy Clause upon which the majority relies ("the Judges in every State shall be bound [by federal law], any Thing in the Constitution or Laws of any state to the Contrary notwithstanding"), expressly embraces that narrower conflict of laws principle. Art. VI, cl. 2. But the Supremacy Clause means far more. As Testa held, because the "Laws of the United States . . . [are] the supreme Law of the Land," state courts of appropriate jurisdiction must hear federal claims whenever a federal statute, such as the Emergency Price Control Act, requires them to do so. Ibid.

Hence, the Court's textual argument is quite misguided. The majority focuses on the Clause's specific attention to the point that "Judges in every State shall be bound." Ibid. That language commands state judges to "apply federal law" in cases that they entertain, but it is not the source of their duty to accept jurisdiction of federal claims that they would prefer to ignore. Our opinions in Testa, and earlier the Second Employers' Liability Cases, rested generally on the language of the Supremacy Clause, without any specific focus on the reference to judges. n31

n31 As the discussion above suggests, the Clause's mention of judges was almost certainly meant as nothing more than a choice of law rule, informing the state courts that they were to apply federal law in the event of a conflict with state authority. The majority's quotation of this language, ante, at 30, is quite misleading because it omits a crucial phrase that follows the mention of state judges. In its entirety, the Supremacy Clause reads: "This Constitution, and the Laws of the United States which shall be made in Pursuance thereof; and all Treaties made, or which shall be made, under the Authority of the United States, shall be the supreme Law of the Land; and the Judges in every State shall be bound thereby, any Thing in the Constitution or Laws of any state to the Contrary notwithstanding." Art. VI, cl. 2 (emphasis added). The omitted language, in my view, makes clear that the specific reference to judges was designed to do nothing more than state a choice of law principle. The fact that our earliest opinions in this area, see Testa; Second Employers' Liability Cases, written at a time when the question was far more hotly contested than it is today, did not rely upon that language lends considerable support to this reading.

The majority's reinterpretation of Testa also contradicts our decision in FERC. In addition to the holding mentioned earlier, see supra, at 30, we also approved in that case provisions of federal law requiring a state utilities commission to "adjudicate disputes arising under [a federal] statute." FERC, 456 U.S. at 760. Because the state commission had "jurisdiction to entertain claims analogous to those" put before it under the federal statute, ibid., we held that Testa required it to adjudicate the federal claims. Although the commission was serving an adjudicative function, the commissioners were unquestionably not "judges" within the meaning of Art. VI, cl. 2. It is impossible to reconcile the Court's present view that Testa rested entirely on the specific reference to state judges in the Supremacy Clause with our extension of that early case in FERC. n32

n32 The Court's suggestion that these officials ought to be treated as "judges" for constitutional purposes because that is, functionally, what they are, is divorced from the constitutional text upon which the majority relies, which refers quite explicitly to "Judges" and not administrative officials. In addition, it directly contradicts the majority's position that early statutes requiring state courts to perform executive functions are irrelevant to our assessment of the original understanding because "Judges" were at issue. In short, the majority's adoption of a proper functional analysis gives away important ground elsewhere without shoring up its argument here.

The notion that the Framers would have had no reluctance to "press state judges into federal service" against their will but would have regarded the imposition of a similar—indeed, far lesser— burden on town constables as an intolerable affront to principles of state sovereignty, can only be considered perverse.

Even if the Court were correct in its suggestion that it was the reference to judges in the Supremacy Clause, rather than the central message of the entire Clause, that dictated the result in Testa, the Court's implied expressio unius argument that the Framers therefore did not intend to permit the enlistment of other state officials is implausible. Throughout our history judges, state as well as federal, have merited as much respect as executive agents. The notion that the Framers would have had no reluctance to "press state judges into federal service" against their will but would have regarded the imposition of a similar--indeed, far lesser-- burden on town constables as an intolerable affront to principles of state sovereignty, can only be considered perverse. If such a distinction had been contemplated by the learned and articulate men who fashioned the basic structure of our government, surely some of them would have said so. n33

n33 Indeed, presuming that the majority has correctly read the Supremacy Clause, it is far more likely that the founders had a special respect for the independence of judges, and so thought it particularly important to emphasize that state judges were bound to apply federal law. The Framers would hardly have felt any equivalent need to state the then well-accepted point, see supra, at 8-10, that the enlistment of state executive officials was entirely proper.

The provision of the Brady Act that crosses the Court's newly defined constitutional threshold is more comparable to a statute requiring local police officers to report the identity of missing children to the Crime Control Center of the Department of Justice than to an offensive federal command to a sovereign state.

The provision of the Brady Act that crosses the Court's newly defined constitutional threshold is more comparable to a statute requiring local police officers to report the identity of missing children to the Crime Control Center of the Department of Justice than to an offensive federal command to a sovereign state. If Congress believes that such a statute will benefit the people of the Nation, and serve the interests of cooperative federalism better than an enlarged federal bureaucracy, we should respect both its policy judgment and its appraisal of its constitutional power.

Accordingly, I respectfully dissent.

JUSTICE SOUTER, dissenting.

I join JUSTICE STEVENS's dissenting opinion, but subject to the following qualifications. While I do not find anything dispositive in the paucity of early examples of federal employment of state officers for executive purposes, for the reason given by JUSTICE STEVENS, ante, at 11-12, neither would I find myself in dissent with no more to go on than those few early instances in the administration of naturalization laws, for example, or such later instances as state support for federal emergency action, see ante, at 12-14; ante, at 5-10, 16-18 (majority opinion). These illustrations of state action implementing congressional statutes are consistent with the Government's positions, but they do not speak to me with much force.

In deciding these cases, which I have found closer than I had anticipated, it is The Federalist that finally determines my position. I believe that the most straightforward reading of No. 27 is authority for the Government's position here, and that this reading is both supported by No. 44 and consistent with Nos. 36 and 45.

Hamilton in No. 27 first notes that because the new Constitution would authorize the National Government to bind individuals directly through national law, it could "employ the ordinary magistracy of each [State] in the execution of its laws." The Federalist No. 27, p. 174 (J. Cooke ed. 1961) (A. Hamilton). Were he to stop here, he would not necessarily be speaking of anything beyond the possibility of cooperative arrangements by agreement. But he then addresses the combined effect of the proposed Supremacy Clause, U.S. Const., Art. VI, cl. 2, and state officers's oath requirement, U.S. Const., Art. VI, cl. 3, and he states that "the Legislatures, Courts and Magistrates of the respective members will be incorporated into the operations of the national government, as far as its just and constitutional authority extends; and will be rendered auxiliary to the enforcement of its laws." The Federalist No. 27, at 174-175 (emphasis in original). The natural reading of this language is not merely that the officers of the various branches of state governments may be employed in the performance of national functions; Hamilton says that the state governmental machinery "will be incorporated" into the Nation's operation, and because the "auxiliary" status of the state officials will occur because they are "bound by the sanctity of an oath," id., at 175, I take him to mean that their auxiliary functions will be the products of their obligations thus undertaken to support federal law, not of their own, or the States', unfettered choices. n1

n1 The Court offers two criticisms of this analysis. First, as the Court puts it, the consequences set forth in this passage (that is, rendering state officials "auxiliary" and "incorporating" them into the operations of the Federal Government) "are said . . . to flow automatically from the officers' oath," ante, at 12; from this, the Court infers that on my reading, state officers' obligations to execute federal law must follow "without the necessity for a congressional directive that they implement it," ibid. But neither Hamilton nor I use the word "automatically"; consequently, there is no reason on Hamilton's view to infer a state officer's affirmative obligation without a textual indication to that effect. This is just what JUSTICE STEVENS says, ante at 11, and n.8.

Second, the Court reads Federalist No. 27 as incompatible with our decision in New York v. United States, 505 U.S. 144, 120 L. Ed. 2d 120, 112 S. Ct. 2408 (1992), and credits me with the imagination to devise a "novel principle of political science," ante at 12-13, n.5, "in order to bring forth disparity of outcome from parity of language," ibid.; in order, that is, to salvage New York, by concluding that Congress can tell state executive officers what to execute without at the same time having the power to tell state legislators what to legislate. But the Court is too generous. I simply realize that "parity of language" (i.e., all state officials who take the oath are "incorporated" or are "auxiliaries") operates on officers of the three branches in accordance with the quite different powers of their respective branches. The core power of an executive officer is to enforce a law in accordance with its terms; that is why a state executive "auxiliary" may be told what result to bring about. The core power of a legislator acting within the legislature's subject-matter jurisdiction is to make a discretionary decision on what the law should be; that is why a legislator may not be legally ordered to exercise discretion a particular way without damaging the legislative power as such. The discretionary nature of the authorized legislative Act is probably why Madison's two examples of legislative "auxiliary" obligation address the elections of the President and Senators, see infra, at 4 (discussing the Federalist No. 44, p. 307 (J. Cooke ed. 1961) (J. Madison), not the passage of legislation to please Congress.

The Court reads Hamilton's description of state officers' role in carrying out federal law as nothing more than a way of describing the duty of state officials "not to obstruct the operation of federal law," with the consequence that any obstruction is invalid. Ante, at 13. But I doubt that Hamilton's English was quite as bad as all that. Someone whose virtue consists of not obstructing administration of the law is not described as "incorporated into the operations" of a government or as an "auxiliary" to its law enforcement. One simply cannot escape from Hamilton by reducing his prose to inapposite figures of speech.

Madison in No. 44 supports this reading in his commentary on the oath requirement. He asks why state magistrates should have to swear to support the National Constitution, when national officials will not be required to oblige themselves to support the state counterparts. His answer is that national officials "will have no agency in carrying the State Constitutions into effect. The members and officers of the State Governments, on the contrary, will have an essential agency in giving effect to the Federal Constitution." The Federalist No. 44, at 307 (J. Madison). He then describes the state legislative "agency" as action necessary for selecting the President, see U.S. Const., Art. II, §1, and the choice of Senators, see U.S. Const., Art. I, §3 (repealed by Amendment XVII). Ibid. The Supremacy Clause itself, of course, expressly refers to the state judges' obligations under federal law, and other numbers of The Federalist give examples of state executive "agency" in the enforcement of national revenue laws. n2

n2 The Court reads Madison's No. 44 as supporting its view that Hamilton meant "auxiliaries" to mean merely "nonobstructors." It defends its position in what seems like a very sensible argument, so long as one does not go beyond the terms set by the Court: if Madison really thought state executive officials could be required to enforce federal law, one would have expected him to say so, instead of giving examples of how state officials (legislative and executive, the Court points out) have roles in the election of national officials. See ante, at 14-16, and n.8. One might indeed have expected that, save for one remark of Madison's, and a detail of his language, that the Court ignores. When he asked why state officers should have to take an oath to support the National Constitution, he said that "several reasons might be assigned," but that he would "content [himself] with one which is obvious & conclusive." The Federalist No. 44, at 307. The one example he gives describes how state officials will have "an essential agency in giving effect to the Federal Constitution." He was not talking about executing congressional statutes; he was talking about putting the National Constitution into effect by selecting the executive and legislative members who would exercise its powers. The answer to the Court's question (and objection), then, is that Madison was expressly choosing one example of state officer agency, not purporting to exhaust the examples possible.

There is, therefore, support in Madison's No. 44 for the straightforward reading of Hamilton's No. 27 and, so, no occasion to discount the authority of Hamilton's views as expressed in The Federalist as somehow reflecting the weaker side of a split constitutional personality. Ante, at 16, n.9. This, indeed, should not surprise us, for one of the Court's own authorities rejects the "split personality" notion of Hamilton and Madison as being at odds in The Federalist, in favor of a view of all three Federalist writers as constituting a single personality notable for its integration:

"In recent years it has been popular to describe Publius [the nominal author of the Federalist] as a 'split personality' who spoke through Madison as a federalist and an exponent of limited government, but through Hamilton as a nationalist and an admirer of energetic government. . . . Neither the diagnosis of tension between Hamilton and Madison nor the indictment of each man for self-contradiction strikes me as a useful of perhaps even fair-minded exercise. Publius was, on any large view--the only correct view to take of an effort so sprawling in size and concentrated in time--a remarkably 'whole personality,' and I am far more impressed by the large area of agreement between Hamilton and Madison than by the differences in emphasis that have been read into rather than in their papers. . . . The intellectual tensions of The Federalist and its creators are in fact an honest reflection of those built into the Constitution it expounds and the polity it celebrates." C. Rossiter, Alexander Hamilton and the Constitution 58 (1964).

While Hamilton and Madison went their separate ways in later years, see id., at 78, and may have had differing personal views, the passages from The Federalist discussed here show no sign of strain.

Two such examples of anticipated state collection of federal revenue are instructive, each of which is put forward to counter fears of a proliferation of tax collectors. In No. 45, Hamilton says that if a State is not given (or declines to exercise) an option to supply its citizens' share of a federal tax, the "eventual collection [of the federal tax] under the immediate authority of the Union, will generally be made by the officers, and according to the rules, appointed by the several States." The Federalist No. 45, at 313. And in No. 36, he explains that the National Government would more readily "employ the State officers as much as possible, and to attach them to the Union by an accumulation of their emoluments," The Federalist No. 36, at 228, than by appointing separate federal revenue collectors.

In the light of all these passages, I cannot persuade myself that the statements from No. 27 speak of anything less than the authority of the National Government, when exercising an otherwise legitimate power (the commerce power, say), to require state "auxiliaries" to take appropriate action. To be sure, it does not follow that any conceivable requirement may be imposed on any state official. I continue to agree, for example, that Congress may not require a state legislature to enact a regulatory scheme and that New York v. United States, 505 U.S. 144, 120 L. Ed. 2d 120, 112 S. Ct. 2408 (1992) was rightly decided (even though I now believe its dicta went too far toward immunizing state administration as well as state enactment of such a scheme from congressional mandate); after all, the essence of legislative power, within the limits of legislative jurisdiction, is a discretion not subject to command. But insofar as national law would require nothing from a state officer inconsistent with the power proper to his branch of tripartite state government (say, by obligating a state judge to exercise law enforcement powers), I suppose that the reach of federal law as Hamilton described it would not be exceeded, cf. Garcia v. San Antonio Metropolitan Transit Authority, 469 U.S. 528, 554, 556-567, 83 L. Ed. 2d 1016, 105 S. Ct. 1005 (1985) (without precisely delineating the outer limits of Congress's Commerce Clause power, finding that the statute at issue was not "destructive of state sovereignty").

I should mention two other points. First, I recognize that my reading of The Federalist runs counter to the view of Justice Field, who stated explicitly in United States v. Jones, 109 U.S. 513, 519-520, 27 L. Ed. 1015, 3 S. Ct. 346 (1883), that the early examples of state execution of federal law could not have been required against a State's will. But that statement, too, was dictum, and as against dictum even from Justice Field, Madison and Hamilton prevail. Second, I do not read any of The Federalist material as requiring the conclusion that Congress could require administrative support without an obligation to pay fair value for it. The quotation from No. 36, for example, describes the United States as paying. If, therefore, my views were prevailing in these cases, I would remand for development and consideration of petitioners' points, that they have no budget provision for work required under the Act and are liable for unauthorized expenditures. Brief for Petitioner in No. 95-1478, pp. 4-5; Brief for Petitioner in No. 95-1503, pp. 6-7.

JUSTICE BREYER, with whom JUSTICE STEVENS joins, dissenting.

the United States is not the only nation that seeks to reconcile the practical need for a central authority with the democratic virtues of more local control.

They do so in part because they believe that such a system interferes less, not more, with the independent authority of the "state," member nation, or other subsidiary government, and helps to safeguard individual liberty as well.

I would add to the reasons JUSTICE STEVENS sets forth the fact that the United States is not the only nation that seeks to reconcile the practical need for a central authority with the democratic virtues of more local control. At least some other countries, facing the same basic problem, have found that local control is better maintained through application of a principle that is the direct opposite of the principle the majority derives from the silence of our Constitution. The federal systems of Switzerland, Germany, and the European Union, for example, all provide that constituent states, not federal bureaucracies, will themselves implement many of the laws, rules, regulations, or decrees enacted by the central "federal" body. Lenaerts, Constitutionalism and the Many Faces of Federalism, 38 Am. J. Comp. L. 205, 237 (1990); D. Currie, The Constitution of the Federal Republic of Germany 66, 84 (1994); Mackenzie-Stuart, Foreward, Comparative Constitutional Federalism: Europe and America ix (M. Tushnet ed. 1990); Kimber, A Comparison of Environmental Federalism in the United States and the European Union, 54 Md. L. Rev. 1658, 1675-1677 (1995). They do so in part because they believe that such a system interferes less, not more, with the independent authority of the "state," member nation, or other subsidiary government, and helps to safeguard individual liberty as well. See Council of European Communities, European Council in Edinburgh, 11-12 December 1992, Conclusions of the Presidency 20-21 (1993); D. Lasok & K. Bridge, Law and Institutions of the European Union 114 (1994); Currie, supra, at 68, 81-84, 100-101; Frowein, Integration and the Federal Experience in Germany and Switzerland, 1 Integration Through Law 573, 586-587 (M. Cappelletti, M. Seccombe, & J. Weiler eds. 1986); Lenaerts, supra, at 232, 263.

Why, or how, would what the majority sees as a constitutional alternative—the creation of a new federal gun-law bureaucracy, or the expansion of an existing federal bureaucracy— better promote either state sovereignty or individual liberty?

Of course, we are interpreting our own Constitution, not those of other nations, and there may be relevant political and structural differences between their systems and our own. Cf. The Federalist No. 20, pp. 134-138 (C. Rossiter ed. 1961) (J. Madison and A. Hamilton) (rejecting certain aspects of European federalism). But their experience may nonetheless cast an empirical light on the consequences of different solutions to a common legal problem--in this case the problem of reconciling central authority with the need to preserve the liberty-enhancing autonomy of a smaller constituent governmental entity. Cf. id., No. 42, p. 268 (J. Madison) (looking to experiences of European countries); id., No. 43, pp. 275, 276 (J. Madison) (same). And that experience here offers empirical confirmation of the implied answer to a question JUSTICE STEVENS asks: Why, or how, would what the majority sees as a constitutional alternative--the creation of a new federal gun-law bureaucracy, or the expansion of an existing federal bureaucracy-- better promote either state sovereignty or individual liberty? See ante, at 7-8, 23 (STEVENS, J., dissenting).

As comparative experience suggests, there is no need to interpret the Constitution as containing an absolute principle--forbidding the assignment of virtually any federal duty to any state official. Nor is there a need to read the Brady Act as permitting the Federal Government to overwhelm a state civil service. The statute uses the words "reasonable effort," 18 U.S.C. §922(s)(2)--words that easily can encompass the considerations of, say, time or cost, necessary to avoid any such result.

Regardless, as JUSTICE STEVENS points out, the Constitution itself is silent on the matter. Ante, at 7, 18, 25 (STEVENS, J., dissenting). Precedent supports the Government's position here. Ante, at 19, 23-25, 26-34 (STEVENS, J., dissenting). And the fact that there is not more precedent--that direct federal assignment of duties to state officers is not common--likely reflects, not a widely shared belief that any such assignment is incompatible with basic principles of federalism, but rather a widely shared practice of assigning such duties in other ways. See, e.g., South Dakota v. Dole, 483 U.S. 203, 97 L. Ed. 2d 171, 107 S. Ct. 2793 (1987) (spending power); Garcia v. United States, 469 U.S. 70, 83 L. Ed. 2d 472, 105 S. Ct. 479 (1984); New York v. United States, 505 U.S. 144, 160, 120 L. Ed. 2d 120, 112 S. Ct. 2408 (1992) (general statutory duty); FERC v. Mississippi, 456 U.S. 742, 72 L. Ed. 2d 532, 102 S. Ct. 2126 (1982) (pre-emption). See also ante, at 4-5 (SOUTER, J., dissenting). Thus, there is neither need nor reason to find in the Constitution an absolute principle, the inflexibility of which poses a surprising and technical obstacle to the enactment of a law that Congress believed necessary to solve an important national problem.

For these reasons and those set forth in JUSTICE STEVENS' opinion, I join his dissent.

ROGERS v. UNITED STATES

(FULL CASE)

522 U.S. 252; 118 S. Ct. 673; 139 L. Ed. 2d 686

November 5, 1997, Argued

January 14, 1998, Decided

GIST: When is a firearm not a firearm? When it is a National Firearms Act firearm, a special category of weapons such as silencers, hand grenades and machine guns, which have been strictly controlled by federal tax law since the 1930s. When this case says "firearm" it is generally referring to the nine-inch silencer the defendant was accused of possessing illegally. At issue was the application of *Staples v. United States.* In *Staples,* "knowing possession" of an NFA "firearm" was interpreted to require that the defendant not only knew he possessed the object but that he knew it had all the characteristics that made it a specially-regulated "firearm." The Court sidestepped the issue by dismissing this appeal, because the record in the case did not clearly present a constitutional issue to be decided. In effect, the Justices said they never should have taken the case in the first place (their consent was "improvidently granted.")

JUSTICE STEVENS announced the decision of the Court and delivered an opinion, in which JUSTICE THOMAS, JUSTICE GINSBURG, and JUSTICE BREYER join.

We granted certiorari to decide whether a district court's failure to instruct the jury on an element of an offense is harmless error where, at trial, the defendant admitted that element. Because we have concluded that the question is not fairly presented by the record, we dismiss the writ as improvidently granted.

I

Petitioner was charged with the knowing possession of an unregistered and unserialized firearm described as "a 9" by 1 3/4 " silencer," in violation of 26 U.S.C. §§5861(d) and (i). n1 Although he claimed that he did not know that the item was in a canvas bag found behind the driver's seat in his pickup truck when he was arrested, he candidly acknowledged that he knew it was a silencer. He repeated this admission during questioning by the police and in his testimony at trial; moreover, it was confirmed by his lawyer during argument to the jury.

n1 Section 5861 provides that "it shall be unlawful for any person . . . (d) to receive or possess a firearm which is not registered to him in the National Firearms Registration and Transfer Record; or . . . (i) to receive or possess a firearm which is not identified by a serial number as required by this chapter." Section 5845(a) provides that "the term 'firearm' means . . . (7) any silencer (as defined in section 921 of title 18, United States Code)."

In a separate count petitioner was charged with the unlawful possession of a machine-gun in violation of 18 U.S.C. §922(o). His conviction on that count was reversed on appeal after the Government conceded that the evidence did not establish that petitioner knew that the gun had been modified to act as a fully automatic weapon. 94 F.3d 1519, 1523 (CA11 1996). Reversal was therefore required under Staples v. United States, 511 U.S. 600, 128 L. Ed. 2d 608, 114 S. Ct. 1793 (1994), which was decided after the trial in this case.

Under our decision in Staples v. United States (1994), the mens rea element of a violation of §5861(d) requires the Government to prove that the defendant knew that the item he possessed had the characteristics that brought it within the statutory definition of a firearm. n2 It is not, however, necessary to prove that the defendant knew that his possession was unlawful, or that the firearm was unregistered. United States v. Freed (1971). Thus, in this case, petitioner's admission that he knew the item was a silencer constituted evidence sufficient to satisfy the mens rea element of the charged offenses. He nevertheless submits that his conviction is unconstitutional because, without an instruction from the trial judge defining that element of the offense, there has been no finding by the jury that each of the elements of the offense has been proved beyond a reasonable doubt. Relying on JUSTICE SCALIA's opinion concurring in the judgment in Carella v. California (1989), petitioner contends that "' "the question is not whether guilt may be spelt out of a record, but whether guilt has been found by a jury according to the procedure and standards appropriate for criminal trials."' "

Congress did not intend "to make outlaws of gun owners who were wholly ignorant of the offending characteristics of their weapons"

n2 See 511 U.S. 600 at 602, 114 S. Ct. 1793, 128 L. Ed. 2d 608 (Government must prove that defendant "knew the weapon he possessed had the characteristics that brought it within the statutory definition of a machine-gun"); id., at 604 ("[Section] 5861(d) requires proof that a defendant knew of the characteristics of his weapon that made it a 'firearm' under the Act"); id., at 609 ("[Section] 5861(d) requires the defendant to know of the features that make his weapon a statutory 'firearm'"); id., at 619 ("Thus, to obtain a conviction, the Government should have been required to prove that petitioner knew of the features of his AR-15 that brought it within the scope of the Act"); id., at 620 (Congress did not intend "to make outlaws of gun owners who were wholly ignorant of the offending characteristics of their weapons").

The Court of Appeals for the Eleventh Circuit rejected petitioner's argument and affirmed his conviction. The Court of Appeals reasoned that the failure to give an instruction on an element of the offense can be harmless error if the "omission related to an element of the crime that the defendant in any case admitted," n3 and that in this case petitioner's unequivocal and repeated admissions made it clear that the error was harmless beyond a reasonable doubt. In view of the fact that petitioner's submission relies on the Due Process Clause of the Fifth Amendment and the Sixth Amendment right to a jury trial, as interpreted in cases like In re Winship (1970), and Sullivan v. Louisiana (1993), it is clear that the Court of Appeals decided an important constitutional question. Given our tradition of avoiding the unnecessary or premature adjudication of such questions, we first consider whether the trial judge failed to give the jury an adequate instruction on the mens rea element of the offense.

n3 94 F.3d at 1526. The court also suggested that an instructional omission could be harmless if "the jury has necessarily found certain other predicate facts that are so closely related to the omitted element that no rational jury could find those facts without also finding the element." Ibid.

II

Count 2 of the indictment charged that the petitioner "knowingly" possessed an unregistered firearm, and Count 3 charged that he "knowingly" possessed a firearm that was not properly identified by a serial number. The trial judge denied petitioner's request for an instruction that defined the Government's burden of establishing "'knowing possession'" as proof that "the defendant willfully and consciously possessed items which he knew to be 'firearms.'" Apparently assuming that our holding in Staples required such an instruction, the Court of Appeals concluded that the trial judge's denial "effectively omitted from the instructions an essential element of the crime charged under §5861(d)." For two reasons, we believe this assumption was unwarranted.

First, the tendered instruction was ambiguous. It might have been interpreted to require proof that the defendant knew that his silencer was a "firearm" as defined by the federal statute, not merely that the item possessed certain offending characteristics. Second, and of greater importance, a fair reading of the instructions as actually given did require the jury to find that petitioner knew that he possessed a silencer.

In his objections to the instruction that the trial judge originally proposed as a definition of the §5861(d) offense charged in Count 2, petitioner complained of "a third essential element in there, that being knowledge or knowing." In response, the trial judge inserted the word "knowingly" between the words "Defendant" and "possessed" in the instruction defining the necessary mens rea. n4 In instructing the jury, the judge first explained that the statute defined the term "firearm" to include a silencer. He then instructed the jury that the defendant could not be found guilty without proof beyond a reasonable doubt that "the Defendant knowingly possessed a 'firearm,' as defined above." Since the term "firearm" had been "defined above" to include a silencer, that instruction required the jury to determine that the defendant knew that the item he possessed was a silencer. n5 A comparable instruction was given on Count 3. n6

n4 "THE COURT: You want me to insert knowingly between defendant and possessed in the first element, I don't care.

"MR. SALANTRIE: Sure. That would work.

"THE COURT: Okay." App. 78-79.

n5 JUSTICE KENNEDY argues that our "novel reading of the instruction," post, at 2, differs from the interpretation of the trial judge and petitioner's counsel. He is incorrect. First, as we point out, n. 4, supra, the judge responded to the defense counsel's objection to the proposed instruction by inserting "knowingly."

Second, the "colloquy," post, at 1, between the defense counsel and the trial court concerning the instruction in fact supports our interpretation. A "fair reading of the record," ibid., reveals the following:

The defense counsel begins his objection to the instruction by arguing that the Government must prove that the defendant knew that the law required registration of the silencer. App. 84. After some discussion, the defense counsel, by referencing the holding in United States v. Anderson, 885 F.2d 1248 (CA5 1989) (en banc), shifts his argument to contend that the defendant had to have knowledge of the offending characteristics of the firearm. App. 86. The trial judge responds to this objection as follows:

"THE COURT: If you'll just read the last sentence [of the instruction] you're adequately protected, sir.

"MR. SALANTRIE: It seems the first sentence and the second sentence are mutually exclusive. One says it's not required for him to have knowledge that it's a firearm. The second says it is. It has firearm in quotes.

"THE COURT: Your client has gotten on the stand and testified that he knew instantly that that silencer was a silencer . . . . We could take that sentence out of there.

"MR. SALANTRIE: He didn't say he knew it should be registered." Id., at 87 (emphasis added).

Thus, the trial judge explicitly interpreted the instruction as satisfying the defense counsel's objection concerning the requirement that the defendant have knowledge of the offending characteristics of the firearm. The defense counsel, whose objection continually shifted between arguing that the defendant must know the offending characteristics of the firearm and that the defendant must know that the law requires the firearm to be registered, also agreed that the instruction "required for him to have knowledge that it's a firearm." Ibid. Ultimately, he merely argued that "the first sentence" -- pertaining to knowledge of the registration requirement -- was inconsistent with the requirement that the jury find that the defendant have knowledge of the offending characteristics of the firearm. Ibid.

n6 Id., at 105. In a footnote, the Court of Appeals noted that although the reasoning in Staples only involved §5861(d), it logically applied equally to §5861(i). 94 F.3d at 1524, n. 8.

Petitioner also has called our attention to the instruction which told the jury that it was not necessary for the Government to prove that petitioner knew that the item "was a 'firearm' which the law requires to be registered." Ibid. Given the fact that the jurors had previously been told that a conviction requires that they find that petitioner knew the item was a silencer, this instruction is best read as merely explaining that a conviction did not require the jury to find that the defendant knew that the law required registration of the silencer. Under our decision in Freed, the Government was entitled to such an instruction.

we are satisfied that the instructions as given did inform the jurors that they must find that the defendant knew that the silencer was in fact a silencer.

We assume that the trial judge would have been more explicit in explaining the mens rea element of these offenses if Staples had been decided prior to submitting the case to the jury. However, in this case, we are satisfied that the instructions as given did inform the jurors that they must find that the defendant knew that the silencer was in fact a silencer. n7 We therefore conclude that the record does not fairly present the question that we granted certiorari to address. Accordingly, the writ is dismissed as improvidently granted.

n7 Of course, if the instruction merely required the jury to find that the defendant knowingly possessed a canvas bag, or knowingly possessed a dangerous item that might not have had the characteristics of a silencer, it would not have complied with Staples. Our disposition is based on our view that the instruction required the jury to find that the defendant knew that he possessed a device having all the characteristics of a silencer. It would be wise for trial courts to explain the Staples requirement more carefully than the instruction used in this case to foreclose any possibility that jurors might interpret the instruction as JUSTICE KENNEDY does in his dissent.

It is so ordered.

JUSTICE O'CONNOR, with whom JUSTICE SCALIA joins, concurring in the result.

As the plurality points out, we granted certiorari to address an important issue of constitutional law, and we ought not to decide the question if it has not been cleanly presented. In my view, it is sufficient to dismiss the writ that the instructions tendered by the District Court were ambiguous on whether the jury was asked to find, as is required by Staples v. United States (1994), that petitioner "knew that the item he possessed was a silencer." As a result, it is at least unclear whether the question we intended to address in this case -- whether a district court's failure to instruct the jury on an element of an offense is harmless error where, at trial, the defendant admitted that element -- is squarely presented. For that reason, I concur in the dismissal of the writ as improvidently granted. I share the plurality's concern that trial courts should structure their instructions in cases implicating Staples in a way that prevents the possible interpretation identified by JUSTICE KENNEDY in his dissent.

JUSTICE KENNEDY, with whom THE CHIEF JUSTICE and JUSTICE SOUTER join, dissenting.

The case was submitted to a jury prior to our decision in Staples v. United States, 511 U.S. 600, 128 L. Ed. 2d 608, 114 S. Ct. 1793 (1994), and there was a colloquy between defense counsel and the trial court about whether the Government was required to show the defendant knew the object was a silencer. See, e.g., App. 84-87. A fair reading of the record indicates that, consistent with then-governing Eleventh Circuit precedent, see 94 F.3d 1519, 1523, n. 7 (1996), the trial court ruled this knowledge was not a necessary part of the Government's case.

Under the trial court's instructions, the defendant could be found guilty if he "knowingly possessed a 'firearm,' as defined above." App. 104. The word "knowingly" in the instruction modifies the word which follows it, viz., "possessed," rather than the instruction's further reference to the statutory definition of "firearm." Although in other circumstances one might argue the instruction was ambiguous, here the trial court agreed with the defendant's understanding of it. The trial court explained to the jury: "What must be proved beyond a reasonable doubt is that the Defendant knowingly possessed the item as charged, that such item was a 'firearm' as defined above, and that [it] was not then registered to the Defendant in the National Firearms Registration and Transfer Record." Ibid. As understood by the trial court, ibid., petitioner's counsel, Brief for Petitioner 2, the Solicitor General, Brief for United States 12, and the Court of Appeals, 94 F.3d 1519 at 1523, the instruction told the jury it had to find the defendant knew he possessed the device in question but not that he knew it was a silencer.

The plurality proceeds, however, to find not even that the instruction was ambiguous, but that it was a satisfactory implementation of our later-announced decision in Staples. And, though the Court in the end does nothing more than order the case dismissed, the plurality by its extensive discussion suggests in effect that all convictions based on this form of instruction must be affirmed. This is a substantive point; it was neither briefed nor argued; it is contrary to a common-sense reading of the instruction; and it tends to diminish the force of Staples itself.

If the plurality wishes to persist in its interpretation of the instruction, it ought to issue a full opinion addressing the merits of the conviction, rather than mask a substantive determination in its opinion supporting dismissal. As things stand, it brings little credit to us to get rid of the case by a strained and novel reading of the instruction -- a reading quite unsupportable on the record -- after we granted certiorari and expended the Court's resources to determine a different and important issue of substantive criminal law. The petitioner, whose conviction now stands based on what is for practical purposes an affirmance on a theory no one has suggested until now, will be hard put to understand the plurality's cavalier refusal to address his substantive arguments.

I dissent from the order dismissing the case.

SPENCER v. KEMNA

(CASE EXCERPT)
523 U.S. 1; 118 S. Ct. 978; 140 L. Ed. 2d 43
November 12, 1997, Argued
March 3, 1998, Decided

GIST: The Court dismissed as moot Spencer's challenge to two felony convictions because his sentence had already expired and he failed to demonstrate any continuing injury. Justice Stevens, dissenting, would have found continuing injury for Spencer because the felony record results in the loss of the right to vote and to bear arms, as well as the possibility of an enhanced sentence for any future crime.

JUSTICE STEVENS, dissenting.

An official determination that a person has committed a crime may cause two different kinds of injury. It may result in tangible harms such as imprisonment, loss of the right to vote or to bear arms, and the risk of greater punishment if another crime is committed.

An official determination that a person has committed a crime may cause two different kinds of injury. It may result in tangible harms such as imprisonment, loss of the right to vote or to bear arms, and the risk of greater punishment if another crime is committed. It may also severely injure the person's reputation and good name.

In holding that petitioner's case is moot, the Court relies heavily on our opinion in Lane v. Williams. Lane, however, is inapposite. In Lane, the respondents did not seek to challenge the factual findings underlying their parole revocations. Instead, they simply sought to challenge their sentences; yet because they had been released by the time the case reached us, the case was moot. "Through the mere passage of time, respondents had obtained all the relief that they sought."

In this case, petitioner challenges the factual findings on which his parole revocation was based. His parole was revoked based on an official determination that he committed the crime of forcible rape. n1 Assuming, as the Court does, that he had standing to bring that challenge while he remained in prison, the mootness question, as framed by the Court, is whether he continues to have "a personal stake in the outcome of the lawsuit" that is likely to be redressed by a favorable decision.

n1 Throughout the parole revocation proceedings, it was alleged that petitioner violated three parole conditions: Parole Condition # 1, because he allegedly was guilty of rape; Parole Condition # 6, because he allegedly used or possessed crack cocaine; and Parole Condition # 7, because he allegedly used or possessed a dangerous weapon (i.e., the screwdriver allegedly used during the rape). App. 60-64 (alleging violations of Conditions # 1, # 6, and # 7); App. id., at 72-76 (same); App. id., at 112-114 (alleging violations of Conditions # 1 and # 6). Thus, when the parole revocation board declared, "after careful consideration of evidence presented," that petitioner violated Parole Conditions # 1, # 6, and # 7, App. id., at 55-56, it found that petitioner was guilty of forcible rape. See also Brief for Respondents 1 ("Spencer violated condition # 1 by committing the crime of rape"). In addition, even apart from the rape finding, it is undisputed that the board found that petitioner used or possessed drugs, and that he used or possessed a dangerous weapon (which was only alleged to have been used during the rape). App. 55-56.

BOUSLEY v. UNITED STATES

(CASE EXCERPT)

523 U.S. 614; 118 S. Ct. 1604; 140 L. Ed. 2d 828

March 3, 1998, Argued

May 18, 1998, Decided

GIST: Bousley pled guilty to using a firearm during and in relation to a drug-trafficking crime. This case challenges the constitutionality of the guilty plea, arguing that under *Bailey v. United States,* there was no factual basis for Bousley's guilty plea, because he did not "use" the firearm as defined by law. The Court held that if Bousley were able to demonstrate that he did not "use" a firearm in relation to the drug offense, he would be entitled to challenge the guilty plea.

CHIEF JUSTICE REHNQUIST delivered the opinion of the Court.

Petitioner pleaded guilty to "using" a firearm in violation of 18 U.S.C. §924(c)(1) in 1990. Five years later we held in Bailey v. United States (1995), that §924(c)(1)'s "use" prong requires the Government to show "active employment of the firearm." Petitioner meanwhile had sought collateral relief under 28 U.S.C. §2255, claiming that his guilty plea was not knowing and intelligent because he was misinformed by the District Court as to the nature of the charged crime. We hold that, although this claim was procedurally defaulted, petitioner may be entitled to a hearing on the merits of it if he makes the necessary showing to relieve the default.

Following his arrest in March 1990, petitioner was charged with possession of methamphetamine with intent to distribute, in violation of 21 U.S.C. §841(a)(1). A superseding indictment added the charge that he "knowingly and intentionally used . . . firearms during and in relation to a drug trafficking crime," in violation of 18 U.S.C. §924(c). Petitioner agreed to plead guilty to both charges while reserving the right to challenge the quantity of drugs used in calculating his sentence.

The District Court accepted petitioner's pleas, finding that he was "competent to enter [the] pleas, that [they were] voluntarily entered, and that there [was] a factual basis for them." Following a sentencing hearing, the District Court sentenced petitioner to 78 months' imprisonment on the drug count, a consecutive term of 60 months' imprisonment on the §924(c) count, and four years of supervised release. Petitioner appealed his sentence, but did not challenge the validity of his plea. The Court of Appeals affirmed.

petitioner sought a writ of habeas corpus under 28 U.S.C. §2241, challenging the factual basis for his guilty plea on the ground that neither the "evidence" nor the "plea allocution" showed a "connection between the firearms in the bedroom of the house, and the garage, where the drug trafficking occurred."

In June 1994, petitioner sought a writ of habeas corpus under 28 U.S.C. §2241, challenging the factual basis for his guilty plea on the ground that neither the "evidence" nor the "plea allocution" showed a "connection between the firearms in the bedroom of the house, and the garage, where the drug trafficking occurred." A magistrate judge recommended that the petition be treated as a motion under 28 U.S.C. §2255 and recommended dismissal, concluding that there was a factual basis for petitioner's guilty plea because the guns in petitioner's bedroom were in close proximity to drugs and were readily accessible. The District Court adopted the magistrate judge's Report and Recommendation and ordered that the petition be dismissed.

we held in Bailey that a conviction for use of a firearm under §924(c)(1) requires the Government to show "active employment of the firearm." As we explained, active employment includes uses such as "brandishing, displaying, bartering, striking with, and, most obviously, firing or attempting to fire" the weapon, but does not include mere possession of a firearm.

Thus, a "defendant cannot be charged under §924(c)(1) merely for storing a weapon

near drugs or drug proceeds," or for "placement of a firearm to provide a sense of security or to embolden."

Petitioner appealed. While his appeal was pending, we held in Bailey that a conviction for use of a firearm under §924(c)(1) requires the Government to show "active employment of the firearm." As we explained, active employment includes uses such as "brandishing, displaying, bartering, striking with, and, most obviously, firing or attempting to fire" the weapon, but does not include mere possession of a firearm. Thus, a "defendant cannot be charged under §924(c)(1) merely for storing a weapon near drugs or drug proceeds," or for "placement of a firearm to provide a sense of security or to embolden."

Following our decision in Bailey, the Court of Appeals appointed counsel to represent petitioner. Counsel argued that Bailey should be applied "retroactively," that petitioner's guilty plea was involuntary because he was misinformed about the elements of a §924(c)(1) offense, that this claim was not waived by his guilty plea, and that his conviction should therefore be vacated. Nevertheless, the Court of Appeals affirmed the District Court's order of dismissal.

We then granted certiorari to resolve a split among the Circuits over the permissibility of post-Bailey collateral attacks on §924(c)(1) convictions obtained pursuant to guilty pleas. Because the Government disagreed with the Court of Appeals' analysis, we appointed amicus curiae to brief and argue the case in support of the judgment below.

A plea of guilty is constitutionally valid only to the extent it is "voluntary" and "intelligent." Brady v. United States (1970). We have long held that a plea does not qualify as intelligent unless a criminal defendant first receives "real notice of the true nature of the charge against him, the first and most universally recognized requirement of due process." Smith v. O'Grady (1941). Amicus contends that petitioner's plea was intelligently made because, prior to pleading guilty, he was provided with a copy of his indictment, which charged him with "using" a firearm. Such circumstances, standing alone, give rise to a presumption that the defendant was informed of the nature of the charge against him. Henderson v. Morgan (1976). Petitioner nonetheless maintains that his guilty plea was unintelligent because the District Court subsequently misinformed him as to the elements of a §924(c)(1) offense. In other words, petitioner contends that the record reveals that neither he, nor his counsel, nor the court correctly understood the essential elements of the crime with which he was charged. Were this contention proven, petitioner's plea would be, contrary to the view expressed by the Court of Appeals, constitutionally invalid.

.....

petitioner need demonstrate no more than that he did not "use" a firearm as that term is defined in Bailey.

In this case, the Government maintains that petitioner must demonstrate that he is actually innocent of both "using" and "carrying" a firearm in violation of §924(c)(1). But petitioner's indictment charged him only with "using" firearms in violation of §924(c)(1). And there is no record evidence that the Government elected not to charge petitioner with "carrying" a firearm in exchange for his plea of guilty. Accordingly, petitioner need demonstrate no more than that he did not "use" a firearm as that term is defined in Bailey.

If, on remand, petitioner can make that showing, he will then be entitled to have his defaulted claim of an unintelligent plea considered on its merits. The judgment of the Court of Appeals is therefore reversed, and the case is remanded for further proceedings consistent with this opinion.

MUSCARELLO v. UNITED STATES

(FULL CASE)

524 U.S. 125; 118 S. Ct. 1911; 141 L. Ed. 2d 111

Argued March 23, 1998

June 8, 1998, Decided

GIST: The Court was again called upon to interpret the federal gun law imposing a mandatory 5-year sentence for using or carrying a firearm in relation to a drug-trafficking crime. Three drug dealers had brought guns along to their deals, but weren't "packing" (the Court's word), they kept the guns in their cars. As a defense, they claimed they weren't actually "carrying," and the Court examined the language of the statute. The Court held that the phrase "carries a firearm" is not limited to carrying a gun on yourself, and includes guns carried in a trunk or locked compartment of your car. They found no difference in the dangerousness of a drug dealer with a gun tucked in a pocket, and a drug dealer with a gun in the trunk.

The clearest legal error detected in any of the Court's decisions compiled in *Supreme Court Gun Cases* appears in this case. Five paragraphs from the end, the majority, relying upon a citation that is off by a single character (the (4) in 18 U.S.C. 921(a)(4)(A) should be a (3)), incorrectly define firearms as destructive devices (grenades, bombs, missiles, rockets and similar), and draw a wholly erroneous conclusion on that basis. The error though, falls in a minor additional argument for their case, and had no discernable effect on the outcome.

In one of the juiciest dissents in all the cases in this book, two quite liberal Justices (Ginsburg and Souter) join two quite conservative Justices (Rehnquist and Scalia) to mock the majority's use of the Bible, great authors and newspaper clippings to make its argument. While the majority holds that the use of the word "carry" in this case is clearly defined, the dissenters carry on until they pretty clearly prove it's not that clear. The citation from the TV show "M*A*S*H" is a contender for one of the most striking phrases in any decision in *Supreme Court Gun Cases* (and perhaps in much of TV too).

Finally, the case includes what may be the most remarkable remark by a politician whose comments enjoyed the unusual honor of inclusion in a published majority decision. Rep. Poff, the chief legislative sponsor of the section about carrying guns while drug trafficking, said in 1968 that the provision seeks "to persuade the man who is tempted to commit a Federal felony to leave his gun at home." The Court was sufficiently enamored of this line to say it six times (three by Poff, and three by other Congressmen). In reply, the dissenters point out that Poff's very next sentence, omitted by the majority, erases the conclusion the Court drew. You just gotta love it.

JUSTICE BREYER delivered the opinion of the Court.

The question before us is whether the phrase "carries a firearm" is limited to the carrying of firearms on the person. We hold that it is not so limited. Rather, it also applies to a person who knowingly possesses and conveys firearms in a vehicle, including in the locked glove compartment or trunk of a car, which the person accompanies.

A provision in the firearms chapter of the federal criminal code imposes a 5-year mandatory prison term upon a person who "uses or carries a firearm" "during and in relation to" a "drug trafficking crime." 18 U.S.C. §924(c)(1). The question before us is whether the phrase "carries a firearm" is limited to the carrying of firearms on the person. We hold that it is not so limited. Rather, it also applies to a person who knowingly possesses and conveys firearms in a vehicle, including in the locked glove compartment or trunk of a car, which the person accompanies.

The question arises in two cases, which we have consolidated for argument. The defendant in the first case, Frank J. Muscarello, unlawfully sold marijuana, which he carried in his truck to the place of sale. Police officers found a handgun locked in the truck's glove compartment. During plea proceedings, Muscarello admitted that he had "carried" the gun "for protection in relation" to the drug offense, though he later claimed to the contrary, and added that, in any event, his "carrying" of the gun in the glove compartment did not fall within the scope of the statutory word "carries."

The defendants in the second case, Donald Cleveland and Enrique Gray-Santana, placed several guns in a bag, put the bag in the trunk of a car, and then traveled by car to a proposed drug-sale point, where they intended to steal drugs from the sellers. Federal agents at the scene stopped them, searched the cars, found the guns and drugs, and arrested them.

In both cases the Courts of Appeals found that the defendants had "carried" the guns during and in relation to a drug trafficking offense. We granted certiorari to determine whether the fact that the guns were found in the locked glove compartment, or the trunk, of a car, precludes application of §924(c)(1). We conclude that it does not.

II

A

Although the word "carry" has many different meanings, only two are relevant here. When one uses the word in the first, or primary, meaning, one can, as a matter of ordinary English, "carry firearms" in a wagon, car, truck, or other vehicle that one accompanies. When one uses the word in a different, rather special, way, to mean, for example, "bearing" or (in slang) "packing" (as in "packing a gun"), the matter is less clear.

We begin with the statute's language. The parties vigorously contest the ordinary English meaning of the phrase "carries a firearm." Because they essentially agree that Congress intended the phrase to convey its ordinary, and not some special legal, meaning, and because they argue the linguistic point at length, we too have looked into the matter in more than usual depth. Although the word "carry" has many different meanings, only two are relevant here. When one uses the word in the first, or primary, meaning, one can, as a matter of ordinary English, "carry firearms" in a wagon, car, truck, or other vehicle that one accompanies. When one uses the word in a different, rather special, way, to mean, for example, "bearing" or (in slang) "packing" (as in "packing a gun"), the matter is less clear. But, for reasons we shall set out below, we believe Congress intended to use the word in its primary sense and not in this latter, special way.

Consider first the word's primary meaning. The Oxford English Dictionary gives as its first definition "convey, originally by cart or wagon, hence in any vehicle, by ship, on horseback, etc." 2 Oxford English Dictionary 919 (2d ed. 1989); see also Webster's Third New International Dictionary 343 (1986) (first definition: "move while supporting (as in a vehicle or in one's hands or arms)"); The Random House Dictionary of the English Language Unabridged 319 (2d ed. 1987) (first definition: "to take or support from one place to another; convey; transport").

The origin of the word "carries" explains why the first, or basic, meaning of the word "carry" includes conveyance in a vehicle.

The origin of the word "carries" explains why the first, or basic, meaning of the word "carry" includes conveyance in a vehicle. See The Barnhart Dictionary of Etymology 146 (1988) (tracing the word from Latin "carum," which means "car" or "cart"); 2 Oxford English Dictionary, supra, at 919 (tracing the word from Old French "carier" and the late Latin "carricare," which meant to "convey in a car"); The Oxford Dictionary of English Etymology 148 (C. Onions ed. 1966) (same); The Barnhart Dictionary of Etymology, supra, at 143 (explaining that the term "car" has been used to refer to the automobile since 1896).

The greatest of writers have used the word with this meaning.

The greatest of writers have used the word with this meaning. See, e.g., the King James Bible, 2 Kings 9:28 ("His servants carried him in a chariot to Jerusalem"); id., Isaiah 30:6 ("They will carry their riches upon the shoulders of young asses"). Robinson Crusoe says, "with my boat, I carry'd away every Thing." D. Defoe, Robinson Crusoe 174 (J. Crowley ed. 1972). And the owners of Queequeg's ship, Melville writes, "had lent him a [wheelbarrow], in which to carry his heavy chest to his boarding-house." H. Melville, Moby Dick 43 (U. Chicago 1952). This Court, too, has spoken of the "carrying" of drugs in a car or in its "trunk." California v. Acevedo (1991); Florida v. Jimeno (1991).

These examples do not speak directly about carrying guns. But there is nothing linguistically special about the fact that weapons, rather than drugs, are being carried. Robinson Crusoe might have carried a gun in his boat

we have surveyed modern press usage, albeit crudely, by searching computerized newspaper databases

We looked for sentences in which the words "carry," "vehicle," and "weapon" (or variations thereof) all appear. We found thousands of such sentences, and random sampling suggests that many, perhaps more than one third, are sentences used to convey the meaning at issue here, i.e., the carrying of guns in a car.

These examples do not speak directly about carrying guns. But there is nothing linguistically special about the fact that weapons, rather than drugs, are being carried. Robinson Crusoe might have carried a gun in his boat; Queequeg might have borrowed a wheelbarrow in which to carry, not a chest, but a harpoon. And, to make certain that there is no special ordinary English restriction (unmentioned in dictionaries) upon the use of "carry" in respect to guns, we have surveyed modern press usage, albeit crudely, by searching computerized newspaper databases -- both the New York Times database in Lexis/Nexis, and the "US News" database in Westlaw. We looked for sentences in which the words "carry," "vehicle," and "weapon" (or variations thereof) all appear. We found thousands of such sentences, and random sampling suggests that many, perhaps more than one third, are sentences used to convey the meaning at issue here, i.e., the carrying of guns in a car.

The New York Times, for example, writes about "an ex-con" who "arrives home driving a stolen car and carrying a load of handguns," Mar. 21, 1992, section 1, p. 18, col. 1, and an "official peace officer who carries a shotgun in his boat," June 19, 1988, section 12WC, p. 2, col. 1; cf. The New York Times Manual of Style and Usage, a Desk Book of Guidelines for Writers and Editors, foreword (L. Jordan rev. ed. 1976) (restricting Times journalists and editors to the use of proper English). The Boston Globe refers to the arrest of a professional baseball player "for carrying a semiloaded automatic weapon in his car." Dec. 10, 1994, p. 75, col. 5. The Colorado Springs Gazette Telegraph speaks of one "Russell" who "carries a gun hidden in his car." May 2, 1993, p. B1, col. 2. The Arkansas Gazette refers to a "house" that was "searched" in an effort to find "items that could be carried in a car, such as . . . guns." Mar. 10, 1991, p. A1, col. 2. The San Diego Union-Tribune asks, "What, do they carry guns aboard these boats now?" Feb. 18, 1992, p. D2, col. 5.

Now consider a different, somewhat special meaning of the word "carry"—a meaning upon which the linguistic arguments of petitioners and the dissent must rest. The Oxford English Dictionary's twenty-sixth definition of "carry" is "bear, wear, hold up, or sustain, as one moves about; habitually to bear about with one."

Black's Law Dictionary defines the entire phrase "carry arms or weapons" as "To wear, bear or carry them upon the person or in the clothing or in a pocket, for the purpose of use, or for the purpose of being armed and ready for offensive or defensive action in case of a conflict with another person."

Now consider a different, somewhat special meaning of the word "carry" -- a meaning upon which the linguistic arguments of petitioners and the dissent must rest. The Oxford English Dictionary's twenty-sixth definition of "carry" is "bear, wear, hold up, or sustain, as one moves about; habitually to bear about with one." 2 Oxford English Dictionary, supra, at 921. Webster's defines "carry" as "to move while supporting," not just in a vehicle, but also "in one's hands or arms." Webster's Third New International Dictionary, supra, at 343. And Black's Law Dictionary defines the entire phrase "carry arms or weapons" as

"To wear, bear or carry them upon the person or in the clothing or in a pocket, for the purpose of use, or for the purpose of being armed and ready for offensive or defensive action in case of a conflict with another person." Black's Law Dictionary 214 (6th ed. 1990).

No one doubts that one who bears arms on his person "carries a weapon." But to say that is not to deny that one may also "carry a weapon" tied to the saddle of a horse or placed in a bag in a car.

These special definitions, however, do not purport to limit the "carrying of arms" to the circumstances they describe. No one doubts that one who bears arms on his person "carries a weapon." But to say that is not to deny that one may also "carry a weapon" tied to the saddle of a horse or placed in a bag in a car.

In this sense a gangster might "carry" a gun (in colloquial language, he might "pack a gun") even though he does not move from his chair.

Nor is there any linguistic reason to think that Congress intended to limit the word "carries" in the statute to any of these special definitions. To the contrary, all these special definitions embody a form of an important, but secondary, meaning of "carry," a meaning that suggests support rather than movement or transportation, as when, for example, a column "carries" the weight of an arch. 2 Oxford English Dictionary, supra, at 919, 921. In this sense a gangster might "carry" a gun (in colloquial language, he might "pack a gun") even though he does not move from his chair. It is difficult to believe, however, that Congress intended to limit the statutory word to this definition -- imposing special punishment upon the comatose gangster while ignoring drug lords who drive to a sale carrying an arsenal of weapons in their van.

We recognize, as the dissent emphasizes, that the word "carry" has other meanings as well. But those other meanings, (e.g., "carry all he knew," "carries no colours"), are not relevant here. And the fact that speakers often do not add to the phrase "carry a gun" the words "in a car" is of no greater relevance here than the fact that millions of Americans did not see Muscarello carry a gun in his car. The relevant linguistic facts are that the word "carry" in its ordinary sense includes carrying in a car and that the word, used in its ordinary sense, keeps the same meaning whether one carries a gun, a suitcase, or a banana.

Given the ordinary meaning of the word "carry," it is not surprising to find that the Federal Circuit Courts of Appeals have unanimously concluded that "carry" is not limited to the carrying of weapons directly on the person but can include their carriage in a car.

Given the ordinary meaning of the word "carry," it is not surprising to find that the Federal Circuit Courts of Appeals have unanimously concluded that "carry" is not limited to the carrying of weapons directly on the person but can include their carriage in a car.

B

We conclude that neither the statute's basic purpose nor its legislative history support circumscribing the scope of the word "carry" by applying an "on the person" limitation.

We now explore more deeply the purely legal question of whether Congress intended to use the word "carry" in its ordinary sense, or whether it intended to limit the scope of the phrase to instances in which a gun is carried "on the person." We conclude that neither the statute's basic purpose nor its legislative history support circumscribing the scope of the word "carry" by applying an "on the person" limitation.

This Court has described the statute's basic purpose broadly, as an effort to combat the "dangerous combination" of "drugs and guns."

the provision's chief legislative sponsor has said that the provision seeks "to persuade the man who is tempted to commit a Federal felony to leave his gun at home."

This Court has described the statute's basic purpose broadly, as an effort to combat the "dangerous combination" of "drugs and guns." Smith v. United States (1993). And the provision's chief legislative sponsor has said that the provision seeks "to persuade the man who is tempted to commit a Federal felony to leave his gun at home." 114 Cong. Rec. 22231 (1968) (Rep. Poff); see Busic v. United States (1980) (describing Poff's comments as "crucial material" in interpreting the purpose of §924(c)); Simpson v. United States (1978) (concluding that Poff's comments are "clearly probative" and "certainly entitled to weight"); see also 114 Cong. Rec. 22243-22244 (statutes would apply to "the man who goes out taking a gun to commit a crime") (Rep. Hunt); id., at 22244 ("Of course, what we are trying to do by these penalties is to persuade the criminal to leave his gun at home") (Rep. Randall); id., at 22236 ("We are concerned . . . with having the criminal leave his gun at home") (Rep. Meskill).

It is difficult to say that, considered as a class, those who prepare, say, to sell drugs by placing guns in their cars are less dangerous, or less deserving of punishment, than those who carry handguns on their person.

From the perspective of any such purpose (persuading a criminal "to leave his gun at home") what sense would it make for this statute to penalize one who walks with a gun in a bag to the site of a drug sale, but to ignore a similar individual who, like defendant Gray-Santana, travels to a similar site with a similar gun in a similar bag, but instead of walking, drives there with the gun in his car? How persuasive is a punishment that is without effect until a drug dealer who has brought his gun to a sale (indeed has it available for use) actually takes it from the trunk (or unlocks the glove compartment) of his car? It is difficult to say that, considered as a class, those who prepare, say, to sell drugs by placing guns in their cars are less dangerous, or less deserving of punishment, than those who carry handguns on their person.

We have found no significant indication elsewhere in the legislative history of any more narrowly focused relevant purpose. We have found an instance in which a legislator referred to the statute as applicable when an individual "has a firearm on his person," Ibid. (Rep. Meskill); an instance in which a legislator speaks of "a criminal who takes a gun in his hand," id., at 22239 (Rep. Pucinski); and a reference in the Senate Report to a "gun carried in a pocket." S. Rep No. 98-225, p. 314, n. 10 (1983); see also 114 Cong. Rec. 21788, 21789 (1968) (references to gun "carrying" without more). But in these instances no one purports to define the scope of the term "carries": and the examples of guns carried on the person are not used to illustrate the reach of the term "carries" but to illustrate, or to criticize, a different aspect of the statute.

One legislator indicates that the statute responds in part to the concerns of law enforcement personnel, who had urged that "carrying short firearms in motor vehicles be classified as carrying such weapons concealed."

Regardless, in other instances, legislators suggest that the word "carries" has a broader scope. One legislator indicates that the statute responds in part to the concerns of law enforcement personnel, who had urged that "carrying short firearms in motor vehicles be classified as carrying such weapons concealed." Id., at 22242 (Rep. May). Another criticizes a version of the proposed statute by suggesting it might apply to drunken driving, and gives as an example a drunken driver who has a "gun in his car." Id., at 21792 (Rep. Yates). Others describe the statute as criminalizing gun "possession" -- a term that could stretch beyond both the "use" of a gun and the carrying of a gun on the person. See id., at 21793 (Rep. Casey); id., at 22236 (Rep. Meskill); id., at 30584 (Rep. Collier); id., at 30585 (Rep. Skubitz).

C

We are not convinced by petitioners' remaining arguments to the contrary. First, they say that our definition of "carry" makes it the equivalent of "transport." Yet, Congress elsewhere in related statutes used the word "transport" deliberately to signify a different, and broader, statutory coverage. The immediately preceding statutory subsection, for example, imposes a different set of penalties on one who, with an intent to commit a crime, "ships, transports, or receives a firearm" in interstate commerce. 18 U.S.C. §924(b). Moreover, §926A specifically "entitles" a person "not otherwise prohibited . . . from transporting, shipping, or receiving a firearm" to "transport a firearm . . . from any place where he may lawfully possess and carry" it to "any other place" where he may do so. Why, petitioners ask, would Congress have used the word "transport," or used both "carry" and "transport" in the same provision, if it had intended to obliterate the distinction between the two?

The short answer is that our definition does not equate "carry" and "transport." "Carry" implies personal agency and some degree of possession, whereas "transport" does not have such a limited connotation and, in addition, implies the movement of goods in bulk over great distances. See Webster's Third New International Dictionary 343 (noting that "carry" means "moving to a location some distance away while supporting or maintaining off the ground" and "is a natural word to use in ref. to cargoes and loads on trucks, wagons, planes, ships, or even beasts of burden," while "transport refers to carriage in bulk or number over an appreciable distance and, typically, by a customary or usual carrier agency"); see also Webster's Dictionary of Synonyms 141 (1942). If Smith, for example, calls a parcel delivery service, which sends a truck to Smith's house to pick up Smith's package and take it to Los Angeles, one might say that Smith has shipped the package and the parcel delivery service has transported the package. But only the truck driver has "carried" the package in the sense of "carry" that we believe Congress intended. Therefore, "transport" is a broader category that includes "carry" but also encompasses other activity.

The dissent refers to §926A and to another statute where Congress used the word "transport" rather than "carry" to describe the movement of firearms. 18 U.S.C. §§925(a)(2)(B); post, at 8-9. According to the dissent, had Congress intended "carry" to have the meaning we give it, Congress would not have needed to use a different word in these provisions. But as we have discussed above, we believe the word "transport" is broader than the word "carry."

And, if Congress intended "carry" to have the limited definition the dissent contends, it would have been quite unnecessary to add the proviso in §926A requiring a person, to be exempt from penalties, to store her firearm in a locked container not immediately accessible. See §926A (quoted in full at post, 8-9) (exempting from criminal penalties one who transports a firearm from a place where "he may lawfully possess and carry such firearm" but not exempting the "transportation" of a firearm if it is "readily accessible or is directly accessible from the passenger compartment of transporting vehicle"). The statute simply could have said that such a person may not "carry" a firearm. But, of course, Congress did not say this because that is not what "carry" means.

As we interpret the statutory scheme, it makes sense. Congress has imposed a variable penalty with no mandatory minimum sentence upon a person who "transports" (or "ships" or "receives") a firearm knowing it will be used to commit any "offense punishable by imprisonment for [more than] . . . one year," §924(b), and it has imposed a 5-year mandatory minimum sentence upon one who "carries" a firearm "during and in relation to" a "drug trafficking crime," §924(c). The first subsection imposes a less strict sentencing regime upon one who, say, ships firearms by mail for use in a crime elsewhere; the latter subsection imposes a mandatory sentence upon one who, say, brings a weapon with him (on his person or in his car) to the site of a drug sale.

Second, petitioners point out that, in Bailey v. United States (1995), we considered the related phrase "uses . . . a firearm" found in the same statutory provision now before us. See 18 U.S.C. §924(c)(1) ("uses or carries a firearm"). We construed the term "use" narrowly, limiting its application to the "active employment" of a firearm. Petitioners argue that it would be anomalous to construe broadly the word "carries," its statutory next-door neighbor.

In Bailey, however, we limited "use" of a firearm to "active employment" in part because we assumed "that Congress . . . intended each term to have a particular, non-superfluous meaning." A broader interpretation of "use," we said, would have swallowed up the term "carry." But "carry" as we interpret that word does not swallow up the term "use." "Use" retains the same independent meaning we found for it in Bailey, where we provided examples involving the displaying or the bartering of a gun. "Carry" also retains an independent meaning, for, under Bailey, carrying a gun in a car does not necessarily involve the gun's "active employment." More importantly, having construed "use" narrowly in Bailey, we cannot also construe "carry" narrowly without undercutting the statute's basic objective. For the narrow interpretation would remove the act of carrying a gun in a car entirely from the statute's reach, leaving a gap in coverage that we do not believe Congress intended.

They <petitioners> add that some lower courts, thinking approximately the same, have limited the scope of "carries" to instances where a gun in a car is immediately accessible, thereby most likely excluding from coverage a gun carried in a car's trunk or locked glove compartment.

Third, petitioners say that our reading of the statute would extend its coverage to passengers on buses, trains, or ships, who have placed a firearm, say, in checked luggage. To extend this statute so far, they argue, is unfair, going well beyond what Congress likely would have thought possible. They add that some lower courts, thinking approximately the same, have limited the scope of "carries" to instances where a gun in a car is immediately accessible, thereby most likely excluding from coverage a gun carried in a car's trunk or locked glove compartment. See, e.g., Foster, 133 F.3d at 708 (concluding that person "carries" a firearm in a car only if the firearm is immediately accessible); Giraldo, 80 F.3d at 676 (same).

In our view, this argument does not take adequate account of other limiting words in the statute—words that make the statute applicable only where a defendant "carries" a gun both "during and in relation to" a drug crime.

In our view, this argument does not take adequate account of other limiting words in the statute -- words that make the statute applicable only where a defendant "carries" a gun both "during and in relation to" a drug crime. §924(c)(1) (emphasis added). Congress added these words in part to prevent prosecution where guns "played" no part in the crime. See S. Rep. No. 98-225, at 314, n. 10; cf. United States v. Stewart, 779 F.2d 538, 539 (CA9 1985) (Kennedy, J.) (observing that "'in relation to'" was "added to allay explicitly the concern that a person could be prosecuted . . . for committing an entirely unrelated crime while in possession of a firearm"), overruled in part on other grounds, United States v. Hernandez, 80 F.3d 1253, 1257 (CA9 1996).

Once one takes account of the words "during" and "in relation to," it no longer seems beyond Congress' likely intent, or otherwise unfair, to interpret the statute as we have done. If one carries a gun in a car "during" and "in relation to" a drug sale, for example, the fact that the gun is carried in the car's trunk or locked glove compartment seems not only logically difficult to distinguish from the immediately accessible gun, but also beside the point.

On petitioners' reading, the "carry" provision would not apply to instances where drug lords, engaged in a major transaction, took with them "firearms" such as these, which most likely could not be carried on the person.

At the same time, the narrow interpretation creates its own anomalies. The statute, for example, defines "firearm" to include a "bomb," "grenade," "rocket having a propellant charge of more than four ounces," or "missile having an explosive or incendiary charge of more than one-quarter ounce," where such device is "explosive," "incendiary," or delivers "poison gas." 18 U.S.C. §921(a)(4)(A). On petitioners' reading, the "carry" provision would not apply to instances where drug lords, engaged in a major transaction, took with them "firearms" such as these, which most likely could not be carried on the person.

petitioners argue that we should construe the word "carry" to mean "immediately accessible." And, as we have said, they point out that several Circuit Courts of Appeals have limited the statute's scope in this way. That interpretation, however, is difficult to square with the statute's language, for one "carries" a gun in the glove compartment whether or not that glove compartment is locked.

Fourth, petitioners argue that we should construe the word "carry" to mean "immediately accessible." And, as we have said, they point out that several Circuit Courts of Appeals have limited the statute's scope in this way. That interpretation, however, is difficult to square with the statute's language, for one "carries" a gun in the glove compartment whether or not that glove compartment is locked. Nothing in the statute's history suggests that Congress intended that limitation. And, for reasons pointed out above, we believe that the words "during" and "in relation to" will limit the statute's application to the harms that Congress foresaw.

Finally, petitioners and the dissent invoke the "rule of lenity." The simple existence of some statutory ambiguity, however, is not sufficient to warrant application of that rule, for most statutes are ambiguous to some degree. Cf. Smith, 508 U.S. at 239 ("The mere possibility of articulating a narrower construction . . . does not by itself make the rule of lenity applicable"). "'The rule of lenity applies only if, "after seizing everything from which aid can be derived," . . . we can make "no more than a guess as to what Congress intended."' " United States v. Wells (1997) (quoting Reno v. Koray (1995), Smith, supra, at 239, and Ladner v. United States (1958)). To invoke the rule, we must conclude that there is a "'grievous ambiguity or uncertainty' in the statute." Staples v. United States (1994) (quoting Chapman v. United States (1991)). Certainly, our decision today is based on much more than a "guess as to what Congress intended," and there is no "grievous ambiguity" here. The problem of statutory interpretation in this case is indeed no different from that in many of the criminal cases that confront us. Yet, this Court has never held that the rule of lenity automatically permits a defendant to win.

In sum, the "generally accepted contemporary meaning" of the word "carry" includes the carrying of a firearm in a vehicle. The purpose of this statute warrants its application in such circumstances. The limiting phrase "during and in relation to" should prevent misuse of the statute to penalize those whose conduct does not create the risks of harm at which the statute aims.

For these reasons, we conclude that the petitioners' conduct falls within the scope of the phrase "carries a firearm." The decisions of the Courts of Appeals are affirmed.

It is so ordered.

JUSTICE GINSBURG, with whom THE CHIEF JUSTICE <REHNQUIST>, JUSTICE SCALIA, and JUSTICE SOUTER join, dissenting.

Section 924(c)(1) of Title 18, United States Code, is a punishment-enhancing provision; it imposes a mandatory five-year prison term when the defendant "during and in relation to any crime of violence or drug trafficking . . . uses or carries a firearm." In Bailey v. United States (1995), this Court held that the term "uses," in the context of §924(c)(1), means "active employment" of the firearm. In today's cases we confront a related question: What does the term "carries" mean in the context of §924(c)(1), the enhanced punishment prescription again at issue.

It is uncontested that §924(c)(1) applies when the defendant bears a firearm, i.e., carries the weapon on or about his person "for the purpose of being armed and ready for offensive or defensive action in case of a conflict."

It is uncontested that §924(c)(1) applies when the defendant bears a firearm, i.e., carries the weapon on or about his person "for the purpose of being armed and ready for offensive or defensive action in case of a conflict." Black's Law Dictionary 214 (6th ed. 1990) (defining the phrase "carry arms or weapons"). The Court holds that, in addition, "carries a firearm," in the context of §924(c)(1), means personally transporting, possessing, or keeping a firearm in a vehicle, anyplace in a vehicle.

I would read the words to indicate not merely keeping arms on one's premises or in one's vehicle, but bearing them in such manner as to be ready for use as a weapon.

Without doubt, "carries" is a word of many meanings, definable to mean or include carting about in a vehicle. But that encompassing definition is not a ubiquitously necessary one. Nor, in my judgment, is it a proper construction of "carries" as the term appears in §924(c)(1). In line with Bailey and the principle of lenity the Court has long followed, I would confine "carries a firearm," for §924(c)(1) purposes, to the undoubted meaning of that expression in the relevant context. I would read the words to indicate not merely keeping arms on one's premises or in one's vehicle, but bearing them in such manner as to be ready for use as a weapon.

I

A

I note first what is at stake for petitioners. The question before the Court "is not whether possession of a gun [on the drug offender's premises or in his car, during and in relation to commission of the offense,] means a longer sentence for a convicted drug dealer. It most certainly does . . . . Rather, the question concerns which sentencing statute governs the precise length of the extra term of punishment," §924(c)(1)'s "blunt 'mandatory minimum'" five-year sentence, or the more finely tuned "sentencing guideline statutes, under which extra punishment for drug-related gun possession varies with the seriousness of the drug crime." United States v. McFadden, 13 F.3d 463, 466 (CA1 1994) (Breyer, C. J., dissenting).

Accordingly, there would be no "gap," no relevant conduct "ignored," were the Court to reject the Government's broad reading of §924(c)(1). To be more specific, as cogently explained on another day by today's opinion writer:

"The special 'mandatory minimum' sentencing statute says that anyone who 'uses or carries' a gun 'during and in relation to any . . . drug trafficking crime' must receive a mandatory five-year prison term added on to his drug crime sentence. 18 U.S.C. §924(c). At the same time, the Sentencing Guidelines, promulgated under the authority of a different statute, 28 U.S.C. §994, provide for a two-level (i.e., a 30% to 40%) sentence enhancement where a 'firearm . . . was possessed' by a drug offender, U.S. S. G. §2D1.1(b)(1), unless the possession clearly was not 'connected with the [drug] offense.'" McFadden, 13 F.3d at 467 (Breyer, C. J., dissenting).

In Muscarello's case, for example, the underlying drug crimes involved the distribution of 3.6 kilograms of marijuana, and therefore carried a base offense level of 12. See United States Sentencing Commission, Guidelines Manual §2D1.1(a)(3) (Nov. 1995). After adjusting for Muscarello's acceptance of responsibility, see id., §3E1.1(a), his final offense level was 10, placing him in the 6-to-12 month sentencing range. See id., ch. 5, pt. A. The two-level enhancement for possessing a firearm, id., §2D1.1(b)(1), would have increased his final offense level to 12 (a sentencing range of 10 to 16 months). In other words, the less rigid (tailored to "the seriousness of the drug crime," McFadden, 13 F.3d at 466) Guidelines regime would have added four months to Muscarello's prison time, in contrast to the five-year minimum addition the Court's reading of §924(c)(1) mandates. n1

n1 The Sentencing Guidelines carry out "a major congressional effort to create a fairly sophisticated . . . system that distinguishes among different kinds of criminal behavior and punishes accordingly." United States v. McFadden, 13 F.3d at 467-468 (Breyer, C. J., dissenting). A "mandatory minimum" statute deviates from the general regime Congress installed. "Given the importance (to Congress) of the Guidelines system, . . . courts should take care not to interpret [with unnecessary breadth] . . . deviations from the basic congressionally-directed effort to rationalize sentencing." Id., at 468.

In sum, drug traffickers will receive significantly longer sentences if they are caught travelling in vehicles in which they have placed firearms. The question that divides the Court concerns the proper reference for enhancement in the cases at hand, the Guidelines or §924(c)(1).

B

Unlike the Court, I do not think dictionaries, surveys of press reports, or the Bible tell us, dispositively, what "carries" means embedded in §924(c)(1).

Surely a most familiar meaning is, as the Constitution's Second Amendment ("keep and bear Arms") and Black's Law Dictionary indicate: "wear, bear, or carry . . . upon the person or in the clothing or in a pocket, for the purpose . . . of being armed and ready for offensive or defensive action in a case of conflict with another person."

Unlike the Court, I do not think dictionaries, n2 surveys of press reports, n3 or the Bible n4 tell us, dispositively, what "carries" means embedded in §924(c)(1). On definitions, "carry" in legal formulations could mean, inter alia, transport, possess, have in stock, prolong (carry over), be infectious, or wear or bear on one's person. n5 At issue here is not "carries" at large but "carries a firearm." The Court's computer search of newspapers is revealing in this light. Carrying guns in a car showed up as the meaning "perhaps more than one third" of the time. One is left to wonder what meaning showed up some two thirds of the time. Surely a most familiar meaning is, as the Constitution's Second Amendment ("keep and bear Arms") (emphasis added) and Black's Law Dictionary, at 214, indicate: "wear, bear, or carry . . . upon the person or in the clothing or in a pocket, for the purpose . . . of being armed and ready for offensive or defensive action in a case of conflict with another person."

n2 I note, however, that the only legal dictionary the Court cites, Black's Law Dictionary, defines "carry arms or weapons" restrictively.

n3 Many newspapers, the New York Times among them, have published stories using "transport," rather than "carry," to describe gun placements resembling petitioners'. See, e.g., Atlanta Constitution, Feb. 27, 1998, p. 9D, col. 2 ("House members last week expanded gun laws by allowing weapons to be carried into restaurants or transported anywhere in cars."); Chicago Tribune, June 12, 1997, sports section, p. 13 ("Disabled hunters with permission to hunt from a standing vehicle would be able to transport a shotgun in an all-terrain vehicle as long as the gun is unloaded and the breech is open."); Colorado Springs Gazette Telegraph, Aug. 4, 1996, p. C10 (British gun laws require "locked steel cases bolted onto a car for transporting guns from home to shooting range."); Detroit News, Oct. 26, 1997, p. D14 ("It is unlawful to carry afield or transport a rifle . . . or shotgun if you have buckshot, slug, ball loads, or cut shells in possession except while traveling directly to deer camp or target range with firearm not readily available to vehicle occupants."); N. Y. Times, July 4, 1993, p. A21, col. 2 ("The gun is supposed to be transported unloaded, in a locked box in the trunk."); Santa Rosa Press Democrat, Sept. 28, 1996, p. B1 ("Police and volunteers ask that participants . . . transport [their guns] to the fairgrounds in the trunks of their cars."); Worcester Telegram & Gazette, July 16, 1996, p. B3 ("Only one gun can be turned in per person. Guns transported in a vehicle should be locked in the trunk.") (emphasis added in all quotations).

n4 The translator of the Good Book, it appears, bore responsibility for determining whether the servants of Ahaziah "carried" his corpse to Jerusalem. Compare with, e.g., The New English Bible, 2 Kings 9:28 ("His servants conveyed his body to Jerusalem."); Saint Joseph Edition of the New American Bible ("His servants brought him in a chariot to Jerusalem."); Tanakh: The Holy Scriptures ("His servants conveyed him in a chariot to Jerusalem."); see also id., Isaiah 30:6 ("They convey their wealth on the backs of asses."); The New Jerusalem Bible ("They bear their riches on donkeys' backs.") (emphasis added in all quotations).

n5 The dictionary to which this Court referred in Bailey v. United States, 516 U.S. 137, 145, 133 L. Ed. 2d 472, 116 S. Ct. 501 (1995), contains 32 discrete definitions of "carry," including "to make good or valid," "to bear the aspect of," and even "to bear (a hawk) on the fist." See Webster's New International Dictionary of English Language 412 (2d ed. 1949).

On lessons from literature, a scan of Bartlett's and other quotation collections shows how highly selective the Court's choices are. If "the greatest of writers" have used "carry" to mean convey or transport in a vehicle, so have they used the hydra-headed word to mean, inter alia, carry in one's hand, arms, head, heart, or soul, sans vehicle.

On lessons from literature, a scan of Bartlett's and other quotation collections shows how highly selective the Court's choices are. If "the greatest of writers" have used "carry" to mean convey or transport in a vehicle, so have they used the hydra-headed word to mean, inter alia, carry in one's hand, arms, head, heart, or soul, sans vehicle. Consider, among countless examples:

"He shall gather the lambs with his arm, and carry them in his bosom." The King James Bible, Isaiah 40:11.

"And still they gaz'd, and still the wonder grew, That one small head could carry all he knew."

O. Goldsmith, The Deserted Village, ll. 215-216, in The Poetical Works of Oliver Goldsmith 30 (A. Dobson ed. 1949).

"There's a Legion that never was 'listed, That carries no colours or crest."

R. Kipling, The Lost Legion, st. 1, in Rudyard Kipling's Verse, 1885-1918, p. 222 (1920).

"There is a homely adage which runs, 'Speak softly and carry a big stick; you will go far.'" T. Roosevelt, Speech at Minnesota State Fair, Sept. 2, 1901, in J. Bartlett, Familiar Quotations 575:16 (J. Kaplan ed. 1992). n6

These and the Court's lexicological sources demonstrate vividly that "carry" is a word commonly used to convey various messages.

These and the Court's lexicological sources demonstrate vividly that "carry" is a word commonly used to convey various messages. Such references, given their variety, are not reliable indicators of what Congress meant, in §924(c)(1), by "carries a firearm."

"You think I am brave because I carry a gun; well, your fathers are much braver because they carry responsibility, for you, your brothers, your sisters, and your mothers."

"I will not carry a gun. . . . I'll carry your books, I'll carry a torch, I'll carry a tune, I'll carry on, carry over, carry forward, Cary Grant, cash and carry, carry me back to Old Virginia, I'll even 'hari-kari' if you show me how, but I will not carry a gun!"

n6 Popular films and television productions provide corroborative illustrations. In "The Magnificent Seven," for example, O'Reilly (played by Charles Bronson) says: "You think I am brave because I carry a gun; well, your fathers are much braver because they carry responsibility, for you, your brothers, your sisters, and your mothers." See http://us.imdb.com/M/search_quotes?for=carry. And in the television series "M * A * S * H," Hawkeye Pierce (played by Alan Alda) presciently proclaims: "I will not carry a gun. . . . I'll carry your books, I'll carry a torch, I'll carry a tune, I'll carry on, carry over, carry forward, Cary Grant, cash and carry, carry me back to Old Virginia, I'll even 'hari-kari' if you show me how, but I will not carry a gun!" See http://www.geocities.com/Hollywood/8915/mashquotes.html.

C

I use a gun to protect my house, but I've never had to use it

Just as "uses" was read to mean not simply "possession," but "active employment," so "carries," correspondingly, is properly read to signal the most dangerous cases—the gun at hand, ready for use as a weapon.

As the Ninth Circuit suggested, it is not apparent why possession of a gun in a drug dealer's moving vehicle would be thought more dangerous than gun possession on premises where drugs are sold: "A drug dealer who packs heat is more likely to hurt someone or provoke someone else to violence. A gun in a bag under a tarp in a truck bed [or in a bedroom closet] poses substantially less risk."

Noting the paradoxical statement, "'I use a gun to protect my house, but I've never had to use it,'" the Court in Bailey emphasized the importance of context -- the statutory context. Just as "uses" was read to mean not simply "possession," but "active employment," so "carries," correspondingly, is properly read to signal the most dangerous cases -- the gun at hand, ready for use as a weapon. n7 It is reasonable to comprehend Congress as having provided mandatory minimums for the most life-jeopardizing gun-connection cases (guns in or at the defendant's hand when committing an offense), leaving other, less imminently threatening, situations for the more flexible guidelines regime. n8 As the Ninth Circuit suggested, it is not apparent why possession of a gun in a drug dealer's moving vehicle would be thought more dangerous than gun possession on premises where drugs are sold: "A drug dealer who packs heat is more likely to hurt someone or provoke someone else to violence. A gun in a bag under a tarp in a truck bed [or in a bedroom closet] poses substantially less risk." United States v. Foster (CA9 1998). n9

n7 In my view, the Government would carry its burden by proving a firearm was kept so close to the person as to approximate placement in a pocket or holster, e.g., guns carried at one's side in a briefcase or handbag, or strapped to the saddle of a horse.

n8 The Court reports that the Courts of Appeals "have unanimously concluded that 'carry' is not limited to the carrying of weapons directly on the person." In Bailey, however, the Government's argument based on a similar observation did not carry the day. See Brief for United States in Bailey v. United States, O. T. 1995, Nos. 94-7448 and 94-7492, p. 16, n. 4. No Court of Appeals had previously adopted an "active employment" construction of "uses . . . a firearm" in §924(c)(1), yet this Court did exactly that.

The "Firearms" statutes indicate that Congress, unlike the Court, recognizes that a gun in the hand is indeed more dangerous than a gun in the trunk.

n9 The "Firearms" statutes indicate that Congress, unlike the Court, recognizes that a gun in the hand is indeed more dangerous than a gun in the trunk. See, e.g., 18 U.S.C. §926A (permitting the transportation of firearms in a vehicle, but only if "neither the firearm nor any ammunition being transported is readily accessible or is directly accessible from the passenger compartment of such transporting vehicle"); see infra, at 8-9.

For indicators from Congress itself, it is appropriate to consider word usage in other provisions of Title 18's chapter on "Firearms." See Bailey (interpreting §924(c)(1) in light of 18 U.S.C. §§922(g), 922(j), 922(k), 922(o)(1), 924(d)(1), 930(a), 930(b)). The Court, however, does not derive from the statutory complex at issue its thesis that "'carry' implies personal agency and some degree of possession, whereas 'transport' does not have such a limited connotation and, in addition, implies the movement of goods in bulk over great distances." Looking to provisions Congress enacted, one finds that the Legislature did not acknowledge or routinely adhere to the distinction the Court advances today; instead, Congress sometimes employed "transports" when, according to the Court, "carries" was the right word to use.

Section 925(a)(2)(B), for example, provides that no criminal sanction shall attend "the transportation of [a] firearm or ammunition carried out to enable a person, who lawfully received such firearm or ammunition from the Secretary of the Army, to engage in military training or in competitions." The full text of §926A, rather than the truncated version the Court presents, is also telling:

"Notwithstanding any other provision of any law or any rule or regulation of a State or any political subdivision thereof, any person who is not otherwise prohibited by this chapter from transporting, shipping, or receiving a firearm shall be entitled to transport a firearm for any lawful purpose from any place where he may lawfully possess and carry such firearm to any other place where he may lawfully possess and carry such firearm if, during such transportation the firearm is unloaded, and neither the firearm nor any ammunition being transported is readily accessible or is directly accessible from the passenger compartment of such transporting vehicle: Provided, That in the case of a vehicle without a compartment separate from the driver's compartment the firearm or ammunition shall be contained in a locked container other than the glove compartment or console."

In describing when and how a person may travel in a vehicle that contains his firearm without violating the law, §§925(a)(2)(B) and 926A use "transport," not "carry," to "imply personal agency and some degree of possession."

Tellingly, when referring to firearms traveling in vehicles, the "Firearms" statutes routinely use a form of "transport"; they never use a form of "carry."

n10 The Court asserts that "'transport' is a broader category that includes 'carry' but encompasses other activity." "Carry," however, is not merely a subset of "transport." A person seated at a desk with a gun in hand or pocket is carrying the gun, but is not transporting it. Yes, the words "carry" and "transport" often can be employed interchangeably, as can the words "carry" and "use." But in Bailey, this Court settled on constructions that gave "carry" and "use" independent meanings. Without doubt, Congress is alert to the discrete meanings of "transport" and "carry" in the context of vehicles, as the Legislature's placement of each word in §926A illustrates. The narrower reading of "carry" preserves discrete meanings for the two words, while in the context of vehicles the Court's interpretation of "carry" is altogether synonymous with "transport." Tellingly, when referring to firearms traveling in vehicles, the "Firearms" statutes routinely use a form of "transport"; they never use a form of "carry."

For example, under §925(a)(2)(B), one could carry his gun to a car, transport it to the shooting competition, and use it to shoot targets.

Under the conditions of §926A, one could transport her gun in a car, but under no circumstances could the gun be readily accessible while she travels in the car.

Reading "carries" in §924(c)(1) to mean "on or about [one's] person" is fully compatible with these and other "Firearms" statutes. n11 For example, under §925(a)(2)(B), one could carry his gun to a car, transport it to the shooting competition, and use it to shoot targets. Under the conditions of §926A, one could transport her gun in a car, but under no circumstances could the gun be readily accessible while she travels in the car. "Courts normally try to read language in different, but related, statutes, so as best to reconcile those statutes, in light of their purposes and of common sense." McFadden, 13 F.3d at 467 (Breyer, C. J., dissenting). So reading the "Firearms" statutes, I would not extend the word "carries" in §924(c)(1) to mean transports out of hand's reach in a vehicle. n12

The Government points to numerous federal statutes that authorize law enforcement officers to "carry firearms" and notes that, in those authorizing provisions, "carry" of course means "both on the person and in a vehicle." Quite right. But as viewers of "Sesame Street" will quickly recognize, "one of these things [a statute authorizing conduct] is not like the other [a statute criminalizing conduct]."

a penal statute is not to be construed generously in the Government's favor.

n11 The Government points to numerous federal statutes that authorize law enforcement officers to "carry firearms" and notes that, in those authorizing provisions, "carry" of course means "both on the person and in a vehicle." Quite right. But as viewers of "Sesame Street" will quickly recognize, "one of these things [a statute authorizing conduct] is not like the other [a statute criminalizing conduct]." The authorizing statutes in question are properly accorded a construction compatible with the clear purpose of the legislation to aid federal law enforcers in the performance of their official duties. It is fundamental, however, that a penal statute is not to be construed generously in the Government's favor. See, e.g., United States v. Bass (1971).

n12 The Court places undue reliance on Representative Poff's statement that §924(c)(1) seeks "'to persuade the man who is tempted to commit a Federal felony to leave his gun at home.'" See ante, at 7 (quoting 114 Cong. Rec. 22231 (1968)). As the Government argued in its brief to this Court in Bailey:

"In making that statement, Representative Poff was not referring to the 'carries' prong of the original Section 924(c). As originally enacted, the 'carries' prong of the statute prohibited only the 'unlawful' carrying of a firearm while committing an offense. The statute would thus not have applied to an individual who, for instance, had a permit for carrying a gun and carried it with him when committing an offense, and it would have had no force in 'persuading' such an individual 'to leave his gun at home.' Instead, Representative Poff was referring to the 'uses' prong of the original Section 924(c)." Brief for United States in Bailey v. United States.

Representative Poff's next sentence confirms that he was speaking of "uses," not "carries": "Any person should understand that if he uses his gun and is caught and convicted, he is going to jail."

Representative Poff's next sentence confirms that he was speaking of "uses," not "carries": "Any person should understand that if he uses his gun and is caught and convicted, he is going to jail." 114 Cong. Rec., at 22231 (emphasis added).

II

Section 924(c)(1), as the foregoing discussion details, is not decisively clear one way or another. The sharp division in the Court on the proper reading of the measure confirms, "at the very least, . . . that the issue is subject to some doubt. Under these circumstances, we adhere to the familiar rule that, 'where there is ambiguity in a criminal statute, doubts are resolved in favor of the defendant.'" Adamo Wrecking Co. v. United States (1978); see United States v. Granderson (1994) ("Where text, structure, and history fail to establish that the Government's position is unambiguously correct -- we apply the rule of lenity and resolve the ambiguity in [the defendant's] favor."). "Carry" bears many meanings, as the Court and the "Firearms" statutes demonstrate. n13 The narrower "on or about [one's] person" interpretation is hardly implausible nor at odds with an accepted meaning of "carries a firearm."

n13 Any doubt on that score is dispelled by examining the provisions in the "Firearms" chapter, in addition to §924(c)(1), that include a form of the word "carry": 18 U.S.C. §922(a)(5) ("carry out a bequest"); §§922(s)(6)(B)(ii), (iii) ("carry out this subsection"); §922(u) ("carry away [a firearm]"); 18 U.S.C. A. §924(a)(6)(B)(ii) (Supp. 1998) ("carry or otherwise possess or discharge or otherwise use [a] handgun"); 18 U.S.C. §924(e)(2)(B) ("carrying of a firearm"); §925(a)(2) ("carried out to enable a person"); §926(a) ("carry out the provisions of this chapter"); §926A ("lawfully possess and carry such firearm to any other place where he may lawfully possess and carry such firearm"); §929(a)(1) ("uses or carries a firearm and is in possession of armor piercing ammunition"); §930(d)(3) ("lawful carrying of firearms . . . in a Federal facility incident to hunting or other lawful purposes") (emphasis added in all quotations).

Overlooking that there will be an enhanced sentence for the gun-possessing drug dealer in any event, the Court asks rhetorically: "How persuasive is a punishment that is without effect until a drug dealer who has brought his gun to a sale (indeed has it available for use) actually takes it from the trunk (or unlocks the glove compartment) of his car?" Correspondingly, the Court defines "carries a firearm" to cover "a person who knowingly possesses and conveys firearms [anyplace] in a vehicle . . . which the person accompanies." Congress, however, hardly lacks competence to select the words "possesses" or "conveys" when that is what the Legislature means. n14 Notably in view of the Legislature's capacity to speak plainly, and of overriding concern, the Court's inquiry pays scant attention to a core reason for the rule of lenity: "Because of the seriousness of criminal penalties, and because criminal punishment usually represents the moral condemnation of the community, legislatures and not courts should define criminal activity. This policy embodies 'the instinctive distaste against men languishing in prison unless the lawmaker has clearly said they should.'" United States v. Bass (1971) (quoting H. Friendly, Mr. Justice Frankfurter and the Reading of Statutes, in Benchmarks 196, 209 (1967)).

n14 See, e.g., 18 U.S.C. A. §924(a)(6)(B)(ii) (Supp. 1998) ("if the person sold . . . a handgun . . . to a juvenile knowing . . . that the juvenile intended to carry or otherwise possess . . . the handgun . . . in the commission of a crime of violence"); 18 U.S.C. §926A ("may lawfully possess and carry such firearm to any other place where he may lawfully possess and carry such firearm"); §929(a)(1) ("uses or carries a firearm and is in possession of armor piercing ammunition"); §2277 ("brings, carries, or possesses any dangerous weapon") (emphasis added in all quotations).

The narrower "on or about [one's] person" construction of "carries a firearm" is consistent with the Court's construction of "uses" in Bailey to entail an immediacy element. It respects the Guidelines system by resisting overbroad readings of statutes that deviate from that system. It fits plausibly with other provisions of the "Firearms" chapter, and it adheres to the principle that, given two readings of a penal provision, both consistent with the statutory text, we do not choose the harsher construction. The Court, in my view, should leave it to Congress to speak "'in language that is clear and definite'" if the Legislature wishes to impose the sterner penalty. Accordingly, I would reverse the judgments of the First and Fifth Circuits.

BRYAN v. UNITED STATES

(FULL CASE)

524 U.S. 184; 118 S. Ct. 1939; 141 L. Ed. 2d 197

March 31, 1998, Argued

June 15, 1998, Decided

GIST: The term *willfully* has many meanings in law. In this case, the Court interprets in great detail what willfully means in the context of a federal gun law that prohibits willfully dealing in firearms without a federal license. The Court held that a person willfully violates this law by knowing the conduct is unlawful. No specific knowledge of the federal license requirement is needed. A legislative history of the 1968 Gun Control Act is included, which mentions the need to subsequently enact the 1986 Firearm Owners' Protection Act (amending the Gun Control Act), to protect law-abiding citizens from flagrant federal abuse with respect to getting, having and using guns for lawful purposes.

The Firearms Owners' Protection Act (FOPA) added 18 U.S.C. §924(a)(1)(D) to the Criminal Code to prohibit anyone from "willfully" violating, inter alia, §922(a)(1)(A), which forbids dealing in firearms without a federal license. The evidence at petitioner's unlicensed dealing trial was adequate to prove that he was dealing in firearms and that he knew his conduct was unlawful, but there was no evidence that he was aware of the federal licensing requirement. The trial judge refused to instruct the jury that he could be convicted only if he knew of the federal licensing requirement, instructing, instead, that a person acts "willfully" if he acts with the bad purpose to disobey or disregard the law, but that he need not be aware of the specific law that his conduct may be violating. The jury found petitioner guilty. The Second Circuit affirmed, concluding that the instructions were proper and that the Government had elicited "ample proof" that petitioner had acted willfully.

Held: The term "willfully" in §924(a)(1)(D) requires proof only that the defendant knew his conduct was unlawful, not that he also knew of the federal licensing requirement.

(a) When used in the criminal context, a "willful" act is generally one undertaken with a "bad purpose." See, e.g., Heikkinen v. United States, 355 U.S. 273, 279, 2 L. Ed. 2d 264, 78 S. Ct. 299. In other words, to establish a "willful" violation of a statute, the Government must prove that the defendant acted with knowledge that his conduct was unlawful. Ratzlaf v. United States, 510 U.S. 135, 137, 126 L. Ed. 2d 615, 114 S. Ct. 655. The Court rejects petitioner's argument that, for two principal reasons, a more particularized showing is required here. His first contention -- that the "knowingly" requirement in §§924(a)(1)(A)-(C) for three categories of acts made unlawful by §922 demonstrates that the Government must prove knowledge of the law -- is not persuasive because "knowingly" refers to knowledge of the facts constituting the offense, as distinguished from knowledge of the law, see, e.g., United States v. Bailey, 444 U.S. 394, 408, 62 L. Ed. 2d 575, 100 S. Ct. 624. With respect to the three §924 "knowingly" categories, the background presumption that every citizen knows the law makes it unnecessary to adduce specific evidence to prove an evil-meaning mind. As regards the "willfully" category here at issue, however, the jury must find that the defendant acted with such a mind, i.e., with knowledge that his conduct was unlawful. Also rejected is petitioner's second argument: that §924(a)(1)(D) must be read to require knowledge of the law in light of this Court's adoption of a similar interpretation in cases concerned with willful violations of the tax laws, see, e.g., Cheek v. United States, 498 U.S. 192, 201, 112 L. Ed. 2d 617, 111 S. Ct. 604, and the willful structuring of cash transactions to avoid a bank reporting requirement, see Ratzlaf, 510 U.S. at 138, 149. Those cases are readily distinguishable because they involved highly technical statutes that threatened to ensnare individuals engaged in apparently innocent conduct. That danger is not present here because the jury found that this petitioner knew that his conduct was unlawful.

(b) Petitioner's additional arguments based on his reading of congressional intent are rejected. FOPA's legislative history is too ambiguous to offer him much assistance, since his main support lies in statements made by opponents of the bill. See, e.g., Schwegmann Brothers v. Calvert Distillers Corp., 341 U.S. 384, 394, 95 L. Ed. 1035, 71 S. Ct. 745. His next argument -- that, at the time FOPA was passed, the "willfulness" requirements in §§923(d)(1)(C)-(D) had uniformly been interpreted to require knowledge of the law -- is

inaccurate because a number of courts had reached different conclusions. Moreover, the cases adopting petitioner's view support the notion that disregard of a known legal obligation is sufficient to establish a willful violation, but in no way make it necessary. Petitioner's final argument -- that §922(b)(3), which is governed by §924(a)(1)(D), indicates that Congress intended "willfully" to include knowledge of the law -- fails for a similar reason.

(c) The trial court's misstatement of law in a jury instruction given after the correct instructions were given -- specifically, a sentence asserting that "the government [need not] prove that [petitioner] had knowledge that he was breaking the law" -- does not provide a basis for reversal because (1) petitioner did not effectively object to that sentence; (2) in the context of the entire instructions, it seems unlikely that the jury was misled; (3) petitioner failed to raise this argument in the Second Circuit; and (4) this Court's grant of certiorari was limited to the narrow legal question hereinbefore decided.

JUSTICE STEVENS delivered the opinion of the Court.

Petitioner was convicted of "willfully" dealing in firearms without a federal license.

Petitioner was convicted of "willfully" dealing in firearms without a federal license. The question presented is whether the term "willfully" in 18 U.S.C. §924(a)(1)(D) requires proof that the defendant knew that his conduct was unlawful, or whether it also requires proof that he knew of the federal licensing requirement.

I

In 1968 Congress enacted the Omnibus Crime Control and Safe Streets Act. 82 Stat. 197-239. In Title IV of that Act Congress made findings concerning the impact of the traffic in firearms on the prevalence of lawlessness and violent crime in the United States n1 and amended the Criminal Code to include detailed provisions regulating the use and sale of firearms. As amended, 18 U.S.C. §922 defined a number of "unlawful acts"; subsection (a)(1) made it unlawful for any person except a licensed dealer to engage in the business of dealing in firearms. n2 Section 923 established the federal licensing program and repeated the prohibition against dealing in firearms without a license, and §924 specified the penalties for violating "any provision of this chapter." Read literally, §924 authorized the imposition of a fine of up to $5,000 or a prison sentence of not more than five years, "or both," on any person who dealt in firearms without a license even if that person believed that he or she was acting lawfully. n3 As enacted in 1968, §922(a)(1) and §924 omitted an express scienter requirement and therefore arguably imposed strict criminal liability on every unlicensed dealer in firearms. The 1968 Act also omitted any definition of the term "engaged in the business" even though that conduct was an element of the unlawful act prohibited by §922(a)(1).

n1 "Sec. 901. (a) The Congress hereby finds and declares --

"(1) that there is a widespread traffic in firearms moving in or otherwise affecting interstate or foreign commerce, and that the existing Federal controls over such traffic do not adequately enable the States to control this traffic within their own borders through the exercise of their police power;

"(2) that the ease with which any person can acquire firearms other than a rifle or shotgun (including criminals, juveniles without the knowledge or consent of their parents or guardians, narcotics addicts, mental defectives, armed groups who would supplant the functions of duly constituted public authorities, and others whose possession of such weapons is similarly contrary to the public interest) is a significant factor in the prevalence of lawlessness and violent crime in the United States;

"(3) that only through adequate Federal control over interstate and foreign commerce in these weapons, and over all persons engaging in the businesses of importing, manufacturing, or dealing in them, can this grave problem be properly dealt with, and effective State and local regulation of this traffic be made possible . . . ." 82 Stat. 225.

n2 82 Stat. 228. The current version of this provision, which is substantially the same as the 1968 version, is codified at 18 U.S.C. §922(a)(1)(A). It states:

"(a) It shall be unlawful --

"(1) for any person --

"(A) except a licensed importer, licensed manufacturer, or licensed dealer, to engage in the business of importing, manufacturing, or dealing in firearms, or in the course of such business to ship, transport, or receive any firearm in interstate or foreign commerce."

n3 " §924. Penalties

"(a) Whoever violates any provision of this chapter . . . shall be fined not more than $5,000 or imprisoned not more than five years, or both." 82 Stat. 233.

The findings in that statute explained that additional legislation was necessary to protect law-abiding citizens with respect to the acquisition, possession, or use of firearms for lawful purposes.

In 1986 Congress enacted the Firearms Owners' Protection Act (FOPA), in part, to cure these omissions. The findings in that statute explained that additional legislation was necessary to protect law-abiding citizens with respect to the acquisition, possession, or use of firearms for lawful purposes. n4 FOPA therefore amended §921 to include a definition of the term "engaged in the business," n5 and amended §924 to add a scienter requirement as a condition to the imposition of penalties for most of the unlawful acts defined in §922. For three categories of offenses the intent required is that the defendant acted "knowingly"; for the fourth category, which includes "any other provision of this chapter," the required intent is that the defendant acted "willfully." n6 The §922(a)(1)(A) n7 offense at issue in this case is an "other provision" in the "willfully" category.

n4 "The Congress finds that --

.....

"(b)(2) additional legislation is required to reaffirm the intent of the Congress, as expressed in section 101 of the Gun Control Act of 1968, that 'it is not the purpose of this title to place any undue or unnecessary Federal restrictions or burdens on law-abiding citizens with respect to the acquisition, possession, or use of firearms appropriate to the purpose of hunting, trapshooting, target shooting, personal protection, or any other lawful activity, and that this title is not intended to discourage or eliminate the private ownership or use of firearms by law-abiding citizens for lawful purposes.'" 100 Stat. 449.

n5 "Section 921 of title 18, United States Code, is amended --

.....

"(21) The term 'engaged in the business' means --

.....

"(C) as applied to a dealer in firearms, as defined in section 921(a)(11)(A), a person who devotes time, attention, and labor to dealing in firearms as a regular course of trade or business with the principal objective of livelihood and profit through the repetitive purchase and resale of firearms, but such term shall not include a person who makes occasional sales, exchanges, or purchases of firearms for the enhancement of a personal collection or for a hobby, or who sells all or part of his personal collection of firearms . . . ." 100 Stat. 449-450.

n6 Title 18 U.S.C. §924(a)(1) currently provides:

"Except as otherwise provided in this subsection, subsection (b), (c), or (f) of this section, or in section 929, whoever --

"(A) knowingly makes any false statement or representation with respect to the information required by this chapter to be kept in the records of a person licensed under this chapter or in applying for any license or exemption or relief from disability under the provisions of this chapter;

"(B) knowingly violates subsection (a)(4), (f), (k), (r), (v), or (w) of section 922;

"(C) knowingly imports or brings into the United States or any possession thereof any firearm or ammunition in violation of section 922(l); or

"(D) willfully violates any other provision of this chapter,

"shall be fined under this title, imprisoned not more than five years, or both."

n7 See n. 2, supra.

II

The jury having found petitioner guilty, we accept the Government's version of the evidence. That evidence proved that petitioner did not have a federal license to deal in firearms; that he used so-called "straw purchasers" in Ohio to acquire pistols that he could not have purchased himself; that the straw purchasers made false statements when purchasing the guns; that petitioner assured the straw purchasers that he would file the serial numbers off the guns; and that he resold the guns on Brooklyn street corners known for drug dealing.

The jury having found petitioner guilty, we accept the Government's version of the evidence. That evidence proved that petitioner did not have a federal license to deal in firearms; that he used so-called "straw purchasers" in Ohio to acquire pistols that he could not have purchased himself; that the straw purchasers made false statements when purchasing the guns; that petitioner assured the straw purchasers that he would file the serial numbers off the guns; and that he resold the guns on Brooklyn street corners known for drug dealing. The evidence was unquestionably adequate to prove that petitioner was dealing in firearms, and that he knew that his conduct was unlawful. n8 There was, however, no evidence that he was aware of the federal law that prohibits dealing in firearms without a federal license.

n8 Why else would he make use of straw purchasers and assure them that he would shave the serial numbers off the guns? Moreover, the street corner sales are not consistent with a good-faith belief in the legality of the enterprise.

Petitioner was charged with a conspiracy to violate 18 U.S.C. §922(a)(1)(A), by willfully engaging in the business of dealing in firearms, and with a substantive violation of that provision. n9 After the close of evidence, petitioner requested that the trial judge instruct the jury that petitioner could be convicted only if he knew of the federal licensing requirement, n10 but the judge rejected this request. Instead, the trial judge gave this explanation of the term "willfully": "A person acts willfully if he acts intentionally and purposely and with the intent to do something the law forbids, that is, with the bad purpose to disobey or to disregard the law. Now, the person need not be aware of the specific law or rule that his conduct may be violating. But he must act with the intent to do something that the law forbids." n11

n9 Although the prohibition against unlicensed dealing in firearms is set forth in §922, see n. 2, supra, the criminal sanction is set forth in §924(a)(1), see n. 6, supra.

n10 "KNOWLEDGE OF THE LAW

"The Federal Firearms Statute which the Defendant is charged with, conspiracy to violate and with allegedly violated [sic], is a specific intent statute. You must accordingly find, beyond a reasonable doubt, that Defendant at all relevant times charged, acted with the knowledge that it was unlawful to engage in the business of firearms distribution lawfully purchased by a legally permissible transferee or gun purchaser.

.....

. . . . .

"You must be persuaded that with the actual knowledge of the federal firearms licensing laws Defendant acted in knowing and intentional violation of them." App. 17 (citing Ratzlaf v. United States, 510 U.S. 135, 126 L. Ed. 2d 615, 114 S. Ct. 655 (1994)).

n11 App. 18-19.

Petitioner was found guilty on both counts. On appeal he argued that the evidence was insufficient because there was no proof that he had knowledge of the federal licensing requirement, and that the trial judge had erred by failing to instruct the jury that such knowledge was an essential element of the offense. The Court of Appeals affirmed. It concluded that the instructions were proper and that the Government had elicited "ample proof " that petitioner had acted willfully. App. 22.

Because the Eleventh Circuit has held that it is necessary for the Government to prove that the defendant acted with knowledge of the licensing requirement, United States v. Sanchez-Corcino, 85 F.3d 549, 553-554 (1996), we granted certiorari to resolve the conflict.

III

As a general matter, when used in the criminal context, a "willful" act is one undertaken with a "bad purpose."

The word "willfully" is sometimes said to be "a word of many meanings" whose construction is often dependent on the context in which it appears. See, e.g., Spies v. United States, 317 U.S. 492, 497, 87 L. Ed. 418, 63 S. Ct. 364 (1943). Most obviously it differentiates between deliberate and unwitting conduct, but in the criminal law it also typically refers to a culpable state of mind. As we explained in United States v. Murdock, 290 U.S. 389, 78 L. Ed. 381, 54 S. Ct. 223 (1933), a variety of phrases have been used to describe that concept. n12 As a general matter, when used in the criminal context, a "willful" act is one undertaken with a "bad purpose." n13 In other words, in order to establish a "willful" violation of a statute, "the Government must prove that the defendant acted with knowledge that his conduct was unlawful." Ratzlaf v. United States, 510 U.S. 135, 137, 126 L. Ed. 2d 615, 114 S. Ct. 655 (1994).

n12 "The word often denotes an act which is intentional, or knowing, or voluntary, as distinguished from accidental. But when used in a criminal statute it generally means an act done with a bad purpose (Felton v. United States, 96 U.S. 699, 24 L. Ed. 875; Potter v. United States, 155 U.S. 438, 39 L. Ed. 214, 15 S. Ct. 144; Spurr v. United States, 174 U.S. 728, 43 L. Ed. 1150, 19 S. Ct. 812); without justifiable excuse (Felton v. United States, supra; Williams v. People, 26 Colo. 272; 57 P. 701; People v. Jewell, 138 Mich. 620; 101 N.W. 835; St. Louis, I. M. & S. Ry. Co. v. Batesville & W. Tel. Co., 80 Ark. 499; 97 S.W. 660; Clay v. State, 52 Tex. Crim. 555; 107 S.W. 1129); stubbornly, obstinately, perversely, Wales v. Miner, 89 Ind. 118, 127; Lynch v. Commonwealth, 131 Va. 762; 109 S.E. 427; Claus v. Chicago Gt. W. Ry. Co., 136 Iowa 7; 111 N.W. 15; State v. Harwell, 129 N.C. 550; 40 S.E. 48. The word is also employed to characterize a thing done without ground for believing it is lawful (Roby v. Newton, 121 Ga. 679; 49 S.E. 694), or conduct marked by careless disregard whether or not one has the right so to act, United States v. Philadelphia & R. Ry. Co., 223 F. 207, 210; State v. Savre, 129 Iowa 122; 105 N.W. 387; State v. Morgan, 136 N.C. 628; 48 S.E. 670." 290 U.S. at 394-395.

n13 See, e.g., Heikkinen v. United States, 355 U.S. 273, 279, 2 L. Ed. 2d 264, 78 S. Ct. 299 (1958) ("There can be no willful failure by a deportee, in the sense of §20(c), to apply to, and identify, a country willing to receive him in the absence of evidence . . . of a 'bad purpose' or '[non-

]justifiable excuse,' or the like . . . . It cannot be said that he acted 'willfully' -- i.e., with a 'bad purpose' or without a 'justifiable excuse'"); United States v. Murdock, 290 U.S. 389, 394, 78 L. Ed. 381, 54 S. Ct. 223 (1933) ("When used in a criminal statue [willfully] generally means an act done with a bad purpose"); Felton v. United States, 96 U.S. 699, 702, 24 L. Ed. 875 (1878) ("Doing or omitting to do a thing knowingly and wilfully, implies not only a knowledge of the thing, but a determination with a bad intent to do it or to omit doing it. 'The word "wilfully,"' says Chief Justice Shaw, 'in the ordinary sense in which it is used in statutes, means not merely "voluntarily," but with a bad purpose.' 20 Pick. 220. 'It is frequently understood,' says Bishop, 'as signifying an evil intent without justifiable excuse.' Crim. Law, vol. i. sect. 428"); 1 L. Sand, J. Siffert, W. Loughlin, & S. Reiss, Modern Federal Jury Instructions 3A.01, p. 3A-18 (1997) ("'Willfully' means to act with knowledge that one's conduct is unlawful and with the intent to do something the law forbids, that is to say with the bad purpose to disobey or to disregard the law").

Petitioner argues that a more particularized showing is required in this case for two principal reasons. First, he argues that the fact that Congress used the adverb "knowingly" to authorize punishment of three categories of acts made unlawful by §922 and the word "willfully" when it referred to unlicensed dealing in firearms demonstrates that the Government must shoulder a special burden in cases like this. This argument is not persuasive because the term "knowingly" does not necessarily have any reference to a culpable state of mind or to knowledge of the law. As Justice Jackson correctly observed, "the knowledge requisite to knowing violation of a statute is factual knowledge as distinguished from knowledge of the law." n14 Thus, in United States v. Bailey, 444 U.S. 394, 62 L. Ed. 2d 575, 100 S. Ct. 624 (1980), we held that the prosecution fulfills its burden of proving a knowing violation of the escape statute "if it demonstrates that an escapee knew his actions would result in his leaving physical confinement without permission." Id., at 408. And in Staples v. United States, 511 U.S. 600, 128 L. Ed. 2d 608, 114 S. Ct. 1793 (1994), we held that a charge that the defendant's possession of an unregistered machinegun was unlawful required proof "that he knew the weapon he possessed had the characteristics that brought it within the statutory definition of a machinegun." Id., at 602. It was not, however, necessary to prove that the defendant knew that his possession was unlawful. See Rogers v. United States, 522 U.S. 252, 254 (1998) (plurality opinion) (slip op., at 1-3). Thus, unless the text of the statute dictates a different result, n15 the term "knowingly" merely requires proof of knowledge of the facts that constitute the offense.

n14 In his opinion dissenting from the Court's decision upholding the constitutionality of a statute authorizing punishment for the knowing violation of an Interstate Commerce regulation, Justice Jackson wrote:

"It is further suggested that a defendant is protected against indefiniteness because conviction is authorized only for knowing violations. The argument seems to be that the jury can find that defendant knowingly violated the regulation only if it finds that it knew the meaning of the regulation he was accused of violating. With the exception of Screws v. United States, 325 U.S. 91, 89 L. Ed. 1495, 65 S. Ct. 1031, which rests on a very particularized basis, the knowledge requisite to knowing violation of a statute is factual knowledge as distinguished from knowledge of the law. I do not suppose the Court intends to suggest that if petitioner knew nothing of the existence of such a regulation its ignorance would constitute a defense." Boyce Motor Lines, Inc. v. United States, 342 U.S. 337, 345, 96 L. Ed. 367, 72 S. Ct. 329 (1952) (dissenting opinion).

n15 Liparota v. United States, 471 U.S. 419, 85 L. Ed. 2d 434, 105 S. Ct. 2084 (1985), was such a case. We there concluded that both the term "knowing" in §2024(c) and the term "knowingly" in §2024(b)(1) of Title 7 literally referred to knowledge of the law as well as knowledge of the relevant facts. See id., at 428-430.

the background presumption that every citizen knows the law makes it unnecessary to adduce specific evidence to prove that "an evil-meaning mind" directed the "evil-doing hand."

With respect to the three categories of conduct that are made punishable by §924 if performed "knowingly," the background presumption that every citizen knows the law makes it unnecessary to adduce specific evidence to prove that "an evil-meaning mind" directed the "evil-doing hand." n16 More is required, however, with respect to the conduct in the fourth category that is only criminal when done "willfully." The jury must find that the defendant acted with an evil-meaning mind, that is to say, that he acted with knowledge that his conduct was unlawful.

n16 Justice Jackson's translation of the terms mens rea and actus reus is found in his opinion for the Court in Morissette v. United States, 342 U.S. 246, 251, 96 L. Ed. 288, 72 S. Ct. 240 (1952).

Petitioner next argues that we must read §924(a)(1)(D) to require knowledge of the law because of our interpretation of "willfully" in two other contexts. In certain cases involving willful violations of the tax laws, we have concluded that the jury must find that the defendant was aware of the specific provision of the tax code that he was charged with violating. See, e.g., Cheek v. United States, 498 U.S. 192, 201, 112 L. Ed. 2d

617, 111 S. Ct. 604 (1991). n17 Similarly, in order to satisfy a willful violation in Ratzlaf, we concluded that the jury had to find that the defendant knew that his structuring of cash transactions to avoid a reporting requirement was unlawful. See 510 U.S. at 138, 149. Those cases, however, are readily distinguishable. Both the tax cases n18 and Ratzlaf n19 involved highly technical statutes that presented the danger of ensnaring individuals engaged in apparently innocent conduct. n20 As a result, we held that these statutes "carve out an exception to the traditional rule" that ignorance of the law is no excuse n21 and require that the defendant have knowledge of the law. n22 The danger of convicting individuals engaged in apparently innocent activity that motivated our decisions in the tax cases and Ratzlaf is not present here because the jury found that this petitioner knew that his conduct was unlawful. n23

n17 Even in tax cases, we have not always required this heightened mens rea. In United States v. Pomponio, 429 U.S. 10, 50 L. Ed. 2d 12, 97 S. Ct. 22 (1976) (per curiam), for example, the jury was instructed that a willful act is one done "with [the] bad purpose either to disobey or to disregard the law." Id., at 11. We approved of this instruction, concluding that "the trial judge . . . adequately instructed the jury on willfulness." Id., at 13.

n18 As we stated in Cheek v. United States, 498 U.S. 192, 199-200, 112 L. Ed. 2d 617, 111 S. Ct. 604 (1991),

"The proliferation of statutes and regulations has sometimes made it difficult for the average citizen to know and comprehend the extent of the duties and obligations imposed by the tax laws. Congress has accordingly softened the impact of the common-law presumption by making specific intent to violate the law an element of certain federal criminal tax offenses. Thus, the Court almost 60 years ago interpreted the statutory term 'willfully' as used in the federal criminal tax statutes as carving out an exception to the traditional rule [that every person is presumed to know the law]. This special treatment of criminal tax offenses is largely due to the complexity of the tax laws."

n19 See Bates v. United States, 522 U.S. 23, 31, n. 6 (1997) (slip op., at 7, n. 6) (noting that Ratzlaf's holding was based on the "particular statutory context of currency structuring"); Ratzlaf, 510 U.S. at 149 (Court's holding based on "particular context" of currency structuring statute).

n20 Id., at 144-145 ("Currency structuring is not inevitably nefarious . . . . Nor is a person who structures a currency transaction invariably motivated by a desire to keep the Government in the dark"; Government's construction of the statute would criminalize apparently innocent activity); Cheek, 498 U.S. at 205 ("In 'our complex tax system, uncertainty often arises even among taxpayers who earnestly wish to follow the law,' and '"it is not the purpose of the law to penalize frank difference of opinion or innocent errors made despite the exercise of reasonable care."' United States v. Bishop, 412 U.S. 346, 360-361, 36 L. Ed. 2d 941, 93 S. Ct. 2008 (1973) (quoting Spies v. United States, 317 U.S. 492, 496, 87 L. Ed. 418, 63 S. Ct. 364 (1943))"); Murdock, 290 U.S. at 396 ("Congress did not intend that a person, by reason of a bona fide misunderstanding as to his liability for the tax, as to his duty to make a return, or as to the adequacy of the records he maintained, should become a criminal by his mere failure to measure up to the prescribed standard of conduct").

n21 Cheek, 498 U.S. at 200; see also Ratzlaf, 510 U.S. at 149 (noting the "venerable principle that ignorance of the law generally is no defense to a criminal charge," but concluding that Congress intended otherwise in the "particular context" of the currency structuring statute).

n22 Even before Ratzlaf was decided, then Chief Judge Breyer explained why there was a need for specificity under those statutes that is inapplicable when there is no danger of conviction of a defendant with an innocent state of mind. He wrote:

"I believe that criminal prosecutions for 'currency law' violations, of the sort at issue here, very much resemble criminal prosecutions for tax law violations. Compare 26 U.S.C. §§6050I, 7203 with 31 U.S.C. §§5322, 5324. Both sets of laws are technical; and both sets of laws sometimes criminalize conduct that would not strike an ordinary citizen as immoral or likely unlawful. Thus, both sets of laws may lead to the unfair result of criminally prosecuting individuals who subjectively and honestly believe they have not acted criminally. Cheek v. United States, 498 U.S. 192, 112 L. Ed. 2d 617, 111 S. Ct. 604 . . . (1991), sets forth a legal standard that, by requiring proof that the defendant was subjectively aware of the duty at issue, would avoid such unfair results." United States v. Aversa, 984 F.2d 493, 502 (CA1 1993) (concurring opinion).

He therefore concluded that the "same standards should apply in both" the tax cases and in cases such as Ratzlaf. 984 F.2d at 503.

FOPA was enacted to protect law-abiding citizens who might inadvertently violate the law.

n23 Moreover, requiring only knowledge that the conduct is unlawful is fully consistent with the purpose of FOPA, as FOPA was enacted to protect law-abiding citizens who might inadvertently violate the law. See n. 4, supra; see also United States v. Andrade, 135 F.3d 104, 108-109 (CA1 1998).

Thus, the willfulness requirement of §924(a)(1)(D) does not carve out an exception to the traditional rule that ignorance of the law is no excuse; knowledge that the conduct is unlawful is all that is required.

IV

the fears and doubts of the opposition are no authoritative guide to the construction of legislation.

In their zeal to defeat a bill, they understandably tend to overstate its reach.

Petitioner advances a number of additional arguments based on his reading of congressional intent. Petitioner first points to the legislative history of FOPA, but that history is too ambiguous to offer petitioner much assistance. Petitioner's main support lies in statements made by opponents of the bill. n24 As we have stated, however, "the fears and doubts of the opposition are no authoritative guide to the construction of legislation." Schwegmann Brothers v. Calvert Distillers Corp., 341 U.S. 384, 394, 95 L. Ed. 1035, 71 S. Ct. 745 (1951). "In their zeal to defeat a bill, they understandably tend to overstate its reach." NLRB v. Fruit Packers, 377 U.S. 58, 66, 12 L. Ed. 2d 129, 84 S. Ct. 1063 (1964). n25

n24 For example, Representative Hughes, a staunch opponent of the bill, stated that the willfulness requirement would "make it next to impossible to convict dealers, particularly those who engage in business without acquiring a license, because the prosecution would have to show that the dealer was personally aware of every detail of the law, and that he made a conscious decision to violate the law." 132 Cong. Rec. 6875 (1986). Even petitioner's amicus acknowledges that this statement was "undoubtedly an exaggeration." Brief for National Association of Criminal Defense Lawyers as Amicus Curiae 14.

n25 See also Andrade, 135 F.3d at 108-109.

Petitioner next argues that, at the time FOPA was passed, the "willfulness" requirements in other subsections of the statute -- §§923(d)(1)(C)-(D) -- had uniformly been interpreted by lower courts to require knowledge of the law; petitioner argues that Congress intended that "willfully" should have the same meaning in §924(a)(1)(D). As an initial matter, the lower courts had come to no such agreement. While some courts had stated that willfulness in §923(d)(1) is satisfied by a disregard of a known legal obligation, n26 willful was also interpreted variously to refer to "purposeful, intentional conduct," n27 "indifference to the requirements of the law," n28 or merely a "conscious, intentional, deliberate, voluntary decision." n29 Moreover, in each of the cases in which disregard of a known legal obligation was held to be sufficient to establish willfulness, it was perfectly clear from the record that the licensee had knowledge of the law n30 ; thus, while these cases support the notion that disregard of a known legal obligation is sufficient to establish a willful violation, they in no way stand for the proposition that it is required. n31

n26 See, e.g., Perri v. Department of the Treasury, 637 F.2d 1332, 1336 (CA9 1981); Stein's Inc. v. Blumenthal, 649 F.2d 463, 467-468 (CA7 1980).

n27 Rich v. United States, 383 F. Supp. 797, 800 (SD Ohio 1974).

n28 Lewin v. Blumenthal, 590 F.2d 268, 269 (CA8 1979); Fin & Feather Sport Shop v. United States Treasury Department, 481 F. Supp. 800, 807 (Neb. 1979).

n29 Prino v. Simon, 606 F.2d 449, 451 (CA4 1979) (internal quotation marks omitted); see also Stein's, 649 F.2d at 467 ("If a person 1) intentionally does an act which is prohibited,- irrespective of evil motive or reliance on erroneous advice, or 2) acts with careless disregard of statutory requirements, the violation is willful" (internal quotation marks omitted)).

n30 Perri, 637 F.2d at 1336 ("The district court found Perri knew a strawman transaction would violate the Act"); Stein's, 649 F.2d at 468 ("The record shows that the plaintiff's agents were instructed on the requirements of the law and acknowledged an understanding of the Secretary's regulations. Nevertheless, and despite repeated warnings from the Secretary, violations continued to occur" (footnote omitted)); Powers v. Bureau of Alcohol, Tobacco and Firearms, 505 F. Supp. 695, 698 (ND Fla. 1980) ("Bureau representatives inspected Powers August 31, 1976. They pointed out his many violations, gave him a copy of the regulations, thoroughly explained his obligations, and gave him a pamphlet explaining his obligations. As of that date Powers knew his obligations"); Shyda v. Director, Bureau of Alcohol, Tobacco and Firearms, 448 F. Supp. 409, 415 (MD Pa. 1977) ("At the formal administrative hearing petitioner admitted on the stand under oath that he was aware of the specific legal obligation at issue"); Mayesh v. Schultz, 58 F.R.D. 537, 540 (SD Ill. 1973) ("The uncontroverted evidence shows clearly that plaintiff was aware of the above holding period requirements. Mr. Mayesh had been previously advised on the requirements under Illinois law, and he clearly acknowledged that he was aware of them"); McLemore v. United States Treasury Department, 317 F. Supp. 1077, 1078 (ND Fla. 1970) (finding that both the owner of the pawnshop, as well as his employees, had knowledge of the law).

n31 In Mayesh, for example, the court stated:

"The uncontroverted evidence shows clearly that plaintiff was aware of the above holding period requirements. Mr. Mayesh had been previously advised on the requirements under Illinois law, and he clearly acknowledged that he was aware of them . . . . Since the material facts are undisputed, as a matter of law the plaintiff clearly and knowingly violated the Illinois holding provisions . . . , and hence, 18 U.S.C. §922(b)(2). This court can only consider such action to have been 'wilful' as a matter of law. There is no basis for trial of any disputed facts in this connection. This is sufficient to justify refusal of license renewal." 58 F.R.D. at 540.

See also, e.g., Perri, 637 F.2d at 1336 (stating that when a dealer understands the requirements of the law, but knowingly fails to follow them or is indifferent to them, willfulness "is established," i.e., is satisfied); Stein's, 649 F.2d at 468 ("Evidence of repeated violations with knowledge of the law's requirements has been held sufficient to establish willfulness" (emphasis added)); McLemore, 317 F. Supp. at 1078-1079.

Finally, petitioner argues that §922(b)(3), which is governed by §924(a)(1)(D)'s willfulness standard, indicates that Congress intended "willfully" to include knowledge of the law. Subsection 922(b)(3) prohibits licensees from selling firearms to any person who the licensee knows or has reasonable cause to believe does not reside in the licensee's State, except where, inter alia, the transaction fully complies with the laws of both the seller's and buyer's State. The subsection further states that the licensee "shall be presumed, . . . in the absence of evidence to the contrary, to have had actual knowledge of the State laws and published ordinances of both States." n32 Although petitioner argues that the presumption in §922(b)(3) indicates that Congress intended willfulness to require knowledge of the law for all offenses covered by §924(a)(1)(D), petitioner is mistaken. As noted above, while disregard of a known legal obligation is certainly sufficient to establish a willful violation, it is not necessary -- and nothing in §922(b)(3) contradicts this basic distinction. n33

n32 18 U.S.C. §922(b)(3).

n33 Petitioner also argues that the statutory language -- "willfully violates any other provision of this chapter" -- indicates a congressional intent to attach liability only when a defendant possesses specific knowledge of the "provisions of [the] chapter." We rejected a similar argument in United States v. International Minerals & Chemical Corp., 402 U.S. 558, 29 L. Ed. 2d 178, 91 S. Ct. 1697 (1971). Although that case involved the word "knowingly" (in the phrase "knowingly violates any such regulation"), the response is the same:

"We . . . see no reason why the word 'regulations' [or the phrase 'any other provision of this chapter'] should not be construed as a shorthand designation for specific acts or omissions which violate the Act. The Act, so viewed, does not signal an exception to the rule that ignorance of the law is no excuse . . . ." Id., at 562.

V

One sentence in the trial court's instructions to the jury, read by itself, contained a misstatement of the law. In a portion of the instructions that were given after the correct statement that we have already quoted, the judge stated: "In this case, the government is not required to prove that the defendant knew that a license was required, nor is the government required to prove that he had knowledge that he was breaking the law." App. 19 (emphasis added). If the judge had added the words "that required a license," the sentence would have been accurate, but as given it was not.

Nevertheless, that error does not provide a basis for reversal for four reasons. First, petitioner did not object to that sentence, except insofar as he had argued that the jury should have been instructed that the Government had the burden of proving that he had knowledge of the federal licensing requirement. Second, in the context of the entire instructions, it seems unlikely that the jury was misled. See, e.g., United States v. Park, 421 U.S. 658, 674-675, 44 L. Ed. 2d 489, 95 S. Ct. 1903 (1975). Third, petitioner failed to raise this argument in the Court of Appeals. Finally, our grant of certiorari was limited to the narrow legal question whether knowledge of the licensing requirement is an essential element of the offense.

Accordingly, the judgment of the Court of Appeals is affirmed.

It is so ordered.

JUSTICE SOUTER, concurring

I join in the Court's opinion with the caveat that if petitioner had raised and preserved a specific objection to the erroneous statement in the jury instructions, see Part V, ante, at 15-16, I would vote to vacate the conviction.

JUSTICE SCALIA, with whom THE CHIEF JUSTICE and JUSTICE GINSBURG join, dissenting.

the Court curiously falls back on "the traditional rule that ignorance of the law is no excuse" to conclude that "knowledge that the conduct is unlawful is all that is required."

In my view, this case calls for the application of a different canon—"the familiar rule that, 'where there is ambiguity in a criminal statute, doubts are resolved in favor of the defendant.'"

Petitioner Sillasse Bryan was convicted of "willfully" violating the federal licensing requirement for firearms dealers. The jury apparently found, and the evidence clearly shows, that Bryan was aware in a general way that some aspect of his conduct was unlawful. See ante, at 4-5 and n. 8. The issue is whether that general knowledge of illegality is enough to sustain the conviction, or whether a "willful" violation of the licensing provision requires proof that the defendant knew that his conduct was unlawful specifically because he lacked the necessary license. On that point the statute is, in my view, genuinely ambiguous. Most of the Court's opinion is devoted to confirming half of that ambiguity by refuting Bryan's various arguments that the statute clearly requires specific knowledge of the licensing requirement. Ante, at 7-15. The Court offers no real justification for its implicit conclusion that either (1) the statute unambiguously requires only general knowledge of illegality, or (2) ambiguously requiring only general knowledge is enough. Instead, the Court curiously falls back on "the traditional rule that ignorance of the law is no excuse" to conclude that "knowledge that the conduct is unlawful is all that is required." Ante, at 11. In my view, this case calls for the application of a different canon -- "the familiar rule that, 'where there is ambiguity in a criminal statute, doubts are resolved in favor of the defendant.'" Adamo Wrecking Co. v. United States, 434 U.S. 275, 284-285, 54 L. Ed. 2d 538, 98 S. Ct. 566 (1978), quoting United States v. Bass, 404 U.S. 336, 348, 30 L. Ed. 2d 488, 92 S. Ct. 515 (1971).

Section 922(a)(1)(A) of Title 18 makes it unlawful for any person to engage in the business of dealing in firearms without a federal license. That provision is enforced criminally through §924(a)(1)(D), which imposes criminal penalties on whoever "willfully violates any other provision of this chapter." The word "willfully" has a wide range of meanings, and "'its construction [is] often . . . influenced by its context.'" Ratzlaf v. United States, 510 U.S. 135, 141, 126 L. Ed. 2d 615, 114 S. Ct. 655 (1994), quoting Spies v. United States, 317 U.S. 492, 497, 87 L. Ed. 418, 63 S. Ct. 364 (1943). In some contexts it connotes nothing more than "an act which is intentional, or knowing, or voluntary, as distinguished from accidental." United States v. Murdock, 290 U.S. 389, 394, 78 L. Ed. 381, 54 S. Ct. 223 (1933). In the present context, however, inasmuch as the preceding three subparagraphs of §924 specify a mens rea of "knowingly" for other firearms offenses, see §§924(a)(1)(A)-(C), a "willful" violation under §924(a)(1)(D) must require some mental state more culpable than mere intent to perform the forbidden act. The United States concedes (and the Court apparently agrees) that the violation is not "willful" unless the defendant knows in a general way that his conduct is unlawful. Brief for United States 7-9; ante, at 9 ("The jury must find that the defendant acted with an evil-meaning mind, that is to say, that he acted with knowledge that his conduct was unlawful").

That concession takes this case beyond any useful application of the maxim that ignorance of the law is no excuse. Everyone agrees that §924(a)(1)(D) requires some knowledge of the law; the only real question is which law? The Court's answer is that knowledge of any law is enough -- or, put another way, that the defendant must be ignorant of every law violated by his course of conduct to be innocent of willfully violating the licensing requirement. The Court points to no textual basis for that conclusion other than the notoriously malleable word "willfully" itself. Instead, it seems to fall back on a presumption (apparently derived from the rule that ignorance of the law is no excuse) that even where ignorance of the law is an excuse, that excuse should be construed as narrowly as the statutory language permits.

Bryan would also be "acting with an evil-meaning mind," and hence presumably be guilty of "willfully" dealing in firearms without a license, if he knew that his street-corner transactions violated New York City's business licensing or sales tax ordinances. (For that matter, it ought to suffice if Bryan knew that the car out of which he sold the guns was illegally double-parked, or if, in order to meet the appointed time for the sale, he intentionally violated Pennsylvania's speed limit on the drive back from the gun purchase in Ohio.) Once we stop focusing on the conduct the defendant is actually charged with (i.e., selling guns without a license), I see no principled way to determine what law the defendant must be conscious of violating.

I do not believe that the Court's approach makes sense of the statute that Congress enacted. I have no quarrel with the Court's assertion that "willfully" in §924(a)(1)(D) requires only "general" knowledge of illegality -- in the sense that the defendant need not be able to recite chapter and verse from Title 18 of the United States Code. It is enough, in my view, if the defendant is generally aware that the actus reus punished by the statute -- dealing in firearms without a license -- is illegal. But the Court is willing to accept a mens rea so "general" that it is entirely divorced from the actus reus this statute was enacted to punish. That approach turns §924(a)(1)(D) into a strange and unlikely creature. Bryan would be guilty of "willfully" dealing in firearms without a federal license even if, for example, he had never heard of the licensing requirement but was aware that he had violated the law by using straw purchasers or filing the serial numbers off the pistols. Ante, at 5, n. 8. The Court does not even limit (for there is no rational basis to limit) the universe of relevant laws to federal firearms statutes. Bryan would also be "acting with an evil-meaning mind," and hence presumably be guilty of "willfully" dealing in firearms without a license, if he knew that his street-corner transactions violated New York City's business licensing or sales tax ordinances. (For that matter, it ought to suffice if Bryan knew that the car out of which he sold the guns was illegally double-parked, or if, in order to meet the appointed time for the sale, he intentionally violated Pennsylvania's speed limit on the drive back from the gun purchase in Ohio.) Once we stop focusing on the conduct the defendant is actually charged with (i.e., selling guns without a license), I see no principled way to determine what law the defendant must be conscious of violating. See, e.g., Lewis v. United States, 523 U.S. 155 (1998) (slip op., at 2-3) (SCALIA, J., concurring in judgment) (pointing out a similar interpretive problem potentially raised by the Assimilative Crimes Act).

Congress is free, of course, to make criminal liability under one statute turn on knowledge of another, to use its firearms dealer statutes to encourage compliance with New York City's tax collection efforts, and to put judges and juries through the kind of mental gymnastics described above. But these are strange results, and I would not lightly assume that Congress intended to make liability under a federal criminal statute depend so heavily upon the vagaries of local law -- particularly local law dealing with completely unrelated subjects. If we must have a presumption in cases like this one, I think it would be more reasonable to presume that, when Congress makes ignorance of the law a defense to a criminal prohibition, it ordinarily means ignorance of the unlawfulness of the specific conduct punished by that criminal prohibition.

That is the meaning we have given the word "willfully" in other contexts where we have concluded it requires knowledge of the law. See, e.g., Ratzlaf, 510 U.S. at 149 ("To convict Ratzlaf of the crime with which he was charged, . . . the jury had to find he knew the structuring in which he engaged was unlawful"); Cheek v. United States, 498 U.S. 192, 201, 112 L. Ed. 2d 617, 111 S. Ct. 604 (1991) ("The standard for the statutory willfulness requirement is the 'voluntary, intentional violation of a known legal duty.' . . . The issue is whether the defendant knew of the duty purportedly imposed by the provision of the statute or regulation he is accused of violating"). The Court explains these cases on the ground that they involved "highly technical statutes that presented the danger of ensnaring individuals engaged in apparently innocent conduct." Ante, at 10-11. That is no explanation at all. The complexity of the tax and currency laws may explain why the Court interpreted "willful" to require some awareness of illegality, as opposed to merely "an act which is intentional, or knowing, or voluntary, as distinguished from accidental." Murdock, 290 U.S. at 394. But it in no way justifies the distinction the Court seeks to draw today between knowledge of the law the defendant is actually charged with violating and knowledge of any law the defendant could conceivably be charged with violating. To protect the pure of heart, it is not necessary to forgive someone whose surreptitious laundering of drug money violates, unbeknownst to him, a technical currency statute. There, as here, regardless of how "complex" the violated statute may be, the defendant would have acted "with an evil-meaning mind."

It seems to me likely that Congress had a presumption of offense-specific knowledge of illegality in mind when it enacted the provision here at issue. Another section of the Firearms Owners' Protection Act, Pub. L. No. 99-308, 100 Stat. 449, prohibits licensed dealers from selling firearms to out-of-state residents unless they fully comply with the laws of both States. 18 U.S.C. §922(b)(3). The provision goes on to state that all licensed dealers "shall be presumed, for purposes of this subparagraph, in the absence of evidence to the contrary, to have had actual knowledge of the State laws and published ordinances of both States." Ibid. Like the dealer-licensing provision at issue here, a violation of §922(b)(3) is a criminal offense only if committed "willfully" within the meaning of §924(a)(1)(D). The Court is quite correct that this provision does not establish beyond doubt that "willfully" requires knowledge of the particular prohibitions violated: the fact that knowledge (attributed knowledge) of those prohibitions will be sufficient does not demonstrate conclusively that knowledge of other prohibitions will not be sufficient. Ante, at 14-15. But though it does not demonstrate, it certainly suggests. To say that only willful violation of a certain law is criminal, but that knowledge of the existence of that law is presumed, fairly reflects, I think, a presumption that willful violation requires knowledge of the law violated.

If one had to choose, therefore, I think a presumption of statutory intent that is the opposite of the one the Court applies would be more reasonable. I would not, however, decide this case on the basis of any presumption at all. It is common ground that the statutory context here requires some awareness of the law for a §924(a)(1)(D) conviction, but the statute is simply ambiguous, or silent, as to the precise contours of that mens rea requirement. In the face of that ambiguity, I would invoke the rule that "'ambiguity concerning the ambit of criminal statutes should be resolved in favor of lenity,'" United States v. Bass, 404 U.S. at 347, quoting Rewis v. United States, 401 U.S. 808, 812, 28 L. Ed. 2d 493, 91 S. Ct. 1056 (1971).

It is founded on the tenderness of the law for the rights of individuals; and on the plain principle that the power of punishment is vested in the legislative, not in the judicial department."

"The rule that penal laws are to be construed strictly, is, perhaps, not much less old than construction itself. It is founded on the tenderness of the law for the rights of individuals; and on the plain principle that the power of punishment is vested in the legislative, not in the judicial department." United States v. Wiltberger, 18 U.S. 76, 5 Wheat. 76, 95, 5 L. Ed. 37 (1820).

In our era of multiplying new federal crimes, there is more reason than ever to give this ancient canon of construction consistent application: by fostering uniformity in the interpretation of criminal statutes, it will reduce the occasions on which this Court will have to produce judicial havoc by resolving in defendants' favor a circuit conflict regarding the substantive elements of a federal crime, see, e.g., Bousley v. United States, 523 U.S. 614, 140 L. Ed. 2d 828, 118 S. Ct. 1604 (1998).

I respectfully dissent.

CARON v. UNITED STATES

(CASE EXCERPT)

524 U.S. 308; 118 S. Ct. 2007; 141 L. Ed. 2d 303

April 21, 1998, Argued

June 22, 1998, Decided

GIST: Under federal law, a person previously convicted of an offense punishable by a penalty of at least one year in jail may not possess any firearm, and a person previously convicted of three or more such serious offenses is subject to a mandatory five-year enhanced penalty. A prior conviction no longer counts however, if the state has restored the defendant's civil rights, unless the restoration of rights expressly provides that the person may not possess firearms.

Caron had a long rap sheet, including four felony priors. Three of these were in Massachusetts, which had automatically restored most of his civil rights after five years and issued him a firearms permit for rifles, shotguns and handguns, but subject to a restriction that he may only possess the handguns in his home or business. This criminal tried to skate by claiming the limited state restoration was a complete remedy, but the Court wasn't buying. The Court held that if the defendant remains subject to any restriction on firearms ownership—that the state considers him too dangerous to have handguns while out and about—the federal government can count the offenses toward application of the enhanced sentence.

The decision comes close to a precarious position that federal controls are fine, tied to a novel though undefined concept of excessive degree of dangerousness. Contrast this concept of dangerousness with one typical of firearms experts who assert that guns are supposed to be dangerous, and wouldn't be much good if they weren't dangerous (Massad Ayoob), and that a gun that's safe isn't worth anything (Col. Jeff Cooper).

In a well-reasoned dissent, three justices argue that it is "bizarre" for the Court to subject a person to an enhanced penalty for behavior their state law allows.

JUSTICE KENNEDY delivered the opinion of the Court.

Under federal law, a person convicted of a crime punishable by more than one year in prison may not possess any firearm. 18 U.S.C. §922(g)(1). If he has three violent felony convictions and violates the statute, he must receive an enhanced sentence. §924(e). A previous conviction is a predicate for neither the substantive offense nor the sentence enhancement if the offender has had his civil rights restored, "unless such . . . restoration of civil rights expressly provides that the person may not . . . possess . . . firearms." §921(a)(20). This is the so-called "unless clause" we now must interpret. As the ellipses suggest, the statute is more complex, but the phrase as quoted presents the issue for our decision.

.....

Petitioner Gerald Caron has an extensive criminal record, including felonies. In Massachusetts state court, he was convicted in 1958 of attempted breaking and entering at night and, in 1959 and 1963, of breaking and entering at night. In California state court, he was convicted in 1970 of assault with intent to commit murder and attempted murder.

In July 1993, petitioner walked into the home of Walter Miller, carrying a semiautomatic rifle. He threatened Miller, brandished the rifle in his face, and pointed it at his wife, his daughters, and his 3-year-old grandson.

In July 1993, petitioner walked into the home of Walter Miller, carrying a semiautomatic rifle. He threatened Miller, brandished the rifle in his face, and pointed it at his wife, his daughters, and his 3-year-old grandson. Police officers disarmed and arrested petitioner.

.....

Massachusetts law allowed petitioner to possess rifles or shotguns, as he had the necessary firearm permit and his felony convictions were more than five years old. The law forbade him to possess handguns outside his home or business.

A federal jury convicted petitioner of four counts of possessing a firearm or ammunition after having been convicted of a serious offense. See 18 U.S.C. §922(g)(1). The District Court enhanced his sentence because he was at least a three-time violent felon, based on his one California and three Massachusetts convictions. See §924(e). Petitioner claimed the Court should not have counted his Massachusetts convictions because his civil rights had been restored by operation of Massachusetts law. Massachusetts law allowed petitioner to possess rifles or shotguns, as he had the necessary firearm permit and his felony convictions were more than five years old. The law forbade him to possess handguns outside his home or business.

.....

Congress meant to keep guns away from all offenders who, the Federal Government feared, might cause harm, even if those persons were not deemed dangerous by States.

The need for this caution is borne out by petitioner's rifle attack on the Miller family, in which petitioner used a gun permitted by state law.

Permission to possess one gun cannot mean permission to possess all.

In Congress' view, existing state laws "provide less than positive assurance that the person in question no longer poses an unacceptable risk of dangerousness." Congress meant to keep guns away from all offenders who, the Federal Government feared, might cause harm, even if those persons were not deemed dangerous by States. If federal law is to provide the missing "positive assurance," it must reach primary conduct not covered by state law. The need for this caution is borne out by petitioner's rifle attack on the Miller family, in which petitioner used a gun permitted by state law. Any other result would reduce federal law to a sentence enhancement for some state-law violations, a result inconsistent with the congressional intent we recognized in Dickerson. Permission to possess one gun cannot mean permission to possess all.

Congress responded to our ruling in Dickerson by providing that the law of the State of conviction, not federal law, determines the restoration of civil rights as a rule.

As to the possession of weapons, however, the Federal Government has an interest in a single, national, protective policy, broader than required by state law. Petitioner's approach would undermine this protective purpose.

Congress responded to our ruling in Dickerson by providing that the law of the State of conviction, not federal law, determines the restoration of civil rights as a rule. While state law is the source of law for restorations of other civil rights, however, it does not follow that state law also controls the unless clause. Under the Government's approach, with which we agree, the federal policy still governs the interpretation of the unless clause. We see nothing contradictory in this analysis. Restoration of the right to vote, the right to hold office, and the right to sit on a jury turns on so many complexities and nuances that state law is the most convenient source for definition. As to the possession of weapons, however, the Federal Government has an interest in a single, national, protective policy, broader than required by state law. Petitioner's approach would undermine this protective purpose.

.....

Massachusetts treats petitioner as too dangerous to trust with handguns, though it accords this right to law-abiding citizens. Federal law uses this state finding of dangerousness in forbidding petitioner to have any guns.

In sum, Massachusetts treats petitioner as too dangerous to trust with handguns, though it accords this right to law-abiding citizens. Federal law uses this state finding of dangerousness in forbidding petitioner to have any guns.

JUSTICE THOMAS, with whom JUSTICE SCALIA and JUSTICE SOUTER join, dissenting.

The only limitation that Massachusetts law imposed on petitioner's possession of firearms was that he could not carry handguns outside his home or business. In my view, Massachusetts law did not "expressly provide" that petitioner "may not . . . possess . . . firearms," 18 U.S.C. §921(a)(20), and thus petitioner cannot be sentenced as an armed career criminal under 18 U.S.C. §924(e). Because the Court holds to the contrary, I respectfully dissent.

Petitioner was permitted by Massachusetts law to possess shotguns, rifles, and handguns. Indeed, Massachusetts provided petitioner with a firearm identification card

By prohibiting petitioner from possessing only certain firearms (handguns) in only certain places (outside his home or office), Massachusetts law did not expressly provide that petitioner could not possess firearms.

Petitioner's prior Massachusetts convictions qualify as violent felonies for purposes of §924(e) only if the "restoration of [his] civil rights" by operation of Massachusetts law "expressly provided that [petitioner] may not . . . possess . . . firearms." 18 U.S.C. §921(a)(20). In 1994, Massachusetts law did not expressly provide that petitioner could not possess firearms. To the contrary: Petitioner was permitted by Massachusetts law to possess shotguns, rifles, and handguns. Indeed, Massachusetts provided petitioner with a firearm identification card that enabled him to possess such firearms. The only restriction Massachusetts law placed on petitioner's possession of firearms was that he could not carry handguns outside his home or business. See §269:10(A). By prohibiting petitioner from possessing only certain firearms (handguns) in only certain places (outside his home or office), Massachusetts law did not expressly provide that petitioner could not possess firearms.

The plain meaning of §921(a)(20) thus resolves this case. The Court, however, rejects this plain meaning on the basis of "a likely, and rational, congressional policy" of prohibiting firearms possession by all ex-felons whose ability to possess certain firearms is in any way restricted by state law. According to the Court, Congress could not have intended the "bizarre result" that a conviction would not count as a violent felony if a State only partially restricts the possession of firearms by the ex-felon. But this would not be a bizarre result at all. Under §921(a)(20), state law limitations on firearms possession are only relevant once it has been established that an ex-felon's other civil rights, such as the right to vote, the right to seek and to hold public office, and the right to serve on a jury, have been restored. In restoring those rights, the State has presumably deemed such ex-felons worthy of participating in civic life. Once a State makes such a decision, it is entirely rational (and certainly not bizarre) for Congress to authorize the increased sentences in §924(e) only when the State additionally prohibits those ex-felons from possessing firearms altogether.

Given the primacy of state law in the statutory scheme, it is bizarre to hold that the legal possession of firearms under state law subjects a person to a sentence enhancement under federal law. That, however, is precisely the conclusion the Court reaches in this case.

Moreover, as the Court concedes, its own interpretation creates "incongruities." Under the statute, whether a prior state conviction qualifies as a violent felony conviction under §924(e) turns entirely on state law. Given the primacy of state law in the statutory scheme, it is bizarre to hold that the legal possession of firearms under state law subjects a person to a sentence enhancement under federal law. That, however, is precisely the conclusion the Court reaches in this case. It is simply not true, as the Court reasons, that federal law "must reach primary conduct not covered by state law." It is entirely plausible that Congress simply intended to create stiffer penalties for weapons possessions that are already illegal under state law. And such a purpose is consistent with the statutory direction that state law controls what constitutes a conviction for a violent felony.

Ex-felons cannot be expected to realize that a federal statute that explicitly relies on state law prohibits behavior that state law allows.

I believe that the plain meaning of the statute is that Massachusetts did not "expressly provide" that petitioner "may not . . . possess . . . firearms." At the very least, this interpretation is a plausible one. Indeed, both the Government and the Court concede as much. See Brief for United States 16 ("grammatically possible" to read statute to say that its condition is not satisfied if the State does permit its felons to possess some firearms); ante, at 8 (this "reading is not plausible enough"). Accordingly, it is far from clear under the statute that a prior state conviction counts as a violent felony conviction for purposes of §924(e) just because the State imposes some restriction, no matter how slight, on firearms possession by ex-felons. The rule of lenity must therefore apply: "The Court will not interpret a federal criminal statute so as to increase the penalty that it places on an individual when such an interpretation can be based on no more than a guess as to what Congress intended." Ex-felons cannot be expected to realize that a federal statute that explicitly relies on state law prohibits behavior that state law allows.

The Court rejects the rule of lenity in this case because it thinks the purported statutory ambiguity rests on a "grammatical possibility" and "an implausible reading of the congressional purpose." But the alleged ambiguity does not result from a mere grammatical possibility; it exists because of an interpretation that, for the reasons I have described, both accords with a natural reading of the statutory language and is consistent with the statutory purpose.

The plain meaning of §921(a)(20) is that Massachusetts law did not "expressly provide that [petitioner] may not . . . possess . . . firearms." This interpretation is, at the very least, a plausible one, and the rule of lenity must apply. I would therefore reverse the judgment below.

PENNSYLVANIA BOARD OF PROBATION AND PAROLE v. SCOTT

(CASE EXCERPT)

524 U.S. 357; 118 S. Ct. 2014; 141 L. Ed. 2d 344

March 30, 1998, Argued

June 22, 1998, Decided

GIST: The exclusionary rule of the 4th Amendment prohibits the use of illegally obtained evidence at a trial. It serves, in part, as a deterrent to official misconduct. This is a 4th Amendment case in which the Court held that the exclusionary rule does not require exclusion of illegally seized evidence at a parole revocation hearing.

Firearms seized from Keith Scott's home in violation of his 4th Amendment rights were therefore properly admitted into evidence at his parole revocation hearing, and his goose was cooked. Scott, a felon on parole (he had just served ten years in prison for third degree murder), had been caught at his mother's home, where he lived, with five firearms, a compound bow and some arrows. He got three more years.

JUSTICE THOMAS delivered the opinion of the Court.

This case presents the question whether the exclusionary rule, which generally prohibits the introduction at criminal trial of evidence obtained in violation of a defendant's Fourth Amendment rights, applies in parole revocation hearings. We hold that it does not.

.....

One of the conditions of respondent's parole was that he would refrain from "owning or possessing any firearms or other weapons."

One of the conditions of respondent's parole was that he would refrain from "owning or possessing any firearms or other weapons." The parole agreement, which respondent signed, further provided:

"I expressly consent to the search of my person, property and residence, without a warrant by agents of the Pennsylvania Board of Probation and Parole. Any items, in [sic] the possession of which constitutes a violation of parole/reparole shall be subject to seizure, and may be used as evidence in the parole revocation process."

About five months later, after obtaining an arrest warrant based on evidence that respondent had violated several conditions of his parole by possessing firearms, consuming alcohol, and assaulting a co-worker, three parole officers arrested respondent at a local diner. Before being transferred to a correctional facility, respondent gave the officers the keys to his residence. The officers entered the home, which was owned by his mother, but did not perform a search for parole violations until respondent's mother arrived. The officers neither requested nor obtained consent to perform the search, but respondent's mother did direct them to his bedroom. After finding no relevant evidence there, the officers searched an adjacent sitting room in which they found five firearms, a compound bow, and three arrows.

At his parole violation hearing, respondent objected to the introduction of the evidence obtained during the search of his home on the ground that the search was unreasonable under the Fourth Amendment. The hearing examiner, however, rejected the challenge and admitted the evidence. As a result, the Pennsylvania Board of Probation and Parole found sufficient evidence in the record to support the weapons and alcohol charges and recommitted respondent to serve 36 months' backtime.

.....

We have long been averse to imposing federal requirements upon the parole systems of the States. A federal requirement that parole boards apply the exclusionary rule, which is itself a "grudgingly taken medicant," United States v. Janis, supra, at 454, n. 29 (1976), would severely disrupt the traditionally informal, administrative process of parole revocation. The marginal deterrence of unreasonable searches and seizures is insufficient to justify such an intrusion. We therefore hold that parole boards are not required by federal law to exclude evidence obtained in violation of the Fourth Amendment. Accordingly, the judgment below is reversed, and the case is remanded to the Pennsylvania Supreme Court.

It is so ordered.

FLORIDA v. J. L.

(CASE EXCERPT)

529 U.S. 266; 120 S. Ct. 1375; 146 L. Ed. 2d 254

February 29, 2000, Argued

March 28, 2000, Decided

GIST: This case relates to the 4th Amendment protection against an arbitrary search. Acting on an anonymous tip, police searched a man and found an unlawfully possessed gun. Because anonymous tips are known to be less reliable information, and because such tips, if allowable as grounds for a frisk could be severely abused by anyone with a grudge, the Court decided such a search was not permissible under the 4th Amendment.

Florida, and the federal government in an amicus brief, also argued that guns are so dangerous a special exemption should be made for allegations of an illegal gun from an anonymous tipster. The Court specifically rejected this request to carve out a firearm exception to the established general rule, that a tip must be reliable in its assertions of illegality, and in its assertions of identity.

Dave Kopel was one of the attorneys who filed an amicus brief in this case. That brief is posted at davekopel.org.

JUSTICE GINSBURG delivered the opinion of the Court.

The question presented in this case is whether an anonymous tip that a person is carrying a gun is, without more, sufficient to justify a police officer's stop and frisk of that person. We hold that it is not.

.....

The safety of the police and the public, they maintained, justifies a "firearm exception" to the general rule barring investigatory stops and frisks on the basis of bare-boned anonymous tips.

Anonymous tips, the Florida Supreme Court stated, are generally less reliable than tips from known informants and can form the basis for reasonable suspicion only if accompanied by specific indicia of reliability, for example, the correct forecast of a subject's "'not easily predicted'" movements. The tip leading to the frisk of J. L., the court observed, provided no such predictions, nor did it contain any other qualifying indicia of reliability. Two justices dissented. The safety of the police and the public, they maintained, justifies a "firearm exception" to the general rule barring investigatory stops and frisks on the basis of bare-boned anonymous tips.

.....

That the allegation about the gun turned out to be correct does not suggest that the officers, prior to the frisks, had a reasonable basis for suspecting J. L. of engaging in unlawful conduct: The reasonableness of official suspicion must be measured by what the officers knew before they conducted their search.

The tip in the instant case lacked the moderate indicia of reliability present in White and essential to the Court's decision in that case. The anonymous call concerning J. L. provided no predictive information and therefore left the police without means to test the informant's knowledge or credibility. That the allegation about the gun turned out to be correct does not suggest that the officers, prior to the frisks, had a reasonable basis for suspecting J. L. of engaging in unlawful conduct: The reasonableness of official suspicion must be measured by what the officers knew before they conducted their search. All the police had to go on in this case was the bare report of an unknown, unaccountable informant who neither explained how he knew about the gun nor supplied any basis for believing he had inside information about J. L. If White was a close case on the reliability of anonymous tips, this one surely falls on the other side of the line.

Florida contends that the tip was reliable because its description of the suspect's visible attributes proved accurate: There really was a young black male wearing a plaid shirt at the bus stop. The United States as amicus curiae makes a similar argument, proposing that a stop and frisk should be permitted "when (1) an anonymous tip provides a description of a particular person at a particular location illegally carrying a concealed firearm, (2) police promptly verify the pertinent details of the tip except the existence of the firearm, and (3) there are no factors that cast doubt on the reliability of the tip . . . ." These contentions misapprehend the reliability needed for a tip to justify a Terry stop.

.....

Under such an exception, a tip alleging an illegal gun would justify a stop and frisk even if the accusation would fail standard pre-search reliability testing. We decline to adopt this position.

A second major argument advanced by Florida and the United States as amicus is, in essence, that the standard Terry analysis should be modified to license a "firearm exception." Under such an exception, a tip alleging an illegal gun would justify a stop and frisk even if the accusation would fail standard pre-search reliability testing. We decline to adopt this position.

Firearms are dangerous, and extraordinary dangers sometimes justify unusual precautions. Our decisions recognize the serious threat that armed criminals pose to public safety

But an automatic firearm exception to our established reliability analysis would rove too far. Such an exception would enable any person seeking to harass another to set in motion an intrusive, embarrassing police search of the targeted person simply by placing an anonymous call falsely reporting the target's unlawful carriage of a gun.

Firearms are dangerous, and extraordinary dangers sometimes justify unusual precautions. Our decisions recognize the serious threat that armed criminals pose to public safety; Terry's rule, which permits protective police searches on the basis of reasonable suspicion rather than demanding that officers meet the higher standard of probable cause, responds to this very concern. But an automatic firearm exception to our established reliability analysis would rove too far. Such an exception would enable any person seeking to harass another to set in motion an intrusive, embarrassing police search of the targeted person simply by placing an anonymous call falsely reporting the target's unlawful carriage of a gun. Nor could one securely confine such an exception to allegations involving firearms. Several Courts of Appeals have held it per se foreseeable for people carrying significant amounts of illegal drugs to be carrying guns as well. If police officers may properly conduct Terry frisks on the basis of bare-boned tips about guns, it would be reasonable to maintain under the above-cited decisions that the police should similarly have discretion to frisk based on bare-boned tips about narcotics. As we clarified when we made indicia of reliability critical in Adams and White, the Fourth Amendment is not so easily satisfied.

The facts of this case do not require us to speculate about the circumstances under which the danger alleged in an anonymous tip might be so great as to justify a search even without a showing of reliability. We do not say, for example, that a report of a person carrying a bomb need bear the indicia of reliability we demand for a report of a person carrying a firearm before the police can constitutionally conduct a frisk. Nor do we hold that public safety officials in quarters where the reasonable expectation of Fourth Amendment privacy is diminished, such as airports, see Florida v. Rodriguez, 469 U.S. 1, 83 L. Ed. 2d 165, 105 S. Ct. 308 (1984) (per curiam), and schools, see New Jersey v. T.L.O., 469 U.S. 325, 83 L. Ed. 2d 720, 105 S. Ct. 733 (1985), cannot conduct protective searches on the basis of information insufficient to justify searches elsewhere.

We hold that an anonymous tip lacking indicia of reliability of the kind contemplated in Adams and White does not justify a stop and frisk whenever and however it alleges the illegal possession of a firearm.

Finally, the requirement that an anonymous tip bear standard indicia of reliability in order to justify a stop in no way diminishes a police officer's prerogative, in accord with Terry, to conduct a protective search of a person who has already been legitimately stopped. We speak in today's decision only of cases in which the officer's authority to make the initial stop is at issue. In that context, we hold that an anonymous tip lacking indicia of reliability of the kind contemplated in Adams and White does not justify a stop and frisk whenever and however it alleges the illegal possession of a firearm.

CASTILLO v. UNITED STATES

(FULL CASE)

530 U.S. 120; 120 S. Ct. 2090; 147 L. Ed. 2d 94

April 24, Argued

June 5, 2000, Decided

GIST: The infamous assault by the Bureau of Alcohol, Tobacco and Firearms, that resulted in the deaths of several federal agents and more than 80 members of the Branch Davidian religious group based near Waco, Texas, lead to this very narrowly focused case on a question of statutory interpretation, and a factor to be used in sentencing based on the type of firearm used. The Court concluded that the type of firearm used in a Gun Control Act violation is an element of the offense and not a mere sentencing factor, which means it must be alleged in the indictment and decided by the jury, not by a judge.

Attorney Stephen Halbrook, representing the surviving Branch Davidians charged in this case, made the winning oral arguments before the Justices.

Justice Breyer delivered the opinion of the Court.*

We conclude that the statute uses the word "machinegun" (and similar words) to state an element of a separate offense.

In this case we once again decide whether words in a federal criminal statute create offense elements (determined by a jury) or sentencing factors (determined by a judge). See Jones v. United States, 526 U.S. 227 (1999); Almendarez-Torres v. United States, 523 U.S. 224 (1998). The statute in question, 18 U.S.C. § 924(c) (1988 ed., Supp. V), prohibits the use or carrying of a "firearm" in relation to a crime of violence, and increases the penalty dramatically when the weapon used or carried is, for example, a "machinegun." We conclude that the statute uses the word "machinegun" (and similar words) to state an element of a separate offense.

I

Petitioners are members of the Branch-Davidian religious sect and are among those who were involved in a violent confrontation with federal agents from the Bureau of Alcohol, Tobacco, and Firearms near Waco, Texas, in 1993.

Petitioners are members of the Branch-Davidian religious sect and are among those who were involved in a violent confrontation with federal agents from the Bureau of Alcohol, Tobacco, and Firearms near Waco, Texas, in 1993. The case before us arises out of an indictment alleging that, among other things, petitioners conspired to murder federal officers. At the time of petitioners' trial, the criminal statute at issue (reprinted in its entirety in the Appendix, infra) read in relevant part:

"(c)(1) Whoever, during and in relation to any crime of violence . . . , uses or carries a firearm, shall, in addition to the punishment provided for such crime of violence . . . , be sentenced to imprisonment for five years, and if the firearm is a short barreled rifle [or a] short-barreled shotgun to imprisonment for ten years, and if the firearm is a machinegun, or a destructive device, or is equipped with a firearm silencer or firearm muffler, to imprisonment for thirty years." 18 U.S.C. § 924(c)(1) (1988 ed., Supp. V).

At sentencing, the judge found that the "firearms" at issue included certain machineguns (many equipped with silencers) and handgrenades that the defendants actually or constructively had possessed.

A jury determined that petitioners had violated this section by, in the words of the trial judge's instruction, "knowingly us[ing] or carr[ying] a firearm during and in relation to" the commission of a crime of violence. App. 29. At sentencing, the judge found that the "firearms" at issue included certain machineguns (many equipped with silencers) and handgrenades that the defendants actually or constructively had possessed. United States v. Branch, Crim. No. W—93—CR—046 (WD Tex., June 21, 1994), reprinted in App. to Pet. for Cert. 119a, 124a—125a. The judge then imposed the statute's mandatory 30-year prison sentence. Id., at 134a.

Petitioners appealed. Meanwhile, this Court decided that the word "use" in §924(c)(1) requires evidence of more than "mere possession." Bailey v. United States, 516 U.S. 137, 143 (1995). The Court of Appeals subsequently held that our decision in Bailey necessitated a remand of the case to determine whether, in Bailey's stronger sense of "use," petitioners had used "machineguns and other enhancing weapons." United States v. Branch, 91 F.3d 699, 740—741 (CA5 1996). The court also concluded that statutory words such as "machinegun" create sentencing factors, i.e., factors that enhance a sentence, not elements of a separate crime. Id., at 738—740. Hence, it specified that the jury "was not required" to determine whether petitioners used or carried "machineguns" or other enhanced weapons. Id., at 740. Rather, it wrote that "[s]hould the district court find on remand that members of the conspiracy actively employed machineguns, it is free to reimpose the 30-year sentence." Id., at 740—741 (emphasis added). On remand, the District Court resentenced petitioners to 30-year terms of imprisonment based on its weapons-related findings. See App. to Pet. for Cert. 119a. The Court of Appeals affirmed. 179 F.3d 321 (CA5 1999).

The Federal Courts of Appeals have different views as to whether the statutory word "machinegun" (and similar words appearing in the version of 18 U.S.C. § 924(c)(1) here at issue) refers to a sentencing factor to be assessed by the trial court or creates a new substantive crime to be determined by the jury. Compare, e.g., United States v. Alborola-Rodriguez, 153 F.3d 1269, 1272 (CA11 1998) (sentencing factor), with United States v. Alerta, 96 F.3d 1230, 1235 (CA9 1996) (element). We granted certiorari to resolve the conflict.

II

consideration of §924(c)(1)'s language, structure, context, history, and such other factors as typically help courts determine a statute's objectives, leads us to conclude that the relevant words create a separate substantive crime.

The question before us is whether Congress intended the statutory references to particular firearm types in §924(c)(1) to define a separate crime or simply to authorize an enhanced penalty. If the former, the indictment must identify the firearm type and a jury must find that element proved beyond a reasonable doubt. If the latter, the matter need not be tried before a jury but may be left for the sentencing judge to decide. As petitioners note, our decision in Jones concluded, in a similar situation, that treating facts that lead to an increase in the maximum sentence as a sentencing factor would give rise to significant constitutional questions. See Jones, supra, at 239—252. Here, even apart from the doctrine of constitutional doubt, our consideration of §924(c)(1)'s language, structure, context, history, and such other factors as typically help courts determine a statute's objectives, leads us to conclude that the relevant words create a separate substantive crime.

First, while the statute's literal language, taken alone, appears neutral, its overall structure strongly favors the "new crime" interpretation. The relevant statutory sentence says: "Whoever, during and in relation to any crime of violence ... , uses or carries a firearm, shall ... be sentenced to imprisonment for five years, and if the firearm is a . . . machinegun, . . . to imprisonment for thirty years." §924(c)(1). On the one hand, one could read the words "during and in relation to a crime of violence" and "uses or carries a firearm" as setting forth two basic elements of the offense, and the subsequent "machinegun" phrase as merely increasing a defendant's sentence in relevant cases. But, with equal ease, by emphasizing the phrase "if the firearm is a ... ," one can read the language as simply substituting the word "machinegun" for the initial word "firearm"; thereby both incorporating by reference the initial phrases that relate the basic elements of the crime and creating a different crime containing one new element, i.e., the use or carrying of a "machinegun" during and in relation to a crime of violence.

The first part of the opening sentence clearly and indisputably establishes the elements of the basic federal offense of using or carrying a gun during and in relation to a crime of violence.

The statute's structure clarifies any ambiguity inherent in its literal language. The first part of the opening sentence clearly and indisputably establishes the elements of the basic federal offense of using or carrying a gun during and in relation to a crime of violence. See United States v. Rodriguez-Moreno, 526 U.S. 275, 280 (1999). Congress placed the element "uses or carries a firearm" and the word "machinegun" in a single sentence, not broken up with dashes or separated into subsections. Cf. Jones, 526 U.S., at 232—233 (noting that the structure of the carjacking statute–a "principal paragraph" followed by "numbered subsections"–makes it "look" as though the statute sets forth sentencing factors). The next three sentences of §924(c)(1) (which appear after the sentence quoted above (see Appendix, infra)) refer directly to sentencing: the first to recidivism, the second to concurrent sentences, the third to parole. These structural features strongly suggest that the basic job of the entire first sentence is the definition of crimes and the role of the remaining three is the description of factors (such as recidivism) that ordinarily pertain only to sentencing.

We concede that there are two other structural circumstances that suggest a contrary interpretation. The title of the entirety of §924 is "Penalties"; and in 1998 Congress reenacted §924(c)(1), separating different parts of the first sentence (and others) into different subsections, see Pub. L. 105—386, §1(a)(1), 112 Stat. 3469. In this case, however, the section's title cannot help, for Congress already has determined that at least some portion of §924, including §924(c) itself, creates, not penalty enhancements, but entirely new crimes. See S. Rep. No. 98—225, pp. 312—314 (1984) ("Section 924(c) sets out an offense distinct from the underlying felony and is not simply a penalty provision"); see also Busic v. United States, 446 U.S. 398, 404 (1980); Simpson v. United States, 435 U.S. 6, 10 (1978). The title alone does not tell us which are which. Nor can a new postenactment statutory restructuring help us here to determine what Congress intended at the time it enacted the earlier statutory provision that governs this case. See Almendarez-Torres, 523 U.S., at 237 (amendments that, among other things, neither "declare the meaning of earlier law" nor "seek to clarify an earlier enacted general term" fail to provide interpretive guidance).

Second, we cannot say that courts have typically or traditionally used firearm types (such as "shotgun" or "machinegun") as sentencing factors, at least not in respect to an underlying "use or carry" crime. See Jones, supra, at 234 ("[S]tatutory drafting occurs against a backdrop ... of traditional treatment of certain categories of important facts"); see also Almendarez-Torres, supra, at 230 (recidivism "is as typical a sentencing factor as one might imagine"). Traditional sentencing factors often involve either characteristics of the offender, such as recidivism, or special features of the manner in which a basic crime was carried out (e.g., that the defendant abused a position of trust or brandished a gun). See 18 U.S.C. § 3553(a)(1) (providing that a sentencing court "shall" consider "the history and characteristics of the defendant" and "the nature and circumstances of the offense"); see also, e.g., United States Sentencing Commission, Guidelines Manual §4A1.1 (Nov. 1998) (sentence based in part on defendant's criminal history); §3B1.3 (upward adjustment for abuse of position of trust); §5K2.6 (same for use of a dangerous instrumentality). Offender characteristics are not here at issue. And, although one might consider the use of a machinegun, or for that matter a firearm, as a means (or a manner) in which the offender carried out the more basic underlying crime of violence, the underlying crime of violence is not the basic crime here at issue. Rather, as we have already mentioned, the use or carrying of a firearm is itself a separate substantive crime. See Busic, supra, at 404; Simpson, supra, at 10.

the difference between carrying, say, a pistol and carrying a machinegun (or, to mention another factor in the same statutory sentence, a "destructive device," i.e., a bomb) is great, both in degree and kind.

It is not surprising that numerous gun crimes make substantive distinctions between weapons such as pistols and machineguns.

we do not have any indication that legislatures or judges typically have viewed the difference between using a pistol and using a machinegun as insubstantial.

the difference between the act of using or carrying a "firearm" and the act of using or carrying a "machinegun" is both substantive and substantial–a conclusion that supports a "separate crime" interpretation.

The Government argues that, conceptually speaking, one can refer to the use of a machinegun as simply a "metho[d]" of committing the underlying "firearms offense." Brief for United States 23. But the difference between carrying, say, a pistol and carrying a machinegun (or, to mention another factor in the same statutory sentence, a "destructive device," i.e., a bomb) is great, both in degree and kind. And, more importantly, that difference concerns the nature of the element lying closest to the heart of the crime at issue. It is not surprising that numerous gun crimes make substantive distinctions between weapons such as pistols and machineguns. See, e.g., 18 U.S.C. § 922(a)(4) (making it unlawful to "transport in interstate or foreign commerce" any "destructive device," "machine gun," or similar type of weapon unless carrier is licensed or authorized, but making no such prohibition for pistols); §922(b)(4) (prohibiting the unauthorized sale or delivery of "machine gun[s]" and similar weapons); §922(o)(1) (making it "unlawful for any person to transfer or possess a machine gun"); §922(v)(1) (making it illegal "to manufacture, transfer, or possess a semiautomatic assault weapon"). And we do not have any indication that legislatures or judges typically have viewed the difference between using a pistol and using a machinegun as insubstantial. Indeed, the fact that (a) the statute at issue prescribes a mandatory penalty for using or carrying a machinegun that is six times more severe than the punishment for using or carrying a mere "firearm," and (b) at least two Courts of Appeals have interpreted §924(c)(1) as setting forth a separate "machinegun" element in relevant cases, see Alerta, 96 F.3d, at 1235; United States v. Melvin, 27 F.3d 710, 714 (CA1 1994); see also Judicial Committee on Model Jury Instructions for the Eighth Circuit, Manual of Model Criminal Jury Instructions ¶6.18.924C (1997 ed.), in L. Sand, J. Siffert, W. Loughlin, & S. Reiss, Modern Federal Jury Instructions: Criminal Pattern Instructions, p. 8—153 (1999), points to the conclusion that the difference between the act of using or carrying a "firearm" and the act of using or carrying a "machinegun" is both substantive and substantial–a conclusion that supports a "separate crime" interpretation.

to ask a jury, rather than a judge, to decide whether a defendant used or carried a machinegun would rarely complicate a trial or risk unfairness.

As a practical matter, in determining whether a defendant used or carried a "firearm," the jury ordinarily will be asked to assess the particular weapon at issue as well as the circumstances under which it was allegedly used.

Third, to ask a jury, rather than a judge, to decide whether a defendant used or carried a machinegun would rarely complicate a trial or risk unfairness. Cf. Almendarez-Torres, supra, at 234—235 (pointing to potential unfairness of placing fact of recidivism before jury). As a practical matter, in determining whether a defendant used or carried a "firearm," the jury ordinarily will be asked to assess the particular weapon at issue as well as the circumstances under which it was allegedly used. Furthermore, inasmuch as the prosecution's case under §924(c) usually will involve presenting a certain weapon (or weapons) to the jury and arguing that the defendant used or carried that weapon during a crime of violence within the meaning of the statute, the evidence is unlikely to enable a defendant to respond both (1) "I did not use or carry any firearm," and (2) "even if I did, it was a pistol, not a machinegun." Hence, a rule of law that makes it difficult to make both claims at the same time to the same decisionmaker (the jury) will not often prejudice a defendant's case.

At the same time, a contrary rule–one that leaves the machinegun matter to the sentencing judge–might unnecessarily produce a conflict between the judge and the jury. That is because, under our case law interpreting the statute here at issue, a jury may well have to decide which of several weapons the defendant actively used, rather than passively possessed. See Bailey, 516 U.S., at 143. And, in such a case, the sentencing judge will not necessarily know which "firearm" supports the jury's determination. Under these circumstances, a judge's later, sentencing-related decision that the defendant used the machinegun, rather than, say, the pistol, might conflict with the jury's belief that he actively used the pistol, which factual belief underlay its firearm "use" conviction. Cf. Alerta, supra, at 1234—1235 (in the absence of a specific jury finding regarding the type of weapon that defendant used, it was possible that jury did not find "use" of a machinegun even though judge imposed the 30-year mandatory statutory sentence). There is no reason to think that Congress would have wanted a judge's views to prevail in a case of so direct a factual conflict, particularly when the sentencing judge applies a lower standard of proof and when 25 additional years in prison are at stake.

Fourth, the Government argues that the legislative history of the statute favors interpreting §924(c) as setting forth sentencing factors, not elements. It points out that §924(c), as originally enacted, provided a mandatory minimum prison term of at least one year (up to a maximum of 10 years) where a person (1) "use[d] a firearm to commit any felony," or (2) "carr[ied] a firearm unlawfully during the commission of any felony." Gun Control Act of 1968, §102, 82 Stat. 1223; see also Omnibus Crime Control Act of 1970, §13, 84 Stat. 1889. In 1984, Congress amended the law, eliminating the range of permissible penalties, setting a mandatory prison term of five years, and specifying that that term was to be added on top of the prison term related to the underlying "crime of violence," including statutory sentences that imposed certain other weapons-related enhancements. See Comprehensive Crime Control Act of 1984, §1005(a), 98 Stat. 2138. In 1986, Congress again amended the law by providing for a 10-year mandatory prison term (20 years for subsequent offenses) "if the firearm is a machinegun, or is equipped with a firearm silencer or firearm muffler." Firearms Owners' Protection Act, §104(a)(2), 100 Stat. 456. In 1988, Congress changed the provision to its here-relevant form. Anti-Drug Abuse Act of 1988, §6460, 102 Stat. 4373.

The Government finds three features of the history surrounding the enactment of the key 1986 version of the statute significant. First, the House Report spoke in terms of a sentence, not an offense. The Report stated, for example, that the relevant bill would create "a new mandatory prison term of ten years for using or carrying a machine gun during and in relation to a crime of violence or a drug trafficking offense for a first offense, and twenty years for a subsequent offense." H. R. Rep. No. 99—495, p. 28 (1986); see also id., at 2 (bill "[p]rovides a mandatory prison term of ten years for using or carrying a machine gun during and in relation to a crime of violence or a drug trafficking offense, and a mandatory twenty years for any subsequent offense"). Second, statements of the bill's sponsors and supporters on the floor of the House also spoke in terms of sentencing, noting, for example, that the proposed law "imposes mandatory prison terms on those [who] would use a machinegun in the commission of a violent offense." 132 Cong. Rec. 3809 (1986) (statement of Rep. Hughes); see also, e.g., id., at 6843 (statement of Rep. Volkmer) (bill "includes stiff mandatory sentences for the use of firearms, including machineguns and silencers, in relation to violent or drug trafficking crimes"); id., at 6850 (statement of Rep. Moore) (machinegun clause "strengthen[s] criminal penalties"); id., at 6856 (statement of Rep. Wirth) (proposed law "would have many benefits, including the expansion of mandatory sentencing to those persons who use a machinegun in the commission of a violent crime"). Third, and similarly, "any discussion suggesting the creation of a new offense" was "[n]oticeably absent" from the legislative record. Branch, 91 F.3d, at 739; Brief for United States 36.

Insofar as this history may be relevant, however, it does not significantly help the Government. That is because the statute's basic "uses or carries a firearm" provision also dealt primarily with sentencing, its pre-eminent feature consisting of the creation of a new mandatory term of imprisonment additional to that for the underlying crime of violence. Cf. Bailey, supra, at 142 ("Section 924(c)(1) requires the imposition of specified penalties"); Smith v. United States, 508 U.S. 223, 227 (1993) (same). In this context, the absence of "separate offense" statements means little, and the "mandatory sentencing" statements to which the Government points show only that Congress believed that the "machinegun" and "firearm" provisions would work similarly. Indeed, the legislative statements that discuss a new prison term for the act of "us[ing] a machine gun," see, e.g., supra, at 10, seemingly describe offense conduct, and, thus, argue against (not for) the Government's position.

Fifth and finally, the length and severity of an added mandatory sentence that turns on the presence or absence of a "machinegun" (or any of the other listed firearm types) weighs in favor of treating such offense-related words as referring to an element. Thus, if after considering traditional interpretive factors, we were left genuinely uncertain as to Congress' intent in this regard, we would assume a preference for traditional jury determination of so important a factual matter. Cf. Staples v. United States, 511 U.S. 600, 619, n. 17 (1994) (rule of lenity requires that "ambiguous criminal statute[s] ... be construed in favor of the accused"); United States v. Granderson, 511 U.S. 39, 54 (1994) (similar); United States v. Bass, 404 U.S. 336, 347 (1971) (same).

we believe that Congress intended the firearm type-related words it used in §924(c)(1) to refer to an element of a separate, aggravated crime.

These considerations, in our view, make this a stronger "separate crime" case than either Jones or Almendarez-Torres–cases in which we were closely divided as to Congress' likely intent. For the reasons stated, we believe that Congress intended the firearm type-related words it used in §924(c)(1) to refer to an element of a separate, aggravated crime. Accordingly, we reverse the contrary determination of the Court of Appeals and remand the case for proceedings consistent with this opinion.

It is so ordered.

Appendix to opinion of the court

"§924. Penalties.

"(c)(1) Whoever, during and in relation to any crime of violence or drug trafficking crime (including a crime of violence or drug trafficking crime which provides for an enhanced punishment if committed by the use of a deadly or dangerous weapon or device) for which he may be prosecuted in a court of the United States, uses or carries a firearm, shall, in addition to the punishment provided for such crime of violence or drug trafficking crime, be sentenced to imprisonment for five years, and if the firearm is a short-barreled rifle [or a] short-barreled shotgun to imprisonment for ten years, and if the firearm is a machinegun, or a destructive device, or is equipped with a firearm silencer or firearm muffler, to imprisonment for thirty years. In the case of his second or subsequent conviction under this subsection, such person shall be sentenced to imprisonment for twenty years, and if the firearm is a machinegun, or a destructive device, or is equipped with a firearm silencer or firearm muffler, to life imprisonment without release. Notwithstanding any other provision of law, the court shall not place on probation or suspend the sentence of any person convicted of a violation of this subsection, nor shall the term of imprisonment imposed under this subsection run concurrently with any other term of imprisonment including that imposed for the crime of violence or drug trafficking crime in which the firearm was used or carried. No person sentenced under this subsection shall be eligible for parole during the term of imprisonment imposed herein." 18 U.S.C. § 924(c)(1) (1988 ed., Supp. V) (footnote omitted).

Notes. 1. *Justice Scalia joins this opinion except as to point Fourth of Part II.

HARRIS v. UNITED STATES

(CASE EXCERPT)

No.536 U.S. 545; 122 S. Ct. 2406; 153 L. Ed. 2d 524

March 25, 2002, Argued

June 24, 2002, Decided

GIST: This is a statutory construction case, an appeal from a conviction for brandishing a firearm during a drug-trafficking offense. The operator of a pawn shop, who routinely wore a gun at his place of business, was dealing small amounts of pot to his friends on the side. In the dissenting opinion, we learn that Harris did not actually wave his gun around, but was nonetheless charged with brandishing, which forces a higher sentence than merely possessing under the same circumstance. Progressively long sentences attach to possession, brandishing and shooting, respectively.

If a condition in a statute is an "element" of a crime, a jury must decide if it has been proven beyond a reasonable doubt, but if the condition is a sentencing "factor" a judge may decide. Harris argued that, because of the extra penalty, it was a separate offense, should have been charged in the indictment (it had not been), and a jury would have had to decide. He faced a mandatory additional seven-year minimum sentence. The Court disagreed and let the additional sentence stand. In a dissent, three of the Court's liberal justices join with a conservative to point out several interesting holes in the Court's reasoning.

Petitioner, who sold illegal narcotics at his pawnshop with an unconcealed semiautomatic pistol at his side, was arrested for violating, inter alia, 18 U.S.C. §924(c)(1)(A), which provides in relevant part that a person who in relation to a drug trafficking crime uses or carries a firearm "shall, in addition to the punishment for such crime" "(i) be sentenced to a term of imprisonment of not less than 5 years; (ii) if the firearm is brandished, be sentenced to ... not less than 7 years; and (iii) if the firearm is discharged, be sentenced to ... not less than 10 years." Because the Government proceeded on the assumption that the provision defines a single crime and that brandishing is a sentencing factor to be found by the judge following trial, the indictment said nothing about brandishing or subsection (ii), simply alleging the elements from the principal paragraph. Petitioner was convicted. When his presentence report recommended that he receive the 7-year minimum sentence, he objected, arguing that brandishing was an element of a separate statutory offense for which he was not indicted or convicted. At the sentencing hearing, the District Court overruled his objection, found that he had brandished the gun, and sentenced him to seven years in prison. Affirming, the Fourth Circuit rejected petitioner's statutory argument and found that McMillan v. Pennsylvania, 477 U.S. 79, 91 L. Ed. 2d 67, 106 S. Ct. 2411, foreclosed his argument that if brandishing is a sentencing factor, the statute is unconstitutional under Apprendi v. New Jersey, 530 U.S. 466, 147 L. Ed. 2d 435, 120 S. Ct. 2348. In Apprendi, this Court held that other than the fact of a prior conviction, any fact that increases the penalty for a crime beyond the prescribed statutory maximum is, in effect, an element of the crime, which must be submitted to a jury, and proved beyond a reasonable doubt (and, in federal prosecutions, alleged in an indictment handed down by a grand jury). But 14 years earlier, McMillan sustained a statute that increased the minimum penalty for a crime, though not beyond the statutory maximum, when the judge found that the defendant had possessed a firearm.

Held: The judgment is affirmed.

JUSTICE KENNEDY delivered the opinion of the Court with respect to Parts I, II, and IV, concluding:

1. As a matter of statutory interpretation, §924(c)(1)(A) defines a single offense, in which brandishing and discharging are sentencing factors to be found by the judge, not offense elements to be found by the jury.

(a) The prohibition's structure suggests that brandishing and discharging are sentencing factors. Federal laws usually list all offense elements in a single sentence and separate the sentencing factors into subsections. Castillo v. United States, 530 U.S. 120, 125, 147 L. Ed. 2d 94, 120 S. Ct. 2090. The instant statute's lengthy principal paragraph lists the elements of a complete crime. Toward the end of the paragraph is the word "shall," which often divides offense-defining provisions from sentence-specifying ones. Jones v. United States, 526 U.S. 227, 233, 143 L. Ed. 2d 311, 119 S. Ct. 1215. And following "shall" are the separate subsections, which explain how defendants are to "be sentenced." Thus this Court can presume that the principal paragraph defines a single crime and its subsections identify sentencing factors.

(b) As Jones illustrates, the statute's text might provide evidence to the contrary, but the critical textual clues here reinforce the single-offense interpretation. Brandishing has been singled out as a paradigmatic sentencing factor, Castillo, supra, at 126. Under the Sentencing Guidelines, moreover, brandishing and discharging are factors that affect sentences for numerous crimes. The incremental changes in the minimum penalty at issue here are precisely what one would expect to see in provisions meant to identify matters for the sentencing judge's consideration.

(c) The canon of constitutional avoidance -- which provides that when a statute is susceptible of two constructions, the Court must adopt the one that avoids grave and doubtful constitutional questions -- plays no role here. The constitutional principle that petitioner says a single-offense interpretation of the statute would violate -- that any fact increasing the statutory minimum sentence must be accorded the safeguards assigned to elements -- was rejected in McMillan. Petitioner's suggestion that the canon be used to avoid overruling one of this Court's own precedents is novel and, given that McMillan was in place when §924(c)(1)(A) was enacted, unsound. Congress would have had no reason to believe that it was approaching the constitutional line by following the instruction this Court gave in McMillan.

2. Reaffirming McMillan and employing the approach outlined in that opinion, the Court concludes that §924(c)(1)(A)(ii) is constitutional. Basing a 2-year increase in the defendant's minimum sentence on a judicial finding of brandishing does not evade the Fifth and Sixth Amendments' requirements. Congress simply dictated the precise weight to be given to one traditional sentencing factor. McMillan, supra, at 89-90.

JUSTICE KENNEDY, joined by THE CHIEF JUSTICE, JUSTICE O'CONNOR, and JUSTICE SCALIA, concluded in Part III that §924(c)(1)(A)(ii) is constitutional under McMillan, which remains sound authority after Apprendi. The Court will not overrule a precedent absent a special justification. The justification offered by petitioner is that Apprendi and McMillan cannot be reconciled. Those decisions are consistent, however, because there is a fundamental distinction between the factual findings at issue in those two cases. Apprendi said that any fact extending the defendant's sentence beyond the maximum authorized by the jury's verdict would have been considered an element of an aggravated crime by the Framers of the Bill of Rights. That cannot be said of a fact increasing the mandatory minimum (but not extending the sentence beyond the statutory maximum), for the jury's verdict has authorized the judge to impose the minimum with or without the finding. This sort of fact is more like the facts judges have traditionally considered when exercising their discretion to choose a sentence within the range authorized by the jury's verdict -- facts that the Constitution does not require to be alleged in the indictment, submitted to the jury, or proved beyond a reasonable doubt.

Read together, McMillan and Apprendi mean that those facts setting the outer limits of a sentence, and of the judicial power to impose it, are elements of the crime for the purposes of the constitutional analysis. Within the range authorized by the jury's verdict, however, the political system may channel judicial discretion -- and rely upon judicial expertise -- by requiring defendants to serve minimum terms after judges make certain factual findings. Legislatures have relied upon McMillan's holding, and there is no reason to overturn these statutes or cast uncertainty upon sentences imposed under them.

JUSTICE BREYER concluded that although Apprendi v. New Jersey, 530 U.S. 466, cannot easily be distinguished from this case in terms of logic, the Sixth Amendment permits judges to apply sentencing factors -- whether those factors lead to a sentence beyond the statutory maximum (as in Apprendi) or the application of a mandatory minimum (as here). This does not mean to suggest approval of mandatory minimum sentences as a matter of policy. Mandatory minimum statutes are fundamentally inconsistent with Congress' simultaneous effort to create a fair, honest, and rational sentencing system through the use of the Sentencing Guidelines. They transfer sentencing power to prosecutors, who can determine sentences through the charges they decide to bring, and who thereby have reintroduced much of the sentencing disparity that Congress created the Guidelines to eliminate. Applying Apprendi in this case would not, however, lead Congress to abolish, or to modify such statutes, and it would take from the judge the power to make a factual determination, while giving that power not to juries, but to prosecutors. The legal consequences of extending Apprendi are also seriously adverse, for doing so would diminish further Congress' otherwise broad constitutional authority to define crimes through specification of elements, to shape criminal sentences through the specification of sentencing factors, and to limit judicial discretion in applying those factors in particular cases.

JUSTICE KENNEDY announced the judgment of the Court and delivered the opinion of the Court with respect to Parts I, II, and IV, and an opinion with respect to Part III, in which THE CHIEF JUSTICE, JUSTICE O'CONNOR, and JUSTICE SCALIA join.

Once more we consider the distinction the law has drawn between the elements of a crime and factors that influence a criminal sentence. Legislatures define crimes in terms of the facts that are their essential elements, and constitutional guarantees attach to these facts. In federal prosecutions, "no person shall be held to answer for a capital, or otherwise infamous crime, unless on a presentment or indictment of a Grand Jury" alleging all the elements of the crime. U.S. Const., Amdt. 5; see Hamling v. United States, 418 U.S. 87, 117, 41 L. Ed. 2d 590, 94 S. Ct. 2887 (1974). "In all criminal prosecutions," state and federal, "the accused shall enjoy the right to ... trial ... by an impartial jury," U.S. Const., Amdt. 6; see Duncan v. Louisiana, 391 U.S. 145, 149, 20 L. Ed. 2d 491, 88 S. Ct. 1444, 45 Ohio Op. 2d 198 (1968), at which the government must prove each element beyond a reasonable doubt, see In re Winship, 397 U.S. 358, 364, 25 L. Ed. 2d 368, 90 S. Ct. 1068, 51 Ohio Op. 2d 323 (1970).

Yet not all facts affecting the defendant's punishment are elements. After the accused is convicted, the judge may impose a sentence within a range provided by statute, basing it on various facts relating to the defendant and the manner in which the offense was committed. Though these facts may have a substantial impact on the sentence, they are not elements, and are thus not subject to the Constitution's indictment, jury, and proof requirements. Some statutes also direct judges to give specific weight to certain facts when choosing the sentence. The statutes do not require these facts, sometimes referred to as sentencing factors, to be alleged in the indictment, submitted to the jury, or established beyond a reasonable doubt.

The Constitution permits legislatures to make the distinction between elements and sentencing factors, but it imposes some limitations as well. For if it did not, legislatures could evade the indictment, jury, and proof requirements by labeling almost every relevant fact a sentencing factor. The Court described one limitation in this respect two Terms ago in Apprendi v. New Jersey, 530 U.S. 466, 490, 147 L. Ed. 2d 435, 120 S. Ct. 2348 (2000): "Other than the fact of a prior conviction, any fact that increases the penalty for a crime beyond the prescribed statutory maximum," whether the statute calls it an element or a sentencing factor, "must be submitted to a jury, and proved beyond a reasonable doubt." Fourteen years before, in McMillan v. Pennsylvania, 477 U.S. 79, 91 L. Ed. 2d 67, 106 S. Ct. 2411 (1986), the Court had declined to adopt a more restrictive constitutional rule. McMillan sustained a statute that increased the minimum penalty for a crime, though not beyond the statutory maximum, when the sentencing judge found, by a preponderance of the evidence, that the defendant had possessed a firearm.

The principal question before us is whether McMillan stands after Apprendi.

I

Petitioner William Joseph Harris sold illegal narcotics out of his pawnshop with an unconcealed semiautomatic pistol at his side. He was later arrested for violating federal drug and firearms laws, including 18 U.S.C. §924 (c)(1)(A). That statute provides in relevant part:

"Any person who, during and in relation to any crime of violence or drug trafficking crime ... uses or carries a firearm, or who, in furtherance of any such crime, possesses a firearm, shall, in addition to the punishment provided for such crime of violence or drug trafficking crime --

"(i) be sentenced to a term of imprisonment of not less than 5 years;
"(ii) if the firearm is brandished, be sentenced to a term of imprisonment of not less than 7 years; and
"(iii) if the firearm is discharged, be sentenced to a term of imprisonment of not less than 10 years."

The Government proceeded on the assumption that §924(c)(1)(A) defines a single crime and that brandishing is a sentencing factor to be considered by the judge after the trial.

The Government proceeded on the assumption that §924(c)(1)(A) defines a single crime and that brandishing is a sentencing factor to be considered by the judge after the trial. For this reason the indictment said nothing of brandishing and made no reference to subsection (ii). Instead, it simply alleged the elements from the statute's principal paragraph: that "during and in relation to a drug trafficking crime," petitioner had "knowingly carried a firearm." At a bench trial the United States District Court for the Middle District of North Carolina found petitioner guilty as charged.

the presentence report recommended that petitioner be given the 7-year minimum because he had brandished the gun.

Following his conviction, the presentence report recommended that petitioner be given the 7-year minimum because he had brandished the gun. Petitioner objected, citing this Court's decision in Jones v. United States, 526 U.S. 227, 143 L. Ed. 2d 311, 119 S. Ct. 1215 (1999), and arguing that, as a matter of statutory interpretation, brandishing is an element of a separate offense, an offense for which he had not been indicted or tried. At the sentencing hearing the District Court overruled the objection, found by a preponderance of the evidence that petitioner had brandished the gun, and sentenced him to seven years in prison.

In the Court of Appeals for the Fourth Circuit petitioner again pressed his statutory argument. He added that if brandishing is a sentencing factor as a statutory matter, the statute is unconstitutional in light of Apprendi -- even though, as petitioner acknowledged, the judge's finding did not alter the maximum penalty to which he was exposed. Rejecting these arguments, the Court of Appeals affirmed. United States v. Harris, 243 F.3d 806 (2001). Like every other Court of Appeals to have addressed the question, it held that the statute makes brandishing a sentencing factor. Id., 243 F.3d at 812; accord, United States v. Barton, 257 F.3d 433, 443 (CA5 2001); United States v. Carlson, 217 F.3d 986, 989 (CA8 2000); United States v. Pounds, 230 F.3d 1317, 1319 (CA11 2000). The court also held that the constitutional argument was foreclosed by McMillan. 243 F.3d at 809.

We granted certiorari, 534 U.S. 1064, 151 L. Ed. 2d 578, 122 S. Ct. 663 (2001), and now affirm.

II

Did Congress make brandishing an element or a sentencing factor in §924(c)(1)(A)?

We must first answer a threshold question of statutory construction: Did Congress make brandishing an element or a sentencing factor in §924(c)(1)(A)? In the Government's view the text in question defines a single crime, and the facts in subsections (ii) and (iii) are considerations for the sentencing judge. Petitioner, on the other hand, contends that Congress meant the statute to define three different crimes. Subsection (ii), he says, creates a separate offense of which brandishing is an element. If petitioner is correct, he was neither indicted nor tried for that offense, and the 7-year minimum did not apply.

So we begin our analysis by asking what §924(c)(1)(A) means. The statute does not say in so many words whether brandishing is an element or a sentencing factor, but the structure of the prohibition suggests it is the latter. Federal laws usually list all offense elements "in a single sentence" and separate the sentencing factors "into subsections." Castillo v. United States, 530 U.S. 120, 125, 147 L. Ed. 2d 94, 120 S. Ct. 2090 (2000). Here, §924(c)(1)(A) begins with a lengthy principal paragraph listing the elements of a complete crime -- "the basic federal offense of using or carrying a gun during and in relation to" a violent crime or drug offense. Id., 530 U.S. at 124. Toward the end of the paragraph is "the word 'shall,' which often divides offense-defining provisions from those that specify sentences." Jones, 526 U.S. at 233. And following "shall" are the separate subsections, which explain how defendants are to "be sentenced." Subsection (i) sets a catchall minimum and "certainly adds no further element." Ibid. Subsections (ii) and (iii), in turn, increase the minimum penalty if certain facts are present, and those subsections do not repeat the elements from the principal paragraph.

When a statute has this sort of structure, we can presume that its principal paragraph defines a single crime and its subsections identify sentencing factors. But even if a statute "has a look to it suggesting that the numbered subsections are only sentencing provisions," id., 526 U.S. at 232, the text might provide compelling evidence to the contrary. This was illustrated by the Court's decision in Jones, in which the federal carjacking statute, which had a similar structure, was interpreted as setting out the elements of multiple offenses.

The critical textual clues in this case, however, reinforce the single-offense interpretation implied by the statute's structure. Tradition and past congressional practice, for example, were perhaps the most important guideposts in Jones. The fact at issue there -- serious bodily injury -- is an element in numerous federal statutes, including two on which the carjacking statute was modeled; and the Jones Court doubted that Congress would have made this fact a sentencing factor in one isolated instance. Id., 526 U.S. at 235-237; see also Castillo, supra, 530 U.S. at 126-127; Almendarez-Torres v. United States, 523 U.S. 224, 230, 140 L. Ed. 2d 350, 118 S. Ct. 1219 (1998). In contrast, there is no similar federal tradition of treating brandishing and discharging as offense elements. In Castillo v. United States, supra, 530 U.S. 120 the Court singled out brandishing as a paradigmatic sentencing factor: "Traditional sentencing factors often involve ... special features of the manner in which a basic crime was carried out (e.g., that the defendant ... brandished a gun)." Id., 530 U.S. at 126. Under the Sentencing Guidelines, moreover, brandishing and discharging affect the sentences for numerous federal crimes. See, e.g., United States Sentencing Commission, Guidelines Manual §§2A2.2(b)(2), 2B3.1(b)(2), 2B3.2(b)(3)(A), 2E2.1(b)(1), 2L1.1(b)(4) (Nov. 2001). Indeed, the Guidelines appear to have been the only antecedents for the statute's brandishing provision. The term "brandished" does not appear in any federal offense-defining provision save 18 U.S.C. §924(c)(1)(A), and did not appear there until 1998, when the statute was amended to take its current form. The numbered subsections were added then, describing, as sentencing factors often do, "special features of the manner in which" the statute's "basic crime" could be carried out. Castillo, supra, 530 U.S. at 126. It thus seems likely that brandishing and discharging were meant to serve the same function under the statute as they do under the Guidelines.

We might have had reason to question that inference if brandishing or discharging altered the defendant's punishment in a manner not usually associated with sentencing factors. Jones is again instructive. There the Court accorded great significance to the "steeply higher penalties" authorized by the carjacking statute's three subsections, which enhanced the defendant's maximum sentence from 15 years, to 25 years, to life -- enhancements the Court doubted Congress would have made contingent upon judicial factfinding. 526 U.S. at 233; see also Castillo, supra, 530 U.S. at 131; Almendarez-Torres, supra, 523 U.S. at 235-236. The provisions before us now, however, have an effect on the defendant's sentence that is more consistent with traditional understandings about how sentencing factors operate; the required findings constrain, rather than extend, the sentencing judge's discretion. Section 924(c)(1)(A) does not authorize the judge to impose "steeply higher penalties" -- or higher penalties at all -- once the facts in question are found. Since the subsections alter only the minimum, the judge may impose a sentence well in excess of seven years, whether or not the defendant brandished the firearm. The incremental changes in the minimum -- from 5 years, to 7, to 10 -- are precisely what one would expect to see in provisions meant to identify matters for the sentencing judge's consideration.

Nothing about the text or history of the statute rebuts the presumption drawn from its structure. Against the single-offense interpretation to which these considerations point, however, petitioner invokes the canon of constitutional avoidance. Under that doctrine, when "a statute is susceptible of two constructions, by one of which grave and doubtful constitutional questions arise and by the other of which such questions are avoided, our duty is to adopt the latter." United States ex rel. Attorney General v. Delaware & Hudson Co., 213 U.S. 366, 408, 53 L. Ed. 836, 29 S. Ct. 527 (1909). It is at least an open question, petitioner contends, whether the Fifth and Sixth Amendments require every fact increasing a federal defendant's minimum sentence to be alleged in the indictment, submitted to the jury, and proved beyond a reasonable doubt. To avoid resolving that question (and possibly invalidating the statute), petitioner urges, we should read §924(c)(1)(A) as making brandishing an element of an aggravated federal crime.

The avoidance canon rests upon our "respect for Congress, which we assume legislates in the light of constitutional limitations."

The avoidance canon played a role in Jones, for the subsections of the carjacking statute enhanced the maximum sentence, and a single-offense interpretation would have implicated constitutional questions later addressed -- and resolved in the defendant's favor -- by Apprendi. See Jones, 526 U.S. at 243, n. 6 ("Any fact (other than prior conviction) that increases the maximum penalty for a crime must be charged in an indictment, submitted to a jury, and proven beyond a reasonable doubt"). Yet the canon has no role to play here. It applies only when there are serious concerns about the statute's constitutionality, Reno v. Flores, 507 U.S. 292, 314, 123 L. Ed. 2d 1, 113 S. Ct. 1439, n. 9 (1993), and petitioner's proposed rule -- that the Constitution requires any fact increasing the statutory minimum sentence to be accorded the safeguards assigned to elements -- was rejected 16 years ago in McMillan. Petitioner acknowledges as much but argues that recent developments cast doubt on McMillan's viability. To avoid deciding whether McMillan must be overruled, he says, we should construe the problem out of the statute. Petitioner's suggestion that we use the canon to avoid overruling one of our own precedents is novel and, given that McMillan was in place when

§924(c)(1)(A) was enacted, unsound. The avoidance canon rests upon our "respect for Congress, which we assume legislates in the light of constitutional limitations." Rust v. Sullivan, 500 U.S. 173, 191, 114 L. Ed. 2d 233, 111 S. Ct. 1759 (1991). The statute at issue in this case was passed when McMillan provided the controlling instruction, and Congress would have had no reason to believe that it was approaching the constitutional line by following that instruction. We would not further the canon's goal of eliminating friction with our coordinate branch, moreover, if we alleviated our doubt about a constitutional premise we had supplied by adopting a strained reading of a statute that Congress had enacted in reliance on the premise. And if we stretched the text to avoid the question of McMillan's continuing vitality, the canon would embrace a dynamic view of statutory interpretation, under which the text might mean one thing when enacted yet another if the prevailing view of the Constitution later changed. We decline to adopt that approach.

The statute regards brandishing and discharging as sentencing factors to be found by the judge, not offense elements to be found by the jury.

As the avoidance canon poses no obstacle and the interpretive circumstances point in a common direction, we conclude that, as a matter of statutory interpretation, §924(c)(1)(A) defines a single offense. The statute regards brandishing and discharging as sentencing factors to be found by the judge, not offense elements to be found by the jury.

.....

IV

Reaffirming McMillan and employing the approach outlined in that case, we conclude that the federal provision at issue, 18 U.S.C. §924(c)(1)(A)(ii), is constitutional. Basing a 2-year increase in the defendant's minimum sentence on a judicial finding of brandishing does not evade the requirements of the Fifth and Sixth Amendments. Congress "simply took one factor that has always been considered by sentencing courts to bear on punishment ... and dictated the precise weight to be given that factor." McMillan, 477 U.S. at 89-90. That factor need not be alleged in the indictment, submitted to the jury, or proved beyond a reasonable doubt.

The Court is well aware that many question the wisdom of mandatory minimum sentencing. Mandatory minimums, it is often said, fail to account for the unique circumstances of offenders who warrant a lesser penalty. These criticisms may be sound, but they would persist whether the judge or the jury found the facts giving rise to the minimum. We hold only that the Constitution permits the judge to do so, and we leave the other questions to Congress, the States, and the democratic processes.

The Court is well aware that many question the wisdom of mandatory minimum sentencing. Mandatory minimums, it is often said, fail to account for the unique circumstances of offenders who warrant a lesser penalty. See, e.g., Brief for Families Against Mandatory Minimums Foundation as Amicus Curiae 25, n. 16; cf. Almendarez-Torres, supra, at 245 (citing United States Sentencing Commission, Mandatory Minimum Penalties in the Federal Criminal Justice System 26-34 (Aug. 1991)). These criticisms may be sound, but they would persist whether the judge or the jury found the facts giving rise to the minimum. We hold only that the Constitution permits the judge to do so, and we leave the other questions to Congress, the States, and the democratic processes.

The judgment of the Court of Appeals is affirmed.

It is so ordered.

JUSTICE THOMAS, with whom JUSTICE STEVENS, JUSTICE SOUTER, and JUSTICE GINSBURG join, dissenting.

The range of punishment to which petitioner William J. Harris was exposed turned on the fact that he brandished a firearm, a fact that was neither charged in his indictment nor proved at trial beyond a reasonable doubt.

The United States Court of Appeals for the Fourth Circuit nonetheless held that the fact that Harris brandished a firearm was a mere sentencing factor to which no constitutional protections attach.

The range of punishment to which petitioner William J. Harris was exposed turned on the fact that he brandished a firearm, a fact that was neither charged in his indictment nor proved at trial beyond a reasonable doubt. The United States Court of Appeals for the Fourth Circuit nonetheless held, in reliance on McMillan v. Pennsylvania, 477 U.S. 79, 91 L. Ed. 2d 67, 106 S. Ct. 2411 (1986), that the fact that Harris brandished a firearm was a mere sentencing factor to which no constitutional protections attach. United

States v. Harris, 243 F.3d 806, 808-812 (2001).

McMillan, however, conflicts with the Court's later decision in Apprendi v. New Jersey, 530 U.S. 466, 147 L. Ed. 2d 435, 120 S. Ct. 2348 (2000), as the dissenting opinion in Apprendi recognized. See id., 530 U.S. at 533 (O'CONNOR, J., dissenting). The Court's holding today therefore rests on either a misunderstanding or a rejection of the very principles that animated Apprendi just two years ago. Given that considerations of stare decisis are at their nadir in cases involving procedural rules implicating fundamental constitutional protections afforded criminal defendants, I would reaffirm Apprendi, overrule McMillan, and reverse the Court of Appeals.

I

At sentencing, the District Court acknowledged that it was a "close question" whether Harris "brandished" a firearm, and noted that "the only thing that happened here is [that] he had [a gun] during the drug transaction."

Harris was indicted for distributing marijuana in violation of 21 U.S.C. §841 and for carrying a firearm "in relation to" a drug trafficking crime in violation of 18 U.S.C. §924(c)(1)(A). Harris pleaded guilty to distributing marijuana but disputed that he had carried a firearm "in relation to" a drug trafficking crime. The District Court disagreed, n1 and he was convicted by the judge, having waived his right to trial by jury. Although the mandatory minimum prison sentence under §924(c)(1)(A)(i) is five years in prison, the presentence report relied on §924(c)(1)(A)(ii), which increases the mandatory minimum prison sentence to seven years when the firearm is brandished. n2 At sentencing, the District Court acknowledged that it was a "close question" whether Harris "brandished" a firearm, and noted that "the only thing that happened here is [that] he had [a gun] during the drug transaction." App. 231-232, 244-247. The District Court nonetheless found by a preponderance of the evidence that Harris had brandished a firearm and as a result sentenced him to the minimum mandatory sentence of seven years' imprisonment for the violation of §924(c)(1)(A).

Harris owned a pawn shop and routinely wore a gun at work; the District Court accepted that it was Harris' ordinary practice to wear a gun whether or not he was selling small amounts of marijuana to his friends.

n1 Harris owned a pawn shop and routinely wore a gun at work; the District Court accepted that it was Harris' ordinary practice to wear a gun whether or not he was selling small amounts of marijuana to his friends. The District Court, however, determined that the gun was carried "in relation to" a drug trafficking offense within the meaning of §924(c) because it was "unable to draw the distinction that if it is [carried] for a legitimate purpose, it cannot be for an illegitimate purpose." App. 163.

n2 The presentence report recommended that Harris be given a term of imprisonment of zero to six months for the distribution charge.

Relying on McMillan, the Court of Appeals affirmed the sentence and held as a matter of statutory interpretation that brandishing is a sentencing factor, not an element of the §924(c)(1)(A) offense. Accordingly, the Court of Appeals concluded that the allegation of brandishing a firearm did not need to be charged in the indictment or proved beyond a reasonable doubt in order for the 7-year mandatory minimum to be triggered.

II

The Court construes §924(c)(1)(A) to "define a single offense," ante, at 8, rather than the multiple offenses the Court found in a similarly structured statute in Jones v. United States, 526 U.S. 227, 143 L. Ed. 2d 311, 119 S. Ct. 1215 (1999). n3 In reliance on McMillan, it then discounts the increasing mandatory minimum sentences set forth in the statutory provision as constitutionally irrelevant. In the plurality's view, any punishment less than the statutory maximum of life imprisonment for any violation of §924(c)(1)(A) avoids the single principle the Court now gleans from Apprendi: "'Other than the fact of a prior conviction, any fact that increases the penalty for a crime beyond the prescribed statutory maximum,' whether the statute calls it an element or a sentencing factor, 'must be submitted to a jury, and proved beyond a reasonable doubt.'" Ante, at 2 (quoting Apprendi, supra, at 490). According to the plurality, the historical practices underlying the Court's decision in Apprendi with respect to penalties that exceed the statutory maximum do not support extension of Apprendi's rule to facts that increase a defendant's mandatory minimum sentence. Such fine distinctions with regard to vital constitutional liberties cannot withstand close scrutiny.

n3 See 18 U.S.C. §2119.

A

The Federal Constitution provides those "accused" in federal courts with specific rights, such as the right "to be informed of the nature and cause of the accusation," the right to be "held to answer for a capital, or otherwise infamous crime" only on an indictment or presentment of a grand jury, and the right to be tried by "an impartial jury of the State and district wherein the crime shall have been committed." Amdts. 5 and 6. Also, no Member of this Court disputes that due process requires that every fact necessary to constitute a crime must be found beyond a reasonable doubt by a jury if that right is not waived. See In re Winship, 397 U.S. 358, 364, 25 L. Ed. 2d 368, 90 S. Ct. 1068 (1970). As with Apprendi, this case thus turns on the seemingly simple question of what constitutes a "crime."

This question cannot be answered by reference to statutory construction alone solely because the sentence does not exceed the statutory maximum. As I discussed at great length in Apprendi, the original understanding of what facts are elements of a crime was expansive:

"If the legislature defines some core crime and then provides for increasing the punishment of that crime upon a finding of some aggravating fact -- of whatever sort, including the fact of a prior conviction -- the core crime and the aggravating fact together constitute an aggravated crime, just as much as grand larceny is an aggravated form of petit larceny. The aggravating fact is an element of the aggravated crime. Similarly, if the legislature, rather than creating grades of crimes, has provided for setting the punishment of a crime based on some fact ... that fact is also an element. No multifactor parsing of statutes, of the sort that we have attempted since McMillan, is necessary. One need only look to the kind, degree, or range of punishment to which the prosecution is by law entitled for a given set of facts. Each fact for that entitlement is an element." 530 U.S. at 501 (concurring opinion).

The fact that a defendant brandished a firearm indisputably alters the prescribed range of penalties to which he is exposed under 18 U.S.C. §924(c)(1)(A). Without a finding that a defendant brandished or discharged a firearm, the penalty range for a conviction under §924(c)(1)(A)(i) is five years to life in prison. But with a finding that a defendant brandished a firearm, the penalty range becomes harsher, seven years to life imprisonment. §924(c)(1)(A)(ii). And if the court finds that a defendant discharged a firearm, the range becomes even more severe, 10 years to life. §924(c)(1)(A)(iii). Thus, it is ultimately beside the point whether as a matter of statutory interpretation brandishing is a sentencing factor, because as a constitutional matter brandishing must be deemed an element of an aggravated offense. See Apprendi, supra, 530 U.S. at 483, n. 10 ("Facts that expose a defendant to a punishment greater than that otherwise legally prescribed were by definition 'elements' of a separate legal offense").

I agree with the Court that a legislature is free to decree, within constitutional limits, which facts are elements that constitute a crime. See ante, at 2. But when the legislature provides that a particular fact shall give rise "'both to a special stigma and to a special punishment,'" ante, at 12 (plurality opinion) (quoting McMillan, 477 U.S. at 103 (STEVENS, J., dissenting)), the constitutional consequences are clear. As the Court acknowledged in Apprendi, society has long recognized a necessary link between punishment and crime, 530 U.S. at 478 ("The defendant's ability to predict with certainty the judgment from the face of the felony indictment flowed from the invariable linkage of punishment with crime"). This link makes a great deal of sense: Why, after all, would anyone care if they were convicted of murder, as opposed to manslaughter, but for the increased penalties for the former offense, which in turn reflect the greater moral opprobrium society attaches to the act? We made clear in Apprendi that if a statute "'annexes a higher degree of punishment'" based on certain circumstances, exposing a defendant to that higher degree of punishment requires that those circumstances be charged in the indictment and proved beyond a reasonable doubt. Id., 530 U.S. at 480 (quoting J. Archbold, Pleading and Evidence in Criminal Cases 51 (15th ed. 1862)).

This constitutional limitation neither interferes with the legislature's ability to define statutory ranges of punishment nor calls into question judicial discretion to impose "judgment within the range prescribed by statute." Apprendi, 530 U.S. at 481. But it does protect the criminal defendant's constitutional right to know, ex ante, those circumstances that will determine the applicable range of punishment and to have those circumstances proved beyond a reasonable doubt:

"If a defendant faces punishment beyond that provided by statute when an offense is committed under certain circumstances but not others, it is obvious that both the loss of liberty and the stigma attaching to the offense are heightened; it necessarily follows that the defendant should not -- at the moment the State is put to proof of those circumstances -- be deprived of protections that have, until that point, unquestionably attached." Id., 530 U.S. at 484.

B

The Court truncates this protection and holds that "facts, sometimes referred to as sentencing factors," do not need to be "alleged in the indictment, submitted to the jury, or established beyond a reasonable doubt," ante, at 2, so long as they do not increase the penalty for the crime beyond the statutory maximum. This is so even if the fact alters the statutorily mandated sentencing range, by increasing the mandatory minimum sentence. But to say that is in effect to claim that the imposition of a 7-year, rather than a 5-year, mandatory minimum does not change the constitutionally relevant sentence range because, regardless, either sentence falls between five years and the statutory maximum of life, the longest sentence range available under the statute. This analysis is flawed precisely because the statute provides incremental sentencing ranges, in which the mandatory minimum sentence varies upward if a defendant "brandished" or "discharged" a weapon. As a matter of common sense, an increased mandatory minimum heightens the loss of liberty and represents the increased stigma society attaches to the offense. Consequently, facts that trigger an increased mandatory minimum sentence warrant constitutional safeguards.

Actual sentencing practices appear to bolster this conclusion. The suggestion that a 7-year sentence could be imposed even without a finding that a defendant brandished a firearm ignores the fact that the sentence imposed when a defendant is found only to have "carried" a firearm "in relation to" a drug trafficking offense appears to be, almost uniformly, if not invariably, five years. Similarly, those found to have brandished a firearm typically, if not always, are sentenced only to 7 years in prison while those found to have discharged a firearm are sentenced only to 10 years. Cf. United States Sentencing Commission, 2001 Datafile, USSCFY01, Table 1 (illustrating that almost all persons sentenced for violations of 18 U.S.C. §924(c)(1)(A) are sentenced to 5, 7, or 10 years' imprisonment). This is true even though anyone convicted of violating §924(c)(1)(A) is theoretically eligible to receive a sentence as severe as life imprisonment. n4 Yet under the decision today, those key facts actually responsible for fixing a defendant's punishment need not be charged in an indictment or proved beyond a reasonable doubt.

n4 Indeed it is a certainty that in virtually every instance the sentence imposed for a §924(c)(1)(A) violation is tied directly to the applicable mandatory minimum. See United States Sentencing Commission, Guidelines Manual §2K2.4, comment., n. 1 (Nov. 2001) (stating clearly that "the guideline sentence for a defendant convicted under 18 U.S.C. §924(c) ... is the minimum term required by the relevant statute .... A sentence above the minimum term ... is an upward departure").

The incremental increase between five and seven years in prison may not seem so great in the abstract (of course it must seem quite different to a defendant actually being incarcerated). However, the constitutional analysis adopted by the plurality would hold equally true if the mandatory minimum for a violation of §924(c)(1) without brandishing was five years, but the mandatory minimum with brandishing was life imprisonment. The result must be the same because surely our fundamental constitutional principles cannot alter depending on degrees of sentencing severity. So long as it was clear that Congress intended for "brandishing" to be a sentencing factor, that fact would still neither have to be charged in the indictment nor proved beyond a reasonable doubt. But if this is the case, then Apprendi can easily be avoided by clever statutory drafting.

It is true that Apprendi concerned a fact that increased the penalty for a crime beyond the prescribed statutory maximum, but the principles upon which it relied apply with equal force to those facts that expose the defendant to a higher mandatory minimum: When a fact exposes a defendant to greater punishment than what is otherwise legally prescribed, that fact is "by definition [an] 'element' of a separate legal offense." 530 U.S. at 483, n. 10. Whether one raises the floor or raises the ceiling it is impossible to dispute that the defendant is exposed to greater punishment than is otherwise prescribed.

This is no less true because mandatory minimum sentences are a 20th-century phenomena. As the Government acknowledged at oral argument, this fact means only that historical practice is not directly dispositive of the question whether facts triggering mandatory minimums must be treated like elements. Tr. of Oral Arg. 47. The Court has not previously suggested that constitutional protection ends where legislative innovation or ingenuity begins. Looking to the principles that animated the decision in Apprendi and the bases for the historical practice upon which Apprendi rested (rather than to the historical pedigree of mandatory minimums), there are no logical grounds for treating facts triggering mandatory minimums any differently than facts that increase the statutory maximum. In either case the defendant cannot predict the judgment from the face of the felony, see 530 U.S. at 478-479, and the absolute statutory limits of his punishment change, constituting an increased penalty. In either case the defendant must be afforded the procedural protections of notice, a jury trial, and a heightened standard of proof with respect to the facts warranting exposure to a greater penalty. See id., 530 U.S. at 490; Jones, 526 U.S. at 253 (SCALIA, J., concurring).

.....

UNITED STATES et al. v. BEAN

(FULL CASE)
537 U.S. 71, 123 S.Ct. 584; 154 L. Ed. 2d 483
October 16, 2002, Argued
December 10, 2002, Decided

GIST: U.S. law allows a person to regain the right to arms, if the right has been lost due to a legal disability, such as a prior felony conviction (see 18 USC §925). The Secretary of the Treasury (acting through the Bureau of Alcohol, Tobacco and Firearms), is to decide if the person is fit to have those rights restored. Since 1992 however, Congress has refused to give BATF any funding with which to investigate requests for restoration of rights (every congressional funding denial is cited in this case) and the process has ground to a halt.

Thomas Bean, a gun dealer attending a gun show in Laredo, Texas, went to dinner with some of his associates after the show, across the border in Nuevo Laredo, Mexico. At the border, a single box of ammunition was found in his car, and a Mexican court convicted him of importing ammunition, a felony with a five-year sentence. He served six months in Mexican detention, and was then transferred to a U.S. facility and immediately paroled.

Devoid of any reflection about his character or intentions, the Mexican felony nonetheless effectively stripped Bean of his American gun rights. He applied for relief to BATF, who returned his application unprocessed, citing Congress' prohibition on spending any money to provide relief. Relying on a judicial-review provision of the rights-restoration law, Bean sued for relief in federal court, and won at the District and Appeals Courts. Some observers believed this heralded a long overdue correction to the rights-restoration problem.

The High Court unanimously overturned the lower courts, observing that the determination of fitness to have gun rights restored was: 1) best handled by BATF, 2) by law had to be handled by BATF, 3) that courts lacked competence to perform the determination, and 4) that without a dispositive denial, the issues the courts were empowered to address were necessarily missing. A failure to process Bean's request did not constitute a denial, so there were no grounds for judicial review, and Bean, along with many other citizens, was plain out of luck. And that was the Supreme Court's last word about your gun rights, as we went to press with this book, six years after we began the project.

Certiorari to the United States Court of Appeals for the Fifth Circuit

Because of respondent's felony conviction, he was prohibited by 18 U.S.C. §922(g)(1) from possessing, distributing, or receiving firearms or ammunition. Relying on §925(c), he applied to the Bureau of Alcohol, Tobacco, and Firearms (ATF) for relief from his firearms disabilities. ATF returned the application unprocessed, explaining that its annual appropriations law forbade it from expending any funds to investigate or act upon such applications. Invoking §925(c)'s judicial review provision, he filed suit, asking the District Court to conduct its own inquiry into his fitness to possess a gun and to issue a judicial order granting relief. The court granted the requested relief, and the Fifth Circuit affirmed.

Held: The absence of an actual denial by ATF of a felon's petition precludes judicial review under §925(c). The Secretary of the Treasury is authorized to grant relief from a firearms disability if certain preconditions are met, and an applicant may seek federal-court review if the Secretary denies his application. Ibid. Since 1992, however, the appropriations bar has prevented ATF, to which the Secretary has delegated this authority, from using appropriated funds to investigate or act upon the applications. Section

925(c)'s text and the procedure it lays out for seeking relief make clear that an actual decision by ATF on an application is a prerequisite for judicial review, and that mere inaction by ATF does not invest a district court with independent jurisdiction. Grammatically, the phrase "denied by the Secretary" references the Secretary's decision on whether an applicant "will not be likely to act in a manner dangerous to public safety," and whether "the granting of the relief would not be contrary to the public interest." Such determination can hardly be construed as anything but a decision actually denying the application. Under §925(c)'s procedure for those seeking relief, the Secretary, i.e., ATF, has broad authority to grant or deny relief, even when the statutory prerequisites are satisfied. This procedure shows that judicial review cannot occur without a dispositive decision by ATF. First, in the absence of a statutorily defined standard of review for action under §925(c), the Administrative Procedure Act (APA) supplies the applicable standard. 5 U.S.C. §§701(a), 706(2)(A). The APA's "arbitrary and capricious" test, by its nature, contemplates review of some action by another entity. Second, both parts of §925(c)'s standard for granting relief--whether an applicant is "likely to act in a manner dangerous to public safety" and whether the relief is in the "public interest"--are policy-based determinations and, hence, point to ATF as the primary decisionmaker. Third, §925(c) allows the admission of additional evidence in district court proceedings only in exceptional circumstances. Congressional assignment of such a circumscribed role to a district court shows that the statute contemplates that a court's determination will heavily rely on the record and the ATF's decision. Indeed, the very use in §925(c) of the word "review" to describe a court's responsibility in this statutory scheme signifies that it cannot grant relief on its own, absent an antecedent actual denial by ATF. Pp. 2-7.

253 F. 3d 234, reversed.

Thomas, J., delivered the opinion for a unanimous Court.

Justice Thomas delivered the opinion of the Court.

We consider in this case whether, despite appropriation provisions barring the Bureau of Alcohol, Tobacco, and Firearms (ATF) from acting on applications for relief from firearms disabilities of persons convicted of a felony, a federal district court has authority under 18 U.S.C. §925(c) to grant such relief.

I

After attending a gun show in Laredo, Texas, respondent, Thomas Lamar Bean, a gun dealer, and his associates drove respondent's vehicle to Nuevo Laredo, Mexico, for dinner. When Mexican officials stopped the vehicle at the border, they found in the back, in plain view, approximately 200 rounds of ammunition.

After attending a gun show in Laredo, Texas, respondent, Thomas Lamar Bean, a gun dealer, and his associates drove respondent's vehicle to Nuevo Laredo, Mexico, for dinner. Bean v. Bureau of Alcohol, Tobacco and Firearms, 253 F. 3d 234, 236 (CA5 2001). When Mexican officials stopped the vehicle at the border, they found in the back, in plain view, approximately 200 rounds of ammunition. Ibid. According to respondent, he had instructed his associates to remove any firearms and ammunition from his vehicle, but inexplicably one box remained. Ibid. Respondent was convicted in a Mexican court of importing ammunition into Mexico and sentenced to five years' imprisonment.

Because of his felony conviction, respondent was prohibited by 18 U.S.C. §922(g)(1) from possessing, distributing, or receiving firearms or ammunition. Relying on §925(c), respondent applied to ATF for relief from his firearms disabilities. ATF returned the application unprocessed, explaining that its annual appropriations law forbade it from expending any funds to investigate or act upon applications such as respondent's.

Relying on the judicial review provision in §925(c), respondent asked the District Court to conduct its own inquiry into his fitness to possess a gun, and to issue a judicial order granting relief from his firearms disabilities.

Respondent then filed suit in the United States District Court for the Eastern District of Texas. Relying on the judicial review provision in §925(c), respondent asked the District Court to conduct its own inquiry into his fitness to possess a gun, and to issue a judicial order granting relief from his firearms disabilities. Respondent attached various affidavits from persons attesting to his fitness to possess firearms. After conducting a hearing, the court entered judgment granting respondent the requested relief. The Court of Appeals for the Fifth Circuit affirmed, concluding that congressional refusal to provide funding to ATF for reviewing applications such as respondent's "is not the requisite direct and definite suspension or repeal of the subject rights." 253 F. 3d, at 239. The Fifth Circuit then proceeded to hold that the District Court had jurisdiction to review ATF's (in)action. We granted certiorari. 534 U. S. 1112 (2002).

II

Under federal law, a person who is convicted of a felony is prohibited from possessing firearms. See §922(g)(1). The Secretary of the Treasury is authorized to grant relief from that prohibition if it is established to his satisfaction that certain preconditions are met. See §925(c).1 An applicant may seek judicial review from a "United States district court" if his application "is denied by the Secretary." Ibid.

Footnote 1. Title 18 U.S.C. §925(c) provides:

"A person who is prohibited from possessing, shipping, transporting, or receiving firearms or ammunition may make application to the Secretary for relief from the disabilities imposed by Federal laws with respect to the acquisition, receipt, transfer, shipment, transportation, or possession of firearms, and the Secretary may grant such relief if it is established to his satisfaction that the circumstances regarding the disability, and the applicant's record and reputation, are such that the applicant will not be likely to act in a manner dangerous to public safety and that the granting of the relief would not be contrary to the public interest. Any person whose application for relief from disabilities is denied by the Secretary may file a petition with the United States district court for the district in which he resides for a judicial review of such denial. The court may in its discretion admit additional evidence where failure to do so would result in a miscarriage of justice. A licensed importer, licensed manufacturer, licensed dealer, or licensed collector conducting operations under this chapter, who makes application for relief from the disabilities incurred under this chapter, shall not be barred by such disability from further operations under his license pending final action on an application for relief filed pursuant to this section. Whenever the Secretary grants relief to any person pursuant to this section he shall promptly publish in the Federal Register notice of such action, together with the reasons therefor."

Since 1992, however, the appropriations bar has prevented ATF, to which the Secretary has delegated authority to act on §925(c) applications,2 from using "funds appropriated herein ... to investigate or act upon applications for relief from Federal firearms disabilities under 18 U.S.C. [§]925(c)." Treasury, Postal Service, and General Government Appropriations Act, 1993, Pub. L. 102-393, 106 Stat. 1732.3 Accordingly, ATF, upon receipt of respondent's petition, returned it, explaining that "[s]ince October 1992, ATF's annual appropriation has prohibited the expending of any funds to investigate or act upon applications for relief from Federal firearms disabilities." App. 33-34. Respondent contends that ATF's failure to act constitutes a "denial" within the meaning of §925(c), and that, therefore, district courts have jurisdiction to review such inaction.

Footnote 2. Respondent contends that congressional denial of funds to ATF did not eliminate the Secretary's power to act on his application. In support, respondent notes that §925(c) refers to the action by "the Secretary." That claim, however, is waived, as respondent raised it for the first time in his brief on the merits to this Court.

Even if considered on the merits, respondent's argument faces several difficulties. First, it appears that the Secretary delegated to ATF the exclusive authority to act on petitions brought under §925(c), see 27 CFR §§178.144(b) and (d) (2002); such delegation is not unreasonable. Second, even assuming the Secretary has retained the authority to act on such petitions, it is not clear that respondent would prevail were he to file a requisite action under 5 U.S.C. §706(1) (providing for judicial review to "compel agency action unlawfully withheld or unreasonably delayed"). Not only does the Secretary, by the explicit terms of the statute, possess broad discretion as to whether to grant relief, see infra, at 6-7, but congressional withholding of funds from ATF would likely inform his exercise of discretion.

Footnote 3. In each subsequent year, Congress has retained the bar on the use of appropriated funds to process applications filed by individuals. Treasury and General Government Appropriations Act, 2002, Pub. L. 107-67, 115 Stat. 519; Consolidated Appropriations Act, 2001, Pub. L. 106-554, 114 Stat. 2763A-129; Treasury and General Government Appropriations Act, 2000, Pub. L. 106-58, 113 Stat. 434; Treasury and General Government Appropriations Act, 1999, Pub. L. 105-277, 112 Stat. 2681-485; Treasury and General Government Appropriations Act, 1998, Pub. L. 105-61, 111 Stat. 1277; Treasury, Postal Service, and General Government Appropriations Act, 1997, Pub. L. 104-208, 110 Stat. 3009-319; Treasury, Postal Service, and General Government Appropriations Act, 1996, Pub. L. 104-52, 109 Stat. 471; Treasury, Postal Service and General Government Appropriations Act, 1995, Pub. L. 103-329, 108 Stat. 2385; Treasury, Postal Service, and General Government Appropriations Act, 1994, Pub. L. 103-123, 107 Stat. 1228.

Inaction by ATF does not amount to a "denial" within the meaning of §925(c).

We disagree. Inaction by ATF does not amount to a "denial" within the meaning of §925(c). The text of §925(c) and the procedure it lays out for seeking relief make clear that an actual decision by ATF on an application is a prerequisite for judicial review, and that mere inaction by ATF does not invest a district court with independent jurisdiction to act on an application.

Grammatically, the phrase "denied by the Secretary" references the Secretary's decision on whether an applicant "will not be likely to act in a manner dangerous to public safety," and whether "the granting of the relief would not be contrary to the public interest." The determination whether an applicant is "likely to act in a manner dangerous to public safety" can hardly be construed as anything but a decision actually denying the application.4 And, in fact, respondent does not contend that ATF actually passed on his the application, but rather claims that "refusal to grant relief constitutes a literal, or at least a constructive, denial of the application because it has precisely the same impact on [the applicant] as denial on the merits." Brief for Respondent 35 (internal quotation marks and citations omitted).

Footnote 4. Also counseling against construing failure to act as a denial for purposes of §925(c) is the fact that while the Administrative Procedure Act (APA) draws a distinction between a "denial" and a "failure to act," see 5 U.S.C. §551(13), an applicant may obtain judicial review under §925(c) only if an application is denied. See 2A N. Singer, Sutherland on Statutes and Statutory Construction §46.06, p. 194 (6th ed. 2000) ("The use of different words within related statutes generally implies that different meanings were intended").

The procedure that §925(c) lays out for those seeking relief also leads us to conclude that an actual adverse action on the application by ATF is a prerequisite for judicial review. Section 925(c) requires an applicant, as a first step, to petition the Secretary and establish to the Secretary's satisfaction that the applicant is eligible for relief. The Secretary, in his discretion, may grant or deny the request based on the broad considerations outlined above. Only then, if the Secretary denies relief, may an applicant seek review in a district court.

This broad authority of the Secretary, i.e., ATF, to grant or deny relief, even when the statutory prerequisites are satisfied, shows that judicial review under §925(c) cannot occur without a dispositive decision by ATF. First, in the absence of a statutorily defined standard of review for action under §925(c), the APA supplies the applicable standard. 5 U.S.C. §701(a). Under the APA, judicial review is usually limited to determining whether agency action is "arbitrary, capricious, an abuse of discretion, or otherwise not in accordance with law." §706(2)(A). Application of the APA standard of review here indicates that judicial review is predicated upon ATF's dispositive decision: the "arbitrary and capricious" test in its nature contemplates review of some action by another entity, rather than initial judgment of the court itself.

Second, both parts of the standard for granting relief point to ATF as the primary decisionmaker. Whether an applicant is "likely to act in a manner dangerous to public safety" presupposes an inquiry into that applicant's background--a function best performed by the Executive, which, unlike courts, is institutionally equipped for conducting a neutral, wide-ranging investigation. Similarly, the "public interest" standard calls for an inherently policy-based decision best left in the hands of an agency.

Third, the admission of additional evidence in district court proceedings is contemplated only in exceptional circumstances. See 18 U.S.C. §925(c) (allowing, "in [district court's] discretion," admission of evidence where "failure to do so would result in a miscarriage of justice"). Congressional assignment of such a circumscribed role to a district court shows that the statute contemplates that a district court's determination will heavily rely on the record and the decision made by ATF. Indeed, the very use in §925(c) of the word "review" to describe a district court's responsibility in this statutory scheme signifies that a district court cannot grant relief on its own, absent an antecedent actual denial by ATF.

we hold that the absence of an actual denial of respondent's petition by ATF precludes judicial review under §925(c)

Accordingly, we hold that the absence of an actual denial of respondent's petition by ATF precludes judicial review under §925(c), and therefore reverse the judgment of the Court of Appeals.

It is so ordered.

THE NEXT CASE

(FULL CASE)
No. 01-001

GIST: As sure as the sun rises, you know there will be more cases on guns, the militia, the right to keep arms, the right to bear arms, self defense, gun crimes and more. To keep this book current, Bloomfield Press plans to post any new cases on our website, gunlaws.com.

While we prepared to go to press, the 5th Circuit's *Emerson* case, and the *Silveira* case from the 9th Circuit both seemed poised for possible review, and both involved the 2nd Amendment head on (Emerson is now off the burner but Silveira is poised to possibly move up). Adding to the tension, the 5th and 9th Circuits take opposite positions on the gun rights protected in the 2nd Amendment (the 5th Circuit says you have rights, the 9th Circuit says you do not have rights; lower courts have been in disarray on this for a long while).

The *Silveira* case is of particular concern because it takes the no-rights position, and in the words of the dissent in that case, "...the panel misses the mark by interpreting the Second Amendment right to keep and bear arms as a collective right, rather than as an individual right. Because the panel's decision abrogates a constitutional right, this case should have been reheard en banc." In addition, "About twenty percent of the American population, those who live in the Ninth Circuit, have lost one of the ten amendments in the Bill of Rights. And, the methodology used to take away the right threatens the rest of the Constitution. The most extraordinary step taken by the panel opinion is to read the frequently used Constitutional phrase, "the people," as conferring rights only upon collectives, not individuals."

This is not unexpectable from the San Francisco-based 9th Circuit, the nation's least conservative, and least frequently upheld federal appeals court. The High Court can let a split in the Circuits fester for decades, or take it up before the ink in this book dries, and other cases are in the judiciary pipeline that keeps on flowing and flowing. We'll just have to wait and see.

Descriptive Index of Cases

by Alan Korwin

All 92 Supreme Court gun cases are posed here as answered questions to help you locate specific proceedings. [Dissents and dismissals appear in brackets.] Only questions related to firearms or self defense are listed even if, as is often the case, they are not the core issues. Many other questions are often addressed in the cases and, because of the terseness of the posed questions, you should rely on the full actual cases for an understanding of the significance of each one. Think of this index as a navigation tool, a memory jogger, and a good read.

• Indicates the 44 cases presented in their entirety
Δ Indicates the 14 self-defense cases

Name — Date — Citation — Page

Acers v. United States • Δ .... 1896 .... 164 U.S. 388 238
Is fear of a deadly attack, without reasonable demonstrated grounds for the fear, sufficient to support a claim of self defense [NO]; Must the danger be immediate [YES]; Can any object be considered as a deadly weapon depending on how it was used [YES].

Adams v. Williams .... 1972 .... 407 U.S. 143 363
Can a peace officer conduct a limited protective search for concealed weapons, if there is reason to believe a suspect is armed and dangerous [YES]; Are 4th Amendment guarantees violated by such a stop and frisk [NO].

Adamson v. California .... 1947 .... 332 U.S. 46 310
[The dissenting opinion in a 5th Amendment case argues that the 14th Amendment was intended to incorporate the Bill of Rights, including the 2nd Amendment, against the states].

Alberty v. United States • Δ .... 1896 .... 162 U.S. 499 231
If a husband sees another man trying to get into his wife's room window at night is it natural for him to investigate further [YES]; Is the husband under a duty to retreat when attacked with a knife under such circumstances [NO]; May the husband use only as much force as is necessary to repel the assault [YES]; If in an ensuing confrontation the husband shoots and kills the other man, then flees, must his flight in and of itself be seen as evidence of his guilt [NO].

Albright v. Oliver .... 1994 .... 510 U.S. 266 481
[The dissenting opinion in a case involving freedom from malicious prosecution cites the right to keep and bear arms as among fundamental freedoms guaranteed by the Constitution].

Allen v. United States • Δ .... 1896 .... 164 U.S. 492 241
Are words alone sufficient provocation to justify an assault [NO]; Are words alone sufficient to reduce murder to manslaughter [NO]; Can premeditation and intent to kill be determined from your actions [YES]; Although flight after a possibly criminal event may suggest guilt, does it prove it conclusively [NO].

the fact that Congress currently provides no way for a felon to restore the right to keep and bear arms matter in this regard [NO].

Biswell, United States v., ... 1972 .... 406 U.S. 311 361
Is the 4th Amendment violated when a federally licensed firearms dealer's business is searched under 18 USC §923(g) without a warrant, and illegally possessed guns are seized [NO]; When a dealer "chooses to engage in this pervasively regulated business" and to accept a federal license, does he do so with the knowledge that his business will be subject to effective inspection [YES].

Bousley v. United States .... 1998 .... 523 U.S. 614 599
Does a defendant need to understand what constitutes "use" of a firearm in relation to a drug-trafficking crime, in order to enter a constitutionally valid guilty plea [YES].

Brown v. United States • Δ .... 1921 .... 256 U.S. 335 285
Is there a duty to retreat when attacked by a man with a knife [NO]; Believing you're in a mortal conflict, if you fire a shot in the heat of combat, which in cool reflection later may be seen as unnecessary, may you still be acquitted on grounds of self defense [YES]; Is your right of self defense roughly similar in your home, on your land, and at your work [YES]; Can detached reflection be demanded in the presence of an uplifted knife [NO].

Brown v. Walker .... 1896 .... 161 U.S. 591 223
Is the object of the first eight amendments to the Constitution to incorporate into the fundamental law of the land certain principles of natural justice [YES]; Are the first eight amendments limitations only upon the powers of Congress and the Federal courts, and not applicable to the several States, except so far as the 14th Amendment may have made them applicable [YES].

Bryan v. United States • .... 1998 .... 524 U.S. 184 613
Are you committing the crime of "willfully" dealing in firearms without a license, if you know your actions are illegal but do not know the licensing law you are violating [YES]; Was the Firearms Owners' Protection Act enacted to protect law-abiding citizens who might inadvertently violate the law [YES].

Burton v. Sills • .... 1969 .... 394 U.S. 812 344
[The New Jersey Supreme Court rejected a 2nd Amendment suit against a discretionary firearm licensing law, citing cases that held the 2nd Amendment inapplicable to the states; the U.S. Supreme Court dismissed the appeal for want of a substantial federal question.]

Busic v. United States .... 1980 .... 446 U.S. 398 410
Can an assault sentence, increased under the armed-assault-of-a-federal-officer law, also be increased under the separate federal armed-felony law [NO].

Caron v. United States .... 1998 .... 524 U.S. 308 623
Can a three-time violent-felony loser avoid a five-year mandatory penalty enhancement for carrying a gun in a subsequent crime he commits, if a state court had partially restored his right to keep and bear arms [NO]; If a state restores a convicted felon's right to keep and bear long guns but not handguns, is the federal ban for felons on possession on all guns removed [NO].

Freed, United States v., • .... 1971 .... 401 U.S. 601 345
Does the regulatory scheme of the amended National Firearms Act violate the 5th Amendment protection against self incrimination, or violate a person's right to due process of law [NO].

Galioto, United States v., • .... 1986 .... 477 U.S. 556 439
[Court dismisses as moot the constitutionality of allowing felons a means to restore their right to obtain firearms but not allowing the same for former mental patients, because Congress, while this case was in process, changed the law to allow any person with firearms disabilities to apply for relief.]

Gonzales, United States v., ... 1997 .... 520 U.S. 1 552
May the federal five-year-sentence enhancement for using or carrying a gun during a drug trafficking crime run concurrently with a state sentence [NO].

Gourko v. United States • Δ .... 1894 .... 153 U.S. 183 189
If you shoot someone who has repeatedly threatened you, and the circumstances of the shooting are not found to be justifiable as self defense, does the fact that you armed yourself in response to the threat automatically make the shooting murder (as opposed to manslaughter) [NO].

Griswold v. Connecticut .... 1965 .... 381 U.S. 479 322
Do the first eight amendments to the Constitution protect fundamental rights of the people [YES].

Hamilton v. Regents of the University of California ..... 1934 .... 293 U.S. 245 294
Do the states have the authority to train their able-bodied male citizens of suitable age, to develop fitness to serve in the state militia [YES]; Is the state the sole judge of the means and amount of training as long as it doesn't conflict with federal law [YES].

Harris v. United States .... 2002 .... 00-10666 634
Is brandishing a gun during a specified drug-trafficking crime a sentencing factor to be determined by a judge, and not an element of the crime to be determined by a jury [YES].

Haynes v. United States • .... 1968 .... 390 U.S. 85 326
Does Congress have the authority to regulate the manufacture, transfer, and possession of firearms, subject to constitutional limitations, and to tax unlawful activities [YES]; Did the registration requirements of the National Firearms Act violate the defendant's 5th Amendment privilege against self incrimination [YES]; Was a proper claim of 5th Amendment protection a complete defense against failure to register or possession of an unregistered NFA weapon [YES]. (Note that Congress redrafted the relevant statute to overcome these findings and continue to require NFA registration.)

Houston v. Moore .... 1820 .... 18 U.S. 1 147
[The first mention of the 2nd Amendment in a High Court decision occurs as a brief remark in a dissent in this case, postulating that the amendment would have little effect on the legitimacy of a state running and arming its militia in the absence of, or subordinate to Congressional regulation. It implies that the amendment was not primarily viewed as a guarantee of state government powers to control state militias.]

Huddleston v. United States • .... 1974 .... 415 U.S. 814 369
Is the return of a gun from a pawnbroker subject to the same requirements as the sale of a gun from a dealer under the Gun Control Act of 1968 [YES]; Is the intention of the GCA to deprive guns to unauthorized juveniles, fugitives, criminals and the mentally incompetent [YES]; Are hunting, target practice, gun collecting, and the legitimate use of guns for individual protection allowed under the GCA [YES]; Did Congress require commerce in firearms to be channeled through a federalized network of dealers in an effort to halt illegal mail-order and interstate consumer traffic in firearms [YES].

Johnson v. Eisentrager .... 1950 .... 339 U.S. 763 313
Does the Constitution confer to Nazi spies captured in China during WWII, subsequently convicted of spying on the U.S. and serving their sentences in post-war Germany, the rights it confers to U.S. citizens [NO]; Do the rights of U.S. citizens include among others the right to bear arms as in the 2nd Amendment [YES].

Kepner v. United States .... 1904 .... 195 U.S. 100 274
Did the adoption in the Philippines of most of the U.S. Bill of Rights omit the right to a trial by jury and the right of the people to bear arms [YES].

Knapp v. Schweitzer .... 1958 .... 357 U.S. 371 314
Do all the first eight amendments of the Bill of Rights apply to the states [NO].

Konigsberg v. State Bar of California .... 1961 .... 366 U.S. 36 315
Does absolute verbiage ("shall make no law," "shall not be infringed") in the 1st and 2nd Amendments allow for some level of regulation, some of which is well established and widely recognized [YES].

Laird v. Tatum .... 1972 .... 408 U.S. 1 368
Was the 2nd Amendment added to the Constitution to authorize a decentralized militia, guaranteeing the right of the people to keep and bear arms [YES].

Lewis v. United States • .... 1980 .... 445 U.S. 55 401
If a person is prohibited from possessing firearms due to a prior felony conviction, does it matter if the prior conviction was unconstitutional [NO].

Logan v. United States Δ .... 1892 .... 144 U.S. 263 180
Does the 2nd Amendment guarantee a preexisting right recognized by the Constitution, and not a right created by the Constitution [YES]; Is a prisoner in legal custody entitled to protection "while he is deprived of the ordinary means of defending and protecting himself" [YES].

Lopez, United States v., • .... 1995 .... 514 U.S. 549 506
Does the Interstate Commerce Clause give Congress the power to regulate personal possession of firearms near local schools [NO]; Is possession of a gun in a school zone an economic activity [NO].

Malloy v. Hogan .... 1964 .... 378 U.S. 1 319
Is it unsettled as to whether the 14th Amendment applies the first eight amendments to the Bill of Rights against the states [YES]; Did *Presser v. Illinois* find that the particular guarantees of the 2nd Amendment were not safeguarded from state action [YES].

Maryland v. United States .... 1965 .... 381 U.S. 41 320
For the purpose of determining liability in an air crash involving a National Guard and commercial aircraft, are National Guard members state employees, and not federal employees, if not specifically called into federal service [YES]; Does it matter if the members were military or civilian members [NO].

Maxwell v. Dow .... 1900 .... 176 U.S. 581 269
Did the court decide in *Presser v. Illinois* that the 2nd Amendment is only a limitation on federal power [YES]. Would incorporation of the privileges and immunities of U.S. citizens against the states entirely destroy the sovereignty of the states [YES]. (Dissent suggests the Bill of Rights should apply to the states.)

Miller v. State of Texas • .... 1894 .... 153 U.S. 535 194
Will the Court accept a 2nd Amendment issue on appeal if it wasn't raised in court prior to the appeal [NO].

Miller, United States v., • .... 1939 .... 307 U.S. 174 300
Without the presentation of evidence or testimony, can the Court determine whether a short-barreled shotgun, as defined in the 1934 NFA law, is a militia weapon and therefore an arm protected by the 2nd Amendment [NO]; Is possession of arms by the people related to the preservation and efficiency of a well regulated militia [YES].

Miranda v. Arizona .... 1966 .... 384 U.S. 436 325
Where rights secured by the Constitution are involved, can there be any rule making or legislation that would abrogate them [NO].

Moore v. E. Cleveland .... 1976 .... 431 U.S. 494 390
Is the right to keep and bear arms among the type of individual rights enumerated in the Bill of Rights [YES].

Muscarello v. United States • .... 1998 .... 524 U.S. 125 600
With regard to a mandatory penalty increase for carrying a firearm in relation to a drug trafficking crime, does "carry" include in the trunk of a car [YES]; Is a drug dealer with a gun in her pocket more dangerous than a drug dealer with a gun in her car trunk [NO].

One Assortment of 89 Firearms, United States v., • ..... 1984 .... 465 U.S. 354 422
Does acquittal from criminal charges for dealing in firearms without a license prevent the government from conducting a separate civil forfeiture action and confiscating the firearms involved [NO]; Is such confiscation a violation of the protection against double jeopardy [NO]; Can the lower threshold of guilt (preponderance of the evidence) allow the government to prevail in the forfeiture, where it could not against the higher threshold (beyond a reasonable doubt) in criminal proceedings [YES]; Is the gun confiscation scheme in the law primarily a civil, non-criminal, remedial action [YES].

Patsone v. Pennsylvania • .... 1914 .... 232 U.S. 138 279
Can a state prohibit possession of rifles or shotguns for hunting by nonresident aliens without violating due process guarantees [YES]; Does such a prohibition violate specified treaty conditions with Italy [NO].

Pennsylvania Bd. of Probation and Parole v. Scott ...... 1998 .... 524 U.S. 357 626

Are firearms seized in a warrantless search of a paroled felon's residence admissible as evidence at a parole revocation hearing, even if the seizure violated the 4th Amendment [YES].

Perpich v. Department of Defense • .... 1990 .... 496 U.S. 334 446

Can members of a state's organized militia be called into federal service, for training outside the United States, without an imminent emergency and without the state Governor's permission [YES]; When members of the state National Guard are federalized, are they still members of their state militia [NO]; When they muster out of federal service do they regain their state status [YES].

Planned Parenthood v. Casey .... 1992 .... 505 U.S. 833 468

Do the protections of the 14th Amendment extend beyond the specifics in the Bill of Rights—such as free speech, press, religion, the right to keep and bear arms and more—and to a freedom from all arbitrary impositions [YES]; Is the right to keep and bear arms among the type of individual rights enumerated in the Bill of Rights [YES].

Poe v. Ullman .... 1961 .... 367 U.S. 497 317

(Justices Douglas and Harlan filed dissenting opinions, asserting that the 14th Amendment applies the Bill of Rights to the states, a position that was later adopted into law.)

Powell, United States v., • .... 1975 .... 423 U.S. 87 378

Is a 22-inch-long sawed-off shotgun capable of being concealed on the person and hence illegal to ship through the U.S. Post Office [YES].

Presser v. Illinois • .... 1886 .... 116 U.S. 252 172

Are all citizens capable of bearing arms the reserve military force in the country [YES]; Can the states deny citizens the right to keep and bear arms, thus depriving the United States of calling forth the militia [NO]; Can states regulate firearms as required for public order [YES].

Printz/Mack v. United States • .... 1997 .... 521 U.S. 898 556

Does the 10th Amendment prohibit the federal government from commanding local police authorities to implement federal police mandates, and conduct background checks on prospective handgun purchasers (the Brady case) [YES].

Robertson v. Baldwin .... 1897 .... 165 U.S. 275 254

Does the Bill of Rights protect "guarantees and immunities" which existed long before the Constitution was adopted [YES]; Are there well-recognized limits on these rights [YES]; Can a state prohibit concealed carry without violating the 2nd Amendment [YES].

Roe v. Wade .... 1973 .... 410 U.S. 113 369

Is the full scope of liberty protected by the 14th Amendment more than a series of isolated points that includes the right to keep and bear arms [YES].

Rogers v. United States • .... 1998 .... 522 U.S. 252 594

[A writ to consider "knowing possession" of an NFA "firearm" (a silencer in this case) is dismissed because the case fails to present the issue sufficiently clearly to merit review.]

Rowe v. United States • Δ .... 1896 .... 164 U.S. 546 247
If a man is provoked into making a minor assault on someone, and then backs off in good faith, is his right to self defense restored if the person he assaulted attacks him with a deadly weapon? [YES]; Is he required to retreat under such circumstances [NO]; Is he under an obligation to try to only wound an attacker when fighting for his life [NO]; Can either party in a mutual combat claim self defense [NO].

Scarborough v. United States • .... 1977 .... 431 U.S. 563 391
With regard to illegal possession of a firearm by a felon, which is federally banned for guns in or affecting commerce, does it matter when the gun moved in commerce, or when the felon was convicted, as long as both conditions occurred [NO].

Schwimmer, United States v., • .... 1929 .... 279 U.S. 644 289
If a person is unwilling to take up arms in military service if called upon, should application for naturalized U.S. citizenship be accepted [NO]; Is a fundamental principle of our Constitution that it is the duty of citizens, by force of arms, to defend our government against all enemies whenever necessity arises [YES].

Simpson v. United States .... 1978 .... 435 U.S. 6 399
Can a bank-robbery sentence, increased under the federal armed-bank-robbery law, also be increased under the separate federal armed-felony law [NO].

Smith v. United States • .... 1993 .... 508 U.S. 223 470
For the purpose of enhancing the sentence in a drug-trafficking crime to a mandatory 30 years, does the phrase "using a gun," in connection with drug trafficking, include offering to barter a MAC-10 with a silencer for two ounces of cocaine [YES].

Sonzinsky v. United States • .... 1937 ...... 300 U. S. 506 296
Is a firearm, as defined in the 1934 NFA law, and a firearm dealer, federally taxable [YES].

Spencer v. Kemna .... 1998 .... 523 U.S. 1 598
[A dissenting opinion says a felon endures tangible harm after his sentence expires because he loses his right to vote or to bear arms, and is at risk for greater penalty in a future offense.].

Staples v. United States • .... 1994 .... 511 U.S. 600 486
If a person is not aware that a firearm he possesses has been modified to fire as a machinegun, is he guilty of violating the ban on possessing an unregistered NFA weapon [NO].

Starr v. United States Δ .... 1894 .... 153 U.S. 614 196
If a law officer legally serving a warrant shoots at a suspect without identifying himself, is the suspect justified in shooting back and killing the officer in self defense [YES].

Stearns v. Wood • .... 1915 .... 236 U.S. 75 283
Does the Court have to interpret the 2nd Amendment or militia aspects of the Constitution for a National Guard officer who has insufficient legal standing to bring a case [NO].

Stinson v. United States .... 1993 .... 508 U.S. 36 480
Is the commentary to the U.S. Sentencing Guidelines, stating that possession of a firearm by a convicted felon is not a crime of violence, binding on the federal courts [YES].

Tennessee v. Garner Δ .... 1985 .... 471 U.S. 1 428
Is the use of deadly force by police to prevent the escape of all felony suspects constitutionally unreasonable [YES]; Is the use of deadly force by a police officer permissible under the 4th Amendment, if necessary to prevent the escape of a felony suspect who threatens the officer with a weapon, or if there is probable cause to believe that the suspect has committed a crime involving the infliction or threatened infliction of serious physical harm, if, where feasible, some warning has been given [YES].

Terry v. Ohio .... 1968 .... 392 U.S. 1 334
Is a limited, protective, non-invasive "pat-down" search for weapons, known as a "stop and frisk," a reasonable search and seizure under the 4th Amendment if an officer observes suspicious behavior and believes it's necessary for the safety of the officer or others nearby [YES]; Is the higher standard of probable cause needed to conduct such a search for weapons [NO]; Is a more complete search reasonable under these conditions [NO]; Is such a stop and frisk a severe but allowable intrusion upon cherished personal security [YES].

Thompson v. United States Δ .... 1894 ...... 155 U.S. 271 203
Does arming yourself after being threatened, and then traveling the only road in the area where you know your adversary may be, turn a subsequent shooting of the adversary during a confrontation into murder? [NO]; Is arming yourself for legitimate self defense premeditation [NO].

Thompson/Center Arms Co., U.S. v., • .... 1992 ...... 504 U.S. 505 458
Is the definition of "making" an NFA firearm sufficiently clear to require registration and payment of the $200 NFA tax on a parts kit that can be assembled into a legal carbine or into a must-be-registered-to-be-legal short-barreled rifle [NO]; Is a carbine together with all the parts needed to convert it to a machinegun a machinegun [YES]; Is an unassembled silencer a silencer [YES]; Is an unassembled machinegun a machinegun [YES]; Is a pistol and attachable shoulder stock found in different drawers of the same dresser a short-barreled rifle [YES].

Tot v. United States • .... 1943 ...... 319 U.S. 463 306
Does possession of a pistol by a person who has a prior felony conviction constitute proof that the person acquired the gun in interstate commerce, or acquired it after the date of the act that would outlaw such possession [NO].

Trono v. United States .... 1905 ...... 199 U.S. 521 276
Is the right of the people to bear arms omitted in the Act of Congress of July 1, 1902, concerning people in the Philippines [YES].

Twining v. New Jersey • .... 1908 .... 211 U.S. 78 277
Are the right of trial by jury, guaranteed by the 7th Amendment, and the right to bear arms, guaranteed by the 2nd Amendment, among the privileges and immunities of citizens of the United States guaranteed by the 14th Amendment against abridgment by the States [NO].

United States v. (various names)
Cases beginning with "United States" are listed alphabetically by the named party, q.v., Bass, Bean, Biswell, Cruikshank, Freed, Galioto, Gonzales, Lopez, Miller, One Assortment of 89 Firearms, Powell, Schwimmer, Thompson/Center Firearms Co., Ursery, Verdugo-Urquidcz.

Ursery, United States v., ... 1996 .... 518 U.S. 267 549
Was the confiscation of guns in the U.S. v. One Assortment of 89 Firearms case remedial, and not criminal in nature, and thus not prohibited under double jeopardy protections [YES].

Verdugo-Urquidez, United States v., ... 1990 .... 494 U.S. 259 444
Does the phrase "the people" used in the 2nd Amendment refer to individual members of the American society, the same as it does in the Constitution's preamble, and its 1st, 4th, 9th and 10th Amendments [YES]; Does the 2nd Amendment protect "the right of the people to keep and bear arms." [YES].

Wallace v. United States • Δ .... 1896 .... 162 U.S. 466 224
Is it up to the jury to decide whether a homicide is murder, manslaughter or justifiable [YES]; Does a perfect right of self defense require blamelessness in the confrontation and an act of necessity only [YES]; Can you claim self defense if you had intentionally brought about a lethal conflict [NO]; Is it up to the jury to decide whether you armed yourself defensively or otherwise [YES]; Is it murder if you enter a quarrel without felonious or malicious intent, and then, under reasonable belief of imminent mortal danger, you kill the assailant [NO]; Does the fact that you deliberately go and arm yourself, for self defense or other innocent purpose, turn a subsequent shooting necessarily from manslaughter to murder [NO].

SUBJECT MATTER INDEX FOR THE CASES

Case name index begins on p. 649

David B. Kopel

Stephen P. Halbrook

Alan J. Korwin

Dave Kopel is Research Director of the Independence Institute, a civil liberties think tank in Golden, Colo., and an Associate Policy Analyst with the Cato Institute, in Washington, D.C. He has served as an Assistant Attorney General for Colorado, enforcing hazardous waste and Superfund law. In 1985 he graduated *magna cum laude* from the University of Michigan Law School, where he served on the law review. In 1982 he graduated from Brown University, with Highest Honors for his history thesis on Arthur M. Schlesinger, Jr. In 1998-99 he was an adjunct professor of law at New York University.

Kopel is a regular panelist on the PBS public affairs show "Colorado Inside-Out" in Denver, a columnist for the *Rocky Mountain News*, and a Contributing Editor for *National Review Online* and *Liberty*. He has testified many times before Congress and state legislatures on topics including gun control, free speech, and criminal justice. His website is davekopel.org.

Kopel's books related to firearms law and policy include, *Gun Control and Gun Rights* (with Andrew McClurg and Brannon Denning), which is the first law school and university textbook on the subject; *No More Wacos: What's Wrong with Federal Law Enforcement, and How to Fix It* (with Paul Blackman), which won the Thomas S. Szasz Award for Outstanding Contributions to the Cause of Civil Liberties; *Guns: Who Should Have Them?*; *Gun Control in Great Britain: Saving Lives or Constricting Liberty?*; and *The Samurai, the Mountie, and the Cowboy: Should America Adopt the Gun Controls of Other Democracies?,* which was named Book of the Year by the International Criminology Division of the American Society of Criminology. He was a member of the Editorial Board for *Guns in American Society: An Encyclopedia of History, Politics, Culture, and the Law.*

He has authored dozens of articles in scholarly journals, including the *University of Pennsylvania Law Review, Brown Journal of World Affairs, Connecticut Law Review, Maryland Law Review, Journal of the Medical Association of Georgia, Quarterly Journal of Ideology, Michigan Law Review, BYU Law Review, Tennessee Law Review, Temple Law Review, Journal of Contemporary Law, Asia-Pacific Law Review, St. Louis University Public Law Review, William and Mary Bill of Rights Journal, Political Communication, Arizona Law Review, Criminal Justice Policy Review,* and the *American Journal of Criminal Law*. Kopel is Editor-in-Chief of the *Journal on Firearms & Public Policy*.

Stephen P. Halbrook is an attorney in private practice with offices in Fairfax, Virginia. He has successfully argued three cases before the U.S. Supreme Court: *Castillo v. United States,* 530 U.S. 120 (2000), which upheld the right to jury trial concerning firearms types in the Branch Davidian prosecution; *Printz v. United States,* 521 U.S. 98 (1997), which struck down federal mandates to the states under the Brady law; and *United States v. Thompson/Center Arms Co.,* 504 U.S. 505 (1992), which applied the rule of lenity to firearms definitions.

His books include, *That Every Man Be Armed: The Evolution of a Constitutional Right; Freedmen, the Fourteenth Amendment, and the Right to Bear Arms; Firearms Law Deskbook; A Right to Bear Arms;* and *Target Switzerland: Swiss Armed Neutrality in World War II,* which has also been published in German, French, and Italian editions.

Halbrook holds a Ph.D. in Philosophy from Florida State University and a J.D. from Georgetown University Law Center. His litigation practice includes representation of the National Rifle Association and other nonprofit organizations, and his pro bono amicus curiae clients include the National Association of Criminal Defense Lawyers and the Cato Institute. He is a Fellow with the Independent Institute. To learn more about Mr. Halbrook, visit stephenhalbrook.com.

Alan Korwin, author of three books and co-author of seven others, is a full-time freelance writer, consultant and businessman with a twenty-five-year track record. He is a founder and two-term past president of the Arizona Book Publishing Association, which has presented him with its Visionary Leadership award, named in his honor, the Korwin Award. He has received national awards for his publicity work as a member of the Society for Technical Communication, and is a past board member of the Arizona chapter of the Society of Professional Journalists.

Working with American Express, Mr. Korwin wrote the executive-level strategic plan that defined its worldwide telecommunications strategy for the 1990s; he wrote the business plan that raised $5 million in venture capital and launched SkyMall; he did the publicity for Pulitzer Prize cartoonist Steve Benson's fourth book; and he had a hand in developing ASPED, Arizona's economic strategic plan. Korwin's writing appears often in a wide spectrum of local and national publications.

Korwin turned his first book, *The Arizona Gun Owner's Guide,* into a self-published best-seller, now in its 20th edition. With his wife Cheryl he operates Bloomfield Press, which has grown into the largest producer and distributor of gun-law books in the country. It is built around six books he has completed on the subject including the unabridged guide *Gun Laws of America,* an expanding line of related items, and countless radio and TV appearances. *Supreme Court Gun Cases* is his 10th book.

Alan Korwin is originally from New York City, where his clients included IBM, AT&T, NYNEX and others, many with real names. He is a pretty good guitarist and singer, with a penchant for parody (his last band was The Cartridge Family). In 1986, finally married, he moved to the Valley of the Sun. It was a joyful and successful move.